Praise for
Songwriter's Market

This annual directory is recognized as one of the most comprehensive guides to music publishers, record companies, managers, agents and more.
—American Songwriter

Every year over 20,000 aspiring music industry individuals pick up this book and use it as a reference point from which they literally seek to build their career. Consider it the foundation of *your* songwriting career.
—Songwriter's Monthly

Provides insight and advice that goes beyond writing good music or lyrics to help aspiring professionals establish themselves in the field.
—American Music Teacher

A bounty of contacts. . . . Highly recommended for songwriters and music industry professionals of all levels. **—Music Connection**

This is required reading for anyone serious about songwriting.
—Country Weekly

2002
SONG WRITER'S MARKET.

1,200 PLACES TO
MARKET YOUR SONGS

EDITED BY **IAN BESSLER**

WRITER'S DIGEST BOOKS
CINCINNATI, OH

If you would like to be considered for a listing in the next edition of *Songwriter's Market*, send a SASE (or SAE and IRC) with your request for a questionnaire to *Songwriter's Market*—QR, 1507 Dana Ave., Cincinnati OH 45207. Please indicate in which section you would like to be included. Questionnaires received after February 1, 2002, will be held for the 2004 edition.

Managing Editor, Annuals Department: Doug Hubbuch
Editorial Director, Annuals Department: Barbara Kuroff

Writer's Market website: www.writersmarket.com

Writer's Digest website: www.writersdigest.com

International Standard Serial Number 0161-5971
International Standard Book Number 1-58297-047-5

Attention Booksellers: This is an annual directory of F&W Publications. Return deadline for this edition is December 31, 2002.

contents at a glance

Articles to Help You Use This Book   3

Articles About the Business of Songwriting   10

The Markets

   Music Publishers   97

   Record Companies   169

   Record Producers   254

   Managers & Booking Agents   291

   Advertising, Audiovisual &
   Commercial Music Firms   343

   Play Producers & Publishers   359

   Classical Performing Arts   376

   Contests & Awards   393

Resources

   Organizations   411

   Workshops & Conferences   439

   Retreats & Colonies   450

Indexes

   Openness to Submissions Index   476

   Film & TV Index   484

   Geographic Index   485

   General Index   502

Contents

1 **From the Editor**

2 *Songwriter's Market* **Feedback**

ARTICLES TO HELP YOU USE THIS BOOK

3 **Quick Start**
A quick and easy plan for using this book to launch your songwriting career.

5 **How to Use *Songwriter's Market* to Get Your Songs Heard**
Step-by-step instructions on how to read and use the listings to get your music to the appropriate markets.
  5 Frequently Asked Questions About This Book
  6 Where Should I Send My Songs?
  7 How Songs Are Recorded and Released
  8 Narrowing Your Search
  8 Openness to Submissions
  9 Sample Listing
  9 How to Send Your Demos

ARTICLES ABOUT THE BUSINESS OF SONGWRITING

10 **Getting Started**
The basics on getting your songwriting career off the ground—how to prepare demos of your songs and begin making contact with industry professionals.
  10 If You Write Lyrics, But Not Music
  10 Improving Your Craft
  11 The Structure of the Music Business
  12 Royalties
  13 Submitting Your Songs
  15 What Music Professionals Look for in a Demo

18 **Quiz: Are You Professional?**
Take this quiz to assess whether you and your submission package are as professional as possible.

20 **The Business of Songwriting**
A look at more advanced music business topics, with tips on how to protect your songs, what to look for when signing a contract and unethical practices to avoid.
  20 Copyright   24 Publishers That Charge
  21 Contracts   24 Record Keeping
  23 The Rip-Offs   24 International Markets

25 **Using the Internet to Get Your Songs Heard** *by Cynthia Laufenberg*
Find out more about new opportunities for non-performing songwriters on the Internet.

29 From Development Deals to Work-For-Hire: What Way of Working with a Producer is Best for Me? *by Scott Mathews*
Get the inside scoop on methods and madness in the world of record production.

34 Taking Stock & Making Plans: Advice for Long-Distance Nashville Songwriters *by Jim Melko*
Thinking of moving to Nashville? Evaluate and compare your craft and industry knowledge to find out if you are ready for the big time.

41 Taking the Labor Out of Collaboration: From Creation to Realization *by Bill Pere*
Use this guide to help you choose and manage your songwriting collaborations.

47 Demo FAQs: Answers to the Frequently Asked Questions About Demos *by Cynthia Laufenberg*
Industry professionals answer the questions most songwriters ask about making and sending demos.

51 Music Publishers: Royalties From Foreign Sources *by Randy Poe*
Find out how music publishers tap the huge potential of overseas music markets.

58 Taking Notes: Music Publishers and Background Research *by Phil Goldberg*
Is that publisher right for your song? Are they legitimate? Become a musical detective and learn how to conduct your own background checks.

64 Music Publishers: The New A&R *by Dan Kimpel*
Launching a new act is an expensive and risky proposition for record labels. Find out how music publishers are picking up the slack.

68 Copyright Law: The Primary Source Of Your Rights *by Kent Klavens*
Learn more about basic copyright issues and terminology with this accessible, yet in-depth guide.

77 Roundtable: Composing for Film and Television *by Anne Bowling*
Do you have what it takes to break in and be competitive in the field of film and TV soundtrack composition? Find out from our panel of industry insiders.

82 Selling Your Own CDs & Cassettes—The How & Why *by Jana Stanfield*
Discusses how to sell your own CDs and cassettes directly to your audience, including how to get them made and how to make money selling them.

86 How to Make Your Submission Stand Out *by Mike Po*
Explains getting and holding the attention of A&R persons without turning them off.

90 Is This the Right Company for Me? *by Don Grierson*
Questions to ask before signing with a company along with red flags to look out for.

THE MARKETS

96 Important Information on Market Listings

96 Key to Abbreviations

96 Complaint Procedure

97 Music Publishers
The music publishers listed here provide a vital link between songwriters and artists.

  📖 *insider* **report**
  113 Carter Wood, published Nashville songwriter, talks about success and the song-writing life in Nashville.

161 Music Publishers Category Index
An index of music publishers according to the types of music they are looking for.

169 Record Companies
If you're a songwriter/performer looking for a record deal, these major and independent labels are interested in hearing what you have to offer.

  📖 *insider* **report**
  187 Randy Thorderson, smooth jazz composer and guitarist, talks about his success as part of a new breed of online independent artists.

246 Record Companies Category Index
An index of record companies according to the types of music they are looking for.

254 Record Producers
This section lists names of producers who are not only responsible for the outcome of a recording project, but also seek new material for their clients.

286 Record Producers Category Index
An index of record producers according to the types of music they are looking for.

291 Managers & Booking Agents
If you're an artist looking for representation or want to get your songs into the hands of a particular artist, the companies listed here can help.

336 Managers & Booking Agents Category Index
An index of managers and booking agents according to the types of music they are looking for.

343 Advertising, Audiovisual & Commercial Music Firms
Explore the opportunities for writing commercial music for TV, radio and film through the listings in this section.

◢ *insider* **report**

349 Gary Chang, veteran film and television composer, shares the insight and experience gained from his long and varied career.

359 Play Producers & Publishers

Writing musicals can be a considerable challenge, but these listings are actively seeking material from aspiring musical playwrights.
359 Play Producers
373 Play Publishers

376 Classical Performing Arts

Here you'll find orchestras, operas, chamber groups and others interested in hearing from classical composers.

393 Contests & Awards

Participation in contests is a good way to gain exposure for your songs. The contests listed here encompass all types of music.

RESOURCES

411 Organizations

Making contacts is imperative in the music business, and these organizations provide opportunities to expand your network of contacts in the industry.

◢ *insider* **report**

425 Mick McEvilley, special events coordinator for the Dayton/Cincinnati chapter of NSAI, shares his thoughts on the benefits of belonging to a songwriting organization like Nashville Songwriters Association International.

439 Workshops & Conferences

Conferences, seminars and workshops are great places to get feedback and advice from industry experts. These listings provide you with national and local dates and details.

450 Retreats & Colonies

These arts councils provide grants and fellowships for area artists, including songwriters.

455 State & Provincial Grants

These arts councils provide grants and fellowships for area artists, including songwriters.

458 Publications of Interest

These periodicals, books and directories will keep you up-to-date on what's going on in the music industry.

463 Websites of Interest

Check out these websites and begin exploring alternative sources of creativity as well as new opportunities to get your music heard on the Internet.

468 Contributors to the Insider Reports

469 **Glossary**
Definitions of terms and abbreviations relating specifically to the music industry.

476 **Openness to Submissions Index**
This index lists music publishers, record companies, producers, managers and booking agents, according to their openness to beginners' submissions.

484 **Film & TV Index**
This index lists companies placing music in film and TV (excluding commercials).

485 **Geographic Index**
An index of listings by state and country.

502 **General Index**
An alphabetical index of all the listings as well as common article topics.

From the Editor

Working on a book of this size and complexity always reminds me of how important collaboration is to the successful outcome of a creative process. As with the recording of an album, a book of this scope requires the active participation of many people, including freelancers, typesetters and other editors, to keep the project on course. Similarly, finding success in the music industry, at all stages, also requires the good will and hard work of others.

In the music industry, you may find yourself collaborating with others in many different ways, from co-writing with another songwriter, to working with a producer or engineer to mold raw tracks into an album. It could also include brainstorming ideas with a graphic designer for your album cover. If you write alone, you will still need to deal with publishers, record company A&R, and people necessary to take your music to the next step.

In this spirit, this year's article about collaboration by **Bill Pere**, **Taking the Labor Out of Collaboration** on page 41, offers a method for analyzing what sort of complementary methods and personality traits you might need for a successful collaboration. For those of you who are considering finding a producer, take a look at the article by multi-platinum producer **Scott Mathews**, **From Development Deals to Work-For-Hire: What Way of Working with a Producer is Best for Me?**on page 29. The working relationship between an artist and a producer is an interweaving of personalities and legal agreements, and Scott passes along numerous bits of wisdom from his extensive experience in record production.

Check out the article by former *Songwriter's Market* editor **Cynthia Laufenberg**, **Using the Internet to Get Your Songs Heard**, on page 25. This article examines online opportunities you may not have heard much about, including online songwriting organizations such as Just Plain Folks and sites for pitching, such as Songlink or Songpitch.com. While online interaction is never going to replace the person-to-person contact you can get at a music industry conference or workshop, it can supplement those approaches and open other doors. Also take a look at the **Websites of Interest** on page 463, featuring 37 new sites.

For those of you who dream of going to Nashville, go to the article by Nashville Songwriters Association International regional coordinator **Jim Melko** entitled **Taking Stock & Making Plans: Advice for Long-Distance Nashville Songwriters** on page 34. Jim has seen many songwriters move to Nashville before they were ready and then leave in disappointment, so read this article and find out whether you are ripe for Nashville.

So, as you work through this book, think about your own goals and level of skill. Where are you now as a songwriter and/or artist, and where do you want to be? No matter where you are on the music industry ladder of success, there are many possibilities available through this book, and I hope it serves you well.

Ian C. Bessler
songmarket@fwpubs.com
www.writersdigest.com

P.S. If you would like to receive the new *Songwriter's Market* newsletter (by either e-mail or regular mail) for updates, tips and news, send an e-mail to songmarket@fwpubs.com or write to my attention at F&W Publications, 1507 Dana Avenue, Cincinnati OH 45207.

Songwriter's Market
Feedback

If you have a suggestion for improving *Songwriter's Market*, or would like to take part in a reader survey we conduct from time to time, please make a photocopy of this form (or cut it out of the book), fill it out, and return it to:

> Songwriter's Market Feedback
> 1507 Dana Ave.
> Cincinnati OH 45207
> Fax: (513)531-2686

☐ Yes! I'm willing to fill out a short survey by mail or online to provide feedback on *Songwriter's Market* or other books on songwriting.

☐ Yes! I would like to subscribe to the *Songwriter's Market* newsletter (be sure to include your e-mail address if you wish to receive it online).

☐ Yes! I have a suggestion to improve *Songwriter's Market* (attach a second sheet if more room is necessary):

_____

_____

_____

_____

_____

_____

_____

_____

Name:_____

Address:_____

City:_____ State:_____ Zip:_____

Phone:_____ Fax:_____

E-mail:_____ Website:_____

I am a
☐ songwriter
☐ performing songwriter
☐ musician
☐ other_____

Quick-Start

If the business of marketing your songs is a new experience, this book may seem overwhelming. This "Quick-Start" will take you step by step through the process of preparing you and your songs to be heard by music industry professionals. It points you to the different places in *Songwriter's Market* that contain information on specific marketing and business subjects.

Use this as a guide to launch your songwriting career. When you are finished looking it over, read through the referred articles in their entirety. They will reinforce what you already know and introduce you to facets of the industry you have yet to encounter. Good luck!

1. Join a songwriting organization. This is the most important first step for a songwriter. Organizations provide opportunities to learn about the music business, polish your craft, and make indispensable contacts who can take you to the next level.

- Organizations, page 411

2. Educate yourself about the music business. Before you leap, read up on what you are getting yourself into. Attend songwriting workshops and music conferences. Don't learn the ins and outs the hard way.

- The Structure of the Music Business, page 11
- Royalties, page 12
- If You Write Lyrics, But Not Music sidebar, page 10
- Frequently Asked Questions About This Book sidebar, page 5
- The Business of Songwriting, page 20
- Copyright Law: The Primary Source of Your Rights, page 68
- Workshops & Conferences, page 439
- Publications of Interest, page 458

3. Prepare yourself and your songs for marketing. Get letterhead, get criticism, make contacts and subscribe to songwriting/music magazines; then start building a following and a strong catalog.

- Improving Your Craft, page 10
- Organizations, page 411
- Workshops & Conferences, page 439
- Publications of Interest, page 458
- Using the Internet to Get Your Songs Heard, page 25
- Taking Stock & Making Plans: Advice for Long-Distance Nashville Songwriters, page 34

4. Choose three songs you feel are ready to be marketed and make a demo.

- Submitting Your Songs, page 13
- What Music Professionals Look for In a Demo sidebar, page 15
- Demo FAQs: Answers to the Frequently Asked Questions About Demos, page 47
- How to Make Your Submission Stand Out, page 86

5. Decide which arm(s) of the music business you will submit your songs to.

- Where Should I Send My Songs?, page 6

6. Find the companies open to your style of music and level of experience or use your contacts to get a referral and permission to submit. Be picky about where you send your material. It's a waste of your effort and money to send to every company listed in this book without regard to whether or not they want to hear your songs.

- Narrowing Your Search, page 8
- Openness to Submissions sidebar, page 8
- Taking Notes: Music Publishers and Background Research, page 58

7. Locate the companies closest to where you live. It's easier to have a relationship when the company is within driving distance.
- Geographic Index, page 485

8. Decide which companies you to want to submit your song to and whether they are appropriate markets for you (pay special attention to the information under the **Music** subhead and also the royalty percentage they pay). Do additional research through trade publications, Internet, other songwriters.
- The Markets, pages 95
- Publications of Interest, page 458
- Websites of Interest, page 463
- Taking Notes: Music Publishers and Background Research, page 58

9. Find out how to submit. Read the information under the **How to Contact** subhead.
- Sample Reply Postcard, page 14
- How to Send Your Demos, page 9
- Quiz: Are You Professional?, page 18

10. Call the companies and verify that their submission policy has not changed; also check to make sure the contact person is still there.

11. Send out your submission package according to each company's directions.
- Quiz: Are You Professional?, page 18
- Submitting Your Songs, page 13

12. Decide whether you want to sign with a company (if they reply and are interested in working with you). Just because they want to sign you doesn't mean you should.
- The Rip-Offs, page 23
- Taking Notes: Music Publishers and Background Research, page 58
- Is This the Right Company for Me?, page 90

13. Have an entertainment attorney look over any contract before you sign.
- Contracts, page 21
- Publishing Contracts, page 99
- Record Company Contracts, page 172

14. After signing, how do you get paid?
- Royalties, page 12
- Music Publishers: Royalties From Foreign Sources, page 57

How to Use *Songwriter's Market* to Get Your Songs Heard

Songwriter's Market is designed to help you make good decisions about submitting your songs—whether you're approaching music publishers, record companies, producers, managers, chamber music groups, or theater companies.

If you're new to the business of marketing your music, a good place to start—after this article, but before you dive into the market listings—is with Quick-Start on page 3 and Getting Started, on page 10. If you're an old hand at this, you might wish to begin with a quick brush-up in The Business of Songwriting, on page 20. In either case, the other articles, Insider Report interviews, and section introductions throughout the book should prove informative and inspiring.

Getting to know this book. *Songwriter's Market* is divided into Markets and Resources. The Markets section contains all the companies (music publishers, record companies, etc.) seeking new material and is the part of the book you will concentrate on when submitting songs. If you're uncertain about which markets might have the most interest in your material, review the introductory explanations at the beginning of each section. They will clarify the various functions of each segment of the music industry and help you narrow your list of possible submissions. The Resources section contains listings and information on organizations, workshops, retreats/colonies, publications and websites to help you learn more about the music industry and the craft of songwriting.

Frequently Asked Questions About This Book

1. What's the deal with listing companies that don't take unsolicited submissions?

We want to provide you with the most complete songwriting resource. To do this, you should be aware of the companies that are not open to unsolicited submissions so you can take one of two actions: either 1) don't submit to them; or 2) work to establish a relationship with them to earn a solicited submission. If the major companies that are closed to submissions weren't in here, wouldn't you wonder what their policy was? Also, it's important to read these listings every year to keep informed about the industry.

2. How do these companies get listed in the book anyway?

No company pays to be included—all listings are free. Every company has to fill out a detailed questionnaire about their services. All questionnaires are screened to make sure the companies meet our requirements (see The Rip-Offs on page 23). Each year we contact every company in the book and have them update their information.

3. Why aren't other companies I know about listed in this book?

We may have sent these companies a questionnaire, but they never returned it. Or if they did return a questionnaire, we may have decided not to include them based on our requirements (see The Rip-Offs on page 23).

4. I sent a company a demo tape, and they said in their listing they take unsolicited submissions. My demo was returned unopened. What happened?

At the time we contacted the company they were open to submissions, but things change fast in this business and their policy may have changed by the time you sent your demo. It's always a good idea to call a company to check on their policy before sending them anything.

WHERE SHOULD I SEND MY SONGS?

It depends. Who are you writing your music for? Are you writing songs for an act you now belong to? Are you hoping to have your music accepted and recorded by an artist? Take a look at the How Songs Are Recorded and Released flow chart on page 7. It shows the different paths a songwriter can take to get her music recorded (the Key to this chart is below).

The performing songwriter. If you are writing songs for an existing group or for yourself as a solo artist, you're probably trying to advance the career of your act. If that's the case, and you're seeking a recording contract, the Record Companies section will be the place to start. Look also at the Record Producers section. Independent record producers are constantly on the lookout for up-and-coming artists. They may also have strong connections with record companies looking for acts, and will pass your demo on or recommend the act to a record company. And if your act doesn't yet have representation, your demo submission may be included as part of a promotional kit sent to a prospective manager listed in the Managers & Booking Agents section.

The nonperforming songwriter. If you are a songwriter seeking to have your songs recorded by other artists, you may submit to some of the same markets as the performing songwriter, but for different reasons. The Record Producers section contains mostly independent producers who work regularly with particular artists, rather than working fulltime for one record company. Because they work closely with a limited number of clients, they may be willing to consider songs written with a specific act in mind. The independent producer is often responsible for picking cuts for a recording project. The Managers & Booking Agents section may be useful for the same reason. Many personal managers are constantly seeking new material for the acts they represent, and a good song sent at the right time can mean a valuable cut for the songwriter. The primary market for songwriters not writing with particular artists in mind will be found in the Music Publishers section. Music publishers are the jacks-of-all-trades in the industry, having knowledge about and keeping abreast of developments in all other segments of the music business. They act as the first line of contact between the songwriter and the music industry.

Key to How Songs Are Recorded and Released (page 7)

A and B—options for non-performing songwriters
C—avenue for both performing and non-performing songwriters
D and E—processes for performing songwriters

Artist—band or singer who performs the music
Artist's Manager—works with the artist to manage her career; locates songs to record if the artist does not write her own material
Independent Producer—not affiliated with a record company; works in the studio and records songs; may have an affiliation with an artist
Producer—affiliated with a record company or music publisher; works in the studio and records songs
Publisher—evaluates songs for commercial potential, finds artists to record them, finds other uses (such as TV or film) for the songs, collects income generated by the songs and protects copyrights from infringement
Record Company—signs artists to its label, finances recording, promotion and touring, and releases songs/albums to radio and TV

How Songs Are Recorded and Released

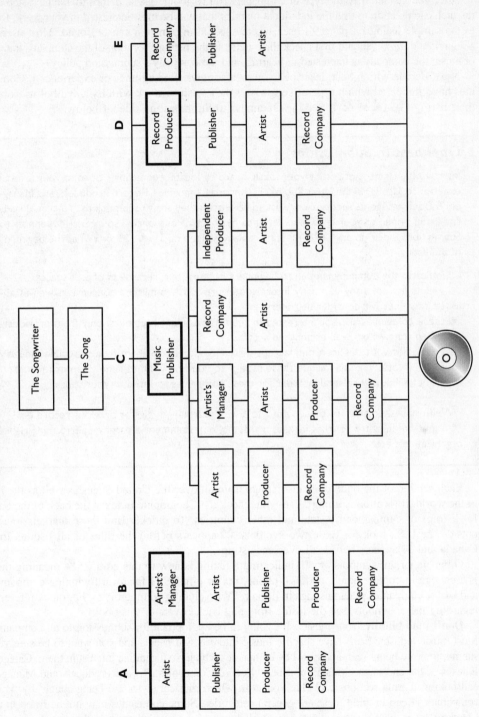

NARROWING YOUR SEARCH

After you've identified the type of companies you're going to send demos to, the next step is to research each section to find the individual markets that will be most interested in your work. Refer to the sample listing on page 9 to see where specific information can be found. Most users of *Songwriter's Market* should first check three items in the listings: location of the company, the type of music the company is interested in hearing, and the company's submission policy.

Next, decide which best describes you as a songwriter: beginner or experienced. Companies have indicated which type of songwriter they wish to work with by a symbol in front of their listing (☐ ☑ ☑ ☑). See the Openness to Submissions sidebar below.

Openness to Submissions

Improve the chances of getting your music heard by locating companies open to your level of experience. Listings in the Music Publishers, Record Companies, Record Producers, and Managers & Booking Agents sections were asked how open they are to submissions. You can quickly find listings open to your level of experience by checking one of two sources: 1. Openness to Submissions Index on page 476; or 2. the openness icon (☐ ☑ ☑ or ☑) at the beginning of the listing.

☐ indicates the company is open to beginners' submissions, regardless of past success.
☑ means the company is mostly interested in previously published songwriters/well-established acts*, but will consider beginners.
☑ these companies are not interested in submissions from beginners, only from previously published songwriters/well-established acts*.
☑ companies with this icon only accept material referred to them by a reputable industry source**. [Note: We still include these listings so you know *not* to send them material. You must get an industry referral in order for these companies to listen to your songs.]

* Well-established acts are those with a following, permanent gigs or previous record deal.
** Reputable industry sources include managers, entertainment attorneys, performing rights organizations, etc.

Each section of the book contains listings from all over the United States as well as the rest of the world. If location is important to you, check the Geographic Index at the back of the book for listings of companies by state and other countries. To quickly find those markets located outside the U.S., look for these two symbols: ☑ appears before the titles of all listings from Canada and ☑ appears before all overseas listings.

Other important symbols are ☑ indicating a listing is new to this edition; ☑ meaning there is a change in contact name, address, phone, fax or e-mail; ☑ for award-winning companies; and ☑ for companies placing songs in film or TV (excluding commercials). For quick reference regarding these symbols, see the inside front and back covers of this book.

Don't mail blindly. Your music isn't going to be appropriate for submission to all companies. Most music industry firms have specific music interests and needs, and you want to be sure your submissions are being seen and heard by companies who have a genuine interest in them. Category Indexes at the end of the Music Publishers, Record Companies, Record Producers and Managers & Booking Agents sections will clue you in to which musical styles are being sought by which companies. (Keep in mind these are general categories. Some companies may not be listed in the Category Index because they either accept all types of music or the music they are looking for doesn't fit into any of the general categories.) Within each listing, under the **Music** subhead, you will find, in **bold** type, a more detailed list of the styles of music a company is seeking.

Pay close attention to the types of music described. For instance, if the music you write fits the category of "rock," there can be many variations on that style. Our sample above is interested in **hard rock**, another listing may be looking for **country rock**, and another, **soft rock**. These are three very different styles of music, but they all fall under the same general category. The Category Index is there to help you narrow down the listings within a certain music genre; it is up to you to narrow them down even further to fit the type of music you write. The music styles in each listing are *in descending order of importance*; if your particular specialty is country music, you may want to seek out those companies that list country as their first priority as your primary targets for submissions.

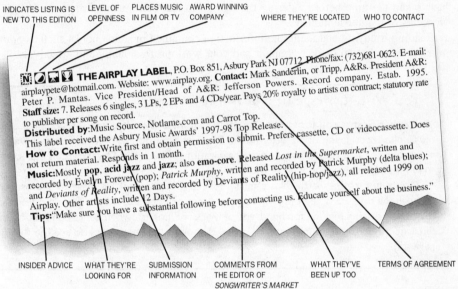

You will note that some market listings contain editorial comments and are marked by a bullet (●). Editorial comments give you additional information such as special submission requirements, any awards a company may have won, and other details that will be helpful in narrowing down your list of companies to submit to.

HOW TO SEND YOUR DEMOS

Finally, when you've placed the most likely listings geographically and identified their music preferences and openness to submissions, read the **How to Contact** subhead. As shown in the sample listing above, it will give you pertinent information about what to send as part of a demo submission, how to go about sending it and when you can expect to hear back from them.

Read carefully! Not all of the markets listed in *Songwriter's Market* accept unsolicited submissions (indicated by ⊘ in front of the listing), so it's important to read this information closely. Most companies have carefully considered their submission policies, and packages that do not follow their directions are returned or discarded without evaluation. Follow the instructions: it will impress upon the market your seriousness about getting your work heard.

You've now identified markets you feel will have the most interest in your work. Read the complete listing carefully before proceeding. Many of the listings include individualized information important for the submitting songwriter. Then, it's time for you to begin preparing your demo submission package to get your work before the people in the industry. For further information on that process, turn to Getting Started on page 10.

Getting Started

Breaking in and thriving in the competitive music industry without being overwhelmed is perhaps the biggest challenge facing songwriters. Those who not only survive but also succeed have taken the time before entering the market to learn as much as they can about the inner workings of the music industry.

Reading, studying and using the information contained in sourcebooks such as *Songwriter's Market* will help you market yourself and your work professionally and effectively.

If You Write Lyrics, But Not Music

You must find a collaborator. The music business is looking for the complete package: music plus lyrics. If you don't write music, find a collaborator who does. The best way to find a collaborator is through songwriting organizations. Check the Organizations section (pages 411) for songwriting groups near you.

Don't get ripped-off. "Music mills" advertise in the back of magazines or solicit you through the mail. For a fee they will set your lyrics or poems to music. The rip-off is that they may use the same melody for hundreds of lyrics and poems, whether it sounds good or not. Publishers recognize one of these melodies as soon as they hear it. (Also see the Rip-Offs on page 23).

IMPROVING YOUR CRAFT

There is no magic formula for success in the music business. If you want to make it, you must begin by believing in yourself and your talent. Develop your own personal vision and stick with it. Why do you write songs? Is it because you want to be rich or because you love the process? Is every song you write an attempt to become famous or a labor of love? Every effort you make to discern your motives and clarify your goals will be a step in the right direction. Successful songwriters usually believe they have a talent that deserves to be heard, whether by 2 or 2,000 people. Songwriting is a craft, like woodworking or painting. Talent is involved, of course, but with time and practice the craft can be improved and eventually mastered.

Organizations. While working on songs, look for support and feedback wherever you can. A great place to start is a local songwriting organization, which can offer friendly advice, support from other writers, and a place to meet collaborators. (For more information on songwriting organizations, see the Organizations section on page 411.) Many organizations offer song critique sessions to help you identify strengths and weaknesses in your material and give you guidance to improve your craft. Use the criticism you receive in such sessions to fine-tune your writing style. Your songwriting will improve, and you will be creating connections within the industry and continuing your education not only in the craft of songwriting but in the business as well.

Books. Books can also be helpful in matters of craft and business. Books are available to help you write better melodies, stronger lyrics and songs that sell. Many books cover the business side of music, explaining the intricacies of how the business works and giving valuable tips on how to network with people in the business. Music catalogs such as Music Books Plus (call (800)265-8481 for a catalog or visit www.musicbooksplus.com) or online booksellers like Amaz on.com and barnesandnoble.com carry hundreds of books about songwriting and the music industry.

Magazines. Magazines can keep you up-to-date on the latest trends and happenings in today's ever-changing music business. From industry trade magazines like *Billboard* and *Variety* to more specific magazines such as *Performing Songwriter* and *JazzTimes*, there is a magazine catering to just about every segment of the industry and type of music you can imagine. Since this is a trend-oriented business, weekly and monthly magazines can help you stay abreast of what's hot and what's not. For some suggestions, see Publications of Interest on page 458.

The Internet. The Internet can be another valuable source of information. Not only are many record companies, publishers and magazines online, but a growing number of music sites exist where artists can showcase their songs for an unlimited audience, chat with other songwriters and musicians from all over the world, and even sell their product online. See Websites of Interest on page 463 for a list of some current music-oriented websites as well as Using the Internet to Get Your Songs Heard on page 25. New ones are popping up every day, so surfing the Web frequently will help you learn what's available.

THE STRUCTURE OF THE MUSIC BUSINESS

The music business in the U.S. revolves around three major hubs: New York, Nashville and Los Angeles. Power is concentrated in those areas because that's where most record companies, publishers, songwriters and performers are. Many people trying to break into the music business move to one of those three cities to be close to the people and companies they want to contact. From time to time a regional music scene will heat up in a non-hub city such as Austin, Chicago or Seattle. When this happens, songwriters and performers in that city experience a kind of musical Renaissance complete with better-paying gigs, a creatively charged atmosphere and intensified interest from major labels.

All this is not to say that a successful career cannot be nurtured from any city in the country, however. It can be, especially if you are a songwriter. By moving to a major music hub, you may be closer physically to major companies, but you'll also encounter more competition than you would back home. Stay where you're comfortable; it's probably easier (and more cost-effective) to conquer the music scene where you are than it is in Los Angeles or Nashville. There are many smaller, independent companies located in cities across the country. Most international careers are started on a local level, and some may find a local career more satisfying, in its own way, than the constant striving to gain the attention of major companies.

For more advice on whether you are ready to move to a major music center, specifically Nashville, see Taking Stock & Making Plans: Advice for Long-Distance Nashville Songwriters on page 34.

Making contact. If you are interested in obtaining a recording contract, you will need to make contact with A&R reps, producers, publishers and managers. Getting your material to these professionals and establishing relationships with as many people in the industry as you can should be your main goal as a songwriter. The more people who hear your songs, the better your chances of getting them recorded.

A&R reps, producers and managers. Consumer support, in the form of money spent on records, concert tickets and other kinds of musical entertainment, keeps the music industry in business. Because of that, record companies, publishers and producers are eager to give the public what they want. To stay one step ahead of public tastes, record companies hire people who have a knack for spotting musical talent and anticipating trends, and put them in charge of finding and developing new talent. These talent scouts are called A&R representatives. "A&R" stands for "artist and repertoire," which simply means they are responsible for discovering new talent and matching songs to particular artists. The person responsible for the recording artist's product—the record—is called the producer. The producer's job is to develop the artist's work and come out of the studio with a good-sounding, saleable product that represents the artist in the best way possible. His duties sometimes include choosing songs for a particular project, so record producers are also great contacts for songwriters. Managers are interested in developing an artist's career as a whole, and are typically on the prowl for material suitable for the performers they represent.

Music publishers. Producers, A&R reps, and managers are aided in their search for talent by the music publisher. A publisher works as a songwriter's advocate who, for a percentage of the profits (typically 50% of all earnings from a particular song), attempts to find commercially profitable uses for the songs he represents. A successful publisher stays in contact with several A&R reps, finding out what upcoming projects are in need of new material, and whether any songs he represents will be appropriate.

ROYALTIES

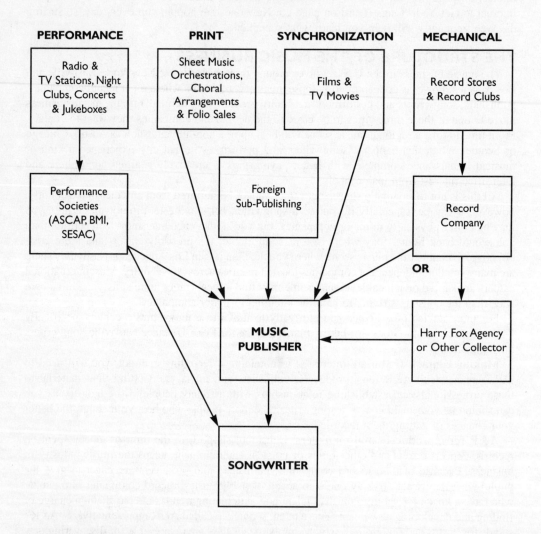

ROYALTIES

When a song is recorded and released to the public, the recording artist, songwriter, record company, producer and publisher all stand to profit. Recording artists earn a negotiated royalty from a record company based on the number of records sold. Producers are usually paid either a negotiated royalty based on sales or a flat fee at the time of recording. Publishers and songwriters earn mechanical royalties (money a record company pays a publisher based on record sales) and performance royalties, which are based on radio airplay and live performances. Look at the royalties flow chart above. It shows where royalties come from and where they go before landing in the songwriter's pocket. As the chart shows, a music publisher is an invaluable resource for songwriters to earn royalties (see the Music Publishers section on page 97).

For More Information

I

Songwriter's Market lists music publishers, record companies, producers and managers (as well as advertising firms, play producers and classical performing arts organizations) along with specifications on how to submit your material to each. If you can't find a certain person or company you're interested in, there are other sources of information you can try. *The Recording Industry Sourcebook*, an annual directory published by Norris-Whitney Communications, lists record companies, music publishers, producers and managers, as well as attorneys, publicity firms, media, manufacturers, distributors and recording studios around the U.S. Trade publications such as *Billboard* or *Variety*, available at most local libraries and bookstores, are great sources for up-to-date information. These periodicals list new companies as well as the artists, labels, producers and publishers for each song on the charts. CD booklets and cassette j-cards can be valuable sources of information, providing the name of the record company, publisher, producer and usually the manager of an artist or group. Use your imagination in your research and be creative—any contacts you make in the industry can only help your career as a songwriter. See Publications of Interest on page 463.

SUBMITTING YOUR SONGS

When it comes to presenting your material, the tool of the music industry is a demonstration recording—a demo. Cassette tapes have been the standard in the music industry for decades because they're so convenient. Songwriters use demos to present their songs, and musicians use them to showcase their performance skills. Demos are submitted to various professionals in the industry, either by mail or in person. Be sure to read the sidebar What Music Professionals Look for in a Demo on page 15 for specifics. Also read Quiz: Are You Professional? on page 18 and Demo FAQs: Answers to Frequently Asked Questions About Demos on page 47.

Demo quality

The production quality of demos can vary widely, but even simple guitar/vocal or piano/vocal demos must sound clean, with the instrument in tune and lyrics sung clearly. Many songwriters invest in home recording equipment, such as multitrack recorders, and record demos themselves. Other writers prefer to book studio time, hire musicians, and get professional input from an engineer or producer. Demo services are also available to record your demo for a fee. It's up to you to decide what you can afford and feel most comfortable with, and what you think best represents your song. Once a master recording is made of your song, you're ready to make cassette copies and start pitching your song to the contacts you've researched.

Some companies indicate that you may send a videocassette of your act in performance or a group performing your songs, instead of the standard cassette demo. Most of the companies listed in *Songwriter's Market* have indicated that a videocassette is not required, but have indicated their preferred format should you decide to send one. Television systems vary widely from country to country, so if you're sending a video to a foreign listing check with them for the system they're using. For example, a VHS format tape recorded using the U.S. system (called NTSC) will not play back on a standard British VCR (using the PAL system), even if the recording formats are the same. It is possible to transfer a video from one system to another, but the expense in both time and money may outweigh its usefulness. Systems for some countries include: NTSC—U.S., Canada and Japan; PAL—United Kingdom, Australia and Germany; and SECAM—France.

SAMPLE REPLY POSTCARD

I would like to hear:
☐ "Name of Song"   ☐ "Name of Song"   ☐ "Name of Song"

I prefer:
☐ cassette   ☐ DAT   ☐ CD   ☐ videocassette

With:
☐ lyric sheet   ☐ lead sheet   ☐ either   ☐ both

☐ I am not looking for material at this time, try me in _____ weeks/months.
☐ I am not interested.

_____
Name   Title

Submitting by mail

When submitting material to companies listed in this book:

☑ Read the listing carefully and submit *exactly* what a company asks for in the exact way it asks that it be submitted. It's always a good idea to call first, just in case a company has changed its submission policy.

☑ Listen to each demo before sending to make sure the quality is satisfactory.

☑ Enclose a brief, typed cover letter to introduce yourself. Indicate what songs you are sending and why you are sending them. If you're a songwriter pitching songs to a particular artist, state that in the letter. If you're an artist/songwriter looking for a recording deal, you should say so. Be specific.

☑ Include typed lyric sheets or lead sheets if requested. Make sure your name, address and phone number appear on each sheet.

☑ Neatly label each tape with your name, address and phone number along with the names of the songs in the sequence in which they appear on the tape.

What Music Professionals Look for in a Demo

- **Format**. The cassette is still the preferable format for demos, although CDs are becoming more popular. Music executives are busy people and whenever they have a chance, they will listen to demos. Cassette players are what they have the easiest access to, whether in their office, car or home. Cassettes are also cheaper to duplicate than CDs or DATs, and are cheaper and easier to mail. If they like what they hear on the cassette they can always ask you for a DAT or CD later.
- **Number, order and length of songs**. The consensus throughout the industry is that three songs is sufficient. Most music professionals don't have time to listen to more than three, and they figure if you can't catch their attention in three songs, your songs probably don't have hit potential.

    Put three complete songs on the tape, not just snippets of your favorites, and remember to put your best, most commercial song first on the tape. If it's an up-tempo number, that makes it even easier to catch someone's attention. All songs should be on the same side of the tape, and none of them should be longer than four minutes. Cue the tape to the beginning of the first song so no time will be wasted fast-forwarding or rewinding.
- **Production**. How elaborate a demo has to be lies in the type of music you write, and what an individual at a company is looking for. Usually, up-tempo pop, rock and dance demos need to be more fully produced than pop ballads and country demos. Many of the companies listed in *Songwriter's Market* tell you what type of demo they prefer to receive, and if you're not sure you can always call and ask what their preference is. Either way, make sure your demo is clean and clear, and the vocals are up front.

    If you are an artist looking for a record deal, obviously your demo needs to be as fully produced as possible to convey your talent as an artist. Many singer/songwriters record their demos as if they were going to be released as an album. That way, if they have already recorded three or four CD-quality demo tapes but haven't heard anything from the labels they've been submitting to, they can put those demos together and release a CD or cassette on their own. They end up with a professional-looking product, complete with album cover graphics and liner notes, to sell at shows and through mail order without spending a lot of money to re-record the songs.
- **Performance**. If you can't sing well, you may want to find someone who can. It pays to find a good vocalist and good musicians to record your demos, and there are many places to find musicians and singers willing to work with you. Check out local songwriting organizations, music stores and newspapers to find musicians in your area you can hire to play on your demo. Many singers who don't write their own songs will sing on demos in exchange for a copy of the tape they can use as their own demo to help further their performing careers.

    If you can't find local musicians, or don't want to go through the trouble of putting together a band just for the purposes of recording your demo, you may want to try a demo service. For a fee, a demo service will produce your songs in their studio using their own singers and musicians. Many of these services advertise in music magazines, songwriting newsletters and bulletin boards at local music stores. If you decide to deal with a demo service, make sure you can hear samples of work they've done in the past. Many demo services are mail-order businesses—you send them either a rough tape of your song or the sheet music and they'll produce and record a demo within a month or two. Be sure you find a service that will let you have creative control over how your demo is to be produced, and make sure you tell them exactly how you want your song to sound. As with studios, shop around and find the demo service that best suits your needs and budget.

☑ If the company returns material (many do not; be sure to read each listing carefully), include a SASE for the return. Your return envelope to countries other than your own should contain a self-addressed envelope (SAE) and International Reply Coupon (IRC), available at your local post office. Be sure the return envelope is large enough to accommodate your material, and include sufficient postage for the weight of the package.

☑ Wrap the package neatly and write (or type on a shipping label) the company's address and your return address so they are clearly visible. Your package is the first impression a company has of you and your songs, so neatness is important.

☑ Mail first class. Stamp or write "First Class Mail" on the package and on the SASE you enclose. Don't send by registered or certified mail unless it is specifically requested by the company.

☑ Keep records of the dates, songs and companies you submit to.

If you are writing to inquire about a company's needs or to request permission to submit (many companies ask you to do this first), your query letter should be typed, brief and pleasant. Explain the kind of material you have and ask for their needs and submission policy.

To expedite a reply, enclose a self-addressed, stamped postcard requesting the information you are seeking. Your typed questions (see the Sample Reply Postcard on the previous page) should be direct and easy to answer. Place the company's name and address in the upper left hand space on the front of the postcard so you'll know which company you queried. Keep a record of the queries you send for future reference.

Simultaneous submissions and holds. It's acceptable to submit your songs to more than one person at a time (this is called simultaneous submission). The exception to this is when a publisher, artist or other industry professional asks if he may put a song of yours "on hold." This means he intends to record it and doesn't want you to give the song to anyone else. Your song may be returned to you without ever having been recorded, even if it's been on hold for months. Or, it may be recorded but not used on an album. If either of these things happens, you're free to pitch your song to other people again. (You can, and should, protect yourself from having a song on hold indefinitely. Establish a deadline for the person who asks for the hold, e.g., "You can put my song on hold for [number of] months." Or modify the hold to specify that you will pitch the song to other people, but you will not sign a deal without allowing the person who has the song on hold to make you an offer.) When someone publishes your song and you sign a contract, you grant that publisher exclusive rights to your song and you may not pitch it to other publishers. You can, however, pitch it to any artists or producers interested in recording the song without publishing it themselves.

Following up. If a company doesn't respond within several weeks after you've sent your demo, don't despair. As long as your demo is in their hands, there is a chance someone is reviewing it. If after a reasonable amount of time you still haven't received word on your submission (check the reporting time each company states in its listing), follow up with a friendly letter or phone call. Many companies do not return submissions, so don't expect a company that states "Does not return material" to send your materials back to you.

Submitting in person

Planning a trip to one of the major music hubs will give you insight into how the music industry works. Whether you decide to visit New York, Nashville or Los Angeles, have specific goals in mind and set up appointments to make the most of your time there. It will be difficult to get in to see some industry professionals as many of them are extremely busy and may not feel meeting out-of-town writers is a high priority. Other people are more open to, and even encourage, face-to-face meetings. They may feel that if you take the time to travel to where they are and you're organized enough to schedule meetings beforehand, you're more professional than many aspiring songwriters who blindly submit inappropriate songs through the mail. (For listings of companies by state, see the Geographic Index at the back of the book.)

What to take. Take several cassette copies and lyric sheets of each of your songs. More than one of the companies you visit may ask that you leave a copy to review. There's also a good chance that the person you have an appointment with will have to cancel (expect that occasionally) but wants you to leave a copy of the songs so he can listen and contact you later. Never give someone the last or only copy of your material—if it is not returned to you, all the hard work and money that went into making that demo will be lost.

Where to network. Another good place to meet industry professionals face-to-face is at seminars such as the yearly South by Southwest Music and Media Conference in Austin, the National Academy of Songwriters' annual Songwriters Expo in Los Angeles, or the Nashville Songwriters Association's Spring Symposium, to name a few (see the Workshops & Conferences section on page 439 for further ideas). Many of these conferences feature demo listening sessions, where industry professionals listen to demos submitted by songwriters attending the seminars.

Dealing with rejection. Many good songs have been rejected simply because they weren't what the particular publisher or record company was looking for at the time, so don't take rejection personally. Realize that if a few people don't like your songs, it doesn't mean they're not good. However, if there seems to be a consensus about your work—for instance, the feel of a song isn't right or the lyrics need work—give the advice serious thought. Listen attentively to what the reviewers say and use their criticism constructively to improve your songs.

Quiz: Are You Professional?

OK, everybody! Take out your submission package and let's take a look. Hmm . . . very interesting. I think you're well on your way, but you should probably change a few things.

We asked record companies, music publishers and record producers, "What do songwriters do in correspondence with your company (by phone, mail or demo) that screams 'amateur'?" Take this quiz and find out how professional you appear to those on the receiving end of your submission. The following are common mistakes songwriters make all the time. They may seem petty, but, really, do you want to give someone an excuse not to listen to your demo? Check off the transgressions you have committed.

BY MAIL YOU SENT:

☐ anything handwritten (lyrics, cover letters, labels for cassettes). Today there is no excuse for handwritten materials. Take advantage of your local library's typewriters or businesses that charge by the hour to use a computer. And don't even think about using notebook paper.

☐ materials without a contact name *and* phone number. Put this information on *everything*.

☐ lyrics only. Music companies want music and words. See the If You Write Lyrics, But Not Music sidebar on page 10.

☐ insufficient return postage, an envelope too small to return materials, no SASE at all, or a "certified mail" package. If you want materials returned, don't expect the company to send it back on their dime with their envelope—give them what they need. Certified mail is unnecessary and annoying; first class will suffice.

☐ long-winded, over-hyped cover letters, or no cover letter at all. Companies don't need (or want) to hear your life story, how many instruments you play, how many songs you've written, how talented you are or how all your songs are sure-fire hits. Briefly explain why you are sending the songs (e.g., your desire to have them published) and let the songs speak for themselves. Double check your spelling too.

☐ over-packaged materials. Do not use paper towels, napkins, foil or a mountain of tape to package your submission. Make the investment in bubble wrap or padded envelopes.

☐ photos of your parents or children. As much as you love them, your family's pictures or letters of recommendation won't increase your chances of success (unless your family is employed by a major music company).

☐ songs in the style the company doesn't want. Do not "shotgun" your submissions. Read the listings carefully to see if they want your style of music.

YOU CALLED THE CONTACT PERSON:

☐ to check on the submission only a couple days after it was received. Read the listings to see how soon (or if) they report back on submissions. Call them only after that time has elapsed. If they are interested, they will find a way to contact you.

☐ excessively. It's important to be proactive, but check yourself. Make sure you have given them enough time to respond before you call again. Calling every week is inappropriate.

☐ armed with an angry or aggressive tone of voice. A bad attitude will get you nowhere.

WITH THE DEMO YOU PROVIDED:

☐ no lyric sheet. A typed sheet of lyrics for each song is required.

☐ poor vocals and instrumentation. Spending a little extra for professionals can make all the difference.

☐ a poor-quality cassette. The tape should be new and have a brand name.

☐ long intros. Don't waste time—get to the heart of the song.

☐ buried vocals. Those vocals should be out front and clear as a bell.

☐ recordings of sneezes or coughs. Yuck.

SCORING

If you checked 1-3: Congratulations! You're well within the professional parameters. Remedy the unprofessional deeds you're guilty of and send out more packages.

If you checked 4 or more: Whoa! Overhaul your package, let someone check it over, and then fire away with those impeccably professional submissions!

The Business of Songwriting

Familiarizing yourself with standard music industry practices will help you toward your goal of achieving and maintaining a successful songwriting career. The more you know, the less likely you'll be to make a mistake when dealing with contracts, agreements and the other legal and business elements that make up the *business* side of your songwriting career.

COPYRIGHT

Copyright protection is extended to your songs the instant they are put down in fixed form. This protection lasts for your lifetime (or the lifetime of the last surviving author, if you co-wrote the song) plus 70 years. When you prepare demos, place notification of copyright on all copies of your song—the lyric sheets, lead sheets and cassette labels. The notice is simply the word "copyright" or the symbol © followed by the year the song was created (or published) and your name: © 2001 by John L. Public.

Registering your copyright

For the best protection, you may want to consider registering your copyright with the Library of Congress. Although a song is copyrighted whether or not it is registered, registration establishes a public record of your copyright and could prove useful in any future litigation involving the song. Registration also entitles you to a potentially greater settlement in a copyright infringement suit.

To register your song, request government form PA from the Copyright Office. Call the 24-hour hotline at (202)707-9100 and leave your name and address on the recorder. Once you receive the PA form, you will be required to return it, along with a registration fee and a tape or lead sheet of your song, to the Register of Copyrights, Copyright Office, Library of Congress, Washington DC 20559. It may take as long as four months to receive your certificate of registration from the Copyright Office, but your songs are protected from the date of creation, and the date of registration will reflect the date you applied for registration. For additional information about registering your songs, call the Copyright Office's Public Information Office at (202)707-3000 or visit their website at http://lcweb.loc.gov/copyright.

> ### For More Information
> The Library of Congress's copyright website is your best source for current, complete information on the subject of copyright. Not only can you learn all you could possibly wish to know about intellectual property rights and U.S. copyright law (the section of the U.S. Code dealing with copyright is reprinted there in its entirety), but you can also download copyright forms directly from the site. The site also includes links to other copyright-related web pages, many of which will be of interest to songwriters, including ASCAP, BMI, SESAC, and the Harry Fox Agency. Check it out at **http://lcweb.loc.gov/copyright**.

Copyright infringement is rarer than most people think, but if you ever feel that one of your songs has been stolen—that someone has unlawfully infringed on your copyright—you must prove that you created the work. Copyright registration is the best proof of a date of creation. You *must* have your copyright registered in order to file a copyright infringement lawsuit. One way writers prove a work is original is to keep their rough drafts and revisions of songs, either on paper or on tape. (For further information in this book on copyright issues, see Copyright Law: The Primary Source of Your Rights, on page 68.)

Be forewarned there is one potential unintended consequence of registering your song with the Library of Congress. Because copyright registration establishes a public record of your songwriting, unethical music companies, or "song sharks" (see the Rip-Offs on page 23), often search the copyright indexes and mail solicitations to songwriters with registered songs who live out away from the major music centers such as Nashville, and who may not know any better and therefore be easy prey for these unethical companies. *Do not allow this possibility to dissuade you from registering your songs with the copyright office!* Simply be aware and educate yourself about what you should expect from a legitimate ethical music company.

CONTRACTS

You will encounter several types of contracts as you deal with the business end of songwriting. You may sign a legal agreement between you and a co-writer establishing percentages of the writer's royalties each of you will receive, what you will do if a third party (e.g., a recording artist) wishes to change your song and receive credit as a co-writer, and other things. As long as the issues at stake are simple and co-writers respect each other and discuss their business philosophy in advance of writing a song, they can write up an agreement without the aid of a lawyer. In other situations— when a publisher, producer or record company wants to do business with you—you should always have the contract reviewed by a knowledgeable entertainment attorney.

Single song contracts

This is a common contract and is likely to be the first you will encounter in your songwriting career. A music publisher offers a single song contract when he wants to sign one or more of your songs but doesn't want to hire you as a staff writer. You assign your rights to a particular song to the publisher for an agreed-upon number of years (usually the life of the copyright).

Typical components. Every single song contract should contain this basic information: the publisher's name, the writer's name, the song's title, the date and the purpose of the agreement. The songwriter also declares that the song is an original work and he is the creator of the work. The contract must specify the royalties the songwriter will earn from various uses of the song, including performance, mechanical, print and synchronization royalties.

Splits and royalties. The songwriter should receive no less than 50% of the income his song generates. That means that whatever the song earns in royalties, the publisher and songwriter should split 50/50. The songwriter's half is called the "writer's share" and the publisher's half is called the "publisher's share." If there is more than one songwriter, the songwriters split the writer's share. Sometimes successful songwriters will bargain for a percentage of the publisher's share, negotiating what is in fact a co-publishing agreement. For a visual explanation of royalties, see the flow chart on page 12.

"Holds" and reversion clauses. Songwriters should also negotiate for a reversion clause. This calls for the rights to the song to revert to the songwriter if some provision of the contract is not met. The typical reversion clause covers the failure to secure a commercial release of a song within a specified period of time (usually one or two years). If nothing happens with the song, the rights will revert back to the songwriter, who can then give the song to a more active publisher if he so chooses. Some publishers will agree to this, figuring that if they don't get some action on the song in the first year, they're not likely to ever have much luck with it. Other publishers are reluctant to agree to this clause. They may invest a lot of time and money in a song, re-demoing it and pitching it to a number of artists; they may be actively looking for ways to exploit the song. If a producer puts a song on hold for a while and goes into a lengthy recording project, by the time the record company (or artist or producer) decides which songs to release as singles, a year can easily go by. That's why it's so important to have a good working relationship with your publisher. You need to trust that he has your best interests in mind and be flexible if the situation calls for it.

Ten Basic Points Your Contract Should Include

The following list, taken from a Songwriters Guild of America publication, enumerates the basic features of an acceptable songwriting contract:

1. **Work for Hire.** When you receive a contract covering just one composition, you should make sure the phrases "employment for hire" and "exclusive writer agreement" are *not* included. Also, there should be no options for future songs.

2. **Performing Rights Affiliation.** If you previously signed publishing contracts, you should be affiliated with either ASCAP, BMI or SESAC. All performance royalties must be received directly by you from your performing rights organization and this should be written into your contract.

3. **Reversion Clause.** The contract should include a provision that if the publisher does not secure a release of a commercial sound recording within a specified time (one year, two years, etc.), the contract can be terminated by you.

4. **Changes in the Composition.** If the contract includes a provision that the publisher can change the title, lyrics or music, this should be amended so that only with your consent can such changes be made.

5. **Royalty Provisions.** You should receive fifty percent (50%) of all publisher's income on all licenses issued. If the publisher prints and sells his own sheet music, your royalty should be ten percent (10%) of the wholesale selling price. The royalty should not be stated in the contract as a flat rate ($.05, $.07, etc.).

6. **Negotiable Deductions.** Ideally, demos and all other expenses of publication should be paid 100% by the publisher. The only allowable fee is for the Harry Fox Agency collection fee, whereby the writer pays one half of the amount charged to the publisher for mechanical rights. The current rate charged by the Harry Fox Agency is 7.55 cents per cut for songs under 5 minutes; and 1.45 cents per minute for songs over 5 minutes.

7. **Royalty Statements and Audit Provision.** Once the song is recorded, you are entitled to receive royalty statements at least once every six months. In addition, an audit provision with no time restriction should be included in every contract.

8. **Writer's Credit.** The publisher should make sure that you receive proper credit on all uses of the composition.

9. **Arbitration.** In order to avoid large legal fees in case of a dispute with your publisher, the contract should include an arbitration clause.

10. **Future Uses.** Any use not specifically covered by the contract should be retained by the writer to be negotiated as it comes up.

Additional clauses. Other issues a contract should address include whether or not an advance will be paid to the songwriter and how much it will be; when royalties will be paid (quarterly or semiannually); who will pay for demos—the publisher, songwriter or both; how lawsuits against copyright infringement will be handled, including the cost of such lawsuits; whether the publisher has the right to sell the song to another publisher without the songwriter's consent; and whether the publisher has the right to make changes in a song, or approve of changes written by someone else, without the songwriter's consent. In addition, the songwriter should have the right to audit the publisher's books if the songwriter deems it necessary and gives the publisher reasonable notice. (For more information on music publishers, see the Music Publishers section introduction on page 97.)

SGA's Popular Songwriter's Contract. While there is no such thing as a "standard" contract, The Songwriters Guild of America (SGA) has drawn up a Popular Songwriter's Contract which it believes to be the best minimum songwriter contract available. The Guild will send a copy of the contract at no charge to any interested songwriter upon request. (See the Songwriters Guild of America listing in the Organizations section on page 434.) SGA will also review free of charge any contract offered to its members, checking it for fairness and completeness. For a thorough discussion of the somewhat complicated subject of contracts, see these two books published by Writer's Digest Books: *The Craft and Business of Songwriting*, by John Braheny and *Music Publishing: A Songwriter's Guide*, by Randy Poe.

THE RIP-OFFS

As in any business, the music industry has its share of dishonest, greedy people who try to unfairly exploit the talents and aspirations of others. Most of them use similar methods of attack that you can learn to identify and avoid. "Song sharks," as they're called, prey on beginners—those writers who are unfamiliar with ethical industry standards. Song sharks will take any songs—quality doesn't count. They're not concerned with future royalties, since they get their money upfront from songwriters who think they're getting a great deal.

Here are some guidelines to help you recognize these "song sharks":

- **Never pay to have your music "reviewed"** by a company that may be interested in publishing, producing or recording it. Reputable companies review material free of charge.
- **Never pay to have your songs published**. A reputable company interested in your songs assumes the responsibility and cost of promoting them, in hopes of realizing a profit once the songs are recorded and released.
- **Avoid paying a fee to have a publisher make a demo of your songs**. Some publishers may take demo expenses out of your future royalties, but you should reconsider paying upfront for demo costs for a song that is signed to a publisher. See the sidebar Publishers That Charge on the next page for more information.
- **No record company should ask you to make or pay for a demo**. Their job is to make records and decide which artists to sign *after* listening to demo submissions.
- **Never pay to have your lyrics or poems set to music**. "Music mills"—for a price—may use the same melody for hundreds of lyrics and poems, whether it sounds good or not. Publishers recognize one of these melodies as soon as they hear it (see the sidebar If You Write Lyrics, But Not Music on page 10.)
- **Avoid CD compilation deals where a record company asks you to pay a fee** to be included on a CD to be sent to radio stations, producers, etc. It's primarily a money-maker for the company involved, and radio station programmers and other industry professionals just don't listen to these things to find new artists.
- **Read all contracts carefully before signing** and don't sign any contract you're unsure about or that you don't fully understand. It is well worth paying an attorney for the time it takes him to review a contract if you can avoid a bad situation that may cost you thousands of dollars in potential income.
- **Don't pay a company to pair you with a collaborator**. A better way is to contact songwriting organizations that offer collaboration services to their members.
- **Don't sell your songs outright**. It's unethical for anyone to offer such a proposition.
- **If you are asked by a record company or other music-industry company to pay expenses upfront, be careful**. A record producer may charge upfront to produce your record, or a small indie label may ask you to pay recording costs. Each situation is different, and it's up to you to decide whether or not it will be beneficial. Talk to other artists who have signed similar contracts before signing one yourself. Research the company and its track record by finding out what types of product they have released, and what kind of distribution they have. Visit their website on the Internet, if they have one. Beware of any

company that won't let you know what it has done in the past. If it has had successes and good working relationships with other writers and artists, it should be happy to brag about them.

- **Before participating in a songwriting contest, read the rules carefully**. Be sure that what you're giving up in the way of entry fees, etc., is not greater than what you stand to gain by winning the contest. See the Contests & Awards section introduction on page 393 for more advice on this.
- **Verify any situation about an individual or company if you have any doubts at all**. Contact the performing rights society with which it is affiliated. Check with the Better Business Bureau in the town where it is located or the state's attorney general's office. Contact professional organizations you're a member of and inquire about the reputation of the company.

Publishers That Charge

Songwriter's Market feels if a publisher truly believes in you and your music, they will invest in a professional demo. This book only lists publishers that do not charge for this service. If you have found a publisher through this book that charges for demo services, write to the editor at: *Songwriter's Market*, 1507 Dana Ave., Cincinnati OH 45207.

There are smaller publishing companies with demo services as part of their organization. They may request a professional demo and give you the option of using their services or those of an outside company. This doesn't necessarily mean the publishing company is ripping you off. Use your best judgement and know there are many other publishing companies that will not charge for this service.

RECORD KEEPING

As your songwriting career continues to grow, you should keep a ledger or notebook containing all financial transactions relating to your songwriting. It should include a list of income from royalty checks as well as expenses incurred as a result of your songwriting business: cost of tapes, demo sessions, office supplies, postage, traveling expenses, dues to organizations, class and workshop fees and any publications you purchase pertaining to songwriting. It's also advisable to open a checking account exclusively for your songwriting activities, not only to make record keeping easier, but to establish your identity as a business for tax purposes.

Any royalties you receive will not reflect taxes or any other mandatory deductions. It is your responsibility to keep track of income and file the appropriate tax forms. Contact the IRS or an accountant who serves music industry clients for specific information.

INTERNATIONAL MARKETS

Everyone talks about the world getting smaller, and it's true. Modern communication technology has brought us to the point at which information can be transmitted around the globe instantly. No business has enjoyed the fruits of this progress more than the music industry. American music is heard in virtually every country in the world, and having a hit song in other countries as well as in the United States can greatly increase a songwriter's royalty earnings.

While these listings may be a bit more challenging to deal with than domestic companies, they offer additional avenues for songwriters looking for places to place their songs. To find international listings, see the Geographical Index at the back of the book. You might also flip through the pages and look for listings preceded by ⊞ which indicates an international market.

Using the Internet to Get Your Songs Heard

BY CYNTHIA LAUFENBERG

Cynthia Laufenberg

If you're a performing songwriter, the Internet provides infinite possibilities to get your songs heard. You can sell your own CDs on Amazon.com, offer free downloads of your music at MP3.com, and strut your stuff for industry bigwigs at sites like Farmclub.com or LoudEnergy.com. But what if you're not a performer? What if you don't have a CD to sell? What if you're just looking for a publishing deal and want to get your songs cut? Are there resources on the Internet for the non-performing songwriter? Sure there are—you just have to know where to look.

Using the Internet for research and networking

First and foremost, you should look at the Internet as a valuable research tool. It's a great place to research the music industry and network with other songwriters and industry professionals. Brian Austin Whitney, founder of Just Plain Folks (www.jpfolks.com), an organization for songwriters, musicians, and industry professionals, says, "Songwriters should view the Net as a tool in their war chest as opposed to an end-all solution for success. It's a great way to make contacts, research opportunities for appropriate submissions, and learn more about the craft and business of songwriting."

Just about any kind of information for songwriters can be found on the Internet, from free music organizations that you can join to informational sites that provide industry news, updates on trends in the industry, and tips on writing a hit song, finding a collaborator, or recording a demo. There are chat rooms and bulletin boards where songwriters can meet other writers from different parts of the country and the world. David Hooper, President of Kathode Ray Music in Nashville, likens logging onto the Internet to visiting a vast library. "The best thing about the Internet is the trading of information," he says. "You can't learn everything you need to know about the music business from the Net, but it is a good primer."

The amount of information about the music industry and the songwriting community available on the Internet grows every day, and it pays to take advantage of all of the free information provided, no matter what type of music you write. According to Whitney, "You can visit great online resource sites like the Muse's Muse (www.musesmuse.com), read information sites like the Mi2N network (www.Mi2N.com), use the vast services of TAXI, one of the earliest music entities on the Internet (www.taxi.com), set up an info page on MP3.com, and learn all you can directly from the sites of music industry educators like Jason Blume (www.jasonblume.com), among many others."

CYNTHIA LAUFENBERG *was editor of* Songwriter's Market *from 1991-1996. She currently lives in Princeton, New Jersey.*

While the Internet can provide songwriters with an introduction to a world that's beyond their front door, it's important to remember that it can never be as effective as actual face-to-face interaction with people in the industry. "The most successful writers use the tools the Internet offers to supplement their in-person visits and phone calls with publishers, labels, artists and other writers. But, these new tools cannot replace that human contact," Whitney says. "Even the best tool in a mechanic's toolbox can't repair an engine alone. The same principle applies to songwriting success. Songwriters need to learn to use all their tools in concert, adding new technology to their existing arsenal for the greatest possible success."

Jodi Krangle, owner of The Muse's Muse, agrees. "Internet services are great, but they shouldn't take the place of networking in person," she says. "This isn't to say that you should move to Nashville, L.A. or New York. It's only to say that if you have a local songwriting association, get involved with it. Audience feedback is essential to writing good songs. Sharing your songs with others and getting them to tell you what works and what doesn't is also a great way to get to know people with the potential to help you get your music heard. As I always say, it's all about relationships. Go after them— nurture them—and you will ultimately be successful, whether you perform your own songs or not."

Sending e-mails and conducting business from the privacy of your own home can be effective and quick, but don't get complacent with the convenience of electronic communication and forget about the human factor that's so important when networking in the music business. "While you're making contacts and promoting your work, never forget to do all the traditional things that many using the Net have stopped doing," Whitney says. "Send an actual letter, typed and signed by hand, in a real envelope sent to a specific real person as a follow-up. Just as e-mail was a novelty three years ago, sending a real letter—not a form letter—to someone is now a novelty itself. Use that to your advantage. A writer on the Net is at her most powerful when she uses the vast array of Internet and technological tools available but never forgets that human interaction—especially face-to-face—can never be replaced and can never be improved on. Never put all your eggs in one basket—and that goes for the Internet. Be sure to balance e-mails with phone calls and in-person meetings. Balance digital files with actual hardcopy CDs. Balance a general mailing list announcement with a simple personal letter to a specific person. Just as a balanced diet positively affects your health, balanced online and off-line efforts will positively affect the health of your career."

Do you need your own website?

Definitely. A website is like a press kit for the new millennium. Design your own website so interested writers, artists, publishers, and industry professionals can learn about your music and hear your songs. "Purchase your name as a domain name and set up a simple and classy info/bio page. Include a nice photograph," Whitney says, "because pictures humanize the face-lessness of the Internet. Also, learning the very simple basics of making your own website is a must," Whitney says. "And don't be intimidated, because it's much easier than anyone initially thinks, in most cases being as simple as using a word processor. Consider this your online business card/press kit." There are literally hundreds of books available now that can help you set up your own website, no matter what your skill level is (see the sidebar at the end of this article for some book suggestions).

Once you've created a killer website with cool graphics, photos, and biographical information about yourself, you can't just post the lyrics to your songs and expect anyone to pay attention. "A non-performing artist still needs a demo," Krangle says. "Just because they don't perform their own material doesn't mean non-performing artists don't have to set their words and music down in some sort of format others can listen to. It's virtually impossible these days to sell a song based on lyrics alone." And if you can't sing, by all means, don't! Find someone who can and record a professional-sounding demo. "The lead vocal on a demo is hugely important," says Krangle. "Let's face it—if you're wincing through a recording, it'll be a great deal more difficult to hear the song's potential. This doesn't have to cost a lot of money. A tape recorder in someone's living room with a guitar and a friend who has a good voice will do it, or consider having a professionally recorded demo of your best songs done." And be sure to copyright your songs before putting them on the Internet. "It's good to know you have some protection when you're putting your songs on the Internet for a lot of anonymous people to hear," Krangle says.

Learn how to add your own digital files to your website so people can hear that fabulous demo you spent your last two months' salary creating. Hooper finds having a website to go to after he's met with a songwriter can be a valuable way to stay on top of what a writer is doing. "Personally, I don't like to take demos over the Net," he says. "It's great if I was talking to you and you had a website that I could go to and listen to your music."

Using the Internet as a song plugger

You've done your research and know which publishers are interested in the music you write. You've made a fabulous, professional demo of your songs. Your website is up and running, featuring info about you and clips of your songs. Now it's time to start sending out those tapes and making visits to publishers' offices, right? Sure it is. But the Web can also help you pitch your songs to interested parties. Brett Perkins, owner of Brett Perkins Presents and former CEO of the National Academy of Songwriters, sees the Internet as yet another way to pitch songs. "I find one of the greatest tools—which I teach in my workshops—is the sending of song submissions by e-mail sound file to companies seeking songs who list in reputable publications," he says. "It saves time and postage, and often generates a faster response in my experience, evidenced recently by a publisher in the Philippines who liked my e-mailed song, and now we're negotiating for usage by one of their groups." Learn how to download your demos onto the Web for easy access. "One tip for this usage," says Perkins, "is to offer up two forms of download—a standard MP3 and also a faster/lower streaming sample—so the receiver isn't kept waiting." Whitney concurs. "Nothing is faster, cheaper or as easy to duplicate to many recipients as e-mail and digital song files," he says.

Using the Internet, you can discover valuable information about companies who use the type of music you write and what kind of writers they work with. Listen to songs from those artists to get an idea of the quality and style of music they are using. This will also give you an idea of the production value each company may expect from you when you send them a demo of your songs.

Research the companies you want to submit to and contact them via email to introduce yourself, along with a link to your website that features your songs. "Explain that you are sending them a CD or cassette copy of your demo, but wanted them to have access to the songs immediately if it was convenient for them to listen via the Internet," Whitney suggests. "Never assume how your listener wants to receive their music. Instead, send them the link and a real-life copy." Continue to use e-mail to follow up, but don't send spam mail or form letters. "Write short personal notes directly to the person you are building your relationship with," Whitney says. "Only send information to your contacts that is specifically applicable for them, and is compelling for them as well. This means they will benefit by having read this information. If only you benefit, it is a waste of their time."

Not only can you post your songs to your own website for anyone to hear, but you can also post your songs on other sites industry professionals visit to search for new songs. These sites multiply daily, so you need to constantly check the Web to see what's out there and to find the right places for you and your songs. There are many services available on the Internet that will list your songs in a database for industry professionals to search through. Start with the established sites and link from there. Some well-known sites include TAXI (www.taxi.com), which has been around since 1992. It offers a yearly subscription to writers and artists along with personal feedback from top industry professionals. Every two weeks, TAXI members receive an updated list of what people in the industry are looking, giving you the opportunity to pitch your songs to those interested parties. SongScope (www.songscope.com), which bills itself as the "World's First On-Line Independent Songwriter's Song Shopping Catalog," and SongCatalog (www.SongCatalog.com) let you list your catalog of songs on their sites for industry profession-als to access. These are just a few of the sites out there that can help you pitch your songs to industry professionals. However, pay close attention to the fees these sites charge; some charge monthly fees, and others charge per song downloaded. It's up to you to decide what will work best for you.

The Internet offers a variety of ways for non-performing songwriters to get their music heard and into the hands of industry professionals who can get their songs recorded. Research your options wisely to find the best sites and contacts that will help you find the songwriting success you've been searching for!

For More Information
PRINT RESOURCES

Here is a list of books to help you learn more about promoting your songs on the Internet and setting up your own website: Building a Web Site for Dummies, by David and Rhonda Crowder (Hungry Minds, Inc., 2000); Creating Web Pages for Dummies, by Bud E. Smith, Arthur Bebak, and Kevin Werbach (Hungry Minds, Inc., 1999); How to Promote Your Music Successfully on the Internet: The Musicians Guide to Effective Music Promotion on the Internet, by David Nevue (Midnight Rain Productions, 2001); MP3 for Musicians: Promote Your Music Career Online, by John V. Hedtke and Sandy Bradley (Top Floor Publishing, 2000); MP3 for Dummies, by Andy Rathbone (Hungry Minds, Inc., 1999)

Web Resources

This select list of websites for songwriters is only the tip of the iceberg when it comes to promoting your songs online. The Internet is constantly growing and changing, so you need to keep up-to-date on the latest sites.

www.getsigned.com
www.indiebiz.com
www.jpfolks.com
www.mp3.com
www.musesmuse.com
www.songcatalog.com
www.songlink.com
www.songpitch.com
www.songscope.com
www.taxi.comwww.unisong.com

From Development Deals to Work-For-Hire: What Way of Working with a Producer is Best for Me?

BY SCOTT MATHEWS

When considering working with a producer, artists/performing songwriters have an abundance of details to consider about the various way producers function in the industry. My intention is to aim you towards a situation and, eventually, a person who puts the "pro" in "producer" as opposed to sticking you with a Record Reducer.

Scott Mathews

THE BASICS

The two most common approaches to production agreements are:

A) Development Deals—also commonly referred to as Production Deals or "Spec" Deals (as in "speculative") and;

B) Work-For-Hire

From here, it boils down to the two big career questions: which road is the least bumpy when you are getting started? And which is in your best long-term interest? Both types of production agreements have successfully matched artists and producers, and they have each resulted in lasting creative relationships. But, each type of agreement is structured differently, and each contains different provisions. In the case of a Development Deal, the artist is contractually obligated to continue with the producer (or a producer assigned to them). In a Work-For-Hire arrangement, the artist can choose to stay with the producer or work with other producers on future projects. No one type of agreement will fit all situations. The production agreement you choose depends on your individual goals as an artist, songwriter and performer.

DEVELOPMENT DEALS

As an artist signing a Development Deal, you ink an agreement with the *production company*. There are definite pros and cons to this course of action, but one important feature must always be understood: by signing, the artist is beholden to whatever deal the producer and his production

---

Multi-platinum contributor **SCOTT MATHEWS** *has produced, recorded or performed with a wide range of artists including John Hiatt, Van Morrison, Ry Cooder and John Lee Hooker. His film music credits include* One Flew Over the Cuckoo's Nest *and* Wag the Dog. *His songs have been cut by Barbra Streisand and Dave Edmunds. See his listing in this book in the Record Producers section.*

company decide to make for release of his or her product. In effect, the production company assigns you to your future by choosing how to get you there. You sign to them and THEY sign with the record company (or in some cases, put it out themselves). Now, if the production company is in the driver's seat with this much control, it follows that in slicing up the royalty pie from a record label, they will serve themselves a hefty portion before dishing out the artist's take, and the flow of royalties is typically something like this: record company to production company to artist to landlord. Other royalty arrangements are rare and not easy to negotiate.

These deals are also usually constructed to be in effect for an extended length of time, sometimes several years. Again, like everything else in this biz, these terms are negotiable, but expect most offers of this type to be a long-term commitment.

But let's have a look at the bright side. A Development Deal offers to get the project up and running. How would you feel if I offered the services of myself, my engineer and staff, as well as all the studio time you needed, but you didn't have to sink any money into the recording costs of your demo, press package, CD duplications and the like? Too good to be true? No. This offer to "front" costs is commonly made available and is by far the most positive aspect of the Development Deal from the artist's point of view. It is, initially, taking the easy (sometimes ONLY) way to get things done—but it can be a complex and trying agreement when you want to maintain creative control and establish a fair artist/producer royalty structure (along with a contract addressing other concerns, including ownership of masters and song publishing rights). It can be a rude awakening for unwary artists when they find their career is essentially in someone else's clutches.

A Warning to the Unwary

As a case in point to illustrate the dangers of signing a Development Deal without careful consideration, I used to teach record production, songwriting and a music industry class at San Francisco State University. One of my most gifted students stayed in touch with me and, at age 23, landed a Development Deal with a major label (labels, sometimes functioning as very large production and development companies, in some cases offer a similar sort of contract). She called me up to ask if I wanted to participate in the record. We got together, did a bit of writing and prepared for what we thought would be a fun project. I found her unique approach to melodies, lyrics and vocals to be stunning. Her stage show was incredible. She was like a new Joni Mitchell!

But, instead of supporting her own vision of her artistic development, her label went right to work on changing her upon signing a deal. She had her own style and the label began watering it down with "safer, more common" approaches, including dance and country. Long story short, she's in a contract she can't get out of, is working a day job again, and owes big bucks to the record company. She is finally working on the record after four years. I hope there is a happy ending.

On the other hand, if we are talking about a successful producer who has been around awhile and worked with some heavyweight artists, they will obviously have some clout and credibility with record companies. A&R and producers have a two-way relationship. Labels constantly bring me artists they want me to produce and, conversely, they often look to me to find new artists to sign. If I show enough enthusiasm to take on an unknown, unsigned artist, labels want to know about it. It is a privileged position that can take years to cultivate but is essential for a long and strong career in the industry as a producer. In some cases, since my company does most of its own A&R work (quite frankly, I trust my own ears to find talent more than most "corporate ears") labels often offer situations where I can bring X amount of artists with finished master recordings, and have their records paid for and released. (In my case, I choose not to get mixed up in the aforementioned Development Deal's strict guidelines—I have my own "artist friendly" formula—but all producers have their own way of working.) In an ideal situation, producers favoring this type of arrangement can pass along their well-earned position to their well-deserving artists, and all can benefit.

WORK-FOR-HIRE

In a Work-For-Hire arrangement, one possible scenario has an artist (with their own funds or with part of their advance from a label deal) paying the producer on a "project rate" basis where the time and services needed to deliver a specific number of finished masters is figured into one lump sum to be paid by the artist (a Work-For-Hire deal brokered by a record label also sometimes includes paying the producer a small part of the artist's subsequent percentage of royalties from record sales—referred to as "points"). This is also sometimes known as an "All-In" deal. But, never forget, whether you are signed to a label or not, the money spent on a producer's fees and points is always out of the artist's end. (The money flow on a Work-For-Hire deal is usually like this: record company to artist to producer to cigars.)

When entering into this type of agreement, a detailed budget and schedule needs to be drawn up. Otherwise, the scam producer could simply phone in a couple of sessions and pronounce his job finished. (On the other hand, the insecure artist could in effect own a producer for life by perpetually claiming the production is unfinished.) The key is to know the producer's history and make sure there have been many successful project rate-type deals under their belt. You should have an entertainment attorney negotiate a fair time schedule, a fair fee and points structure (usually 3 or 4 points—considerably less than Development Deals) and all other areas of concern, defining both parties' interests and expectations.

In some cases, productions can get bigger as time goes on. The London Philharmonic might not have been part of the plan at first, but if you wish to continue adding more things than were originally stated and budgeted for, most producers will continue with the project by charging a "day rate."

PRODUCERS—WHO NEEDS THEM ANYWAY?

So, you're a cool artist, maybe even a great songwriter. But do you know how to take what you've got and make the most brilliant presentation on record? You might, but it takes a whole lot more than simply having a focused direction on songs, style and approach.

Most artists find it overly taxing to deal with much of the extra work involved in running a session—all the, shall we say, "less than creative" administrative drone labor, including but not limited to: scheduling, choosing studios, recording formats, studio players/singers, guest artists, rental cars, cartage, food, accommodations, flights—and of course being the accountant/point person to pay all of these parties and keep within the limitations of the recording budget and serve as liaison to the label (that alone is sometimes a full-time job!). Early in the process, one realizes it is an ongoing, time-consuming effort to maintain happy relations, report back on the progress of the sessions and keep the almighty dollar flowing. As a producer, I work hard to protect my artists from all the outside distractions that can creep into their creative bubble. Time spent in the studio is golden and I know if it is spent unwisely, it is money out of the artist's pocket and possibly a career out of their reach. So, to see that through, collaborating with a like-minded producer is often key to a successful outcome.

Still, some artists want to produce themselves and some of them absolutely should. As a producer, I need to know which of my artists lean that way before I go into the studio with them. I have had the experience where the pre-production meetings go smoothly and everyone is in agreement, but when the sessions begin and it's time to roll tape, things change and every-thing goes south. I may find out the bass player (or better yet, the girlfriend) resents that he is forced to listen to someone else's opinion or, in other words, be put in the position of being produced. It may be this person has previously produced some serious four-track cassette masters in his closet and now secretly sees himself as Sir George Martin. In short, an artist's ego can be bigger than our common goal if their position is that it's their music therefore no one else has the right to stick their nose (let alone ear) in it.

I've become good at detecting this huff early on, because if I miss it, helping them subsequently focus their music and energy is like pulling teeth without laughing gas. I am in the business (and I hope to speak for all reputable producers) of collaboration, so that the artist may shine the brightest, but that takes the artist's participation and cooperation.

In other circumstances, labels and artists are interested in name recognition of the producer, regardless of the producer's actual level of participation. It's like, "Here take this sack of money, we are going to list you as producer so people will take notice of us. No need to show up. Oh yeah, how many points do you want?"

To be fair, the reverse happens as well. Some producers (I know of more than a couple) who still have some kind of "name," take huge advances, limo the artist around, make the photo ops, pick up the tab at the restaurant, and yet somehow can't find time in their hectic schedule to be physically present at the artist's recording sessions.

Do your homework. It may be the producer you are seeking to sign with is overseeing four or five other projects at once. Production is a day-to-day, moment-to-moment gig. You deserve and should demand your producer's sole attention during your involvement with him or her.

WHO DO YOU LOVE?

There are as many different producers as there are versions of Michael Jackson's nose and each one has a different way of working and getting results. Bob Dylan doesn't need the same producer as Britney Spears, or vice versa.

When choosing a producer, it's like any other important partner—mutual respect is the big feature. One has to be nothing short of an absolute fan of the other's gifts and work. But, when it all boils down, there has to be chemistry. Great chemistry in the studio is what makes great records. I have seen far too many big budget deals fall into the hands of the wrong producer and the fallout is scary. What looks good on paper may sound dreadful on CD.

So, if you come up with the right stuff with your producer, my best advice is to hold on to him or her for as long as things keep working. Labels love to see teams already formed (more on that in a bit), and holding that partnership together after signing can be crucial, because the sound, vibe and feel you conjure with this person is part of what the label is signing. When a band abruptly switches producers, it can upset the apple cart because the "fifth member" of the band is missing. As a producer, I become a trusted new ear and helping hand within the band when I come on board. If by some slip the winning team falls apart, it can get real ugly real quick.

As an illustration, I once produced a "baby" band for next to nothing. In doing so, we ended up with a hot little tape that made the rounds and started a bidding war between major labels. The band and I were thrilled with all that had happened. After all, when they (the oldest member being twenty, only a handful of songs to their name, and even less gigs ever played) signed a multi-record deal for well in excess of $1,000,000, what's not to dig? I figured logic would prevail and I would naturally be continuing my role as producer of the band, since in fact the signing was based on the strength of the work we had done together.

The band that just a week before had been bumming for bus fare was soon in LA on their way to their first official A&R meeting, sans producer, in the back of a well-stocked limo. Fair to say the band is slightly seduced by the time their A&R man opens that week's *Billboard* magazine and marks brackets around the Top 10. He says, "OK, let's pick your new producer! We believe so much in this band, the sky's the limit, our whole team is behind you." All fingers point to the #1 spot. "Let's get that guy!"

They place a call to "that guy's" manager and discover "that guy" is committed to other projects for months to come. But, how lucky they were, the engineer on the #1 record is readily available and "knows all the tricks they used."

"We'll take him! More champagne!" With stars in their eyes, that band ends up spending the better part of a year laboring over their big debut. Advance copies are sent to radio stations. No action. An instant stiff. Stand-in Producer Mr. #1 had somehow, through the miracles of modern recording, siphoned every nuance, hook, charm and appeal out of the music and delivered a vapid, "who cares?" version of a once compelling and promising band.

Next, I got a call from the label. "We're in a spot. The band and label likes your demos better than the finished record and would like to release them as singles." I agreed to the release of one song. The song charted, but they needed to sell beyond platinum to get out of the "Rock Star" hole they had dug.

In the end, their budget was spent and so were their careers. A million-and-a-half in the red, the band was dropped from the label, imploded under the pressure and disbanded. That was their shot. With that short but sordid past, nobody would touch them after that.

THE 'FIT' or, IF IT DON'T FIT, IT'LL SOUND LIKE ****

If an artist can align with the right producer and sound before making a record deal, things run much smoother and there is much less chance of losing creative control, money and time. More and more, there is an emphasis on "self-contained" artists. This used to mean strictly artists that wrote their own material, but is now broadening to include artists with their own signature sound, which usually means a producer is already in place. Most labels see a good marriage between an artist and a producer as a great plus. They don't have to waste time setting up artists on expensive dates or use up their "imagination" on trying to pair up artists and producers.

The Fix in the Mix

As a side note, much of what happens in the studio by the producer to shape the band's sound ends up being used on stage when the band tours. Obviously, arrangement ideas and such are used, but sometimes actual backing tracks and vocals are sampled from the CD and stuck in to beef up what would otherwise be a weaker sound without some help. It's actually getting quite common. Hey, I want a percentage of the gate now!

But, it's all about the right fit. Don't be tricked into working (and especially signing!) with someone your instincts tell you not to. There are indeed scummy scam artists out there, preying on desperate artists who will soon be praying to get out of their deals!

So, go out and get a reputable producer who "gets" you. That means they see the potential you have and can make real strides to help you realize it. The right producer could be a newcomer just starting out, or it might be some grey geezer with a track record as long as James Brown's arrest record. But, no matter what, you must "get" each other and enjoy each other's company. Good chemistry between any artist and producer is a must. Find someone you can trust, give your best to, communicate freely with and (important to me) share a sense of humor with (it comes in handy). Hours are long and rooms are small. Bathe before each session, show up fed, choose your battles well, wear cool clothes, don't record until you have songs that are worthy, and when you connect and feel you've cut a hit, immediately go on a massive shopping spree for good luck.

See ya on the charts, baby!

Taking Stock & Making Plans: Advice for Long-Distance Nashville Songwriters

BY JIM MELKO

"If you want to become a successful songwriter in Nashville, you gotta move here!" If you're an aspiring songwriter who has ever visited or even called Nashville, you have undoubtedly heard that statement many times. But if you're never going to make that move, must you give up the dream of success at songwriting?

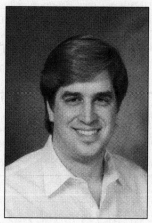

Jim Melko

No, but recognize that no one gives any special breaks to the out-of-towner, that you have to compete with the very best professional songwriters in Nashville, and you have much less access to the people you need to see. To make it in "Music City" without actually living there, you must:

- make a careful assessment of where you stand,
- figure out what you need to achieve,
- and plan carefully for achieving it.

Success in Nashville is rarely just around the corner. It lies at the top of a long flight of stairs. This article is intended to help you figure out where you are on that staircase and what steps you need to take to move closer to the top. In the following sections, *choose the level for each category that best describes you, and develop realistic goals and deadlines based upon the recommendations for that level.*

CRAFT & QUALITY
Level one

You enjoy your own songs, but you have never played them for anyone other than family and friends. You do not belong to any songwriters' groups, and your songs have never been critiqued by someone truly knowledgeable in the craft.

What to Do

☑ If you haven't already joined NSAI, that should be your first step. The Nashville Songwriters Association International (NSAI) is dedicated to educating songwriters around the world in the craft and business of songwriting, and it provides a wealth of resources and information. I believe becoming a member of NSAI is critical to the long-distance writer's chances of success.

JIM MELKO *has been a staff writer for a Nashville publisher and has also been a co-ordinator since 1993 for the Songwriters Workshop at SouthBrook, the Dayton/Cincinnati chapter for NSAI (Nashville Songwriters Association International). See the NSAI listing in the Organizations section of this book.*

☑ If you are an NSAI member, you need to make regular use of the NSAI critiquing service. NSAI members may send in a song on cassette along with a lyric sheet, and a professional songwriter will record his or her critique on the tape itself.

☑ Set the goal of having a song submitted for critiquing at all times; as soon as one is returned, send the next one in. If necessary, submit even old songs of dubious quality; you may find that the critiquer finds something worth salvaging from them.

☑ Consult with NSAI and find out if there is a local area workshop in proximity to you. If not, then consider forming your own (contact NSAI for more information). There may also be non-NSAI local groups in your area (check with your local colleges, newspapers, music stores, and radio stations); the important thing is to find one that maintains high standards for song critiques.

☑ If there is a workshop nearby, attend regularly. If you truly want to become successful in songwriting, don't confuse inconvenient with impossible! Make your personal schedule bend around your workshop schedule, and do not allow your non-songwriting obligations to limit your ability to attend on a regular basis.

Level two

You have been submitting songs fairly often to NSAI, and you present songs regularly at a local workshop. The feedback almost always includes suggestions for improvement, often requiring major structural changes.

What to Do

☑ Rewrite! Rewrite! Rewrite! Then, resubmit! Far too many writers go on to write new songs without seriously attempting to rewrite songs that were critiqued. Until you learn to improve your songs, you will not learn how to write them properly from the start.

☑ Collaborate with other writers at your level or slightly above your level of writing.

☑ Visit Nashville and get feedback from publishers and the performing rights organizations (ASCAP, BMI, and SESAC).

Level three

You have been submitting songs fairly often to NSAI and to your local group, and the feedback is positive. The criticisms you receive don't tend to require major rewrites, and the NSAI critiques keep saying things like, "This one is almost there."

What to Do

☑ Attend one of the NSAI Song Camps.

☑ Start working with collaborators who are better in some ways than you. (Skip down to the sections below concerning discipline and Nashville networking.)

☑ Remember: *You may be "almost there" but there are probably many new levels of development ahead of you.*

PRODUCTIVITY

Level one

You love to write a song but can't find the time to do it often. You must feel inspired to write. You are amazed to hear of professionals who write a song or more a day. Your biggest problem seems to be your inability to finish a song, which you manage to do only every two or three months. You believe you have creative cycles that at their peaks allow you to be highly productive, and at their lows render you incapable of writing anything.

What to Do

☑ Set aside one night a week—or more—that is absolutely your time to work on music.

☑ Ask your family or friends to challenge you to make effective use of that time, to help you avoid procrastinating or being lazy.

☑ If you can collaborate with someone, meet regularly and agree upon the mutual goal of finishing what you start.

☑ Work on revisions as soon as possible after receiving critiques.

☑ Attend local workshops on a regular basis.

☑ Remember: *If you can write songs, you can become a disciplined writer. It's simply a behavior, a habit, not an innate talent or disposition.*

Level two

You have several unfinished songs at any time, but you also finish at least a song or two a month. You maintain a regular time for writing and squeeze more writing in at other times. You have a few collaborators at your level of quality, and hopefully at least one who is much better. You still cope with "creative cycles," but they are shorter in duration and you can "turn on" your creativity when you collaborate. You have at least one or two songs that received positive critiques suggesting only minor revisions, but you have not made professional demos of your songs.

What to Do

☑ Set up a regular routine just for finishing projects—late at night after everyone is in bed, or extra early in the morning, maybe an hour before you go to work.

☑ Discipline yourself either to finish a song or to make significant progress every time.

☑ Get your finished songs professionally demoed. Demos provide a sense of completion, allowing you to look ahead to the new songs you will write.

Level three

You either have a regular work schedule for songwriting, or you spend a significant amount of writing throughout the week. Several projects are underway at any time, but you are also adept at finishing them. Most writers you know are willing to collaborate with you because they respect your craft and ability. You have several professionally produced demos.

What to Do

☑ If most of your best songs are already published through single-song contracts, concentrate on writing new and better songs to build your available catalog.

☑ Use your contacts to find Nashville collaborators.

☑ When your catalog is better developed, meet with the writer relations professional at your performing rights organization and ask for referrals and advice.

☑ Develop friendships within the music business, at least one professional contact willing to meet with you over a meal or after business hours.

BUSINESS KNOWLEDGE
Level one

You know little about the music business. You're not sure how much money a hit song makes, but you suspect that one could set you up for life. You don't really know how a staff writing position works. If you were to make a trip to Nashville, you wouldn't know what to do. You are unable to name many hit songwriters or publishers.

What to Do

☑ Browse through the music business sections in your local bookstore, buy books and read them. NSAI offers several books to its members through its bookstore.

☑ Look through *Songwriter's Market* for publishers with cuts by recognizable artists, and read the articles.

☑ Attend an NSAI Symposium this year. The Symposium is rich in information about the music business, and you'll be surrounded by long-distance songwriters like yourself. NSAI also sponsors Tin Pan South, a week in which the very best songwriters perform every night in several clubs throughout Nashville, allowing you to become familiar with the most respected songwriters in the industry.

Level two

You've read a few books and understand how the business works. You've attended at least one NSAI symposium and met with one or two publishers, or with someone at the performing rights organizations.

What to Do

☑ Attend more Symposiums in Nashville.

☑ Read the trade journals such as *Billboard* and track writers and publishers whose songs appear on the charts. Try to see those publishers.

☑ Set up appointments to get feedback and talk about your aspirations with writers relations staff at ASCAP, BMI, and SESAC.

☑ Get a "feel" for the competition. Visit Nashville as frequently as possible and go to see acts at the Bluebird Café and other establishments that feature songwriters.

Level three

You know the business directly through your relationships with publishers and the performing rights organizations. You've attended several NSAI symposiums, and much of what's presented is "old hat" to you.

What to Do

☑ Start using your connections. Determine the kind of publisher you want to have, and begin cultivating the relationships which interest you most. Remember that *Nashville is built on friendships*. It's not enough to be a name or face the publisher will recognize; you need to become friends with the publisher.

☑ Have an entertainment attorney lined up now to consult with quickly if you are offered a contract.

EXPOSURE
All levels

You should be able to play an instrument and perform your songs if at all possible. There are professional writers who are unable to play an instrument or perform, but none of them would regard their lack of skill as an advantage.

☑ Perform locally and learn to entertain and read how your audiences react to your songs. Once you're comfortable on stage, participate in open mic nights in Nashville and audition for establishments like the Bluebird Café where writers can showcase their material.

☑ Consider entering songwriting contests. While such contests are not likely to make you an overnight success, they can improve your confidence, win you the attention of other writers and any involved reputable publishers, and of course earn you money or prizes. However, Songwriting contests can create problems with your copyright ownership if they are not reputable, so be very cautious about entering them.

☑ It is likewise unlikely you will earn a hit record through "cassette roulette" — sending song submissions to publishers through the mail with their permission. Nevertheless, it is possible that you might capture the interest of a publisher and begin a relationship that could prove beneficial later on. If you aren't visiting Nashville regularly and you have no special contacts, cassette roulette is certainly better than nothing. However, *never submit through the mail without first obtaining permission.* Your call to obtain that permission can be the start of a relationship.

NETWORKING
Level one
You've never visited publishers or the performing rights organizations in Nashville.

What to Do

☑ If the quality of your work is at Level One as described earlier, this is probably not the time for you to visit publishers or the performing rights organizations. You need to be writing songs of sufficient quality to show a publisher that you are serious and have some promise. Instead, use the NSAI critiquing process and your local workshop critiques to improve your quality to Level Two. If you have good contacts, save them; *don't blow them by presenting inferior material!*

☑ If you are at higher levels of quality, start making the trip. Make an appointment with writer's relations staff at BMI, ASCAP, and SESAC. If one believes you're ready, he or she will refer you to publishers. At the least you'll get some good advice.

☑ Use *Songwriter's Market* to find publishers who will meet with you and listen to your songs. Even if you are not offered a contract, you should consider your visit a success if you are at least invited to come back when you have new material.

☑ If you can get in to see the publisher at companies with major hits, be careful to present yourself well. Cultivate those relationships as well as the ones you establish with the still struggling publishers. You never know which relationships could pay off later.

☑ If you've been procrastinating about visiting Nashville, ask yourself why. Is it because you are afraid to face rejection? If so, then you are indeed facing a major crisis because you will not find success without making the visits, and you will suffer a lot of rejection. *Rejection is the only constant in the business of songwriting!*

Level two
You've made some visits to Nashville and you've been invited to revisit some publishers when you have new material. You have contacts in the performing rights organizations who will meet with you when you're in town. You've not yet earned a publishing contract.

What to Do

☑ Work hard on developing the quality of your songs, and maintain regular contact with your publishing contacts both by phone and in person. Your publishing contacts want to know if you are serious, so don't disappoint them or procrastinate.

☑ If you are eventually offered a single-song contract, enjoy the experience and the excitement of knowing that success could happen at any time. But keep in mind, too, that publishers sometimes offer such contracts more for the sake of encouraging you to come back and to see what you will be able to do next.

Level three
You've earned a few single-song contracts either with a single publisher or with several, but no staff contract seems to be on the horizon. You may be frustrated that no one has heard your

entire catalog because the best songs have been awarded contracts and scattered among various publishers.

What to Do

☑ Your contacts at your performing rights organization would probably be willing at this stage to sit down and review a more comprehensive presentation of your work, including already published songs. Nevertheless, you need to have a catalog of both strong and available songs if you are going to earn a staff contract.

☑ Stop signing individual contracts and work hard on developing your catalog.

☑ When your catalog is ready, use your résumé of publishing contracts to open new doors to other publishers.

Conclusion

There is a saying in Nashville that "a good song will find its way." In that philosophy is hope for the long-distance songwriter who believes that merit can prevail over geographical location. But a good song isn't really "good" unless it's heard—and it will only find its way among the people who hear it. For the Nashville resident, it's much easier to believe in that saying because the song is already in the right place to be heard. But if you don't live there, you need to make your own way before your song will ever have the chance it needs to break through the long-distance barrier.

Taking the Labor Out of Collaboration: From Creation to Realization

BY BILL PERE

Look at the credits for a song and you most likely see more than one name. Having multiple writers, artists, producers and engineers is not unusual in navigating the path from creation to realization. The music business, like any entertainment industry, is a business based on people interacting to shape and market the products of a creative process.

Bill Pere

WHAT IS COLLABORATION

Collaboration literally means "working together." Any time two or more people combine their efforts toward a common goal, they are collaborating. This happens at all phases in the life of a song—writing, revision, arranging, performance, recording and marketing. No one person is likely to do all of these things with great success. Collaboration is most often mentioned in terms of creating the music and lyrics of a song, but any time a writer interacts in a mutual way with an artist, arranger, studio engineer, agent, etc., they are collaborating. But, it is important not to confuse the *process* of collaboration with the *form* of the agreement governing that process.

Whenever multiple people contribute to any part of the marketable property, some kind of understanding is necessary as to how credit and payments are to be shared. If you simply hire someone to record your song, arrange it or market it, you typically negotiate a work-for-hire arrangement. This means the person you hire has no ownership interest in the actual copyright. However, your interaction with that person can certainly be collaborative in nature if it involves mutual input. When you work together with a studio engineer and a vocalist to record your song, you are collaborating with them even though they receive a one-time flat fee and have no claim of ownership on the song.

In the actual writing of a song, all the contributors have an ownership in the copyright, but if a creator agrees to exchange his or her interest for an up-front payment, there is nothing wrong with that. Thus, the nature of a collaborative interaction may be governed by whatever business terms the parties agree to. The important things are to be sure that:

BILL PERE *is an official Connecticut State Troubador, serves as Director of Special Projects for the* Connecticut Songwriters Association, *edits* Connecticut Songsmith, *and also is a member of the Music Educators National Conference.*

- all parties feel they are being treated fairly
- the value of their contribution is adequately recognized and compensated
- agreements are written down in clear and precise language

WHERE DO I FIND A COLLABORATOR?

Ideal places to meet collaborators include:
- Songwriter Associations
- Songwriter conferences and workshops
- Trade magazines and newsletters
- Internet bulletin boards
- Local music stores
- Local performance venues

Geography need not be a factor. Collaboration can occur by phone, fax, mail or e-mail. However, when it comes to resolving the inevitable differences of opinion, there is no substitute for face-to-face interaction.

THE HUMAN FACTORS

In addition to the business side of collaborating, there is the all-important human side. The process of collaboration can go a long way toward enhancing your creative output, but it can also be a source of great stress and frustration. How can you attune yourself to spot potential collaborators who will raise the quality of your creative endeavors while avoiding partnerships that will simply raise your blood pressure? Just because a person has a proven track record, does not necessarily make them a good collaborator for you. Can a person who has never had a song published be the catalyst you need to write the next chart-topper? Bands are by nature, collaborative units. Bands tend to break up or be held back because of human interaction issues probably more than for any other reason.

There are several keys to success in the human aspects of collaboration:
- aligned goals
- complementary skills
- compatible personalities
- respect for different views and approaches

Goals

Before entering into a collaboration agreement with someone, be absolutely sure you both are working toward the same goals. If you want a commercial hit while your partner wants a self-expressive classical symphony, it is going to be difficult to have a satisfactory final product. You may not want to formally collaborate with someone who is heading in a different direction than you are, but be aware that talking and bouncing ideas off someone who is of a different mind-set can give you new ideas as well. Differentiate between a collaborative partner and people who are good sources of creative inspiration.

Skills

Collaboration causes the least friction when the strengths of each participant are complementary, i.e. each contributes something the others cannot. If you are only a lyricist, you need a composer. If you can write and play but not sing, you need a vocalist. If you can write and perform but are not technologically adept, you need an engineer. Those are obvious pairings, but can two people with the same skills work together? The answer is yes, if they approach their craft from different perspectives, and if each sees the different view as a source of new ideas rather than as an obstacle. In short, it's a matter of understanding and respecting the differences between people, which of course leads to . . .

Personalities

People are obviously quite complex, but based on decades of extensive research, there are four dimensions which, when taken in their various combinations, explain a wide range of human interaction.

These four aspects of personality have a profound effect on how we relate to people and to the world around us, both as a giver and receiver of communications and actions. For people who communicate through songwriting and/or performing, who give or receive critique, and who interact with the business aspects of music, these dimensions play a crucial role.

In each of the four areas shown below, people have a natural preference for being on one side or the other, much like being left-handed or right-handed. Neither is "better" than the other—they are just different. Many situations in life require we act in a manner opposite our natural preference. The stronger the preference is for one style over the other, the more effort it takes to act the other way, and sometimes it is just not possible, despite our best effort.

Thus, a person's preference profile can be represented by four letters, one from each area described in the shaded sidebar below. There are sixteen combinations in all. This does not mean there are only sixteen types of people. Two folks with the same four preferences can be very different based on their values and life experiences. Still, there will be certain tendencies in common that clue us in as to what it might be like to work with a particular person. The importance of these four areas is widely researched and based on the Myers-Briggs Type Indicator (MBTI). See the references at the end of this article for further information. As you read the brief descriptions, think of how many people you know, including yourself, whom they reflect.

The four personality preference dimensions (Extroversion vs. Introversion/Sensing vs. Intuition/Thinking vs. Feeling/Judging vs. Perceiving), represented by pairs of letters, are described in the sidebar below:

It's no surprise people with different preferences may have difficulty dealing with each other. Introverts often say extroverts talk too much, are draining and don't mind their own business. Extroverts often say introverts are uncommunicative, unsociable or just plain strange.

Sensors may say iNtuitives are impractical and have their heads in the clouds. Intuitives may say Sensors are boring, hung up on trivia, full of 'small talk' and lacking in vision. The S/N difference can drive a great wedge between people—how can they communicate if they don't see the same things to begin with, yet are both right in what they see?

Feelers can view Thinkers as cold, distant, aloof and uncaring. Thinkers can view Feelers as irrational, illogical, emotional, inconsistent and trying hopelessly to please everybody.

For Judgers and Perceivers, just think of The Odd Couple, Oscar Madison and Felix Ungar.

Before being too quick to criticize someone who is your opposite, keep in mind that if they are weak in an area where you are strong, then they are strong in an area where you are weak. For example, all Judging and no Perceiving is a ship at full sail with no rudder. *It takes qualities of all eight facets to write good songs and market them to an audience.*

- **Introversion** provides the internal reflection that allows ideas to form and a song to be born.
- **Extroversion** provides the drive to share that song with others and want others to relate to it.
- **Sensing** provides information about the world that gives concrete subject matter for songs; it also provides the detail that makes a lyric accessible to the senses.
- **Intuition** provides creative association for presenting a topic in a new and fresh way, for giving a lyric depth of meaning, and for providing a coherent, overarching metaphor. Intuition is a wellspring of the creative process for songwriting.
- **Feeling** provides the emotion that is a centerpiece of most lyrics and is a universal form of expression, despite its subjective imprecision.
- **Thinking** provides the analysis and crafting needed to give polish an impact to a song; it

The Four Dimensions of Personality Preference

HOW WE FOCUS OUR ENERGY: EXTROVERSION(E) VS. INTROVERSION(I)

Extroversion: 50% of the population	Introversion: 50% of the population
☑ Outward focus	☑ Inward focus
☑ Speaks and acts first, thinks later	☑ Thinks before speaking or acting
☑ Seeks social interaction for energy	☑ Social interaction is draining
☑ At ease in crowds	☑ Recharges self by turning inward
☑ Action-oriented	☑ Reflective, has "inner voice"
☑ Talks loudly	☑ Speaks softly
☑ Deals with conflicts openly	☑ Deals with conflict privately
☑ Many broad friendships	☑ Fewer, deeper friendships
☑ Prefers talking to writing	☑ Prefers writing to talking

WHAT WE PAY ATTENTION TO OR PERCEIVE: SENSING(S) VS. INTUITION(N)

Sensing: 70% of the population	iNuition: 30% of the population
☑ Pays attention to details	☑ Pays attention to "big picture"
☑ Focus on trees instead of forest	☑ Focus on forests instead of trees
☑ Focus on the concrete, specific	☑ Focus on concepts and abstraction
☑ Sensory data taken at face value	☑ Sensory data associated with other data to make ideas ("What if . . .?")
☑ Follows established ways of working	☑ Improvises own methods, procedures
☑ Likes what is real and tangible	☑ Likes what is possible
☑ Lives in the present	☑ Looks to the future
☑ Prefers sequential steps to big leaps	☑ Takes leaps of faith
☑ Language is for practical use	☑ Language is a toy—puns, paradoxes

HOW WE MAKE DECISIONS OR JUDGE: THINKING(T) VS. FEELING(F)

Thinking: 50% of Males, 40% of Females	Feeling: 50% of Males, 60% of Females
☑ Makes decisions based on logic	☑ Logic is optional
☑ Evaluates things rationally	☑ Evaluates based on how people will feel
☑ Objective	☑ Subjective
☑ Justice and fairness	☑ Compassion and humanity
☑ Words and actions are measured	☑ Words and actions show emotion
☑ Rules and laws, then circumstances	☑ Circumstances, then rules and laws
☑ "What do you think about this?"	☑ "How do you feel about this?"
☑ Detached	☑ Involved
☑ Critiques things	☑ Appreciates things
☑ Seeks what is true	☑ Seeks what is involved
☑ Direct	☑ Tactful

WHAT WE SHOW THE OUTSIDE WORLD: JUDGING(J) VS. PERCEIVING(P)

Judging: 50% of the population	Perceiving: 50% of the population
☑ Planning and scheduling	☑ Spontaneity
☑ Resolve pending tasks	☑ Leave things "open-ended"
☑ One sequential task at a time	☑ Bounce between many tasks at once
☑ Makes lists and sticks to them	☑ Makes lists, loses or changes them
☑ Draws conclusions and makes decisions based on available data	☑ Delays conclusions and decisions to wait for more data

The Four Dimensions of Personality Preference—Continued

WHAT WE SHOW THE OUTSIDE WORLD: JUDGING(J) VS. PERCEIVING(P)

Judging: 50% of the population	Perceiving: 50% of the population
☑ Harder to change direction once decided	☑ Changes direction easily
☑ Needs order; bothered by things out of place	☑ Not bothered by disorder or randomness
☑ Things filed, not piled	☑ Things piled, not filed
☑ Feels pressure of time	☑ Elastic sense of time
☑ Punctual, dislikes being late	☑ "You mean it's that late already?"
☑ Stays focused	☑ Easily distracted

also lends precision to change expression into communication.

- **Judging** provides the desire for structure and order in the song, and the drive to get it done.
- **Perception** provides the openness to new ideas and the ability to change and rewrite as better words and phrases come along.

Can one person do all eight things effectively? We inevitably do four of them better than the other four, and usually one of those emerges as our primary strength. It requires collaboration to cover all the bases.

Preference profiles and pairing up

When all four dimensions are taken together, a person's preference profile can be represented by four letters, one from each area. For each of the sixteen possible combinations of preferences there is a quintessential persona associated with it, as the four dimensions act together. Any of the sixteen types can successfully enter any profession, however there is a correlation between a person's approach to life and the demands of certain professions. Let's look at some combinations which are relevant to a business driven by creative and performing artists:

- **Introverted/iNtuitive/Thinking/Judging(INTJ)**—An INTJ is the quintessential scientist. A person of this type is driven to know *why* things are as they are, and lives to shape abstract ideas, symbols and concepts (including words and metaphors). This does not mean an INTJ must become a professional chemist or physicist. It just means that most aspects of his or her pursuits will be approached scientifically, conceptually and inventively, always seeking innovation. This is not a matter of good, bad, right or wrong. It is simply how this kind of person is wired inside.
- **Extroverted/Sensing/Feeling/Perceiving(ESFP)**—The ESFP, the opposite profile of the INTJ, is a quintessential entertainer. An ESFP is always "on stage," no matter what he or she is doing. Performing is as natural as breathing. ESFPs live for each moment, squeezing all they can from it. Stage and screen careers are natural magnets for these folks; they exude energy, are down-to-earth, are spontaneous and show their feelings. Billy Joel's "Big Shot" is a perfect portrait of an ESFP.
- **Introverted/iNtuitive/Feeling/Perceiving(INFP)**—The INFP preference represents the quintessential idealist. These folks are always committed to a noble cause and to performing service to aid society. A hallmark of the INFP is to reflect endlessly on the all-important question "Who am I?" (e.g., Am I an artist? Am I a writer? Am I a parent? Am I a lover? I am all of these things, but what does that mean? Who am I?) INFPs, well-represented on stage and on screen, are also natural wordsmiths, writing in many fields. Think of how many song lyrics are based on the question "Who am I?"
- **Extroverted/Sensing/Thinking/Judging(ESTJ)**—When thinking of the ESTJ preference,

ask yourself "What are the key qualities for a successful business manager?" As a matched opposite to the INFP preference, the ESTJ is oriented toward interacting with others, focusing on practical, "real" issues, quick and objective decision-making, and a preference for order, scheduling, planning and closure. It is no coincidence that more than half of business managers are TJs, with ESTJs being the quintessential "administrators of life." If you are an introverted writer, an ESTJ is a great partner if you need someone to pitch a song and negotiate on your behalf.

Now, none of these profiles is inherently "good/bad" or "better/worse" than the other. They are simply different. The music business thrives only through the interaction and cooperation of writers, performers, engineers, managers, businessmen, lawyers, agents, producers, promoters, roadies, consumers, etc. In this light, the key to successful collaboration is understanding and respecting the differences between people, and seeing those differences as positive rather than negative.

Each of the sixteen possible profiles has very specific gifts and strengths which lead them into areas of endeavor where success flows from those strengths. Just as INFP idealists cannot turn off their need to champion a cause, whether good or misguided, the ESTJ corporate managers cannot turn off their need to make decisions, whether good or misguided. Just as an INTJ scientist cannot turn off the need to discover things, some memorable and some forgettable, the ESFP entertainer cannot turn off the need to give performances, both memorable and forgettable.

Interactions between different types has the potential to be mutually strengthening if the opposite preferences are appreciated and recognized, or mutually antagonistic if either party thinks the other isn't the kind of person they "should" be. In writer-writer collaborations, Sensing/Intuitive pairs complement each other because both perspectives—concrete references and an overarching metaphor—are needed for an enduring lyric. But it's not always easy for Sensing and Perceiving types to "get on the same page" with each other.

In a Thinking/Feeling collaboration, the Thinking type's input provides the analysis of structure, meter, language and logic, while the Feeling input provides effective communication through emotion. Introverts usually don't collaborate with other introverts, because they have an "inner voice" which they would rather listen to, but in so doing may limit their sources of ideas and feedback. Extroverts love to collaborate with others, but two extroverts collaborating miss the dimension of quiet introspection so important for depth, meaning and emotion in a song. An Extroverted/Introverted team can produce great results if each respects the needs and quirks of the other.

A Judging/Judging collaboration is usually the type where a specific time and agenda are decided in advance. A Perceiving/Perceiving collaboration means either party can call the other at any hour of the night when an inspiration strikes. Both of these methods seem to work well.

In a Judging/Perceiving collaboration, assuming the partners can get along, the Judging-oriented partner forces the Perceiver to focus energy on the task of writing, and usually pushes to get things finished. The Perceiver opens the Judging type to the possibilities of developing inspirations outside of the appointed time and topic, and is more open to rewriting and revising. ESFP entertainers and ESTJ agents make a good collaboration. The ES qualities allow easy communication, while the SP/TJ differences provide complementary strengths.

IN CONCLUSION

Collaboration is more than just two writers getting together. It's a mutual effort among any group of people who share a common goal, be it artistic, business, legal or technical, who are getting together in a way so each can use their strengths to shine a light where the others might have a blind spot. Viewed in this way, reaching the pinnacle of art, craft and commercial reward will be far less of a battle, the music industry will be healthier, and the world will be richer for what is produced.

Demo FAQs: Answers to the Frequently Asked Questions About Demos

BY CYNTHIA LAUFENBERG

In today's music business, the demonstration tape, or demo, is the accepted way of getting your songs heard by industry professionals. Unless you already have established contacts at major publishing and record companies in the industry, you're going to need a demo to display your talents as a songwriter or performer. Demos can range from a simple, two-track guitar/vocal arrangement to a fully produced 24-track recording by an 8-piece band. How do you know what type of demo will best represent your songs? What will make your demo stand out? What do music business professionals look for in a demo? We've compiled some of the most frequently asked questions (FAQs) songwriters ask about submitting demos and asked several A&R reps and publishing professionals their opinions on the subject. They gave us tips on what they look for in the demos they receive, and offered advice on how to make your demos stand out and attract attention.

How elaborate does a demo have to be? Do I need a full arrangement, or is a simple guitar or piano/vocal sufficient?

The answer to this question lies in the type of music you write, and what an individual at a company is looking for. Usually, up-tempo pop, rock and dance demos need to be more fully produced than pop ballads and country demos. "The type of demo depends on the type of song," says Carla Berkowitz, director of creative affairs at EMI Music Publishing in Los Angeles. "A great ballad is best represented by a simple piano/vocal (with a good vocal) to show off the lyric and melody. A great pop/rock song may be served well by a 'fully realized' demo." Julie Gordon, A&R representative at The Enclave in New York, agrees: "I think the type of demo depends to some extent on the type of artist submitting the demo. Certainly a techno/artist needs quite a sophisticated/produced demo, whereas for a singer/songwriter type, a basic demo will suffice." Many of the companies listed in *Songwriter's Market* tell you what type of demo they prefer to receive, and if you're not sure you can always call and ask what their preference is. Either way, make sure your demo is clean and clear, and the vocals are up front.

If you are an artist looking for a record deal, obviously your demo needs to be as fully produced as possible to convey your talent as an artist. Many singer/songwriters record their demos as if they were going to be released as an album. That way, if they have already recorded three or four CD-quality demo tapes but haven't heard anything from the labels they've been submitting to, they can put those demos together and release a CD or cassette on their own. They end up with a professional-looking product, complete with an album cover graphics and liner notes, to sell at shows and through mail order without spending a lot of money to re-record the songs.

CYNTHIA LAUFENBERG *was editor of* Songwriter's Market *from 1991-1996. She currently lives in Princeton, New Jersey.*

Whether your demo is produced with a full band or just a solo piano, it is the quality of the writing that will get your songs noticed. "If a song is great you can tell even without production, and if the song is not there, all the production in the world won't help," says Julie Gordon.

How many songs should there be on a demo? Should they be in any particular order? Should the demo have complete songs, or just portions of songs?

The consensus throughout the industry is that three songs is sufficient. Most music business professionals don't have time to listen to more than three, and they figure if you can't catch their attention in three songs, your songs probably don't have hit potential. "A common mistake [many songwriters make] is sending too many songs," says Julie Gordon. "I think three songs is a good amount to start with to introduce yourself. Even if you have recorded an entire CD, you can send that later if you get a request for more material."

Put three complete songs on the tape, not just snippets of your favorites, and remember to put your best, most commercial song first on the tape. If it's an up-tempo number, that makes it even easier to catch someone's attention. "I prefer complete songs," says Lonn Friend, vice president of A&R at Arista Records in Los Angeles. "Always put your strongest track first on the tape. Most A&R people don't have the patience or time to get past the first couple of tracks if an impression isn't made early." Some individuals don't even need to hear three songs; for Carla Berkowitz at EMI, "one or two is enough." Whether two or three songs, all songs should be on the same side of the tape, and none of them should be longer than five minutes. Most professional managers and A&R reps are looking for hit songs, and hit songs are usually between three and four minutes long. David McPherson, senior director of A&R at Jive Records in New York, advises, "Don't talk on the tape—just music! Don't make the songs longer than five minutes each unless it's really necessary. And don't have long introductions for your songs."

What's the most preferable format: cassette, DAT or CD?

The cassette is still the most widely-preferred format for demos. David McPherson prefers cassettes because "I can listen to it in my car/house/office or almost anywhere. CDs and DATs are only more convenient because you can skip to the next song faster and the sound is better, but hits are hits on whatever configuration. A fully produced full-length CD only impresses me if it is full of hit records, which does not usually happen." Carla Berkowitz also prefers the ease of cassettes over other formats. "I prefer a traditional cassette, so I can toss it in my bag and listen to it in my car. CDs do not impress me or cause me to listen quicker or like the music more. Also, if I do like what I hear, I can always request a DAT or better recording." Cassettes are also cheaper to duplicate than CDs or DATs (although the recordable CDR format is quickly catching up to cassettes in terms of low cost and ease of duplication), and are cheaper and easier to mail.

Do I have to record my demo in a studio? What are my options if I can't afford to record at a studio?

With the advances in home recording technology, it's very acceptable—as well as affordable—to record your demos at home. Lonn Friend has received home-recorded demos, and finds them to be "very acceptable. When I received demos from alternative rock band the Eels, they were home recordings and, still to this day, the best demos I've ever heard."

It's up to you to decide how many tracks you think you need to record your songs. If you're recording a simple guitar/vocal demo, a four-track recording made in your living room would work just fine. The more instruments, vocals and effects you want to add, the more tracks you need. Home recording equipment has become quite affordable in recent years, and for the same amount of money it would cost you to have a few demos recorded at a studio, you could invest in a good home studio setup in 4-, 8- and 16-track formats. You might even want to get together with other songwriters or performers in your area and pool your resources, buying equipment together you can all use to record demos.

If you decide you can't do it at home and want to go into the studio to record, be sure to find the right studio for your music and your budget. Shop around for studios (you can find them listed in the Yellow Pages or in your local newspaper), and remember that not only will you have to pay for recording time but also for any additional, a producer or engineer, and the tapes you are recording on. Base your decision on what studio will work best for the type of music you write, and be sure to hear samples of work that have been recorded at the studio

Yet another option is to consider using a demo service—see the next question for more information.

I'm a songwriter, not a performer. Where do I find someone to sing and/or perform on my demo? What about demo services?

Finding a good vocalist who can adequately convey the meaning of your songs is important, so if you can't sing that well, you may want to find someone who can. Pat Fincher, senior creative director at Famous Music in Nashville, says, "For me, [a demo] has to be performed by competent singers and players. I don't have time to struggle through poorly recorded demos." Carla Berkowitz finds "bad vocalists to be really distracting from the song itself." Julie Gordon agrees. "Obviously, the performance and the material are what make a good demo stand out. If I can't remember anything about a song after I have heard it, can't find a hook, can't hear the vocals or am presented with sub-par material, it stands out as bad." It pays to find a good vocalist and good musicians to record your demos, and there are many places to find musicians and singers willing to work with you. Check out local songwriting organizations, music stores and newspapers to find musicians in your area you can hire to play on your demo. Many singers who don't write their own songs will sing on demos in exchange for a copy of the tape they can use as their own demo to help further their performing careers.

If you can't find local musicians, or don't want to go through the trouble of putting together a band just for the purposes of recording your demo, you may want to try a demo service. For a fee, a demo service will produce your songs in their studio using their own singers and musicians. Many of these services advertise in music magazines, songwriting newsletters and bulletin boards at local music stores. If you decide to deal with a demo service, make sure you can hear samples of work they've done in the past. Many demo services are mail-order business—you send them either a rough tape of your song or the sheet music and they produce and record a demo within a month or two. Be sure you find a service that will let you have creative control over how your demo is produced, and make sure you tell them exactly how you want your song to sound. As with studios, shop around and find the demo service that best suits your needs and budget.

What's the most effective way to package my demo? Does it need graphics, or should it be just a cassette with my name, address and telephone number on it?

"The simpler the better!" says Pat Finch, and most agree. A demo package doesn't have to be elaborate—most professionals aren't looking for slick graphics but a simple tape with the appropriate contact information. Brian Malouf, A&R representative and producer at RCA Records in New York, looks for a "simple package, no graphics necessary. Three songs, picture and short bio/press release are sufficient. According to Julie Gordon, "Presentation should be neat and professional, but an expensive press kit is not necessary. Remember, it's not the package that matters, it's the materials. A cassette is fine, as long as it has a label on it—all unlabeled cassettes go straight in the trash." Since your tape may become separated from the box it came in, it's imperative to have your name, address and telephone number on the cassette box as well as the cassette itself. The cassette label should provide your name and phone number, the titles of the songs, the name of your publisher (if you have one), and copyright information. Cue your tape to the beginning of the first song, and keep about 6 seconds between songs. A neat, professionally done package may be just enough to make your tape stand out from the hundreds of others that arrive on the desks of publisher and A&R reps.

What information should go with the demo when I send it out?

Your package should be as complete as possible, without overwhelming the listener with unnecessary information. A cover letter and lyric sheet along with the demo tape are fine if you're a songwriter looking for a publisher. If you're an artist looking for a record deal, a biography, photo and press clippings should be included in the package as well. Lonn Friend advises, "Prepare a good package with photo, lyrics, bio, etc., like a press kit. If it's impressive, it sets itself aside from the rest—and getting attention is the hardest part."

Include a short, to-the-point cover letter addressed to a specific person in the company, and briefly state why you're sending the tape. Are you a writer looking for a publishing deal, an artist looking for a record deal, or a writer wanting to have a song recorded by a particular artist? Add any important professional credits you may have, and ask for feedback if you want it. Be sure to thank the individual for their time and consideration, and don't forget to include your name, address and phone number. If you have professionally printed letterhead, use it. It makes you look as though you take your career seriously.

Your lyric sheets should be neatly typed and inserted in the package in the order they appear on the tape. Include the names of all the writers of each song, as well as a copyright notice on the first page of the lyric sheet. It is not necessary to send lead sheets with your demo tape, unless they are specifically requested.

The outside of you package should be as neat as everything on the inside. Make sure you have adequate postage, and don't send your tape in a regular business envelope. Use an envelope that's large enough to accommodate your tape and your lyric sheets/press kit, one that's padded or insulated so your tape does not get damaged in mailing. Have a specific contact name to mail your tape to, and type your mailing label. Extra tape is not necessary to seal your envelope; the harder it is to open, the less likely it is to be listened to. The idea is to make your package as friendly as possible.

Many songwriters include SASEs in their packages so they can have their materials returned to them. Even if you include return postage, there is no guarantee your tape will actually be returned, so it's up to you to decide if you want to risk spending the extra money. If you think the price of return postage is worth the price of the returned tape (if it is returned at all), include the SASE. If you do, make sure it's big enough and has sufficient postage for the materials you want returned.

When asked the question "What makes a good demo stand out?" all of the professionals interviewed for this article said the same thing: "Great songs!" No matter how professional your demo package is, and no matter how closely you follow submission guidelines, it's important the songs you are sending are able to compete with the songs and artists currently on the radio. Ray McKenzie, president of indie label Zero Hour Records in New York, notes that he sees, "too much time spent on production and packaging, and not enough on songcraft" in many of the submissions he receives. If you can combine well-crafted songs with an attractive, professional demo package, you and your songs stand a good chance of being noticed and listened to.

Music Publishers: Royalties From Foreign Sources

BY RANDY POE

It has been said the popular songs created in this country are America's greatest ambassadors to the rest of the world. Since American music is listened to around the globe, royalties are generally being earned wherever that music is played.

Not wanting to miss out on opportunities to earn income from a song's use, music publishers have devised methods by which they can be compensated for their works gathering royalties on foreign soil, just as foreign copyright owners receive royalties when their songs are recorded and performed in the United States.

Of course, our government helped pave the way by having the United States become a member of the Universal Copyright Convention and—more recently—the Berne Convention. These multinational treaties cause many countries to recognize copyrights created in the United States as having the same protection as their own domestic copyrights.

There are some countries that don't belong to either of the conventions mentioned above. Some of these nonmember nations have direct treaties with the United States; some countries' copyright relationships with the United States are officially listed as "unclear" by the Copyright Office; and a few countries have no copyright agreements with the United States at all.

Going through detailed explanations of which countries recognize U.S. copyrights under which specific treaties would be a lengthy and boring exercise. Germany, Spain, the United Kingdom, France, Japan, Belgium, Holland, Italy, Australia, Mexico, Argentina and Brazil all recognize U.S. copyrights. Countries such as Iran, Iraq, Oman and Qatar don't. At this point in history, it's a safe assumption there aren't too many American pop songs being played in Iran, so U.S. publishers probably aren't missing out on large sums of royalties there.

The main method of acquiring royalties from countries that do recognize U.S. copyrights is through a process called "subpublishing." For example, if my publishing company owns a copyright that becomes a hit in England, I need to have an agreement with a British publishing company so it can collect royalties earned on the song in the United Kingdom. Based on the conditions provided by my company's agreement with the British firm, that company (referred to as the subpublisher) will pay my publishing company a percentage of all the monies earned by the song originally published by my company in the United States.

The concept of subpublishing is actually rather simple. It tends to become confusing because there are a variety of different routes a U.S. publishing company can take to have proper foreign representation. On top of that, subpublishing agreements can vary widely. Add to this the difficulty of dealing with a language barrier, foreign currencies and "partners" who are thousands of miles away, and you can begin to see how the simple concept of subpublishing can become extremely complicated.

TWO MAIN AVENUES OF FOREIGN REPRESENTATION

When a song is a hit in the United States, there is frequently foreign activity on the work as well. If a hit song belongs to a new publishing company in the United States, the new publisher will seek to determine how he wishes to have his company represented in other countries. The U.S. Publisher has two main choices for foreign representation, either:

1) country-by-country subpublishing agreements, or

2) a single worldwide subpublishing agreement with a multinational subpublisher—a company that already has subpublishing agreements in place or owns its own subpublishing companies around the world.

There are advantages and disadvantages to both choices. First, let's consider the advantages of country-by-country subpublishing agreements. If a song originating in the United States becomes a hit in England, the U.S. publisher can negotiate an agreement with a British subpublisher whereby the British company will agree to pay a large advance to the American publisher. If the song becomes a hit in Germany a few weeks later, the U.S. publisher can then enter into a subpublishing agreement with a German publisher, acquiring another advance from the German publisher for the right to represent the song in his territory. As the song becomes a hit around the world, the U.S. publisher can continue to negotiate deals with publishers in each new country the song reaches, collecting advances from the individual subpublishers until the song has achieved worldwide representation.

Since there will probably be several companies in each country vying for subpublishing rights to the song, the U.S. publisher will usually have the upper hand in the negotiating procedures. In the end, he will come away with advances from each country and—if he has a good entertainment lawyer—the best possible deal from each of the subpublishers.

On the other hand, the U.S. publisher will now have over a dozen subpublishing agreements to keep track of, complicated by the fact each agreement may have different terms and different percentages to be collected. Also, if there is a dispute about payments due from, say, Scandinavia, a lawsuit would probably prove to be impractical.

The U.S. publisher's other choice for representation would be a single administration agreement with a large, multinational publishing company that already has representation outside of the United States. If a song becomes a hit abroad, the song's U.S. publisher would need to sign only one agreement that would cover the entire world. If a problem arose in a particular foreign country, the U.S. publishers could require the administering publisher to resolve the problem. Also, the single subpublishing administration agreement is usually uniform for all of the countries involved, rather than the group of assorted contracts possible in a country-by-country situation.

The major disadvantage of a single administration agreement is there would be only one advance for the entire world, which would—in all likelihood—be substantially less than the total of all advances the song's U.S. publisher could have acquired on a country-by-country basis. Then there is the matter of how much attention the U.S. publisher's song will receive. After all, the administrating publisher has a catalog of its own songs to worry about—songs that may be making far more money for them than they will earn from simply representing your song in foreign countries for a small percentage.

Of course, the fact the U.S. publisher might be receiving less money doesn't negate the fact that having several subpublishers is also a very costly exercise. Therefore, the U.S. publisher might end up with essentially the same amount of money in either situation after the song's success has run its course.

A THIRD AVENUE OF FOREIGN REPRESENTATION

The U.S. publisher has a third option for collecting foreign royalties due, although it is not a common route chosen by many publishers. A U.S. publisher affiliated with the Harry Fox Agency may request that Fox collect foreign royalties via HFA's agreements with foreign collection societies and agencies. The advantage to using Harry Fox Agency is there is no percentage to give up to a subpublisher. However, there are several disadvantages, including that there are no advances offered, no exploitation of the publisher's songs, and no attempts to acquire foreign language recordings. Most U.S. publishers are willing to allow subpublishers a percentage of foreign income in the subpublisher's territory in exchange for an advance and the other available amenities.

THE COUNTRY-BY-COUNTRY APPROACH

If a U.S. publisher decides to take the country-by-country approach to subpublishing, he will be entering into a series of agreements with various subpublishers. For each agreement there will be several points of negotiation to consider.

If a song is released in the United Kingdom, the U.S. publisher will probably be contacted by several British publishers wishing to represent the song in the territory they usually cover (United Kingdom, Republic of Eire, etc.). Determining which one of these companies will act as a subpublisher for the song is a process usually based on which company has the best reputation or which one offers the best deal. Ideally, both qualities will belong to the same company.

Some issues that should be considered by the U.S. publisher are:
- the amount of the advance; the term (or duration) of the subpublishing agreement; and
- the percentage of royalties to be retained by the subpublisher in exchange for services rendered.

Regarding the advance, the amount offered will depend on the country in question. Obviously, the U.K. subpublisher will offer more than another much less active country's subpublisher. It will be up to the U.S. publisher to determine if any of the U.K. firms are offering a reasonable advance based on recent offers to other American publishers in similar circumstances. If the U.S. publisher doesn't have knowledge of other recent deals, he will either have to assume the highest offer is a reasonable advance or rely on the expertise of an entertainment attorney who is familiar with the current advances being negotiated in the United Kingdom.

However, the highest advance doesn't necessarily dictate the best deal. The U.S. publisher must also negotiate the type of royalties the subpublisher will be able to claim and the percentages of those royalties the subpublisher will be able to retain.

According to Gary Ford, Director of International Services for ASCAP, and former manager of foreign administration for Warner/Chappell Music, "In an ideal situation, a publisher should actually visit the office of the intended subpublisher, meet the administrative and creative staff, and get an overall feeling for how they communicate and transact business. He should check their computer systems, royalty statement formats, etc.

"Also, if the publisher wants his catalog exploited in the local market, it is often best to go with independent subpublishers as they focus primarily on exploitation of their clients' catalogs and have excellent track records for obtaining local 'covers.' [In music publishing lingo, exploitation is synonmous with plugging or promoting a song in an attempt to get it recorded and/or performed.]

"However, the independents also have a reputation for not being the best administrators; hence the reasoning for either visiting the particular office *or* relying on an attorney you can trust to choose the best independent to suit your needs."

Gary feels these points "are equally as important as an advance when deciding to do deals on a country-by-country basis. Each publisher has different needs and an advance or rate split should not be the sole determining factor in choosing a subpublisher."

Subpublishers generally issue licenses for and collect on mechanical reproductions, synch uses, printed editions, and—sometimes—the publisher's share of performance royalties. The amount of royalties the subpublisher retains can usually be anywhere from 10-25 percent. If the subpublisher causes a recording to be made in his territory (this is generally referred to as a "local cover" version), he frequently is allowed to keep anywhere from 25-40 percent of the royalties earned on that particular release.

THE SUBPUBLISHING SCENARIO

S. Mackenzie Music Publishing Company owns the song "I Love My Dog." Mr. Mackenzie makes a subpublishing deal for his catalog with a French company in which the original French subpublisher will retain 10 percent of the royalties it collects on the original American recording of "I Love My Dog" in France. The French publisher is also given the right to adapt or translate the song into French so that he can have a better opportunity to exploit the song in his country. Although the foreign language version will still be copyrighted in the name of the U.S. publisher, the French publisher will be able to retain 25 percent of the royalties on *either* the English or French version of the song if he causes a recording of it to be made in his territory.

Let's say "I Love My Dog," as recorded by the American band Herman's Mutts, is an international hit (originating in the United States). If the Mutts' recording is released in France, that wouldn't qualify the French publisher to retain 25 percent of the royalties earned in France.

However, if the French publisher gets another act to record "I Love My Dog" (the English language version) in France, he would retain 25 percent of the mechanical royalties received on that local cover. The same holds true if the French publisher gets Jacques Beagle to record "J'aime mon Bow Wow"—the French version of the song.

Assuming S. Mackenzie Music Publishing Company has a contract with the writer of "I Love My Dog" that calls for the songwriter to receive 50 percent of the mechanical income received by the publisher from foreign sources, the royalty payments would go like this:

Let's say the subpublisher in France receives the equivalent of $1,000 in mechanical royalties for Hermans' Mutts' recording of "I Love My Dog." According to the subpublishing agreement, he retains $100 and pays the remaining $900 to S. Mackenzie's company. S. Mackenzie then pays $450 (50 percent of the mechanical income from the foreign sources) to the writer of "I Love My Dog."

When Jacques Beagle's recording of "J'aime mon Bow Wow" becomes a hit in France, the French publisher receives another $1,000 in mechanical royalties—this time for Jacque's local cover recording of the song. the subpublisher now retains $250 (25 percent of the local cover version income) and pays $750 to S. Mackenzie. S. Mackenzie then pays $375 to the composer of "I Love My Dog" (once again, 50 percent of income from a foreign source received by the American publisher).

What about the French writer who turned "I Love My Dog" into "J'aime mon Bow Wow"? He receives mechanical royalties from the 25 percent retained by the French publisher according to whatever deal the two of them have negotiated. He will also receive a portion of the song's performance royalty income reported in France, but only on the French language version of the song.

THE SUBPUBLISHING AGREEMENT TERM

Another area of consideration is the term of the agreement. In earlier days, subpublishers often acquired a song for the life of copyright (which, in many countries, was already "life-plus-fifty"). As you can see, if a U.S. publisher became unhappy with a particular subpublisher, the results could be pretty devastating, and since the life of a copyright is now "life-plus-seventy" in many foreign countries, the U.S. publisher who entered into a "life of copyright" deal a few decades ago has lost the song outside the U.S. for twenty more years than he originally thought he would.

In more recent times, the subpublishing deals have taken on more reasonable durations. Today, the common subpublishing term is usually around three years. The philosophy behind the three-year term is that the subpublisher will have plenty of time to show he can exploit the song in his market, but not so much time the remaining points of the deal have a chance to become antiquated.

There was a time when the subpublisher retained 50 percent of all income collected as opposed to the 10-20 percent usually retained today. Many American publishers now find themselves locked into those old 50/50 deals for the life of their copyrights because those types of deals were very common not too many years ago. Luckily for U.S. publishers and songwriters, such deals don't happen anymore when dealing with legitimate subpublishers.

Another point of negotiation is the rights being granted to the subpublisher. We already know the subpublisher has the right to collect mechanical, synch and print royalties (and sometimes performance royalties). However, in a normal, pro-U.S. publisher deal, the subpublisher does not acquire the copyright itself in the subpublisher's territory. The publisher is merely allowing the subpublisher to act on the publisher's behalf.

In non-English-speaking countries, as pointed out in "The Subpublishing Scenario," the American publisher will usually allow the subpublisher to have translations or adaptations of the lyrics created (to be approved by the publisher and, sometimes, the songwriter) so the sub-publisher will be in a better position to promote the song. The publisher should own the copyright to these new versions of the works; otherwise, if he decides to change subpublishers, the original subpublisher may claim to own rights to the adapted versions of the songs in the catalog. Two versions of the same song in the same country would not only be difficult to exploit, but payments of royalties would be confusing at best.

The number of songs the subpublisher acquires depends on the individual deal. A subpublisher may be granted the rights to a single song, to all of the songs the U.S. publisher acquires during the term of the subpublishing agreement, or to any or all of the songs in the publisher's catalog that haven't already been assigned to another subpublisher in a particular territory.

If a subpublisher is acquiring the rights to an American publisher's catalog containing several hits, that publisher should be able to strike a much better deal than another American publisher who is offering only one song for subpublication.

Of course, a U.S. publisher with several hits could make deals with various subpublishers in the same territory on a song-by-song basis, acquiring advances from each subpublisher that might total more than the single advance offered by one subpublisher for all of the songs. But, once again, the U.S. publisher might find himself buried under tons of paperwork while trying to keep track of who subpublishes what song in which territory—which leads us to the other main subpublishing option available to the U.S. publisher.

THE SINGLE WORLDWIDE SUBPUBLISHING APPROACH

This type of agreement is usually made with a multinational subpublisher—a major publishing company that either already has subpublishing deals in place throughout the world or owns its own subpublishing companies around the globe.

Although the publisher would receive only one overall advance—as opposed to advances from each country—a major benefit of the single worldwide subpublishing agreement is it is much simpler and easier to maintain. Also, by going with this approach, the publisher only has one deal to negotiate, and he will usually receive one foreign royalty statement twice a year that covers the entire world, rather than receiving many different statements from various territories at different times during a twelve-month period.

As Gary Ford explains, "There are many other advantages of going with a multinational subpublisher: They usually have a better working relationship with their local performing rights societies due to their size; their computer systems are normally more up to date; and their professional staff is better equipped to deal with areas not usually addressed by the independent subpublisher."

The various negotiating points of the worldwide subpublishing agreements are very similar to a single subpublishing agreement. However, the U.S. publisher has to protect himself from allowing the worldwide subpublisher to pay less than the U.S. publisher is expecting by avoiding accounting for royalties "at the source."

Sound confusing? It is. Many U.S. publishers have been duped by subpublishers with whom they have entered into worldwide agreements. Although this is not a practice among the well-known and well-respected multinational subpublishers, it does still take place among a few companies. Here's how it works:

U.S. publisher A enters into a worldwide subpublishing agreement with publisher B, who owns publishing companies around the world. B agrees to pay A 80 percent of the royalties B receives from its subpublishers. (Remember, these are companies that B owns.) Meanwhile, B has agreements with all of its subpublishers (essentially, agreements with itself) stating the subpublishers will retain 50 percent of all sums received in their territories. So, if English subpublisher C receives $200 in royalties for a song in A's catalog, C retains $100 and sends $100 (50 percent) to B in the United States. B then pays $80 to A. Meanwhile, A was expecting to receive $160 (80 percent of $200).

There are several variations on this theme, the end result of which is that publisher A receives substantially less subpublishing royalties than his agreement would seem to indicate. To avoid this problem—known in the industry as "double dipping"—a good entertainment lawyer makes certain the worldwide subpublishing agreement calls for royalties to be computed "at the source." In other word, each subpublisher must report the amount earned in his territory, of which 80 percent is to be received by publisher A when royalties are paid.

A FINAL WORD ON SUBPUBLISHING

Subpublishing is more important today than it has ever been before. The amount of royalties earned abroad on an international hit originating in the United States can sometimes be as much or more than the amount earned in this country.

In the past, American publishers put the most emphasis on the amount of the advance they could get from a subpublisher without worrying about how much that song might eventually earn in a foreign territory. In fact, after the initial large advance, the publishers often left the subpublisher to his own devices.

Today, subpublishers have become very competitive. Due to the shortened term of most subpublishing agreements, subpublishers work harder to exploit U.S. publishers' songs so their agreements will be renewed on a continuing basis.

Finally, it is interesting to note the Internet might prove to be an extremely important factor in the future of subpublishing. By virtue of the fact the World Wide Web is, indeed, worldwide, U.S. publishers are now capable of promoting their catalogs over the Internet. With that in mind, it's concievable the day will come when U.S. publishers will also be able to administer and collect royalties from foreign sources without the help of today's conventional subpublisher. What will happen to the entire concept of subpublishing in the years ahead depends almost entirely upon where expanding technology will lead us.

Performance Royalty Income from Foreign Sources

The U.S. publisher's share of foreign performance royalties is usually a point of discussion in subpublishing deals because there are two possible ways for the publisher to receive foreign performance income.

One way payment is handled is for the subpublisher to collect the U.S. publisher's foreign performance royalties directly from the foreign performing rights society with which the sub-publisher is affiliated. The subpublisher then pays the publishing company its share of foreign performance income when he accounts to the publisher for all types of royalties due.

The other possible method of payment is for the foreign performing rights society to pay the publisher's (and songwriter's) share of foreign performance royalties directly to the proper performing rights society in America. That society then pays the publisher and songwriter.

Which of these two methods is best for the publisher is open to debate. In the first case mentioned above, the subpublisher is going to get to keep a portion of the U.S. publisher's performance royalty income, which—on the surface—would appear to be a disadvantage to the publisher.

On the other hand, the publisher is more likely to receive his foreign performance royalties sooner with this method, since the foreign performing rights society is paying the publisher's performance royalties directly to the subpublisher, which in turn pays the publisher the next time royalty accountings are due.

In the second scenario, the American publisher doesn't have to lose the percentage of performance royalty income that would have been taken out by the subpublisher. The disadvantage, though, is that foreign performing rights societies generally take a long time to pay U.S. performing rights societies. It also takes time for the U.S. societies to enter all of the foreign information into their computer systems. By the time the publisher finally receives the foreign performance royalties from his affiliated U.S. performing rights society, those royalties can be monies owed from the previous year or even earlier.

In the end, if this is a negotiable deal point in the U.S. publisher's agreement with his subpublisher, the publisher will have to determine which method he prefers. Of course, the subpublisher is going to want to collect the foreign performance royalties himself, since this means more money will go into his pocket.

Meanwhile, notwithstanding the manner in which the publisher is paid performance royalties, the U.S. songwriter receives his foreign performance royalties direct from his domestic performing rights society.

Taking Notes: Music Publishers and Background Research

BY PHIL GOLDBERG

So now that you have this book, what are you going to do with it? I know, I know. You're about to make copies of your songs and send them off to the companies listed.

Hopefully you've read up on how to present and package your songs and how to network and make contacts with people in the music business. These are indeed essential skills to develop, but it's also essential you be able to size up the companies you are dealing with. Too many aspiring songwriters operate in the dark.

Let's say you're calling a major company such as Sony Records or Warner/Chappell Music. The odds are you will be met with a firm "no," no matter what request you make. You might call Sony Records and start the conversation with "What does your company do? Do you

Phil Goldberg (and Rusty)

have any singers I've heard of?" Begin a call that way—and some people do!—and you're likely to mark yourself as an absolute amateur. Any chance of ever hearing a "yes" has instantly evaporated. At the other end of the continuum, if you're making calls straight out of the phone book and you don't know how to judge a company's credibility, you increase the odds you could be taken advantage of.

The answer is RESEARCH. The music business can be a tough nut to crack under any circumstance. *Songwriter's Market* is a tool. Learn how to use it and other tools, and you'll lower your level of frustration.

HOW MANY PUBLISHERS ARE OUT THERE?

Songwriter's Market contains a representative sample of music publishers in major music centers such as Los Angeles, New York and Nashville. There are also publishers from out of the way places you wouldn't immediately associate with the music business. But, this is a sample, not a totality. *Songwriter's Market* is not a complete listing of every music publisher that exists. If you're looking for a total listing of publishers, this isn't it.

But you know what? That list doesn't exist.

If what you want is a long list, the next best thing is to access the Yellow Pages from every major music center, and then look under "Music Publishers." In Los Angeles, where the music business is not centralized, you're going to need more than one Yellow Pages. Some libraries may

PHIL GOLDBERG *is currently a membership consultant for Nashville Songwriters Association International. As NSAI's members services director, he managed the NSAI bookstore and song evaluation service, counseled songwriters, and answered many, many questions. And, yes, Phil is a songwriter.*

have collections of Yellow Pages from across the country. You may also find some equivalents to the Yellow Pages online.

But, just having a long, long list of publishers isn't particularly helpful, either. For example, if you get the Nashville Yellow Pages, you'll find about 400 music publishers listed, compared to less than a hundred listed in *Songwriter's Market* for the entire state of Tennessee.

Are you better off with 400 names? I guess so, if you are wealthy and plan on running up a lengthy long-distance phone bill! Otherwise, the phone book doesn't tell you anything other than a company's name, phone number and usually an address. Sure, you could save yourself the 400 phone calls and "shotgun" 400 letters to 400 strangers. It's cheaper, but it's a variation on the same problem: you don't know anything about these companies.

One asset of *Songwriter's Market* is it supplies you with information you need to know about the companies listed. If you learn how to use this information and this book, you'll be better prepared when you broaden your investigation.

TRACKING DOWN INFORMATION—SOURCES

Look at the big picture. What you need is to get a sense of who the "players" are for the type of music you're creating. You'll need to start checking and compiling publishing credits. Where do you look?

CD booklets

Most CD booklets include the names of the music publishers who control copyrights to those songs. Publishing credits are usually in small print, often following the titles of the songs. You should start compiling this information. If you're lucky, the songwriters' names will also be listed, and you should start compiling that information as well.

A credit in a CD booklet might read "Acuff-Rose Music (ASCAP)/John Doe Music (ASCAP)/Irving Music (BMI)/Jane Doe Music (BMI)." In this example, the publishing is administered or owned by four companies: Acuff-Rose Music, John Doe Music, Irving Music and Jane Doe Music. Get a 3-ring binder or enter this information in a computer. Every time you find a listing for Acuff-Rose, you can enter the information on the song title, the songwriters, the artist, the record company, the year the song was released, whether the artist was also the writer, etc.

However, before you go through your CD collection, think about the songs YOU are writing. If you write country songs, your best bet is to start with your country albums. If you're writing hip-hop, go through your hip-hop albums. *The purpose of this is to give you an initial database specific to your genre of music.* The more information you compile, the more background you will get on who is doing what.

Now a few warnings:

• **PRO Affiliation:** ASCAP, BMI and SESAC (mentioned in the previous example) are Peforming Rights Organizations (PROs). The PROs collect money from performances and distribute it to songwriters and music publishers. A large music publisher may have one staff writer affiliated with ASCAP, another with BMI and yet another affiliated with SESAC. That music publisher may have three distinct company names, one name associated with each PRO, and only one of those names may show up in the phone book or *Songwriter's Market*.

• **Co-Publishing Arrangements:** Successful songwriters also tend to have co-publishing arrangements. This means they are still signed to a music publisher, but are successful enough to keep some of the publishing money themselves. To collect these extra royalties, they have to form companies of their own and affiliate with a PRO. So, if a well-known songwriter wrote a song by himself, you would probably see two companies listed, not just one, and the name of the second company wouldn't show up in the phone book or *Songwriter's Market*, and that is because the songwriter's own company serves only to collect money for the songwriter. A traditional publisher may sign "outside" songs, but a songwriter in a co-publishing situation usually doesn't.

This means you may be compiling information that is initially going to confuse you. But, the more experience you have and the more information you gather, the more you will start to see patterns. "Oh, look! These two publishing companies have the same address. One is affiliated with ASCAP and one is affiliated with BMI! I bet it's really the same company!" "Oh, look! I think this company must be a pretty active company 'cause they have credits for several different songwriters!"

Billboard

Another source of publishing credits is *Billboard Magazine. Billboard* is a weekly business publication focused on the music industry. For major genres of music, such as pop, country, Latin and R&B/hip-hop, *Billboard* lists the music publishers for that week's hit songs. For example, there are publishing credits listed for each of the 100 songs on the "Hot R&B/Hip-Hop Singles & Tracks" chart.

Now, for the aspiring songwriter, I don't recommend subscribing to *Billboard.* Why? A subscription is quite expensive, but you may find it worthwhile to buy an occasional issue. Also, the biggest hit songs stay on the charts for a long time, so you may be able to compile publishing credits on most hit songs if you buy one issue every three or four months.

There are also specific issues that can be helpful. For example, the final issue each year is a recap and ranking of that year's biggest songs and artists. Not surprisingly, that year-end issue also ranks music publishers. Other issues occasionally spotlight publishers, either in articles or in the ads. For example, the Nashville-based Country Music Association (CMA) gives out awards every fall. Usually *Billboard* runs special articles the week of the CMA Awards. That issue may include more publishing information than you'd normally find. In addition, during the week of the CMA Awards, the PROs (ASCAP, BMI and SESAC) also give awards to their writers and publishers, and those awards are spotlighted in the *Billboard* printed the next week.

The same thing applies periodically in the pop and R&B fields. If you're trying to figure out when such articles and ads might appear, you might check with the PROs or the *Billboard* staff.

I'm singling out *Billboard* only because publishing credits are available in every issue. But keep in mind the *Billboard* credits typically appear only for major musical genres. If you discover a music-business magazine relevant to your style of songwriting or your geographic market, give the magazine a call. See if they ever spotlight publishers and songwriters. (For example: *Music Connection* magazine from Los Angeles and *Music Row* magazine from Nashville usually run publisher-oriented issues once a year.) And let me just emphasize I'm talking about business magazines, not fan-oriented magazines.

Performing rights organizations

Remember ASCAP, BMI and SESAC? Each of these organizations collects performance royalty money for both publishers and songwriters. In this modern Internet age, you shouldn't be surprised to learn each has a website. So when you have time, check out the following (listed alphabetically):

www.ascap.com

www.bmi.com

www.sesac.com

Each PRO website has an area where you can research song titles, songwriters and music publishers. You might find a few details on what artists recorded the songs as well. The ASCAP site will have details on ASCAP titles, writers and publishers. Similarly, the BMI site focuses on BMI affiliates, while the SESAC site focuses on SESAC affiliates. So, assuming you're dealing with companies and writers within the United States, you may have to proceed through all three websites to track down what you're looking for. (Songwriters do sometimes change their PRO affiliations, so the same songwriter may have credits with multiple PROs.)

There are two difficulties with this source of information:

- There's no guarantee you'll find what you want. These websites are updated periodically, but they're not always up-to-date, and the information can be incomplete or inconsistent. You might find last year's hits, but finding this year's hits might be hit-or-miss. I've found addresses and phone numbers listed for some publishers, and no real in-depth information for others.
- Looking up song titles can be problematic if the song title is relatively generic. You won't find too many songs called "Bridge Over Troubled Water." You will find a great many songs called "Hold On." In that case, if you don't know the writers or the publisher, you may not be able to figure out who did what. So pull out that CD booklet!

Other songwriters and musicians

Talk to other songwriters and musicians. Have they heard of a particular publisher? Do they know anything about the publisher's reputation? Do they have any recommendations for publishers you should talk to or publishers you should avoid?

I can't stress enough how much you can learn from your peers! People who have been where you want to go - even if they're just a step or two ahead of you - can teach you so much. This is the reason why you should be a part of your local music community.

Ask the publisher directly

Sometimes songwriters are reluctant to ask direct questions. But, this is a business. You have a right to know some facts about the people you'll be working with. (Can you imagine taking a job and not knowing anything at all about your employer?) Mind you, sometimes you have to carefully choose when to ask. Asking for a publisher's credentials may not be important in an initial conversation. That question may possibly wait until you see how the publisher responds to your songs.

Sure, you might make a fool of yourself by asking the publisher questions, but if you've done your homework and still don't have an inkling about the company you're researching, you still made a good faith effort. You can't know everything, and sometimes the information is just not available. Or maybe the publisher hasn't done anything.

Just be prepared. Have a pencil and paper handy when you ask the publisher for the company's history. What songs did the publisher pitch and get recorded? Who recorded those songs? (And if you don't recognize the artist's name, try to get the name of the artist's record label!) Afterward, check those credits out, and see what they tell you about the company.

CHECKING OUT CREDITS—FURTHER STEPS

Check to see if the credits are real

Unfortunately, in the entertainment business, people sometimes take credit for that which they did not do. If the publisher claims a recent Faith Hill cut, look at the CD booklet and check out *Billboard* and the PRO websites. Which companies are cited? His or somebody else's? Remember, the PRO sites are not always complete, and the multiple-name syndrome I referred to earlier may make it difficult to verify publishing information. Also, companies are often bought and sold, so a publisher's past name may not match the current company name.

Also, if a publisher is touting credits from long, long ago, that may be a sign the company is no longer vital. A publisher whose heyday was in the 1960s may not know anybody still active in the new millennium.

Check on the relative importance of the credits

Let's say you write power ballads suitable for Celine Dion. If a publisher has only placed songs with his Aunt Celine from Idaho, his ability to get your songs to Celine Dion may be a long shot. Not impossible, but not probable!

Suppose you usually write R&B songs, and you just wrote your first country song. You know a few things about hip-hop, but country is alien territory. You talk to a few publishers who claim they have country credits. They tell you those credits and you take good notes.

- **Visit a record store.** How do you decide if these credits have credibility? A little common sense goes a long way. I might pay a visit to a record store, probably a local store with a wide selection or a specialty store handling country, and then I would look for the artist in question and talk to the sales clerks. I probably wouldn't go to the record section in a discount or department store, because those stores often carry only the biggest and most recent hits, and their salespeople are rarely music experts.

- **Check out artists' record labels.** If I know the artist's record label, I have another resource. If I can't find this artist, can I find other performers on the same record label. Not every new artist is as successful as the Dixie Chicks, but if the publisher got a cut with an unknown artist on the same label as the Dixie Chicks, that's a good sign. It indicates the publisher knows somebody, and ideally, you want to be working with people who have access to decision-makers.

- **Access music websites.** In these days of Internet access, you can also access websites such as CDNow or Amazon.com. These websites carry thousands upon thousands of albums, searchable by artist, title or label. You can't have the same one-on-one conversation you might have with the clerk at the record store, but online you can easily check for one artist after another.

- **Read trade magazines.** For mainstream types of music, the charts and articles in trade magazines such as *Billboard* will teach you an incredible amount about the market. Let's assume again that your song is a mainstream country song. If you look at the current country charts, you'll see almost all of the charted acts record for a handful of record labels. It's practically impossible in today's mainstream country market for an unknown label to get any action, so if you're aiming straight for the mainstream, you'll want a publisher with access to the bigwigs or who is willing to put the energy into cultivating those contacts.

That doesn't mean you should necessarily avoid a small country record company or independent country performer. That independent label or artist may provide you with a learning opportunity. The key thing is, hopefully, you'll enter into any business deals with an educated perspective.

But, every genre of music is not like country. That's why your research needs to be tailor-made to your field of music. If you're researching hip-hop, you'll soon discover independent artists and independent labels play a much larger part. This is true in many niche markets - bluegrass, dance, left-field college rock, etc. That's not to say you or a music publisher will have an easy time accessing a small independent label, but as you tailor-make your research, you tailor-make your approaches based on your knowledge of the marketplace.

YOUR FRIEND—COMMON SENSE

Suppose a music publishing company is owned by Jack Xyz, all the publisher's recorded songs were written by Jill Xyz, and all the recordings were performed by the Xyz Brothers and released on Xyz Records. What does that tell you?

The company might be legitimate. Everybody in the Xyz family might have genius level talent or be the next Jackson family, complete with Janet, Michael, Jermaine, and the rest. Or maybe you're writing Zydeco, and there are no other options to pursue. Maybe it's this company, or nobody.

Don't you want to make sure the situation makes sense? Do a little research before you tie up your songs for a few years (or perhaps a lifetime).

This doesn't mean you should only deal with companies with long lists of publishing credits. A large company with a dozen number one hits may not give you the time of day, but pursuing access to that company may motivate you to write great songs and network like crazy. On the other hand, a publisher with few or no credits may be extremely aggressive and eager to find undiscovered talent. Such a publisher may be willing to listen to your songs and take time to develop you as a songwriter. Or, a publisher with few or no credits may be lazy and a bad judge of songs. That's when knowledge becomes your friend. As you understand The Biz better, you can make better judgment calls.

REALITY CHECK

Getting feedback from a publisher can be a reality check. If you've never approached a music publisher before, getting cuts is good, but it's also important to get feedback and build relationships. That way, you can develop some perspective on your songwriting. (That's also the reason why belonging to a songwriters organization can be so helpful. You may be able to get an evaluation without risking much, other than your ego.)

If you sense your songwriting is not yet of Grammy-winning caliber, you may want to focus on smaller companies with limited credentials. Your research can guide you through the maze of company names.

If you're smart, you'll take inventory as you get more feedback. Constantly. Are your songs getting a good reaction? If not, are you sending them to the wrong companies? Or is it because the songs aren't good enough? Maybe it's the demo recording. Maybe it's how you come across on the phone.

And if your songs get a great reaction, you still need to ask yourself questions. Do they love my songs because they don't know any better? Are they trying to rip me off? Do they have a verifiable track record? Do I need to set my marketing and songwriting goals even higher?

IN CONCLUSION

When it comes down to it, most of us write songs because we love to. Never forget that. Keep your dreams alive. We need those dreams to keep us going, especially when conditions get rough.

But, this book is a business book, and you now have a responsibility to yourself and your songs. Take the music business seriously. Do your homework, and you'll have a better chance of making those dreams come true.

Music Publishers: The New A&R

BY DAN KIMPEL

With the British Invasion of the 1960s, rock acts began generating their own songs. Suddenly, the role of the outside songwriter in pop music was substantially diminished. In the decades that followed, other formats—most notably R&B and country—still required outside songs, but the pop music market grew increasingly tight.

Previous generations of songwriters had labored in the employ of music publishers. In New York's famed Brill Building, teams of writers toiling in tiny cubicles turned out songs on demand. Today, many music publishing firms cut lucrative co-publishing and administration deals with successful writers and artists in lieu of retaining a stable of staff songwriters.

This is the era of the multi-hyphenate: the artist/writer, the writer/producer, the artist/writer/producer/entrepreneur. Creative publishers are now in the business of doing what record companies used to do: finding, nurturing and promoting artists. In some cases, they also shop them for label deals.

What makes a band or artist attractive to a record label is often what will interest a publishing company: a strong vision, regional success and a proactive team (manager, lawyer, etc.). But time is the crucial factor: because a publishing company has a good chance of recouping its investment, either through record sales or film and television outlets, it may often take a chance on an unknown artist that a record company simply cannot afford to take.

In preparing this article, I spoke with representatives of the ten most powerful music publishers in the United States. One viewpoint remained consistent, from the top executives to the creative directors to the on-the-street reps: this is a talent-driven business and they are always on the lookout for something new and potentially profitable.

Talk from the top

Ira Jaffe, president of Famous Music Publishing Companies asserts, "We're very aggressive, but we work very specifically. This is a company that doesn't sign every act. We look at a lot of acts, and try to see if we can get them at our price, but we haven't signed that many. Last year we only signed five bands; that is, five *new bands* from clubs, in addition to major bands."

Danny Strick, president of BMG Songs, the U.S. division of BMG Music Publishing Worldwide, says, "There was a time not so many years ago when an act would be signed by a label with the thought that by the third album X amounts of units would be sold. But in today's world, you need an immediate result.

"As a music publisher," says Strick, "we can get involved with things very early, put acts through our own A&R process and then, depending on what each act needs, keep them alive, get them on the road, get them with collaborators and producers and do all the things you do on an A&R level to help things develop."

The record or the publishing deal?

"We negotiate many types of deals," says Judy Stakee, Warner/Chappell VP of creative affairs. "We sign everything from developing writers to developing artists/writers (in hopes of

---

DAN KIMPEL *is a Los Angeles-based personal manager, PR consultant, journalist and author. Dan has served as director of the National Academy of Songwriters and the Los Angeles Songwriters Showcase. He is also author of* Networking in the Music Business (*Writer's Digest Books*).

getting them a record deal) to established writers and artists/writers.''

"It's timing: the project gets a life of it's own," says Jim Vellutato, director of creative affairs at Sony Music. "You get someone who can write great songs or someone with a great vocal and you begin working with them to develop a sound. I play demos for friends in the industry and try to get a feeling of their either liking or not liking what they hear. If I get good reactions, I'll pull back and have the artist or songwriter write five or six songs. Then we have a project."

Valerie Patton, senior director urban for Chrysalis Music adds, "It's fun for me to do deals and work with writers who are up and coming. It's easy to look at *Billboard* and see music by Puffy, Jermaine Dupree and Dallas Austin on the charts—any publisher would love to be in that position. But it's also rewarding to sign writers early in their careers."

Doing the deal

Jaffe says, "At Famous Music we take a careful look at how we do development deals and, as far as supporting bands, we make tapes and put together packages. We also put them together with managers and legal teams so the people making the deals on their behalf are formidable.

"In two instances, we've made videos, so that when we shop the artists around we're walking in with more than just a tape. It's not a state of the art video, but it's enough to give the idea we're serious. It makes a whole presentation that helps us get artists a deal."

"As a creative publisher working with the developing act or someone who's just gotten a deal," says Stakee, "when you're in the trenches fighting for tour support for them, it creates a strong bond. Our writers stay here for a long time. We're the parents and we have all these kids—you make them happy and they stay."

Ron Moss is Director of A&R for North America at Rondor Music, a company which includes Almo-Irving Music and is affiliated with Almo Sounds. The company has an in-house recording studio which Moss uses to his advantage. "I'm empowered to give away studio time to upcoming artists and bands," he says. "They get into the building and get a vibe as far as who we are and what we do."

Tracking the trends

"Sometimes radio forces a 'cookie-cutter' mentality with artists," says Damon Booth, creative director West Coast for EMI Music Publishing. "Radio stations are not in the business of breaking artists. Labels have to pander to radio, and sometimes they miss the talent. A publisher should be good at things that fall through the cracks. A writer/artist can pitch songs to other artists, score films and do this until they get the attention of a bigger label."

John Lloyd, director of talent acquisition at Peer Music, agrees. "The main reason I think publishers have been involved in A&R development is that the A&R guys at the major labels are not given these opportunities. They've pretty much got to have instant results happen for them. I've been willing to spend time —sometimes a year or more—making sure that, when a band is signed to a record deal, it is absolutely ready to go."

Neil Portnow, senior VP of West Coast operations for Zomba Group adds, "I think there are two elements involved in today's music industry. One, there is a need on behalf of the record companies for sources of A&R. But in the corporate environment, where you have bigger companies and fewer creative staff people, it becomes more difficult to be freewheeling and always available for new talent and the new music out there. So it's useful to have another resource such as publishers performing a talent-scouting function."

"I think it's scary times for record companies right now," says Moss. "The price of breaking a band is about a million dollars. Once you get a video out there, sign a band like Garbage, have three videos, a tour, ads in *Billboard*, chart hits and indie promotion, it's a very expensive proposition. Unfortunately, that's created an environment where the label turns off the tap if a band does not get an immediate reaction at radio to their first record."

What's next?

"Pop is here," says Stakee. "It's in the rock market, it's in the country market, and it's in the alternative market. Since the 1950s, we have not had as many teenagers as we do now and they are the ones buying records. And they are buying pop records."

"Pop in all forms is going to be very substantial," says Jaffe. "Traditional rock & roll is going to be there. It's one genre that may change it's face, but it never goes away. The kids still want to go to arenas and concerts and jump up and down and get crazy."

Vellutato agrees: "I think the teen thing is going to get a little edge. Pop will wear itself out and people will want more depth in the lyric. Either you'll find pop-rock or a little more urban pop a la 'N Sync meets TLC, if you can imagine that."

Says Strick, "If you look at the charts, there's a hunger for music. You have the same buyer interested in differing genres—it's not genre specific. When I go to a record store, it's interesting to see a kid buying both Limp Bizkit and Christina Aguilera."

"I can't make a crystal ball prediction," says Portnow. "Our job is to spot a trend when it develops. Obviously the current teen pop trend is filling a void and a niche that's needed. I think there's been a tendency to look down one's nose at what hasn't been judged to be hip, cool or groovy, or to be a pop music maven. But this is changing."

"My philosophy is: listen to the music. Don't put a tag on it. A great song is a great song," says Jaffe.

The dotted line—who and why?

"I just recently signed Angela Via, a seventeen-year-old Tejano artist—like Selena—who writes," says Vellutato. "She's doing Latin-tinged R&B/pop. She's signed with Jason Flom and Kevin Weaver at LAVA/Atlantic. I met with her when she was sixteen. She was sent over by her attorney, Sandy Fox. She came into my office with a couple of demos. She'd tried writing— I gave her three tracks to write to and she wrote a couple of great songs."

Booth says, "I'm working with Tim Easton who was previously signed to a publishing deal. We developed a record and a marketing fund and did a grassroots thing. He's not the Backstreet Boys. He's a real troubadour. John Prine meets Steve Earle. He's not trendy, so instead of trying to convince A&R people at major labels, we've been doing soundtracks. Also, he did his own record which we helped market, and we got him an agent. As a publisher, we are doing everything a label would do. Eventually the major labels can't ignore him. It's the most fun I have."

Patton says, "I signed Johnta' Austin, who is eighteen. He was signed to RCA at thirteen, but it wasn't his time. When he was fifteen, he wrote 'Sweet Lady,' which was recorded by Tyrese. He wants to be an artist - now he's affiliated with a publisher who can actually hook him up with major producers to hone his writing and vocal skills. He's got cuts with Toni Braxton and Aaliyah and a no. 2 R&B cut, 'Get Gone,' with Ideal."

"Our publishing company is proud of Macy Gray," adds Portnow. "She had a previous publishing and record arrangement and, for whatever reason, nothing came of it. We signed her to the publishing company. Macy is off to a real good start. We're particularly pleased to be involved with someone as talented as she is.

"We also signed Korn and Limp Bizkit so we're seeing amazing success," he continues. "We're extremely happy in our association with Mutt Lange, since we participate in half of Shania Twain's success. We have the lion's share of writing and publishing on Backstreet Boys and Britney Spears. We were kind of looking over the market share—which we don't get into in terms of corporate culture—but it's pretty staggering. We also have R. Kelly and Teddy Riley. For an indie company our success has been incredible."

"Justin Clayton is an English gentleman I signed two years ago," says Stakee. "We gave him enough to live on and bought him a four-track to put in his room. He made demos and we shopped them around and showcased him and got him a deal with Ultimatum. He just made his record and got on CMJ and the MP3 tour. It's a little record—we didn't spend a million dollars. This is someone I've worked with from the very beginning. I spent a lot of time going over his songs and taking his demos to the record companies."

Says John Lloyd, "The projects I've recently worked on include Joe 90, who is signed to Adam Duritz' label, E Pluribus Unum, which is through Interscope. We actually recorded the album at his studio in Los Angeles. We are also working with Jimmy's Chicken Shack, a band from the East Coast."

"We do development in all our offices, but the area where we've probably had the greatest success is in Nashville," says Jaffe. "But the people we are signing are not country just because they're from there. Hillary Lindsay is one of our brightest stars—she's signed to Epic 550, but she is a pop act who happens to live in Nashville."

Search mode

Stakee says, "Sheryl Crow was introduced to me by Robert Kraft, president of Fox Music, who was a producer at the time. Jewel was introduced to me in San Diego by a longtime agent friend, Darrin Murphy. He made me stay the night to see her perform at a little coffee shop." Though Stakee is open to submissions from attorneys, managers and industry contacts, she doesn't listen to unsolicited material.

"No unsolicited material," echoes Vellutato. "It has to come in through an attorney, a manager or someone I know in the record industry."

Says Moss, "Managers and attorneys I have relationships with will notify me about a new client they're repping. Every once in a while I'll get out on the road and look for something. I got in a car in Cincinnati, Ohio, and drove around. I had a few leads, but I didn't know where I'd be the next night. I researched it by talking to people and finding out what the main bands were in those areas. It was a great networking experience."

"I listen to everything; I'm open to meeting with people, but obviously material needs to come through a legitimate source," says Patton. "As much as we like to rely on managers and attorneys, I got one package through my accountant. It took me three months to get to it, but I'm glad I did. The writer's name is Arvel McClinton and he's written with Brandy and Eric Benet. People I meet in real life are sources, too. My friend's neighbor's son across the street who cuts hair is a rapper."

"We find acts in every way imaginable," says Portnow. "We find many through the obvious channels: managers, attorneys, producers. But then we have our own folks who like to think they have a pretty good network feeding them information, and they're out there looking all the time."

In conclusion

"The art of songwriting has grown to include many creative elements: producing, discovering, engineering and performing," says Tom Sturges executive VP creative affairs for the Universal Music Publishing Group. "The more a writer can be, the more that writer can become. The music business is the artist development business. Everybody has to be involved."

Copyright Law: The Primary Source of Your Rights

BY KENT KLAVENS

No matter what your level of songwriting experience or success, you should make an effort to tackle at least the basic concepts of the copyright laws. Virtually all of the legal rights you own in your songs come from these laws, and whenever you sign any kind of agreement affecting your songs, you will be dealing with some or all of these rights.

When is a song protected?

The Copyright Law of the United States provides a variety of legal rights and protections to the creator of an original work of authorship. For your songs, then, it is important to understand the meaning of originality and what constitutes a work of authorship.

Originality for a song simply requires that you create original music and lyrics. If you create original lyrics alone or original music alone, these can be separately protected under the copyright law. To be original, your music and lyrics must not have been substantially copied from any other song that is protected by copyright and must also contain some degree of novelty or distinctiveness. As to what is substantial copying, juries and judges determine that on a case-by-case basis. There are no maximum or minimum numbers of notes, words, or musical bars that may or may not be copied. If you think that you may be copying someone else's work, don't do it!

As long as you have not substantially copied lyrics or music from a protected song, it is not really difficult to meet the originality criteria for copyright. Be aware, however, that if you create a distinctive melody line with lyrics that include nothing more than a repetition of the same two words throughout the song (for example, "Let's dance! Let's dance!"), those lyrics will not be protected by the copyright law unless someone uses them with the same melodic notes and rhythm contained in your song.

For your creation to be considered a work of authorship, there must be an expression of your original musical or lyrical creation that has been fixed in tangible form. This simply means that a mere idea for a song (such as one about two next-door neighbors who fall in love) will not be protected until actually expressed with specific lyrics and music embodied in some medium of recorded expression (for example, written down on paper or recorded on tape). Even when expressed in tangible form, however, titles, phrases, and other short expressions are not protected by copyright, so don't attempt to register and protect two lines of lyrics or a few bars of music as a separate work of authorship.

Remember that your song is protected under the copyright laws immediately upon its fixation in tangible form. Formal registration in Washington, D.C., only provides evidence of your claim and makes available to you certain other legal procedural advantages if you sue someone for copying (infringing) your work.

The term (duration) of copyright protection is for the life of the author plus seventy years (in the case of songs created by two or more songwriters, this is marked from the death of the last surviving writer). For works made for hire (I'll describe this later), the duration of copyright is seventy-five years from publication (a legal term specifically defined in the law that I'll also discuss later) or one hundred years from creation, whichever is shorter.

What parts of a song are protected?

For purposes of copyright protection, the primary source of originality usually involves only the melody line and lyrics. Rhythm has rarely been found to be original enough in itself to be protected by copyright, although the rhythm is certainly taken into consideration in determining the degree of similarity between two melody lines. Harmony is also virtually never protected.

A musical arrangement may be protected by copyright, but a very high degree of originality is required. Also, an arrangement of a song is a derivative right (a right derived from the original song), so the copyright owner of the song must consent to ownership of a separate copyright for the arrangement. Most copyright owners will not permit this. Assuming sufficient originality, an arrangement of a song in the public domain (that is, a song not protected by copyright) is the most likely type of arrangement to merit separate copyright protection for the arranger.

The other most common copyright in the music industry, a sound recording copyright, is a different matter because it protects the actual sounds on a recording against unauthorized reproduction. These copyrights are most often held by record companies, who have usually obtained all rights to the performances of the musical and vocal performers on the sound recording as well as to the services of the record producer who processed and compiled all of the performances and other sounds and put them in the final recording.

What songs are not protected?

Besides mere ideas for music or lyrics, or certain forms of expression that do not constitute original works of authorship, there are many existing songs that may not be protected by copyright. These are considered to be in the public domain, and anyone may use as much as they like from such songs in creating a new song (of course, the "free" elements taken from the prior song will not be protected in the new song either). For example, compositions written by Mozart are not protected by the copyright laws, so you could use a pretty melody from one of his works for your love ballad without needing anyone's permission. If someone else later wanted to copy the same melody line from your song, however, they would not need your permission either, although they could not take any of the original, protectible lyrics or music you created for the song.

Whether or not a song is in the public domain can be a difficult question. This is because the U.S. Copyright Law was revised substantially in the late 1970s (effective on January 1, 1978), drastically changing the term of copyright protection and the registration requirements, and was further revised when the United States joined the Berne Convention (an international copyright treaty) in 1989. Prior to these revisions to the law, for example, a song was not protected under federal copyright law at all until it was properly registered in the Copyright Office (although certain state laws may have protected these songs); a song could have been in the public domain if it was published prior to proper registration without an appropriate copyright notice. Now a song is protected from the moment it is fixed in tangible form, regardless of registration, and a song published without proper copyright notice cannot "fall" into the public domain . Also, there used to be an initial copyright term of twenty-eight years and a separate renewal term of an additional twenty-eight years as opposed to the present term described earlier.

To confuse matters more, under the revised copyright laws, there is one set of rules and requirements for the copyright term of songs that were in their initial copyright term on January 1, 1978, another set of rules for songs that were in their renewal term on that date, and a third set of rules for works created thereafter. So a determination of whether a song is in the public domain could depend upon when it was created, when it was registered for copyright, when it was published, and whether its copyright was properly renewed.

If you need to know whether an old song is still protected by copyright, contact either an attorney or the Copyright Office regarding investigation of the copyright status of that song.

Who owns a song's copyright?

The creator of a song owns the copyright unless that copyright has been transferred either by operation of law (without a written agreement) or by the terms of a written document. It's important to know that it's not always necessary for you to have signed a contract for there to have been a partial or complete transfer of ownership rights to your song. These types of automatic transfers of rights include the following:

- **Collaboration:** The most common partial transfer of rights by operation of law occurs when a song is created jointly by more than one songwriter. Without a written document specifying otherwise, all of the songwriters are equal, joint owners.
- **Work-for-hire:** Another way in which a song copyright is transferred by operation of law is when a song was created as a work made for hire. Unless a song was created by the songwriter as an employee within the "scope" of employment, this type of transfer will not occur without a written agreement specifying that a songwriter is creating (or has created) a work made for hire. Typically, to avoid any dispute as to whether a particular creative relationship was really one of employment, a written agreement usually will be requested in this situation.

  In all work made for hire relationships, the employer (whether a person or company) acquiring the song is considered the author for all purposes.

  If a situation like this is proposed to you, you must be careful to retain both the right to future royalties from exploitation of the song and a guarantee of printed or visual credit for writing the song. An appropriate contractual provision might specify that the credit appear "wherever such credit normally appears for songwriters in the entertainment industry."

  Aside from exclusive or staff songwriter agreements, or agreements with film, television, home video, or commercial advertising production companies to compose scores or songs for a specific project in exchange for an advance fee, you should virtually never agree that a song you've created will be considered written for hire. For example, a song you create before you present it for consideration in a film, television, home video, or commercial project should not be characterized as work made for hire. Even though you might agree to assign (transfer ownership) the copyright for the song to the production company anyway, you will retain greater rights if the song is not deemed created for hire. You should have work made for hire language deleted from any songwriting agreement where it appears to be inappropriate.
- **Spousal rights:** A third way in which a song copyright may apparently be partially transferred by operation of law is under the community property laws that exist in various states. In states with such laws, property created or acquired by either a husband or wife during the marriage automatically becomes the joint property of the spouses.

Other than by operation of law, a transfer of the copyright in a song must be made in a written document. Oral agreements to transfer ownership are void and unenforceable.

What rights are involved in copyright?

The rights involved in copyright are simply your exclusive rights to do anything you want with your song (assuming you don't violate some other law in the process, such as performing a song with obscene lyrics over public airwaves). You should always remember that, with certain limited exceptions (such as fair use for purposes of education, criticism, or commentary), no one can exercise any of these rights without your permission. The most common rights include:

- **Mechanical Rights:** These are the rights to mechanically reproduce the song on records, tapes, compact discs, and other recorded products. It is important to know about compulsory mechanical licenses, because it's the major area in music copyrights where someone does not need your permission to use your song. Once a song has been distributed for sale to the public in the U.S. in the form of phonorecords (a term specifically defined in the Copyright Law that includes virtually all recorded products now commonly exploited except audiovisual products), anyone can produce and record that song (not the original recorded performance, though) for other phonorecords without approval, as long as they comply with the law regarding proper notice, payment, and accounting to the music publisher or songwriter controlling the rights.

The royalty paid is known as the statutory royalty (under current law that rate will adjust periodically under a formula tied to the Consumer Price Index). So if you want to "cover" a particular song of a major artist that you really love, you can do it without permission if you follow the legal requirements and pay the statutory royalty.

- **Synchronization Rights:** These are the rights to synchronize the song with visual action for a television program, theatrical motion picture, home video device, or other filmed, taped, or reproduced visual action.
- **Print Rights:** These are the rights to print sheet music and other visual copies of the song.
- **Small Performing Rights:** These are certain, specifically defined performances of your music that are distinguished from other performing rights primarily because two major performing rights "societies" (ASCAP and BMI) collect the vast majority of these sums for their songwriter and publisher members. Small performances mostly include performances on radio and television, and in motion picture theaters outside the U.S., nightclubs, concert halls, and commercial businesses (for example, recorded music performed in jukeboxes, elevators, and department stores). As a practical matter, you will not be paid for these rights unless you have become a member of some performing rights society, because it would be difficult for you to go around the country suing everyone who is performing your hit song without your permission. By joining either ASCAP or BMI (you can't belong to both as a songwriter), or by using some other collection organization (for example, SESAC), you have a collection agent granting permission for these performances and collecting money on your behalf.
- **Grand Performing Rights:** This term is most often applied to the dramatic performance of music in musical plays. It is also sometimes described to include the dramatic performance of a song in any manner that advances the plot or story line of the "work" in which it is performed. As a practical matter, though, the dramatic performance of songs in a theatrical motion picture or television program (for example, a motion picture or television performance of a musical such as *Fiddler on the Roof*) usually generates separate small performing rights payments. The grand performing right for such programs is most often covered in the fee paid for the synchronization right for the song.
- **Derivative Rights:** These are the rights to create other works derived from the song, such as television commercials and new foreign lyrical versions. In the case of "Ode to Billie Joe," an entire motion picture was based upon a song. All of these derivative "works" require the permission of the copyright owner of the original song.
- **General Exploitation and Administration Rights:** These are the rights to issue the licenses (permissions) for all of the uses described above, as well as to collect the money from the exercise of all of the rights to the song. These rights are commonly transferred if you are assigning your song's copyright to a music publisher. It is also common to assign these rights to a foreign subpublisher for a particular country or region of the world.

What is copyright infringement?

For songs, an infringement is generally any unauthorized use of a substantial part of a song that is not within some exception in the Copyright Law allowing that use (such as fair use for educational purposes). For this section, though, I will concentrate only on infringement in the creation of a song, because situations such as the sale of "bootleg" copies by record counterfeiters or some other unlawful use of an entire song without authorization are too obvious to merit discussion. In the most basic sense, copyright infringement with respect to creation of a song is the copying of one legally protected song in the creation of another song. A legal finding of this kind of infringement generally requires proof of both access to the copyrighted song and substantial similarity between the protected song and the later song.

Proof of access, or at least proof that an infringing songwriter had the reasonable opportunity to hear and copy the protected song, can be critical. Some courts have permitted two songs to have striking similarity (that is, the two songs were even more than substantially similar) without a legal finding of copyright infringement because the copyright laws theoretically permit two different songwriters, creating songs independently of each other, to create virtually identical songs, both capable of copyright protection.

A songwriter named Selle once sued the Bee Gees for copyright infringement, claiming "How Deep Is Your Love" infringed his song "Let It End." A musical expert testified that twenty-four of the first thirty-four notes of the Bee Gee's song were identical to Selle's song. In fact, the similarity between the songs was so blatant that one of the Bee Gees, while on the witness stand, mistakenly identified music from "Let It End" as music from "How Deep Is Your Love!" The judge in that case reversed a jury finding of copyright infringement primarily because Selle could offer only speculation and conjecture as to how the Bee Gees had the opportunity to hear and copy his song.

The importance of this principle to the songwriter is obvious: *Keep an accurate, precise record of every person and company where you have sent a demo tape of your songs, as well as the names of the songs on each tape.* All of this evidence could prove crucial if you ever sue someone for copyright infringement.

Of course, if a hit song is widely known and performed, no particular evidence that an infringing songwriter heard or copied the song will be necessary. George Harrison was held liable for copyright infringement in creating "My Sweet Lord" based on its substantial similarity to the hit song "He's So Fine." The widespread popularity of "He's So Fine" led to a finding that, even if George Harrison did not intentionally copy it, he must have heard the song at some point and copied it subconsciously.

What is substantial similarity between two songs? Contrary to the belief of many songwriters that they can safely use up to two or three bars or eight notes of another song (or some other absolute number), this is not the case. There is no definite test. For most courts in this country, even though the testimony of musical experts will virtually always be introduced as evidence during a trial involving copyright infringement, the test will be a question of fact for a judge or a jury to decide after hearing both songs.

What is publication of a song?

The legal concept of publication is important in the copyright law, because the actual date of publication will affect the copyright registration procedure for the song, the "presumption" of legal validity for the facts stated in the copyright registration, the necessity of copyright notice, the proper form of notice, the term of copyright protection, the availability of certain legal "remedies" in case of infringement, and various other legal rights you will have to your song. The most important of these are discussed throughout this chapter. The actual legal definition is the following:

Publication is the distribution of copies or phonorecords of a work to the public by sale or other transfer of ownership, or by rental, lease, or lending. The offering to distribute copies of phonorecords to a group of persons for purposes of further distribution, public performance, or public display constitutes publication. A public performance or display of a work does not of itself constitute publication.

The first commonly misunderstood aspect of this concept is that merely signing your song to a music publisher is not publication and does not mean your song has been published within the meaning of the copyright law. Also, a single performance of your song, whether on radio or television, or the multiple performances of the song live at local nightclubs, does not, by itself, constitute publication. If you distribute multiple copies for purposes of public performance, though, that would be considered publication (for example, sending copies of records to many radio stations or copies of videos to many television stations).

Limited distribution of demo tapes to music publishers or record companies for promotional purposes is not considered legal publication. Even though the eventual purpose of that kind of promotion is the distribution and public performance of the songs on the tapes to the public, that kind of distribution is limited both as to specific people to whom they are being sent and to the immediate purpose of promotion. If the distribution were for the direct purpose of further distribution (for example, distribution of actual sale copies to a record distributor for further distribution to retailers for further sale to the public) or for the direct purpose of public perform-ance (for example, distribution of a motion picture containing the song to movie theaters for exhibition to the public), then publication will have legally occurred.

Bear in mind that, despite the discussion in the paragraph above, if a songwriter were to send hundreds of copies of a song over a long period of time to various publishers, managers, record companies, producers, and recording artists, a court would likely find that a legal publication had occurred. There is no precise dividing line as to how many copies would have to be sent for this to occur. If you are in doubt, consider the song to have been published and follow all of the copyright registration and copyright notice procedures described in this chapter and in the informational materials available from the Copyright Office.

How are copyrights registered?

Registration of copyright in a song is accomplished by filing the proper form with the Register of Copyrights in Washington, D.C., paying the filing fee (currently $30), and submitting either one or two copies of the work to be registered. Generally, one copy is required if the song is unpublished, and two are required if the song has been published. Copyright forms and information pamphlets may be obtained by writing to the Copyright Office, Library of Congress, Washington, D.C., 20559-6000, by phone at (202)707-3000, or online at http://lcweb.loc.gov/copyright.

Form PA is usually the proper form to use for a song. A form SR should be used to obtain a sound recording copyright if you wish to protect the actual sounds on your tape or record in addition to the music and lyrics registered. For example, you may have used some unique synthesizer sounds on your track that you programmed after weeks of work. Although individual sounds are not protected under a song copyright, a sound recording copyright, or under the copyright laws in general, the collection and compilation of various sounds in an original manner would be protected. Anyone could imitate those sounds without consequences, but if they copy (dub) a substantial part of the actual sounds from your tape, you would have a right of legal action against them.

The copyright office does not require either a lead sheet or lyric sheet along with your tape. It is usually best to submit these as extra protection, however, because your registration is only effective for exactly what you register. If any of the lyrics or melody line to your song are not clear on the tape you submit with your registration form, and if you are later involved in a legal action concerning those unclear elements in particular, it's possible you will have totally lost the advantages of copyright registration relating to those elements.

To save money, multiple songs can be registered on one tape as a collection for one fee, and you can use a title such as The Best of (your name), Part I or Songs of Love. The Copyright Office requires that, to register two or more unpublished musical compositions with one application and fee, all of the following conditions must be met:
- the songs must be assembled in an orderly form;
- the combined songs must bear a single title identifying the collection as a whole;

- the copyright "claimant" or claimants must be the same for each song (that is, the owner or owners of the copyright for each song must be the same);
- all of the songs must be by the same songwriter, or, if they are by different songwriters, at least one songwriter must have contributed to each song as a co-writer.

There are potential disadvantages to registering a collection that you should understand. In theory, a song collection, as opposed to each individual song in that collection, is only protected by copyright to the extent that there has been sufficient originality in the selection and arrangement of the songs put together as one "work." If it's obvious that you randomly selected the songs with no apparent theme (such as by registering every song you've ever written under one copyright form or registering groups of songs that have no relationship to each other), theoretically the copyright in the collection could be challenged. If the validity of that copyright and its registration is later denied by a court, it's possible that you would no longer be able to use that registration as a source of evidence of the date of your authorship. In that case, all of the statutory advantages of registration would be lost for each individual song in the collection, and each song would only be protected as though it had never been registered for copyright at all. This is really a fairly obscure legal possibility, and I know of no major cases on this subject, but when you register a collection, it's a good idea to use a title that implies at least some minimal overall concept (for example, *Songs of Love*; *Dance Tunes, Volume I*; *Songs from 1998*; *Ballads*; *Songs for Laura*; *The Best of (your name), Volume I*).

Another issue in registering multiple songs is the indexing of titles by the Copyright Office. This indexing procedure is one of the advantages of copyright registration, because it's legally deemed public notice of your registration (discussed below), and it makes searches of the copyright office records much easier (for example, to find the name of an author, a copyright owner, or the date of registration). A collective work will only be indexed by the title of the collection (not by individual song titles), unless you later file a CA registration form (a supplemental copyright form designed to correct or amplify a prior registration) listing all of the separate song titles that were registered as part of the collection. You should wait until the Copyright Office sends you a copy of your original PA registration form with a registration number and date, because in completing your CA form, you will have to refer to the number and registration date entered on the original PA form by the Copyright Office.

What is the effect of registration?

Copyright registration only establishes a public record of your copyright claim. Many songwriters mistakenly believe that it firmly establishes their claim. For example, just because one writer of a jointly written song decides to register a copyright form PA without the names of the other writers doesn't mean the other writers do not still own equal shares of the copyright. The omitted writers should, however, for best protection, file a form CA to claim that a correction of the original PA form should be made, and that their names should be added to the basic registration.

Copyright registration is also usually necessary before any legal action for infringement can be initiated. If the registration is made within three months after publication of the song or, in the case of infringement of an unpublished song, prior to any infringement, and if the copyright owner wins an infringement case, the owner may be entitled to a court award of attorneys' fees and statutory damages. Otherwise, the copyright owner would be limited to only the actual damages suffered and the profits made by the person or company that infringed the copyright.

An additional advantage of copyright registration is that it constitutes constructive notice to the public of the facts of your claim of authorship and ownership. This means that the public is deemed to have knowledge of your claim whether or not a particular person or company has searched the records of the Copyright Office. For example, if one of your collaborators for a particular song attempts to assign the entire song to a music publisher without your knowledge, your registration will enable you to "void" and nullify the transfer of your interest unless the publisher or collaborator can initially prove you did not co-write the song. Without the registration, it would be up to you to prove initially that you did co-write the song.

That brings up another advantage of registration—the legal burden of proof in court for copyright disputes. If copyright registration has been made either before legal publication or within five years after publication, it constitutes "prima facie" evidence of the facts in the registration. This means that someone contesting a registration, whether an accused infringer or otherwise, has the initial burden to introduce sufficient evidence to prove the registration is invalid, by either establishing that:

- the registering owner did not properly obtain ownership from the author or a prior owner;
- the author did not create the song;
- the song was copied from another source;
- the song was otherwise not an original work of authorship.

The registering owner has no burden to prove anything until the opposing party has produced such evidence.

From this discussion, you should see why registration of your song in the Copyright Office of the Library of Congress is by far the best registration and protection. There are independent registration services (such as that offered by the National Academy of Songwriters in Los Angeles), but they should be used only for short-term purposes, for example, to offer some formal evidence of protection when you may be ready to present your song to someone but haven't had time to register a copyright in Washington, D.C.

Independent registration services, if they are reliable and efficient, do provide an independent source of evidence of your claim of creation on or before the date of registration, but they provide none of the important statutory advantages discussed in this section. It is also important to remember that, as with copyright registration, registration with independent services does not establish your claim—it just provides a dated record of your claim.

Do-it-yourself methods, such as sending a self-addressed letter in the mail, are virtually worthless and should never be used to protect your songs! When in doubt, do it the right way: File a copyright registration form with the Copyright Office!

What about copyright notice?

Under present law for published works, a notice on all "visually perceptible copies" (for example, lead sheets, other sheet music, demo tapes, records), in "such manner and location as to give reasonable notice of the claim or copyright, " is still required to obtain the maximum benefit of copyright protection. The proper copyright notice is either a C in a circle or the word "Copyright," followed by the year of first publication and the name of the original copyright owner. The omission of any element of that notice results in an incorrect notice, having the same legal effect as if there were no copyright notice at all.

Always remember that the proper copyright notice date is not the date of creation, and it's not the date of registration. As you learned earlier in this chapter, the date of publication has a specific legal meaning. No copyright notice is technically required for unpublished works. The Copyright Office, however, recommends that to avoid inadvertant publication without notice, a notice such as "Unpublished Work Copyright 1989 John Doe" should be placed on any copies or phonorecords that leave the possession and control of the creator. Until legal publication has occurred, you can continue to update your unpublished copyright notice. That means if you're positive your song hasn't been published, you will not have to send tapes with copyright notices that make it appear you're promoting an old song! (Be careful, however. As I discussed earlier, the dividing line between preliminary distribution and legal publication is sometimes difficult to determine. Therefore, if you believe publication may have occurred for a particular song, continue to use the same year in all of your copyright notices.)

As I've already mentioned, in previous versions of the copyright laws, under certain circumstances, the publication of a work without copyright notice could have resulted in that work being in the public domain, free to be used by anyone forever without penalty. Under present law, however, revised to bring the United States in line with the requirements of the Berne Convention, publication without notice cannot invalidate your copyright and put your song in the public domain under any circumstances. Despite that safeguard, it's important you realize that infringers who innocently rely on an authorized copy or a phonorecord without a copyright notice may be found by a court to have no liability whatsoever for the infringement if they prove they were misled by the omission of notice. *Without a proper copyright notice, your work could still be used by someone without payment!*

Make it a habit to place the correct copyright notice on all lead sheets and demo tapes of your songs. The rights you protect and save may be your own!

International copyright protection

Copyright protection for your songs in foreign countries can be a complex issue, as there is no international copyright law that applies everywhere. Protection in a particular country depends solely upon the laws of that country.

Countries offering the best protection to U.S. songwriters are usually those having agreed to particular copyright treaties or conventions. These include countries with private, direct, bilateral treaties with the U.S. and countries that have joined a major, multi-country copyright convention to which we also belong.

The United States is now a member of both the Berne Convention and the Universal Copyright Convention, the two most widely accepted international copyright treaties. Under both treaties, as a general rule, a song written at least partially by a U.S. citizen or other person who normally lives in the United States is entitled to protection in each member country in accordance with the same copyright laws that would protect the works of that country's own citizens. Under the Berne Convention, such protection is also offered to any song first published in a Berne member country on or after March 1, 1989. The Berne Convention provides additional protection by virtue of minimum standards established uniformly for all of its member countries.

Most major foreign countries that commonly exploit songs and records of U.S. artists and songwriters are members with us under either Berne or the UCC (for example, Canada, Japan, Australia, and most countries in western Europe). If you are concerned about the protection of your songs in a particular distant foreign country, however, the Copyright Office recommends that you investigate the extent of protection of foreign works in that country before publication anywhere, because protection in that country may depend upon certain facts about your registration, copyright status, or form of publication only at the time of first publication.

If you want more specific information concerning copyrights, contact either a copyright attorney or the Copyright Office, Library of Congress, Washington, D.C., 20559. Request a copy of their current list of application forms, regulations, and circulars. These materials explain registration and protection in much greater detail.

Roundtable: Composing for Film and Television

BY ANNE BOWLING

Soundtrack music is the underappreciated workhorse of the recording industry. Music written for feature films, television shows and commercials doesn't enjoy center stage, but performs a supporting role for storylines and advertising messages. When it works, soundtrack music can both evoke subtle emotional reactions and help prompt us to spend our hard-earned cash. But those compositions—barring perhaps John Williams' highly recognizable work on *Jaws* or the *Star Wars* series, for example—usually don't get too much attention, other than at Academy, Emmy and Clio awards time.

But there is steady work and a good deal of money to be made in the field. Just ask our experts. Here we've collected three industry pros to discuss breaking into the field of writing music for film, television and commercial jingles: film composer Mark Isham; television and film composer Roger Neill; and Jack Streitmarter, president/creative director of the music production house Sound Images. The fields are as competitive now as ever, they say, but as Neill says, "people who are talented will always shine through, eventually."

So whether you want to supplement your solo career with work in commercial jingles, or you dream of composing orchestral scores like Rachel Portman's Academy Award nominated score for *The Cider House Rules*, pay attention. Our experts may save you a few steps or missteps on your road to success.

Mark Isham is an Academy Award-winning film composer who has scored more than 50 feature films, among them *A River Runs Through It* and *Nell*, for which he received a Golden Globe nomination. Named one of the "top three composers of the 1980s" by the American Film Institute, Isham has also recorded more than fifty albums, and has received seven Grammy nominations including his Grammy Award for *Mark Isham*. He has also scored for television, and won an Emmy Award for his work on the drama *EZ Streets*.

Award-winning composer **Roger Neill** has written extensively for television, feature films and the concert stage. During his ten-year career, Neill has written scores for network dramas and comedies from *Silk Stalkings* to *Chicago Hope* to *King of the Hill*. His film credits include the black comedy *Bury Me in Kern County*, which was recognized for excellence at the 1998 South by Southwest Film Fest. Neill also teaches film scoring at the University of Southern California.

Jack Streitmarter is president/creative director of the music production company Sound Images, based in Cincinnati and Los Angeles. He has produced over 2,000 musical scores and jingles for clients across the world, and his work has been recognized with more than 150 Addy, Emmy and Clio awards.

ANNE BOWLING *is editor of* Novel & Short Story Writer's Market, *and a Cincinnati-based freelance writer.*

Mark Isham on composing for film

You've been writing music for films for nearly twenty years now. How has the field changed since you wrote the score for Disney's *Never Cry Wolf* in 1982?

In the last couple of years I've seen a lot of new names pop up, which I think is good. It brings a lot of fresh ideas. Also, because technology has changed a lot, it's pretty much essential that you be able to demo things now. When I started, it was not really possible to demo without a multi-track tape machine or an ensemble to record. Now, of course, you can mock it all up in a room by yourself, and that's pretty much considered mandatory.

Also, I had felt that scores were getting less adventuresome for a while. But again, over the last couple of years I think that's changed. There seems to be a new crop of young filmmakers being given a chance these days, and they are bringing with them a lot of new, exciting approaches to scoring.

For a composer trying to break into the field, which is more important: connections in the field, or perseverance?

I'd say perseverance. With perseverance you can gain connections in the field. If you don't have perseverance, you're not going to survive. You can be connected to Michael Eisner, but if you don't persevere through the politics and even the work itself, you won't survive. Connections don't hurt, but perseverance is absolutely key.

What route would you recommend songwriters go to break into the field?

Well, after the perseverance comes promotion: letting everyone know who you are and what you do, and that you can do it well and are going to continue to do it no matter what. That would include all music supervisors and as many people as you can get your music to.

You have said "the successful film composers are those who begin with a distinct style," and broaden their abilities from that base. Is that still the case?

I still very much think that's the case. You look at someone like Tom Newman, who's pretty much at the top of his game. He started out with a very unique sound and has brought that right up to the top of his profession. Younger guys like Mychael Danna I see doing the same thing—he's working his way with a very specific musical point of view, and it's serving him well. I still think that's much better than being able to do so many different things that no one remembers exactly what it is you do.

Aside from the ability to write evocative music and production experience, what other skills should a composer be prepared to bring to the job?

Communication with the director and producers is the most important aspect of being a film composer. If you know how to talk to somebody, listen to somebody, and can get through whatever evaluations are made about your work by somebody else, that is 80 percent of this job, because filmmaking is a collaborative art form.

You recorded music for more than five feature films in 1998. How long does a typical job take? Are you able to work on your solo projects at the same time, or are they pretty mutually exclusive in terms of your time and creative focus?

I certainly don't like to do films in less than four weeks, although I can—I've done it in less than that! Some jobs you'll start and then the film will move, and you'll end up working on it for three months, but not continuously. So I can work on my solo projects during that time. But if I have to finish a project in four or five weeks, it pretty much becomes the only thing I can do. But I take great care in scheduling my time so that I don't ever completely lose track of my solo projects.

Roger Neill, on composing for television

What common misconceptions do students bring to your course about the field?

Almost everything they think is a misconception. One is that you need to be adept at writing for orchestra. I know a lot of students who are very good orchestral writers coming out of the conservatory and they think that's going to get them some sort of leg up in the industry, but it has become less and less important. Fewer television shows use orchestra, and even of those that do, fewer use orchestras in ways that are applicable to the way you study orchestra in the conservatory. The way the orchestra was used in a movie like *Shawshank Redemption* is a completely original, idiosyncratic approach to using orchestra, and it has nothing to do with studying Stravinsky.

Also, young composers need to know that when you're trying to get on a certain TV show, you are not trying to convince somebody you're a talented composer. That's completely unimportant. You're trying to get a job from somebody who has a problem to solve. The problem is that they have this story that first of all needs music, and what you're trying to do is convince that person you can help them with their problem. They're really uninterested in how talented you are—all they're interested in is their problem and how to solve it.

Were there any real turning points on your way to breaking in?

I got a BMI fellowship in film scoring set up to bring student composers from around the country to L.A. to learn something about the industry. That gave me the last push I needed to enter the field. So I wrote letters to people I had worked with in L.A., and TV composer Mike Post called me and said if you're going to move here, work for me. And as soon as I got there, there was an opportunity for a low budget TV show called *Silk Stalkings*, and he gave me the show to score. It was so simple, and part of the reason it was easy was because the music industry was going through a technological revolution. MIDI technology was new, and my being involved with electronic music in school gave me skills that were valuable. Older composers were becoming outmoded very quickly, because there were no longer any big recording sessions where you'd have thirty guys show up at a session and the score would happen. It became one guy with a lot of synthesizers. So I came in at a time when a lot of people found themselves lacking the basic technical skills that were needed to continue in the industry. And I had them, so I was hired.

Do you see any other mini-revolutions on the horizon in the industry?

I think the Internet is where the new opportunities will be. Very quickly, networks and TV producers are going to be providing Internet content themselves, and making programs for broadcast on the Internet, and they'll be hiring writers and actors and composers. So whoever's in the right place at the right time when that happens is going to find themselves very much in demand.

How valuable and or necessary classroom is instruction for those interested in breaking in?

I have a glib answer, but it's more or less true: despite my PhD, the skills I use most in what I do are the skills I learned as a garage guitarist when I was 17. Knowing the technology, having an understanding of pop music—you don't need to know 20th Century compositional techniques to do this. Just understanding basic harmony and how people hear music is more important, and I think that's why a lot of pop writers have become very fine film composers.

How competitive would you say the field is now?

It's very competitive now. I bet there are probably more bodies here trying to do it just because the technology that's out there makes it possible to create good sounding music without a whole lot of expertise in the basics of music, like harmony. But certainly it was my own misconception that all I had to do was be a really good composer and I would be in demand, but it's not as simple as that. There are plenty of good composers who are trying to make a living doing what I'm doing and can't.

There are other parts which are at least equally important, including being a good business person, being able to work well with people, but even more important probably is really understanding drama, and how films work, and how stories are told—that aspect of the art form. I'll often work with directors who say, "I don't know anything about music, so I don't know how I'm going to communicate to you what I want." And I'll say to them, "It doesn't matter that you don't know anything about music. That's what I'm here for. But hopefully you do know something about your story. Let's talk about the story you're trying to tell, and I'll add what I think I can do for it."

In terms of contracts, are these jobs typically work-for-hire, or do you retain some rights?

Generally, they're works-for-hire. There are exceptions. If you're a particularly in-demand composer and they don't have enough money to pay you your regular fee, you might be given publishing rights, or you might be given profit-sharing points in the movie. Also, particularly for television, a huge part of my income is not the fees I get paid upfront by the producers, but the broadcast royalties I get paid by BMI.

If you could choose one personality trait that is indispensable to success in the field, what would it be?

You can't do this unless you can be a very hard worker, someone who can work hour after hour. You have to have that kind of constitution. If you want a career that's going to have you working 35 hours per week, this isn't going to work out for you.

Is there less personal investment in composing for TV or movies? Do you have to remove yourself from it, and give ownership of parts of it to the other people who are involved in the creative process with you?

Young composers in particular get themselves in trouble with this. I've heard so many times about composers working on a movie, and the director doesn't like what they're doing, so they get in big fighting matches.

I am not less emotionally attached to the music. But I have also developed the ability to completely turn my back on a piece of music if it's not going to work for the director, and start with something totally fresh. It's tough to learn that skill, because you might write something you think is really great, and they don't like it. If that's the case, I will just say, "Okay, I'll put that in my back pocket and write something else for you." We can get ourselves in trouble if we start liking the music, so much that we're blinding ourselves to whether it's working for the project.

Jack Streitmarter on commercial jingle writing

How important is it to be versatile in a range of musical styles?

We're dealing with clients who will demand hip-hop one day and a Brazilian swing the next day, and folk or a garage band the next day. So the more you understand a variety of different musical styles the better it is, so people think of you as being capable of doing more.

Does it help a songwriter to have a very distinctive style as well?

I think it's more true in TV work, and film work, than in our business. Because we tend to have more than one person work on the spot, it's very difficult to think of it as just one style, or one person with one style. On the other hand, don't overstate what you can do. So many people try to be all things to all people, and it's a big mistake because the agency people can see through it. And if you try to be all things to all people and you can't pull it off, you don't get a second opportunity at anything, even what might be your strength. In film and TV, you can be more focused.

Are there a couple of key things a jingle writer can do to make himself more in demand?

First, understand a variety of music—be as eclectic as possible. That helps because the ad agencies don't typically know exactly where they're going, but they can describe the emotions or a piece of music they've heard before. So if you understand that music and can replicate the tone and emotion but not the song itself, that's important.

Secondly, you have to know where to find the best talent for it. I think this is many times not understood in the business. You can write a great piece but if you don't have a great performer sing it, if you don't have that really great pianist or guitar player, then the piece isn't going to be what it should be. It's important for the jingle writer to know where to find the right talent. It's not necessary for that jingle writer to be the pianist simply because he plays keyboard. You should find that perfect talent for the job. Jingle writers should spend a lot of time developing talent lists as well.

Are there common misconceptions that jingle writers bring into the field?

Probably the biggest misconception that any writer has is that anything they write is good. Once you're in the competitive business of music, you have to be able to analyze what truly is a great piece of music, and what is average. If people can't do that, they tend not to be able to sell their product. It's such a competitive business—we go through what I call 'demo wars,' where our music is competing against two or three other jingle houses, and may the best win. And if you don't go through the process of eliminating the average work so you can submit the best, they'll do it for you. And you'll be one of those people left out.

I think we have to able to recognize when we're not writing the best piece. We might have to throw something away that we may have spent hours or even days on, and start from scratch because it didn't develop the way it should. I look at it as a two-part process: I want great creative people, but I also want appropriate pieces. If it's the most creative piece but it doesn't fit the product and it doesn't fit the audience, then it's not appropriate, and it won't sell.

Is now a good time to break into the field?

Sure—it's as good as any. Because there's so much going on—the medium has expanded so much from when I got into the business. Now it's very rare that you see a spot that doesn't require some type of musical effect, or musical score. And in the early days, that required a tremendous budget, and people had to really think about that necessity. And now I think it's pretty standard. The technology in video has changed so drastically. So many spots have computer or cell animation. Because of the rapid speed of the images, so many layers of activities going on, something needs to support that, and that generally is music and sound design.

How do you recommend songwriters break in?

To break into the business, the best thing to do is join organizations where you will find your clients. In my business, it's the ad clubs and the art directors clubs and the marketing clubs. You have to learn how to network with these people, and find some common interests. You're more likely to get work from people who become your friends than people with whom you have strictly a business relationship.

Selling Your Own CDs & Cassettes— The How & Why

BY JANA STANFIELD

Have you ever heard of me? Probably not. That's because I'm relatively famous. In other words, famous to my relatives. Most of us think that in order to make a living with our music we have to be well-known, well-financed or well-connected. No way. With no club dates, festivals or stadium shows last year I sold over $75,000 worth of albums. Most of those gigs were at fellowship halls, schools, house concerts and Tupperware events. If you are capable of entertaining audiences in similar settings, you are capable of making a great living with your music.

ADJUST YOUR ATTITUDE

We used to think record companies and radio stations were the guards at the gateway to our dreams. If we could charm them into opening the gate for us, we could get our music out to the vast record-buying public. These two entities stand tall and tough at the gate, but you know what?

There's no fence.

The record-buying public is just a fancy name for the people all around you: your former teachers, your mechanic, your kids' soccer coach. There are enough people in your life already to help you make a living doing what you love. The trick is to stop thinking our music has to be distributed on a huge scale. Adjust your attitude. Let your new motto be: Start small, dream big, live large.

RECORD YOUR MUSIC

When you record your music it's like a painter putting a frame around an artwork instead of throwing each painting in the trash. You are making it possible for people to enjoy and share your music when you're not there. In terms of marketing you and what you do, it's like putting your pebble in the water so the ripples can multiply. The first people who buy your music will be your friends and family. They will begin to tell *their* friends and family. As that second ring of people becomes interested in your music they'll create the third ring.

Start with just a hundred cassettes if that's all you can afford. Keep your first album simple because you'll be learning as you go. You can make a good quality album without being extravagant. Consider recording it on a 4-track or 8-track. You can get fancier on the next album. I've made all four of my CDs on 8-track and I've never had an album buyer complain that I didn't use enough tracks. People are not buying your albums for the number of tracks or the number of horn players you used. They are buying it to recapture the way they felt when you sang those songs.

You can do a studio album for less than $5,000 these days by budgeting $300 each to produce ten songs and $2,000 for graphics and duplication. If you don't know how to find the right

---

JANA STANFIELD *is the author of* The Musician's Guide to Making & Selling Your Own CDs & Cassettes *(Writer's Digest Books). She has toured with best-selling authors including Wayne Dyer, Bernie Siegal and Deepak Chopra. Jana facilitates workshops for songwriters and performers called "Start Small, Think Big, Live Large."*

studio and musicians for you, ask for recommendations at your local music stores. Call those people and tell them you want to make a good album for the lowest price and then ask what they charge. Some studios will provide a package price that includes the studio time, the engineer and all the musicians. Most studios will also provide you with a checklist of things you can do to keep your costs at a minimum.

The cost of your album will go up according to:

- the amount of time you use, so be sure you and your songs are completely ready for recording. Go over the studio's checklist carefully. Your neighbor's guitar playing may be fine in the living room, but if he's never played in the studio before, it will be cheaper to hire a professional than to pay studio time while your neighbor learns the ropes.
- the number of tracks you use. The 4-track and 8-track studios are less expensive than 24-track studios.
- the number of instrumentalists and vocalists.
- the number of songs you record. Many studios give a volume discount if you're recording ten songs instead of just one.
- the size and reputation of the studio. Expect the huge famous studio overlooking the bay to be more expensive than the home studio where you sing your vocals in the coat closet.
- the complexity of the graphics. Simple black-and-white printing with no song lyrics included is less expensive than full color. Every extra page and every photo in your CD booklet is an additional charge so you can save money by keeping it simple.

For information about cassette and CD duplication, check the ads in the latest musicians' magazines. Currently you can get 500 cassettes and 500 CDs for about $2,000 if you're going for simple graphics. Some duplicators provide the graphic designer with this price and some don't, so be sure to read the fine print. After you've paid your recording costs in this example, each album costs you $2. Even if you give away 100 promo CDs and 100 promo cassettes, you can still make a good profit. Selling 400 CDs for $15 each will bring in $6,000. Selling 400 cassettes for $10 each will bring in $4,000. So you've got $10,000, enough to pay your entire investment with a good chunk left over.

RETHINK YOUR GIGS

So how do you sell a thousand cassettes? Maybe you're wondering how to sell a hundred. It's easy and it's fun. In the beginning of our musical journeys, we sing for enthusiastic gatherings of family and friends. As soon as we start to think those audiences are "easy" because they love us, we think we have to get gigs that will give us "exposure." Not necessarily. Once you have recordings of your music to sell, the one factor that will determine your financial success is your ability to place yourself in front of audiences of people who would potentially buy your albums regardless of the venue.

LET PEOPLE SUPPORT YOUR CAREER BY BUYING ALBUMS

You already have a strong base of "fans" among friends and family. If you will allow those people to support you by buying your albums, they can help you live your dreams. Wouldn't you be willing to help make a dream come true for one of them? Especially if all it took was the purchase of a $10 cassette?

Go for easy. Think of the people who love your music, either in your home town or a town nearby. Play a backyard barbecue for 30 friends and go away with a few hundred dollars in album sales. Can you think of at least one person who would sponsor a house concert? A house concert is a gathering of at least 20 people that can take place in a living room, a backyard, or even on someone's driveway. You provide the music. Those invited are told that there's a $5 suggested donation to the performer. You do the concert and make your albums available on the dining room table, the picnic table or the trampoline next to the blue Impala.

Organize an album release concert, or a series of album release concerts if you have family and friends in different towns. Ask your family and friends to invite other family and friends who might like your music. Tell all the people there that your dream is to support yourself with your music. Tell them you're looking for people who might like this kind of music, and you're looking for places to play. Let them be the first to own your new album. Let them be part of creating your success.

Believe me, the people who like your music will be proud to own your first album. They want to support you. By helping you become all that you can be, they are affirming that their faith in you is well-founded. They want to prove they have a good eye for talent, and they will go to amazing lengths to help you be successful in making your living by performing and selling your albums. They'll even buy albums for their friends.

You may think you could never sell albums to family and friends. If a friend or relative owned a store or a restaurant, would you expect to shop there/eat there for free? No. Once you let everyone know you are still paying off recording costs and are striving to make a living/get out of debt/build your own business with these albums, they will graciously offer to pay. Your challenge is to graciously accept (unless you owe them money). Once you get this thing going, you can give away lots of CDs and still make a living. Until then, just promise yourself that for each person who has generously paid, you will generously pass their kindness on down the road.

WHAT NOT TO SAY ONSTAGE

"Oh, by the way, if you really want one, I have some cassettes with me tonight. They're just some little things that I made up myself. No big deal. They're not on a major label or anything. I didn't even work with a producer. It was just me and the band messing around in the studio. I can't blame you if you don't buy them. I know you'd have to feel about as foolish carrying one out of here tonight as I feel telling you about them. I know you probably don't want one anyway, but my husband/wife said he'd/she'd kill me if I didn't mention them this time. I don't know . . . just forget about them."

Don't get me wrong. This technique is very effective. It is very effective in NOT SELLING YOUR ALBUM.

SUCCESSFUL SELLING FROM THE STAGE

The most important tool in selling your albums is helping audience members feel that by buying your album, they are supporting someone in living a dream. Here are some ways to announce your album sales from the stage without sounding money-hungry:

- "At the risk of jeopardizing my current level of obscurity, I will point out that all the songs you've heard tonight can be found on my albums at the back of the room. I've also got a mailing list you can sign if you'd like for me to let you know when I'll be back this way."
- "If you think these songs sound pretty good here tonight, you won't believe how great they'll sound coming out of your own stereo. All the songs you've heard tonight can be found on my albums which will be available and can be enjoyed in the privacy of your own home or car."
- "If there are any songs you've heard tonight you'd like to hear again or share with a friend, they are all available on my new album, which I'm really proud of. I'll be back there signing albums during the break, and if you've got time I'd love to have you sign my mailing list."
- "We've shared a special evening tonight, so even if you don't have a cassette player or a mailing address, at least come back so we can meet and I can personally thank you for making this a great evening for me."
- "Even if you don't want a cassette and don't particularly want me to know where you live, I hope you'll come back during the break to say hello."

START SMALL, DREAM BIG, LIVE LARGE
The beauty of creating CDs and cassettes is you can:
- automatically move your music career to the next level.
- create your own music on your own terms.
- increase your income and notoriety without moving to a major music center.
- have a successful music career based in your own home town.
- allow your songs to be heard, shared and "pitched" to other artists when you're not even there.
- work your day job for as long as you need or want to.
- start your own small business with about a $5,000 investment.

If all this is not enough, I personally promise your musical self-esteem will receive a major boost every time someone hands you $10 or $15 for your album. For all the rejection musicians endure, each album sold means someone is saying, "I like what you do. I don't care if you're famous. Your music moves me and this is my way of supporting you in making more." So go out there and make your own music, make your own circuit, make your own fame. You will not regret it.

Checklist for a successful sales table

☐ **Cassettes and CDs**. Make sure the front of the cases are facing forward, not facing up toward the ceiling, to allow greater visibility. You can buy cardboard display boxes for a few dollars apiece from your CD manufacturer.

☐ **Solid color tablecloth**. Thin, bright-colored plastic ones cost less than a dollar each at party supply stores and will show off your music better than a dark-colored, scratched or stained table.

☐ **Photo, posters or backdrop sign**. Put your promo photo, poster or logo sign on the table to add visual pizzazz and draw attention from across the room. Frame them or back them with stiff foam-core board, or stand them up with an L-shaped stand.

☐ **Mailing list**. If the line to sign your mailing list is causing a traffic jam and keeping potential buyers from getting to your cassettes and CDs, move the sign-up sheet away from your sales table. Be sure to write "Please Print" in the handwriting of a first grade teacher to model what you want.

☐ **A bowl for business cards**. This prevents mailing list sign-up table clog.

☐ **Your business cards**. If you think people are serious about wanting to book you, take *their* business cards and call them to explore the possibility.

☐ **A Sharpie brand permanent marker**. These markers will write on anything—even the CD itself. Always offer to sign your albums. It may seem hokey to you but buyers value this.

☐ **Price list**. Put as much info as you can on your signs so people get their questions answered even when you're not there. Include the names of the songs that they're most likely to ask for. Print the letters as big as possible.

☐ **Change ($50)**. Charge easy amounts for your albums, like $10 for cassettes and $15 for CDs. Numbers like $7.50 and $13.95 become complicated to make change for. Keep it simple, and then you'll only need fives or tens for change.

How to Make Your Submission Stand Out

BY MIKE PO

A common misconception is that, in order for a demo package to stand out, it must be the brightest, loudest, most attention-grabbing package of them all. In reality, this couldn't be further from the truth. Amidst a desk full of odd-shaped packages, fluorescent-colored paper and obnoxiously screaming press releases, what really shines is a demo submission presented in a concise, professional manner—one that says, "take me seriously."

The A&R rep, booking agent or radio programmer on the other end of your demo package is, above all, *busy*. With that in mind, then, the most successful way to make a first impression is to show you have done your homework, followed submission guidelines, and can present a complete package that needs no apologies—in short, to showcase your professionalism, as well as your musical talent!

MINIMIZE THE HYPE

Consider this: Yes, without question, the general public responds to hype, cheap gimmicks, fads, hucksterism and relentless hyperbole. For most performers, these are the key components of a successful rise to stardom (musical talent notwithstanding). Unfortunately, though, at this level the general public isn't your target audience—bored, jaded, "seen-it-all" music business professionals are. This is not to say everyone who receives your promo package is entirely immune to hype tactics. But, in addition to the countless unsolicited packages received from complete unknowns, nearly everyone at every level of the music business is constantly bombarded with press releases, gimmicks, the latest "hottest new act of the year," all crafted by some of the most clever advertising execs in the country.

This sort of hype is unstoppable, unbeatable and, frankly, numbing. You can gauge for yourself. Just consider how often you listen to glowing reviews and the like in magazines, on television and over the Internet. Now, can you put yourself in the position of someone who is immersed in this hype machine for a living, like a local club promoter, a disc jockey, an A&R rep for a big label? Face it, it's extremely difficult to compete with the big-label, big-money promotional machine!

More importantly, you've got to redefine your conception of who your target audience is. Music industry professionals are now prospective *business partners*, not potential new *fans*. This is, indeed, the music *business*, and that's exactly how it needs to be approached. You're not trying to sell tickets or T-shirts to your industry contacts; you are asking them to enter into a high-risk financial arrangement with you.

Just forget that concept of *hype* for a moment. Yes, like every other aspect of your career, there is plenty of room in your promotional presentation for sheer, unadulterated hype. For the most part, however, bear in mind that at this stage of your professional life, just getting out the raw *information* is absolutely crucial. This might be an entirely new way of thinking, compared

---

MIKE PO, *as president and A&R of Limited Potential Records, discovered acts such as Smashing Pumpkins, Brainiac and Catherine. He is a regular columnist for www.getsigned.com and is the author of his self-published book* The Press Kit-A Rock Band's Survival Guide.

to the "must be on stage all the time, must be a master showman" mentality, but: It's time to start thinking of yourself as more of a newscaster than a talk-show host.

COVER THE BASICS

The typical demo submission is centered around the *press kit*—a package of promotional materials generally accompanying a review copy of an album release or demo tape. Different versions of the press kit include materials suited for different recipients, as in music columnists, promoters, radio programmers or A&R reps. A typical press kit for a recording artist is composed of several basic components:

- artist biography
- fact sheet
- promotional photo
- reprints of press "clippings"

In addition, it's not unusual to include a song list, lyric sheet, gig sheet and reports of radio airplay and chart positions. These elements are almost always accompanied by a cassette or CD "demo," packaged in an outer folder or binder, along with a traditional, personalized cover letter.

The press kit

The goal of the press kit is twofold: The factual information within is sufficient for journalists to base an article or review upon, while the editorial content of the artist's biography leaves enough room for a certain element of *hype*. Above all else, the end result of the press kit is to generate interest for the artist. The press kit serves as the "mouthpiece," the salesman pitching the performer.

You can consider a press kit, then, to be either of two things: A) a promo package full of existing press clippings, or B) a promo package to be used by the press to produce clippings. For a larger, national act, a press kit contains reprints of interviews, reviews and articles—a representation of the overall persona of the performer. In this case, the purpose is more likely to promote a new release, a new tour, or perhaps put a new spin on the artist's public image— maybe even an attempt to completely overhaul an image.

For the as-yet-undiscovered act, though, the press kit is a much different animal. Rather than compiling review and interview clippings, its mission is to *generate* some of these write-ups. The press kit for a start-up act is also the promotional device used to get the first live bookings, radio play, reviews, and "shop" for the goal of every hungry artist: that huge record deal.

The fact sheet

This most useful element of the kit is also the easiest to compose. Just what the name implies, the fact sheet contains no hyperbole, no salesmanship and no filler. It's a concise overview of the factual information of who and what is involved. For a band or group project, it's the place to list individual members' names, instruments played and musical backgrounds (involvements in previous bands, side projects, awards, etc.). For solo artists, perhaps the focus will be on the specifies of a recent release or recording session. There are no hard and fast rules on what exactly should be in a fact sheet, but in general, it should at least contain:

- artist's hometown
- members' names and instruments played
- album release information
- touring, recent dates, upcoming shows of note
- management and record label (indie or otherwise) contact information
- producer and recording studios involved

The fact sheet can contain just about any relevant information you would like, as long as it is, indeed, *fact*. "We totally rocked every audience we played for last year" may or may not be entirely factual. However, "The band recently completed a 22-date Midwest college tour, supporting . . ." is verifiable information.

Why is the fact sheet so important? Basically, because numbers don't lie. If your act has been receiving consistent regional airplay, for example, it might serve you well to show the stations and chart positions, almost in spreadsheet format. The same rule applies to live performances. Show the attendance figures and capacities of venues played, rather than employing hype-filled "we're HUGE on the radio!" Music statements such as "we consistently sell out shows" or industry folks are surrounded by numbers, and pay attention to them: sales figures, attendance figures, chart positions, etc. If you can chart the progress of your act from playing to crowds of 50, all the way up to playing to crowds of 500, then you're able to show tangible proof of your act's audience appeal.

TOO MUCH? TOO LITTLE?

Generally, it's wise to avoid the temptation to cram absolutely everything relating to your act into the first promotional mailing. Attempts to "pad" the press kit with multiple pages of clippings are usually taken as an amateur mistake, particularly if the enclosed clippings are repetitive or contain multiple mentions from the same publication. By and large, a well-written kit need not be more than several pages in length—particularly in the case of an unsolicited mailing. The old show biz adage of "leave 'em wanting more" is somewhat appropriate. While you don't want to leave out any of the vital information, the goal isn't to overwhelm with every imaginable detail. Quality, and not quantity, is the approach that will net the best results.

THE GIMMICK

Promotional gimmicks are another touchy issue. Again, most recipients of these tactics have seen it all, and aren't likely to be impressed. Worse than that, an ill-planned gimmick can work against you, by evidencing a desperation to be noticed, as opposed to letting the music speak for itself. From odd-shaped boxes, to glitter-covered cassette cases, to any sort of non-standard promotional item, there is no evidence gimmicks help get your music heard. In fact, if anything, these items are a hindrance, cluttering desks and making a mess, and more likely to be thrown away to make space.

SUBMISSION QUALITY

Above all else—above *anything* else—from the solo singer/songwriter to the full performing group, the single most important thing to consider in the promotional mailing is "*do I need to make apologies for any of this material?*" Ask yourself:

- Is the cassette or CD of the best quality?
- Is all of the necessary contact information clearly visible on EVERY element of the mailing (all pages of the press kit, the cassette or CD itself, the folder it's packaged in)?
- Are there any handwritten elements, or is everything clearly typewritten or laser printed?
- Have posted submission guidelines been followed *exactly*?
- Is the photo clean and sharp?
- Would you have any reservations about the material, from the performance, to the recording, if this was your only chance at being reviewed by a top A&R exec?

THE ALL-IMPORTANT CONTACT INFO

Lastly, if you are to read this, file it away, ignore it, forget it—do anything, but learn from it, at least remember only this one tip: Put your contact info on EVERYTHING. Worse even than being summarily rejected, imagine if your band missed out on a prime opportunity because a promoter couldn't figure out how to call you! It can, and does, happen. Tapes and CDs are quickly separated from their packing in a messy, busy office. Demos are often reviewed in the car, and club promoters leave a stack of demos next to the tape deck on the mixing board. When your demo really does get its 15-second shot at glory, you had better hope that whoever is "discovering" it will know whom to call! The same principle applies to your press kit, in that you shouldn't assume your cover letter will stay attached, or even that all your pages will stay stapled together.

Follow these guidelines. Make your submission concise, fact-filled and keep the hype to a minimum. Prove you've taken a professional approach to your career, and your demo submission truly will stand out from the rest.

Is This the Right Company for Me?

BY DON GRIERSON

The absolute ideal in asking the above question would be for you to have created such responsive music and an identifiable image that a multitude of record labels or publishers would be aware, excited and on the phone demanding you sign a deal immediately. Ideal, but not often the case, unfortunately!

THE "PERFECT" DEAL

Without question, the *perfect* record or publishing company does not exist. Sometimes, these deals are determined by relationships managers or attorneys have with label executives, connections which obviously can be valuable. But there are certain relevant criteria that should become part of any serious, decision-making process to find the "right" company for you. These include looking for a company that has a proven record for responding to the needs of its artists and writers, fostering innovation, planning wisely and following through with those plans to deliver results. It also means finding the company that will provide the most supportive "creative family" for you. Although many artists and writers may never have the luxury of making such choices, I hope you will pursue your dream no matter what. And when you are one of the lucky ones who must decide which dotted line to entrust your dream to, I hope you remember the following considerations.

ARTISTS & RECORD DEALS

Once a "buzz—i.e., hype, media attention has been created (various ways and means of getting to this point have been explored in previous editions of *Songwriters Market*) and there are potential choices available to the artist, numerous questions need to be addressed and "red flags" need to be watched out for.

Investigate the company track record

Let's assume that you as an artist are secure in your musical vision and have several labels interested in you. The first challenge is identifying the companies that, from known history, are most likely to best relate to your type of music and have a greater understanding of promoting, marketing and selling that creativity. Also crucial is evaluating the style and image of the label:

☑ Are they known to be a "big checkbook" company that might agree to a hefty contract but then lets the act end up just one of many names on a busy release schedule?

☑ Or, is the label more boutique in style and roster size with a reputation for selectivity and development of talent?

Give serious consideration to the history of each label, whether they have or don't have

DON GRIERSON *has headed the A&R departments of Epic Records, Capitol Records and EMI-America Records. He is directly responsible for signing some of the world's most noted artists including Celine Dion, Kate Bush, Joe Cocker and George Clinton.*

proven successes in working with and maximizing talent similar to yours. Some labels have proven strengths with certain categories of music and not with others, even though they may have artists signed in several different genres. Arista Records, for example, has always been extremely successful with pop and R&B music but hasn't had the same level of success with rock. Warner Bros. Records has always been a label respected for being artist-friendly with a long history of unique, self-defining talent, but lacks the same results with R&B. Research the style, strengths, history and even staff stability and reputation of any label showing interest in signing a deal.

Learn the position of your company contact

Is your initial connection to the label a junior A&R staff member or a senior A&R executive? The junior A&R person might be the daily go-to in-house champion and excitement trigger. However, the senior executive is more likely to be involved in the planning process for a new release and is included in the decision-making department meetings. In turn she is in a stronger position to speak on your behalf and help define the numerous, crucial commitments made.

Evaluate staff enthusiasm

I have, unfortunately, seen situations where artists have been lost in the shuffle after:

☑ being signed for political or other non-A&R reasons;

☑ not communicating or creating a "working" relationship with appropriate staff members; or

☑ lacking that daily in-house champion.

A key objective is having as many department heads as possible be knowledgeable about you and your music. The more excitement created within the company the better! It is not at all beneficial to sign with a label and be scheduled for release without the decision makers knowing and understanding your personality and vision. If these key decision makers at the label don't show legitimate interest in spending real time, or have to be pushed to do so, then perhaps this is not the company to do business with.

Meet with the creative departments

Ask questions of staff members of all the creative departments.

☑ How do they perceive the general imaging of your act and the type of approach they might take to establish you in the marketplace?

☑ What are their marketing philosophies? Get a feel for their "flair" and desire to bring innovation to their campaigns.

☑ Ask about their approach to video usage and their knowledge and exploitation via the ever-growing Internet.

Confer with the sales and press departments

Meet with the national sales staff. Analyze how they deal with the retail community and especially their understanding, and ability, to address nontraditional sales and distribution (e.g., a tie-in with a nontypical retail chain like The Gap or McDonald's). Again, see if they are idea-oriented people who consistently attempt to find new ways to reach potential customers. The same applies to the press department:

☑ How connected are they to key influential journalists?

☑ What kind of thinking goes into their planning of press campaigns if there is no unique story "hook" (which frequently happens)?

☑ Does it appear the staff involved has the time to personalize a campaign for each artist they are responsible for?

☑ Do they hire independent people to augment current staff?

I have seen the press folk definitely unable to spend necessary time working an artist, usually due to overload, but won't or can't outsource for help unless the artist pays for it.

Meet with the promotion department

Promotion is perhaps the most important segment of the company team, and also the most difficult to relate to. Promotion people usually concentrate on radio exposure and often lead the company on whether a record "has it" or not. I have never accepted the attitude that if a record doesn't make it at radio then all is lost. This is, unfortunately, often the case. A *good* record company will fight for radio exposure but will also strive to find other ways to connect to an audience. Try as best you can to relate with the promotion department but know they generally live and die by what radio tells them. There can be much more to the big picture than just that medium, making it critical to work with the other departments, to ensure *all* avenues for exposure are explored.

Ask about touring

Touring can be very important, depending on music style (see the When to Tour sidebar below). If touring is appropriate and will be beneficial in the early stages of an album's life, or even prior to release, ask about relationships the label has that can potentially enhance the right touring opportunities. Knowledgeable artist management and a good booking agency will be crucial in this mix. Check the label's ability to make things happen with agencies and what similar touring packages they have been involved with.

When to Tour

- Being able to play live and develop a "buzz' prior to a release can really enhance an act's interest level with labels, especially if the music is rock, alternative or metal. Once an album is released from those categories touring becomes a very important part of the marketing plan.
- If the music is adult contemporary, dance or "pure pop"—singles driven—touring doesn't become part of the equation until after the hits have been established.
- Jazz artists can sometimes tour (usually clubs) without a label.
- Generally, R&B and rap artists don't use touring as a key element of a career until after a record has been exposed.
- With country music, touring has always, and probably always will be, a big part of an artist's life, contract or not. It's a lifestyle!

Determine commitment to international exposure

With the United States now only one-third of the world market, it is important to check the company's understanding and support for international exposure. Though it's usually necessary to jumpstart a successful release domestically before it has relevance overseas, it is smart to know about the various key markets outside the U.S. and the differentials that come into play in those locales.

With clever planning and the right timing, international presence and success can really extend your career. There is much more loyalty shown to artists overseas, and less emphasis on trends. Once you are accepted there and you show a commitment to them by a steady pattern of touring and doing the necessary press and promotion, an act can have a very long and rewarding career— U.S. longevity or not. For example, Tina Turner reigns as queen in Europe, selling out arenas and in some cases stadiums, but cannot come close to matching that status here.

Making the decision

Once you and the label feel you want to partner, the attorneys (including your entertainment attorney) take over and then the "deal points" become part of the total package.

☑ If it is the biggest deal you are interested in, then much of the above philosophy won't apply. This article's overview is really about making creative decisions, not dollar ones.

☑ If it is the best "fair" offer that drives you, then your instincts and information gleaned from the relationships at the label and the belief in the staff's ability to identify with the act and its place in the market will be as important as the deal. A contract and no success is a very short term positive!

SONGWRITERS & PUBLISHING DEALS

For the songwriter in a similar situation to the artist (these days they can often be the same), the approach isn't so different. Usually a writer, and often the artist, enters into a separate agreement with a music publisher. Sometimes that contract is basically a collection agreement for all writer income for which the publisher takes an administration fee. That approach can be appropriate, but if you wish to have a professional team work on your behalf, this exercise will pertain to some of the elements that should be evaluated in considering a full publishing agreement. Assuming a record deal is in place, a publisher is likely to be anxious to lock in a relationship because it guarantees an album, and probably singles, will be released. Will the publisher support the label in any way to help promote the record upon release?

Inquire about song placement outlets

Some publishers will augment the record company's promotional efforts with added dollars to hire independent "consultants." How aggressive are they in working with the film and television community to create placement for songs, and sometimes exciting opportunities in upcoming movie and TV shows? In this era of heavy music involvement in these mediums, the more creative publishers spend a great deal of time and manpower attempting to initiate these types of usage, especially when a soundtrack is involved. Record labels are also active in this respect. It has become more difficult to work the traditional placement of songs with artists, primarily because the great majority of artists are self-contained (country music being the obvious exception). A good publishing entity must seek additional ways to maximize usage of signed writers.

Ask about co-writing partnerships

The aggressive publisher will be active in generating co-write liaisons, sometimes with fellow signed writers, but more often with artists who are readying new material. Contemporary recording artists, in general, are very reluctant to record outside songs, but are more open to a creative co-write. Knowing schedules, who's interested, and whose music might fit with an outside writer's style is part of the publisher's day-to-day activity. Having the instincts to plan such combinations is a real expertise, as is the ability to actually make them happen.

Identify relationships with international markets

How interactive is the publisher with their overseas affiliates? As with record sales, the international marketplace constitutes approximately two thirds of the total publishing revenues earned. Does the publisher attempt to initiate co-writing opportunities with overseas artists and writers? This question applies much more to the basic songwriter than the recording artist whose publishing they represent. A big international hit can obviously stimulate serious cash flow, but it can also create new territories where your writing skills can be utilized, no matter your success, or lack of, at home.

Numerous songwriters have more success getting "cuts" overseas than here in the U.S. There are various international markets where the local recording scene is extremely active and where there is a very open mind to using "outside" songs. One Los Angeles-based songwriter I know has 20 songs (some co-written) recently recorded, or scheduled to be, by local artists in such diverse countries as Norway, Holland, England, Hungary, South Africa, Germany, Hong Kong and Japan. Many of these records create only small income but collectively it adds up. And, one big hit can mean not only a big payday but establish a much higher profile for future collaborations and covers.

Making the decision

A good publisher can open doors, make connections and initiate opportunities. Finding that publisher involves being proactive by asking questions and learning to trust your instincts. Remember, if a deal sounds fishy, it probably is. Do not enter into any agreement lightly and be sure to have an entertainment attorney look over any contract before signing. Understanding the possibilities and having a well-rounded overview of the broad spectrum of the music business will be invaluable in determining the right company to align with.

The Markets

Music Publishers... 97

    Category Index.................................... 161

Record Companies...................................... 169

    Category Index.................................... 246

Record Producers....................................... 254

    Category Index.................................... 286

Managers & Booking Agents............... 291

    Category Index.................................... 336

**Advertising, Audiovisual &
Commercial Music Firms**......................... 343

Play Producers.. 359

    Play Publishers.................................. 373

Classical Performing Arts....................... 376

Contests & Awards.................................... 393

Important Information on Market Listings

- Although every listing in *Songwriter's Market* is updated, verified or researched prior to publication, some changes are bound to occur between publication and the time you contact any listing. You may want to call a company before sending them material to make sure their submission policy has not changed.
- Listings are based on interviews and questionnaires. They are not advertisements, nor are markets reported here necessarily endorsed by the editor.
- Every listing in *Songwriter's Market* is screened for unethical practices. If a listing does not meet our ethical requirements, they will be excluded from the book.
- Companies that appeared in the 1999 edition of *Songwriter's Market*, but do not appear this year, are listed in the General Index at the back of the book along with a code explaining why they do not appear in this edition.
- A word of warning. Don't pay to have your song published and/or recorded or to have your lyrics—or a poem—set to music. Read "Rip-Offs" in The Business of Songwriting section to learn how to recognize and protect yourself from the "song shark."
- If you have found a song shark through this book, write to us at 1507 Dana Ave., Cincinnati OH 45207, with an explanation and copies of documentation of the company's unethical practices.
- *Songwriter's Market reserves the right to exclude any listing which does not meet its requirements.*

Key to Abbreviations

SASE—self-addressed, stamped envelope
SAE—self-addressed envelope
IRC—International Reply Coupon, for use in countries other than your own.

- For definitions of terms and abbreviations relating specifically to the music industry, see the Glossary in the back of the book.
- For explanations of symbols, see the inside front and back covers of the book. Also see pages 8.

Complaint Procedure

If you feel you have not been treated fairly by a listing in *Songwriter's Market*, we advise you to take the following steps:

- First try to contact the listing. Sometimes one phone call or a letter can quickly clear up the matter.
- Document all your correspondence with the listing. When you write to us with a complaint, provide the details of your submission, including the date of your first contact with the listing, the nature of your subsequent correspondence, and copies of any documentation.
- We will enter your letter into our files and attempt to contact the listing.
- The number and severity of complaints will be considered in our decision whether or not to delete the listing from the next edition.

Music Publishers

Finding songs and getting them recorded—that's the main function of a music publisher. Working as an advocate for you and your songs, a music publisher serves as a song plugger, administrator, networking resource and more. The knowledge and personal contacts a music publisher can provide may be the most valuable resources available for a songwriter just starting in the music business.

HOW MUSIC PUBLISHERS WORK

Music publishers attempt to derive income from a song through recordings, use in TV and film soundtracks and other areas. While this is their primary function, music publishers also handle administrative tasks such as copyrighting songs, collecting royalties for the songwriter, negotiating and issuing synchronization licenses for use of music in films, television programs and commercials, arranging and administering foreign rights, auditing record companies and other music users, suing infringers, and producing new demos of the music submitted to them. In a small, independent publishing company, one or two people may handle all these jobs. Larger publishing companies are more likely to be divided into the following departments: creative (or professional), copyright, licensing, legal affairs, business affairs, royalty, accounting and foreign.

The *creative department* is responsible for finding talented writers and signing them to the company. Once a writer is signed, it is up to the creative department to develop and nurture the writer so he will write songs that create income for the company. Staff members often put writers together to form collaborative teams. And, perhaps most important, the creative department is responsible for securing commercial recordings of songs and pitching them for use in film and other media. The head of the creative department, usually called the professional manager, is charged with locating talented writers for the company. Once a writer is signed, the professional manager arranges for a demo to be made of the writer's songs. Even though a writer may already have recorded his own demo, the publisher will often re-demo the songs using established studio musicians in an effort to produce the highest-quality demo possible.

Once a demo is produced, the professional manager begins shopping the song to various outlets. He may try to get the song recorded by a top artist on his or her next album or get the song used in an upcoming film. The professional manager uses all the contacts and leads he has to get the writer's songs recorded by as many artists as possible. Therefore, he must be able to deal efficiently and effectively with people in other segments of the music industry, including A&R personnel, recording artists, producers, distributors, managers and lawyers. Through these contacts, he can find out what artists are looking for new material, and who may be interested in recording one of the writer's songs.

WHERE THE MONEY COMES FROM

After a writer's songs are recorded, the other departments at the publishing company come into play.

- The *licensing and copyright departments* are responsible for issuing any licenses for use of the writer's songs in film or TV and for filing various forms with the copyright office.
- The *legal affairs department and business affairs department* works with the professional department in negotiating contracts with its writers.
- The *royalty and accounting departments* are responsible for making sure that users of music are paying correct royalties to the publisher and ensuring the writer is receiving the

proper royalty rate as specified in the contract and that statements are mailed to the writer promptly.

- Finally, the *foreign department*'s role is to oversee any publishing activities outside of the United States, to notify subpublishers of the proper writer and ownership information of songs in the catalogue and update all activity and new releases, and to make sure a writer is being paid for any uses of his material in foreign countries.

LOCATING A MUSIC PUBLISHER

How do you go about finding a music publisher that will work well for you? First, you must find a publisher suited to the type of music you write. If a particular publisher works mostly with alternative music and you're a country songwriter, the contacts he has within the industry will hardly be beneficial to you. Each listing in this section details, in order of importance, the type of music that publisher is most interested in; the music types appear in **boldface** to make them easier to locate. It's also very important to submit only to companies interested in your level of experience (see the Openness to Submissions sidebar on page 4). You will also want to refer to the Category Index at the end of this section, which lists companies by the type of music they work with. Publishers placing music in film or TV will be proceded by a ▨ (see the Film & TV Index for a complete list of these companies).

Additional Publishers

There are **MORE PUBLISHERS** located in other sections of the book! On page 160 use the list of Additional Publishers to find listings within other sections who are also music publishers.

Do your research!

It's important to study the market and do research to identify which companies to submit to.

- Many record producers have publishing companies or have joint ventures with major publishers who fund the signing of songwriters and who provide administration services. Since producers many times have an influence over what is recorded, targeting the producer/publisher can be a useful avenue.
- Since most publishers don't open unsolicited material, try to meet the publishing representative in person (at conferences, speaking engagements, etc.) or try to have an intermediary intercede on your behalf (for example, an entertainment attorney; a manager, an agent, etc.).
- As to demos, submit no more than 3 songs.
- As to publishing deals, co-publishing deals (where a writer owns part of the publishing share through his or her own company) are relatively common if there is interest in a writer.
- Are you targeting a specific artist to sing your songs? If so, find out if that artist even considers outside material. Get a copy of the artist's latest album, and see who wrote most of the songs. If they were all written by the artist, he's probably not interested in hearing material from outside writers. If the songs were written by a variety of different writers, however, he may be open to hearing new songs.
- Check the album liner notes, which will list the names of the publishers of each writer. These publishers obviously have had luck pitching songs to the artist, and they may be able to get your songs to that artist as well.
- If the artist you're interested in has a recent hit on the *Billboard* charts, the publisher of that song will be listed in the "Hot 100 A-Z" index. Carefully choosing which publishers will work best for the material you write may take time, but it will only increase your

chances of getting your songs heard. "Shotgunning" your demo packages (sending out many packages without regard for music preference or submission policy) is a waste of time and money and will hurt, rather than help, your songwriting career.

Once you've found some companies that may be interested in your work, learn what songs have been successfully handled by those publishers. Most publishers are happy to provide you with this information in order to attract high-quality material. Ask the publisher for the names of some of their staff writers, and give them a call. Ask their opinion of how the publisher works. Keep in mind as you're researching music publishers how you get along with them personally. If you can't work with a publisher on a personal level, chances are your material won't be represented as you would like it to be. A publisher can become your most valuable connection to all other segments of the music industry, so it's important to find someone you can trust and feel comfortable with. Also read the article Taking Notes: Music Publishers and Background Research on page 58.

Independent or major company?

Also consider the size of the publishing company. The publishing affiliates of the major music conglomerates are huge, handling catalogs of thousands of songs by hundreds of songwriters. Unless you are an established songwriter, your songs probably won't receive enough attention from such large companies. Smaller, independent publishers offer several advantages. First, independent music publishers are located all over the country, making it easier for you to work face-to-face rather than by mail or phone. Smaller companies usually aren't affiliated with a particular record company and are therefore able to pitch your songs to many different labels and acts. Independent music publishers are usually interested in a smaller range of music, allowing you to target your submissions more accurately. The most obvious advantage to working with a smaller publisher is the personal attention they can bring to you and your songs. With a smaller roster of artists to work with, the independent music publisher is able to concentrate more time and effort on each particular project.

I **For More Information**

For more instructional information on the listings in this book, including explanations of symbols ( ), read the article How to Use *Songwriter's Market* to Get Your Songs Heard on page 5.

SUBMITTING MATERIAL TO PUBLISHERS

When submitting material to a publisher, always keep in mind that a professional, courteous manner goes a long way in making a good impression. When you submit a demo through the mail, make sure your package is neat and meets the particular needs of the publisher. Review each publisher's submission policy carefully, and follow it to the letter. Disregarding this information will only make you look like an amateur in the eyes of the company you're submitting to.

Listings of companies in Canada are preceded by a ☑ , and international markets are designated with a ⊕ . You will find an alphabetical list of these companies at the back of the book, along with an index of publishers by state.

PUBLISHING CONTRACTS

Once you've located a publisher you like and he's interested in shopping your work, it's time to consider the publishing contract—an agreement in which a songwriter grants certain rights to a publisher for one or more songs. The contract specifies any advances offered to the writer, the rights that will be transferred to the publisher, the royalties a songwriter is to receive and the length of time the contract is valid.

- When a contract is signed, a publisher will ask for a 50-50 split with the writer. This is standard industry practice; the publisher is taking that 50% to cover the overhead costs of running his business and for the work he's doing to get your songs recorded.
- It is always a good idea to have a publishing contract (or any music business contract) reviewed by a competent entertainment lawyer.
- There is no "standard" publishing contract, and each company offers different provisions for their writers.

Make sure you ask questions about anything you don't understand, especially if you're new in the business. Songwriter organizations such as the Songwriters Guild of America (SGA) provide contract review services, and can help you learn about music business language and what constitutes a fair music publishing contract. Be sure to read The Business of Songwriting on page 20 for more information on contracts. See the Organizations section of this book for more information on the SGA and other songwriting groups.

When signing a contract, it's important to be aware of the music industry's unethical practitioners. The "song shark," as he's called, makes his living by asking a songwriter to pay to have a song published. The shark will ask for money to demo a song and promote it to radio stations; he may also ask for more than the standard 50% publisher's share or ask you to give up all rights to a song in order to have it published. Although none of these practices is illegal, it's certainly not ethical, and no successful publisher uses these methods. *Songwriter's Market* works to list only honest companies interested in hearing new material. (For more on "song sharks," see The Rip-Offs on page 23.)

N ⊘ A TA Z MUSIC, P.O. Box 1014, St. George VT 84771-1014. Phone/fax: (435)688-1818. E-mail: info@aecrazy.com. Website: www.acecrazy.com. **Contact:** Kyle Garrett, professional manager (pop/r&b/hip-hop). Music publisher. Estab. 1999. Publishes 8 songs/year; publishes 2 new songwriters/year. Staff size: 4. Pays standard royalty.
How to Contact: *We only accept material referred to us by a reputable industry source (manager, entertainment attorney, etc.)* Prefers CD/CDR or VHS videocassette with lyric sheet. "Be sure to include lyric sheets!" Include SASE. Responds only if interested.
Music: Mostly **pop**, **r&b** and **hip-hop**; also **rock**, **dance** and **alternative**. Does not want country. Published "Weekend Crush" (single), "Body Heat" (single), written and recorded by Ace (pop/r&b); "Edge of Time" (single), written and recorded by Ron Broad (pop/rock), all from *Weekend Crush* (album), released 2000 on Diferent Records.
Tips: "Put a lot of effort into your submission . . . it'll show. Never take a submission lightly . . . it'll show! Go to as many songwriter workshops as possible and refine your craft. Send only great songs . . . *not* good songs."

✓ ◯ ABALONE PUBLISHING, 29355 Little Mack, Roseville MI 48066. (810)775-6533. E-mail: ruffprod@aol.com. Website: members.aol.com/jtrupi4539/index.html. President: Jack Timmons. Music Director: John Dudick. Music publisher and record company (L.A. Records). Estab. 1984. Publishes 20-30 songs/year; publishes 20-30 new songwriters/year. Staff size: 12. Hires staff songwriters. Pays standard royalty.
Affiliate(s): BGM Publishing, AL-KY Music and Bubba Music (BMI).
How to Contact: Submit demo tape by mail. Unsolicited submissions are OK. Prefers cassette with 1-5 songs and lyric sheet. "Include cover letter describing your goals." Include SASE with first class postage. All others, please include $1 to cover fluctuating postal rates. Responds in 3 months.

Music: Mostly **rock**, **pop** and **alternative**; also **dance**, **pop/rock** and **country**. Does not want rap, alternative or rave. Published *The Torch* (album by Robbi Taylor/The Sattellites), recorded by The Sattellites (rock); "The Web" (single by Jay Collins), recorded by The Net (rock); and "Passion" (single by R. Gibb), recorded by Notta (blues), all on L.A. Records.

Tips: "Follow stipulations for submission 'to a tee.' Not conforming to our listing exactly constitutes return of your submission. Write what you feel; however, don't stray too far from the trends that are currently popular. Lyrical content should depict a definite story line and paint an accurate picture in the listener's mind."

ACTIVATE ENTERTAINMENT LLC, (formerly Solid Discs), 11328 Magnolia Blvd., Suite 3, N. Hollywood CA 91601. Fax: (818)508-1101. President: James Warsinske. Music publisher. Estab. 1988. Publishes 30-60 songs/year; publishes 10-20 new songwriters/year. Pays standard royalty.

Affiliate(s): Harmonious Music (BMI).

How to Contact: Submit demo tape by mail. Unsolicited submissions are OK. Prefers CD, cassette or VHS videocassette with 2-5 songs and lyric sheet. "Clearly label tapes with phone numbers." SASE. Responds in 1 month.

Music: Mostly **hip-hop**, **rock** and **pop**.

ALCO MUSIC (BMI), P.O. Box 18197, Panama City Beach FL 32417. Professional Manager: Ann McEver (country, alternative, rock). **Contact:** A&R Dept. Music publisher. Estab. 2000. Staff size: 2. Pays standard royalty.

How to Contact: Submit demo tape by mail. Unsolicited submissions are OK. Prefers cassette or CD with 3 songs, lyric sheet and cover letter. SASE. Responds in 3 weeks.

Music: Mostly **pop/rock**, **country** and **alternative**; also **gospel**. Does not want instrumentals.

Tips: "Make sure your submission meets our submission requirements. We are looking for songs that can compete at a Nashville or Los Angeles level and strong enough for major artists."

ALLRS MUSIC PUBLISHING CO. (ASCAP), P.O. Box 1545, Smithtown NY 11787. (718)767-8995. E-mail: allrsmusic@aol.com. Website: www.geocities.com/allrsmusic. **Contact:** Renee Silvestri, president. Music publisher. Voting member of NARAS, CMA, SGMA, SGA. Estab. 1994. Staff size: 6. Publishes 3 songs/year; publishes 2 new songwriters/year. Pays standard royalty.

Affiliate(s): Midi-Track Publishing Co. (BMI).

How to Contact: *Write, call or e-mail for permission to submit.* Prefers CD or cassette with 3 songs, lyric sheet and a #10 business-size SASE. "Make sure CD or cassette tape is labeled with your name, address and telephone number." Does not return material. "Include SASE for reply . . . even if we decide to pass on your song, we will keep cassette on file. In the future there could be a need for your song." Responds in 2 months.

Film & TV: Places 1 song in film/year. Recently published "Why Can't You Hear My Prayer" (single by F. John Silvestri), recorded by Iliana Medina in a documentary on anxiety disorders.

Music: Mostly **pop**, **country** and **gospel**; also **MOR**, **R&B** and **top 40**. Does not want jazz, classical or rap. Published "Debide A Ti" (single by F. John Silvestri/Leslie Silvestri), from *Nancy Raven Sings Her Favorites in Spanish* (album), recorded by Nancy Raven (Latin country), released 2000 on KMA Records; and "Because of You" (single by F. John Silvestri/Leslie Silvestri), from *Ernie Ashworth and Friends* (album), recorded by Vicki Leigh (country gospel), released March 2001 on KMA Records.

**FOR EXPLANATIONS OF THESE SYMBOLS,
SEE THE INSIDE FRONT AND BACK COVERS OF THIS BOOK.**

Tips: "Attend workshops, seminars, join songwriters organizations and keep writing, you will achieve your goal."

✓ ▨ ◻ **ALEXANDER SR. MUSIC (BMI)**, PMB 364, 7100 Lockwood Blvd., Boardman OH 44512. (330)782-5031. Fax: (330)782-6954. E-mail: dap@netdotcom.com. Website: www.dapenterta inment.com. **Contact:** LaVerne Chambers, promotions. Owner: Darryl Alexander. Music publisher, record company (DAP Entertainment), music consulting, distribution and promotional services and record producer. Estab. 1992. Publishes 12-22 songs/year; publishes 2-4 new songwriters/year. Staff size: 3. Pays standard royalty.

How to Contact: *Write first and obtain permission to submit.* Prefers cassette with 4 songs and lyric sheet. "We will accept finished masters (cassette or CD) for review." SASE. Responds in 2 months. "No phone calls or faxes please."

Film & TV: Places 2 songs in TV/year. Music Supervisor: Darryl Alexander. Recently published "Feel Your Love" and "You Are So Beautiful" for the film *The Doctor Is Upstairs*, both written and recorded by Darryl Alexander.

Music: Mostly **contemporary jazz** and **urban gospel**; also **R&B**. Does not want rock, gangsta rap, heavy metal or country. Published "Take A Chance" (single by Darryl Alexander/Shiela Hayes), recorded by Shiela Hayes (urban jazz), released 2001.

Tips: "Send only music in styles that we review. Submit your best songs and follow submission guidelines. Finished masters open up additional possibilities. Lead sheets may be requested for material we are interested in. Must have SASE if you wish to have cassette returned. No phone calls, please."

◻ **ALEXIS (ASCAP)**, P.O. Box 532, Malibu CA 90265. (323)463-5998. **Contact:** Lee Magid, president. Music publisher, record company, personal management firm, and record and video producer. Member AIMP. Estab. 1950. Publishes 50 songs/year; publishes 20-50 new songwriters/year. Pays standard royalty.

Affiliate(s): Marvelle (BMI), Lou-Lee (BMI), D.R. Music (ASCAP) and Gabal (SESAC).

How to Contact: Submit a demo tape by mail. Unsolicited submissions are OK. Prefers cassette or VHS videocassette with 1-3 songs and lyric sheet. "Try to make demo as clear as possible—guitar or piano should be sufficient. A full rhythm and vocal demo is always better." Does not return material. Responds in 2 months only if interested.

Music: Mostly **R&B**, **jazz**, **MOR**, **pop** and **gospel**; also **blues**, **church/religious**, **country**, **dance-oriented**, **folk** and **Latin**. Published "Jesus Is Just Alright" (single by Reynolds), recorded by D.C. Talk on Forefront Records (pop); "Blues For the Weepers" (single by Rich/Magid), recorded by Lou Rawls on Capitol Records (pop/blues); and "What Shall I Do" (single by Q. Fielding), recorded by Tramaine Hawkins on EMI/Sparrow Records (ballad).

Tips: "Try to create a good demo, vocally and musically. A good home-recorded tape will do."

✓ ◻ **ALIAS JOHN HENRY TUNES (BMI)**, 11 Music Square E. #101, Nashville TN 37203. (615)259-2012. Fax: (615)259-2148. E-mail: bobbyjohn@spencemanor.com/BJH. Website: spencem anor.com. **Contact:** Bobby John Henry, owner. Music publisher, record producer and music hotel (The Spence Manor Suites). Estab. 1996. Publishes 3 songs/year; publishes 1 new songwriter/year. Staff size: 3. Pays standard royalty.

How to Contact: *Call first and obtain permission to submit a demo.* Prefers cassette with 3 songs and lyric sheet. Does not return material. Responds in 6 months only if interested.

Music: Mostly **country**, **rock** and **alternative**. Does not want rap. Published *Mr. Right Now* (album by Kari Jorgensen), recorded by "Hieke" on Warner Bros. (rock); and *Nothing to Me* (album by B.J. Henry), recorded by Millie Jackson on Spring.

Tips: "Focus and rewrite, rewrite, rewrite."

🌐 ✓ ◻ **ALL ROCK MUSIC**, . Phone: (31) 186-604266. Fax: (32) 0186-604366. E-mail: sales@ collectorrec.com. Website: www.collectorrec.com. **Contact:** Cees Klop, president. Music publisher, record company (Collector Records) and record producer. Estab. 1967. Publishes 40 songs/year; publishes several new songwriters/year. Staff size: 3. Pays standard royalty.

Affiliate(s): All Rock Music (England).
How to Contact: Submit demo tape by mail. Unsolicited submissions are OK. Prefers cassette. SAE and IRC. Responds in 2 months.
Music: Mostly **'50s rock**, **rockabilly** and **country rock**; also **piano boogie woogie**. Published "The Brush" (single), from *Boogie Woogie Special* (album), written and recorded by André Valkering (piano boogie), released 2000 on Down South Records; "Playtoy" (single), from *R & R with Piano* (album), written and recorded by Mike Cushman ('50s rock), released 2000 on Collector Records; and "Bingo Boogie" (single by R. Turner) from *High Steppin' Daddy* (album), recorded by Tommy Mooney ('50s hillbilly), released 2000 on Collector Records.
Tips: "Send only the kind of material we issue/produce as listed."

◯ **ALLEGHENY MUSIC WORKS**, 306 Cypress Ave., Johnstown PA 15902. (814)535-3373. E-mail: TunedOnMusic@aol.com. Website: www.alleghenymusicworks.com. **Contact:** Al Rita, managing director. Music publisher and record company (Allegheny Records). Estab. 1991. Staff size: 2. Pays standard royalty.
Affiliate(s): Allegheny Music Works Publishing (ASCAP) and Tuned on Music (BMI).
How to Contact: *Write first and obtain permission to submit.* "Include SASE for reply. E-mail queries are acceptable. Responds in 1 week to regular mail requests and usually within 48 hours to e-mail queries."
Music: Mostly **country**; also **pop**, **A/C**, **R&B**, **novelty**, **Halloween** and **inspirational**. Does not want rap, metal or x-rated lyrics. Published "Flying In the Sky" (single by Penny Towers Wilber) from *Halloween Bash* (album), recorded by Victor R. Vampire (pop/novelty/Halloween), released 2000 on Allegheny.
Tips: "Bookmark our website and check it regularly, clicking on *Songwriter Opportunities.* Each month, as a free service to songwriters, we list a new artist or company looking for songs. Complete contact information is included. For a deeper insight into the type of material our company publishes, we invite you to read the customer reviews on amazon.com to our 2000 best seller Halloween album release, *Halloween Bash.*"

◯ **ALLISONGS INC. (ASCAP, BMI)**, 1603 Horton Ave., Nashville TN 37212. (615)292-9899. Website: www.allisongs.com. President: Jim Allison. Professional Manager: Bill Renfrew. Music publisher, record company (ARIA Records) and record producer (Jim Allison). Estab. 1985. Publishes 50 songs/year. Staff size: 4. Pays standard royalty.
Affiliate(s): Jim's Allisongs (BMI), Songs of Jim Allison (BMI) and Annie Green Eyes Music (BMI).
 • Reba McEntire's "What Am I Gonna Do About You," published by AlliSongs, Inc., was included on her triple-platinum album, *Greatest Hits.*
How to Contact: Submit demo tape by mail. Unsolicited submissions are OK. Send CD and lyric sheet. Does not return material. Responds in 6 weeks only if interested.
Music: Mostly **country** and **pop**. Published "Fade To Blue" (single by Reeves/Scott/Allison), recorded by LeAnn Rimes on Curb Records (country); "Preservation of the Wild Life" (single by Allison/Young), recorded by Earl Thomas Conley on RCA Records (country); and "Cowboys Don't Cry" (single by Allison/Simon/Gilmore/Raymond), recorded by Daron Norwood on Giant Records.
Tips: "Send your best—we will contact you if interested. No need to call us. It will be listened to."

✓ 📷 ◯ **ALPHA MUSIC INC. (BMI)**, 747 Chestnut Ridge Rd., Chestnut Ridge NY 10977. (845)356-0800. Fax: (845)356-0895. E-mail: info@trfmusic.com. **Contact:** Michael Nurko. Music publisher. Estab. 1931. Pays standard royalty.
Affiliate(s): Dorian Music Corp. (ASCAP) and TRF Music Inc.
How to Contact: "We accept submissions of new compositions. Submissions are not returnable."
Music: All categories, mainly **instrumental** and **acoustic**; also **theme music** for television and film. "Have published over 50,000 titles since 1931."

◯ **AMEN, INC.** (Spanish only), 2035 Pleasanton Rd., San Antonio TX 78221-1306. (210)932-AMEN. E-mail: amen@txdirect.net/. Music publisher and record company (AMC Records). Estab. 1963. Pays standard royalty.

Affiliate(s): CITA Music (BMI).
How to Contact: Submit demo tape by mail. Unsolicited submissions are OK. Prefers cassette and lyric sheet. "Allow three to four weeks before calling to inquire about submission." SASE. Responds in 4 months.
Music: Evangelical Christian gospel in Spanish. Published "Imponme Tus Manos" (by Jesus Yorba Garcia), recorded by Rudy Guerra; "Jesucristo" (by Enrique Alvarez), recorded by Kiko Alvarez; and "Hey, Hey, Hey" (by Manny R. Guerra), all on AMC Records.

✓ ○ **AMERICAN HEARTSTRING PUBLISHING (ASCAP)**, 25300 Heather Vale St., Santa Clorita CA 91350. E-mail: amh@amhpublish.com. Website: www.amhpublish.com. **Contact:** Tim Howell, president. Music publisher. Estab. 1994. Publishes 10-20 songs/year; publishes 1-2 new songwriters/year. Staff size: 1. Pays standard royalty.
How to Contact: *Contact first and obtain permission to submit.* Prefers "radio ready" CDs. SASE. Responds in up to 2 months.
Music: Mostly **pop**, **MOR**, **R&B** and **duets any style**. Does not want rap. Published "Highly Insensitive Comments," recorded by Rob Carter and the Blueprints, released 1999 on Salt Mine.
Tips: "Lyrics are king and good melodies make the magic happen. Make sure your song is 'singable' with a good hook and contemporary theme anyone can identify with."

[N] ○ **AMERICATONE INTERNATIONAL**, 1817 Loch Lomond Way, Las Vegas NV 89102-4437. (702)384-0030. Fax: (702) 382-1926. President: Joe Jan Jaros. Estab. 1975. Publishes 25 songs/year. Pays variable royalty.
Affiliate(s): Americatone Records International, Christy Records International USA, Rambolt Music International (ASCAP).
How to Contact: Submit demo tape by mail. Unsolicited submissions OK. Prefers cassettes, "studio production with top sound recordings." SASE. Responds in 1 month.
Music: Mostly **country**, **R&B**, **Spanish** and **classic ballads**. Published "Romantic Music," written and recorded by Chuck Mymit; "Explosion" (by Ray Sykora), recorded by Sam Trippe; and "From Las Vegas" (by Ladd Staide), recorded by Robert Martin, all on Americatone International Records.

○ **ANTELOPE PUBLISHING INC.**, P.O. Box 55, Rowayton CT 06853. **Contact:** Tony LaVorgna, president. Music publisher. Estab. 1982. Publishes 5-10 new songs/year; publishes 3-5 new songwriters/year. Pays standard royalty.
How to Contact: Submit demo tape by mail. Unsolicited submissions are OK. Prefers cassette with lead sheet. Does not return material. Responds in 1 month "only if interested."
Music: Only **bebop** and **1940s swing**. Does not want anything electronic. Published *Inspiration* (album), written and recorded by T. LaVorgna (jazz); *Please Stay* (album by Nicole Pasternak), recorded by Cathy Gale (1940s swing), both on Antelope; and *Nightcrawler* (album by Tommy Dean), recorded by Swing Fever on Alto Sound (jazz).
Tips: "Put your best song first with a short intro."

⊕ ○ **AQUARIUS PUBLISHING**, Servitengasse 24, Vienna A-1090 Austria. Phone: (+43)1-7684380. Fax:(+43)1-7677573. **Contact:** Peter Jordan, owner. Music publisher and record company (World Int'l Records). Estab. 1987. Publishes 100-200 songs/year; publishes 10 new songwriters/year.
How to Contact: Submit demo tape by mail. Unsolicited submissions are OK. Prefers cassette with up to 10 songs. "Lyric sheets not important; send photo of artist." Does not return material. Responds in 1 month.
Music: Mostly **country, pop** and **rock/ballads**; also **folk, instrumental** and **commercial**. Published *Sehnsucht ist ein Feuer* (album), recorded by Emanuela, released 2000 on WIR.

✓ ○ **ARAS MUSIC (ASCAP)**, P.O. Box 100215, Palm Bay FL 32910-0215. Phone/fax: (208)441-6559. E-mail: savmusic@juno.com. Website: www.zyworld.com/arasmusic/aras.htm. President: Bill Young. **Contact:** Amy Young (country, contemporary Christian, pop, alternative, jazz and latin) or Bruce Marion (piano and instrumental). Music publisher and record company (Outback Records). Member Academy of Country Music, Country Music Association. Estab. 1996. Pays standard royalty.

Affiliate(s): SAV Music (BMI), Outback Records, Stone Age Records and PARDO Music (SESAC).

How to Contact: Submit demo tape by mail. Unsolicited submissions are OK. Prefers cassette or CD with 3 songs and typed lyric sheet. SASE. "Make sure enough postage is included to return demo." Responds in 6 weeks.

Music: Mostly **country**, **contemporary Christian** and **jazz**; also music suitable for motion pictures. Does not want rap or classical. Published *Disturbing Behavior*, written and recorded by Chokehold (heavy metal), released 2000 on Stone Age Records; *Now and Forever*, written and recorded by Charlie Allen (country), released 2000 on CBS Records; and *Reflections*, written and recorded by Carl Sanders (country), released 2000 on Outback Records.

Tips: "When recording a demo, have an artist in mind. We pitch to major labels and major artists, so please submit studio-quality demos with typed lyric sheets. If you submit a marketable product, we will put forth 100% effort for you."

AUDIO IMAGES TWO THOUSAND MUSIC PUBLISHING (BMI), P.O. Box 250806, Holly Hill FL 32125-0806. (904)238-3820. **Contact:** D.L. Carter, submissions department. Music publisher. Estab. 1995. Pays standard royalty.

Affiliate(s): Sun Queen Publishing (ASCAP).

How to Contact: *Write first and obtain permission to submit.* "No phone calls, please." Does not return material. Responds in 6 weeks.

Music: Mostly **MOR**, **country** and **contemporary Christian**; also **gospel**. Published "Every Dog Has His Day" (single by Dianne Carter/BJ Shawd), recorded by Dianne Carter (country); "Do You Care" (single by Dorothy J. Smith/Vincent Survinski), recorded by B.J. Shawd (country); and "All Ya Gotta Do Is Pray" (single by Barbara Jean Smith), recorded by Sunshine Singers (gospel), all on BJ's Records.

AUDIO MUSIC PUBLISHERS (ASCAP), 449 N. Vista St., Los Angeles CA 90036. (818)362-9853. Fax: (323)653-7670. E-mail: parlirec@aol.com. Website: www.parlirec@bigstep.com. **Contact:** Lew Weisman, professional manager. Owner: Ben Weisman. Music publisher, record company and record producer (The Weisman Production Group). Estab. 1962. Publishes 25 songs/year; publishes 10-15 new songwriters/year. Staff size: 10. Pays standard royalty.

How to Contact: Submit demo tape by mail. Unsolicited submissions are OK. "No permission needed." Prefers cassette with 3-10 songs and lyric sheet. "We do not return unsolicited material without SASE. Don't query first; just send tape." Responds in 6 weeks. "We listen; we don't write back. If we like your material we will telephone you."

Music: Mostly **pop**, **R&B** and **rap**; also **dance**, **funk**, **soul** and **gospel**. Does not want heavy metal. "Crazy About You" (single) and *Where Is Love* (album), both written by Curtis Womack; and *Don't Make Me Walk Away* (album by Debe Gunn), all recorded by Valerie (R&B) on Kon Kord.

AVALON MUSIC (ASCAP, BMI), P.O. Box 121626, Nashville TN 37212. **Contact:** A&R Review Department. Professional Manager: Avalon Hughs. Music publisher, record company (Avalon Recording Group) and record producer (Avalon Productions). Estab. 2001. Staff size: 3. Pays standard royalty.

How to Contact: Submit demo tape by mail. Unsolicited submissions are OK. Prefers cassette or CD with 3 songs and lyric sheet. Include SASE. Responds in 3 weeks.

Music: Mostly **rock**, **country**, and **alternative**; also **R&B** and **hip hop**.

Tips: "Send songs suitable for today's market."

BAGATELLE MUSIC PUBLISHING CO. (BMI), P.O. Box 925929, Houston TX 77292. (713)680-2160 or (800)845-6865. **Contact:** Byron Benton, president. Music publisher, record company and record producer. Publishes 40 songs/year; publishes 2 new songwriters/year. Pays standard royalty.

Affiliate(s): Floyd Tillman Publishing Co.

How to Contact: Submit demo tape by mail. Unsolicited submissions are OK. Prefers cassette (or videocassette) with any number of songs and lyric sheet. SASE.

Music: Mostly **country**; also **gospel** and **blues**. Published "Everything You Touch" (single), written and recorded by Johnny Nelms; "This Is Real" and "Mona from Daytona" (singles), written and recorded by Floyd Tillman, all on Bagatelle Records.

⟨N⟩ ◐ BAIRD MUSIC GROUP (BMI), P.O. Box 42, 1 Main St., Ellsworth PA 15331. E-mail: ronssong@charterpa.net. **Contact:** Ron Baird, president. Vice President: Ed Bailes. Music publisher, record company (La Ron Ltd. Records), record producer (Ron Baird Enterprises). Estab. 1999. Publishes 5-12 songs/year. Pays standard royalty.

Affiliate(s): Baird Family Music (ASCAP).

How to Contact: Submit demo tape by mail. Unsolicited submissions are OK. "No certified mail." Prefers cassette only with 2-4 songs and lyric sheet. Does not return submissions. Responds only if interested.

Music: Mostly **country** and **country rock**. Does not want hip-hop, gospel/religious or R&B.

Tips: "Don't give up!"

◐ BAITSTRING MUSIC (ASCAP), 2622 Kirtland Rd., Brewton AL 36426. (334)867-2228. **Contact:** Roy Edwards, president. Music publisher and record company (Bolivia Records). Estab. 1972. Publishes 20 songs/year; publishes 10 new songwriters/year. Hires staff songwriters. Pays standard royalty.

Affiliate(s): Cheavoria Music Co. (BMI)

How to Contact: Submit demo tape by mail. Unsolicited submissions are OK. Prefers cassette with 3 songs and lyric sheet. Does not return material. Responds in 1 month.

Music: Mostly **R&B, pop** and **easy listening**; also **country**. Published "Forever and Always," written and recorded by Jim Portwood (pop); and "Make Me Forget" (by Horace Linsley) and "Never Let Me Go" (by Cheavoria Edwards), both recorded by Bobbie Roberson (country), all on Bolivia Records.

◐ BAL & BAL MUSIC PUBLISHING CO. (ASCAP), P.O. Box 369, LaCanada CA 91012-0369. (818)548-1116. E-mail: balmusic@pacbell.net. **Contact:** Adrian P. Bal, president. Music publisher, record company (Bal Records) and record producer. Member AGAC and AIMP. Estab. 1965. Publishes 2-6 songs/year; publishes 2-4 new songwriters/year. Staff size: 2. Pays standard royalty.

Affiliate(s): Bal West Music Publishing Co. (BMI).

How to Contact: *Write or call first and obtain permission to submit.* Prefers cassette with 3 songs and lyric sheet. SASE. Responds in 3 months.

Music: Mostly **MOR, country, rock** and **gospel**; also **blues, church/religious, easy listening, jazz, R&B, soul** and **top 40/pop**. Does not want heavy metal or rap. Published *Special Day* (album), written and recorded by Rhonda Johnson on Bal Records (gospel).

Tips: "Send what you believe to be commercial—who will buy the product?"

◻ BARKIN' FOE THE MASTER'S BONE, 1111 Elm St. #520, Cincinnati OH 45210-2271. (513)721-4965. Website: www.1stbook.com. Company Owner (rock, R&B): Kevin Curtis. Professional Managers: Shonda Barr (country, jazz, pop, rap); Betty Barr (gospel, soul, soft rock). Music publisher. Estab. 1989. Publishes 4 songs/year; publishes 1 new songwriter/year. Staff size: 4. Pays standard royalty.

Affiliate(s): Beat Box Music (ASCAP) and Feltstar (BMI).

How to Contact: Submit demo tape by mail. Unsolicited submissions are OK. Prefers cassette (or VHS videocassette) with 3 songs. SASE. Responds in 2 weeks.

TO HELP YOU UNDERSTAND and use the information in these listings, see "How to Use *Songwriter's Market* to Get Your Songs Heard," on page 5.

Music: Mostly **country**, **soft rock** and **pop**; also **soul**, **gospel**, **rap** and **jazz**. Does not want classical. Published "Close to the Son" (single by Sean Stewart), recorded by Young Souls on God's Garden Records (gospel).

[N] ○ BARREN WOOD PUBLISHING (BMI), 2426 Auburn Ave., Dayton OH 45406-1928. Phone/fax: (937)275-4221. President: Jack Froschauer. Music publisher and record company (Emerald City Records). Estab. 1992. Publishes 5-6 songs/year; publishes 3-4 new songwriters/year. Staff size: 1. Pays standard royalty.
Affiliate(s): MerryGold Music Publishing (ASCAP).
How to Contact: Submit demo tape by mail. Unsolicited submissions are OK. Prefers cassette or CD with 1-4 songs and lyric or lead sheet. "Studio quality demo please." SASE. Responds in 3 months.
Music: Mostly **country**, **A/C** and **Christian**. Does not want alternative. Published "We Can't Go Home" and "She's Married" (singles by D. Walton) from *Relish* (album), recorded by My 3 Sons (rock), released 2000 on Emerald City.
Tips: "Recognize that songwriting is a business. Present yourself and your material in a professional, businesslike mannner."

○ BAY RIDGE PUBLISHING CO. (BMI), P.O. Box 5537, Kreole Station, Moss Point MS 39563-1537. (228)475-0059. Estab. 1974. **Contact:** Doris M. Mitchell, president. Vice President: Justin F. Mitchell. Vice President/Manager: Joe F. Mitchell. Music publisher and record company (Missile Records).
How to Contact: *Write first and obtain permission to submit.* Include #10 business-size SASE, with sufficient postage to return all materials. "No collect calls; not reviewing unsolicited material. All songs sent for review MUST include sufficient return postage. Do not send reply postcards, only SASE. If you only write lyrics, do not submit. We only accept completed songs, so you must find a musical collaborator." Responds in 2 months.
Music: Mostly **country**, **hardcore**, **folk**, **contemporary**, **alternative**, **gospel**, **rap**, **heavy metal**, **jazz**, **bluegrass**, **R&B**; also **ballads**, **reggae**, **world**, **soul**, **MOR**, **blues**, **rock** and **pop**. Published "Excuse Me, Lady," "When She Left Me" (singles by Rich Wilson), "Everyone Gets A Chance (To Lose in Romance)" and "I'm So Glad We Found Each Other" (singles by Joe F. Mitchell), recorded by Rich Wilson (country), released on Missile Records.
Tips: "We will give consideration to new exceptionally talented artists with a fan base and some backing."

◪ HAL BERNARD ENTERPRISES, INC., 2612 Erie Ave., P.O. Box 8385, Cincinnati OH 45208. (513)871-1500. Fax: (513)871-1510. E-mail: umbrella@one.net. **Contact:** Elaine Diehl, assistant. President: Stan Hertzman. Professional Manager: Pepper Bonar. Music publisher, record company (Strugglebaby), record producer and management firm (Umbrella Artists Management). Publishes 12-24 songs/year; 1-2 new songwriters/year. Pays standard royalty.
Affiliate(s): Sunnyslope Music (ASCAP), Bumpershoot Music (BMI), Apple Butter Music (ASCAP), Carb Music (ASCAP), Saiko Music (ASCAP), Smorgaschord Music (ASCAP), Clifton Rayburn Music (ASCAP) and Robert Stevens Music (ASCAP).
How to Contact: *Write or call first and obtain permission to submit.* Prefers cassette with 3 songs and lyric sheet. SASE. Responds in 6 weeks only if interested.
Music: Mostly **rock**, **R&B** and **top 40/pop**. Published *Heaven in Your Eyes* (album by Paul Bromwell), recorded by Bromwell-Diehl Band, released 1999 on Bash; *Inner Man* (album), written and recorded by Adrian Belew, released 1999 on ABP; and *Show Me Love* (album), written and recorded by The Greenhornes, released 1999 on Prince.
Tips: "Best material should appear first on demo. Cast your demos. If you, as the songwriter, can't sing it—don't. Get someone who can present your song properly, use a straight rhythm track and keep it as naked as possible. If you think it still needs something else, have a string arranger, etc. help you but still keep the *voice up* and the *lyrics clear*."

☑ 🖾 🖉 **BETTER THAN SEX MUSIC (ASCAP)**, 110 W. 26th St., Third Floor South, New York NY 10001-6805. Fax: (212)989-6459. E-mail: betterthansexmus@aol.com or betterthansexmusic@hotmail.com. **Contact:** James Citkovic, president. Music publisher. Estab. 1996. Publishes 14 songs/year; publishes 2 new songwriters/year. Staff size: 3. Pays standard royalty.
Affiliate(s): PolySutra Music (ASCAP) and Deerbrook Music (ASCAP).
How to Contact: Submit demo tape by mail, "first class only. Will not accept 'certified or registered' mail." Unsolicited submissions are OK. Prefers cassette, CD, DAT or VHS videocassette with 4 songs and lyric sheet. "No phone calls. Put the best song first on the tape. Include any information that can help us evaluate you and your music." Does not return material. Responds in 3 weeks.
Film & TV: Places 17 songs in film and 3 songs in TV/year.
Music: Mostly **pop**, **R&B** and **dance**; also **modern rock**, **electronica** and **acid house/hip-hop/funk**. Published "Love, Let Me Go" (single by Jo Gabriel/Rob Surace) from *Song For All Time* (album), recorded by Amanda (pop), released 2000 on Pacific Records.
Tips: "We are looking for leaders, not followers."

🖾 🖉 **BIG FISH MUSIC PUBLISHING GROUP**, 11927 Magnolia Blvd. #3, N. Hollywood CA 91607. (818)984-0377. CEO: Chuck Tennin. Professional Manager: Cathy Carlson (country, adult contemporary, pop). Producer: Gary Black (country, pop, adult contemporary, crossover songs, other styles). Music publisher, record company (California Sun Records) and production company. Estab. 1971. Publishes 10-20 songs/year; publishes 5-10 new songwriters/year. Staff size: 6. Pays standard royalty.
Affiliate(s): Big Fish Music (BMI) and California Sun Music (ASCAP).
How to Contact: *Write first and obtain permission to submit.* Include SASE for reply. "*Please do not call.* After permission to submit, we will assign you a submission code number allowing you to submit up to 4 songs maximum, preferably on cassette or CD. Include a cover letter, dated and signed, with your source of referral (*Songwriter's Market*) with your assigned submission code number and SASE for reply and/or return of material. Unsolicited material will not be accepted. That is our Submission Policy to review outside and new material." Responds in 2 weeks.
Film & TV: Places 6 songs in TV/year. Recently published "Even the Angels Knew" (by Cathy Carlson/Craig Lackey/Marty Axelrod); "Stop Before We Start" (by J.D. Grieco); and "Oh Santa" (by Christine Bridges/John Deaver), all recorded by The Black River Girls in *Passions* (NBC).
Music: **Country**, including **country pop**, **country A/C** and **country crossover** with a cutting edge; also **pop**, **pop ballads**, **uplifting**, **inspirational contemporary gospel** with a message, **instrumental background music** for TV & films and **novelty type songs** for all kinds of commercial use. Published "If Wishes Were Horses" (single by Billy O'Hara); "Purple Bunny Honey" (single by Robert Lloyd/Jim Love); and "Stop Before We Start" (single by J.D. Grieco), all recorded by Black River Girls on California Sun Records.
Tips: "Demo should be professional, high quality, clean, simple, dynamic, and must get the song across on the first listen. Good clear vocals, a nice melody, a good musical feel, good musical arrangement, strong lyrics and chorus—a unique, catchy, clever song that sticks with you. Looking for unique country songs with a different edge that can crossover to the mainstream market for ongoing Nashville music projects and songs for a female country trio that crosses over to adult contemporary and pop with great harmonies. Also catchy uptempo songs (Shania Twain style)."

🖾 🖉 **BIXIO MUSIC GROUP/IDM VENTURES, LTD. (ASCAP)**, 111 E. 14th St., Suite 140, New York NY 10003. (212)695-3911. Fax: (212)967-6284. E-mail: sales@bixio.com. Website: www.bixio.com. General Manager: Miriam Westercappel (all styles). A&R Director: Tomo (all styles). Office Manager: Karlene Evans (soundtracks). Creative Director: Robert Draghi (all styles). A&R: Claudene Neysmith (world/New Age). Music publisher, record company and rights clearances. Estab. 1985. Publishes a few hundred songs/year; publishes 2 new songwriters/year. Staff size: 6. Pays standard royalty.
How to Contact: *Does not accept unsolicited material.*
Music: Mostly **soundtracks**. Published "La Strada Nei Bosco," included in the motion picture *Big Tease*, released on Virgin Records; "Vivere," included in the motion picture *Titus*, released on Sony Classical; and "Violino Tzigano," included in the motion picture *Mickey Blue Eyes*, released on Milan Records.

◐ **BLACK STALLION COUNTRY PUBLISHING (BMI)**, P.O. Box 368, Tujunga CA 91043. (818)352-8142. Fax: (818)364-1250. E-mail: kenn.king@verizon.net. **Contact:** Kenn Kingsbury, president. Music publisher, management firm and book publisher (*Who's Who in Country & Western Music*). Member CMA, CMF. Publishes 2 songs/year; publishes 1 new songwriter/year. Pays standard royalty.
How to Contact: Submit demo tape by mail. Unsolicited submissions are OK. Prefers cassette with 3 songs and lyric sheet. SASE. Responds in 1 month.
Music: Mostly **jazz** and **country**.

◐ **BLUE DOG PUBLISHING AND RECORDS**, P.O. Box 3438, St. Louis MO 63143. (314)646-0191. Fax: (314)646-8005. E-mail: chillawack@worldnet.att.net. Website: www.bluedogpublishing.com. **Contact:** James Pedigo, president (rock/pop/commercial/alternative). Music publisher and record company. Estab. 1999. Publishes 3 songs/year; publishes 3 new songwriters/year. Staff size: 5. Pays standard royalty or payment negotiable.
How to Contact: Submit demo tape by mail. Unsolicited submissions are OK. Prefers cassette or CD with 3 songs, lyric sheet and cover letter. "Call to make sure we received material. We do call back." Does not return material. Responds in 1 month.
Music: Mostly **rock**, **pop/commercial** and **alternative**. Published "All Fall Down" (single by Bob Bender/Matt Davis/Steve Gendron) from *Phone Home* (album), recorded by 5th Degree (heavy/hard); "Still in Love With You" (single by Tiffany Kappler) from *Ariel* (album), recorded by Ariel (pop); and *All That and More* (album), written and recorded by Jeff Reulback (country/ballad), all released 2000 on Blue Dog Publishing and Records.
Tips: "Send a quality demo. Even a two-track demo is fine. Vocals should be clear and upfront. Be professional and stay motivated."

⊕ ✓ ◐ **BME PUBLISHING**, P.O. Box 450224, Cologne Germany 50877. Phone: (049)221-9472000. Fax: (049)221-9502278. E-mail: info@BME-Records.de. Website: www.BME-Records.de. **Contact:** Dr. Dietmar Barzen. Music publisher, record company and record producer. Estab. 1993. Pays standard royalty to artists on contract.
How to Contact: Submit demo tape by mail. Unsolicited submissions are OK. Prefers cassette, DAT or CDR with 3-5 songs and lyric sheet. SAE and IRC. Responds in 1 month.
Music: Mostly **pop/AC**, **rock** and **commercial dance/hip-hop**; also **MOR**.

◐ **BMG MUSIC PUBLISHING**, 1540 Broadway, 39th Floor, New York NY 10036-4098. (212)930-4000. Fax: (212)930-4263. Website: www.bmgentertainment.com. Beverly Hills office: 8750 Wilshire Blvd., Beverly Hills CA 90211. (310)358-4700. Fax: (310)358-4727. **Contact:** Danny Strick. Vice President of Film & Music: Art Ford. Nashville office: One Music Circle N., Suite 380, Nashville TN 37203. (615)780-5420. Fax: (615)780-5430. Music publisher.
How to Contact: BMG Music Publishing does not accept unsolicited submissions.
Music: Published "All Night Long" (single by F. Evans/R. Lawrence/S. Combs/S. Crawford), recorded by Faith Evans featuring Puff Daddy on Bad Boy; and "Ain't Enough Roses" (single by L. Brokop/S. Hogin/B. Reagan), recorded by Lisa Brokop on Columbia (country).

◐ **BOURNE CO. MUSIC PUBLISHERS (ASCAP)**, 5 W. 37th St., New York NY 10018. (212)391-4300. Fax: (212)391-4306. E-mail: bournemusic@worldnet.att.net. Website: www.bournemusic.com. **Contact:** Professional Manager. Music publisher. Estab. 1917. Publishes educational material and popular music.
Affiliate(s): ABC Music, Ben Bloom, Better Half, Bogat, Burke & Van Heusen, Goldmine, Harborn, Lady Mac and Murbo Music.
How to Contact: *Does not accept unsolicited submissions.*
Music: **Piano/vocal**, **band pieces** and **choral pieces**. Published "Amen" and "Mary's Little Boy Child" (singles by Hairston); "When You Wish Upon a Star" (single by Washington/Harline); and "Unforgettable" (single by Irving Gordon).

☐**ALLAN BRADLEY MUSIC (BMI)**, 1325 Marengo Ave., South Pasadena CA 91030. (626)441-4453. E-mail: melodi4ever@aol.com. Website: http://allanlicht.ontheweb.com. **Contact:** Allan Licht, owner. Music publisher, record company (ABL Records) and record producer. Estab. 1993. Publishes 10 songs/year; publishes 5 new songwriters/year. Staff size: 2. Pays standard royalty. **Affiliate(s):** Holly Ellen Music (ASCAP).

How to Contact: Submit demo tape by mail. Unsolicited submissions are OK. Prefers cassette with 3 songs and lyric sheet. "Send only unpublished works." Does not return material. Responds in 2 weeks only if interested.

Music: Mostly **A/C, pop** and **R&B**; also **country** and **Christian contemporary**. Does not want hard rock. Published *Time to Go* (album), written and recorded by Alan Douglass; *The Sun that Follows the Rain* (album by R.K. Holler/Rob Driggers), recorded by Michael Cavanaugh (pop), released 1999; and *Only In My Mind* (album by Jonathon Hansen), recorded by Allan Licht, all on ABL Records.

Tips: "Be open to suggestions from well-established publishers. Please send only songs that have Top 10 potential. Only serious writers are encouraged to submit."

☑ ☐ **BRANSON COUNTRY MUSIC PUBLISHING (BMI)**, P.O. Box 2527, Broken Arrow OK 74013. (918)455-9442. Fax: (918)451-1965. E-mail: bransoncm@aol.com. **Contact:** Betty Branson, general partner. Music publisher. Estab. 1997. Publishes 25 songs/year; publishes 4-5 new songwriters/year. Pays standard royalty.

How to Contact: Submit demo tape by mail with photo and bio. Unsolicited submissions are OK. Prefers cassette with 3-5 songs and lyric sheet. Does not return material. Responds in 2 weeks only if interested.

Music: Mostly **traditional country** and **upbeat country**. Published "That Cowboy Hat's on a Little Too Tight" (single by Carla J), recorded by Christine Clark (country), released 2000; "Smokey Bars and Steel Guitars" (single by Danny Davis) from *Maximum Country CD* (album), recorded by Danny Davis and the Detours (country), released 2000; and "Montana Cowboy," (single written and recorded by Wess Cooke) (country), released 2000.

Tips: "Send good quality demo of traditional or upbeat country songs capable of competing with current top 40. Put your 'attention getter' up front and build from that point as your listener will give you about 10-15 seconds to continue listening or turn you off. Use a good hook and keep comming back to it."

☐ ☐ **BRENTWOOD-BENSON MUSIC PUBLISHING (ASCAP,BMI,SESAC)**, 741 Cool Springs Blvd., Franklin TN 37067. (615)261-3300. Fax: (615)261-3384. Professional Managers: Todd Moore, creative director (AC/Christian); Holly Zabka, creative director (praise & worship/inspirational/southern gospel); Marty Wheeler, vice president of creative affairs (all genres). **Contact:** Leslie Linebaugh, assistant to vice president. Music publisher. Estab. 1901. Publishes 600 songs/year; publishes 5 new songwriters/year. Staff size: 16 (10 staff writers). Hires staff songwriters. Pays standard royalty.

Affiliate(s): New Spring Publishing, Inc. (ASCAP), Bridge Building Music, Inc. (BMI) and Designer Music, Inc. (SESAC).

How to Contact: *Only accepts material referred by a reputable industry source.* "Do not call and say someone is referring you; have the person make the reference call." SASE.

Film & TV: Places 7 songs in film and 3 songs in TV/year. Music Supervisor: Marty Wheeler, vice president of creative affairs (all/gospel/Christian/AC). Recently published "Unforgetful You" (single), written and recorded by Jars of Clay in *Drive Me Crazy*; "Do We Dare" (single), written and recorded by Carolyn Arends in *Providence* (album); and "Damaged" (single by Tiffany Arbuckle), recorded by Plumb in *Brokedown Palace*(album).

Music: Mostly **praise** and **worship**. Published "Can't Live A Day" (single by Joe Beck), recorded by Avalon (AC) on Sparrow; "I Will Go the Distance" (single by Joel Lindsey), recorded by The Martins (inspirational); and "You Have Been Good" (single by Tony Wood), recorded by Scott Krippagne (inspirational), both on Spring Hill.

Tips: "Get a reference!"

🌐 ⭕ KITTY BREWSTER SONGS, "Norden," 2 Hillhead Rd., Newtonhill Stonehaven AB39 3TS Scotland. Phone: 01569 730962. **Contact:** Doug Stone, managing director. Music publisher, record company (KBS Records), record producer and production company (Brewster & Stone Productions). Estab. 1989. Staff size: 6. Pays standard royalty.

How to Contact: Submit demo tape by mail. Unsolicited submissions are OK. Prefers cassette or VHS videocassette with any number of songs and lyric or lead sheet. Does not return material. Responds in 4 months.

Music: Mostly **AOR, pop, R&B** and **dance**; also **country, jazz, rock** and **contemporary**. Published *Sleepin' Alone* (album by R. Donald); *I Still Feel the Same* (album by R. Greig/K. Mundie); and *Your Love Will Pull Me Thru* (album by R. Greig), all recorded by Kitty Brewster on KBS Records (AOR).

◓ BRIAN SONG MUSIC CORP. (BMI), P.O. Box 1376, Pickens SC 29671. (864)878-7217. Fax: (864)878-8398. E-mail: braines105@aol.com. **Contact:** Brian E. Raines, president. Music publisher, record company (Palmetto Records), record producer and artist management. Estab. 1985. Publishes 5 songs/year; publishes 2-3 new songwriters/year. Staff size: 3. Pays standard royalty.

How to Contact: Write first and obtain permission to submit a demo. Prefers cassette, CD or VHS videocassette with 3 songs and lyric sheet. "Unsolicited material not accepted, and will be returned. Demo must be good quality, lyrics typed. Send photo if an artist; send bio on writer or artist." Does not return material. Responds in 1 month.

Music: Mostly **country, gospel** and **country/gospel**; also **country/blues**. Published *I Wasn't There* (album), written and recorded by Dale Cassell on Mark V (gospel); and *From the Heart* (album), written and recorded by Jim Hubbard on Hubbitt (gospel).

✅ 🐾 ♀ ⭕ BSW RECORDS (BMI), P.O. Box 2297, Universal City TX 78148. (210)599-0022. Fax: (210)653-3989. E-mail: bswr18@txdirect.net. Website: www.bswrecords.com. **Contact:** Frank Willson, president. Music publisher, record company and record producer (Frank Willson). Estab. 1987. Publishes 26 songs/year; publishes 14 new songwriters/year. Staff size: 7. Pays standard royalty.

Affiliate(s): WillTex Music and Universal Music Marketing (BMI).

● This company has been named Record Label of the Year ('94-'99) by the Country Music Association of America.

How to Contact: Submit demo tape by mail. Unsolicited submissions are OK. Prefers cassette or CD with 3 songs, lyric sheet and cover letter. SASE. Responds in 2 months.

Film & TV: Places 3 songs in film/year.

Music: Mostly **country, blues** and **soft rock**. Does not want rap. Published *These Four Walls* (album), written and recorded by Dan Kimmel (country); and *I Cried My Last Tear* (album by T. Toliver), recorded by Candeeland (country), both released 1999 on BSW Records.

⭕ BURIED TREASURE MUSIC (ASCAP), 524 Doral Country Dr., Nashville TN 37221. **Contact:** Scott Turner, owner/manager. Music publisher and record producer (Aberdeen Productions). Estab. 1972. Publishes 30-50 songs/year; publishes 3-10 new songwriters/year. Pays standard royalty.

Affiliate(s): Captain Kidd Music (BMI).

How to Contact: Submit demo tape by mail. Unsolicited submissions are OK. Prefers cassette or VHS videocassette with 1-4 songs and lyric sheet. Responds in 2 weeks. "Always enclose SASE if answer is expected."

Music: Mostly **country, country/pop** and **MOR**. Does not want rap, hard rock, metal, hip-hop or alternative. "One Heart" (single by Scott Turner/Doc Pomus) and "September Hearts" (single by Buddy Holly/Scott Turner) both from *September Hearts* (album), recorded by Colin Cook (pop/MOR), released 2001; and "Please Mr. Music Man" (single by Audie Murphy/Scott Turner) from *The Entrance* (album), recorded by Lea Brennan (country), released 2000.

Tips: "*Don't* send songs in envelopes that are 15″x 20″, or by registered mail. The post office will not accept tapes in regular business-size envelopes."

N ○ CALIFORNIA COUNTRY MUSIC (BMI), 112 Widmar Pl., Clayton CA 94517. (925)833-4680. **Contact:** Edgar J. Brincat, owner. Music publisher and record company (Roll On Records). Estab. 1985. Publishes 30 songs/year; publishes 2-4 new songwriters/year. Staff size: 1. Pays standard royalty.
Affiliate(s): Sweet Inspirations Music (ASCAP).
How to Contact: Submit demo tape by mail. Unsolicited submissions are OK. Do not call or write. Prefers cassette with 3 songs and lyric sheet. Any calls will be returned collect to caller. SASE. Responds in 6 weeks.
Music: Mostly **MOR**, **contemporary country** and **pop**; also **R&B**, **gospel** and **light rock**. Does not want rap, metal or rock. Published *For Realities Sake* (album by F.L. Pittman/R. Barretta) and *Maddy* (album by F.L. Pittman/M. Weeks), both recorded by Ron Banks & L.J. Reynolds on Life & Bellmark Records; and *Quarter Past Love* (album by Irwin Rubinsky/Janet Fisher), recorded by Darcy Dawson on NNP Records.

N ○ CHEAVORIA MUSIC CO. (BMI), 2622 Kirtland Rd., Brewton AL 36426. (334)867-2228. **Contact:** Roy Edwards, president. Music publisher, record company (Bolivia Records) and record producer (Known Artist Production). Estab. 1972. Publishes 20 new songwriters/year. Pays standard royalty.
Affiliate(s): Baitstring Music (ASCAP).
How to Contact: *Write first and obtain permission to submit.* Prefers cassette with 3 songs and lyric sheet. Does not return material. Responds in 1 month.
Music: Mostly **R&B**, **pop** and **country**; also **ballads**. Published "Forever and Always" (single), written and recorded by Jim Portwood on Bolivia Records (country).

☑ ⌧ ○ CHERRI/HOLLY MUSIC INC. (BMI), 1859 Acton Court, Simi Valley CA 93065-2205. (805)527-4082. Professional Managers: John G. Goske (MOR, top 40, jazz); Holly Rose Lawrence (R&B, new and traditional country, dance/pop); Pat (Big Red) Silzer (Southern gospel, Christian contemporary). Vice President: Helen Goske; Engineer/A&R: Cherri (meat and potato Bob Seger-type rock). Music publisher, record company (Whirlwind Label) and record producer (Helen and John G. Goske). Estab. 1961. Publishes 200-300 songs/year; publishes 75-100 new songwriters/year. Staff size: 3-7. Pays standard royalty.
Affiliate(s): Blue Sapphire Music (ASCAP).
How to Contact: Submit professional studio demo by mail with SASE. Unsolicited submissions are OK. Prefers cassette or CD with 3 songs and typed lyric sheet and cover letter. Must be copyrighted. "Absolutely no phone calls. Put name, address and phone number on everything. Important to hear lyrics above music. Please submit cover letter overview with cassette. Lyrics should be typed. Photo would be good. Please include SASE." Does not return material. Responds in 2 months only if interested.
Music: Mostly **traditional country**, **contemporary country with crossover edge**, **dance/pop**, **Latin pop** ala Ricky Martin, **pop ballads** ala Diane Warren; also **Southern Christian and contemporary Christian gospel** and **film and TV music**. No grunge or gangster rap. Published "Regina" (single by Ron McManaman), recorded by Ronnie Kimbal, released on WIR Records; "Dance Like You Love Her" (single by Ron McManaman), recorded by Ronnie Kimbal, released on Woodrich Records; "Morocco" (single), written and recorded by Joe Striffolino on Retrieve Records; and "I Want Everyone to Know" (single by John G. Goske/John Wm. LaRocca), recorded by various artists in Germany, Netherlands, Switzerland and Austria.
Tips: "Submit well-crafted songs with killer hooks ala hits on radio. Must be copyrighted with symbol and year."

☑ ⌧ ○ CHRISTMAS & HOLIDAY MUSIC (BMI), 3517 Warner Blvd., Suite 4, Burbank CA 91505. (323)849-5381. Fax: (818)848-7234. E-mail: justinwilde@christmassongs.com. Website: www.christmassongs.com. **Contact:** Justin Wilde, president. Music publisher. Estab. 1980. Publishes 8-12 songs/year; publishes 8-12 new songwriters/year. Staff size: 1. "All submissions must be complete songs (i.e., music and lyrics)." Pays standard royalty.

insider report

Songwriter realizes dreams in Nashville

Having a song recorded by country superstar George Strait would be a dream come true for any self-respecting country songwriter, and that dream has recently come true for songwriter Carter Wood. Her song "Don't Make Me Come Over There and Love You," co-written with songwriting veteran Jim Lauderdale, was picked by Strait to be included on his 2000 release *George Strait* (UNI/MCA Nashville) and, believe it or not, it was the first song by Wood to be cut by an artist other than herself.

Carter Wood

Hailing from Louisville, Kentucky, Wood started writing songs while attending Connecticut College in New London, Connecticut. "I grew up singing musicals and performing locally, but in college I really became interested in songwriting. Mary Chapin Carpenter and the Indigo Girls were on the scene and I started getting into that." Soon after, Nashville beckoned. "I was full of romantic notions in college," she says. "At the end of my senior year I was thinking, 'What am I going to do?' I have a psychology degree, but I didn't think about making a career in music until I moved to Nashville and observed the different options for obtaining a publishing deal and actually making it a career. I really didn't know a lot about it before I moved there, I just knew that I wanted to be involved in music." She started off by getting a job as an intern at a Nashville record company. "I thought it would be a good way to learn more about the business and kind of study songwriting around town."

Moving to Nashville was important for Wood, especially since she wasn't looking for a recording deal but a publishing deal. "If you are an artist/writer and you create a local following and have a buzz going, I think maybe you can be successful outside of Nashville," she says. "But as far as attaining a publishing deal in Nashville goes, whether you're writing for yourself or the country music market, I think you really need to be in Nashville. I've been really lucky and I've had a lot of nice people sort of take me under their wing, but you have to have the goods. You can't be full of air—you have to really show your persistence and determination."

Through networking and playing her songs in Nashville clubs for anyone who would listen, Wood eventually signed with publisher Carnival Music. "I met with a lot of different publishers once I had a decent catalog of songs I felt confident playing for people," she says. "Publishers kept telling me to come back in a month and show them what else I was working on, and relationships developed. Somebody I met with at one of the companies wasn't in need of a female songwriter at the time, but he knew of someone who was interested, so just through networking, I met with Carnival."

Wood finds co-writing to be a particularly productive part of the songwriting process, and plays off the inspiration of other writers to feed her creativity. "Songwriting is really organic for me," she explains. "I do a lot of co-writing, and in Nashville, I think, business-wise it's a smart thing to do for a couple of reasons. Your collaborator or your publisher might have more connections to an artist or to a record label. And I also really feed off others creatively. Being around other creative people stimulates a lot of good ideas. With co-writing, I try to be structured and schedule appointments, but the people I work with are so creative that, even though we say we're going to meet at 10 on Tuesday, it's not that uptight. It's still so fun and creative just being around the people I get to work with. A lot of times just listening to music I've never heard before can be inspiring."

"Don't Make Me Come Over There and Love You" was co-written with Jim Lauderdale, a veteran Nashville songwriter who has not only released seven of his own albums but has had songs recorded by more than twenty-five different artists, including Mark Chesnutt, the Dixie Chicks, Dave Edmunds, Vince Gill, Shelby Lynne, Patty Loveless, and George Strait. Hooking up with Lauderdale was a combination of networking and being in the right place at the right time, as Wood explains. "I write with a fellow named Rory Burke, who's been around a very long time. He had a lot of big hits in the 70s and 80s and is still doing well today. I met him through a family friend who came to hear me perform at the Bluebird, and we started writing together. Rory and I were at lunch one day and ran into Jim Lauderdale. Rory knows Jim just from being in the business, so they started talking and he joined us for lunch. It turns out that Jim is very close to my publisher, so when I told him I wrote for Carnival Music, I think it gave me some credibility, and he gave me his number. After about two weeks I got up the nerve to call him. We wrote three or four songs, and "Don't Make Me Come Over There and Love You" was probably the fourth or fifth song we wrote together. We finished it in January 2000, it was put on hold in February 2000, and was picked up by George Strait in late March. It was my first song that was recorded, and it was a great way to start."

Now that she's had some success with songwriting, Wood wants to take her career to the next level by performing her own songs and looking for a record deal. "I'm definitely pursuing the artist thing," she says. "I've always played live because I love the performance side of it, but now I think I'm doing it with songs that are more suited for me versus singing any old song I hope someone will record. It's more enjoyable and fulfilling for me as an artist when I perform. I'm performing a lot and recording with some really neat performers. I'm looking to perform outside Nashville, and right now I'm finishing up some more recording in hopes of getting more attention from labels." Some of her songs also appeared in an HBO movie released in March

2001 called *Nice Guys Sleep Alone*, and Wood continues to pursue all avenues to get her music heard. "I hope to continue to make great music and connect with a lot of different people, artists and listeners, and hopefully get more songs recorded that way," Wood says. "Having a song recorded by George Strait helps me in the Nashville arena, and now I would like to reach a broader base artistically with my own stuff to get a record deal and start touring."

Wood encourages songwriters trying to make it in Nashville to be true to their music. "It sounds kind of dramatic," she says, "but you should stay true to yourself. Everybody needs their uniqueness to shine, because there's too much of the same thing in this industry. It really shows when you're genuinely doing your own thing. Whether that works with a broad group of people or a small group of people, however it works it will work. You also need persistence. There's so much rejection in this business, so you have to find a way to look at that positively. Every day I try to approach it all in a more humble way and learn from everything and everybody and every artist."

—*Cynthia Laufenberg*

● Christmas & Holiday Music is relocating their office this year. See their website for most current address before mailing.

Affiliate(s): Songcastle Music (ASCAP).

How to Contact: Submit demo tape by mail. Unsolicited submissions are OK. Do *not* call. "First class mail only. Registered or certified mail not accepted." Prefers cassette with no more than 3 songs and lyric sheet. Do not send lead sheets or promotional material, bios, etc." SASE but does not return material out of the US. Responds only if interested.

Film & TV: Places 4-5 songs in TV/year. Published "Mr. Santa Claus" in *Casper's Haunted Christmas.*

Music: Strictly **Christmas music** (and a little Hanukkah and Halloween) in every style imaginable: easy listening, rock, R&B, pop, blues, jazz, country, reggae, rap, children's secular or religious. *Please do not send anything that isn't a holiday song.* Published "What Made the Baby Cry?" (single by William Golay) and "You've Just Missed Christmas" (single by Penny Lea/Buzz Smith/Bonnie Miller) from *The Vikki Carr Christmas Album* (album), recorded by Vikki Carr (holiday/Christmas), released 2000 on Delta; and "Mr. Santa Claus" (single by James Golseth) from *Casper's Haunted Christmas* soundtrack (album), recorded by Scotty Blevins (Christmas), released 2000 on Koch International.

Tips: "We only sign one out of every 100 submissions. Please be selective. If a stranger can hum your melody back to you after hearing it twice, it has 'standard' potential. Couple that with a lyric filled with unique, inventive imagery, that stands on its own, even without music. Combine the two elements, and workshop the finished result thoroughly to identify weak points. Only when the song is polished to perfection, then cut a master quality demo that sounds like a record or pretty close to it. Submit positive lyrics only. Avoid negative themes like 'Blue Christmas.' "

REMEMBER: Don't "shotgun" your demo tapes. Submit only to companies interested in the type of music you write. For more submission hints, refer to Getting Started on page 10.

☑ SONNY CHRISTOPHER PUBLISHING (BMI), P.O. Box 9144, Ft. Worth TX 76147-2144. (817)367-0860. **Contact:** Sonny Christopher, CEO. Music publisher, record company and record producer. Estab. 1974. Publishes 20-25 new songs/year; publishes 3-5 new songwriters/year. Staff size: 1. Pays standard royalty.
How to Contact: Write first, then call and obtain permission to submit. Prefers cassette with lyric sheet. SASE (#10 or larger). Responds in 3 months.
Music: Mostly **country**, **rock** and **blues**. Published *Did They Judge Too Hard* (album by Sonny Christopher), recorded by Ronny Collins on Sonshine Records.
Tips: "Be patient. I will respond as soon as I can. A songwriter should have a studio-cut demo with a super vocal. I am one who can hear a song with just acoustic guitar. Don't be hesitant to do a rewrite. To the young songwriter: *never, never* quit."

⊕ ☑ ○ R.D. CLEVÈRE MUSIKVERLAG, Postfach 2145, D-63243 Neu-Isenburg, Germany. Phone: (0180)5052-5920-3291. Fax: (0180)5052-5320-6508. E-mail: rdc.in@web.de. **Contact:** Tony Hermonez, professional manager. Music publisher. Estab. 1967. Publishes 700-900 songs/year; publishes 40 new songwriters/year. Pays standard royalty.
Affiliate(s): Big Sound Music, Hot Night Music, Lizzy's Blues Music, Max Banana Music, R.D. Clevère-Cocabana-Music, R.D. Clevère-Far East & Orient-Music, and R.D. Clevère-America-Today-Music.
How to Contact: Submit demo tape by mail. Unsolicited submissions are OK. Prefers cassette or MD, CD, DAT with "no limit" on songs and lyric sheet. SAE and 2 IRCs. Responds in 2 months.
Music: Mostly **pop**, **disco**, **rap**, **rock**, **R&B**, **country**, **ethno** and **folk**; also **musicals** and **classic/opera**. "No jazz, free style or instrumental music."

☑ ○ CORELLI'S MUSIC BOX (BMI), P.O. Box 2314, Tacoma WA 98401-2314. (253)846-2226. E-mail: corellimusic@usa.net. Website: www.corellimusic.com. **Contact:** Jerry Corelli, owner. Music publisher. Estab. 1996. Publishes 10 songs/year; publishes 3 new songwriters/year. Staff size: 2. Pays standard royalty.
How to Contact: Submit demo tape by mail. Unsolicited submissions are OK. Prefers cassette or DAT with 1-3 songs and lyric sheet. "We want songs with a message and overtly Christian. Make sure all material is copyrighted." SASE. Responds in 2 months.
Music: Mostly **contemporary Christian** and **Christmas**. Does not want rap. Published *This Child* (album by Bert Boone), recorded by Jerry Corelli (Christmas); *Easter Sunday* (album), written and recorded by Earl Richards and Dave Gonzalez (contemporary Christian); and *Too Good for This World* (album by Stuart Logan), recorded by Jerry Corelli (Christian), all released 2000 on Omega III Records.

Ⓝ ☑ THE CORNELIUS COMPANIES (BMI, ASCAP, SESAC), Dept. SM, 1719 West End Ave., Suite 805-E, Nashville TN 37203. (615)321-5333. Website: www.corneliuscompanies.com. **Contact:** Ron Cornelius, owner/manager. Music publisher and record producer (Ron Cornelius). Estab. 1986. Publishes 60-80 songs/year; publishes 2-3 new songwriters/year. Occasionally hires staff writers. Pays standard royalty.
Affiliate(s): RobinSparrow Music (BMI), Strummin' Bird Music (ASCAP) and Bridgeway Music (SESAC).
How to Contact: Write or call first and obtain permission to submit. Submit demo tape by mail. Unsolicited submissions are OK. Prefers CD, DAT or cassette with 2-3 songs. SASE. Responds in 2 months.
Music: Mostly **country** and **pop**; also **positive country**, **gospel** and **alternative**. Published songs by Confederate Railroad, Faith Hill, David Allen Coe, Alabama and over 50 radio singles in the positive Christian/country format.
Tips: "Looking for material suitable for film."

☑ ○ COUNTRY RAINBOW MUSIC (BMI), 9 Music Square S., PMB 225, Nashville TN 37203-3203. (513)755-6666. Fax: (513)489-8944. E-mail: countryRbw@aol.com. **Contact:** Samuel D. Rogers, owner. Music publisher. Estab. 1995. Publishes 10-12 songs/year; publishes 4-6 new songwriters/year. Staff size: 1. Pays standard royalty.

Affiliate(s): Venture South Music (ASCAP).
How to Contact: "Please do not call first." Submit demo tape by mail. Unsolicited submissions are OK. Prefers cassette with 1-3 songs and lyric sheet. "No lead sheets." SASE. Responds in 2 weeks.
Music: Mostly **country** (contemporary and traditional). Published "Sleepwalking Avenue" (single by Lionel deBernard), on Spree Productions.
Tips: "If you don't include a self-addressed stamped envelope we don't reply. Professional studio demos preferred . . . on good quality tape, please (not normal bias.) Your submission should sound better than what is currently on the charts."

⊕ 🖼 ⃠ CTV MUSIC (GREAT BRITAIN), Television Centre, St. Helier, Jersey JE1 3ZD Channel Islands Great Britain. Phone: (1534)816816. Fax: (1534)816817. Website: www.channeltv.co .uk. **Contact:** Gordon De Ste. Croix, managing director. Music publisher of music for TV commercials, TV programs and corporate video productions. Estab. 1986. Staff size: 1. Pays standard royalty.
How to Contact: *Does not accept unsolicited submissions.*
Music: Mostly **instrumental**, for TV commercials and programs.

✔ 🎤 ○ CUPIT MUSIC (ASCAP, BMI), P.O. Box 121904, Nashville TN 37212. (615)731-0100. Fax: (615)731-3005. E-mail: jerrycupit@cupitmusic.com. Website: www.cupitmusic.com. **Contact:** Denise Roberts, creative assistant. Music publisher, record producer and recording studio. Estab. 1986. Staff size: 4. Pays standard royalty.
Affiliate(s): Cupit Memaries (ASCAP) and Cupit Music (BMI).
  • Cupit Music's "What If He's Right" was number 1 on CCRB Christian Country Chart for ten consecutive weeks, and was named Song of the Year."
How to Contact: *Write first and obtain permission to submit.* Prefers cassette with lyric sheet. "We will return a response card." SASE. Responds in 2 months.
Music: Mostly **country**. Does not want rap, hard rock or metal. Published "What If He's Right" (single by Jerry Cupit) from *Memarie* (album), recorded by Memarie (Christian country), released 2000 on HotSong.com Records; and "I'm Not Homeless" (single by Jerry Cupit/Ken Mellons/Randy Roberts) from *Wings of a Dove* (album), recorded by Ken Mellons (Christian country), released 2000 on Curb Records.

Ⓝ ○ DAGENE MUSIC (ASCAP), P.O. Box 410851, San Francisco CA 94141. (415)822-1530. President: David Alston. Music publisher, record company (Cabletown Corp.), management firm (Golden City) and record producer (Classic Disc Production). Estab. 1988. Hires staff songwriters. Pays standard royalty.
Affiliate(s): 1956 Music.
How to Contact: Call first and obtain permission to submit. Prefers cassette with 2 songs and lyric sheet. "Be sure to obtain permission before sending any material." SASE. Responds in 1 month.
Music: Mostly **R&B/rap**, **dance** and **pop**. Published "Maxin" (single by Marcus Justice/Bernard Henderson), recorded by 2 Dominatorz on Dagene Records; "To Know You Better" (single by David Alston), recorded by Rare Essence on Cabletown Records; and "High On You" (single), written and recorded by David Alston on E-lect-ric Recordings.

○ DAPMOR PUBLISHING (ASCAP, BMI, SESAC), Box 121, Kenner LA 70065. (504)468-9820. **Contact:** Kelly Jones, president. Music publisher, record company and record producer. Estab. 1977. Publishes 10 songs/year. Publishes 3 new songwriters/year. Hires staff songwriters. Pays standard royalty.
How to Contact: *Write first and obtain permission to submit.* "Submit only through an attorney or another publisher." Prefers 10-song professionally-recorded CD. Does not return material. Responds in 6 weeks.
Music: Mostly **R&B**, **soul**, and **pop**; also **top 40**, **country** and **rap**. Published "Tell Me, Tell Me" (single) (R&B); and "Sisco" (single) (R&B), both written and recorded by Kelly Jones on Justice Recordings.

☑ ◙ **JOF DAVE MUSIC (ASCAP)**, 1055 Kimball Ave., Kansas City KS 66104. (888)295-2006. Fax: (816)584-9916. **Contact:** David Johnson, owner. Music publisher, record company (Cymbal Records). Estab. 1984. Publishes 10 songs/year; publishes 2 new songwriters/year. Pays standard royalty.
How to Contact: *Contact first and obtain permission to submit.* Prefers cassette or CD. SASE. Responds in 1 month.
Music: Mostly **gospel**, **blues** and **R&B**. Published "The Woman I Love" (single) from *Sugar Bowl* (album), written and recorded by King Alex, released 2001 on Cymbal Records.

▨ ◙ **THE EDWARD DE MILES MUSIC COMPANY (BMI)**, 117 W. Harrison Bldg., Suite S627, Chicago IL 60605-1709. (773)509-6381. Fax: (312)922-6964. **Contact:** Professional Manager. Music publisher, record company (Sahara Records), record producer, management, bookings and promotions. Estab. 1984. Publishes 50-75 songs/year; publishes 5 new songwriters/year. Hires staff songwriters. Pays standard royalty.
How to Contact: *Write first and obtain permission to submit.* Prefers cassette with 1-3 songs and lyric sheet. Does not return material. Reponds in 1 month.
Music: Mostly **top 40 pop/rock**, **R&B/dance** and **country**; also **musical scores for TV, radio, films and jingles**. Published "Dance Wit Me" and "Moments" (singles), written and recorded by Steve Lynn on Sahara Records (R&B).
Tips: "Copyright all songs before submitting to us."

☑ �‍◯ **DELEV MUSIC COMPANY**, 7231 Mansfield Ave., Philadelphia PA 19138-1620. (215)276-8861. Fax: (215)276-4509. E-mail: delevmusic@cs.com. President/CEO: W. Lloyd Lucas. A&R: Darryl Lucas. Music publisher and management. Publishes 6-10 songs/year; publishes 6-10 new songwriters/year. Pays standard royalty.
Affiliate(s): Sign of the Ram Music (ASCAP), Gemini Lady Music (SESAC) and Delev Music (BMI).
How to Contact: *Write first and obtain permission to submit.* Prefers cassette or VHS videocassette with 1-3 songs and lyric sheet. "Video must be in VHS format and as professionally done as possible. It does not necessarily have to be done at a professional video studio, but should be a very good quality production showcasing artist's performance. We will not accept certified mail." Does not return material. Responds in 3 months.
Music: Mostly **R&B ballads** and **dance-oriented**; also **pop ballads**, **crossover** and **country/western**. Published "Angel Love" (single by Barbara Heston/Geraldine Fernandez) from *The Silky Sounds of Debbie G* (album), recorded by Debbie G (light R&B/easy listening), released 2000 on Rosebudd Records.
Tips: "Persevere regardless if it is sent to our company or any other company. Believe in yourself."

☑ ◯ **DOOR KNOB MUSIC PUBLISHING**, 3950 N. Mt. Juliet Rd., Mt. Juliet TN 37122. (615)754-0417. E-mail: geneken@usit.net. Professional Manager: Gene Kennedy, president (country/gospel); **Contact:** Karen Kennedy, vice president (country/gospel). Music publisher. Estab. 1975. Staff size: 3. Pays standard royalty.
How to Contact: *Write or call first and obtain permission to arrange personal interview or submit demo tape by mail.* Unsolicited submissions are OK. Prefers cassette with 1-2 songs and lyric sheet. SASE for tape return or response. "Use regular mail; no FedEx, certified, etc." Responds in 3 weeks if SASE included.
Music: Mostly **country** and **gospel**. Does not want rock, rap or anything not listed. Published "You'll Always Have a Home" (single by Jerry Roberson) from *From Norway to Nashville* (album), recorded by Tom Brathen (country), released 2000 on Bergen.

LISTINGS OF COMPANIES within this section which are either commercial music production houses or music libraries will have that information printed in **boldface** type.

☑ DORÉ RECORDS (ASCAP), P.O. Box 7156, Beverly Hills CA 90212. (323)462-6614. Fax: (323)462-6197. **Contact:** Stephanie Bedell, president. Music publisher and record company. Estab. 1960. Publishes 15 songs/year; publishes 15 new songwriters/year. Pays standard royalty.
How to Contact: Submit demo tape by mail. Unsolicited submissions are OK. Prefers cassette and lyric sheet. Does not return unsolicited material. Responds in 2 weeks.
Music: Mostly **all kinds**; also **novelty** and **comedy**. Published *Percolator* (album by Bideu/Freeman), recorded by the Billy Joe and the Checkmates/the Ventures on EMI Records; and *Ten-Uh-See* (album), written and recorded by Steve Rumph on Doré Records.
Tips: "Currently seeking an R&B group with male lead vocals. No rap."

☐ BUSTER DOSS MUSIC (BMI), 341 Billy Goat Hill Rd., Winchester TN 37398. (931)649-2577. Fax: (615)649-2732. E-mail: cbb@vallnet.com. Website: http://stardustcountrymusic.com. **Contact:** Buster Doss, president. Music publisher, record producer, management firm and record company (Stardust). Estab. 1959. Publishes 500 songs/year; publishes 50 new songwriters/year. Staff size: 62. Pays standard royalty.
How to Contact: *Write or call first and obtain permission to submit.* Prefers cassette with 2 songs and lyric sheet. SASE. Responds in 1 week.
Music: Mostly **country**; also **rock**. Does not want rap or hard rock. Published *The Heart* (album), written and recorded by Bryant Miller (country); *Do I Ever Cross Your Mind* (album), written and recorded by Michael Apidgian; and *Down South* (album), written and recorded by Rooster Quantrell, all on Stardust Records.

☐ DREAM SEEKERS PUBLISHING (BMI), 403 Brunswick Lane, Danville IL 61832. (615)822-1160. **Contact:** Jerry Webb, professional manager. President: Sally Sidman. Music publisher. Estab. 1993. Publishes 25-50 songs/year; publishes 15-20 new songwriters/year. Hires staff songwriters. Pays standard royalty.
Affiliate(s): Dream Builders Publishing (ASCAP).
How to Contact: Submit demo tape by mail. Unsolicited submissions are OK. "Please do not call to request permission—just submit your material. There are no code words. We listen to everything." Prefers cassette or CD with 2 songs and lyric sheet. "If one of your songs is selected for publishing, we prefer to have it available on DAT or CD for dubbing off copies to pitch to artist. Do not send your DAT until you have received a publishing contract." SASE. Responds in 6 weeks.
Music: Mostly **country** and **pop**. Does not want rap, jazz, classical, children's, hard rock, instrumental or blues. Published "Starting Tonight" (single by Sam Storey), recorded by Wayne Horsburgh on Rotation Records (country); "I Can Still See it From Here" (single by John Pearson), recorded by Matt Caldwell on RMC Records; and "An Elvis Night Before Christmas" (single by Keith Collins), recorded by C.C. McCartney on Rotation Records (country).
Tips: "Be willing to work hard to learn the craft of songwriting. Be persistent. Nobody is born a hit songwriter. It often takes years to achieve that status."

☐ DUANE MUSIC, INC. (BMI), 382 Clarence Ave., Sunnyvale CA 94086. (408)739-6133. **Contact:** Garrie Thompson, president. Music publisher and record producer. Publishes 10-20 songs/ year; publishes 1 new songwriter/year. Pays standard royalty.
Affiliate(s): Morhits Publishing (BMI).
How to Contact: Submit demo tape by mail. Unsolicited submissions are OK. Prefers cassette with 1-2 songs. SASE. Responds in 2 months.
Music: Mostly **blues**, **country**, **disco** and **easy listening**; also **rock**, **soul** and **top 40/pop**. Published "Little Girl" (single), recorded by The Syndicate of Sound & Ban (rock); "Warm Tender Love" (single), recorded by Percy Sledge (soul); and "My Adorable One" (single), recorded by Joe Simon (blues).

☐ EARITATING MUSIC PUBLISHING (BMI), P.O. Box 1101, Gresham OR 97030. Music publisher. Estab. 1979. Pays individual per song contract, usually greater than 50% to writer.

How to Contact: Submit demo tape by mail. Unsolicited submissions are OK. Prefers CD or CD-R with lyric sheet. "Submissions should be copyrighted by the author. We will deal for rights if interested." Does not return material. Responds only if interested.
Music: Mostly **rock**, **country** and **folk**. Does not want rap.
Tips: "Melody is most important, lyrics second. Style and performance take a back seat to these. A good song will stand with just one voice and one instrument. Also, don't use staples on your mailers."

[N] ☑ EARTHSCREAM MUSIC PUBLISHING CO. (BMI), 8377 Westview Dr., Houston TX 77055. (713)464-GOLD. E-mail: sarsjef@aol.com. Website: www.soundartsrecording.com. Contact: Jeff Wells; Peter Verheck. Music publisher, record company and record producer. Estab. 1975. Publishes 12 songs/year; publishes 4 new songwriters/year. Pays standard royalty.
Affiliate(s): Reach For The Sky Music Publishing (ASCAP).
How to Contact: Submit demo tape by mail. Unsolicited submissions are OK. Prefers cassette or videocassette with 2-5 songs and lyric sheet. Does not return material. Responds in 6 weeks.
Music: Mostly **new rock**, **country**, **blues** and **top 40/pop**. Published "Baby Never Cries" (single by Carlos DeLeon), recorded by Jinkies on Surface Records (pop); "Telephone Road" (single), written and recorded by Mark May on Icehouse Records (blues); and "Do You Remember" (single by Barbara Pennington), recorded by Perfect Strangers on Earth Records (rock).

☑ ☐ EAST COAST MUSIC PUBLISHING (BMI), P.O. Box 12, Westport MA 02790-0012. (508)679-4272. Fax: (508)673-1235. E-mail: eastcoastmusic@hotmail.com. Website: www.ecmp.com or www.keytomusicsuccess.com. President: Mary-Ann Thomas. Professional Managers: Michael Thomas (hip-hop, rock, jazz); Lisa Medeiros (pop, electronic, dance, country); Noel James (R&B, rap, alternative). Music publisher. Estab. 1996. Publishes 20 songs/year; publishes 10 new songwriters/year. Staff size: 9. Pays standard royalty.
Affiliate(s): New England Sound (BMI).
How to Contact: Submit demo tape by mail. Unsolicited submissions are OK. Prefers cassette with 3-5 songs and lyric or lead sheet. "If you send a SASE I will get back to you within one month. If no SASE I will only respond if interested. We keep submissions in case we decide to publish the song at a future date." Does not return material. Responds only if interested.
Music: Mostly **pop**, **country** and **rock**; also **R&B**, **alternative**, **dance**, **hip-hop** and **rap**. Published "Innocent Girl" (single by Narihiko Habino), recorded by Christine Mills, released November 1999 on the *Dearest Lizzie Musical Soundtrack*; "Did It 4 You" (single by Jackson/Gould), recorded by Streetwise (hip-hop), released January 2000 on East Coast Records; and "Hard to Believe" (single by Joel Greene), recorded by Blackstreet Dolls (r&b), released on Prolific Records.
Tips: "We are seeking very radio friendly songs like Britney Spears, Destiny's Child or N*Sync. Something real now. We are not seeking non-commercial material. We also have a free monthly newsletter with over 1,000 members. It tells people what's going on at East Coast Music Publishing, gives helpful music business advice and allows members to announce things. The way to subscribe is online and it's absolutely free. Just send e-mail to: eastcoastmusic-subscribe@yahoogroups.com."

⊕ ☑ ☐ EDITION ROSSORI, Hietzinger Hptstr 94, Vienna A-1130 Austria. Phone: (01)8762400. Fax: (01)8795464. E-mail: mario_rossori@compuserve.com. Website: www.poppate.com. **Contact:** Mario Rossori, manager. Music publisher and management agency. Estab. 1990. Publishes 150 songs/year; publishes 10 new songwriters/year. Staff size: 2. Pays negotiable royalty.
How to Contact: Submit demo tape by mail. Unsolicited submissions are OK. Does not return material. Responds in 2 months.
Music: Mostly **pop, dance** and **rock**. Does not want jazz. Published *Welsfischer au Wolpedelta* (album), written and recorded by Heinz on Universal (rock).

☐ EMANDELL TUNES, 10220 Glade Ave., Chatsworth CA 91311. (818)341-2264. Fax: (818)341-1008. **Contact:** Leroy C. Lovett, Jr., president/administrator. Music Publisher. Estab. 1979. Publishes 6-12 songs/year; publishes 3-4 new songwriters/year. Pays standard royalty.

Affiliate(s): Ben-Lee Music (BMI), Birthright Music (ASCAP), Em-Jay Music (ASCAP), Northworth Songs, Chinwah Songs, Gertrude Music (all SESAC), Alvert Music (BMI), Andrask Music, Australia (BMI), Nadine Music, Switzerland.

How to Contact: *Write first and obtain permission to submit.* Prefers cassette, videocassette or CD with 4-5 songs and lead or lyric sheet. Include bio of writer, singer or group. SASE. Responds in 6 weeks.

Music: Mostly **inspirational**, **contemporary gospel** and **choral**; also **strong country** and **light top 40**. Published "Under My Skin" and "Colorada River (singles by Diana/Kim Fowley), recorded by Diana, released 2001 on WFL Records; and "Runaway Love" (single by Gil Askey), recorded by Linda Clifford (new gospel), released 2001 on Sony Records.

Tips: "We suggest you listen to current songs. Imagine how that song would sound if done by some other artist. Keep your ear tuned to new groups, bands, singers. Try to analyze what made them different, was it the sound? Was it the song? Was it the production? Ask yourself these questions: Do they have that 'hit' feeling? Do you like what they are doing?"

○ **EMSTONE, INC. MUSIC PUBLISHING (BMI)**, P.O. Box 1287, Hallandale FL 33008. (305)936-0412. E-mail: emstoneinc@yahoo.com. **Contact:** Michael Gary, creative director. President: Mitchell Stone. Vice President: Madeline Stone. Music publisher. Estab. 1997. Pays standard royalty.

How to Contact: Submit demo tape by mail. Unsolicited submissions are OK. Prefers cassette with any number of songs and lyric sheet. Does not return material. Responds in 2 months.

Music: Mostly **pop**, **rock**, **country** and **R&B**. Published "Offer Me Your Love" (single by Harvey G. Gross), recorded by Shawn Rains (country) on Cimarron Music; "I Love What I've Got" (single by Paul and Heather Turner), recorded by Gypsy (pop/rock); and "I've Seen Everything" (single by David Holiday), recorded by Bob Browning (contemporary country) on Universal Sound Records.

Tips: "Send the most polished-sounding demo you can, with songs that have clever hooks and memorable melodies. Make sure that all songs have been registered with the U.S. Copyright Office."

⊕ ✓ ○ **EVER-OPEN-EYE MUSIC (PRS)**, Wern Fawr Farm, Pencoed, MID, Glam CF356NB United Kingdom. Phone: (01656)860041. **Contact:** M.R. Blanche, managing director. Music publisher and record company (Red-Eye Records). Member PPL and MCPS. Estab. 1980. Publishes 6 songs/year. Staff size: 3. Pays negotiable royalty.

How to Contact: Submit demo tape by mail. Unsolicited submissions are OK. Prefers cassette or VHS videocassette. Does not return material. Responds in 2 months.

Music: Mostly **R&B**, **gospel** and **pop**; also **swing**. Published "Snake Hips" and "Eclection" (singles by Burton/Jones); and "Life Insurance" (single by Steve Finn), all recorded by Tiger Bay on Red-Eye Records.

✓ 🖻 ○ **FAMOUS MUSIC PUBLISHING COMPANIES**, 10635 Santa Monica Blvd., Suite 300, Los Angeles CA 90025. (310)441-1300. Fax: (310)441-4722. Website: www.syncsite.com. President: Ira Jaffe. Vice President, Film and TV: Stacey Palm. Director Film & TV Licensing: Delly Ramin. Vice President/Urban: Brian Postelle. Senior Creative Director: Carol Spencer (rock/pop/alternative). Senior Creative Director/Latin: Claribell Cuevas. New York office: 1633 Broadway, 11th Floor, New York NY 10019. Vice President, Catalogue Development: Mary Beth Roberts. Creative Director: Tanya Brown. Nashville office: 65 Music Square East, Nashville TN 37212. Vice President: Pat Finch (country). Senior Creative Director: Curtis Green. Music Publisher. Estab. 1929. Publishes 500 songs/year. Hires staff songwriters. Staff size: 100. Pays standard royalty.

Affiliate(s): Famous Music (ASCAP) and Ensign Music (BMI).

How to Contact: *Famous Music does not accept unsolicited submissions.*

Film & TV: Famous Music is a Paramount Pictures' company. Music Supervisors: Stacey Palm and Delly Ramin. Published "My Heart Will Go On" (by James Homer/Wil Jennings), recorded by Celine Dion in *Titanic*.

Music: Mostly **rock**, **urban**, **R&B**, **country** and **Latin**. Published "I Hope You Dance" (single by Tia Sellers/Michael Dulaney), recorded by Lee Ann Womack; and "He Wasn't Man Enough" (single by Fred Jerkins III), recorded by Toni Braxton.

☑ ◯ **FAVERETT GROUP**, 1502 18th Ave. S., Nashville TN 37212. (615)292-2474. Fax: (615)292-9117. E-mail: FaverettGroup@aol.com. **Contact:** Dan Schafer, creative director. Music publisher and record company (Bridge Records, Inc.). Estab. 1994. Pays standard royalty.
Affiliate(s): Faverett Tracks (BMI).
How to Contact: *Write or call first and obtain permission to submit a demo.* Prefers cassette or CDR with up to 5 songs and lyric sheet. SASE. Responds ASAP.
Music: Accepts **all styles**.

☑ ◯ **FIFTH AVENUE MEDIA, LTD.**, 19 W. 21st St., #603A, New York NY 10010. (516)295-3922. Fax: (516)295-6872. E-mail: fifthavmed@aol.com. Website: www.thefirm.com/fifthavenue. Professional Managers: Bruce E. Colfin (rootsy bluesy rock/reggae); Jeffrey E. Jacobson (hip-hop/ R&B/dance); Daniel Weiss (alternative rock/heavy metal). Music publisher and record company (Fifth Avenue Media, Ltd.). Estab. 1995. Publishes 2 songs/year. Staff size: 4. Pays standard royalty.

🌐 📺 ☑ **FIRST TIME MUSIC (PUBLISHING) U.K. (PRS)**, Sovereign House, 12 Trewartha Road, Praa Sands, Penzance, Cornwall TR20 9ST United Kingdom. Phone: (01736)762826. Fax: (01736)763328. E-mail: panamus@aol.com. Website: www.songwriters-guild.com. **Contact:** Roderick G. Jones, managing director. Music publisher, record company (First Time Records), record producer (Panama Music Library) and management firm (First Time Management and Production Co.). Member MCPS. Estab. 1986. Publishes 500-750 songs/year; 20-50 new songwriters/year. Staff size: 6. Hires staff writers. Pays standard royalty; "50-60% to established and up-and-coming writers with the right attitude."
Affiliate(s): Scamp Music Publishing, Panama Music Library, Musik Image Library, Caribbean Music Library, Psi Music Library, ADN Creative Music Library, Heraldic Production Music Library, Promo Sonor International, Eventide Music.
How to Contact: Submit demo tape by mail. Unsolicited submissions are OK. Prefers cassette, CD/CDR or VHS videocassette "of professional quality" with unlimited number of songs and lyric or lead sheets. Responds in 1 month. SAE and IRC required for reply.
Film & TV: Places 58 songs in film and TV/year. Published "Atmos," written and recorded by Bob Brimley for the BBC; "Maciek," written and recorded by Henryk Wozniacki for World Wide Pictures; and "Haunted House" (by Frank Millum), recorded by Colin Eade for Carlton Television.
Music: All styles. Published *Spring* (album), written and recorded by Kevin Kendle (New Age), released 2000 on Eventide Records; and *The Phoenix Rises* (album by Mike Porterfield/Michael Cook), recorded by Jet Harris (pop/instrumental), released 2000 on Mustang Records.
Tips: "Have a professional approach—present well produced demos. First impressions are important and may be the only chance you get. Writers are advised to join the Guild of International Songwriters and Composers in the United Kingdom."

☑ ◍ **FLYING RED HORSE PUBLISHING (BMI)**, 2932 Dyer St., Dallas TX 75205. (214)691-5318. Fax: (214)692-1392. E-mail: barbe@texasmusicgroup.com. Website: texasmusicgroup.com. **Contact:** Barbara McMillen, creative director. Music publisher, record company (Remarkable Records) and record producer (Texas Fantasy Music). Estab. 1993. Publishes 15-30 songs/year; publishes 6-10 new songwriters/year. Pays standard royalty.
Affiliate(s): Livin' the Life Music (ASCAP).
How to Contact: Submit demo tape by mail between March and July only. Unsolicited submissions are OK. Prefers cassette with 3 songs and lyric sheet. SASE. Responds in 6 months.
Music: Mostly **children's and special occasion songs and stories**. Published *Teardrops to Rainbows* (album by Rollie Anderson/Richard Theisen); *Little Last Note* (album by Lauren Shipird/Richard Theisen); and *First Star* (album by Joe Dickinson/Richard Theisen), all on Remarkable Records.
Tips: "Even when a song is written for children, it should still meet the criteria for a well-written song—and be pleasing to adults as well."

☑ 📺 ◯ **FRESH ENTERTAINMENT (ASCAP)**, 1315 Simpson Rd., Atlanta GA 30314. Phone/fax: (770)642-2645. E-mail: whunter1122@yahoo.com. **Contact:** Willie W. Hunter, managing director. Music publisher and record company. Publishes 5 songs/year. Staff size: 4. Hires staff songwriters. Pays standard royalty.

Affiliate(s): !Hserf Music (ASCAP), Blair Vizzion Music (BMI) and Santron Music (BMI).
How to Contact: Submit demo tape by mail. Unsolicited submissions are OK. Prefers cassette or videocassette with 3 songs and lyric sheet. "Send photo if available." SASE. Responds in 6 weeks.
Film & TV: Places 1 song in TV/year. Published the theme song for BET's *Comic Vue* (by Charles E. Jones), recorded by Cirocco.
Music: Mostly **rap**, **R&B** and **pop/dance**. Published "We Hate Pastor Troy" (single by W. Jackson/Javou/Chosen One) from *Ready For War* (album), recorded by Swat Team (rap/hip-hop), released 2000 on Armageddon/Milltyme; "Erase the Color Line" (single by M. Warner/J. Smith/J. Lewis) from *EMQ-Non Pilation* (album), recorded by Michael Warner/JS-1/Noray (R&B/hip-hop), released 2000 on EMQ Entertainment; and "Live Your Fantasy" (single by B. Miles/E. Davis) from *Nubian Woman* (album), recorded by Bob Miles (jazz), released 2000 on Sheets of Sounds.

⬛ **BOB SCOTT FRICK ENTERPRISES**, 404 Bluegrass Ave., Madison TN 37115-5307. (615)865-6380. Fax: (615)865-6380. **Contact:** Bob Frick, owner. Music publisher, record company (R.E.F.) and record producer. Estab. 1961. Publishes 25 songs/year; publishes 2 new songwriters/year. Staff size: 2. Pays standard royalty.
Affiliate(s): Sugarbakers Music (ASCAP) and Frick Music Publishing Co. (BMI).
How to Contact: Submit demo tape by mail. Unsolicited submissions are OK. Prefers cassette with 2 songs and lyric sheet. SASE. Responds in 3 weeks.
Music: Mostly **Christian** and **country**. Does not want rock. Published *Come Home Daddy* (album by Bill Herold) (country); *It's All Right* (album by Gerald Cunningham) (country); and *If You Need A Miracle* (album by Don Blunkall) (gospel), all recorded by Bob Scott Frick on R.E.F.

✅ ⬛ **FRICON MUSIC COMPANY (BMI)**, 11 Music Square E, Suite 301, Nashville TN 37203. (615)726-0090. Fax: (615)826-0500. E-mail: fricon@home.com. President: Terri Fricon. **Contact:** Madge Benson, professional manager. Music publisher. Estab. 1981. Publishes 25 songs/year; publishes 1-2 new songwriters/year. Staff size: 6. Pays standard royalty.
Affiliate(s): Fricout Music Company (ASCAP) and Now and Forever Songs (SESAC).
How to Contact: *Contact first and obtain permission to submit.* Prefers cassette with 1-2 songs and lyric or lead sheet. "Prior permission must be obtained or packages will be returned." SASE. Responds in 2 months.
Music: Mostly **country**.

✅ ⬛ **FROZEN INCA MUSIC**, P.O. Box 20387, Atlanta GA 30325. (404)931-9049. Fax: (404)351-2786. E-mail: mrland@mindspring.com. Website: www.landsliderecords.com. President: Michael Rothschild. Professional Manager: Eddie Cleveland. Music publisher, record company (Landslide Records) and record producer. Estab. 1981. Publishes 12 songs/year; publishes 3 new songwriters/year. Pays standard royalty.
Affiliate(s): Landslide Records.
How to Contact: Submit demo tape by mail. Unsolicited submissions are OK. Prefers cassette with 3-12 songs. SASE. Responds in 2 months.
Music: Mostly **blues**, **swing**, **rock** and **roots music**. Published "A Quitter Never Wins" (single by Ellis/Sampson); "Cold Cold Ground" (single by Sean Costello); and "Who's Been Cheating Who" (single by Costello/Cleveland), all recorded by Sean Costillo (blues/rock).

⬛ **FURROW MUSIC (BMI)**, P.O. Box 4121, Edmond OK 73083-4121. **Contact:** G.H. Derrick, owner/publisher. Music publisher, record company (Gusher Records) and record producer. Estab. 1984. Publishes 10-15 songs/year. Staff size: 1. Pays standard royalty.
How to Contact: Submit demo tape by mail. Unsolicited submissions are OK. Prefers cassette or VHS videocassette with 1 song and lyric sheet. "One instrument and vocal is OK for demo." SASE. Responds in 2 weeks.
Music: Mostly **country** and **cowboy**. Released 5 original songs on Devin Derrick's CD in 2000. Looking for original songs for his second CD for 2001.

Tips: "Have your song critiqued by other writers (or songwriter organizations) prior to making the demo. Only make and send demos of songs that have a universal appeal. Make sure the vocal is out front of the music. Never be so attached to a lyric or tune that you can't rewrite it. Don't forget to include your SASE."

G MAJOR MUSIC (BMI), P.O. Box 3331, Fort Smith AR 72913-3331. Fax: (501)782-0842. E-mail: JerryGlidewell@juno.com. Professional Managers: Alex Hoover (country/southern rock/gospel); Jerry Glidewell (contemporary country/pop). Music publisher. Estab. 1992. Publishes 10 songs/year; publishes 3 new songwriters/year. Staff size: 2. Pays standard royalty.
How to Contact: Submit demo tape by mail. Unsolicited submissions are OK. Prefers cassette or CD. Submit up to 3 songs. SASE. Responds in 3 weeks.
Music: Mostly **country**, **traditional country** and **pop**; also **contemporary Christian**. Published *In Competition With a Truck* (album by Elaine Woolsey), recorded by Libby Benson (country); "Question of Heart" (single by Jerry Glidewell), recorded by Brian Bateman (country); and "Step Out Into the Sun" (single by Chad Little/Jerry Glidewell), recorded by Libby Benson (Christian contemporary), all on MBS.
Tips: "We are looking for radio-friendly hits for the country market. We use a top songplugger in Nashville. Remember, your song has to be so good that people will spend their hard earned money to hear it over and over again."

ALAN GARY MUSIC (ASCAP, BMI), P.O. Box 179, Palisades Park NJ 07650. President: Alan Gary. Creative Director: Fran Levine. Creative Assistant: Harold Green. Music publisher. Estab. 1987. Publishes a varying number of songs/year. Staff size: 3. Pays standard royalty.
How to Contact: Submit demo tape by mail. Unsolicited submissions are OK. Prefers cassette or VHS videocassette with lyric sheet. SASE.
Music: Mostly **pop**, **R&B** and **dance**; also **rock**, **A/C** and **country**. Published "Liberation" (single by Gary/Julian), recorded by Les Julian on Music Tree Records (A/C); "Love Your Way Out of This One" (single by Gary/Rosen), recorded by Deborah Steel on Bad Cat Records (contemporary country); and "Dueling Rappers" (single by Gary/Free), recorded by Prophets of Boom on You Dirty Rap! Records (rap/R&B).

GLAD MUSIC CO. (ASCAP, BMI, SESAC), 14340 Torrey Chase, Suite 380, Houston TX 77014. (281)397-7300. Fax: (281)397-6206. E-mail: wesdaily@gladmusicco.com. Website: www.gladmusicco.com. **Contact:** Wes Daily, A&R director (country). Professional Managers: Don Daily (traditional country); "Bud" Daily (traditional country). Music publisher, record company and record producer. Estab. 1958. Publishes 10 songs/year; publishes 10 new songwriters/year. Staff size: 4. Pays standard royalty.
Affiliate(s): Bud-Don (ASCAP) and Rayde (SESAC).
How to Contact: *Write first and obtain permission to submit a demo or to arrange personal interview.* Prefers cassette or CD with 3 songs, lyric sheet and cover letter. Does not return material. Responds in 2 weeks.
Music: Mostly **country**. Does not want weak songs. Published *Love Bug* (album by C. Wayne/W. Kemp), recorded by George Strait, released 1995 on MCA; *Walk Through This World With Me* (album), written and recorded by George Jones and *Race Is On* (album by D. Rollins), recorded by George Jones, both released 1999 on Asylum.

AUGUST GOLDEN MUSIC (BMI), 6666 Brookmont Terrace #705, Nashville TN 37205. Phone/fax: (615)353-8134. **Contact:** Marie Golden (pop/film/country). Music publisher. Estab. 1998. Staff size: 3.
How to Contact: *Write, call or fax first and obtain permission to submit a demo.* Prefers cassette or CD with 3 songs and lyric sheet. Does not return material. Responds in 3 weeks.

THE TYPES OF MUSIC each listing is interested in are printed in **boldface**.

Music: Mostly **country**, **pop** and **rock**; also **film music** and **Latin music**. Does not want rap.
Tips: "Have a professional studio demo and the guts to be different."

THE GOODLAND MUSIC GROUP INC., P.O. Box 24454, Nashville TN 37202. (615)269-7074. Fax: (615)269-0131. E-mail: jonwalk@aristomedia.com. Website: www.aristomedia. com. **Contact:** John Walker, publishing coordinator. Music publisher. Estab. 1988. Publishes 50 songs/year; 5-10 new songwriters/year. Pays standard royalty.
Affiliate(s): Goodland Publishing Company (ASCAP), Marc Isle Music (BMI) and Gulf Bay Publishing (SESAC).
How to Contact: Submit demo tape by mail. Unsolicited submissions are OK. Include SASE with first class postage "for reply only."
Music: Mostly **country/Christian**, but open to **all styles**. Published "Where Does Love Go When It's Gone?" (single by Barton/Byram), recorded by Warren Johnson on MDL Records; "Swingin' for the Fences" (single by Myers/Meier) and "The Best Mistake" (single by Primamore), both recorded by Daniel Glidwell on Starborn Records.

GOODNIGHT KISS MUSIC (BMI), 10153½ Riverside Dr. #239, Toluca Lake CA 91601. (323)969-9993. E-mail: staff@goodnightkiss.com. Website: www.goodnightkiss.com. **Contact:** Janet Fisher, managing director. Music publisher, record company and record producer. Estab. 1986. Publishes 8-10 songs/year; publishes 5-7 new songwriters/year. Pays standard royalty.
● Goodnight Kiss Music specializes in placing music in movies and TV, but also pitches major label acts.
Affiliate(s): Scene Stealer Music (ASCAP).
How to Contact: "Check our website or subscribe to free newsletter (www.egroups.com/group/goodnightkiss) to see what we are looking for." Prefers CD or cassette with 1-3 songs and lyric sheet. Send SASE for reply. Does not return material. Responds in 6 months.
Film & TV: Places 3-5 songs in film/year. Published "I Do, I Do, Love You" (by Joe David Curtis), recorded by Ricky Kershaw in *Road Ends*; "Bee Charmer's Charmer" (by Marc Tilson) for the MTV movie *Love Song*; "Right When I Left" (by B. Turner/J. Fisher) in the movie *Knight Club*.
Music: **All modern styles**. Published *I'm Gonna Lasso Santa* (album) and *When Sunny Gets Blues, Scarlet Ribbons, and Other Songs I Wrote* (album by Jack Segal), both released 2000 on Goodnight Kiss Records.
Tips: "The absolute best way to keep apprised of the company's needs is to subscribe to the online newsletter. Only specifically requested material is accepted, as listed in the newsletter (what the industry calls us for is what we request from writers). We basically use an SGA contract, and there are never fees to be considered for specific projects or albums. However, we are a real music company, and the competition is just as fierce as with the majors."

GREEN ONE MUSIC (BMI), Rockin' Chair Center Suite 102, 1033 W. State Highway 76, Branson MO 65616. (417)334-2336. Fax: (417)334-2306. **Contact:** George J. Skupien, president. Music publisher, record label and recording studio. Estab. 1992. Publishes 6-12 songs/year. Pays standard royalty.
How to Contact: *Write or fax first and obtain permission to submit.* Prefers CD, cassette or DAT with 2-4 songs. "We *only* accept professional studio demo tapes. This means that your tape has been performed, recorded and produced by someone with music industry experience, who will represent your songs with the quality of a master recording." Does not return material. "For your protection, all tapes, lyrics or other material that is received, that are not accepted, are immediately destroyed to protect the songwriters." Responds in 3 months.
Music: Mostly **country**, **MOR** and **light rock**; also **American polka music**, **waltzes** and **comedy—fun songs**. Published "Today May Be Too Late" (single by Billy Rice/Matt Row'd), recorded by Billy Rice, released 2000 on Green Bear Records; and "Love Is Why I Feel This Way" (single by G. Skupien/Sara Wright), from *Country Compilation 102* (album), recorded by Buddy Thomas, released 2000 on Green Bear Records.
Tips: "Always put your best song first on your tapes submitted. Be sure your vocal is clear!"

☐**R.L. HAMMEL ASSOCIATES, INC.**, P.O. Box 531, Alexandria IN 46001-0531. E-mail: rlh@rlhammel.com. Website: www.rlhammel.com. **Contact:** A&R Department. President: Randal Hammel. Music publisher, record producer and consultant. Estab. 1974. Staff size: 3-5. Pays standard royalty.
Affiliate(s): Ladnar Music (ASCAP) and Lemmah Music (BMI).
How to Contact: Submit demo tape by mail. Unsolicited submissions are OK. Prefers cassette, DAT or VHS/8mm videocassette with 3 songs and typed lyric sheet. Does not return material. Responds ASAP.
Music: Mostly **pop**, **Christian** and **R&B**; also **MOR**, **rock** and **country**. Published *Lessons For Life* (album by Kelly Hubbell/Jim Boedicker) and *I Just Want Jesus* (album by Mark Condon), both recorded by Kelly Connor on Impact Records.

⊡ ⊕ ☐**HAPPY MELODY**, VZW, Paul Gilsonstraat 31, 8200 St-Andries, Belgium. Phone: (050)31-63-80. **Contact:** Eddy Van Mouffaert, general manager. Music publisher, record company (Jump Records) and record producer (Jump Productions). Member SABAM S.V., Brussels. Publishes 100 songs/year; publishes 8 new songwriters/year. Staff size: 2. Pays standard royalty via SABAM S.V.
How to Contact: Submit demo tape by mail. Unsolicited submissions are OK. Prefers cassette. Does not return material. Responds in 2 weeks.
Music: Mostly **easy listening**, **disco** and **light pop**; also **instrumentals**. Published *Dikke Berta* and *Da Da Da* (albums by Ricky Mondes), both recorded by Guy Dumon on BM Studio (Flemish); and *Onze Vader* (album by David Linton), recorded by De Korenaar on Korenaar (profane).
Tips: "Music wanted with easy, catchy melodies (very commercial songs)."

⊕ ▦ ☐**HEUPFERD MUSIKVERLAG GmbH**, Ringwaldstr. 18, Dreieich 63303 Germany. Phone/fax: (06103)86970. E-mail: heupferd@t-online.de. **Contact:** Christian Winkelmann, general manager. Music publisher and record company (Viva La Difference). GEMA. Publishes 60 songs/year. Staff size: 3. Pays "royalties after GEMA distribution plan."
Affiliate(s): Song Bücherei (book series).
How to Contact: *Does not accept unsolicited submissions.*
Film & TV: Places 1 song in film/year. Published "El Grito Y El Silencio" (by Thomas Hickstein), recorded by Tierra in *Frauen sind was Wunderbares.*
Music: Mostly **folk**, **jazz** and **fusion**; also **New Age**, **rock** and **ethnic music**. Published "Neddle Park" (single), written and recorded by Mike Hanraham; and *Mozarts Mazurka* (album), written and recorded by Tom Daun, both on Wundertüte; and "West Coast of Clare" (single by Andy Irvine), recorded by Geraldine MacGowan on Magnetic.

▨ ☑ ⊘**HICKORY LANE PUBLISHING AND RECORDING (ASCAP, SOCAN)**, 19854 Butternut Lane, Pitt Meadows, British Columbia V3Y 2S7 Canada. (604)465-1258. E-mail: cmu@3web.net. Website: keywordsearch:HickoryLaneRecords. **Contact:** Chris Urbanski, president. Music publisher, record company and record producer. Estab. 1988. Hires staff writers. Publishes 30 songs/year; publishes 5 new songwriters/year. Pays standard royalty.
How to Contact: *Does not accept unsolicited submissions.*
Music: Mostly **country** and **country rock**. Published *All Fired Up* (album), "Ask Me" (single) and "That's How Life Goes" (single), all written and recorded by Chris Michaels (country), released 2000 on Hickory Lane Records.
Tips: "Send us a professional quality demo with the vocals upfront. We are looking for hits, and so are the major record labels we deal with. Be original in your approach, don't send us a cover tune."

☐**HICKORY VALLEY MUSIC (ASCAP)**, 10303 Hickory Valley, Ft. Wayne IN 46835. E-mail: alstraten@aol.com. **Contact:** Allan Straten, president. Music publisher, record company (Yellow Jacket Records) and record producer (Al Straten Productions). Estab. 1988. Publishes 10 songs/year; publishes 5 new songwriters/year. Staff size: 3. Pays standard royalty.
Affiliate(s): Straten's Song (BMI).

How to Contact: Submit demo tape by mail. Unsolicited submissions are OK. Prefers cassette with 3-4 songs and typed lyric sheets. Use a 6×9 envelope with no staples. Does not return material. Responds in 1 month.
Music: Mostly **country**, **MOR** and **contemporary Christian**. Does not want rap, hip-hop or hard/acid rock. Published "My Dream Come True" (single by Robert Kraft/S); and "Our God is Everywhere" and "Christ Came Down" (singles by Sylvia Grogg).

◖ HIGH-MINDED MOMA PUBLISHING & PRODUCTIONS (BMI), P.O. Box 959, Coos Bay OR 97420. **Contact:** Kai Moore Snyder, president. Music publisher and production company. Pays standard royalty.
How to Contact: Prefers 7½ ips reel-to-reel, CD or cassette with 4-8 songs and lyric sheet. SASE. Responds in 1 month.
Music: Mostly **country**, **MOR**, **rock (country)**, **New Age** and **top 40/pop**.

⊠ ◯ HIS POWER PRODUCTIONS AND PUBLISHING (ASCAP, BMI), 1304 Canyon, Plainview TX 79072-4740. (806)296-7073. Fax: (806)296-7111. E-mail: dcarter@o-c-s.com. Website: www.o-c-s.com/hispowerproductions or www.hppp.com. Professional Managers: Darryl Carter (R&B, gospel, country rock); T. Lee Carter (pop, new rock, classic rock). Music publisher, record company (Lion and Lamb), record producer and management and booking agency (End-Time Management & Booking Agency). Estab. 1995. Publishes 4-10 songs/year; publishes 3 new songwriters/year. Staff size: 4. Hires staff songwriters. Pays negotiable royalty.
Affiliate(s): Love Story Publishing (BMI).
  • The song "Heal Me," published by His Power, was awarded a 1998, 1999 and 2000 ASCAP Popular Award.
How to Contact: Write or call first and obtain permission to submit a demo. Prefers cassette, CD or DAT with 1-5 songs and lyric sheet. SASE. Responds in 3 months.
Music: Mostly **power gospel**, **pop**, **new rock**, **classic rock**, **country rock gospel** and **adult contemporary gospel**; also **R&B**, **jazz**, **Christ-oriented Christmas music**, **pro-life and family** and **southern gospel**. Does not want negative-based lyrics of any kind. Published "She Used to Be Me" (single), written and recorded by Crystal Cartier on Love Story (blues); "It's His Life" (single), written and recorded by Mike Burchfield (country gospel), released on Lion and Lamb Records; and "I Didn't Say That I Love You" (single), written and recorded by Joe Copeland (country), released on Tex Sound Records.
Tips: "Be serious. We are only interested in those who have meaning and substance behind what is created. Music is an avenue to change the world. Submit what comes from the heart. Don't be in a hurry. Good music has no time limits. And yet, time will reward the desire you put into it. Be willing to embark on newly designed challenges that will meet a new century of opportunity and needs never before obtainable through conventional music companies."

ℕ ⊕ HIT-FABRIK MUSIKVERLAG, Mühlgasse 1, Obj. 20, Guntramsdorf A-2353 Austria. Phone: + +43-2236/53006. Fax: + +43-2236/53006-90. E-mail: hit.fabrik@magnet.at. Director: Franz Groihs. Music publisher, record company and record producer. Estab. 1985. Publishes 150-200 songs/year; publishes 12 new songwriters/year. Hires staff songwriters. Pays standard royalty.
How to Contact: Submit demo tape by mail. Unsolicited submissions are OK. Prefers cassette, DAT, VHS videocassette or CD with lyric sheet. Does not return material. Responds in 1 month.
Music: Mostly **jazz**, **rock** and **pop**; also **classical** and **instrumental**. Published "Jazzline" (single), written and recorded by Jon Bechert (jazz); "Girls" (single), written and recorded by Rohan Sillip (piano ballad) and "Runner" (single), written and recorded by Peter Paul (rock), all on EAR Records.

◯ HITSBURGH MUSIC CO. (BMI), P.O. Box 1431, 233 N. Electra, Gallatin TN 37066. (615)452-0324. Promotional Director: Kimolin Crutcher. A&R Director: K'leetha Gilbert. Executive Vice President: Kenneth Gilbert. **Contact:** Harold Gilbert, president/general manager. Music publisher. Estab. 1964. Publishes 12 songs/year. Staff size: 4. Pays standard royalty.
Affiliate(s): 7th Day Music (BMI).

How to Contact: Submit demo tape by mail. Unsolicited submissions are OK. Prefers cassette or quality videocassette with 2-4 songs and lead sheet. Prefers studio produced demos. SASE. Responds in 6 weeks.

Music: Mostly **country gospel** and **MOR**. Published "Georgia Boy" (single by Donald Layne), recorded by The Swingsters (MOR), released 2000 on Southern City.

⬤HITSOURCE PUBLISHING (BMI), 1324 Oakton, Evanston IL 60202. (847)328-4203. Fax: (847)328-4236. E-mail: hitsrce@wwa.com. **Contact:** Al Goldberg, president. Music publisher. Estab. 1986. Publishes 3-12 songs/year; publishes 1-2 new songwriters/year. Pays standard royalty.
Affiliate(s): Grooveland Music (ASCAP) and KidSource Publishing (BMI).
How to Contact: *Write or e-mail first and obtain permission to submit.* Prefers cassette with 3 songs and lyric sheet. Does not return material. Responds in 2 months.
Music: Mostly **pop**, **country** and **rock**.
Tips: "Ask yourself the following questions: Does this song come from the heart? Will an artist be willing to risk his career by recording this song? Have you critiqued the song yourself and rewritten it yet?"

🎬 ⬜ HOLY SPIRIT MUSIC (BMI), P.O. Box 31, Edmonton KY 42129. (270)432-3183. **Contact:** W. Junior Lawson, president. Music publisher. Member GMA, International Association of Gospel Music Publishers and Southern Gospel Music Association. Estab. 1973. Publishes 4 songs/year; publishes 2 new songwriters/year. Staff size: 1. Pays standard royalty.
How to Contact: Submit demo tape by mail. Unsolicited submissions are OK. Prefers cassette with 2 songs and lyric sheet. SASE. Responds in 3 weeks.
Film & TV: Places 1 song in film and 1 song in TV/year. Published "I'm Making Plans To See Jesus" (by Gregory A. Pollard), recorded by The Florida Boys in *Saved By Grace*.
Music: Mostly **Southern gospel** and **country gospel**. Does not want rock gospel or contemporary gospel. Published "Just Imagine" and "The Letter" (singles by Carl L. Smoker) from *Somebody Touched the Lord* (album), recorded by Higher Ground Trio (gospel), released 2000 on Independent; and "Excuses" (single by Harold S. Leake) from *Live . . . In the Smokies* (album), recorded by Kingdom Heirs, released 2000 on Sonlite Video.
Tips: Send "good clear cut tape with typed copy of lyrics."

⬜ INDIE-GO MUSIC (ASCAP), 200 Main St., Binghamton NY 13905. (607)655-2175. E-mail: guinnsang@yahoo.com. **Contact:** Chris Guinn, professional manager. Music publisher. Estab. 1999. Staff size: 2. Pays standard royalty.
Affiliate(s): Subterranean Songs (BMI).
How to Contact: Submit demo tape by mail. Unsolicited submissions are OK. Prefers cassette or CD with maximum 3 songs, lyric sheet and cover letter. Send copyrighted material only. SASE. Responds in 1 month.
Music: All genres except rap, jazz, hip-hop, classical.
Tips: "Be very selective—send hit songs only!"

🌐 ⬤ INSIDE RECORDS/OK SONGS, St.-Jacobsmarkt 76, 2000 Antwerp 6 Belgium. Phone: (32)+3+226-77-19. Fax: (32)+3+226-78-05. **Contact:** Jean Ney, MD. Music publisher and record company. Estab. 1989. Publishes 50 songs/year; publishes 30-40 new songwriters/year. Hires staff writers. Royalty varies "depending on teamwork."
How to Contact: Submit demo tape by mail. Unsolicited submissions are OK. Prefers cassette with complete name, address, telephone and fax number. SAE and IRC. Responds in 2 months.
Music: Mostly **dance, pop** and **MOR contemporary**; also **country, reggae** and **Latin**. Published *Fiesta De Bautiza* (album by Andres Manzana); *I'm Freaky* (album by Maes-Predu'homme-Robinson); and *Heaven* (album by KC One-King Naomi), all on Inside Records.

[N] ⬜ INTERPLANETARY MUSIC (BMI), 584 Roosevelt, Gary IN 46404. (219)886-2003. Fax: (219)886-1000. CEO: James R. Hall III. A&R Director (hip-hop, R&B, jazz): Martin Booker. A&R

(R&B, gospel): Bryant Henderson. Music publisher, record company (Interplanetary Records) and record producer. Estab. 1972. Staff size: 5. Publishes 10 songs/year; publishes 4 new songwriters/year. Pays standard royalty.

How to Contact: Call first and obtain permission to submit. Prefers cassette. SASE. Responds in 1 month.

Music: Mostly **R&B**, **rap** and **Top 40/urban contemporary**. Does not want country. Published "Beneath the Sheets" (single by James Hall) and "Good Times" (single by Bernard Tucker), both recorded by Subliminal on Interplanetary Records.

Tips: "Please submit a good quality cassette recording of your best work."

☑ ○ **IRON SKILLET MUSIC**, 229 Ward Circle, #A21, Brentwood TN 37027. (615)371-0646. Fax: (615)370-0353. E-mail: jschneiderasspc@aol.com. **Contact:** Jack Schneider, president. Vice President: Claude Southall. Office Manager: Nell Tolson. Music publisher, record company (Rustic Records Inc.) and record producer. Estab. 1984. Publishes 20 songs/year. Pays standard royalty.

Affiliate(s): Covered Bridge Music (BMI), Town Square Music (SESAC).

How to Contact: Submit demo tape by mail. Unsolicited submissions are OK. Prefers cassette with 3 songs and lyric sheet. SASE. Responds in 3 months.

Music: Mostly **country**. Published "Hey You" (single by Liz Real/T. Strawbridge), recorded by T. Strawbridge; "Now You See Him Now You Don't" and "Fire and Thunder" (singles), both written and recorded by T. Strawbridge, all released 2000 on Rustic Records.

Tips: "Send three or four traditional country songs, story songs or novelty songs with strong hook. Enclose SASE (manilla envelope)."

○ **JANA JAE MUSIC (BMI)**, P.O. Box 35726, Tulsa OK 74153. (918)786-8896. Fax: (918)786-8897. E-mail: janajae@janajae.com. Website: www.janajae.com. **Contact:** Kathleen Pixley, secretary. Music publisher, record company (Lark Record Productions, Inc.) and record producer (Lark Talent and Advertising). Estab. 1980. Publishes 5-10 songs/year; publishes 1-2 new songwriters/year. Staff size: 8. Pays standard royalty.

How to Contact: Submit demo tape by mail. Unsolicted submissions are OK. Prefers cassette or VHS videocassette with 3-4 songs and typed lyric and lead sheet if possible. Does not return material. Responds only if accepted for use.

Music: Mostly **country**, **bluegrass**, **jazz** and **instrumentals** (**classical** or **country**). Published *Mayonnaise* (album by Steve Upfold), recorded by Jana Jae; and *Let the Bible Be Your Roadmap* (album by Irene Elliot) recorded by Jana Jae, both on Lark Records.

Ⓝ ⊕ **JAMMY MUSIC PUBLISHERS LTD.**, The Beeches, 244 Anniesland Rd., Glasgow G13 1XA, Scotland. Phone: (041)954-1873. E-mail: 100734.2674@compuserve.com. Managing Director: John D. R. MacCalman. Music publisher and record company. PRS. Estab. 1977. Publishes 45 songs/year; publishes 2 new songwriters/year. Pays royalty "in excess of 50%."

How to Contact: Contact by e-mail only and obtain permission to submit. Does not return material. Responds in 3 months.

Music: Mostly **rock**, **pop**, **country** and **instrumental**; also **Scottish**. Published "The Wedding Song" (single by Bill Padley/Grant Mitchell), recorded by True Love Orchestra on BBC Records (pop); *The Old Button Box* (album by D. McCrone), recorded by Foster & Allen on Stylus Records; and "Absent Friends" (single by D. McCrone), recorded by Dominic Kirwan on Ritz Records.

Tips: "We are not currently taking any new writers, although we will consider material in traditional Scottish and Irish styles. We will give faster responses by e-mail. We cannot accept music across the net, but if you convince us we should listen to your stuff we will ask for a tape by snail mail."

Ⓝ ⊕ ○ **JA/NEIN MUSIKVERLAG GMBH**, Hallerstr. 72, D-20146 Hamburg Germany. Fax: (+49)40 448850. E-mail: janeinmv@aol.com. General Manager: Mary Dostal. Music publisher, record company and record producer. GEMA. Publishes 100 songs/year; publishes 20 new songwriters/year. Staff size: 3. Pays 60% royalty.

Affiliate(s): Pinorrekk Mv., Star-Club Mv., Wunderbar Mv. and Sempex Mv. (GEMA).

How to Contact: Submit demo tape by mail. Unsolicited submissions are OK. Prefers cassette, CDR or VHS videocassette and lyric sheet. SAE and IRC. Responds in 2 months.
Music: Mostly **jazz**, **klezmer**, **pop**, **rap** and **rock**. Published "Dem Melekh's Nigh" (single by Alan Bern), recorded by Brave New World (klezmer), released on ÿ Pinorrekk Records; "Wenn Ich Robert DeNiro Waer" (single), written and recorded by Bernd Huber (pop), released on Lux Records; and "Just Before the Break of Day" (single), written and recorded by Axel Zwingenberger and Big Joe Duskin (boogie woogie), released on Vagabond Records.
Tips: "If IRC is not included, we only react if we fall in love. Single, A-Side songs only or extraordinary ideas, please. If artist, include photo. Leave three seconds between songs. Enclose lyrics. Be fantastic!"

N: ☐ JASPER STONE MUSIC (ASCAP)/JSM SONGS (BMI), 10 Deepwell Farms Rd., South Salem NY 10590. E-mail: gcrecords@aol.com. Website: members.aol.com/gcrecords. President: Chris Jasper. Vice President/General Counsel: Margie Jasper. Music publisher. Estab. 1986. Publishes 20-25 songs/year. "Each contract is worked out individually and negotiated depending on terms." Staff size: 5. Pays standard royalty.
How to Contact: Submit demo tape by mail. Unsolicited submissions are OK. Prefers cassette, CD or DAT with maximum of 3 songs and lyric sheets. SASE. Responds in 6 weeks.
Music: Mostly **R&B/pop**, **rap** and **rock**. Does not want country, classical or children's. Published "And I Love Her" (single by J. Lennon/P. McCartney), recorded by Brothaz By Choice on Gold City Records (R&B).
Tips: "Keep writing. Keep submitting tapes. Be persistent. Don't give up. Send your best songs in the best form (best production possible)."

☐ JERJOY MUSIC (BMI), P.O. Box 1264, 6020 W. Pottstown Rd., Peoria IL 61654-1264. (309)673-5755. Fax: (309)673-7636. E-mail: uarltd@unitedcyber.com. Website: www.unitedcyber.com/uarltd. **Contact:** Jerry Hanlon, professional manager. Music publisher and record company (Universal-Athena Records). Estab. 1978. Publishes 6 songs/year; publishes 6 new songwriters/year. Staff size: 3. Pays standard royalty.
How to Contact: "We accept unsolicited submissions. We do not return phone calls." Prefers cassette or CD with 4-8 songs and lyric sheet. SASE. "We do not critique work unless asked." Responds in 2 weeks.
Music: Mostly **country**. Published "The Girl From Central High" (single by Ron Czikall) from *Right Here In Tennessee* (album), recorded by Tracy Wells (country); "Too Late to Put the Bottle Down" (single by Cliff Thigpen) from *Hello Mr. Heartache* (album), recorded by Jerry Hanlon (country); and "New Jerusalem" (single by Diane Kemp Pantel) from *Country Nights* (album), recorded by Garry Johnson (country), all released 2000 on UAR.
Tips: "Don't submit any song that you don't honestly feel is well constructed and strong in commercial value. Be honest and sincere."

☑ AL JOLSON BLACK & WHITE MUSIC (BMI), 116 17th Ave. S., Nashville TN 37203. (615)244-5656. **Contact:** Albert Jolson, president. Music publisher. Estab. 1981. Publishes 600 songs/year; publishes 50 new songwriters/year. Pays standard royalty.
Affiliate(s): Jolie House Music (ASCAP).
How to Contact: Submit a demo tape by mail. Unsolicited submissions are OK. Prefers cassette with 3 songs and lyric sheet. Send: Attn. Johnny Drake. SASE. Responds in 6 weeks.
Music: Mostly **country crossover**, **light rock** and **pop**. Published "Come Home to West Virginia" (single by Scott Phelps), recorded by Kathy Mattea; "Ten Tiny Fingers, Ten Tiny Toes" (single by David John Hanley), recorded by Kelly Dawn; and "Indiana Highway" (single), recorded by Staggerlee, both on ASA Jolson Records (country).

REFER TO THE CATEGORY INDEX (at the end of this section) to find exactly which companies are interested in the type of music you write.

Tips: "Make sure it has a strong hook. Ask yourself if it is something you would hear on the radio five times a day. Have good audible vocals on demo tape."

○ **JPMC MUSIC INC. (BMI)**, 80 Pine St., 33rd Floor, New York NY 10005. (212)344-5588. Fax: (212)344-5566. E-mail: music@jpmc.com. Website: www.jpmc.com. **Contact:** Jane Peterer, president. Music publisher, record company (JPMC Records) and book publisher. Estab. 1989. Publishes 20 songs/year; publishes 10 new songwriters/year. Pays standard royalty.
Affiliate(s): GlobeSound Publishing (ASCAP) and GlobeArt Publishing Inc. (BMI).
How to Contact: Submit a demo tape by mail. Unsolicited submissions are OK. Prefers "professional" cassette or CD with 3 songs and lyric sheet. "If submitting a CD, indicate which three tracks to consider, otherwise only the first three will be considered." SASE. Responds in 2 months.
Music: Mostly **pop/R&B**, **jazz** and **gospel**; also **country** and **instrumental**. Published "Ode to Ireland" (single by Breschi), recorded by Breschi/Cassidy on Pick Records (instrumental); and "Ici Paris" (single), written and recorded by Michael Ganian.
Tips: "We are in constant communication with record and film producers and will administer your work on a worldwide basis. We also publish songbooks for musicians and fans, as well as educational and method books for students and teachers."

✓ ○ **JUKE MUSIC (BMI)**, P.O. Box 120277, Nashville TN 37212. **Contact:** Becky Gibson, songwriter coordinator. Professional Manager: Jack Cook. Music publisher. Estab. 1987. Publishes 60-150 songs/year; publishes 3-25 new songwriters/year. Pays standard royalty.
How to Contact: Submit demo tape by mail. Unsolicited submissions are OK. Prefers cassette with 3 songs and lyric sheet. "Send only radio-friendly material." Does not return material. Responds in 8 months.
Music: Mostly **country/pop** and **rock**; also **alternative adult** and **Christian**. Does not want theatrical, improperly structured, change tempo and feel, poor or music with no hook. Published "Cross on the Highway" (single) from *Summer Country Drive Inn* (album), written and recorded by Ronnie McDowell, released 2001 on Portland; "April Fool" (single by Phil Delberg) from *Georgia Rockitt* (album), recorded by Tuscaloosa (southern rock/country), released 2000 on Blackstone; and "King & Queen of Love" (single by Ralph Lake) from *Running Scared 2001*, recorded by Michael Sheahan (pop/rock), released 2001 on Daydreamer.
Tips: "Do your homework, craft the song, be sure you're willing to gamble your songwriting integrity on this song or songs you're sending. We recommend songwriters attend workshops or conferences before submitting material. Help us cut through the junk. Send *positive, uptempo, new country* for best results. It seems most of our submitters read what we *do not* want and send that! *Please* listen to country radio."

[N] ○ **KANSA RECORDS CORPORATION**, 11716 Manor Rd., Leawood KS 66211. (913)661-0233. **Contact:** Kit Johnson, secretary and treasurer/general manager. Music publisher, record company and record producer. Estab. 1972. Publishes 50-60 songs/year; publishes 8-10 new songwriters/year. Pays standard royalty.
Affiliate(s): Great Leawood Music, Inc. (ASCAP) and Twinsong Music (BMI).
How to Contact: Submit demo tape by mail. Unsolicited submissions are OK. Prefers cassette with 4 songs and lyric sheet. Does not return material. Responds in 2 months.
Music: Mostly **country**, **MOR** and **country rock**; also **R&B** (leaning to country) and **Christian**. Does not want hard rock. Published *Louisiana Hop*; *Big Hurt*; *Seasons of Our Love* (albums by Walter Leise), all recorded by Jerry Piper on Kansas Records.

✓ ○ **KAUPPS & ROBERT PUBLISHING CO. (BMI)**, P.O. Box 5474, Stockton CA 95205. (209)948-8186. Fax: (209)942-2163. Website: www.makingmusic4u.com. **Contact:** Kristy Ledford, A&R coordinator (all styles). Production Manager (country, pop, rock): Rick Webb. Professional Manager (country, pop, rock): Bruce Boun. President: Nancy L. Merrihew. Music publisher, record company (Kaupp Records), manager and booking agent (Merri-Webb Productions and Most Wanted Bookings). Estab. 1990. Publishes 15-20 songs/year; publishes 5 new songwriters/year. Pays standard royalty.

How to Contact: *Write first and obtain permission to submit.* Prefers cassette or VHS videocassette (if available) with 3 songs maximum and lyric sheet. "If artist, send PR package." SASE. Responds in 6 months.

Music: Mostly **country**, **R&B** and **A/C rock**; also **pop**, **rock** and **gospel**. Published "Prisoner of Love" (single by N. Merrihew/Rick Webb), recorded by Nanci Lynn (country/rock/pop); "Excuse Me, But That Ain't Country" (single by N. Merrihew/B. Bolin), recorded by Bruce Bolin (country/rock/pop); and "Did You Think That I Thought That You Liked Me" (single by N. Merrihew/B. Bolin), recorded by Nanci Lynn (country/rock/pop), all released on Kaupp Records.

Tips: "Know what you want, set a goal, focus in on your goals, be open to constructive criticism, polish tunes and keep polishing."

N ⃝ **KEYSHAVON MUSIC PUBLISHING (BMI)**, 530 Broadway St., Platteville WI 53818. (608)348-7419. E-mail: Topcat@mhct.net. **Contact:** Christopher Isabell, owner. Music Publisher. Estab. 2001. Pays standard royalty.

How to Contact: Submit demo tape by mail. Unsolicited submissions are OK. Prefers cassette or CD with 5 songs and lyric and lead sheet. "Please copyright your songs." Include SASE. Responds in 1 month.

Music: All types.

Tips: "Make sure your song is well written with a professional demo. We need hits. Also, please read all you can about the music industry."

N ⃝ **LAKE TRANSFER PRODUCTIONS & MUSIC (ASCAP, BMI)**, 11300 Hartland St., North Hollywood CA 91605. (818)508-7158. **Contact:** Jim Holvay, professional manager (pop, R&B, soul); Tina Antoine (hip-hop, rap); Steve Barri Cohen (alternative rock, R&B). Music publisher and record producer (Steve Barri Cohen). Estab. 1989. Publishes 11 songs/year; publishes 3 new songwriters/year. Staff size: 6. Pay "depends on agreement, usually 50% split."

Affiliate(s): Lake Transfer Music (ASCAP) and Transfer Lake Music (BMI).

How to Contact: *Does not accept unsolicited submissions.*

Music: Mostly **alternative pop**, **R&B/hip-hop** and **dance**. Does not want country & western, classical, New Age, jazz or swing.

Tips: "All our staff are songwriters/producers. Jim Holvay has written hits like 'Kind of a Drag' and 'Hey Baby They're Playin our Song' for the Buckinghams. Steve Barri Cohen has worked with every one from Evelyn 'Champaigne' King, Patrice Rushen to Phantom Planets (Geffen)."

N ▣ ⃝ **LARGO MUSIC PUBLISHING (ASCAP, BMI)**, 425 Park Ave., New York NY 10022. (212)756-5080. Fax: (212)207-8167. E-mail: largomp@aol.com. Website: www.largomusic.c om. Creative Manager (all music genres): Peter Oriol. Professional Manager (hip-hop, rap, R&B): Walter Velesquez. A&R (A/C, pop): John M. Murro. Music publisher. Estab. 1980. Staff size: 10. Pays variable royalty.

Affiliate(s): Catharine Hiren Music, American Compass Music Corp., Diplomat Music Corp., Larry Shayne Enterprises (ASCAP), Largo Cargo Music (BMI), X-Square Music and Three White Boys Music, Rap Music (BMI), Rock-Logic Music (ASCAP).

How to Contact: Write first and obtain permission to submit or to arrange personal interview. Prefers cassette or CD with 4 songs and lyric sheet. "Spend money on recording well, not packaging." Does not return material. Responds in 1 month.

Film & TV: Places 10 songs in film and 10 songs in TV/year. Music Supervisors: Peter Oriol (all); Walter Velesquez (hip-hop, rap, R&B).

Music: Mostly **alternative rock**, **AOR** and **R&B**; also **hip-hop** and **rap**; "good music that transcends categories." Published "Drama" (single by Ty Macklin), recorded by Erykah Badu on Universal (R&B); "Step Into a World" (single by Jesse West), recorded by KRS-One on Jive (rap); and "24/7" (single by Jesse West), recorded by 24/7 on Loud (rap).

Tips: "Good songs are not enough—you must be a complete artist and writer."

⊘ **LARI-JON PUBLISHING (BMI)**, 325 W. Walnut, Rising City NE 68658. (402)542-2336. **Contact:** Larry Good, owner. Music publisher, record company (Lari-Jon Records), management firm (Lari-Jon Promotions) and record producer (Lari-Jon Productions). Estab. 1967. Publishes 20 songs/year; publishes 2-3 new songwriters/year. Staff size: 1. Pays standard royalty.

How to Contact: Submit demo tape by mail. Unsolicited submissions are OK. Prefers cassette with 5 songs and lyric sheet. "Be professional." SASE. Responds in 2 months.

Music: Mostly **country, Southern gospel** and **'50s rock**. Does not want rock, hip-hop, pop or heavy metal. Published "Glory Bound Train" (single), written and recorded by Tom Campbell; "Nebraskaland" and "Jesus Is My Hero" (singles), written and recorded by Larry Good, all on Lari-Jon Records.

☑ ○ **TRIXIE LEIGH MUSIC**, 1717 Crimson Tree Way #A, Edgewood MD 21040. (410)676-5841. Music publisher: Rick Solimini. E-mail: cherasnyelijah@webtv.net. Music publisher and record company (Cherasny Records). Estab. 1997. Publishes 4 songs/year; publishes 4 new songwriters/year. Hires staff writers. Staff size: 4. Pays standard royalty.

How to Contact: *Write first and obtain permission to submit.* Prefers cassette with 3 songs and lyric and lead sheets. SASE. Responds in 1 month.

Music: Contemporary Christian. Does not want secular, rap, opera or hard rock. Published *Paid In Full* (album), recorded by Redemption (contemporary Christian), released 2001 on Cherasny Records.

Tips: "Be consistent in learning the craft of songwriting."

☑ ○ **LES MUSIC GROUP**, 6301 N. O'Connor, Irving TX 75039. E-mail: chris@dallastexas.cc. Website: www.studiosatlascolinas.com. Professional Managers: Chris Christian (pop/Christian); Shannon Megallson. Music publisher, record company and record producer. Estab. 1981. Publishes 2,000 songs/year. Staff size: 35. Hires staff songwriters. Pays standard royalty.

Affiliate(s): Home Sweet Home Music/Bug and Bear Music (ASCAP), Chris Christian Music (BMI) and Monk and Tid (SESAC).

How to Contact: Submit demo tape by mail. Unsolicited submissions are OK. Prefers cassette, CD, DAT or videocassette. Include name, phone number and e-mail on CD or tape. Does not return material. Responds in up to 1 year.

Music: Does not want quartet music.

Tips: "Keep writing until you get good at your craft. Co-write with the best you can—always put phone number on tape or CD's."

Ⓝ ⊘ **LEXINGTON ALABAMA MUSIC PUBLISHING (BMI)**, 3596 County Rd. 136, Lexington AL 35648. Phone/fax: (256)229-8814. Email: LampMusic@cs.com. **Contact:** Darrell Glover, owner. Professional Managers: Roy Crabb (R&B); Ann Glover (country); Grady Glover (rock). Music publisher and record company (Lamp Records). Estab. 1981. Publishes 35 songs/year; publishes 5 new songwriters/year. Staff size: 4. Pays standard royalty.

Affiliate(s): Northwest Alabama Music Publishing (BMI).

How to Contact: Submit demo tape by mail. Unsolicited submissions are OK. Prefers CD or CD-R with 3 songs, lyric sheet and cover letter. "Find a new way of expressing old ideas." Does not return material. Responds only if interested.

Music: Mostly **country, southern rock** and **R&B**; also **comedy, gospel** and **Christmas**. Does not want rap, hard rock and classical. Published "Candlelight Opera" (single), written and recorded by Mark Narmore (country); *Let's Make the World Noisy* (album by Curtis Hall), recorded by Apul (rock), both released 2000 on Lamp Records; and "He Pours Out His Spirit" (single), written and recorded by Gary Springer (gospel), released 2001 on Lamp Records.

🕷 🖼 ⊘ **LILLY MUSIC PUBLISHING (SOCAN)**, 61 Euphrasia Dr., Toronto, Ontario M6B 3V8 Canada. (416)782-5768. Fax: (416)782-7170. **Contact:** Panfilo DiMatteo, president. Music publisher and record company (P. & N. Records). Estab. 1992. Publishes 20 songs/year; publishes 8 new songwriters/year. Staff size: 3. Pays standard royalty.

Affiliate(s): San Martino Music Publishing and Paglieta Music Publishing (CMRRA).

How to Contact: Submit demo tape by mail. Unsolicited submissions are OK. Prefers cassette (or videocassette if available) with 3 songs and lyric and lead sheets. "We will contact you only if we are interested in the material." Responds in 1 month.
Film & TV: Places 12 songs in film/year.
Music: Mostly **dance**, **ballads** and **rock**; also **country**. Published *Only This Way* (album), recorded by Zoe Skylar (dance), released on P&N Records.

○ **DORIS LINDSAY PUBLISHING (ASCAP)**, P.O. Box 35005, Greensboro NC 27425. (336)882-9990. **Contact:** Doris Lindsay, president. Music publisher and record company (Fountain Records). Estab. 1979. Publishes 20 songs/year; publishes 4 songwriters/year. Pays standard royalty.
Affiliate(s): Better Times Publishing (BMI).
How to Contact: Submit demo tape by mail. Unsolicited submissions are OK. Prefers cassette with 2 songs. "Submit good quality demos." SASE. Responds in 2 months.
Music: Mostly **country**, **pop** and **contemporary gospel**. Published "Grandma Bought a Harley" (single by Susan and Frank Rosario) on Fountain Records.
Tips: "Present a good quality demo (recorded in a studio). Positive clean lyrics and up-tempo music are easiest to place."

○ **LINEAGE PUBLISHING CO. (BMI)**, P.O. Box 211, East Prairie MO 63845. (314)649-2211. **Contact:** Tommy Loomas, professional manager. Staff: Alan Carter and Joe Silver. Music publisher, record producer, management firm (Staircase Promotions) and record company (Capstan Record Production). Pays standard royalty.
How to Contact: Submit demo tape by mail. Unsolicited submissions are OK. Prefers cassette with 2-4 songs and lyric sheet; include bio and photo if possible. SASE. Responds in 2 months.
Music: Mostly **country**, **easy listening**, **MOR**, **country rock** and **top 40/pop**. Published "Let It Rain" (single by Roberta Boyle), recorded by Vicarie Arcoleo on Treasure Coast Records; "Country Boy" (single), written and recorded by Roger Lambert; and "Boot Jack Shuffle" (single by Zachary Taylor), recorded by Skid Row Joe, both on Capstan Records.

N: ○ **HAROLD LUICK & ASSOCIATES MUSIC PUBLISHER (BMI)**, P.O. Box 368, Carlisle IA 50047. (515)989-3748. Fax: (515)989-0235. E-mail: haroldl@cmshowcase.org. Website: www.cmshowcase.org. President (country, bluegrass, blues, contemporary Christian): Harold L. Luick. Vice President (cajun, gospel, country, blues): Barbara A. Luick. Professional Manager: Frank Gallagher (MOR, contemporary country). Music publisher, record company, record producer and music industry consultant. Publishes 25-30 songs/year; publishes 5-10 new songwriters/year. Pays standard royalty.
How to Contact: *Write or call first about your interest, or for more information on CMSI.* Prefers cassette with 3-5 songs and lyric sheet. SASE. Responds in 3 weeks.
   • Harold Luick & Associates is now owned and operated by Country Music Showcase International Inc.
Music: Mostly **traditional country** and **hard core country**. Does not want hip-hop or rap. Published "Ballad of Deadwood L.P." (single), written and recorded by Don Laughlin on Kajac Records (historical country); "He Thought She Always Knew" (single by Frank Gallagher/Scott Hoff), recorded by Scott Hoff (country), released 2000 on Door Knob Records; and "Adios, Sayonara, Goodbye" (single by Hank Sasaki/Frank Gallagher), recorded by Hank Sasaki (Japanese EMI country artist), released 2000 on EMI Japan. (Note: mp3 samples available at www.cmshowcase.org/setarecord.htm.)
Tips: "It takes just as much of your time and money to pitch a good song as a bad one, so concentrate on the potential of the good ones. Join nonprofit educational songwriters associations (like CMSI) that can help you write better songs through critiques, evaluations, seminars and workshops."

✓ ⚑ ○ **LYRICK STUDIOS (ASCAP, BMI, SESAC)**, 830 S. Greenville Ave., Allen TX 75002-3320. (972)390-6080. Fax: (972)390-6001. E-mail: jsmith@lyrick.com. Website: www.lyricks tudios.com. **Contact:** Jonathan E. Smith, administrator, music publishing and clearances. Music publisher and record company. Estab. 1996.

• Lyrick Studios produces and distributes music, products and TV programming for the characters Barney and Wishbone.

How to Contact: "Send only a résumé with a list of songwriting accomplishments." SASE. Responds only if interested.

Music: Mostly **children's**. Controls Barney catalog of music for television, film, radio, home video, toy, Internet and albums.

N **MAGIC MESSAGE MUSIC (ASCAP)**, P.O. Box 9117, Truckee CA 96162. (530)587-0111. E-mail: alanred@telis.org. Website: www.alanredstone.com. Owner: Alan Redstone. Music publisher and record company (Sureshot Records). Estab. 1979. Publishes 6 songs/year; publishes 1 new songwriter/year. Staff size: 1. Pays standard royalty.

How to Contact: Write or call first and obtain permission to submit or submit demo tape by mail. Unsolicited submissions are OK. SASE. Responds in 1 week.

Music: Mostly **comedy**, **novelty** and **parody**; also **blues**. Does not want rap, soul, top 40, New Age or instrumental.

N **MAKERS MARK GOLD (ASCAP)**, P.O. Box 42751, Philadelphia PA 19101. (215)236-4817. Website: www.prolificrecords.com. Producer: Paul Hopkins. Music publisher and record producer. Estab. 1991. Pays standard royalty.

How to Contact: Submit demo tape by mail. Unsolicited submissions are OK. Prefers cassette with 2-4 songs. Does not return material. Responds in 6 weeks if interested.

Music: Mostly **R&B**, **hip-hop**, **gospel**, **pop**, **country** and **house**. Published "Last Kiss" and "Top of the World" (singles by C. Foreman/P. Hopkins), recorded by Rachel Scarborough; "All Eyes on the Philosopher" (single by Norman Gilliam/P. Hopkins), recorded by Norman Gilliam; and "In the Still of the Night" (single), recorded by Emerge, all on Prolific Records.

Tips: "I prefer to work with those with representation."

MANUITI L.A. (ASCAP), 4007 W. Magnolia Blvd., Burbank CA 91505. (818)843-2628. Fax: (818)843-4480. E-mail: manuitila@aol.com. **Contact:** Steven Rosen, president. Music publisher and record producer.

How to Contact: Submit demo tape by mail. Unsolicited submissions OK. Prefers CD with 3 songs, lyric sheet, cover letter and photo/bio. Does not return material. Responds in 1 month.

Film & TV: Recently published "As If," recorded by Blaque in *Bring It On* and "What A Girl Wants," recorded by Christina Aguilera in *What Women Want*.

Music: Mostly **pop** and **R&B**. Does not want heavy metal. Published "Almost Doesn't Count," recorded by Brandy (R&B) on Atlantic; "Beauty," recorded by Dru Hill (R&B) on Island; and "Under My Tree," recorded by *NSync on RCA.

Tips: "Do your homework on who you are contacting and what they do. Don't waste yours or their time by not having that information."

MARKEA MUSIC/GINA PIE MUSIC (BMI, SESAC), P.O. Box 121396, Nashville TN 37212. (615)329-1111. Fax: (615)329-4121. E-mail: keatonmusic@mindspring.com. Professional Managers: Chris Keaton (country/folk/R&B); Kent Martin (folk/pop). Music publisher. Estab. 1995. Publishes 19 songs/year; publishes 1 new songwriter/year. Staff size: 2. Hires staff songwriters. Pays standard royalty.

Affiliate(s): Markea Music (BMI) and Gina Pie Music (SESAC).

How to Contact: *Call first and obtain permission to submit a demo.* Prefers cassette or CD with 3 songs and lyric sheet. Does not return material. Responds in 6 weeks.

Film & TV: Places 1 song in film and 1 song in TV/year. Published "Keep Coming Back," written and recorded by Mike Younger in *Time of Your Life*; and "If By Chance . . .," written and recorded by Mike Younger in *A Galaxy, Far, Far Away*.

Music: Mostly **country**, **folk** and **pop**; also **R&B**. Published "I'm Happy" (single by Ronna Reeves/Tom McHugh) from *Ronna Reeves* (album), recorded by Ronna Reeves (pop/country), released 2000 on Hello.

Tips: "Send your best."

N: ⊘ JOHN WELLER MARVIN PUBLISHING (ASCAP), 863 Sarcee Ave., Suite 1, Akron OH 44305. (330)733-8585. Fax: (216)589-5823. E-mail: stephanie_jwm@yahoo.com. **Contact:** Stephanie Arble, president. Music Publisher. Estab. 1996. Pays standard royalty.
How to Contact: Submit demo tape by mail. Unsolicited submissions are OK. Prefers cassette, CD or VHS and lyric or lead sheet. Responds in 6 weeks.
Music: All genres, mostly **pop, R&B, rap**; also **rock**, and **country**. Published "Downloading Files" (single by S. Arble/R. Scott), recorded by Ameritech Celebration Choir (corporate promotional). "We work with a promoter booking major label artists and with some television and corporate promotional recordings."

⊘ MAVERICK MUSIC, 8730 Sunset Blvd., Suite 420, Los Angeles CA 90069. (310)652-6300. Contact: Lionel Conway. Music publisher and record company (Maverick).
How to Contact: *Maverick Music does not accept unsolicited submissions.*

♣ ✓ ◻ MAYFAIR MUSIC (BMI), (formerly Berandol Music Ltd.), 2600 John St., Unit 219, Markham, Ontario L3R 3W3 Canada. (905)475-1848. **Contact:** Ralph Cruickshank, A&R director. Music publisher, record company (MBD Records), music print publisher (Music Box Dancer Publications), record producer and distributor. Member CMPA, CIRPA, CRIA. Estab. 1979. Publishes 20-30 songs/year; publishes 3-5 new songwriters/year. Pays standard royalty.
How to Contact: Submit demo CD/CDR by mail. Unsolicited submissions are OK. Prefers CD/CDR with 2-5 songs. Does not return material. Responds in 3 weeks.
Music: Mostly **instrumental** and **children's**.
Tips: "Strong melodic choruses and original-sounding music receive top consideration."

✓ ☒ ◻ McCONKEY ARTISTS AGENCY MUSIC PUBLISHING (BMI), Hollywood Media Center Blgd., 1604 N. Cahuenga, Suite 108, Hollywood CA 90028-6267. (323)463-7141. Fax: (323)463-2558. E-mail: info@vinegowerrecords.com. Website: www.vinegowerrecords.com. **Contact:** Mack K. McConkey, managing director. Director of A&R: Steve Fazio. Music publisher. Estab. 1998. Publishes 13 songs/year; publishes 5 new songwriters/year. Staff size: 10. Hires staff songwriters (part time only). Pays standard royalty.
Affiliate(s): Vinegower Music (ASCAP).
How to Contact: Submit demo tape by mail. Unsolicited submissions are OK. Prefers cassette or CD with 1-5 songs and lyric sheet and cover letter. "Please send us a professional tape or CD, as well as a typed or computer-printed lyric sheet and cover letter." Does not return material. Responds in 2 months.
Film & TV: Places 1 song in TV/year. Recently published "August" (single by Em Kitterman), recorded by Pat Noland in an HBO Movie of The Month (untitled at press time).
Music: **All types**. Published *Somewhere Inside* (album by F.T. Tolbert), recorded by FLYNN (hot AC), released 2000 on Vinegower Records; and "Think About Me" (single by Al Villanueva) from *Red Fish Blue Fish* (album) by Red Fish Blue Fish (alternative rock), released 2000 on Vinegower Records.
Tips: "Provide the best quality package on your songs. Also send the songs you feel are hits. Do not bother sending album filler material."

◻ JIM McCOY MUSIC (BMI), Rt. 2, Box 2910, Berkeley Springs WV 25411. (304)258-9381. **Contact:** Bertha and Jim McCoy, owners. Music publisher, record company (Winchester Records) and record producer (Jim McCoy Productions). Estab. 1973. Publishes 20 songs/year; publishes 3-5 new songwriters/year. Pays standard royalty.
Affiliate(s): New Edition Music (BMI).

● **A BULLET** introduces comments by the editor of *Songwriter's Market* indicating special information about the listing.

How to Contact: Submit demo tape by mail. Unsolicited submissions are OK. Prefers cassette, 7½ or 15 ips reel-to-reel (or VHS or Beta videocassette) with 6 songs. SASE. Responds in 1 month.
Music: Mostly **country, country/rock** and **rock**; also **bluegrass** and **gospel**. Published "One Time" (single by T. Miller), recorded by J.B. Miller on Hilton Records (country); and "Like Always" (single by J. Alford), recorded by Al Hogan on Winchester Records (country).

☐ MELLOW HOUSE MUSIC (BMI), P.O. Box 423618, San Francisco CA 94142. (415)776-8430. **Contact:** Darren Brown, president. Music publisher, record company (Mellow House Recordings) and record producer. Estab. 1992. Publishes 10 songs/year; publishes 10 new songwriters/year. Hires staff writers. Staff size: 7. Pays standard royalty.
How to Contact: Submit demo tape by mail. Unsolicited submissions are OK. Prefers cassette, DAT or CD with 3 songs and lyric sheet. SASE. Responds in 2 months.
Music: Mostly **funk, R&B** and **hip-hop**; also **pop/rock, alternative jazz** and **gospel**. Published "Soul Reflection" and "Love Parade" (singles), both written and recorded by Bobby Beale on Mellow House Recordings (jazz).

⊘ MELODY HILLS RANCH PUBLISHING CO. (BMI), 804 N. Trenton, Ruston LA 71270. (318)255-7127. Fax: (318)255-3050. E-mail: melodyhills@altavista.com. Owners: Jim Ball and Jane Ball. Music publisher. Estab. 1996. Publishes 2-3 songs/year; publishes 1-2 new songwriters/year. Staff size: 5. Pays standard royalty.
How to Contact: *Write first and obtain permission to submit.* Prefers cassette with 3-4 songs and lyric sheet. Does not return material. Responds in 6 weeks.
Music: Mostly **traditional country, southern rock** and **pop**. Does not want rap or rock. Published *Hungover Heart* and *Last Call for Alcohol* (albums), both written and recorded by Jim Ball; and *Peter Filed Chapter 13* and *Lovin' On* (albums), both written and recorded by Monty Russell on Melody Hills (traditional country).

🌐 ⊘ MENTO MUSIC GROUP, Winterhuder Weg 142, D-22085, Hamburg Germany. Phone: (040)22716552 + -53. Fax: (040)22716554. E-mail: mento_music@t-online.de. **Contact:** Arno H. Van Vught, general manager. Professional Manager: Michael Frommhold. Music publisher and record company (Playbones Records). Estab. 1970. Pays standard royalty.
Affiliate(s): Auteursunie, Edition Lamplight, Edition Melodisc, Massimo Jauch Music Productions and Marathon Music.
How to Contact: Submit demo tape by mail. Unsolicited submissions are OK. Prefers cassette with 3-4 songs. "Put your strongest/best song first. Put your name and address on the inside sleeve of the tape. If you have a fax number, inform us. Tell us in a typed cover letter what you want/what you are looking for." Does not return material. Responds in 3 weeks.
Music: Mostly **instrumental, pop, MOR, country, background music** and **film music**. Does not want classical. Published "Remember Jaco" (single by D. Krauser) from *Bass & Fusion* (album), recorded by Dixi Krauser (pop); "LA Palma-sinfonia (from the mara-mediarama)" (single by W. Bauer) from *Earthviews-Special Edition* (album), recorded by Wolfgang v. Wolpertshausen (soft melodic); and "Horner Marie" (single) from *The best of . . .* (album), written and recorded by Volker Frank (pop), all released 2000 on Playbones Records.

✓ ☐ THE MIGHTY BLUE MUSIC MACHINE, 2016 Douglas Ave., Clearwater FL 33755. Fax: (727)449-8814. E-mail: mightyblue@earthlink.net. **Contact:** Tony Blue, president. Music publisher. Estab. 1995. Staff size: 3-5. Pays standard royalty.
Affiliate(s): Earth Groovz (ASCAP) and Songs From Out of the Blue (BMI).
How to Contact: *Write first and obtain permission to submit.* Include SASE. "No phone calls, please." Prefers cassette or CD with 1-3 songs and lyric sheets. "Send 'studio' quality demo with typed lyric sheets." SASE. Responds in 3 months.
Music: Mostly **rock (acoustic), country** and **pop**; also **blues, Christian/gospel, R&B, jazz** and **dance**. Does not want violent lyrics. "Be positive—be original."
Tips: "Submit only professional 'studio' quality demos (invest in your craft) and be very patient."

◆ ◑ **MONTINA MUSIC (SOCAN)**, Box 702, Snowdon Station, Montreal, Quebec H3X 3X8 Canada. **Contact:** David P. Leonard, professional manager. Music publisher and record company (Monticana Records). Estab. 1963. Pays negotiable royalty.
Affiliate(s): Saber-T Music (SOCAN).
How to Contact: Write first and obtain permission to submit or submit demo tape by mail. Unsolicited submissions are OK. Prefers CD, cassette, phonograph record or VHS videocassette. SAE and IRC. Responds in 3 months.
Music: Mostly **top 40**; also **bluegrass**, **blues**, **country**, **dance-oriented**, **easy listening**, **folk**, **gospel**, **jazz**, **MOR**, **progressive**, **R&B**, **rock** and **soul**. Does not want heavy metal, hard rock, jazz, classical or New Age.
Tips: "Maintain awareness of styles and trends of your peers who have succeeded professionally. Understand the markets to which you are pitching your material. Persevere at marketing your talents. Develop a network of industry contacts, first locally, then regionally, nationally and internationally."

◻ **MOON JUNE MUSIC (BMI)**, 4233 SW Marigold, Portland OR 97219. (507)777-4621. Fax: (503)277-4622. **Contact:** Bob Stoutenburg, president. Music publisher. Estab. 1971. Staff size: 1. Pays standard royalty.
How to Contact: Submit demo tape by mail. Unsolicited submissions are OK. Prefers cassette or CD with 2-10 songs. SASE. Responds in 6 weeks.
Music: Mostly **country**, **top 40**, **blues**, **Christmas** and **novelty**. Does not want rap, Christian, world, folk or New Age.

◙ **THE MUSIC BRIDGE (ASCAP, BMI)**, P.O. Box 661918, Los Angeles CA 90066-1918. (310)398-9650. Fax: (310)398-4850. E-mail: thebridge@aol.com. Website: http://themusicbridge.com. **Contact:** David G. Powell, president. Music publisher and music supervision. Estab. 1992.
How to Contact: *Only accepts material referred by a reputable industry source.* Does not return material. Responds in 2 months.

◙ **THE MUSIC ROOM PUBLISHING GROUP**, P.O. Box 219, Redondo Beach CA 90277. (310)316-4551. **Contact:** John Reed, president/owner. Music publisher and record producer. Estab. 1982. Pays standard royalty.
Affiliate(s): MRP (BMI).
How to Contact: *Not accepting unsolicited material.*
Music: Mostly **pop/rock/R&B** and **crossover**.

◙ **MUSIKUSER PUBLISHING (ASCAP)**, 15030 Ventura Blvd., Suite 425, Sherman Oaks CA 91403. (818)783-2182. Fax: (818)783-3204. E-mail: musikuser@aol.com. **Contact:** John Sloate, president. Music publisher. Estab. 1974. Publishes 20 songs/year; publishes 3 new songwriters/year. Pays standard royalty.
How to Contact: *Write first and obtain permission to submit.* "No phone calls." Prefers DAT with lyric and lead sheet. Does not return material.
Music: **All styles**. Published *Thief of Hearts* (album by Hattler/Kraus), recorded by Tina Turner on Virgin Records.

◻ **CHUCK MYMIT MUSIC PRODUCTIONS (ASCAP)**, 9840 64th Ave., Flushing NY 11374. Professional Managers: Chuck Mymit (pop, soft rock); Monte Mymit (A/C). Music publisher and record producer (Chuck Mymit Music Productions). Estab. 1978. Publishes 3-5 songs/year; publishes 2-4 new songwriters/year. Pays standard royalty.
Affiliate(s): Viz Music (BMI), Chargo Music (ASCAP) and Tore Music (BMI).
How to Contact: Submit demo tape by mail. Unsolicited submissions are OK. Prefers cassette or CD with 3-5 songs and lyric and lead sheets. "Bio and picture would be helpful." SASE. Responds in 6 weeks.
Music: Mostly **pop**, **soft rock** and **A/C**. Published "Never More" (single by C. Mymit/M. Asuaje) from *Romance* (album), recorded by Chuck Mymit (A/C), released 2000 on CMP; "Give It To Me"

(single by R. Rose/L. Spencer/F.W. Stein) from *Dance the Night Away* (album), recorded by Marci Michaels (dance), released 2000 on LSI; and "It's Over Now" (single by C. Mymit), from *Everything* (album), recorded by Delana (soft rock), released 2000 on Excalibur Sound.

Tips: "We are a small company. We have to be selective. Only send us your best work and make sure that it is as professional-sounding as possible. No cheap tapes. No weak productions."

☑ 🐾 ⊘ **NAKED JAIN RECORDS (ASCAP)**, P.O. Box 4132, Palm Springs CA 92263-4132. (760)325-8663. Fax: (760)320-4305. E-mail: info@nakedjainrecords.com. Website: www.nakedjainr ecords.com. **Contact:** Dena Banes, vice president/A&R. Music publisher, record company and record producer (Dey Martin). Estab. 1991. Publishes 40 songs/year; publishes 2 new songwriters/year. Staff size: 5. Pays standard royalty.

Affiliate(s): Aven Deja Music (ASCAP).

How to Contact: *Write or call first and obtain permission to submit a demo or to arrange personal interview.* Prefers cassette or CD with 3 songs, lyric sheet and cover letter. Does not return material. Responds in 2 weeks.

Film & TV: Places 10 songs in TV/year. Music Supervisors: Dey Martin (alternative). Recently published "Yea Right" (single), written and recorded by Lung Cookie in Fox Sports TV; "Just Ain't Me" (single), written and recorded by Lung Cookie in ESPN-TV; and "Speak Easy" (single), written and recorded by Lung Cookie in ESPN-TV.

Music: Mostly **alternative rock**. Does not want country.

Tips: "Write a good song."

🌀 **A NEW RAP JAM PUBLISHING**, P.O. Box 683, Lima OH 45802. Professional Managers: William Roach (rap, clean); James Milligan (country, 70s music, pop). **Contact:** A&R Dept. Music publisher and record company (New Experience/Grand Slam Records and Pump It Up Records). Estab. 1989. Publishes 30 songs/year; publishes 2-3 new songwriters/year. Hires staff songwriters. Staff size: 6. Pays standard royalty.

Affiliate(s): Party House Publishing (BMI) and Creative Star Management.

How to Contact: *Write first to arrange personal interview or submit demo tape by mail.* Unsolicited submissions are OK. Prefers cassette with 3-5 songs and lyric or lead sheet. SASE. Responds in 5 weeks.

Music: Mostly **R&B**, **pop** and **rock/rap**; also **contemporary**, **gospel**, **country** and **soul**. Published *Experiences* (album), written and recorded by Jayhson Rodgers (R&B/rap); and "Brothers Striving" (single) from *Rap Music* (album), written and recorded by William Roach (rap), both released 2001 on Pump It Up Records.

Tips: "We are seeking hit artists of the 1970s and 1980s who would like to be re-signed, as well as new talent and female solo artists. Send any available information supporting the group or act. We are a label that does not promote violence, drugs or anything that we feel is a bad example for our youth. Establish music industry contacts, write and keep writing and most of all believe in yourself. Use a good recording studio but be very professional. Just take your time and produce the best music possible. Sometimes you only get one listen. Make sure you place your best song on your demo first. This will increase your chances greatly. If you're the owner of your own small label and have a finished product, please send it. And if there is interest we will contact you."

🌑 **NEWCREATURE MUSIC (BMI)**, P.O. Box 1444, Hendersonville TN 37077-1444. (615)452-3234. Fax: (615)206-9136. E-mail: lmarkcom@aol.com. **Contact:** Bill Anderson, Jr., president. Professional Manager: G.L. Score. Music publisher, record company, record producer (Landmark Communications Group) and radio and TV syndicator. Publishes 25 songs/year; publishes 2 new songwriters/year. Pays standard royalty.

Affiliate(s): Mary Megan Music (ASCAP).

How to Contact: *Contact first and obtain permission to submit.* Prefers cassette or videocassette with 4-10 songs and lyric sheet. SASE. Responds in 6 weeks.

Music: Mostly **country**, **gospel**, **jazz**, **R&B**, **rock** and **top 40/pop**. Published *Glory* and *Popcorn, Peanuts and Jesus* (albums by Harry Yates), both recorded by Joanne Cash Yates on Angel Too Records (gospel); and *Were You Thinkin' Of Me* (album), written and recorded by Jack Mosley on Landmark Records (country).

[N] [Ø] NORTHWEST ALABAMA MUSIC PUBLISHING CO. (BMI), 3596 County Rd. 136, Lexington AL 35648. Phone/fax: (256)229-8814. E-mail: LampMusic@cs.com. **Professional Managers:** Erica Hand (country, soft rock); Kimberley Glover (gospel, R&B); D. Glover (rock, pop). Music Publisher and record company (Harmony House Records). Estab. 2000. Publishes 10 songs/year; publishes 2 new songwriters/year. Staff size: 3. Hires staff writers. Pays standard royalty.
Affiliate(s): Lexington Alabama Music Publishing (BMI).
How to Contact: Submit demo tape by mail. Unsolicited submissions are OK. Prefers cassette or CD with 3 songs, a lyric sheet and cover letter. "If you send unsolicited materials please label it as such in correspondence. List the name of your manager or contact person and the phone number as well as address with SASE for response." Does not return material. Responds only if interested.
Music: Mostly **country, pop** and **rock**; also **R&B, gospel** and **southern rock**. Does not want classical. Published "Let It Go" (single by Mark Terry), recorded by Mark Anthony (country); "Heirlooms" (single), written and recorded by Kellie Flippo (pop); and "Southern Girls" (single by Teena Hartsfield), recorded by Rex & the Rockets (R&B), all released 2000 on Harmony House Records.
Tips: "Don't try to critique your own songs."

[N] [▨] [Ø] OLD SLOWPOKE MUSIC (BMI), P.O. Box 52681, Tulsa OK 74152. (918)742-8087. E-mail: ryoung@cherrystreetrecords.com. Website: www.cherrystreetrecords.com. **Contact:** Steve Hickerson, professional manager. **President:** Rodney Young. Music publisher and record producer. Estab. 1977. Publishes 24-36 songs/year; publishes 2-3 new songwriters/year. Staff size: 2. Pays standard royalty.
How to Contact: Does not accept unsolicited submissions.
Film & TV: Places 1 song in film/year. Recently published "Samantha," written and recorded by George W. Carroll in *Samantha.*
Music: Mostly **rock, country** and **R&B**; also **jazz**. Published *Promise Land* (album), written and recorded by Richard Neville on Cherry Street Records (rock).
Tips: "Write great songs. We sign only artists who play an instrument, sing and write songs."

[✓] [Ø] OMNI 2000, INC., 413 Cooper St., Camden NJ 08102. (609)963-6400. Fax: (856)964-3291. E-mail: omniplex@erols.com. Website: www.omniplex413.com. **Contact:** Michael Nise, president/executive producer. Music publisher, record company (Power Up-Sutra), recording studio (Studio 2000) and production company. Publishes 10 songs/year; publishes 5 new songwriters/year. Pays standard royalty.
How to Contact: *Write or call first and obtain permission to submit.* Prefers cassette or videocassette with 3 songs. Send Attention: Michael Nise. SASE. Responds in 3 months.
Music: Mostly **dance, R&B, country rock** and **pop**, all with pop crossover potential; also **children's, church/religious, easy listening, folk, gospel** and **jazz**.

[○] ONTRAX COMPANIES (ASCAP), P.O. Box 769, Crown Point IN 46308. (219)736-5815. **Contact:** Professional Manager. Music publisher and record producer. Estab. 1991. Publishes 30 songs/year; 7 new songwriters/year. Staff size: 7. Pays standard royalty.
How to Contact: Submit demo tape by mail. Unsolicited submissions are OK. Prefers CD (but will accept cassette) with 1-6 songs. "Tapes should be mailed in as small a package as possible, preferrably in a small bubble mailer. All items must be labeled and bear the proper copyright notice. We listen to all submissions in the order they arrive. No phone calls please." Does not return submissions. Responds only if interested.
Music: Mostly **pop/rock, country** and **crossover country**. Does not want heavy metal or rap. Published "Thirteenth Floor" (single by J. Russell/B. Powell) from *The Humble Crow* (album), recorded by The Mann Act (crossover country), released 2000 on Formality Records; "Fever Pitch" (single by M. Grzb/L. Tonkinson) from *Leverage* (album), recorded by The Glen Park Consortium (pop/rock), released 2000 on 28IF Records; and "Why Laugh? It's Tuesday!" (single by W. Shenson/T. Bonner/T. Kirkland) from *Tunes From Prock's Ditch* (album), recorded by 43,560 Square Feet (new traditionalist), released 2000 on Trax Tracks.
Tips: "Please do not include SASEs or response cards. We will not respond unless interested in publishing the song."

◐ **ORCHID PUBLISHING (BMI)**, Bouquet-Orchid Enterprises, P.O. Box 1335, Norcross GA 30091. (770)814-2420. **Contact:** Bill Bohannon, president. Music publisher, record company, record producer (Bouquet-Orchid Enterprises) and artist management. Member: CMA, AFM. Publishes 10-12 songs/year; publishes 3 new songwriters/year. Pays standard royalty.
How to Contact: Submit demo tape by mail. Unsolicited submissions are OK. Prefers cassette or CD with 3-5 songs and lyric sheet. "Send biographical information if possible—even a photo helps." SASE. Responds in 1 month.
Music: Mostly **religious** ("Amy Grant, etc., contemporary gospel"); **country** ("Garth Brooks, Trisha Yearwood-type material"); and **top 100/pop** ("Bryan Adams, Whitney Houston-type material"). Published "Blue As Your Eyes" (single), written and recorded by Adam Day; "Spare My Feelings" (single by Clayton Russ), recorded by Terri Palmer; and "Trying to Get By" (single by Tom Sparks), recorded by Bandoleers, all on Bouquet Records.

◯ **OTTO PUBLISHING CO. (ASCAP)**, P.O. Box 16540, Plantation FL 33318. (954)741-7766. President (pop, gospel): Frank X. Loconto. Professional Manager (country western, bluegrass): Bill Dillon. Professional Manager (top 40, contemporary): Dennis Bach. Music publisher, record company (FXL Records) and record producer (Loconto Productions). Estab. 1978. Publishes 25 songs/year; publishes 1-5 new songwriters/year. Pays standard royalty.
Affiliate(s): Betty Brown Music Co. (BMI), Clara Church Music Co. (SESAC) and True Friends Music (BMI).
How to Contact: Submit demo tape by mail. Unsolicited submissions are OK. Prefers cassette or CD/CDR with 1-4 songs and lyric sheet. SASE. Responds in 4 months.
Music: Mostly **country**, **MOR**, **religious** and **gospel**. Published "Silent Waters" (by various), recorded by Irena Kofman (inspirational); and "Holy Spirit" (by Frank X. Loconto), recorded by Kaye Stevens (gospel), both on FXL; and "Finally" (by various), recorded by Miracle Lights on RLB (gospel).
Tips: "The more you write the better you get. If you are a good writer, it will happen."

◑ **PADEN PLACE MUSIC (BMI)**, 3803 Bedford Ave., Nashville TN 37215. (615)292-5848. Fax: (615)292-9598. E-mail: t.paden@worldnet.att.net. **Contact:** Tedd French, song plugger/creative manager (country/AC). Music publisher. Estab. 1986. Publishes 30 songs/year; publishes 2 new songwriters/year. Staff size: 4. Pays statutory royalty.
Affiliate(s): Bedford Ave. Music (SESAC).
How to Contact: *Write first and obtain permission to submit a demo.* Prefers cassette or CD with 3 songs and lyric sheet. SASE. Responds in 2 weeks.
Music: Mostly **country**, **adult contemporary** and **light rock**. Does not want rap, Christian or hard rock.

🌐 ✔ 🖼 ⊘ **PAS MAL PUBLISHING SARL**, 283 Fbg St. Antoine, Paris 75020 France. Phone: 011(33)1 43485151. Fax: 011(33)1 43485753. E-mail: patrickjammes@compuserve.com. Website: www.intoxygene.com or www.theyounggods.com. **Contact:** Jammes Patrick, managing director. Music publisher. Estab. 1990. Staff size: 2. Publishes 5-10 songs/year. Pays 60% royalty.
How to Contact: Does not accept unsolicited submissions.
Film & TV: Places 3 songs in film and 2 songs in TV/year.
Music: Mostly **new industrial** and **metal**. Does not want country, pop or jazz. Published *Second Nature Lucidogen Astromic* (album), written and recorded by The Young Gods (alternative), released October 2000 on Intoxygene.

✔ ◯ **PECOS VALLEY MUSIC (BMI)**, 2709 W. Pine Lodge, Roswell NM 88201. (505)622-2008. E-mail: willmon@bigfoot.com. **Contact:** Ray Willmon, president. Professional Managers: Jack Bush; Lance Law. Music publisher. Estab. 1989. Publishes 15-20 songs/year; publishes 4-5 new songwriters/year. Staff size: 3. Pays standard royalty.
How to Contact: Submit demo tape by mail. Unsolicited submissions are OK. "No phone calls please." Prefers cassette, CD or VHS videocassette with 1-2 songs and lyric sheet. SASE. Responds in 3 months.

Music: Mostly **country**. Does not want rock & roll. Published "Wait on Me" (single), written and recorded by Mel Farmer (country); and "Till the Sun Sets" (single), written and recorded by Joe Farmer (country), both on SunCountry Records.

Tips: "Listen to what's playing on radio and TV and write with these in mind. Use proper song format (AAAA, ABAB, AABA, etc.) Also, please follow submission instruction. Do not phone. Learn proper song structure and proper meter. Make a good demo."

N ⊕ ♥ PEGASUS MUSIC, P.O. Box 127, Otorohanga 2564, New Zealand. E-mail: peg.music @voyager.co.nz. Professional Managers: Errol Peters (country, rock); Ginny Peters (gospel, pop). Music publisher and record company. Estab. 1981. Publishes 20-30 songs/year; publishes 5 new songwriters/year. Pays standard royalty.

How to Contact: Submit demo tape by mail. Unsolicited submissions are OK. Prefers cassette with 3-5 songs and lyric sheet. SAE and IRC. Responds in 1 month.

Music: Mostly **country**; also **bluegrass**, **easy listening** and **top 40/pop**. Published "Angel Things" (single by Kevin Johnston/Don Breeden) from *My Girl* (album), recorded by Craig Byrne (country), released 2000 (Top Ten in Australia) on Windsong; "What Does It All Really Mean" (single by Bob Carey) from *Sooner Than You Thought* (album), recorded by Graeme McCardle (country), released 2000 on Manuka; and "Meet Me In the Middle" (single by Michael F. Eck) from *Leavin' Made Easy* (album), recorded by Dan Mureau (country), released 2000 on Nashgrill.

Tips: "Get to the meat of the subject without too many words. Less is better."

☑ ▨ ☐ PEN MUSIC GROUP, INC. (ASCAP, BMI, SESAC, CCLI), 1608 N. Las Palmas Ave., Los Angeles CA 90028-6112. (323)993-6542. Fax: (323)468-0519. E-mail: submission@penm usic.com. Website: www.penmusic.com. Professional Managers: Jennifer Herbig, manager film & TV (film & TV); Michael Eames, president (all styles). **Contact:** Karri Bowman, office manager. Music publisher and publishing administrator. Estab. 1994. Publishes 100 songs/year; publishes 15 new songwriters/year. Staff size: 5. Pay varies depending on situation.

Affiliate(s): Pensive Music (ASCAP) and Penname Music (BMI).

How to Contact: *E-mail or write first and obtain permission to submit a demo.*

Film & TV: Places over 200 songs in various projects per year.

Music: Publishes **all styles** of music with songs on both major label and independent releases world-wide.

Tips: "Present yourself professionally and then let the music speak for itself."

⊘ PERLA MUSIC (ASCAP), 122 Oldwick Rd., Whitehouse Station NJ 08889-5014. (908)439-2336. Fax: (908)439-9119. E-mail: gperla@ccinyc.com. Website: www.pmrecords.org. **Contact:** Gene Perla (jazz). Music publisher, record company (P.M. Records, Inc.), record producer (Gene Perla) and Internet Design and Hosting. Estab. 1971. Publishes 5 songs/year. Staff size: 1. Pays 75%/25% royalty.

Music: Mostly **jazz**.

☑ ☐ JUSTIN PETERS MUSIC (BMI), P.O. Box 271056, Nashville TN 37227. (615)269-8682. Fax: (615)269-8929. Website: http://songsfortheplanet.com. **Contact:** Justin Peters, president. Music publisher. Estab. 1981.

Affiliate(s): Platinum Planet Music and Tourmaline (BMI).

How to Contact: Submit demo tape by mail. Unsolicited submissions are OK. Prefers cassette with 5 songs and lyric sheet. Does not return material. "Place code '2002' on each envelope submission."

Music: Mostly **religious**. Published "Saved By Love," recorded by Amy Grant on A&M Records; "Love's Still Changing Hearts," recorded by Imperials on Starsong Records; and "Wipe a Tear," recorded by Russ Taff and Olanda Draper on Word Records, all singles written by Justin Peters.

☑ ⊘ PIANO PRESS (ASCAP), P.O. Box 85, Del Mar CA 92014-0085. (858)481-5650. Fax: (858)755-1104. E-mail: pianopress@aol.com. Website: www.pianopress.com. **Contact:** Elizabeth C.

Axford, M.A., owner. Music publisher. Publishes songbooks & CD's for music students and teachers. Estab. 1999. Publishes 32 songs/year; publishes 1-15 new songwriters/year. Staff size: 5. Pays standard print music and/or mechanical royalty; composer retains rights to songs.

How to Contact: *Write or call first and obtain permission to submit a demo.* Prefers cassette or CD with 1-3 songs, lyric and lead sheet, cover letter and sheet music/piano arrangements. "Looking for children's songs for young piano students and arrangements of public domain folk songs of any nationality." Currently accepting submissions for *Kidtunes*. SASE. Responds in 2 months.

Music: Mostly **children's**, **folk songs** and **funny songs**; also **piano arrangements**, **lead sheets with melody, chords and lyrics** and **songbooks**. Does not want commercial pop, R&B, etc. Published "Lots & Lotsa Latkes" and "Eight Little Candles in a Window" (singles both by Katherine Dines) from *Merry Christmas Happy Hanukkah—A Multilingual Songbook & CD* (album), both recorded and arranged by Elizabeth C. Axford on Piano Press.

Tips: "Songs should be simple, melodic and memorable. Lyrics should be for a juvenile audience and well-crafted."

✔ 🎵 **POLLYBYRD PUBLICATIONS LIMITED (ASCAP, BMI, SESAC)**, P.O. Box 8442, Universal CA 91608. (818)506-8533. Fax: (818)506-8534. E-mail: pplzmi@aol.com. Branch office: 333 Proctor St., Carson City NV 89703. (818)884-1946. Fax: (818)882-6755. **Contact:** Dakota Hawk, vice president. Professional Managers: Cisco Blue (country, pop, rock); Tedford Steele (hip-hop, R&B). Music publisher, record company (PPL Entertainment) and Management firm (Sa'mall Management). Estab. 1979. Publishes 100 songs/year; publishes 25-40 new songwriters/year. Hires staff writers. Pays standard royalty.

Affiliate(s): Kellijai Music (ASCAP), Pollyann Music (ASCAP), Ja'Nikki Songs (BMI), Velma Songs International (BMI), Lonnvanness Songs (SESAC), PPL Music (ASCAP), Zettitalia Music, Butternut Music (BMI), Zett Two Music (ASCAP), Plus Publishing and Zett One Songs (BMI).

How to Contact: *Write first and obtain permission to submit.* Prefers cassette or VHS videocassette with 4 songs and lyric and lead sheet. SASE. Responds in 2 months.

Music: Published "Believe" (single by J. Jarrett/S. Cuseo) from *Time* (album), recorded by Lejenz (pop), released 2001 on PRL/Credence; *Rainbow Gypsy Child* (album), written and recorded by Riki Hendrix (rock), released 2001 on PRL/Sony; and "What's Up With That" (single by Brandon James/Patrick Bouvier) from *Outcast* (album), recorded by Condottieré (hip-hop), released 2001 on Bouvier.

Tips: "Make those decisions—are you really a songwriter? Are you prepared to starve for your craft? Do you believe in delayed gratification? Are you commercial or do you write only for yourself? Can you take rejection? Do you want to be the best? If so, contact us—if not, keep your day job."

Ⓝ 🔾 **PORTAGE MUSIC (BMI)**, 16634 Gannon W., Rosemount MN 55068. (952)432-5737. President: Larry LaPole. Music publisher. Publishes 5-20 songs/year. Pays standard royalty.

How to Contact: Submit demo tape by mail. Unsolicited submissions are OK. Prefers cassette with 3 songs and lyric sheet. Does not return material. Responds in 3 months.

Music: Mostly **country** and **country rock**. Published "Lost Angel," "Think It Over" and "Congratulations to Me" (by L. Lapole), all recorded by Trashmen on Sundazed.

Tips: "Keep songs short, simple and upbeat with positive theme."

🔾 **PREJIPPIE MUSIC GROUP (BMI)**, Box 312897, Penobscot Station, Detroit MI 48231. E-mail: prejippie@aol.com. Website: www.prejippie.com. Professional Manager: Victoria Henderson. **Contact:** Bruce Henderson, president. Music publisher, record company (PMG Records) and record producer (PMG Productions). Estab. 1990. Publishes 50-75 songs/year; publishes 2-3 new songwriters/year. Hires staff writers. Staff size: 3. Pays standard royalty.

How to Contact: Submit demo tape by mail. Unsolicited submissions are OK. Prefers cassette or CD with 3-4 songs and lyric sheet. "No phone calls please." SASE. Responds in 6 weeks.

REFER TO THE GEOGRAPHIC INDEX (at the back of this book) to find listings of companies by state, as well as foreign listings.

Music: Mostly **alternative R&B, alternative rock, techno/house** and **experimental**. Does not want country, gospel, show tunes or lyrics only. Published "Do What I Can Do Right" (single), written and recorded by Bourgeoisie Paper Jam (funk/rock); and "2001 Bass Blizzard" (single), written and recorded by Tony Webb (jazz) all on PMG Records.

Tips: "We're always looking for new approaches to traditional genres. We want to hear vocals, lyrics and music that is passionate and takes a chance, but still keeps hooks that are solid."

○ **PRESCRIPTION COMPANY (BMI)**, Box 222249, Great Neck NY 11021. (415)553-8540. Fax: (415)553-8541. E-mail: medmike525@aol.com. President: David F. Gasman. Vice President of A&R: Kirk Nordstrom. Vice President of Sales: Bruce Brennan. Vice President of Finance: Robert Murphy. Music publisher and record producer. Staff size: 7. Pays standard royalty.

How to Contact: Write or call first and obtain permission to submit. Prefers cassette with any number of songs and lyric sheet. "Send all submissions with SASE (or no returns)." Responds in 1 month.

Music: Mostly **bluegrass, blues, children's** and **country, dance-oriented**; also **easy listening, folk, jazz, MOR, progressive, R&B, rock, soul** and **top 40/pop**. Published "Good Lookin' Thing" (single by Giant/Baum/Kaye), recorded by Medicine Mike on Prescription Records (rock).

Tips: "Songs should be good and written to last. Forget fads—we want songs that'll sound as good in ten years as they do today. Organization, communication and exploration of form are as essential as message (and sincerity matters, too)."

☑ ⚑ ○ **THEODORE PRESSER CO. (ASCAP, BMI, SESAC)**, 588 N. Gulph Rd., King of Prussia PA 19406. (610)525-3636. Fax: (610)527-7841. E-mail: presser@presser.com. Website: www.presser.com. **Contact:** Brett Rosenau, editorial assistant. Music publisher. Estab. 1783. Publishes 200 songs/year; publishes 3 new songwriters/year. Staff size: 51. Pays standard royalty; 10% on print.

Affiliate(s): Theodore Presser, Beekman, Oliver Ditson, John Church, Elkan-Vogel (ASCAP), Merion Music (BMI) and Mercury Music (SESAC).

How to Contact: Submit demo tape by mail. Unsolicited submissions are OK. Prefers cassette and score. SASE. Responds in 2 months.

Film & TV: Places 12 songs in film and 14 songs in TV/year.

Music: Mostly **serious concert music, sacred and secular choral** and **educational music**. Does not want popular music.

Tips: "Write honest, high quality music and send it to us, following our submission guidelines which you can receive via e-mail."

☑ ◑ **PRITCHETT PUBLICATIONS (BMI)**, P.O. Box 725, Daytona Beach FL 32114-0725. (904)252-4848. Fax: (904)252-4849. E-mail: CharlesVickers@USALink.com. Website: www.ZYWorld.com/CharlesVickers. **Contact:** Charles Vickers, vice president. Music publisher and record company (King of Kings Record Co., Pickwick/Mecca/International Records). Estab. 1975. Publishes 21 songs/year; publishes 12 new songwriters/year.

Affiliate(s): Alison Music (ASCAP), Charles H. Vickers Music Associates (BMI) and QuickSilver Encrease Records Inc.

How to Contact: *Write first and obtain permission to submit.* Prefers cassette with 6 songs and lyric or lead sheet. Does not return material.

Music: Mostly **gospel, rock-disco** and **country**.

☑ ⚑ ○ **QUARK, INC.**, P.O. Box 7320, New York NY 10150-7320. (212)741-2888. Fax: (212)807-9501. E-mail: quarkent@aol.com. **Contact:** Curtis Urbina, manager. Professional Manager: Michelle Harris (alternative/pop). Music publisher, record company (Quark Records) and record producer (Curtis Urbina). Estab. 1984. Publishes 12 songs/year; 2 new songwriters/year. Staff size: 4. Pays standard royalty.

Affiliate(s): Quarkette Music (BMI), Freedurb Music (ASCAP), Pacific Time Entertainment and Quark Records.

How to Contact: Call first and obtain permission to submit. Prefers cassette with 2 songs. SASE. Responds in 2 months.

Film & TV: Places 10 songs in film/year. Music Supervisor: Curtis Urbina (pop/dance).

Music: Mostly **pop**. Does not want anything short of a hit. Published "Which Way To Go" (single by A. Reynolds/D. Grassie/C. Grayston) from *Inverse Catch-22* (album), recorded by Cynical Blend (pop), released 2001 on Pacific Time Entertainment; and "Weight Of The World" (single by K. Katafigiotis) from *Fearless* (album), recorded by Kimon (pop), released 2001 on Quark Records.

Tips: "Write strong songs with commercial appeal. Trust your instincts."

⌨ Ⓞ RAINBOW MUSIC CORP. (ASCAP), 45 E. 66 St., New York NY 10021. (212)988-4619. **Contact:** Fred Stuart, vice president. Music publisher. Estab. 1990. Publishes 25 songs/year. Staff size: 2. Pays standard royalty.

Affiliate(s): Tri-Circle (ASCAP).

How to Contact: *Only accepts material referred by a reputable industry source.* Prefers cassette with 2 songs and lyric sheet. SASE. Responds in 1 week.

Film & TV: Published "Break It To Me Gently" (by Diane Lampert/Joe Seneca), recorded by Brenda Lee in *Trees Lounge*; and "Nothin' Shakin' (But Leaves on the Tree)" (by Diane Lampert/Eddie Fontaine), recorded by The Beatles in *Beatles TV Special*.

Music: Mostly **pop**, **R&B** and **country**; also **jazz**.

⌨ Ⓞ REN ZONE MUSIC (ASCAP), P.O. Box 3153, Huntington Beach CA 92605. (714)846-4470. Fax: (714)846-2816. E-mail: renzone@socal.rr.com. Website: www.renzonemusic.com. **Contact:** Keith Wolzinger, president. Music publisher. Estab. 1998. Publishes 14 songs/year; publishes 2 new songwriters/year. Staff size: 2. Pays standard royalty.

• This company won a Parents Choice 1998 Silver Honor Shield.

How to Contact: *Does not accept unsolicited submissions.*

Music: Mostly **children's**. Does not want rap or punk. Published "Walk Like the Animals" (single by Dayle Lusk) from *Tumble 'n' Tunes* (album), recorded by Dayle Lusk/Danielle Ganya (children's); "Surf Town" (single by Dayle Lusk) from *City Song at Huntington Beach* (album), recorded by Lisa Worshaw (pop); and "Snowboardin' (single by Stephanie Donatoni) from *Sea Cliff Tunes*, recorded by Lisa Worshaw (children's), all released 2000 on Ren Zone.

Tips: "Submit well-written lyrics that convey important concepts to kids on good quality demos with easy to understand vocals."

🌐 ✓ Ⓞ R.J. MUSIC, 'The Return', 10A Margaret Rd., Barnet, Herts. EN4 9NP United Kingdom. Phone: (020)440-9788. **Contact:** Roger James and Susana Boyle, managing directors. Music publisher and management firm (Roger James Management). PRS. Pays negotiable royalty (up to 50%).

How to Contact: Submit demo tape by mail. Unsolicited submissions are OK. Prefers cassette with 1 song and lyric or lead sheet. "Will return cassettes, but only with correct *full* postage!"

Music: Mostly **MOR**, **blues**, **country** and **rock**; also **chart material**. Does not want disco or rap.

Ⓞ ROCK N METAL MUSIC PUBLISHING CO., P.O. Box 325, Fort Dodge IA 50501-0325. **Contact:** James E. Hartsell Jr., owner. Music publisher. Estab. 1996. Publishes 1-4 songs/year. Pays standard royalty.

How to Contact: *Write first and obtain permission to submit a demo.* Prefers cassette and bio with 3 songs and lead sheet. SASE. Responds in 3 weeks.

Music: Heavy metal, **hard rock** and **hard alternative** only.

Tips: "We are looking for new and established songwriters and artists. We will help musicians who need to collaborate with a lyricist. Please follow the guidelines and be patient. Remember the louder, the faster, the better."

✓ Ⓞ ROCKER MUSIC/HAPPY MAN MUSIC (BMI, ASCAP), 4696 Kahlua Lane, Bonita Springs, FL 34134. (941)947-6978. E-mail: obitts@aol.com. **Contact:** Dick O'Bitts, executive pro-

ducer. Estab. 1960. Music publisher, record company (Happy Man Records, Condor Records and Air Corp Records), record producer (Rainbow Collections Ltd.) and management firm (Gemini Complex). Publishes 25-30 songs/year; publishes 8-10 new songwriters/year. Staff size: 2. Pays standard royalty.
How to Contact: Submit demo tape by mail. Unsolicited submissions are OK. Prefers cassette or VHS videocassette with 4 songs and lyric or lead sheet. SASE. Do not call. Responds in 1 month.
Music: Mostly **country**, **rock**, **pop**, **gospel**, **Christian** and **off-the-wall**. Does not want hip-hop. Published *Got the T Shirt* (album), recorded by The Thorps, released 2001 on Happy Man; and *In The Distance* (album), recorded by 4 Harmonee, released 2001 on Happy Man.

N **🖉** **ROCKFORD MUSIC CO. (ASCAP, BMI)**, 150 West End Ave., Suite 6-D, New York NY 10023. (212)873-5968. **Contact:** Danny Darrow, manager. Music publisher, record company (Mighty Records), record and video tape producer (Danny Darrow). Publishes 1-3 songs/year; publishes 1-3 new songwriters/year. Staff size: 3. Pays standard royalty.
Affiliate(s): Corporate Music Publishing Company (ASCAP) and Stateside Music Company (BMI).
How to Contact: Submit demo tape by mail. Unsolicited submissions are OK. "No phone calls and do not write for permission to submit." Prefers cassette with 3 songs and lyric sheet. Does not return material. Responds in 2 weeks.
Music: Mostly **MOR** and **top 40/pop**; also **adult pop**, **country**, **adult rock**, **dance-oriented**, **easy listening**, **folk** and **jazz**. Does not want rap. Published *Falling In Love* (album by Brian Dowen); *A Part of You* (album by Brian Dowen/Randy Lakeman); and *For My Tomorrow* (album by Steven Schoenbeng/Michael Greer), all recorded by Danny Darrow on Mighty Records (easy listening).
Tips: "Listen to Top 40 and write current lyrics and music."

🌐 **✅** **◐** **R.T.L. MUSIC**, White House Farm, Shropshire TF9 4HA England. Phone: (01630)647374. Fax: (01630)647612. A&R Manager: Tanya Woof. Professional Managers: Ron Lee (rock/rock 'n roll); Katrine LeMatt (MOR/dance); Xavier Lee (heavy metal); Tanya Lee (classical/other types). Music publisher, record company (Le Matt Music) and record producer. Estab. 1971. Publishes approximately 30 songs/year. Pays standard royalty.
Affiliate(s): Lee Music (publishing), Swoop Records, Grenouille Records, Check Records, Zarg Records, Pogo Records, R.T.F.M. (all independent companies).
How to Contact: Submit demo tape or CD by mail. Unsolicited submissions are OK. Prefers CD, cassette or MDisc (also VHS 625/PAL system videocassette) with 1-3 songs and lyric and lead sheets; include still photos and bios. "Make sure name and address are on CD or cassette." SAE and IRC. Responds in 6 weeks.
Music: **All types.** Published "Time Bombs" (single by Phill Dunn), recorded by Orphan (rock), released 2000 on Pogo; *Phobias* (album), recorded by Orphan (rock), released 2000 on Pogo; and *The Best Of* (album), recorded by Emmitt Till (rock/blues), released 2000 on Swoop.

✅ **◐** **RUSTRON MUSIC PUBLISHERS (BMI)**, 1156 Park Lane, West Palm Beach FL 33417-5957. (561)686-1354. E-mail: gordon_whims@juno.com. **Contact:** any professional manager. Professional Managers: Rusty Gordon (adult contemporary, acoustic, New Age, children's, cabaret); Ron Caruso (all styles); Davilyn Whims (folk fusions, country, blues). Music publisher, record company, management firm and record producer (Rustron Music Productions). Estab. 1972. Publishes 100-150 songs/year; publishes 10-20 new songwriters/year. Staff size: 9. Pays standard royalty.
Affiliate(s): Whimsong Publishing (ASCAP).
How to Contact: Submit demo tape by mail. Unsolicited submissions are OK. Prefers cassette with 1-3 songs and typed lyric or lead sheet. "Clearly label your tape and container. Include cover letter. We don't review songs on websites." SASE required for all correspondence. Responds in 4 months.
Music: Mostly **pop** (ballads, blues, theatrical, cabaret), **progressive country** and **folk/rock**; also **R&B** and **New Age** instrumental fusions with classical, jazz or pop themes and women's music. Does not want rap, hip-hop, new wave, youth music, hard rock, heavy metal or punk. Published "Never Always" (single) from *Shades of Reason* (album), written and recorded by Jayne Margo Reby (folk/rock), released 2000 on MSB Records; "A Country Song for America" (single by Star Smiley/Delia Foley) from *Anthem in Harmony* (album), recorded by Star Smiley (country), released

2000 on Whimsong Records; and "Tropical Trouble" (single by Rusty Gordon/Linda Davis) from *Florida Fresh* (album), recorded by Song on a Whim (folk/country), released 2000 on Rustron Records.

Tips: "Accepting songwriter's CD for full product review of all songs on CD. Write strong hooks. Keep song length 3½ minutes or less. Avoid predictability—create original lyric themes. Tell a story. Compose definitive melody. Tune in to the trends and fusions indicative of commercially viable new music for the new millennium."

☑ ◻ **SABTECA MUSIC CO. (ASCAP)**, P.O. Box 10286, Oakland CA 94610. (510)465-2805. Fax: (510)832-0464. Professional Managers: Sean Herring (pop, R&B, jazz); Lois Shayne (pop, R&B, soul, country). **Contact:** Duane Herring, president. Music publisher and record company (Sabteca Record Co., Andre Romare). Estab. 1980. Publishes 8-10 songs/year; 1-2 new songwriters/year. Pays standard royalty.
Affiliate(s): Toyiabe Publishing (BMI).
How to Contact: *Write first and obtain permission to submit a tape.* Prefers cassette with 2 songs and lyric sheet. SASE. Responds in 1 month.
Music: Mostly **R&B**, **pop** and **country**. Published "On the Good Side" (single by Tom Roller), recorded by Larry Johnson (country), released 2000.
Tips: "Listen to music daily, if possible. Keep improving writing skills."

◻ **SALT WORKS MUSIC (ASCAP, BMI)**, 80 Highland Dr., Jackson OH 45640-2074. (740)286-1514 or (740)286-6561. Professional Managers: Jeff Elliott (country/gospel); Mike Morgan (country). Music publisher and record producer (Mike Morgan). Staff size: 2. Pays standard royalty.
Affiliate(s): Salt Creek Music (ASCAP) and Sojourner Music (BMI).
How to Contact: Submit demo tape by mail. Unsolicited submissions are OK. Prefers cassette or CD. SASE. Responds in 2 weeks.
Music: Mostly **country**, **gospel** and **pop**. Does not want rock, jazz or classical.

◼ ◻ **R. SAMUELS PUBLISHING**, 318 Acacia Ave., Suite A, Carlsbad CA 92008. (760)434-0815. E-mail: coral@richardsamuels.com. Website: www.coralrecords.com. President: Richard Samuels. Personal Management: Mike Davies. Music publisher, record company (Coral Records Inc. in Canada and Coral Records LLC in the US). Estab. 1993. Publishes 10-15 songs/year. Record producers available for hire.
How to Contact: Submit demo tape by mail. Unsolicited submissions are OK. Prefers CD/CDR or cassette. "Make sure to include typed lyric sheet."
Music: Mostly *pop*, *country*, *R&B* and *rock*.
Tips: "We are looking for well-crafted songs with 'single' potential."

◼ ◻ **SCI-FI MUSIC (SOCAN)**, P.O. Box 941, N.D.G., Montreal Quebec H4A 3S3 Canada. (514)487-8953. **Contact:** Gary Moffet (formerly guitarist/composer with April Wine), president. Music publisher and record producer. Estab. 1984. Publishes 10 songs/year; publishes 2 new songwriters/year. Pays standard royalty.
How to Contact: Submit demo tape by mail. Unsolicited submissions are OK. Submit cassette with 3-10 songs and lyric sheet. Does not return material.
Music: Mostly **rock** and **pop**.

☑ ◻ **TIM SCOTT MUSIC GROUP (BMI)**, P.O. Box 91079, Springfield MA 01139. Phone/fax: (509)351-4379. E-mail: simpleandsafe@aol.com. **Contact:** Timothy Scott, president. Vice President: Sylvia Edson (country, R&B). Music publisher and record company (Keeping It Simple and Safe). Estab. 1993. Publishes 20-50 songs/year. Staff size: 20. Hires staff writers. Pays standard royalty.
Affiliates: Tim Scott Music (ASCAP).
How to Contact: Submit demo tape by mail. Unsolicited submissions are OK. Prefers cassette with 3-5 songs and lyric sheet. SASE. Responds in 3 months.
Music: Mostly **R&B** and **pop**; also **country**, **rock** and **gospel**. Published "As We Touch" (single) from *Morning Star*(album), writtern and recorded by Terry Adams; "Thoughts in the Rain" (single)

from *Thoughts in the Rain* (album), written and recorded by Billy Johnson/Linda Jenkins; and "Here Comes the Pain (Again)" (single by Greg Harrison/James McDougal) from *Here I Go Again* (album), recorded by 3 Plus One, all released 2000 on Night Owl Records.

◖ **SCRUTCHINGS MUSIC (BMI)**, 429 Homestead St., Akron OH 44306. (330)773-8529. **Contact:** Walter E. L. Scrutchings, owner/president. Music publisher. Estab. 1980. Publishes 35 songs/year; publishes 10-20 new songwriters/year. Hires staff songwriters. Pays standard royalty.
How to Contact: Submit demo tape by mail. Unsolicited submissions are OK. Prefers cassette or videocassette with 2 songs, lyric and lead sheet. Does not return material. "We will return calls only if selection is to be used."
Music: Mostly **gospel**, **contemporary** and **traditional**. Published "God Can Fix It For You" (single by R. Hinton), recorded by Raymond Hinton and the Voices of Praise Ensemble; "Just Call On Jesus" (single by W. Scrutchings), recorded by Walter Scrutchings and Company; and "Follow Jesus" (single by W. Scrutchings), recorded by Akron City Family Mass Choir.
Tips: "Music must be clear and uplifting in message."

◖ **SEGAL'S PUBLICATIONS (BMI)**, P.O. Box 507, Newton MA 02159. (617)969-6196. **Contact:** Charles Segal. Music publisher and record producer (Segal's Productions). Estab. 1963. Publishes 80 songs/year; publishes 6 new songwriters/year. Pays standard royalty.
Affilate(s): Charles Segal's Publications (BMI) and Charles Segal's Music (SESAC).
How to Contact: Submit demo tape by mail. Unsolicited submissions are OK. Prefers CD or VHS videocassette with 3 songs and lyric or lead sheet. Does not return material. Responds only if interested.
Music: Mostly **rock**, **pop** and **country**; also **R&B**, **MOR** and **children's songs**. Published "A Time to Care" (by Brilliant/Segal), recorded by Rosemary Wills (MOR); "Go to Bed" (by Colleen Segal), recorded Susan Stark (MOR); and "Only In Dreams" (by Chas. Segal), recorded by Rosemary Wills (MOR), all on Spin Records.
Tips: "Besides making a good demo cassette, include a lead sheet of music—words, melody line and chords. Put your name and phone number on CD."

◖ **SELLWOOD PUBLISHING (BMI)**, 170 N. Maple, Fresno CA 93702. Phone/fax: (559)255-1717. E-mail: tracsell@aol.com. **Contact:** Stan Anderson, owner. Music publisher, record company (TRAC Record Co.) and record producer. Estab. 1972. Publishes 10 songs/year; publishes 3 new songwriters/year. Pays standard royalty.
How to Contact: Submit demo tape—unsolicited submissions are OK. Prefers cassette or VHS videocassette with 2 songs and lyric sheet. SASE. Responds in 3 weeks. "Submit professional studio demos only."
Music: Mostly **traditional country**, **southern gospel** and **country**. Does not want rock 'n' roll, rap or heavy metal. Published *Reno* (album); *Let the Music Play* (album); and *Remember the Love* (album), all written and recorded by Kevin B. Willard (country), all released 2000 on TRAC Records.
Tips: "We're looking for all styles of country, especially uptempo dance types."

☑ ◖ **SHAWNEE PRESS, INC.**, 49 Waring Dr., Delaware Water Gap PA 18327. (570)476-0550. Fax: (570)476-5247. E-mail: shawneepress@noln.com. Website: www.shawneepress.com. Editor (church music): Joseph M. Martin. Professional Managers: Greg Gilpin (educational choral); Ed Esposito (instrumental); David Angerman (handbell music, organ-sacred only); Joseph Martin (piano). **Contact:** Cherie Troester, assistant. Music publisher. Estab. 1917. Publishes 150 songs/year. Staff size: 35. Pays negotiable royalty.
Affilate(s): Glory Sound and Harold Flammer Music.

OPENNESS TO SUBMISSIONS: ◻ beginners; ◪ beginners and experienced; ◖ experienced only; ◓ no unsolicited submissions/industry referrals only.

How to Contact: Submit manuscript. Unsolicited submissions are OK. Prefers manuscript. SASE. Responds in 4 months.

Music: Mostly **church/liturgical**, **educational choral** and **instrumental**.

Tips: "Submission guidelines appear on our website."

☑ 🔳 ⊘ **SHU'BABY MONTEZ MUSIC**, P.O. Box 28816, Philadelphia PA 19151. (215)473-5527. Fax: (215)473-8895. E-mail: schubaby@aol.com. Website: www.geocities.com/SunsetStrip/Cabaret/2810. President: Leroy Schuler. Music publisher. Estab. 1986. Publishes 25 songs/year; publishes 10 new songwriters/year. Pays standard royalty.

How to Contact: *Contact first and obtain permission to submit.* Prefers cassette with 3 songs and lyric sheet. SASE. Responds in 5 weeks.

Film & TV: Places 9 songs in film/year. Music Supervisor: Paul Roberts. Recently published "Sweaty and Nakey" (single by Martin "Martygraw" Schuler), recorded by Color Blind; "Baby With Blues" and "A Chance to Love Again" (singles by Lou Leggerie), recorded by Marie Davenport.

Music: Mostly **R&B**, **dance**, **hip-hop** and **pop**. Does not want country. Published "Luv Groove" (single), recorded by Wilson Lambert (R&B); "Theme from The Groove Cousins" (single by Ralph Brown), recorded by Freestyle (R&B); and "Asphalt Jungle" (single) (pop), recorded by Lou Leggerie, all on Urban Logic Records.

Tips: "Keep the music simple, but with nice changes. Don't be afraid to use altered chords."

◑ **SILICON MUSIC PUBLISHING CO. (BMI)**, 222 Tulane St., Garland TX 75043-2239. President: Gene Summers. Vice President: Deanna L. Summers. Public Relations: Steve Summers. Music publisher and record company (Front Row Records). Estab. 1965. Publishes 10-20 songs/year; publishes 2-3 new songwriters/year. Pays standard royalty.

How to Contact: Submit demo tape by mail. Unsolicited submissions are OK. Prefers cassette with 1-2 songs. Does not return material. Responds ASAP.

Music: Mostly **rockabilly** and **'50s material**; also **old-time blues/country** and **MOR**. Published "Almost Persuaded," "Someone Somewhere," and "Who Stole The Marker," all recorded by Gene Summers on Crystal Clear Records (rockabilly). New CD to be released in 2001 with 10 newly published Silicon songs.

Tips: "We are very interested in '50s rock and rockabilly *original masters* for release through overseas affiliates. If you are the owner of any '50s masters, contact us first! We have releases in Holland, Switzerland, England, Belgium, France, Sweden, Norway and Australia. We have the market if you have the tapes! Our staff writers include James McClung, Gary Mears (original Casuals), Robert Clark, Dea Summers, Shawn Summers, Joe Hardin Brown, Bill Becker and Dan Edwards."

🔳 ⊘ **SILVER BLUE MUSIC/OCEANS BLUE MUSIC**, 3940 Laurel Canyon Blvd., Suite 441, Studio City CA 91604. (818)980-9588. E-mail: jdiamond20@aol.com. **Contact:** Joel Diamond, president. Music publisher and record producer (Joel Diamond Entertainment). Estab. 1971. Publishes 50 songs/year. Pays standard royalty.

How to Contact: Does accept unsolicited material. "No tapes returned."

Film & TV: Places 4 songs in film and 6 songs in TV/year.

Music: Mostly **pop** and **R&B**; also **rap**. Does not want country, jazz or classical. Published "After the Lovin" (by Bernstein/Adams), recorded by Engelbert Humperdinck. Other artists include David Hasselhof, Kari (Curb Records), Ike Turner, Andrew Dice Clay and Gloria Gaynor.

⊘ **SILVER THUNDER MUSIC GROUP**, P.O. Box 41335, Nashville TN 37204. (615)391-5035. **Contact:** Rusty Budde, president. Music publisher and record producer (Rusty Budde Productions). Estab. 1985. Publishes 200 songs/year. Publishes 5-10 new songwriters/year. Hires staff songwriters. Pays standard royalty.

How to Contact: *Write first and obtain permission to submit.* Prefers cassette or VHS videocassette. Does not return material.

Music: Mostly **country**, **pop** and **R&B**. Published *Rock N Cowboys* (album), written and recorded by Jeff Samules on STR Records; *This Ain't the Real Thing* (album by Rusty Budde), recorded by Les Taylor on CBS Records; and "Feel Again" (single by Rusty Budde/Shara Johnson), recorded by Shara Johnson on Warner Bros. Records.

Tips: "Send clear, clean recording on cassette with lyric sheets."

[N] [symbol] SIMPLY GRAND MUSIC, INC. (ASCAP, BMI), P.O. Box 41981, Memphis TN 38174-1981. (901)763-4787. Fax: (901)763-4883. E-mail: wahani@aol.com. President: Linda Lucchesi. Music publisher. Estab. 1965. Pays standard royalty.
Affiliate(s): Memphis Town Music, Inc. (ASCAP) and Beckie Publishing Co. (BMI).
How to Contact: Submit demo tape by mail. Unsolicited submissions are OK. Prefers cassette with 1-3 songs and lyric sheet. SASE. Responds in 1 month. "Please do not send demos by certified or registered mail. Include enough postage for return of materials."
Music: Mostly **pop**, **soul**, **country**, **soft rock**, **children's songs**, **jazz** and **R&B**.

[symbol] [symbol] SINUS MUSIK PRODUKTION, ULLI WEIGEL, Geitnerweg 30a, D-12209, Berlin Germany. +49-30-7159050. Fax: +49-30-71590522. E-mail: ulli.weigel@t-online.de. Website: www.sinusmusik.de. **Contact:** Ulli Weigel, owner. Music publisher, record producer and producer of radio advertising spots. Member: GEMA, GVL. Estab. 1976. Publishes 20 songs/year; publishes 6 new songwriters/year. Staff size: 3. Pays standard royalty.
Affiliate(s): Sinus Musikverlag H.U. Weigel GmbH.
How to Contact: Submit demo tape by mail. Unsolicited submissions are OK. Prefers cassette or CD-R with up to 10 songs and lyric sheets. SASE. Responds in 2 months.
Music: Mostly **rock**, **pop** and **New Age**; also **background music for movies/advertising**. Does not want hip-hop or techno. Published "Simple Story" (single), recorded by MAANAM on RCA (Polish rock); *Die Musik Maschine* (album by Klaus Lage), recorded by CWN Productions on Hansa Records (pop/German); and "Maanam" (single by Jakowskyl/Jakowska), recorded by CWN Productions on RCA Records (pop/English).
Tips: "Take more time working on the melody than on the instrumentation. Since December of 1999, I am a provider of 'Music-On-Demand.' This is an online record service of the Deutsche Telekom in Germany, Austria and Switzerland. I am also looking for master-quality recordings for non-exclusive release on my label."

[symbol] [symbol] SLANTED CIRCLE MUSIC (BMI), 13413 Delaney Rd., Woodbridge VA 22193. Phone/fax: (703)670-8092. E-mail: sllavey@mailcity.com. **Contact:** Pete Lawrence, A&R dept. Music publisher and record producer. Estab. 1993. Publishes 15 songs/year; publishes 10 new songwriters/year. Pays standard royalty.
How to Contact: *Write first and obtain permission to submit.* Prefers cassette or CD-R with 2 songs and lyric sheet. "Only fully produced band demos." Does not return material. Responds in 6 weeks if interested.
Music: Mostly **go cat rockabilly**; also **Chicago blues**, **Christian pop** and **contemporary jazz**. Does not want country or bluegrass. Published *Rockin Till The Break of Dawn* (album by Kingery/LaVey), recorded by Larry LaVey on RHM (blues); and "Another Empty Table For Two" (single by LaVey/Kingery), recorded by Teri Schaeffer on Trend Records (blues).
Tips: "Have a good clear demo made and use the best tape when pitching material. A demo should sound authentic to the style the publisher wants. Research the style before sending."

[N] [symbol] [symbol] [symbol] S.M.C.L. PRODUCTIONS, INC., P.O. Box 84, Boucherville, Quebec J4B 5E6 Canada. (514)641-2266. **Contact:** Christian Lefort, president. Music publisher and record company. SOCAN. Estab. 1968. Publishes 25 songs/year. Pays standard royalty.
Affiliate(s): A.Q.E.M. Ltee, Bag Enrg., C.F. Music, Big Bazaar Music, Sunrise Music, Stage One Music, L.M.S. Ltee, ITT Music, Machine Music, Dynamite Music, Danava Music, Coincidence Music, Music and Music, Cinemusic Inc., Cinafilm, Editions La Fete Inc., Groupe Concept Musique, Editions Dorimen, C.C.H. Music (PRO/SDE) and Lavagot Music.
How to Contact: *Write first and obtain permission to submit.* Prefers cassette with 4-12 songs and lead sheet. SAE and IRC. Responds in 3 months.
Film & TV: Places songs in film and TV. Recently published songs in French-Canadian TV series and films, including *Young Ivanhoe*, *Twist of Terror* and *More Tales of the City*.

Music: Mostly **dance**, **easy listening** and **MOR**; also **top 40/pop** and **TV and movie soundtracks**. Published *Always and Forever* (album by Maurice Jarre/Nathalie Carien), recorded by N. Carsen on BMG Records (ballad); *Au Noy De La Passion* (album), written and recorded by Alex Stanke on Select Records.

☑ ◻ **SOUND CELLAR MUSIC**, 703 N. Brinton Ave., Dixon IL 61021. (815)288-2900. E-mail: tjoos@essexl.com. Website: www.cellarrecords.net. **Contact:** Todd Joos (country, pop, Christian), president. Professional Managers: James Miller (folk, adult contemporary); Mike Thompson (metal, hard rock, alternative). Music publisher, record company (Sound Cellar Records), record producer and recording studio. Estab. 1987. Publishes 15-25 songs/year. Publishes 5 or 6 new songwriters/year. Staff size: 7. Pays standard royalty.
How to Contact: Submit demo tape by mail. Unsolicited submissions are OK. Prefers cassette with 3 or 4 songs and lyric sheet. Does not return material. "We contact by phone in 3-4 weeks only if we want to work with the artist."
Music: Mostly **metal**, **country** and **rock**; also **pop** and **blues**. Published "Problem of Pain" (single by Shane Sowers) from *Before the Machine* (album), recorded by Junker Jorg (alternative metal/rock), released 2000; "Vaya Baby" (single by Joel Ramirez) from *It's About Time* (album), recorded by Joel Ramirez and the All-Stars (latin/R&B), released 2000; and "X" (single by Jon Pomplin) from *Project 814* (album), recorded by Project 814 (progressive rock), released 2001, all on Cellar Records.

☑ ◻ **SOUTHERN MOST PUBLISHING COMPANY (BMI)**, P.O. Box 1461446, Laurie MO 65038. (573)374-1111. Fax: (275)522-1533. E-mail: mashred@yahoo.com. **Contact:** Dann E. Haworth, president/owner. Music publisher and record producer (Haworth Productions). Estab. 1985. Publishes 10 songs/year; 3 new songwriters/year. Hires staff songwriters. Pays standard royalty.
Affiliate(s): Boca Chi Key Publishing (ASCAP).
How to Contact: Submit demo tape by mail. Unsolicited submissions are OK. Prefers cassette with 3 songs and lyric sheet. SASE. Responds in 2 weeks.
Music: Mostly **rock**, **R&B** and **country**; also **gospel** and **New Age**.
Tips: "Keep it simple and from the heart."

◪ **SPRADLIN/GLEICH PUBLISHING (BMI)**, 4234 N. 45th St., Phoenix AZ 85018-4307. **Contact:** Lee Gleich (rock, pop, movie, country); Paul Spradlin (country), managers. Music publisher. Estab. 1988. Publishes 4-10 songs/year; 2-4 new songwriters. Staff size: 2. Pays standard royalty.
Affiliate(s): Paul Lee Publishing (ASCAP).
How to Contact: *Write first and obtain permission to submit.* Prefers cassette with 3 songs and lyric or lead sheet. "It must be very good material, as I only have time for promoting songwriters who really care." SASE. Responds in 6 weeks.
Music: Mostly **country** geared to the US and European country markets; also **pop**, **rock** and **movie**. Published "Going Slow" (single by Paul Spradlin) from *Goosecreek* (album), recorded by Goosecreek Symphony, released 2000 on Capital; and "Blue Ain't As Blue" and "Frosty Morning" (singles by Kurt McFarland) from *Big Sky* (album), recorded by Kurt McFarland, released 2000 on Big Sky Records.
Tips: "I need radio type songs. Please send me only your best. I have pitches to major stars but need great songs. I cannot train writers!"

🄽 ◪ **STARBOUND PUBLISHING CO. (BMI)**, Dept. SM, 207 Winding Rd., Friendswood TX 77546. Phone/fax: (281)482-2346. E-mail: bh207@msn.com. **Contact:** Buz Hart, president. Music

---

THE OPENNESS TO SUBMISSIONS INDEX at the back of this book lists all companies in this section by how open they are to submissions.

publisher, record company (Juke Box Records, Quasar Records and Eden Records) and record producer (Lonnie Wright and Buz Hart). Estab. 1970. Publishes 35-100 songs/year; publishes 5-10 new songwriters/year. Pays standard royalty.

How to Contact: *Write or call first and obtain permission to submit.* Prefers cassette with 3 songs and lyric sheet. SASE. Responds in 2 months.

Music: Mostly **country, R&B** and **gospel**. Does not want rap. Published "If I Had Another Heart" (single by Larry Wheeler/Buz Hart) from *Day One* (album), recorded by Waylon Adams (country), released 1999 on Jukebox Records; "My Biggest Thrill" and "Old Fashioned Girl" (singles by Phil Hamm/Buz Hart) from *This and That* (album), recorded by Raiders of the Lost Heart (country), released 2000 on MP3.com.

☑ ◎ **STELLAR MUSIC INDUSTRIES (ASCAP, BMI)**, P.O. Box 54700, Atlanta GA 30308-0700. (770)454-1011. Fax: (770)454-8088. E-mail: goldwaxrec@aol.com. Website: www.goldwax.com. President: E.W. Clark. Vice President: Elliot Clark. Music publisher and record company (Goldwax Record Corporation). Estab. 1963. Staff size: 4. Publishes 100 songs/year; publishes 60 new songwriters/year. Hires staff songwriters. Pays standard royalty.

Affiliate(s): Rodanca Music (ASCAP), Bianca Music (BMI) and Urban Assault Records.

How to Contact: Write or call first and obtain permission to submit a demo. Prefers cassette, CD/CDR, DAT or videocassette with 4 songs and lyric sheet. SASE. Responds in 6 weeks.

Music: Mostly **R&B/hip hop, pop/rock** and **jazz**; also **blues, contemporary country** and **contemporary gospel**. Published "Rude" (by A. Clark), recorded by 3-4-U, released 2000 on Urban Assault Records; *Long Journey* (by G. Harris), released 2000 on Gold Wax Records; and *We're Rollin* (by J.&C. Harris), released 1999 on Rap/N/Wax Records.

◎ **JEB STUART MUSIC CO. (BMI)**, P.O. Box 6032, Station B, Miami FL 33101-6032. (305)547-1424. **Contact:** Jeb Stuart, president. Music publisher, record producer (Esquire International) and management firm. Estab. 1975. Publishes 4-6 songs/year. Pays standard royalty.

How to Contact: Submit demo tape by mail. Unsolicited submissions are OK. Prefers cassette or CD with 2-4 songs and lead sheet. SASE. Responds in 1 month.

Music: Mostly **gospel, jazz/rock, pop, R&B** and **rap**; also **blues, church/religious, country, disco** and **soul**. Published "Love in the Rough," "Guns, Guns (No More Guns)" and "Come On Cafidia" (singles), all written and recorded by Jeb Stuart on Esquire Int'l Records.

⊕ ▣ ○ **SUCCES**, Pijnderslaan 84, 9200 Dendermonde Belgium. (052)21 89 87. Fax: (052)21 89 87. **Contact:** Deschuyteneer Hendrik, director. Music publisher, record company and record producer. Estab. 1978. Publishes 400 songs/year. Hires staff songwriters. Staff size: 4. Pays standard royalty.

How to Contact: Submit demo tape by mail. Unsolicited submissions are OK. Prefers cassette or VHS videocassette with 3 songs. SAE and IRC. Responds in 2 months.

Film & TV: Places songs in TV. Recently released "Werkloos" (by Deschuyteneer), recorded by Jacques Vermeire in *Jacques Vermeire Show*.

Music: Mostly **pop, dance** and **variety**; also **instrumental** and **rock**. Published "Bobbejaan" (single by Henry Spider), recorded by Guy Dumon (country), released 2000 on Scorpion; "Rock and Roll is OK" (single by Ricky Mondes), recorded by Rudy Silvester, released 2000 on Scorpion; and "Palmyre" (single), written and recorded by Henry Spider (pop), released 2000 on Privat.

◐ **SUN STAR SONGS**, P.O. Box 1387, Pigeon Forge TN 37868. (865)428-4121. Fax: (865)908-4121. E-mail: sunstarsng@aol.com. **Contact:** Tony Glenn Rast, president. Music publisher. Estab. 1965. Pays standard royalty.

How to Contact: Submit demo tape by mail. Unsolicited submissions are OK. Prefers cassette with 3 songs and lyric sheets. SASE. Responds in 3 weeks.

Music: Mostly **country, Christian country-gospel** and **bluegrass**; also **comedy**. Published "Tonight Is Mine" (single by Stampley/Shirley/Alderman), from *Rockin' Country Party* (album), recorded by Confederate Railroad (country), released 2000 on Atlantic.

Tips: "Submit quality demos. Also interested in good lyrics for co-writing."

✔ ◙ **SUNSONGS MUSIC (BMI)/DARK SUN MUSIC (SESAC)**, 52 N. Evarts Ave., Elmsford NY 10523. (914)592-2563. Fax: (914)592-6905. E-mail: mberman438@aol.com. **Contact:** Michael Berman (pop, country, rock); John Henderson (R&B, hip-hop), professional managers. Music publisher, record producer and talent agency (Hollywood East Entertainment). Estab. 1981. Publishes 20 songs/year; publishes 10 new songwriters/year. Staff size: 6. Pays standard royalty; co-publishing deals available for established writers.
How to Contact: Submit demo tape by mail. Unsolicited submissions are OK. Prefers CD, cassette with 3-4 songs and lyric sheet. SASE. Responds in 1 month.
Music: Mostly **dance-oriented, techno-pop** and **R&B**; also **rock (all styles)** and **top 40/pop**. Does not want hard core rap or heavy metal. Published "What Kind of Man" (single by Kevin Ceballo/John Henderson/Jeff Germain) and "Quiero Bailar" (single by Kevin Ceballo/John Henderson/William Duval), both from *Mi Primer Amor* (album), recorded by Kevin Ceballo (latin), released 2000 on RMM Records; and "Love Overload" (single by John Henderson/Amad Henderson/J. Riccifelli) from *G.T. & the Big Arrival* (album), recorded by The Joneses (R&B), released 2000 on J. President Records/Japan.
Tips: "Submit material with strong hook and know the market being targeted by your song."

◙ **T.C. PRODUCTIONS/ETUDE PUBLISHING CO. (BMI)**, 121 Meadowbrook Dr., Somerville NJ 08876. (908)359-5110. Fax: (908)359-1962. E-mail: tcproductions@ren.com. Website: www.vmgmusic.com. President: Tony Camillo. Professional Manager (R&B): Jacqui Collins. Professional Manager (dance): Gene Serina. Music publisher and record producer. Estab. 1992. Publishes 25-50 songs/year; publishes 3-6 new songwriters/year. Pays negotiable royalty.
Affiliate(s): We Iz It Music Publishing (ASCAP) and Etude/Barcam (BMI).
How to Contact: Write or call first and obtain permission to submit a demo. Prefers cassette with 3-4 songs and lyric sheet. SASE. Responds in 1 month.
Music: Mostly **R&B** and **dance**; also **country** and **outstanding pop ballads**. Published "One of a Kind" (single by Sandy Farina/Lisa Ratner), recorded by Vanessa Williams; "Waiting for Last Goodbye" and "I Feel a Song" (singles by Tony Camillo/Mary Sawyer), recorded by Gladys Knight, all on P.A.R. Records (R&B).

▣ ◯ **DALE TEDESCO MUSIC CO. (BMI)**, 16020 Lahey St., Granada Hills CA 91344. (818)360-7329. Fax: (818)832-4292. **Contact:** Dale T. Tedesco, president. General Manager: Betty Lou Tedesco. Music publisher. Estab. 1981. Publishes 20-40 songs/year; publishes 20-30 new songwriters/year. Staff size: 2-3. Pays standard royalty.
Affiliate(s): Tedesco Tunes (ASCAP).
How to Contact: Submit demo tape by mail. Unsolicited submissions are OK. Prefers cassette or CD with 1 song and lyric sheet. SASE or postcard for critique. "Dale Tedesco Music hand-critiques all material submitted. Only reviews 1 song. Free evaluation." SASE. Responds in 1 month.
Film & TV: Places 15 songs in film and 8 songs in TV/year. Published "Trouble on Your Mind," "Redneck Man" and "Logger Time," all written and recorded by Doug Ellis in *Sunset Beach*.
Music: Mostly **pop, R&B** and **A/C**; also **dance-oriented, instrumentals** (for TV and film), **jazz, MOR, rock, soul** and **ethnic instrumentals**. Does not want rap. Published *One Child* (album by David Brisbin), recorded by Ernestine Anderson on Quest Records (jazz).

▨ ▧ ◯ **THIRD WAVE PRODUCTIONS LIMITED**, P.O. Box 563, Gander, Newfoundland A1V 2E1 Canada. (709)256-8009. Fax: (709)256-7411. Website: www.buddywashisname.com. **Contact:** Arch. Bonnell, president. Music publisher, record company (Third Wave/Street Legal), distribution and marketing company. Estab. 1986. Publishes 20 songs/year; publishes 2 new songwriters/year.
How to Contact: Submit demo tape by mail. Unsolicited submissions are OK. Prefers cassette or DAT with lyric sheet. SASE. Responds in 2 months.
Music: Mostly **traditional Newfoundland, Celtic/Irish, folk**; also **bluegrass, country** and **pop/rock**. Published *Salt Beef Junkie* and *He's a Part of Me* (albums by Buddy Wosisname), recorded by The Other Fellers (traditional); and *Nobody Never Told Me* (album), written and recorded by The Psychobilly Cadillacs (country), all on Third Wave Productions.

◘ **TIKI ENTERPRISES, INC. (ASCAP, BMI)**, 195 S. 26th St., San Jose CA 95116. (408)286-9840. Fax: (408)286-9845. **Contact:** Gradie O'Neal, president. Professional Manager: Jeannine O'Neil. Music publisher, record company (Rowena Records) and record producer (Jeannine O'Neal and Gradie O'Neal). Estab. 1967. Publishes 40 songs/year; publishes 12 new songwriters/year. Staff size: 3. Pays standard royalty.
Affiliate(s): Tooter Scooter Music (BMI), Janell Music (BMI) and O'Neal & Friend (ASCAP).
How to Contact: Submit demo tape by mail. Unsolicited submissions are OK. Prefers cassette with 3 songs and lyric or lead sheets. SASE. Responds in 2 weeks.
Music: Mostly **country**, **Mexican**, **rock/pop gospel**, **R&B** and **New Age**. Does not want atonal music. Published *Blessed—Instrumental Worship Hymns* (album), written and recorded by Jeannine O'Neal; and *Come Play With Me* (album), written and recorded by Amanda Shelby.
Tips: "Keep writing and sending songs in. Never give up—the next hit may be just around the bend."

▨ ◘ **TOWER MUSIC GROUP** 50 Music Square W., Suite 201, Nashville TN 37203. (615)320-7003. Fax: (615)320-7006. E-mail: castlerecord@earthlink.net. Website: www.castlerecords.com. **Contact:** Dave Sullivan, A&R director. Professional Managers: Ed Russell; Eddie Bishop. Music publisher, record company (Castle Records) and record producer. Estab. 1969. Publishes 50 songs/year; publishes 10 new songwriters/year. Staff size: 15. Pays standard royalty.
Affiliate(s): Cat's Alley Music (ASCAP) and Alley Roads Music (BMI).
How to Contact: *Call first and obtain permission to submit or to arrange personal interview.* Prefers cassette with 3 songs and lyric sheet. Does not return material. "You may follow up via e-mail." Responds in 3 months only if interested.
Film & TV: Places 2 songs in film and 26 songs in TV/year. Published "Run Little Girl" (by J.R. Jones/Eddie Ray), recorded by J.R. Jones in *Roadside Prey.*
Music: Mostly **country** and **R&B**; also **blues**, **pop** and **gospel**. Does not want rap. Published "If You Broke My Heart" (single by Condrone) from *If You Broke My Heart* (album), recorded by Kimberly Simon (country); "I Wonder Who's Holding My Angel Tonight" (single) from *Up Above* (album), written and recorded by Carl Butler (country); and "Psychedelic Fantasy" (single by Paul Sullivan/Priege) from *The Hip Hoods* (album), recorded by The Hip Hoods (power/metal/y2k), all released 2001 on Castle Records.
Tips: "Please contact us via e-mail with any other demo submissions questions."

▨ ▦ ▨ ◘ **TRANSAMERIKA MUSIKVERLAG KG**, Wilhelmstrasse 10, 23611 Bad Schwartau, Germany. Phone: 0049-451-21530. E-mail: transamerika@online.de. Website: www.TRANSAM ERIKA.de. General Manager: Pia Kaminsky. **Hamburg**: Isestrasse 77, 20149 Hamburg, Germany. Phone: 0049-40-46961527. E-mail: transamerika@t-online.de. Professional Manager: Kirsten Jung. Member: GEMA, PRS, KODA, NCB, APRA. Music publisher and administrator. Estab. 1978. Staff size: 3. Pays 50% royalty if releasing a record; 85% if only administrating.
Affiliate(s): German Fried Music, Screen Music Services Ltd. (London), Cors Ltd. (London), MCI Ltd. (London) and Leosong Music Australia Rty. Ltd. (Sydney).
How to Contact: "We accept only released materials—no demos!" Submit CD or VHS videocassette. Does not return material. Responds only if interested.
Film & TV: Places several songs in film and 2 songs in TV/year. Recently published "Nice 'N' Nasty" (single by Vincent Montana) in *La Verité si Qe Mens*; and "Wilde" (single) written and recorded by Debbie Wiseman in *Oscar Wilde.*
Music: Mostly **pop**; also **rock**, **country**, **film music** and **reggae**. Published "T'estimo (I Love you")" (single), written and recorded by José Carreras.
Tips: "We are specializing in administering (filing, registering, licensing and finding unclaimed royalties, and dealing with counter-claims) publishers worldwide."

THE FILM & TV INDEX found at the back of this book lists companies placing music in film and TV (excluding TV commercials).

⚄ ◑ **TRANSITION MUSIC CORPORATION (ASCAP, BMI, SESAC)**, 11328 Magnolia, N. Hollywood CA 91601. (818)760-1001. Fax: (818)760-7625. E-mail: onestopmus@aol.com. Director of Film and Television Music: Jennifer Brown. President: Donna Ross-Jones. Vice President: David Jones. Administration: Mike Dobson. Music publisher. Estab. 1988. Publishes 250 songs/year; publishes 20 new songwriters/year. Variable royalty based on song placement and writer.
Affiliate(s): Pushy Publishing (ASCAP), Creative Entertainment Music (BMI) and One Stop Shop Music (SESAC).
How to Contact: Address submissions to: New Submissions Dept. Submit demo tape by mail. Unsolicited submissions are OK. Prefers cassette, DAT or CD with 3 songs. SASE. Responds in 3 weeks.
Film & TV: "TMC provides music for film, TV and commercials."
Music: All styles.
Tips: "Supply master quality material with great songs."

✅ ◯ **ULTIMATE PEAK MUSIC (BMI)**, P.O. Box 707, Nashville TN 37076. E-mail: greenzebra @home.com. Website: http://members.home.net/greenzebra/. **Contact:** Danny Crader, creative manager. Music publisher. Estab. 1992. Publishes 35 songs/year; publishes 4 new songwriters/year. Hires staff writers. Staff size: 4. Pays standard royalty.
How to Contact: Submit demo tape by mail. Unsolicited submissions are OK. Prefers cassette with 1-6 songs and lyric sheet. SASE. Responds in 6 weeks.
Music: Mostly **country** and **MTV pop/rock**. Published "Tell" (single by Anderson Page/Stephany Delray) from *Eleven-Eleven* (album), recorded by Eleven-Eleven (rock/alternative), released 2000 on Green Zebra; and "Blue Paper, Blue Ink" (single by Frankie Moreno/Billy Herzig/Stephany Delray), recorded by Frankie Moreno (retro R&B/rock), released 2001 on Primo.
Tips: "Listen to the radio and compare your songs to the hits—not for recording quality, but for substance and content and structure—and be objective and realistic and honest with yourself."

◑ **VAAM MUSIC GROUP (BMI)**, P.O. Box 29550, Hollywood CA 90029-0550. Phone/fax: (323)664-7765. E-mail: pmarti3636@aol.com. **Contact:** Pete Martin, president. Music publisher and record producer (Pete Martin/Vaam Productions). Estab. 1967. Publishes 9-24 new songs/year. Pays standard royalty.
Affiliate(s): Pete Martin Music (ASCAP).
How to Contact: Prefers cassette with 2 songs and lyric sheet. SASE. Responds in 1 month. "Small packages only."
Music: Mostly **top 40/pop**, **country** and **R&B**. "Submitted material must have potential of reaching top 5 on charts."
Tips: "Study the top 10 charts in the style you write. Stay current and up-to-date with today's market."

✅ ◑ **VALET PUBLISHING CO. (BMI)**, 2442 N.W. Market St., Suite 273, Seattle WA 98107. (253)396-1055. Fax: (256)396-1029. **Contact:** Buck Ormsby, publishing director. Music publisher, record producer (John "Buck" Ormsby) and record company (Etiquette/Suspicious Records). Estab. 1961. Publishes 5-10 songs/year. Pays standard royalty.
How to Contact: Call first and obtain permission to submit a demo tape. Prefers cassette with 3-4 songs and lyric sheets. Does not return material. Responds only if interested.
Music: Mostly **R&B**, **rock** and **pop**; also **dance**.
Tips: "Production of tape must be top quality and lyric sheets professional."

⟦N⟧ ◑ **VOKES MUSIC PUBLISHING (BMI)**, Box 12, New Kensington PA 15068-0012. (724)335-2775. President: Howard Vokes. Music publisher, record company, booking agency and promotion company.
How to Contact: Submit cassette with 3 songs and lyric or lead sheet. SASE. Responds in 1 week.
Music: Mostly **traditional country/bluegrass** and **gospel**. Published "A Million Tears" (single by Duke & Null), recorded by Johnny Eagle Feather on Vokes Records; "I Won't Be Your Honky Tonk Queen" (single by Vokes/Wallace), recorded by Bunnie Mills on Pot-Of-Gold Records; and "Break The News" (single by Vokes/Webb), recorded by Bill Beere on Oakhill Records.

Tips: "We're always looking for country songs that tell a story, and only interested in hard-traditional-bluegrass, country and country gospel songs. Please no 'copy-cat songwriters.' "

🎵 📷 ⊘ WARNER/CHAPPELL MUSIC CANADA LTD. (SOCAN), 40 Sheppard Ave. W. #800, Toronto, Ontario M2N 6K9 Canada. (416)227-0566, ext. 216. Fax: (416)227-0573. E-mail: john_robertson@warnerchappell.com. Website: www.warnerchappell.com. **Contact:** Anne-Marie Smith, creative manager. General Manager: Pat Campbell. Copyright Manager: Linda Worden. Film/TV Manager: Andrew Meck. Music publisher.
How to Contact: *Call first and obtain permission to submit a demo.* Prefers cassette with 3 songs with bio and lyric sheet. SAE and IRC. Responds in 2 months.
Music: All genres with music and lyrics completed. Published "Arriba" (single), written and recorded by Joee (pop), released 1999 on UMG; *Heaven Coming Down* (album), written and recorded by Tea Party (rock); and "Rallyin' " (single), written and recorded by Jully Black (R&B), both released 1999 on EMI.
Tips: "We are looking for hard-working people with honesty and professionalism."

⊘ WEAVER OF WORDS MUSIC (BMI), P.O. Box 803, Tazewell VA 24651. (540)988-6267. **Contact:** H.R. Cook, president. Music publisher and record company (Fireball Records). Estab. 1978. Publishes 12 songs/year. Pays standard royalty.
Affiliate(s): Weaver of Melodies Music (ASCAP).
How to Contact: Submit demo tape by mail. Unsolicited submissions are OK. Prefers cassette with 3 songs and lyric or lead sheets. SASE. Responds in 3 weeks.
Music: Mostly **country**. Published "Winds of Change" (single), written and recorded by Cecil Surrett; "Texas Saturday Night" and "Old Flame Burning" (singles), written and recorded by H.R. Cook, all on Fireball Records (country).

◖ WEMAR MUSIC CORP. (BMI), 836 N. La Cienega Blvd., #276, W. Hollywood CA 90069. Phone/fax: (323)692-1037. **Contact:** Stuart Wiener, president. Music publisher. Estab. 1940. Publishes 30 songs/year; publishes 30 new songwriters/year. Pays standard royalty.
Affiliate(s): Grand Music Corp. (ASCAP).
How to Contact: Submit demo tape by mail. Unsolicited submissions are OK. "No phone calls." SASE. Responds in 2 months.
Music: Mostly **pop**, **country**, **R&B** and **dance**. Published "Pearl" and "Heavy Hitter" (singles), written and recorded by Geri Verdi on Mills Records (blues); and "Meat Street" (single), written and recorded by Neal Fox on Gravity Records (Broadway Show).

🌐 ◖ BERTHOLD WENGERT (MUSIKVERLAG), Waldstrasse 27, D-76327, Pfinztal-Sollingen, Germany. **Contact:** Berthold Wengert. Music publisher. Pays standard GEMA royalty.
How to Contact: Prefers cassette and complete score for piano. SAE and IRC. Responds in 1 month. "No cassette returns!"
Music: Mostly **light music** and **pop**.

✅ 📷 ⊘ WESTWOOD MUSIC GROUP (ASCAP, BMI), 1031 Amboy Ave., Suite 202, Edison NJ 08837. (732)225-8600. Fax: (732)225-8644. E-mail: music@westwoodmusicgroup.com. Website: www.westwoodmusicgroup.com. President: Victor Kaply. Vice President/Creative Services: Steve Willoughby. **Film & TV Dept.:** 521 Fifth Ave., Suite 1700, New York NY 10175. (212)619-3500. Fax: (212)619-3588. E-mail: filmmusic@westwoodmusicgroup.com. **Contact:** Steve Willoughby, director of film/TV music. Music publisher. Publishes 30 songs/year; publishes 2 new songwriters/year. Staff size: 4. Pays standard royalty.
How to Contact: *Write first and obtain permission to submit.* Prefers CD with 3 songs and lyric sheet. SASE. Responds in 6 weeks.
Music: Mostly **rock**; also **pop**. Published "Burlesque" (single) from *Anywhere USA* (album), written and recorded by Skip Denenberg (pop/country), released 2000 on Westwood; "Sometimes Lover" (single by Steve Kaminski/Dan Amabile) from *Westwood Presents Original Music for Film/TV* (al-

bum), recorded by Renee Grace and Dan Amabile (pop), released 2000 on Westwood; and "Best From This Man" (single by Simmons) from *Best From This Man* (album), recorded by Chaz Wesley (R&B/soul), released 2000 on Sweet Tone.

Tips: Submit a "neat promotional package with bio and lyrics."

[N] ☐ WHITE CAT MUSIC, P.O. Box 19720, Fountain Hills AZ 85269. (480)951-3115. Fax: (480)951-3074. Professional Manager: Frank Fara. Producer: Patty Parker. Music publisher, record company and record producer. Member CMA, CCMA, BCCMA and BBB. Estab. 1978. Publishes 20 songs/year; publishes 10 new songwriters/year. Staff size: 2. "50% of our published songs are from non-charted and developing writers." Pays standard royalty.

Affiliate(s): Rocky Bell Music (BMI), How The West Was Sung Music (BMI) and Crystal Canyon Music (ASCAP).

• Fara and Parker are authors of the book *How to Open Doors in the Music Industry—the Independent Way.*

How to Contact: Submit demo tape by mail. Unsolicited submissions are OK. Prefers cassettes with 2-4 songs and include lyric sheet. SASE. Responds in 2 weeks.

Music: All styles of **country**—traditional to crossover. Published "Stop, Look and Listen" (single by Roy Ownbey), recorded by Valerie Joy (country); "Ain't No One In Love With Me" (single by Michael Ray/Rand Rich), recorded by Howdy (country rock); and "If You Say It With A Country Song" (single by David Scott), recorded by Gary Mahnken (country traditional), all released 2000 on Comstock Records.

Tips: "Have an out front vocal presentation so lyric can be heard. Go easy on long instrumental intros and breaks which distract. Send only two to four songs—medium to up tempo are always in demand. This helps stack the odds in your favor for getting heard."

☑ WHITING MUSIC (ASCAP, BMI), P.O. Box 110002, Nashville TN 37211. (615)331-8945. Fax: (615)315-9391. E-mail: musicnash@aol.com. Website: www.whitingmusic.com. Publisher: James Whiting. **Contact:** Lisa Dey, professional manager. Music publisher and record producer (Jamey Whiting). Estab. 1982. Publishes 12 songs/year; publishes 4 new songwriters/year. Staff size: 2. Hires staff songwriters. Pays standard royalty.

Affiliate(s): James Whiting Music (ASCAP) and Moody Judy Music (BMI).

How to Contact: Submit demo tape by mail. Unsolicited submissions are OK. Prefers cassette or CD with 3 songs, lyric sheet and cover letter. SASE. Responds in 3 weeks.

Music: Mostly **country**, **pop** and **rock**; also **blues**, **jazz** and **reggae**. Published "Long Haul" (single), written and recorded by Marcus Vickers (country) on Viking; *Guilty* (album by B. Loomis/P. Loomis), recorded by B. Loomis (country); and *Hear Me Now (For All the Things Never Said)* (album by J. Fischer/J. Whiting), recorded by Joice Walton (blues) on Pinnacle.

Tips: "Songs should be less than 3½ minutes long, should have a clear title or hook, and should be presented with a clean vocal with simple demo."

☑ ☑ WILCOM PUBLISHING (ASCAP), Box 4456, West Hills CA 91308. (661)395-3950. Fax: (661)285-8032. E-mail: info@wilcompublishing.com. Website: www.wilcompublishing.com. **Contact:** William Clark, owner. Music publisher. Estab. 1989. Publishes 10-15 songs/year; publishes 1-2 new songwriters/year. Staff size: 2. Pays standard royalty.

How to Contact: *Write or call first and obtain permission to submit a tape.* Prefers cassette with 1-2 songs and lyric sheet. SASE. Responds in 3 weeks.

Music: Mostly **R&B**, **pop** and **rock**; also **country**. Does not want rap. Published "Girl Can't Help It" (single by W. Clark/D. Walsh/P. Oland), recorded by Stage 1 on Rockit Records (top 40).

☑ ☒ ☑ WINSTON & HOFFMAN HOUSE MUSIC PUBLISHERS (ASCAP, BMI), P.O. Box 1415, Burbank CA 91507-1415. Fax: (323)462-8342. E-mail: sixties1@aol.com. **Contact:** Lynne Robin Green, president. Music publisher. Estab. 1958. Publishes 25 songs/year. Staff size: 2. Pays standard royalty.

Affiliate(s): Lansdowne Music Publishers (ASCAP), Bloor Music (BMI) and Ben Ross Music (ASCAP), "also administer 15 other firms."

How to Contact: Submit demo tape by mail. Unsolicited submissions are OK. "Do not query first. Do not call." Prefers cassette with 3 songs maximum and lyric sheet. "*Must* include SASE, or *no* reply!" Responds in 1 month.

Film & TV: Places 45 songs in film and 25 songs in TV/year. Recently published "Dooley" (by Dillard/Jayne) in *Baby Blues*; "Closer Walk With Thee" (by Craver/Henderson) in *Smiling Fish and Goat on Fire*; and "Born to Jump" (by Larry Dunn) in *Olympics 2000*.

Music: Mostly **R&B dance**, **ballads**, **hip hop**, **vocal jazz**, **alternative rock** and **R&B**; also **bluegrass**, **Spanish pop** and **pop ballads**. Published "What I Know Now" (single by Larry Dunn) from *Suspicion* (album), recorded by CoCo Montoya (blues), released 2000 on Alligator Records; "Old Home Place" (single by Dean Webb/Mitch Jayne) from *Retrograss* (album), recorded by David Grisman/John Hartford/Mike Seeger (bluegrass), released 2000 on Acousti-Disc; and "Azuca Pa Tu Amargura" (single by Albita) from *Son* (album), written and recorded by Albita (latin tropicale), released 2000 on Times Square Records.

Tips: "Be selective in what you send. Be realistic about which artist it suits! Be patient in allowing time to place songs. Be open to writing for films—be interesting lyrically and striking melodically."

N 🌐 ⊘ **WIPE OUT MUSIC LTD.**, P.O. Box 1NW, Newcastle-Upon-Tyne NE99 1NW England. Phone: (0191)2326700. Fax: (0191)2666073. E-mail: john@overground.co.uk. Managing Director (punk, indie, garage): John Esplen. Music publisher. Estab. 1995. Staff size: 3. Pays standard royalty.

How to Contact: *Contact first and obtain permission to submit. No unsolicited submissions accepted.* Prefers cassette or CD with cover letter. SAE and IRC. Responds in 1 week.

Music: Mostly **punk**, **indie** and **garage**; also **lo-fi**, **power pop** and **instrumentals**. Does not want anything mainstream.

Tips: "As we are connected to a radio/TV plugging company, artists must have some potential in those areas."

○ WORLD FAMOUS MUSIC CO. (ASCAP), 1364 Sherwood Rd., Highland Park IL 60035. (847)831-3123. E-mail: getchip@interacess.com. **Contact:** Chip Altholz, president. Music publisher and record producer. Estab. 1986. Publishes 25 songs/year; 3-4 new songwriters/year. Pays standard royalty.

How to Contact: Submit demo tape by mail. Unsolicited submissions are OK. Prefers cassette with 3 songs and lyric sheet. SASE. Responds in 1 month.

Music: Mostly **pop**, **R&B** and **rock**. Published "Harmony" (single by Altholz/Faldner), recorded by Barry Faldner on Amertel Records (ballad); and "Running" and "Serious" (singles), both written and recorded by Nick Bak on Pink Street Records.

Tips: "Have a great melody, a lyric that is visual and tells a story and a commercial arrangement."

N ○ YORGO MUSIC (BMI), 615 Valley Rd., Upper Montclair NJ 07043. (973)746-2359. President: George Louvis. Affiliated with Warner/Chappell Music Publishing. Music publisher. Estab. 1987. Publishes 5-10 songs/year; publishes 3-5 new songwriters/year. Pays standard royalty.

How to Contact: Submit demo tape by mail. Unsolicited submissions are OK. Prefers cassette with 1-3 songs and lyric or lead sheets. "Specify if you are a writer/artist or just a writer." Does not return material. Responds in 3 months.

Music: Mostly **gospel**, **contemporary Christian**, **R&B** and **pop ballads**.

✔ 🖼 ⊘ ZETTITALIA MUSIC INTERNATIONAL (ASCAP, BMI), P.O. Box 8442, Universal City CA 91618. Phone/fax: (818)506-8533. E-mail: pplzmi@aol.com. Website: www.pplzmi.com. **Contact:** Cheyenne Phoenix, A&R. Assistant, A&R: Kaitland Diamond. Music publisher. Estab. 1995. Publishes 40 songs/year; publishes 2 new songwriters/year. Staff size: 2. Hires staff songwriters. Pays standard royalty.

Affiliate(s): Zett One Songs (ASCAP) and Zett Two Music (BMI).

How to Contact: *Write to obtain permission to submit.* "Include SASE or e-mail." Prefers cassette or CD with 3 songs. SASE. Responds in 6 weeks.

Film & TV: Places 2 songs in film and 4 songs in TV/year.

Music: Mostly **pop**, **film music**, **country**, **instrumental** and **R&B**. Does not want gangster rap or heavy metal. Published *Wings of Faith* (album), written and recorded by Karen Heart (Christian), released 2000 on KGM Records.

Tips: "In art, be a good student and stay true to your instincts. In business, be thorough, realistic, flexible and straightforward. Finally, The Golden Rule rules."

✔ ◐ **ZOMBA MUSIC PUBLISHING (ASCAP, BMI)**, 137-139 W. 25th St., New York NY 10001. (212)727-0016. Fax: (212)242-7462. West Hollywood office: 9000 Sunset Blvd., Suite 300, West Hollywood CA 90069. (310)247-8300. Fax: (310)247-8366. **Contact:** Neil Portnow or Andrea Torchia. Music publisher. Publishes 5,000 songs/year; publishes 25 new songwriters/year.

Affiliate(s): Zomba Enterprises, Inc. (ASCAP); Zomba Songs, Inc. (BMI).

How to Contact: *Zomba Music Publishing does not accept unsolicited material.* "Contact us through management or an attorney."

Music: Mostly **R&B**, **pop** and **rap**; also **rock** and **alternative**. Published ". . . Baby One More Time" (single by M. Martin), recorded by Britney Spears on Jive; "Home Alone" (single by R. Kelly/K. Price/K. Murray), recorded by R. Kelly featuring Keith Murray on Jive; and "Taking Everything" (single by G. Levert/D. Allamby/L. Browder/A. Roberson), recorded by Gerald Levert on EastWest.

MARKETS THAT WERE listed in the 2001 edition of *Songwriters Market* but do not appear this year are listed in the General Index with a notation explaining why they were omitted.

Additional Music Publishers

The following companies are also music publishers, but their listings are found in other sections of the book. See the General Index for page numbers, then read the listings for submission information.

"A" Major Sound Corporation
A.A.M.I. Music Group
Aberdeen Productions
ACR Productions
Afterschool Publishing Company/
    Records, Inc.
American Artists Entertainment
A.P.I. Records
Arkadia Entertainment Corp.
Atlan-Dec/Grooveline Records
Avalon Productions/Recording
    Group
Avita Records
Bagatelle Record Company
Bal Records
Belham Valley Records
Bernard Enterprises, Inc., Hal
Black Stallion Country, Inc.
Blue Gem Records
Blue Wave Productions
Blues Alley Records
Butler Music, Bill
Cambria Records & Publishing
Capital Entertainment
CBA Artists
Celt Musical Services, Jan
Chattahoochee Records
Cherry Street Records
Chucker Music Inc.
Circuit Rider Talent & Manage-
    ment Co.
Class Act Productions/Management
Coffee and Cream Productions
Collector Records
Cosmotone Records
Crawfish Productions
Criss-Cross Industries
DAP Entertainment
Dagene/Cabletown Company
Dapmor Records
De Miles, Edward
Discmedia
Eiffert, Jr., Leo J.
Ellis International Talent Agency,
    The
Emerald City Records
Enterprize Records-Tapes
Eternal Song Agency, The
Final Mix Music
Fireant
Fish of Death Records and Manage-
    ment
Front Row Records
Garrett Entertainment, Marty
GCI, Inc.
Gig Records
Golden Triangle Records
Groove Makers' Recordings

Gueststar Entertainment Agency
Gueststar Records, Inc.
Hailing Frequency Music Produc-
    tions
Happy Man Records
Hardison International Entertainment
    Corporation
Heads Up Int., Ltd.
Heart Consort Music
Heart Music, Inc.
Hi-Bias Records Inc.
Horizon Records, Inc.
Hot Wings Entertainment
Hottrax Records
J & V Management
Jag Studio, Ltd.
Jay Jay Publishing & Record Co.
Kingston Records and Talent
KMA
Knight Agency, Bob
Known Artist Productions
Kuper Personal Management
L.A. Entertainment, Inc.
L.A. Records (Michigan)
Lamar Music Marketing
Lawrence, Ltd., Ray
Lazy Bones Productions/Recordings,
    Inc.
Levy Management, Rick
Lock
Lowell Agency
Lucifer Records, Inc.
Mac-Attack Productions
Magid Productions, Lee
Magnetic Oblivion Music Co.
Magnum Music Corp. Ltd.
Magnum Music Corporation Ltd.
Major Entertainment, Inc.
Mathews, d/b/a Hit or Myth Produc-
    tions, Scott
Montgomery Management, Gary F.
Noteworthy Enterprises
NPO Records, Inc.
OCP Publications
On the Level Music!
Only New Age Music, Inc.
Orillyon Entertainment
Permanent Press Recordings/Perma-
    nent Wave
PGE Platinum Groove Entertainment
Philly Breakdown Recording Co.
Pierce, Jim
Platinum Entertainment, Inc.
Precision Management
Presence Records
RA Records
RAVE Records, Inc.
Rainbow Collection Ltd.

Rampant Records
R&D Productions
Riohcat Music
Rival Records
Robbins Entertainment LLC
Roll On Records®
Ruf Records
SAS Productions/Hit Records
    Network
Safire Records
Sahara Records and Filmworks
    Entertainment
Satellite Music
Sea Cruise Productions, Inc.
Serge Entertainment Group
Silver Thunder Music Group
Songgram Music
Sound Arts Recording Studio
Sound Management Direction
Sound Works Entertainment Produc-
    tions Inc.
Stardust
Stormin' Norman Productions
Street Records
Strugglebaby Recording Co.
Studio Seven
Sureshot Records
Surface Records
Sweet June Music
Swift River Productions
Tangent® Records
Tari, Roger Vincent
Tas Music Co./Dave Tasse Enter-
    tainment
Thump Records, Inc.
T.J. Booker Ltd.
TMC Productions
Tutta Forza Music
UAR Records
Umpire Entertainment Enterprizes
Universal Music Marketing
Van Pol Management, Hans
Wall Street Music
Warehouse Creek Recording Corp.
Warner Productions, Cheryl K.
Weisman Production Group, The
Wemus Entertainment
WIR (World International Records)
Wilder Artists' Management, Shane
Williams Management, Yvonne
World Wide Management
Worldwide Recordings Limited/
    Worldrecords.com
X.R.L. Records/Music
Young Country Records/Plain
    Country Records

Category Index

The Category Index is a good place to begin searching for a market for your songs. Below is an alphabetical list of 20 general music categories. If you write country songs and are looking for a publisher to pitch them, check the Country section in this index. There you will find a list of music publishers interested in hearing country songs. Once you locate the entries for those publishers, read the music subheading *carefully* to determine which companies are most interested in the type of country music you write. Some of the markets in this section do not appear in the Category Index because they have not indicated a specific preference. Most of these said they are interested in "all types" of music. Listings that were very specific, or whose description of the music they're interested in doesn't quite fit into these categories, also do not appear here.

Adult Contemporary (also easy listening, middle of the road, AAA, ballads, etc.)
ALLRS Music Publishing Co.
Alexis
Allegheny Music Works
American Heartstring Publishing
Antelope Publishing Inc.
Audio Images Two Thousand Music Publishing
Baitstring Music
Bal & Bal Music Publishing Co.
Barkin' Foe the Master's Bone
Barren Wood Publishing
Bay Ridge Publishing Co.
Big Fish Music Publishing Group
BME Publishing
Bradley Music, Allan
Buried Treasure Music
California Country Music
Clevère Musikverlag, R.D.
Duane Music, Inc.
Emstone, Inc. Music Publishing
Gary Music, Alan
Green One Music
Hammel Associates, Inc., R.L.
Happy Melody
Hickory Valley Music
High-Minded Moma Publishing & Productions
Hitsburgh Music Co.
Inside Records/OK Songs
Ja/Nein Musikverlag GmbH
Kansa Records Corporation
Kaupps & Robert Publishing Co.
Largo Music Publishing
Lineage Publishing Co.
Mento Music Group
Montina Music
Mymit Music Productions, Chuck
New Rap Jam Publishing, A
Omni 2000, Inc.

Otto Publishing Co.
Paden Place Music
Pegasus Music
Prescription Company
R.J. Music
Rockford Music Co.
S.M.C.L. Productions, Inc.
Segal's Publications
Silicon Music Publishing Co.
Tedesco Music Co., Dale

Alternative (also modern rock, punk, college rock, new wave, hardcore, new music, industrial, ska, indie rock, garage, etc.)
A Ta Z Music
Abalone Publishing
Alco Music
Alias John Henry Tunes
Avalon Music
Bay Ridge Publishing Co.
Blue Dog Publishing and Records
Cornelius Companies, The
East Coast Music Publishing
Faverett Group
Juke Music
Lake Transfer Productions & Music
Largo Music Publishing
Mellow House Music
Montina Music
Pas Mal Publishing Sarl
Prejippie Music Group
Prescription Company
Rock N Metal Music Publishing Co.
Winston & Hoffman House Music Publishers
Wipe Out Music Ltd.
Zomba Music Publishing

Blues
Alexis
Bagatelle Music Publishing Co.

Bal & Bal Music Publishing Co.
Bay Ridge Publishing Co.
Brian Song Music Corp.
BSW Records
Christopher Publishing, Sonny
Dave Music, Jof
Duane Music, Inc.
Earthscream Music Publishing Co.
Frozen Inca Music
Ja/Nein Musikverlag GmbH
Magic Message Music
Mighty Blue Music Machine, The
Montina Music
Moon June Music
Prescription Company
R.J. Music
Silicon Music Publishing Co.
Slanted Circle Music
Sound Cellar Music
Stellar Music Industries
Stuart Music Co., Jeb
Tower Music Group
Whiting Music

Children's
Flying Red Horse Publishing
Lyrick Studios
Mayfair Music
Omni 2000, Inc.
Piano Press
Prescription Company
Ren Zone Music
Segal's Publications
Simply Grand Music, Inc.

Classical (also opera, chamber music, serious music, choral, etc.)
Clevère Musikverlag, R.D.
Hit-Fabrik Musikverlag
Jae Music, Jana
Presser Co., Theodore

Country (also western, C&W, bluegrass, cowboy songs, western swing, honky-tonk, etc.)
Abalone Publishing
ALLRS Music Publishing Co.
Alco Music
Alexis
Alias John Henry Tunes
All Rock Music
Allegheny Music Works
AlliSongs Inc.
Americatone International
Aquarius Publishing
ARAS Music
Audio Images Two Thousand Music Publishing
Avalon Music

Bagatelle Music Publishing Co.
Baird Music Group
Baitstring Music
Bal & Bal Music Publishing Co.
Barkin' Foe the Master's Bone
Barren Wood Publishing
Bay Ridge Publishing Co.
Big Fish Music Publishing Group
Black Stallion Country Publishing
Bradley Music, Allan
Branson Country Music Publishing
Brewster Songs, Kitty
Brian Song Music Corp.
BSW Records
Buried Treasure Music
California Country Music
Cheavoria Music Co. (BMI)
Cherri/Holly Music Inc.
Christopher Publishing, Sonny
Clevère Musikverlag, R.D.
Cornelius Companies, The
Country Rainbow Music
Cupit Music
Dapmor Publishing
De Miles Music Company, The Edward
Delev Music Company
Door Knob Music Publishing
Doss Music, Buster
Dream Seekers Publishing
Duane Music, Inc.
Earitating Music Publishing
Earthscream Music Publishing Co.
East Coast Music Publishing
Emandell Tunes
Emstone, Inc. Music Publishing
Famous Music Publishing Companies
Faverett Group
Frick Enterprises, Bob Scott
Fricon Music Company
Furrow Music
G Major Music
Gary Music, Alan
Glad Music Co.
Golden Music, August
Goodland Music Group Inc., The
Green One Music
Hammel Associates, Inc., R.L.
Hickory Lane Publishing and Recording
Hickory Valley Music
High-Minded Moma Publishing & Productions
Hitsburgh Music Co.
Hitsource Publishing
Inside Records/OK Songs
Iron Skillet Music
Jae Music, Jana
Jammy Music Publishers Ltd.
Jerjoy Music
Jolson Black & White Music, Al

JPMC Music Inc.
Juke Music
Kansa Records Corporation
Kaupps & Robert Publishing Co.
Lari-Jon Publishing
Lexington Alabama Music Publishing
Lilly Music Publishing
Lindsay Publishing, Doris
Lineage Publishing Co.
Luick & Associates Music Publisher, Harold
Makers Mark Gold
Markea Music/Gina Pie Music
Marvin Publishing, John Weller
McConkey Artists Agency Music Publishing
McCoy Music, Jim
Melody Hills Ranch Publishing Co.
Mento Music Group
Mighty Blue Music Machine, The
Montina Music
Moon June Music
New Rap Jam Publishing, A
Newcreature Music
Northwest Alabama Music Publishing
Old Slowpoke Music
Omni 2000, Inc.
Ontrax Companies
Orchid Publishing
Otto Publishing Co.
Paden Place Music
Pecos Valley Music
Pegasus Music
PEN Music Group, Inc.
Portage Music
Prescription Company
Pritchett Publications
R.J. Music
Rainbow Music Corp.
Rocker Music/Happy Man Music
Rockford Music Co.
Rustron Music Publishers
Sabteca Music Co.
Salt Works Music
Samuels Publishing, R.
Scott Music Group, Tim
Segal's Publications
Sellwood Publishing
Silicon Music Publishing Co.
Silver Thunder Music Group
Simply Grand Music, Inc.
Sound Cellar Music
Southern Most Publishing Company
Spradlin/Gleich Publishing
Starbound Publishing Co.
Stellar Music Industries
Stuart Music Co., Jeb
Sun Star Songs
T.C. Productions/Etude Publishing Co.
Third Wave Productions Limited

Tiki Enterprises, Inc.
Tower Music Group
Transamerika Musikverlag KG
Ultimate Peak Music
Vaam Music Group
Valet Publishing Co.
Vokes Music Publishing
Warner/Chappell Music Canada Ltd.
Weaver of Words Music
Wemar Music Corp.
White Cat Music
Whiting Music
Wilcom Publishing
Winston & Hoffman House Music Publishers
Zettitalia Music International

Dance (also house, hi-NRG, disco, club, rave, techno, trip-hop, trance, etc.)
A Ta Z Music
Abalone Publishing
Alexis
Audio Music Publishers
Better Than Sex Music
BME Publishing
Brewster Songs, Kitty
Cherri/Holly Music Inc.
Clevère Musikverlag, R.D.
Dagene Music
De Miles Music Company, The Edward
Delev Music Company
Duane Music, Inc.
East Coast Music Publishing
Edition Rossori
Fresh Entertainment
Gary Music, Alan
Happy Melody
Inside Records/OK Songs
Lake Transfer Productions & Music
Lilly Music Publishing
Makers Mark Gold
Mighty Blue Music Machine, The
Montina Music
Omni 2000, Inc.
Prejippie Music Group
Prescription Company
Pritchett Publications
Rockford Music Co.
S.M.C.L. Productions, Inc.
Shu'Baby Montez Music
Stuart Music Co., Jeb
Succes
Sunsongs Music/Dark Son Music
T.C. Productions/Etude Publishing Co.
Tedesco Music Co., Dale
Valet Publishing Co.
Wemar Music Corp.
Winston & Hoffman House Music Publishers

Folk (also acoustic, Celtic, etc.)
Alexis
Aquarius Publishing
Bay Ridge Publishing Co.
Clevère Musikverlag, R.D.
Earitating Music Publishing
Heupferd Musikverlag GmbH
Markea Music/Gina Pie Music
Montina Music
Omni 2000, Inc.
Piano Press
Prescription Company
Rockford Music Co.
Rustron Music Publishers
Third Wave Productions Limited

Instrumental (also background music, musical scores, etc.)
Alpha Music Inc.
Aquarius Publishing
Big Fish Music Publishing Group
CTV Music
Happy Melody
Hit-Fabrik Musikverlag
Jae Music, Jana
JPMC Music Inc.
Mayfair Music
Mento Music Group
PEN Music Group, Inc.
Rustron Music Publishers
Shawnee Press, Inc.
Succes
Tedesco Music Co., Dale
Wipe Out Music Ltd.
Zettitalia Music International

Jazz (also fusion, bebop, swing, etc.)
Alexander Sr. Music
Alexis
Antelope Publishing Inc.
ARAS Music
Bal & Bal Music Publishing Co.
Barkin' Foe the Master's Bone
Bay Ridge Publishing Co.
Brewster Songs, Kitty
Heupferd Musikverlag GmbH
His Power Productions and Publishing
Hit-Fabrik Musikverlag
Jae Music, Jana
JPMC Music Inc.
McConkey Artists Agency Music Publishing
Mellow House Music
Mighty Blue Music Machine, The
Montina Music
Newcreature Music
Old Slowpoke Music
Omni 2000, Inc.
Perla Music

Prescription Company
Rainbow Music Corp.
Rockford Music Co.
Simply Grand Music, Inc.
Slanted Circle Music
Stellar Music Industries
Stuart Music Co., Jeb
Tedesco Music Co., Dale
Whiting Music
Winston & Hoffman House Music Publishers

Latin (also Spanish, salsa, Cuban, conga, Brazilian, cumbja, rancheras, Mexican, merengue, Tejano, Tex Mex, etc.)
Alexis
Amen, Inc.
Americatone International
Famous Music Publishing Companies
Golden Music, August
Inside Records/OK Songs
Tiki Enterprises, Inc.

Metal (also thrash, grindcore, heavy metal, etc.)
Bay Ridge Publishing Co.
Pas Mal Publishing Sarl
Rock N Metal Music Publishing Co.
Sound Cellar Music

New Age (also ambient)
Heupferd Musikverlag GmbH
High-Minded Moma Publishing & Productions
Rustron Music Publishers
Sinus Musik Produktion
Southern Most Publishing Company
Tiki Enterprises, Inc.

Novelty (also comedy, humor, etc.)
Allegheny Music Works
Big Fish Music Publishing Group
Doré Records
Green One Music
Lexington Alabama Music Publishing
Magic Message Music
Moon June Music
Piano Press
Sun Star Songs

Pop (also top 40, top 100, popular, chart hits, etc.)
A Ta Z Music
Abalone Publishing
Activate Entertainment LLC
ALLRS Music Publishing Co.
Alco Music
Alexis
Allegheny Music Works
AlliSongs Inc.

American Heartstring Publishing
Aquarius Publishing
Audio Music Publishers
Baitstring Music
Bal & Bal Music Publishing Co.
Barkin' Foe the Master's Bone
Bay Ridge Publishing Co.
Bernard Enterprises, Inc., Hal
Better Than Sex Music
Big Fish Music Publishing Group
Blue Dog Publishing and Records
BME Publishing
Bradley Music, Allan
Brewster Songs, Kitty
Buried Treasure Music
California Country Music
Cheavoria Music Co.
Cherri/Holly Music Inc.
Clevère Musikverlag, R.D.
Cornelius Companies, The
Dagene Music
Dapmor Publishing
De Miles Music Company, The Edward
Delev Music Company
Dream Seekers Publishing
Duane Music, Inc.
Earthscream Music Publishing Co.
East Coast Music Publishing
Edition Rossori
Emandell Tunes
Emstone, Inc. Music Publishing
Ever-Open-Eye Music
Faverett Group
Fresh Entertainment
G Major Music
Gary Music, Alan
Golden Music, August
Hammel Associates, Inc., R.L.
Happy Melody
High-Minded Moma Publishing & Productions
Hit-Fabrik Musikverlag
Hitsource Publishing
Inside Records/OK Songs
Interplanetary Music
Jammy Music Publishers Ltd.
Ja/Nein Musikverlag GmbH
Jasper Stone Music/JSM Songs
Jolson Black & White Music, Al
JPMC Music Inc.
Juke Music
Kaupps & Robert Publishing Co.
Lake Transfer Productions & Music
Lindsay Publishing, Doris
Lineage Publishing Co.
Makers Mark Gold
Manuiti L.A.
Markea Music/Gina Pie Music
Marvin Publishing, John Weller

Mellow House Music
Melody Hills Ranch Publishing Co.
Mento Music Group
Mighty Blue Music Machine, The
Montina Music
Moon June Music
Music Room Publishing Group, The
Mymit Music Productions, Chuck
New Rap Jam Publishing, A
Newcreature Music
Northwest Alabama Music Publishing
Omni 2000, Inc.
Ontrax Companies
Orchid Publishing
Pegasus Music
PEN Music Group, Inc.
Prescription Company
QUARK, Inc.
Rainbow Music Corp.
R.J. Music
Rocker Music/Happy Man Music
Rockford Music Co.
Rustron Music Publishers
S.M.C.L. Productions, Inc.
Sabteca Music Co.
Salt Works Music
Samuels Publishing, R.
Sci-Fi Music
Scott Music Group, Tim
Segal's Publications
Shu'Baby Montez Music
Silver Blue Music/Oceans Blue Music
Silver Thunder Music Group
Simply Grand Music, Inc.
Sinus Musik Produktion
Sound Cellar Music
Stellar Music Industries
Stuart Music Co., Jeb
Succes
Sunsongs Music/Dark Son Music
T.C. Productions/Etude Publishing Co.
Tedesco Music Co., Dale
Third Wave Productions Limited
Tiki Enterprises, Inc.
Tower Music Group
Transamerika Musikverlag KG
Ultimate Peak Music
Vaam Music Group
Valet Publishing Co.
Warner/Chappell Music Canada Ltd.
Wemar Music Corp.
Wengert, Berthold (Musikverlag)
Westwood Music Group
Whiting Music
Wilcom Publishing
Winston & Hoffman House Music Publishers
Wipe Out Music Ltd.
World Famous Music Co.

Yorgo Music
Zettitalia Music International
Zomba Music Publishing

R&B (also soul, black, urban, etc.)
A Ta Z Music
ALLRS Music Publishing Co.
Alexander Sr. Music
Alexis
Allegheny Music Works
American Heartstring Publishing
Americatone International
Audio Music Publishers
Avalon Music
Baitstring Music
Bal & Bal Music Publishing Co.
Barkin' Foe the Master's Bone
Bay Ridge Publishing Co.
Bernard Enterprises, Inc., Hal
Better Than Sex Music
Bradley Music, Allan
Brewster Songs, Kitty
California Country Music
Cheavoria Music Co.
Clevère Musikverlag, R.D.
Dagene Music
Dapmor Publishing
Dave Music, Jof
De Miles Music Company, The Edward
Delev Music Company
Duane Music, Inc.
East Coast Music Publishing
Emstone, Inc. Music Publishing
Ever-Open-Eye Music
Famous Music Publishing Companies
Fresh Entertainment
Frozen Inca Music
Gary Music, Alan
Hammel Associates, Inc., R.L.
His Power Productions and Publishing
Interplanetary Music
Jasper Stone Music/JSM Songs
JPMC Music Inc.
Kansa Records Corporation
Kaupps & Robert Publishing Co.
Lake Transfer Productions & Music
Largo Music Publishing
Lexington Alabama Music Publishing
Makers Mark Gold
Manuiti L.A.
Markea Music/Gina Pie Music
Marvin Publishing, John Weller
McConkey Artists Agency Music Publishing
Mellow House Music
Mighty Blue Music Machine, The
Montina Music
Music Room Publishing Group, The
New Rap Jam Publishing, A

Newcreature Music
Northwest Alabama Music Publishing
Old Slowpoke Music
Omni 2000, Inc.
PEN Music Group, Inc.
Prejippie Music Group
Prescription Company
Rainbow Music Corp.
Rustron Music Publishers
Sabteca Music Co.
Samuels Publishing, R.
Scott Music Group, Tim
Segal's Publications
Shu'Baby Montez Music
Silver Blue Music/Oceans Blue Music
Silver Thunder Music Group
Simply Grand Music, Inc.
Southern Most Publishing Company
Starbound Publishing Co.
Stellar Music Industries
Stuart Music Co., Jeb
Sunsongs Music/Dark Son Music
T.C. Productions/Etude Publishing Co.
Tedesco Music Co., Dale
Tiki Enterprises, Inc.
Tower Music Group
Vaam Music Group
Valet Publishing Co.
Wemar Music Corp.
Wilcom Publishing
Winston & Hoffman House Music Publishers
World Famous Music Co.
Yorgo Music
Zettitalia Music International
Zomba Music Publishing

Rap (also hip-hop, bass, etc.)
A Ta Z Music
Activate Entertainment LLC
Audio Music Publishers
Avalon Music
Barkin' Foe the Master's Bone
Bay Ridge Publishing Co.
Better Than Sex Music
BME Publishing
Clevère Musikverlag, R.D.
Dagene Music
Dapmor Publishing
East Coast Music Publishing
Fresh Entertainment
Interplanetary Music
Jasper Stone Music/JSM Songs
Lake Transfer Productions & Music
Largo Music Publishing
Makers Mark Gold
Marvin Publishing, John Weller
Mellow House Music
New Rap Jam Publishing, A

PEN Music Group, Inc.
Shu'Baby Montez Music
Silver Blue Music/Oceans Blue Music
Stellar Music Industries
Stuart Music Co., Jeb
Winston & Hoffman House Music Publishers
Zomba Music Publishing

Religious (also gospel, sacred, Christian, church, hymns, praise, inspirational, worship, etc.)
ALLRS Music Publishing Co.
Alco Music
Alexander Sr. Music
Alexis
Allegheny Music Works
Amen, Inc.
ARAS Music
Audio Images Two Thousand Music Publishing
Audio Music Publishers
Bagatelle Music Publishing Co.
Bal & Bal Music Publishing Co.
Barkin' Foe the Master's Bone
Barren Wood Publishing
Bay Ridge Publishing Co.
Big Fish Music Publishing Group
Bradley Music, Allan
Brentwood-Benson Music Publishing
Brian Song Music Corp.
California Country Music
Cherri/Holly Music Inc.
Corelli's Music Box
Cornelius Companies, The
Dave Music, Jof
Door Knob Music Publishing
Emandell Tunes
Ever-Open-Eye Music
Frick Enterprises, Bob Scott
G Major Music
Goodland Music Group Inc., The
Hammel Associates, Inc., R.L.
Hickory Valley Music
His Power Productions and Publishing
Hitsburgh Music Co.
Holy Spirit Music
JPMC Music Inc.
Juke Music
Kansa Records Corporation
Kaupps & Robert Publishing Co.
Lari-Jon Publishing
Leigh Music, Trixie
Lexington Alabama Music Publishing
Lindsay Publishing, Doris
Makers Mark Gold
McCoy Music, Jim
Mellow House Music
Mighty Blue Music Machine, The
Montina Music

New Rap Jam Publishing, A
Newcreature Music
Northwest Alabama Music Publishing
Omni 2000, Inc.
Orchid Publishing
Otto Publishing Co.
Peters Music, Justin
Pritchett Publications
Rocker Music/Happy Man Music
Salt Works Music
Scott Music Group, Tim
Scrutchings Music
Sellwood Publishing
Shawnee Press, Inc.
Southern Most Publishing Company
Starbound Publishing Co.
Stellar Music Industries
Stuart Music Co., Jeb
Sun Star Songs
Tiki Enterprises, Inc.
Tower Music Group
Vokes Music Publishing
Yorgo Music

Rock (also rockabilly, AOR, rock 'n' roll, etc.)
A Ta Z Music
Abalone Publishing
Activate Entertainment LLC
Alco Music
Alias John Henry Tunes
All Rock Music
Americatone International
Aquarius Publishing
Avalon Music
Baird Music Group
Bal & Bal Music Publishing Co.
Bay Ridge Publishing Co.
Bernard Enterprises, Inc., Hal
Better Than Sex Music
Blue Dog Publishing and Records
BME Publishing
Brewster Songs, Kitty
BSW Records
California Country Music
Christopher Publishing, Sonny
Clevère Musikverlag, R.D.
De Miles Music Company, The Edward
Doss Music, Buster
Duane Music, Inc.
Earitating Music Publishing
Earthscream Music Publishing Co.
East Coast Music Publishing
Edition Rossori
Famous Music Publishing Companies
Frozen Inca Music
Gary Music, Alan
Golden Music, August
Green One Music

Hammel Associates, Inc., R.L.
Heupferd Musikverlag
Hickory Lane Publishing and Recording
High-Minded Moma Publishing & Productions
Hit-Fabrik Musikverlag
Hitsource Publishing
Jammy Music Publishers Ltd.
Ja/Nein Musikverlag
Jasper Stone Music/Songs (BMI)
Jolson Black & White Music, Al
Juke Music
Kaupps & Robert Publishing Co.
Largo Music Publishing
Lari-Jon Publishing
Lexington Alabama Music Publishing
Lilly Music Publishing
Marvin Publishing, John Weller
McConkey Artists Agency Music Publishing
McCoy Music, Jim
Mellow House Music
Melody Hills Ranch Publishing Co.
Mighty Blue Music Machine, The
Montina Music
Music Room Publishing Group, The
Mymit Music Productions, Chuck
New Rap Jam Publishing, A
Newcreature Music
Northwest Alabama Music Publishing
Old Slowpoke Music
Ontrax Companies
PEN Music Group, Inc.
Portage Music
Prejippie Music Group
Prescription Company
Pritchett Publications
R.J. Music

Rocker Music/Happy Man Music
Rockford Music Co.
Samuels Publishing, R.
Sci-Fi Music
Scott Music Group, Tim
Segal's Publications
Silicon Music Publishing Co.
Simply Grand Music, Inc.
Sinus Musik Produktion
Sound Cellar Music
Southern Most Publishing Company
Stellar Music Industries
Stuart Music Co., Jeb
Succes
Sunsongs Music/Dark Son Music
Tedesco Music Co., Dale
Third Wave Productions Limited
Tiki Enterprises, Inc.
Transamerika Musikverlag KG
Ultimate Peak Music
Valet Publishing Co.
Warner/Chappell Music Canada Ltd.
Westwood Music Group
Whiting Music
Wilcom Publishing
World Famous Music Co.
Zomba Music Publishing

World Music (also reggae, ethnic, calypso, international, world beat, etc.)
Bay Ridge Publishing Co.
Heupferd Musikverlag GmbH
Inside Records/OK Songs
Tedesco Music Co., Dale
Transamerika Musikverlag KG
Whiting Music

Record Companies

Record companies release and distribute records, cassettes and CDs—the tangible products of the music industry. They sign artists to recording contracts, decide what songs those artists will record, and determine which songs to release. They are also responsible for providing recording facilities, securing producers and musicians, and overseeing the manufacture, distribution and promotion of new releases.

MAJOR LABELS & INDEPENDENT LABELS

Major labels and independent labels—what's the difference between the two? Major labels are defined as those record companies distributed by one of the "Big 5" distribution companies: BMG Distribution, EMI Music Distribution (EMD), Sony Music Distribution, Warner/Elektra/Atlantic Distribution (WEA) and Universal Music and Video Distribution (UMVD). (UMVD is the result of the 1998 acquisition of PolyGram Distribution by Universal parent Seagram, making UMVD the world's largest record company.) Distribution companies are wholesalers that sell records to retail outlets. If a label is distributed by one of these major companies, you can be assured any release coming out on that label has a large distribution network behind it. It will most likely be sent to most major retail stores in the United States. Independent labels go through smaller distribution companies to distribute their product. They usually don't have the ability to deliver records in massive quantities as the major distributors do. However, that doesn't mean independent labels aren't able to have hit records just like their major counterparts. A record label's distributors are found in the listings after the **Distributed by** heading.

Many of the companies listed in this section are independent labels. They are usually the most receptive to receiving material from new artists. Major labels spend more money than most other segments of the music industry; the music publisher, for instance, pays only for items such as salaries and the costs of making demos. Record companies, at great financial risk, pay for many more services, including production, manufacturing and promotion. Therefore, they must be very selective when signing new talent. Also, the continuing fear of copyright infringement suits has closed avenues to getting new material heard by the majors. Most don't listen to unsolicited submissions, period. Only songs recommended by attorneys, managers and producers who record company employees trust and respect are being heard by A&R people at major labels (companies with a referral policy have a ⊘ preceding their listing). But that doesn't mean all major labels are closed to new artists. With a combination of a strong local following, success on an independent label (or strong sales of an independently produced and released album) and the right connections, you could conceivably get an attentive audience at a major label.

But the competition is fierce at the majors, so you shouldn't overlook independent labels. Since they're located all over the country, indie labels are easier to contact and can be important in building a local base of support for your music (consult the Geographic Index at the back of the book to find out which companies are located near you). Independent labels usually concentrate on a specific type of music, which will help you target those companies your submissions should be sent to. And since the staff at an indie label is smaller, there are fewer channels to go through to get your music heard by the decision makers in the company.

The Case for Independents

If you're interested in getting a major label deal, it makes sense to look to independent record labels to get your start. Independent labels are seen by many as a stepping stone to a major recording contract. Very few artists are signed to a major label at the start of their careers; usually, they've had a few independent releases that helped build their reputation in the industry. Major labels watch independent labels closely to locate up-and-coming bands and new trends. In the current economic atmosphere at major labels—with extremely high overhead costs for developing new bands and the fact that only 10% of acts on major labels actually make any profit—they're not willing to risk everything on an unknown act. Most major labels won't even consider signing a new act that hasn't had some indie success.

But independents aren't just farming grounds for future major label acts; many bands have long term relationships with indies, and prefer it that way. While they may not be able to provide the extensive distribution and promotion that a major label can (though there are exceptions), indie labels can help an artist become a regional success, and may even help the performer to see a profit as well. With the lower overhead and smaller production costs an independent label operates on, it's much easier to "succeed" on an indie label than on a major.

HOW RECORD COMPANIES WORK

Independent record labels can run on a small staff, with only a handful of people running the day-to-day business. Major record labels are more likely to be divided into the following departments: A&R, sales, marketing, promotion, product management, artist development, production, finance, business/legal and international.

- The *A&R department* is staffed with A&R representatives (reps) who search out new talent. They go out and see new bands, listen to demo tapes, and decide which artists to sign. They also look for new material for already signed acts, match producers with artists and oversee recording projects. Once an artist is signed by an A&R rep and a record is recorded, the rest of the departments at the company come into play.
- The *sales department* is responsible for getting a record into stores. They make sure record stores and other outlets receive enough copies of a record to meet consumer demand.
- The *marketing department* is in charge of publicity, advertising in magazines and other media, promotional videos, album cover artwork, in-store displays, and any other means of getting the name and image of an artist to the public.
- The *promotion department*'s main objective is to get songs from a new album played on the radio. They work with radio programmers to make sure a product gets airplay.
- The *product management department* is the ringmaster of the sales, marketing and promotion departments, assuring that they're all going in the same direction when promoting a new release.
- The *artist development department* is responsible for taking care of things while an artist is on tour, such as setting up promotional opportunities in cities where an act is performing.
- The *production department* handles the actual manufacturing and pressing of the record and makes sure it gets shipped to distributors in a timely manner.
- People in the *finance department* compute and distribute royalties, as well as keep track of expenses and income at the company.
- The *business/legal department* takes care of contracts, not only between the record company and artists but with foreign distributors, record clubs, etc.
- And finally, the *international department* is responsible for working with international companies for the release of records in other countries.

LOCATING A RECORD LABEL

With the abundance of record labels out there, how do you go about finding one that's right for the music you create? First, it helps to know exactly what kind of music a record label releases. Become familiar with the records a company has released, and see if they fit in with what you're doing. Each listing in this section details the type of music a particular record company is interested in releasing. You will want to refer to the Category Index, located at the end of this section, to help you find those companies most receptive to the type of music you write. You should only approach companies open to your level of experience (see the Openness to Submissions sidebar on page 8). Visiting a company's website can also provide valuable information about a company's philosophy, the artists on the label and the music they work with.

Networking

Recommendations by key music industry people are an important part of making contacts with record companies. Songwriters must remember that talent alone does not guarantee success in the music business. You must be recognized through contacts, and the only way to make contacts is through networking. Networking is the process of building an interconnecting web of acquaintances within the music business. The more industry people you meet, the larger your contact base becomes, and the better are your chances of meeting someone with the clout to get your demo into the hands of the right people. If you want to get your music heard by key A&R representatives, networking is imperative.

Networking opportunities can be found anywhere industry people gather. A good place to meet key industry people is at regional and national music conferences and workshops. There are many held all over the country for all types of music (see the Workshops and Conferences section for more information). You should try to attend at least one or two of these events each year; it's a great way to increase the number and quality of your music industry contacts.

Creating a buzz

Another good way to attract A&R people is to make a name for yourself as an artist. By starting your career on a local level and building it from there, you can start to cultivate a following and prove to labels that you can be a success. A&R people figure if an act can be successful locally, there's a good chance they could be successful nationally. Start getting booked at local clubs, and start a mailing list of fans and local media. Once you gain some success on a local level, branch out. All this attention you're slowly gathering, this "buzz" you're generating, will not only get to your fans but to influential people in the music industry as well.

For More Information

For more instructional information on the listings in this book, including explanations of symbols (N ✔ ⬇ ⬇ ⊕ ◯ ◒ ◓ ◒), read the article How to Use *Songwriter's Market* to Get Your Songs Heard on page 5.

SUBMITTING TO RECORD COMPANIES

When submitting to a record company, major or independent, a professional attitude is imperative. Be specific about what you are submitting and what your goals are. If you are strictly a songwriter and the label carries a band you believe would properly present your song, state that in your cover letter. If you are an artist looking for a contract, showcase your strong points as a performer. Whatever your goals are, follow submission guidelines closely, be as neat as possible and include a top-notch demo. If you need more information concerning a company's requirements, write or call for more details. (For more information on submitting your material, see the article Getting Started on page 10, What Music Professionals Look for in a Demo sidebar on page 15 and Quiz: Are You Professional? on page 18.)

Additional Record Companies

There are **MORE RECORD COMPANIES** located in other sections of the book! On page 245 use the list of Additional Record Companies to find listings within other sections who are also record companies.

RECORD COMPANY CONTRACTS

Once you've found a record company that is interested in your work, the next step is signing a contract. Independent label contracts are usually not as long and complicated as major label ones, but they are still binding, legal contracts. Make sure the terms are in the best interest of both you and the label. Avoid anything in your contract that you feel is too restrictive. It's important to have your contract reviewed by a competent entertainment lawyer. A basic recording contract can run from 40-100 pages, and you need a lawyer to help you understand it. A lawyer will also be essential in helping you negotiate a deal that is in your best interest.

Recording contracts cover many areas, and just a few of the things you will be asked to consider will be: What royalty rate is the record label willing to pay you? What kind of advance are they offering? How many records will the company commit to? Will they offer tour support? Will they provide a budget for video? What sort of a recording budget are they offering? Are they asking you to give up any publishing rights? Are they offering you a publishing advance? These are only a few of the complex issues raised by a recording contract, so it's vital to have an entertainment lawyer at your side as you negotiate.

A.A.M.I. MUSIC GROUP, Maarschalklaan 47, 3417 SE Montfoort, The Netherlands. Fax: 31-384-471214. E-mail: aamimus@wxs.nl. Website: www.klikenklaar.nl/aamimusic.nl. Release Manager: Joop Gerrits. Manager (pop, R&B): Iris Gabeler. Manager (dance, rap): Carlo Bonti. Labels include Associated Artists, Disco-Dance Records and Italo. Record company, music publisher (Hilversum Happy Music/BUMA-STEMRA, Intermedlodie/BUMA-STEMRA and Hollands Glorie Productions), record producer (Associated Artists Productions) and TV promotions. Estab. 1975. Releases 10 singles, 25 12″ singles, 6 LPs and 6 CDs/year. Pays 14% royalty to artists on contract; variable amount to publishers.
How to Contact: Submit demo tape by mail. Unsolicited submissions are OK. Prefers CD or VHS videocassette with any number of songs and lyric or lead sheets. Records also accepted. SAE and IRC. Responds in 6 weeks.
Music: Mostly **dance**, **pop**, **house**, **hip-hop** and **rock**. Released "Black Is Black" (single by Gibbons/Hayes), recorded by Belle Epoque (dance); *Pocket Full of Whishes* (single by Robert Jones), recorded by Assault Team (dance), both on Movin' Novelties; and "Let Me Be Free" (single), written and recorded by Samantha Fox on LLP (pop). Other artists include Robert Ward, Yemisi, F.R. David and Black Nuss.

FOR BOOKS ON THE CRAFT AND BUSINESS of songwriting, check out the website for Writer's Digest Books at www.writersdigest.com.

Tips: "We invite producers and independent record labels to send us their material for their entry on the European market. Mark all parcels as 'no commercial value—for demonstration only.' We license productions to record companies in all countries of Europe and South Africa. Submit good demos or masters."

☑ ○ **A.P.I. RECORDS**, P.O. Box 7041, Watchung NJ 07061-0741. (908)753-1601. Fax: (908)753-3724. E-mail: apirecord@aol.com. Website: www.apirecords.com. **Executive Vice President:** Meg Poltorak. Vice President: Kevin Ferd. Record company, music publisher (Humbletunes, Inc.) and record producer (August Productions, Inc.). Estab. 1989. Staff size: 5. Releases 5 singles, 6 LPs and 6 CDs/year. Pays negotiable royalty to artists on contract; statutory rate to publisher per song on record.
How to Contact: Submit demo tape by mail. Unsolicited submissions are OK. Prefers cassette, CD, DAT or VHS videocassette with 3 songs and lyric sheet. Does not return material. Responds in 6 months if interested.
Music: Mostly **pop/rock**, **jazz** and **classical**. Released *Children of Promise* (album), written and recorded by Tom Gavornik (jazz), released 2000; *Nativitas* (album), written by Tim Keyes and recorded by The Tim Keyes Consort (classical), released 2000; and "When Will I See You" (single by Micheals/Keyes) from *Kassy Micheals* (album), recorded by Kassy Micheals (pop), released 2000, all on API.
Tips: "Looking for well-crafted material. Packaging and production are not important."

⊘ **A&M RECORDS**, 825 Eighth Ave., 29th Floor, New York NY 10019.
• As a result of the PolyGram and Universal merger, A&M Records has been folded into Interscope Records. See the Interscope/Geffen/A&M Records listing is this section for further information.

⊘ **AFTERSCHOOL RECORDS, INC.**, P.O. Box 14157, Detroit MI 48214. (313)894-8855.
Contact: Genesis Act, MCP, director/producer. Record company, music publisher (Afterschool Publishing Co., Inc.) and record producer (Feel Production, MCP). Estab. 1969. Releases 6 singles, 1 LP and a variable number of CDs/year. Pays negotiable royalty to artists on contract; statutory rate to publisher per song on record.
Distributed by: Afterschool, Fermata, Cancopy, CMRAA, NCB, AMRA, MCPS and BMG.
How to Contact: Submit demo tape by mail. Unsolicited submissions are OK. Prefers cassette, CD, DAT or videocassette with 1 song and lyric and lead sheets. SASE. Responds in 1 month.
Music: **All types.** Mostly **pop**, **dance** and **rap**; also **jazz**. Artists include P.M. Dawn, 2 Hyped Brothers and a Dog, 2 Live Crew, Beats International, Miss Jones, Luke, Cut-N-Move, Rockman, Kinsui, Jazzy Jeff & Fresh Prince, Whodini, M.C. Hammer, Betty Wright, Body & Soul, Gloria Estefan & Miami Sound Machine.
Tips: "Contracts are non-exclusive. Artists must have legal representation when submitting. Afterschool Records does not have pre-drafted documents."

☑ ○ **THE AIRPLAY LABEL**, P.O. Box 851, Asbury Park NJ 07712. Phone/fax: (732)681-0623. E-mail: airplaypete@hotmail.com. Website: www.airplay.org. Head of A&R: Mark Sanderlin, or Tripp, A&Rs. President A&R: Peter P. Mantas. Vice President/Head of A&R: Jefferson Powers. Record company. Estab. 1995. Staff size: 7. Releases 6 singles, 3 LPs, 2 EPs and 4 CDs/year. Pays 20% royalty to artists on contract; statutory rate to publisher per song on record.
Distributed by: Music Source, Notlame.com, Valley and Redeye.
• This label received the Asbury Music Awards' 1997-98 Top Release.
How to Contact: *Write first and obtain permission to submit.* Prefers cassette, CD or videocassette. Does not return material. Responds in 1 month.
Music: Mostly **pop**, **acid jazz** and **jazz**; also **emo-core**. Released *Good to Be Alive* (album), written and recorded by Evelyn Forever (pop), released 2001 on Airplay; and *Pop 2K* (album), written and recorded by various artists (pop), released 2000 on Airplay/Pop 2K label.
Tips: "Hard work pays off."

N ◯ ALBATROSS RECORDS, P.O. Box 540102, Houston TX 77254-0102. (713)521-2616. Fax: (713)529-4914. E-mail: rpds2405@aol.com. Website: www.rndproductions.com. A&R: Byron Gates. Labels include R&D Productions and Fanatic Records. Record company. Estab. 1990. Staff size: 4. Releases 20 singles, 10 LPs and 10 CDs/year. Pays negotiable royalty to artists on contract; statutory rate to publisher per song on record.
Distributed by: Select-O-Hits and Bayside.
How to Contact: Submit demo tape by mail. Unsolicited submissions are OK. Prefers CD and pictures. Does not return material. Responds in 3 weeks.
Music: Mostly **R&B**, **rap** and **Latino/TexMex pop**; also **jazz**, **country**, **rock** and **blues**. Released *Lines & Spaces* (album), recorded by Shades of Brown (jazz); *Remi n Alize* (album), recorded by Mr. International (rap); and *Screw Theory Vol. 2* (album), recorded by various (rap), all on Albatross Records. Other artists include Nu Ground, D.G.I. Posse, Hollister Fraucus and 4-Deep.

◯ ALCO RECORDINGS, P.O. Box 18197, Panama City Beach FL 32417. **Contact:** Ann McEver, president. Record company. Estab. 2000. Staff size: 2. Pays standard royalty to artists on contract; statutory rate to publisher per song on record.
How to Contact: Submit demo tape by mail. Unsolicited submissions are OK. Prefers cassette or CD with 2-3 songs, lyric sheet and cover letter. SASE. Responds in 3 weeks.
Music: Mostly **pop/rock**, **country** and **alternative**. Also **gospel**. Does not want instrumentals.
Tips: "Think about your submission. Make sure it meets our submission requirements. We are looking for artists or groups who could compete at a national level."

N ◯ ALL STAR RECORD PROMOTIONS, 1229 S. Prospect St., Marion OH 43302-7267. (740)382-5939. E-mail: allstarmanage@msn.com. **Contact:** John Simpson, president. Record promoter. Estab. 1980.
How to Contact: *Contact and obtain permission to submit.*
Music: Mostly **top 40**, **country**, **alternative**, **smooth jazz**, **jazz**, **active rock**, **rap and college**.

◯ ALLEGHENY MUSIC WORKS, 306 Cypress Ave,. Johnstown PA 15902. (814)535-3373. E-mail: TunedOnMusic@aol.com. Website: www.alleghenymusicworks.com. **Contact:** Al Rita, managing director. Labels include Allegheny Records. Record company and music publisher (Allegheny Music Works Publishing/ASCAP and Tuned on Music/BMI). Estab. 1991. Pays 10-12% royalty to artists on contract; statutory rate to publisher per song on record.
How to Contact: *Write first and obtain permission to submit.* "Include SASE for reply. E-mail queries are acceptable. Responds in 1 week to regular mail requests and usually within 48 hours to e-mail queries."
Music: Mostly **country (all styles)**; also **pop**, **A/C**, **R&B**, **inspirational**, **novelty** and **Halloween**. Released "That's My Jack O'Lantern" (single), written and recorded by Neil Hartenburg) from *Halloween Bash* (album) (country), released 2000 on Allegheny.
Tips: "Bookmark our website and check it regularly, clicking on *Songwriter Opportunities*. Each month, as a free service to songwriters, we list a new artist or company looking for songs. Complete contact information is included. For a deeper insight into the type of material our company publishes, we invite you to read the customer reviews on amazon.com to our 2000 best seller Halloween album release *Halloween Bash*."

N ⊕ ◯ ALPHABEAT, Box 12 01, D-97862 Wertheim/Main, Germany. Phone/fax: (49)9342-84155. E-mail: alphabeat@t-online.de. **Contact:** Stephan Dehn, owner. A&R Managers (all styles): Marga Zimmermann, Ottmar Simon and Wolfgang Weinmann. Record company and record producer. Payment to artists on contract "depends on product."
How to Contact: Submit demo tape by mail. Unsolicited submissions are OK. Prefers cassette or PAL videocassette with maximum of 3 songs and lyric sheet. "When sending us your demo tapes, please advise us of your ideas and conditions." SAE and IRC. Responds in 1 month.

Music: Mostly **dance/disco/pop**, **synth/pop** and **electronic**; also **R&B**, **hip-hop/rap** and **ballads**.
Tips: "We are a distributor of foreign labels. If foreign labels have interest in distribution of their productions in Germany (also Switzerland and Austria) they can contact us. We distribute all styles of music of foreign labels. Please contact our 'Distribution Service' department."

☑ ☺ **AMERICAN RECORDINGS**, 2100 Colorado Ave., Santa Monica CA 90404. (310)449-2190. Website: www.american.recordings.com. A&R: Dino Paredes, George Drakoulias, Antony Bland, Brendon Mendoza. Labels include Too Pure, Infinite Zero, UBL, Venture and Onion. Record company.
Distributed by: Sony.
How to Contact: Submit demo tape by mail. Unsolicited submissions are OK. Prefers CD, cassette or videocassette with lyric and lead sheet.
Music: Released *Unchained*, recorded by Johnny Cash on American Recordings. Other artists include Slayer, System of a Down, The Black Crowes, Jayhawks, Loudermilk, Unida, American Head Charge, Man Made God, Saul Williams, Nusvat Fatch Ali Khan, Rohat Fetch Ali Khan.

☑ ◐ **AMERICATONE RECORDS INTERNATIONAL USA**, 1817 Loch Lomond Way, Las Vegas NV 89102-4437. (702)384-0030. Fax: (702)382-1926. E-mail: jjj@americatone.com. Website: www.americatone.com. Estab. 1985. **Contact:** A&R Director. Labels include The Rambolt Music International (ASCAP), Americatone (BMI) and Christy Records International. Record company, producer and music publisher. Releases 8 CDs and cassettes/year. Pays 10% royalty.
Distributed by: Big Band, Otter, Dist., North County, General, Harbor Export, International Dist., Twinbrook Dist., Gibson Dist.
How to Contact: Submit demo tape by mail. Unsolicited submissions are OK. Prefers cassette or CD. SASE. Responds in 1 month.
Music: Mostly **jazz**, **rock**, **Spanish** and **classic ballads**. Released *After All These Years*, written and recorded by Brent Blount; and *The Ramblers*, written and recorded by Brad Sauders, both on Americatone International Records. Other artists include Mark Masters Jazz Orchestra, Raoul Romero and His Jazz Stars Orchestra, Ladd McIntosh Big Band, Dick Shearer and His Stan Kenton Spirits, Gabriel Rosati from Roma Italy, Lee Gibson with John Reddick and his Jazz Orchestra from BBC London, Explosion Sam Trippe, Bill Perkins Jazz Quintet, Caribbean Jazz, Jazz in the Rain, Americatone is also music published of Top Sheet Music Orchestrations and Piano Publishers.

☑ ◑ **AMIGOS MUSIC & MARKETING**, 81 Pondfield Rd., Suite 266, Bronxville NY 10708. Phone/fax: (718)548-7366. E-mail: amigosrcd@aol.com or andygrullon@yolandaduke.com. Website: www.yolandaduke.com. **Contact:** Andy Grullon, director. Labels include Amigos, Tataiba, 3×2 Son, and Flamenco. Record company. Estab. 1990. Staff size: 10. Releases 5 singles, 3 LPs and 3 CDs/year. Pays 6¼% royalty to artists on contract or negotiable; statutory rate to publisher per song on record.
Distributed by: Ace Music Distributors, GB Records and J + N Records.
How to Contact: Submit demo tape by mail. Unsolicited submissions are OK. Prefers cassette, CD or VHS videocassette with 3 songs and lyric sheet. Does not return materials. Responds in 6 weeks if interested.
Music: Mostly **Latin**. Released *Experiencias* (album by Jose L. Perales and Juan Lanfranco), recorded by Yolanda Duke (salsa); *Todo*, (album by Roberto Carlos), recorded by Fernando Villalona (merengue), both on Amigos Records; and *Te Quiero* (album), written and recorded by Juan Lanfranco (ballad) on Flamenco Records.
Tips: "Put together lyrics that make sense with a good melody. We are noted for releasing Latin music."

N ⊕ ◐ **AMP RECORDS & MUSIC**, Box BM Fame, London WC1N 3XX United Kingdom. Phone/fax: (0044)(0)208 889 0616. E-mail: info@ampmusic.demon.co.uk. Website: www.ampmusic. demon.co.uk. **Contact:** Mark Jenkins, A&R (New Age, instrumental, ambient, progressive, rock). Record company. Estab. 1985. Staff size: 10. Releases 12 CDs/year. Pays negotiable royalty to artists on contract; negotiable rate to publisher per song on record.

Distributed by: Shellshock (UK), Eurock/ZNR/NSA (USA), MP (Italy) and Crystal Lake (France).
How to Contact: Submit demo tape by mail. Unsolicited submissions are OK. Prefers cassette, CD or DAT with cover letter and press clippings. Does not return material. Responds in 2 months.
Music: Mostly **New Age**, **instrumental** and **ambient**; also **progressive rock**, **synthesizer** and **ambient dance**. Does not want ballads, country or AOR. Released *Changing States*, recorded by Keith Emerson (progressive rock); *Tyranny of Beauty*, written and recorded by Tangerine Dream (synthesizer); and *Spirit of Christmas*, written and recorded by various artists (instrumental compilation), all on AMP Records.
Tips: "Send a relevant style of music."

☑ ◯ **ANISETTE RECORDS**, 8 Garrison St., #601, Boston MA 02116. Phone/fax: (213)365-9495. E-mail: anisette@earthlink.net. Website: home.earthlink.net/~anisette. A&R Chief: M-K O'Connell. Record company. Estab. 1998. Staff size: 2. Releases 2 CDs/year. Pays negotiable royalty to artists on contract; statutory rate to publisher per song on record.
Distributed by: NAIL, Darla, Carrot Top, Surefire, Scratch and Parasol.
How to Contact: Submit demo tape by mail. Unsolicited submissions are OK. Prefers cassette or CD. Does not return material. Responds in 2 weeks.
Music: Mostly **rock**, **pop** and **rap**. Released *Greatest Moments of Doubt* (album by Kevin Castillo), recorded by Retriever; *The Miracle of Flight* (album), written and recorded by Stratotanker; and *El Rey* (album), recorded by The Lassie Foundation (rock), all on Anisette.
Tips: "Send the material and follow up with an e-mail."

☑ ◯ **ARIANA RECORDS**, 1336 S. Avenida Polar #C-208, Tucson AZ 85710. (520)790-7324. E-mail: jimigas1@earthlink.net. **Contact:** James M. Gasper, president. Vice President (pop, rock): Tom Dukes. Partners: Tom Privett (funk, experimental, rock); Scott Smith (pop, rock, AOR). Labels include Egg White Records. Record company, music publisher (Myko Music/BMI) and record producer. Estab. 1980. Staff size: 4. Releases 2 singles, 4 LPs and 1 compilation/year. Pays negotiable royalty to artists on contract; negotiable rate to publisher per song on record.
Distributed by: Impact Music Distributors and Care Free Music.
How to Contact: Submit demo tape by mail. Unsolicited submissions are OK. Prefers cassette or CD. SASE. Responds in 6 months.
Music: Mostly **rock**, **funk** and **jazz**; also **anything weird or strange**. Released "B.T.B.A." (single by Scott Seleny), recorded by Baby Fish Mouth on Ariana (funk); and *Stompbox* (album by Michael West/Tom James), recorded by Larry's Limo on Egg White (space funk). Other artists include Radiant Grub, The Rakeheads, Mary's Purse and New World Slavery.
Tips: "We're a small company, but working your material is our job. If we like it, we'll sell it!"

⊘ **ARISTA RECORDS**, 6 W. 57th St., New York NY 10019. (212)489-7400. Fax: (212)977-9843. Website: www.aristarec.com. Vice President A&R: Joshua Sarubin. Vice President A&R: Joey Arbagey. Beverly Hills office: 8750 Wilshire Blvd., 3rd Floor, Beverly Hills CA 90211. (310)358-4600. Vice President A&R: Pete Farmer. Senior Director A&R: Michelle Ozbourn. Nashville office: 7 Music Circle North, Nashville TN 37203. (615)846-9100. Fax: (615)846-9192. Senior Director A&R: Steve Williams. Director of A&R: Mike Sistad. Manager of A&R: Kerri Pauley Edwards. Labels include LaFace Records, Bad Boy Records, Arista Nashville and Time Bomb Recordings. Record company.
Distributed by: BMG.
How to Contact: Does not accept unsolicited material.
Music: Released *Harem World* by Mace on Bad Boy; *Surfacing* by Sarah McLachlan on Arista; and *Soul Food* soundtrack on LaFace. Other artists include Kenny G, Brooks & Dunn, Alan Jackson and OutKast.

◖ **ARKADIA ENTERTAINMENT CORP.**, 34 E. 23rd St., New York NY 10010. (212)533-0007. Fax: (212)979-0266. E-mail: info@arkadiarecords.com. Website: www.arkadiarecords.com.

Contact: A&R Song Submissions. Labels include Arkadia Jazz, Arkadia Classical, Arkadia Now and Arkadia Allworld. Record company, music publisher (Arkadia Music), record producer (Arkadia Productions) and Arkadia Video. Estab. 1995.
How to Contact: Write or call first and obtain permission to submit.
Music: Mostly **jazz**, **classical** and **pop/R&B**; also **world**.

ASTRALWERKS, (formerly Caroline Records, Inc.), 104 W. 29th St., 4th Floor, New York NY 10001. (212)886-7500. Fax: (212)643-5573. Website: www.astralwerks.com. **Contact:** Todd Roberts, A&R director. Exclusive manufacturing and distribution of EG, Astralwerks (electronic) and Real World (world music), Vernon Yard (alternative rock), Instant Mayhem (alternative rock), Scamp (retrocool), Mercator (world) and Gyroscope (eclectic). Record company and independent record distributor (Caroline Records Inc.). Estab. 1979. Releases 10-12 12″ singles and 100 CDs/year. Pays varying royalty to artists on contract; statutory rate to publisher per song.
How to Contact: Does not accept unsolicited submissions.
Music: Mostly **alternative/indie/electronic**. Released *You've Come A Long Way* (album), recorded by Fatboy Slim; *Surrender* (album), recorded by Chemical Brothers; and *3 eps* (album), recorded by Beta Band, all on Astralworks.
Tips: "We are open to artists of unique quality and enjoy developing artists from the ground up. We listen to all types of 'alternative' rock, metal, funk and rap but do not sign mainstream hard rock or dance. We send out rejection letters so do not call to find out what's happening with your demo."

ATLAN-DEC/GROOVELINE RECORDS, 2529 Green Forest Court, Snellville GA 30078-4183. (770)985-1686. Fax: (877)751-5169. E-mail: atlandec@prodigy.net. Website: www.ATLAN-DEC.com. President/Senior A&R Rep: James Hatcher. A&R Rep: Wiletta J. Hatcher. Record company, music publisher and record producer. Estab. 1994. Staff size: 2. Releases 3-4 singles, 3-4 LPs and 3-4 CDs/year. Pays 10-25% royalty to artists on contract; statutory rate to publisher per song on record.
Distributed by: ATLAN-DEC Records and Baker & Taylor Entertainment.
How to Contact: Submit demo tape by mail. Unsolicited submissions are OK. Prefers cassette and lyric sheet. Does not return material. Responds in 3 months.
Music: Mostly **R&B/urban**, **hip-hop/rap** and **contemporary jazz**; also **soft rock**, **gospel**, **dance** and **new country**. Released "Dog I Will" (single by Lamar Brown) from *Temptation* (album), recorded by Shawnee (rap/hip-hop), released 2001 on Atlan-Dec/Grooveline Records; and "Da Best" (single by Donyelle Whitehead) from *Skilz 2 Make Milz* (album), recorded by B-Double-O (rap/hip-hop), released 2001 on Atlan-Dec/Grooveline Records. Other artists include R.I.P., Family Tiez, Furious D (rap/hip-hop), Paul Carroll (jazz), Mark Cocker (new country).

ATLANTIC RECORDS, 1290 Avenue of the Americas, New York NY 10104. (212)707-2000. Fax: (212)581-6414. Los Angeles office: 9229 Sunset Blvd., 9th Floor, Los Angeles CA 90069. (310)205-7450. Fax: (310)205-7411. Senior Vice President A&R: Mike Caren. Vice President of A&R: Tom Storms. Vice President (soundtracks): Darren Higman. Nashville office: 20 Music Square East, Nashville TN 37203. (615)272-7990. A&R: Al Cooley. Website: www.atlantic-records.com. Labels include Big Beat Records, LAVA, Nonesuch Records, Atlantic Classics and Rhino Records. Record company. Pays negotiable royalty to artists on contract; negotiable rate to publisher per song on record.
Distributed by: WEA.
How to Contact: Does not accept unsolicited material. "No phone calls please."

SENDING TO A COUNTRY other than your own? Be sure to send International Reply Coupons (IRCs) instead of stamps for replies or return of your materials.

Music: Released *Yourself or Someone Like You* (album), recorded by Matchbox 20 on LAVA; *Pieces of You* (album), recorded by Jewel on Atlantic; and *Greatest Hits* (album), recorded by John Michael Montgomery on Atlantic (Nashville). Other artists include Sugar Ray, Kid Rock and Brandy.

:N: ◯ AVALON RECORDING GROUP, P.O. Box 121626, Nashville TN 37212. **Contact:** A&R Review Department. Director: Avalon Hughs. Record company, music publisher (Avalon Music) and record producer (Avalon Productions). Estab. 2001. Staff size: 3. Pays standard royalty to artists on contract.
How to Contact: Submit demo tape by mail. "We do not accept unsolicited material. No phone calls, please." Prefers cassette or CD with 3 songs and lyric sheet. Include SASE. Responds in 3 weeks.
Music: Mostly **rock**, **country**, and **alternative**; also **R&B**, **hip hop** and **gospel**.
Tips: "Send songs suitable for today's market. We are looking for singers, singer/songwriters and bands that have the potential to go large."

:N: ◯ AVENUE COMMUNICATIONS, P.O. Box 1432, Menlo Park CA 94026-1432. (650)321-8291 or (800)5AVENUE. Fax: (650)321-7491. Website: www.5avenue.com. Vice President: Erik Nielsen. Record company. Estab. 1989. Releases 5 singles and 3 CDs/year. Pays negotiable royalty to artists on contract; statutory rate to publisher per song on record.
Distributed by: CRD, Valley, Bayside and CD One-Stop.
How to Contact: Submit demo tape by mail. Unsolicited submissions are OK. Prefers cassette, CD, DAT or VHS videocassette. Does not return material. Responds "next day if we like it."
Music: Mostly **American/international**. Released "Got the Whole Night," (single), recorded by Denny Brown.

✔ ⊘ AVITA RECORDS, P.O. Box 764, Hendersonville TN 37077-0764. (615) 824-9313. Fax: (615)824-0797. E-mail: Tachoir@bellsouth.net. Website: www.tachoir.com. **Contact:** Robert Kayre, manager. Record company, music publisher (Riohcat Music, BMI) and record producer (Jerry Tachoir). Estab. 1976. Staff size: 8. Releases 2 LPs and 2 CDs/year. Pays negotiable royalty to artists on contract; statutory rate to publisher per song on record.
How to Contact: *Contact first and obtain permission to submit.* We only accept material referred to us by a reputable industry source. Prefers cassette, CD or DAT. Does not return materials. Responds only if interested.
Music: Mostly **jazz**. Released *Improvised Thoughts* (album by Marlene Tachoir/Jerry Tachoir/Van Marakas), recorded by Jerry Tachoir and Van Marakas (jazz), released 2001 on Avita Records. Other artists include Van Marakas.

✔ ◑ AWAL.COM, P.O. Box 879, Ojai CA 93024. (805)640-7399. Fax: (805)646-6077. E-mail: info@awal.com. Website: www.awal.com. **Contact:** A&R Department. President: Denzyl Feigelson. Record company. Estab. 1996. Staff size: 7. Releases 6 singles, 12 LPs and 12 CDs/year. Pays 50% or negotiable royalty to artists on contract.
Distributed by: Valley and on the Internet.
How to Contact: Submit demo tape by mail. Unsolicited submissions are OK. Prefers CD with 5 songs, lyric sheet, cover letter and press clippings. Does not return materials. Responds in 1 month if interested.
Music: Mostly **pop**, **world** and **jazz**; also **techno**, **teen** and **children's**. Released *Go Cat Go* (album by various), recorded by Carl Perkins on ArtistOne.com; *Bliss* (album), written and recorded by Donna Delory (pop); and *Shake A Little* (album), written and recorded by Michael Ruff, both on Awal Records.

✔ ◯ AWARE RECORDS, P.O. Box 803817, Chicago IL 60680. (773)248-4210. Fax: (773)248-4211. E-mail: aware@awarerecords.com. Website: www.awarerecords.com. A&R: Steve Smith. President: Gregg Latterman. Record company. Estab. 1993. Staff size: 8. Releases 5 LPs, 1 EP and 3 CD/year. Pays negotiable royalty to artists on contract; statutory rate to publisher per song on record.
Distributed by: Sony and RED.

How to Contact: Submit demo tape by mail. Unsolicited submissions are OK. Prefers CD with lead sheet, cover letter and press clippings. Does not return material. Responds back only if interested.
Music: Mostly **rock/pop**. Released *Aware 7* (album), written and recorded by various artists (pop/rock); and *More Sounds from Spaghetti Westerns* (album), recorded by Red Elephant, both on Aware Records. Other artists include Dovetail Joint, Five for Fighting, Mile Porcelain and Cary Pierce.

○ **babysue**, P.O. Box 8989, Atlanta GA 31106. (404)320-1178. Website: www.babysue.com. **Contact:** Don W. Seven, president/owner. Record company and management firm. Estab. 1983. Staff size: 1. Releases 2 singles, 5 LPs, 2 EPs and 7 CDs/year. Pays 5-20% royalty to artists on contract; varying royalty to publisher per song on record.
Distributed by: Not Lame Distribution.
How to Contact: Submit demo tape, CD or CDRW by mail. Unsolicited submissions are OK. Prefers submisison with any number of songs. Does not return material. Responds in 3 months. "We only report back if we are interested in the artist or act."
Music: Mostly **rock**, **pop** and **gospel**; also **heavy metal**, **punk** and **classical**. Released *Mnemonic* (album), recorded by LMNOP on babysue records (rock/pop). Other artists include the Mushcakes, The Shoestrings and The Mommy.
Tips: "We're just into sincere, good stuff."

◑ **BAGATELLE RECORD COMPANY**, P.O. Box 925929, Houston TX 77292. **Contact:** Byron Benton, president. Record company, record producer and music publisher (Bagatelle Music, Floyd Tillman Music Co.). Releases 20 singles and 10 LPs/year. Pays negotiable royalty to artists on contract.
How to Contact: Submit demo tape by mail. Prefers cassette and lyric sheet. SASE. Responds in 2 weeks.
Music: Mostly **country**; also **gospel**. Released "This is Real" (single by Floyd Tillman) (country); "Lucille" (single by Sherri Jerrico) (country); and "Everything You Touch" (single by Johnny Nelms) (country). Other artists include Jerry Irby, Bobby Beason, Bobby Burton, Donna Hazard, Danny Brown, Sonny Hall, Ben Gabus, Jimmy Copeland and Johnny B. Goode.

N ◑ **BANKROLL RECORDS INC.**, P.O Box 3861, Chicago IL 60654. (312)635-5143. E-mail: bankroll@mobil.att.net. Website: www.bankroll.com. **Contact:** William Gaston, A&R. Record Company. Estab. 1994. Staff size: 3. Pays 12-13% royalty.
Distributed by: "We sell direct to Best Buy, Circuit City, Sam Goody, Camelot Music and some one stops."
How to Contact: Submit demo by mail. Prefers cassette or CD/CDR. Include SASE. Responds in 1 month, only if interested.
Music: Mostly **rap**, **R&B** and **rock**; also **house** and **dance**.

○ **BELHAM VALLEY RECORDS**, P.O. Box 12367, Lahaina HI 96761. Fax: (808)669-5719. E-mail: info@TheArtsContest.com. Website: www.TheArtsContest.com. **Contact:** Gary Robilotta, owner/producer. Owner/Producer: Carrll Robilotta. A&R Director: Garbaldo. Labels include Isles Bay Music, Volcano, Montserrat Records and Rivermouth Records. Record company, music publisher (Belham Valley Records Publishing) and record producer (Gary Robilotta). Estab. 1993. Releases 1 LP and 1 CD every 2 years. Pays standard royalty to artists on contract; statutory rate to publisher per song on record.
Distributed by: Belham Valley Records.
How to Contact: *Write first and obtain permission to submit.* Prefers cassette or CD with any number of songs and lyric sheet. SASE. Responds in 3 weeks.
Music: Mostly **instrumental (pop/jazz/reggae)** and **neo-classical/jazz**; also **solo piano**. Released *Project: Montserrat*; *Once Around The Island*; and *Jungle Junge* (albums), all written and recorded by Gary Robilotta on Belham Valley Records (instrumental).
Tips: "Be original but not to the point of sacrificing musical integrity. That is, there's lots of original stuff out there, but lots of it shouldn't really be called 'music.' Above all else, strive for mellifluous-

ness—regardless of your chosen genre. We release music that transcends generational boundaries because it is music that speaks to the soul—the type of music Mannheim Steamroller is noted for. See our website for contest information."

☑ Ø **BELMONT RECORDS**, 484 Lexington St., Waltham MA 02452. (781)891-7800. Fax: (781)891-7800. E-mail: jpennycw@aol.com. **Contact:** John Penny, president. Labels include Waverly Records. Record company and record producer. Pays standard royalty to artists on contract; statutory rate to publisher per song on record.
How to Contact: *Write first and obtain permission to submit.* Prefers cassette with 3 songs and lyric sheet. SASE. Responds in 3 weeks.
Music: Mostly **country**. Released *Barbara Lawrence* (album), recorded by Barbara Lawrence (c&w), released 1999; and *Listen To Me* (album), recorded by Barbara Lawrence (c&w), released 2000, both on Belmont Records. Other artists include Stan Jr., Tim Barrett, Jackie Lee Williams, Robin Right, Mike Walker and Dwain Hathaway.

N̲ ○ **BELUGA RECORDS**, 1532 N. Milwaukee Ave., #202, Chicago IL 60622. Website: www.belugarecords.com. Mastermind: Scott Beluga. Record company. Estab. 1994. Staff size: 1. Releases 4-8 CDs/year. Pays negotiable royalty to artists on contract; statutory rate to publisher per song on record.
Distributed by: Carrot Top, Southern and Choke.
How to Contact: Submit demo tape by mail. Unsolicited submissions are OK. Prefers cassette or CD. "Please don't call." Does not return material. Responds back only if interested.
Music: Mostly **indie pop**, **indie rock** and **derivatives thereof**. Does not want heavy metal, goth, ska, country or singer/songwriters looking for publishing deals. Released *After School Special* (album), written and recorded by Cats and Jammers (garage pop); *13 Electric Turn-Ons* (album), written and recorded by Big Angry Fish (indie rock); and *Volume* (album), recorded by Dragstrip Syndicate (rock), all on Beluga Records. Other artists include Zipperhead, Today's My Super Spaceout Day and Mustache.
Tips: "Research the record company before wasting your time and product. For example, if you knew that Beluga Records only works with rock bands that write their own music, would it be appropriate to send us your music?"

○ **BIG BEAT RECORDS**, 9229 Sunset Blvd., Los Angeles CA 90069. (310)205-5717. Fax: (310)205-5721. E-mail: mike.caren@atlantic-recording.com. Website: www.atlantic-recordings.com. **Contact:** Michael Caren, director of A&R/staff producer. Record company. Labels include Undeas Records, CWAL and Slip-N-Slide.
Distributed by: WEA.
How to Contact: Submit demo tape by mail. Unsolicited submissions are OK. Prefers cassette, CD or DAT with bio and photo.
Music: Released *www.thug.com* (album), written and recorded by Trick Daddy (rap) on Slip-n-Slide; *Causin' Drama* (album), written and recorded by Drama (rap) on Tight IV Life; and *Any Given Sunday* (album soundtrack), written and recorded by various artists (rap/rock) on Atlantic.

☑ ♛ Ø **BIG HEAVY WORLD**, P.O. Box 428, Burlington VT 05402-0428. (802)865-1140 or (800)303-1590. E-mail: groundzero@bigheavyworld.com. Website: www.bigheavyworld.com. **Contact:** James Lockridge, founder/A&R director. Record company. Estab. 1996. Staff size: 4. Releases 3 CDs/year. Pays negotiable royalty to artists on contract; pay varies by project to publisher per song on record.
Distributed by: Redeye USA.
   ● This company was given the 1998 Visionary Award by the Women's Rape Crisis Center. Big Heavy World promotes the music of Burlington, Vermont, and its region. Their compilation CDs vary in genre and theme and often benefit humanitarian services.
How to Contact: Big Heavy World does not accept unsolicited submissions.

Music: Compilation projects vary in genre. Released *Pop Pie* (pop); *Pulsecuts Vol II* (alternative); *No Secrets* and *Tonic Two: Core Breach Burlington* (rock/alternative), (albums), all written and recorded by various artists on Big Heavy World. Other artists include ChinHo! (pop) and chainsaws.and.children (industrial).

Tips: "Vermont-based artists are welcome to contact us, both as a record label and online music retail venue."

⏏ BIG WIG PRODUCTIONS, 14088 W. Wrigley St., Boise ID 83713. Phone/fax: (208)938-1176. **Contact:** Bryan Lass, A&R representative. Record company. Estab. 1992. Releases 3 singles and 2 CDs/year. Pays negotiable royalty to artists on contract; statutory rate to publisher per song on record.

How to Contact: *Call first and obtain permission to submit.* Prefers cassette or CD with 4 songs and lyric sheet. "Enclose any information regarding recent radio airtime and album sales if available." Does not return material. Responds in 6 weeks.

Music: Mostly **pop/top 40**, **contemporary** and **country**; also **gospel**, **folk** and **rock**. Released "Something's Missing" and "Day of Reckoning" (singles), both written and recorded by Memory Garden; and "Digital Madness" (single by Bryan Lass), recorded by Hyperdigits on Big Wig Records (alternative).

◯ BLUE GEM RECORDS, P.O. Box 29550, Hollywood CA 90029. (323)664-7765. E-mail: pmarti3636@aol.com. **Contact:** Pete Martin. Record company, music publisher (Vaam Music Group) and record producer (Pete Martin/Vaam Productions). Estab. 1981. Pays 6-15% royalty to artists on contract; statutory rate to publisher per song on record.

How to Contact: Submit demo tape by mail. Unsolicited submissions are OK. Prefers cassette with 2 songs. SASE. Responds in 3 weeks.

Music: Mostly **country** and **R&B**; also **pop/top 40** and **rock**. Released "The Greener Years" (single), written and recorded by Frank Loren (country); "It's a Matter of Loving You" (single by Brian Smith), recorded by Brian Smith & The Renegades (country); and "Two Different Women" (single by Frank Loren/Greg Connor), recorded by Frank Loren (country), all on Blue Gem Records. Other artists include Sherry Weston (country).

☑◯ BLUE WAVE, 3221 Perryville Rd., Baldwinsville NY 13027. (315)638-4286. Fax: (315)635-4757. Website: www.bluewaverecords.com. **Contact:** Greg Spencer, president/producer. Labels include Blue Wave/Horizon. Record company, music publisher (G.W. Spencer Music/ASCAP) and record producer (Blue Wave Productions). Estab. 1985. Staff size: 1. Releases 3 LPs and 3 CDs/year. Pays variable royalty to artists on contract; statutory rate to publisher per song on record.

Distributed by: MS Distribution, Select-O-Hits, United and Valley.

How to Contact: Submit demo tape by mail. Unsolicited submissions are OK. Prefers cassette or videocassette (live performance only) and as many songs as you like. SASE. Responds in 1 month only if interested.

Music: Mostly **blues/blues rock**, **roots rock** and **roots R&B/soul**; also **roots country/rockabilly** or **anything with "soul."** Released "Find the Truth" (single by Kim Lembo/Terry Mulhauser) from *Paris Burning* (album), recorded by Kim Lembo (blues); "It's Been So Long" (single by Don Walsh) from *A Matter of Time* (album), recorded by Downchild Blues Band (blues); and "Solitaire" (single) from *Blue Wave 15th Anniversary Collection* (album), written and recorded by Kim Simmonds (blues), all released 2000 on Blue Wave. Other artists include Kim Simmonds and Backbone Slip.

Tips: "Be able to put the song across vocally."

[N] ⏏ BOLIVIA RECORDS, 2622 Kirtland Rd., Brewton AL 36246. (334)867-2228. President: Roy Edwards. Labels include Known Artist Records. Record company, record producer (Known Artist Productions) and music publisher (Cheavoria Music Co.). Estab. 1972. Releases 10 singles and 3 LPs/year. Pays 5% royalty to artists on contract; statutory rate to publishers for each record sold.

   ● Bolivia Records' publishing company, Cheavoria Music, is listed in the Music Publishers section and Known Artist Productions is listed in the Record Producers section.

How to Contact: Submit demo tape by mail. Unsolicited submissions are OK. Prefers cassette with 3 songs and lyric sheet. SASE for reply. All tapes will be kept on file. Responds in 1 month.
Music: Mostly **R&B**, **country** and **pop**; also **easy listening**, **MOR** and **soul**. Released "If You Only Knew" (single by Horace Linsky), recorded by Roy Edwards; "Make Me Forget" (single by Horace Linsky), recorded by Bobbie Roberson, both on Bolivia Records; and "We Make Our Reality" (single), written and recorded by Brad Smiley on Known Artist Records. Other artists include Jim Portwood.

BRENTWOOD RECORDS/DIADEM RECORDS, 741 Cool Springs Blvd., Franklin TN 37067. (615)261-6500. Fax: (615)261-5903. Website: providentmusic.com. Director of A&R: Ed Kee (Christian concept, instrumental). Co-Vice President/General Manager: Dean Diehl (A/C, Christian). Labels include Brentwood Jazz, Diadem Records and Brentwood Kids Company. Record company and music publisher (Brentwood-Benson Publishing). Estab. 1981. Staff size: 9. Releases 18 CDs/year. Pays statutory rate to publisher per song on record "except when negotiated otherwise."
Distributed by: Provident Music Distribution and BMG.
● Music released by Brentwood Records has been certified Gold by the RIAA; and won the Gospel Music Association's Dove Award.
How to Contact: *Does not accept unsolicited material.*
Music: Mostly **Christian praise and worship**, **A/C** and **inspirational**; also **concept-driven projects**. Does not want country, rap, reggae, dance, hip-hop, etc. Released *Acoustic Worship & Acoustic Hymns Series* (album), (praise and worship), released 2000 on Brentwood Records; *Big Songs for Little Kids* (album), (children's), released 2000 on Brentwood Records; and *Glad Voices of Christmas* (album by Glad), (A/C and pop), recorded 2000 on Diadem Records.

BROKEN NOTE RECORDS, 3925 Pierce St., #531, Riverside CA 92505. (909)343-4196. **Contact:** Tony Avitia, A&R. Record company. Estab. 1993. Staff size: 3. Releases 4 singles, 6 LPs and 6 CDs/year. Pays negotiable royalty to artists on contract; statutory rate to publisher per song on record.
Distributed by: Southwest and Crystal Clear.
● Awarded 1999 Best Local Label by Houston Press
How to Contact: Submit demo tape by mail. Unsolicited submissions are OK. Prefers cassette, CD or VHS videocassette with lyric sheet, cover letter and press clippings. Does not return materials. Responds in 2 months if interested.
Music: Mostly **heavy rock**, **rap** and **techno-rock**; also **surf-instrumental**, **hip hop** and **folk**. Released *The Sultry Sounds of Collision* (album), written and recorded by Cult Ceavers (jazzcore); *The Regal Beagle* (album), written and recorded by I-45 (rap); and *Pogo Au-go-go* (album), written and recorded by Bickley (punk), all on Broken Note.
Tips: "Be persistent."

BROKEN RECORDS INTERNATIONAL, 940 S. Grace St., Lombard IL 60148. Phone/fax: (630)693-0719. E-mail: roy@mcguitar.com. Website: www.mcguitar.com/BrokenRecords.htm. International A&R: Roy Bocchieri. Vice President: Jeff Murphy. Record company. Estab. 1984. Payment negotiable.
How to Contact: Write first and obtain permission to submit. Prefers cassette or CD with at least 2 songs and lyric sheet. Does not return material. Responds in 2 months.
Music: Mostly **rock**, **pop** and **dance**; also **acoustic** and **industrial**. Released *Figurehead* (album by LeRoy Bocchieri), recorded by Day One (pop/alternative); and *Eitherway* (album by Jeff Murphy/Herb Eimerman), recorded by The Nerk Twins (pop/alternative), both on Broken Records.

BSW RECORDS, P.O. Box 2297, Universal City TX 78148. (210)599-0022. Fax: (210)653-3989. E-mail: bswr18@txdirect.net. Website: www.bswrecords.com. President: Frank Willson. Vice Presidents: Verdi Williams (pop); Frank Weatherly (country, jazz); Regina Willson (blues). Record company, music publisher (BSW Records/BMI), management firm (Universal Music Marketing) and record producer (Frank Willson). Estab. 1987. Staff size: 3. Releases 18 albums/year. Pays standard royalty to artists on contract; statutory rate to publisher per song on record.

How to Contact: Submit demo tape by mail. Unsolicited submissions are OK. Prefers cassette (or ¾″ videocassette) with 3 songs and lyric sheet. SASE. Responds in 6 weeks.
Music: Mostly **country**, **rock** and **blues**. Released *Follow the Roses* (album), written and recorded by Larry Butler; *Slow Dance* (album by Joseph Mast), recorded by Paul Carter; and *I'll Get All the Sleep I Need When I Die* (album), written and recorded by Curtis Wayne, all on BSW Records (country). Other artists include Peter Coulton, Candee Land, Vince Hopkins, Shawn DeLorme, Buddy Hodges, Kenny Post, Davis Bueschler and Celeste.

● C.P.R., 4 West St., Massapequa Park NY 11762. Phone/fax: (516)797-7752. **Contact:** Denise Yannacone, A&R. Record company. Estab. 1997. Pays negotiable royalty to artists on contract; statutory rate to publisher per song on record.
How to Contact: Submit demo tape by mail. Unsolicited submissions are OK. Prefers cassette, CD or DAT with 4 songs and lyric sheet. Does not return material. Responds in 3 months.
Music: Mostly **uptempos**, **R&B**, **rap**, **rock**, **pop** and **soundtrack**.
Tips: "Keep in mind the sky's the limit. Remember when you feel like quitting, there are no short cuts to success. So please submit songs that are well produced."

● CAMBRIA RECORDS & PUBLISHING, P.O. Box 374, Lomita CA 90717. (310)831-1322. Fax: (310)833-7442. E-mail: cambruamus@aol.com. **Contact:** Lance Bowling, director of recording operations. Labels include Charade Records. Record company and music publisher. Estab. 1979. Staff size: 3. Pays 5-8% royalty to artists on contract; statutory rate to publisher for each record sold.
Distributed by: Albany Distribution.
How to Contact: *Write first and obtain permission to submit.* Prefers cassette. SASE. Responds in 1 month.
Music: Mostly **classical**. Released *Songs of Elinor Remick Warren* (album) on Cambria Records. Other artists include Marie Gibson (soprano), Leonard Pennario (piano), Thomas Hampson (voice), Mischa Leftkowitz (violin), Leigh Kaplan (piano), North Wind Quintet and Sierra Wind Quintet.

N ● CANDYSPITEFUL PRODUCTIONS, 4202 Co. Rt. 4, Oswego NY 13126. (315)342-3129. E-mail: WilliamF@northnet.org. Website: www.candyspiteful.com. President: William Ferraro. Professional Managers: Lori Wall (all styles), Maxwell Frye (jazz, rock). Record company, music publisher (Candyspiteful Productions), record producer (Candyspiteful Productions). Estab. 2000. Staff size: 3. Produces 6 singles, 2 albums per year. Pays negotiable royalty to artists; statutory to publisher per song on record.
How to Contact: Submit demo tape by mail. Unsolicited submissions are OK. Prefers CD/CDR with 3 songs, lyric sheet and cover letter. "Please include a fact sheet, bio, current play dates, etc." Does not return material. Responds only if interested.
Music: Mostly **progressive rock**, **rock/pop/R&B** and **smooth jazz/rock**. Produced "Endless Night" (single by Maxwell Frye) from *Mandrake*, recorded by Mandrake (rock), released 2001 on Candyspiteful Productions.

✔ ● CANTILENA RECORDS, 6548 Via Sereno, Rancho Murieta CA 95683-9226. (916)354-8651. E-mail: llzz@aol.com. Website: members.aol.com/ufonia/zucker.html. A&R: Laurel Zucker. A&R: Davis Sapper. Record company. Estab. 1993. Releases 5 CDs/year. Pays Harry Fox standard royalty to artists on contract; statutory rate to publishers per song on record.
How to Contact: *Write first and obtain permission to submit or to arrange personal interview.* Prefers cassette, CD or DAT. Does not return material.
Music: Mostly **classical**. Released *Answer to a Poem* (album by Alec Wilder) (classical); *Kokopeli* (album by Katherine Hoover) (classical); and *Senario Musicale II* (album by David Kingman) (classical), all recorded by Laurel Zucker. Other artists include Tim Gorman, Prairie Prince, Dave Margen, Israel Philharmonic, Erkel Chamber Orchestra, Samuel Magill, Renee Siebert, Robin Sutherland and Gerald Ranch.

✔ ● CAPITOL RECORDS, 1750 N. Vine St., Hollywood CA 90028-5274. (323)462-6252. Fax: (323)469-4542. Website: www.hollywoodandvine.com. Senior Vice President A&R: Perry Watts-

Russell; Vice President of A&R: Steve Schnur; Vice President A&R: Ron Laffite; Associate Director A&R: Holly Hutchinson. New York office: 304 Park Ave. S., 3rd Floor, New York NY 10010. (212)253-3000. Website: www.hollywoodandvine.com. Vice President of A&R: Dave Ayers; A&R: Amy Ingber. Nashville office: 3322 West End Ave., 11th Floor, Nashville TN 37203. (615)269-2000. Vice President of A&R: Larry Willoughby. A&R: Tracy Cox. Labels include Blue Note Records, Grand Royal Records, Pangaea Records, The Right Stuff Records and Capitol Nashville Records. Record company.

Distributed by: EMD.

How to Contact: *Capitol Records does not accept unsolicited submissions.*

Music: Released *Double Live* (album), recorded by Garth Brooks; *Two Teardrops* (album), recorded by Steve Wariner; and *OK Computer* (album), recorded by Radiohead, all on Capitol Records. Other artists include Bonnie Raitt, Robbie Williams and Beastie Boys.

CAPP RECORDS, P.O. Box 150871, San Rafael CA 94915-0871. (415)457-8617. Fax: (415)453-6990. E-mail: submissions@capprecords.com. Website: www.capprecords.com. Publisher/ International Manager: Dominique Toulon (pop, dance, New Age); Creative Manager/A&R: Mark D'Elicio (dance, techno). Vice President/Publisher: Marc Oshry (pop, rock, dance). Music publisher (CAPP Company, BMI) and record company. Member: NARAS, NCSA, Songwriter's Guild of America. Estab. 1993. Publishes 100 songs/year; publishes 25 new songwriters/year. Staff size: 8. Pays standard royalty.

Affiliate(s): Cary August Publishing Co./CAPP Company (BMI).

How to Contact: Submit demo by mail. Unsolicited submissions are OK. Prefers CD, NTSC videocassette or CD-R with 3 songs and cover letter. "E-mail us in advance for submissions, if possible." SASE. Responds in 2 weeks.

Film & TV: Places 20 songs in film and 7 songs in TV/year. Music Supervisors: Dominique Toulon (pop, dance, New Age); Mark D. D'Elicio (dance, techno). Published "Wish You Were Here" (by Cary August/Marc Oshry/Brian Wood/Tom Finch), recorded by Cary August for "Café Froth" TV/ ad; "Indian Dream" and "Song For the Earth," both written and recorded by Steven Buckner in "Deep Encounters."

Music: Mostly **pop**, **dance** and **techno**; also **New Age**. Does not want country. Released "It's Not a Dream" (single by Cary August/André Pessis), recorded by Cary August on CAPP Records (dance).

CAPRICORN RECORDS, 83 Walton St., Atlanta GA 30303. (404)954-6600. Fax: (404)954-6688. Website: www.capri.corn.com. Vice President A&R: G. Scott Waldon. Vice President: Amantha Walden. Record company.

How to Contact: *Write first and obtain permission to submit.*

Music: Released *Fashion Nugget* (album), recorded by Cake; *311* (album), recorded by 311; and *Bombs & Butterflies* (album), recorded by Widespread Panic, all on Capricorn Records. Other artists include Fiji Mariners, Freddy Jones Band and Speaker.

CAPSTAN RECORD PRODUCTION, P.O. Box 211, East Prairie MO 63845. (314)649-2211. Contact: Joe Silver or Tommy Loomas. Labels include Octagon and Capstan Records. Record company, music publisher (Lineage Publishing Co.), management firm (Staircase Promotion) and record producer (Silver-Loomas Productions). Pays 3-5% royalty to artists on contract.

How to Contact: *Write first and obtain permission to submit.* Prefers cassette or VHS videocassette with 2-4 songs and lyric sheet. "Send photo and bio." SASE. Responds in 1 month.

**FOR EXPLANATIONS OF THESE SYMBOLS,
SEE THE INSIDE FRONT AND BACK COVERS OF THIS BOOK.**

Music: Mostly **country, easy listening, MOR, country rock** and **top 40/pop**. Released "Country Boy" (single by Alden Lambert); and "Yesterday's Teardrops" and "Round & Round" (single), written and recorded by The Burchetts. Other artists include Bobby Lee Morgan, Skidrow Joe, Vicarie Arcole, Fleming and Scarlett Britoni.

☑ ◯ **CELLAR RECORDS**, 703 N. Brinton Ave., Dixon IL 61021. (815)288-2900. E-mail: tjoos @essex1.com. Website: www.cellarrecords.net. **Contact:** Todd Joos, president (rock, pop, country). Vice President (rock): Bob Brady. Vice President Sales and Marketing: Albert Hurst. A&R: Mike Thompson (metal); Jim Miller (adult contemporary, pop, country); Mark Summers. Record company, music publisher (Sound Cellar Music/BMI) and record producer (Todd Joos). Estab. 1987. Staff size: 7. Releases 6-8 CDs/year. Pays 15-100% royalty to artists on contract; statutory rate to publisher per song on record. Charges in advance "if you use our studio to record."
Distributed by: V&R Distribution, Valley One Stop, Amazon.com and cdnow.com.
How to Contact: Submit demo tape by mail. Unsolicited submissions are OK. Prefers CD with 3-4 songs and lyric sheet. Does not return material. Responds in 1 month only if interested. "If we like it we will call you."
Music: Mostly **metal, country** and **rock**; also **pop** and **blues**. "No rap." Released "Interesting Life" (single by Hylton Valentine/John Steele) from *Interesting Life* (album), recorded by The Animals (rock/classic), released 2000 on A2/Cellar Records; "Problem of Pain" (single by Sharie Sowers) from *Before the Machine* (album), recorded by Junker Jorg (alternative metal), released 2000 on Cellar Records; and "Vaya Baby" (single by Joel Ramirez) from *It's About Time* (album), recorded by Joel Ramirez and the All-Stars (latin/R&B), released 2000 on Cellar Records. Other artists include Eric Topper, Jim Miller, Snap Judgment, Ballistic, Dago Red, Sea of Monsters, Twist of Fate, Rogue, Fusion, Famous Nobodies, Kings, 11¢ Junk, James Miller, Vehement and Noopy Wilson.
Tips: "Make sure that you understand that your band is business and you must be willing to self invest time, effort and money just like any other new business. We can help you but you must also be willing to help yourself."

◯ **CHATTAHOOCHEE RECORDS**, 2544 Roscomare Rd., Los Angeles CA 90077. (818)788-6863. Fax: (310)471-2089. **Contact:** Chris Yardum. Music Director: Robyn Meyers. Record company and music publisher (Etnoc/Conte). Member NARAS. Releases 4 singles/year. Pays negotiable royalty to artists on contract.
How to Contact: Submit demo tape by mail. Unsolicited submissions are OK. Prefers cassette with 2-6 songs and lyric sheet. Does not return material. Responds in 2 months only if interested.
Music: Mostly **rock**. Released *Don't Touch It Let It Drip* (album), recorded by Cream House (hard rock), released 2000 on Chattahoochee Records. Artists include DNA.

🅽 ◯ **CHERRY STREET RECORDS**, P.O. Box 52681, Tulsa OK 74152. (918)742-8087. E-mail: ryoung@cherrystreetmusic.com. Website: www.cherrystreetrecords.com. President: Rodney Young. Vice President: Steve Hickerson. Record company and music publisher. Estab. 1990. Staff size: 2. Releases 2 CD/year. Pays 50% royalty to artists on contract; statutory rate to publisher per song on record.
Distributed by: Internet.
How to Contact: Write first and obtain permission to submit. Prefers cassette or videocassette with 4 songs and lyric sheet. SASE. Responds in 4 months.
Music: **Rock, country** and **R&B**; also **jazz**. Released *Promise Land* (album), written and recorded by Richard Neville on Cherry Street (rock). Other artists include George W. Carroll and Chris Blevins.
Tips: "We sign only artists who play an instrument, sing and write songs. Send only your best four songs."

☑ ◯ **CHIAROSCURO RECORDS**, 830 Broadway, New York NY 10003. (212)473-0479. Fax: (849)279-5025. E-mail: jon@chiaroscurojazz.com. Website: www.ChiaroscuroJazz.com. **Contact:** Jon Bates, A&R. Labels include Downtown Sound. Record company and record producer (Hank O'Neal, Andrew Sordoni, Jon Bates). Estab. 1973. Releases 12 CDs/year. Pays negotiable royalty to artists on contract; statutory rate to publisher per song on record.

Distributed by: D.N.A. and Bayside.

How to Contact: Submit demo tape by mail. Unsolicited submissions are OK. Prefers cassette, CD, DAT or videocassette with 1-3 songs. SASE. Responds in 6 weeks.

Music: Mostly **jazz** and **blues**. "A full catalog listing is available on the web at www.chiarascurojazz. com or by calling (800)528-2582. New releases scheduled for 2001 include Jade Wilkins with the Brecker Brothers, Bill Charlap with Phil Woods, and a new Clark Terry CD."

Tips: "We are not a pop label. Our average release sells between 3,000-5,000 copies in the first three years. We do not give cash advances or tour support, and our average budget per release is about $15,000 including all production, printing and manufacturing costs."

☑ ◑ **CKB RECORDS/HELAPHAT ENTERTAINMENT**, 1908 Estrada Pkwy., Apt. 231, Irving TX 75061-1105. (972)870-1720. Fax: (972)243-7749. E-mail: spoonfedmusik@juno.com. **Contact:** Tony Briggs, A&R director. Record company and record producer (Tony Briggs). Estab. 1999. Staff size: 6. Pays negotiable royalty to artists on contract.

Distributed by: Southwest Distributing.

How to Contact: Submit demo tape by mail. Unsolicited submissions are OK. Prefers cassette, CD or DAT with 4 songs, cover letter and press clippings. Does not return materials. Responds only if interested.

Music: Mostly **rap**, **R&B** and **pop**; also **country**, **jazz** and **adult contemporary**. Artists include Tha 40oz Clique, T-Spoon, Baby Boo and Laticia Love.

Tips: "Be confident, honest and open to ideas."

☑ ◑ **CLEOPATRA RECORDS**, 13428 Maxella Ave., PMB 251, Marina del Rey CA 90292. (310)823-0337. Fax: (310)823-5497. **Contact:** Timothy Dooner or Jason Myers. Labels include Hypnotic, Deadline, X-Ray, Cult, Stardust and Purple Pyramid. Record company. Estab. 1991. Releases 5 singles, 10 LPs, 5 EPs and 100 CDs/year. Pays 10-14% royalty to artists on contract; negotiable rate to publisher per song on record.

How to Contact: Submit demo tape by mail. Unsolicited submissions are OK. Prefers CD with 3 songs. Does not return material. Responds in 1 month.

Music: Mostly **industrial**, **gothic** and **trance**; also **heavy metal**, **space rock** and **electronic**.

⊕ ☑ ◖ **COLLECTOR RECORDS**, P.O. Box 1200, 3260 AE oud beyerland Holland. Phone: (31)186 604266. Fax: (31)186 604366. E-mail: cees@collectorrec.com. Website: www.collectorrec.c om. **Contact:** Cees Klop, president. Manager: John Moore. Labels include All Rock, Downsouth, Unknown, Pro Forma and White Label Records. Record company, music publisher (All Rock Music Publishing) and record producer (Cees Klop). Estab. 1967. Staff size: 4. Release 25 LPs/year. Pays 10% royalty to artist on contract.

How to Contact: Submit demo tape by mail. Unsolicited submissions are OK. Prefers cassette. SAE and IRC. Responds in 2 months.

Music: Mostly **'50s rock**, **rockabilly**, **hillbilly boogie** and **country/rock**; also **piano boogie woogie**. Released "Mind Your Own Business" (single by Williams) from *High Steppin' Daddy* (album), recorded by Evelyn White ('50s rock); "Tuesday Shuffle" (single) from *Boogie Woogie Special* (album), written and recorded by André Valkering (piano boogie); and "Bingo Boogie" (single by R. Turner) from *High Steppin' Daddy* (album), recorded by Tommy Mooney ('50s hillbilly), all released 2000 on Collector Records. Other artists include Teddy Redell and Henk Pepping.

◑ **COLUMBIA RECORDS**, 550 Madison Ave., 24th Floor, New York NY 10022-3211. (212)833-4000. Fax: (212)833-4389. Senior Vice President A&R: Mitchell Cohen; Senior Vice President A&R: Don Devito; Vice President A&R: Kevin Patrick. Santa Monica office: 2100 Colorado Ave., Santa Monica CA 90404. (310)449-2100. Fax: (310)449-2743. Senior Vice President A&R: John David Kalodner; Senior Vice President A&R: Tim Devine; Manager A&R: Barry Squire. Nashville office: 34 Music Square E., Nashville TN 37203. (615)742-4321. Fax: (615)244-2549. E-mail: sonymusiconl ine@sonymusic.com. Website: www.sony.com/Music/Columbia. Labels include So So Def Records and Ruffhouse Records. Record company.

Distributed by: Sony.

insider report

Smooth jazz artist finds an audience—and some money!— on the Internet

When you hear the words "downloadable music on the Internet," the first thing that most likely pops into your head is the ongoing debate about artists' rights and websites such as Napster. But while the mainstream record industry struggles with the Internet, there is a growing group of artists who aren't waiting for the outcome and who are actually making money by putting their music in cyberspace. One such artist is smooth jazz musician Randy Thorderson.

Randy Thorderson

Thorderson wasn't looking for fame and fortune in the music business, but simply an outlet for the music he was making. "I believe many musicians have no choice but to create music or they personally short-circuit," he says. "I spent many years as a full-time professional musician, but it takes a great deal of discipline. I made plenty of money, just not with any consistency." After stints as a studio engineer, producer and arranger to pay the bills, he ended up working for an audio equipment manufacturer, which offered him a rewarding job with benefits and a steady paycheck. He gave up on music, but was pulled back into it after attending the Catalina JazzTrax Festival. "I returned home anxious to compose and create again," he says. "I began working on *Smile for Me*, my first full-length CD, a few months after returning, without any clue as what to do with the finished product. There was no record deal pending, so I figured I would press a few copies and give them to family and friends." Thorderson was looking for ways to promote his CD when he stumbled across MP3.com, the website that allows artists to make their music available for downloading online.

To date, Thorderson has made nearly $10,000 through MP3.com. For every CD sold through the site, he splits the $10 sale price with MP3.com, making $5 per CD. But the real money comes through the downloads and the revenue-sharing program MP3.com implemented, called Pay-for-Play. "I realized that the rules had changed," Thorderson says. "It wasn't about selling CDs. It was about people listening to your music online. Coming from the old school of music sales, I was very concerned that making my music available for free downloading might hurt my CD sales. But MP3.com has a program that seems so fair, it can't possibly be true. MP3.com makes much of their money from online advertising. They actually thought that since it was the artist's music that brought listeners to the MP3.com pages, the artist should share the advertising revenues. My songs climbed the MP3.com music charts and more and more people listened in. Meanwhile, the money just kept trickling steadily in. I was amazed—people were actually listening to my music!"

"In my mind, MP3.com runs two businesses," he says, "one that distributes mainstream music—music you buy in the store—and another that offers something completely different, a distribution method that eliminates the record company and the distribution company. The MP3.com store takes its cut, but the rest goes to the artist."

According to Thorderson, one of the benefits of MP3.com is that there are no startup costs for the artist; the CD itself is not produced until the CD is sold. "There is never an unsold CD sitting on a shelf somewhere, nor is there a need to invest in thousands of CDs to get started," Thorderson explains. "I finished the music in May 2000 and uploaded the music files and CD artwork to MP3.com. The CD was ready to sell in about a week's time. MP3.com provided me with a personal web page (www.mp3.com/randyt) that I could customize and my CD appeared there, ready to sell. Also, I was able to make any songs from the CD available for free listening online. And I had not paid MP3.com a penny."In addition to featuring his music on MP3.com, Thorderson also created his own site (www.thorderson.com) and continued promoting himself through an electronic mailing list. "I mainly tickle my e-mail list now and then and keep my site active with new info," he says. "I designed my main site to be helpful to other artists trying to make their music work. I take personal joy in seeing other musicians succeed in their early efforts. So I put tons of how-to's and recording tips on the site hoping that would attract an additional base of loyal fans."

With a background in producing, Thorderson has seen the toll that waiting for that "big deal" can take on his fellow artists. "I have produced/arranged dozens of CD projects for new artists hoping to hit it big," he says, "but I always felt bad because I knew that if they didn't find a distribution method, they were done before they even started." And with MP3.com, Thorderson found a way to promote his music without relying on a recording or distribution company to do it for him. "MP3.com answers that need perfectly," he says. "If an artist isn't able to find a way to be successful in the MP3.com world, they need to 1) revamp their product, 2) improve their skills, or 3) find a new career path. It is the perfect testing ground . . . all at no cost to the artist! There have even been artists signed to record deals right out of the MP3.com pool."

Thorderson is thrilled with the success he's found on the Internet, and is amazed at the number of people who have been exposed to his music. "My music has been downloaded over 150,000 times in a period of about 6 months," he says. "I sell CDs all over the world. I have a few musician friends with record deals who were not too happy with my success. They did the math and realized it was probable that more people had listened to my music in six months than they had fans in their entire career. Without MP3.com, I would still have a music project looking for a label. My situation is such that I don't know what I would do with a record deal anyway. I have a wonderfully steady and fulfilling job that keeps the family happy. Stability is a good thing for some musicians . . . and I am no exception. I have found a way to create, distribute and actually make a little money with my musical efforts. I had hoped that was possible but never allowed myself to actually believe it could be."

"MP3.com makes earning a living with music a little more possible," Thorderson continues. "I remember the days of playing bars, clubs and weddings, but my personal music wasn't earning a dime. Today, a working musician can do both . . . and possibly even make a decent living. Even though I have years of professional music experience, I still feel like an aspiring rookie songwriter/artist. I am so excited to be able to make music and have people actually enjoy it. I get e-mails from people all over who took the time to say they enjoyed my work. That is so incredibly fulfilling—I just wish I had discovered all this earlier!"

MP3.com has not only helped Thorderson find an audience; it's also helped him meet other musicians who love jazz as much as he does. "I was picked up by a couple of smooth jazz artists, Sam Cardon and Michael Dowdle, to help in their respective bands," he says. "I was able to return to Catalina the next year and play on the main stage with them . . . the same stage that inspired *Smile for Me* in the first place. I still dream of being able to play my own material at some jazz or folk festivals in the future. But above all, I feel balanced right now, which is where I want to stay. I just love making music and having people listen in, and making a little money with the music is quite nice too!"

—*Cynthia Laufenberg*

How to Contact: Columbia Records does not accept unsolicited submissions.
Music: Released *The Writing's on the Wall* (album), recorded by Destiny's Child; *Marc Anthony* (album), recorded by Marc Anthony; *Affirmation* (album), recorded by Savage Garden; *J.E. Heartbreak* (album), recorded by Jagged Edge; *Ricky Martin* (album), recorded by Ricky Martin; and *Rainbow* (album), recorded by Mariah Carey, all on Columbia Records. Other artists include Aerosmith and Bob Dylan.

N ◯ COM-FOUR DISTRIBUTION, 7 Dunham Place, Brooklyn NY 11211. (718)599-2205. Distribution Manager: Albert Garzon. Distribution company. Estab. 1985. Distributes over 100,000 different titles including imports.
How to Contact: "Please visit our website for submission information."
Music: All genres.
Tips: "Be original and have some talent. Be willing and ready to work hard touring, promoting, etc."

✓ ◻ ◯ COMSTOCK RECORDS LTD., P.O. Box 19720, Fountain Hills AZ 85269. (480)951-3115. Fax: (480)951-3074. Production Manager/Producer: Patty Parker. President: Frank Fara. Record company, music publisher (White Cat Music/ASCAP, Rocky Bell Music/BMI, How the West Was Sung Music/BMI), record producer (Patty Parker) and radio promotion. Member CMA, BBB, CCMA, BCCMA, British CMA and AF of M. "Comstock Records, Ltd. has three primary divisions: Production, Promotion and Publishing. We distribute and promote both our own Nashville productions, as well as already completed country or pop/rock CDs. We also offer CD design and mastering and

manufacturing for products we promote. We can master from a copy of your DAT master or CD."
Staff size: 2. Releases 15-20 CD singles, 10-12 albums/year and 5-6 international sampler CDs. Pays
10% royalty to artists on contract; statutory rate to publishers for each record sold. "Artists pay
distribution and promotion fee to press and release their masters."

- Comstock Records was named indie Label of the Year at ECMA of Europe's Country Music
  Awards for 1998 and 1999. Fara & Parker are also authors of the book *How To Open Doors
  in the Music Industry—The Independent Way* (available through amazon.com).

How to Contact: Submit demo tape by mail. Unsolicited submissions are OK. Prefers CD or
cassette. SASE. "Enclose stamped return envelope if demo is to be returned." Responds in 2 weeks.
Music: Released "The Shoulder You Cry On" (single by Frank M. Pahl), recorded by Beth Hogan
(country), released 2001; "Giving and Losing" (single), written and recorded by R.J. McClintock
and Lorena Prater (traditional country), released 2000; and "Good Morning Sunshine" (single by
Suzy Kim/Tomi Fujiyama), recorded by Tomi Fujiyama (traditional country), released 2000, all on
Comstock Records. Other artists include Derek Carle, John Hargett, Maria Carmin, McNasty Brothers.
Tips: "Go global—good songs and good singers are universal. Country acts from North America
will find a great response in the overseas radio market. Likewise U.S. Radio is open to the fresh new
sounds that foreign artists bring to the airwaves."

N □ CORAL RECORDS LLC, 318 Acacia Ave., Suite A, Carlsbad CA 92008. (760)434-0815.
E-mail: coral@richardsamuels.com. Website: www.coralrecords.com. President: Richard Samuels.
Personal Management: Mike Davies. Record company, music publisher (R. Samuels Publishing).
Estab. 1993. Record producers available for hire.
How to Contact: Submit demo tape by mail. Unsolicited submissions are OK. Prefers CD/CDR
or cassette. "Make sure to include typed lyric sheet."
Music: Mostly *pop*, *country*, *R&B* and *rock*.
Tips: "We are looking for well-crafted songs with 'single' potential."

⊘ COSMOTONE RECORDS, PMB 412, 3350-A Highway 6 S., Sugar Land TX 77478. E-
mail: marianland@earthlink.net. Website: www.marianland.com/music.html. Record company, music
publisher (Cosmotone Music, ASCAP) and record producer (Rafael Brom). Estab. 1984.
Distributed by: marianland.com.
How to Contact: "We do not accept material at this time." Does not return materials.
Music: All types.

□ CREATIVE IMPROVISED MUSIC PROJECTS (CIMP) RECORDS, Cadence Building,
Redwood NY 13679. (315)287-2852. Fax: (315)287-2860. Website: www.cadencebuilding.com.
Contact: Bob Rusch, producer. Labels include Cadence Jazz Records. Record company and record
producer (Robert D. Rusch). Estab. 1980. Releases 25-30 CDs/year. Pays negotiable royalty to artists
on contract; pays statutory rate to publisher per song on record.
Distributed by: North Country Distributors.
- CIMP specializes in jazz and creative improvised music.
How to Contact: Submit demo tape by mail. Unsolicited submissions are OK. Prefers cassette or
CD. "We are not looking for songwriters but recording artists." SASE. Responds in 1 week.
Music: Mostly **jazz** and **creative improvised music**. Released *Mark 'N' Marshall* (album), recorded
by Marshall Allen; and *Tag* (album), recorded by Yukofujiyama, both on CIMP (improvised jazz).
Other artists include Arthur Blyme, John McPhee & David Prentice, Anthony Braxton and Roswell
Rudd.
Tips: "CIMP Records are produced to provide music to reward repeated and in-depth listenings.
They are recorded live to two-track which captures the full dynamic range one would experience in

TO HELP YOU UNDERSTAND and use the information in these listings, see "How
to Use *Songwriter's Market* to Get Your Songs Heard," on page 5.

a live concert. There is no compression, homogenization, eq-ing, post-recording splicing, mixing, or electronic fiddling with the performance. Digital recording allows for a vanishingly low noise floor and tremendous dynamic range. This compression of the dynamic range is what limits the 'air' and life of many recordings. Our recordings capture the dynamic intended by the musicians. In this regard these recordings are demanding. Treat the recording as your private concert. Give it your undivided attention and it will reward you. CIMP Records are not intended to be background music. This method is demanding not only on the listener but on the performer as well. Musicians must be able to play together in real time. They must understand the dynamics of their instrument and how it relates to the others around them. There is no fix-it-in-the-mix safety; either it works or it doesn't. What you hear is exactly what was played. Our main concern is music not marketing."

✔ ◎ **CURB RECORDS**, 47 Music Square E., Nashville TN 37203. (615)321-5080. Fax: (615)327-1964. Website: www.curb.com. **Contact:** Michelle Metzgar, director A&R. Record company.
How to Contact: Curb Records does not accept unsolicited submissions; accepts previously published material only. *Do not submit without permission.*
Music: Released *Everywhere* (album), recorded by Tim McGraw; *Sittin' On Top of the World* (album), recorded by LeAnn Rimes; and *I'm Alright* (album), recorded by Jo Dee Messina, all on Curb Records. Other artists include Mary Black, Bananarama, Junior Brown, Merle Haggard, Kal Ketchum, David Kersh, Lyle Lovett, Tim McGraw, Wynonna and Sawyer Brown.

Ⓝ ◯ **DAGENE/CABLETOWN COMPANY**, P.O. Box 410851, San Francisco CA 94141. (415)822-1530. President: David Alston. Record company, music publisher (Dagene Music), management firm (Golden City International) and record producer (David-Classic Disc Productions). Estab. 1993. Pays standard royalty to artists on contract; statutory rate to publisher per song on record.
How to Contact: Write or call first and obtain permission to submit. Prefers cassette (or VHS videocassette) with 2 songs and lyric sheet. SASE. Responds in 1 month.
Music: Mostly **R&B/rap**, **dance** and **pop**; also **gospel**. Released "Maxin" (single by Marcus Justice/Bernard Henderson), recorded by 2 Dominatorz on Dagene Records; "To Know You Better" (single by David Alston), recorded by Rare Essence on Cabletown Records; and "High On You" (single), written and recorded by David Alston on E-lect-ric Recordings. Other artists include Chapter 1.

✔ ◯ **ALAN DALE PRODUCTIONS**, 1630 Judith Lane, Indianapolis IN 46227. (317)786-1630. E-mail: AlanDale22@aol.com. **Contact:** Alan D. Heshelman, president. Labels include ALTO Records. Record company. Estab. 1990. Pays 10% royalty to artists on contract.
How to Contact: *Write or call first and obtain permission to submit* or to arrange personal interview. Prefers cassette with 3 songs. Does not return material. Responds in 10 weeks.
Music: Mostly A/C, **country**, **jazz**, **gospel** and **New Age**.
Tips: "At the present time, we are only looking for vocalists to promote as we promote the songs we write and produce."

◎ **DAPMOR RECORDS**, 3031 Acorn St., Kenner LA 70065. (504)468-9820. Fax: (504)466-2896. **Contact:** Kelly Jones, president. Record company and music publisher (Dapmor Music). Estab. 1996.
How to Contact: "Submit professionally done CDs through an attorney or another publisher."
Music: Mostly **R&B**, **jazz** and **country**; also **blues**, **rap**, **reggae** and **rock**.
Tips: "Learn to accept rejection and keep trying."

✔ ◯ **DEADEYE RECORDS**, P.O. Box 2607, Capistrano Beach CA 92624. (714)768-0644. E-mail: deadeye@deadeye.com. Website: www.deadeyerecords.com. **Contact:** James Frank, A&R. Record company, record producer and management firm (Danny Federici's Shark River Music). Estab. 1992. Staff size: 2. Releases 3 CDs/year. Pays varying royalty to artists on contract; statutory rate to publisher per song on record.
How to Contact: *Write or e-mail first and obtain permission to submit.* Prefers cassette or videocassette with 3 songs and lyric sheet. Does not return material. Responds in 3 months.

Music: Mostly **country**, **rock** and **blues**. Released *Ragin' Wind* (album by Frank Jenkins), recorded by Diamondback on Deadeye Records (country); and *Flemington*, (album) recorded by Danny Federici (of the E Street Band).

☑ ◖ **DEARY ME RECORDS**, P.O. Box 19315, Cincinnati OH 45219. (513)557-2930. E-mail: dearyme@one.net. Website: www.dearymerecords.com. **Contact:** Jim Farmer, director of business & A&R. Record company. Estab. 1995. Staff size: 2. Releases 1 single and 3 CDs/year. Pays 50% royalty "after we break even."
Distributed by: Redeye Distribution, Valley and AEC.
How to Contact: Unsolicited submissions are OK. "Please check our website for submission policy."
Music: Mostly **indie rock** and **off-beat punk**. Does not want top 40. Released *This Is Our ~ Music* (album by Matt Hart/Darren Callahan), recorded by Travel (off-beat punk), released 2000 on Deary Me Records. Other artists include Chalk and Fairmount Girls.
Tips: "We are typically not impressed with gimmicks, or interested in trends. Be simple and direct. You have to be willing to work your album. You work for us, we will work for you. Touring is a major plus."

◖ **DEEP SOUTH ENTERTAINMENT**, P.O. Box 17737, Raleigh NC 27619-7737. (919)877-0098. Fax: (919)877-9698. E-mail: amy@deepsouthrecords.com. Website: www.deepsouthrecords.com. Director of Artist Relations: Amy Cox. Director of A&R: Steve Williams. Record company and management company. Estab. 1996. Staff size: 7. Pays negotiable royalty to artists on contract; statutory rate to publisher per song on record.
Distributed by: Redeye Distribution, Valley, Select-O-Hits, City Hall, AEC/Bassin, Northeast One Stop, Pollstar and Koch International.
How to Contact: Submit demo tape by mail. Unsolicited submissions are OK. Prefers cassette or CD with 3 songs, cover letter and press clippings. Does not return material. Responds only if interested.
Music: Mostly **pop**, **modern rock** and **alternative**; also **swing**, **rockabilly** and **heavy rock**. Does not want rap or R&B. Released *One Night of Sin Live* (album), recorded by The Belmont Playboys (rockabilly); *White Lies and Cigarettes* (album), recorded by Nickel Slots (aternative country/pop rock); and *Once A Jerk Always A Jerk* (album), recorded by Kamal (formerly of The Jerky Boys), all released on Deep South Records. Other artists include Collapsis, Cigar Store Indians and Radiostar.

◖ **DEL-FI RECORDS, INC.**, 8271 Melrose Ave., Suite 103, Los Angeles CA 90046. (800)993-3534. Fax: (323)966-4805. E-mail: info@del-fi.com. Website: www.del-fi.com. Director of A&R: Bryan Thomas. **Contact:** Bob Keane, owner and president. Labels include Del-Fi, Del-Fi Nashville, Donna, Mustang, Bronco and others. Record company. Estab. 1957. Releases 5-10 LPs and 40 CDs/year. Pays negotiable royalty to artists on contract; statutory rate to publisher per song on record.
Distributed by: Paulstarr Distribution.
  • Del-Fi's open door policy is legendary.
How to Contact: Submit demo tape by mail. Unsolicited submissions are OK. Prefers cassette or CD. "Please enclose bio information and photo if possible. Send a résumé via fax." Does not return material "unless specified. Allow several weeks." Responds in 1 month.
Music: Mostly **rock**, **surf/drag** and **exotica**. Recently released *Out There in the Dark* (album), written and recorded by Outrageous Cherry (rock); and *Cloud Eleven* (album), written and recorded by Cloud Eleven (rock/pop), both released 1999 on Del-Fi. Other artists include The El Caminos.
Tips: "Be sure you are making/writing music that specifically meets your own artistic/creative demands, and not someone else's. Write/play music from the heart and soul and you will always succeed on a personal rewarding level first. We are *the* surf label . . . home of the 'Delphonic' sound. We've also released many of the music world's best known artists, including Ritchie Valens and the Bobby Fuller Four."

☑ ◯ **DISCMEDIA**, 2134 Newport Blvd., Costa Mesa CA 92627. (949)631-8597. Fax: (949)515-7499. E-mail: irma@discmedia.com. Website: www.discmedia.com. **Contact:** Irma Moller, manager. Producers: Glenn Moller (rock, dance) and Henry Moller (pop). Record company, music publisher (Discmedia) and record producer (Moller Digital Studios). Estab. 1989.
How to Contact: Submit demo tape by mail. Unsolicited submissions are OK. Prefers cassette, CD or VHS with 3 songs, lyric sheet and cover letter. "Do not call after submitting." Does not return materials. Responds only if interested.
Music: Mostly **rock**, **pop** and **dance**; also **bilingual Spanish material** (dance, pop-merengue, rock ballads).

◯ **DISCOS FUENTES/MIAMI RECORDS & EDIMUSICA USA**, (formerly Miami Records), % Music Group, 254 W. 54th St., 13th Floor, New York NY 10019. (212)246-3333. E-mail: info@arc music.com. Website: www.arcmusic.com. **Contact:** Juan Carlos Barguil. Vice President: Jorge Fuentes. President: Alejandro Fuentes. Labels include Discos Fuentes. Record company, music publisher (Edimusica-USA). Estab. 1936. Staff size: 14. Releases 13 singles and 89 CDs/year. Pays negotiable royalty to artists on contract; statutory rate to publisher per song on record.
   • Edimusica-USA, Discos Fuentes/Miami Publishing Division entered into an administration deal effective August 18, 2000 with Arc Music Group.
Distributed by: Miami Records.
How to Contact: Submit demo CD/CDR by mail. Unsolicited submissions are OK. Prefers CD/CDR with lyric sheet. Does not return material. Responds only if interested.
Music: Mostly **salsa**, **cumbia** and **vallenato**; also **grupera**, **merengue** and **tropical**. Released *Que Lindo Cu* (album) by Rafael Benitez), recorded by Sonora Dinamita (cumbia); *Mi Libertad* (album by Saulo Sanchez), recorded by Fruko y Sostesos (salsa); and *El Majedro (El Viagra)* (album by Elkin Garcia), recorded by Embajadores Vallenatos (vallenato). Other artists include Sonora Carruseles, The Latin Brothers, Los Chiches Vallenatos, Latinos En La Casa, Chambacu, Pastor Lopez, Grupo Mayoral, Los Titanes and Frank La P & Anthony.
Tips: "Please keep sending us material. Don't give up if we do not use your first demo."

Ⓝ ◯ **DM/BELLMARK/CRITIQUE RECORDS**, (formerly DM Records), 1791 Blount Rd., Suite 712, Pompano Beach FL 33069. (954)969-1623. Fax: (954)969-1997. Website: www.dmrecords .com. President: Mark Watson. Record company, music publisher (Bass Tracks & Ashley Watson Publishing) and record producer (Bass 305). Estab. 1992. Releases 16-20 CDs/year. Pays negotiable royalty to artists on contract; 75% statutory rate to publisher per song on record.
Distributed by: Ryko/WEA.
How to Contact: Submit CD/CDR by mail. Unsolicited submissions are OK. Prefers CD/CDR. Does not return material. Responds in 2 weeks, if interested.
Music: Mostly **southern rap**, **R&B** and **gospel**; also **dance**.

Ⓝ ◯ **DON'T RECORDS**, P.O. Box 11513, Milwaukee WI 53211. (414)224-9023. Fax: (414)224-8021. E-mail: dont@execpc.com. A&R: Bryan Utech. Record company. Estab. 1991. Releases 6 LPs/year. Pays negotiable royalty to artists on contract; statutory rate to publisher per song on record.
How to Contact: Submit demo tape by mail. Unsolicited submissions are OK. Prefers cassette. "Send studio quality material." Does not return material. Responds in 2 months.
Music: Mostly **pop/rock** and **alternative**. Released *Upstroke for Downfolk* (album), written and recorded by Paul Cebar & The Milwaukeeans (pop); *Star of Desire* (album by Scott & Brian Wooldridge), recorded by Wooldridge Brothers (pop); and *Gag Me with Spoon* (album), written and recorded by various (pop), all on Don't Records. Other artists include Pet Engine, Citizen King. The Gufs, Comet 9 and Yell Leaders.
Tips: "Play a lot and be selling your own release when you send us material."

☑ 🎵 ◯ **DREAMWORKS RECORDS**, 9268 W. Third St., Beverly Hills CA 90210. (310)288-7700. Fax: (310)288-7750. Website: www.dreamworksrec.com. A&R: Michael Goldstone. A&R: Beth Halper. Nashville office: 1516 16th Ave. S., Nashville TN 37203. (615)463-4600. Fax: (615)463-

4601. **A&R:** Allison Jones. New York office: 575 Broadway, 6th Floor, New York NY 10012. (212)588-6600. Fax: (212)588-6611. **A&R:** Will Langolf; Tommy Regisford. Record company and music publisher (DreamWorks SKG Music Publishing).

- DreamWorks' John Williams won a 1998 Grammy Award for Best Instrumental Composition Written for a Motion Picture.

How to Contact: Material must be submitted through an agent or attorney. *Does not accept unsolicited submissions.*

Music: Released *Forces of Nature* (album soundtrack); *XO* (album), recorded by Elliott Smith; and *The Sound of Wet Paint* (album), recorded by Forest for the Trees, all on DreamWorks Records.

✓◻ DROOL RECORDS, 8306 Wilshire Blvd., #645, Beverly Hills CA 90211. (310)652-1744. Fax: (310)652-1744. E-mail: droolrecords@earthlink.net. **President:** Kenny Kerner. **CEO:** Boi. Record company and record producer (Boi). Estab. 1998. Staff size: 4. Releases 3 LPs and 3 CDs/year. Pays negotiable royalty to artists on contract.

Distributed by: City Hall.

How to Contact: Submit demo tape by mail. Unsolicited submissions are OK. Prefers cassette or CD with cover letter. Does not return materials. Responds only if interested.

Music: Mostly **pop**, **glam** and **alternative**; also **electronica**. Does not want jazz, new age or classical. Released *Nipples* (album), recorded by Cartoon Boyfriend (pop), released 2000 on Drool Records; and "The End of the World" (single by Joey Rosa/Boi), recorded by Joey Rosa (alternative), released 2000 on Drool Records.

Tips: "Send in CD with cover letter and be patient."

◑ DRUMBEAT INDIAN ARTS, INC., 4143 N. 16th St., Suite 1, Phoenix AZ 85016. (602)266-4823. **Contact:** Bob Nuss, president. Labels include Indian House and Sweet Grass. Record company and distributor of American Indian recordings. Estab. 1984. Staff size: 8. Releases 50 cassettes and 50 CDs/year. Royalty varies with project.

- Note that Drumbeat Indian Arts is a very specialized label, and only wants to receive submissions by Native American artists.

How to Contact: *Call first and obtain permission to submit.* Prefers cassette or VHS videocassette. SASE. Responds in 2 months.

Music: Music by American Indians—any style (must be enrolled tribal members). Does not want New Age "Indian style" material. Released *Pearl Moon* (album), written and recorded by Xavier (native Amerindian), released 2000 on Sweet Grass. Other artists include Black Lodge Singers, R. Carlos Nakai, Lite Foot, Kashtin and Joanne Shenandoah.

Tips: "We deal only with American Indian performers. We do not accept material from others. Please include tribal affiliation."

◑ DWELL RECORDS, P.O. Box 39439, Los Angeles CA 90039. Fax: (323)669-1470. Website: www.dwellrecords.com. **Label Managers:** Rex Quick. Record company. Estab. 1991. Staff size: 11. Releases 15 CDs/year.

Distributed by: DNA, Navarre, Handleman, BMG and Columbia House.

How to Contact: Submit demo tape by mail. Unsolicited submissions are OK. Prefers CD, bio and photo with press clippings. Does not return materials. Responds only if interested.

Music: Mostly **extreme heavy music**. Released *Procession to the Infraworld* (album), written and recorded by The Chasm (dark metal); and *Gods of Creation, Death, and Afterlife* (album).

Tips: "Submit quality music."

◼ ◻ EDMONDS RECORD GROUP, (formerly Yab Yum Records), 1635 N. Cahenga Blvd., 6th Floor, Los Angeles CA 90028. (323)860-1520. Fax: (323)860-1537. Record company.

Distributed by: Elektra Entertainment.

How to Contact: Submit demo tape by mail. Unsolicited submissions are OK. Any format accepted.

✓◎ ELEKTRA RECORDS, (formerly Elektra Entertainment Group), 345 N. Maple Dr., Suite 123, Beverly Hills CA 90210. (310)288-3800. Fax: (310)246-0347. Website: www.elektra.com. Vice

President A&R: Jerry Brown. Director of A&R: John Kirkpatrick. New York office: 75 Rockefeller Plaza, 17th Floor, New York NY 10019. (212)275-4000. Fax: (212)581-4650. Website: www.elektra.com. Director of A&R: Leigh Lust. Labels include Elektra Records, Eastwest Records and Asylum Records. Record company.
Distributed by: WEA.
How to Contact: *Elektra does not accept unsolicited submissions.*
Music: Mostly **alternative/modern rock**. Released *Reload*, recorded by Metallica; *Ophelia*, recorded by Natalie Merchant; and *When Disaster Strikes*, recorded by Busta Rhymes, all on Elektra Entertainment. Other artists include Tracy Chapman, Bryan White, Phish, Björk, Spacehog, Pantera, The Cure, Silk and Natalie Cole.

EMERALD CITY RECORDS, 2426 Auburn Ave., Dayton OH 45406-1928. Phone/fax: (937)275-4221. President: Jack Froschauer. Record company and publishing company (Barren Wood Publishing). Estab. 1992. Staff size: 1. Pays negotiable royalty to artists on contract; statutory rate to publisher per song on record.
Distributed by: Rotation Record Distributors, Dream Machine Entertainment and GEM.
How to Contact: Submit demo tape by mail. Unsolicited submissions are OK. Prefers cassette or CD with 1-4 songs and lyric or lead sheet. "If sending cassette, studio quality please." SASE. Responds in 3 months.
Music: Mostly **A/C**, **country** and **contemporary Christian**. Released *Relish* (album by D. Walton), recorded by My 3 Sons (rock), released 2000 on Emerald City Records. Other artists include Cadillac Jack, Mark Vanluvender and Dale Walton.

EMF PRODUCTIONS, 1000 E. Prien Lake Rd., Suite D, Lake Charles LA 70601. Phone/fax: (318)474-0435. Website: www.etatrilogy.com. **Contact:** Ed Fruge, owner. Record company, music publisher and record producer. Estab. 1977. Releases 3 singles, 3 LPs and 3 CDs/year. Pays 10-14% royalty to artists on contract; statutory rate to publisher per song on record.
● See their listing in the Music Publishers section.
How to Contact: Submit demo tape by mail. Unsolicited submissions are OK. Prefers cassette and lyric sheet. Does not return material. Responds in 6 weeks.
Music: Mostly **pop**, **R&B** and **country**. Released *Trilogy* (album), recorded by ETA (contemporary jazz/New Age/pop), released 2000 on EMF Productions.

EMF RECORDS & AFFILIATES, 633 Post, Suite #145, San Francisco CA 94109. (415)273-1421. Fax: (415)752-2442. **Contact:** Steven Lassiter, director of operations. Vice President, A&R (all styles): Michael Miller. A&R Supervisor (commercial): Ed Jones. International Producer (world artists): Kimberly Nakamori. Producer/Writer (all or most styles): Joe Tsongo. Labels include Richland Communications, Sky Bent and Urbana Sounds. Record company. Estab. 1994. Staff size: 11. Releases 5 LPs and 5 CDs/year. Pays negotiable royalty to artists on contract; statutory rate to publisher per song on record.
Distributed by: GTI Marketing and Songo Publishing International.
How to Contact: Submit demo tape by mail. Unsolicited submissions are OK. Prefers cassette, CD or DAT with 3 songs and lyric and lead sheets. Does not return material. Responds in 4 months.
Music: Mostly **urban/pop/rock**, **jazz/Latin** and **New Age/classical (crossover)**; also **country**, **world beat** and **ethnic (world)**. Released *Mutual Impact*, written and recorded by Joe Tsongo on EMF Records (New Age); *If I Had Your Love*, written and recorded by Flamé on Richland Communications (soft jazz); and *From The Source* (by B. Flores/A. Jiminez), recorded by Orchestra de Sabor on Urbana Sounds (salsa/Latin jazz). Other artists include Slam Jam.
Tips: "Build your fan base and present good images or professional packages as much as possible."

◐ **ENTERPRIZE RECORDS-TAPES**, 1507 Scenic Dr., Longview TX 75604-2319. (903)759-0300. Fax: (903)234-2944. **Contact:** Johnny Patterson, studio manager/A&R (country, gospel). Owner: Jerry Haymes (all styles). Record company and music publisher (Enterprize Entertainment). Estab. 1960. Staff size: 2. Releases 2 singles, 5 LPs and 5 CDs/year. Pays negotiable royalty to artists on contract.

Distributed by: Warner Bros Europe.

How to Contact: *Write or call first and obtain permission to submit a demo.* Prefers cassette, CD or videocassette with lyric and lead sheet, cover letter and press clippings. Does not return material. Responds in 1 month.

Music: Mostly **pop (AC)**, **country** and **gospel**; also **rock**. Does not want rap.

☑ ◑ **EPIC RECORDS**, 550 Madison Ave., 21st Floor, New York NY 10022. (212)833-8000. Fax: (212)833-4054. Website: www.epicrecords.com. Senior Vice President: Michael Caplan; Senior Vice President A&R: Peter Robinson; Vice President A&R: Ben Goldman; Vice President A&R: Rose Noone. Santa Monica office: 2100 Colorado Ave., Santa Monica CA 90404. (310)449-2100. Fax: (310)449-2848. E-mail: sonymusiconline@sonymusic.com. Website: www.epicrecords.com. Senior Vice President A&R: Kaz Utsunomiya; Vice President of A&R: Matthew Marshall; Vice President A&R: David Field. Nashville office: 34 Music Square E., Nashville TN 37203. (615)742-4321. Fax: (615)244-2549. Labels include Epic Soundtrax, LV Records, Immortal Records, Word Records, Work Records and 550 Music. Record company.

• Epic's *Iron Man*, released by Sabbath won a 1999 Grammy for Best Metal Performance.

Distributed by: Sony Music Distribution.

How to Contact: *Write or call first and obtain permission to submit* (New York office only). Does not return material. Responds only if interested. *Santa Monica and Nashville offices do not accept unsolicited submissions.*

Music: Released *All the Way . . . A Decade of Song* (album), recorded by Celine Dion on 550 Music; *On How Life Is* (album), recorded by Macy Gray on Epic; and *Issues* (album), recorded by Korn on Epic. Other artists include Ghostface Killah, Cappadonna, 7 Mile, Amel Larrieux, TQ and Cha Cha.

Tips: "Do an internship if you don't have experience or work as someone's assistant. Learn the business and work hard while you figure out what your talents are and where you fit in. Once you figure out which area of the record company you're suited for, focus on that, work hard at it and it shall be yours."

◐ **EVIL TEEN RECORDS**, P.O. Box 651, Village Station, New York NY 10014. (212)337-0760. Fax: (212)337-0708. E-mail: info@evilteen.com. Website: www.evilteen.com. **Contact:** Stefani Scamardo, president. Record company. Estab. 1996. Releases 2 singles, 1 LP and 4-6 CDs/year. Pays negotiable royalty to artists on contract; statutory rate to publisher per song on record.

Distributed by: Select-O-Hits.

How to Contact: Submit demo tape by mail. Unsolicited submissions are OK. Prefers cassette, CD, DAT or VHS videocassette. "Send latest musical product with press kit and tour schedule." SASE. Responds in 1 month.

Music: Mostly **rock/alternative**, **drum & bass** and **Americana**. Released *The Dumbest Magnets* (album), recorded by Dolly Varden (Americana); *Wintertime Blues* (benefit CD for Habitat for Humanity), recorded by various artists (blues/Americana); and *Flower and the Knife* (album), recorded by Kevn Kinney (Americana), all released 2000 on Evil Teen Records. Other artists include Shaft, Benna, Pen Pal and Random.

[N] ◐ FIREANT, 2009 Ashland Ave., Charlotte NC 28205. Phone/fax: (704)335-1400. E-mail: lewh@fireantmusic.com. Website: www.fireantmusic.com. **Contact:** Lew Herman, owner. Record company, music publisher (Fireant Music) and record producer (Lew Herman). Estab. 1990. Releases several CDs/year. Pays negotiable royalty to artists on contract; statutory royalty to publisher per song on record.

Distributed by: CityHall, North Country and Redeye.

How to Contact: Submit demo tape by mail. Unsolicited submissions are OK. Prefers cassette, DAT or videocassette. Does not return material.

Music: Mostly **progressive**, **traditional** and **musical hybrids**. "Anything except New Age and MOR." Released *Loving the Alien: Athens Georgia Salutes David Bowie* (album), recorded by various artists (rock/alternative/electronic), released 2000 on Fireant; and *Good Enough* (album), recorded by Zen Frisbee. Other artists include Mr. Peters' Belizean Boom and Chime Band.

◐ FIRST POWER ENTERTAINMENT GROUP, 5801 Riverdale Rd., Suite 105, Riverdale MD 20737. (301)277-1671. Fax: (301)277-0173. E-mail: powerpla@mail.erols.com. **Contact:** Adrianne Harris, vice president/A&R. Labels include Power Play Records and First Power Records. Record company, recording studio and television show (*StreetJam* and *Phat Trax*). Estab. 1992. Releases 3-5 singles, 2-3 LPs and a variable number of EPs and CDs/year. Pays negotiable royalty to artists on contract; statutory rate to publisher per song on record.
Distributed by: Independent Distributor.
How to Contact: Submit demo tape by mail. Unsolicited submissions are OK. Prefers cassette, CD, DAT or VHS videocassette. "Send name and contact number and address. Please write clearly. Also, it is imperative to include a photo of the artist or group." Does not return material. Responds in 3 months.
Music: Mostly **R&B**, **rap** and **rock**; also **alternative**, **gospel** and **children's**. "We prefer r&b, urban rap, rock and alternative. We do not accept 'gansta rap' artists or material. We prefer 'dance, love, reality and positive' song material and artists." Released *Bunwatcher* (by J. McCoy/M. Butler), recorded by Bad Influence on Power Play (rap/R&B). Other artists include Mothership, Provenwyze, Coffee and The Hylandas.
Tips: "Have patience, a professional attitude and devoted commitment to your career. You must also be creative, open to explore new ways to improve your songs from producers and appear at scheduled events in a timely manner. Artists should be focused and ready to work. We also love groups who have a creative and unique gimmick or image."

⊕ ✔ ◐ FIRST TIME RECORDS, Sovereign House, 12 Trewartha Rd., Praa Sands, Penzance, Cornwall TR20 9ST England. Phone: (01736)762826. Fax: (01736)763328. E-mail: panamus@aol.com. Website: www.songwriters-guild.co.uk. **Contact:** Roderick G. Jones, managing director A&R. Labels include Pure Gold Records, Rainy Day Records and Mohock Records. Registered members of Phonographic Performance Ltd. (PPL). Record company, music publisher (First Time Music Publishing U.K./MCPS/PRS), management firm and record producer (First Time Management & Production Co.). Estab. 1986. Staff size: 6. Pays variable royalty to artists on contract; statutory rate to publisher per song on record subject to deal.
Distributed by: Media U.K. Distributors.
How to Contact: Submit demo tape by mail. Unsolicited submissions are OK. Prefers cassette with unlimited number of songs and lyric or lead sheets, but not necessary. SAE and IRC. Responds in 3 months.
Music: Released *Turn the Lights Down When You Go* (album by Peter Arnold/Steve Leather), recorded by A Band Called Frank (folk), released 2000 on First Time Records/Frank Records; *The Voice of Cornwall* (album by Brenda Wootton/Richard Gendall/Bob Bartlett), recorded by Brenda Wootton (cornish/celtic folk), released 2000 on First Time Records/Sentimental Records/Keltia Musique; and *Gigantic Days* (album by Neville Atkinson/Stephen Robson/Malcolm Eltringham), recorded by Punishment of Luxury (new wave), released 2000 on First Time Records/Overground Records. Other artists include A Band Called Frank and Brenda Wooten.

Ⓝ ◐ FISH OF DEATH RECORDS AND MANAGEMENT, P.O. Box 245, Westwood MA 02090. (781)326-0143. E-mail: fod@earthlink.net. Website: www.fishofdeath.com. President: Michael D. Andelman. Record company, music publisher and management firm. Estab. 1994. Releases 2-4 singles, 1-2 EPs and 2-4 CDs/year. Pays 18% royalty to artists on contract; statutory rate to publisher per song on record.
Distributed by: MS Distributing, Carrot Top, Nail, Dutch East India and Surefire.
   ● This label is noted for releasing fun, happy music.
How to Contact: Submit demo tape by mail. Unsolicited submissions are OK. Prefers cassette or CD with 3 songs. Does not return material. Responds in 3 weeks.

Music: Mostly **alternative**, **rock** and **hip-hop**; also **top 40**, **modern rock** and **AAA**. Released *American Made* (album), written and recorded by Hal Lovejoy Circus (alternative/rock); "Kitty Kat Max" (single by Kevin Krakower), recorded by 1000 Clowns (rap/pop); and *430 N. Harper Ave* (album by Jude Cristodal), recorded by Jude (folk), all on Fish of Death Records. Other artists include All Miserable Times, The Ghost of Tony Gold, Tiny Buddy and Brown Betty.

Tips: "Be persistent, professional, focused, and not too annoying."

✓ ◻ **FLOOD RECORDING CORP.**, 3210 21st St., San Francisco CA 94110. (415)282-4466. Fax: (415)282-4474. E-mail: info@solomusicgroup.com. **Contact:** Jay Siegan, vice president of A&R. Head of A&R: Jeffrey Wood. Record company. Estab. 1995. Releases 2-5 LPs and 2-5 CDs/year. Pays negotiable royalty to artists on contract; statutory rate to publisher per song on record.

Distributed by: ADA and BMG.

How to Contact: Submit demo tape by mail. Unsolicited submissions are OK. Prefers cassette or CD with 2-3 songs and lyric sheet. Does not return material. Responds only if interested.

Music: Mostly **pop**; also **alternative**. Released *Fly* (album), recorded by Hopscotch (pop), released 2001 on Flood Media.

◻ **FLYING HEART RECORDS**, Dept. SM, 4026 NE 12th Ave., Portland OR 97212. (503)287-8045. E-mail: flyheart@teleport.com. Website: www.teleport.com/~flyheart. **Contact:** Jan Celt, owner. Record company and record producer (Jan Celt). Estab. 1982. Releases 2 LPs and 1 EP/year. Pays variable royalty to artists on contract; negotiable rate to publisher per song on record.

Distributed by: Burnside Distribution Co.

How to Contact: Submit demo tape by mail. Unsolicited submissions are OK. Prefers cassette with 1-10 songs and lyric sheets. Does not return material. "SASE required for *any* response." Responds in 3 months.

Music: Mostly **R&B**, **blues** and **jazz**; also **rock**. Released *Vexatious Progr.* (album), written and recorded by Eddie Harris (jazz); *Juke Music* (album), written and recorded by Thara Memory (jazz); and *Lookie Tookie* (album), written and recorded by Jan Celt (blues), all on Flying Heart Records. Other artists include Janice Scroggins, Tom McFarland, Obo Addy, Snow Bud and The Flower People.

Ⓝ ◻ **FOUNTAIN RECORDS**, P.O. Box 35005 AMC, Greensboro NC 27425. (336)882-9990. President: Doris W. Lindsay. Record company, music publisher (Better Times Publishing/BMI, Doris Lindsay Publishing/ASCAP) and record producer. Estab. 1979. Releases 3 singles and 1 LP/year. Pays standard royalty to artists on contract; statutory rate to publisher per song on record.

How to Contact: Submit demo tape by mail. Unsolicited submissions are OK. Prefers cassette with 2 songs and lyric sheets. SASE. Responds in 2 months.

Music: Mostly **country**, **pop** and **gospel**. Released *Two Lane Life* (album by D. Lindsay), recorded by Mitch Snow; "Grandma Bought A Harley" (single by S. Rosario), recorded by Glenn Mayo; *Service Station Cowboy* (album by Hoss Ryder), recorded by David Johnson, all on Fountain Records.

Tips: "Have a professional demo and include phone and address on cassette."

✓ ◻ **FRESH ENTERTAINMENT**, 1315 Simpson Rd. NW, Suite 5, Atlanta GA 30314. Phone/fax: (770)642-2645. E-mail: w.hunter@yahoo.com. **Contact:** Willie Hunter, managing director. Record company and music publisher (Hserf Music/ASCAP, Blair Vizzion Music/BMI). Releases 5 singles and 2 LPs/year. Pays 7-10% royalty to artists on contract; statutory rate to publisher per song on record.

Distributed by: Ichiban International and Intersound Records.

How to Contact: Submit demo tape by mail. Unsolicited submissions are OK. Prefers cassette or VHS videocassette with at least 3 songs and lyric sheet. SASE. Responds in 2 months.

Music: Mostly **R&B**, **rock** and **pop**; also **jazz**, **gospel** and **rap**. Released "We Hate Pastor Troy" (single by W. Jackson/Javou/Chosen One) from *Ready For War*, recorded by Swat Team (rap/hip-hop), released 2000 on Armageddon/Milltyme; "Erase The Color Line" (single by M. Warner/J. Smith/J. Lewis) from *EMG-Non Pilation*, recorded by Michael Warner/JS-1/Noray (R&B/hip-hop),

released 2000 on EMQ Entertainment; and "Live Your Fantasy" (single by B. Miles/E. Davis) from *Nubian Woman* (album), recorded by Bob Miles (jazz), released 2000 on Sheets of Sounds. Other artists include Cirocco and Invisible Men.

⚫ **FRONT ROW RECORDS**, Ridgewood Park Estates, 222 Tulane St., Garland TX 75043. Website: www.athenet.net/~genevinc/GeneSummers.html. **Contact:** Gene or Dea Summers. Public Relations/Artist and Fan Club Coordinator: Steve Summers. A&R: Shawn Summers. Labels include Juan Records. Record company and music publisher (Silicon Music/BMI). Estab. 1968. Releases 5-6 singles and 2-3 LPs/year. Pays negotiable royalty to artists on contract; standard royalty to songwriters on contract.
Distributed by: Crystal Clear Records.
How to Contact: Submit demo tape by mail. Unsolicited submissions are OK. Prefers cassette or VHS videocassette with 1-3 songs. *"We request a photo and bio with material submission."* Does not return material. Responds ASAP.
Music: Mostly **'50s rock/rockabilly**; also **country**, **bluegrass**, **old-time blues** and **R&B**. Released "Domino" (single), recorded by Gene Summers on Pollytone Records (rockabilly); "Goodbye Priscilla" and "Cool Baby" (singles), both recorded by Gene Summers on Collectables Records.
Tips: "If you own masters of 1950s rock and rockabilly, contact us first! We will work with you on a percentage basis for overseas release. We have active releases in Holland, Switzerland, Belgium, Australia, England, France, Sweden, Norway and the US at the present. We need original masters. You must be able to prove ownership of tapes before we can accept a deal. We're looking for little-known, obscure recordings. We have the market if you have the tapes! We are also interested in country and rockabilly *artists* who have not recorded for awhile but still have the voice and appeal to sell overseas."

⚫ **MARTY GARRETT ENTERTAINMENT**, 111 E. Canton St., Broken Arrow OK 74012-7140. (800)210-4416. Website: www.telepath.com/bizbook. **Contact:** Marty R. Garrett, president. Labels include Lonesome Wind Records. Record company, record producer, music publisher and entertainment consultant. Estab. 1988. Releases 3-4 EPs and 1 CD/year. Pays negotiable royalty to artists on contract; statutory rate to publisher per song on record.
How to Contact: *Call or check Internet site first and obtain permission to submit.* Prefers cassette with 4-5 songs and lyric or lead sheet with chord progressions listed. Does not return material. Responds in 6 weeks.
Music: Mostly **Honky tonk**, **progressive/traditional country** or **scripturally-based gospel**. Released *I'm Not Over You* (album by Drake/McGuire), recorded by Darla Drake on Comstock Records; *Too Free Too Long* (album by Cliff Voss), recorded by Mark Cypert on Stormy Heart Records; and *Carry Me Over* (album), written and recorded by The Cripple Jimmi Band on Kid Mega Records.
Tips: "We help artists secure funding to record and release major label quality CD products to the public for sale through 1-800 television and radio advertising and on the Internet. Although we do submit finished products to major record companies for review, our main focus is to establish and surround the artist with their own long-term production, promotion and distribution organization. We do not require professional studio demos, but make sure vocals are distinct, up-front and up-to-date. I personally listen and respond to each submission received, so check website to see if we are reviewing for an upcoming project."

⚫ **GEFFEN/DGC RECORDS**, 10900 Wilshire Blvd., Suite 1230, Los Angeles CA 90024. (310)208-6547. Fax: (310)824-3927. New York office: 825 Eighth Ave., 29th Floor, New York NY 10019. (212)445-3235. Fax: (212)445-3686.
 • As a result of the PolyGram and Universal merger, Geffen has been folded into Interscope Records. See the Interscope/Geffen/A&M Records listing in this section for further information.

⚫ **GIG RECORDS**, 520 Butler Ave., Point Pleasant NJ 08742. (732)701-9044. Fax: (732)701-9777. E-mail: Indian@gigrecords.com. Website: www.gigrecords.com. **Contact:** Indian, president. Labels include AMPED. Record company and music publisher (Gig Music). Estab. 1998. Staff size: 8. Releases 1 single, 9 LPs, 1 EP and 9 CDs/year. Pays negotiable royalty to artists on contract; statutory rate to publisher per song on record.

Distributed by: Valley, Amazon, E-Music, CD Now, The Orchard, Nail and Sumthing.
How to Contact: Submit demo tape by mail. Unsolicited submissions are OK. Prefers cassette, CD or VHS videocassette with lyric sheet and cover letter. Does not return materials. Responds ASAP if interested.
Music: Mostly **rock** and **electronic**; also **drum & bass**, **trip-hop** and **hip-hop**. Does not want country. Released *Sweet Conscience* (album by Virginia Traut), recorded by Virginia (pop); *5 Songs* (album), written and recorded by Miles Hunt (pop rock); and *Grace's Period* (album), written and recorded by Michael Ferentino (pop rock), all released 2000 on Gig Releases. Other artists include Virginia, The Vibrators, Groundswell UK, Nebula Nine, The Youth Ahead, Dryer and Red Engine Nine.
Tips: "No egos."

⊘ **GOLD CITY RECORDS, INC.**, 10 Deepwell Farms Rd., S. Salem NY 10590. (914)533-5096. Fax: (914)533-5097. E-mail: gcrecords@aol.com. Website: members.aol.com/GCRecords. President: Chris Jasper. Vice President/General Counsel: Margie Jasper. Labels include Gold City Label. Record company. Estab. 1986. Staff size: 5. Releases 5-10 singles and 3-5 CDs/year. Pays negotiable royalty to artists on contract; statutory rate to publisher per song on record.
How to Contact: Submit demo tape by mail. Unsolicited submissions are OK. Prefers cassette, DAT or CD with 3 songs and lyric sheets. SASE. Responds in 6 weeks.
Music: Mostly **R&B**, **contemporary gospel** and **pop**; also **rap**. Released "And I Love Her" (single by P. McCartney/J. Lennon), recorded by Brothaz By Choice (R&B); *Faithful and True* (album), recorded by Chris Jasper (contemporary gospel), released 2001, both on Gold City Records.

☑ ☐ **GOLDEN TRIANGLE RECORDS**, 5501 Camelia St., Pittsburgh PA 15201. E-mail: marc els@salsgiver.com. Website: www.salsgiver.com/people/marcels/mair.html. **Contact:** Sunny James Cvetnic, producer. Labels include Rockin Robin and Shell-B. Record company, music publisher (Golden Triangle/BMI) and record producer (Sunny James). Estab. 1987. Staff size: 2. Releases 1 CD/year. Pays standard royalty to artists on contract; statutory rate to publishers per song on record.
How to Contact: Submit demo tape by mail. Unsolicited submissions are OK. Prefers cassette or ½" VHS videocassette with 3 songs and lyric or lead sheets. Does not return material. Responds in 1 week.
Music: Mostly **progressive R&B**, **rock** and **A/C**; also **jazz** and **country**. Released "My True Story" (single) from *Moon to Millennium* (album), written and recorded by The Marcels on Golden Triangle. Other artists include the T. Jack (blues), Weetman (r&b) and Sunny James (pop/rock).
Tips: "Have patience."

☐ **GOLDWAX RECORD CORPORATION**, P.O. Box 54700, Atlanta GA 30308-0700. (770)454-1011. Fax: (770)454-8088. E-mail: goldwaxrec@aol.com. Website: www.goldwax.com. **Contact:** Jimmy McClendon, A&R. Labels include Abec, Bandstand USA and Beale Street USA. Record company and music publisher (Stellar Music Industries). Estab. 1963. Staff size: 4. Releases 15 singles, 12 LPs, 4 EPs and 2 CDs/year. Pays negotiable royalty to artists on contract; statutory rate to publisher per song on record.
Distributed by: City Hall Records, Goldwax Distributing.
How to Contact: Write or call first and obtain permission to submit a demo. Prefers cassette, CD, DAT or VHS videocassette with 4 songs and lyric sheet. SASE. Responds in 6 weeks.
Music: Mostly **R&B/hip-hop**, **pop/rock** and **jazz**; also **blues**, **contemporary country** and **contemporary gospel**. Released *Clifford & Co.* (album) (soul) on Beale Street Records and *Double Deuce* (album) (rap) on Urban Assault Records. Other artists include Double Deuce, Elvin Spenser and Margie Alexander.
Tips: "Songwriters need to provide great melodies; artists need to have commercial appeal."

REMEMBER: Don't "shotgun" your demo tapes. Submit only to companies interested in the type of music you write. For more submission hints, refer to Getting Started on page 10.

■ ○ **GONZO! RECORDS INC.**, P.O. Box 3688, San Dimas CA 91773. Phone/fax: (909)598-9031. E-mail: gonzorcrds@aol.com. Website: members.aol.com/gonzorcrds. **Contact:** Jeffrey Gonzalez, president. Record company. Estab. 1993. Staff size: 3. Releases 3 singles and 1-6 CDs/year. Pays negotiable royalty to artists on contract; statutory rate to publisher per song on record.

• Gonzo! Records was awarded Best Indie Label, and Full Frequency was awarded Best Techno/Industrial Band at the 1999 Los Angeles Music Awards.

How to Contact: Submit demo tape by mail. Unsolicited submissions are OK. Prefers cassette or CD. "When submitting, please specify that you got the listing from *Songwriter's Market*." Does not return material. Responds in 6 weeks.

Music: Mostly **commercial industrial**, **dance** and **techno**; also **commercial alternative** and **synth pop**. Released *Hate Breeds Hate* (album), written and recorded by BOL (hard industrial); *Momentum* (album), written and recorded by Full Frequency (commerical industrial); and *Ruth in Alien Corn* (album), written and recorded by Pinch Point (alternative pop), all on Gonzo! Records. Other artists include Turning Keys.

Tips: "If you're going to submit music to me, it must be because you love to write music, not because you want to be a rockstar. That will eventually happen with a lot of hard work."

Ⓝ ○ **GOTHAM RECORDS**, P.O. Box 20188, New York NY 10014. Phone/fax: (212)517-9192. E-mail: gothamrec@aol.com. Website: www.gothamrecords.com. **Contact:** John Cross, vice president A&R/retail. Record company. Estab. 1994. Staff size: 3. Releases 8 LPs and 8 CDs/year. Pays negotiable royalty to artists on contract; statutory rate to publisher per song on record.

Distributed by: Dutch East India and MS Distributing.

How to Contact: Submit demo tape by mail "in a padded mailer or similar package." Unsolicited submissions are OK. Prefers cassette or CD and bios, pictures and touring information. Does not return material. Responds in 6 weeks.

Music: Mostly **rock**, **pop**, **alternative** and **AAA**. Released *Nineteenth Soul*, recorded by Liquid Gang (rock); *Supafuzz*, written and recorded by Supafuzz (rock); and *Oh God! Help Our Fans!*, written and recorded by The Loose Nuts (ska), all on Gotham Records. Other artists include Love Huskies.

Tips: "Send all submissions in regular packaging. Spend your money on production and basics, not on fancy packaging and gift wrap."

Ⓝ ○ **GRASS ROOTS RECORD & TAPE/LMI RECORDS**, P.O. Box 532, Malibu CA 90265. (213)463-5998. **Contact:** Lee Magid, president. Record company, record producer (Lee Magid), music publisher (Alexis/ASCAP, Marvelle/BMI, Lou-Lee/BMI) and management firm (Lee Magid Management Co.). Member AIMP, NARAS. Estab. 1967. Releases 4 LPs and 4 CDs/year. Pays 50% royalty per record sold to artists on contract; statutory rate to publishers per song on record.

• Grass Roots Record's publishing company, Alexis, is listed in the Music Publishers section, and President Lee Magid is listed in the Record Producers section.

How to Contact: Submit demo tape by mail. Unsolicited submissions are OK. Prefers cassette with 3 songs and lyric sheet. "Please, no 45s." Does not return material. Responds in 2 months.

Music: Mostly **pop/rock**, **R&B**, **country**, **gospel**, **jazz/rock** and **blues**; also **bluegrass**, **children's** and **Latin**. Released "Mighty Hand" (single by C. Rhone), recorded by Cajun Hart on LMI Records (R&B); *Don't You Know* (album by B. Worth), recorded by Della Reese on RCA Records (pop); and *Blues For The Weepers* (album by L. Magid/M. Rich), recorded by Lou Rawls on Capitol Records (R&B). Other artists include John Michael Hides, Julie Miller, Tramaine Hawkins and ZAD.

Ⓩ **GREEN BEAR RECORDS**, Rockin' Chair Center Suite 103, 1033 W. Main St., Branson MO 65616. Phone/fax: (417)334-2306. **Contact:** George J. Skupien, president. Labels include Green One Records and Green Bear Records. Record company, music publisher (Green One Music/BMI) and record producer (George Skupien). Estab. 1992. Releases 3-4 singles, 1-10 LPs and 2-6 CDs/year. Pays negotiable royalty to artists on contract; statutory rate to publisher per song on record.

How to Contact: *Write or fax first and obtain permission to submit.* Does not accept unsolicited submissions. "Please send request to submit to address above by mail or fax. If you are approved to send material, songs must be professionally performed and produced. We no longer accept homemade demos. For your protection, all tapes, lyrics and other material that is received and/or rejected will be shredded and destroyed. We do not return material!" Responds on accepted material.

Music: Mostly **country** and **light rock**; also **American polkas**, **southern gospel**, **waltzes**, **comedy** and **fun songs**. Released "Our Last Cowboy Song" (single by Matt Row'd/G. Skupien) from *Memories* (album), recorded by Matt Row'd; and "Love Is Why I Feel This Way" (single by G. Skupien/Sara Wright) from *Country Compilation 102* (album), recorded by Buddy Thomas, both released 2000 on Green Bear Records. Other artists include D. Mack, B. Jackson, Ted Thomas, Rudy Negron and The Mystics.

☑ ◐ **GRIFFIN MUSIC (a Division of Tango Music LLC)**, P.O. Box 1952, Lombard IL 60148. (630)424-0801. Fax: (630)424-0806. E-mail: grifmus@aol.com. Website: griffinmusic.com. **Contact:** Ginger Lord, A&R. Labels include Tango Music and Lakeshore. Record company. Estab. 1992. Staff size: 8. Releases 2 singles, 4 LPs and 24 CDs/year. Pays negotiable royalty to artists on contract; pay to publisher per song on record "depends on artist."
Distributed by: Alliance, Baker & Taylor, Action, Norwalk, Pacific Coast, H.L. Distribution, Valley and MDI.
How to Contact: Submit demo tape by mail. Unsolicited submissions are OK. Prefers cassette or CD with cover letter and press clippings. Does not return material. Responds in 6 weeks.
Music: Mostly **classic rock**, **pop** and **various artists compilations**. Released *Mile By Blues Mile* (album), written and recorded by various artists (blues); *Thrilling Hawkwind Stories* (album), recorded by Hawkwind (space rock); and *The Pearls Concert* (album), recorded by Elrie Brooks (pop), all released 2000 on Griffin.
Tips: "Have some sort of track history."

◉ **GROOVE MAKERS' RECORDINGS**, P.O. Box 271170, Houston TX 77227-1170. Phone/fax: (281)403-6279. E-mail: lmistamadd@aol.com. Website: www.paidnphull.com. **Contact:** Ben Thompson (R&B, rap), CEO. Labels include Paid In Full Entertainment. Record company, music publisher and record producer (Crazy C). Estab. 1994. Staff size: 4. Releases 3 singles, 2 LPs and 2 CDs/year. Pays negotiable royalty to artists on contract; statutory rate to publisher per song on record.
Distributed by: S.O.H., Big Easy and Southwest Wholesale.
How to Contact: *Write first and obtain permission to submit.* Prefers cassette or CD. Does not return material.
Music: Mostly **rap** and **R&B**. Released "We Thoed" (single by various artists) from *Can I Live* (album), recorded by Mista Madd (rap), released 2000 on Paid In Full Entertainment; and *Soulology: The Genesis* (album), recorded by Sounds of Urban Life (R&B), released 2000 on Soul Muzick Recordings. Other artists include S.O.U.L. and Heather Barrett.

Ⓝ ◯ **GUESTSTAR RECORDS, INC.**, 17321 Ritchie Ave. NE, Sand Lake MI 49343-9475. (616)636-5068. Fax: (775)743-4169. E-mail: gueststarww.wingsisp.com. Website: www.wingsisp.com/mountainmanww/. **Contact:** Raymond G. Dietz, Sr., president. Record company, management firm (Gueststar Entertainment Agency), record producer and music publisher (Sandlake Music/BMI). Estab. 1967. Staff size: 3. Releases 8 singles, 2 LPs and 2 CDs/year. Pays variable royalty to artist on contract, "depending on number of selections on product; 3½¢/per record sold; statutory rate to publisher per song on record."
Distributed by: Guestar Worldwide Music Distributors.
How to Contact: Submit demo tape by mail. Unsolicited submissions are OK. Prefers cassette or VHS videocassette with lyric and lead sheet. "Send a SASE with submissions." Does not return material. Responds in 3 weeks.
Music: Mostly **traditional country**. Released *Best of Mountain Man #2* (album), recorded by Mountain Man (traditional country), released 2000 on Gueststar Records, Inc. Other artists include Jamie "K" and Sweetgrass Band.
Tips: "Songwriters: send songs like you hear on the radio. Keep updating your music to keep up with the latest trends. Artists: send VHS video and press kit."

☑ ◯ **HACIENDA RECORDS & RECORDING STUDIO**, 1236 S. Staples St., Corpus Christi TX 78404. (361)882-7066. Fax: (361)882-3943. E-mail: info@haciendarecords.com. Website: www.haciendarecords.com. **Contact:** Rick Garcia, executive vice president. Producers: Carlos Acevedo.

Record company, music publisher, record producer. Estab. 1979. Staff size: 19. Releases 12 singles, 20 LPs and 20 CDs/year. Pays negotiable royalty to artists on contract; negotiable rate to publisher per song on record.
How to Contact: Submit demo tape by mail. Unsolicited submissions are OK. Prefers cassette with cover letter. Does not return material. Responds in 6 weeks.
Music: Mostly **latin pop/rock**, **tejano** and **salsa**. Released *Sola* and *Puro Candela* (albums), both written and recorded by Marlissa Vela (salsa); and "Chica Bonita" (single), recorded by Albert Zamora and D.J. Cubanito, released 2001 on Hacienda Records. Other artists include Albert Zamora Y Talento, Mango Punch, Victoria Y Sus Chikos, Peligro and La Traizion.
Tips: "Submit your best."

☑ ◑ **HAPPY MAN RECORDS**, 4696 Kahlua Lane, Bonita Springs FL 34134. (941)947-6978. E-mail: obitts@aol.com. **Contact:** Dick O'Bitts, executive producer. Labels include Condor and Con Air. Record company, music publisher (Rocker Music/BMI, Happy Man Music/ASCAP) and record producer (Rainbow Collection Ltd.). Estab. 1972. Releases 4-6 singles, 4-6 12″ singles, 4-6 LPs and 4 EPs/year. Pays negotiable royalty to artists on contract; statutory rate to publisher per song on record.
Distributed by: V&R.
   ● Happy Man's publishing company, Rocker Music/Happy Man Music, can be found in the Music Publishers section.
How to Contact: Submit demo tape by mail. Unsolicited submissions are OK. Prefers cassette, CD or VHS videocassette with 3-4 songs and lyric sheet. SASE. Responds in 1 month.
Music: All types. Released *Got the T-Shirt* (album by Jake Thorp), recorded by The Thorp's; and *In the Distance* (album), written and recorded by 4 Harmonee, both released 2001 on Happy Man Records. Other artists include Ray Pack, Crosswinds, Overdue, The Thorps, Okeefenokee Joe and Colt Gipson.

☑ ◐ **HEADS UP INT., LTD.**, 23309 Commerce Park Dr., Cleveland OH 44122. (216)765-7381. Fax: (216)464-6037. E-mail: dave@headsup.com. Website: www.headsup.com. **Contact:** Dave Love, president. Record company, music publisher (Heads Up Int., Buntz Music, Musica de Amor) and record producer (Dave Love). Estab. 1980. Staff size: 57. Releases 10 LPs/year. Pays negotiable royalty to artists on contract.
Distributed by: Telarc Int. Corp.
How to Contact: Submit demo tape by mail. Unsolicited submissions are OK. Prefers CD. Does not return material. Responds in one month.
Music: Mostly **jazz**, **R&B** and **pop**. Does not want anything else. Released *Keeping Cool* (album), written and recorded by Joyce Cooling (jazz); *Another Side of Midnight* (album), written and recorded by Marion Meadows (jazz); and *Love Letters* (album), written and recorded by Gerald Veasley (jazz). Other artists include Philip Bailey, Joe McBride, Richard Smith, Robert Perera, Spyro Gyra and Pieces of a Dream.

◐ **HEART MUSIC, INC.**, P.O. Box 160326, Austin TX 78716-0326. (512)795-2375. Fax: (512)795-9573. E-mail: info@heartmusic.com. Website: www.heartmusic.com. **Contact:** Mimi Alidor, promotions director. Record company and music publisher (Coolhot Music). Estab. 1989. Staff size: 2. Releases 3 CDs/year. Pays 75% royalty to artists on contract; statutory rate to publisher per song on record.
How to Contact: *Not interested in new material at this time.* Does not return material. Responds only if interested.
Music: Mostly **rock**, **pop** and **jazz**; also **blues**, **urban** and **contemporary folk**. Does not want New Age jazz, smooth jazz or Christian/religious. Released *Mirror* (album), recorded by Monte Montgomery (pop/rock), released June 1999; and *Be Cool Be Kind* (album), recorded by Carla Helmbrecht (jazz), released January 2001, both on Heart Music.

▣ ▨ ◯ **HI-BIAS RECORDS INC.**, 20 Hudson Dr., Maple, Toronto, Ontario L6A 1X3 Canada. Phone/fax: (905)303-9611. E-mail: info@hibias.ca. Website: www.hibias.ca/~hibias. **Contact:** Nick

Fiorucci, director. Labels include Toronto Underground, Remedy and Club Culture. Record company, music publisher (Bend 60 Music/SOCAN) and record producer (Nick Fiorucci). Estab. 1990. Staff size: 2. Releases 30-40 singles, 4-8 LPs, 10 EPs and 5-10 CDs/year. Pays negotiable royalty to artists on contract; statutory rate to publisher per song on record.

Distributed by: PolyGram/Universal.

How to Contact: Submit demo tape by mail. Unsolicited submissions are OK. Prefers cassette or DAT with 3 songs and lyric sheet. Does not return material. Responds in 6 weeks.

Music: Mostly **dance, pop** and **R&B**; also **acid jazz** and **house**. Released "Hands of Time" (single by N. Fiorucci/B. Cosgrove), recorded by Temperance; "Now That I Found You" (single by B. Farrinco/Cleopatra), recorded by YBZ; and "Lift Me Up" (single), written and recorded by Red 5, all on Hi-Bias (dance/pop). Other artists include DJ's Rule.

✓ ⊘ **HOLLYWOOD RECORDS**, 500 S. Buena Vista St., Old Team Bldg., Burbank CA 91521-1840. (818)560-5670. Fax: (818)845-4313. Website: www.hollywoodrec.com. Senior Vice President of A&R: Rob Cavallo. Senior Vice President of A&R (soundtracks): Mitchell Lieb. Vice President: Julian Raymond. New York office: 170 Fifth Ave., 9th Floor, New York NY 10010. (212)645-2722. Fax: (212)741-3016. Website: www.hollywoodrec.com. Director A&R: Jason Jordan. Labels include Acid Jazz Records, Mountain Division Records and Bar/None Records. Record company.

How to Contact: *Hollywood Records does not accept unsolicited submissions.* Queries accepted only from a manager or lawyer.

Music: Released *All the Pain Money Can Buy*, recorded by Fastball. Other artists include Brian May, Khaleel, Caroline's Spine, Fishbone, Leroy & Loudmouth, Jesse Camp, Roger McGuinn and Pistoleros.

N ⊘ **HORIZON RECORDS, INC.**, P.O. Box 610487, San Jose CA 95161-0487. E-mail: info@ horizonrecords.com. (408)782-1501. Fax: (408)778-3567. Website: www.horizonrecords.com. **Contact:** Jennifer Linn, vice president. Record company and music publisher (Horizon Music West). Estab. 1996. Staff size: 6. Pays negotiable royalty to artists on contract; statutory rate to publisher per song on record.

Distributed by: Red Eye Distribution.

How to Contact: *Horizon records does not accept unsolicited material.*

Music: Mostly **rock/pop**, **singer/songwriter** and **blues**; also **jazz** and techno. Released *Bohemia* (album), written and recorded by Tommy Elskes on Horizon Records (rock/pop).

⊘ **HOT WINGS ENTERTAINMENT**, 429 Richmond Ave., Buffalo NY 14222. (716)884-0248. E-mail: dahotwings@aol.com. **Contact:** Dale Anderson, president. Record company and music publisher (Buffalo Wings Music/BMI). Estab. 1994. Staff size: 1. Releases 2 CDs/year. Pays 10-15% to artists on contract; statutory rate to publisher per song on record.

How to Contact: *Call first and obtain permission to submit.* Prefers cassette or CD with 3 or more songs. Does not return material. Responds in 2 months.

Music: Mostly **folk/acoustic**, **alternative rock** and **jazz**. (Preference to artists from Upstate New York.) Released *Like Being Born* (album), written and recorded by Alison Pipitone (folk/rock); *Flavor* (album by Geoffrey Fitzhugh Perry), recorded by Fitzhugh and the Fanatics (blues/rock); and *Everything Counts* (album), written and recorded by Gretchen Schulz (pop/R&B), all on Hot Wings Records.

◻ **HOTTRAX RECORDS**, 1957 Kilburn Dr., Atlanta GA 30324. (770)662-6661. E-mail: hotwax @hottrax.com. Website: www.hottrax.com. **Contact:** Oliver Cooper, vice president, A&R. Labels include Dance-A-Thon and Hardkor. Record company and music publisher (Starfox Publishing). Staff size: 3. Releases 12 singles and 3-4 CDs/year. Pays 5-15% royalty to artists on contract.

Distributed by: Get Hip Inc.

How to Contact: *Write first and obtain permission to submit.* Prefers cassette with 3 songs and lyric sheet. Does not return material. Responds in 6 months. "When submissions get extremely heavy, we do not have the time to respond/return material we pass on. We do notify those sending the most promising work we review, however."

Music: Mostly **top 40/pop**, **rock** and **country**; also **hardcore punk** and **jazz-fusion**. Released *Starfoxx* (album), written and recorded by Starfoxx (rock); "Cherie, Cherie" (single by A. Janoulis), recorded by Blues Mafia (rock); and *Vol. III, Psychedelic Era* (album by various), recorded by Night Shadows (rock), all released 2000 on Hottrax. Other artists include Big Al Jano.

IDOL RECORDS, P.O. Box 720043, Dallas TX 75372. (214)826-4365. Fax: (214)370-5417. E-mail: info@idol-records.com. Website: www.Idol-Records.com. **Contact:** Erv Karwelis, president. Record company. Estab. 1992. Releases 2-3 singles, 30 LPs, 2-3 EPs and 15-20 CDs/year. Pays negotiable royalty to artists on contract; statutory rate to publisher per song on record.
Distributed by: Choke, Crystal Clear, Smash, Southern, Carrot Top, Nail and Parasol.
How to Contact: *Write first and obtain permission to submit a demo.* Does not return material.
Music: Mostly **rock**, **pop** and **alternative**; also **country** and **experimental**. Released *Use Your Powers for Good, Not Evil* (album), recorded by The May Seven; *Center of Attention Deficit Disorder* (album), recorded by Clumsey; and *South Sam Gabriel Songs/Music* (album), recorded by Centro-Matic, all released 2001 on Idol Records. Other artists include Pervis, Billyclub, Old 97's, Hoarse, Feisty Cadavers, The American Fuse and Watershed.

IMAGINARY RECORDS, P.O. Box 66, Whites Creek TN 37189-0066. Phone/fax: (615)299-9237. E-mail: townsend@imaginaryrecords.com. Website: www.imaginaryrecords.com. **Contact:** Lloyd Townsend, proprietor. Labels include Imaginary Records, Imaginary Jazz Records. Record company. Estab. 1981. Staff size: 1. Releases 1-3 CDs/year. Pays negotiable royalty to artists on contract; statutory rate to publisher per song on record.
Distributed by: North Country, Harbor Record Export and Imaginary Distribution.
How to Contact: *Write first to obtain permission to submit a demo.* Prefers cassette or CD with 3-5 songs, cover letter and press clippings. SASE. Responds in 4 months if interested.
Music: Mostly **mainstream jazz**, **swing jazz** and **classical**. Does not want country, rap, hip-hop or metal. Released *Triologue* (album), recorded by Stevens, Sigel & Ferguson (jazz); *Tennessee Jazz, Vol. 1* (album), recorded by various artists (jazz); and *Cool Conception of Love* (album), recorded by Susan Fiering (pop), all released 2000 on Imaginary/Firesong.
Tips: "Be patient, I'm slow. I'm primarily considering mainstream jazz or classical—other genre submissions are much less likely to be responded to."

INTERSCOPE/GEFFEN/A&M RECORDS, 2220 Colorado Ave., Santa Monica CA 90404. (310)855-1000. Fax: (310)855-7908. A&R: Tony Ferguson; A&R: Jon Sidel; A&R: Ben Gordon. New York office: 825 Eighth Ave., 29th Floor, New York NY 10019. (212)333-8000. Fax: (212)445-3686. E-mail: interscope@interscoperecords.com. Website: www.interscoperecords.com. President: Ron Fair; A&R Director: Debbie Southwood-Smith. Labels include Death Row Records, Nothing Records, Rock Land, Almo Sounds, Aftermath Records and Trauma Records. Record company.
  • As a result of the PolyGram and Universal merger, Geffen and A&M Records have been folded into Interscope Records. A&M's Sting won 2000 Grammy Awards for Best Pop Album and Best Male Vocal Pop Performance. Geffen's Beck won a 2000 Grammy for Best Alternative Music Performance.
How to Contact: *Does not accept unsolicited submissions.*

**FOR EXPLANATIONS OF THESE SYMBOLS,
SEE THE INSIDE FRONT AND BACK COVERS OF THIS BOOK.**

Music: Released *Fush Yu Mang*, recorded by Smash Mouth; *The Dirty Boogie*, recorded by The Brian Setzer Orchestra; and *Bulworth—The Soundtrack*, all on Interscope Records. Other artists include U2, Garbage and Marilyn Manson.

☑ ⊘ **ISLAND/DEF JAM MUSIC GROUP**, (formerly Mercury Records), 825 Eighth Ave., 19th Floor, New York NY 10019. (212)333-8000. Fax: (212)603-7654. Website: www.defjam.com. Executive Vice President A&R: Jeff Fenster; Senior Vice President A&R: Tina Davis; Vice President A&R: Randy Acker. Los Angeles office: 8920 Sunset Blvd, 2nd Floor, Los Angeles CA 90069. (310)276-4500. Fax: (310)278-5862. Executive A&R: Paul Pontius; A&R Billy Clark. Nashville office: 66 Music Square W., Nashville TN 37203. (615)320-0110. Fax: (615)327-4856. A&R Director: Gary Harrison. Labels include Mouth Almighty Records, Worldly/Triloka Records, Blackheart Records, Private Records, Slipdisc Records, Thirsty Ear, Blue Gorilla, Dubbly, Little Dog Records, Rounder and Capricorn Records. Record company.

* In 2000, Island/Def Jam Music Groups' Shania Twain won a Grammy Award for Best Female Vocal Award ("Man! I Feel Like A Woman!" from *Come On Over*) and "Come On Over," written by Robert John "Mutt" Lange and Shania Twain and recorded on Mercury won a Grammy for Best Country Song.

How to Contact: *Island/Def Jam Music Group does not accept unsolicited submissions. Do not send material unless requested.*
Music: Released *Come On Over* (album), recorded by Shania Twain on Mercury Nashville. Other artists include Gina Thompson, Crystal Waters, Cardigans, James, Elvis Costello, Bon Jovi and downset.

⊘ **JIVE RECORDS**, 137-139 W. 25th St., 9th Floor, New York NY 10001. (212)727-0016. Fax: (212)337-0990. Senior Vice President of A&R: Peter Thea. Director of A&R: David Lighty. West Hollywood office: 9000 Sunset Blvd., Suite 300, West Hollywood CA 90069. (310)247-8300. Fax: (310)247-8366. Vice President of A&R: Andy Goldmark. Vice President of Creative Development: Jonathan McHugh. Chicago office: 700 N. Green St., Suite 200, Chicago IL 60622. (312)942-9700. Fax: (312)942-9800. Vice President of A&R: Wayne Williams. Nashville office: 914-916 19th Ave. S., Nashville TN 37212. (615)321-4850. Fax: (615)321-4616. London office: Zomba House, 165-167 High Rd., Willesden, London NW 10 2SG England. Phone: (44) 81-459-8899. Fax: (31) 2153-16785. Record company. Estab. 1982. Releases 23 singles and 23 CDs/year.
Distributed by: BMG.
How to Contact: *Does not accept unsolicited material.* "Contact us through management or an attorney."
Music: Mostly **R&B**, **pop** and **rap**. Artists include Backstreet Boys, Joe, KRS-One, R. Kelly, Britney Spears, Too Short and Imajin.
Tips: "Make the best material possible."

◖ **KAUPP RECORDS**, Box 5474, Stockton CA 95205. (209)948-8186. **Contact:** Nancy L. Merrihew, president. Record company, music publisher (Kaupps and Robert Publishing Co./BMI), management firm (Merri-Webb Productions) and record producer (Merri-Webb Productions). Estab. 1990. Releases 1 single and 4 LPs/year. Pays standard royalty to artists on contract; statutory rate to publisher per song on record.
Distributed by: Merri-Webb Productions and Cal-Centron Distributing Co.
How to Contact: Write first and obtain permission to submit or to arrange personal interview. Prefers cassette or VHS videocassette with 3 songs. SASE. Responds in 3 months.
Music: Mostly **country**, **R&B** and **A/C rock**; also **pop**, **rock** and **gospel**. Released "He's Alive" and "Little Do You Know" (singles by N. Merrihew/B. Bolin), recorded by Nanci Lynn; and "(Since I Started to Believin') My Own B.S." (single by N. Merrihew/B. Bolin), recorded by Bruce Bolin, all on Kaupp Records.

☑ ○ **KEEPING IT SIMPLE AND SAFE, INC.**, P.O. Box 91079, Springfield MA 01139-1079. (509)351-4379. Fax: (509)351-4379. E-mail: simpleandsafe@aol.com. **Contact:** Timothy Scott, president. Vice President: Sylvia Edson. A&R Directors: Tony Martin; Robert Perry. Labels include Night

Owl Records, Grand Jury Records, Second Time Around Records and Southend-Essex Records. Record company and music publisher (Tim Scott Music Group). Estab. 1993. Releases 3 singles, 2 LPs and 2 CDs/year. Pays 12-20% royalty to artists on contract; statutory rate to publisher per song on record.

How to Contact: Write first to obtain permission to submit. Prefers cassette, CD or VHS videocassette with 3-5 songs and lyric sheet. SASE. Responds in 2 months.

Music: Mostly **pop**, **R&B**, and **rap**; also **country**, **rock** and **gospel**. Released "As We Touch" (single) from *Morning Star*(album), writtern and recorded by Terry Adams; "Thoughts in the Rain" (single) from *Thoughts in the Rain* (album), written and recorded by Billy Johnson/Linda Jenkins; and "Here Comes the Pain (Again)" (single by Greg Harrison/James McDougal) from *Here I Go Again* (album), recorded by 3 Plus One, all released 2000 on Night Owl Records.

Tips: "Always explain what you are asking for."

🅜 **KINGSTON RECORDS**, 15 Exeter Rd., Kingston NH 03848. (603)642-8493. E-mail: kingston records@ttlc.net. **Contact:** Harry Mann, coordinator. Record company, record producer and music publisher (Strawberry Soda Publishing/ASCAP). Estab. 1988. Releases 3-4 singles, 2-3 12″ singles, 3 LPs and 2 CDs/year. Pays 3-5% royalty to artists on contract; statutory rate to publisher per song.

How to Contact: Write first and obtain permission to submit. Prefers cassette, DAT, 15 ips reel-to-reel or videocassette with 3 songs and lyric sheet. Does not return material. Responds in 2 months.

Music: Mostly **rock**, **country** and **pop**; "no heavy metal." Released *Two Lane Highway* and *Armand's Way* (albums), written and recorded by Armand Learay (rock); and *Count the Stars* (album), written and recorded by Doug Mitchell, released 1999, all on Kingston Records.

Tips: "Working only with N.E. and local talent."

🍁 ☑ 🅞 **L. A. RECORDS (CANADA)**, P.O. Box 1096, Hudson, Quebec J0P 1H0 Canada. Phone/fax: (450)458-2819. Pager: (514)869-3236. E-mail: la_records@excite.com. Website: http:// www.radiofreedom.com. Manager (alternative): Tonya Hart. Producer (rock): M. Lengies. Record company, management firm (M.B.H. Music Management), music publisher (G-String Publishing) and record producer (M. Lengies). Estab. 1991. Releases 20-40 singles and 5-8 CDs/year. Pays negotiable royalty to artists on contract; statutory rate to publishers per song on record.

Distributed by: L.A. Records and Radiofreedom.com.

How to Contact: Submit demo tape by mail. Unsolicited submissions are OK. Prefers cassette or DAT with 3 songs and lyric sheet. Does not return material. Responds in 6 months.

Music: Mostly **commercial rock**, **alternative** and **A/C**; also **country** and **dance**. Released "First Off" (single), written and recorded by Brittany on L.A. Records. Other artists include El Vache, General Panic, Jessica Ehrenworth, Brittany and Joe King.

☑ 🅞 **L.A. RECORDS**, 29355 Little Mack, Roseville MI 48066. (810)775-6533. E-mail: ruffprod @aol.com. Website: www.abchosting.com/lotto or http://members.aol.com/jtrupi4539/index.html. President: Jack Timmons. Music Director: John Dudick. Labels include Stark Records, R.C. Records and Fearless. Record company, record producer and music publisher (Abalone Publishing). Estab. 1984. Staff size: 12. Releases 20-30 singles, 1-10 12″ singles, 20-30 LPs, 1-5 EPs and 2-15 CDs/ year. Pays 5% royalty to artists on contract; statutory rate to publisher per song on record.

How to Contact: Submit demo tape by mail. Unsolicited submissions are OK. Prefers cassette with 1-10 songs and lyric sheet. "It is very important to include a cover letter describing your objective goals." Responds in 3 months. "Due to fluctuation of postal rates include $1 to cover postage overage above 34¢. All others SASE is acceptable. Packages with 34¢ SASE are not acceptable."

LISTINGS OF COMPANIES within this section which are either commercial music production houses or music libraries will have that information printed in **boldface** type.

Music: Mostly **rock/hard rock**, **heavy metal** and **pop/rock**; also **country/gospel**, **MOR/ballads**, **R&B**, **jazz**, **New Age**, **dance** and **easy listening**. Released *The Torch* (album by Robbi Taylor/The Sattellites), recorded by The Sattellites (rock); "The Web" (single by Jay Collins), recorded by The Net (rock); and "Passion" (single by R. Gibb), recorded by Notta (blues), all on L.A. Records. Other artists include The Simmones, Kevin Stark, The Comets and Fearless.

LAFACE RECORDS, One Capitol City Plaza, 3350 Peachtree Rd., Suite 1500, Atlanta GA 30326-1040. (404)848-8050. Fax: (404)848-8051. **Contact:** Kawan Prather, vice president A&R director. Beverly Hills office: 8750 Wilshire Blvd., 2nd Floor West, Beverly Hills CA 90211-2713. (310)358-4980. Fax: (310)358-4981. Website: www.laface.com. A&R Director: Pete Farmer. Record company.
   • In 2000, LaFace recording artist TLC won Grammies for Best R&B Song and Best R&B Performance By A Duo or Group With Vocal for "No Scrubs."
Distributed by: BMG.
How to Contact: *Does not accept unsolicited material.*
Music: Released *Aquemini* (album), recorded by OutKast; *Soul Food* (album soundtrack); and *My Way* (album), recorded by Usher, all on LaFace Records. Other artists include Az Yet, TLC, Toni Braxton and Donell Jones.

LAMAR MUSIC MARKETING, % 104 Pearsall Dr., Mt. Vernon NY 10552. (914)699-1744 or 973-7385. Fax: (914)668-3119. Executive Director: Darlene Barkley. Operations Director: Vernon Wilson. Music Producer: M3. Labels include Lamar, MelVern, Wilson, Pulse Music Publications. Record company, music publisher and workshop organization. Estab. 1984. Staff size: 4. Releases 4 CD singles and 1 LP/year. Pays standard royalty to artists on contract; statutory rate to publisher per song. "We charge only if we are hired to do 'work-for-hire' projects."
How to Contact: "Videotape submissions of actual performance only."
Music: Mostly **R&B**, **rap** and **pop**. Released "I Am So Confused" (single), written and recorded by Eemense; and "Heavenly" (single), recorded by Vern Wilson, both on Lamar Records; and "Feel Like a Woman" (single by Wilson/Johnson), recorded by Sandra Taylor on MelVern Records (R&B/ballad). Other artists include Barry Manderson and J-Son. Clients include: Hollywood Records, Riviera Film Company and Warner Bros.
Tips: "Unsolicited demo submissions are a waste of time. We need to *see* what you can do as well as hear what you can do. We are aware that there are extremely talented producers, but we are looking for extremely talented performers! Those selected will become a part of our music business program. Funding is available for those in the program."

LANDMARK COMMUNICATIONS GROUP, P.O. Box 1444, Hendersonville TN 37077. E-mail: lmarkcom@aol.com. **Contact:** Bill Anderson, Jr., president (all styles). Professional Manager (western): Dylan Horse. Labels include Jana and Landmark Records. Record company, record producer, music publisher (Newcreature Music/BMI and Mary Megan Music/ASCAP) and management firm (Landmark Entertainment). Releases 10 singles, 8 LPs and 8 CDs/year. Pays 5-7% royalty to artists on contract; statutory rate to publisher for each record sold.
How to Contact: Submit demo tape by mail. Unsolicited submissions are OK. Prefers 7½ ips reel-to-reel or cassette with 4-10 songs and lyric sheet. SASE. Responds in 1 month.
Music: Mostly **country/crossover**, **gospel**, **jazz**, **R&B**, **rock** and **top 40/pop**. Released *The Gospel Truth* (album by various artists), recorded by Vernon Oxford on Rocade (country); *The Yates Family 25 Year Anniversary* (album by various artists), recorded by Joanne Cash Yates on Jana (gospel); and *Nothin' Else Feels Quite Like It* (album), written and recorded by various artists on Landmark (positive country).
Tips: "Be professional in presenting yourself."

LANDSLIDE RECORDS, P.O. Box 20387, Atlanta GA 30325. (404)931-9049. E-mail: mrland @mindspring.com. Website: http://www.landsliderecords.com. President A&R: Michael Rothschild. Promotions Director/A&R: Eddie Cleveland. Record company, music publisher (Frozen Inca Music/BMI) and record producer. Estab. 1981. Releases 4 LPs and 4 CDs/year. Pays negotiable royalty to artists on contract; negotiable rate to publisher per song on record.

Distributed by: Rock Bottom, Action, Paul Starr and Twin Brook.
How to Contact: Submit demo tape by mail. Unsolicited submissions are OK. Prefers cassette with 6-12 songs and lyric sheet. SASE. Responds in 2 months.
Music: Mostly **blues** and **roots music**; also **jazz** and **swing**. Released *Derek Trucks Band* (album by Derek Trucks), recorded by Derek Trucks Band (rock); *The Lost Continentals* (album), written and recorded by Amy Pike; and *New Orleans Big Beat* (album), written and recorded by Dave Bartholomew, all on Landslide Records. Other artists include The Steam Donkeys, Colonel Bruce Hampton and Paul McCandless.

◖ LARI-JON RECORDS, 325 W. Walnut, Rising City NE 68658. (402)542-2336. **Contact:** Larry Good, owner. Record company, management firm (Lari-Jon Promotions), music publisher (Lari-Jon Publishing/BMI) and record producer (Lari-Jon Productions). Estab. 1967. Staff size: 1. Releases 15 singles and 5 LPs/year. Pays varying royalty to artists on contract.
How to Contact: Submit demo tape by mail. Unsolicited submissions are OK. Prefers cassette with 5 songs and lyric sheet. SASE. Responds in 2 months.
Music: Mostly **country**, **gospel-Southern** and **'50s rock**. Released "Glory Bound Train" (single), written and recorded by Tom Campbell; *The Best of Larry Good* (album), written and recorded by Larry Good (country); and *Her Favorite Songs* (album), written and recorded by Johnny Nace (country), all on Lari-Jon Records. Other artists include Kent Thompson and Brenda Allen.

◖ LARK RECORD PRODUCTIONS, INC., P.O. Box 35726, Tulsa OK 74153. (918)786-8896. Fax: (918)786-8897. E-mail: janajae@janajae.com. Website: www.janajae.com. **Contact:** Kathleen Pixley, vice president. Record company, music publisher (Jana Jae Music/BMI), management firm (Jana Jae Enterprises) and record producer (Lark Talent and Advertising). Estab. 1980. Staff size: 8. Pays negotiable royalty to artists on contract; statutory rate to publisher per song on record.
How to Contact: Submit demo tape by mail. Unsolicited submissions are OK. Prefers cassette or VHS videocassette with 3 songs and lead sheets. Does not return material. Responds only if interested.
Music: Mostly **country**, **bluegrass** and **classical**; also **instrumentals**. Released "Fiddlestix" (single by Jana Jae); "Mayonnaise" (single by Steve Upfold); and "Flyin' South" (single by Cindy Walker), all recorded by Jana Jae on Lark Records (country). Other artists include Syndi, Hotwire and Matt Greif.

✔ ◎ LEATHERLAND PRODUCTIONS, 2301 Atlantic St., Hopewell VA 23860. (804)458-1612. E-mail: leatherlandprod@firstsaga.com. Website: www.spudmanfoo.com. **Contact:** Tammy Alexander, owner. Record company, music publisher (Leatherland Productions) and books on tape. Estab. 1997. Pays negotiable royalty to artists on contract; statutory rate to publisher per song on record.
Distributed by: Leatherland Productions.
How to Contact: *No unsolicited submissions accepted.*
Music: Contemporary Christian.

N ⊕ ◻ LOCK, (formerly Plastic Surgery), Coachhouse, Mansion Farm, Liverton Hill, Sandway, Maidstone, Kent ME172NJ England. Phone/fax: (01622)858300. E-mail: info@eddielock.com. **Contact:** Eddie Lock, A&R. Record company, music publisher (Lock 'n' S) and record producer (Carpe Diem). Estab. 1988. Staff size: 2. Releases 5 singles/year. Pays negotiable royalty to artists on contract; statutory rate to publisher per song on record.
Distributed by: "Varies, as we mainly license to majors."
How to Contact: Submit demo tape by mail. Unsolicited submissions are OK. Prefers cassette. Does not return material. Responds in 1 week.
Music: Mostly **dance**, **house** and **trance**. Released "Camels" (single), written and recorded by Santos (dance), released 2001 on Lock; and "Phuture" (single by E. Lock/S. McGuire/J. Davis), recorded by Eddie Lock vs. Priest (dance), released 2000 on Portent.

◻ LOCONTO PRODUCTIONS/SUNRISE STUDIO, 10244 NW 47 St., Sunrise FL 33351. (954)741-7766. President: Frank X. Loconto. Producer (country/western, gospel): Bill Dillon. Producer (pop, top 40): Dennis Bach. Labels include FXL Records. Record company, music publisher (Otto Music Publishing/ASCAP) and record producer. Estab. 1978. Releases 10 singles, 10 cassettes/ albums and 5 CDs/year. Pays negotiable royalty to artists on contract; statutory rate to publisher per song on record.

Distributed by: FXL Record Distribution.

How to Contact: Submit demo tape by mail. Unsolicited submissions are OK. Prefers cassette or CD/CDR with lyric sheet or lead sheet. SASE. Responds in 4 months.

Music: Released *Palm Beach Society Feeling* (album), written and recorded by Michael Moog (pop); *Ballet Techniques Music* (album), written and recorded by Vladimir Issaek (classical), both released 1999 on FXL; and *Love and Joy* (album), written and recorded by Irena Kofman (sacred), released 1999 on MDI. Other artists include Roger Bryant, Bill Dillon, Bob Orange, The New Redemption Singers (gospel), Back In Bimini (calypso) and Arcangel Piano Quartet (classical).

Tips: "Be sure to prepare a professional demo of your work and don't hesitate to seek 'professional' advice."

⊘ LONDON SIRE RECORDS, 7381 Beverly Blvd., Los Angeles CA 90036. (323)937-4660. Fax: (323)933-7277. Website: www.sirerecords.com. A&R: Jonathon Paley, Andy Paley. New York office: 936 Broadway, New York NY 10010. (212)253-3900. (212)253-2950. Director of A&R: Greg Glover; Director A&R: Greg Glover. Record company.

Distributed by: WEA.

How to Contact: *Does not accept unsolicited submissions.*

Music: Mostly **rock** and **alternative**. Artists include Spacehog, Morcheeba, Everything, Guster, The Tragically Hip, Aphex Twin and Jolene.

◍ LUCIFER RECORDS, INC., P.O. Box 263, Brigantine NJ 08203-0263. (609)266-2623. Fax: (609)266-4870. **Contact:** Ron Luciano, president. Labels include TVA Records. Record company, music publisher (Ciano Publishing and Legz Music), record producer (Pete Fragale and Tony Vallo), management firm and booking agency (Ron Luciano Music Co. and TVA Productions). "Lucifer Records has offices in South Jersey; Palm Beach, Florida; and Las Vegas, Nevada."

How to Contact: *Call or write to arrange personal interview.* Prefers cassette with 4-8 songs. SASE. Responds in 3 weeks.

Music: Mostly **dance**, **easy listening**, **MOR**, **rock**, **soul** and **top 40/pop**. Released "I Who Have Nothing," (single), by Spit-N-Image (rock); "Lucky" (single), by Legz (rock); and "Love's a Crazy Game" (single), by Voyage (disco/ballad). Other artists include Bobby Fisher, Jerry Denton, FM, Zeke's Choice, Al Caz, Joe Vee and Dana Nicole.

🅽 ⬆ ⊘ MAGNUM MUSIC CORP. LTD., 8607 128th Ave., Edmonton, Alberta T5E 0G3 Canada. (780)476-8230. Fax: (780)472-2584. General Manager: Bill Maxim. Record company, management firm and music publisher (High River Music Publishing/ASCAP and Ramblin' Man Music Publishing/BMI). Estab. 1982. Pays standard royalty.

How to Contact: Write or call first and obtain permission to submit. Prefers cassette or VHS videocassette with 3 songs and lyric sheet. Does not return material. Responds in 2 months.

Music: Mostly **country, gospel** and **contemporary**; also **pop, ballads** and **rock**. Published *Pray for the Family* and *Emotional Girl* (albums), both written and recorded by C. Greenly (country); and *Don't Worry 'Bout It* (album), written and recorded by T. Anderson (country), all on Magnum Records.

✅ ⊘ MAJOR ENTERTAINMENT, INC., 331 W. 57th St., #173, New York NY 10019. (212)489-1500. Fax: (212)489-5660. E-mail: majcrentertain@aol.com. **Contact:** Tatiana Sampson, president. A&R Department: Matt "½ Pint" Davis. Record company, music publisher (Major Entertainment/BMI), artist management, distribution and consulting. Estab. 1997.

How to Contact: Submit demo tape by mail. Unsolicited submissions are OK. Prefers cassette with 3 songs. SASE. Responds in 2 months.

Music: Mostly **rap** and **R&B**. Released *2 Hot Fa TV* (album by Walter McCullon), recorded by Tre-8 (rap), released 2000 on Smoke 1; and *No Secrets* (album by Timothy Brown), recorded by Father MG (rap), released 2000 Street Solid.

[icons] MAKOCHÉ RECORDING COMPANY, 208 N. Fourth St., Bismarck ND 58501. (701)223-7316. Fax: (701)255-8287. E-mail: makoche@aol.com. Website: www.makoche.com. **Contact:** Jennifer Swap, A&R assistant. Labels include Chairmaker's Rush, Scoria and Tellurian. Record company and recording studio. Estab. 1995. Staff size: 7. Releases 4 CDs/year. Pays negotiable royalty to artists on contract; statutory rate to publisher per song on record.
Distributed by: DNA, Music Design, Four Winds Trading, Zango Music and New Leaf Distribution.
 • Makoché is noted for releasing quality music based in the Native American tradition. Recognized by the NAmmy's, New Age Voice Music Awards and C.O.V.R. Music Awards.
How to Contact: *Call first and obtain permission to submit demo.* "Please submit only fiddle and American Indian-influenced music." SASE. Responds in 2 months.
Music: Mostly **Native American**, **flute** and **fiddle**. Released *The Heron Smiled* (album), written and recorded by Annie Humphrey (folk), released 2000; and *Cheyenne Nation* (album), writter and recorded by Joseph Fire Crow (Native American flute), both released 2000 on Makoché. Other artists include Gary Stroutsos, Bryan Akipa, Keith Bear, Joseph Fire Crow, Sissy Goodhouse and Kevin Locke.
Tips: "We are a small label with a dedication to quality. Be persistent but patient."

[icons] MALACO RECORDS, 3023 W. Northside Dr., Jackson MS 39213. (601)982-4522. Executive Director: Jerry Mannery. Record company. Estab. 1986. Releases 20 projects/year. Pays 8% royalty to artists on contract; statutory rate to publisher per song.
How to Contact: Submit demo tape by mail. Unsolicited submissions are OK. Prefers cassette or VHS videocassette. Does not return material.
Music: Mostly **traditional** and **contemporary gospel**. Artists include Mississippi Mass Choir, Willie Neal Johnson & the Gospel Keynotes, Rev. James Moore, Mississippi Children's Choir, Bryan Wilson, The Pilgrim Jubilees, Lillian Lilly, Ruby Terry, Jackson Southernaires, Dorothy Norwood, The Sensational Nightengales, The Angelic Gospel Singers, Carolyn Traylor, Christopher Brinson and Rudolph Stanfield & New Revelation.

[icons] MAVERICK RECORDS, 9348 Civic Center Dr., Beverly Hills CA 90210. (310)385-7800. Fax: (310)385-8033. Website: www.maverickrc.com. Head of A&R: Guy Oseary. A&R: Jason Bentley; Russ Rieger. New York office: 1290 Avenue of the Americas, 9th Floor, New York NY 10019. (212)229-0337. Fax: (212)315-5590. Director A&R: Michael Taylor. Record company.
Distributed by: WEA.
 • In 2000, Maverick's Madonna won a Grammy Award for Best Song Written for A Motion Picture ("Beautiful Stranger"), and Lenny Kravitz won a Grammy for Best Male Rock Performance ("American Woman"), both from *Austin Powers' The Spy Who Shagged Me*.
How to Contact: *Maverick Records does not accept unsolicited submissions.*
Music: Released *The Wedding Singer Volume 2* (soundtrack); *Supposed Former Infatuation Junkie* (album), recorded by Alanis Morissette; and *Ray of Light* (album), recorded by Madonna. Other artists include Candlebox, Deftones, Love Spit Love, Me'shell Ndegeocello, Neurotic Outsiders, The Rentals, Rule 62 and Summercamp.

[icons] MAYFAIR MUSIC, (formerly Berandol Music), 2600 John St., Unit 219, Markham, Ontario L3R 3W3 Canada. (905)475-1848. **Contact:** Ralph Cruickshank, A&R. Record company, music publisher (MBD Records). Estab. 1979. Pays 10% royalty to artists on contract; statutory rate to publisher per song on record.
 • Mayfair Music is also listed in the Music Publishers section.
How to Contact: Submit demo CD/CDR by mail. Unsolicited submissions are OK. Prefers CD/CDR only with 4 songs. Does not return material. Responds in 3 weeks.
Music: Mostly **instrumental** and **children's**. Current acts include Frank Mills and Paul Saulnier.

[icons] MCA RECORDS, 1755 Broadway, 8th Floor, New York NY 10019. (212)841-8000. Fax: (212)841-8146. Website: www.mca.com/mca_records. Vice President A&R-urban: Wendy Goldstein. Santa Monica office: 2220 Colorado Ave., Santa Monica CA 90404. (310)865-4000. Senior

Vice President A&R: Randy Jackson; Senior Vice President A&R: Michael Rosenblatt. Nashville office: 60 Music Square E., Nashville TN 37203. (615)244-8944. Fax: (615)880-7447. A&R Senior Manager: Renee White. Record company and music publisher (MCA Music).

● In 2000, MCA's The Roots featuring Erykah Badu won a Grammy Award for Best Rap Performance By A Duo or Group ("You Got Me," from *Things Fall Apart*).

How to Contact: MCA Records cannot accept unsolicited submissions. Have your demo recommended to their A&R Department by a well-known manager, agent, producer, radio DJ or other music industry veteran. Create a buzz in your local community at the club label, through local music publications and at your local radio station.

Music: Released *Love Always* (album), recorded by K-Ci & JoJo; *Acquarium* (album), recorded by Aqua; and *Sublime* (album), recorded by Sublime, all on MCA Records. Other artists include Tracy Byrd, George Strait, Vince Gill, The Mavericks and Trisha Yearwood.

⬤ MCB RECORDS/PEPE, 1437 Central G-1, Memphis TN 38104. (901)725-4940. E-mail: peper ecords@excelonline.com. **Contact:** Ms. Boswell, president. Record company, music publisher (In the Green/BMI) and record producer (Ms. Boswell). Estab. 1991. Releases 4 singles and 2 CDs/year. Pays standard royalty to artists on contract; statutory rate to publisher per song on record.

Distributed by: Select-O-Hits.

How to Contact: Write first and obtain permission to submit a demo. Prefers cassette with 3 songs and lyric sheet. "Full production, please. No home recordings." SASE. Responds in 3 months.

Music: Mostly **country**, **pop** and **alternative country**; also **rock**, **gospel** and **blues**. Released *Only In It For the Money* (album), recorded by Gary Williams; *It Must Be Love* (album), recorded by Alan Hall (pop); and *Gone to the Dogs* (album), written and recorded by Jeremiah Lucker (alternative county), both on MCB. Other artists include Scott Elwood.

Tips: "Read every book you can on songwriting."

[N] ⬤ MEGAFORCE WORLDWIDE ENTERTAINMENT, P.O. Box 779, New Hope PA 18938. (215)862-5411. Fax: (215)862-9470. E-mail: contact@megaforcerecords.com. Website: www. megaforcerecords.com. **Contact:** Greg Caputo, A&R. President: Marsha Zazula. CEO: Jon Zazula. General Manager: Missi Callazzo. Labels include Megaforce Records Inc. Record company. Estab. 1983. Staff size: 2. Releases 5 LPs, 2 EPs and 5 CDs/year. Pays various royalties to artists on contract; ¾ statutory rate to publisher per song on record.

Distributed by: Alternative Distribution Alliance.

How to Contact: *Contact first and obtain permission to submit.*

Music: Mostly **rock**. Released *Matinee Idols* (album), written and recorded by Ominous Seapods (rock); *They Missed the Perfume* (album), recorded by The Disco Bisquits (rock), released 2001; and *Let's Get It Right* (album), written and recorded by SNFU (rock) on Megaforce. Other artists include Gouds Thumb and Wolfpack.

🍁 ✓ ⬤ MERLIN RECORDS OF CANADA, (formerly Merlin Productions), P.O. Box 5087 VMPO, Vancouver British Columbia V6B 4A9 Canada. Phone/fax: (604)434-9129. E-mail: merlin.m erlin@home.com. President: Wolfgang Hamann (dance, R&B). Vice Presidents of A&R: Martin E. Hamann (rock); Leslie Bishko (world, reggae). Record company, record producer and management firm (Merlin Management). Estab. 1979. Staff size: 5. Releases 5 singles, 3 LPs, 1 EP and 3 CDs/year. Pays negotiable royalty to artists on contract; statutory rate to publisher per song on record.

How to Contact: Write or call first and obtain permission to submit. Prefers cassette with 3 songs and lyric sheet. SAE and IRC. Responds in 2 weeks.

Music: Mostly **rock/pop**, **R&B** and **dance**; also **modern rock**. Released *None Too Soon* (album), written and recorded by None Too Soon; *Died and Gone to Heaven* (album), written and recorded by Donner & Blitzen; and *Every Day's A New Day* (album), written and recorded by Lady Jane, all released on Merlin Records of Canada. Other artists include Wolfgang-Wolfgang.

THE TYPES OF MUSIC each listing is interested in are printed in **boldface**.

Tips: "Learn what it takes to be a professional! Developing your art also means learning about the business side."

N⃞ ⃞ MIGHTY RECORDS, 150 West End, Suite 6-D, New York NY 10023. (212)873-5968. Manager: Danny Darrow. Labels include Mighty Sounds & Filmworks. Record company, music publisher (Rockford Music Co./BMI, Stateside Music Co./BMI and Corporate Music Publishing Co./ ASCAP) and record producer (Danny Darrow). Estab. 1958. Releases 1-2 singles, 1-2 12″ singles and 1-2 LPs/year. Pays standard royalty to artists on contract; statutory rate to publisher per song on record.

How to Contact: Submit demo tape by mail. Unsolicited submissions are OK. "No phone calls." Prefers cassette with 3 songs and lyric sheet. Does not return material. Responds in 1 month only if interested.

Music: Mostly **pop**, **country** and **dance**; also **jazz**. Released *Impulse* (album by D. Darrow); *Corporate Lady* (album by Michael Green); and *Falling In Love* (album by Brian Dowen), all recorded by Danny Darrow on Mighty Records.

✓⃞ ⃞ MISSILE RECORDS, Box 5537, Kreole Station, Moss Point MS 39563-1537. (228)475-0059. "No collect calls." **Contact:** Doris M. Mitchell, president. Vice President: Justin F. Mitchell. Vice President/Manager: Joe F. Mitchell. Record company, music publisher (Bay Ridge Publishing/ BMI) and record producer. Estab. 1974. Releases 28 singles and 10 LPs/year. Pays "10-16¢ per song to new artists, higher rate to established artists"; statutory rate to publisher for each record sold.

Distributed by: Select-O-Hits, Total Music Distributors, Music Network, Impact Music, Universal Record Distributing Corporation, Dixie Rak Records & Tapes, KY Imports/Exports, Curtis Wood Distributors, Valley Media Distributors, ATM Distributors.

How to Contact: *Write first and obtain permission to submit.* Include #10 business-size SASE, with sufficient postage to return all materials. "All songs sent for review MUST include sufficient return postage. No collect calls. Do not send reply post cards, only SASE. If you only write lyrics, do not submit. We only accept completed songs, so you must find a musical collaborator." Prefers cassette with 3-6 songs and lyric sheet. Responds in 2 months.

Music: Mostly **country**, **alternative**, **gospel**, **rap**, **heavy metal**, **hardcore**, **folk**, **contemporary**, **jazz**, **bluegrass** and **R&B**; also **soul**, **MOR**, **blues**, **ballads**, **reggae**, **world**, **rock** and **pop**. Released "Excuse Me, Lady," "When She Left Me" (singles by Rich Wilson), "Everyone Gets A Chance (To Lose in Romance)" and "I'm So Glad We Found Each Other" (singles by Joe F. Mitchell), recorded by Rich Wilson (country/western); "Rose Up On A Stem" (single by Joe F. Mitchell), recorded by Jerry Piper (country/western), all on Missile Records. Other artists include Sarah Cooper (pop/R&B), Charlene White (country & western), Della Reed (contemporary Christian), Matellica (heavy metal), Coco Hodge (alternative) and Lady Love (rap).

Tips: "We will give consideration to new exceptionally talented artists with a fan base and some backing."

⃞ MODAL MUSIC, INC.™, P.O. Box 6473, Evanston IL 60204-6473. (847)864-1022. E-mail: modalmusic@juno.com. Website: www.modalmusic.com. President: Terran Doehrer. Assistant: J. Distler. Record company and agent. Estab. 1988. Staff size: 2. Releases 1-2 LPs/year. Pays negotiable royalty to artists on contract; negotiable rate to publisher per song on record.

How to Contact: Submit demo tape by mail. Unsolicited submissions are OK. Prefers cassette with bio, PR, brochures, any info about artist and music. Does not return material. Responds in 4 months.

Music: Mostly **ethnic** and **world**. Released *Dance The Night Away* (album by T. Doehrer), recorded by Balkan Rhythm Band™; and *Sid Beckerman's Rumanian (D. Jacobs)* (album), recorded by Jutta & The Hi-Dukes™, both on Modal Music Records. Other artists include Ensemble M'Chaiya™, Nordland Band™ and Terran's Greek Band™.

Tips: "Please note our focus is ethnic. You waste your time and money by sending us any other type of music. If you are unsure of your music fitting our focus, please call us before sending anything. Put your name and contact info on every item you send!"

MONTICANA RECORDS, P.O. Box 702, Snowdon Station, Montreal, Quebec H3X 3X8 Canada. **Contact:** David P. Leonard, general manager. Labels include Dynacom. Record company, record producer (Monticana Productions) and music publisher (Montina Music/SOCAN). Estab. 1963. Staff size: 1. Pays negotiable royalty to artists on contract.
How to Contact: Submit demo tape by mail. Unsolicited submissions are OK. Prefers CD, phonograph record or VHS videocassette. SASE.
Music: Mostly **top 40**, **blues**, **country**, **dance-oriented**, **easy listening**, **folk** and **gospel**; also **jazz**, **MOR**, **progressive**, **R&B**, **rock** and **soul**.
Tips: "Be excited and passionate about what you do. Be professional."

DOUG MOODY PRODUCTIONS, P.O. Box 6271, Oceanside CA 92058-6271. E-mail: dmprodx@aol.com. Website: www.MysticRecordsHQ.com. Labels include Clock. Music publisher (Mystic Records USA & UK), music producer (Doug Moody Music USA & UK). Estab. 1968. Releases 8 LPs, 6 EPs and 6 CDs/year. Pays 10% royalty to artists on contract.
How to Contact: Only open to groups who perform. SASE.
Music: Mostly **mystic thrash** and **punk** ; also **blues**, **50s** and **60s** music for Clock Records. Does not want pop, classical, religious. Released *Maximum Rock 'n' Roll* (album), written and recorded by NOFX (mystic); and *Happy Organ* (album), written and recorded by Dave Baby Cortez (clock).
Tips: "Make a master ready for release."

MOR RECORDS, 17596 Corbel Court, San Diego CA 92128. (858)485-1550. Fax: (858)485-1883. E-mail: stuart@glassman.org. President: Stuart L. Glassman. A&R (pop): Don Smith. Engineer: Dan Milner. Record company and record producer. Estab. 1980. Staff size: 2. Releases 3 singles/year. Pays 4% royalty to artists on contract; negotiable rate to publisher per song on record.
Affiliate(s): MOR Jazztime (country M.O.R. Americana).
How to Contact: Submit demo tape by mail. Unsolicited submissions are OK. Prefers cassette or CD. SASE. Responds in 1 month.
Music: Mostly **pop instrumental/vocal MOR**; also **country**.
Tips: "We are looking for commercially sounding product with a 'hook' and a clean lyric with 'outstanding' melody."

MOTOWN RECORDS, 825 Eighth Ave., New York NY 10019. (212)373-0600. Senior Vice President A&R: Bruce Carbone. Los Angeles office: 11150 Santa Monica Blvd. #1000, Los Angeles CA 90025. (310)996-7200. Website: www.motown40.com. Labels include BIV Records, Illtown Records and MoJazz Records. Record company.
How to Contact: *Motown Records does not accept unsolicited submissions.*
Music: Artists include Brian McKnight and Erykah Badu.

NATION RECORDS INC., 6351 W. Montrose #333, Chicago IL 60634. (312)458-9888. Fax: (773)645-2025. E-mail: info@nationrecords.com. Website: www.nationrecords.com. **Contact:** Phil Vaughan, A&R. Record company. Estab. 1996. Releases 5 CDs/year. Pays negotiable royalty to artists on contract; statutory rate to publisher per song on record.
Distributed by: Midwest Artist Distribution.
How to Contact: Submit demo tape by mail. Unsolicited submissions are OK. Prefers cassette or CD with lyric sheet. Does not return material. Responds in 3 months.
Music: All types. Released *American Stories* (album by Bob Young); and *Steve & Johnnie Present* "Life After Dark" (album), both on Nation Records Inc. Other artists include The Buckinghams, Dick Holiday and The Bamboo Gang.

NEURODISC RECORDS, INC., 4592 N. Hiatus Rd., Ft. Lauderdale FL 33351. (954)572-0289. Fax: (954)572-2874. E-mail: neurodisc@aol.com. Website: www.neurodisc.com. President: Tom O'Keefe. Label Manager: John Wai. Record company and music publisher. Estab. 1990. Releases 3 singles, 10 LPs and 10 CDs/year. Pays negotiable royalty to artists on contract; 75% "to start" to publisher per song on record.
Distributed by: Priority/EMI.

How to Contact: Submit demo tape by mail. Unsolicited submissions are OK. Prefers cassette, CD, DAT or VHS videocassette. SASE. Responds in 2 months.
Music: Mostly **electronic**, **dance** and **New Age**; also **rap**. Released *The Chemical Box* (electronic); and *Acid Breaks & Brat* (albums), both written and recorded by various artists (electronic); and *Holiday Moods* (album), recorded by NuSound (ambient). Other artists include Level X and Get Some Crew.

NORTH STAR MUSIC, 22 London St., E. Greenwich RI 02818. (401)886-8888. Website: www.northstarmusic.com. **Contact:** Richard Waterman, president. Record company. Estab. 1985. Staff size: 15. Releases 12-16 LPs/year. Pays 9% royalty to artists on contract; ¾ statutory rate to publisher per song on record.
Distributed by: Valley Media Inc., Goldenrod and Lady Slipper.
How to Contact: Submit demo CD by mail. Unsolicited submissions are OK. Prefers finished CD. Does not return material. Responds in 2 months.
Music: Mostly **instrumental**, **traditional** and **contemporary jazz**, **New Age**, **traditional world (Cuban, Brasilian, singer/songwriter, Hawaiian and Flamenco)** and **classical**. Released *Mother* (album), written and recorded by Susan McKeown/Cathie Ryan/Robin Spielberg (instrumental); *Mysts of Time* (album), written and recorded by Aine Minogue (Celtic chant); and *Crossing the Waters* (album by Steve Schuch), recorded by Steve Schuch and the Night Heron Consort (contemporary Celtic), all on North Star Music. Other artists include Judith Lynn Stillman, David Osborne, Emilio Kauderer, Gerry Beaudoin, Cheryl Wheeler and Nathaniel Rosen.

NPO RECORDS, INC., P.O. Box 41251, Staten Island NY 10304. Phone/fax: (718)967-6121. E-mail: nporecords@hotmail.com. Website: www.nporecords.com or www.Anomos.com. **Contact:** Erin McCavatelli, vice president. Record company and music publisher (NPO Records and Music Publishing). Estab. 1996. Releases 6 singles, 2 LPs, 2 CDs/year. Pays negotiable royalty to artists on contract; statutory rate to publisher per song on record.
How to Contact: We only accept material referred to us by a reputable industry source (manager, entertainment attorney, etc.).
Music: Mostly **hip-hop** and **dance**. Released "Playing No Games" (single by Anomes/Stealth/Potent Pete) from *From Here On* (album), recorded by Anomos/Stealth (hip-hop); "Show Gee The Money" (single by Gee Money/Potent Pete) from *Show Gee The Money* (album), recorded by Gee Money (hip-hop); and "Something" (single by Allie Gally/Potent Pete) from *The EP* (album), recorded by Allie (R&B), all released 2000 on NPO Records.
Tips: "Be open minded and accepting of constructive criticism. Self-discipline and professionalism are essential."

OCP PUBLICATIONS, 5536 NE Hassalo, Portland OR 97213. (503)281-1191. Fax: (503)282-3486. **Contact:** Dave Island, marketing manager. Labels include Candleflame and NALR. Record company, music publisher and record producer. Estab. 1977. Releases 20 LPs and 10 CDs/year. Pays 10% royalty to artists on contract; negotiable rate to publisher per song on record.
How to Contact: Submit demo tape or CD by mail. Unsolicited submissions are OK. Requires lead sheets (with chords, melody line and text minimum) with *optional* demo tape/CD. Prefers cassette with lead sheet. "Detailed submission information available upon request." SASE. Responds in 3 months.
Music: Mostly **liturgical, Christian/listening** and **children's Christian**; also **choral Christian anthems** and **youth Christian anthems**. Released *You Are the Way* (album), written and recorded by Steve Angrisano (youth gospel); *Cry the Gospel* (album), written and recorded by Tom Booth (youth gospel); and *Spirit & Song* (hymnal with 9 CDs), written and recorded by various (youth gospel), all released 1999 on OCP. "There are over 80 artists signed by OCP."
Tips: "Know the Catholic liturgy and the music needs therein."

OMEGA RECORD GROUP, INC., 27 W. 72nd St., New York NY 10023. (212)769-3060. Fax: (212)769-3195. E-mail: info@omegarecords.com. Website: www.omegarecords.com. Sales

Manager (pop, jazz, dance): Duane Martuge. Operations Manager (classical, jazz): Frank Burton. Labels include Vanguard Classics and Everest. Record company. Estab. 1989. Releases 5 singles and 60-70 CDs/year. Pays negotiable royalty to artists on contract.

Distributed by: Allegro Corporation.

How to Contact: Submit demo tape by mail. Unsolicited submissions are OK. Prefers cassette, CD or DAT. SASE. Responds in 3 weeks.

Music: Mostly **classical** and **jazz**.

☑ ◑ **OMNI 2000 INC.**, 413 Cooper St., Camden NJ 08102. (609)963-6400. Fax: (609)964-FAX-1. E-mail: omniplex@erols.com. Website: www.omniplex413.com. **Contact:** Michael Nise, president/executive producer. Record company, music publisher and record producer. Estab. 1995. Pays 50% royalty to artists on contract; statutory rate to publisher per song on record.

Distributed by: Sutra and Sema.

How to Contact: *Write first and obtain permission to submit.* Prefers cassette. SASE. Responds in 2 months.

Music: Mostly **R&B**, **gospel** and **pop**; also **children's**.

Tips: "Send music with great hooks, magnetizing lyrics and commercial appeal. Quantity is not as important as quality."

🅽 ◻ **ONLY NEW AGE MUSIC, INC.**, 8033 Sunset Blvd. #472, Hollywood CA 90046. (323)851-3355. Fax: (323)851-7981. E-mail: onam@loop.com. Website: www.newagemusic.com or www.newageuniverse.com. **Contact:** Suzanne Doucet, president. Record company, music publisher and consulting firm. Estab. 1987.

How to Contact: Call first and obtain permission to submit. Does not return material.

Music: Mostly **New Age**; also **world music**.

Tips: "You should have a marketing strategy and at least a small budget for markteing your product."

◑ **ORILLYON ENTERTAINMENT**, P.O. Box 8414, Washington DC 20336-8414. E-mail: orillyon@email.msn.com. Website: www.orillyonentertainment.com. President/CEO (rap, hip-hop): Lex Orillyon. Vice President A&R (R&B, blues, gospel): J. Bishop. Record company, music publisher and record producer (Donneat B. [Lex Orillyon]). Estab. 1997. Releases 3 singles and 2 CDs/year. Pays 9-15% royalty to artists on contract; statutory rate to publisher per song on record.

How to Contact: Submit demo tape by mail. Unsolicited submissions are OK. Prefers cassette, CD or videocassette with 1-6 songs, lyric sheet, bio and picture. SASE. Responds in 6 weeks.

Music: Mostly **rap**, **hip-hop** and **R&B**; also **jazz**, gospel and **blues**. Released *Da Chameleon* (album), written and recorded by Lex Orillyon (hip-hop), released 1999; and *Genesis Da Beginning* (album), written and recorded by Legend (hip-hop), released 2000, both on Orillyon Entertainment.

Tips: "If you think your music is ready for the world, then it is. But it takes lots of time and preparation to be competitive on the next level."

☑ ◑ **OUTSTANDING RECORDS**, P.O. Box 2111, Huntington Beach CA 92647. (714)377-7447. Fax: (714)377-7468. **Contact:** Earl Beecher, owner. Labels include Morrhythm. Record company, music publisher (Earl Beecher Publishing) and record producer (Earl Beecher). Estab. 1968. Staff size: 1. Releases 20 CDs/year. Pays $2/CD royalty to artists on contract; statutory rate to publisher per song on record.

Distributed by: Sites on the Internet.

How to Contact: Submit demo tape by mail. Unsolicited submissions are OK. Prefers cassette, CD or videocassette (VHS) with 3 songs, lyric sheet, photo and cover letter. SASE. Responds in 3 weeks.

Music: Mostly **jazz**, **rock** and **country**; also **everything else especially Latin.** Does not want music with negative, anti-social or immoral messages. Released "Stay With Me" (single by Vic Garcia) from *Sounds of Love* (album), recorded by Ron Brown and Mike Sharp's Balboa Brass (pop), released 2000 on Outstanding; "Hey Mr. Eastwood" (single) from *Gator Brown* (album), written and recorded by Richard Murray (country); and "Timidez" (single) from *Love for the World* (album), written and recorded by Vic Garcia (Latin), both released 2001 on Morrhythm. Other artists include Ron Brown, Paul Smith, Varouge Merjanian, Greg Doamanian and James Long.

Tips: "Keep selections short (three to three and a half minutes). Short intros and fade outs (if any). No dirty language. Do not encourage listeners to use drugs, alcohol or engage in immoral behavior. I'm especially looking for upbeat, happy, danceable music."

○ **P.M. RECORDS**, P.O. Box 19332, Indianapolis IN 46219-0100. (317)897-2545. E-mail: justtony @indy.net. Website: www.simplytony.com. A&R Directors: John Pelfrey Jr. (country/blues); Tony Mansour (pop, rock). Assistant A&R: Lisa Jack (country); Lori Ellis (rock). Labels include Tomahawk Records. Record company and record producer. Estab. 1998. Staff size: 10. Releases 5 singles, 4 LPs and 4 CDs/year. Pays negotiable royalty to artists on contract; statutory rate to publisher per song on record.

How to Contact: Submit demo tape by mail. Unsolicited submissions are OK. Prefers cassette, CD or videocassette with 3 songs, lyric sheet and lead sheet. "Please specify music style on envelope. Vocals must be clear." SASE. Responds in 6 weeks.

Music: Mostly **rock**, **country** and **blues**; also **pop**. Does not want rap. Released "Alibi" (single by Tony Manseur) from *The "Simply Tony" Show* (album), recorded by Simply Tony (pop/rock), released 2000 on P.M. Records; and "All I Wanna Do . . . Is You" (single by John Pelfrey Jr.) from *Cherokee* (album), recorded by J.W. Bach (country rock), released 2000 on Tomahawk.

Tips: "Remember, music is a business. Only serious-minded individuals need apply. Supply as much information as possible."

▨ ○ **P. & N. RECORDS**, 61 Euphrasia Dr., Toronto, Ontario M6B 3V8 Canada. (416)782-5768. Fax: (416)782-7170. **Contact:** Panfilo Di Matteo and Nicola Di Matteo, presidents, A&R. Record company, record producer and music publisher (Lilly Music Publishing). Estab. 1993. Staff size: 2. Releases 10 singles, 20 12″ singles, 15 LPs, 20 EPs and 15 CDs/year. Pays 25-35% royalty to artists on contract; statutory rate to publisher per song on record.

How to Contact: Submit demo tape by mail. Unsolicited submissions are OK. Prefers cassette or videocassette with 3 songs and lyric or lead sheet. Does not return material. Responds in 1 month only if interested.

Music: Mostly **dance**, **ballads** and **rock**. Released *Only This Way* (album), written and recorded by Angelica Castro; and *The End of Us* (album), written and recorded by Putz, both on P. & N. Records (dance).

▨ ◨ **PACIFIC TIME ENTERTAINMENT**, 4 E. 12th St., New York, NY 10003. (212)741-2888. Fax: (212)807-9501. E-mail: pactimeco@aol.com. Website: www.pactimeco.com. **Contact:** Curtis Urbina, president. Record company. Estab. 1998. Staff size: 4. Releases 2 singles and 20 CDs/ year. Pays negotiable royalty to artists on contract; ¾ rate to publisher per song on record.

Distributed by: Navarre Corporation.

How to Contact: *Call first and obtain permission to submit demo.* Prefers CD with 3 songs. Responds in 1 month.

Music: Film scores. Released *Fever (Original Motion Picture Soundtrack)* (album), recorded by Joe Delia (soundtrack), released 2000; *What's Cooking (Original Motion Picture Soundtrack)* (album), recorded by Craig Pruess (soundtrack), released 2001; and *Shadow of the Vampire (Original Motion Picture Soundtrack)* (album), recorded by Dan Jones (soundtrack), released 2001, all on Pacific Time Entertainment. Other artists include Nana Simpoulos, Jimmy Earl, Psonica, Mark P. Adler and Scotch Egg.

◨ **PAINT CHIP RECORDS**, P.O. Box 12401, Albany NY 12212. (518)765-4027. E-mail: paintch ipr@aol.com. **Contact:** Dominick Campana, owner/producer. Record/production company. Estab. 1992. Staff size: 1. Releases 2 CDs/year. Pays negotiable royalty to artists on contract; statutory rate to publisher per song on record.

Distributed by: Dutch East India Trading.

How to Contact: Submit demo tape by mail. Unsolicited submissions are OK. Prefers cassette with 4 songs. Does not return material. Responds in several weeks only if interested.

Music: Mostly **"alternative" guitar rock** (bands). Released *Dear Soul* (album by Pendergrast/ Barnum), recorded by The Wait (alternative rock), released 1999; *Pink As Hell* (album by Conners/ Campana), recorded by MK4 (alternative rock), both on Paint Chip; and *Take Her To The Zoo* (album by Powell), recorded by Vodkasonics (alternative rock) on Cacophone.

Tips: "Do not submit music if you haven't heard of any of the artists on this label. Do not submit music if you are not currently performing. Do not submit music if you don't think your work is absolutely amazing. Do not phone without written permission."

◑ **PERMANENT PRESS RECORDINGS/PERMANENT WAVE**, 14431 Ventura Blvd. #311, Sherman Oaks CA 91423. Phone/fax: (818)981-7760. E-mail: pop@permanentpress.net. Website: www.permanentpress.net. **Contact:** Ray Paul Klimek, president/director of A&R. Labels include Permanent Wave. Record company, music publisher (Permanent Pop Music/BMI) and record producer (Ray Paul). Releases 8-10 CDs/year. Pays negotiable royalty to artists on contract; negotiable rate to publisher per song on record.

Distributed by: Burnside Distributing Corp., Phantom/Digital Waves, Paulstarr Distributing Group, Action Music and The Song Corporation (Canada).

How to Contact: Unsolicited submissions are OK. Mostly interested in well-established acts, but will consider beginners.

Music: Mostly **pop/power pop**, **rock/pop reissues** and **alternative pop**; also **smooth jazz** and **modern instrumental**. Released *The Charles Beat* (album), written and recorded by Ray Paul (pop/ rock); *20/20 Hindsight* (album by Robbie Sinclair/Donald McDonald), recorded by Yogi; and *Spklanng!* (album by Maury Lafoy/Graham Powell), recorded by The Supers (pop/rock), all released 2000 on Permanent Press. Other artists include Badfinger, The Breetles, Brown Eyed Susans, The Carpet Frogs, Chewy Marble, The City Beat, Walter Clevenger & The Dairy Kings, Terry Draper, Richard X. Heyman, Klaatu, Bob Segarini, The Spongetones, The Van DeLecki's, Vivabeat, Bobby Wells and William Pears.

Tips: "Permanent Press is known for signing well-known or established artists. New artists are considered by referral only, the strength of their songwriting, and the recordings submitted, which should be a finished master recording. We are known to release high-quality product with excellent packaging. Permanent Press is a nationally distributed label with close ties to retail, industry trades, AAA, AC and NAC radio. We service radio, most music publications, and the majority of weekly, daily and specialty newspapers."

☑ ◑ **PGE PLATINUM GROOVE ENTERTAINMENT**, P.O. Box 2877, Palm Beach FL 33480. (561)775-4561. Fax: (561)775-4562. E-mail: Brian@PGEcd.com. Website: www.PGEcd.com or www.561.net. Record company and music publisher (Advantage 1000 Music). Estab. 1993. Staff size: 5. Releases 8 singles, 8 LPs and 7 CDs/year. Pays negotiable royalty to artists on contract; statutory rate to publisher per song on record.

How to Contact: Submit demo tape by mail. Unsolicited submissions are OK. Prefers CD. Does not return material. Responds in 1 month.

Music: Mostly **hip hop**, **R&B** and **dance**; also **drum n bass** and **alternative**. Does not want rock, country or garbage. Released *Face Off II* (album), written and recorded by various (rap); *Cali Things* (album), written and recorded by various (rap); and *Double Platinum* (album), written and recorded by DJ X. Travagant, all released on Platinum Groove Entertainment (funky breaks/dance).

☑ ◑ **PICKWICK/MECCA/INTERNATIONAL RECORDS**, P.O. Box 725, Daytona Beach FL 32115. (904)252-4849. Fax: (904)252-7402. E-mail: CharlesVickers@USALink.com. Website: www.ZYWorld.com/CharlesVickers. **Contact:** Clarence Dunklin, president. Record company and music publisher (Pritchett Publications). Estab. 1980. Releases 20 singles, 30 LPs and 30 CDs/year. Pays 5-10% royalty to artists on contract; negotiable rate to publisher per song on record.

How to Contact: Submit demo tape by mail. Unsolicited submissions are OK. Prefers cassette with 12 songs and lyric or lead sheet. Does not return material.

Music: Mostly **gospel**, **disco** and **rock/pop**; also **country**, **ballads** and **rap**. Released *Give It To Me Baby* (album by Loris Doby), recorded by Gladys Nighte; *Baby I Love You* (album), written and recorded by Joe Simmon; and *I Love Sweetie* (album by Doris Doby), recorded by Bobby Blane.

◯ PLATEAU MUSIC, P.O. Box 947, White House TN 37188. (615)654-8131. Fax: (615)654-8207. E-mail: nville93@aol.com. Website: www.sbshow.com/TN/PlateauMusicEnterprises/. **Contact:** Tony Mantor, owner. Record company and record producer. Estab. 1990. Staff size: 1. Pays negotiable royalty to artists on contract; statutory rate to publisher per song on record.
How to Contact: Submit demo tape by mail. Unsolicited submissions are OK. Prefers cassette with 4 songs and lyric sheet. Does not return material. Responds in 6 weeks.
Music: Mostly **country**, **R&B** and **rock/pop**. Released *Somewhere in the Neighborhood* (album), recorded by Dobie Toms, released 1999; and *I've Got Love* (album by Sara Majors), recorded by The Weeds, both on PMI Records (country). Other artists include Mark Knight.
Tips: "We are a music producer that develops talent and shops them to the major labels. We do very few independent releases. Our focus is on getting the artist ready to compete in the major arena. Have dedication and be prepared to work."

Ⓝ ◪ PLATINUM ENTERTAINMENT, INC., 11415 Old Roswell Rd., Alpharetta GA 30004. (770)664-9262. Fax: (770)664-7316. Website: www.platinumcd.com. A&R Rep (gospel): Claudius Craig; (classical/other): Lynne Hoffman-Engle. Labels include CGI Intersound and Platinum. Record company, music publisher and distributor. Estab. 1982. Releases 6-10 singles and 150 CDs/year. Pays negotiable royalty to artists on contract; negotiable rate to publisher per song on record.
How to Contact: *Write or call first and obtain permission to submit.* Prefers cassette with 3 songs. "We will contact the songwriter when we are interested in the material." Does not return material. Responds in 2 months.
Music: Mostly **gospel** and **classical**. Released *B2K: Prophetic Songs of Promise* (album), recorded by William Becton (gospel); and *Best of James Hall & Worship* (album), recorded by James Hall & Worship (gospel), both released 2000 on CGI.

🌐 ✓ ◪ PLAYBONES RECORDS, Winterhuder Weg 142, D-22085 Hamburg Germany. Phone: (040)22716552 + -53. Fax: (040)22716554. E-mail: mento_music@t-online.de. **Contact:** Michael Frommhold, head of A&R. Producer: Arno van Vught. Labels include Rondo Records. Record company, music publisher (Mento Music Group) and record producer (Arteg Productions). Estab. 1975. Releases 30 CDs/year. Pays 8-16% royalty to artists on contract; statutory rate to publisher per song on record.
How to Contact: Submit demo tape by mail. Unsolicited submissions are OK. Prefers cassette with 3-4 songs. Put your strongest/best song first. "Put your name and address on the inside sleeve of the tape. If you have a fax number, inform us. Tell us in a typed cover letter what you want/what you are looking for." Does not return material. Responds in 3 weeks.
Music: Mostly **instrumentals**, **country** and **jazz**; also **background music**, **rock** and **gospel**. Released "Geesthus" (single) from *The Best of* . . . (album), written and recorded by Volker Frank (pop); "Earthviews 4" (single by W. Bauer) from *Earthview/Special Edition* (album), recorded by Wolfgang v. Wolpertshausen (soft melodic); and "Longing for Djerba" (single) from *Bass & Fusion* (album), written and recorded by Dixi Krauser (pop), all released 2000 on Playbones Records. Other artists include H.J. Knipphals, Gaby Knies, Jack Hals, H. Hausmann, Crabmeat and M. Frommhold.

◯ PMG RECORDS, P.O. Box 312897, Penobscot Station, Detroit MI 48231. E-mail: prejippie@aol.com. Website: www.presjippie.com. **Contact:** Bruce Henderson, president. Record company, music

---

REFER TO THE CATEGORY INDEX (at the end of this section) to find exactly which companies are interested in the type of music you write.

publisher (Prejippie Music Group/BMI) and record producer (PMG Productions, Prejippie Music Group). Estab. 1990. Staff size: 3. Releases 6-12 12″ singles, 2 LPs and 2 EPs/year. Pays 40% royalty to artists on contract; statutory rate to publisher per song on record.

- Publishes *Direct Hitz*, a newsletter "where other independents can learn how to work effectively in the music business today."

Distributed by: Dancefloor and Win.

How to Contact: Submit demo tape by mail. Unsolicited submissions are OK. Prefers CD or VHS videocassette with 3-4 songs and lyric sheet. "Include photo if possible. No calls please." SASE. Responds in 6 weeks.

Music: Mostly **funk/rock**, **alternative R&B**, **alternative rock**, **experimental** and **techno/dance**. Released *Tony Webb's Bass Christmas* (album), written and recorded by Tony Webb (alternative jazz) on PMG Records. Other artists include Urban Transit and the Prejippies.

Tips: "Be very original in your approach to a song: concentrate on creating an interesting arrangement; concentrate on having at least one good hook; and put some thought into creating interesting lyrical themes."

[N] [Ø] POINTBLANK RECORDS, 338 N. Foothill Rd., Beverly Hills CA 90210. (310)288-1420. Fax: (310)288-1494. Website: www.virginrecords.com. **Contact:** John Wooler, president. Pointblank is owned by Virgin Records America. Record company. Estab. 1989. Releases 2 CDs/year.

Distributed by: EMD.

How to Contact: *Only accepts material from managers and attorneys.* "Do not call—we will get in touch with you when the demo has been listened to." Does not return material. Responds in 1 year.

Music: Mostly **blues**, **roots** and **soul**. Released *Best of Blues Guitar* (album), written and recorded by various artists; *Found True Love* (album), written and recorded by John Hammond; and *Duke's Blues* (album), written and recorded by Duke Robillard, all on Pointblank Records. Other artists include John Lee Hooker, Pops Staples, Roy Rogers, Hadda Brooks, Marva Wright, Bill Perry, Johnny Winter, The Boneshakers, Charlie Musselwhite and Jon Cleary.

[N] [Ø] POP RECORD RESEARCH, 10 Glen Ave., Norwalk CT 06850. (203)847-3085. Director: Gary Theroux. Labels include Surf City, GTP and Rock's Greatest Hits. Record company, music publisher (Surf City Music/ASCAP), record producer and archive of entertainment-related research materials (files on hits and hitmakers since 1877). Estab. 1962. Pays statutory rate to publisher per song on record.

- See their listing in the Organizations section.

How to Contact: Submit demo tape by mail. Unsolicited submissions are OK. Prefers cassette or VHS videocassette. Does not return material.

Music: Mostly **pop**, **country** and **R&B**. Released "The Declaration" (single by Theroux-Gilbert), recorded by An American; "Thoughts From a Summer Rain" (single), written and recorded by Bob Gilbert, both on Bob Records; and "Tiger Paws" (single), written and recorded by Bob Gilbert on BAL Records. Other artists include Gary and Joan, The Nightflight Singers and Ruth Zimmerman.

Tips: "Help us keep our biographical file on you and your career current by sending us updated bios/press kits, etc. They are most helpful to writers/researchers in search of accurate information on your success."

[✓] [○] POWERBLAST RECORDINGS, P.O. Box 12911, Cincinnati OH 45212. (513)691-2788. E-mail: ewc@powerblastworldwide.com. Website: www.powerblastworldwide.com. CEO: Ernest W. Coleman. Vice President: M.L. Rogers. Record company. Estab. 1992. Staff size: 6. Releases 4 CDs/year. Pays negotiable royalty to artists on contract; statutory rate to publisher per song on record.

Distributed by: Various one-stop distributors and online e-commerce sites on the Internet.

How to Contact: Submit demo tape by mail. Unsolicited submissions are OK. Prefers CD, cassette or videotape (VHS) with 3 songs and cover letter. SASE. Responds in 1 month if interested.

Music: Mostly **hip-hop/rap**, **alternative** and **metal**; also **jazz**, **r&b** and **New Age**. Does not want country. Released *Destructive Communication* (album), written and recorded by Bombthreat (hardcore hip hop); *Death Becomes All of 'Em* (album), written and recorded by Cutty B. Spooky; *Explosive*

Material (album), written and recorded by Bombthreat (hardcore hip hop); and *Heat* (album), written, produced and recorded by The G. Other artists include Skin Curtain, Architect Sound Design, DJ Abstrakt, Short Body and Mayhem Stompabitch.

Tips: "Be professional when making contact or approaching our company."

☑ ◎ **PPL ENTERTAINMENT GROUP**, P.O. Box 8442, Universal City CA 91608. Phone/fax: (818)506-8534. E-mail: pplzmi@aol.com. Website: www.polzmi.com. **Contact:** Cisco Crowe, vice president A&R. Vice President A&R: Jaeson Effantic. Vice President, A&R: Kaitland Diamond. General Manager: Jim Sellavain. President, Creative: Suzette Cuseo. Labels include Bouvier and Credence. Record company, music publisher (Pollybyrd Publications) and management firm (Sa'mall Management). Estab. 1979. Staff size: 3. Releases 10-30 singles, 12 12″ singles, 6 LPs and 6 CDs/year. Pays 10-15% royalty to artists on contract; statutory rate to publisher per song on record.

Distributed by: Sony and The Malibu Trading Company.

How to Contact: *E-mail and obtain permission to submit.* Prefers cassette or videocassette with 2 songs. SASE. Responds in 6 weeks.

Music: Released "I Am Sorry" (single) from *JR Perry* (album), written and recorded by JR Perry (gospel), released 2001 on PPL/Sony; "I Don't Want to Be Alone" (single by Jarrett/Cuseo) from *Phyne I Can B.* (album), recorded by Phyne (pop), released 2001 on PPL/Sony; and "Steel Hat, Cold Heart" (single by Ken Allen) from *Destiny* (album), recorded by Buddy Wright (blues), released 2001 on PPL. Other artists include Phuntaine, Condottiere and D.M. Groove.

🅽 ◎ **PRAVDA RECORDS**, 6311 N. Neenah, Chicago IL 60631. (773)763-7509. Fax: (773)763-3252. E-mail: pravdausa@aol.com. Website: pravdamusic.com. **Contact:** Mo Goodman, director of A&R. A&R (pop/rock): Matt Favazza. Labels include Bughouse. Record company. Estab. 1985. Releases 3-6 singles, 1 EP and 5-6 CDs/year. Pays 10-15% royalty to artists on contract; statutory rate to publisher per song on record.

Distributed by: Hep Cat, Columbia House and Carrot Top.

How to Contact: Submit demo tape by mail. Unsolicited submissions are OK. Prefers cassette or CD with 3-4 songs. Does not return material. "Will contact only if interested."

Music: Mostly **rock**. Released "Slipped Away" (single by Dag Juhlin) from *Junior* (album), recorded by The Slugs (pop); "Paralyzed" (single) from *Live In Chicago* (album), written and recorded by Legendary Stardust Cowboy (psychobilly); and "The Freshman 15 (fifteen)" (single) from *Sticky* (album), written and recorded by The New Duncan Imperials (alternative rock), all released 2000 on Pravda. Other artists include Tiny Tim, Frantic Flattops, Gringo, Javelin Boot and cheer-accident.

Tips: "Be nice! Tour behind your release, don't take yourself too seriously."

◻ **PRESENCE RECORDS**, 67 Candace Lane, Chatham NJ 07928-1115. (201)701-0707. **Contact:** Paul Payton, president. Record company, music publisher (Paytoons/BMI) and record producer (Presence Productions). Estab. 1985. Staff size: 1. Pays 1-2% royalty to artists on contract; statutory rate to publisher per song on record.

Distributed by: Clifton Music.

How to Contact: Submit demo tape by mail. Unsolicited submissions are OK. "No phone calls." Prefers cassette with 2-4 songs and lyric sheet. SASE. Responds in 1 month. "Tapes and CDs not returned without prepaid mailer."

Music: Mostly **doo-wop ('50s)**, **rock** and **new wave rock**. "No heavy metal, no 'Christian' or religious rock." Released "Ding Dong Darling," "Bette Blue Moon" and "Davilee/Go On" (singles by Paul Payton/Peter Skolnik), recorded by Fabulous Dudes (doo-wop), all on Presence Records. "No heavy metal, Christian or religious rock."

Tips: "Would you press and distribute it if it was *your* money? Only send it here if the answer is yes."

☑ ◎ **PRIORITY RECORDS**, 6430 Sunset Blvd., Suite 900, Hollywood CA 90028. (323)467-0151. Fax: (323)856-8796. Website: www.priorityrec.com. Senior Vice President of A&R: Andrew Shack. National Director A&R: Marvin Watkins. Manager A&R: Mark Brown. New York office: 32

W. 18th St., 12th Floor, New York NY 10011. (212)627-8000. Fax: (212)627-5555. A&R: Ray/Rae. Labels include No Limit Records, Rawkus Records, Hoo-Bangin' Records and Duck Down Records. Record company.
Distributed by: EMD.
How to Contact: Does not accept unsolicited submissions.
Music: Released *MP Da Last Don*, recorded by Master P; *Life or Death*, recorded by C-Murder; and *I Got the Hook-Up!* (soundtrack), all on No Limit. Other artists include Ice Cube, Young Bleed and Kane & Abel.

☑️ ◩ **Q RECORDS**, 1200 Wilson Dr., West Chester PA 19380-4262. (484)701-1580. Fax: (484)701-1988. Senior Director: Jonathan P. Fine. General Manager: Alan Rubens. A&R: Dana Kasha-Murray. Record company, music publisher. Estab. 1999. Staff size: 9. Releases 16 CDs/year. Pays negotiable royalty to artists on contract; negotiable rate to publisher per song on record.
Distributed by: Atlantic Records/WEA.
How to Contact: *Write first and obtain permission to submit a demo.* Prefers CD with press clippings. Does not return material. Responds only if interested.
Music: Mostly **rock**, **pop**, **jazz** and **classical**. Released *Footloose: Original Bradway Cast Recording* (album), recorded by the original Broadway cast (soundtrack); and *"American Bandstand" Library of Rock 'n' Roll*, written and recorded by various.

◩ **QUARK RECORDS**, P.O. Box 7320, FDR Station, New York NY 10150 or 4 E. 12th St., New York NY 10003. Phone/fax: (212)741-2888. E-mail: quarkent@aol.com. **Contact:** Curtis Urbina, president (pop, dance). A&R: Michelle Harris (alternative). Labels include Pacific Time Entertainment. Record company and music publisher (Quarkette Music/BMI and Freedurb Music/ASCAP). Estab. 1984. Releases 6 singles and 3 LPs/year. Pays negotiable royalty to artists on contract; ¾ statutory rate to publisher per song on record.
How to Contact: *Call first and obtain permission to submit.* Prefers cassette with 2 songs. SASE. Responds in 6 weeks.
Music: Mostly **dance/pop** and **movie soundtracks**. Released "Which Way To Go" (single by A. Reynolds/D. Grassie/C. Grayston) from *Inverse Catch-22* (album), recorded by Cynical Blend (pop), released 2001 on Pacific Time Entertainment; and "Weight of the World" (single by K. Katafigidtis) from *Fearless* (album), recorded by Kimon (pop), released 2001 on Quark Records.

◩ **QWEST RECORDS**, 3800 Barham Blvd., Suite 503, Los Angeles CA 90068. (323)874-7770. Fax: (323)874-5049. Vice President of A&R: Fade Duvernay; A&R: Marcia Johnson. New York office: 75 Rockefeller Plaza, 20th Floor, New York NY 10019-6908. (212)275-4800. Fax: (212)258-3036. Website: www.qwestrecords.com. Record company.
Distributed by: WEA.
How to Contact: *Qwest Records does not accept unsolicited submissions.*
Music: Released *Tamia* (album), recorded by Tamia on Qwest Records.

🅽 ☑️ ◩ **RA RECORDS**, P.O. Box 72087, 1562 Danforth Ave., Toronto, Ontario M4J 5C1 Canada. (416)693-1609. Fax: (416)693-0688. E-mail: ra@ican.net. Website: www.janilanzon.com. **Contact:** Josephine Nyholm, manager. Record company and music publisher (Soda Jerks Melodies). Estab. 1993. Releases 1-2 singles and 1 CD/year. Pays negotiable royalty to artists on contract; statutory rate to publisher per song on record.
Distributed by: Indie Pool Toronto and Canyon Records U.S.A.
How to Contact: Write or call first and obtain permission to submit a demo. Prefers cassette or CD with 3 songs, lyric and lead sheet, press kit and bio information. SAE and IRC. Responds in 2 months.
Music: Mostly **world beat**, **women's** and **native/indigenous**. Released *Songs for Chiapas; Off the Record*, recorded by various artists.

☑️ ◯ **RADICAL RECORDS**, 77 Bleecker St., Suite C2-21, New York NY 10012. (212)475-1111. Fax: (212)475-3676. E-mail: info@radicalrecord.com. Website: www.radicalrecords.com. **Contact:**

Johnny Chiba, A&R. Record company. "We also do independent retail distribution for punk, hardcore and oi! music." Estab. 1986. Staff size: 7. Releases 1 single, 2 LPs and 4 CDs/year. Pays 14% royalty to artists on contract; statutory rate to publisher per song on record.
Distributed by: Caroline, City Hall, Revelation, Select-O-Hits, Revolver.
How to Contact: Submit demo tape by mail. Unsolicited submissions are OK. Prefers cassette or CD. Does not return material. Responds in 1 month.
Music: Mostly **punk**, **hardcore** and **oi! music**. Released *Too Legit for the Pit—Hardcore Takes the Rap* (album), recorded by various; *Punk's Not Dead—A Tribute to the Exploited* (album), recorded by various; *Fresh Out of Give-a-Fucks* (album), recorded by Submachine; and *East Coast of Oi!* (album), recorded by various. Other artists include The Agents, The Cuffs, Social Scare, Sturgeon General and Inspector 7.
Tips: "Create the best possible demos you can and show a past of excellent self-promotion."

☑ ◑ **RADIOACTIVE RECORDS**, 8570 Hedges Place, Los Angeles CA 90069. (310)659-6598. Fax: (310)659-1679. E-mail: lowfi99@aol.com. Website: www.radioactive.net. A&R Director/Promotion (rock, alternative): Michelle Needy. A&R: Veronica Gretton (New York (212)595-8066) and Gary Kurfirst. Record company.
Distributed by: UVMD.
How to Contact: Submit demo tape by mail. Unsolicited submissions are OK. Does not return material.
Music: Released *Let Me Take You on A Journey* (album), recorded by Big Audio Dynamite; and *Please God* (album), recorded by Ana Voog, both on Radioactive Records. Other artists include Snow Pony, Live, Ramones, Shirley Manson, Elysian Fields and Black Grape.

☑ ◐ **RAGS TO RECORDS, INC.**, P.O. Box 42523, Washington DC 20015. (301)806-3070. Fax: (202)829-5590. E-mail: info@ragstorecords.com. Website: www.ragstorecords.com. **Contact:** John Meyer, president, A&R. Record company. Estab. 1997. Releases 1-2 single per CD and 1-4 CDs/year. Pays 10-80% royalties to artists on contract based on sliding scale of total sales and initial company outlay (see website for details); statutory rate to publisher per song on record.
How to Contact: Submit CD or tape by mail. Unsolicited submissions are OK. Prefers CD or tape with 3 or more songs. Does not return material. Responds only if interested.
Music: Mostly **rock**; also **anything loosely classifiable as rock**. Released *Six Pack of Shame* (album), written and recorded by Battery Apple; and *Dakota Floyd* (album), written and recorded by Dakota Floyd, both released 2001, both on Rags To Records.
Tips: "Be confident and be good. RTR is not in the business of holding people's hands while they get their acts together. It is a small company that invests extremely small amounts of money into acts which have already spent considerable time and effort making their music sound good. If you suck, we're not going to call you in the hopes that you get better later on; we're going to ignore you and possibly laugh at you."

▦ ◐ **RAMPANT RECORDS**, 2406 Gates Ave., Redondo Beach CA 90278. (310)546-2896. Fax: (520)396-2515. E-mail: rampant@earthlink.net. Website: www.rampantrecords.com. Vice President of A&R: Paul Grogan. Labels include Slinkey Recordings. Record company, music publisher (Nipple Fish Music Company) and record producer (Paul Grogan). Estab. 1993. Releases 3 LPs, 10 EPs and 2 CDs/year. Pays negotiable royalty to artists on contract; 75% rate to publisher per song on record.
Distributed by: Watts Music, Nemesis Distribution, T.R.C., Syntax, Intergroove and Magestic.
How to Contact: *Check website before submitting.* Submit demo tape by mail. Unsolicited submissions are OK. Prefers cassette with 3 songs. "Supply contact info on cassette and cassette box cover." Does not return material. Responds in 3 weeks.
Music: Mostly **progressive house**, **trance** and **big beat**; also **techno**, **jungle** and **funky breaks**. Does not want pop or electronica. Released *Tempest* (by J. Scotts/J. Blum), recorded by Deepsky (progressive house); and *Hush*, written and recorded by Joshua Ryan and Forefield (trance), both on Slinkey; and *Fly Mutha Beatz* (by Chris Brown), recorded by Brownie on Rampant (big beat/funky breaks). Other artists include Pablo, The Coffee Boys and Ascendance.

Tips: "We are looking for tracks that will rock a dance floor. Solid, well produced, underground tracks only."

⊘ RAVE RECORDS, INC., 13400 W. Seven Mile Rd., Detroit MI 48235. (248)540-RAVE. Fax: (248)338-0739. E-mail: info@raverecords.com. Website: www.raverecords.com. **Contact:** Carolyn and Derrick, production managers. Record company and music publisher (Magic Brain Music/AS-CAP). Estab. 1992. Staff size: 2. Releases 2-4 singles and 2 CDs/year. Pays various royalty to artists on contract; statutory rate to publisher per song on record.
Distributed by: Action Music Sales.
How to Contact: *Does not accept unsolicited submissions.*
Music: Mostly **alternative rock** and **dance**. Artists include Cyber Cryst, Dorothy, Nicole and Bukimi 3.

⊘ RAZOR & TIE ENTERTAINMENT, 214 Sullivan St., Suite 4A, New York NY 10012. E-mail: info@razorandtie.com. Website: www.razorandtie.com. Record company.
How to Contact: *Does not accept unsolicited material.*
Music: Released *Cry, Cry, Cry* by Dar Williams; *The Sweetheart Collection* by Frankie & The Knockouts; and *Everybody's Normal But Me* by Stuttering John, all on Razor & Tie Entertainment. Other artists include Cledus T. Judd, Graham Parker and Mare Winningham.

▼ ⊘ RCA RECORDS, 1540 Broadway, 36th Floor, New York NY 10036. (212)930-4000. Fax: (212)930-4447. Website: www.bmg.com/labels/rca.html. A&R: David Bendeth; David Novik; Brian Malouf; Steve Ferrera; Steve Ralbovsky. Beverly Hills office: 8750 Wilshire Blvd., Beverly Hills CA 90211. (310)358-4000. Fax: (310)358-4040. Senior Vice President of A&R: Bruce Flohr. Nashville office: 1 Music Circle N., Nashville TN 37203. (615)301-4300. Website: www.twangthis.com. A&R Director: Sam Ramage. Director of Artist Development: Debbie Schwartz. Labels include Loud Records, Deconstruction Records and Judgment/RCA Records. Record company.
Distributed by: BMG.
  • In 2000, RCA won Grammy Awards for Best Instrumental Arrangement ("Chelsea Bridge," by Don Sebesky); Best Historical Album (*The Duke Ellington Centennial Edition*); and Best Classical Engineered Album (*Stravinsky: Firebird; The Rite of Spring; Persephone*).
How to Contact: RCA Records does not accept unsolicited submissions.
Music: Released *'N Sync* (album), recorded by 'N Sync; and *Capitol Punishment* (album), recorded by Big Punisher, both on RCA Records. Other artists include Foo Fighters, Vertical Horizon, Eve 6, Robyn and Dave Matthews Band.

⊕ ⊘ RED-EYE RECORDS, Wern Fawr Farm, Pencoed, Mid-Glam CF35 6NB United Kingdom. Phone: (01656)86 00 41. **Contact:** M.R. Blanche, managing director. Record company and music publisher (Ever-Open-Eye Music/PRS). Estab. 1979. Releases 4 singles and 2-3 LPs/year. Pays negotiable royalty to artists on contract; statutory rate to publisher per song on record.
How to Contact: Submit demo tape by mail. Unsolicited submissions are OK. Prefers cassette, VHS videocassette or 7½ or 15 ips reel-to-reel with 4 songs. SAE and IRC. Does not return material.
Music: Mostly **R&B**, **rock** and **gospel**; also **swing**. Released "River River" (single by D. John), recorded by The Boys; and "Billy" (single by G. Williams); and "Cadillac Walk" (single by Moon Martin), both recorded by the Cadillacs, all on Red-Eye Records. Other artists include Cartoon and Tiger Bay.

🅝 ◯ REDEMPTION RECORDS, P.O. Box 3244, Omaha NE 68103-0244. (712)328-2771. Los Angeles: (323)651-0221. Fax: (712)328-9732. E-mail: rkuper@redemption.net. Website: www.redem

---

● **A BULLET** introduces comments by the editor of *Songwriter's Market* indicating special information about the listing.

ption.net. **A&R Czar:** Ryan D. Kuper (hardcore punk, indie rock, power pop). Record company. Estab. 1990. Staff size: varies. Releases 2-3 singles, 2-3 EPs and 2-3 CDs/year. Pays standard royalty to artists on contract; statutory rate to publisher per song on record.
Distributed by: Redemption Distribution Alliance, Lumberjack and Revelation.
How to Contact: Submit demo tape by mail. Unsolicited submissions are OK. "We accept links to websites too. Include band's or artist's goals." Does not return material. Responds only if interested.
Music: Mostly **indie rock** and **power pop**. Artists include Not From Space (members of Sunny Day Real Estate, Seaweed, and Verbal Assault), The Eye, Real (members of Supertouch and American Standard), The Show-offs, N.F.S./Real, Citrus, Grasshopper Takeover, Andy Dick & The Bitches of the Century and The Heavyweight Champions.
Tips: "If you think your music is the right genre, submit by mail. Be prepared to tour to support the release. Make sure the current line-up is secure."

REITER RECORDS LTD., 308 Penn Estates, East Stroudsburg PA 18301. (570)424-9599. Fax: (570)424-0452. E-mail: stewrose@aol.com. Website: www.reiterrecords.com. **Contact:** Greg Macmillan, vice president of A&R. Record company. Estab. 1990. Releases 5 singles, 5-10 LPs and 5-10 CDs/year. Pays negotiable royalty to artists on contract; 75% of statutory rate to publisher per song on record for covered compositions.
How to Contact: Submit demo tape by mail. Unsolicited submissions are OK. Does not return material.
Music: Mostly **pop**, **jazz** and **rock**. Released *Battery Operated Orange* (album), recorded by Paul Tripp (rock); and *There Was A Time in America* (album), recorded by Paul Val and Corinne Gotti (pop/dance).

RELATIVITY RECORDS, 79 Fifth Ave., 16th Floor, New York NY 10003. (212)337-5300. **Contact:** A&R Dept. **A&R Administrator:** John Trumpadour. Website: www.relativityrecords.com. Labels include Ruthless Records. Record company.
Distributed by: Sony.
How to Contact: Submit demo tape by mail. Unsolicited submissions are OK. Prefers cassette, CD or DAT. Submit to Attn: A&R Dept.
Music: Released *Heaven'z Movie* (album), recorded by Bizzy Bone on Mo Thugs Records.

REPRISE RECORDS, 3300 Warner Blvd., 4th Floor, Burbank CA 91505. (818)846-9090. Fax: (818)840-2389. **Vice President A&R:** Matt Aberle; **Vice President A&R:** Mio Vukovic; **Manager A&R:** Tripp Walker. New York office: 75 Rockefeller Plaza, 21st Floor, New York NY 10019. (212)275-4500. Fax: (212)275-4596. Website: www.repriserec.com. **A&R:** Craig Pizzella. Labels include Duck. Record company.
Distributed by: WEA.
How to Contact: *Reprise Records does not accept unsolicited submissions.*
Music: Released *The Dance* (album), recorded by Fleetwood Mac; *Stunt* (album), recorded by Barenaked Ladies on Reprise; and *Pilgrim* (album), recorded by Eric Clapton on Duck. Other artists include Wilco, Paul Brandt, Chaka Khan, Brady Seals, Arkarna, Dinosaur Jr., Depeche Mode, Faith No More and Green Day.

RHIANNON RECORDS, 20 Montague Rd., London, E8 2HW United Kingdom. (020)7275 8292. Fax: (020)7503 8034. E-mail: rhiannonmusic@appleonline.net. Website: www.rhiannonrecords.co.uk. **Owner:** Colin Jones. Record company, music publisher (Rhiannon Music) and record producer (Colin Jones). Estab. 1993. Releases 4-6 CDs/year. Pays negotiable royalty to artists on contract; pays according to agreement rate to publisher per song on record.
Distributed by: Rhiannon Distribution.
How to Contact: Submit demo tape by mail. Unsolicited submissions are OK. "We only publish writers we also record. No separate publishing deals!" Prefers cassette or DAT with press writings, bio and photo. "Please ensure material submitted meets label requirements." SAE and IRC. Responds in 1 month.

Music: Mostly **acoustic**, **ethnic-based folk**, **folk rock**, **singer/songwriter**, **folk/country** and **contemporary**. Released *Wings of the Sphinx* (album), recorded by Barry Dransfield (British folk); *Sin É* (album), recorded by Sin É (contemporary Irish folk); and *By Heart* (album), by Maggie Holland (contemporary acoustic), all on Rhiannon Records. Other artists include Calico, Bob Pegg and Felicity Buirski.

Tips: "Don't imitate—originate! I'm not looking for imitation Chieftains or Nanci Griffith. I want to hear talented artists using their background and imagination to offer new ideas. One of my former artists said, 'Most singer/songwriters are putting down on record what they should be telling their therapist.' If this is you, please don't send me your material!"

☑ ☯ **RIVAL RECORDS**, 204 W. Fifth St., Lorain OH 44052-1610. (440)244-5324. Fax: (440)244-5349. E-mail: scotti@rivalrecords.com. Website: www.RivalRecords.com. **Contact:** Scotti C. Campana, president. Record company, music publisher (Campana Music Publishing/ASCAP) and record producer. Estab. 1998. Staff size: 8.

How to Contact: Submit demo tape by mail. Unsolicited submissions are OK. Prefers CD with 3 songs, lyric sheet, cover letter, photo and press clippings. Does not return submissions. Responds in 6 weeks.

Music: Mostly **R&B**, **hip-hop** and **pop**. Released "You Played Me" (single by David Tolliver), recorded by Men at Large; and "Something About You" (single by Scotti Campana), recorded by Soul, both on Rival Records (R&B). Other artists include Danny and S.O.S.C.

🅽 ◯ **ROAD RECORDS**, P.O. Box 2620, Victorville CA 92393. Website: www.roadrecords.com. **Contact:** Conrad Askland, president. Record company, record producer (Road Records) and music publisher (Askland Publishing). Estab. 1989. Produces 6 singles and 10 albums/year.

How to Contact: *Write or call first and obtain permission to submit a demo.* Prefers at least 3 songs with lyric and lead sheet. "We are looking for people that have a different, original sound." Does not return submissions. Responds in 3 weeks.

Music: Mostly **alternative**, **modern country** and **dance**; also **orchestral instrumental**. Does not want jazz. "We supply music to Grand Ole Opry, United Airlines, Knoxbury Farm and G.T.E."

Tips: "Do not submit what you think we are looking for. A lot of our projects are 'on the edge.'"

🅽 ☯ **ROBBINS ENTERTAINMENT LLC**, 159 W. 25th St., 4th Floor, New York NY 10001. (212)675-4321. Fax: (212)675-4441. E-mail: info@robbinsent.com. **Contact:** John Parker, director of A&R. Record company and music publisher (Rocks, No Salt). Estab. 1996. Staff size: 7. Releases 25 singles and 12-14 CDs/year. Pays negotiable royalty to artists on contract; statutory rate to publisher per song on record.

Distributed by: BMG.

How to Contact: Does not accept unsolicited submissions.

Music: Mostly **dance** and **pop**. Released "This Kind of Love" (single by Meg Hentges/Jude O'Nym), and *Brompton's Cocktail* (album by Meg Hentges/Jude O'Nym/Adam Schlesinger), both recorded by Meg Hentges (modern rock); and "When I'm Gone" (single by A. Hammond/H. Payne), recorded by Rockell (dance/pop), all on Robbins Entertainment. Other artists include Marco Polo, Nikisha Grier, Victoria Angeles and Lovatux.

Tips: "We are looking for original, but accessible music, with crossover potential."

🅽 ◯ **ROLL ON RECORDS**®, 112 Widmar Pl., Clayton CA 94517. (925)833-4680. E-mail: rollonrecords@aol.com. **Contact:** Edgar J. Brincat, owner. Record company and music publisher (California Country Music). Estab. 1985. Releases 2-3 LPs/cassettes/year. Pays 10% royalty to artists on contract; statutory rate to publisher per song on record.

Distributed by: Tower.

How to Contact: Submit demo tape by mail. Unsolicited submissions are OK. Do not call or write. Prefers cassette with 3 songs and lyric sheet. SASE. Responds in 6 weeks.

Music: Mostly **contemporary/country**, **MOR** and **R&B**; also **pop**, **light rock** and **modern gospel**. Released "Broken Record" (single by Horace Linsley/Dianne Baumgartner), recorded by Edee Gordon on Roll On Records; *Maddy* and *For Realities Sake* (albums both by F.L. Pittman/Madonna Weeks), recorded by Ron Banks/L.J. Reynolds on Life Records/Bellmark Records.

Tips: "Be patient and prepare to be in it for the long haul. A successful songwriter does not happen overnight. It's rare to write a song today and have a hit tomorrow. If you give us your song and want it back, then don't give it to us to begin with."

N ○ ROTTEN RECORDS, P.O. Box 2157, Montclair CA 91763. (909)624-2332. Fax: (909)624-2392. E-mail: rotten@rottenrecords.com. Website: www.rottenrecords.com. President: Ron Peterson. Promotions/Radio/Video: Andi Jones. Record company. Estab. 1988. Releases 3 LPs, 3 EPs and 3 CDs/year.
Distributed by: Shock (Australia), Sonic Rendezvous (UK), DNA, Smash (US) and St. Clair (Canada).
How to Contact: Submit demo tape by mail. Unsolicited submissions are OK. Prefers CD. Does not return material.
Music: Mostly **rock**, **alternative** and **commercial**; also **punk** and **heavy metal**. Released *Paegan Terrorism . . .* (album), written and recorded by Acid Bath; *Kiss the Clown* (album by K. Donivon), recorded by Kiss the Clown; and *Full Speed Ahead* (album by Cassidy/Brecht), recorded by D.R.T., all on Rotten Records.
Tips: "Be patient."

○ ROWENA RECORDS, 195 S. 26th St., San Jose CA 95116. (408)286-9840. Fax: (408)286-9845. E-mail: onealproduction@juno.com. Owner/A&R (country, Mexican, gospel): Grady O'Neal. A&R (all styles): Jeannine O'Neal. Record company and music publisher (Tiki Enterprises). Estab. 1967. Staff size: 3. Releases 8-12 LPs and 8-12 CDs/year. Pays negotiable royalty to artists on contract; pays statutory rate to publisher per song on record.
How to Contact: Submit demo tape by mail. Unsolicited submissions are OK. Prefers cassette with 2 songs and lyric sheet. SASE. Responds in 2 weeks.
Music: Mostly **gospel**, **country** and **pop**; also **Mexican** and **R&B**. Released "Amazing Grace" (single by Jeannine O'Neal) from *Blessed-Celebration*, recorded by Jeannine O'Neal (worship music/ *Up Lift'N Music*); "Style Of Our Own" (single by Art Kelly Glavin) from *I Like the Way You Dance*, recorded by Kool Katz (Latin groove); and "La Ultima Carta" (single by Jose Luis/Guitro'n Rodriquez) from *Fugitivos del Stress*, recorded by Jose Luis Guitron Rodriquez (Mexican music), all released 2000 on Rowena.

N ○ RUF RECORDS, 162 N. 18th St., Kenilworth NJ 07033. (908)653-9700. E-mail: intumg@a ol.com. **Contact:** Mike DeUrso, marketing manager. General Manager: Ira Leslie. Record company, music publisher and record producer (Thomas Ruf). Estab. 1993. Releases 12 CDs/year. Pays negotiable royalty to artists on contract; statutory rate to publisher per song on record.
Distributed by: IDN.
  ● Ruf is known for releasing heavy blues.
How to Contact: Submit demo tape by mail. Unsolicited submissions are OK. Prefers CD with 4 songs. Does not return material. Responds in 1 week.
Music: Mostly **blues**, **rock** and **R&B**. Released *Joy and Rain* (album), recorded by Mighty Sam McCain (blues), released 2001 on Ruf. Other artists include Luther Allison, John Mooney, Larry Garner, Friends n Fellow, Hans Theessink, Hank Shizzoe and Joanna Connor.

✓ ○ RUSTRON MUSIC PRODUCTIONS, 1156 Park Lane, West Palm Beach FL 33417-5957. (561)686-1354. E-mail: gordon-whims@juno.com. **Contact:** A&R. Executive Director: Rusty Gordon (folk fusions, blues, women's music, adult contemporary, electric, acoustic, New Age instrumentals, children's, cabaret). Director A&R: Ron Caruso. Associate Director of A&R: Kevin Reeves (pop, country, blues, R&B, jazz). Labels include Rustron Records and Whimsong Records. "Rustron administers 20 independent labels for publishing and marketing." Record company, record producer, management firm and music publisher (Whimsong/ASCAP and Rustron Music/BMI). Estab. 1970. Releases 5-10 cassettes and CDs/year. Pays variable royalty to artists on contract. "Artists with history of product sales get higher percent than those with no sales track record." Pays statutory rate to publisher.

How to Contact: *Write or call first to obtain permission to submit or submit* demo tape or CD by mail. Unsolicited submissions are OK. Prefers cassette with 3 songs and typed lyric sheet. "If singer/songwriter has independent product (cassette or CD) produced and sold at gigs—send this product." SASE required for all correspondence, no exceptions. Responds in 4 months.

Music: Mostly **mainstream** and **women's music**, **A/C**, **electric acoustic**, **pop (cabaret, blues)** and **blues (R&B, country and folk)**; also **New Age fusions** (instrumentals), **modern folk fusions**, **environmental** and **socio-political**. Released "Sunrise In the Mountains" (single by Ron Caruso/Rusty Gordon) from *Florida Fresh* (album), recorded by Song on A Whim (folk/country), released 2000 on Whimsong Records; "Never Always" (single) from *Shades of Reason* (album), written and recorded by Jayne Margo-Reby (folk/rock), released 2000 on MSB Records; and "Everybody Counts" (single by Susan Mosely) from *Children on the Brink* (album), recorded by Helen Hannah (children's), released 2000 on Rustron Records. Other artists include Star Smiley, Boomslang Swampsinger, Lisa Cohen, Ellen Hines and Robin Plitt.

Tips: "Find your own unique style; write well crafted songs with unpredictable concepts, strong hooks and definitive melody. New Age composers: evolve your themes and add multi-cultural diversity with instruments. Don't be predictable. Don't over-produce your demos and don't drown vocals. Send cover letter clearly explaining your reasons for submitting."

◻ **SABRE PRODUCTIONS**, P.O. Box 10147, San Antonio TX 78210. **Contact:** E.J. Henke, producer. Labels include Fanfare, Satin and Legacy. Record company and record producer. Estab. 1965. Staff size: 2. Releases 4 CDs/year. Pays 10% royalty to artists on contract; statutory rate to publisher per song on record.

How to Contact: Submit demo tape by mail. Unsolicited submissions are OK. Prefers cassette with 4 songs and lyric sheet. SASE. Responds in 1 month.

Music: Mostly **country** (all styles), **gospel** and **rock/R&B**. Released "Heaven's Telephone Line," "The Crushed Rose" and "Your Mansion Is Waiting" (singles by Wynona Kuntz), all recorded by Robert Beckom on Legacy Records.

☑◻ **SABTECA RECORD CO.**, P.O. Box 10286, Oakland CA 94610. (510)465-2805. Fax: (510)832-0464. E-mail: vitaminsun@aol.com. **Contact:** Duane Herring, president. Production Coordinator (pop, R&B, jazz): Sean Herring. Secretary (pop, R&B, country): Lois Shayne. Labels include André Romare Records. Record company and music publisher (Sabteca Music Co./ASCAP, Toyiabe Music Co./BMI). Estab. 1980. Releases 3 singles and 1 12″ single/year. Pays 10% royalty to artists on contract; statutory rate to publisher per song on record.

Distributed by: Sabteca.

How to Contact: *Write first and obtain permission to submit.* Prefers cassette with lyric sheet. SASE. Responds in 1 month.

Music: Mostly **R&B**, **pop** and **country**. Released "On the Good Side" (single by Thomas Roller), recorded by Johnny B (pop), released 2000 on Sabteca. Other artists include Walt Coleman, Lil Brown, Reggie Walker and Lois Shayne.

Tips: "Determination and persistence are vital."

☑◻ **SAFIRE RECORDS**, 5617 W. Melvina, Milwaukee WI 53216. Phone/fax: (414)444-3385. **Contact:** Darnell Ellis, president. A&R Representatives: Darrien Kingston (country, pop); Reggie Rodriqez (world, Latin, Irish). Record company, music publisher (Buzz Duzz Duzz), record producer (Darnell Ellis) and management firm (The Ellis International Talent Agency). Estab. 1997. Staff size: 2. Releases 3 singles, 3 LPs, 1 EP and 3 CDs/year. Pays negotiable royalty to artists on contract; statutory rate to publisher per song on record.

How to Contact: Submit demo tape by mail. Unsolicited submissions are OK. Prefers cassette with 3-4 songs. Does not return material. Responds in 2 months. "We will respond only if we are interested."

Music: Mostly **world**, **Latin** and **Irish**, **pop** and **country pop**. Artists include Magen Cory (country/pop). "Anything else except rap and metal."

Tips: "Songwriters need to get back to the basics of songwriting: great hooklines, strong melodies. We would love to hear from artists and songwriters from all over the world. And remember, just because someone passes on a song it doesn't mean that it's a bad song. Maybe it's a song that the label is not able to market or the timing is just bad."

SAHARA RECORDS AND FILMWORKS ENTERTAINMENT, 117 W. Harrison Bldg. #S627, Chicago IL 60605-1709. (773)509-6381. Fax: (312)922-6964. **Contact:** Edward De Miles, president. Record company, music publisher (EDM Music/BMI, Edward De Miles Music Company) and record producer (Edward De Miles). Estab. 1981. Releases 15-20 CD singles and 5-10 CDs/year. Pays 9½-11% royalty to artists on contract; statutory rate to publishers per song on record.
How to Contact: *Does not accept unsolicited submissions.*
Music: Mostly **R&B/dance**, **top 40 pop/rock** and **contemporary jazz**; also **TV-film themes**, **musical scores** and **jingles**. Released "Hooked on U," "Dance Wit Me" and "Moments" (singles), written and recorded by Steve Lynn (R&B) on Sahara Records. Other artists include Lost in Wonder, Dvon Edwards and Multiple Choice.
Tips: "We're looking for strong mainstream material. Lyrics and melodies with good hooks that grab people's attention."

SALEXO MUSIC, P.O. Box 18093, Charlotte NC 28218-0093. (704)392-2477. E-mail: salexo@bellsouth.net. **Contact:** Samuel Obie, president. Record company. Estab. 1992. Releases 1 CD/year.
How to Contact: *Write first and obtain permission to submit.* Prefers cassette with 3 songs and lyric sheet. SASE. Responds in 1 month.
Music: Mostly **contemporary gospel** and **jazz**. Released "Make A Joyful Noise" (single by Samuel Obie) from *Edwin Hawkins Music & Arts Seminar/Los Angeles*, recorded by Edwin Hawkins (gospel), released 2001 on World Class Gospel Records.
Tips: "Make initial investment in the best production."

SATELLITE MUSIC, 34 Salisbury St., London NW8 8QE United Kingdom. Phone: (+44)207-402-9111. Fax: (+44)207-723-3064. E-mail: eliot@amimedia.co.uk. Website: www.amime dia.co.uk. **Contact:** Eliot Cohem, CEO. Director: Ray Dorset. Labels include Saraja and Excalibur. Record company and music publisher. Estab. 1976. Staff size: 10. Releases 5 singles, 3 LPs and 3 CDs/year. Pays negotiable royalty to artists on contract; statutory rate to publisher per song on record.
Distributed by: S. Gold & Sons and Total Home Entertainment.
 • Satellite Music won two ASCAP awards in 1996 for Top R&B Song of the Year and Top Rap Song of the Year in the U.S.
How to Contact: Submit demo tape by mail. Unsolicited submissions are OK. Prefers cassette, CD, DAT or VHS videocassette with 4 songs, cover letter and press clippings. SAE and IRC. Responds in 6 weeks.
Music: Mostly **dance**, **disco** and **pop**. Does not want blues, jazz or country. Released "In the Snow" (by Ray Dorset), recorded by Mungo Jerry on BME (pop).

SEALED FATE RECORDS, 955 Massachusetts Ave., PMB 120, Cambridge MA 02139. E-mail: submit@sealedfate.com. Website: www.sealedfate.com. A&R: Eric Masunaga. Record company. Estab. 1995. Staff size: 3. Releases 3 singles, 1 EP and 3 CDs/year. Pays 15% royalty to artists on contract; statutory rate to publisher per song on record.
Distributed by: Revolver, Nail, CTD, Choke, Bayside, Red Eye, Sure Fire and Darla.
How to Contact: *Does not accept unsolicited submissions.* Prefers cassette or CD. Does not return material.
Music: Mostly **suburban underground rock**, **pop/techno** and **synth soul/mood**. Released *The Brighter Shore* (album), recorded by Sleepyhead (rock); *Carousel* (album), recorded by the Fly Seville (rock); and *Far Places* (album), recorded by The Pushkings (pop/soul), all on Sealed Fate Records.
Tips: "Send quality material."

SILTOWN RECORDS, 5 Park Plaza, Suite 870, Irvine CA 92614. (949)474-9684. Fax: (949)367-1078. E-mail: asp@siltown.com. Website: www.siltown.com. **Contact:** Alban Silva, CEO. Vice President/A&R: Greg Jensen. A&R, Christian/Gospel: Barbara Anderson. A&R, Rap/Hip Hop: Robert Davis. Record company. Estab. 1998. Staff size: 5. Releases 2 singles and 2 CDs/year.
Distributed by: On website.
How to Contact: Submit demo tape by mail. Unsolicited submissions are OK. Prefers CD, DAT with lyric sheet, cover letter and press clipping. Does not return material. Responds in 6 weeks.
Music: Mostly **pop/rock**, **Christian** and **country**; also **rap**, **hip-hop**, **all genres**.
Tips "Submit songs and music that are preferably in digital mode. Submit lyric sheet and send only your best CD. If your are interested in free exposure of your music, submit CD, a recent color photograph of band, and a short biography of thirty words or less. Please visit our website for format."

N: SILVER WAVE RECORDS, P.O. Box 7943, Boulder CO 80306. (303)443-5617. Fax: (303)443-0877. E-mail: info@silverwave.com. Website: www.silverwave.com. **Contact:** James Marienthal. Record company. Estab. 1986. Releases 4-5 CDs/year. Pays varying royalty to artists on contract and to publisher per song on record.
How to Contact: Write first and obtain permission to submit. Prefers CD. SASE. Responds only if interested.
Music: Mostly **world** and **Native American**.

N: SILVERTONE RECORDS, 137-139 W. 25th St., New York NY 10001. (212)727-0016. Fax: (212)620-0048. Label Director: Michael Tedesco. Hollywood office: 9000 Sunset Blvd., Suite 300, W. Hollywood CA 90069. Fax: (213)247-8366. Labels include Essential Records. Record company.
Distributed by: BMG.
How to Contact: *Does not accept unsolicited materials.* "Contact us through management or an attorney."
Music: Released *Jars of Clay* (album), recorded by Jars of Clay on Essential Records. Other artists include Chris Duarte, Buddy Guy, Hed, Livingstone, John Mayall, Metal Molly and Solar Race.

JERRY SIMS RECORDS, P.O. Box 648, Woodacre CA 94973. (415)789-8322. Fax: (415)456-9197. **Contact:** Jerry Sims, owner. Record company. Estab. 1984. Releases 6-7 CDs/year. Pays negotiable royalty to artists on contract; statutory rate to publisher per song on record.
Distributed by: New Leaf, LeFon, DeVorss and Top (Hong Kong).
How to Contact: Submit demo tape by mail. Unsolicited submissions are OK. Prefers cassette or CD. Does not return material. Responds in 1 month only if interested.
Music: Mostly **instrumental**, **Celtic** and **pop**. Released *Viaggio* and *December Days* (albums), both written and recorded by Coral (Celtic); and *King of California* (album), written and recorded by Chuck Vincent (rock), all on Jerry Sims Records. Other artists include Disfunctional Family, Kim Y. Han and Mike Lovelace.
Tips: "We are currently looking for ethnic music for movie soundtracks."

N: SIN KLUB ENTERTAINMENT, INC., P.O. Box 2507, Toledo OH 43606. (419)475-1189. President/A&R: Edward Shimborske III. Labels include Sin-Ka-Bob Records. Record company, music publisher (Morris St. James Publishing) and record producer (ES3). Estab. 1990. Releases 1 single, 1 LP and 5 CDs/year. Pays negotiable royalty to artists on contract; statutory rate to publisher per song on record.
Distributed by: MAD.

REFER TO THE GEOGRAPHIC INDEX (at the back of this book) to find listings of companies by state, as well as foreign listings.

How to Contact: Submit demo tape by mail. Unsolicited submissions are OK. Prefers cassette or CD with 3 songs and lyric sheet. "Send a good press kit (photos, bio, articles, etc.)." Does not return material. Responds in 1 month.

Music: Mostly **harder-edged alternative**, **punk** and **metal/industrial**; also **rap**, **alternative** and **experimental**. Released *Urban Witchcraft* (album), recorded by Thessalonian Dope Gods (industrial), released 1994; *All Balled Up* (album), recorded by Bunjie Jambo (punk), released 1996, both on Sin Klub. Other artists include Kid Rock, Dan Hicks, Lucky Boys Confusion, Chicken Dog, Crashdog, Section 315, The Geminus Sect, Evolotto, Kitchen Conspiracy, Valve and Three Below.

✓ ◎ **SMITHSONIAN FOLKWAYS RECORDINGS**, 750 9th St. NW, Suite 4100, Washington DC 20560. (202)275-1153. Fax: (202)275-1164. E-mail: folkways@aol.com. Website: www.si.edu/folkways. **Contact:** Daniel Sheehy, curator/director. Labels include Smithsonian Folkways, Dyer-Bennet, Cook and Paredon. Record company and music publisher. Estab. 1948. Releases 25 CDs/year. Pays negotiable royalty to artists on contract and to publisher per song on record.

Distributed by: Koch International.

How to Contact: *Write first and obtain permission to submit or to arrange personal interview.* Prefers CD or DAT. Does not return material. Responds in 6 months.

Music: Mostly **traditional US folk music, world music** and **children's music**. Released *Best of Broadside* (album), recorded by various artists (folk); *Vocal Music in Crete* (album), recorded by various artists (world/folk); and *Songs, Rhythms & Chants for the Dance* (album), recorded by Della Jenkins (children's), all released 2000 on Smithsonian Folkways Recordings. "We only are interested in music publishing associated with recordings we are releasing. Do not send demos of songwriting only."

Tips "If you are a touring artist and singer/songwriter, consider carefully the advantages of a non-museum label for your work. We specialize in ethnographic and field recordings from people around the world."

✓ ◯ **SONAR RECORDS & PRODUCTION**, P.O. Box 8095, Fort Worth TX 76112-0001. (817)531-9979. Fax: (817)451-1066. E-mail: sonarrecords@hotmail.com. Website: http://sonarproductions.com. Producer: Ken Moody (Moodini). Vice President Urban Music: Marvin Henderson. A&R: Marvin Shankle. Artist Development: Chris Dials. Labels include Sounds of New Artist Recordings. Record producer (Sonar, Moodini). Estab. 1994. Staff size: 4. Releases 3 singles, 1 LP, and 1 CD/year. Pays 12% royalty to artists on contract; statutory rate to publisher per song on record.

Distributed by: WEA.

How to Contact: Submit demo tape by mail. Unsolicited submissions are OK. Prefers cassette or CD. Does not return material. Responds in 1 month if interested.

Music: Mostly **r&b**, **positive rap** and **hip-hop gospel**; also **contemporary gospel**. Artists include Locaine, XL, OX, Peaches and Huzzy, Sons of Abraham and Shank.

Tips "Invest in yourself and others will follow."

◯ **SONGGRAM MUSIC**, 2500 E. State St., Hamilton Township NJ 08619. (609)586-4600. Fax: (609)586-8705. Director A&R: Tom Marolda. Supervisor: Tom Jason. Labels include Antra, The Bomb Factory, Leaky Penn. Record company, music publisher (Songgram Music), record producer (Tom Marolda) and distributor. Estab. 1979. Staff size: 45. Releases 5 singles, 6 LPs and 6 CDs/year. Pays negotiable royalty to artists on contract; statutory rate to publisher per song on record.

Distributed by: Red (Sony), Scorpio (Independent).

How to Contact: Submit demo tape by mail. Unsolicited submissions are OK. Prefers cassette, CD with sample songs and cover letter. Does not return material. Responds only if interested.

Music: Mostly **rap, female vocals, rock** and **pop**. Released "Dream" (single by Marolda/Jackson/Bryant/Johnson/Travis) from *Kats R Kummin* (album), recorded by Big Kats (rap), released 2000 on Bombfactory. Other artists include Horizontal Ladies Club, The Toms.

Tips: "Write hit songs in any genre. Love your craft."

Ⓝ ◎ **SONIC RECORDS, INC./SRI RECORDS, INC.**, 157 Woodburn Place, Advance NC 27006. (336)940-5736. Fax: (336)940-5736. E-mail: srecords@bellsouth.net. Website: www.sonicrec

ords.com. President: Doug Thurston. Vice President: Bobby Locke. Vice President, Public Relations: Debbie Anderson Locke. Record company and music publisher (Sonrec Music Publisher/BMI). Estab. 1964. Pays negotiable royalty to artists under contract.

Distributed by: Bertus and Self.

How to Contact: Submit demo tape or CD/CDR by mail. Unsolicited submissions are OK. Prefers cassette, CD, DAT or VHS videocassette with up to 3 songs and lyric or lead sheet. Does not return material. Responds ASAP.

Music: Mostly **country**, **gospel alternative** and **rock**. Released over 20 chart songs in the past year, including "Blindsided" (single by Austin Roberts), recorded by Donna Goodhart (country); "Hey Houston" (single), written and recorded by Jon Thomas (country); and "Tell It To My Heart" (single by Bill Hall), recorded by Tina Stevens (country). Other artists include Jerri Holiday (gospel) and Scott Human (country).

Tips: "Sonic and SRI are associated with a national television show 'Fast Track To Fame' which is aired weekly via satellite and the AmericaOne television network. Fast Track also has 'Specials' which appear approximately every 4 weekss on 'The National Network' which was formerly the Nashville Network. They also have clips on 'Great American Country' as well as their own network on www.fasttracktofame.tv with live shows Sunday through Wednesday nights at 9:30 eastern/6:30 pacific and continuous music video programming 24 hours a day. Only independent and new artists are broadcast."

[N] [⌂] [○] sonic unyon records canada, P.O. Box 57347, Jackson Station, Hamilton, Ontario L8P 4X2 Canada. (905)777-1223. Fax: (905)777-1161. E-mail: jerks@sonicunyon.com. Website: www.sonicunyon.com. Co-owners: Tim Potocic; Mark Milne; Andy McIntosh. Record company. Estab. 1992. Releases 2 singles, 2 EPs and 6 CDs/year. Pays negotiable royalty to artists on contract; statutory rate to publisher per song on record.

Distributed by: Caroline, Revolver and Smash.

How to Contact: Call first and obtain permission to submit. Prefers cassette or CD. "Research our company before you send your demo. We are small; don't waste my time and your money." Does not return material. Responds in 4 months.

Music: Mostly **rock**, **heavy rock** and **pop rock**. Released *Doberman* (album), written and recorded by Kittens (heavy rock); *What A Life* (album), written and recorded by Smoother; and *New Grand* (album), written and recorded by New Grand on sonic unyon records (pop/rock). Other artists include Siansphere, gorp, Hayden and Poledo.

Tips: "Know what we are about. Research us. Know we are a small company. Know signing to us doesn't mean that everything will fall into your lap. We are only the beginning of an artist's career."

[⌂] SOUND GEMS, P.O. Box 801, South Eastern PA 19339. (215)552-8889. Website: www.soundgems.com. CEO: Frank Fioravanti. A&R Director: Trish Wassel. Record company and music publisher (Melomega Music, Meloman Music). Estab. 1972. Staff size: 3. Pays negotiable royalty to artists on contract; statutory rate to publisher per song on record.

Distributed by: EMI, Sony, Warner.

How to Contact: Submit demo tape by mail. Unsolicited submissions are OK. Prefers cassette, CD with lyric sheet, cover letter and press clipping. "Do not send registered or certified mail." Does not return material. Responds only if interested.

Music: Mostly **r&b**, **pop** and **dance**; also **electronica**. Does not want rock, metal. Released *Be Thankful For What You've Got* (album), written and recorded by William DeVaughn (r&b).

Tips: "Be sure your style fits our catagories."

[✓] [○] SOUTHLAND RECORDS, INC., P.O. Box 1547, Arlington TX 76004-1547. (817)461-3280. E-mail: SteveReed@SouthlandRecords.com. Website: www.SouthlandRecords.com. **Contact:** Steve Reed, president. Record company and record producer (Steve Reed). Estab. 1980. Releases 3 CDs/year. Pays negotiable royalty to artists on contract; statutory rate to publisher per song on record.

How to Contact: Submit demo tape by mail. Unsolicited submissions are OK. Prefers cassette or CD with 4 songs, lyric and lead sheet, cover letter and press clippings. Does not return material. Responds in 3 months.

Music: Country only. Released *Close to You* (by Cindy Walker), recorded by Leon Rausch (country); and *Through Her Eyes*, written and recorded by Rob Dixon (country), all Southland Records, Inc..

SPINBALL MUSIC AND VIDEO, (formerly Draft Records), 7611 St. Denis, Montreal, Quebec H2R 2E7 Canada. (514)274-0816. President: Martin Gagnon. Labels include Storm Productions. Record company and record producer. Estab. 1994. Releases 3 singles and 5 CDs/year. Pays negotiable royalty to artists on contract.
Distributed by: Independence.
How to Contact: Submit demo tape by mail. Unsolicited submissions are OK. Prefers CD. Does not return material. Responds in 1 month.
Music: Mostly **dance**, **techno/house** and **rap/R&B**; also **world beat**.

SPOTLIGHT RECORDS, P.O. Box 6055, Hilliard OH 43026-6055. (614)771-5242. Fax: (614)771-5401. E-mail: spotlight3@prodigy.net. Website: www.abwy.net/spotlight3. **Contact:** James Bruce, owner. Record company. Estab. 1994. Staff size: 7. Releases 2 CDs/year. Pays negotiable royalty to artists on contract; statutory rate to publisher per song on record.
How to Contact: Submit demo tape by mail. Unsolicited submissions are OK. Prefers cassette with lyric sheet. Does not return material. Responds only if interested.
Music: Mostly **country**, **pop** and **Christian**. Released *Only In a Picture* (album by various), recorded by Debbie Collins (country); and *Sings the Hits* (by various), recorded by Brandi Lynn Howard (country).
Tips: "Submit your best work. Be very professional."

ST. FRANCIS RECORDS, 808¾ N. Detroit St., Los Angeles CA 90046. Phone/fax: (323)932-1040. Minister of Noise: Leland Leard. Record company. Estab. 1994. Releases 2 singles, 1 EP and 3 CDs/year. Pays negotiable royalty to artists on contract; statutory rate to publisher per song on record.
Distributed by: Nail, K, Darla, Bayside and Revolver.
How to Contact: Submit demo tape by mail. Unsolicited submissions are OK. Prefers cassette or CD with 4 songs and lead sheet. Does not return material. Responds in 2 months.
Music: Mostly **alternative**, **electronic** and **pop**; also **jazz**. Released *El Camino Real* (album), written and recorded by Carmaig de Forest (pop); *Strikes the Earth* (album), written and recorded by Deathstar (pop/alternative); and *Superwinners Summer Rock Academy* (album), written and recorded by various artists (alternative/pop), all on St. Francis Records.
Tips: "Commitment to performance is key."

STARDUST, 341 Billy Goat Hill Rd., Winchester TN 37398. (931)649-2577. Fax: (615)649-2732. E-mail: cbd@vallnet.com. Website: www.stardustcountrymusic.com. **Contact:** Barbara Doss, president. Labels include Stardust, Wizard, Doss, Kimbolon, Thunder Hawk, Flaming Star. Record company, music publisher (Buster Doss Music/BMI), management firm (Buster Doss Presents) and record producer (Colonel Buster Doss). Estab. 1959. Releases 50 singles and 25 CDs/year. Pays 8-10% royalty to artists on contract; statutory rate to publisher per song on record.
How to Contact: Write first and obtain permission to submit. Prefers cassette with 2 songs and lyric sheet. SASE. Responds "on same day received."
Music: Mostly **country**; also **rock**. Released "Come On In" (single), recorded by Duane Hall on Stardust Records and "Rescue Me" (single), recorded by Tommy D on Doss Records. Other artists include Linda Wunder, Rooster Quantrell, Don Sky, James Bryan, "Red" Reider, Holmes Bros., Donna Darlene, Jerri Arnold, "Bronco" Buck Cody and Dwain Gamel.

STONE AGE RECORDS, P.O. Box 100215, Palm Bay FL 32910-0215. Phone/fax: (208)441-6559. E-mail: savmusic@juno.com. President/Project Manager: Amy Young. Vice President/General Manager: Bill Young. Labels include SAV Music, ARAS Music, PARDO Music, Outback Records. Record company. Estab. 2000. Pays negotiable royalty to artists on contract; statutory rate to publisher per song on record.

How to Contact: Submit demo tape by mail. Unsolicited submissions are OK. Prefers finished CD projects with promo package (photo and bio). SASE.

Music: Mostly **country** and **film music** (any genre). Released *Disturbing Behavior* (album), written and recorded by Chokehold (heavy metal).

Tips: "We are an independent record company going places fast. We seek serious bands and artists ready to make a commitment to the label and to their career."

STREET RECORDS, P.O. Box 1356, Folly Beach SC 29439. (843)588-4024. Fax: (843)588-6030. E-mail: rock@streetrecords.com. Website: www.streetrecords.com. Director of A&R: Tasos. A&R: Conner Lewis; MJ Shutrump; Bettina Torello. Labels include Kretan Sea Records. Record company, music publisher (Kretan Sea Music) and record producer (Tasos). Estab. 1983. Staff size: 5. Releases 4 singles, 2 EPs and 5 CDs/year. Pays negotiable or 13% royalty to artists on contract; statutory rate to publisher per song on record.

Distributed by: Southern Records (USA), Southern Studios (UK and parts of Europe), Sonic Unyon (Canada), Hitch-Hyke (Greece) and WEA (parts of Europe/select releases).

How to Contact: *No unsolicited material. Check website for submission policy.*

Music: Mostly **rock**, **pop** and **punk**; also **folk**, **garage** and **indie**. Does not want rap, metal or country. Released *You Should Enjoy Getting Screamed At!* (album by Thomas Crouch/Bryan Biggart), recorded by F13 (punk); *The Rock Garden* (album by band collective), recorded by Eurogression (rock); and *Hutches of Gunch* (album by Eric Baylies), recorded by Baylies Band (rock), all on Street Records. Other artists include Aberdeen Lizards, Desaru, the Cigs, Onassis and Wax American, Tampered and DeadMeat.

Tips: "Are you ready to tour and give up most luxuries for two years?"

STRUGGLEBABY RECORDING CO., 2612 Erie Ave., P.O. Box 8385, Cincinnati OH 45208-8385. (513)871-1500. Fax: (513)871-1510. E-mail: umbrella@one.net or elaine@one.net. **Contact:** Sam Richman, A&R/professional manager. Record company, music publisher and record producer (Hal Bernard Enterprises). Estab. 1983. Releases 3-4 CDs/year. Pays negotiable royalty to artists on contract; statutory (per contract) rate to publisher per song on record.

How to Contact: Submit demo tape by mail. Prefers cassette or CD with 3 songs and lyric sheet. "Positive responses only—no materials returned."

Music: Mostly **modern rock**, **rock** and **R&B**. Released *Heaven in Your Eyes* (album), written and recorded by Bromwell-Diehl Band (AAA), released 1999 on Bash; *Coming Attractions* (album), written and recorded by Adrian Belew (modern rock), released 1999 on ABP; and *Gun for You* (album), written and recorded by The Greenhornes (rock), released 1999 on Prince, all distributed by Strugglebaby Recording Co.

Tips: "Keep it simple, honest, with a personal touch. Show some evidence of market interest and attraction and value as well as the ability to tour."

SUISONIC RECORDS, 1245 W. Guadalupe Rd., Suite B6-290, Mesa AZ 85202. Phone/fax: (480)491-3642. E-mail: grimm2@home.com. **Contact:** B. Grimm, A&R director. Labels include Tremble Rose. Record company. Estab. 1996. Releases 2 singles, 4 LPs, 4 EPs and 4 CDs/year. Pays negotiable royalty to artists on contract; statutory rate to publisher per song on record.

How to Contact: Submit demo CD/CDR by mail. Unsolicited submissions are OK. Prefers CD. "Must fill out application at darkmusic.com. All music must be dark oriented." Does not return material. Responds in 2 weeks, "immediately if we like it a lot. Please do not call."

Music: Mostly **rock** and **dance**. "No glam metal, '80s metal, satanic worshipping music or gangsta please!" Released *Grace Overthrone* (album), written and recorded by Grace Overthrone (industrial); *Visual Purple* (album), written and recorded by Visual Purple (pop/punk), both on Suisonic Records; and *Raylene Emerson*, written and recorded by Raylene Baker on Tremble Rose Records (goth rock).

SUNCOUNTRY RECORDS, 2709 W. Pine Lodge, Roswell NM 88201. (505)622-2008. E-mail: willmon@bigfoot.com. Website: www.angelfire.com/wi/pecosvalleymusic/index.html. **Con-**

tact: Ray Willmon, president, A&R. A&R: Jack Burns. Record company and music publisher (Pecos Valley Music). Estab. 1989. Releases 1-2 singles, 1 CD/year. Pays 2-10% royalty to artists on contract; statutory rate to publisher per song on record.

How to Contact: Submit demo tape by mail. Unsolicited submissions are OK. "No phone calls please—we will accept by mail." Prefers cassette, CD or VHS videocassette with 2 songs maximum and lyric sheet. SASE. Responds in 3 months.

Music: Mostly **C&W** and **gospel (country)**. Released "I'll See You" and "Wait on Me" (singles), both written and recorded by Joe Farmer (country), released 2000 on SunCountry Records (country). Other artists include Sam Means and Jack Taylor.

N **J** **O** **SUN-SCAPE ENTERPRISES LIMITED**, P.O. Box 793, Station F, Toronto, Ontario M4Y 2N7 Canada. (905)951-3155. Fax: (905)951-9712. E-mail: info@sun-scape.com. Website: www .sun-scape.com. Estab. 1973. Releases 2 LPs and 2 CDs/year. Pays negotiable royalty to artists on contract.

Distributed by: Christie and Christie, Music Design, Valley Records, New Leaf Distributing and Backroads.

● See the listing for Star-Scape in the Classical & Performing Arts section.

How to Contact: Call first and obtain permission to submit. Call for submission requirements. Does not return material. Responds in 1 month.

Music: Mostly **choral**, **new age** and **contemporary classical**. Released *Promethean Fire*, *Arrival of the Unexpected* and *Let Robots Melt* (albums), all written and recorded by Kenneth G. Mills (New Age); and *Tonal Persuasions, Vol. II* (album), written by Kenneth G. Mills/various, recorded by New Star-Scape Singers (choral), all on Sun-Scape Records.

N **O** **SURESHOT RECORDS**, P.O. Box 9117, Truckee CA 96162. (530)587-0111. E-mail: alanr ed@telis.org. Website: www.alanredstone.com. **Contact:** Alan Redstone, owner. Record company, record producer and music publisher. Estab. 1979. Releases 1 LP/year. Pays statutory rate to publisher per song on record.

How to Contact: *Write or call first and obtain permission to submit.* SASE. Responds in 1 week.

Music: Mostly **country**, **comedy**, **novelty** and **blues**.

Tips: "Read up and learn to submit properly. Submit like a pro."

O **SURFACE RECORDS**, 8377 Westview, Houston TX 77055. (713)464-4653. Fax: (713)464-2622. E-mail: sarsjef@aol.com. Website: www.soundartsrecording. **Contact:** Jeff Wells, president. A&R: Peter Verkerk. Record company, music publisher (Earthscream Music Publishing Co./BMI) and record producer (Jeff Wells). Estab. 1996. Releases 4 CDs/year. Pays negotiable royalty to artists on contract; statutory rate to publisher per song on record.

Distributed by: Earth Records.

How to Contact: Submit demo tape by mail. Unsolicited submissions are OK. Prefers cassette or CD with 4 songs and lyric sheet. Does not return material. Responds in 6 weeks.

Music: Mostly **country**, **blues** and **pop/rock**. Released *Everest* (album), recorded by The Jinkies; *Joe "King" Carrasco* (album), recorded by Joe "King" Carrasco; and *Perfect Strangers* (album), recorded by Perfect Strangers, all on Surface Records (pop). Other artists include Rosebud.

O **SWEET JUNE MUSIC**, P.O. Box 669, Fulton TX 78358-0669. Phone/fax: (361)729-4249. E-mail: musicdirector@classicctrymusicclub.com. Website: www.classicctrymusicclub.com. Owner/ Producer: Tom Thrasher. Music Critiquer: Doris June. Labels include TBS Records and CMI Records. Record company, music publisher, record producer and music marketing. Estab. 1978. Staff size: 1. Releases 2 singles, 2 LPs and 2 CDs/year. Pays standard royalty to artists on contract; statutory rate to publisher per song on record.

OPENNESS TO SUBMISSIONS: ☐ beginners; ◪ beginners and experienced; ◪ experienced only; ∅ no unsolicited submissions/industry referrals only.

Distributed by: World Wide Web.

How to Contact: Submit demo tape by mail. Unsolicited submissions are OK. Prefers cassette, CD or DAT with 3 songs, lyric sheet and cover letter. Does not return material. Responds in 2 months.

Music: Mostly **traditional country**, **bluegrass** and **gospel**; also **traditional Big Band**, **Dixieland** and **quartet (barbershop/gospel)**. Does not want rock or contemporary. Released "Beautiful Angel" (single by Tom Thrasher), recorded by Jackie Larrivee (Big Band ballad), released 2000 on TBS Records.

Tips: "Looking for new artists. Must have marketing knowledge of who their customers are and what they buy or won't buy. Learn how to be a salesperson. All the exposure in the world won't do any good if the artist/songwriter drops the ball!"

☘️ 🔾 SYNERGY RECORDS, 1609 Harwood St., Suite 7, Vancouver, British Columbia V6G 1Y1, Canada. (604)687-5747. Fax: (604)687-8528. E-mail: darren@synergyrecords.com. Website: www.synergyrecords.com. Project Manager: Darren Staten. Creative Director: Deena Melon. A&R/ Hip Hop/R&B: Kari Staten. Record company, music publisher (Nubian Music) and record producer (Darren Staten). Estab. 1998. Staff size: 6. Releases 2 singles and 2 LPs. Pays negotiable royalty to artists on contract; statutory rate to publisher per song on record.

Distributed by: Indiepool and Amazon.com.

How to Contact: Submit demo tape by mail. Unsolicited submissions are OK. Prefers cassette, CD with 3-4 songs, lyric sheet, cover letter and press clipping. Does not return material. Responds in 3 weeks.

Music: Mostly **pop**, **dance**, **rock**, and **R&B**; also **electronica** and **hip-hop**. Does not want punk, hard rock, traditional country or singer/songwriters. Released *I Don't Look Like You* (album by Carmelian Cupo/Darren Staten/Antonio Cupo/Keith Staten), recorded by Carmelina Cupo (pop); and *This Day* (album by Zoe Fox/Chuck Brickley/Darren Staten/Jeff Silbar/Taura Jackson/Bruce Sugar), recorded by Teena Davis (pop/AC).

Tips: "We are looking for great songs with memorable melodies that are perfect for radio and for pop writers/artists. Production is not that important for pop writers/artists. For club-oriented artists, you must be innovative and unique. All potential artists must be *driven, committed, talented* and have an interesting image."

🅽 🔾 TAKE 2 RECORDS, (formerly PBM Records), 3868 Dickerson Rd., Suite 101, Nashville TN 37207. (615)865-9550. Fax: (615)865-9330. Owner: Michele Gauvin. A&R (country): Barbara Cole. Record company. "PBM also coordinates talent for a country-variety TV show from Nashville and assists in casting for local movies shot in Nashville, TN." Estab. 1990. Releases 1-2 products/ year. Pays negotiable royalty to artists on contract; pays statutory rate to publisher per song on record.

Distributed by: Hit 1, Take 2.

How to Contact: *Write or call first and obtain permission to submit.* Prefers cassette or VHS videocassette with lyric sheet, photo and bio. Does not return material. Responds in 8 months. "We do not respond to or return unrequested material."

Music: Mostly **country**. Released "Big Tennessee River" (single), written and recorded by T. Greggs (country), released on Take 2 Records; "Don't Touch Me" (single by Hank Cochran), "Half A Mind" (single by Roger Miller) and "You're Not the Only Heart In Town" (single by Lonnie Wilson), all recorded by Michele Gauvin (country), released on PBM Records. Other artists include Jim Woodrum.

Tips: "Please pull shrink wrap from CDs and cassettes submitted."

🔾 TANGENT® RECORDS, 1888 Century Park E., Suite 1900, Los Angeles CA 90067. (310)204-0388. Fax: (310)204-0995. E-mail: tangent@ix.netcom.com. **Contact:** Andrew Batchelor, president. Director of Marketing: Elisa Batchelor. Record company and music publisher (ArcTangent Music/ BMI). Estab. 1988. Staff size: 3. Releases 10-12 CDs/year. Pays negotiable royalty to artists on contract; statutory rate to publisher per song on record.

How to Contact: Submit demo tape or CD by mail. Unsolicited submissions are OK. Prefers cassette, CD, DAT or VHS videocassette with minimum of 3 songs and lead sheet if available. "Please include a brief biography/history of artist(s) and/or band, including musical training/education, performance experience, recording studio experience, discography and photos (if available)." Does not return material. Responds in 3 months.

Music: Mostly **artrock** and **contemporary instrumental/rock instrumental**; also **contemporary classical**, **world music**, **smooth jazz**, **acid jazz**, **jazz/rock**, **ambient**, **electronic**, and **New Age**.
Tips: "Take the time to pull together a quality cassette or CD demo with package/portfolio, including such relevant information as experience (on stage and in studio, etc.), education/training, biography, career goals, discography, photos, etc. Should be typed. We are *not* interested in generic sounding or 'straight ahead' music. We are seeking music that is innovative, pioneering and eclectic with a fresh, unique sound."

◻ **TEXAS ROSE RECORDS**, P.O. Box 726, Terrell TX 75160-6765. (972)563-3161. Fax: (972)563-2655. E-mail: txrr1@aol.com. Website: www.texasroserecords.com. **Contact:** Nancy Baxendale, president. Record company, music publisher (Yellow Rose of Texas Publishing, Yellow Rose Petal) and record producer (Nancy Baxendale). Estab. 1994. Staff size: 3. Releases 3 CDs/year. Pays negotiable royalty to artists on contract; statutory rate to publisher per song on record.
Distributed by: Honky Tonkin' Music and self distribution.
How to Contact: Submit demo tape by mail. Unsolicited submissions are OK. Prefers CD with 2 songs, lyric sheet and cover letter. Does not return material. Responds in 6 weeks.
Music: Mostly **country**, **soft rock** and **blues**; also **pop** and **gospel**. Does not want hip-hop, rap, heavy metal. Released *It Ain't Likely* (album), written and recorded by Jeff Elliot (country); *High on the Hog* (album), written and recorded by Steve Harr (country); and *The Prayer Telephone* (album), written and recorded by Dusty Martin (country/gospel).
Tips: "We are interested in songs written from the heart and with a strong hook. Always use a good vocalist."

Ⓝ ✿ ◻ **THIRD WAVE PRODUCTIONS LTD.** P.O. Box 563, Gander Newfoundland A1V 2E1 Canada. (709)256-8009. Fax: (709)256-7411. Website: www.buddywasisname.com. Manager: Wayne Pittman. President: Arch Bonnell. Labels include Street Legal Records. Record company, music publisher, distributor and agent. Estab. 1986. Releases 2 singles, 2 LPs and 2 CDs/year. Pays negotiable royalty to artists on contract; statutory rate to publisher per song on record.
How to Contact: Submit demo tape by mail. Unsolicited submissions are OK. Prefers cassette, DAT and lyric sheet. SASE. Responds in 2 months.
Music: Mostly **folk/traditional**, **bluegrass** and **country**; also **pop**, **Irish** and **Christmas**. Released *Salt Beef Junkie* (album), written and recorded by Buddy Wasisname and Other Fellers (folk/traditional); *Newfoundland Bluegrass* (album), written and recorded by Crooked Stovepipe (bluegrass); and *Nobody Never Told Me* (album), written and recorded by The Psychobilly Cadillacs (rockabilly/country), all on Third Wave Productions. Other artists include Lee Vaughn.
Tips: "We are not really looking for songs but are always open to take on new artists who are interested in recording/producing an album. We market and distribute as well as produce albums. Not much need for 'songs' per se, except maybe country and rock/pop."

Ⓝ ◙ **THUMP RECORDS, INC.**, 3101 Pomona Blvd., Pomona CA 91768. (909)595-2144. Fax: (909)598-7028. E-mail: info@thumprecords.com. Website: www.thumprecords.com. President A&R: Bill Walker. Vice President of A&R and General Manager: Pebo Rodriguez. Labels include Thump Street and Fama Records. Record company and music publisher (Walk-Lo/ASCAP, On the Note/BMI). Estab. 1990. Releases 10 singles, 36 LPs, 6 EPs and 36 CDs/year. Pays 10% (negotiable) royalty to artists on contract; ¾ statutory rate to publisher per song on record.
How to Contact: Submit demo tape by mail. Unsolicited submissions are OK. Prefers CD/CDR—do not send mp3s—lyric sheet, biography and 8×10 photo. SASE. Responds in 1 month.
Music: Mostly **dance**, **rap** and **ballads**; also **oldies**, **classic rock** and **regional Mexican**. Released "DJ Girl" (single by Katalina). Other artists include Art Banks TDWY, Don Cisco and Jonny Z.
Tips: "Provide Thump with positive upbeat music that has universal appeal."

◙ **TOMMY BOY RECORDS**, 902 Broadway, 13th Floor, New York NY 10010-6002. (212)388-8300. E-mail: mail@tommyboy.com. Website: www.tommyboy.com. A&R: Eddie O'Loughlin; Kim Spike; Max Siegel; Victor Lee. Fax: (212)388-8465. Record company. Labels include Penalty Recordings, Outcaste Records, Timber and Tommy Boy Gospel.

Distributed by: WEA.
How to Contact: Call to obtain current demo submission policy.
Music: Artists include Everlast, Screwball, Amber and Capone-N-Noreaga.

N **TOPCAT RECORDS**, P.O. Box 670234, Dallas TX 75367. (972)484-4141. Fax: (972)620-8333. E-mail: blueman@computek.net. Website: www.texasblues.com/topcat. President: Richard Chalk. Record company and record producer. Estab. 1991. Staff size: 1. Releases 3-4 CDs/year. Pays 10-15% royalty to artists on contract; statutory rate to publisher per song on record.
Distributed by: City Hall.
How to Contact: Call first and obtain permission to submit. Prefers cassette or CD. Does not return material. Responds in 1 month.
Music: Mostly **blues**, **swing** and **R&B**. Released *If You Need Me* (album), written and recorded by Robert Ealey (blues); *Texas Blueswomen* (album by 3 Female Singers), recorded by various (blues/R&B); and *Jungle Jane* (album), written and recorded by Holland K. Smith (blues/swing), all on Topcat. Other artists include Grant Cook, Muddy Waters, Big Mama Thornton, Big Joe Turner, Geo. "Harmonica" Smith, J.B. Hutto and Bee Houston.
Tips: "Send me blues (fast, slow, happy, sad, etc.) or good blues oriented R&B. No pop."

M **TRAC RECORD CO.**, 170 N. Maple, Fresno CA 93702. Phone/fax: (209)255-1717. E-mail: tracsell@aol.com. **Contact:** Stan Anderson, owner. Record company, record producer and music publisher (Sellwood Publishing/BMI). Estab. 1972. Staff size: 1. Releases 5 singles, 5 LPs and 2 CDs/year. Pays 13% royalty to artists on contract; statutory rate to publisher per song on record.
How to Contact: Submit demo tape by mail. Unsolicited submissions are OK. Prefers cassette or VHS videocassette with 2-3 songs and lyric sheet. "Demo must be clear and professionally recorded." SASE. Responds in 3 weeks.
Music: **Country, all styles** and **southern gospel**. Released *Sweet Love* (album), written and recorded by Kevin B. Willard, released 2000 on TRAC Records (country). Other artists include Jessica James and Jimmy Walker.

N **TRIPLE X RECORDS**, P.O. Box 862529, Los Angeles CA 90086-2529. (323)221-2204. Fax: (323)221-2778. E-mail: duffxxx@usa.net. Website: www.triple-x.com. A&R Director: Bruce Duff (pop, goth, rock). Co-owner (punk, skate, ska, reggae): Dean Naleway. Record company. Estab. 1986. Staff size: 5. Releases 25 CDs/year. Royalties not disclosed.
Distributed by: Navarre.
How to Contact: "See our web page for submission policy." Does not return material. Responds in 2 months.
Music: Mostly **rock**, **industrial/goth** and **punk**; also **blues**, **roots** and **noise**.
Tips: "Looking for self-contained units that generate their own material and are willing and able to tour."

28 RECORDS, 19700 NW 86 Court, Miami FL 33015-6917. Phone/fax: (305)829-8142. E-mail: rec28@aol.com. **Contact:** Eric Diaz, president/CEO/A&R. Record company. Estab. 1994. Staff size: 1. Releases 2 LPs and 4 CDs/year. Pays 12% royalty to artists on contract; statutory rate to publisher per song on record.
Distributed by: Rock Bottom-USA.
How to Contact: *Contact first and obtain permission to submit.* Submit demo tape by mail. Unsolicited submissions are OK. Prefers cassette, VHS videocassette or CD (if already released on own label for possible distribution or licensing deals). If possible send promo pack and photo. "Please put Attn: A&R on packages." Does not return material. Responds in 6 weeks.
Music: Mostly **hard rock/modern rock**, **metal** and **alternative**; also **punk** and **death metal**. Released *Julian Day* (album), recorded by Helltown's Infamous Vandal (modern/hard rock); *Fractured Fairy Tales* (album), written and recorded by Eric Knight (modern/hard rock); and *Mantra*, recorded by Derek Cintron (modern rock), all on 28 Records.
Tips: "Be patient and ready for the long haul. We strongly believe in nurturing you, the artist/songwriter. If you're willing to do what it takes, and have what it takes, we will do whatever it takes

to get you to the next level. We are looking for artists to develop. We are a very small label but we are giving the attention that is a must for a new band as well as developed and established acts. Give us a call."

◐ **UAR RECORDS (Universal-Athena Records)**, Box 1264, 6020 W. Pottstown Rd., Peoria IL 61654-1264. (309)673-5755. Fax: (309)673-7636. E-mail: uarltd@unitedcyber.com. Website: www.unitedcyber.com/uarltd. **Contact:** Jerry Hanlon, A&R director. Record company and music publisher (Jerjoy Music/BMI). Estab. 1978. Staff size: 1. Releases 1-2 singles and 1 LP/year. Pays standard royalty to artists on contract; statutory rate to publisher for each record sold.

How to Contact: Unsolicited submissions are OK. Does not return telephone calls. Prefers cassette with 4-8 songs and lyric sheet. SASE. "We do not critique work unless asked." Responds in 2 weeks.

Music: Mostly **country**. Released "Hello Mr. Heartache" (single by Harvey Gates) from *Hello Mr. Heartache* (album), recorded by Jerry Hanlon (country); "Country Nights" (single by Matt Dorman) from *Country Nights* (album), recorded by Kent Johnson (country); and "Bang, Bang Goes the Thunder" (single) from *Country Nights* (album), written and recorded by Tim Rehmer (country), all released 2000 on UAR. Other artists include Garry Johnson, Jackie Nelson, Willie Morrissey, Tracy Wells and David Clayton Mize.

✔ ⊘ **UNIVERSAL RECORDS**, 1755 Broadway, 7th Floor, New York NY 10019. (212)373-0600. Fax: (212)373-0688. Website: www.universalrecords.com. Senior Vice President: Jaclyn Cooper. Vice President A&R: Dino Delvaille. Vice President A&R: Angelique Miles. Universal City office: 70 Universal City Plaza, 3rd Floor, Universal City CA 91608. (818)777-1000. Contact: A&R Director. Labels include Uptown Records, Mojo Records, Republic Records, Bystorm Records and Gut Reaction Records. Record company.

• As a result of the 1998 PolyGram and Universal merger, Universal is the world's largest record company.

How to Contact: Universal Records in California does not accept unsolicited submissions. The New York office *only* allows you to call first and obtain permission to submit.

Music: Released *Baduizm* (album), recorded by Erykah Badu on Kedar Records; *Lost* (album), recorded by Eightball on Suave House; and *Spiders* (album), recorded by Space on Gut Reaction Records. Other artists include Boyz II Men and Merrill Bainbridge.

⬛ ⊘ **VAI DISTRIBUTION**, 109 Wheeler Ave., Pleasantville NY 10570. (914)769-3691. Fax: (914)769-5407. President: Ernest Gilbert. Record company, video label and distributor. Estab. 1983. Pays negotiable royalty to artists on contract; other amount to publisher per song on record.

How to Contact: Does not accept unsolicited material.

Music: Mostly **opera (classical vocal)**, **classical (orchestral)** and **classical instrumental/piano**. Released *Susannah* (album by Carlisle Floyd), recorded by New Orleans Opera Orchestra and Chorus, on VAI Audio. Other artists include Jon Vickers, Rosalyn Tureck, Evelyn Lear and Thomas Stewart.

◐ **VALTEC PRODUCTIONS**, P.O. Box 2642, Santa Maria CA 93457. (805)934-8400. **Contact:** J. Anderson and J. Valenta, owner/producers. Record company and record producer (Joe Valenta). Estab. 1986. Releases 20 singles, 15 LPs and 10 CDs/year. Pays negotiable royalty to artists on contract; statutory rate to publisher per song on record.

How to Contact: Submit demo tape by mail. Unsolicited submissions are OK. Prefers DAT with 4 songs and lyric sheet. Does not return material. Responds in 2 months.

Music: Mostly **country**, **top 40** and **A/C**; also **rock**. Released *Just Me* (album by Joe Valenta) and *Hold On* (album by Joe Valenta/J. Anderson), both recorded by Joe Valenta (top 40); and *Time Out (For Love)* (album by Joe Valenta), recorded by Marty K. (country), all on Valtec Records.

THE OPENNESS TO SUBMISSIONS INDEX at the back of this book lists all companies in this section by how open they are to submissions.

☑ ⊘ **VANDER-MOON ENTERTAINMENT**, P.O. Box 331951, Nashville TN 37203. (615)256-0895. E-mail: VanderMoon@1MusicRow.com. Website: www.VanderMoon@1MusicRow. com. **Contact:** Craig Alan, A&R director. Record company and management agency. Estab. 1995. Releases 1 CD/year. Pays negotiable royalty to artists on contract; statutory rate to publisher per song on record.

How to Contact: Submit demo tape by mail. Unsolicited submissions are OK. Prefers cassette, DAT or CD with any number of songs, lyric sheet and press kit. Does not return material. Responds only if interested.

Music: Mostly **rock**, **alternative** and **pop**; also **rap** and **new country**. Released *Texas Vampires* (album), written and recorded by Texas Vampires (rock), released 1996; *McAffe's Breeze* (album), written and recorded by Boo Boo McAfee (hip-hop), released 2000; and *The Millennium Hippie Tour* (album), written and recorded by Guitonga Whisper (pop), released 1999, all on Vander-Moon Entertainment.

☑ ⚓ ⊘ **THE VERVE MUSIC GROUP**, 1755 Broadway, 3rd Floor, New York NY 10019. (212)331-2000. Fax: (212)331-2064. Website: www.vervemusicgroup.com. Senior Vice President of A&R: Richard Seidel. A&R Manager: Jason Olaine. A&R Assistant: Leslie Carr. Los Angeles office (Impulse, Blue Thumb): 100 N. First St., Burbank CA 91502. (818)729-4804. Fax: (818)845-2564. Vice President A&R: Bud Harner. A&R Assistant: George Stamatakis. Record company. Labels include Verve, GRP, Blue Thumb and Impulse! Records.

• Verve's Diana Krall won a 1999 Grammy Award for Best Jazz Vocal Performance; Wayne Shorter won Best Jazz Instrumental Solo; and the Charlie Haden Quartet West won Best Instrumental Arrangement with Vocals.

How to Contact: *The Verve Music Group does not accept unsolicited submissions.*

Music: Artists include George Benson, Ray Hargroy, Spyro Gyra, Roy Haynes, Keith Jarrett and Nicholas Payton.

☑ ⊘ **VIRGIN RECORDS**, 338 N. Foothill Rd., Beverly Hills CA 90210. (310)278-1181. Fax: (310)278-6231. A&R Director (hip-hop, R&B): Alexander Mejia. A&R Director: David Wolter. Executive Vice President A&R: Tony Berg. Vice President A&R: Gemma Corfield. New York office: 304 Park Ave. S., New York NY 10010. (212)253-3100. Fax: (212)253-3099. Director of A&R: Aaron Seawood. Executive Vice President; A&R: Keith Wood. Senior Vice President, A&R: Patrick Moxey. Website: www.virginrecords.com. Labels include Rap-A-Lot Records, Pointblank Records, SoulPower Records, AWOL Records, Astralwerks Records, Cheeba Sounds and Noo Trybe Records. Record company.

Distributed by: EMD.

• Virgin Records' artist Lenny Kravitz won a 1998 Grammy Award for Best Male Rock Vocal Performance.

How to Contact: Virgin Records does not accept recorded material or lyrics unless submitted by a reputable industry source. "If your act has received positive press or airplay on prior independent releases, we welcome your written query. Send a letter of introduction accompanied by all pertinent artist information. Do not send a tape until requested. All unsolicited materials will be returned unopened."

Music: Released *Tribute* (album), recorded by Yanni; *Adore* (album), recorded by The Smashing Pumpkins; and *Bridges to Babylon* (album), recorded by The Rolling Stones, all on Virgin Records. Other artists include Tina Turner, David Bowie, Isaac Hayes, Enigma, dc Talk and Boz Scaggs.

Ⓝ ⚓ ⊘ **VOKES MUSIC RECORD CO.**, P.O. Box 12, New Kensington PA 15068. (724)335-2775. President: Howard Vokes. Labels include Country Boy Records. Record company, booking agency (Vokes Booking Agency) and music publisher (Vokes Music Publishing). Releases 8 singles and 5 LPs/year. Pays 2½-4½% song royalty to artists and songwriters on contract.

• Mr. Vokes is an inductee of the Country Music Organizations of America's American Eagle Awards' Hall of Fame.

How to Contact: Submit cassette only and lead sheet. SASE. Responds in 2 weeks.

Music: Mostly **country**, **bluegrass** and **gospel-old time**. Released *Songs of Tragedy and Disaster* (album), written and recorded by Howard Vokes (country), released on Vokes Records.

✅ 🅾 **WALL STREET MUSIC**, 28545 Greenfield, Suite 200, Southfield MI 48075. (248)353-7733. Fax: (248)353-5985. E-mail: a&r@wallstreetmusic.com. Website: www.wallstreetmusic.com. **Contact:** A&R director. Record company, record distributor, record producer and music publisher (Burgundy Bros.). Estab. 1985.
How to Contact: Submit demo tape by mail. Unsolicited submissions are OK. Also include photo, bio, performance history and sales history. "Be sure to completely label all items." Does not return material. Responds only if interested.
Music: Mostly **urban**, **rap**, **adult contemporary**, **dance** and **gospel**. Released *Downcity* (album), written and recorded by Mary Ann Rossoni (folk/rock), released 2000 on Wall Street Music. Other artists include Mary Ann Rossoni and Tracey Francione.
Tips: "The most important attribute we look for is a track record of local performance and any product sales. We are motivated by artists who perform often and have produced and marketed their music locally. You should keep us informed of your success in the industry as a way of helping us keep an eye on you."

🅽 🅾 **WAREHOUSE CREEK RECORDING CORP.**, P.O. Box 102, Franktown, VA 23354. (757)442-6883. Fax: (757)442-3662. E-mail: warehouse@esva.net. Website: www.warehousecreek.c om. President: Billy Sturgis. Record company, music publisher (Bayford Dock Music) and record producer (Billy Sturgis). Estab. 1993. Staff size: 1. Releases 11 singles and 1 CD/year. Pays negotiable royalty to artists on contract; statutory rate to publisher per song on record.
Distributed by: City Hall Records.
How to Contact: Submit demo tape by mail. Unsolicited submissions are OK. Prefers cassette, CD, DAT or VHS videocassette with lyric sheet. Does not return material.
Music: Mostly **R&B**, **blues** and **gospel**. Released *Greyhound Bus* (album by Arthur Crudup); *Going Down in Style* (album by Tim Drummond); and *Something On My Mind* (album by George Crudup), all recorded by Crudup Brothers on Warehouse Creek Records (blues).

🅽 ✅ 🅾 **WARNER BROS. RECORDS**, 3300 Warner Blvd., 4th Floor, N. Bldg., Burbank CA 91505-4694. (818)846-9090. Fax: (818)953-3423. Vice President of A&R (urban): Alison Ball-Gabriel. Executive Vice President A&R: David Kahne. Vice President A&R: Jeff Blue. Senior Director A&R: Paula Moore. Director A&R (urban): Eddie Singleton. New York office: 75 Rockefeller Plaza, New York NY 10019. (212)275-4500. Fax: (212)275-4595. Vice President of A&R: Che Pope. Senior Vice President A&R: James Dowdall. Director A&R: Brad Kaplan. Nashville office: 20 Music Square E., Nashville TN 37203. (615)748-8000. Fax: (615)214-1523. Website: www.wbr.com. Senior Vice President of A&R: Paige Levy. A&R Director: Danny Kee. Labels include American Recordings, Eternal Records, Imago Records, Mute Records, Giant Records, Malpaso Records and Maverick Records. Record company.
Distributed by: WEA.
● In 2000, "Scar Tissue," written by Flea, John Frusciante, Anthony Kiedis and Chud Smith, recorded by Red Hot Chili Peppers on Warner Bros. Records received a Grammy Award for Best Rock Song.
How to Contact: Warner Bros. Records does not accept unsolicited material. All unsolicited material will be returned unopened. Those interested in having their tapes heard should establish a relationship with a manager, publisher or attorney that has an ongoing relationship with Warner Bros. Records.
Music: Released *Van Halen 3* (album), recorded by Van Halen; *Evita* (soundtrack); and *Dizzy Up the Girl* (album), recorded by Goo Goo Dolls, both on Warner Bros. Records. Other artists include Faith Hill, Tom Petty & the Heartbreakers, Jeff Foxworthy, Porno For Pyros, Travis Tritt, Yellowjackets, Bela Fleck and the Flecktones, Al Jarreau, Joshua Redmond, Little Texas and Curtis Mayfield.

🅾 **WATERDOG MUSIC**, (formerly Waterdog Records), 329 W. 18th St., #313, Chicago IL 60616-1120. (312)421-7499. Fax: (312)421-1848. E-mail: waterdog@waterdogmusic.com. Website:

www.waterdogmusic.com. **Contact:** Rob Gillis, label manager. Labels include Whitehouse Records. Record company. Estab. 1994. Staff size: 1. Releases 6 CDs/year. Pays negotiable royalty to artists on contract; statutory rate to publisher per song on record.

Distributed by: Big Daddy Music.

How to Contact: *E-mail first and obtain permission to submit.* Prefers cassette or CD. Include cover letter, brief bio, itinerary and picture. Does not return material. Responds in 3 weeks.

Music: Mostly **rock**, **pop** and **folk**. Released *Pigeon's Throat* (album), written and recorded by Al Rose (rock); *Live Music in the Apartment* (album by Carey OTT), recorded by Torben Floor (rock); and *Framing Caroline* (album), written and recorded by Kat Parsons (rock), all released 1999 on Waterdog Music. Other artists include MysteryDriver, Joel Frankel, Al Rose, Coin, The Good, Spelunkers, The Bad Examples, Ralph Covert, Middle 8, Peter Bernas, Matt Tiegle and Slink Moss and His Flying Aces.

Tips: "We are primarily interested in artists who write their own material and perform live regularly."

N 🖉 **WINCHESTER RECORDS**, % McCoy, Route 2, Box 114, Berkeley Springs WV 25411. (304)258-9381. Contact: A&R Director. Labels include Master Records and Real McCoy Records. Record company, music publisher (Jim McCoy Music, Clear Music, New Edition Music/BMI), record producer (Jim McCoy Productions) and recording studio. Releases 20 singles and 10 LPs/year. Pays standard royalty to artists; statutory rate to publisher for each record sold.

How to Contact: *Write first and obtain permission to submit.* Prefers 7½ ips reel-to-reel or cassette with 5-10 songs and lead sheet. SASE. Responds in 1 month.

Music: Mostly **bluegrass**, **church/religious**, **country**, **folk**, **gospel**, **progressive** and **rock**. Released *Touch Your Heart* (album), written and recorded by Jim McCoy; "Leavin' " (single), written and recorded by Red Steed, both on Winchester Records; and "The Taking Kind" (single by Tommy Hill), recorded by J.B. Miller on Hilton Records. Other artists include Carroll County Ramblers, Bud Arnel, Nitelifers, Jubilee Travelers and Middleburg Harmonizers.

✓ 🖉 **WINDHAM HILL RECORDS**, 8750 Wilshire Blvd., 3rd Floor, Beverly Hills CA 90211. (310)358-4800. Fax: (310)358-4127. Website: www.windham.com. Director A&R: Jonathan Miller. Record company.
  ● Windham Hill has been folded into RCA Records.

🖉 **WIND-UP ENTERTAINMENT**, 72 Madison Ave., 8th Floor, New York NY 10016. (212)251-9665. Website: www.winduprecords.com. Contact: A&R. Labels include Surefire. Record company. Estab. 1997. Releases 1-2 CDs/year. Pays negotiable royalty to artists on contract; statutory rate to publisher per song on record.

Distributed by: BMG.

How to Contact: Write first and obtain permission to submit a demo. Prefers cassette, CD, DAT or videocassette. Does not return material or respond to submissions.

Music: Mostly **rock**, **folk** and **hard rock**. Released *Human Clay* (album), written and recorded by Creed (rock), released 1999; *Figure 8* (album), written and recorded by Julia Darling (folk/rock), released 1999; and *Stretch Princess* (album), written and recorded by Stretch Princess (rock), released 1998, all on Wind-Up.

Tips: "We rarely look for songwriters as opposed to bands, so writing a big hit single would be the rule of the day."

🖉 **WORD RECORDS & MUSIC**, 25 Music Square W, Nashville TN 37203. (615)457-2000. Website: www.wordrecords.com. Vice President A&R: Brent Bourgeois. Record company.

Distributed by: Epic/Sony.

How to Contact: Word Records does not accept unsolicited submissions.

Music: Released *Blaze*, recorded by Code of Ethics; *Steady On*, recorded by Point of Grace; and *Past the Edges*, recorded by Chris Rice, all on Word.

✓ ◻ **WORLD BEATNIK RECORDS**, 20 Amity Lane, Rockwall TX 75087. Fax: (972)771-0853. E-mail: tropikalproductions@juno.com. Website: www.tropikalproductions.com. Producers: J.

Towry (world beat, reggae, ethnic, jazz); Jembe (reggae, world beat, ethnic); Arik Towry (ska, pop, ragga, rock). Labels include World Beatnik Records. Record company and record producer (Jimi Towry). Estab. 1983. Staff size: 4. Releases 6 singles, 6 LPs, 6 EPs and 6 CDs/year. Pays negotiable royalty to artists on contract; statutory rate to publisher per song on record.

Distributed by: Midwest Records, Southwest Wholesale, Reggae OneLove, Ejaness Records, Ernie B's, CD Waterhouse and Borders.

How to Contact: Submit demo tape by mail. Unsolicited submissions are OK. Prefers cassette, DAT, mini disk or VHS videocassette with 3 songs and lyric sheet. SASE. Responds in 2 weeks.

Music: Mostly **world beat, reggae** and **ethnic**; also **jazz, hip-hop/dance** and **pop**. Released *SKYA FYA* (album by Arik Miles), recorded by SKYA (ska/pop/rock), released 2001; *Ron Weaver* (album), written and recorded by Ron Weaver (roots rock), released 2000; and *Roots Ram* (album by Kumba/Ras/Jahbo), recorded by One Love Uprising (reggae), released 2000, all on World Beatnik Records. Other artists include Jimi Towry, Wisdom Ogbor (Nigeria), Joe Lateh (Ghana), Dee Dee Cooper, Ras Lyrix (St. Croix), Ras Kumba (St. Kitts), Gary Mon, Darbo (Gambia), Ricki Malik (Jamaica), Arik Miles, Narte's (Hawaii), Gavin Audagnotti (South Africa) and Bongo (Trinidad).

N ⬛ 🖉 WORLDWIDE RECORDINGS LIMITED/WORLDRECORDS.COM, 1459 Hunter St., North Vancouver, British Columbia V7H 1H3 Canada. E-mail: info@worldrecords.com. Website: www.worldrecords.com. **Contact:** Jim Rota, president. Record company, music publisher, and Internet search engine ("worldrecords.com—A search engine for information about music. There is more music here than anywhere else in the world.") Estab. 1995. Staff size: 5. Releases 200 CDs/year.

How to Contact: *You must be a subscriber of worldrecords.com before submitting material.* Prefers press kit, reviews and contact info. "If you have Internet access, please read the following page before sending CDs: www.worldrecords.com/aandr/index.html." Does not return material. Responds in 3 days.

Music: Mostly **rock**, **blues** and **jazz**; also **world**, **country** and **folk**. Released *Volumes I, II & III* (albums), written and recorded by various artists on Worldwide Recordings Limited. Other artists include The Unified Theorists, Colourise, Ghost Like Sun, Daniel Rhodes, Shakamoraine, Moon Soup, Lyrical Eaze and others.

Tips: "Be patient. We promote each artist for free at our website which receives over 100,000 visitors per year. We create compilation CDs each year with those artists who sign our licensing and shipping agreement that gives us a 20% commission on deals we bring to the table, but, because we promote a lot of independent artists, we don't have the resources or interest in producing any one of them."

⬤ ✓ ◯ X.R.L. RECORDS/MUSIC, White House Farm, Shropshire TF9 4HA England. Phone: (01630)647374. Fax: (01630)647612. A&R: Tanya Woof. International A&R Manager: Xavier Lee. UK A&R Manager: Cathrine Lee. Labels include Swoop, Zarg Records, Genouille, Pogo and Check Records. Record company, record producer and music publisher (Le Matt Music, Lee Music, R.T.F.M. and Pogo Records). Member MPA, PPL, PRS, MCPS, V.P.L. Estab. 1972. Staff size: 11. Releases 30 12″ singles, 20 LPs and 20 CDs/year. Pays negotiable royalty to artists on contract; negotiable rate to publisher for each record sold. Royalties paid to US songwriters and artists through US publishing or recording affiliate.

Distributed by: Lematt Music.

How to Contact: Submit demo tape by mail. Unsolicited submissions are OK. Prefers CD, cassette, MD or VHS 625 PAL standard videocassette with 1-3 songs and lyric sheet. Include bio and still photos. SAE and IRC. Responds in 6 weeks.

Music: Mostly **pop/top 40**; also **bluegrass**, **blues**, **country**, **dance-oriented**, **easy listening**, **MOR**, **progressive**, **R&B**, **'50s rock**, **disco**, **new wave**, **rock** and **soul**. Released *Now and Then* (album), written and recorded by Daniel Boone (pop rock), released 2000 on Swoop; *The Creepies* (album),

---

THE FILM & TV INDEX found at the back of this book lists companies placing music in film and TV (excluding TV commercials).

recorded by Nightmare (horror rock), released 2000 on Zarg; and *It's a Very Nice* (album), recorded by Groucho (pop), released 2000 on Swoop. Other artists include Orphan, The Chromatics, Mike Sheriden and the Nightriders, Johnny Moon, Dead Fish, Sight 'N' Sound and Mush.
Tips: "Be original."

◢ XEMU RECORDS, 34 W. 17th St., 5th Floor, New York NY 10011. (212)807-0290. Fax: (212)807-0583. E-mail: xemu@xemu.com. Website: www.xemu.com. **Contact:** Dr. Claw, vice president A&R. Record company. Estab. 1992. Staff size: 4. Releases 4 CDs/year. Pays negotiable royalty to artists on contract; statutory rate to publisher per song on record.
Distributed by: Sumthing Distribution.
How to Contact: *Write first and obtain permission to submit.* Prefers cassette with 3 songs. Does not return material. Responds in 2 months.
Music: Mostly **alternative**. Released *A is for Alpha* (album), recorded by Alpha Bitch (alternative rock); *Hold the Mayo* (album), recorded by Death Sandwich (alternative rock); and *The Real Guy Smiley* (album), recorded by Guy Smiley (alternative rock), all released 2000 on Xemu Records. Other artists include Malvert P. Redd, Death Sandwich and Baby-Face Finster.

◻ YELLOW JACKET RECORDS, 10303 Hickory Valley, Ft. Wayne IN 46835. E-mail: alstraten @aol.com. **Contact:** Allan Straten, president. Record company and music publisher (Hickory Valley Music). Estab. 1985. Staff size: 3. Releases 8-10 singles, 1 LP and 1 CD/year. Pays 10% royalty to artists on contract; statutory rate to publisher per song on record.
How to Contact: Submit demo tape by mail. Unsolicited submissions are OK. Prefers cassette with 3-4 songs and typed lyric sheet. Does not return material. Responds in 1 month.
Music: Mostly **country** and **MOR**. Released "Countin' Down to Love," "Love Is" and "Thank You" (singles by S. Gregg/A. Straten), recorded by April on *April Love* (album). Other artists include Roy Allan, Robert "Raven," Rick Hartman and Davin Crisman.
Tips: "Be professional. Be prepared to rewrite. When sending material use 6×9 envelope—no staples."

Ⓝ ◢ YOUNG COUNTRY RECORDS/PLAIN COUNTRY RECORDS, P.O. Box 5412, Buena Park CA 90620. (909)941-8216. E-mail: swampbasque@msn.com. **Contact:** Leo J. Eiffert, Jr., owner. Labels include Eiffert Records and Napoleon Country Records. Record company, music publisher (Young Country Music Publishing Co./BMI, Eb-Tide Music/BMI) and record producer (Leo J. Eiffert, Jr). Releases 10 singles and 5 LPs/year. Pays negotiable royalty to artists on contract; negotiable rate to publishers per song on record.
How to Contact: Submit demo tape by mail. Unsolicited submissions are OK. "Please make sure your song or songs are copyrighted." Prefers cassette with 2 songs and lyric sheet. Does not return material. Responds in 1 month.
Music: Mostly **country, easy rock** and **gospel music**. Released *Like A Fool* (album), written and recorded by Pam Bellows; *Something About Your Love* (album by Leo J. Eiffert, Jr.), recorded by Chance Waite Young (country); and *Cajunland* (album), written and recorded by Leo J. Eiffert, Jr., all on Plain Country Records. Other artists include Brandi Holland, Homemade, Crawfish Band and Larry Settle.

Additional Record Companies

The following companies are also record companies, but their listings are found in other sections of the book. See the General Index for page numbers, then read the listings for submission information.

ACR Productions
Alert Music, Inc.
Alexander Sr. Music
AlliSongs Inc.
Amen, Inc.
American Artists Entertainment
Angel Films Company
Aquarius Publishing
Audio Music Publishers
Avalon Music
Avalon Productions
Bagatelle Music Publishing Co.
Baird Enterprises, Ron/Baird Music
  Group
Bal & Bal Music Publishing Co.
Big Fish Music Publishing Group
Birthplace Productions
Bixio Music Group/IDM Ventures,
  Ltd.
Blue Dog Publishing and Records
Blues Alley Records
BME Publishing
Brewster Songs, Kitty
Brian Song Music Corp.
Celt Musical Services, Jan
Cherri/Holly Music Inc.
Christopher Publishing, Sonny
Coffee and Cream Productions
Conscience Music
Dapmor Publishing
EAO Music Corporation of Canada
Eternal Song Agency, The
Faverett Group
Fifth Avenue Media, Ltd.
Final Mix Music
Flying Red Horse Publishing
Frick Enterprises, Bob Scott
Furrow Music
GCI, Inc.
Glad Music Co.
Hailing Frequency Music Produc-
  tions
Hale Enterprises

Happy Melody
Hardison International Entertainment
  Corporation
Heart Consort Music
Heupferd Musikverlag GmbH
Hickory Lane Publishing and Record-
  ing
His Power Productions and Publish-
  ing
Inside Records/OK Songs
Interplanetary Music
Iron Skillet Music
Jag Studio, Ltd.
Ja/Nein Musikverlag GmbH
Jay Jay Publishing & Record Co.
John Productions, David
JPMC Music Inc.
JSB Groupe Management Inc.
Kansa Records Corporation
Kickstart Music Ltd.
L.A. Entertainment, Inc.
Lazy Bones Productions/Recordings,
  Inc.
Leigh Music, Trixie
Les Music Group
Levy Management, Rick
Lexington Alabama Music Publish-
  ing
Luick & Associates Music Publisher,
  Harold
Lyrick Studios
Magic Message Music
Magnetic Oblivion Music Co.
Makers Mark Music Productions
Martin, Pete/Vaam Music Produc-
  tions
Maverick Music
Mayfair Music
Mayo & Company, Phil
Mega Truth Records
Mellow House Music
Naked Jain Records
Neu Electro Productions

New Experience Records
New Rap Jam Publishing, A
Northwest Alabama Music Publish-
  ing
Outland Productions
Pacific North Studios Ltd.
Pegasus Music
Philly Breakdown Recording Co.
Pierce, Jim
Renaissance Entertainment Group
Road Records
R.T.L. Music
SAS Productions/Hit Records Net-
  work
Satkowski Recordings, Steve
Sea Cruise Productions, Inc.
Segal's Productions
Sellwood Publishing
Shute Management Pty. Ltd., Phill
Silver Thunder Music Group
Sound Works Entertainment Produc-
  tions Inc.
Starbound Publishing Co.
Stormin' Norman Productions
Strictly Forbidden Artists
Studio Seven
Succes
Swift River Productions
Tari, Roger Vincent
Tas Music Co./Dave Tasse Entertain-
  ment
TMC Productions
Tower Music Group
Trac Record Co.
Tutta Forza Music
Valet Publishing Co.
Van Pol Management, Hans
Warner Productions, Cheryl K.
WIR (World International Records)
Williams Management, Yvonne
World Records

Category Index

The Category Index is a good place to begin searching for a market for your songs. Below is an alphabetical list of 20 general music categories. If you write rock songs and are looking for a record company to submit your songs to, check the Rock section in this index. There you will find a list of record companies interested in hearing rock songs. Once you locate the entries for those record companies, read the music subheading *carefully* to determine which companies are most interested in the type of rock music you write. Some of the markets in this section do not appear in the Category Index because they have not indicated a specific preference. Most of these said they are interested in "all types" of music. Listings that were very specific, or whose description of the music they're interested in doesn't quite fit into these categories, also do not appear here.

Adult Contemporary (also easy listening, middle of the road, AAA, ballads, etc.)
Allegheny Music Works
Bolivia Records
Brentwood Records/Diadem Records
Capstan Record Production
Dale Productions, Alan
Emerald City Records
Enterprize Records-Tapes
Fish of Death Records and Management
Golden Triangle Records
Green Bear Records
Kaupp Records
L.A. Records (Canada)
L.A. Records (Michigan)
Leatherland Productions
Lucifer Records, Inc.
Missile Records
MOR Records
Monticana Records
Permanent Press Recordings/Permanent Wave
Roll On Records®
Rustron Music Productions
Valtec Productions
Wall Street Music
X.R.L. Records/Music
Yellow Jacket Records

Alternative (also modern rock, punk, college rock, new wave, hardcore, new music, industrial, ska, indie rock, garage, etc.)
Alco Recordings
AMP Records & Music
Astralwerks
Avalon Recording Group
babysue
Cleopatra Records
Deary Me Records

Deep South Entertainment
Don't Records
Drool Records
Elektra Records
Evil Teen Records
First Power Entertainment Group
Fish of Death Records and Management
Flood Recording Corp.
Gonzo! Records Inc.
Gotham Records
Hot Wings Entertainment
Hottrax Records
Idol Records
L.A. Records (Canada)
London Sire Records
Merlin Records of Canada
Monticana Records
Moody Productions, Doug
Paint Chip Records
PGE Platinum Groove Entertainment
PMG Records
Powerblast Recordings
RAVE Records, Inc.
Radical Records
Redemption Records
Road Records
Rotten Records
Sin Klub Entertainment, Inc.
Sonic Records, Inc./SRI Records, Inc.
St. Francis Records
Street Records
Strugglebaby Recording Co.
Triple X Records
28 Records
Vander-Moon Entertainment
X.R.L. Records/Music
Xemu Records

Blues

Albatross Records
Blue Wave
BSW Records
Cellar Records
Chiaroscuro Records
Dapmor Records
Deadeye Records
Flying Heart Records
Front Row Records
Goldwax Record Corporation
Grass Roots Record & Tape/LMI Records
Heart Music, Inc.
Horizon Records, Inc.
Landslide Records
MCB Records/Pepe
Monticana Records
Moody Productions, Doug
Orillyon Entertainment
P.M. Records
Pointblank Records
Ruf Records
Rustron Music Productions
Sureshot Records
Surface Records
Texas Rose Records
Topcat Records
Triple X Records
Warehouse Creek Recording Corp.
Worldwide Recordings Limited/Worldrecords.com
X.R.L. Records/Music

Children's

Awal.com
First Power Entertainment Group
Grass Roots Record & Tape/LMI Records
Leatherland Productions
Omni 2000 Inc.
Smithsonian Folkways Recordings

Classical (also opera, chamber music, serious music, choral, etc.)

A.P.I. Records
Arkadia Entertainment Corp.
babysue
Belham Valley Records
Cambria Records & Publishing
Cantilena Records
EMF Records & Affiliates
Imaginary Records
Lark Record Productions, Inc.
North Star Music
Omega Record Group, Inc.
Platinum Entertainment, Inc.
Q Records
Sun-Scape Enterprises Limited
Tangent® Records
VAI Distribution

Country (also western, C&W, bluegrass, cowboy songs, western swing, honky-tonk, etc.)

Afterschool Records, Inc.
Albatross Records
Alco Recordings
All Star Record Promotions
All Star Record Promotions
Allegheny Music Works
Americatone Records International USA
Atlan-Dec/Grooveline Records
Avalon Recording Group
Bagatelle Record Company
Belmont Records
Big Wig Productions
Blue Gem Records
Blue Wave
Bolivia Records
BSW Records
Capstan Record Production
Cellar Records
Cherry Street Records
Collector Records
Coral Records LLC
Dale Productions, Alan
Dapmor Records
Deadeye Records
Deep South Entertainment
EMF Productions
EMF Records & Affiliates
Emerald City Records
Enterprize Records-Tapes
Fountain Records
Front Row Records
Garrett Entertainment, Marty
Golden Triangle Records
Goldwax Record Corporation
Grass Roots Record & Tape/LMI Records
Green Bear Records
Guestar Records, Inc.
Hottrax Records
Idol Records
Kaupp Records
Keeping It Simple and Safe, Inc.
Kingston Records
L.A. Records (Canada)
L.A. Records (Michigan)
Landmark Communications Group
Lari-Jon Records
Lark Record Productions, Inc.
Magnum Music Corp. Ltd.
MCB Records/Pepe
Mighty Records
Missile Records
MOR Records
Monticana Records
Outstanding Records
P.M. Records

Pickwick/Mecca/International Records
Plateau Music
Playbones Records
Pop Records Research
Rhiannon Records
Road Records
Roll On Records®
Rowena Records
Rustron Music Productions
Sabre Productions
Sabteca Record Co.
Safire Records
Siltown Records
Sonic Records, Inc./SRI Records, Inc.
Southland Records, Inc.
Spotlight Records
Stardust
Stone Age Records
SunCountry Records
Sureshot Records
Surface Records
Sweet June Music
Take 2 Records
Texas Rose Records
Third Wave Productions Ltd.
Trac Record Co.
UAR Records
Valtec Productions
Vander-Moon Entertainment
Vokes Music Record Co.
Winchester Records
Worldwide Recordings Limited/Worldrecords.com
X.R.L. Records/Music
Yellow Jacket Records
Young Country Records/Plain Country Records

Dance (also house, hi-NRG, disco, club, rave, techno, trip-hop, trance, etc.)
A.A.M.I. Music Group
Alpha-Beat
AMP Records & Music
Atlan-Dec/Grooveline Records
Awal.com
Bankroll Records Inc.
Broken Note Records
Broken Records International
CAPP Records
Dagene/Cabletown Company
Discmedia
DM/Bellmark/Critique Records
Drool Records
Gig Records
Gonzo! Records Inc.
Hi-Bias Records Inc.
Horizon Records, Inc.
L.A. Records (Canada)
L.A. Records (Michigan)
Lock

Lucifer Records, Inc.
Merlin Records of Canada
Mighty Records
Monticana Records
Neurodisc Records, Inc.
NPO Records, Inc.
P. & N. Records
PGE Platinum Groove Entertainment
Pickwick/Mecca/International Records
PMG Records
Quark Records
RAVE Records, Inc.
Rampant Records
Road Records
Robbins Entertainment LLC
Sahara Records and Filmworks Entertainment
Satellite Music
Sealed Fate Records
Sound Gems
Spinball Music and Video
Suisonic Records
Synergy Records
Thump Records, Inc.
Wall Street Music
World Beatnik Records
X.R.L. Records/Music

Folk (also acoustic, Celtic, etc.)
Afterschool Records, Inc.
Big Wig Productions
Broken Note Records
Heart Music, Inc.
Hot Wings Entertainment
Missile Records
Monticana Records
Rhiannon Records
Rustron Music Productions
Sims Records, Jerry
Smithsonian Folkways Recordings
Street Records
Third Wave Productions Ltd.
Waterdog Music
Winchester Records
Wind-Up Entertainment
Worldwide Recordings Limited/Worldrecords.com

Instrumental (also background music, musical scores, etc.)
AMP Records & Music
Belham Valley Records
Broken Note Records
Lark Record Productions, Inc.
Makoché Recording Company
Mayfair Music
MOR Records
North Star Music
Permanent Press Recordings/Permanent Wave
Playbones Records

Road Records
Sims Records, Jerry
Tangent® Records

Jazz (also fusion, bebop, swing, etc.)
A.P.I. Records
Afterschool Records, Inc.
Airplay Label, The
Albatross Records
Americatone Records International USA
Ariana Records
Arkadia Entertainment Corp.
Atlan-Dec/Grooveline Records
Avita Records
Awal.com
Belham Valley Records
Candyspiteful Productions
Cherry Street Records
Chiaroscuro Records
CKB Records/Helaphat Entertainment
Creative Improvised Music Projects (CIMP)
Dale Productions, Alan
Dapmor Records
EMF Records & Affiliates
Flying Heart Records
Fresh Entertainment
Golden Triangle Records
Goldwax Record Corporation
Grass Roots Record & Tape/LMI Records
Heads Up Int., Ltd.
Heart Music, Inc.
Hi-Bias Records Inc.
Horizon Records, Inc.
Hot Wings Entertainment
Hottrax Records
Imaginary Records
L.A. Records (Michigan)
Landmark Communications Group
Landslide Records
Mighty Records
Missile Records
Monticana Records
North Star Music
Omega Record Group, Inc.
Orillyon Entertainment
Outstanding Records
Permanent Press Recordings/Permanent Wave
Playbones Records
Powerblast Recordings
Q Records
Reiter Records Ltd.
Rival Records
Sahara Records and Filmworks Entertainment
Salexo Music
St. Francis Records
Tangent® Records
Topcat Records
World Beatnik Records

Worldwide Recordings Limited/Worldrecords.com

Latin (also Spanish, salsa, Cuban, conga, Brazilian, cumbja, rancheras, Mexican, merengue, Tejano, Tex Mex, etc.)
Albatross Records
Americatone Records International USA
Amigos Music & Marketing
Discmedia
Discos Fuentes/Miami Records & Edimusica USA
EMF Records & Affiliates
Grass Roots Record & Tape/LMI Records
Hacienda Records & Recording Studio
Rowena Records
Thump Records, Inc.

Metal (also thrash, grindcore, heavy metal, etc.)
babysue
Cellar Records
Cleopatra Records
Dwell Records
L.A. Records (Michigan)
Missile Records
Powerblast Recordings
Rotten Records
Sin Klub Entertainment, Inc.
28 Records
Wind-Up Entertainment

New Age (also ambient)
AMP Records & Music
CAPP Records
Dale Productions, Alan
EMF Records & Affiliates
L.A. Records (Michigan)
Neurodisc Records, Inc.
North Star Music
Only New Age Music, Inc.
Powerblast Recordings
Rustron Music Productions
Sun-Scape Enterprises Limited
Tangent® Records

Novelty (also comedy, humor, etc.)
Leatherland Productions
Sureshot Records

Pop (also top 40, top 100, popular, chart hits, etc.)
A.A.M.I. Music Group
A.P.I. Records
Afterschool Records, Inc.
Airplay Label, The
Alco Recordings
Allegheny Music Works
Alpha-Beat
Anisette Records

CATEGORY INDEX: RECORD COMPANIES

Arkadia Entertainment Corp.
Awal.com
Aware Records
babysue
Belham Valley Records
Beluga Records
Big Wig Productions
Blue Gem Records
Bolivia Records
Broken Records International
C.P.R.
CAPP Records
Candyspiteful Productions
Capstan Record Production
Cellar Records
Coral Records LLC
Dagene/Cabletown Company
Deep South Entertainment
Discmedia
Don't Records
Drool Records
EMF Productions
EMF Records & Affiliates
Enterprize Records-Tapes
Fish of Death Records and Management
Flood Recording Corp.
Fountain Records
Fresh Entertainment
Gold City Records, Inc.
Goldwax Record Corporation
Gonzo! Records Inc.
Gotham Records
Grass Roots Record & Tape/LMI Records
Griffin Music
Hacienda Records & Recording Studio
Heads Up Int., Ltd.
Heart Music, Inc.
Hi-Bias Records Inc.
Horizon Records, Inc.
Hottrax Records
Idol Records
Jive Records
Kaupp Records
Keeping It Simple and Safe, Inc.
Kingston Records
L.A. Records (Michigan)
Lamar Music Marketing
Landmark Communications Group
Lucifer Records, Inc.
Magnum Music Corp. Ltd.
Mayfair Music
MCB Records/Pepe
Merlin Records of Canada
Mighty Records
Missile Records
MOR Records
Monticana Records
Nation Records Inc.

Omni 2000 Inc.
P.M. Records
Permanent Press Recordings/Permanent Wave
Pickwick/Mecca/International Records
Plateau Music
Pop Records Research
Q Records
Quark Records
Redemption Records
Reiter Records Ltd.
Rival Records
Robbins Entertainment LLC
Roll On Records®
Rowena Records
Rustron Music Productions
Sabteca Record Co.
Safire Records
Sahara Records and Filmworks Entertainment
Satellite Music
Sealed Fate Records
Siltown Records
Sims Records, Jerry
Songgram Music
sonic unyon records canada
Sound Gems
Spotlight Records
St. Francis Records
Street Records
Surface Records
Synergy Records
Texas Rose Records
Third Wave Productions Ltd.
Valtec Productions
Vander-Moon Entertainment
Waterdog Music
World Beatnik Records
X.R.L. Records/Music

R&B (also soul, black, urban, etc.)
Albatross Records
Allegheny Music Works
Alpha-Beat
Arkadia Entertainment Corp.
Atlan-Dec/Grooveline Records
Avalon Recording Group
Bankroll Records Inc.
Blue Gem Records
Blue Wave
Bolivia Records
C.P.R.
Candyspiteful Productions
Cellar Records
Cherry Street Records
CKB Records/Helaphat Entertainment
Coral Records LLC
Dagene/Cabletown Company
Dapmor Records
DM/Bellmark/Critique Records

EMF Productions
EMF Records & Affiliates
First Power Entertainment Group
Flying Heart Records
Fresh Entertainment
Front Row Records
Gold City Records, Inc.
Golden Triangle Records
Goldwax Record Corporation
Grass Roots Record & Tape/LMI Records
Groove Makers' Recordings
Heads Up Int., Ltd.
Hi-Bias Records Inc.
Jive Records
Kaupp Records
Keeping It Simple and Safe, Inc.
L.A. Records (Michigan)
Lamar Music Marketing
Landmark Communications Group
Lucifer Records, Inc.
Major Entertainment, Inc.
Merlin Records of Canada
Missile Records
Monticana Records
Nation Records Inc.
Omni 2000 Inc.
Orillyon Entertainment
PGE Platinum Groove Entertainment
Plateau Music
PMG Records
Pointblank Records
Pop Records Research
Powerblast Recordings
Red-Eye Records
Rival Records
Roll On Records®
Rowena Records
Ruf Records
Rustron Music Productions
Sabre Productions
Sabteca Record Co.
Sahara Records and Filmworks Entertainment
Sealed Fate Records
Sonar Records & Production
Sound Gems
Spinball Music and Video
Strugglebaby Recording Co.
Synergy Records
Topcat Records
Warehouse Creek Recording Corp.
X.R.L. Records/Music

Rap (also hip-hop, bass, etc.)
A.A.M.I. Music Group
Albatross Records
Alpha-Beat
Anisette Records
Atlan-Dec/Grooveline Records

Avalon Recording Group
Bankroll Records Inc.
Broken Note Records
C.P.R.
CKB Records/Helaphat Entertainment
Dagene/Cabletown Company
Dapmor Records
DM/Bellmark/Critique Records
First Power Entertainment Group
Fish of Death Records and Management
Fresh Entertainment
Gig Records
Gold City Records, Inc.
Goldwax Record Corporation
Groove Makers' Recordings
Heart Music, Inc.
Jive Records
Keeping It Simple and Safe, Inc.
Lamar Music Marketing
Major Entertainment, Inc.
Missile Records
Neurodisc Records, Inc.
NPO Records, Inc.
Orillyon Entertainment
PGE Platinum Groove Entertainment
Pickwick/Mecca/International Records
Powerblast Recordings
Rival Records
Siltown Records
Sin Klub Entertainment, Inc.
Sonar Records & Production
Songgram Music
Spinball Music and Video
Synergy Records
Thump Records, Inc.
Triple X Records
Vander-Moon Entertainment
Wall Street Music
World Beatnik Records

Religious (also gospel, sacred, Christian, church, hymns, praise, inspirational, worship, etc.)
Alco Recordings
All Star Record Promotions
Allegheny Music Works
Atlan-Dec/Grooveline Records
Avalon Recording Group
babysue
Bagatelle Record Company
Big Wig Productions
Brentwood Records/Diadem Records
Dagene/Cabletown Company
Dale Productions, Alan
DM/Bellmark/Critique Records
Emerald City Records
Enterprize Records-Tapes
First Power Entertainment Group

Fountain Records
Fresh Entertainment
Garrett Entertainment, Marty
Gold City Records, Inc.
Goldwax Record Corporation
Grass Roots Record & Tape/LMI Records
Green Bear Records
Kaupp Records
Keeping It Simple and Safe, Inc.
L.A. Records (Michigan)
Landmark Communications Group
Lari-Jon Records
Leatherland Productions
Magnum Music Corp. Ltd.
Malaco Records
MCB Records/Pepe
Missile Records
Monticana Records
OCP Publications
Omni 2000 Inc.
Orillyon Entertainment
Pickwick/Mecca/International Records
Platinum Entertainment, Inc.
Playbones Records
Red-Eye Records
Roll On Records®
Rowena Records
Sabre Productions
Salexo Music
Siltown Records
Sonar Records & Production
Sonic Records, Inc./SRI Records, Inc.
Spotlight Records
SunCountry Records
Sweet June Music
Texas Rose Records
Trac Record Co.
Vokes Music Record Co.
Wall Street Music
Warehouse Creek Recording Corp.
Winchester Records
Young Country Records/Plain Country Records

Rock (also rockabilly, AOR, rock 'n' roll, etc.)

A.A.M.I. Music Group
A.P.I. Records
Albatross Records
Alco Recordings
Americatone Records International USA
Anisette Records
Ariana Records
Arkadia Entertainment Corp.
Atlan-Dec/Grooveline Records
Avalon Recording Group
Aware Records
babysue
Bankroll Records Inc.
Beluga Records

Big Wig Productions
Blue Gem Records
Blue Wave
Broken Note Records
Broken Records International
BSW Records
C.P.R.
Candyspiteful Productions
Capstan Record Production
Cellar Records
Chattahoochee Records
Cherry Street Records
Collector Records
Coral Records LLC
Dapmor Records
Deadeye Records
Deary Me Records
Deep South Entertainment
Del-Fi Records, Inc.
Discmedia
Don't Records
Drool Records
Dwell Records
EMF Records & Affiliates
Enterprize Records-Tapes
Evil Teen Records
First Power Entertainment Group
Fish of Death Records and Management
Flying Heart Records
Fresh Entertainment
Front Row Records
Gig Records
Golden Triangle Records
Goldwax Record Corporation
Gotham Records
Grass Roots Record & Tape/LMI Records
Green Bear Records
Griffin Music
Hacienda Records & Recording Studio
Heart Music, Inc.
Horizon Records, Inc.
Hottrax Records
Idol Records
Kaupp Records
Keeping It Simple and Safe, Inc.
Kingston Records
L.A. Records (Canada)
L.A. Records (Michigan)
Landmark Communications Group
Lari-Jon Records
London Sire Records
Lucifer Records, Inc.
Magnum Music Corp. Ltd.
MCB Records/Pepe
Megaforce Worldwide Entertainment
Merlin Records of Canada
Missile Records
Monticana Records

Outstanding Records
P. & N. Records
P.M. Records
Permanent Press Recordings/Permanent Wave
Pickwick/Mecca/International Records
Plateau Music
Playbones Records
PMG Records
Pravda Records
Presence Records
Q Records
Radical Records
Rags to Records, Inc.
Red-Eye Records
Reiter Records Ltd.
Roll On Records®
Rotten Records
Ruf Records
Sabre Productions
Sealed Fate Records
Siltown Records
Songgram Music
Sonic Records, Inc./SRI Records, Inc.
sonic unyon records canada
Stardust
Street Records
Strugglebaby Recording Co.
Suisonic Records
Surface Records
Synergy Records
Tangent® Records

Texas Rose Records
Thump Records, Inc.
Triple X Records
28 Records
Valtec Productions
Vander-Moon Entertainment
Waterdog Music
Winchester Records
Wind-Up Entertainment
Worldwide Recordings Limited/Worldrecords.com
X.R.L. Records/Music
Young Country Records/Plain Country Records

World Music (also reggae, ethnic, calypso, international, world beat, etc.)
Arkadia Entertainment Corp.
Awal.com
Belham Valley Records
Dapmor Records
EMF Records & Affiliates
Makoché Recording Company
Missile Records
Modal Music, Inc.™
North Star Music
Only New Age Music, Inc.
RA Records
Silver Wave Records
Smithsonian Folkways Recordings
Spinball Music and Video
Tangent® Records
World Beatnik Records
Worldwide Recordings Limited/Worldrecords.com

Record Producers

The independent producer can best be described as a creative coordinator. He's usually the one with the most creative control over a recording project and is ultimately responsible for the finished product. Some record companies have in-house producers who work with the acts on that label (although, in more recent years, such producer-label relationships are often non-exclusive). Today, most record companies contract out-of-house, independent record producers on a project-by-project basis.

WHAT RECORD PRODUCERS DO

Producers play a large role in deciding what songs will be recorded for a particular project and are always on the lookout for new songs for their clients. They can be valuable contacts for songwriters because they work so closely with the artists whose records they produce. They usually have a lot more freedom than others in executive positions and are known for having a good ear for potential hit songs. Many producers are songwriters and musicians themselves. Since they wield a great deal of influence, a good song in the hands of the right producer at the right time stands a good chance of being cut. And even if a producer is not working on a specific project, he is well-acquainted with record company executives and artists and can often get material through doors not open to you.

Additional Record Producers

There are **MORE RECORD PRODUCERS** located in other sections of the book! On page 285 use the list of Additional Record Producers to find listings within other sections who are also record producers.

SUBMITTING MATERIAL TO PRODUCERS

It can be difficult to get your tapes to the right producer at the right time. Many producers write their own songs and even if they don't write, they may be involved in their own publishing companies so they have instant access to all the songs in their catalogs. Also, some genres are more dependent on finding outside songs than others. A producer working with a rock group or a singer-songwriter will rarely take outside songs. It's important to understand the intricacies of the producer/publisher situation. If you pitch your song directly to a producer first, before another publishing company publishes the song, the producer may ask you for the publishing rights (or a percentage thereof) to your song. You must decide whether the producer is really an active publisher who will try to get the song recorded again and again or whether he merely wants the publishing because it means extra income for him from the current recording project. You may be able to work out a co-publishing deal, where you and the producer split the publishing of the song. That means he will still receive his percentage of the publishing income, even if you secure a cover recording of the song by other artists in the future. Even though you would be giving up a little bit initially, you may benefit in the future.

Some producers will offer to sign artists and songwriters to "development deals." These can range from a situation where a Svengali-like producer auditions singers and musicians with the intention of building a group from the ground up, to development deals where a producer signs a band or singer-songwriter to his production company, with the intention of developing an act and producing an album to shop to labels (sometimes referred to as a "baby record deal"). You must carefully consider whether such a deal is right for you. In some cases, such a deal will open doors and propel an act to the next level. In other worst-case scenarios, such a deal can result in loss of artistic and career control, with some acts held in contractual bondage for years at a time. Before you consider any such deal, be clear about your goals, the producer's reputation, and the sort of compromises you are willing to make to reach those goals. If you have any reservations whatsoever, don't do it.

The listings that follow outline which aspects of the music industry each producer is involved in, what type of music he is looking for, and what records and artists he's recently produced. Study the listings carefully, noting the artists each producer works with, and consider if any of your songs might fit a particular artist's or producer's style. Then determine whether they are open to your level of experience (see the Openness to Submissions sidebar on page 8).

Consult the Category Index at the end of this section to find producers who work with the type of music you write, and the Geographic Index at the back of the book to locate producers in your area.

For More Information

For more instructional information on the listings in this book, including explanations of symbols (🗷 ✓ ▼ ☠ ⊕ ◯ ◑ ☯ ∅), read the article How to Use *Songwriter's Market* to Get Your Songs Heard on page 5.

☠ ✓ ⊘ **"A" MAJOR SOUND CORPORATION**, 80 Corley Ave., Toronto, Ontario M4E 1V2 Canada. (416)690-9552. Fax: (416)690-9482. E-mail: pmilner@sympatico.ca. **Contact:** Paul C. Milner, producer. Record producer and music publisher. Estab. 1989. Produces 2 EPs and 12 CDs/year. Fee derived from sales royalty when song or artist is recorded, or outright fee from recording artist or record company, or investors.
How to Contact: Submit demo tape by mail. Unsolicited submissions are OK. Prefers cassette, DAT or VHS videocassette with 5 songs and lyric sheet (lead sheet if available). Does not return material. Responds in 3 months.
Music: Mostly **rock, A/C, alternative** and **pop**; also **Christian** and **R&B**. Produced *Art of Survival* (album), written and recorded by Nashun (funk/hip-hop), released 2000 on LoFish; *The Sydneys* (album by G. Fayer), recorded by The Sydneys (pop/rock), released 2000 on American Nouveux; and *Innocent Child* (album), written and recorded by Carole Pope (alternative/pop), released 1999 on 077.

◯ **ABERDEEN PRODUCTIONS**, 524 Doral Country Dr., Nashville TN 37221. (615)646-9750. **Contact:** Scott Turner, executive producer. Record producer and music publisher (Buried Treasure Music/ASCAP, Captain Kidd/BMI). Estab. 1971. Produces 10 singles, 15-20 12″ singles, 8 LPs and 8 CDs/year. Fee derived from outright fee from recording artist.
How to Contact: Submit demo tape by mail. Unsolicited submissions OK. Prefers cassette with maximum 4 songs and lead sheet. SASE. "No SASE, no reply." Responds in 2 weeks. No "lyrics only."
Music: Mostly **country, MOR** and **rock**; also **top 40/pop**. Produced "All of the Above" (single by Douglas Bush) from *The Entrance* (album), recorded by Lea Brennan (country/MOR), released 2000. Other artists include Jimmy Clanton.
Tips: "Start out on an independent basis because of the heavy waiting period to get on a major label."

☐ **ACR PRODUCTIONS**, 505 N. A St., Midland TX 79701. (615)826-9233 or (915)687-2702. **Contact:** Dwaine Thomas, owner. Record producer, music publisher (Joranda Music/BMI) and record company (ACR Records). Estab. 1986. Produces 120 singles, 8-15 12″ singles, 25 LPs, 25 EPs and 25 CDs/year. Fee derived from sales royalty when song or artist is recorded. "We charge for in-house recording only. Remainder is derived from royalties."
How to Contact: Submit demo tape by mail. Unsolicited submissions are OK. Prefers cassette or VHS videocassette with 5 songs and lyric sheet. Does not return material. Responds in 6 weeks if interested.
Music: Mostly **country swing, pop** and **rock**; also **R&B** and **gospel**. Produced *Bottle's Almost Gone* (album) and "Black Gold" (single), written and recorded by Mike Nelson (country), both released 1999 on ACR Records; and *Nashville Series* (album), written and recorded by various (country), released 1998 on ProJam Music.
Tips: "Be professional. No living room tapes!"

☑ **ALCO PRODUCTIONS**, P.O. Box 18197, Panama City Beach FL 32417. **Contact:** Ann McEver, president. Record producer. Estab. 2000. Produces 6 singles and 3 CDs/year. Fee derived from sales royalty when song or artist is recorded.
How to Contact: Submit demo tape by mail. Unsolicited submissions are OK. Prefers cassette with 3 songs and lyric sheet. SASE. Responds in 3 weeks.
Music: Mostly **pop/rock, country** and **alternative**; also **gospel**. Produced "Snack Time for Slip" (single by Jack Bennion) from *Snacktime* (album), recorded by Snack Bar (alternative), released 2000 on Alco.
Tips: "Submit your best material. We are looking for artists and groups that are unique and are strong enough to compete at a national level. We are also looking for artists and bands that are different yet ones that would fit into the existing Nashville or Los Angeles music formats."

☑ ⊘ **STUART J. ALLYN**, 250 Taxter Rd., Irvington NY 10533. (212)486-0856. E-mail: adrstudios@adrinc.org. Associate: Jack Walker. **Contact:** Jack Davis, general manager. President: Stuart J. Allyn. Record producer. Estab. 1972. Produces 6 singles and 3-6 CDs/year. Fee derived from sales royalty and outright fee from recording artist and record company.
How to Contact: *Does not accept unsolicited submissions.*
Music: Mostly **pop, rock, jazz** and **theatrical**; also **R&B** and **country**. Produced *Thad Jones Legacy* (album), recorded by Vanquard Jazz Orchestra (jazz), released 2000 on New World Records. Other artists include Billy Joel, Aerosmith, Carole Demas, Bob Stewart, The Dixie Peppers, Nora York, Buddy Barnes and various video and film scores.

☑ ☐ **ANGEL FILMS COMPANY**, 967 Hwy. 40, New Franklin MO 65274-9778. Phone/fax: (573)698-3900. E-mail: angelfilm@aol.com. Website: www.phoenix.org. **Contact:** Lord Sackville, president. Owner: William H. Hoehne, Jr. Record producer, motion picture company and record company (Angel One). Estab. 1980. Produces 5 LPs, 5 EPs and 5 CDs/year. Fee derived from sales royalty when song or artist is recorded.
How to Contact: Submit demo tape or CD by mail. Unsolicited submissions are OK. Prefers cassette or VHS videocassette with 3 songs. "Send only original material, not previously recorded, and include a bio sheet on artist." SASE. Responds in 6 weeks.
Music: Mostly **pop, rock** and **rockabilly**; also **jazz** and **R&B**. Produced *Nemo* (album), written and recorded by Nemo (MOR), released 2000; "Shelter" (single), written and recorded by Clam (rock); and "Palm Coaster" (single), written and recorded by Le Gee (MOR), all released on Angel One. Other artists include Julian James, Patrick Donovon, Euttland, B.D.K. and Teddies.
Tips: "Actually listen to what you're doing and ask, 'would I buy that?' "

⊘ **JONATHAN APPELL PRODUCTIONS, INC.**, 400 Second Ave., #13A, New York NY 10010. (212)725-5613. E-mail: appellproductions@rcn.com. Website: www.erols.com/appellproductions. **Contact:** Jonathan Appell, producer/engineer. Record producer and audio engineer. Estab. 1989. Produces 2 singles and 5 LPs/year. Fee derived from sales royalty when song or artist is recorded, or outright fee from recording artist or record company.

How to Contact: *Does not accept unsolicited submissions.*
Music: Mostly **rock**, **pop** and **R&B**; also **jazz** and **reggae**. Produced *Piranha Brothers* (album), written and recorded by Piranha Brothers (rock); *Blue Eyed Soul* (album by Chris and Tom O'Connor), recorded by Blue Eyed Soul (pop); and *Roseanne Drucker* (album by Jan Polkson), recorded by Roseanne Drucker (pop), all on Reload. Other artists include Matt Cohler Band, Lee Drutman Band, YNot and Eric Fleischman.
Tips: "Learn your craft. Ask yourself (honestly), 'Am I good enough to perform alongside whomever the biggest stars are in my genre of music?' If you aren't convinced that you've attained that level of professionalism, you'll never convince a producer or a record company. If you're not ready, get back in there and practice, practice, practice!"

N ○ AVALON PRODUCTIONS, P.O. Box 121626, Nashville TN 37212. **Contact:** A&R Review Department. Record producer, record company (Avalon Recording Group) and music publisher (Avalon Music). Estab. 2001. Produces 6 singles and 3 albums/year. Fee derived from sales royalty when song or artist is recorded, from outright fee from recording artist, or outright fee from record company.
How to Contact: Submit demo tape by mail. Unsolicited submissions are OK. Prefers cassette or CD with 3 songs and lyric sheet. Include SASE. Responds in 3 weeks.
Music: Mostly **rock**, **country**, and **alternative**; also **R&B**, **rap** and **gospel**.
Tips: "Send songs suitable for today's market."

N ○ RON BAIRD ENTERPRISES, P.O. Box 42, 1 Main St., Ellsworth PA 15331. E-mail: ronssong@charterpa.net. **Contact:** Ron Baird, executive producer. Record producer, record company (La Ron Ltd. Records), music publisher (Baird Music Group). Estab. 1999. Produces 2-5 singles and 1-2 LPs/year.
How to Contact: Submit demo tape by mail. Unsolicited submissions are OK. "No certified mail." Prefers cassette only with 2-4 songs and lyric sheet. Does not return submissions. Responds only if interested.
Music: Mostly **country** and **country rock**. Does not want hip-hop, gospel/religious or R&B.
Tips: "Our goal is to produce finished masters and shop these for major label deals. We want to produce legitimate hits."

○ BAL RECORDS, P.O. Box 369, LaCanada CA 91012-0369. (818)548-1116. E-mail: Balmusic@pacbell.net. **Contact:** Adrian Bal, president or Berdella M. Bal, vice president. Record producer and music publisher (Bal & Bal Music). Estab. 1965. Produces 1-3 CDs/year. Fee derived from sales royalty when song or artist is recorded.
How to Contact: Write or call first and obtain permission to submit. Prefers cassette with 3 songs and lyric sheet. SASE. Responds in 3 months.
Music: Mostly **MOR**, **country**, **jazz**, **R&B**, **rock** and **top 40/pop**; also **blues**, **church/religious**, **easy listening** and **soul**. Produced "What's the Matter With Me?" (single) and "Lord You Been So Good to Me" (single), both written and recorded by Rhonda Johnson on BAL Records (gospel). Other artists include Kathy Simmons, Paul Richards and Terry Fischer.

○ HAL BERNARD ENTERPRISES, INC., P.O. Box 8385, Cincinnati OH 45208. (513)871-1500. Fax: (513)871-1510. E-mail: umbrella@one.net. **Contact:** Stan Hertzman, president. Record producer, record company (Strugglebaby Recording Co.), management firm (Umbrella Artists Management) and music publisher (Sunnyslope Music Inc. and Bumpershoot Music Inc.). Produces 5 singles and 3-4 LPs/year. Fee derived from sales royalty.
How to Contact: Prefers cassette with 1-3 songs and lyric sheet. SASE. Responds in 1 month only if interested.

MARKETS THAT WERE listed in the 2001 edition of *Songwriters Market* but do not appear this year are listed in the General Index with a notation explaining why they were omitted.

Music: Produced *Gun For You*, written and recorded by The Greenhornes (rock), released on Prince Records; *Get Me Off Or Get Off Me*, written and recorded by Cicada (rock); and *From the Westside*, written and recorded by Pepper Bonar (rock), both released on Strugglebaby Records.

N☐ BIG SKY AUDIO PRODUCTIONS, 1035 E. Woodland Ave. #2, Springfield PA 19064. (610)328-4709. Fax: (610)328-7728. Website: www.bigskyaudio.com. **Contact:** Drew Raison, producer. Record producer. Estab. 1990. Produces 20-30 CDs/year. Fee derived from sales royalty when song or artist is recorded or outright fee from recording artist or record company.
How to Contact: Submit demo tape by mail. Unsolicited submissions are OK. Prefers CD/CDR with 3 songs and lyric sheet. "Don't send it to us if it isn't copyrighted!" Does not return material. Responds in 6 weeks.
Music: Mostly **rock**, **R&B**, **pop** and **gospel**; also **anything with strong vocals**.

☑ ◑ BIRTHPLACE PRODUCTIONS, P.O. Box 1651, Bristol TN 37621. (423)878-3535. E-mail: stevenp8@prodigy.net. Website: http://pages.prodigy.net/stevenp8. **Contact:** Steve Patrick, president. Record producer and record company (Riverbend Records). Estab. 1994. Produces 12 singles, 10 LPs and 20 CDs/year. Fee derived from outright fee from recording artist or record company.
How to Contact: Write or call first and obtain permission to submit or to arrange personal interview. Prefers cassette or videocassette with 10 songs and lyric sheet. SASE. Responds in 3 weeks.
Music: Mostly **country**, **gospel** and **folk**. Produced "Jinny Rose" (single), written and recorded by Garry Johnson on Sabteca Records; *Power and Grace* (album), written and recorded by Tommy Bradford on Riverbend Records; and *Light of the World* (album), written and recorded by Steve Warren on S&B Records.
Tips: "Stay focused. Be willing to accept that the commitment you make is determined by your understanding of the business itself."

☑ ☐ BLUES ALLEY RECORDS, Rt. 1, Box 288, Clarksburg WV 26301. (304)599-1055. **Contact:** Joshua Swiger, producer. Record producer, record company and music publisher (Blues Alley Publishing/BMI). Produces 2 singles, 1-2 LPs and 2 EPs/year. Fee derived from sales royalty when song or artist is recorded.
How to Contact: Submit demo tape by mail. Unsolicited submissions are OK. Prefers cassette with 4 songs and lyric and lead sheets. Does not return material. Responds in 6 weeks.
Music: Mostly **Christian**, **alternative** and **pop**. Produced *Imaginary Friends* (album by Mike Arbogast), recorded by Imaginary Friends (rock) on Blues Alley Records; "I'll Fly Away" (single), written and recorded by J. Nicholson (Christian), released on Blues Alley Records.

N ◑ CANDYSPITEFUL PRODUCTIONS, 4202 Co. Rt. 4, Oswego NY 13126. (315)342-3129. E-mail: WilliamF@northnet.org. Website: www.candyspiteful.com. **Contact:** William Ferraro, president. Record producer, record company (Candyspiteful Productions), music publisher (Candyspiteful Productions). Estab. 2000. Produces 12 singles, 2 albums per year. Fee derived from outright fee from recording artist.
How to Contact: Submit demo tape by mail. Unsolicited submissions are OK. Prefers CD/CDR with 3 songs and lyric sheet and cover letter. Does not return material. Responds only if interested.
Music: Mostly **progressive rock**, **rock/pop/R&B**and **smooth jazz/rock**. Produced "Endless Night" (single by Maxwell Frye) from *Mandrake*, recorded by Mandrake (rock), released 2001 on Candyspiteful Productions.

☐ JAN CELT MUSICAL SERVICES, 4026 NE 12th Ave., Portland OR 97212. (503)287-8045. E-mail: flyheart@teleport.com. Website: www.teleport.com/~flyheart. **Contact:** Jan Celt, owner. Record producer, music publisher (Wiosna Nasza Music/BMI) and record company (Flying Heart Records). Estab. 1982. Produces 3-5 CDs/year.
How to Contact: Submit demo tape by mail. Unsolicited submissions are OK. Prefers high-quality cassette with 1-10 songs and lyric sheet. "SASE required for any response." Does not return materials. Responds in 4 months.

Music: Mostly **R&B**, **rock** and **blues**; also **jazz**. Produced "Vexatious Progressions" (single), written and recorded by Eddie Harris (jazz); "Bong Hit" (single by Chris Newman), recorded by Snow Bud & the Flower People (rock); and "She Moved Away" (single by Chris Newman), recorded by Napalm Beach, all on Flying Heart Records. Other artists include The Esquires and Janice Scroggins.

COFFEE AND CREAM PRODUCTIONS, 1138 E. Price St., Philadelphia PA 19138. (215)842-3450. **Contact:** Bolden Abrams, Jr., producer. Record producer, music publisher (Coffee and Cream Publishing Company/ASCAP) and record company (Coffee and Cream Records). Produces 12 singles, 12 12″ singles and 6 LPs/year. Fee derived from sales royalty or outright fee from recording artist or record company.
How to Contact: Submit demo tape by mail. Unsolicited submissions are OK. Prefers cassette with 1-4 songs and lyric sheet. SASE. Responds in 2 weeks.
Music: Mostly **R&B**, **pop** and **country**; also **gospel** and **dance**. Produced "Si Me Dejo Llevar" (by Jose Gomez/Sheree Sano/Julio Hernandez); and "I Can't Wait" (by Abrams/Degrazio/Urbach), both recorded by Melissa Manjom on Misa Records; and "If I Let Myself Go" (by Gomez/Sano), recorded by Ron Hevener on RMB Records. Other artists include Michal Beckham, Robert Benjamin, Darrall Campbell, Elektra, Christopher Shirk, Tony Gilmore, Janine Whetstone, Kissie Darnell and Debra Spice.

COACHOUSE MUSIC, P.O. Box 1308, Barrington IL 60011. (847)382-7631. Fax: (847)382-7651. E-mail: coachouse1@aol.com. **Contact:** Michael Freeman, president. Record producer. Estab. 1984. Produces 6-8 CDs/year. Fee derived from sales royalty when song or artist is recorded.
How to Contact: *Write first and obtain permission to submit.* Prefers cassette, DAT or CD with 3-5 songs and lyric sheet. SASE. Responds in 6 weeks.
Music: Mostly **rock**, **pop** and **blues**; also **alternative rock** and **country/roots**. Produced *Casque Nu* (album), written and recorded by Charlelie Couture on Chrysalis EMI France (contemporary pop); *Time Will Tell* (album by various/John Grimaldi), recorded by Studebaker John on Blind Pig Records (blues); *Where Blue Begins* (album by various/D. Coleman), recorded by Deborah Coleman on Blind Pig Records (contemporary blues) and *Floobie* (album by Dan Ruprecht), recorded by The Pranks on Coachouse Records (pop). Other artists include Maybe/Definitely, Eleventh Dream Day, Magic Slim, Amarillo Kings, The Tantrums, The Pranks, Allison Johnson, The Bad Examples, Mississippi Heat and Supermint.
Tips: "Be honest, be committed, strive for excellence."

COLLECTOR RECORDS, P.O. Box 1200, 3260 AE oud beyerland, Holland, The Netherlands. Phone: 186-604266. Fax: 186-604366. E-mail: sales@collectorrec.com. Website: www.collectorrec.com. **Contact:** Cees Klop, president. Record producer and music publisher (All Rock Music). Produces 25 CDs/year. Fee derived from outright fee from record company.
How to Contact: Submit demo tape by mail. Unsolicited submissions are OK. Prefers cassette. SAE and IRC. Responds in 2 months.
Music: Mostly **'50s rock**, **rockabilly** and **country rock**; also **piano boogie woogie**. Produced "The Brush" (single) from *Boogie Woogie Special* (album), written and recorded by André Valkering/Eric-Jan Overbeek (boogie woogie piano), released 2000 on Down South Records. Other artists include Rob Hoeke and Teddy Redell.
Tips: "Only send the kind of music we produce."

DOUGLAS CRAIG, (formerly Bewildering Music, Inc.), P.O. Box 302, Locust Valley NY 11560. (516)759-5560. E-mail: bminc@aol.com. Website: http://members.aol.com/bminc/homepage.htm. **Contact:** Douglas W. Craig, producer. Record producer. Estab. 1992. Produces 1 or 2 EPs and 3-5 CDs/year. Fee derived from flat fee or hourly rate.
How to Contact: Prefers cassette, CD or VHS videocassette with photo. All submissions are kept on file.
Music: Mostly **solo artists**, **rock**, **electronic world beat**; also **remix**, **soundtrack work** (melodic preferred). Artist must live in the New York area and travel to the producer's studio. Other artists include Breakthru and Cuentos Blancos.

☑ ⊘ **JERRY CUPIT PRODUCTIONS**, Box 121904, Nashville TN 37212. (615)731-0100. Fax: (615)731-3005. E-mail: jerrycupit@cupitmusic.com. Website: www.cupitmusic.com. **Contact:** Denise Roberts, creative assistant. Record producer and music publisher (Cupit Music). Estab. 1984. Fee derived from sales royalty when song or artist is recorded or outright fee from artist.
How to Contact: *Write first and obtain permission to submit.* Prefers cassette with bio and photo. SASE. Responds in 2 months.
Music: Mostly **country**, **Southern rock** and **gospel**; also **R&B**. Produced "What If He's Right" (single by Jerry Cupit) from *Memarie* (album), recorded by Memarie (Christian country), released 2000 on HotSong.com Records; and "I'm Not Homeless" (single by Jerry Cupit/Ken Mellons/Randy Roberts) from *Wings of a Dove* (album), recorded by Ken Mellons (Christian country), released 2000 on Curb Records. Other artists include Jack Robertson and Jon Nicholson.
Tips: "Be prepared to work hard and be able to take constructive/professional criticism."

☑ ○ **DAP ENTERTAINMENT**, PMB 364, 7100 Lockwood Blvd., Boardman OH 44512. (330)782-5031. Fax: (330)782-6954. Website: www.mp3.com/DarrylAlexanderSr or www.dapenterta inment.com. **Contact:** Darryl Alexander, producer. Record Producer and music publisher (Alexander Sr. Music, BMI). Estab. 1997. Produces 12 singles and 2-4 CDs/year. Fee derived from sales royalty (producer points) when song or artist is recorded or outright fee from recording artist or record company.
How to Contact: *Write first and obtain permission to submit.* Prefers cassette with 2-4 songs and lyric sheet. SASE. Responds in 1 month. "No phone calls or faxes will be accepted."
Music: Mostly **contemporary jazz**, **urban contemporary gospel**; also **R&B**. Produced "Take A Chance" (single by Darryl Alexander/Sheila Hayes), recorded by Sheila Hayes (urban jazz), released 2001; and "Feel Your Love" and "You Are So Beautiful" (singles), written recorded by Darryl Alexander Sr. (urban jazz), released 2001 on DAP Entertainment. Other artists include Kathryn Williams.

☒ ⊘ **EDWARD DE MILES**, 117 W. Harrison Bldg. #S627, Chicago IL 60605-1709. (773)509-6381. Fax: (312)922-6964. **Contact:** Edward De Miles, president. Record producer, music publisher (Edward De Miles Music Co./BMI) and record company (Sahara Records and Filmworks Entertainment). Estab. 1981. Produces 5-10 CDs/year. Fee derived from sales royalty when song or artist is recorded.
How to Contact: *Does not accept unsolicited submissions.*
Music: Mostly **R&B/dance**, **top 40 pop/rock** and **contemporary jazz**; also **country, TV and film themes—songs and jingles**. Produced "Moments" and "Dance Wit Me" (singles) (dance), both written and recorded by Steve Lynn; and "Games" (single), written and recorded by D'von Edwards (jazz), all on Sahara Records. Other artists include Multiple Choice.
Tips: "Copyright all material before submitting. Equipment and showmanship a must."

☒ ⊘ **AL DELORY AND MUSIC MAKERS**, 3000 Hillsboro Rd. #11, Nashville TN 37215. (615)292-2140. Fax: (615)297-6031. **Contact:** Al DeLory, president. Record producer and career consultant (DeLory Music/ASCAP). Estab. 1987. Fee derived from outright fee from recording artist.
   • Al DeLory has won two Grammy Awards and has been nominated five times.
How to Contact: *Write or call first and obtain permission to submit or to arrange personal interview.* Prefers cassette or VHS videocassette. SASE. Responds in 1 month.
Music: Mostly **pop** and **Latin**. Produced "Gentle On My Mind" (single), "By the Time I Get to Phoenix" (single) and "Wichita Lineman" (single), all recorded by Glen Campbell. Other artists include Letter Men and Gary Puckett.
Tips: "Seek advice and council only with professionals with a track record."

⊘ **JOEL DIAMOND ENTERTAINMENT**, Dept. SM, 3940 Laurel Canyon Blvd., Suite 441, Studio City CA 91604. (818)980-9588. Fax: (818)980-9422. E-mail: jdiamond20@aol.com. **Contact:** Joel Diamond. Record producer, music publisher and manager. Fee derived from sales royalty when song is recorded or outright fee from recording artist or record company.

How to Contact: *Contact first and obtain permission to submit.* Does not return material. Responds only if interested.

Music: Mostly **dance**, **easy listening**, **country**, **R&B**, **rock**, **soul** and **top 40/pop**. Produced "One Night In Bangkok" (single by Robey); "Love is the Reason" (single by Cline/Wilson), recorded by E. Humperdinck and G. Gaynor on Critique Records (A/C); "After the Loving" (single), recorded by E. Humperdinck; I Am What I Am" (single), recorded by Gloria Gaynor; and "Paradise" (single), recorded by Kair.

✓ ⃝ **PHILIP D. DIXON III, ATTORNEY AT LAW**, 2501 Parkview Dr. #500, Ft. Worth TX 76102. (817)332-8553. Fax: (817)332-2834. E-mail: pdixon3@yahoo.com. **Contact:** Philip D. Dixon III, attorney. Record producer, artist representative; trademark/copyright protection for artists. Estab. 1995. Fee derived from sales royalty when song or artist is recorded or outright fee from record company. "We do charge for statutory payments made to third parties."

How to Contact: *Write first and obtain permission to submit a demo or write first to arrange personal interview.* Prefers CD with any number of songs and lyric sheet; although cassette and videocassette are OK. SAE ("we pay return postage"). Responds in 1 month.

Music: Mostly **rock**, **country** and **Latino**; also **rap**.

Tips: "Protect your work from a legal standpoint before making any disclosures to anyone. Be vigilant in your creative and business affairs."

⊘ **COL. BUSTER DOSS PRESENTS**, 341 Billy Goat Hill Rd., Winchester TN 37398. **Contact:** Col. Buster Doss, producer. Fax: (931)649-2732. E-mail: cbd@vallnet.com. Website: http://stardustco untrymusic.com. Record producer, record company (Stardust, Wizard), management firm and music publisher (Buster Doss Music/BMI). Estab. 1959. Produces 100 singles, 10 12″ singles, 20 LPs and 20 CDs/year. Fee derived from sales royalty when song or artist is recorded.

How to Contact: *Write first and obtain permission to submit.* Prefers cassette with 2 songs and lyric sheet. SASE. Responds in 1 week if interested.

Music: Mostly **country** and **gospel**. Produced *Miss Y2K* (album), written and recorded by Brant Miller; *Ahead of His Time* (album), written and recorded by Rooster Quantrell; and *Lying Again* (album), written and recorded by Bronco Buck Cody, all released 1999 on Stardust Records. Other artists include Cliff Archer, Linda Wunder, Honey James, Don Sky, Shelly Streeter, Rooster Quantrell, Dwain Gamel, Donna Darlene and Jersey Outlaw.

Ⓝ ⃝ **LEO J. EIFFERT, JR.**, P.O. Box 5412, Buena Park CA 90620. (760)245-8473. **Contact:** Leo J. Eiffert, Jr., owner. Record producer, music publisher (Eb-Tide Music/BMI, Young Country Music/BMI), management firm (Crawfish Productions) and record company (Plain Country). Estab. 1967. Produces 15-20 singles and 5 LPs/year. Fee derived from sales royalty when song or artist is recorded.

How to Contact: Submit demo tape by mail. Unsolicited submissions are OK. Prefers cassette with 2-3 songs, lyric and lead sheet. SASE. Responds in 1 month.

Music: Mostly **country** and **gospel**. Produced "Flying High" (single by Leo J. Eiffert, Jr.), recorded by Pigeons, released 2001 on Young Country Records. Other artists include Homemade, Crawfish Band, Brandi Holland, Mary T. Eiffert, Stiff Racoons, Steel Promises, Southern Spirit and David Busson.

Tips: "Just keep it real country."

⊘ **ESQUIRE INTERNATIONAL**, P.O. Box 6032, Station B, Miami FL 33101-6032. (305)547-1424. **Contact:** Jeb Stuart, president. Record producer, music publisher (Jeb Stuart Music) and management firm. Produces 6 singles and 2 LPs/year. Fee derived from sales royalty or independent leasing of masters and placing songs.

FOR BOOKS ON THE CRAFT AND BUSINESS of songwriting, check out the website for Writer's Digest Books at www.writersdigest.com.

How to Contact: Submit demo tape by mail. Unsolicited submissions are OK. Prefers cassette or CD with 2-4 songs and lead sheet. SASE. Responds in 1 month.

Music: Mostly **blues, church/religious, country, dance, gospel, jazz, rock, soul** and **top 40/pop**. Produced "Go to Sleep, Little Baby" (single by Jeb Stuart), recorded by Cafidia and Jeb Stuart; "Guns Guns (No More Guns)" (single) and "No One Should Be Alone on Christmas" (single), both written and recorded by Jeb Stuart, all on Esquire Int'l Records. Other artists include Moments Notice and Night Live.

☑ ⊘ **THE ETERNAL SONG AGENCY,** P.O. Box 121, Worthington OH 43085. E-mail: songagency@hotmail.com. Website: www.eternal-song-agency.com. **Contact:** Attn: A&R. Executive Producer: Leopold Xavier Crawford. Record producer, record company and music publisher (Fragrance Records, Song of Solomon Records, Emerald Records, Lilly Records, Ancient of Days Music and Anastacia Music). Estab. 1986. Produces 7-15 singles and 5 CDs/year. Fee derived from sales royalty when song or artist is recorded or outright fee from recording artist or record company.

How to Contact: *Write first and obtain permission to submit.* Prefers cassette or videocassette with 3 songs and lyric or lead sheet. "Type all printed material. Professionalism of presentation will get you an ear with us." SASE. Responds in 6 weeks.

Music: Mostly **contemporary Christian, Christian inspirational** and **southern gospel music**. Produced "The Ultimate Answer" (single by Michael Higgins), recorded by Anna Jackson, released 2001 on Fragrance Records. Other artists include Bloodbought, Seventh Dynasty, Streets of Gold and Jerry Waters.

⊘ **FINAL MIX MUSIC,** 2219 W. Olive Ave., Suite 102, Burbank CA 91506. (818)840-9000. E-mail: finalmix@aol.com. **Contact:** Theresa Frank, A&R. Record producer/remixer/mix engineer, record company (3.6 Music, Inc.) and music publisher (Roachi World Music). Estab. 1989. Releases 12 singles and 3-5 LPs and CDs/year. Fee derived from sales royalty when song or artist is recorded.

How to Contact: Does not accept unsolicited submissions.

Music: Mostly **pop, dance, R&B** and **rap**. Produced Michael Bolton, K-Ci and Jo Jo (of Jodeci), Will Smith, Janet Jackson, Ice Cube, Queen Latifah, Tatyana Ali, Jennifer Paige and The Corrs.

Ⓝ ⊘ **GALLWAY BAY MUSIC,** 136 S. Roxbury Dr., #8, Beverly Hills CA 90212. (310)550-7334. E-mail: gallbay@aol.com. Website: www.petergallway.com. **Contact:** Peter Gallway. Record producer, production company and recording artist. Estab. 1983. Produces 4-5 CDs/year. Fee derived from sales royalty when song or artist is recorded or outright fee from recording artist or record company.

How to Contact: *Write first and obtain permission to submit.* Prefers CD/CDR with 4 songs. Does not return material. "Responds only if interested in further information."

Music: Great songwriters of all kinds specializing in **contemporary folk** and **alternative pop**. Produced *Mona Lisa Cafe* (album), written and recorded by Cliff Eberhardt on Shanachie Records (folk/pop); *Time and Love (the music of Laura Nyro)*, featuring Suzanne Vega, Rosanne Cash, Jane Siberry, Jonatha Brooke and ten other contemporary women artists, on Astor Place Records; *Written in Red* (album), recorded by Louise Taylor, released on Signature Sounds; and eleven solo CDs by Peter Gallway on Gadfly Records (www.gadflyrecords.com).

⊘ **HAILING FREQUENCY MUSIC PRODUCTIONS,** 7438 Shoshone Ave., Van Nuys CA 91406. (818)881-9888. Fax: (818)881-0555. E-mail: blowinsmokeband@ktb.net. Website: www.blowinsmokeband.com. President: Lawrence Weisberg. Vice President: Larry Knight. Record producer, record company (Blowin' Smoke Records), management firm (Blowin' Smoke Productions) and music publisher (Hailing Frequency Publishing). Estab. 1992. Produces 3 LPs and 3 CDs/year. Fee derived from sales royalty when song or artist is recorded or outright fee from artist.

How to Contact: *Write or call first and obtain permission to submit.* Prefers cassette or VHS ½" videocassette. "Write or print legibly with complete contact instructions." SASE. Responds in 1 month.

Music: Mostly **contemporary R&B**, **blues** and **blues-rock**; also **songs for film**, **jingles for commercials** and **gospel (contemporary)**. Produced *100% Pure R&B* (album by various), recorded by Blowin' Smoke Rhythm & Blues Band (R&B), released 2000 on Blowin' Smoke Records. Other artists include the Fabulous Smokettes.

☑ ◯ **HAWORTH PRODUCTIONS**, Box 1446, Laurie MO 65038. (573)374-1111. Fax: (775)522-1533. E-mail: mashred@yahoo.com. Website: www.geocities.com/mashred. **Contact:** Dann E. Haworth, president/producer. Record producer and music publisher (Southern Most Publishing/BMI). Estab. 1985. Produces 5 singles, 3 12″ singles, 10 LPs, 5 EPs and 10 CDs/year. Fee derived from sales royalty when song or artist is recorded or outright fee from recording artist.
How to Contact: Submit demo tape by mail. Unsolicited submissions are OK. Prefers cassette or 7½ ips reel-to-reel with 3 songs and lyric or lead sheets. SASE. Responds in 2 weeks.
Music: Mostly **rock**, **country** and **gospel**; also **jazz**, **R&B** and **New Age**. Produced *Christmas Joy* (album by Esther Kreak) on Serene Sounds Records. Other artists include The Hollowmen, Jordan Border, Jim Wilson, Tracy Creech and Tony Glise.
Tips: "Keep it simple and from the heart."

☑ ◐ **HEART CONSORT MUSIC**, 410 First St. W., Mt. Vernon IA 52314. E-mail: hrtcnsrtms@aol.com. Website: www.heartconsortmusic.com. **Contact:** Catherine Lawson, manager. Record producer, record company and music publisher. Estab. 1980. Produces 2-3 CDs/year. Fee derived from sales royalty when song or artist is recorded.
How to Contact: Submit demo tape by mail. Unsolicited submissions are OK. Prefers cassette or VHS videocassette with 3 songs and 3 lyric sheets. SASE. Responds in 3 months.
Music: Mostly **jazz**, **New Age** and **contemporary**. Produced *New Faces* (album), written and recorded by James Kennedy on Heart Consort Music (world/jazz).
Tips: "We are interested in jazz/New Age artists with quality demos and original ideas. We aim for an international audience."

Ⓝ ◐ **INTEGRATED ENTERTAINMENT**, 3333 Walnut St. #209, Philadelphia PA 19104-3408. (215)417-6921. E-mail: gelboni@aol.com. **Contact:** Lawrence Gelburd, president. Record producer. Estab. 1991. Produces 6 EPs and 6 CDs/year. Fee derived from sales royalty when song or artist is recorded or outright fee from recording artist or record company.
How to Contact: Submit demo tape by mail. Unsolicited submissions are OK. Prefers cassette or CD with 3 songs. "Draw a guitar on the outside of envelope so we'll know it's from a songwriter." SASE. Responds in 2 months.
Music: Mostly **rock** and **AAA**. Produced *Gold Record* (album), written and recorded by Dash Rip Rock on Ichiban Records (rock); *Virus* (album), written and recorded by Margin of Error on Treehouse Records (modern rock); and *I Divide* (album), written and recorded by Amy Carr on Evil Twin Records (AAA). Other artists include Land of the Blind, Grimace, Harpoon, Sprawl, Lockdown and Tripe.

☑ ◐ **INTERSTATE RECORDS (ISR)**, P.O. Box 291991, Nashville TN 37229. (615)360-2331. Fax: (615)361-4438. E-mail: dklittle007@earthlink.net. Website: www.amst.homestead.com/amst.html or www.tcmt.com. CEO/Executive Producer: Deke Little. Director of A&R: Jack Batey. Record producer and record company. Estab. 1993. Produces 10 singles and 2 CDs/year. Fee derived from sales royalty when song or artist is recorded.
How to Contact: Submit demo tape by mail. Unsolicited submissions are OK. Prefers cassette with 3-5 songs and lyric and lead sheet. "Submit original material only. This allows an opportunity to listen for originality in vocal delivery and judge the strength of writing capabilities. (Please no cover songs or karaoke voice overs)." Does not return material. Responds in 2 months.
Music: Mostly **traditional country** and **Texas swing**. Produced "Bad Love" (single), written and recorded by Barbi Presley; and "Us Cowboys Know How to Take a Fall" (by Larry and Rob Matson), recorded by Bart McEntire, all on Ameri-Star.
Tips: "Be original in your vocals, lyrics and melodies. Submitting a full-blown demo is not necessary as we prefer a tape with acoustic guitar and bass or piano and bass."

JAG STUDIO, LTD., 3801-C Western Blvd., Raleigh NC 27606. (919)821-2059. **Contact:** Joy Cook, general manager. Record producer and recording studio. Estab. 1981. Produces 8 CDs/year. Fee derived from outright fee from recording artist.

How to Contact: *Write first and obtain permission to submit.* Does not return material. Responds in 2 months.

Music: Mostly **rock**, **Americana** and **roots** (**country, blues, jazz**). Produced *Six String Drag* (album), written and recorded by Six String Drag (rock/country), released 1999; and *Brother* (album), written and recorded by Cry of Love (rock); and *Apartment 635* (album), written and recorded by Dag, all on Columbia. Other artists include John Custer, Hootie and the Blowfish and Dan Baird (of Georgia Satellites).

Tips: "Be prepared. Learn something about the *business* end of music first."

ALEXANDER JANOULIS PRODUCTIONS/BIG AL JANO PRODUCTIONS, 1957 Kilburn Dr., Atlanta GA 30324. (770)662-6661. E-mail: ajproductions@hottrax.com. **Contact:** Oliver Cooper, vice president of A&R. CEO: Alex Janoulis. Record producer. Produces 6 singles and 2 CDs/year. Fee derived from sales royalty when song or artist is recorded or outright fee from recording artist or record company.

How to Contact: *Write first and obtain permission to submit.* "Letters should be short, requesting submission permission." Prefers cassette with 1-3 songs. Does not return material. Responds in 6 months.

Music: Mostly **top 40**, **rock** and **pop**; also **black** and **disco**. Produced *Everythang & Me* (album), written and recorded by Sammy Blue (blues); and *Blues You Can't Refuse* (album), written and recorded by Big Al (blues), both released 2000 on Hottrax Records. Other artists include Bullitthead, Roger Hurricane Wilson, The Bob Page Project, Mike Lorenz and Chesterfield Kings.

JAY BIRD PRODUCTIONS, 5 Highpoint Dr., RR #3, Stouffville, Ontario L4A 7X4 Canada. (905)640-4104. E-mail: jaybird0@home.com. **Contact:** William Wallace, president. Record producer and music publisher (Smokey Bird Publishing). Estab. 1981. Produces 4 singles/year. Fee derived from sales royalty when song or artist is recorded or outright fee from recording artist.

How to Contact: *Write first and obtain permission to submit.* Prefers cassette or VHS videocassette with 3 songs and lyric sheet. Does not return material. Responds in 3 weeks.

Music: Mostly **country**; also **pop/rock**. Produced "Little Lies" (single by W. Wallace), "Dreamin'" (single by Steve Earle) and "Fine Line" (single by W.W.H.G.), all recorded by Lawnie Wallace on MCA Records (country).

JAY JAY PUBLISHING & RECORD CO., P.O. Box 41-4156, Miami FL 33141. Phone/fax: (305)758-0000. Owner: Walter Jagiello. Associate: J. Kozak. Record producer, music publisher (BMI) and record company (Jay Jay Record, Tape and Video Co.). Estab. 1951. Produces 12 singles, 12 LPs and 12 CDs/year. Fee derived from sales royalty when song or artist is recorded.

How to Contact: Submit demo tape by mail. Unsolicited submissions are OK. Prefers cassette or VHS videocassette with 6 songs and lyric and lead sheet. "Quality cassette or reel-to-reel, sheet music and lyrics." Does not return material. Responds in 2 months.

Music: Mostly **ballads**, **love songs**, **country music** and **comedy**; also **polkas**, **hymns**, **gospel** and **waltzes**. Produced *The Best Co Jest* (album by Li'l Wally Jagiello), recorded by Living Legends; and *Animal Ditties for the Kiddies* (album by Al Trace), recorded by Capt. Stubby-Buccaneers, both on Jay Jay Records. Other artists include Eddie & The Slovenes, Johnny Vandal, Wisconsin Dutchmen and Eddie Zima.

DAVID JOHN PRODUCTIONS, 36 Union Dr., Ashford CT 06278. (860)487-3614. Fax: (860)727-3251. E-mail: davidjohn78@hotmail.com. Producer: David John. Vice President, A&R: Kirsten. Record producer and record company (Rock-It Records). Estab. 1983. Produces 2 singles, 8-12 LPs, 4 EPs and 10 CDs/year. Fee derived from outright fee from recording artist or record company.

How to Contact: Submit demo tape by mail. Unsolicited submissions are OK. Prefers cassette with 4 songs. Does not return material. Responds in 4 months.

Music: Mostly **original rock**, **alternative** and **computer-generated**; also **anything good**! Produced *Red Ruff N Sore* (album by Jeff Rose), recorded by Iron Horses (rock); *Meteor Storm* (album by Jeff Rose), recorded by Iron Horses (rock/metal); and *Ultra Violette* (album by Joni Redd), recorded by Ultra Violette (rock/dance), all released 2000 on Rock-It Records. Other artists include New Johnny 5, Silicone Safari, Guy Walker, Jay Bird, Jeff Weir and Jane Long.

N ☑ ◑ JSB GROUPE MANAGEMENT INC., 1307 Noire-Fontaine Place, Cap-Rouge, Quebec G1Y 3C9 Canada. Phone/fax: (418)651-4917. E-mail: jsbol@videotron.ca. President: Jean-Sebastien Boucher. Record producer, record company (Productions JSB) and management. Estab. 1994. Produces 1 LP and 1 CD/year. Fee derived from sales royalty when song or artist is recorded or outright fee from record company.
How to Contact: Submit demo tape by mail. Unsolicited submissions are OK. Prefers cassette, VHS videocassette or C.V. Does not return material. Responds in 2 months.
Music: Mostly **classical**, **children's** and **pop/rock**. Produced *Eric Laporte, The Tenor II* (album), recorded by Eric Laporte (classical) on JSB.
Tips: "We are very interested in classical music: tenors, instrumentalists and conductors. Be well prepared and have an independent structure of management."

N ⊕ JUMP PRODUCTIONS, 39 Paul Gilsonstraat, 8200 St-Andries Belgium. Phone: (050)137-63-80. **Contact:** Eddy Van Mouffaert, general manager. Record producer and music publisher (Jump Music). Estab. 1976. Produces 25 singles and 2 CDs/year. Fee derived from sales royalty when song or artist is recorded.
   ● See the listing for Jump Music in the Music Publishers section.
How to Contact: Submit demo tape by mail. Unsolicited submissions are OK. Prefers cassette. Does not return material. Responds in 2 weeks.
Music: Mostly **ballads**, **up-tempo**, **easy listening**, **disco** and **light pop**; also **instrumentals**. Produced *Evelien* (album by Eddy Govert), recorded by Evelien on Quartz Records (Flemish); *Liefde Komt En Liefde Gaat* (album by Les Reed), recorded by Lina on Scorpion Records; and "Father Damiaan" (single by Jan De Vuyst), recorded by Eigentijdse Jeugd on Youth Sound Records.

⊕ ☑ ◑ JUNE PRODUCTIONS LTD., "Toftrees," Church Rd., Woldingham, Surrey CR3 7JH England. Fax: 44(0)1883 652457. E-mail: mackay@dircon.co.uk. **Contact:** David Mackay, producer. Record producer and music producer (Sabre Music). Estab. 1970. Produces 6 singles, 3 LPs and 3 CDs/year. Fee derived from sales royalty.
How to Contact: Submit demo tape by mail. Unsolicited submissions are OK. Prefers cassette with 1-2 songs and lyric sheet. SAE and IRC. Responds in 2 months.
Music: Mostly **MOR**, **rock** and **top 40/pop**. Produced *Web of Love* (by various), recorded by Sarah Jory on Ritz Records (country rock). Other artists include Bonnie Tyler, Cliff Richard, Frankie Miller, Johnny Hallyday, Dusty Springfield, Charlotte Henry and Barry Humphries.

☑ ☑ ◑ KAREN KANE PRODUCER/ENGINEER, 185 Jones Ave., Toronto, Ontario M4M 3A2 Canada. (416)466-8562. Fax: (416)252-0464. E-mail: mixmama@total.net. Website: www.total.net/~mixmama. **Contact:** Karen Kane, producer/engineer. Record producer and recording engineer. Estab. 1978. Produces 5-10 singles and 5-10 CDs/year. Fee derived from sales royalty when song or artist is recorded or outright fee from recording artist or record company.
How to Contact: *Write or call first and obtain permission to submit.* Unsolicited submissions are *not* OK. "Please note: I am not a song publisher. My expertise is in album production." Does not return material. Responds in 3 weeks.
Music: Mostly **pop**, **alternative**, **R&B/reggae** and **acoustic**. Produced *Permanent Marker*, written and recorded by Ember Swift on Few'll Ignite Sound (alternative/folk/pop); *Topless* (Juno-nominated by various artists), recorded by Big Daddy G on Reggie's Records (blues); and *Dance the Spiral Dance* (album), written and recorded by Ubaka Hill on Ladyslipper Records (African percussion with vocals). Other artists include Tracy Chapman (her first demo), Jack Grunsky, Kyn, Chad Mitchell and Kay Gardner.

Tips: "Get proper funding to be able to make a competitive, marketable product."

◐ KINGSTON RECORDS AND TALENT, 15 Exeter Rd., Kingston NH 03848. (603)642-8493. E-mail: kingstonrecords@ttlc.net. **Contact:** Harry Mann, coordinator. Record producer, music publisher (Strawberry Soda Publishing/ASCAP) and record company (Kingston Records). Estab. 1988. Produces 3-4 singles, 2-3 12″ singles, 2-3 LPs and 1-2 CDs/year. Fee derived from sales royalty when song or artist is recorded. Deals primarily with NE and local artists.
How to Contact: Write first and obtain permission to submit. Prefers cassette with 1-2 songs and lyric sheet. Does not return material. Responds in 2 months.
Music: Mostly **rock**, **country** and **pop**; "no heavy metal." Produced *Count the Stars* (album), written and recorded by Doug Mitchell; *Time Machine* (album), written and recorded by Gratefull Ted, both released 1999 on Kingston Records. Other artists include Bob Moore, Candy Striper Death Orgy, Pocket Band, Jeff Walker, J. Evans, NTM, Miss Bliss, Ted Solovicus, Armand LeMay, Four On The Floor and Sumx4.

Ⓝ ◐ KMA, 1650 Broadway, Suite 900, Dept. SM, New York NY 10019-6833. (212)265-1570. Website: www.kmamusic.com. **Contact:** Morris Levy, A&R director. Record producer and music publisher (Block Party Music/ASCAP). Estab. 1987. Produces 2 12″ singles, 3 LPs and 3 CDs/year. Fee derived from sales royalty or outright fee from recording artist or record company.
How to Contact: Does not accept unsolicited material.
Music: Mostly **R&B**, **dance** and **rap**; also **movie** and **ethnic**. Produced "I Found It" (single), recorded by Daphne on Maxi Records; "Through the Day" (single), recorded by Millenium on 143/Atlantic Records; and "I Want You for Me" (single), recorded by Raw Stilo on dv8/A&M Records.
Tips: "*Original* lyrics a huge plus. We are starting a movie soundtrack. Send reggae and dance hall submissions."

Ⓝ ◐ KNOWN ARTIST PRODUCTIONS, 2622 Kirtland Rd., Brewton AL 36426. (334)867-2228. President: Roy Edwards. Record producer, music publisher (Cheavoria Music Co./BMI, Baitstring Music/ASCAP) and record company (Bolivia Records, Known Artist Records). Estab. 1972. Produces 10 singles and 3 LPs/year. Fee derived from sales royalty when song or artist is recorded.
How to Contact: Write first and obtain permission to submit. Prefers cassette with 3 songs and lyric sheet. Responds in 1 month. "All tapes will be kept on file."
Music: Mostly **R&B**, **pop** and **country**; also **easy listening**, **MOR** and **soul**. Produced "Got To Let You Know," "You Are My Sunshine" and "You Make My Life So Wonderful" (singles), all written and recorded by Roy Edwards on Bolivia Records (R&B). Other artists include Jim Portwood, Bobbie Roberson and Brad Smiley.

☑ ◯ ROBERT R. KOVACH, P.O. Box 7018, Warner Robins GA 31095-7018. (478)953-2800. **Contact:** Robert R. Kovach, producer. Record producer. Estab. 1976. Produces 6 singles, 2 cassettes and 1 CD/year. Fee derived from sales royalty when song or artist is recorded, or outright fee from record company.
How to Contact: Submit demo tape by mail. Unsolicited submissions are OK. Prefers cassette or CD with 4 songs and lyric sheet. SASE. Responds in 4 months.
Music: Mostly **country** and **pop**; also **easy listening**, **R&B**, **rock** and **gospel**. Produced "Pots & Pans" (single), recorded by Theresa Justus (country); and "You Learn A Heart to Break" (single), recorded by Wayne Little (country), both by Roy Robert Dunten (country); and "Lord I've Been Prayin" (single by Robert R. Kovach), recorded by Napolean Starke (gospel), all on Scaramouche. Other artists include Little Rudy.
Tips: "Submit a demo and be patient."

◪ ⊕ SENDING TO A COUNTRY other than your own? Be sure to send International Reply Coupons (IRCs) instead of stamps for replies or return of your materials.

☑ ◐ **L.A. ENTERTAINMENT, INC.**, 6367 Selma Ave., Hollywood CA 90028. (323)467-1496. Fax: (323)467-0911. E-mail: info@warriorrecords.com. Website: www.warriorrecords.com. **Contact:** Jim Ervin, A&R. Record producer, record company (Warrior Records) and music publisher (New Entity Music/ASCAP). Estab. 1988. Fee derived from sales royalty when song or artist is recorded.
How to Contact: Submit demo tape by mail. Unsolicited submissions are OK. Prefers cassette or videocassette with 3 songs, lyric and lead sheet if available. "All written submitted materials (e.g., lyric sheets, letter, etc.) should be typed." Does not return material. Responds in 2 months.
Music: Mostly **alternative** and **R&B**.

◐ **LANDMARK COMMUNICATIONS GROUP**, P.O. Box 1444, Hendersonville TN 37077. E-mail: lmarkcom@aol.com. **Contact:** Bill Anderson Jr., producer. Record producer, record company, music publisher (Newcreature Music/BMI) and TV/radio syndication. Produces 12 singles and 12 LPs/year. Fee derived from sales royalty.
How to Contact: *Write first and obtain permission to submit.* Prefers 7½ ips reel-to-reel, cassette or videocassette with 4-10 songs and lyric sheet. SASE. Responds in 1 month.
Music: Mostly **country crossover**; also **blues**, **country**, **gospel**, **jazz**, **rock** and **top 40/pop**. Produced *Vernon Oxford* (album), written and recorded by Vernon Oxford (country), released 1999 on Norway; *Cowboy Church* (album), written and recorded by various (Christian country), released 1999 on Landmark; and "Nothin' Else Feels Quite Like It" (single by B. Nash/K. Nash/B. Anderson), recorded on TV Theme Records (country). Other artists include Skeeter Davis, Gail Score and Joanne Cash Yates.

◐ **LARI-JON PRODUCTIONS**, 325 W. Walnut, Rising City NE 68658. (402)542-2336. **Contact:** Larry Good, owner. Record producer, music publisher (Lari-Jon Publishing/BMI), management firm (Lari-Jon Promotions) and record company (Lari-Jon Records). Estab. 1967. Produces 10 singles and 5 LPs/year. Fee derived from sales royalty when song or artist is recorded.
How to Contact: Submit demo tape by mail. Unsolicited submissions are OK. "Must be a professional demo." SASE. Responds in 2 months.
Music: Mostly **country**, **gospel-Southern** and **'50s rock**. Produced *Jesus is my Hero* (album), written and recorded by Larry Good on Lari-Jon Records (gospel). Other artists include Brenda Allen, Tom Campbell and Tom Johnson.

◐ **LARK TALENT & ADVERTISING**, P.O. Box 35726, Tulsa OK 74153. (918)786-8896. Fax: (918)786-8897. E-mail: janajae@janajae.com. Website: www.janajae.com. **Contact:** Kathleen Pixley, vice president. Owner: Jana Jae. Record producer, music publisher (Jana Jae Music/BMI) and record company (Lark Record Productions, Inc.). Estab. 1980. Fee derived from sales royalty when song or artist is recorded.
How to Contact: Submit demo tape by mail. Unsolicited submissions are OK. Prefers cassette or VHS videocassette with 3 songs and lead sheet. Does not return material. Responds in 1 month only if interested.
Music: Mostly **country**, **bluegrass** and **classical**; also **instrumentals**. Produced "Bussin' Ditty" (single by Steve Upfold); "Mayonnaise" (single by Steve Upfold); and "Flyin' South" (single by Cindy Walker), all recorded by Jana Jae on Lark Records (country). Other artists include Sydni, Hotwire and Matt Greif.

◐ **LAZY BONES PRODUCTIONS/RECORDINGS, INC.**, 9594 First Ave. NE, Suite 449, Seattle WA 98115-2012. (206)447-0712. Fax: (425)821-5720. E-mail: lbrinc@earthlink.net. Website: www.lazybones.com. **Contact:** Scott Schorr, president. Record producer, record company and music publisher (Lazy Bones Music/BMI, Cat from Guatemala Music/ASCAP). Estab. 1992. Produces 4-6 CDs/year. Fee derived from sales royalty when song or artist is recorded or outright fee from recording artist (if unsigned) or outright fee from record company (if signed) or publishing royalties when co-songwriting with artist.
How to Contact: Submit demo tape by mail. Unsolicited submissions are OK. Prefers cassette, DAT or CD with 3 songs (minimum) and lyric sheet. "If you honestly believe you can do better,

improve your project to its greatest potential before submitting. With the number of projects received, if the material is not truly special and unique, it will not be taken seriously by a legitimate company." Does not return material. Responds in 1 month only if interested.

Music: Mostly **alternative** and **rock**; also **hip-hop**. Produced *No Samples* (album by Da Blasta/Ratboy), recorded by Turntable Bay (hip-hop); and *Headland II* (album by Dave Hadland), recorded by Headland (pop), both on Lazy Bones. Other artists include Blackhead, MFTJ, B. Chestnut and Alan Charing.

Tips: "Have outstanding and unique talent!"

☐ LINEAR CYCLE PRODUCTIONS, P.O. Box 2608, Sepulveda CA 91393-2608. Phone/fax: (818)347-9880. E-mail: LCP@wgn.net. Website: www.westworld.com/lcp/. **Contact:** Manny Pandanceski, producer. Record producer. Estab. 1980. Produces 15-25 singles, 6-10 12″ singles, 15-20 LPs and 10 CDs/year. Fee derived from sales royalty when song or artist is recorded.

How to Contact: Submit demo tape by mail. Unsolicited submissions are OK. Prefers cassette, 7⅜ ips reel-to-reel or ½″ VHS or ¾″ videocassette. SASE. Responds in 6 months.

Music: Mostly **rock/pop**, **R&B/blues** and **country**; also **gospel** and **comedy**. Produced "FOP It" (single by Poon), recorded by No Cents (alternative); "My Truck Hasn't Got No Room for You" (single by Hay), recorded by The Tumbleweeds (country), both on Grime Recordings; and "Gim 'M' Shee" (single by Jailboy), recorded by PL238A17 (rap), on Moto Records.

Tips: "We only listen to songs and other material recorded on quality tapes and CDs. We will not accept anything that sounds distorted, muffled and just plain bad! If you cannot afford to record demos on quality stock, or in some high aspects, shop somewhere else!"

☐ LOCONTO PRODUCTIONS, 10244 NW 47 St., Sunrise FL 33351. (954)741-7766. (305)741-7766. **Contact:** Frank X. Loconto, president. Record producer, record company and music publisher. Estab. 1978. Produces 10 cassettes/albums and 10 CDs/year. Fee derived from sales royalty or outright fee from songwriter/artist and/or record company.

How to Contact: Submit demo tape by mail. Unsolicited submissions are OK. Prefers cassette or CD/CDR. SASE. Responds in 4 months.

Music: Produced *Aurore* (album by various), recorded by Aurore (gospel); *Vodec* (album by various), recorded by Vodec (gospel); and *Total Package* (album), written and recorded by Jos. E. Ford, all on FXL Records. Other artists include Roger B. Bryant, Mark Goldman and Chris Risi.

Ⓝ ☐ HAROLD LUICK & COUNTRY MUSIC SHOWCASE INTL. ASSOCIATES, Box #368, Carlisle IA 50047. (515)989-3748. Fax: (515)989-0235. E-mail: haroldl@cmshowcase.org. Website: www.cmshowcase.org. Producers: Robbie Wittkowski; Harold L. Luick. Artist Management: Aaron Kerns. Record producer, music industry consultant, music print publisher and music publisher. Produces 20 singles and 6 LPs/year. Fee derived from sales royalty, outright fee from artist/songwriter or record company, and from consulting fees for information or services.

How to Contact: Write or call first and obtain permission to submit. Prefers cassette with 3-5 songs and lyric sheet. SASE. Responds in 3 weeks.

Music: Mostly **traditional country**, **gospel**, **contemporary country** and **MOR**. Produced *I Want to Forget You* (album by Bill Anderson/Sharon Rice/Al Anderson), recorded by Stacey Kerns on Kid Kody Records (country). "Over a 12-year period, Harold Luick has produced and recorded 412 singles and 478 albums, 7 of which charted and some of which have enjoyed independent sales in excess of 30,000 units."

Tips: "If you are looking to place a song with us and have it considered for a recording, make sure you have a decent demo, and all legals in order."

☐ MAC-ATTACK PRODUCTIONS, 8101 NE 8 Court, Miami FL 33138. (305)949-1422. Fax: (305)673-2389. E-mail: gomacster@aol.com. **Contact:** Michael McNamee, engineer/producer. Record producer and music publisher (Mac-Attack Publishing/ASCAP). Estab. 1986. Fee derived from outright fee from recording artist or record company.

How to Contact: Submit demo tape by mail. Unsolicited submissions are OK. Prefers cassette or VHS videocassette with 3-5 songs, lyric sheet and bio. Does not return material. Responds in up to 3 months.

Music: Mostly **pop**, **alternative rock** and **dance**. Produced *Caution Automatc* (album by Emmanuel Canaté), recorded by Caution Automatc (alternative rock), released 2000; and *The Golden Age of Classical Guitar* (album by various artists), recorded by MBHS Classical Guitar Ensemble (classical), released 2001 on MBHS Records. Other artists include Blowfly, Forget the Name, Nine Llopis, The Lead and Girl Talk.

◯ **LEE MAGID PRODUCTIONS**, P.O. Box 532, Malibu CA 90265. (323)463-5998. **Contact:** Lee Magid, president. Record producer, music publisher (Alexis Music, Inc./ASCAP, Marvelle Music Co./BMI and Gabal Music Co./SESAC), record company (Grass Roots Records, LMI Records) and management firm (Lee Magid Management). Estab. 1950. Produces 4 singles, 4 12″ singles, 8 LPs and 8 CDs/year. Fee derived from sales royalty when song or artist is recorded.
How to Contact: Submit demo tape by mail. Unsolicited submissions are OK. "Send cassette giving address and phone number." Prefers cassette or VHS videocassette with 3-6 songs and lyric sheet. "Please only one cassette, and photos if you are an artist/writer." Does not return material. Responds in 6 weeks only if accepted.
Music: Mostly **R&B**, **rock**, **jazz** and **gospel**; also **pop**, **bluegrass**, **church/religious**, **easy listening**, **folk**, **blues**, **MOR**, **progressive**, **soul**, **instrumental** and **top 40**. Produced *I'll Be Seeing You Around* (album by Lorna McGough/John Scott/Mark Newbar), recorded by 2AD on LMI Records (R&B); *It's Only Money* (album by John M. Hides), recorded by J. Michael Hides on Grass Roots Records (pop); and *Blues For the Weepers* (album by Lee Magid/Max Rich), recorded by Bob Stewart on VWC Records (jazz). Other artists include Tramaine Hawkins, Della Reese, Rod Piazza, "Big Joe" Turner, Tom Vaughn and Laura Lee.

◙ **MAGNETIC OBLIVION MUSIC CO.**, P.O. Box 1446, Eureka CA 95502. Phone/fax: (707)445-2698. E-mail: magob@aol.com. Website: www.magneticoblivion.com. **Contact:** Eppilido Torres, director of A&R. President: Matthew Knight. Record producer, record company (Magnetic Oblivion Records) and music publisher. Estab. 1984. Produces 3 singles, 1 EP and 6-10 CDs/year. Fee derived from publishing royalty.
How to Contact: Submit demo tape by mail. Unsolicited submissions are OK. Prefers cassette, DAT or videocassette. "All material must be copyrighted. Non-copyrighted material will be trashed without review." Does not return material. Responds in 6 weeks.
Music: Mostly **experimental**, **early music** and **alternative**; also **Celtic**, **novelty** and **acid jazz**. Produced *Prophecies* (album), written and recorded by Hermetic Science (progressive), released 2000; *Negative Bouancy* (album by Matty Dread), recorded by Troubled Loners (pop), released 1999, both on Magnetic Oblivion Records. Other artists include Goofus & Gallant, Country Matters, Chowderhead, Tama, The Fifth, All For a Lark and Tim Fouts.
Tips: "Either the songwriting is there or it isn't. Don't send us trite material about your girlfriend leaving you—unless it's the best damn 'love lost' song ever written. Last year we received at least ten 'Fiona Apples.' It's great to admire successful performers—but there's only one Fiona (thank God!). Be yourself. Take some risks."

Ⓝ ◙ **MAKERS MARK MUSIC PRODUCTIONS (ASCAP)**, 534 W. Queen Lane, Philadelphia PA 19144. (215)849-7633. E-mail: prolific007@aol.com. Website: www.prolificrecords.com or www.mp3.com/paulhopkins. **Contact:** Paul E. Hopkins, producer. Record producer, music publisher and record company (Prolific Records). Estab. 1991. Produces 15 singles, 5 12″ singles and 4 LPs/year. Fee derived from outright fee from recording artist or record company.
How to Contact: Submit demo tape by mail. Unsolicited submissions are OK. Prefers cassette with 2-4 songs and bio. "Explain concept of your music and/or style, and your future direction as an artist or songwriter." Does not return material. Responds in 6 weeks if interested.
Music: Mostly **R&B**, **gospel**, **dance**, **pop**, **country** and **rap**. Produced "When Will My Heart Beat Again" and "Last Kiss" (singles by Cheryl Forman/Paul Hopkins), both recorded by Rachel Scarborough; and *All Eyes on the Philosopher* (album by Norman Gilliam/Paul Hopkins), recorded by Norman Gilliam on Prolific Records. Other artists include Larry Larr, Paul Hopkins, Nardo Ranks (international Jamaican artist), Elaine Monk (R&B), Andy Romano (R&B/pop), Enon Mass Choir (from Philadelphia *Live at the Tabernacle*), New Jerusalem (drama ministry) and Tatiana (R&B).

COOKIE MARENCO, P.O. Box 874, Belmont CA 94002. E-mail: otrstudios@aol.com. Record producer/engineer. Estab. 1981. Produces 10 CDs/year. Fee derived from sales royalty and outright fee from recording artist or record company.

How to Contact: *Write first and obtain permission to submit.* Does not return material. Responds only if interested.

Music: Mostly **alternative modern rock**, **country**, **folk**, **rap**, **ethnic** and **avante-garde**; also **classical**, **pop** and **jazz**. Produced *Winter Solstice II* (album), written and recorded by various artists; *Heresay* (album by Paul McCandless); and *Deep At Night* (album by Alex DeGrassi), all on Windham Hill Records (instrumental). Other artists include Tony Furtado Band, Praxis, Oregon, Mary Chapin Carpenter, Max Roach and Charle Haden & Quartet West.

PETE MARTIN/VAAM MUSIC PRODUCTIONS, P.O. Box 29550, Hollywood CA 90029-0550. (323)664-7765. E-mail: vaampubl@aol.com or pmarti3636@aol.com. **Contact:** Pete Martin, president. Record producer, music publisher (Vaam Music/BMI and Pete Martin Music/ASCAP) and record company (Blue Gem Records). Estab. 1982. Produces 12 singles and 5 LPs/year. Fee derived from sales royalty when song or artist is recorded.

How to Contact: Prefers cassette with 2 songs and lyric sheet. Send small packages only. SASE. Responds in 1 month.

Music: Mostly **top 40/pop**, **country** and **R&B**. Produced Shay Lynn, Sherry Weston, Vero, Frank Loren, Brian Smith & The Renegades, Victoria Limon, Brandy Rose and Cory Canyon.

Tips: "Study the market in the style that you write. Songs must be capable of reaching top 5 on charts."

SCOTT MATHEWS, D/B/A HIT OR MYTH PRODUCTIONS, 246 Almonte Blvd., Mill Valley CA 94941. Fax: (415)389-9682. E-mail: hitormyth@aol.com. **Contact:** Mary Ezzell, A&R Director. President: Scott Mathews. Assistant: Mary Ezzell. Record producer, song doctor, studio owner and music publisher (Hang On to Your Publishing/BMI). Estab. 1990. Produces 6-9 CDs/year. Fee derived from sales royalty when artist is recorded, or from recording artist or record company (with royalty points).

• Scott Mathews has several gold and platinum awards for sales of over 12 million records. He has worked on several Grammy and Oscar winning releases. See his article on page 29.

How to Contact: Submit demo tape by mail. Unsolicited submissions are OK. Prefers DAT (cassette and CD accepted). SASE. Responds in 2 months. "No phone calls or publishing submissions, please."

Music: Mostly **rock/pop**, **alternative** and **singer/songwriters of all styles**. Produced "The Way We Make a Broken Heart" (single by John Hiatt), recorded by John Hiatt with Rosanne Cash on Capitol (pop); *Slideways* (album), written and recorded by Roy Rogers on E Music (blues); and *How Else Can the Story Go?* (album by Roger Clark), recorded by Lucy Lee on Island (pop). Has produced Roy Orbison, Rosanne Cash, John Hiatt and many more. Has recorded platinum records with everyone from Barbra Streisand to John Lee Hooker, including Keith Richards, George Harrison, Mick Jagger, Van Morrison, Elvis Costello, Bonnie Raitt and Eric Clapton to name but a few, plus several Grammy and Oscar-winning projects.

Tips: "Waiting for a major label to come tap you on the shoulder and say, 'It's your turn,' is the last thing a new artist should even be thinking of. In my humble opinion, today's A&R stands for 'Afraid & Running.' Sorry to all my friends in that department, but the cold truth is, huge corporations are interested only in pleasing the shareholders. It's all about the bottom line, not the music. Recently, I had a president of a major label admit to me that he hates his job because he's not allowed to sign

**FOR EXPLANATIONS OF THESE SYMBOLS,
SEE THE INSIDE FRONT AND BACK COVERS OF THIS BOOK.**

and develop what he wants! So, it's our job to develop our careers by making incredible masters on our own. Believe me, fair deals are born from artists being in control. Set your goal (single, EP, etc.) and budget, find the right producer, and make a stellar CD that can compete with anything on the radio. Early on, you can do more for yourself than a label can. When you prove yourself, they offer the moon. Let me know if I can help."

☑ ◐ **MEGA TRUTH RECORDS**, P.O. Box 4988, Culver City CA 90231. E-mail: jonbare@aol. com. Website: www.jonbare.com. **Contact:** Jon Bare, CEO. Record producer and record company. Estab. 1994. Produces 2 CDs/year. Fee negotiable.
How to Contact: Submit demo tape by mail. Unsolicited submissions are OK. Prefers CD. "We specialize in recording world-class virtuoso musicians and bands with top players." Does not return material. Responds in 2 weeks only if interested.
Music: Mostly **rock**, **blues** and **country rock**; also **swing**, **dance** and **instrumental**. Produced *Party Platter* recorded by Hula Monsters (swing); and *Killer Whales, Shredzilla and Orcastra* (by Jon Bare and the Killer Whales) (rock), all on Mega Truth Records. Other artists include The Rich Harper Blues Band, Aeon Dream & the Dream Machine and Techno Dudes.
Tips: "Create a unique sound that blends great vocals and virtuoso musicianship with a beat that makes us want to get up and dance."

🍁 ☑ ○ **MERLIN PRODUCTIONS**, P.O. Box 5087 V.M.P.O., Vancouver, British Columbia V6B 4A9 Canada. Phone/fax: (604)434-9129. E-mail: merlin.music@home.com. **Contact:** Martin E. Hamann, vice president, A&R. President: Wolfgang Hamman. Record producer, record company and manager. Estab. 1979. Produces 5 singles, 3 LPs, 1 EP and 3 CDs/year. Fee derived from sales royalty when song or artist is recorded.
• See their listing in the Record Companies section, as well as Merlin Management in the Managers & Booking Agents section.
How to Contact: Submit demo tape by mail. Unsolicited submissions are OK. Prefers cassette with 3 songs and lyric and/or lead sheet. "Best songs first. Target your songs, e.g., Whitney Houston." SAE and IRC. Responds in 3 weeks.
Music: Mostly **modern rock**, **dance** and **R&B**; also **pop**. Produced "Pleasure" (single), written and recorded by The Mode to Joy, released on East/West; "Died and Gone to Heaven" (single by Donner & Blitzen), released on Merlin Records; and "Every Day's a New Day" (single by Lady Jane), released on Merlin Records.

◐ **A.V. MITTELSTEDT**, 9717 Jensen Dr., Houston TX 77093. (713)695-3648. **Contact:** A.V. Mittelstedt, producer. Record producer and music publisher (Sound Masters). Produces 100 singles, 10 LPs and 20 CDs/year. Fee derived from sales royalty and outright fee from recording artist.
How to Contact: Prefers cassette. SASE. Responds in 3 weeks.
Music: Mostly **country**, **gospel** and **crossover**; also **MOR** and **rock**. Produced "Too Cold at Home" (single by Bobby Harding), recorded by Mark Chestnutt on Cherry Records (country); "Two Will Be One" (single), written and recorded by Kenny Dale on Axbar Records (country); and "Shake Your Hiney" (single by Gradual Taylor), recorded by Roy Head on Cherry Records (crossover country). Other artists include Randy Cornor, Bill Nash, Ron Shaw, Borderline, George Dearborne and Good, Bad and Ugly.

Ⓝ 🍁 ◐ **GARY MOFFET**, P.O. Box 941 N.D.G., Montreal, Quebec H4A 3S3 Canada. (514)487-8953. Website: www.garymoffet.com. **Contact:** Gary Moffet, president. Record producer and music publisher (Sci-Fi Music). Estab. 1985. Produces 3 LPs, 4 EPs and 3 CDs/year. Fee derived from sales royalty when song or artist is recorded.
How to Contact: Submit demo tape by mail. Unsolicited submissions are OK. Prefers cassette with 6 songs and lyric sheet. SAE and IRC.
Music: Mostly **rock, pop** and **acoustic**. Produced *Back to Reality* (album by T. Mitchell), recorded by Mindstorm on Aquarius Records (heavy rock); *See Spot Run* (album by C. Broadbeck), recorded by See Spot Run on Primer Records (rock); and *The Storm* (album), written and recorded by Ray Lyell on Spy Records (rock). Other artists include Marie Carmen, Marjo and Manon Brunet.

☑ ○ **MONA LISA RECORDS/BRISTOL STUDIOS**, 169 Massachusetts Ave., Boston MA 02115. (617)247-8689. E-mail: bristol@thecia.net. Website: www.BristolStudios.com. **Contact:** Ric Poulin, producer. Record producer. Estab. 1987. Produces 50 singles and 10 CDs/year. Fee derived from outright fee from recording company or artist.
How to Contact: Submit through e-mail. Prefers CD and lyric sheet. Responds in 6 weeks.
Music: Mostly **dance**, **R&B** and **pop**; also **jazz** and **rock**. Produced *Future Classics* (album by Ric Poulin/Sean Cooper), recorded by various artists on Mona Lisa Records (dance); "Call the Doctor" (single by Poulin/Yeldham/Poulin), recorded by Bijou on Critique/Atlantic Records (dance); and "Dance to the Rhythm of the Beat" (single by Ric Poulin), recorded by Jennifer Rivers on Associated Artists Int'l (dance). Other artists include Never Never, Sherry Christian, Zina, Damien, Aaron Brown, Amy Silverman and Leah Langfeld.
Tips: "Develop the frame of mind that whatever you do, you are doing it as a professional."

☀ ◉ **MONTICANA PRODUCTIONS**, P.O. Box 702, Snowdon Station, Montreal, Quebec H3X 3X8 Canada. **Contact:** David Leonard, executive producer. Record producer, music publisher (Montina Music) and record company (Monticana Records). Estab. 1963. Fee derived from sales royalty when song or artist is recorded.
How to Contact: Submit demo tape by mail. Unsolicited submissions are OK. Prefers cassette, phonograph record or VHS videocassette with maximum 10 songs and lyric sheet. "Demos should be as tightly produced as a master." SASE.
Music: Mostly **top 40**; also **bluegrass**, **blues**, **country**, **dance-oriented**, **easy listening**, **folk**, **gospel**, **jazz**, **MOR**, **progressive**, **R&B**, **rock** and **soul**.
Tips: "Work creatively and believe passionately in what you do and aspire to be. Success comes to those who persevere, have talent, develop their craft and network."

☑ ○ **MUSICLAND PRODUCTIONS, INC.**, P.O. Box 2048, Belleview FL 34426. Phone/fax: (352)347-9779. Fax: (352)629-1523. E-mail: musicland@aol.com. Website: www.musiclandproducti onsinc.com. **Contact:** Christine McKimmey and Wally Strawder, owners. Record producer. Estab. 1986. Produces 2 singles and 2 CDs/year. Fee derived from associated producers.
How to Contact: Submit demo by mail. Unsolicited submissions are OK. Prefers cassette with 4 songs and lyric sheet. "Professional demos only." Does not return material. Responds in 2 weeks.
Music: Mostly **pop** and **gospel**. Produced "Cowboy Lady," written and recorded by Curt Powers on MPR Records.
Tips: "Don't get in such a hurry. It takes time."

☑ ○ **NEU ELECTRO PRODUCTIONS**, P.O. Box 1582, Bridgeview IL 60455. (630)257-6289. E-mail: neuelectro@email.com. Website: http://members.nbci.com/neuelectro/index.htm. **Contact:** Bob Neumann, owner. Record producer and record company. Estab. 1984. Produces 16 singles, 16 12″ singles, 20 LPs and 4 CDs/year. Fee derived from outright fee from record company or recording artist.
How to Contact: Submit demo tape by mail. Unsolicited submissions are OK. Prefers cassette or CD with 3 songs and lyric sheet or lead sheet. "Provide accurate contact phone numbers and addresses, promo packages and photos." SASE. Responds in 2 weeks. "A production fee estimate will be returned to artist."
Music: Mostly **dance**, **house**, **techno**, **rap** and **rock**; also **experimental**, **New Age** and **top 40**. Produced "Juicy" (single), written and recorded by Juicy Black on Dark Planet International Records (house); "Make Me Smile" (single), written and recorded by Roz Baker (house); and *Reactovate-6* (album by Bob Neumann), recorded by Beatbox-D on N.E.P. Records (dance). Other artists include Skid Marx and The Deviants.

◉ **NEW EXPERIENCE RECORDS**, P.O. Box 683, Lima OH 45802. **Contact:** A&R Department. Music Publisher: James L. Milligan Jr. Record producer, music publisher (A New Rap Jam Publishing/ASCAP), management firm (Creative Star Management) and record company (New Experience Records, Grand-Slam Records and Pump It Up Records). Estab. 1989. Produces 15-20 12″ singles, 2 LPs, 3 EPs and 2-5 CDs/year. Fee derived from sales royalty when song or artist is recorded or outright fee from record company, "depending on services required."

How to Contact: *Write first to arrange personal interview.* Address material to A&R Dept. or Talent Coordinator. Prefers cassette with a minimum of 3 songs and lyric or lead sheet (if available). "If tapes are to be returned, proper postage should be enclosed and all tapes and letters should have SASE for faster reply." Responds in 6 weeks.

Music: Mostly **pop**, **R&B** and **rap**; also **gospel**, **contemporary gospel** and **rock**. Produced *Experiences* (album), written and recorded by Jayhson Rodgers (R&B/rap), released 2001 on Pump It Up Records. Other artists include Qutina Milligan, Melvin Milligan and Venesta Compton.

Tips: "Do your homework on the music business. There are too many sound alikes. Be yourself. I look for what is different, vocal ability, voice range and sound stage presence, etc."

☑ ◯ THE NEW VIZION STUDIOS, 14 Pinney, Unit 42, Corporate Center, Ellington CT 06029. (860)871-0178, ext. 3. E-mail: Vizionmusi@aol.com. Website: http://hometown.aol.com/vizio nmusi/index.html. **Contact:** Steve Sossin, founder/producer. Executive Assistant to the Producer: Aurore St. Germain. Vice President Marketing: Caroline Hayes. Record producer. Estab. 1990. Produces 2-3 singles, 3-5 LPs and 3-5 CDs/year. Fee derived from outright fee from recording artist or producer/artist development contract.

How to Contact: *Write or call first and obtain permission to submit.* Prefers cassette or CD with 2-9 songs and lyric sheet. "We are an artist development company. Do not send photocopies or black and white promos. Originals and color promos only. Unlike most of the clichés in our industry, we are interested in the color of your eyes! Just because most people copy each other does not mean we all do. We set trends and break new ground." Does not return material. Responds in 2 months.

Music: Mostly **pop**, **A/C**, **pop/rock** and **crossover styles**; also **rock**, **R&B** and **New Age**. Produced "If We Meet Again" (single by Steve Marks) from *Soundtrack* (album), recorded by Julliette Price (pop/rock), released 2000 on Vizion-Capitol; "I Know the Feeling" (single by Marks/Sossin) from *Because the Night Goes on Forever* (album), recorded by Talia (adult contemporary), released 2000 on Vizion Records; and "Through It All" (single by Sossin/Marks) from *We Can Survive* (album), recorded by Kaitlin Thomas (adult contemporary), released 2000 on Vizion-Europe.

Tips: "We are a 'rarity' in the recording industry. We are highly specialized as an artist development company and seek to work with emerging artists. All the talent in the world means nothing if you have a substance abuse problem. Attitude, professionality and quality of character count here. Our aim is to seek out truly gifted persons who are honest and dedicated to a goal and are willing to learn from experienced industry pros."

☑ ◯ OMNI 2000 INC., 413 Cooper St., Camden NJ 08102. (856)963-6400. Fax: (856)964-FAX-1 (3291). E-mail: omniplex@erols.com. Website: www.omniplex413.com. **Contact:** Michael Nise, president/executive producer. Record producer, music publisher and record company. Estab. 1995. Produces 1-5 singles and 1-5 LPs/year. Fee derived from sales royalty when song or artist is recorded.

How to Contact: *Write first and obtain permission to submit.* Include SASE. Prefers cassette with 3 songs and lyric sheet. SASE. Responds in 3 months.

Music: Produced Brothers 2, Coalitions, Ghetto Children and Joy Stamford.

Tips: "Your music must have great hooks, imaginative lyrics and commercial appeal."

☑ ◯ JOHN "BUCK" ORMSBY/ETIQUETTE PRODUCTIONS, 2442 NW Market, Suite 273, Seattle WA 98107. E-mail: nie@eskimo.com. **Contact:** John Ormsby, publishing director. Record producer and music publisher (Valet Publishing). Estab. 1980. Fee varies.

How to Contact: *Call first and obtain permission to submit.* Prefers cassette or CD/CDR with lyric or lead sheet. Does not return material. Responds in 2 months only if interested.

Music: Mostly **R&B**, **rock**, **pop** and **blues**.

Tips: "Tape production must be top quality; lead or lyric sheet professional."

❖ ☑ ◯ PACIFIC NORTH STUDIOS LTD., 257 W. 28th St., North Vancouver, British Columbia V7N 2H9 Canada. (604)990-9146. Fax: (604)990-9178. E-mail: pjewer@home.com. Website:

www.lynnvalleymusic.com. **Contact:** David Jewer, director. Record producer and record company (Lynn Valley Music). Estab. 1993. Produces 4 CDs/year. Fee derived from sales royalty when song or artist is recorded or outright fee from recording artist.

How to Contact: Submit demo tape by mail. Unsolicited submissions are OK. Prefers cassette or CD. "Include a bio." Does not return material. Responds in 1 month.

Music: Mostly **world music**, **jazz** and **blues**; also **country** and **pop**. Produced *Songs From the Seahorse Hall* (album), written and recorded by David Cory (children's); *Mandala* (album by J. Keating/D. Ritter), recorded by Locos Bravos (world), both on LVM; and *Change In the Weather* (album), written and recorded by Michael Dixon (country).

Tips: "Be a live performer."

PANIO BROTHERS LABEL, P.O. Box 99, Montmartre, Saskatchewan S0G 3M0 Canada. **Contact:** John Panio, Jr., executive director. Record producer. Estab. 1977. Produces 1 single and 1 LP/year. Fee derived from sales royalty or outright fee from artist/songwriter or record company.

How to Contact: Submit demo tape by mail. Unsolicited submissions are OK. Prefers cassette with any number of songs and lyric sheet. SAE and IRC. Responds in 1 month.

Music: Mostly **country**, **dance**, **easy listening** and **Ukrainian**. Produced *Ukranian Country* (album), written and recorded by Vlad Panio on PB Records.

PATTY PARKER, Comstock Records, Ltd., P.O. Box 19720, Fountain Hills AZ 85269. (480)951-3115. Fax: (480)951-3074. **Contact:** Patty Parker, producer. Record producer, music publisher (White Cat Music) and record company (Comstock Records). Estab. 1978. Produces 6-8 CD singles and 3-4 albums/year. Fee derived from outright fee from recording artist or recording company.

How to Contact: Submit demo tape by mail. Unsolicited submissions are OK. Prefers CD or cassette with 2-4 songs and lyric sheet. Voice up front on demos. SASE. Responds in 2 weeks.

Music: Mostly **country—traditional** to **crossover**. Produced "It All Adds Up to the Blues" (single by Jimmie Crane/Jean Loving), recorded by Beth Hogan (country crossover); "Are You Ready to Rock" (single by Charles Ingram) from *Reason to Believe* (album), recorded by Derek Carle (country); and "Daddy's Lavender" (single by Roxanne Hall), recorded by Roxanne Hall (country), all released 2000 on Comstock Records. Other artists include Colin Clark.

Tips: "To catch the ears of radio programmers worldwide, I need good medium to uptempo songs for all the artists coming from Europe, Canada and the U.S. that I produce sessions on in Nashville."

PHILLY BREAKDOWN RECORDING CO., 216 W. Hortter St., Philadelphia PA 19119. (215)848-6725. E-mail: mattcozar@juno.com. **Contact:** Matthew Childs, president. Music Director: Charles Nesbit. Record producer, music publisher (Philly Breakdown/BMI) and record company. Estab. 1974. Produces 3 singles and 2 LPs/year. Fee derived from sales royalty when song or artist is recorded.

How to Contact: *Contact first and obtain permission to submit.* Prefers cassette with 4 songs and lead sheet. Does not return material. Responds in 2 months.

Music: Mostly **R&B**, **hip-hop** and **pop**; also **jazz**, **gospel** and **ballads**. Produced "Can I" (single), written and recorded by Clearence Patterson (gospel); *H Factor II* (album), recorded by Rob Henderson (jazz); and "Mother's Love" (single by Stan Roane), recorded by Dottie Jackson (inspirational), all released 2000 on Philly Breakdown. Other artists include Leroy Christy, Gloria Clark, Jerry Walker, Nina Bundy, Mark Adam, Emmit King, Betty Carol, The H Factor and Four Buddies.

Tips: "If you fail, just learn from your past experience and keep on trying, until you get it done right. Never give up."

JIM PIERCE, Dept. SM, 101 Hurt Rd., Hendersonville TN 37075. (615)824-5900. Fax: (615)824-8800. E-mail: jimpierce@bellsouth.net. Website: www.jimpierce.net. **Contact:** Jim Pierce, president. Record producer, music publisher (Strawboss Music/BMI) and record company (Round Robin Records). Estab. 1974. Fee derived from sales royalty or outright fee from recording artist. "Some artists pay me in advance for my services." Has had over 200 chart records to date.

How to Contact: *Write or e-mail first and obtain permission to submit or to arrange personal interview.* Prefers cassette with any number of songs and lyric sheet. Will accept CDs and cassettes. Does not return material. Responds only if interested.

Music: Mostly **country**, **contemporary**, **country/pop** and **traditional country**. Artists include Tommy Cash, George Jones, Jimmy C. Newman, Margo Smith, Bobby Helms, Sammi Smith, Roy Drusky, Charlie Louvin and Melba Montgomery.

Tips: "Industry is seeking good singers who can write songs. Viewing our website is suggested."

🎵 ✅ ⊘ **POKU PRODUCTIONS**, 176-B Woodridge Crescent, Nepran Ontario K2B 759 Canada. (613)820-5715. Fax: (613)820-8736. E-mail: jshakka@hotmail.com. Website: http://stop.at/shak kastop.at/shakka. **Contact:** Jon E. Shakka, president. Record producer. Estab. 1988. Produces 1 album/year. Fee derived from sales royalty when song or artist is recorded.

How to Contact: *Does not accept unsolicited submissions.*

Music: Mostly **funk**, **rap** and **house music**; also **pop**, **ballads** and **funk-rock**. Produced *I'm My Brother's Keeper* (album), recorded by The Jon E. Shakka Project (funk rap), released 2001 on Poku Records. Other artists include Kim Warnock and James T. Flash.

◯ **PREJIPPIE MUSIC GROUP**, P.O. Box 312897, Penobscot Station, Detroit MI 48231. E-mail: prejippie@aol.com. Website: www.prejippie.com. **Contact:** Bruce Henderson, president. Record producer, music publisher and record company (PMG Records). Estab. 1990. Produces 5 12″ singles, 2 LPs and 2 EPs/year. Fee derived from sales royalty when song or artist is recorded.

How to Contact: Submit demo tape by mail. Unsolicited submissions are OK. No phone calls please. Prefers cassette or CD with 3-4 songs and lyric sheet. SASE. Responds in 6 weeks.

Music: Mostly **alternative R&B**, **experimental**, **alternative rock** and **techno/house**. Produced "Is That Life Good?" (single) and "Why Me?" (single), written and recorded by Bourgeoisie Paper Jam (funk/rock); and "Astral Traveler (Part 1)" (single), written and recorded by Synthetic Living Organism (techno), all released 1999 on PMG Records. Other artists include Tony Webb.

◯ **THE PRESCRIPTION CO.**, P.O. Box 222249, Great Neck NY 11021. (516)808-4053. Fax: (415)553-8541. E-mail: mcdmike525@aol.com. President: David F. Gasman. Vice President A&R: Kirk Nordstrom. San Francisco office: 525 Ashbury St., San Francisco CA 94117. (415)553-8540. VP Sales (West Coast warehouse): Bruce Brennan. Record producer and music publisher. Fee derived from sales royalty when artist or song is recorded or outright fee from record company.

How to Contact: *Write or call first about your interest then submit demo.* Prefers cassette with any number of songs and lyric sheet. SASE. "Does not return material without SASE and sufficient postage."

Music: Mostly **bluegrass**, **blues**, **children's**, **country**, **dance**, **easy listening**, **jazz**, **MOR**, **progressive**, **R&B**, **rock**, **soul** and **top 40/pop**. Produced "You Came In," "Rock 'n' Roll Blues" and *Just What the Doctor Ordered* (singles), all recorded by Medicine Mike.

Ⓝ ◑ **RAINBOW RECORDING**, 113 Shamrock Dr., Mankato MN 56001. Phone/fax: (507)625-4027. E-mail: mtotman@prairie.lakes.com. **Contact:** Michael Totman. Record producer and recording studio. Estab. 1986. Produces 4 singles and 4 CDs/year. Fee derived from outright fee from recording artist or record company.

How to Contact: Submit demo tape by mail. Unsolicited submissions are OK. Prefers cassette, DAT or CD with 4 songs and lyric sheet or lead sheet. Does not return material. Responds only if interested.

Music: Mostly **rock**, **country** and **top 40**; also **old time**, **alternative** and **R&B**. Produced *Collection* (album), written and recorded by Scott Wilson (top 40), released 2000.

✅ ◯ **R&D PRODUCTIONS**, P.O. Box 540102, Houston TX 77254-0102. (713)521-2616. Fax: (713)529-4914. E-mail: rpds2405@aol.com. Website: www.rndproductions.com. **Contact:** Byron Gates, A&R director. National Sales Director: Jeff Troncoso. Record producer, record company (Albatross Records) and music publisher (Ryedale Publishing). Estab. 1986. Produces 25 singles, 20 LPs, 4 EPs and 21 CDs/year. Fee derived from sales royalty when song or artist is recorded.

How to Contact: Submit demo CD by mail. Unsolicited submissions are OK. Prefers CD with 4 songs and lyric sheet. Does not return material. Responds in 1 month.
Music: **All types**. Produced "Untitled" by Nu Ground (pop), released 2000.

☐ REEL ADVENTURES, 9 Peggy Lane, Salem NH 03079. (603)898-7097. **Contact:** Rick Asmega, chief engineer/producer. Record producer. Estab. 1972. Produces 100 12" singles, 200 LPs, 5 EPs and 40 CDs/year. Fee derived from sales royalty when song or artist is recorded, or outright fee from recording artist or record company.
How to Contact: Submit demo tape by mail. Unsolicited submissions are OK. Prefers cassette or CD. SASE. Responds in 6 weeks.
Music: Mostly **pop**, **funk** and **country**; also **blues**, **reggae** and **rock**. Produced *Funky Broadway* (album), recorded by Chris Hicks; *Testafye* (album), recorded by Jay Williams; and "Acoustical Climate" (single by John G.). Other artists include Larry Sterling, Broken Men, Melvin Crockett, Fred Vigeant, Monster Mash, Carl Armand, Cool Blue Sky, Ransome, Backtrax, Push, Too Cool for Humans and Burn Alley.

N☐ ROAD RECORDS, P.O. Box 2620, Victorville CA 92393. Website: www.roadrecords.com. **Contact:** Conrad Askland, president. Record producer, record company (Road Records) and music publisher (Askland Publishing). Estab. 1989. Produces 6 singles and 10 albums/year. Fee derived from sales royalty when song or artist is recorded.
How to Contact: *Write or call first and obtain permission to submit a demo.* Prefers at least 3 songs with lyric and lead sheet. "We are looking for people that have a different, original sound." Does not return submissions. Responds in 3 weeks.
Music: Mostly **alternative**, **modern country** and **dance**; also **orchestral instrumental**. Does not want jazz. "We supply music to Grand Ole Opry, United Airlines, Knoxbury Farm and G.T.E."
Tips: "Do not submit what you think we are looking for. A lot of our projects are 'on the edge.'"

✓☐ RUSTRON MUSIC PRODUCTIONS, 1156 Park Lane, West Palm Beach FL 33417-5957. (561)686-1354. E-mail: gordon-whims@juno.com. **Contact:** A&R Dept. Executive Director: Rusty Gordon. A&R Director: Ron Caruso. Assistant A&R Director: Kevin Reeves. Record producer, record company, manager and music publisher (Rustron Music Publishers/BMI and Whimsong Publishing/ASCAP). Estab. 1970. Produces 6-10 LP/cassettes and 6 CDs/year. Fee derived from sales royalty when song or artist is recorded or outright fee from record company. "This branch office reviews all material submitted for the home office in Ridgefield, CT."
How to Contact: *Write or call first and obtain permission to submit or submit demo tape by mail.* Prefers cassette with 1-3 songs and typed lyric or lead sheet. Also send cover letter clearly explaining your reason for submitting. "Songs should be 3½ minutes long or less and must be commercially viable for today's market. Exception: New Age fusion compositions 3-10 minutes each, ½ hour maximum. Singer/songwriters and collaborators are preferred." SASE required for all correspondence. Responds in 4 months.
Music: Mostly **progressive country**, **pop** (ballads, blues, theatrical, cabaret), **folk/rock**, and **A/C electric acoustic**; also **R&B**, **New Age folk fusion**, **women's music** and **New Age instrumentals**. Produced "Sunrise In The Mountains" (single by Ron Caruso/Rusty Gordon) from *Florida Fresh* (album), recorded by Song on A Whim (folk/country), released 2000 on Whimsong Records; "Never Always" (single) from *Shades of Reason* (album), written and recorded by Jayne Margo-Reby (folk/rock), released 2000 on MSB Records; and "Everybody Counts" (single by Susan Mosely) from *Children on the Brink* (album), recorded by Helen Hannah (children's), released 2000 on Rustron Records. Other artists include Eric Shaffer, Bill Buck, Dianne Mower, Christian Camilo, Richard Collins and Diane Marra.

TO HELP YOU UNDERSTAND and use the information in these listings, see "How to Use *Songwriter's Market* to Get Your Songs Heard," on page 5.

Tips: "Be open to developing your own unique style. Write well-crafted songs with unpredictable concepts, strong hooks and definitive melodies. New Age composers: evolve your themes and use multiculturally diverse instruments to embellish your compositions/arrangements. Don't be predictable. Experiment with instrumental fusion with jazz and/or classical themes, pop themes and international styles. Send cover letter clearly explaining your reason for submitting."

✅ ◐ **SAS PRODUCTIONS/HIT RECORDS NETWORK**, (formerly SM Recording/Hit Records Network), P.O. Box 6235, Santa Barbara CA 93160. (805)964-3035. E-mail: cms@silcom.com. **Contact:** Greg Lewolt, Ernie Orosco, Cory Orosco and J.C. Martin, producers. Record producer, record company (Night City Records, Warrior Records and Tell International Records), radio and TV promotion and music publisher. Estab. 1984. Produces 4 singles, 2 12″ singles, 4 LPs, 2 EPs and 2-4 CDs/year. Fee derived from outright fee from record company.
How to Contact: Submit demo tape by mail. Unsolicited submissions are OK. Prefers cassette, CD or VHS videocassette with 4-8 songs, photos, bio and lyric sheet. Does not return material. SASE. Responds in 2 months.
Music: Mostly **pop-rock**, **country** and **top 40**; also **top 40 funk**, **top 40 rock** and **top 40 country**. Produced "Sundance" (single by J.C. Martin) from *Black Angel* (album), recorded by Black Angel (R&B/rock), released 2001 on Outsider Records; "I've Been Bad" (single by J.C. Martin/Ronnie Turner/Audry Madison) from *Life in L.A.* (album), recorded by The Prophets, featuring Ronnie Turner of Ike Turner Review (rock/soul), released 2001 on Hit Records Network/Outsider Records; and "Under the Chessnut Tree" (single) from *Under the Chessnut Tree* (album), written and recorded by Johnny Padz and Brian Faith (alternative rock), released 2001 on Hit Records Network. Other artists include New Vision, Jade, Ernie and the Emperors, Hollywood Heros, Tim Bogert (Vanilla Fudge, Jeff Beck), Peter Lewis, Jim Calire (America), Mike Kowalski, Ernie Knapp (Beach Boys) and Jewel.
Tips: "Keep searching for the infectious chorus hook and don't give up."

◐ **STEVE SATKOWSKI RECORDINGS**, P.O. Box 3403, Stuart FL 34995. (561)781-4657. Fax: (561)283-2374. Engineer/producer: Steven Satkowski. Record producer, recording engineer, management firm and record company. Estab. 1980. Produces 20 CDs/year. Fee derived from outright fee from recording artist or record company.
How to Contact Submit demo tape by mail. Unsolicited submissions are OK. Prefers cassette. Does not return material. Responds in 2 weeks.
Music: Mostly **classical**, **jazz** and **big band**. Produced recordings for National Public Radio and affiliates. Engineered recordings for Steve Howe, Patrick Moraz, Kenny G and Michael Bolton.

◑ **SEGAL'S PRODUCTIONS**, 16 Grace Rd., Newton MA 02159. (617)969-6196. Fax: (617)969-6614. **Contact:** Charles Segal. Record producer, music publisher (Segal's Publications/BMI and Samro South Africa) and record company (Spin Records). Produces 6 singles and 6 LPs/year. Fee derived from sales royalty when song or artist is recorded.
How to Contact: Write first and obtain permission to submit or to arrange personal interview. Prefers cassette, CD or videocassette with 3 songs and lyric sheet or lead sheet of melody, words, chords. "Please record keyboard/voice or guitar/voice if you can't get a group." Does not return material. Responds in 3 months only if interested.
Music: Mostly **rock**, **pop** and **country**; also **R&B** and **comedy**. Produced "What Is This Love" (single by Paul/Motou), recorded by Julia Manin (rock); "Lovely Is This Memory" (single by Segal/Paul), recorded by Nick Chosn on AU.S. (ballad); and *There'll Come A Time* (album by Charles Segal), recorded by Jill Kirkland on Spin Records (ballad). Other artists include Art Heatley, Dan Hill and Melanie.
Tips: "Make a good and clear production of cassette even if it is only piano rhythm and voice. Also do a lead sheet of music, words and chords."

✅ ◐ **SHU'BABY MONTEZ MUSIC**, 1447 N. 55th St., Philadelphia PA 19131-3901. (215)473-5527. Fax: (215)473-8895. E-mail: schubaby@aol.com. Website: www.geocities.com/SunsetStrip/cabaret/2810/. **Contact:** Shubaby, owner. Record producer. Estab. 1986. Produces 6 singles, 6 12″ singles and 3 LPs/year. Fee derived from outright fee from record company.

How to Contact: Submit demo tape by mail. Unsolicited submissions are OK. Prefers cassette with 4 songs and lyric sheet. SASE. Responds in 5 weeks.
Music: Mostly **R&B**, **hip-hop** and **funk**. Produced "Woo Me" (single), written and recorded by Qadir Moore (R&B), released 2001 on Urban Logic Records; "Show Love in the Club" (single by Greg Davis/Seth Simpson Davis/Hasson Davis), recorded by H.A.F.A. (hip-hop), released 2000 on Philly Devine Records; and "My Request" (single by Lou Leggerie), recorded by Marie Davenport (pop), released 2001 on Urban Logic Records. Other artists include Ralph Brown, Wilson Lambert, Martin "Martygraw" Schuler and Waller Wee.
Tips: "Be on time with all projects."

N ☐ SILVER THUNDER MUSIC GROUP, P.O. Box 41335, Nashville TN 37204. (615)391-5035. President: Rusty Budde. Record producer, record company (Silver Thunder Records), music publisher (Silver Thunder Publishing) and management firm. Estab. 1982. Produces 20 singles, 5-7 LPs and 5-7 CDs/year. Fee derived from sales royalty when song or artist is recorded or outright fee from recording artist or record company.
How to Contact: Write first and obtain permission to submit or to arrange personal interview. Prefers cassette. "Artists should submit 8 × 10 photo along with demo tape." Does not return material. Responds in 4 months.
Music: Mostly **country**, **rock** and **R&B**; also **gospel** and **pop**. Produced *What's Not To Love* (album by D.J. Music), recorded by Heather Hartsfield (country); and *Radio Active* (album by G. McCorkel), recorded by J.D. Treece (country), both on STR Records. Other artists include Rod Woodson, Jeff Samules, Jodi Collins and Hank Thompson.

☐ SOUND ARTS RECORDING STUDIO, 8377 Westview Dr., Houston TX 77055. (713)464-GOLD. E-mail: sarsjef@aol.com. Website: soundartsrecording.com. **Contact:** Jeff Wells, president. Record producer and music publisher (Earthscream Music). Estab. 1974. Produces 12 singles and 3 LPs/year. Fee derived from sales royalty when song or artist is recorded.
How to Contact: Submit demo tape by mail. Unsolicited submissions are OK. Prefers cassette with 2-5 songs and lyric sheet. Does not return material. Responds in 6 weeks.
Music: Mostly **pop/rock**, **country** and **blues**. Produced *Texas Johnny Brown* (album), written and recorded by Texas Johnny Brown on Quality (blues). Other artists include Tim Nichols, Perfect Strangers, B.B. Watson, Jinkies, Joe "King" Carasco (on Surface Records), Mark May (on Icehouse Records), The Barbara Pennington Band (on Earth Records), Tempest Under the Sun and Attitcus Finch.

☑ ☐ SOUND WORKS ENTERTAINMENT PRODUCTIONS INC., P.O. Box 26691, Las Vegas NV 89126-0691. (702)878-1870 or (615)480-8580 (Nashville). Fax: (702)878-2284. E-mail: music@wizard.com. Website: www.musicjones.com. **Contact:** Michael E. Jones, president. Record producer, record company (Sound Works Records) and music publisher (Sound Works Music). Estab. 1989. Produces 16 singles, 2 LPs and 20 CDs/year. Fee derived from sales royalty when song or artist is recorded or outright fee from recording artist or record company.
How to Contact: Submit demo tape by mail. Unsolicited submissions are OK. Prefers cassette with 3-6 songs and lyric sheet. "Please include short bio and statement of goals and objectives." Does not return material. Responds in 6 weeks.
Music: Mostly **country**, **folk** and **pop**; also **rock**. Produced "Lonelyville," and "Alabama Slammer" (singles), both written and recorded by Wake Eastman; and "Good Looking Loser" (single), written and recorded by Renee Rubach, all on Sound Works Records (country). Other artists include Matt Dorman, Steve Gilmore, The Tackroom Boys, The Los Vegas Philharmonic and J.C. Clark.
Tips: "Put your ego on hold. Don't take criticism personally. Advice is meant to help you grow and improve your skills as an artist/songwriter. Be professional and business-like in all your dealings."

☑ ☐ SPHERE GROUP ONE, P.O. Box 991, Far Hills NJ 07931-0991. (908)781-1650. Fax: (908)781-1693. E-mail: spheregroupone@att.net. **Contact:** Tony Zarrella, president. Talent Manager: Louisa Pazienza. Record producer, artist development and management firm. Produces 5-6 singles and 3 CDs/year. Estab. 1986.

How to Contact: Submit demo tape by mail. Unsolicited submissions are OK. Prefers cassette, CD or VHS videocassette with 3-5 songs and lyric sheets. "Must include: photos, press, résumé, goals and specifics of project submitted, etc." Does not return material.

Music: Mostly **pop/rock (mainstream)**, **progressive/rock**, **New Age** and **crossover country/pop**; also **film soundtracks**. Produced *Take This Heart*, *It's Our Love* and *You and I* (albums by T. Zarrella), recorded by 4 of Hearts (pop/rock) on Sphere Records. Other artists include Frontier 9 and Bombay Green.

Tips: "Be able to take direction and have trust and faith in yourself, your producer and manager. Currently seeking artists/groups incorporating various styles into a focused mainstream product. Groups with a following are a plus."

⊡ **STUDIO SEVEN**, 417 N. Virginia, Oklahoma City OK 73106. (405)236-0643. Fax: (405)236-0686. E-mail: cope@okla.net. Website: www.lunacyrecords.com. **Contact:** Dave Copenhaver, producer. Record producer, record company (Lunacy Records) and music publisher (VenDome Music). Estab. 1990. Produces 10 LPs and CDs/year. Fee is derived from sales royalty when song or artist is recorded or outright fee from recording artist or record company. "All projects are on a customized basis."

How to Contact: *Contact first and obtain permission to submit.* Prefers cassette with lyric sheet. SASE. Responds in 6 weeks.

Music: Mostly **rock**, **jazz-blues** and **world-Native American**; also **country** and **blues**. Produced *Let's Go* (album), written and recorded by Joe Merrick (western); and *Warren Peace: The Elements* (album), written and recorded by Warren Peace (rock), both released 2000 on Lunacy Records. Other artists include Harvey Shelton, Steve Pryor and Ken Taylor.

N̄ ⊡ **STUDIO VOODOO MUSIC**, (formerly Gary John Mraz), 1324 Cambridge Dr., Glendale CA 91205. E-mail: studiovoodoo@earthlink.net. Website: www.studiovoodoomusic.com. **Contact:** Gary Mraz, producer. Estab. 1984. Record producer. Produces 6-12 12″ singles and 2-6 LPs/year. Fee derived from sales royalty or outright fee from record company.

How to Contact: Submit demo tape by mail. Unsolicited submissions are OK. Prefers cassette or CD/CDR with 3 songs and lyric sheet. Does not return material. Responds in 2 months.

Music: Mostly **dance**, **pop** and **electronica**. Produced "Studio Voodoo," the world's first dts-es surround dvd-audio disc. Other artists include Bush Baby.

Tips: "With today's technology, we are only limited by our own imaginations."

⊡ **SWIFT RIVER PRODUCTIONS**, P.O. Box 231, Gladeville TN 37071. (615)316-9479. E-mail: office@andymay.com. Website: www.swiftrivermusic.com. **Contact:** Andy May, producer/owner. Record producer, record company and music publisher. Estab. 1979. Produces 40 singles and 8 CDs/year. Fee derived from outright fee from recording artist or record company.

How to Contact: *Write or call first and obtain permission to submit.* Prefers cassette or CD with 3 songs and lyric sheet. "Demo should be clear and well thought out. Vocal plus guitar or piano is fine. Let us know your present goals and reason for contacting us and include a short bio." Does not return material. Responds in up to 2 months.

Music: Mostly **country**, **singer/songwriters** and **"roots" (folk, acoustic, bluegrass and rock)**; also **instrumental**. Produced "Leap Frog" (single) from *Curtis McPeake: The View from McPeake* (album), written and recorded by Curtis McPeake (bluegrass); "The Long Way Home to You" (single by Bromley/May/May) from *Brycen Fast* (album), recorded by Brycen Fast (country); and "Dreamin' the Blues" (single) from *Henry May: Dreamin' the Blues* (album), written and recorded by Henry May (acoustic blues/guitar), all released 2000 on Swift River Music. Other artists include Marinda Flom, Robert Bromley, Ron Young, Bryce Fast and Crossties.

Tips: "I'm interested in artists/writers who are accomplished, self-motivated and able to accept direction. I'm looking for music that is intelligent, creative and in some way contributes something positive."

N̄ ⊡ **SYNDICATE SOUND, INC.**, 475 Fifth St., Struthers OH 44471. (330)755-1331. President: Jeff Wormley. Producer: Billy Moyer. Record producer, audio and video production company and record and song production company. Estab. 1981. Produces 6-10 CDs and 15-20 singles/year. Fee derived from sales royalty when song or artist is recorded or outright fee from recording artist or record company.

How to Contact: Submit demo tape by mail. Unsolicited submissions are OK. "Please send a promo package or biography (with pictures) of artist, stating past and present concerts and records." Does not return material. Responds in 6 weeks.

Music: Mostly **rock**, **pop** and **Christian rock**; also **country**, **R&B**, **rap** and **alternative**. Produced "Time to Bowl" (single by Gregg Wormley), recorded by Larry Shankman (rock); "The Shining" (single by Jason Hairston), recorded by Jas the Ace (rap); and *Remember Me* (album by Robert Noble), recorded by Lost Then Found (Christian rock), all on SS&VW. Other artists include Falling Down, Marc Tipton, Severence and Vessel.

☑ ◯ **TAMJAM PRODUCTIONS**, 101 N. Citrus Ave., Suite 2, Covina CA 91723-2029. E-mail: tamjam1111@aol.com. **Contact:** John Maellaro, producer. Record producer. Estab. 1985. Produces 10 singles and 5 CDs/year. Fee derived from sales royalty when song or artist is recorded, outright fee from recording artist and record company, depending on project.

How to Contact: Submit demo tape by mail. Unsolicited submissions are OK. Prefers CD with 3 songs and lyric sheet. Clearly label contact name and number on all items submitted. Does not return material. Responds in 3 months.

Music: Mostly **adult contemporary**, **pop** and **R&B**; also **Latin**, **jazz** and **blues**. Produced *If Only I Could Touch You* (album by Arizaga/Maellaro), recorded by Anthony Arizaga (Latin/jazz) on Duende; *Window Seat* (album by Dorsey/Maellaro), recorded by Patty Dorsey (AC/pop) on Saudade; and *Common Ground* (album by Maellaro), recorded by Oddcat (pop/jazz) on Tamjam. Other artists include Magnetic Mary and Kingman.

Tips: "Have a clear idea of your direction and handle things in a business-like manner."

☑ ◯ **ROGER VINCENT TARI**, P.O. Box 576, Piscataway NJ 08855. Phone/fax: (908)222-8978. E-mail: mroze714@aol.com. **Contact:** Roger Vincent Tari, president/producer. Vice President/A&R: Mike Roze. Record producer, record company (VT Records), music publisher (Vintari Music/ASCAP) and magazine publisher. Estab. 1979. Produces 6-8 singles/year. Fee derived from sales royalty when song or artist is recorded or outright fee from recording artist.

How to Contact: Submit demo tape by mail. Unsolicited submissions are OK. Prefers cassette or VHS videocassette with 3 songs and lyric sheet (videocassette is optional). "The artist should send any relevant literature and a simple black and white picture along with the 3-song cassette and lyric sheet." SASE. Responds in 1 month.

Music: Mostly **creative pop**, **electronic exotica** and **avant-jazz**; also **world music**, **J-pop**, **Korean pop**, and **indie rock**. Produced "System 27 (The Hidden Camera)" (single), written and recorded by Roger Vincent Tari/Mark Sonnenfeld (psychedelic); and "She Wore Blue" (single by Dennis Tirch/Ecco) from *VT Music Sampler Vol. 1* (album), recorded by Ecco (exotica), both released 2001 on VinTari Music. Other artists include Mind Dope 63, Yaag Yang, Leeji Young, Fractured Glass, N.F. Inc., Ling Ling and East Coast Project (midi inc).

Tips: "We seek artists from around the world. The music should be new and creative regardless of style."

☑ ☒ ◯ **TEXAS FANTASY MUSIC GROUP**, 2932 Dyer St., Dallas TX 75205. (214)691-5318. Fax: (214)692-1392. E-mail: barbc@texasmusicgroup.com. Website: www.texasmusicgroup.com. **Contact:** Don Ashley, director of film & TV music. Director of New Age, World and Classical: Richard Theisen. Director of Country, Rock and Classic Rock: Billy Jack Simpson. Creative Director: Barbara McMillen. Record producer and music publisher (Showcat Music and Flying Red Horse Publishing). Estab. 1982. Produces 35 singles/year. Fee derived from sales royalty when song or artist is recorded, or outright fee from record company or recording artist, also sync fees for film/TV.

How to Contact: Submit demo tape by mail. Unsolicited submissions are OK. Prefers cassette with 2 songs and lyric sheet (if applicable). SASE. Responds in 6 months. "Submissions accepted between March and July only."

Music: Mostly **instrumental for film** and **all styles**. Produced *When I Was a Dinosaur* (album), written and recorded by Dixie Chicks and various artists; and *Teardrops To Rainbows & Other New Classic Tales* (album by Richard Theisen/Rollie Anderson), recorded by various artists, both on Remarkable Records (children's).

✔ ○ **THEORETICAL REALITY** 52323 Harrisburg, Chesterfield MI 48051. E-mail: erickilgore @msn.com. **Contact:** Eric Kilgore, chief producer/owner. Record producer. Produces 6 EPs and 2-4 CDs/year. Fee derived from sales royalty when song or artist is recorded, or individual arrangements with artist.
How to Contact: *Write first and obtain permission to submit.* Prefers cassette with 1-3 songs and legibly printed lyric sheet. SASE. Responds in 6 weeks.
Music: Mostly **folk/rock**, **folk** and **acoustic rock**; also **novelty** and **hard to define style combinations**. Produced *New Years Revolution* (album), written and recorded by Bouncing Perversions (techno); and *Black Out the Sun* (album), written and recorded by Fatt Haxx (rock), both released 2000, all on Schizophrenic Records. Other artists include Pantheon June, reductive synthesis and O.C. Tolbert.
Tips: "We are a small company that works with a limited amount of acts. We work as hard as we can for our clients, but they must be willing to help themselves also!"

✔ ○ **TMC PRODUCTIONS**, P.O. Box 12353, San Antonio TX 78212. (210)829-1909. Website: www.axbarmusic.com. **Contact:** Joe Scates, producer. Record producer, music publisher (Axbar Productions/BMI, Scates & Blanton/BMI and Axe Handle Music/ASCAP), record company (Axbar, Trophy, Jato, Prince and Charro Records) and record distribution and promotion. Produces 3-5 CDs/year. Fee derived from sales royalty.
How to Contact: *Write or call first and obtain permission to submit.* Prefers cassette with 1-5 songs and lyric sheet. Does not return material. Responds "as soon as possible, but don't rush us."
Music: Mostly **traditional country**; also **blues**, **novelty** and **rock (soft)**. Produced "Chicken Dance" (single) (traditional), recorded by George Chambers and "Hobo Heart" (single), written and recorded by Juni Moon, both on Axbar Records. Other artists include Jim Marshall, Caroll Gilley, Rick Will, Wayne Carter, Kathi Timm, Leon Taylor, Mark Chestnutt and Kenny Dale.

○ **TRAC RECORD CO.**, 170 N. Maple, Fresno CA 93702. (209)255-1717. E-mail: tracsell@aol.c om. **Contact:** Stan Anderson, Bev Anderson, owners. Record producer, music publisher (Sellwood Publishing/BMI) and record company (TRAC Records). Estab. 1972. Produces 5 12" singles, 5 LPs and 5 CDs/year. Fee derived from outright fee from recording artist or outside investor.
How to Contact: Submit demo tape by mail. Unsolicited submissions are OK. Prefers cassette with 3 songs and lyric sheet. "Send professional studio demo." SASE. Responds in 3 weeks.
Music: Mostly **country, all styles** and **southern gospel**. Produced *All Time Low* (album), written and recorded by Jimmy Walker on TRAC Records (country). Other artists include Jessica James and Kevin Blake Willard.

✔ ○ **THE TRINITY STUDIO**, P.O. Box 1417, Corpus Christi TX 78403. (361)854-SING. E-mail: info@trinitystydio.com. Website: www.trinitystudio.com. **Contact:** Jim Wilken, owner. Record producer and recording studio. Estab. 1988. Fee derived from outright fee from recording artist or record company.
How to Contact: Submit demo tape by mail. Unsolicited submissions are OK. Prefers cassette, CD or VHS videocassette. Does not return material. Responds in 1 month.

MARKET CONDITIONS are constantly changing! If you're still using this book and it is 2003 or later, buy the newest edition of *Songwriter's Market* at your favorite bookstore or order directly from Writer's Digest Books at (800)289-0963.

Music: Mostly **Christian-country**. Produced *Miracle Man* (album), written and recorded by Merrill Lane (country Christian) on TC Records; and *Higher Love* (album by Merrill Lane/Becky Redels), recorded by Becky Redels (country Christian). Other artists include Kerry Patton, Patty Walke, Leah, Lofton Kline, Jesse Bishop and Charlotte McGee.

VALTEC PRODUCTIONS, P.O. Box 2642, Santa Maria CA 93457. (805)934-8400. **Contact:** Joe Valenta, producer. Record producer. Estab. 1986. Produces 20 singles and 10 CDs/year. Fee derived from sales royalty when song or artist is recorded.

How to Contact: Submit demo tape by mail. Unsolicited submissions are OK. Prefers cassette, DAT or 8mm videocassette with 3 songs and lyric or lead sheet. Send photo. Does not return material (kept on file for 2 years). Responds in 6 weeks.

Music: Mostly **country**, **pop/AC** and **rock**. Produced *Lisa Sanchez* (album), written and recorded by Lisa Sanchez (country); *John Jacobson* (album), written and recorded by John Jacobson on Valtone Records (pop); and *Taxi* (album), written and recorded by Groupe Taxi on Tesoro Records (Spanish/pop).

CHARLES VICKERS MUSIC ASSOCIATION, P.O. Box 725, Daytona Beach FL 32015-0725. (904)252-4849. Fax: (904)252-7402. E-mail: CharlesVickers@USALink.com. Website: www.ZYWorld.com/CharlesVickers. President: Harold Vickers. Manager: Loris Doby. President/Producer: Dr. Charles H. Vickers D.M. Record producer, music publisher (Pritchett Publication/BMI and Alison Music/ASCAP) and record company (King of Kings Records, L.A. International Records, Quicksilvers/Increase Records Inc. and Bell Records International). Produces 3 singles and 6 LPs/year. Fee derived from sales royalty when song or artist is recorded.

How to Contact: Call first and obtain permission to submit. Prefers 7½ ips reel-to-reel or cassette with 1-6 songs. Does not return material. Responds in 6 months.

Music: Mostly **church/religious**, **gospel** and **hymns**; also **bluegrass**, **blues**, **classical**, **country**, **easy listening**, **jazz**, **MOR**, **progressive**, **reggae (pop)**, **R&B**, **rock**, **soul** and **top 40/pop**. Produced *Run to Jesus While You Can* (album), written and recorded by Charles Vickers on Quicksilvers/Increase Records Inc. Other artists include James Franklin, Gladys Nighton and Charles Gardy.

THE WEISMAN PRODUCTION GROUP, 449 N. Vista St., Los Angeles CA 90036. (213)653-0693. E-mail: unclelenny@aol.com. **Contact:** Ben Weisman, owner. Record producer and music publisher (Audio Music Publishers). Estab. 1965. Produces 10 singles/year. Fee derived from sales royalty when song or artist is recorded.

How to Contact: Submit demo tape by mail. Unsolicited submissions are OK. Prefers cassette with 3-10 songs and lyric sheet. SASE. "Mention *Songwriter's Market*. Please make return envelope the same size as the envelopes you send material in, otherwise we cannot send everything back. Just send tape." Responds in 6 weeks.

Music: Mostly **R&B**, **soul**, **dance**, **rap** and **top 40/pop**; also **gospel** and **all types of rock**.

WESTWIRES DIGITAL USA, 1042 Club Ave., Allentown PA 18103. (610) 435-1924. E-mail: wayne.becker@westwires.com. Website: www.westwires.com. **Contact:** Wayne Becker, owner/producer. Record producer and production company. Fee derived from outright fee from record company or artist retainer.

How to Contact: Submit demo tape by mail. Unsolicited submissions are OK. Prefers cassette, CD or VHS videocassette with 3 songs and lyric sheet. Does not return material. Responds in 1 month.

Music: Mostly **R&B**, **dance**, **alternative**, **folk** and **improvisation**. Produced *Innocence Lost*, written and recorded by Nooner (alternative), released 1999 on Pinball Records. Other artists include Weston, Anne Le Baron and Gary Hussay.

Tips: "We are interested in singer/songwriters and alternative artists living in the mid-Atlantic area. Must be able to perform live and take chances."

⊕ ◐ **WIR (WORLD INTERNATIONAL RECORDS)**, A-1090 Vienna, Servitengasse 24, Austria. Phone: (+43)1-7684380. Fax: (+43)1-7677573. **Contact:** Peter Jordan, general manager. Record producer, music publisher (Aquarius Publishing) and record company (WIR). Estab. 1986. Produces 5-10 singles and 5-8 LPs/year. Fee derived from sales royalty when song or artist is recorded.
How to Contact: Submit demo tape by mail. Unsolicited submissions are OK. Prefers cassette. Does not return material. Responds in 1 month.
Music: Produced "All Over Me" (single) from *David London* (album), written and recorded by David London (pop); "Das Leben ist schön" (single by Brachner) from *Das Leben ist schön* (album), recorded by Joannis Raymond (commercial); and *Country Pure-Valleys 17* (album), written and recorded by various artists (country), all released 2000 on WIR. Other artists include Bill Roberts, Madmen, John Velora, Full Circle, Veronica Martell, Magaly, Ted Lang, Cindi Cain and John Lake.

Ⓝ ◐ **WILBUR PRODUCTIONS**, 159 W. Fourth St. #10, New York NY 10014. (212)255-5544. E-mail: demo@pilotrecording.com. Website: www.pilotrecording.com. **Contact:** Will Schillinger, president. Record producer and recording engineer/studio owner. Estab. 1989. Produces 50 singles, 20 LPs and 20 CDs/year. Fee derived from sales royalty when song or artist is recorded or outright fee from record company.
How to Contact: Submit demo tape by mail. Prefers CD with 3-5 songs. Does not return material. Responds in 2 weeks.
Music: Mostly **rock** and **jazz**. Produced Marshall Crenshaw, Jack Walrath & Band and In The Groove.
Tips: "Don't worry about your demo quality. Send good songs. Very interested in new bands as well."

✅ ◐ **FRANK WILLSON**, P.O. Box 2297, Universal City TX 78148. (210)659-2557. E-mail: bswr18@txdiret.net. Website: www.BSWRecords.com. **Contact:** Frank Willson, producer. Record producer, management firm (Universal Music Marketing) and record company (BSW Records/Universal Music Records). Estab. 1987. Produces 20-25 albums/year. Fee derived from sales royalty when song or artist is recorded.
● Frank Willson's record company, BSW Records, can be found in the Record Companies section and his management firm, Universal Music Marketing, is in the Managers & Booking Agents section.
How to Contact: Submit demo tape by mail. Unsolicited submissions are OK. Prefers cassette with 3-4 songs and lyric sheets. SASE. Responds in 1 month.
Music: Mostly **country**, **blues**, **jazz** and **soft rock**. Produced *Follow the Roses* (album), written and recorded by Larry Butler on BSW Records (country). Other artists include Candee Land, Laurie Hayes, Dan Kimmel, Brad Lee and Bobby Boyd.

◐ **WLM MUSIC/RECORDING**, 2808 Cammie St., Durham NC 27705-2020. (919)471-3086. Fax: (919)471-4326. E-mail: wlm.musicrecording@worldnet.att.net. **Contact:** Watts Lee Mangum, owner. Record producer. Estab. 1980. Fee derived from outright fee from recording artist. "In some cases, an advance payment requested for demo production."
How to Contact: Submit demo tape by mail. Unsolicited submissions are OK. Prefers cassette with 2-4 songs and lyric or lead sheet (if possible). SASE. Responds in 6 months.
Music: Mostly **country**, **country/rock** and **blues/rock**; also **pop**, **rock**, **blues**, **gospel** and **bluegrass**. Produced "911," and "Petals of an Orchid" (singles), both written and recorded by Johnny Scoggins (country); and "Renew the Love" (single by Judy Evans), recorded by Bernie Evans (country), all on Independent. Other artists include Southern Breeze Band and Heart Breakers Band.

✅ ◐ **WORLD RECORDS**, 5798 Deer Trail Dr., Traverse City MI 49684. E-mail: jack@worldrec.org. Website: www.worldrec.org. **Contact:** Jack Conners, producer. Record producer, engineer/technician and record company (World Records). Estab. 1984. Produces 1 CD/year. Fee derived from outright fee from recording artist.
How to Contact: *Write first and obtain permission to submit.* Prefers cassette with 1 or 2 songs. SASE. Responds in 6 weeks.

Music: Mostly **classical**, **folk** and **jazz**. Produced *Penny Arcade* (album by Jim Davenport/Dave Davenport/Paul Schultz), recorded by The Burdons (pop), released 2000 on World Records. Other artists include The Murphy Brothers and The Burdons.

⬛ STEVE WYTAS PRODUCTIONS, Dept. SM, 11 Custer St., West Hartford CT 06110. (860)953-2834. Contact: Steven J. Wytas. Record producer. Estab. 1984. Produces 4-8 singles, 3 LPs, 3 EPs and 4 CDs/year. Fee derived from outright fee from recording artist or record company.
How to Contact: Submit demo tape by mail. Unsolicited submissions are OK. Prefers CD or VHS ¾" videocassette with several songs and lyric or lead sheet. "Include live material if possible." Does not return material. Responds in 3 months.
Music: Mostly **rock**, **pop**, **top 40** and **country/acoustic**. Produced *Already Home* (album), recorded by Hannah Cranna on Big Deal Records (rock); *Under the Rose* (album), recorded by Under the Rose on Utter Records (rock); and *Sickness & Health* (album), recorded by Legs Akimbo on Joyful Noise Records (rock). Other artists include King Hop!, The Shells, The Gravel Pit, G'nu Fuz, Tuesday Welders and Toxic Field Mice.

⬛ Y-N-A/C.D.T. PRODUCTIONS, Dept. SM, 170 Rosedale Rd., Yonkers NY 10710. (914)961-1051. Fax: (914)961-5906. E-mail: niftrik@aol.com. Website: www.youthnasia.com. **Contact:** Rikk Angel, producer. Record producer. Estab. 1984. Produces 30 singles, 5 LPs, 5 EPs and 5 CDs/year. Fee derived from outright fee from record company or contractual fees.
How to Contact: *Write or call first to arrange personal interview or submit demo tape by mail.* Prefers DAT or VHS videocassette with 3 songs, photo and lyric or lead sheet. Does not return material. Responds in 2 weeks.
Music: Mostly **R&B/dance**, **soul** and **house**. Produced "Sinoa's World" (by Sinoa/Y-N-A), recorded by Sinoa (R&B/house) on T.O. Records. Other artists include Rikk Angel, Ray Tabano (formerly of Aerosmith), D'Angelo, Bob Mayo (of Foreigner, Hall & Oates), Skatelites (1996-'97 Grammy nominated album), Sturken & Rogers (N'Sync, Lara Fabian, etc.) and Angeles.

Additional Record Producers

The following companies are also record producers, but their listings are found in other sections of the book. See the General Index for page numbers, then read the listings for submission information.

A.A.M.I. Music Group
A.P.I. Records
Afterschool Records, Inc.
Alias John Henry Tunes
AlliSongs Inc.
Alpha-Beat
Ariana Records
Arkadia Entertainment Corp.
Atlan-Dec/Grooveline Records
Avalon Music
Avalon Recording Group
Avita Records
Bacchus Group Productions, Ltd.
Bagatelle Music Publishing Co.
Bagatelle Record Company
Belham Valley Records
Belmont Records
Bernard Enterprises, Inc., Hal
Big Fish Music Publishing Group
Blue Wave Productions
BME Publishing
Bradley Music, Allan
Brewster Songs, Kitty
Brian Song Music Corp.
Capstan Record Production
Cellar Records
Cherri/Holly Music Inc.
Chiaroscuro Records
Christopher Publishing, Sonny
Chucker Music Inc.
CKB Records/Helaphat Entertainment
Collector Records
Coral Records LLC
Cornelius Companies, The
Cosmotone Records
Creative Improvised Music Projects (CIMP) Records
Dagene Music
Dagene/Cabletown Company
Dapmor Publishing
Deadeye Records
Discmedia
Drool Records
Duane Music, Inc.
Ellis International Talent Agency, The
Fireant
First Time Music (Publishing) U.K.
First Time Records
Fountain Records
Frick Enterprises, Bob Scott
Frozen Inca Music
Furrow Music

Garrett Entertainment, Marty
GCI, Inc.
Glad Music Co.
Golden Triangle Records
Green Bear Records
Groove Makers' Recordings
Gueststar Entertainment Agency
Gueststar Records, Inc.
Hammel Associates, Inc., R.L.
Happy Man Records
Hardison International Entertainment Corporation
Heads Up Int., Ltd.
Hi-Bias Records Inc.
Hickory Lane Publishing and Recording
Hickory Valley Music
His Power Productions and Publishing
Interplanetary Music
Iron Skillet Music
Ja/Nein Musikverlag GmbH
Kansa Records Corporation
Kaupp Records
L.A. Records (Canada)
L.A. Records (Michigan)
Lake Transfer Productions & Music
Landmark Communications Group
Landslide Records
Les Music Group
Lineage Publishing Co.
Lock
Loggins Promotion/Backstage Entertainment
Lucifer Records, Inc.
Makers Mark Gold
Manuiti L.A.
Martin Productions, Rick
Mayfair Music
McCoy Music, Jim
Mellow House Music
Merlin Records of Canada
Missile Records
MOR Records
Music Room Publishing Group, The
Mymit Music Productions, Chuck
Naked Jain Records
OCP Publications
Ontrax Companies
Orchid Publishing
Orillyon Entertainment
Outland Productions
P. & N. Records
P.M. Records

Perla Music
Permanent Press Recordings/Permanent Wave
Plateau Music
Playbones Records
Prescription Company
Presence Records
QUARK, Inc.
R.T.L. Music
Rampant Records
Renaissance Entertainment Group
Rival Records
Road Records
Rocker Music/Happy Man Music
Ruf Records
Sabre Productions
Safire Records
Salt Works Music
Sea Cruise Productions, Inc.
Sinus Musik Produktion, Ulli Weigel
Slanted Circle Music
Songgram Music
Sound Cellar Music
Sound Management Direction
Southland Records, Inc.
Sphere Group One
Starbound Publishing Co.
Street Records
Succes
Sunsongs Music/Dark Son Music (Sesac)
Sureshot Records
Sweet June Music
T.C. Productions/Etude Publishing Co.
Tiger's Eye Entertainment Management & Consulting
Tiki Enterprises, Inc.
Topcat Records
Tower Music Group
Twentieth Century Promotions
Valtec Productions
Wagner Agency, William F.
Wall Street Music
Warehouse Creek Recording Corp.
Warner Productions, Cheryl K.
Whiting Music
Wilder Artists' Management, Shane
Williams Management, Yvonne
World Beatnik Records
World Famous Music Co.
X.R.L. Records/Music

Category Index

The Category Index is a good place to begin searching for a market for your songs. Below is an alphabetical list of 19 general music categories. If you write dance music and are looking for a record producer to pitch them, check the Dance section in this index. There you will find a list of record producers who work with dance music. Once you locate the entries for those producers, read the music subheading *carefully* to determine which companies are most interested in the type of dance music you write. Some of the markets in this section do not appear in the Category Index because they have not indicated a specific preference. Most of these said they are interested in "all types" of music. Listings that were very specific, or whose description of the music they're interested in doesn't quite fit into these categories, also do not appear here.

Adult Contemporary (also easy listening, middle of the road, AAA, ballads, etc.)
"A" Major Sound Corporation
Aberdeen Productions
Bal Records
Diamond Entertainment, Joel
Integrated Entertainment
Jump Productions
June Productions Ltd.
Known Artist Productions
Kovach, Robert R.
Luick & Country Music Showcase Intl. Associates, Harold
Magid Productions, Lee
Mittelstedt, A.V.
Monticana Productions
New Vizion Studios, The
Panio Brothers Label
Prescription Co., The
Rustron Music Productions
Tamjam Productions
Valtec Productions
Vickers Music Association, Charles

Alternative (also modern rock, punk, college rock, new wave, hardcore, new music, industrial, ska, indie rock, garage, etc.)
"A" Major Sound Corporation
Alco Productions
Avalon Productions
Blues Alley Records
Coachouse Music
Craig, Douglas
John Productions, David
Kane Producer/Engineer, Karen
L.A. Entertainment, Inc.
Lazy Bones Productions/Recordings, Inc.
Mac-Attack Productions
Magnetic Oblivion Music Co.

Marenco, Cookie
Mathews, d/b/a Hit or Myth Productions, Scott
Merlin Productions
Monticana Productions
Prejippie Music Group
Rainbow Recording
Road Records
Studio Voodoo Music
Syndicate Sound, Inc.
Tari, Roger Vincent
Vickers Music Association, Charles
Westwires Digital USA

Blues
Bal Records
Celt Musical Services, Jan
Coachouse Music
Esquire International
Hailing Frequency Music Productions
Jag Studio, Ltd.
Landmark Communications Group
Linear Cycle Productions
Magid Productions, Lee
Mega Truth Records
Monticana Productions
Ormsby, John "Buck"/Etiquette Productions
Pacific North Studios Ltd.
Prescription Co., The
Reel Adventures
Sound Arts Recording Studio
Studio Seven
Tamjam Productions
TMC Productions
Vickers Music Association, Charles
Willson, Frank
WLM Music/Recording

Children's
JSB Groupe Management Inc.
Prescription Co., The

Classical (also opera, chamber music, serious music, choral, etc.)
JSB Groupe Management Inc.
Lark Talent & Advertising
Marenco, Cookie
Satkowski Recordings, Steve
Vickers Music Association, Charles
World Records

Country (also western, C&W, bluegrass, cowboy songs, western swing, honky-tonk, etc.)
Aberdeen Productions
ACR Productions
Alco Productions
Allyn, Stuart J.
Avalon Productions
Baird Enterprises, Ron
Bal Records
Birthplace Productions
Coachouse Music
Coffee and Cream Productions
Cupit Productions, Jerry
De Miles, Edward
Diamond Entertainment, Joel
Dixon III, Philip D., Attorney at Law
Doss Presents, Col. Buster
Eiffert, Jr., Leo J.
Esquire International
Eternal Song Agency, The
Haworth Productions
Interstate Records
Jag Studio, Ltd.
Jay Bird Productions
Jay Jay Publishing & Record Co.
Kingston Records and Talent
Known Artist Productions
Kovach, Robert R.
Landmark Communications Group
Lari-Jon Productions
Lark Talent & Advertising
Linear Cycle Productions
Luick & Country Music Showcase Intl. Associates, Harold
Magid Productions, Lee
Makers Mark Music Productions
Marenco, Cookie
Martin, Pete/Vaam Music Productions
Mega Truth Records
Mittelstedt, A.V.
Monticana Productions
Pacific North Studios Ltd.
Panio Brothers Label
Parker, Patty
Pierce, Jim
Prescription Co., The
Rainbow Recording
R&D Productions

Reel Adventures
Road Records
Rustron Music Productions
SAS Productions/Hit Records Network
Segal's Productions
Silver Thunder Music Group
Sound Arts Recording Studio
Sound Works Entertainment Productions Inc.
Sphere Group One
Studio Seven
Swift River Productions
Syndicate Sound, Inc.
TMC Productions
Trac Record Co.
Trinity Studio, The
Valtec Productions
Vickers Music Association, Charles
Willson, Frank
WLM Music/Recording
Wytas Productions, Steve

Dance (also house, hi-NRG, disco, club, rave, techno, trip-hop, trance, etc.)
Coffee and Cream Productions
De Miles, Edward
Diamond Entertainment, Joel
Esquire International
Final Mix Music
Janoulis Productions, Alexander/Big Al Jano Productions
Jump Productions
KMA
Mac-Attack Productions
Makers Mark Music Productions
Mega Truth Records
Merlin Productions
Mona Lisa Records/Bristol
Monticana Productions
Neu Electro Productions
Panio Brothers Label
Poku Productions
Prejippie Music Group
Prescription Co., The
Road Records
Studio Voodoo Music
Weisman Production Group, The
Westwires Digital USA
Y-N-A/C.D.T. Productions

Folk (also acoustic, Celtic, etc.)
Birthplace Productions
Gallway Bay Music
Magid Productions, Lee
Marenco, Cookie
Monticana Productions
Rustron Music Productions
Sound Works Entertainment Productions Inc.
Swift River Productions

Theoretical Reality
Westwires Digital USA
World Records

Instrumental (also background music, musical scores, etc.)
Eternal Song Agency, The
Jump Productions
Lark Talent & Advertising
Magid Productions, Lee
Mega Truth Records
Road Records
Swift River Productions
Texas Fantasy Music Group

Jazz (also fusion, bebop, swing, etc.)
Allyn, Stuart J.
Angel Films Company
Appell Productions, Inc., Jonathan
Bal Records
Candyspiteful Productions
Celt Musical Services, Jan
DAP Entertainment
De Miles, Edward
Esquire International
Haworth Productions
Heart Consort Music
Jag Studio, Ltd.
Landmark Communications Group
Magid Productions, Lee
Magnetic Oblivion Music Co.
Marenco, Cookie
Mona Lisa Records/Bristol
Monticana Productions
Pacific North Studios Ltd.
Philly Breakdown Recording Co.
Prescription Co., The
R&D Productions
Studio Seven
Tamjam Productions
Tari, Roger Vincent
Vickers Music Association, Charles
Wilbur Productions
Willson, Frank
World Records

Latin (also Spanish, salsa, Cuban, conga, Brazilian, cumbja, rancheras, Mexican, merengue, Tejano, Tex Mex, etc.)
DeLory and Music Makers, Al
Dixon III, Philip D., Attorney at Law
Satkowski Recordings, Steve
Tamjam Productions

New Age (also ambient)
Big Sky Audio Productions
Haworth Productions
Heart Consort Music

Neu Electro Productions
New Vizion Studios, The
Rustron Music Productions
Sphere Group One

Novelty (also comedy, humor, etc.)
Jay Jay Publishing & Record Co.
Linear Cycle Productions
Magnetic Oblivion Music Co.
Segal's Productions
Theoretical Reality
TMC Productions

Pop (also top 40, top 100, popular, chart hits, etc.)
"A" Major Sound Corporation
Aberdeen Productions
ACR Productions
Alco Productions
Allyn, Stuart J.
Angel Films Company
Appell Productions, Inc., Jonathan
Bal Records
Blues Alley Records
Candyspiteful Productions
Coachouse Music
Coffee and Cream Productions
De Miles, Edward
DeLory and Music Makers, Al
Diamond Entertainment, Joel
Esquire International
Eternal Song Agency, The
Final Mix Music
Gallway Bay Music
Janoulis Productions, Alexander/Big Al Jano Productions
Jay Bird Productions
JSB Groupe Management Inc.
Jump Productions
June Productions Ltd.
Kane Producer/Engineer, Karen
Kingston Records and Talent
Known Artist Productions
Kovach, Robert R.
Landmark Communications Group
Linear Cycle Productions
Mac-Attack Productions
Magid Productions, Lee
Marenco, Cookie
Martin, Pete/Vaam Music Productions
Mathews, d/b/a Hit or Myth Productions, Scott
Merlin Productions
Moffet, Gary
Mona Lisa Records/Bristol
Monticana Productions
Musicland Productions, Inc.
Neu Electro Productions
New Experience Records

New Vizion Studios, The
Ormsby, John "Buck"/Etiquette Productions
Pacific North Studios Ltd.
Philly Breakdown Recording Co.
Poku Productions
Prescription Co., The
Rainbow Recording
Reel Adventures
Rustron Music Productions
SAS Productions/Hit Records Network
Segal's Productions
Silver Thunder Music Group
Sound Arts Recording Studio
Sound Works Entertainment Productions Inc.
Sphere Group One
Studio Voodoo Music
Syndicate Sound, Inc.
Tamjam Productions
Tari, Roger Vincent
Valtec Productions
Vickers Music Association, Charles
Weisman Production Group, The
WLM Music/Recording
Wytas Productions, Steve

R&B (also soul, black, urban, etc.)
"A" Major Sound Corporation
ACR Productions
Allyn, Stuart J.
Angel Films Company
Appell Productions, Inc., Jonathan
Avalon Productions
Bal Records
Big Sky Audio Productions
Candyspiteful Productions
Celt Musical Services, Jan
Coffee and Cream Productions
Cupit Productions, Jerry
DAP Entertainment
De Miles, Edward
Diamond Entertainment, Joel
Esquire International
Final Mix Music
Hailing Frequency Music Productions
Haworth Productions
Janoulis Productions, Alexander/Big Al Jano Productions
Kane Producer/Engineer, Karen
KMA
Known Artist Productions
Kovach, Robert R.
L.A. Entertainment, Inc.
Lazy Bones Productions/Recordings, Inc.
Linear Cycle Productions
Magid Productions, Lee
Makers Mark Music Productions
Martin, Pete/Vaam Music Productions
Merlin Productions

Mona Lisa Records/Bristol
Monticana Productions
New Experience Records
New Vizion Studios, The
Ormsby, John "Buck"/Etiquette Productions
Philly Breakdown Recording Co.
Prejippie Music Group
Prescription Co., The
Rainbow Recording
Rustron Music Productions
Segal's Productions
Shu'Baby Montez Music
Silver Thunder Music Group
Syndicate Sound, Inc.
Tamjam Productions
Vickers Music Association, Charles
Weisman Production Group, The
Westwires Digital USA
Y-N-A/C.D.T. Productions

Rap (also hip-hop, bass, etc.)
Avalon Productions
Dixon III, Philip D., Attorney at Law
Final Mix Music
KMA
Makers Mark Music Productions
Marenco, Cookie
Neu Electro Productions
New Experience Records
Philly Breakdown Recording Co.
Poku Productions
R&D Productions
Shu'Baby Montez Music
Syndicate Sound, Inc.
Weisman Production Group, The

Religious (also gospel, sacred, Christian, church, hymns, praise, inspirational, worship, etc.)
"A" Major Sound Corporation
ACR Productions
Alco Productions
Avalon Productions
Bal Records
Birthplace Productions
Blues Alley Records
Coffee and Cream Productions
Cupit Productions, Jerry
DAP Entertainment
Doss Presents, Col. Buster
Eiffert, Jr., Leo J.
Esquire International
Eternal Song Agency, The
Hailing Frequency Music Productions
Haworth Productions
Jay Jay Publishing & Record Co.
Kovach, Robert R.
Landmark Communications Group

Lari-Jon Productions
Linear Cycle Productions
Luick & Country Music Showcase Intl. Associates, Harold
Magid Productions, Lee
Makers Mark Music Productions
Mittelstedt, A.V.
Monticana Productions
Musicland Productions, Inc.
New Experience Records
Philly Breakdown Recording Co.
Silver Thunder Music Group
Syndicate Sound, Inc.
Trac Record Co.
Trinity Studio, The
Vickers Music Association, Charles
Weisman Production Group, The
WLM Music/Recording

Rock (also rockabilly, AOR, rock 'n' roll, etc.)
"A" Major Sound Corporation
Aberdeen Productions
ACR Productions
Alco Productions
Allyn, Stuart J.
Angel Films Company
Appell Productions, Inc., Jonathan
Avalon Productions
Baird Enterprises, Ron
Bal Records
Big Sky Audio Productions
Candyspiteful Productions
Celt Musical Services, Jan
Coachouse Music
Collector Records
Craig, Douglas
Cupit Productions, Jerry
Diamond Entertainment, Joel
Dixon III, Philip D., Attorney at Law
Esquire International
Hailing Frequency Music Productions
Haworth Productions
Integrated Entertainment
Jag Studio, Ltd.
Janoulis Productions, Alexander/Big Al Jano Productions
Jay Bird Productions
John Productions, David
JSB Groupe Management Inc.
June Productions Ltd.
Kingston Records and Talent
Kovach, Robert R.

Landmark Communications Group
Lari-Jon Productions
Lazy Bones Productions/Recordings, Inc.
Linear Cycle Productions
Magid Productions, Lee
Mathews, d/b/a Hit or Myth Productions, Scott
Mega Truth Records
Mittelstedt, A.V.
Moffet, Gary
Mona Lisa Records/Bristol
Monticana Productions
Neu Electro Productions
New Experience Records
New Vizion Studios, The
Ormsby, John "Buck"/Etiquette Productions
Poku Productions
Prejippie Music Group
Prescription Co., The
Rainbow Recording
R&D Productions
Reel Adventures
Rustron Music Productions
SAS Productions/Hit Records Network
Segal's Productions
Silver Thunder Music Group
Sound Arts Recording Studio
Sound Works Entertainment Productions Inc.
Sphere Group One
Studio Seven
Swift River Productions
Syndicate Sound, Inc.
Theoretical Reality
TMC Productions
Valtec Productions
Vickers Music Association, Charles
Weisman Production Group, The
Wilbur Productions
Willson, Frank
WLM Music/Recording
Wytas Productions, Steve
Y-N-A/C.D.T. Productions

World Music (also reggae, ethnic, calypso, international, world beat, etc.)
Appell Productions, Inc., Jonathan
Craig, Douglas
Kane Producer/Engineer, Karen
KMA
Pacific North Studios Ltd.
Reel Adventures
Studio Seven
Tari, Roger Vincent
Vickers Music Association, Charles

Managers & Booking Agents

Before submitting to a manager or booking agent, be sure you know exactly what you need. If you're looking for someone to help you with performance opportunities, the booking agency is the one to contact. They can help you book shows either in your local area or throughout the country. If you're looking for someone to help guide your career, you need to contact a management firm. Some management firms may also handle booking; however, it may be in your best interest to look for a separate booking agency. A manager should be your manager—not your agent, publisher, lawyer or accountant.

MANAGERS

Of all the music industry players surrounding successful artists, managers are usually the people closest to the artists themselves. The artist manager can be a valuable contact, both for the songwriter trying to get songs to a particular artist and for the songwriter/performer. A manager and his connections can be invaluable in securing the right publishing deal or recording contract if the writer is also an artist. Getting songs to an artist's manager is yet another way to get your songs recorded, since the manager may play a large part in deciding what material his client uses. For the performer seeking management, a successful manager should be thought of as the foundation for a successful career.

The relationship between a manager and his client relies on mutual trust. A manager works as the liaison between you and the rest of the music industry, and he must know exactly what you want out of your career in order to help you achieve your goals. His handling of publicity, promotion and finances, as well as the contacts he has within the industry, can make or break your career. You should never be afraid to ask questions about any aspect of the relationship between you and a prospective manager. Always remember that a manager works *for the artist*. A good manager is able to communicate his opinions to you without reservation, and should be willing to explain any confusing terminology or discuss plans with you before taking action. A manager needs to be able to communicate successfully with all segments of the music industry in order to get his client the best deals possible. He needs to be able to work with booking agents, publishers, lawyers and record companies. Keep in mind that you are both working together toward a common goal: success for you and your songs. Talent, originality, professionalism and a drive to succeed are qualities that will attract a manager to an artist—and a songwriter.

BOOKING AGENTS

The function of the booking agent is to find performance venues for their clients. They usually represent many more acts than a manager does, and have less contact with their acts. A booking agent charges a commission for his services, as does a manager. Managers usually ask for a 15-

---

Additional Managers & Booking Agents

There are **MORE MANAGERS & BOOKING AGENTS** located in other sections of the book! On page 335 use the list of Additional Managers & Booking Agents to find listings within other sections who are also managers/booking agents.

20% commission on an act's earnings; booking agents usually charge around 10%. In the area of managers and booking agents, more successful acts can negotiate lower percentage deals than the ones set forth above.

SUBMITTING MATERIAL TO MANAGERS & BOOKING AGENTS

The firms listed in this section have provided information about the types of music they work with and the types of acts they represent. You'll want to refer to the Category Index at the end of this section to find out which companies deal with the type of music you write, and the Geographic Index at the back of the book to help you locate companies near where you live. Then determine whether they are open to your level of experience (see the Openness to Submissions sidebar on page 8). Each listing also contains submission requirements and information about what items to include in a press kit and will also specify whether the company is a management firm or a booking agency. Remember that your submission represents you as an artist, and should be as organized and professional as possible.

For More Information

For more instructional information on the listings in this book, including explanations of symbols (𝕹 ✔ ☑ ☒ ⊕ ◯ ◔ ◖ ◑), read the article How to Use *Songwriter's Market* to Get Your Songs Heard on page 5.

◯ AFTERSCHOOL PUBLISHING COMPANY, P.O. Box 14157, Detroit MI 48214. (313)894-8855. President: Herman Kelly. Manager: Genesis Act. Management firm, booking agency, record company (Afterschool Co.) and music publisher (Afterschool Pub. Co.). Estab. 1978. Represents individual artists, songwriters, producers, arrangers and musicians from anywhere; currently handles 20 acts. Reviews material for acts.
How to Contact: Submit demo tape by mail. Unsolicited submissions are OK. Prefers cassette with 3 songs and lyric or lead sheet. If seeking management, include cover letter, résumé, proposal, photo, demo tape, lyric sheets, press clippings, video and bio in press kit. SASE. Responds in 2 weeks.
Music: Mostly **pop**, **jazz**, **rap**, **country** and **folk**. Works primarily with small bands and solo artists. Current acts include L.L. Cool J, P.M. Dawn, Miss Jones, Whodini, Kinsui, KC and Jimmy B. Horne, T Baby, MC Hammer, Beats International, Cut N Move, Fresh Prince and Jazzy Jeff, 2 Hype, Brothers and a Dog, Brownstone, 2 Live Crew/Luke, Rockman and Gloria Estefan & Miami Sound Machine.

☑ ◖ AIR TIGHT MANAGEMENT, 115 West Rd., P.O. Box 113, Winchester Center CT 06094. (860)738-9139. Fax: (860)738-9135. E-mail: mainoffice@airtightmanagement.com. Website: www.airtightmanagement.com. **Contact:** Jack Forchette, president. A&R: Scott Fairchild. Management firm. Estab. 1969. Represents individual artists, groups or songwriters from anywhere; currently handles 6 acts. Receives 15-20% commission. Reviews material for acts.
How to Contact: *Write first and obtain permission to submit.* Prefers cassette or VHS videocassette. If seeking management, press kit should include photos, bio and recorded material. "Follow up with a fax, not a phone call." Does not return material. Responds in 2 weeks.
Music: Mostly **rock**, **country** and **jazz**. Current acts include Johnny Colla (songwriter/producer, and guitarist/songwriter for Huey Lewis and the News), Jason Scheff (lead singer/songwriter for the

---

REMEMBER: Don't "shotgun" your demo tapes. Submit only to companies interested in the type of music you write. For more submission hints, refer to Getting Started on page 10.

group "Chicago"), Gary Burr (Nashville songwriter/producer), Cassandra Reed (R&B/pop singer/ songwriter), Nathan East (singer/songwriter/bassist—Eric Clapton, Michael Jackson, Madonna, 4-Play and others) and Peter Mayer (guitarist, singer/songwriter for Jimmy Buffett's band).

N ♫ ⊘ ALERT MUSIC INC., 41 Britain St., Suite 305, Toronto Ontario M5A 1R7 Canada. (416)364-4200. Fax: (416)364-8632. E-mail: contact@alertmusic.com. Website: www.alertmusic.c om. **Contact:** W. Tom Berry, president. Management firm, record company and recording artist. Represents local and regional individual artists and groups; currently handles 4 acts. Receives 15% commission. Reviews material for acts.
How to Contact: Write first and obtain permission to submit. Prefers cassette or CD. If seeking management, press kit should include finished CD or 3-4 song cassette, photo, press clippings and bio. SASE.
Music: All types. Works primarily with bands and singer/songwriters. Current acts include Holly Cole (pop vocalist), Kim Mitchell (rock singer/songwriter), Johnny Favourite Swing Orchestra (swing band) and Bet E and Stef (bossanova).

⊘ ALL STAR MANAGEMENT, 1229 S. Prospect St., Marion OH 43302-7267. (740)382-5939. E-mail: allstarmanage@msn.com. **Contact:** John Simpson, president. Management firm. Estab. 1980. Represents individual artists, groups and songwriters from anywhere; currently handles 9 acts. Receives 20% commission. Reviews material for acts.
How to Contact: Submit demo tape by mail. Unsolicited submissions are OK. Prefers cassette or videocassette with 3 songs and lyric or lead sheet. If seeking management, press kit should include audio cassette with 3 songs, bio, 8 × 10 photo or any information or articles written about yourself or group, and video if you have one. Does not return material. Responds in 2 months.
Music: Mostly **country**, **Christian**, **adult contemporary** and **smooth jazz**. Works primarily with bands and singers/songwriters. Current acts include Patricia Hoch (singer/songwriter, adult contemporary), Allen Austin (singer/songwriter, country) and Kenney Polson (songwriter/musician, smooth jazz).

✓ ⊘ ALL STAR TALENT AGENCY, P.O. Box 717, White House TN 37188. (615)643-4208. Fax: (615)643-2228. **Contact:** Joyce Kirby, owner/agent. Booking agency. Estab. 1966. Represents professional individuals, groups and songwriters; currently handles 6 acts. Receives 15% commission. Reviews material for acts.
How to Contact: Submit demo tape by mail. Unsolicited submissions are OK. Prefers cassette or VHS videocassette with 4 songs (can be cover songs) and lead sheet. If seeking management, press kit should include bios, cover letter, press clippings, demo and photos. Does not return material. Responds in 1 month.
Music: Mostly **country**; also **bluegrass**, **gospel**, **MOR**, **rock (country)** and **top 40/pop**. Works primarily with dance, show and bar bands, vocalists, club acts and concerts. Current acts include Alex Houston (MOR), Chris Hartley (country) and Jack Greene (country).

✓ ▣ ⊘ AMERICAN ARTISTS ENTERTAINMENT, 21 Chews Landing Rd., Clementon NJ 08021-3843. (856)566-1232. Fax: (856)435-7453. E-mail: ardept@aaeg.com. Website: www.aaeg.c om. **Contact:** A&R Department. Management firm, music publisher (David Music, BMI), record company (East Coast Records) and record and motion picture distribution. Represents individual artists, groups, actors and models from anywhere; currently handles 3 acts. Receives 20% commission. Reviews material for acts.
How to Contact: Submit demo tape by mail. Unsolicited submissions are OK. Prefers cassette, videocassette or CD with 3 songs. If seeking management, press kit should include bio, press releases, photos, performing, training and background. SASE. Responds in 1 month.
Music: Mostly **R&B**, **top 40** and **rap**; also **modern** and motion picture scores. Current acts include The Blue Notes (R&B), The Trammps (disco), Benjamin Falk (pop singer) and Derrick Simmons (actor/rapper).

✓ ⊘ AMERICAN INDEPENDENT ARTISTS, (formerly Sirius Entertainment), 13531 Clairmont Way #8, Oregon City OR 97045-8450. Phone/fax: (503)657-1813. E-mail: danblair@home.c

om. Website: www.danblair.com. **Contact:** Dan Blair, owner. Management firm and booking agency. Estab. 1991. Represents individual artists and/or groups and songwriters from anywhere; currently handles 65 acts. Receives 10-15% commission. Reviews material for acts.
How to Contact: Submit demo tape by mail. Unsolicited submissions are OK. Prefers cassette with 3 songs and lyric sheet. If seeking management, press kit should include cover letter, bio, 8×10 photo, résumé, CD or cassette, video if available, copies of press clippings and a list of past performances and credits. "Résumé should include total career progress from beginning with all schooling listed." SASE. Responds in 5 weeks.
Music: Mostly **R&B** and **rock**; also **jazz**, **blues**, **classical** and **country**. Current acts include Christopher Loid (country), Mac Charles (A/C rock) and Dorothy Moore (R&B).
Tips: "If you can't afford the services of a good studio and good studio musicians to play your material, then use one acoustic instrument (guitar or piano). Send lyric sheet with original material."

ANDERSON ASSOCIATES COMMUNICATIONS GROUP, 9291 NW 13th Place, Coral Spring FL 33071. (954)753-5440. Fax: (954)753-9715. E-mail: rjppny@aol.com. Website: http://andersonassociates.com. **Contact:** Richard Papaleo, CEO. Management firm. Estab. 1992. Represents individual artists and groups "only on the East Coast of the US." Currently handles 3 acts. Receives 20% commission. Reviews material for acts.
How to Contact: *Call first and obtain permission to submit.* Submit demo tape by mail. "Call before submitting package." Prefers cassette, bio and/or picture with 3 songs and lead sheet. If seeking management, press kit should include cassette with 3 songs (video OK), bio, cover letter and picture. Does not return material. Responds in 2 months.
Music: Mostly **R&B**, **pop/dance** and **pop/rock**; also **A/C**, **pop/mainstream** and **mainstream rock**. Current acts include Josie D'ambola, Joyce Sims (R&B/dance) and Jim Walsh (pop/rock).

ARDENNE INT'L INC., 1800 Argyle St., Suite 444, Halifax, Nova Scotia B3J 3N8 Canada. (902)492-8000. Fax: (902)423-2143. E-mail: mardenne@ardenneinternational.com. Website: www.ArdenneInternational.com. **Contact:** Michael Ardenne, president. Management firm. Estab. 1988. Represents local, individual artists and songwriters from anywhere; currently handles 2 acts. Receives 20-25% commission. Reviews material for acts.
How to Contact: Write, call or fax first and obtain permission to submit. Prefers cassette with lyric sheet. "Put name, address, phone number and song list on the tape. Send maximum 3 songs." If seeking management, press kit should include cover letter, bio, photo, demo tape/CD, lyric sheets and video. Does not return material. Responds in 2 months.
Music: Mostly **country**, **pop** and **soft rock**. Works primarily with vocalists/songwriters. Current acts include Kris Taylor (pop/rock) and Kim Gould (country).
Tips: "Periodically we get asked to search for country material for independent artists."

BACCHUS GROUP PRODUCTIONS, LTD., 5701 N. Sheridan Rd., Suite 8-U, Chicago IL 60660. (773)334-1532. Fax: (773)334-1531. E-mail: bacchusgrp@compuserve.com. Website: www.BacchusGroup.com. **Contact:** D. Maximilian, managing director and executive producer. Senior Vice President: M. Margarida Rainho. Management firm and record producer (D. Maximilian). Estab. 1990. Represents individual artists or groups from anywhere; currently handles 9 acts. Receives 15-25% commission. Reviews material for acts.
How to Contact: *Does not accept unsolicited submissions.*
Music: Mostly **pop**, **R&B/soul** and **jazz**; also **Latin** and **world beat**. Works primarily with singer/songwriters, composers, arrangers, bands and orchestras. Current acts include Orchestra of the Americas (international dance orchestra), Sorcerers of Swing (big band jazz dance orchestra) and Samba Samba 2000 (Carnival/Mardi Gras worldbeat dance orchestra).

BARNARD MANAGEMENT SERVICES (BMS), 228 Main St., Suite 3, Venice CA 90291. (310)399-8886. Fax: (310)450-0470. E-mail: bms@barnardus.com. **Contact:** Russell Barnard, president. Management firm. Estab. 1979. Represents artists, groups and songwriters; currently handles 2 acts. Receives 10-20% commission. Reviews material for acts.

How to Contact: *Write first and obtain permission to submit.* Prefers cassette with 3-10 songs and lead sheet. Artists may submit VHS videocassette (15-30 minutes) by permission only. If seeking management, press kit should include cover letter, bio, photo, demo tape/CD, lyric sheets, press clippings, video and résumé. Does not return material. Responds in 2 months.

Music: Mostly **country crossover**, **blues**, **country**, **R&B**, **rock** and **soul**. Current acts include Mark Shipper (songwriter/author) and Sally Rose (R&B band).

Tips: "Semi-produced demos are of little value. Either save the time and money by submitting material 'in the raw,' or do a finished production version."

✔ ◯ **BASSLINE ENTERTAINMENT, INC.**, P.O. Box 2394, New York NY 10185. (212)769-6956. E-mail: newbassinc@aol.com. Website: www.basslineinc.com. **Contact:** Clarence Williams, vice president. Senior Consultant for Artist Development: Sharon Williams. General Manager: Sincir Johnson. Management firm. Estab. 1993. Represents local and regional individual artists, groups and songwriters. Receives 20-25% commission. Reviews material for acts.

How to Contact: Submit demo tape by mail. Unsolicited submissions are OK. Prefers cassette, CD or VHS videocassette. If seeking management, press kit should include cover letter, press clippings, bio, demo (cassette, CD or VHS video), picture and accurate contact telephone number. SASE. Responds in 3 weeks.

Music: Mostly **pop**, **R&B**, **club/dance** and **hip-hop/rap**; some **Latin**. Works primarily with singer/songwriters, producers, rappers and bands. Current acts include Michael Anthony (Latin pop), Skandalus (rap) and Sincir (rap).

◖ **BIG J PRODUCTIONS**, 2516 S. Sugar Ridge, Laplace LA 70068. (504)652-2645. **Contact:** Frankie Jay, agent. Booking agency. Estab. 1968. Represents individual artists, groups and songwriters; currently handles over 50 acts. Receives 15-25% commission. Reviews material for acts.

How to Contact: Call first and obtain permission to submit. Prefers cassette or VHS videocassette with 3-6 songs and lyric or lead sheet. "It would be best for an artist to lip-sync to a prerecorded track. The object is for someone to see how an artist would perform more than simply assessing song content." Artists seeking management should include pictures, biography, tape or CD and video. Does not return material. Responds in 2 weeks.

Music: Mostly **rock**, **pop** and **R&B**. Works primarily with groups with self-contained songwriters. Current acts include Zebra (original rock group), Crowbar (heavy metal) and Kyper (original dance).

✔ ◯ **BLACK STALLION COUNTRY, INC.**, P.O. Box 368, Tujunga CA 91043. (818)352-8142. Fax: (818)364-1250. E-mail: kenn.king@verizon.net. **Contact:** Kenn E. Kingsbury, Jr., president. Management firm, production company and music publisher (Black Stallion Country Publishing/BMI). Estab. 1979. Represents individual artists from anywhere; currently handles 20 acts. Receives 15-20% commission. Reviews material for acts.

How to Contact: Submit demo tape by mail. Unsolicited submissions are OK. Prefers cassette with 3 songs and lyric sheet. If seeking management, press kit should include picture/résumé and audio and/or video tape. "I would also like a one-page statement of goals and why you would be an asset to my company or me." SASE. Responds in 2 months.

Music: Mostly **country**, **R&B** and **A/C**. Works primarily with country acts, variety acts and film/TV pictures/actors. Current acts include Lane Brody (singer country), Thom Bresh (musician), Barbara Nickell (film/TV actress), B.J. Thomas, Jerry Reed and Peter Breck.

◖ **BLACKGROUND**, 14724 Ventura Blvd., Suite 440, Sherman Oaks CA 91403. (818)995-4683. Fax: (818)995-4398. **Contact:** Gio Hallah, A&R. Management firm and record company. Estab. 1993. Represents individual artists, groups, songwriters and producers from anywhere; currently handles 4 acts. Reviews material for acts.

How to Contact: Call first and obtain permission to submit. Prefers cassette or DAT with 3 or 4 songs. If seeking management or record deal, press kit should include picture, bio, 3 or 4 songs, name and contact number on cassette or DAT. Does not return material. Responds in 3 weeks.

Music: Mostly **R&B**, **hip hop** and **gospel**. Works primarily with songwriters/producers, musicians. Current acts include R. Kelly (R&B singer, producer and songwriter), Aaliyah (R&B singer) and The Winans (gospel singers, producers and songwriters).

Tips: "Submit complete songs with original music. Emphasis should be on strong hooks with commercial R&B appeal."

☑ ◑ **BLANK & BLANK**, 1 Belmont Ave., Suite 320, Bala Cynwyd PA 19004-1604. (610)664-8200. Fax: (610)664-8201. **Contact:** E. Robert Blank, manager. Management firm. Represents individual artists and groups. Reviews material for acts.
How to Contact: *Contact first and obtain permission to submit.* Prefers videocassette. If seeking management, press kit should include cover letter, demo tape/CD and video. Does not return material.

◑ **BLOWIN' SMOKE PRODUCTIONS/RECORDS**, 7438 Shoshone Ave., Van Nuys CA 91406-2340. (818)881-9888. Fax: (818)881-0555. E-mail: blowinsmokeband@ktb.net. Website: www.blowinsmokeband.com. **Contact:** Larry Knight, president. Management firm and record producer. Estab. 1990. Represents local and West Coast individual artists and groups; currently handles 7 acts. Receives 15-20% commission. Reviews material for acts.
How to Contact: *Write or call first and obtain permission to submit.* Prefers cassette or CD. If seeking management, press kit should include cover letter, demo tape/CD, lyric sheets, press clippings, video if available, photo, bios, contact telephone numbers and any info on legal commitments already in place. SASE. Responds in 1 month.
Music: Mostly **R&B**, **blues** and **blues-rock**. Works primarily with single and group vocalists and a few R&B/blues bands. Current acts include Larry "Fuzzy" Knight (blues singer/songwriter), King Floyd (R&B artist), The Blowin' Smoke Rhythm & Blues Band and The Fabulous Smokettes.

◑ **THE BLUE CAT AGENCY**, P.O. Box 4036, San Rafael CA 94913-4036. Phone/fax: (415)507-9722. E-mail: klkindig@marin.k12.ca.us. Website: http://web.csuchico.edu/~klkindig/bluecat.html. **Contact:** Karen Kindig, owner/agent. Management firm and booking agency. Estab. 1989. Represents individual artists and/or groups from anywhere; currently handles 2 acts. Receives 10-15% commission. Reviews material for acts.
How to Contact: *E-mail only for permission to submit.* Prefers cassette or CD. If seeking management, press kit should include demo, CD or tape, bio, press clippings and photo. SASE. Responds in 2 months.
Music: Mostly **rock/pop "en español."** Works primarily with bands. Current acts include Dermis Tatú (rock-en-español) and La Muda (rock-en-español).

◐ **BLUE WAVE PRODUCTIONS**, 3221 Perryville Rd., Baldwinsville NY 13027. (315)638-4286. Fax: (315)635-4757. **Contact:** Greg Spencer, owner/president. Management firm, music publisher (G.W. Spencer Music/ASCAP), record company (Blue Wave Records) and record producer (Blue Wave Productions). Estab. 1985. Represents individual artists and/or groups and songwriters from anywhere; currently handles 5 acts. Receives 10% commission. Reviews material for acts.
How to Contact: Submit demo tape by mail. Unsolicited submissions are OK. Prefers cassette or VHS videocassette with 3-6 songs. "Just the music first, reviews and articles are OK. No photos or lyrics until later." If seeking management, press kit should include cover letter and demo tape/CD. SASE. Responds in 1 month.
Music: Mostly **blues**, **blues/rock** and **roots rock**. Current acts include Kim Lembo (female blues vocalist), Kim Simmonds (blues guitarist and singer/songwriter) and Downchild Bluesband (blues).
Tips: "I'm looking for great singers with soul. Not interested in pop/rock commercial material."

◑ **BOUQUET-ORCHID ENTERPRISES**, P.O. Box 1335, Norcross GA 30091. (770)814-2420. **Contact:** Bill Bohannon, president. Management firm, booking agency, music publisher (Orchid Publishing/BMI) and record company (Bouquet Records). Represents individuals and groups; currently handles 4 acts. Receives 10-15% commission. Reviews material for acts.
How to Contact: Submit demo tape by mail. Unsolicited submissions are OK. Prefers cassette, CD or videocassette with 3-5 songs, song list and lyric sheet. Include brief résumé. If seeking management, press kit should include current photograph, 2-3 media clippings, description of act, and background information on act. SASE. Responds in 1 month.

Music: Mostly **country**, **rock** and **top 40/pop**; also **gospel** and **R&B**. Works primarily with vocalists and groups. Current acts include Susan Spencer, Jamey Wells, Adam Day and the Bandoleers.

◑ BROTHERS MANAGEMENT ASSOCIATES, 141 Dunbar Ave., Fords NJ 08863. (732)738-0880. Fax: (732)738-0970. E-mail: bmaent@cs.com. Website: www.bmaent.com. **Contact:** Allen A. Faucera, president. Management firm and booking agency. Estab. 1972. Represents artists, groups and songwriters; currently handles 25 acts. Receives 15-20% commission. Reviews material for acts.
How to Contact: *Write first and obtain permission to submit.* Prefers cassette/CD or VHS videocassette with 3-6 songs and lyric sheets. Include photographs and résumé. If seeking management, include photo, bio, tape and return envelope in press kit. SASE. Responds in 2 months.
Music: Mostly **pop**, **rock**, **MOR** and **R&B**. Works primarily with vocalists and established groups. Current acts include Waterfront (R&B), Glen Burtnik (pop rock) and Alisha (pop/dance).
Tips: "Submit very commercial material—make demo of high quality."

N ◯ BILL BUTLER MUSIC, P.O. Box 20, Hondo TX 78861-0020. Phone/fax: (830)426-2112. E-mail: bpbutler@aol.com. Owner: Bill Butler. Management firm and music publisher. Estab. 1982. Represents regional (Texas) individual artists, groups and songwriters; currently handles 2 acts. Receives 15% commission. Reviews material for acts.
   • Bill Butler Music only handles artists from Texas. They have received a special Citation of Achievement from BMI for National Popularity of "Baby Blue" and "Love Without End, Amen" by George Strait.
How to Contact: Submit demo tape by mail. Unsolicited submissions are OK. Prefers cassette with 3 songs and lyric sheet. If seeking management, press kit should include bio, photo, tape or CD with 5 unreleased songs. "No cover tunes please." Does not return material. Responds in 3 months only if interested.
Music: Mostly **country**, **R&B** and **tejano**. Works primarily with singer/songwriters, groups and songwriters. Current acts include Rick Reyna (country) and Keith Lutz (country).
Tips: "Send quality demos that allow the lyric to be clearly understood. Include lyric sheets. Make sure your name, address and phone number are on both tape and J-card. Don't try to contact us—we will contact you if we're interested."

⊕ ◑ BUXTON WALKER P/L, (formerly Mr. Walker's Company), P.O. Box 2197, St. Kilda West, Vic 3182 Australia. Phone: (+61)3 9537-7155. Fax: (+61)3 9537-7166. E-mail: andrew@buxt onwalker.com. Website: www.buxtonwalker.com. **Contact:** Andrew Walker. Management firm, music publisher (Head Records Publishing) and record company (Head Records). Estab. 1995. Represents individual artists and groups from anywhere; currently handles 5 acts. Management company receives 20% commission.
How to Contact: Submit demo tape by mail. Unsolicited submissions are OK. Cassette or CD only. If seeking management, press kit should include CD, bio and history. "Processing takes time. Contact by fax or e-mail is best as it allows for time differences to be no obstacle." SAE and IRC. Responds in 2 months.
Music: Mostly **rock/pop**, **jazz** and **acoustic**; also **reggae**, **blues** and **world**. Works primarily with singers/songwriters and bands. Current acts include The Jaynes (rock), Black Sorrows (blues and jazz), The Revelators (blues), Tess McKenna (alt rock) and Jen Anderson (scores).
Tips: "We have low need for songs to be supplied to our artists. We are mostly interested in recorded artists/writers looking for distribution/release in Australia/New Zealand."

▼ ◑ CAPITAL ENTERTAINMENT, 1201 N St., N.W. #A, Washington DC 20005. (202)986-0693. Fax: (202)986-7992. E-mail: youngvince@capitalentertainment.com. Website: www.capital

---

LISTINGS OF COMPANIES within this section which are either commercial music production houses or music libraries will have that information printed in **boldface** type.

entertainment.com. **Contact:** Vincent Young, co-founder. Music publisher and public relations firm/entertainment services. Estab. 1996. Represents individual artists, groups or songwriters from anywhere; currently handles 20 acts. Receives 15-20% commission. Reviews material for acts.

• This company manages CeCe Winans, nine-time Grammy winner.

How to Contact: Submit demo tape by mail. Unsolicited submissions are OK. Prefers cassette and lyric sheet. "Not accepting management submissions." SASE. Responds in 3 weeks.

Music: Mostly **gospel** and **pop**. Current acts include CeCe Winans (gospel singer), Candi Staton (legendary soul singer of "Young Hearts Run Free" fame), Edwin Hawkins (gospel singer), Rob Kensly (singer) and The Staple Singers (soul/gospel group who were inducted into the Rock & Roll Hall of Fame, March 1999).

Tips: "Learn as much as you can. Read about the music industry."

CBA ARTISTS, P.O. Box 1495, Hilversum Netherlands 1200BL. Phone: (31)35 683 0515. Fax: (31)35 683 57 59. E-mail: dex_wessels@cba.nl. Website: www.cbaartists.ne. Management firm, booking agency and music publisher (Altitude Music). Estab. 1982. Represents individual artists, groups or songwriters from anywhere; currently handles 10 acts. Commission varies. Reviews material for acts.

How to Contact: *Write or call first and obtain permission to submit a demo.* Prefers CD or videocassette with 5 songs and lyric and lead sheet. If seeking management, press kit should include bio, photo, reviews. Does not return material. Responds in 2 weeks.

Music: Mostly **dance**. Current acts include Nance (singer/host), Bob Fosk (singer/actor/host) and E'velyne (singer).

CHUCKER MUSIC INC., 345 E. 80th St., 15H, New York NY 10021. Fax: (212)879-9621. E-mail: chuckermusic@earthlink.net. Website: www.musiccounselor.com. **Contact:** Chuck Dembrak, president. Management firm, music publisher (Cool 1) and record producer (Chuck Dembrak). Estab. 1984. Represents individual artists, groups and songwriters from anywhere; currently handles 5 acts. Receives 20% commission. Reviews material for acts.

How to Contact: *Write first and obtain permission to submit.* Prefers cassette, VHS videocassette or CD. If seeking management, press kit should include cover letter, bio, demo tape/CD, press clippings, video and photos. Does not return material. Responds in 2 months.

Music: Mostly **R&B**, **top 40** and **dance**; also **jazz**, **rock** and **A/C**. Works primarily with singer/songwriters. Current acts include Kim Waters (jazz), Dr. Zoot (swing), Louis Love (rock) and GAB (rap).

CIRCUIT RIDER TALENT & MANAGEMENT CO., 123 Walton Ferry Rd., Hendersonville TN 37075. (615)824-1947. Fax: (615)264-0462. E-mail: circuitridertalent@usa.net. **Contact:** Linda S. Dotson, president. UK office: 45 Gladstone Road, Melrose Villa House, Watford, Herts WD1 2RA UK. Phone: 011-44-1923-819415. Consultation firm, booking agency and music publisher (Channel Music, Cordial Music). Represents individual artists, songwriters and actors; currently handles 8 acts. Works with a large number of recording artists, songwriters, actors, producers. (Includes multi Grammy-winning producer/writer Skip Scarborough.) Receives 10-15% commission (union rates). Reviews material for acts (free of charge).

How to Contact: *Write or call first and obtain permission to submit.* Prefers cassette or videocassette with 3 songs and lyric sheet. If seeking consultation, press kit should include bio, cover letter, résumé, lyric sheets if original songs, photo and tape with 3 songs. Videocassettes required of artist's submissions. SASE. Responds in 2 months.

Music: Mostly **pop**, **country** and **gospel**; also **R&B** and **comedy**. Works primarily with vocalists, special concerts, movies and TV. Current acts include Shauna (R&B dance), Willie John Ellison (blues), Frank White (blues), Alton McClain (gospel), Trina Davis (urban gospel), Sheb Wooley (country) and Todd Taylor (pop/rock instrumentalist).

Tips: "Artists, have your act together. Have a full press kit, videos and be professional. Attitudes are a big factor in my agreeing to work with you (no egotists). This is a business, and we will be building your career."

◐ CLASS ACT PRODUCTIONS/MANAGEMENT, P.O. Box 55252, Sherman Oaks CA 91413. (818)980-1039. Fax: (209)821-4408. E-mail: pkimmel@gr8gizmo.com. **Contact:** Peter Kimmel, president. Management firm, music publisher and production company. Estab. 1985. Currently handles 3 acts. Receives 20% commission. Reviews material for acts.
How to Contact: Submit demo tape by mail. Unsolicited submissions are OK. Include cover letter, pictures, bio, lyric sheets (essential), cassette tape or CD and video in press kit. SASE. Responds in 1 month.
Music: All styles. Current acts include Terpsichore (cyber dance/pop) and Don Cameron (new country).

◐ CLOCKWORK ENTERTAINMENT MANAGEMENT AGENCY, 227 Concord St., Haverhill MA 01830. (508)373-5677. **Contact:** William J. Macek, esq., entertainment attorney, president. Management firm. Represents groups and songwriters throughout New England with mastered product who are looking for label deals and licensing in US and internationally. Fee is negotiated individually; currently handles multiple acts. Commissions vary. Reviews material for acts.
How to Contact: Submit demo tape by mail. Unsolicited submissions are OK. Prefers cassette or CD with 3-12 songs. "Also submit promotion and cover letter with interesting facts about yourself." If seeking management, press kit should include cover letter, tape or CD, photo, bio and press clippings. SASE. Responds in 1 month.
Music: Mostly **rock (all types)** and **top 40/pop**. Works primarily with bar bands and original acts.

◐ CLOUSHER PRODUCTIONS, P.O. Box 1191, Mechanicsburg PA 17055. (717)766-7644. Fax: (717)766-1490. E-mail: clousher@webtv.net. Website: www.clousherentertainment.com. **Contact:** Fred Clousher, owner. Booking agency and production company. Estab. 1972. Represents groups from anywhere; currently handles over 100 acts.
How to Contact: Submit demo tape by mail. Unsolicited submissions are OK. Prefers VHS videocassette. If seeking management, press kit should include press clippings, testimonials, letters, credits, glossies, video demo tape, references, cover letter, résumé and bio. Does not return material. "Performer should check back with us!"
Music: Mostly **country**, **old rock** and **ethnic** (German, Italian, etc.); also **dance bands** (regional) and **classical quartets**. "We work mostly with country, old time R&R, regional variety dance bands, tribute acts, and all types of variety acts." Current acts include Robin Right (country vocalist), Mike Bishop and Sweet & Sassy with Country Time (variety show) and Island Breeze (Hawaiian show).
Tips: "The songwriters we work with are entertainers themselves, which is the aspect we deal with. They usually have bands or do some sort of show, either with tracks or live music. We engage them for stage shows, dances, strolling, etc. We do not publish music or submit performers to recording companies for contracts. We strictly set up live performances for them."

◐ CODY ENTERTAINMENT GROUP, P.O. Box 456, Winchester VA 22604. Phone/fax: (540)722-4625. E-mail: codyent@visuallink.com. **Contact:** Phil Smallwood, president. Management firm and booking agency. Estab. 1975. Represents individual artists and groups from anywhere; currently handles 11 acts. Receives 20% commission. Reviews material for acts.
How to Contact: Submit demo tape by mail. Unsolicited submissions are OK. Prefers cassette, DAT or videocassette with 3 songs and lead sheet. If seeking management, press kit should include cover letter, bio, photo, demo tape/CD and video. Does not return material. Responds in 2 months.
Music: Mostly **show acts** and **writers of love songs**. Current acts include The Hutchens (country), Daron Norwood (country), Rivers Edge (country) and Arlo Haines (writer/performer).

◐ CONCEPT 2000 INC., P.O. Box 2950, Columbus OH 43216-2950. (614)276-2000. Fax: (614)275-0163. Florida office: P.O. Box 2070, Largo FL 33779-2070. (727)585-2922. Fax: (727)585-3835. E-mail: info2k@concept2k.com. Website: www.concept2k.com. **Contact:** Brian Wallace, president. Management firm and booking agency. Estab. 1981. Represents international individual artists, groups and songwriters; currently handles 4 acts. Receives 20% commission. Reviews material for acts.

How to Contact: Submit demo tape by mail. Unsolicited submissions are OK. Prefers cassette with 4 songs. If seeking management, include demo tape, press clips, photo and bio. Does not return material. Responds in 2 weeks.

Music: Mostly **country**, **gospel** and **pop**; also **jazz**, **R&B** and **soul**. Current acts include Bryan Hitch (contemporary gospel), Shades of Grey (R&B/soul), Dwight Lenox (show group) and Gene Walker (jazz).

Tips: "Send quality songs with lyric sheets. Production quality is not necessary."

☑ CONCERTED EFFORTS, INC./FOGGY DAY MUSIC, P.O. Box 600099, Newtonville MA 02460. (617)969-0810. Fax: (617)969-6761. Owner: Paul Kahn. Management firm, booking agency and music publisher (Foggy Day Music). Represents individual artists, groups and songwriters from anywhere; currently handles 5 acts. Commission varies. Reviews material for acts.

How to Contact: Submit demo tape by mail. Unsolicited submissions are OK. Prefers CD, will accept cassette, with lyric sheet. "No management submissions." Does not return material.

Music: **Folk**, **country** and **rock**; also **world music**, **zydeco** and **blues**. Current acts include Luther Johnson (blues singer), Holmes Brothers and Paul Kahn.

Tips: "Simple recorded demo is OK, with lyrics."

◯ CONSCIENCE MUSIC, P.O. Box 617667, Chicago IL 60661. (312)226-4858. E-mail: towreco rds@aol.com. **Contact:** Karen M. Smith, consultant/personal manager. Management firm and record company (TOW Records). Estab. 1985. Represents individual artists, groups and songwriters from anywhere; currently handles 1 act. Receives 20% commission. Reviews material for acts.

How to Contact: *Write first and obtain permission to submit.* Prefers cassette or current release with 2-3 songs and lyric sheet. If seeking management, press kit should include current reviews, demo tape/CD, lyric sheets, list of performance locations, and bio or letter with band or artist objectives. "Cannot overemphasize the importance of having objectives you are ready to discuss with us." SASE. Responds in 4 months.

Music: Mostly **rock** and **pop**; also **visual artists**, **writers** and **models**. Works primarily with indie bands in the States and Great Britain. Currently represents Lance Porter (drummer with Tal Bachman). "Many clients are on a consulting basis only."

☑ ◯ CORVALAN-CONDLIFFE MANAGEMENT, 1702 Clark Lane, Unit B, Redondo Beach CA 90278. (310)318-2574. Fax: (310)318-6574. E-mail: convcond@earthlink.com. Website: www.tir anharecords.com. **Contact:** Brian Condliffe, manager. Management firm. Estab. 1982. Represents individual artists, groups and songwriters from anywhere; currently handles 2 acts. Receives 15% commission.

How to Contact: *Write or call first and obtain permission to submit.* Prefers cassette with 4-6 songs. If seeking management, press kit should include bio, professional photo, press reviews and demo. SASE. Responds in 2 months.

Music: Mostly **pop** and **rock**; also **Latin**. Works primarily with alternative rock and pop/rock/world beat bands. Current acts include Ramiro Medina and Blue Tarantula.

Tips: "Be professional in all aspects of your kit and presentation. Check your grammar and spelling in your correspondence/written material. Know your music and your targeted market (rock, R&B, etc.)."

☑ ◯ COUNTDOWN ENTERTAINMENT, 110 W. 26th St., 3rd Floor S., New York NY 10001-6805. (212)645-3068. Fax: (212)989-6459. E-mail: countdownent@netzero.net. Website: www w.countdownentertainment.com. **Contact:** Music Review Department. President: James Citkovic. Management firm and consultants. Estab. 1983. Represents local, regional and international individual artists, groups, songwriters and producers; currently handles 3 acts. Receives 20% commission. Reviews material for acts.

How to Contact: Submit demo tape by mail. "We will not accept certified or registered mail." Unsolicited submissions are OK. "Please, no phone calls." Prefers CDs, cassette and VHS (SP speed) videocassette with lyric sheet. If seeking management, press kit should include cassette tape or CD of best songs, 8 × 10 pictures, "live" VHS performance, lyrics, press and radio playlists. Does not return material. Responds in 3 weeks.

Music: Mostly **pop**, **modern rock** and **electronica/dance**; also **R&B**, **hip-hop** and **funk**. Deals with all styles of artists/songwriters/producers. Current acts include Irene Cara (multi-platinum singer/songwriter/performer/screenwriter/actress), Petra Luna (female Latina pop/crossover bilingual singing group) and Alcohol (earthly, hard-hitting rock/country).

Tips: "Leaders, not followers."

COUNTRYWIDE PRODUCERS, 2466 Wildon Dr., York PA 17403. (717)741-2658. **Contact:** Bob Englar, president. Booking agency. Represents individuals and groups; currently handles 8 acts. Receives 15% commission. Reviews material for acts.

How to Contact: Query or submit demo tape by mail. Unsolicited submissions are OK. If seeking management, press kit should include photo and demo tape. SASE. Responds in 1 week.

Music: Bluegrass, **blues**, **classical**, **country** and **disco**; also **folk**, **gospel**, **jazz**, **polka**, **rock (light)**, **soul** and **top 40/pop**. Works primarily with show bands. Current acts include Majestics (50s/60s), Jeff Williams Show (c/w) and Osborn Bros.

STEPHEN COX PROMOTIONS & MANAGEMENT, 6708 Mammoth Ave., Van Nuys CA 91405. (818)377-4530. Fax: (818)782-5305. E-mail: stephencox@earthlink.net. **Contact:** Stephen Cox, president. Management firm. Estab. 1993. Represents individual artists, groups or songwriters from anywhere; currently handles 5 acts. Receives 15% commission. Reviews material for acts.

How to Contact: *Call first and obtain permission to submit a demo.* Prefers cassette or CD. If seeking management, press kit should include biographies, performance history and radio play. "Include a clear definition of goals in a thoughtful presentation." SASE. Responds in 2 weeks.

Music: Mostly **rock**, **New Age/world** and **alternative**; also **blues**, **folk** and **progressive**. Works primarily with bands. Current acts include Joe Sherbanee (jazz), Val Ewell & Pulse (blues rock) and Paul Micich & Mitch Espe (New Age/jazz).

Tips: "Establish goals based on research, experience and keep learning about the music business. Start the business as though it will always be you as an independent. Establish a foundation before considering alternative commitments. We aim to educate and consult to a level that gives an artist the freedom of choice to choose whether to go to the majors etc., or retain independence. Remember, promote, promote and promote some more. Always be nice to people, treat them as you would wish to be treated."

CRAWFISH PRODUCTIONS, P.O. Box 5412, Buena Park CA 90620. (619)245-2920. E-mail: swampbasque@msn.com. Producer: Leo J. Eiffert, Jr. Management firm, music publisher (Young Country/BMI), record producer (Leo J. Eiffert) and record company (Plain Country Records). Estab. 1968. Represents local and international individual artists and songwriters; currently handles 4 acts. Commission received is open. Reviews material for acts.

How to Contact: Submit demo tape by mail. Unsolicited submissions are OK. Prefers cassette with 2-3 songs and lyric sheet. SASE. Responds in 3 weeks.

Music: Mostly **country** and **gospel**. Works primarily with vocalists. Current acts include Brandi Holland, Teeci Clarke, Joe Eiffert (country/gospel), Mary T. Vertiz (songwriter), Crawfish Band (country) and Homemade.

CREATIVE STAR MANAGEMENT, 615 E. Second St., Lima OH 45804. President/Owner: James Milligan. Vice President: Sonya Koger. Management firm, booking agency, music publisher (Party House Publishing/BMI, A New Rap Jam Publishing/ASCAP), record company (New Experience Records/Grand Slam Records). Estab. 1989. Represents individual artists, groups and songwriters from anywhere; currently handles 6 acts. Receives 15-20% commission. Reviews material for acts.

● Creative Star Management's publishing company, A New Rap Jam Publishing (ASCAP), is listed in the Music Publishers section, and their record label, New Experience Records/Grand Slam Records, is listed in the Record Companies section.

How to Contact: *Contact first and obtain permission to submit.* Prefers cassette or VHS videocassette with 3-5 songs and lyric sheet. If seeking management, press kit should include press clippings, bios, résumé, 8×10 glossy photo, any information that will support material and artist. SASE. Responds in 6 weeks.

Music: Mostly **R&B**, **pop** and **country**; also **rap**, **contemporary gospel** and **soul/funk**. Current acts include T.M.C. (R&B/group), Jayhson Rodgers (gospel/R&B solo artist) and Terry Henderson (solo artists).

Tips: "We are seeking '70s and '80s groups looking to re-sign and for management."

⬛ CRISS-CROSS INDUSTRIES, 24016 Strathern St., West Hills CA 91304. (818)710-6600. Fax: (818)719-0222. **Contact:** Doc Remer, president. Management firm and music publisher (Menachan's Music/ASCAP, Eyenoma Music/BMI). Estab. 1984. Represents individual artists, groups and songwriters from anywhere. Reviews material for acts.

How to Contact: Write first and obtain permission to submit. Prefers cassette or VHS videocassette with 3 songs and lyric sheet. If seeking management, press kit should include photo, bio, cover letter, demo tape/CD, video and credits. SASE. Responds in 1 month.

Music: Mostly **R&B** and **pop**. Works primarily with vocalists and self contained bands.

Tips: "You must currently be a working act. Make the words to the songs so they can be understood. The music should not be as loud as the vocals."

⬛ CROSSFIRE PRODUCTIONS, 304 Braeswood, Austin TX 78704-7200. (512)442-5678. Fax: (512)442-1154. E-mail: vicky@wcclark.com. **Contact:** Vicky Moerbe, president. Management firm. Estab. 1990. Represents local, individual artists and songwriters; currently handles 3 acts. Receives 15% commission. Reviews material for acts.

How to Contact: *Write or call first and obtain permission to submit.* Prefers cassette with any number of songs and lyric sheet. If seeking management, press kit should include biography, press releases/articles/reviews, photograph/discography and copy of current release or demo. SASE. Responds in 1 month.

Music: Mostly **blues**, **swing** and **country**; also **soul** and **contemporary rock**. Works primarily with singers and songwriters. Current acts include W.C. Clark (singer/songwriter/touring act; blues/soul), Rusty Weir (songwriter) and Steven Fromholz (songwriter).

Tips: "Please submit only material to be considered for recordings for blues/soul, swing or country recordings. Our artists are looking for material to be considered for recordings for national releases."

⬛ D&M ENTERTAINMENT AGENCY, P.O. Box 19242, Johnston RI 02919. (401)782-0239. **Contact:** Ray DiMillio, president. Management firm and booking agency. Estab. 1968. Represents local groups; currently handles 28 acts. Receives 15% commission. Reviews material for acts.

How to Contact: Submit demo tape by mail. *Write or call to arrange personal interview.* Unsolicited submissions are OK. Prefers cassette or VHS videocassette with 3 songs and lyric or lead sheet. If seeking management, include photo. Does not return material. Responds in 3 weeks.

Music: Mostly **R&B** and **pop**; also **rock**. Current acts include Clique (top 40), Absolute (top 40) and xpo (top 40).

◻ D&R ENTERTAINMENT, 308 N. Park, Broken Bow OK 74728. (580)584-9429. **Contact:** Don Walton, president. Management firm. Estab. 1985. Represents individual artists from anywhere; currently handles 2 acts. Receives 15% commission. Reviews material for acts. Also reviews for other country singers.

How to Contact: Submit demo tape by mail. Unsolicited submissions are OK. Prefers cassette and videocassette with lyric and lead sheet. If seeking management, press kit should include brief background of artist, videotape of performance, cover letter, résumé, photo, press clippings and cassette or CD. "Indicate whether you have any financial or prospective financial backing." Does not return material. Responds in 3 months.

Music: Mostly **country**; also **gospel** and **pop**. Works primarily with young beginning singers. Current acts include Kristi Reed (positive country) and Thomas Wells (contemporary Christian).

Tips: "I need songs (country) that would fit a young singer under 20. In other words no drinking, cheating, marrying songs. A pretty tough choice. Also Christian contemporary songs."

◐ **DAS COMMUNICATIONS, LTD.**, 83 Riverside Dr., New York NY 10024. (212)877-0400. Fax: (212)595-0176. Management firm. Estab. 1975. Represents individual artists, groups and producers from anywhere; currently handles 25 acts. Receives 20% commission.
How to Contact: Responds in 2 months. Prefers demo with 3 songs, lyric sheet and photo. Does not return material.
Music: Mostly **rock**, **pop**, **R&B** and **alternative**. Current acts include Joan Osborne (rock), Wyelef Jean (hip-hop) and 98° (pop).

◑ **DCA PRODUCTIONS**, 330 W. 38th St., Suite 303, New York NY 10018. (212)245-2063. Fax: (212)245-2367. Website: www.dcaproductions.com. **Contact:** Lauren Pellegrino, office manager. President: Daniel Abrahamsen. Vice President: Geraldine Abrahamsen. Management firm. Estab. 1975. Represents individual artists, groups and songwriters from anywhere; currently handles 14 acts.
How to Contact: If seeking management, press kit should include cover letter, bio, photo, demo tape/CD and video. Prefers cassette or VHS videocassette with 2 songs. "All materials are reviewed and kept on file for future consideration. Does not return material. We respond only if interested."
Music: Mostly **acoustic**, **rock** and **mainstream**; also **cabaret** and **theme**. Works primarily with acoustic singer/songwriters, top 40 or rock bands. Current acts include The Word (singers/songwriters), Amelia's Dream (melodic rock) and Fourth Avenue (a cappella).
Tips: "Please do not call for a review of material."

✔ ◐ **THE EDWARD DE MILES COMPANY**, 117 W. Harrison Bldg. #S627, Chicago IL 60605-1709. (773)509-6381. Fax: (312)922-6964. **Contact:** Edward de Miles, president. Management firm, booking agency, entertainment/sports promoter and TV/radio broadcast producer. Estab. 1984. Represents film, television, radio and musical artists; currently handles 15 acts. Receives 10-20% commission. Reviews material for acts. Regional operations in Chicago, Dallas, Houston and Nashville through marketing representatives. Licensed A.F. of M. booking agent.
How to Contact: *Write first and obtain permission to submit or to arrange personal interview.* Prefers cassette with 3-5 songs, 8x10 b&w photo, bio and lyric sheet. "Copyright all material before submitting." If seeking management, include cover letter, bio, demo cassette with 3-5 songs, 8×10 b&w photo, lyric sheet, press clippings and video if available in press kit. SASE. Does not return material. Responds in 1 month.
Music: Mostly **country**, **dance**, **R&B/soul**, **rock**, **top 40/pop** and **urban contemporary**; also looking for material for television, radio and film productions. Works primarily with dance bands and vocalists. Current acts include Steve Lynn (R&B/dance), Multiple Choice (rap) and D'vou Edwards (jazz).
Tips: "Performers need to be well prepared with their presentations (equipment, showmanship a must)."

○ **BILL DETKO MANAGEMENT**, 378 Palomares Ave., Ventura CA 93003. (805)644-0447. Fax: (805)644-0469. **Contact:** Bill Detko, president. Management firm. Estab. 1984. Represents individual artists, groups and songwriters from anywhere; currently handles 4 acts. Receives 15-20% commission. Reviews material for acts.
How to Contact: *Contact first and obtain permission to submit.* Prefers CD with 3-6 songs and lyric sheet. If seeking management, press kit should include bio, cover letter, résumé, photo, plus above items and any press or radio action. Does not return material. "Artist must call back."
Music: All styles. Current acts include Jennifer Terran (recording artist), Elvis Schoenberg's Orchestre Surreal (performance/recording artist) and Terry Michael Hurd (film composer).

THE TYPES OF MUSIC each listing is interested in are printed in **boldface**.

☉ ✓ ◐ ANDREW DINWOODIE MANAGEMENT, P.O. Box 5052, Victoria Point QLD 4165 Australia. Phone: (07)32070502. E-mail: adinwoodie@bigpond.com. **Contact:** Andrew Dinwoodie, director. Management firm and booking agency. Estab. 1983. Represents regional (Australian) individual artists, groups and songwriters; currently handles 4 acts. Receives 10-20% commission. Reviews material for acts.

How to Contact: Submit demo tape by mail. Unsolicited submissions are OK. Prefers CD/CDR, cassette or VHS PAL videocassette with lyric sheet. If seeking management, press kit should include cover letter, résumé, bio, photo, goals, audio or videotape and CD if available and anything the artist thinks will help. SAE and IRC. Responds in 1 month.

Music: Mostly **adult contemporary folk**, **country**, **R&B** and **rock/pop**; also **bluegrass**, **swing** and **folk**. Current acts include Spot the Dog (cool and cruisy adult contemporary folk), Bullamakanka (good time Australian music), Donna Heke (blues/soul) and Bluey the Bastard (feral folk).

[N] ◐ DIRECT MANAGEMENT, 645 Quail Ridge Rd., Aledo TX 76008-2835. Owner: Danny Wilkerson. Management firm and booking agency. Estab. 1986. Represents individual artists and/or groups from anywhere; currently handles 4 acts. Receives 10-20% commission. Reviews material for acts.

How to Contact: Submit demo tape by mail. Unsolicited submissions are OK. Prefers CD, cassette or VHS videocassette with 3 songs. If seeking management, press kit should include bio, cassette or CD, photo, lyric sheets, press clippings and video. Does not return material. Responds in 1 month.

Music: Mostly **college rock**, **Christian** and **children's**. Current acts include Waltons (pop/rock), The EPs (rock) and Emily Rogers (country).

◐ DMR AGENCY, Galleries of Syracuse, Suite 250, Syracuse NY 13202-2416. (315)475-2500. E-mail: dmr@ican.net. Website: www.dmrbooking.net. **Contact:** David M. Rezak. Booking agency. Represents individuals and groups; currently handles 50 acts. Receives 15% commission.

How to Contact: Submit demo tape by mail. Unsolicited submissions are OK. Submit cassette or videocassette with 1-4 songs and press kit. Does not return material.

Music: Mostly **rock (all styles)**, **pop** and **blues**. Works primarily with cover bands. Current acts include Prime Time (R&B), Tom Townsley and the Backsliders (blues) and Los Blancos (blues).

Tips: "You might want to contact us if you have a cover act in our region. Many songwriters in our area have a cover group in order to make money."

◐ COL. BUSTER DOSS PRESENTS, 341 Billy Goat Hill Rd., Winchester TN 37398. (931)649-2577. Fax: (615)649-2732. **Contact:** Col. Buster Doss, producer. Management firm, booking agency, record company (Stardust Records), record producer and music publisher (Buster Doss Music/BMI). Estab. 1959. Represents individual artists, groups, songwriters and shows; currently handles 14 acts. Receives 15% commission. Reviews material for acts.

How to Contact: *Write first and obtain permission to submit.* Prefers cassette with 2-4 songs and lyric sheet. If seeking management, press kit should include demo, photos, video if available and bio. SASE. Responds back on day received.

Music: Mostly **country**, **gospel** and **progressive**. Works primarily with show and dance bands, single acts and package shows. Current acts include "Rooster" Quantrell, Linda Wunder, The Border Raiders, "Bronco" Buck Cody, Jerri Arnold, Bob Norman, Cindy Lee, John Hamilton and Brant Miller.

♣ ✓ ◐ EAO MUSIC CORPORATION OF CANADA, P.O. Box 1240, Station "M," Calgary, Alberta T2P 2L2 Canada. (403)228-9388. Fax: (403) 229-3598. E-mail: eao@telusphonet.net. **Contact:** Edmund A. Oliverio, president. Management firm and record company. Estab. 1985. Represents individual artists, groups and songwriters from western Canada (aboriginal artists); currently handles 52 acts. Receives 15-20% commission. Reviews material for acts.

How to Contact: Submit demo tape by mail. Unsolicited submissions are OK. Prefers cassette with 3 songs and lyric and lead sheets. If seeking management, press kit should include cover letter, résumé, b&w glossy photo, cassette tape, bio, media clippings and list of venues and festivals performed. SAE and IRC. Responds in 2 weeks.

Music: Mostly **folk** and **native (aboriginal)**; also **rock**. Works primarily with singer/songwriters. Current acts include Activate (funky reggae), Feeding Like Butterflies (folk rock/Celtic), Katrina (country/folk) and Gloria K. MacRae (adult contemporary).

Tips: "Be upfront and honest. Establish your long term goals and short term goals. Have you joined your music associations (i.e., CMA, etc.)? Recent demand for cowboy artists rather than country."

○ **EARTH TRACKS ARTISTS AGENCY**, 4809 Ave. N., Suite 286, Brooklyn NY 11234. E-mail: jewelblues@aol.com. **Contact:** David Krinsky, managing director-artist relations. Management firm. Estab. 1990. Represents individual artists, groups and songwriters from anywhere; currently handles 2 acts. Receives 15% commission. Reviews material for acts.

How to Contact: Submit demo tape by mail. Unsolicited submissions are OK. Prefers cassette or CD with 3-6 songs and lyric sheet. If seeking management, press kit should include cover letter, bio, video (if available), 1 group photo, all lyrics with songs, a cassette/CD of original songs and the ages of the artists. Does not return material. Responds in 1 month. "We will contact artist if interested. Include e-mail address for reply."

Music: Mostly **commercial rock** (all kinds), **pop** and **alternative**; also **blues**. No rap, R&B or metal. Works primarily with commercial, original, solo artists and groups, songwriters in the rock and pop areas (no country, thrash or punk). Current acts include Candid (pop/folk-rock) and Rocketransferwarehouse (pop/rock).

Tips: "I am not an industry 'insider' with extensive contacts. I ask artists 'Give me a Chance.' I am dedicated to artists I believe in. I act strictly as a personal manager for an artist which means I help them choose songs, submit songs, find a publisher, and/or a record company. I ask a 3 year management contract but if I can't get the artist a deal within 9 months of signing, the contract is cancelled. Artists signed should supply promotion packages to submit to publishers or record labels. I prefer artists who write and perform their own songs but will consider songwriters who can write 'hit' songs for pop/rock markets."

☑ ○ **THE ELLIS INTERNATIONAL TALENT AGENCY**, 5617 W. Melvina, Milwaukee WI 53216. Phone/fax: (414)444-3385. **Contact:** Darnell Ellis, A&R rep. Management firm, booking agency, music publisher (Buzz Duzz Duzz Music/ASCAP) record company (Safire Records) and record producer (Darnell Ellis). Estab. 1997. Represents individual artists, groups and songwriters from anywhere; currently handles 2 acts. Receives 15-20% commission. Reviews material for acts.

How to Contact: Submit demo tape by mail. Unsolicited submissions are OK. Prefers cassette or videocassette with 4-6 songs and press kit. If seeking management, press kit should include cassette tape or CD with 4-6 songs (demo), 8×10 photo, video tape and reviews. Does not return material. Responds in 6 weeks. "We will respond only if we are interested."

Music: Mostly **contemporary**, **country**, **world**, **Latin** and **celtic**. Works primarily with singers, singer/songwriters, songwriters and bands. Current acts include Magen Cory (country pop) and Anthony Vincent (country).

☑ ○ **ENDANGERED SPECIES ARTIST MANAGEMENT**, 4 Berachah Ave., South Nyack NY 10960-4202. (845)353-4001. Fax: (845)353-4332. E-mail: endanger@bellatlantic.net. Website: www.endangers.com. President: Fred Porter. Vice President: Suzanne Buckley. Management firm. Estab. 1979. Represents individual artists, groups and songwriters from anywhere; currently handles 3 acts. Receives 20% commission. Reviews material for acts.

How to Contact: Call first and obtain permission to submit. Prefers cassette or CD with 10 songs and lyric sheet. "Please include a demo of your music, a clear, recent photograph as well as any current press, if any. A cover letter indicating at what stage in your career you are and expectations for your future. Please label the cassette and/or CD with your name and address as well as the song titles." If seeking management, press kit should include cover letter, bio, photo, demo tape/CD, lyric sheet and press clippings. SASE. Responds in 6 weeks.

Music: Mostly **pop**, **rock** and **world**; also **Latin/heavy metal**, **R&B**, **jazz** and **instrumental**. Current acts include Tabarruk (pop/reggae), Reggie May (R&B singer/songwriter), Eminence (Brazilian heavy metal), Terry Cole (pop a la N'Sync).

Tips: "Listen to everything, classical to country, old to contemporary, to develop an understanding of many writing styles. Write with many other partners to keep the creativity fresh. Don't feel your style will be ruined by taking a class or a writing seminar. We all process moods and images differently. This leads to uniqueness in the music."

☑○ **SCOTT EVANS PRODUCTIONS**, P.O. Box 814028, Hollywood FL 33081-4028. (954)963-4449. E-mail: evansprod@aol.com. Website: www.theentertainmentmail.com. **Contact:** Ted Jones, new artists. Management firm and booking agency. Estab. 1979. Represents local, regional or international individual artists, groups, songwriters, comedians, novelty acts and dancers; currently handles over 200 acts. Receives 10-50% commission. Reviews material for acts.

How to Contact: Submit demo tape by mail. Unsolicited submissions are OK. Prefers cassette and/or ½" videocassette with 3 songs. If seeking management, include picture, résumé, flyers, cassette or video tape. Does not return material.

Music: Mostly **pop**, **R&B** and **Broadway**. Deals with "all types of entertainers; no limitations." Current acts include Scott Evans and Company (variety song and dance), Dorit Zinger (female vocalist), Jeff Geist, Actors Repertory Theatre, Entertainment Express, Perfect Parties, Joy Deco (dance act), Flashback 2000 Revue (musical song and dance), Everybody Salsa (Latin song and dance) and Around the World (international song and dance).

Tips: "Submit a neat, well put together, organized press kit."

☑◐ **EVERGREEN ENTERTAINMENT SERVICES**, (formerly Professional Artist Management, Ltd.), P.O. Box 755, Shelburne VT 05482. (800)610-7625. Fax: (888)610-7625. E-mail: hughestj@together.net. Website: www.rockandrollacountant.com. **Contact:** Tom Hughes, general manager. Management firm. Estab. 1994. Represents Northeast, New York, Tennessee and California individual artists and groups; currently handles 10 acts. Receives 10-15% commission. Reviews material for acts.

How to Contact: Submit demo tape by mail. Unsolicited submissions are OK. Prefers cassette, DAT, mini disc or CD. If seeking management, press kit should include cover letter, bio, demo tape/CD, any commercial releases, reviews and airplay. Does not return material. Responds in 2 months.

Tips: "We are not a booking agency. We don't shop material to labels."

○ **EXCLESISA BOOKING AGENCY**, 716 Windward Rd., Jackson MS 39206. (601)366-0220. Fax: (601)987-8777. E-mail: exclesis@bellsouth.net. **Contact:** Roy and Esther Wooten, booking managers/owners. Booking agency. Estab. 1989. Represents groups from anywhere; currently handles 8 acts. Receives 15% commission. Reviews material for acts.

How to Contact: *Call first and obtain permission to submit.* Submit demo tape by mail. Unsolicited submissions are OK. Prefers CD or videocassette. If seeking management, press kit should include CD or cassette, videocassette, pictures, address and telephone contact and bio. Does not return material. Responds in 2 months.

Music: Gospel only. Current acts include The Jackson Southernaires, Slim & The Supreme Angels, The Mississippi Seminar Choir, The Christianaires, Charles Woolfolk & Covenant, Carolyn Traylor, The Pilgrim Jubilees, Spencer Taylor & the Highway QC's, The Sweet Singing Cavaliers and David R. Curry, Jr.

Tips: "Make sure your demo is clear with a good sound so the agent can make a good judgement."

◐ **FRED T. FENCHEL ENTERTAINMENT AGENCY**, 2104 S. Jefferson Avenue, Mason City IA 50401. (515)423-4177. Fax: (515)423-8662. **Contact:** Fred T. Fenchel, general manager. Booking agency. Estab. 1964. Represents local and international individual artists and groups; currently handles up to 10 acts. Receives 20% commission.

How to Contact: Submit demo tape by mail. Unsolicited submissions are OK. Prefers cassette or videocassette. Does not return material. Responds in 3 weeks.

Music: Mostly **country**, **pop** and some **gospel**. Works primarily with dance bands and show groups; "artists we can use on club dates, fairs, etc." Current acts include The Memories (vocal/musical trio), The Suby's (karaoke) and Black Diamonds (country group). "We deal primarily with established name acts with recording contracts, or those with a label and starting into popularity."

Tips: "Be honest. Don't submit unless your act is exceptional rather than just starting out, amateurish and with lyrics that are written under the pretense of coming from qualified writers."

⊕ ✓ ⊘ **FIRST TIME MANAGEMENT**, Sovereign House, 12 Trewartha Rd., Praa Sands-Penzance, Cornwall TR20 9ST England. Phone: (01736)762826. Fax: (01736)763328. E-mail: panamus @aol.com. Website: www.songwriters-guild.co.uk. **Contact:** Roderick G. Jones, managing director. Management firm, record company (First Time Records) and music publisher (First Time Music). Estab. 1986. Represents local, regional and international individual aritsts, groups and songwriters; currently handles 114 acts. Receives 15-25% commission. Reviews material for acts.
How to Contact: Submit demo tape by mail. Unsolicited submissions are OK. Prefers cassette, 15 ips reel-to-reel or VHS videocassette with 3 songs and lyric sheets. If seeking management, press kit should include cover letter, bio, photo, demo tape/CD, press clippings and anything relevant to make an impression. Does not return material. Responds in 1 month.
Music: Mostly **dance**, **top 40**, **rap**, **country**, **gospel** and **pop**; also **all styles**. Works primarily with songwriters, composers, vocalists, groups and choirs. Current acts include Willow (pop), Colin Eade and Bob Brimley.
Tips: "Become a member of the Guild of International Songwriters and Composers. Keep everything as professional as possible. Be patient and dedicated to your aims and objectives."

⊘ **GCI, INC.**, P.O. Box 56757, New Orleans LA 70156. (504)299-9000. Fax: (504)581-1188. **Contact:** John Shoup, CEO. Management firm, music publisher, record company, record producer and television producer (network). Estab. 1990. Represents groups and songwriters from anywhere; currently handles 1 act. Reviews material for acts.
How to Contact: *Does not accept unsolicited material.*
Music: Mostly **jazz**. Current acts include Dukes of Dixieland.

⊘ **ERIC GODTLAND MANAGEMENT, INC.**, 5715 Claremont, Suite C, Oakland CA 94618. (510)596-8990. Fax: (510)596-8690. **Contact:** Wayne Ledbetter, manager. Management firm. Estab. 1995. Represents individual artists, groups or songwriters from anywhere; currently handles 5 acts. Reviews material for acts.
How to Contact: Submit demo tape by mail. Unsolicited submissions are OK. Prefers cassette, DAT or CD. If seeking management, press kit should include brief information on how to reach you. Does not return material.
Music: Mostly **pop**, **rock** and **hip-hop**. Works primarily with bands, producers and songwriters. Current acts include Third Eye Blind (rock band), Brougham (alternative/hip-hop group), The KGB (pop rock), Loni Rose (pop) and Dakona (rock band).

Ⓝ ◯ **GOLDEN CITY INTERNATIONAL**, Box 410851, San Francisco CA 94141. (415)822-1530. Fax: (415)695-1845. A&R Rep: Mr. Alston. Management firm, music publisher (Dagene Music/ ASCAP) and record company (Dagene/Cabletown Records). Estab. 1993. Represents regional (California area) individual artists and groups; currently handles 3 acts. Receives 15-20% commission. Reviews material for acts.
How to Contact: Write or call first and obtain permission to submit. Prefers cassette or VHS videocassette with 2-3 songs. If seeking management, press kit should include a complete bio and current photo along with cassette or CD of recent material. SASE. Responds in 1 month.
Music: Mostly **R&B/dance**, **rap** and **pop**; also **gospel** and **dance**. Current clients include Rare Essence (vocal group), Marcus Justice (writer/artist) and David Alston (producer).

⊘ **GREIF-GARRIS MANAGEMENT**, 2112 Casitas Way, Palm Springs CA 92264. (760)322-8655. Fax: (760)322-7793. **Contact:** Sid Garris, vice president. Management firm. Estab. 1961. Represents individual artists and/or groups and songwriters from anywhere; currently owns 1 act. Reviews material for acts.
How to Contact: Write first to obtain permission to submit and/or to arrange a personal interview. Submit demo tape by mail. Unsolicited submissions are OK. Prefers cassette. If seeking management, press kit should include demo, cover letter, bio and photo. SASE. Responds in 3 weeks.

Music: All types. Current acts include The New Christy Minstrels (folk/pop).

☑ ◻ **GUESTSTAR ENTERTAINMENT AGENCY**, 17321 Ritchie Ave. NE, Sand Lake MI 49343-9475. (616)636-5068. Fax: (775)743-4169. E-mail: gueststarww@wingsisp.com. Website: www.wingsisp.com/mountainmanww/. **Contact:** Raymond G. Dietz, Sr., president. Management firm, booking agency, music publisher (Sandlake Music/BMI), record company (Gueststar Records, Inc.), record producer and record distributor (Gueststar Music Distributors). Represents individual artists, groups, songwriters and bands from anywhere; currently handles 3 acts. Receives 20% commission. Reviews material for acts.
 • Mr. Dietz is also the editor of several music books, including *Everything You Should Know Before You Get into the Music Business*.
How to Contact: Submit demo tape by mail. Unsolicited submissions are OK. Prefers cassette or VHS videocassette with unlimited songs, but send your best with lyric or lead sheet. If seeking management, press kit should include photo, demo tape, bio, music résumé and VHS videocassette (live on stage) if possible and press clippings. Does not return material. Responds in 3 weeks. SASE required.
Music: Mostly **traditional country**. Current acts include Mountain Man (singer), Jamie "K" (singer) and Sweetgrass (band).

◪ **HALE ENTERPRISES**, Rt. 1, Box 49, Worthington IN 47471-9310. (812)875-3664. E-mail: haleenterprises@earthlink.net. **Contact:** Rodger Hale, CEO. Management firm, record company (Projection Unlimited) and recording studio. Estab. 1976. Represents artists, groups, songwriters and studio musicians; currently handles 11 acts. Receives 15% commission for booking, 20% for management. Reviews material for acts.
How to Contact: Submit demo tape by mail. Unsolicited submissions are OK. Prefers cassette or videocassette with 2-10 songs and lyric sheet. If seeking management include cover letter, résumé, lyric sheets, press clippings, current promo pack *or* photo, video-audio tape, clubs currently performing, short performance history and equipment list (if applicable). Does not return material. Responds in 1 week.
Music: Mostly **country** and **top 40**; also **MOR**, **progressive**, **rock** and **pop**. Works primarily with show bands, dance bands and bar bands. Current acts include Indiana (country show band), Seventh Heaven (top 40 show) and Cotton (show band).

◪ **BILL HALL ENTERTAINMENT & EVENTS**, 138 Frog Hollow Rd., Churchville PA 18966-1031. (215)357-5189. Fax: (215)357-0320. **Contact:** William B. Hall III. Booking agency and production company. Represents individuals and groups; currently handles 20-25 acts. Receives 15% commission. Reviews material for acts.
How to Contact: Submit demo tape by mail. Unsolicited submissions are OK. Prefers cassette or videocassette of performance with 2-3 songs "and photos, promo material and record or tape. We need quality material, preferably before a 'live' audience." Does not return material. Responds only if interested.
Music: Marching band, **circus** and **novelty**. Works primarily with "unusual or novelty attractions in musical line, preferably those that appeal to family groups." Current acts include Fralinger and Polish-American Philadelphia Championship Mummers String Bands (marching and concert group), Erwin Chandler Orchestra (show band), "Mr. Polynesian" Show Band and Hawaiian Revue (ethnic group), the "Phillies Whiz Kids Band" of Philadelphia Phillies Baseball team, Paul Richardson (Phillies' organist/entertainer), Mummermania Musical Quartet, Philadelphia German Brass Band (concert band), Vogelgesang Circus Calliope, Kromer's Carousel Band Organ, Reilly Raiders Drum & Bugle Corps, Hoebel Steam Calliope, Caesar Rodney Brags Band, Rohe Calliope, Philadelphia Police & Fire Pipes Band, Larry Rothbard's Circus Band and Tim Laushey Pep & Dance Band.

REFER TO THE CATEGORY INDEX (at the end of this section) to find exactly which companies are interested in the type of music you write.

Tips: "Please send whatever helps us to most effectively market the attraction and/or artist. Provide something that gives you a clear edge over others in your field!"

📺 ⓓ **HANSEN ENTERPRISES, LTD.**, 855 E. Twain #123411, Las Vegas NV 89109. (702)896-8115. Fax: (702)792-1363. **Contact:** J. Malcom Baird. Management firm. Estab. 1971. Represents individual artists, groups and songwriters from anywhere; currently handles 3 acts. Receives 15-25% commission "or contracted fee arrangement." Reviews material for acts.
How to Contact: Submit demo tape by mail. Unsolicited submissions are OK. Prefers cassette. SASE. Responds in 3 weeks. We are looking for potential *hit songs* only: top 40, pop and Spanish. From time to time we need music for TV shows, commercials and films. Send SASE for requirements, which change from time to time depending upon the project(s).
Music: Mostly **'50s & '60s rock** and **Spanish adult contemporary**. Current acts include The Ronettes, Pilita Corrales (top selling female Spanish recording star) and Jackie-Lou Blanco.

✅ ⓞ **HARDISON INTERNATIONAL ENTERTAINMENT CORPORATION**, P.O. Box 1732, Knoxville TN 37901-1732. (865)688-5210. Fax: (865)688-5285. E-mail: alt1010@aol.com. **Contact:** Dennis K. Hardison, CEO/founder. Management firm, booking agency, music publisher (Denlatrin Music), record company (Denlatrin Records) and record producer. Estab. 1984. Represents individual artists from anywhere; currently handles 3 acts. Receives 20% commission. Reviews material for acts.
   • This company has promoted acts including New Edition, Freddie Jackson, M.C. Lyte and Kool Moe Dee.
How to Contact: Submit demo tape by mail. Unsolicited submissions are OK. Prefers cassette or CD with 3 songs. If seeking management, press kit should include bio, promo picture and cassette. Does not return material. Responds in 6 weeks.
Music: Mostly **R&B**, **hip-hop** and **rap**. Current acts include Dynamo (hip-hop) and Lil Cela (hip-hop).
Tips: "We have an in-house production staff to critique your music."

ⓞ **M. HARRELL & ASSOCIATES**, 5444 Carolina, Merrillville IN 46410. (219)887-8814 or (219)219-5294. Fax: (219)947-5255 or (219)602-3455. **Contact:** Mary Harrell and Bobby Brooks, owners. Management firm and booking agency. Estab. 1984. Represents individual artists, groups, songwriters, all talents—fashion, dancers, etc.; currently handles 40-50 acts. Receives 10-20% commission. Reviews material for acts.
How to Contact: *Call first and obtain permission to submit.* Submit demo tape by mail. Unsolicited submissions OK. Prefers cassette or videocassette with 2-3 songs. If seeking management, press kit should include cover letter, résumé, bio, photo, demo tape/CD and press clippings. "Keep it brief and current." Does not return material. Responds in 1 month.
Music: **All types**, **country**, **R&B**, **jazz**, **gospel**, **Big Band** and **light rock**. Current acts include Bill Shelton ('50s music), 11th Ave. ('50s music), Larger than Life (variety), Tony Alang Sensation (R&B), Bang (r&b), Country Rodeo (country) and Old Habits (country).

ⓞ **HAWKEYE ATTRACTIONS**, 102 Geiger St., Huntingburg IN 47542. (812)683-3657. **Contact:** David Mounts, agent. Booking agency. Estab. 1982. Represents individual artists and groups; currently handles 2 acts. Receives 10% commission. Reviews material for acts.
How to Contact: Call first and obtain permission to submit. Prefers cassette with 4 songs and lyric sheet. SASE. If seeking management, press kit should include bio, press clippings, 8×10 b&w glossy and cassette. Responds in 9 weeks.
Music: Mostly **country** and **western swing**. Works primarily with show bands, Grand Ole Opry style form of artist and music. Current acts include Bill Mounts and His Midwest Cowboys (country/western swing).

ⓞ **HORIZON MANAGEMENT INC.**, P.O. Box 8770, Endwell NY 13762. (607)785-9120. Fax: (607)785-4516. E-mail: horizonmgtinc@aol.com. Website: www.musicalonline.com/management/ho

rizon. **Contact:** New Talent Department. Management firm, booking agency and concert promotion. Estab. 1967. Represents regional, national and international artists, groups and songwriters; currently handles over 1,500 acts. Receives 20% commission. Reviews material for acts.

How to Contact: *Call first and obtain permission to submit.* Prefers CD, cassette or VHS videocassette with 1-4 songs and lead sheet. Send cover letter, résumé, lead sheets, photo, bio, lyric sheets, equipment list, demo tape/CD, video, press clippings, reviews, etc. Does not return material. Responds in 1 week.

Music: **All styles**, originals or covers. Current acts include Pete Best Band, Sons of Cream, Blessed Foundation (gospel) and "Desert Wind" (Native American Band of the Year 2000).

IMMIGRANT MUSIC INC., 4859 Rue Garnier, Montreal, Quebec H2J 3S8 Canada. Phone/fax: (514)523-5857. E-mail: immigrant@videotron.ca. **Contact:** Dan Behrman, president. Management firm, booking agency and music publisher. Estab. 1979. Represents individual artists, groups and songwriters from anywhere; currently handles 6 acts. Receives 20% commission. Reviews material for acts.

How to Contact: *Call first and obtain permission to submit or to arrange personal interview.* Prefers cassette, VHS videocassette, CD or vinyl with 4 songs. If seeking management, press kit should include bio, press clippings, photo, references, recordings, technical and personal rider and requirements if known. Does not return material. ("I also may use material on my radio program.") Responds in 1 month.

Music: Mostly **world music**, **original ethnic** and **new acoustic music**; also **singer/songwriters**, **folk** and **ethnic/ambient**. Current acts include Simbi (Xenophile Records, vodou-roots band), B'net Houariyat (Gnawa trance music, women ensemble from Morocco), Regis Gizavo (Malagasy accordionist), Kristi Stassinopoulou (contemporary Greek world/folk/electronica) and Robert David & the Mighty Mardi-Gras (swamp-roots music).

INTERNATIONAL ENTERTAINMENT BUREAU, 3612 N. Washington Blvd., Indianapolis IN 46205-3592. (317)926-7566. E-mail: ieb@prodigy.net. Booking agency. Estab. 1972. Represents individual artists and groups from anywhere; currently handles 146 acts. Receives 20% commission.

How to Contact: *No unsolicited submissions.*

Music: Mostly **rock**, **country** and **A/C**; also **jazz**, **nostalgia** and **ethnic**. Works primarily with bands, comedians and speakers. Current acts include Five Easy Pieces (A/C), Doug Lawson (country) and Lordsmen (gospel).

J & V MANAGEMENT, 143 W. Elmwood, Caro MI 48723. (517)673-2889. Manager/Publisher: John Timko. Management firm, booking agency and music publisher. Represents local, regional or international individual artists, groups and songwriters; currently handles 3 acts. Receives 10% commission. Reviews material for acts.

How to Contact: Write first and obtain permission to submit. Prefers cassette with 3 songs maximum and lyric sheet. If seeking management, include short reference bio, cover letter and résumé in press kit. SASE. Responds in 2 months.

Music: Mostly **country**. Works primarily with vocalists and dance bands. Current acts include John Patrick (country), Alexander Depue (fiddle) and Most Wanted (country).

JACOBSON TALENT MANAGEMENT (JTM), P.O. Box 0740, Murrieta CA 92564-0740. (909)461-9923. Fax: (909)461-9913. E-mail: jim4097@aol.com. Website: www.jtm-ink.com. **Contact:** Jake Jacobson, owner. Senior Associate: Randi Morgan. Management firm and online consultation service. Estab. 1981. Represents individual artists and groups from anywhere; currently handles 2 acts. Receives 15-20% commission. Reviews material for acts.

How to Contact: Call first and obtain permission to submit. Prefers cassette or CD with 5 songs and lyric sheet. If seeking management, press kit should include photo, bio and "anything else you think will help your cause." SASE. Responds in 3 weeks.

Music: Mostly **rock**, **R&B/hip-hop** and **country**; also **adult contemporary**. Works primarily with bands and singer/songwriters. Current acts include The Quiet Room (heavy metal) and Glenn Rottmann (guitar instrumental).

Tips: "Work hard. Hold up your end so we can do our jobs. In addition, we find it much easier to work with artists who have a basic working knowledge of the music industry and personal management. Our website provides educational tips for artists and music industry entrepreneurs. Consulting is available for those that do not need full time management, but may be in need of occasional advice and counsel or career direction."

JANA JAE ENTERPRISES, P.O. Box 35726, Tulsa OK 74153. (918)786-8896. Fax: (918)786-8897. E-mail: janajae@janajae.com. Website: www.janajae.com. **Contact:** Kathleen Pixley, agent. Booking agency, music publisher (Jana Jae Publishing/BMI) and record company (Lark Record Productions, Inc.). Estab. 1979. Represents individual artists and songwriters; currently handles 12 acts. Receives 15% commission. Reviews material for acts.
How to Contact: Submit demo tape by mail. Unsolicited submissions are OK. Prefers cassette or videocassette of performance. If seeking management, press kit should include cover letter, bio, photo, demo tape/CD, lyric sheets and press clippings. Does not return material.
Music: Mostly **country**, **classical** and **jazz instrumentals**; also **pop**. Works with vocalists, show and concert bands, solo instrumentalists. Represents Jana Jae (country singer/fiddle player), Matt Greif (classical guitarist), Sydni (solo singer) and Hotwire (country show band).

ROGER JAMES MANAGEMENT, 10A Margaret Rd., Barnet, Herts EN4 9NP England. Phone: 020 844 9788. **Contact:** Susana Boyle, professional manager. Management firm and music publisher (R.J. Music/PRS). Estab. 1977. Represents songwriters. Receives 50% commission (negotiable). Reviews material for acts.
How to Contact: Submit demo tape by mail. Unsolicited submissions are OK. Prefers cassette with 3 songs and lyric sheet. Does not return material.
Music: Mostly **pop**, **country** and "any good song."

SHELDON KAGAN INTERNATIONAL, 35 McConnell, Dorval, Quebec H9S 5L9 Canada. (514)631-2160. Fax: (514)631-4430. E-mail: sheldon@sheldonkagan.com. Website: www.sheldonkagan.com. **Contact:** Sheldon Kagan, president. Booking agency. Estab. 1965. Represents local individual artists and groups; currently handles 17 acts. Receives 10-20% commission. Reviews materials for acts.
How to Contact: Submit demo tape by mail. Unsolicited submissions are OK. Prefers cassette or VHS videocassette with 6 songs. SASE. Responds in 5 weeks.
Music: Mostly **top 40**. Works primarily with vocalists and bands. Current acts include Quazz (jazz trio), City Lights (top 40 band), Jeux de Cordes (violin and guitar duo), The Soulmates (top 40) and After Hours (top 40).

KICKSTART MUSIC LTD., 10 Park House, 140 Battersea Park Rd., London SW11 4NB England. Phone: (020)7498 9696. Fax: (020)7498 2064. E-mail: cms@cmsi.demon.co.uk. **Contact:** Frank Clark, director. Management/publishing Company. Estab. 1994. Represents individual artists, groups or songwriters from anywhere; currently handles 10 acts. Receives 20-40% commission, "depends on contract." Reviews material for acts.
How to Contact: Submit demo by mail. Unsolicited submissions are OK. Prefers CD, cassette or DAT with 3 songs and lyric and lead sheet. If seeking management, press kit should include photograph and bio. SAE and IRC. Responds in 2 weeks.
Music: All genres including **pop**, **dance**, **rock**, **country** and **blues**. Works primarily with bands who perform a live set of original music and talented singer/songwriters who can cross over to all types of music. Current acts include Kris & Paul Walker (artists/songwriters), Pal Joey (rave band) and Simon Fox (songwriter).
Tips: "We prefer songwriters whose songs can cross over to all types of music, those who do not write in one style only."

KKR ENTERTAINMENT GROUP, 2 Embarcadero Centre, Suite 200, San Francisco CA 94111. Fax: (510)769-8024. E-mail: jkrashna@kke-co.com. Director of Operations: Keith Washington. Management firm. Estab. 1989. Represents individual artists, groups and producers from anywhere; currently handles 5 acts. Receives 20% commission. Reviews material for acts.

How to Contact: *E-mail first and obtain permission to submit.* Prefers CD. If seeking management, press kit should include CD and photo (if available). "We do not accept unsolicited material." SASE. Responds in 1 month.

Music: Mostly **R&B**, **rap** and **rock**. Current acts include E-A-Ski & CMT (DreamWorks/Sony Music), Christion (R&B group, Def Jam Records), The Lab-Producers and Katherina Ramirez.

Tips: "Always learn who you are working with and stay involved in everything."

☑ JOANNE KLEIN, 130 W. 28 St., New York NY 10001. Phone/fax: (212)741-3949. **Contact:** Joanne Klein. Management firm and music publisher. Estab. 1982. Represents individual artists and songwriters from anywhere; currently handles 8 acts. Receives 15-20% commission. Reviews material for acts.

How to Contact: *Write first and obtain permission to submit.* Prefers cassette or CD. If seeking management, press kit should include bio, photos, press/reviews, discography, information on compositions. Does not return material. Responds in 1 month.

Music: Mostly **jazz**. Works primarily with instrumentalist/composers. Current acts include Kenny Barron (jazz), Victor Lewis (jazz), Terell Stafford (jazz), Alex Blake (jazz) and Eddie Henderson (jazz).

☑ BOB KNIGHT AGENCY, 185 Clinton Ave., Staten Island NY 10301. (718)448-8420. **Contact:** Bob Knight, president. Management firm, booking agency, music publisher and royalty collection firm. Estab. 1971. Represents artists, groups and songwriters; currently handles 4 acts. Receives 10-20% commission. Reviews material for acts and for submission to record companies and producers.

How to Contact: Submit demo tape by mail. Unsolicited submissions are OK. Prefers cassette or videocassette (if available) with 5 songs and lead sheet "with bio and references." If seeking management, press kit should include bio, videocassette and audio cassette. SASE. Responds in 2 months.

Music: Mostly **top 40/pop**; also **easy listening**, **MOR**, **R&B**, **soul**, **rock** (nostalgia '50s and '60s), **alternative**, **country**, **country/pop**, **jazz**, **blues** and **folk**. Works primarily with recording and name groups and artists—'50s, '60s and '70s acts, high energy dance and show groups. Current acts include Delfonics (R&B nostalgia), B.T. Express, Brass Construction and Main Ingredient.

Tips: "We're seeking artists and groups with completed albums/demos."

☑ ○ KUPER PERSONAL MANAGEMENT, P.O. Box 66274, Houston TX 77266. (713)520-5791. Fax: (713)523-1048. E-mail: kuper@wt.net. Website: www.kupergroup.com. **Contact:** Ivan Kuper, owner. Management firm and music publisher (Kuper-Lam Music/BMI and Uvula Music/BMI). Estab. 1979. Represents individual artists, groups and songwriters from Texas; currently handles 4 acts. Receives 20% commission. Reviews material for acts.

How to Contact: Submit demo tape by mail. Unsolicited submissions are OK. Prefers cassette. If seeking management, press kit should include cover letter, press clippings, photo, bio (1 page) tearsheets (reviews, etc.) and demo tape/CD. Does not return material. Responds in 2 months.

Music: Mostly **singer/songwriters**, **triple AAA**, **hip-hop** and **Americana**. Works primarily with self-contained and self-produced artists. Current acts include Philip Rodriguez (singer/songwriter), Champ X (rap artist), The Hit Squad (hip-hop) and U.S. Representative for The Watchman (Dutch singer/songwriter).

Tips: "Create a market value for yourself, produce your own master tapes, create a cost-effective situation."

☑ LARI-JON PROMOTIONS, 325 W. Walnut, P.O. Box 216, Rising City NE 68658. (402)542-2336. **Contact:** Larry Good, owner. Management firm, music publisher (Lari-Jon Publishing Co./BMI) and record company (Lari-Jon Records). Represents individual artists, groups and songwriters; currently handles 3 acts. Receives 15% commission. Reviews material for acts.

How to Contact: Submit demo tape by mail. Unsolicited submissions are OK. Prefers cassette with 5 songs and lyric sheet. If seeking management, press kit should include 8 × 10 photos, cassette, videocassette and bio sheet. SASE. Responds in 2 months.

Music: Mostly **country**, **gospel** and **'50s rock**. Works primarily with dance and show bands. Represents Kent Thompson (singer), Nebraskaland 'Opry (family type country show) and Brenda Allen (singer and comedienne).

◐ **RAY LAWRENCE, LTD.**, P.O. Box 1987, Studio City CA 91614. (818)508-9022. Fax: (818)508-5672. **Contact:** Ray Lawrence, president. Management firm, booking agency and music publisher (Boha Music/BMI). Estab. 1963. Represents individual artists from anywhere; currently handles 15 acts. Receives 10-15% commission.
How to Contact: Submit demo tape by mail. Unsolicited submissions are OK. Prefers VHS videocassette. If seeking management, press kit should include 8×10 professional photographs and bio. Does not return material. Responds in 2 weeks.
Music: **All types**. Works primarily with musical and variety acts. Current acts include Trini Lopez (recording artist), Wayland Pickard (recording artist) and Glenn Ash (recording artist).

◐ **LEVINSON ENTERTAINMENT VENTURES INTERNATIONAL, INC.**, 1440 Veteran Ave., Suite 650, Los Angeles CA 90024. (323)663-6940. E-mail: leviinc@aol.com. President: Bob Levinson. **Contact:** Jed Leland, Jr. Management firm. Estab. 1978. Represents national individual artists, groups and songwriters; currently handles 4 acts. Receives 15-25% commission. Reviews material for acts.
How to Contact: *Write first and obtain permission to submit.* Prefers cassette or VHS videocassette with 6 songs and lead sheet. If seeking management, press kit should include bio, pictures and press clips. SASE. Responds in 1 month.
Music: Mostly **rock**, **MOR**, **R&B** and **country**. Works primarily with rock bands and vocalists.
Tips: "Should be a working band, self-contained and, preferably, performing original material."

◑ **RICK LEVY MANAGEMENT**, 4250 A1AS, D-11, St. Augustine FL 32084. (904)460-1225. Fax: (904)460-1226. E-mail: ricklevymgt@webtv.net. Website: www.ricklevy.com. **Contact:** Rick Levy, president. Management firm, music publisher (Flying Governor Music/BMI) and record company (Luxury Records). Estab. 1985. Represents local, regional or international individual artists and groups; currently handles 7 acts. Receives 15-20% commission. Reviews material for acts.
How to Contact: Write or call first and obtain permission to submit. Prefers cassette or VHS videocassette with 3 songs and lyric sheet. If seeking management, press kit should include cover letter, bio, demo tape/CD, VHS video, photo and press clippings. SASE. Responds in 2 weeks.
Music: Mostly **R&B** (no rap), **pop**, **country** and **oldies**. Current acts include Jay & the Techniques ('60s hit group), The Original Box Tops ('60s), The Limits (pop), Barbara Lewis ('60s) and Steel Dog Cafe (modern rock).

N ◐ **DORIS LINDSAY PRODUCTIONS/SUCCESSFUL PRODUCTIONS**, P.O. Box 35005 AMC, Greensboro NC 27425. (336)882-9990. President: Doris Lindsay. Management firm and music publisher (Doris Lindsay Publishing/ASCAP, Better Times/BMI). Estab. 1979. Represents individual artists and/or songwriters from anywhere; currently handles 2 acts. Receives 15% commission. Reviews material for acts.
   • Doris Lindsay Publishing is listed in the Music Publishers section.
How to Contact: Submit demo tape by mail. Unsolicited submissions are OK. Prefers cassette or VHS videocassette with 2-3 songs and lyric sheet. If seeking management, press kit should include photo, cassette and bio. SASE. Responds in 4 months.
Music: Mostly **country**, **contemporary Christian** and **pop**; also **children's**. Primarily works with singers, songwriters. Current acts include Mitch Snow (country).
Tips: "Have a professional studio type demo. Don't send too many songs at one time. Be patient."

◐ **LIVE-WIRE MANAGEMENT**, P.O. Box 653, Morgan Hill, CA 95038. (408)778-3526. Fax: (408)778-3567. E-mail: bruce@L-WM.com. Website: www.L-WM.com. **Contact:** Bruce Hollibaugh, president. Management firm. Estab. 1990. Represents individual artists and groups from anywhere; currently handles 2 acts. Receives 15-25% commission. Reviews material for acts.

How to Contact: Submit demo tape by mail. Unsolicited submissions are OK. Prefers CD or cassette with 3-6 songs and lyric sheet. If seeking management, press kit should include what region you are currently performing in; how often you are doing live shows; any reviews; photos. Does not return material. Responds in 1 month.

Music: Mostly **pop**, **acoustic pop** and **New Age**; also **jazz**, **R&B** and **country**. Works primarily with bands and singer/songwriters. Current acts include Tommy Elskes (singer/songwriter) and Janny Choi (jazz).

□ LOGGINS PROMOTION/BACKSTAGE ENTERTAINMENT, 26239 Senator Ave., Harbor City CA 90710. (310)325-2800. Fax: (310)325-2560. E-mail: promo@logginspromotion.com. Website: www.logginspromotion.com. **Contact:** Paul Loggins, CEO. Management firm and radio promotion. Represents individual artists, groups and songwriters from anywhere; currently handles 6 acts. Receives 20% commission. Reviews material for acts.

How to Contact: If seeking management, press kit should include picture, short bio, cover letter, press clippings and CD (preferred). "Mark on CD which cut you, as the artist, feel is the strongest." Does not return material. Responds in 2 weeks.

Music: Mostly **adult**, **top 40** and **AAA**; also **urban**, **rap**, **alternative**, **college**, **smooth jazz** and **Americana**. Works primarily with bands and solo artists. Current acts include Andi Harrison (A/C/top 40 crossover solo musician), Kenny Loggins (Columbia Records), Silent Opera (Coast Records), Bill Zucker and Joe's Band.

□ LOWELL AGENCY, 4043 Brookside Court, Norton OH 44203. (330)825-7813. Website: www. rfwm.com/leon/. **Contact:** Leon Seiter, agent. Booking agency and song publisher (Lanies Pride/BMI). Estab. 1985. Represents regional (Midwest and Southeast) individual artists; currently handles 2 acts. Receives 10% commission. Reviews material for acts.

How to Contact: Submit demo tape by mail. Unsolicited submissions are OK. Prefers cassette with 4 songs and lyric sheet. If seeking management, press kit should include demo cassette tape, bio and picture. Does not return material. Responds in 2 months.

Music: Mostly **country**. Works primarily with country vocalists. Current acts include Leon Seiter (country singer/entertainer/songwriter) and Marvin Rainwater (country singer/songwriter).

□ M.E.G. MANAGEMENT, 5900 Wilshire Blvd., #560, Los Angeles CA 90036. (323)932-6500. **Contact:** Ty Ronald Supancic, vice president artist development. Management firm. Estab. 1996. Represents individual artists, groups and songwriters from anywhere; currently handles 5 acts. Receives 20% commission. Reviews material for acts.

How to Contact: Submit demo tape by mail. Unsolicited submissions are OK. Prefers cassette or VHS videocassette and lyric sheet. If seeking management, press kit should include cover letter, demo tape/CD, lyric sheets, video, press clippings, photos and bio. "We believe in first impressions. Make it professional." Responds in 3 months.

Music: Mostly **alternative rock**. Current acts include ON (alternative/dance, signed to Warner Bros.), Nick Frost (folk/alternative), Sallie B (rap) and Simple Intrigue (R&B).

□ MAGNUM MUSIC CORPORATION LTD., 8607-128 Avenue, Edmonton, Alberta Canada T5E 0G3. (780)476-8230. Fax: (780)472-2584. **Contact:** Bill Maxim, manager. Booking agency, music publisher (Ramblin' Man Music Publishing/PRO and High River Music Publishing/ASCAP) and record company (Magnum Records). Estab. 1984. Represents individual artists, groups and songwriters from anywhere; currently handles 5 acts. Receives 15% commission. Reviews material for acts.

● **A BULLET** introduces comments by the editor of *Songwriter's Market* indicating special information about the listing.

How to Contact: *Write or call first and obtain permission to submit.* Prefers cassette with 3-4 songs. If seeking management, press kit should include tape or CD, photo, press clippings, bio, résumé and video. Does not return material. Responds in 2 months.
Music: Mostly **country** and **gospel**. Works primarily with "artists or groups who are also songwriters." Current acts include Catheryne Greenly (country), Thea Anderson (country) and Gordon Cormier (country).
Tips: "Prefers finished demos."

N ☮ MANAGEMENT BY JAFFE, 1560 Broadway, Suite 1103, New York NY 10036-0000. (212)869-6912. Fax: (212)869-7102. E-mail: jerjaf@aol.com. President: Jerry Jaffe. Management firm. Estab. 1987. Represents individual artists and groups from anywhere; currently handles 2 acts. Receives 20% commission. Reviews material for acts "sometimes."
How to Contact: *Write or call first to arrange personal interview.* Prefers CD or cassette and videocassette with 3-4 songs and lyric sheet. Does not return material. Responds in 2 months.
Music: Mostly **rock/alternative**, **pop** and **AAA**. Works primarily with groups and singers/songwriters. Current acts include Joe McIntrye (pop) and Ann Marie Montads (rock).
Tips: "Create some kind of 'buzz' first."

✓ ◑ MANAGEMENT PLUS, P.O. Box 65089, San Antonio TX 78265. (210)698-8181, ext. 202. Fax: (210)223-3251. E-mail: bangeliniz@prodigy.net. Website: www.ynotcall.com. **Contact:** Bill Angelini, owner. Management firm and booking agency. Estab. 1980. Represents individual artists and groups from anywhere; currently handles 6 acts. Receives 10-15% commission. Reviews material for acts.
How to Contact: Submit demo tape by mail. Unsolicited submissions are OK. Prefers cassette, VHS videocassette and bio. If seeking management, press kit should include pictures, bio, résumé and discography. Does not return material. Responds in 1 month.
Music: Mostly **Latin American**, **Tejano** and **international**; also **Norteño** and **country**. Current acts include Jay Perez (Tejano), Ram Herrera (Tejano), Rodeo (Tejano) and Grupo Vida (Tejano).

❀ ✓ ◑ THE MANAGEMENT TRUST LTD., 411 Queen St. W, 3rd Floor, Toronto, Ontario M5V 2A5 Canada. (416)979-7070. Fax: (416)979-0505. E-mail: mail@mgmtrust.ca. **Contact:** Sarah Barker Tonge; Bernie Breen; Jake Gold; Allan Gregg; Shelley Stertz; Daniel Buckman. Management firm. Estab. 1986. Represents individual artists and/or groups; currently handles 6 acts.
How to Contact: Submit demo tape by mail. Unsolicited submissions are OK. If seeking management, press kit should include CD or tape, bio, cover letter, photo and press clippings. Does not return material. Responds in 2 months.
Music: **All types**. Current acts include The Tragically Hip (rock band), Big Wreck (rock), The Headstones (rock), Alex Slate (guitar rock), The Watchmen (rock band) and Colin Cripps (producer).

◐ RICK MARTIN PRODUCTIONS, 125 Fieldpoint Road, Greenwich CT 06830. (203)661-1615. E-mail: ezwayrick@aol.com. **Contact:** Rick Martin, president. Personal manager and independent producer. Held the Office of Secretary of the National Conference of Personal Managers from 1975-1997. Represents actresses and vocalists; currently handles 4 acts. Receives 15-25% commission.
How to Contact: *Write first and obtain permission to submit.* SASE.
Music: Mostly **top 40**, **dance** and **rock**. Produces vocal groups and female vocalists. Current acts include Marisa Mercedes (vocalist/songwriter) and Jackie Tohn (vocalist/songwriter/actress).
Tips: "The tape does not have to be professionally produced—it's really not important what you've done—it's what you can do now that counts."

◐ PHIL MAYO & COMPANY, P.O. Box 304, Bomoseen VT 05732. (802)468-2554. Fax: (802)468-8884. E-mail: pmcamgphil@aol.com. **Contact:** Phil Mayo, president. Management firm and record company (AMG Records). Estab. 1981. Represents individual artists, groups and songwriters from anywhere; currently handles 4 acts. Receives 15-20% commission. Reviews material for acts.

How to Contact: *Contact first and obtain permission to submit.* Prefers CD with 3 songs and lyric or lead sheet. If seeking management, include bio, photo and lyric sheet in press kit. Does not return material. Responds in 2 months.

Music: Mostly **rock**, **pop** and **country**; also **blues** and **Christian pop**. Works primarily with dance bands, vocalists and rock acts. Current acts include The Drive (R&B), John Hall, Guy Burlage, Souell Mosser and Pam Buckland.

☑ ◑ **THE McDONNELL GROUP**, 27 Pickwick Lane, Newtown Square PA 19073. (610)353-8554. E-mail: fmcdonn@aol.com. **Contact:** Frank McDonnell. Management firm. Estab. 1985. Represents individual artists, groups and songwriters from anywhere; currently handles 6 acts. Receives 20% commission. Reviews material for acts.

How to Contact: *Write first and obtain permission to submit.* Prefers cassette or VHS videocassette with 4 songs and lyric sheet. If seeking management, include cover letter, lyric sheets, press, tape or video, recent photos and bio. SASE. Responds in 1 month.

Music: Mostly **rock**, **pop** and **R&B**; also **country** and **jazz**. Current acts include Johnny Bronco (rock group), Mike Forte (producer/songwriter) and Pat Martino (jazz guitarist).

☑ ◑ **MEDIA MANAGEMENT**, P.O. Box 3773, San Rafael CA 94912-3773. (415)457-0700. Fax: (415)457-0964. E-mail: mediamanagement9@aol.com. **Contact:** Eugene, proprietor. Management firm. Estab. 1990. Represents local, regional or international individual artists, groups and songwriters; currently handles 4 acts. Receives 20% commission. Reviews material for acts.

How to Contact: Submit demo tape by mail. Unsolicited submissions are OK. Prefers cassette or VHS videocassette with lyric sheet. If seeking management, include lyric sheets, demo tape, photo and bio. Does not return material.

Music: Mostly **rock**, **blues** and **pop**; also **jazz** and **R&B**. Works primarily with songwriting performers/bands (rock). Current acts include Zakiya Hooker (r&b/blues/singer/songwriter), Richard Linley and Mike Gorman (singer/songwriters) and Horace Heidt, Jr. (swing/Big Band leader/singer/songwriter).

Tips: "Write great *radio-friendly* songs."

◑ **MEGA MUSIC PRODUCTIONS**, 290 Sunrise Dr., Unit #3-K, Key Biscayne FL 33149. (309)365-8551. Fax: (305)365-8552. E-mail: megamusic1@aol.com. **Contact:** Marco Vinicio Carvajal, general manager. Management firm and booking agency. Represents individual artists and groups from anywhere; currently handles 8 acts. Receives 20% commission. Reviews material for acts.

How to Contact: Submit demo tape by mail. Unsolicited submissions are OK. Prefers cassette, CD or VHS videocassette with 5 songs and lyric sheet. If seeking management, press kit should include cover letter, demo tape/CD, video, photos and bio. Does not return material. Responds in 1 month.

Music: Mostly **rock**, **techno-dance** and **Latin rock**; also **Latin** and **pop**. Works primarily with bands and singers. Current acts include David Summers (Latin pop), Miguel Majeos and Vilma Palma e Vampiros.

Tips: "Send us compact information and describe your goals."

☒ ☑ ○ **MERLIN MANAGEMENT CORP.**, P.O. Box 5087 V.M.P.O., Vancouver, British Columbia V6B 4A9 Canada. Phone/fax: (604)434-9129. E-mail: merlin.music@home.com. **Contact:** Wolfgang Hamman, president. Management firm, record company (Merlin) and record producer. Estab. 1979. Represents individual artists, groups, songwriters and producers from anywhere; currently handles 3 acts. Receives 20-25% commission. Reviews material for acts.

How to Contact: *Write or call first and obtain permission to submit.* Prefers cassette with 3 songs and lyric and/or lead sheet. If seeking management, press kit should include photo, demo tape/CD, cover letter and bio. SASE. Responds in 2 weeks.

Music: Mostly **modern rock**, **dance** and **pop**; also **techno** and **alternative**. Current acts include Wolfgang-Wolfgang (dance), Lady Jane (pop/R&B) and Donner & Blitzen (electro pop).

Tips: "Write daily, study successful writers."

◐ **MERRI-WEBB PRODUCTIONS**, P.O. Box 5474, Stockton CA 95205. (209)948-8186. E-mail: merri-webb@calcentron.com. **Contact:** Kristy Ledford, A&R coordinator. Management firm, music publisher (Kaupp's & Robert Publishing Co./BMI) and record company (Kaupp Records). Represents regional (California) individual artists, groups and songwriters; currently handles 13 acts. Receives 10-15% commission. Reviews material for acts.
How to Contact: Write first and obtain permission to submit or to arrange personal interview. Prefers cassette or VHS videocassette with 3 songs maximum and lyric sheet. SASE. Responds in 3 months.
Music: Mostly **country, A/C rock** and **R&B**; also **pop, rock** and **gospel**. Works primarily with vocalists, bands and songwriters. Current acts include Bruce Bolin (rock/pop singer), Nanci Lynn (country/pop singer) and Rick Webb (country/pop singer).

☑ ◐ **MIRKIN MANAGEMENT**, 906½ Congress Ave., Austin TX 78701. (512)472-1818. Fax: (512)472-6915. E-mail: mirk1@aol.com. **Contact:** Sue Mortaccia, administrative assistant. Management firm, ASCAP regional representative. Estab. 1986. Represents individual artists, groups and songwriters from anywhere. Reviews material for acts.
How to Contact: *Write or call first and obtain permission to submit a demo.* Prefers CD with 4 songs. If seeking management, press kit should include photo, press clippings and music. SASE.
Music: All types. Current acts include Ian Moore Band (blues/rock) and Kitty Gordon (rock).

Ⓝ ◐ **GARY F. MONTGOMERY MANAGEMENT**, P.O. Box 5106, Macon GA 31208. (478)749-7259. Fax: (478)757-0002. E-mail: gfmmusic@aol.com. **Contact:** Gary F. Montgomery, president. Management firm, music publisher (g.f.m. Music/ASCAP and 12/31/49 Music/BMI) and production company. Estab. 1981. Represents individual artists, groups, songwriters, record producers and engineers; currently handles 4 acts. Receives 10-20% commission (it varies depending on the act). Reviews material for acts.
How to Contact: *Write or call first and obtain permission to submit a demo.* Prefers cassette with 3-5 songs and lyric sheet. If seeking management, press kit should include cover letter, bio, résumé, photo, demo tape/CD, lyric sheets, press clippings and video. "Call first to see if we are accepting new clients." Does not return material. Responds in 2 months only if interested.
Music: All types. Works primarily with singer/songwriters. Current acts include Davis Causey (New Age guitarist).

🌐 ☑ ◯ **MUSIC MARKETING & PROMOTIONS**, (formerly Music Man Promotions), P.O. Box 956, South Perth 6951 Australia. Phone: (618)9450 1199. Fax: (618)9450 8527. E-mail: mmp@global.net.au. Website: www.global.net.au/~mmp/. **Contact:** Eddie Robertson. Booking agency. Estab. 1991. Represents individual artists and/or groups; currently handles 50 acts. Receives 20% commission. Reviews material for acts.
How to Contact: *Write first and obtain permission to submit or submit demo tape by mail.* Unsolicited submissions are OK. Prefers cassette or videocassette with photo, information on style and bio. If seeking management, press kit should include photos, bio, cover letter, résumé, press clippings, video, demo, lyric sheets and any other useful information. Does not return material. Responds in 1 month.
Music: Mostly **top 40/pop, jazz** and **'60s-'90s**; also **reggae** and **blues**. Works primarily with show bands and solo performers. Current acts include Faces (dance band), N.R.G. (show band) and C.J. & the Thorns (soul).
Tips: "Send as much information as possible. If you do not receive a call after four to five weeks, follow up with letter or phone call."

◯ **NASH-ONE MANAGEMENT, INC.**, 4555 Hickory Ridge Rd., Lebanon TN 37087. (615)449-7818. Fax: (615)443-3218. E-mail: bquisenb@bellsouth.net. **Contact:** Bill Quisenberry, president. Management firm and booking agency (Talent Group Intercontinental, Inc.). Estab. 1990. Represents local individual artists and groups; currently handles 1 act. Receives 10% commission. Reviews material for acts.

How to Contact: *Call first and obtain permission to submit.* Prefers cassette. If seeking management, press kit should include photo, cover letter, bio and 4-song tape. SASE. Responds in 2 weeks.
Music: Mostly **country** and **some rock**. Current acts include David Allan Coe (country).

◉ NORTHERN LIGHTS MANAGEMENT, 437 Live Oak Loop NE, Albuquerque NM 87122-1406. (505)856-7100. Fax: (505)856-2566. E-mail: nlightsmgt@aol.com. Website: www.northernligh tsmgt.com. **Contact:** Linda Bolton, owner/manager. Booking agency. Estab. 1989. Represents individual artists, groups and songwriters from anywhere; currently handles 4 acts. Receives 10-15% commission.
How to Contact: *Write or call first and obtain permission to submit.* Prefers cassette or CD with 3-4 songs and lyric sheet. "Please specify which artist the song(s) should be submitted to." Does not return material. Response time varies.
Music: Mostly **bluegrass** and **folk**. Works primarily with 1 "newgrass" band and 3 singer/songwriters. Current acts include Jonathan Edwards (folk/pop/rock singer), Dave Mallett (Maine singer/songwriter), Northern Lights (bluegrass/newgrass band) and Lisa McCormick (contemporary folk rock singer).

◉ NOTEWORTHY ENTERPRISES, 3741 Sunny Isles Blvd., N. Miami Beach FL 33160. (305)949-9192. Fax: (305)949-9492. E-mail: ss@noteworthy.net. Website: www.Noteworthy.net. **Contact:** Sheila Siegel, president. Booking agency, music publisher (On the Water Publications/BMI) and talent buyer. Estab. 1987. Represents individual artists, groups and songwriters from anywhere. Receives 20% commission. Reviews material for acts.
How to Contact: *Does not accept unsolicited submissions.*
Music: Mostly **big band**. Works primarily with jazz artists. Current acts include Noteworthy Orchestra (big band), Southlanders Traditional Jazz Band, David Siegel and Jack Siegel.

✓ ◉ NOTEWORTHY PRODUCTIONS, 124½ Archwood Ave., Annapolis MD 21401. (410)268-8232. Fax: (410)268-2167. E-mail: mcshane@mcnote.com. Website: www.mcnote.com. **Contact:** McShane Glover, president. Management firm and booking agency. Estab. 1985. Represents individual artists, groups and songwriters from everywhere; currently handles 6 acts. Receives 15-20% commission. Reviews material for acts.
How to Contact: *Write first and obtain permission to submit.* Prefers CD/CDR with lyric sheet. If seeking management, press kit should include cassette or CD, photo, bio, venues played and press clippings (preferably reviews). "Follow up with a phone call 3-5 weeks after submission." Does not return material. Responds in 1 month.
Music: Mostly **Americana**, **folk**, and **celtic**. Works primarily with performing singer/songwriters. Current acts include Seamus Kennedy (Celtic/contemporary), Tanglefoot (Canadian) and Clandestine (Texas celtic).

◯ ON STAGE MANAGEMENT, P.O. Box 679, Bronx NY 10469. E-mail: onstagemgt@aol.com. Management firm and production. Estab. 1988. Represents individual artists and/or groups and songwriters from anywhere; currently handles 4 acts. Receives 15-20% commission. Reviews material for acts.
How to Contact: Submit demo tape by mail. Unsolicited submissions are OK. Prefers cassette or VHS videocassette with at least 2 songs, "the more the better." If seeking management, press kit should include cassette or VHS video tape, picture and bio. Does not return material. Responds in 2 weeks only if interested.
Music: Mostly **dance music**, **rock**, and **pop**; also **R&B**. Current acts include Choir of the Damned (rock group), Luna Eclipse (ambient dance), AVA (dance) and Psychosis (techno).
Tips: "Our artists sing songs with positive messages. We don't want songs that glorify violence or are too risqué."

◯ ON THE LEVEL MUSIC!, P.O. Box 508, Owego NY 13827. (607)689-0122. Fax: (607)687-0928. **Contact:** Fred Gage, CEO/president. Management firm, booking agency and music publisher (On The Level Music! Publishing). Estab. 1970. Represents individual artists, groups and songwriters from anywhere; currently handles 30 acts. Receives 15% commission. Reviews material for acts.

How to Contact: Submit demo tape by mail. Unsolicited submissions are OK. Prefers CDs, DAT or VHS videocassette with 4 songs and lyric or lead sheet. If seeking management, press kit should include cover letter, bio, demo tape/CD, lyric sheets, press clippings, 8×10 photo and video. Does not return material. Responds in 1 month.

Music: Mostly **rock**, **alternative** and **jazz**. Current acts include Mule in the Corn, Reynolds and Chase (rock).

✔️ 🎵 **ORIGINAL ARTISTS' AGENCY**, 1031 E. Battlefield Rd., Suite 224, Springfield MO 65807. (417)881-4174. Fax: (417)881-3185. **Contact:** James R. Doran, manager. Management firm and booking agency. Estab. 1984. Represents individual artists, groups and songwriters from anywhere; currently handles 7 acts. Commission varies. Reviews materials for acts.

How to Contact: Submit demo tape by mail. Unsolicited submissions are OK. Prefers cassette. If seeking management, press kit should include demo tape, picture and bio. Does not return material.

Music: Mostly **country**, **blues** and **rock**. Works primarily with individual artists and bands. Current acts include Ray Price (country artist), Johnny Paycheck (country artist) and Ozark Jubilee (country show).

Tips: "Please submit initial demo with your three top songs. We can go from there."

✔️ 🎵 **OUTLAND PRODUCTIONS**, 8511 Hurst Ave., Savannah GA 31406-6013. (912)920-6208. **Contact:** John R. Brookshire, producer/manager. Management firm, record company (Outland Records) and record producer (John R. Brookshire). Estab. 1973. Represents individual artists and groups from anywhere; currently handles 2 acts. Receives 15% commission. Reviews material for acts.

How to Contact: Submit demo tape by mail. Unsolicited submissions are OK. Prefers cassette, videocassette or CD with 5 songs and lead sheet. If seeking management, press kit should include cover letter, demo tape/CD, lyric sheets, press clippings, résumé, bio and pictures or video. Does not return material. Responds in 3 months.

Music: Mostly **hard rock**, **heavy metal** and **hardcore**; also **punk rock**, **death metal** and **death black metal**. Works primarily with all metal bands. Current acts include Requiem (hardcore thrash), Grip (hip-hop) and Fist (death metal).

🔄 ⭕ **OUTLAW ENTERTAINMENT INTERNATIONAL**, #101-1001 W. Broadway, Dept. 400, Vancouver, British Columbia V6H 4E4 Canada. (604)878-1494. Fax: (604)878-1495. E-mail: info@outlawentertainment.com. Website: www.outlawentertainment.com. CEO/President: Tommy Floyd. Assistant President: Suzanne Funke. Management firm. Estab. 1995. Represents individual artists, groups and songwriters from anywhere; currently handles 3 acts. Receives 20% commission. Reviews material for acts.

How to Contact: Submit demo tape by mail. Unsolicited submissions are OK. Prefers cassette with 2-3 songs and lyric sheet. If seeking management, press kit should include 8×10 photo, bio and written statement of goals. SAE and IRC. Responds in 1 month.

Music: Mostly **rock**, **metal** and **punk**; also **pop** and **dance**. Works primarily with bands, "but welcomes dynamic singer/songwriters." Current acts include The Cartels (punk rock act), American Dog (hard rock act) and Shuvel Head (heavy metal act).

Tips: "Clearly define your target market. Write simple, emotional, primal songs."

🆕 🎵 **PILLAR RECORDS**, P.O. Box 858, Carlisle PA 17013-0858. Phone/fax: (717)249-2536. E-mail: mail@v-domains.com. Website: www.craigkelley.com. **Contact:** A&R Department. Management firm, music publisher and record company. Estab. 1994. Represents individual artists, groups and songwriters from anywhere; currently handles 2 acts. Receives 20% commission. Reviews material for acts.

REFER TO THE GEOGRAPHIC INDEX (at the back of this book) to find listings of companies by state, as well as foreign listings.

How to Contact: Submit demo tape by mail. Unsolicited submissions are OK. Prefers CD/CDR with 3 songs and lyric sheet. If seeking management, press kit should include bio, photo, reviews, mailing list, tape or CD. "Please be neat and as professional as possible." Does not return material. Responds in 6 weeks.
Music: Mostly **pop/rock** and **folk/rock**. Works primarily with solo artists and bands. Current acts include the Craig Kelley Band (mainstream rock).
Tips: "Currently looking for a vocals/guitar or vocal/piano act. No band needed."

◯ **PRECISION MANAGEMENT**, 110 Coliseum Crossing, #158, Hampton VA 23666-5902. Phone/fax: (757)875-0323. E-mail: pmmuzic@aol.com. Website: www.angelfire.com/on2/Precision Management. **Contact:** Cappriccieo Scates, operations director. Management firm and music publisher (Mytrell/BMI). Estab. 1990. Represents individual artists and/or groups and songwriters from anywhere; currently handles 3 acts. Receives 20% commission. Reviews material for acts.
How to Contact: Submit demo tape by mail. Unsolicited submissions are OK. Prefers cassette or VHS videocassette with 3-4 songs and lyric sheet. If seeking management, press kit should include photo, bio, demo tape/CD, lyric sheets, press clippings and all relevant press information. SASE. Responds in 6 weeks.
Music: Mostly **R&B**, **rap** and **gospel**; also **all types**. Current acts include Surface (R&B act), Joe'I Chancellor (rap artist) amd Desire (R&B).

▦ ☑ ◐ **PRESTIGE ARTISTES**, HighRidge Bath Rd., Farmborough NR Bath BA3 1BR United Kingdom. Phone: 07050 277053. E-mail: drees15066@aol.com. **Contact:** David Rees, proprietor. Management firm and booking agency. Associate company: Lintern Rees Organisation. Estab. 1983. Represents individual artists, groups, songwriters, comedians and specialty acts; currently handles 20 acts. Receives 10-15% commission. Reviews material for acts.
How to Contact: Submit demo tape by mail. Unsolicited submissions are OK. Prefers cassette with 3 songs and lyric sheet. If seeking management, press kit should include good demo tape, cover letter, any references, bio, press clippings, publicity photos and video if available (UK format). Artist should be based in the UK. Does not return material. Responds in 1 month.
Music: Mostly **MOR**, **pop**, **'60s style**, **country** and **rock**. Works primarily with vocal guitarists/keyboards, pop groups, pub/club acts and guitar or keyboard duos. Current acts include Legend (duo), Elvis Presley Junior (vocalist) and Fran DeVere (vocalist).
Tips: "Do not send more than three songs, your best available. Tell us what you want in the UK—be realistic."

◯ **PRO TALENT CONSULTANTS**, P.O. Box 233, Nice CA 95464. Phone/fax: (707)274-2625. E-mail: jemusic@hotmail.com. **Contact:** John Eckert, coordinator. Management firm and booking agency. Estab. 1979. Represents individual artists and groups; currently handles 9 acts. Receives 20% commission. Reviews material for acts.
How to Contact: Submit demo tape by mail. Unsolicited submissions are OK. Prefers cassette or VHS videocassette with at least 4 songs and lyric sheet. "We prefer audio cassette (4 songs). Submit videocassette with live performance only." If seeking management, press kit should include an 8×10 photo, a cassette or CD of at least 4-6 songs, a bio on group/artist, references, cover letter, press clippings, video and business card or a phone number with address. Does not return material. Responds in 5 weeks.
Music: Mostly **country**, **country/pop** and **rock**. Works primarily with vocalists, show bands, dance bands and bar bands. Current acts include Jon Richards (country singer), The Golden Leaders of the Rockin' '60s (variety show, various performers) and Jewel Akens "Mr. Birds and Bees" (pop singer).

☑ ◯ **RADIOACTIVE**, 350 Third Ave., Suite 400, New York NY 10010. (917)733-4700. E-mail: info@radiotv.com. Website: radiotv.com. **Contact:** Kenjamin Franklin, agent. Booking and talent agency. Estab. 1983. Represents individual artists, groups and broadcasters from anywhere; currently handles 20 acts. Receives 10% commission. Reviews material for acts.
How to Contact: Submit demo tape by mail. Unsolicited submissions are OK. "Please do not phone." Prefers CD, cassette or VHS video with 3 songs and lyric sheet. Press kit should include

bio, press clippings, photo, cover letter, résumé, video, e-mail address and 3 radio-friendly original songs on cassettes/CD. "Label all cassettes with phone number and e-mail address." Does not return material. Responds in 3 weeks. "We only call upon further interest."

Music: Mostly **modern rock**, **ballads** and **AAA**; also **A/C** and **CHR/pop**. Current acts include Ambrosia (rock), Les Lokey (alternative) and Kati Mac (AAA).

☑ ◖ **RAINBOW COLLECTION LTD.**, 4696 Kahlua Lane, Bonita Springs FL 34134. (941)947-6978. E-mail: obitts@aol.com. **Contact:** Richard (Dick) O'Bitts, executive producer. Management firm, record company (Happy Man Records) and music publisher (Rocker Music and Happy Man Music). Represents individual artists, groups, songwriters and producers; currently handles 3 acts. Receives 10-20% commission. Reviews material for acts.

How to Contact: Submit demo tape by mail. Unsolicited submissions are OK. Prefers cassette or VHS videocassette of live performance with 4 songs and lyric sheet. If seeking management, press kit should include photos, bio and tapes. SASE. Responds in 1 month.

Music: Mostly **country**, **pop** and **rock**. Works primarily with writer/artists and groups of all kinds. Current acts include 4 Harmonee (country/pop), The Thorps (country pop) and Okefenokee Joe (nature writer and vocalist).

☑ ◖ **RAINBOW TALENT AGENCY**, (formerly M & M Talent Agency Inc.), 146 Round Pond Lane, Rochester NY 14662. (716)723-3334. **Contact:** Carl Labate. Management firm and booking agency. Represents artists and groups; currently handles 3 acts. Receives 15-25% commission.

How to Contact: Submit demo tape by mail. Unsolicited submissions are OK. Prefers cassette, CD/CDR with minimum 3 songs and lyric sheet. May send video if available; "a still photo would be good enough to see the type of performance; if you are a performer, it would be advantageous to show yourself or the group performing live. Theme videos are not helpful." If seeking management, include photos, bio, markets established, tape and/or videos. Does not return material. Responds in 1 month.

Music: **Blues**, **rock** and **R&B**. Works primarily with touring bands and recording artists. Current acts include The Frantic Flattops (rockabilly) and Artimus Pyle Band (southern rock/R&B).

Tips: "My main interest is with groups or performers that are currently touring or ready to do so. And are at least 60% percent original. Strictly songwriters should apply elsewhere."

☑ ◯ **RENAISSANCE ENTERTAINMENT GROUP**, P.O. Box 1222, Mountainside NJ 07092-1222. E-mail: regroup@hotmail.com. **Contact:** Kevin A. Joy, president/CEO. Management firm, booking agency, record company (Suburan Records) and record producer (Onyx Music and Bo²Legg Productions). Estab. 1992. Represents individual artists, groups and songwriters from anywhere; currently handles 10 acts. Receives 20% commission. Reviews material for acts.

How to Contact: *Write first and obtain permission to submit.* Prefers cassette with 3 songs and lyric or lead sheet. If seeking management, press kit should include cover letter, demo tape/CD, lyric sheets, press clippings, pictures and bio. Does not return material. Responds in 5 weeks.

Music: Mostly **R&B**, **rap** and **rock**. Works primarily with R&B groups, rap and vocalists. Current acts include Hillside Strangler (rap), Lori Stephens (R&B/pop) and A Mother's Child (rock).

◖ **DIANE RICHARDS WORLD MANAGEMENT, INC.** E-mail: drworldmgm@aol.com. **Contact:** Diane Richards, president. Management firm. Estab. 1994. Represents individual artists, groups, songwriters and producers from anywhere; currently handles 8 acts. Receives 20% commission. Reviews material for acts.

How to Contact: *Write first (via e-mail) and obtain permission to submit.* If seeking management, press kit should include cover letter, photograph, biography, cassette tape, telephone number and address. Does not return material. Responds in 1 month.

Music: Mostly **dance**, **pop** and **rap**; also **New Age**, **A/C** and **jazz**. Works primarily with pop and dance acts, and songwriters who also are recording artists. Current acts include Sappho (songwriter/artist), Menace (songwriter/producer/artist) and Babygirl (R&B/rap artist).

◖ **RIGHT-ON MANAGEMENT**, P.O. Box 2627, Dearborn MI 48123. (313)274-7000. Fax: (313)274-9255. E-mail: angel@angelgomez.com. Website: www.angelgomez.com. **Contact:** Angel

Gomez, president. Management firm. Estab. 1979. Represents local and international individual artists, groups and songwriters; currently handles 9 acts. Receives 15-20% commission. Reviews material for acts.

How to Contact: *Write first and obtain permission to submit.* Prefers cassette or videocassette of performance with 3-5 songs. If seeking management, include photo, tape/CD, bio, cover letter, press clippings and itinerary of dates. Does not return material. Responds in 2 months.

Music: Mostly **rock**, **pop** and **top 40**; also **funk**. Works primarily with individual artists, groups (bar bands) and songwriters. Current artists include Deena (soulful funk), The Rev. Right Time and the First Cuzins of Funk (new funk) and Greg Isles (rock).

☑ ◗ **RIOHCAT MUSIC**, P.O. Box 764, Hendersonville TN 37077-0764. (615)824-9313. Fax: (615)824-0797. E-mail: tachoir@bellsouth.net. Website: www.tachoir.com. **Contact:** Robert Kayne, manager. Management firm, booking agency, record company (Avita Records) and music publisher. Estab. 1975. Represents individual artists and groups; currently handles 4 acts. Receives 15-20% commission.

How to Contact: *Contact first and obtain permission to submit.* Prefers cassette and lead sheet. If seeking management, press kit should include cover letter, bio, photo, demo tape/CD and press clippings. Does not return material. Responds in 6 weeks.

Music: Mostly **contemporary jazz** and **fusion**. Works primarily with jazz ensembles. Current acts include Group Tachoir (jazz), Tachoir/Manakas Duo (jazz) and Marlene Tachoir.

☑ ◗ **A.F. RISAVY, INC.**, 1312 Vandalia, Collinsville IL 62234. (618)345-6700. Fax: (618)235-0004. Website: www.swingcitymusic.com. **Contact:** Art Risavy, president. Management firm and booking agency. Divisions include Artco Enterprises, Golden Eagle Records, Swing City Music and Swing City Sound. Estab. 1960. Represents artists, groups and songwriters; currently handles 50 acts. Receives 10% commission. Reviews material for acts.

How to Contact: Submit demo tape by mail. Unsolicited submissions are OK. Prefers CD/CDR, cassette or VHS videocassette with 2-6 songs and lyric sheet. If seeking management, press kit should include pictures, bio and VHS videocassette. SASE. Responds in 3 weeks.

Music: Mostly **rock**, **country**, **MOR** and **top 40**.

Ⓝ ◗ **ROCK OF AGES PRODUCTIONS**, 1001 W. Jasmine Dr., Suite K, Lake Park FL 33403-2119. (561)848-1500. Fax: (561)848-2400. President/Agency Director: Joseph E. Larson. Booking agent, literary agency and publisher. Estab. 1980. Represents individual artists and groups from anywhere; currently handles 500 acts. Receives 15-25% commission. Reviews material for acts.

How to Contact: Submit demo tape by mail. Unsolicited submissions are OK. Prefers cassette or VHS videocassette with 3 or more songs and lead sheet. If seeking management, press kit should include videocassette and/or audio cassette, lyric sheets, relevant press, bio, cover letter, résumé and recent photo. SASE. Responds in 3 months.

Music: Mostly **top 40**, **country/western** and **rock**; also **gospel** and **opera**. Works primarily with bands, singers, singer/songwriters. Current acts include Andrew Epps (ballad singer/songwriter), John Michael Ferrari (singer/songwriter) and Paola Semprini (opera star).

◗ **ROCK WHIRLED MUSIC MANAGEMENT**, 1423 N. Front St., Harrisburg PA 17102. (717)236-2386. E-mail: phil.clark@rockwhirled.com. Website: www.rockwhirled.com. **Contact:** Philip Clark, director. Management firm, booking agency and publicists. Estab. 1987. Represents individual artists and/or groups from anywhere; currently handles 12 acts. Receives 10-25% commission. Reviews material for acts.

How to Contact: *Contact first and obtain permission to submit.* Prefers cassette. If seeking management, press kit should include bio, cover letter, demo tape/CD, photo, song list, venue list, description of performance frequency, equipment needed, goals. SASE. Responds in 6 weeks.

Music: Mostly **rock**, **alternative** and **folk**. Works primarily with soloist singer/instrumentalists, duo acoustic acts, bands. Current acts include My World (modern rock), Cameron Molloy (country fusion) and Adria (celtic).

Tips: "Be brief, clear, focused in approach. Approach a variety of other agents and managers to get a feel for which companies make the best match. We look for clients who wish to work specifically with us, not just any firm."

CHARLES R. ROTHSCHILD PRODUCTIONS INC., 330 E. 48th St., New York NY 10017. (212)421-0592. **Contact:** Charles R. Rothschild, president. Booking agency. Estab. 1971. Represents individual artists, groups and songwriters from anywhere; currently handles 25 acts. Receives 25% commission. Reviews material for acts.

How to Contact: *Call first and obtain permission to submit.* Prefers cassette, CD or VHS videocassette with 1 song and lyric and lead sheet. If seeking management, include cassette, photo, bio and reviews. SASE. Responds in 6 weeks.

Music: Mostly **rock**, **pop**, **family** and **folk**; also **country** and **jazz**. Current acts include Richie Havens (folk singer), Leo Kottke (guitarist/composer), Emmylou Harris (country songwriter), Tom Chapin (kids' performer and folksinger) and John Forster (satirist).

RUSTRON MUSIC PRODUCTIONS, Send all artist song submissions to: 1156 Park Lane, West Palm Beach FL 33417-5957. (561)686-1354. E-mail: gordon-whims@juno.com. Main Office: 42 Barrack Hill Rd., Ridgefield CT 06877. ("Main office does not review new material—only South Florida Branch office does.") Executive Director: Rusty Gordon. Artist Consultants: Rusty Gordon and Davilyn Whims. Composition Management: Ron Caruso. Management firm, booking agency, music publisher (Rustron Music Publishers/BMI and Whimsong Publishing/ASCAP), record company and record producer. Estab. 1970. Represents individuals, groups and songwriters; currently handles 20 acts. Commissions vary. Reviews material for acts.

How to Contact: Write first and obtain permission to submit. Send cassette with 3-6 songs (CD/cassette produced for sale preferred). Provide typed lyric or lead sheet for every song in the submission. If seeking management, press kit should include cover letter, bio, demo tape/CD, typed lyric sheets and press clippings. "SASE required for all correspondence." Responds in 4 months.

Music: Mostly **blues** (**country folk/urban**, **Southern**), **country** (**rock**, **blues**, **progressive**), **easy listening**, **Cabaret**, **soft rock** (**ballads**), **women's music**, **R&B**, **folk/rock**; also **New Age instrumentals** and **New Age folk fusion**. Current acts include Jayne Margo-Reby (folk rock), Vic Bersok (folk fusions/soft rock), Star Smiley (country), Lynn Thomas and Dorothy Hirsh (music comedy), Robin Plitt (historical folk), Lisa Cohen (Cabaret/pop/acapella) and Song on A Whim (folk/world music).

Tips: "Send cover letter, typed lyric sheets for all songs. Carefully mix demo, don't drown the vocals, 3-6 songs in a submission. Prefer a for-sale CD made to sell at gigs. Send photo if artist is seeking marketing and/or production assistance. Very strong hooks, definitive melody, evolved concepts, unique and unpredictable themes. Flesh out a performing sound unique to the artist."

SAFFYRE MANAGEMENT, 400 Paula Ave., #306, Glendale CA 91201. (818)842-4368. E-mail: ebsaffyre@yahoo.com. **Contact:** Esta G. Bernstein, president. Management firm. Estab. 1990. Represents individual artists, groups and songwriters from anywhere; currently handles 3 acts. Receives 15% commission.

How to Contact: *Call first and obtain permission to submit.* If seeking management, press kit should include cover letter, bio, photo, cassette with 3-4 songs and lyric sheets. Does not return material. Responds in 2 weeks only if interested.

Music: Mostly **alternative/modern rock** and **top 40**. "We work only with bands and solo artists who write their own material; our main objective is to obtain recording deals and contracts, while advising our artists on their careers and business relationships." Current artists include Scott Moss (top 40 singer/songwriter), Will Postell (alternative singer/songwriter) and Jason Blair (R&B singer/songwriter).

SA'MALL MANAGEMENT, P.O. Box 8442, Universal City CA 91608. (310)317-4338. Fax: (818)506-8534. E-mail: samusa@aol.com. Website: www.pplzmi.com. **Contact:** Ted Steele, vice president of talent. Management firm, music publisher (Pollybyrd Publications) and record company (PPL Entertainment Group). Estab. 1990. Represents individual artists, groups and songwriters from anywhere; currently handles 10 acts. Receives 10-25% commission. Reviews material for acts.

How to Contact: *E-mail first and obtain permission to submit.* Prefers cassette with 2 songs and lyric and lead sheet. If seeking management, press kit should include picture, bio and tape. SASE. Responds in 2 months.

Music: All types. Current acts include Riki Hendrix (rock), Buddy Wright (blues), Fhyne, Suzette Cuseo, The Band Aka, LeJenz, B.D. Fuoco and Jay Sattiewhite.

○ SEA CRUISE PRODUCTIONS, INC., P.O. Box 1875, Gretna LA 70054-1875. (504)392-4615. Fax: (504)392-4512. E-mail: kenkeene@aol.com. Website: www.frankieford.com. **Contact:** Ken Keene, president/general manager. Management firm, booking agency, music publisher (Sea Cruise Music/BMI), record company (Briarmeade Records) and record producer (Sea Cruise Productions). Estab. 1970. Represents individual artists, groups and songwriters from anywhere; currently handles 12 acts. Receives 15% commission. Reviews material for acts.

How to Contact: Submit demo tape by mail. Unsolicited submissions are OK. Prefers cassette or VHS videocassette with 5-6 songs and lyric or lead sheet. If seeking management, press kit should include cassette, videocassette, CD, publicity photos, bio and press clipping, cover letter, résumé and lyric sheets. Does not return material. "No phone calls." Responds in 2 months "if we are interested in the act."

Music: Mostly **nostalgia '50s/'60s**, **country rock** and **R&B**; also **ballads**, **double entendre** and **novelty songs**. "Most of our acts are '50s, '60s and '70s artists, all of whom have had million selling records, and who are still very active on the concert/night club circuit." Current acts include Frankie Ford (legendary rock 'n' roll singer/pianist), Troy Shondell (singer/songwriter), Jean Knight (Grammy nominated R&B singer) and Narvel Felts (country/rockabilly legend).

⊘ SENDYK, LEONARD & CO. INC., 532 Colorado Ave., Santa Monica CA 90401. (310)458-8860. Fax: (310)458-8862. **Contact:** Gerri Leonard, partner. Business management. Represents individual artists, groups and songwriters from anywhere; currently handles 15 acts. Receives 5% commission.

How to Contact: "We do not solicit any songwriters for works to be submitted to artists, but are certainly interested in representing songwriters with respect to their financial affairs. We can also monitor their royalties; we have an extensive royalty administration department."

Music: Current acts include Marilyn Manson (hard rock), Jonathon Butler (jazz/urban), Great White (hard rock) and The Cranberries (alternative).

📺 ⊘ SERGE ENTERTAINMENT GROUP, P.O. Box 672216, Marietta GA 30006-0037. (770)850-9560. Fax: (770)850-9646. E-mail: sergeent@aol.com. Website: www.serge.org. **Contact:** Sandy Serge, president. Management and PR firm and song publishers. Estab. 1987. Represents individual artists, groups, songwriters from anywhere; currently handles 15 acts. Receives 15-25% commission. Reviews materials for acts.

How to Contact: Submit demo tape or CD by mail. Unsolicited submissions are OK. Prefers cassette or CD with 4 songs and lyric sheet. If seeking management, press kit should include 8 × 10 photo, bio, cover letter, lyric sheets, max of 4 press clips, VHS videocassette, performance schedule and CD. "All information submitted must include name, address and phone number on each item." Does not return material. Responds in 6 weeks if interested.

Music: Mostly **rock**, **pop** and **country**; also **New Age**. Works primarily with singer/songwriters and bands. Current acts include Rene (New Age), Dominic Gaudious (New Age) and Ted Winn (country).

Tips: "We specialize in synchronication licensing with TV/firm."

🌐 ⊘ PHILL SHUTE MANAGEMENT PTY. LTD., Box 273, Dulwich Hill NSW 2203 Australia. Phone: +61 2 95692152. Fax: +61 2 95692152. Website: www.big-rock.com.au. **Contact:** Phill

---

OPENNESS TO SUBMISSIONS: ○ beginners; ⊘ beginners and experienced; ⊘ experienced only; ⊘ no unsolicited submissions/industry referrals only.

Shute, CEO. Management firm, booking agency and record company (Big Rock Records). Estab. 1979. Represents local individual artists and groups; currently handles 8 acts. Receives 10% commission. Reviews material for acts.

How to Contact: Submit demo tape by mail. Unsolicited submissions are OK. Prefers cassette with 4 songs and lyric sheet. If seeking management, press kit should include cover letter, bio, photo, demo tape/CD, press clippings and résumé. Does not return material. Responds in 1 month.

Music: Mostly **rock**, **pop** and **R&B**; also **country rock**. Works primarily with rock bands, pop vocalists and blues acts (band and vocalists). Current acts include Phill Simmons (country), Two R More (pop/rock) and Now Hear This (rock).

Tips: "Make all submissions well organized (e.g., bio, photo and experience of the act). List areas in which the act would like to work, complete details for contact."

✔ ◑ **SIDDONS & ASSOCIATES**, 584 N. Larchmont Blvd., Hollywood CA 90004. (323)462-6156. Fax: (323)462-2076. E-mail: siddons@earthlink.net. A&R: Lexa Nicoletti. President: Bill Siddons. Management firm. Estab. 1972. Represents individual artists and groups from anywhere; currently handles 2 acts. Receives 15-20% commission. Reviews material for acts.

How to Contact: Write first and obtain permission to submit a demo. Prefers CD or VHS videocassette with 3 songs and lyric sheet. If seeking management, press kit should include cassette of 3 songs, lyric sheet, VHS videocassette if available, biography, past credits and discography. Does not return material. Responds in 3 months.

Music: **All styles.** Current acts include Elayne Boosler (comedian) and Kurt Bestor (singer/songwriter).

◑ **T. SKORMAN PRODUCTIONS, INC.**, 3660 Maguire Blvd., Suite 250, Orlando FL 32803. (407)895-3000. Fax: (407)895-1422. E-mail: ted@talentagency.com. Website: www.talentagency.com. **Contact:** Ted Skorman, president. Management firm and booking agency. Estab. 1983. Represents groups; currently handles 40 acts. Receives 10-25% commission. Reviews material for acts.

How to Contact: *Write or call first for permission to send tape.* Prefers cassette with 3 songs, or videocassette of no more than 15 minutes. "Live performance—no trick shots or editing tricks. We want to be able to view act as if we were there for a live show." If seeking management, press kit should include cover letter, bio, photo and demo tape/CD. Does not return material. Responds in 2 months.

Music: Mostly **top 40**, **techno**, **dance**, **MOR** and **pop**. Works primarily with high-energy dance acts, recording acts, and top 40 bands. Current acts include Steph Carse (pop), Kimberly Spears (country) and Michael Behm (rock).

Tips: "We have many pop recording acts and are looking for commercial material for their next albums."

◑ **SOUND MANAGEMENT DIRECTION**, 152-18 Union Turnpike, Flushing NY 11367. (718)969-0166. Fax: (718)969-8914. E-mail: sounddirection@aol.com. **Contact:** Bob Currie, president. Management firm, consultant, music publisher (Sun Face Music/ASCAP, Shaman Drum/BMI) and record producer. Estab. 1986. Represents individual artists and/or groups, songwriters, producers and engineers from anywhere; currently handles 6 acts. Receives 20% commission. Reviews material for acts.

How to Contact: Submit demo tape by mail. Unsolicited submissions are OK. Prefers CD or VHS videocassette with 2 songs and lyric sheet. If seeking management, press kit should include 3 song demo, photo and contact information including phone numbers. "If you want material returned, include SASE." Responds in 3 weeks.

Music: Seeking commercial, contemporary and radio-oriented **rock**, **dance**, **jazz** and **urban**. Works primarily with singer/songwriters and self-contained bands.

Tips: "We only want your best, and be specific with style. Quality, not quantity."

🅽 ◑ **SOUTHEASTERN ATTRACTIONS**, 181 W. Valley Ave., Suite 105, Birmingham AL 35209. (205)942-6600. Fax: (205)942-7700. E-mail: seattractions@mindspring.com. **Contact:** Agent. Booking agency. Estab. 1967. Represents groups from anywhere; currently handles 200 acts. Receives 20% commission.

How to Contact: Submit demo tape by mail. Unsolicited submissions are OK. Prefers cassette or VHS videocassette. Does not return material. Responds in 2 weeks.

Music: Mostly **rock**, **alternative** and **oldies**; also **country**. Works primarily with bands. Current acts include Second Hand Jive (contemporary rock), Telluride (Southern rock) and Undergrounders (variety to contemporary).

SP TALENT ASSOCIATES, P.O. Box 475184, Garland TX 75047. **Contact:** Richard Park, talent coordinator. Management firm and booking agency. Represents individual artists and groups; currently handles 7 acts. Receives 15% commission. Reviews material for acts.

How to Contact: Submit demo tape by mail. Unsolicited submissions are OK. Prefers VHS videocassette with several songs. Send photo and bio. Does not return material. Responds as soon as possible.

Music: Mostly **rock**, **nostalgia rock** and **country**; also **specialty acts** and **folk/blues**. Works primarily with vocalists and self-contained groups. Current acts include Joe Hardin Brown (country), Rock It! (nostalgia), Renewal (rock group) and Juan Madera & the Supple Grain Seeds.

SPHERE GROUP ONE, P.O. Box 991, Far Hills NJ 07931-0991. (908)781-1650. Fax: (908)781-1693. E-mail: spheregroupone@att.net. President: Tony Zarrella. Talent Manager: Louisa Pazienza. Management firm and record producer. Estab. 1987. Represents individual artists and groups from anywhere; currently handles 5 acts. Receives 20-25% commission.

How to Contact: Send all new submissions to Vision 2000. Submit demo tape by mail. Unsolicited submissions are OK. Prefers CD, cassette or VHS videocassette with 3-5 songs. All submissions must include cover letter, lyric sheets, tape/CD, photo, bio and all press. "Due to large number of submissions we can only respond to those artists which we may consider working with." Does not return material

Music: Mostly **pop/rock**, **pop/country** and **New Age**; also **R&B**. Works primarily with bands and solo singer/songwriters. Current acts include 4 of Hearts (pop/rock), Oona Falcon (pop/rock), Frontier 9 (pop/rock), Viewpoint (experimental) and Bombay Green (hybrid pop).

Tips: "Develop and create your own style, focus on goals and work as a team and maintain good chemistry with all artists and business relationships."

THE SPOON AGENCY L.L.C., (formerly Bread & Butter Productions), P.O. Box 92075, Austin TX 78709-2075. (512)301-7117. Fax: (888)647-4010. E-mail: steve@spoonagency.com. **Contact:** Steve Gladson, managing partner. Management firm and booking agency. Estab. 1969. Represents individual artists, songwriters and groups from anywhere; currently handles 6 acts. Receives 10-20% commission. Reviews material for acts.

How to Contact: Submit demo tape by mail. Unsolicited submissions OK. Prefers cassette, videocassette or CD and lyric sheet. If seeking management, press kit should include cover letter, demo tape/CD, lyric sheets, press clippings, video, résumé, picture and bio. Does not return material. Responds in 1 month.

Music: Mostly **alternative rock**, **country** and **R&B**; also **classic rock**. Works primarily with singer/songwriters and original bands. Current acts include Lou Cabaza (songwriter/producer/manager), Duck Soup (band) and Gaylan Ladd (songwriter/singer).

Tips: "Remember why you are in this biz. The art comes first."

STAIRCASE PROMOTION, P.O. Box 211, East Prairie MO 63845. (573)649-2211. **Contact:** Tommy Loomas, president. Vice President: Joe Silver. Management firm, music publisher (Lineage Publishing) and record company (Capstan Record Production). Estab. 1975. Represents individual artists and groups from anywhere; currently handles 6 acts. Receives 25% commission. Reviews material for acts.

How to Contact: Submit demo tape by mail. Unsolicited submissions are OK. Prefers cassette with 3 songs and lyric sheet. If seeking management, press kit should include bio, photo, audio cassette and/or video and press reviews, if any. "Be as professional as you can." SASE. Responds in 2 months.

Music: Mostly **country**, **pop** and **easy listening**; also **rock**, **gospel** and **alternative**. Current acts include Skidrow Joe (country comedian, on Capstan Records), Vicarie Arcoleo (pop singer, on Treasure Coast Records) and Scarlett Britoni (pop singer on Octagon Records).

STANDER ENTERTAINMENT, 6309 Ben Ave., N. Hollywood CA 91606. Phone/fax: (818)769-6365. E-mail: stander@earthlink.net. **Contact:** Jacqueline Stander, manager. Management firm, music publisher (DocRon Publishing), record company (Soaring Records) and consulting firm. Estab. 1970. Represents local individual artists, groups, film composers and songwriters; currently handles 6 acts. Receives 15% commission. Charges $50/hour consulting fee. Reviews material for acts.
How to Contact: Call first and obtain permission to submit. Prefers cassette or VHS videocassette with 3-5 songs and lyric sheet. If seeking management, press kit should include photo, bio, press publicity, CD or cassette. SASE. Responds in 3 weeks.
Music: Mostly **jazz**, **pop** and **R&B** (no rap); also **world music** and **Broadway**. Works primarily with national recording artists, film composers and singer/songwriters. Current acts include Bill Cunliffe (jazz pianist/producer), Freddie Ravel (contemporary Latin jazz keyboardist), Lauren Wood (vocalist/songwriter) and Ruby (blues singer).
Tips: "Always looking for long term professionals who have worked to establish themselves in their market, yet want to go to the next level. For those who have something to offer and are just starting out, I am available for consulting by phone or in person. Please call for submission request."

STARKRAVIN' MANAGEMENT, 20501 Ventura Blvd., 217, Woodland Hills CA 91364. (818)587-6801. Fax: (818)587-6802. E-mail: bcmclane@aol.com. **Contact:** B.C. McLane, Esq. Management and law firm. Estab. 1994. Represents individual artists, groups and songwriters. Receives 20% commission (management); $175/hour as attorney.
How to Contact: Submit demo tape by mail. Unsolicited submissions are OK. Does not return material. Responds in 1 month.
Music: Mostly **rock**, **pop** and **R&B**. Works primarily with bands.

OBI STEINMAN MANAGEMENT, 5627 Sepulveda Blvd., #230, Van Nuys CA 91411. (818)787-4065. Fax: (818)787-4194. E-mail: obistmgmt@aol.com. **Contact:** Obi Steinman, manager. Management firm. Represents individual artists and groups from anywhere; currently handles 4 acts. Receives 15-20% commission.
How to Contact: Submit demo tape by mail. Unsolicited submissions are OK. Prefers cassette with 4 songs and lyric sheet. If seeking management, press kit should include 8×10 picture, press clippings and bio. "Concentrate more on the material enclosed than the flashy package." SASE. Responds in 5 weeks.
Music: Mostly **pop R&B**, **pop rock**, **alternative** and **hard rock**. Works primarily with bands and self-contained artists (write own material, have own backing band). Current acts include Warrant (hard rock), Slaughter (hard rock) and L.A. Guns (hard rock).
Tips: "We are street level. We are looking for new acts."

STEVENS & COMPANY MANAGEMENT, P.O. Box 6368, Corpus Christi TX 78411. (361)888-7311. Fax: (361)888-7360. E-mail: steveco@flash.net. Website: www.fidelHernandez.co. **Contact:** Matt Stevens, owner. Management firm. Estab. 1995. Represents individual artists from anywhere. Currently handles 3 acts. Receives 20% commission. Reviews material for acts.
How to Contact: Submit demo tape by mail. Unsolicited submissions are OK. Prefers cassette with lyric sheet. SASE. Responds in 3 weeks.
Music: Mostly **Latin**, **Mexican regional** and **tejano**; also **country**. Works primarily with singers and individual artists. Current acts include Fidel Hernandez (Mexican regional vocalist/Universal Music Latino) and Victoria Y Sus Chickos (Gupero-Tejano).
Tips: "Send material every time you have something new, always leave phone number on tapes."

☑ ◑ **STEVE STEWART MANAGEMENT**, 8225 Santa Monica Blvd., Los Angeles CA 90046. (323)650-9700. Fax: (323)650-2690. E-mail: scout@stevestewart.com. Website: www.stevestewart.c om. **Contact:** Steve Stewart, president. Management firm. Estab. 1993. Represents individual artists and/or groups from anywhere; currently handles 9 acts. Receives 20% commission.
How to Contact: Submit demo tape by mail. Unsolicited submissions are OK. Prefers cassette. If seeking management, press kit should include CD, photo and bio if available. "Mail first, call 4-6 weeks later. Cannot return any material." Responds in 2 months.
Music: Mostly **alternative** and **rock**. Works primarily with bands. Current acts include Hometown Hero, Bluebird and Screaming Trees.

☑ ◑ **STORMIN' NORMAN PRODUCTIONS**, 2 Front, Red Bank NJ 07701. (732)741-8733. (732)741-5353. E-mail: normanseldin@aol.com. Website: www.storminnormanproductions.com. **Contact:** Norman Seldin, owner. Management firm, booking agency, music publisher (Noisy Joy Music/BMI) and record company (Ivory Records). Estab. 1967. Represents individual artists, groups and songwriters from anywhere; currently handles 6 acts. Receives 15-20% commission. Reviews material for acts.
How to Contact: Submit demo tape by mail. Unsolicited submissions are OK. Prefers cassette with 2-4 songs and lyric sheet. If seeking management, press kit should include demo cassette with cover and original songs, photo, song list, appearance credits, home base area, phone and address. SASE. Responds in 5 weeks.
Music: Mostly **country, rock** and **reggae**; also **soft rock, dynamic blues** and **folk**. Current acts include Stormin' Norman Band (R&B/nostalgia/adult contemporary), Steel Breeze (Caribbean/Latin/ blues) and Bobby Vac & Everyone (adult contemporary).

♣ ◑ **STRICTLY FORBIDDEN ARTISTS**, 320 Avenue Rd., Suite 144, Toronto, Ontario M4V 2H3 Canada. (416)926-0818. Fax: (416)926-0811. E-mail: brad.black@sympatico.ca. Website: http:// brad2001.homestead.com/1.html. **Contact:** Brad Black, vice president of A&R. Management firm, booking agency and record company. Estab. 1986. Represents individual artists and groups from anywhere; currently handles 8 acts. Receives 20-30% commission. Reviews material for acts.
How to Contact: Submit demo tape by mail. Unsolicited submissions are OK. Prefers cassette with 3-6 songs and lyric sheet. If seeking management, press kit should include biography, press clippings, 8×10, photo and demo tape/CD. "Once you've sent material, don't call us, we'll call you." Does not return material. Responds in 6 weeks.
Music: Mostly **alternative rock, art rock** and **grindcore**; also **electronic, hip-hop** and **experimental**. Works primarily with performing bands, studio acts and performance artists. Current acts include Sickos (experimental/art-rock), Lazer (coldwave/electronica) and Andy Warhead (punk rock/noise).
Tips: "As long as you have faith in your music, we'll have faith in promoting you and your career."

🅽 ◑ **SURFACE MANAGEMENT INC.**, 200 Shearwater Court W., Suite #23, Jersey City NJ 10008. Phone/fax: (201)369-9784. E-mail: patti@surfacemgmt.com. Website: www.surfacemgmt.c om. **Contact:** Patti Beninati, president. Management firm. Estab. 1990. Represents local individual solo artists and groups; currently handles 3 acts. Receives 20% commission. Reviews material for acts.
How to Contact: Submit demo tape by mail or website. Unsolicited submissions are OK. Prefers CD/CDR with 5 songs and lyric sheet. If seeking management, press kit should include cover letter, bio, photo, demo, lyric sheets and press clippings. Does not return material. Responds in 1 month.
Music: Mostly **alternative pop** and **heavy rock**. Current acts include Nick Douglas.

♣ ☑ ◯ **T.J. BOOKER LTD.**, P.O. Box 969, Rossland, British Columbia V0G 1Y0 Canada. (250)362-7795. E-mail: winterland@netidea.com. **Contact:** Tom Jones, owner. Management firm, booking agency and music publisher. Estab. 1976. Represents individual artists, groups and songwriters from anywhere; currently handles 6 acts. Receives 15% commission. Reviews material for acts.
How to Contact: Submit demo tape by mail. Unsolicited submissions are OK. Prefers cassette or videocassette with 3 songs. If seeking management, include demo tape or CD, picture, cover letter and bio in press kit. Does not return material. Responds in 1 month.

Music: Mostly **MOR**, **crossover**, **rock**, **pop** and **country**. Works primarily with vocalists, show bands, dance bands and bar bands. Current acts include Kirk Orr (folk/country), Mike Hamilton (rock/blues) and Larry Hayton (rock/blues).

✓ ◖ **T.L.C. BOOKING AGENCY**, 37311 N. Valley Rd., Chattaroy WA 99003. (509)292-2201. Fax: (509)292-2205. E-mail: tlcagent@yahoo.com. Website: www.tlcagency.com. **Contact:** Tom or Carrie Lapsansky, agent/owners. Booking agency. Estab. 1970. Represents individual artists and groups from anywhere; currently handles 17 acts. Receives 10-15% commission. Reviews material for acts.
How to Contact: *Call first and obtain permission to submit.* Prefers cassette with 3-4 songs. Does not return material. Responds in 3 weeks.
Music: Mostly **rock**, **country** and **variety**; also **comedians** and **magicians**. Works primarily with bands, singles and duos. Current acts include Nobody Famous (variety), Menagerie (variety-duo) and Soul Patrol (variety/top 40).

◖ **TAS MUSIC CO./DAVE TASSE ENTERTAINMENT**, N2467 Knollwood Dr., Lake Geneva WI 53147-9731. E-mail: baybreeze@idcnet.com. Website: www.baybreezerecords.com. **Contact:** David Tasse. Booking agency, record company and music publisher. Represents artists, groups and songwriters; currently handles 21 acts. Receives 10-20% commission. Reviews material for acts.
How to Contact: Submit demo tape by mail. Unsolicited submissions are OK. Prefers cassette with 2-4 songs and lyric sheet. Include performance videocassette if available. If seeking management, press kit should include tape, bio and photo. Does not return material. Responds in 3 weeks.
Music: Mostly **pop** and **jazz**; also **dance**, **MOR**, **rock**, **soul** and **top 40**. Works primarily with show and dance bands. Current acts include Max Kelly (philosophic rock) and L.J. Young (rap).

◖ **TEXAS SOUNDS ENTERTAINMENT**, P.O. Box 1644, Dickinson TX 77535. (281)337-2473. Fax: (281)534-1127. Website: www.texas-sounds.com. **Contact:** Mike Sandberg or George M. DeJesus, co-owners. Management firm, booking agency. Estab. 1980. Represents individual artists, groups and songwriters from anywhere. Currently handles 60 acts. Receives 10% commission.
How to Contact: *Write first and obtain permission to submit a demo.* Prefers cassette with 3-4 songs and lyric and/or lead sheet. If seeking management, press kit should include bio, photo, accomplishments, demo tape. Does not return material.
Music: Mostly **country**, **R&B** and **Latin pop**. Works primarily with bands, orchestras, singer/songwriters. Current acts include Johnny Lee (country singer), Chris Chitsey (country singer/songwriter), Patrick Murphy (country singer/songwriter) and Hamilton Loomis (R&B singer/musician).

𝕹 ◖ **315 BEALE STUDIOS/TALIESYN ENTERTAINMENT**, P.O. Box 382638, Memphis TN 38183. (901)751-4189. Fax: (901)753-8323. E-mail: escrugas@wspice.com. **Contact:** Eddie Scruggs, president. Management firm and music publisher. Estab. 1972. Represents individual artists and/or groups and songwriters from anywhere; currently handles 12 acts. Receives 20% commission. Reviews material for acts.
How to Contact: *Contact first and obtain permissions to submit.* Prefers cassette. If seeking management, press kit should include bio, picture, tape and clippings. Does not return material. Responds in 3 weeks.
Music: Mostly **rock**, **urban** and **country**. Current acts include Curtis Lance.

◖ **TIGER'S EYE ENTERTAINMENT MANAGEMENT & CONSULTING**, 1876 Memorial Drive, Green Bay WI 54303. (920)494-1588. **Contact:** Thomas C. Berndt, manager/CEO. Management firm and record producer. Estab. 1992. Represents individual artists, groups and songwriters from anywhere; currently handles 3 acts. Receives 20% commission. Reviews material for acts.

THE OPENNESS TO SUBMISSIONS INDEX at the back of this book lists all companies in this section by how open they are to submissions.

How to Contact: Submit demo tape by mail. Unsolicited submissions are OK. Prefers cassette or VHS videocassette with 3-4 songs and lyric sheet. If seeking management, press kit should include tape, lyric sheet, photo, relevant press and bio. "Artist should follow up with a call after 2 weeks." Does not return material. Responds in 2 weeks.

Music: Mostly **alternative**, **hard rock** and **R&B**; also **pop**, **rap** and **gothic groove**. Works primarily with vocalists, singer/songwriters and fresh alternative grunge. Current acts include Dusk (ambient gothic groove), Arlo Leach (folksinger) and C.J. Mack (R&B).

A TOTAL ACTING EXPERIENCE, Dept. Rhymes-1, 20501 Ventura Blvd., Suite 399, Woodland Hills CA 91364. **Contact:** Dan A. Bellacicco, agent. Talent agency. Estab. 1984. Represents vocalists, lyricists, composers and groups; currently handles 30 acts. Receives 10% commission. Reviews material for acts. Agency License: TA-0698.

How to Contact: Submit demo tape by mail. Unsolicited submissions are OK. Prefers cassette or VHS videocassette with 3-5 songs and lyric or lead sheets. Please include a revealing "self talk" at the end of your tape. "Singers or groups who write their own material must submit a VHS videocassette with photo and résumé." If seeking management, press kit should include VHS videotape, five 8×10 photos, cover letter, professional résumé, bio, demo tape/CD, lyric sheets, press clippings and business card. Does not return material. Responds in 3 months only if interested. "Please include your e-mail address."

Music: Mostly **top 40/pop**, **jazz**, **blues**, **country**, **R&B**, **dance** and **MOR**; also "theme songs for new films, TV shows and special projects."

Tips: "No calls please. We will respond via your SASE. Your business skills must be strong. Please use a *new/fresh* tape and keep vocals up front. We welcome young, sincere talent who can give total commitment, and most important, *loyalty*, for a long-term relationship. We are seeking female vocalists (a la Streisand or Whitney Houston) who can write their own material, for a major label recording contract. Your song's story line must be as refreshing as the words you skillfully employ in preparing to build your well-balanced, orchestrated, climactic last note! Try to eliminate old, worn-out, dull, trite rhymes. A new way to write/compose or sing an old song/tune will qualify your originality and professional standing. We welcome young fresh talent who appreciate old fashioned agency nurturing, and strong guidance, in return, your honesty, commitment and growth."

TUTTA FORZA MUSIC, 34 Haviland St. #310, Norwalk CT 06854. Phone/fax: (203)855-0095. Proprietor: Andrew Anello. Management firm, booking agency, music publisher (Tutta Forza Publishing/ASCAP) and record company. Estab. 1990. Represents New York Metro Area artists; currently handles 6 acts. Receives 10% commission. Reviews material for acts.

How to Contact: Submit demo tape by mail. Unsolicited submissions are OK. Prefers cassette, VHS videocassette or CD with 3 songs. If seeking management, press kit should include recent press releases, music reviews, biography and cover letter. SASE. Responds in 3 weeks.

Music: Mostly **jazz fusion**, **classical** and **modal combat jazz**; also **instrumentalists**, **composers** and **improvisors**. Works primarily with single artists, composers, improvisors and instrumentalists. Current acts include Andrew Anello (clarinetist/composer) and The Jazz X-Centrix.

Tips: "Looking for self-sufficient individualists; musicians who bring their own unique artistic qualities to work with. Genre of music not nearly as important as quality and taste in their style!"

TWENTIETH CENTURY PROMOTIONS, 155 Park Ave., Cranston RI 02905. (401)467-1832. Fax: (401)467-1833. **Contact:** Gil Morse, president. Management firm, booking agency and record producer (20th Century). Estab. 1972. Represents individual artists and groups from anywhere; currently handles 9 acts. Receives 15% commission. Reviews material for acts.

How to Contact: Call first and obtain permission to submit or to arrange personal interview. Prefers cassette. If seeking management, press kit should include photo and bio. Does not return material. Responds in 3 weeks.

Music: Mostly **country** and **blues**. Works primarily with individuals and groups. Current acts include Robbin Lynn, Charlie Brown's Costars and Bobby Buris Pickett (Monster Mash).

Tips: "Don't give up."

⊘UMPIRE ENTERTAINMENT ENTERPRIZES, 1507 Scenic Dr., Longview TX 75604. (903)759-0300. Fax: (903)234-2944. **Contact:** Jerry Haymes, owner/president. Management firm, music publisher (Golden Guitar, Umpire Music) and record company (Enterprize Records). Estab. 1974. Represents individual artists, groups, songwriters and rodeo performers from anywhere; currently handles 6 acts. Receives 15% commission. Reviews material for acts.
How to Contact: *Contact first and obtain permission to submit.* Prefers cassette with lyric and lead sheets. If seeking management, press kit should include cover letter, bio, picture, lyric sheets, video and any recordings. Does not return material. "Submissions become part of files for two years, then disposed of." Responds in 1 month.
Music: Mostly **country, pop** and **gospel**. Artists include Kelly Grant (country/pop artist), Over the Hill Gang (Golden Oldies group) and Jerry Haymes (cross-over country/rock-a-billy).

☑○ UNIVERSAL MUSIC MARKETING, P.O. Box 2297, Universal City TX 78148. (210)599-0022. E-mail: bswrl8@txdirect.net. Website: www.bswrecords.com. **Contact:** Frank Willson, president. Management firm, record company (BSW Records), booking agency, music publisher and record producer (Frank Wilson). Estab. 1987. Represents individual artists and groups from anywhere; currently handles 12 acts. Receives 15% commission. Reviews material for acts.
How to Contact: Submit demo tape by mail. Unsolicited submissions are OK. Prefers cassette or ¾″ videocassette with 3 songs and lyric sheet. If seeking management, include tape/CD, bio, photo and current activities. SASE. Responds in 6 weeks.
Music: Mostly **country** and **light rock**; also **blues** and **jazz**. Works primarily with vocalists, singer/songwriters and bands. Current acts include Candee Land, Darlene Austin and Larry Butler.

⊕☑♡ HANS VAN POL MANAGEMENT, Utrechtseweg 39, 1381 GS Weesp, Netherlands. Phone: (0)294-413-633. Fax: (0)294-480-844. E-mail: osgood-morely@wxs.nl. Managing Director: Hans Van Pol. A&R/Producer: Jochem Fluitsma. Management firm, consultant (Hans Van Pol Music Consultancy), record company (J.E.A.H.! Records) and music publisher (Blue & White Music). Estab. 1984. Represents regional (Holland/Belgium) individual artists and groups; currently handles 7 acts. Receives 20% commission. Reviews material for acts.
How to Contact: Submit demo tape by mail. Unsolicited submissions are OK. Prefers cassette or VHS videocassette with 3 songs and lyric sheets. If seeking management, press kit should include demo, possible video (VHS/PAL), bio, press clippings, photo and release information. SAE and IRC. Responds in 1 month.
Music: Mostly **MOR**, dance: **rap/swing beat/hip house/R&B/soul/c.a.r.** Current acts include George Bakker Selection (MOR), Fluitsma & Van Tÿn (production, commercials, MOR), Tony Scott (rap) and MC Miker "G" (rap/R&B).

☑⊘ RICHARD VARRASSO MANAGEMENT, P.O. Box 387, Fremont CA 94537. (510)792-8910. Fax: (510)792-0891. E-mail: richard@varrasso.com. Website: www.varrasso.com. President: Richard Varrasso. A&R: Saul Vigil. Management firm. Estab. 1976. Represents individual artists, groups and songwriters from anywhere; currently handles several acts. Receives 10-20% commission. Reviews material for acts.
How to Contact: Submit demo tape by mail. Unsolicited submissions are OK. Prefers cassette or CD. If seeking management, press kit should include photos, bios, cover letter, cassette, lyric sheets, press clippings, video, résumé and contact numbers. Good kits stand out. Does not return material. Responds in 2 months.
Music: Mostly **rock, blues** and **young country**. Works primarily with concert headliners and singers. Current acts include Gary Cambra of the Tubes, Dave Meniketti Group, Famous Hits Band featuring Rich Varasso, Alameda Allstars (Greg Allman's backup band), Richie Barron of HWY2000, Tongue N Groove, Greg Douglass (songwriter) and Blunt Force Trauma.

Ⓝ⊘ VOKES BOOKING AGENCY, P.O. Box 12, New Kensington PA 15068-0012. (724)335-2775. President: Howard Vokes. Booking agency, music publisher (Vokes Music Publishing) and record company (Vokes Record Co.). Represents individual traditional country and bluegrass artists. Books name acts in on special occasions. For special occasions books nationally known acts from Grand Ole Opry, Jamboree U.S.A., Appalachian Jubliee, etc. Receives 10-20% commission.

How to Contact: New artists send 45 rpm record, cassette, LP or CD. Responds in 1 week.
Music: Mostly traditional **country**, **bluegrass**, **old time** and **gospel**; definitely no rock or country rock. Current acts include Howard Vokes & His Country Boys (country) and Mel Anderson.
Tips: "We work mostly with traditional country bands and bluegrass groups that play various bars, hotels, clubs, high schools, malls, fairs, lounges, or fundraising projects. We work at times with other booking agencies in bringing acts in for special occasions. Also we work directly with well-known and newer country, bluegrass and country gospel acts not only to possibly get them bookings in our area, but in other states as well. We also help 'certain artists' get bookings in the overseas marketplace."

◻ **WILLIAM F. WAGNER AGENCY**, 14343 Addison St. #221, Sherman Oaks CA 91423. (818)905-1033. **Contact:** Bill Wagner, owner. Management firm and record producer (Bill Wagner). Estab. 1957. Represents individual artists and groups from anywhere; currently handles 2 acts. Receives 15% commission. Reviews materials for acts.
How to Contact: Submit demo tape by mail. Unsolicited submissions are OK. Prefers cassette or CD with 5 songs and lead sheet. If seeking management, press kit should include cover letter, bio, picture, tape or CD with 5 songs. "If SASE and/or return postage are included, I will reply in 30 days. I will not reply by telephone or fax." SASE. Responds in 1 month.
Music: Mostly **jazz**, **contemporary pop** and **contemporary country**; also **classical**, **MOR** and **film and TV background**. Works primarily with singers, with or without band, big bands and smaller instrumental groups. Current acts include Page Cavanaugh (jazz/pop/contemporary/pianist) and Sandy Graham (jazz singer).
Tips: "Indicate in first submission what artists you are writing for, by name if possible. Don't send material blindly. Be sure all material is properly copyrighted. Be sure package shows 'all material herein copyrighted' on outside."

◻ **WALLS & CO. MANAGEMENT/SHOWBIZ KIDZ!**, 4237 Henderson Blvd., Tampa FL 33629. (813)288-2022. Fax: (813)639-1164. E-mail: prinkey@mindspring.com. **Contact:** M. Susan Walls, director/personal manager. Management firm. Estab. 1988. Represents individual artists from anywhere; currently handles 4 acts. Receives 15% commission. Reviews material for acts.
How to Contact: *Call first and obtain permission to submit a demo or submit demo tape by mail.* Prefers cassette or CD with up to 5 songs and lyric sheet. If seeking management, press kit should include appearance schedules, press releases, bio/picture, publicist's name, articles/reviews. Does not return material. Responds in 2 weeks.
Music: Mostly **country**, **jazz** and **pop**. Works primarily with bands with lead vocalists, individual artists and some songwriters. Current acts include Brandy Taylor (17-year-old country artist), Darcy McClaren (15-year-old country artist) and Nick Pellito (14-year-old musical theatre artist).
Tips: "Listen, learn from experience and write every day."

☑ ◻ **CHERYL K. WARNER PRODUCTIONS**, P.O. Box 127, Hermitage TN 37076-0127. Phone/fax: (615)847-1286. E-mail: cherylkwarner@home.com. Website: www.cherylkwarner.com. **Contact:** Cheryl K. Warner and David M. Warner, owners. Management firm, booking agency, music publisher (Cheryl K. Warner Music), record company (CKW Records) and record producer (Cheryl K. Warner). Estab. 1988. Currently handles 3 acts. Receives 20-25% commission. Reviews material for acts.
How to Contact: Submit demo tape by mail. Unsolicited submissions are OK. Prefers cassette or VHS videocassette with 3 best songs, lyric or lead sheet, bio and picture. If seeking management, press kit should include CD or cassette with up-to-date bio, cover letter, lyric sheets, press clippings, video and picture. Does not return material. Responds in 6 weeks if interested.
Music: Mostly **country/traditional and contemporary**, **Christian/gospel** and **A/C/pop**. Works primarily with singer/songwriters and bands with original and versatile style. Current acts include Cheryl K. Warner (Nashville recording artist/entertainer), Cheryl K. Warner Band (support/studio alt) and Veronica (developmental/contemporary artist).

☑ ◻ **WEMUS ENTERTAINMENT**, 4301 Arroyo, Suite 2, Midland TX 79707. (972)444-9040. Fax: (972)869-1173. E-mail: wemus@aol.com. Website: www.wemus.com. **Contact:** Dennis Grubb, president. Management firm, booking agency and music publisher (Wemus Music, Inc.). Estab. 1983. Represents local and regional individual artists and groups; currently handles 10 acts. Receives 15-20% commission. Reviews material for acts.

How to Contact: Submit demo tape by mail. Unsolicited submissions are OK. Prefers cassette or VHS videocassette with 3-5 songs and lyric sheet. If seeking management, press kit should include glossy head and full body shots and extensive biography. "Make sure address, phone number and possible fax number is included in the packet, or a business card." Does not return material. Responds in 1 month if possible.

Music: Mostly **country**. Current acts include The Image (variety), The Big Time (variety) and The Pictures (variety).

Tips: "We preview and try to place good songs with national artists who are in need of good materials. We have a very tough qualification process. We refuse to forward sub-par materials to major artists or artists management."

✔ ◯ **SHANE WILDER ARTISTS' MANAGEMENT**, P.O. Box 335678, North Las Vegas NV 89033-0012. (702)395-5624. **Contact:** Shane Wilder, president. General Manager: Aaron Wilder. Management firm, music publisher (Shane Wilder Music/BMI) and record producer (Shane Wilder Productions). Represents artists and groups; currently handles 3 acts. Receives 10% commission. Reviews material for acts.

How to Contact: Submit demo tape by mail. Unsolicited submissions are OK. Prefers cassette or videocassette of performance with 4-10 songs and lyric sheet. If seeking management, send cover letter, bio, lyric sheets, cassette with 4-10 songs, photos of individuals or groups, video if possible and any press releases. "Submissions should be highly commercial." SASE. Responds in 2 weeks.

Music: Country. Works primarily with single artists and groups. Current acts include Isabel Marie (country), Craig Dodson (country), Darren Collier (rock) and Ann Lee (country).

✔ ◖ **YVONNE WILLIAMS MANAGEMENT**, 6433 Topanga Blvd. #142, Canoga Park CA 91303. (818)366-0510. Fax: (818)366-0520. E-mail: yvonne1940@aol.com. **Contact:** Yvonne Williams, president. Management firm, music publisher (Jerry Williams Music), record company (S.D.E.G.) and record producer (Jerry Williams). Estab. 1978. Represents individual artists and songwriters from anywhere; currently handles 12 acts. Receives 10-20% commission. Reviews material for acts.

How to Contact: Submit demo tape by mail. Unsolicited submissions are OK. Prefers CD/CDR only with any number of songs and lyric sheet. If seeking management, press kit should include cover letter, bio, photo, CD, press clippings, video and résumé. Include SASE, name, phone and any background in songs placed. Responds in 2 months.

Music: Mostly **rap**, **R&B**, **rock** and **country**; also **gospel** and **blues**. Works primarily with singer/songwriters and singers. Current acts include Swamp Dogg (R&B, rock, soca), Wilson Williams (blues), Clarence Carter (R&B/blues) and 20 Mill Kasino (rap).

Tips: "Make a good clean demo, with a simple pilot vocal that is understandable."

◯ **RICHARD WOOD ARTIST MANAGEMENT**, 69 North Randall Ave., Staten Island NY 10301. (718)981-0641. Fax: (718)273-0797. **Contact:** Richard Wood. Management firm. Estab. 1974. Represents musical groups; currently handles 3 acts. Receives 20% commission. Reviews material for acts.

How to Contact: Submit demo tape by mail. Unsolicited submissions are OK. Prefers cassette and lead sheet. If seeking management, press kit should include demo tape, photo, cover letter and résumé. SASE. Responds in 1 month.

Music: Mostly **dance**, **R&B** and **top 40/pop**; also **MOR**. Works primarily with "high energy" show bands, bar bands and dance bands. Current acts include Forces of Nature (rap).

◖ **WORLD PARK PRODUCTIONS**, P.O. Box 1571, Providence RI 02901-1571. (617)278-9968. Fax: (401)944-4755. E-mail: worldpark@aol.com. **Contact:** Eric Sanzen, director/president. Management firm and booking agency. Estab. 1985. Represents individual artists, groups and songwriters from anywhere; currently handles 8-15 acts. Receives 10-15% commission. Reviews material for acts.

How to Contact: *Write first and obtain permission to submit.* Prefers CD. If seeking management, press kit should include cover letter, press clippings, photo, bio, CD and video (if available). Does not return material. Responds in 2 months.

Music: Mostly **world/roots**, **jungle/techno** and **folk**; also **electronica**, **vocals** and **jazz**. Works primarily with established acts. Current acts include Vinx (singer/songwriter major releases), Capercaillie (Scottish/Celtic rock band), Brian Hughes (jazz guitarist/producer) and Master Musicians of Jajouka (traditional Moroccan).

Tips: "Have an organized presentation and attitude."

WORLD WIDE MANAGEMENT, P.O. Box 536, Bronxville NY 10708. (914)337-5131. Fax: (914)337-5309. **Contact:** Jared Lloyd, A&R. Director: Steve Rosenfeld. Management firm and music publisher (Neighborhood Music/ASCAP). Estab. 1971. Represents artists, groups, songwriters and actors; currently handles 6 acts. Receives 15-20% commission. Reviews material for acts.

How to Contact: *Write first and obtain permission to submit.* Prefers CD, cassette or videocassette of performance with 3-4 songs. If seeking management, press kit should include cover letter, bio, reviews, press clippings, CD or cassette with lyrics and photo. Does not return material. Responds in 1 month.

Music: Mostly **contemporary pop**, **folk**, **folk/rock** and **New Age**; also **A/C**, **rock**, **jazz**, **bluegrass**, **blues**, **country** and **R&B**. Works primarily with self-contained bands and vocalists. Current acts include Small Things Big (alternative), Sandi Rose (country/pop) and Levi Byrd (blues).

WORLDSOUND, LLC, (formerly Wyatt Management Worldwide, Inc.), 17860 New Hope St., #160, Fountain Valley CA 92708. (714)839-7700. Fax: (425)988-0294. E-mail: wmw@wyattworld.com. Website: www.wyattworld.com. **Contact:** Marysia Kolodziet, A&R manager. Management firm. Estab. 1976. Represents individual artists, groups and songwriters from anywhere; currently handles 8 acts. Receives 20% commission. Reviews material for acts.

How to Contact: Submit demo tape by mail. Unsolicited submissions are OK. Prefers CD, cassette or VHS videocassette with 2-10 songs and lyric sheet. If seeking management, press kit should include band biography, photos, video, members' history, press and demo reviews. SASE. Responds in 1 month.

Music: Mostly **rock**, **pop** and **world**; also **heavy metal**, **hard rock** and **top 40**. Works primarily with pop/rock groups. Current acts include Carmine Appice (rock), Keali'i Reichel (world music) and Carbon 9 (tribal rock/industrial pop metal).

Tips: "Always submit new songs/material, even if you have sent material that was previously rejected; the music biz is always changing."

ZANE MANAGEMENT, INC., The Land Title Building, 100 S. Broad St., Suite 630, Philadelphia PA 19110. (215)640-9770. Fax: (215)640-9769. **Contact:** Lloyd Z. Remick, Esq., president. Entertainment/sports consultants and managers. Represents artists, songwriters, producers and athletes; currently handles 7 acts. Receives 10-15% commission.

How to Contact: Submit demo tape by mail. Unsolicited submissions are OK. Prefers cassette, CD and lyric sheet. If seeking management, press kit should include cover letter, bio, photo, demo tape and video. Does not return material. Responds in 3 weeks.

Music: Mostly **dance**, **easy listening**, **folk**, **jazz** (fusion), **MOR**, **rock** (hard and country), **soul** and **top 40/pop**. Current acts include Bunny Sigler (disco/funk), Peter Nero and Philly Pops (conductor), Cast in Bronze (rock group) and Pieces of a Dream (jazz/crossover).

THE FILM & TV INDEX found at the back of this book lists companies placing music in film and TV (excluding TV commercials).

Additional Managers & Booking Agents

The following companies are also managers/booking agents, but their listings are found in other sections of the book. See the General Index for page numbers, then read the listings for submission information.

Alexis
Bernard Enterprises, Inc., Hal
Brian Song Music Corp.
babysue
De Miles Music Company, The Edward
Deadeye Records
Deep South Entertainment
Delev Music Company

Diamond Entertainment, Joel
Edition Rossori
Esquire International
Fish of Death Records and Management
His Power Productions and Publishing
JSB Groupe Management Inc.
Lucifer Records, Inc.

Magid Productions, Lee
Major Entertainment, Inc.
Modal Music, Inc.™
Satkowski Recordings, Steve
Silver Thunder Music Group
Sphere Group One
Stuart Music Co., Jeb
Third Wave Productions Ltd.

Category Index

The Category Index is a good place to begin searching for a market for your songs. Below is an alphabetical list of 20 general music categories. If you write pop songs and are looking for a manager or booking agent to submit your songs to, check the Pop section in this index. There you will find a list of managers and booking agents who work with pop performers. Once you locate the entries for those publishers, read the music subheading *carefully* to determine which companies are most interested in the type of pop music you write. Some of the markets in this section do not appear in the Category Index because they have not indicated a specific preference. Most of these said they are interested in "all types" of music. Listings that were very specific, or whose description of the music they're interested in doesn't quite fit into these categories, also do not appear here.

Adult Contemporary (also easy listening, middle of the road, AAA, ballads, etc.)
All Star Talent Agency
Anderson Associates Communications Group
Black Stallion Country, Inc.
Brothers Management Associates
Chucker Music Inc.
Dinwoodie Management, Andrew
Hale Enterprises
International Entertainment Bureau
Jacobson Talent Management (JTM)
Knight Agency, Bob
Kuper Personal Management
Levinson Entertainment Ventures International, Inc.
Loggins Promotion/Backstage Entertainment
Management by Jaffe
Merri-Webb Productions
Prestige Artistes
RadioActive
Richards World Management, Inc., Diane
Risavy, Inc., A.F.
Rustron Music Productions
Skorman Productions, Inc., T.
Staircase Promotion
Stormin' Norman Productions
T.J. Booker Ltd.
Tas Music Co./Dave Tasse Entertainment
Total Acting Experience, A
Van Pol Management, Hans
Wagner Agency, William F.
Warner Productions, Cheryl K.
World Wide Management
Zane Management, Inc.

Alternative (also modern rock, punk, college rock, new wave, hardcore, new music, industrial, ska, indie rock, garage, etc.)
American Artists Entertainment
Countdown Entertainment

Cox Promotions & Management, Stephen
DAS Communications, Ltd.
Direct Management
Doss Presents, Col. Buster
Earth Tracks Artists Agency
Knight Agency, Bob
Kuper Personal Management
Loggins Promotion/Backstage Entertainment
M.E.G Management
Management by Jaffe
Merlin Management Corp.
On the Level Music!
Outland Productions
Outlaw Entertainment International
Pillar Records
RadioActive
Rock Whirled Music Management
Saffyre Management
Southeastern Attractions
Spoon Agency L.L.C., The
Staircase Promotion
Stewart Management, Steve
Strictly Forbidden Artists
Surface Management Inc.
Tiger's Eye Entertainment Management & Consulting

Blues
American Independent Artists
Barnard Management Services (BMS)
Blowin' Smoke Productions/Records
Blue Wave Productions
Buxton Walker P/L
Concerted Efforts, Inc./Foggy Day Music
Countrywide Producers
Cox Promotions & Management, Stephen
Crossfire Productions
DMR Agency

Kickstart Music Ltd.
Knight Agency, Bob
Mayo & Company, Phil
Media Management
Music Marketing & Promotions
Noteworthy Productions
Original Artists' Agency
Pillar Records
Rustron Music Productions
SP Talent Associates
Stormin' Norman Productions
Total Acting Experience, A
Twentieth Century Promotions
Universal Music Marketing
Williams Management, Yvonne
World Wide Management

Children's
Direct Management
Lindsay Productions, Doris/Successful Productions

Classical (also opera, chamber music, serious music, choral, etc.)
American Independent Artists
Clousher Productions
Countrywide Producers
Jae Enterprises, Jana
Rock of Ages Productions
Tutta Forza Music
Wagner Agency, William F.

Country (also western, C&W, bluegrass, cowboy songs, western swing, honky-tonk, etc.)
Afterschool Publishing Company
Air Tight Management
All Star Management
All Star Talent Agency
American Independent Artists
Ardenne Int'l Inc.
Barnard Management Services (BMS)
Black Stallion Country, Inc.
Bouquet-Orchid Enterprises
Butler Music, Bill
Circuit Rider Talent & Management Co.
Clousher Productions
Concept 2000 Inc.
Concerted Efforts, Inc./Foggy Day Music
Countrywide Producers
Crawfish Productions
Creative Star Management
Crossfire Productions
D&R Entertainment
De Miles Company, The Edward
Dinwoodie Management, Andrew
Doss Presents, Col. Buster
Ellis International Talent Agency, The
Fenchel Entertainment Agency, Fred T.

First Time Management
Gueststar Entertainment Agency
Hale Enterprises
Harrell & Associates, M.
Hawkeye Attractions
International Entertainment Bureau
J & V Management
Jacobson Talent Management (JTM)
Jae Enterprises, Jana
James Management, Roger
Kickstart Music Ltd.
Knight Agency, Bob
Lari-Jon Promotions
Levinson Entertainment Ventures International, Inc.
Levy Management, Rick
Lindsay Productions, Doris/Successful Productions
Live-Wire Management
Lowell Agency
Magnum Music Corporation Ltd.
Management Plus
Mayo & Company, Phil
McDonnell Group, The
Merri-Webb Productions
Nash-One Management Inc.
Northern Lights Management
Noteworthy Productions
Original Artists' Agency
Pillar Records
Prestige Artistes
Pro Talent Consultants
Rainbow Collection Ltd.
Risavy, Inc., A.F.
Rock of Ages Productions
Rothschild Productions Inc., Charles R.
Rustron Music Productions
Sea Cruise Productions, Inc.
Serge Entertainment Group
Shute Management Pty. Ltd., Phill
Southeastern Attractions
SP Talent Associates
Sphere Group One
Spoon Agency L.L.C., The
Staircase Promotion
Stevens & Company Management
Stormin' Norman Productions
T.J. Booker Ltd.
T.L.C. Booking Agency
Texas Sounds Entertainment
315 Beale Studios/Taliesyn Entertainment
Total Acting Experience, A
Twentieth Century Promotions
Umpire Entertainment Enterprizes
Universal Music Marketing
Varrasso Management, Richard
Vokes Booking Agency
Wagner Agency, William F.
Walls & Co. Management/Showbiz Kidz!
Warner Productions, Cheryl K.

Wemus Entertainment
Wilder Artists' Management, Shane
Williams Management, Yvonne
World Wide Management

Dance (also house, hi-NRG, disco, club, rave, techno, trip-hop, trance, etc.)

Anderson Associates Communications Group
Bassline Entertainment, Inc.
CBA Artists
Chucker Music Inc.
Clousher Productions
Countdown Entertainment
Countrywide Producers
De Miles Company, The Edward
First Time Management
Golden City International
Kickstart Music Ltd.
Martin Productions, Rick
Mega Music Productions
Merlin Management Corp.
On Stage Management Inc.
Outlaw Entertainment International
Richards World Management, Inc., Diane
Skorman Productions, Inc., T.
Sound Management Direction
Strictly Forbidden Artists
Tas Music Co./Dave Tasse Entertainment
Total Acting Experience, A
Van Pol Management, Hans
Varrasso Management, Richard
Wood Artist Management, Richard
World Park Productions
Zane Management, Inc.

Folk (also acoustic, Celtic, etc.)

Afterschool Publishing Company
Concerted Efforts, Inc./Foggy Day Music
Countrywide Producers
Cox Promotions & Management, Stephen
Dinwoodie Management, Andrew
EAO Music Corporation of Canada
Immigrant Music Inc.
Knight Agency, Bob
Northern Lights Management
Noteworthy Productions
Rock Whirled Music Management
Rothschild Productions Inc., Charles R.
Rustron Music Productions
SP Talent Associates
Stormin' Norman Productions
World Park Productions
World Wide Management
Zane Management, Inc.

Instrumental (also background music, musical scores, etc.)

Endangered Species Artist Management
Jae Enterprises, Jana

Pillar Records
Tutta Forza Music
Wagner Agency, William F.

Jazz (also fusion, bebop, swing, etc.)

Afterschool Publishing Company
Air Tight Management
American Independent Artists
Bacchus Group Productions, Ltd.
Buxton Walker P/L
Chucker Music Inc.
Concept 2000 Inc.
Countrywide Producers
Crossfire Productions
Endangered Species Artist Management
GCI, Inc.
Harrell & Associates, M.
International Entertainment Bureau
Jae Enterprises, Jana
Klein, Joanne
Knight Agency, Bob
Live-Wire Management
Loggins Promotion/Backstage Entertainment
McDonnell Group, The
Media Management
Music Marketing & Promotions
Noteworthy Enterprises
On the Level Music!
Richards World Management, Inc., Diane
Riohcat Music
Rothschild Productions Inc., Charles R.
Stander Entertainment
Tas Music Co./Dave Tasse Entertainment
Total Acting Experience, A
Tutta Forza Music
Universal Music Marketing
Wagner Agency, William F.
Walls & Co. Management/Showbiz Kidz!
World Park Productions
World Wide Management
Zane Management, Inc.

Latin (also Spanish, salsa, Cuban, conga, Brazilian, cumbja, rancheras, Mexican, merengue, Tejano, Tex Mex, etc.)

Bacchus Group Productions, Ltd.
Bassline Entertainment, Inc.
Blue Cat Agency, The
Butler Music, Bill
Corvalan-Condliffe Management
Ellis International Talent Agency, The
Endangered Species Artist Management
Hansen Enterprises, Ltd.
Management Plus
Mega Music Productions
Stevens & Company Management
Texas Sounds Entertainment

Metal (also thrash, grindcore, heavy metal, etc.)
Endangered Species Artist Management
Outland Productions
Outlaw Entertainment International
Strictly Forbidden Artists
WorldSound, LLC

New Age (also ambient)
Cox Promotions & Management, Stephen
Live-Wire Management
Richards World Management, Inc., Diane
Rustron Music Productions
Serge Entertainment Group
Sphere Group One
World Wide Management

Novelty (also comedy, humor, etc.)
Circuit Rider Talent & Management Co.
Hall Entertainment & Events, Bill
Sea Cruise Productions, Inc.

Pop (also top 40, top 100, popular, chart hits, etc.)
Afterschool Publishing Company
Alert Music, Inc.
All Star Talent Agency
American Artists Entertainment
Anderson Associates Communications Group
Ardenne Int'l Inc.
Bacchus Group Productions, Ltd.
Bassline Entertainment, Inc.
Big J Productions
Blue Cat Agency, The
Bouquet-Orchid Enterprises
Brothers Management Associates
Buxton Walker P/L
Capital Entertainment
Chucker Music Inc.
Circuit Rider Talent & Management Co.
Clockwork Entertainment Management Agency
Concept 2000 Inc.
Conscience Music
Corvalan-Condliffe Management
Countdown Entertainment
Countrywide Producers
Creative Star Management
Criss-Cross Industries
D&M Entertainment Agency
D&R Entertainment
DAS Communications, Ltd.
De Miles Company, The Edward
Dinwoodie Management, Andrew
DMR Agency
Earth Tracks Artists Agency
Endangered Species Artist Management
Evans Productions, Scott
Fenchel Entertainment Agency, Fred T.

First Time Management
Godtland Management, Inc., Eric
Golden City International
Hale Enterprises
Jae Enterprises, Jana
James Management, Roger
Kagan International, Sheldon
Kickstart Music Ltd.
Knight Agency, Bob
Levy Management, Rick
Lindsay Productions, Doris/Successful Productions
Live-Wire Management
Loggins Promotion/Backstage Entertainment
Management by Jaffe
Martin Productions, Rick
Mayo & Company, Phil
McDonnell Group, The
Media Management
Mega Music Productions
Merlin Management Corp.
Merri-Webb Productions
Music Marketing & Promotions
On Stage Management Inc.
Outlaw Entertainment International
Pillar Records
Prestige Artistes
Pro Talent Consultants
RadioActive
Rainbow Collection Ltd.
Richards World Management, Inc., Diane
Right-On Management
Risavy, Inc., A.F.
Rock of Ages Productions
Rothschild Productions Inc., Charles R.
Saffyre Management
Serge Entertainment Group
Shute Management Pty. Ltd., Phill
Skorman Productions, Inc., T.
Sphere Group One
Staircase Promotion
Stander Entertainment
Starkravin' Management
Steinman Management, Obi
Surface Management Inc.
T.J. Booker Ltd.
Tas Music Co./Dave Tasse Entertainment
Tiger's Eye Entertainment Management & Consulting
Total Acting Experience, A
Umpire Entertainment Enterprizes
Wagner Agency, William F.
Walls & Co. Management/Showbiz Kidz!
Warner Productions, Cheryl K.
Wood Artist Management, Richard
World Wide Management
WorldSound, LLC
Zane Management, Inc.

R&B (also soul, black, urban, etc.)
American Artists Entertainment
American Independent Artists
Anderson Associates Communications Group
Bacchus Group Productions, Ltd.
Barnard Management Services (BMS)
Bassline Entertainment, Inc.
Big J Productions
Black Stallion Country, Inc.
Blackground
Blowin' Smoke Productions/Records
Bouquet-Orchid Enterprises
Brothers Management Associates
Butler Music, Bill
Chucker Music Inc.
Circuit Rider Talent & Management Co.
Concept 2000 Inc.
Countdown Entertainment
Countrywide Producers
Creative Star Management
Criss-Cross Industries
Crossfire Productions
D&M Entertainment Agency
DAS Communications, Ltd.
De Miles Company, The Edward
Dinwoodie Management, Andrew
Endangered Species Artist Management
Evans Productions, Scott
Golden City International
Hardison International Entertainment Corporation
Harrell & Associates, M.
Jacobson Talent Management (JTM)
KKR Entertainment Group
Knight Agency, Bob
Levinson Entertainment Ventures International, Inc.
Levy Management, Rick
Live-Wire Management
McDonnell Group, The
Media Management
Merri-Webb Productions
On Stage Management Inc.
Precision Management
Rainbow Talent Agency
Renaissance Entertainment Group
Right-On Management
Rustron Music Productions
Sea Cruise Productions, Inc.
Shute Management Pty. Ltd., Phill
Sound Management Direction
Sphere Group One
Spoon Agency L.L.C., The
Stander Entertainment
Starkravin' Management
Steinman Management, Obi
Tas Music Co./Dave Tasse Entertainment
Texas Sounds Entertainment
315 Beale Studios/Taliesyn Entertainment

Tiger's Eye Entertainment Management & Consulting
Total Acting Experience, A
Van Pol Management, Hans
Williams Management, Yvonne
Wood Artist Management, Richard
World Wide Management
Zane Management, Inc.

Rap (also hip-hop, bass, etc.)
Afterschool Publishing Company
American Artists Entertainment
Bassline Entertainment, Inc.
Blackground
Countdown Entertainment
Creative Star Management
First Time Management
Godtland Management, Inc., Eric
Golden City International
Hardison International Entertainment Corporation
Jacobson Talent Management (JTM)
KKR Entertainment Group
Kuper Personal Management
Precision Management
Renaissance Entertainment Group
Richards World Management, Inc., Diane
Sound Management Direction
Strictly Forbidden Artists
Tiger's Eye Entertainment Management & Consulting
Van Pol Management, Hans
Williams Management, Yvonne

Religious (also gospel, sacred, Christian, church, hymns, praise, inspirational, worship, etc.)
All Star Management
All Star Talent Agency
Blackground
Bouquet-Orchid Enterprises
Capital Entertainment
Circuit Rider Talent & Management Co.
Concept 2000 Inc.
Countrywide Producers
Crawfish Productions
Creative Star Management
D&R Entertainment
Direct Management
Doss Presents, Col. Buster
Exclesisa Booking Agency
Fenchel Entertainment Agency, Fred T.
First Time Management
Golden City International
Harrell & Associates, M.
Lari-Jon Promotions
Lindsay Productions, Doris/Successful Productions
Magnum Music Corporation Ltd.
Mayo & Company, Phil

Merri-Webb Productions
Precision Management
Rock of Ages Productions
Staircase Promotion
Umpire Entertainment Enterprizes
Vokes Booking Agency
Warner Productions, Cheryl K.
Williams Management, Yvonne

Rock (also rockabilly, AOR, rock 'n' roll, etc.)
Air Tight Management
Alert Music, Inc.
All Star Talent Agency
American Independent Artists
Anderson Associates Communications Group
Ardenne Int'l Inc.
Barnard Management Services (BMS)
Big J Productions
Blowin' Smoke Productions/Records
Blue Cat Agency, The
Blue Wave Productions
Bouquet-Orchid Enterprises
Brothers Management Associates
Buxton Walker P/L
Chucker Music Inc.
Clockwork Entertainment Management Agency
Clousher Productions
Concerted Efforts, Inc./Foggy Day Music
Conscience Music
Corvalan-Condliffe Management
Countdown Entertainment
Countrywide Producers
Cox Promotions & Management, Stephen
Crossfire Productions
D&M Entertainment Agency
DAS Communications, Ltd.
DCA Productions
De Miles Company, The Edward
Dinwoodie Management, Andrew
DMR Agency
Doss Presents, Col. Buster
EAO Music Corporation of Canada
Earth Tracks Artists Agency
Endangered Species Artist Management
Godtland Management, Inc., Eric
Hale Enterprises
Hansen Enterprises, Ltd.
Harrell & Associates, M.
International Entertainment Bureau
Jacobson Talent Management (JTM)
Kickstart Music Ltd.
KKR Entertainment Group
Knight Agency, Bob
Lari-Jon Promotions
Levinson Entertainment Ventures International, Inc.
Loggins Promotion/Backstage Entertainment
Management by Jaffe
Martin Productions, Rick

Mayo & Company, Phil
McDonnell Group, The
Media Management
Mega Music Productions
Merri-Webb Productions
Nash-One Management Inc.
On Stage Management Inc.
On the Level Music!
Original Artists' Agency
Outland Productions
Outlaw Entertainment International
Pillar Records
Prestige Artistes
Pro Talent Consultants
RadioActive
Rainbow Collection Ltd.
Rainbow Talent Agency
Renaissance Entertainment Group
Right-On Management
Risavy, Inc., A.F.
Rock of Ages Productions
Rock Whirled Music Management
Rothschild Productions Inc., Charles R.
Rustron Music Productions
Saffyre Management
Sea Cruise Productions, Inc.
Serge Entertainment Group
Shute Management Pty. Ltd., Phill
Sound Management Direction
Southeastern Attractions
SP Talent Associates
Sphere Group One
Spoon Agency L.L.C., The
Staircase Promotion
Starkravin' Management
Steinman Management, Obi
Stewart Management, Steve
Stormin' Norman Productions
Strictly Forbidden Artists
Surface Management Inc.
T.J. Booker Ltd.
T.L.C. Booking Agency
Tas Music Co./Dave Tasse Entertainment
315 Beale Studios/Taliesyn Entertainment
Tiger's Eye Entertainment Management & Consult-
    ing
Universal Music Marketing
Varrasso Management, Richard
Williams Management, Yvonne
World Wide Management
WorldSound, LLC
Zane Management, Inc.

**World Music (also reggae, ethnic, calypso,
international, world beat, etc.)**
Bacchus Group Productions, Ltd.
Buxton Walker P/L
Concerted Efforts, Inc./Foggy Day Music

Cox Promotions & Management, Stephen
Ellis International Talent Agency, The
Endangered Species Artist Management
Immigrant Music Inc.
Management Plus
Music Marketing & Promotions

Noteworthy Productions
Stander Entertainment
Stormin' Norman Productions
World Park Productions
WorldSound, LLC

Advertising, Audiovisual & Commercial Music Firms

It's happened a million times—you hear a jingle on the radio or television and can't get it out of your head. That's the work of a successful jingle writer, writing songs to catch your attention and make you aware of the product being advertised. But the field of commercial music consists of more than just memorable jingles. It also includes background music that many companies use in videos for corporate and educational presentations, as well as films and TV shows.

SUBMITTING MATERIAL

More than any other market listed in this book, the commercial music market expects composers to have made an investment in the recording of their material before submitting. A sparse, piano/vocal demo won't work here; when dealing with commercial music firms, especially audiovisual firms and music libraries, high quality production is important. Your demo may be kept on file at one of these companies until a need for it arises, and it may be used or sold as you sent it. Therefore, your demo tape or reel must be as fully produced as possible.

The presentation package that goes along with your demo must be just as professional. A list of your credits should be a part of your submission, to give the company an idea of your experience in this field. If you have no experience, look to local television and radio stations to get your start. Don't expect to be paid for many of your first jobs in the commercial music field; it's more important to get the credits and exposure that can lead to higher-paying jobs.

Commercial music and jingle writing can be a lucrative field for the composer/songwriter with a gift for writing catchy melodies and the ability to write in many different music styles. It's a very competitive field, so it pays to have a professional presentation package that makes your work stand out.

Three different segments of the commercial music world are listed here: advertising agencies, audiovisual firms and commercial music houses/music libraries. Each looks for a different type of music, so read these descriptions carefully to see where the music you write fits in.

ADVERTISING AGENCIES

Ad agencies work on assignment as their clients' needs arise. Through consultation and input from the creative staff, ad agencies seek jingles and music to stimulate the consumer to identify with a product or service.

When contacting ad agencies, keep in mind they are searching for music that can capture and then hold an audience's attention. Most jingles are short, with a strong, memorable hook. When an ad agency listens to a demo, it is not necessarily looking for a finished product so much as for an indication of creativity and diversity. Many composers put together a reel of excerpts of work from previous projects, or short pieces of music that show they can write in a variety of styles.

AUDIOVISUAL FIRMS

Audiovisual firms create a variety of products, from film and video shows for sales meetings, corporate gatherings and educational markets, to motion pictures and TV shows. With the increase of home video use, how-to videos are a big market for audiovisual firms, as are spoken word educational videos. All of these products need music to accompany them. For your quick reference, companies working to place music in movies and TV shows (excluding commercials) have a ▣ preceding their listing (also see the Film & TV Index on page 484 for a complete list of these companies).

Like ad agencies, audiovisual firms look for versatile, well-rounded songwriters. When submitting demos to these firms, you need to demonstrate your versatility in writing specialized background music and themes. Listings for companies will tell what facet(s) of the audiovisual field they are involved in and what types of clients they serve. Your demo tape should also be as professional and fully produced as possible; audiovisual firms often seek demo tapes that can be put on file for future use when the need arises.

COMMERCIAL MUSIC HOUSES & MUSIC LIBRARIES

Commercial music houses are companies contracted (either by an ad agency or the advertiser) to compose custom jingles. Since they are neither an ad agency nor an audiovisual firm, their main concern is music. They use a lot of it, too—some composed by inhouse songwriters and some contributed by outside, freelance writers.

Music libraries are different in that their music is not custom composed for a specific client. Their job is to provide a collection of instrumental music in many different styles that, for an annual fee or on a per-use basis, the customer can use however he chooses.

In the following listings, commercial music houses and music libraries, which are usually the most open to works by new composers, are identified as such by **bold** typeface.

The commercial music market is similar to most other businesses in one aspect: experience is important. Until you develop a list of credits, pay for your work may not be high. Don't pass up opportunities if a job is non- or low-paying. These assignments will add to your list of credits, make you contacts in the field, and improve your marketability.

Money and rights

Many of the companies listed in this section pay by the job, but there may be some situations where the company asks you to sign a contract that will specify royalty payments. If this happens, research the contract thoroughly, and know exactly what is expected of you and how much you'll be paid.

Depending on the particular job and the company, you may be asked to sell one-time rights or all rights. One-time rights involve using your material for one presentation only. All rights means the buyer can use your work any way he chooses, as many times as he likes. Be sure you know exactly what you're giving up, and how the company may use your music in the future.

In the commercial world, many of the big advertising agencies have their own publishing companies where writers assign their compositions. In these situations, writers sign contracts whereby they do receive performance and mechanical royalties when applicable.

ⓘ For More Information

For additional names and addresses of ad agencies that may use jingles and/or commercial music, refer to the *Standard Directory of Advertising Agencies* (National Register Publishing). For a list of audiovisual firms, check out the latest edition of *AV Marketplace* (R.R. Bowker). Both these books may be found at your local library. To contact companies in your area, see the Geographic Index at the back of this book.

THE AD AGENCY, P.O. Box 470572, San Francisco CA 94147. **Contact:** Michael Carden, creative director. Advertising agency and **jingle/commercial music production house**. Clients include business, industry and retail. Estab. 1971. Uses the services of music houses, independent songwriter/ composers and lyricists for scoring of commercials, background music for video production, and jingles for commercials. Commissions 20 composers and 15 lyricists/year. Pays by the job or by the hour. Buys all or one-time rights.

How to Contact: Submit demo tape of previous work. Prefers cassette with 5-8 songs and lyric sheet. SASE. Responds in 3 weeks.

Music: Uses variety of musical styles for commercials, promotion, TV, video presentations.

Tips: "Our clients and our needs change frequently."

ADVERTEL, INC., P.O. Box 18053, Pittsburgh PA 15236-0053. (412)886-1400. Fax: (412)886-1411. E-mail: pberan@advertel.com. Website: www.advertel.com. **Contact:** Paul Beran, president/ CEO. Telephonic/Internet production company. Clients include small and multi-national companies. Estab. 1983. Uses the services of music houses and independent songwriters/composers for scoring of instrumentals (all varieties) and telephonic production. Commissions 3-4 composers/year. Pay varies. Buys all rights and phone exclusive rights.

How to Contact: Submit demo tape of previous work. Prefers CD or cassette. "Most compositions are 2 minutes strung together in 6, 12, 18 minute length productions." Does not return material; prefers to keep on file. Responds "right away if submission fills an immediate need."

Music: Uses all varieties, including unusual; mostly subdued music beds. Radio-type production used exclusively in telephone and Internet applications.

Tips: "Go for volume. We have continuous need for all varieties of music in two minute lengths."

N **AGA CREATIVE COMMUNICATIONS**, (formerly AGA Communications), 2400 E. Bradford Ave., Suite 206, Milwaukee WI 53211-4165. (414)962-9810. E-mail: greink@juno.com. CEO: Arthur Greinke. Advertising agency, public relations/music artist management and media relations. Clients include small business, original music groups and special events. Estab. 1984. Uses the services of music houses, independent songwriters/composers and lyricists for independent productions and scoring of motion picture and video productions; background music for commercial release, special events; jingles for TV and radio. Commissions 4-6 composers and 4-6 lyricists/year. Pays on a per job basis. Buys all rights and one-time rights.

How to Contact: Submit demo tape of previous work. Prefers CD, cassette, DAT or VHS videocassette with any number of songs and lyric sheet. "We will contact only when job is open, but will keep submissions on file." Does not return material. Responds only if interested.

Music: Uses original rock, pop and heavy rock for recording groups, commercials and video projects.

Tips: "Try to give as complete a work as possible without allowing us to fill in the holes. High energy, unusual arrangements, be creative, different and use strong hooks! Strong knowledge of popular music history/production and having it as an influence is a major plus."

ANGEL FILMS COMPANY, 967 Hwy. 40, New Franklin MO 65274-9778. Phone/fax: (573)698-3900. E-mail: angelfilm@aol.com. **Contact:** Linda G. Grotzinger, vice president/marketing. Motion picture and record production company (Angel One Records). Estab. 1980. Uses the services of music houses, independent songwriters/composers and lyricists for scoring of feature films, animation, TV programs and commercials, background music for TV and radio commercials and jingles for commercials. Commissions 12-20 composers and 12-20 lyricists/year. Payment depends upon budget; each project has a different pay scale. Buys all rights.

How to Contact: Submit demo tape of previous work or query with résumé of credits. Prefers cassette or VHS videocassette with 3 pieces and lyric and lead sheet. "Do not send originals." SASE, but prefers to keep material on file. Responds in 6 weeks.

Music: Uses basically MOR, but will use anything (except country and religious) for record production, film, television and cartoon scores. Uses jazz—modern, classical for films.

Tips: "Send new material, not material that has old copyrights on it. Don't copy others, just do the best you can. We freelance all our work for our film and television production company, and are always looking for that one break-through artist for Angel One Records."

BRg MUSIC WORKS, P.O. Box 202, Bryn Mawr PA 19010. (610)825-5656. E-mail: jandron@ voicenet.com. Creative Director: Doug Reed. **Contact:** Lee Napier. **Jingle producers/music library**

producers. Uses independent composers and music houses for background music for radio, TV and commercials and jingles for radio and TV. Commissions 20 songwriters/year. Pays per job. Buys all rights.

How to Contact: Submit demo tape of previous work. Prefers cassette. "We are looking for quality jingle tracks already produced, as well as instrumental pieces between 2 and 3 minutes in length for use in AV music library." SASE. Responds in 2 weeks.

Music: All types.

Tips: "Send your best and put your strongest work at the front of your demo tape."

BRIDGE ENTERPRISES, P.O. Box 789, Marshall TX 75671-0789. (903)935-5524. Fax: (903)935-6789. **Contact:** H.A. (Tony) Bridge, Jr., sales/marketing. Hotel, restaurant and bar operator. Clients include hospitality industry. Estab. 1970. Uses the services of music houses, independent songwriters/composers and lyricists for jingles and commercials for radio and TV. Pays per job. Buys all rights.

How to Contact: Submit demo tape of previous work. Prefers cassette with lyric sheet. "No phone calls, please." SASE. Responds in 3 weeks.

Music: Uses various styles of music for commercials and jingles.

Tips: "Develop a good track record with radio/TV, ad agencies and hospitality industry."

☑ **BUTWIN & ASSOCIATES, INC.**, 8700 Westmoreland Lane, Minneapolis MN 55426. Phone/fax: (952)545-3886. **Contact:** Ron Butwin, president. Advertising agency. Clients include restaurants, banks, manufacturers, retail. Estab. 1977. Uses the services of music houses, independent songwriters/composers and lyricists for background music for videos and corporate presentations, jingles for radio and TV commercials and shows and commercials for radio and TV. Commissions 5-6 composers and 5-6 lyricists/year. Pays per job. Buys all rights "generally."

How to Contact: Submit demo tape of previous work. Prefers CD, cassette or VHS videocassette with 8-12 songs and lyric sheet. Does not return material. Prefers to keep submitted material on file. "We only respond if we're interested and either want more information or have a project in place."

Music: Uses up-tempo, pop, jazz, classical and New Age for slide presentations, jingles and commercials.

Tips: "Send us good, clean work that is truly representative of your skills. We are interested in knowing your experience and skill level. Give us some background on you and your business."

CALDWELL VANRIPER/MARC, 1314 N. Meridian, Indianapolis IN 46202. (317)638-9155. Website: www.cvrmarc.com. **Contact:** Sherry Boyle, senior vice president/executive producer. Advertising agency and public relations firm. Clients include industrial, financial and consumer/trade firms. Uses the services of music houses for scoring of radio, TV and A/V projects, jingles and commercials for radio and TV.

How to Contact: Submit demo tape of previously aired work on audio cassette. Does not return material. "Sender can follow up on submission. Periodic inquiry or demo update is fine."

Tips: "We do not work directly with composers, we work with music production companies. Composers should contact the production companies directly."

▨ **CANTRAX RECORDERS**, Dept. CM, 2119 Fidler Ave., Long Beach CA 90815. **Contact:** Richard Cannata, owner. Recording studio. Clients include anyone needing recording services (i.e., industrial, radio, commercial). Estab. 1980. Uses the services of independent songwriters/composers and lyricists for scoring of independent features and films and background music for radio, industrials and promotions, commercials for radio and TV and jingles for radio. Commissions 10 composers/year. Pays fees set by the artist. "We take 15%."

How to Contact: Query with résumé of credits or submit demo CD of previous work. Prefers CD with lyric sheets. Does not return material. Responds in 2 weeks.

MARKETS THAT WERE listed in the 2001 edition of *Songwriters Market* but do not appear this year are listed in the General Index with a notation explaining why they were omitted.

Music: Uses jazz, New Age, rock, easy listening and classical for slide shows, jingles and soundtracks.
Tips: "You must have a serious, professional attitude."

☑ ⛰ **CINEVUE/STEVE POSTAL PRODUCTIONS**, P.O. Box 428, Bostwick FL 32007. (904)325-9356. E-mail: steve@postalproductions.com. Website: www.postalproductions.com. **Contact:** Steve Postal, director/producer. Motion picture production company. Estab. 1955. Serves all types of film distributors. Uses the services of music houses, independent songwriters, composers and lyricists for scoring and background music for films and nature documentaries. Commissions 10 composers and 5 lyricists/year. Pays by the job. Buys all rights.
How to Contact: Query with résumé of credits or submit demo tape of previous work ("good tape only!"). Submit manuscript showing music scoring skills. Prefers cassette with 10 pieces and lyric or lead sheet. Only returns material if accompanied by SASE with sufficient postage for return of all materials. "Send good audio-cassette, then call me in a week." Responds in 2 weeks.
Music: Uses all styles of music for features (educational films and slide presentations). "Need horror film music on traditional instruments—no electronic music."
Tips: "Be flexible, fast—do first job free to ingratiate yourself and demonstrate your style. Follow up with two phone calls."

COMMUNICATIONS FOR LEARNING, 395 Massachusetts Ave., Arlington MA 02474. (781)641-2350. E-mail: comlearn@thecia.net. **Contact:** Jonathan L. Barkan, executive producer/director. Video, multimedia, exhibit and graphics design firm. Clients include multi-nationals, industry, government, institutions, local, national and international nonprofits. Uses services of music houses and independent songwriters/composers as theme and background music for videos and multimedia. Commissions 1-2 composers/year. Pays $2,000-5,000/job and one-time fees. Rights purchased varies.
How to Contact: Submit demo tape of previous work. Prefers CD. Does not return material; prefers to keep on file. "For each job we consider our entire collection." Responds in 3 months.
Music: Uses all styles of music for all sorts of assignments.
Tips: "Please don't call. Just send good material and when we're interested, we'll be in touch. Make certain name and phone number are on all submitted work itself, not only cover letter."

CREATIVE SUPPORT SERVICES, 1950 Riverside Dr., Los Angeles CA 90039. (323)666-7968. E-mail: info@mail.cssmusic.com. Website: www.cssmusic.com. **Contact:** Michael M. Fuller, creative director. **Music/sound effects library**. Clients include audiovisual production houses. Estab. 1978. Uses the services of independent songwriters and musicians for production library. Commissions 3-5 songwriters and 1-2 lyricists/year. Buys all rights.
How to Contact: Submit demo tape of previous work. Prefers CD/CDR or DAT with 3 or more pieces. Does not return material; prefers to keep on file. "Will call if interested."
Music: Uses "industrial music predominantly, but all other kinds or types to a lesser degree."
Tips: "Don't assume the reviewer can extrapolate beyond what is actually on the demo."

⛰ **D.S.M. PRODUCERS INC.**, 161 W. 54th St., Suite 803, New York NY 10019. (212)245-0006. President, CEO: Suzan Bader. CFO, CPA: Kenneth R. Wiseman. Submit to: Elba T. Maldonado, Director A&R. Vice President, National Sales Director: Doris Kaufman. Scoring service, **jingle/commercial music production house** and original stock library called "All American Composers Library (administered world wide except USA by Warner/Chappell Music, Inc.)" Clients include networks, corporate, advertising firms, film and video, book publishers (music only). Estab. 1979. Uses the services of independent songwriters/composers for scoring of TV and feature films, background music for feature films and TV, jingles for major products and commercials for radio and TV. Pays 50% royalty. Buys all rights.
How to Contact: Write first and enclose SASE for return permission. Prefers cassette or VHS videocassette with 2 songs and lyric or lead sheet. "Use a large enough return envelope to put in a standard business reply letter." Responds in 3 months.
Music: Uses all styles including alternative, dance, New Age, country and rock for adventure films and sports programs.

Tips: "Carefully label your submissions. Include a short bio/résumé of your works. Lyric sheets are very helpful to A&R. Only send your best tapes and tunes. Invest in your profession and get a local professional to help you produce your works. A master quality tape is the standard today. This is your competition so if you really want to be a songwriter, act like the ones who are successful—get a good tape of your tune. This makes it easier to sell overall. Never use 'samples' or any other copyrighted material in your works without a license."

☑ **dbF A MEDIA COMPANY**, P.O. Box 2458, Waldorf MD 20604. (301)843-7110. E-mail: produ ction@dbfmedia.com. Website: www.dbfmedia.com. **Contact:** Randy Runyon, general manager. Advertising agency, audiovisual and media firm and audio and video production company. Clients include business and industry. Estab. 1981. Uses the services of music houses, independent songwriters/ composers and lyricists for background music for industrial, training, educational and promo videos, jingles and commercials for radio and TV. Commissions 5-12 composers and 5-12 lyricists/year. Pays by the job. Buys all rights.
How to Contact: Submit demo tape of previous work. Prefers cassette or CD or VHS videocassette with 5-8 songs and lead sheet. SASE, but prefers to keep material on file. Responds in 6 months.
Music: Uses up-tempo contemporary for industrial videos, slide presentations and commercials.
Tips: "We're looking for commercial music, primarily A/C."

☑ ▣ **DISK PRODUCTIONS**, 1100 Perkins Rd., Baton Rouge LA 70802. Fax: (225)343-0210. E-mail: joey_decker@hotmail.com. **Contact:** Joey Decker, director. **Jingle/production house.** Clients include advertising agencies, slide production houses and film companies. Estab. 1982. Uses the services of music houses, independent songwriters/composers and lyricists for scoring and background music for TV spots, films and jingles for radio and TV. Commissions 7 songwriters/composers and 7 lyricists/year. Pays by the job. Buys all rights.
How to Contact: Submit demo tape of previous work. Prefers CD, cassette or DAT (or ½″ videocassette). Does not return material. Responds in 2 weeks.
Music: Needs all types of music for jingles, music beds or background music for TV and radio, etc.
Tips: "Advertising techniques change with time. Don't be locked in a certain style of writing. Give me music that I can't get from pay needle-drop."

ENSEMBLE PRODUCTIONS, P.O. Box 2332, Auburn AL 36831. (334)703-5963. E-mail: ensem bleproductions@usa.net. **Contact:** Barry J. McConatha, owner/producer/director. Interactive multimedia and video production/post production. Clients include corporate, governmental and educational. Estab. 1984. Uses services of music houses and independent songwriters/composers for background music for corporate public relations, educational and training videos. Commissions 0-5 composers/year. Pays $25-250/job depending upon project. Buys one-time rights or all rights.
How to Contact: Send e-mail or submit demo tape of previous work demonstrating composition skills. "Needs are sporadic, write first if submission to be returned." Prefers cassette, CD or VHS videocassette with 3-5 songs. "Most needs are up-beat industrial sound but occasional mood setting music also. Inquire for details." Does not return material; prefers to keep on file. Responds in 3 months if interested. "Usually does not reply unless interested."
Music: Uses up-beat, industrial, New Age, and mood for training, PR, education and multi-media.
Tips: "Make sure your printed material is as precise as your music."

☑ ▣ **ENTERTAINMENT PRODUCTIONS, INC.**, 2118 Wilshire Blvd. PMB 744, Santa Monica CA 90403. (310)456-3143. Fax: (310)456-8950. **Contact:** Edward Coe, president/producer. Motion picture and television production company. Clients include motion picture and TV distributors. Estab. 1972. Uses the services of music houses and songwriters for scores, production numbers, background and theme music for films and TV and jingles for promotion of films. Commissions/ year vary. Pays by the job or by royalty. Buys motion picture and video rights.
How to Contact: Query with résumé of credits. Demo should show flexibility of composition skills. "Demo records/tapes sent at own risk—returned if SASE included." Responds by letter in 1 month, "but only if SASE is included."
Tips: "Have résumé on file. Develop self-contained capability."

insider report

Composer finds home in world of film scoring

Gary Chang's timing could be called impeccable, even if it wasn't by design. Seventeen years ago, the fledgling film composer was just doing what he loved, creating electronic music, when opportunity knocked, and led him into a career that has spanned more than fifty feature films, from John Hughes's *The Breakfast Club* to John Frankenheimer's *The Island of Dr. Moreau* and through many disparate points in between. And he's still hard at work, doing what he loves.

Gary Chang

"The only thing I consciously did with my career was jump from one stepping stone to the next, when the next stone appeared," Chang says of his entry into the business. The son of Chinese immigrants, Chang was born in Minneapolis and raised in Pittsburgh, where he first found his interest in music, "idolizing The Band and Leon Russell," he says. "People have a hard time believing I cut my teeth transcribing Butterfield Blues Band arrangements. It's hard for them to see the years of R&B and jazz experience—those were the musicians in Pittsburgh I respected the most."

But like his music, Chang is anything but predictable. "Until I moved to Los Angeles, I was often asked where I was from. Whenever I answered, 'Why, I'm from around here,' I would get the reply, 'I mean, where are you *really* from?' At the time, ethnic was black, Italian or Jewish—Chinese was off the map. I now identify with the film *The Man Who Fell to Earth*, in which David Bowie portrays an alien who gets stuck on Earth and ends up succeeding in the business making electronic music!"

Chang earned a masters degree in composition from CalArts, where he studied with Morton Subotnik, the electronic composer who created some of the first electronic music records in the 1960s. Once out of school, Chang worked as a session musician until his first break came along, the opportunity to work with film composer Giorgio Moroder on the scores for *The Neverending Story* and *Electric Dreams*. It was then he developed his signature world music sound, a blend of cultures punctuated by use of instruments and treatments, from bowed wine glasses to digeridoos to string quartet pizzicatos. Experimentation continues to color his work, which he now produces in a state-of-the-art studio in his home in Calabasas, California, where he works on Synclaviers, Pro Tools, and an assortment of G4 digital equipment.

The field has changed as electronic music has matured as a film score medium, Chang says. "Things became dicey when the musician's domain crossed over into the engineer's domain," he says of his early days in the business. "It was very compartmentalized—artist, producer, musician, engineer, second engineer. I never really got comfortable with that situation—I wanted to play with all the knobs. Now, when I'm composing film scores or producing artists, they come to my home. I do it all. There is no pressure. There is my family, there is my dog, there is time, there is life." Here Chang talks about his musical influences, his professional path, and offers his advice for composers starting out.

You studied with Morton Subotnick while earning your MFA at CalArts. To what extent did having a mentor of that caliber impact your career?
Subotnick was the first composer I knew who did everything—program, perform, record, etc. He utilized techniques such as his "player piano" technique of recording control tracks to totally automate the studio in the analog world years before it was common practice. He promoted the idea of a total integration of all the devices in the recording studio, not just synthesizers. Engineers in the 1980s thought they were innovative when they would record a guitar "returns only," recording only the reverb outputs, with no direct sound. I told them I had been doing that for ten years! They thought they were clever using "gated reverb," but Pierre Schaefer was doing that in the 1950s.

Is there a formula for "breaking in," or are there as many ways in as there are artists who break in? Is there a 'typical' path—commercial work to TV to feature films?
Composing is an apprenticeship craft. If you really look into it, you will find that many of the prominent film composers today worked for other composers initially. There is too much to learn about film, music, music for film, and business to cram it all into a two- or four-year program—especially the business aspects. The apprentice stands in the room when a composer argues for his music, when he talks to a musician while producing a recording, when he revises orchestrations with the orchestrator. So it's more likely that someone from a famous composer's group will succeed before someone who started doing industrial films, trying to work his way up. By virtue of being in the heat of the battle he has more experience.

You've said, "Becoming a film composer is not a linear kind of career choice." So your path to this profession wasn't a straight line?
My extensive computer music background paid off, leading to a job as the product specialist for the then new Fairlight CMI (Computer Music Instrument). It was one of the first computer music instruments, used by Peter Gabriel and Kate Bush. I met everyone in the industry during the two years I worked for Fairlight. This led me to the next step of freelancing as a session computer music programmer.

In 1982, this was a bizarre, unique job, and I found myself working with jazz greats like Chick Corea, Weather Report and Herbie Hancock (the heroes of my youth), and mainstream recording artists like Supertramp, Al Jarreau and Kansas. Being a programmer instead of a keyboardist was an unchallenging position for me with my artist-clients. I witnessed many aspects of their process—creative, political, business, you name it.

The people who helped me in my career were different from the ones who influenced me artistically. After accruing over fifty record credits, with various artists all over the board, I met Patrick Williams, a great film composer who also was a jazz composer. Working with Pat found me on the scoring stage with some of the finest studio players in Los Angeles—which I am not! Although it was somewhat embarrassing being the worst player on the bandstand, the experience was an important one for me as a composer. I like to think that many of those musicians who later saw me behind the glass respected my courage to endure such stressful events in order to be a better musician. I look on those sessions now as very special times.

The man who gave me my big opportunity was Giorgio Moroder. I worked for him in 1984 on two films, *The Neverending Story* and *Electric Dreams*. The result of this work—aside from being paid handsomely—was that Giorgio recommended me to Keith Forsey, who with Giorgio won an Oscar for *Flashdance*, to assist in scoring *The Breakfast Club*. Keith left the project before its completion, leaving me to finish it; hence, my first feature film credit. So, band member becomes product specialist becomes session musician becomes ghostwriter becomes composer.

When you first broke into composing for film, what was your biggest surprise, positive or negative?
When I first went out in Los Angeles, I got two reactions: first, "Your portfolio is shit. It will never sell."; and second, "This is brilliant! Let's go into the studio *tomorrow* and record ten new ones!" This reminds me of the current IBM TV ads about the young Web company starting their business, which say the only thing worse than no business is too much business. The thing I was most afraid of was not being prepared for a big opportunity.

You were fortunate in that your world music approach to composition became highly marketable—a sort of "right place at the right time" story. But to what extent should composers keep the market in mind, and to what extent should they follow their own creative muses?
I have been asked, "What kind of music would you write if you didn't write film music?" I would write obscure, ambient electronic pieces, Anthony Braxton-esque jazz pieces and John Adams-esque minimalist chamber pieces. In other words, I would write music that fewer people would understand. This doesn't work in the music business. I'll keep that for later in life. Maybe that is the virtue of getting a college

education—having something to do when my phone stops ringing. Back then, I was really never aware that there were trends going on. I was just trying to make music I liked. Keeping the market in mind has its pitfalls.

You've scored action films, coming-of-age films, thrillers, war dramas, historical pieces—is there anything you would turn down? And what does that say about the need for versatility in the field?
Many people's music experience, especially young people, is more and more diverse today. The accessibility to different music is hugely improved from my youth, vastly changed from my father's youth. Now, I think that everybody is aesthetically versatile, to a certain extent. You know, the global village.

Despite the variety of genres you work in, there must be common elements in your approach to each job. Would you synopsize what you're trying to accomplish, generally, with each score?
I approach film scoring in a similar manner to a screenwriter who is writing an additional character into the script. There must be justification for this character's presence in a scene; continuity is critical. A certain theme may be "the storyteller's theme." In a violent scene, perhaps the music becomes a friend sitting next to you, saying, "It's violent, but there's a reason we are watching this." I think the filmmakers who enjoy working with me appreciate my approach; it is an approach that creates importance for the music in the film.

Your home studio is described as state-of-the-art. I would imagine it took some years to build such a facility. At minimum, what would a composer need to be able to equip a professional level home studio?
It is really amazing how affordable stuff has gotten. I would recommend Logic Platinum. It has synthesizer and sampler plug-ins, with digital audio recording and mixing included. Of course, you need a reasonable room, monitor speakers, and some outboard gear, mics, etc. But at least these recent digital audio/sequencer software packages did away with tape machines and mixing consoles, which were always the most expensive devices in the studio.

In an interview with film composer Mark Isham last year, he said he's seeing a lot of fresh and exciting things happening in scoring now—would you agree, and if so, would you elaborate?
There are a lot of exciting things happening in music in general right now. Many of the techniques considered avant-garde in the 60s and 70s are common practice in today's music. I remember, as a kid, going to the New York World's Fair in the 60s and seeing the RCA exhibit where Edgar Varese had created a piece of *musique concrète* utilizing fifty speakers. The sounds he chose were the sounds of America. Among those sounds were recordings of Joan Baez—sounds a lot like sampling, doesn't it?

Is there any parting advice you'd like to share with composers/musicians eyeing work in the field during the next five years?
When I first started out, a friend of mine knew Billy Cobham, who was then drummer for the Mahavishnu Orchestra. I called him several times, and when I finally got him on the phone, he was rather short with me. He said, "Look—this is what you have to do. First, go out and do what you do. After a while, people will start to notice that you are doing it. Then, keep on doing it." These are the most prophetic words ever spoken to me on the topic of careers in art. If you quit, then you are just like everyone else. Survival is the gestalt of the artist.
—*Anne Bowling*

N **⊡** **FILM CLASSIC EXCHANGE**, 143 Hickory Hill Circle, Osterville MA 02655-1322. Phone/fax: (508)428-7198. E-mail: moviecast@mediaone.net. Vice President: Jeffrey Aikman. Motion picture production company. Clients include motion picture industry/TV networks and affiliates. Estab. 1916. Uses the services of music houses, independent songwriters/composers and lyricists for scoring and background music for motion pictures, TV and video projects. Commissions 10-20 composers and 10-20 lyricists/year. Pays by the job. Buys all rights.
How to Contact: Submit demo tape of previous work. Prefers cassette or VHS videocassette. SASE, but prefers to keep material on file. Responds in 2 months.
Music: Uses pop and up-tempo for theatrical films/TV movies.
Tips: "Be persistent."

☑ **⊡** **FINE ART PRODUCTIONS/RICHIE SURACI PICTURES, MULTIMEDIA, INTERACTIVE**, 67 Maple St., Newburgh NY 12550-4034. Phone/fax: (845)561-5866. E-mail: rs7fap @idsi.net. Website: www.idsi.net/OPPS5.html **Contact:** Richard Suraci, owner. Advertising agency, audiovisual firm, scoring service, **jingle/commercial music production house**, motion picture production company (Richie Suraci Pictures) and **music sound effect library**. Clients include corporate, industrial, motion picture and broadcast firms. Estab. 1987. Uses services of independent songwriters/ composers for scoring, background music and jingles for various projects and commercials for radio and TV. Commissions 1-2 songwriters or composers and 1-3 lyricists/year. Pays by the job, royalty or by the hours. Buys all rights.
How to Contact: Submit demo tape of previous work or tape demonstrating composition skills, query with résumé of credits or write or call first to arrange personal interview. Prefers cassette (or ½″, ¾″, or 1″ videocassette) with as many songs as possible and lyric or lead sheets. SASE, but prefers to keep material on file. Responds in 1 year.
Music: Uses all types of music for all types of assignments.

FITZMUSIC, 208 W. 30th St., Suite 1006, New York NY 10001. (212)695-1992. **Contact:** Gary Fitzgerald, composer/producer. **Commercial music production house and music/sound effects library**. "We service the advertising, film and television community." Estab. 1987. Uses the services of independent composers for scoring of TV, radio and industrials, background music for film and television, and jingles and commercials for radio and TV. Commissions 4-5 composers/year. "*New York talent only.*" Pays per project. Buys all rights. Stock music royalties on back end.

FOR BOOKS ON THE CRAFT AND BUSINESS of songwriting, check out the website for Writer's Digest Books at www.writersdigest.com.

How to Contact: Call first to obtain permission to submit demo tape of previous work. Will not open unsolicited submissions. Prefers CD. SASE, but prefers to keep on file. "A follow-up call must follow submission."
Music: Uses all styles of music.
Tips: "Complete knowledge of how the advertising business works is essential. Currently looking for music for stock library."

☑ **FREDRICK, LEE & LLOYD**, 235 Elizabeth St., Landisville PA 17538. (717)898-6092. E-mail: fll235@aol.com. **Contact:** Dusty Rees, vice president. **Jingle/commercial music production house.** Clients include advertising agencies. Estab. 1976. Uses the services of independent songwriters/composers and staff writers for jingles. Commissions 2 composers/year. Pays $650/job. Buys all rights.
How to Contact: Submit tape demonstrating composition skills. Prefers cassette, CD or 7½ ips reel-to-reel with 5 jingles. "Submissions may be samples of published work or original material." SASE. Responds in 3 weeks.
Music: Uses pop, rock, country and MOR.
Tips: "The more completely orchestrated the demos are, the better."

GETER ADVERTISING INC., 75 E. Wacker Dr. #410, Chicago IL 60601-3708. (312)782-7300. **Contact:** Rosemary Geter, creative director. Advertising agency. Clients include retail-direct response. Estab. 1978. Uses the services of music houses, independent songwriters/composers and lyricists for jingles for clients, commercials for radio and TV. Pays per job. Buys all rights.
How to Contact: Write or call first to arrange personal interview or submit demo tape of previous work. Prefers cassette, ¾" or ½" videocassette with 8 songs. Does not return material.
Music: Uses all styles of music for jingles, commercials.

☑ **HODGES ASSOCIATES, INC.**, P.O. Box 53805, 912 Hay St., Fayetteville NC 28305. (910)483-8489. Fax: (910)483-7197. Website: www.hodgesassoc.com. **Contact:** Anna Smith or Wanda Bullard, presidents. Advertising agency. Clients include industrial, retail and consumer. ("We handle a full array of clientele.") Estab. 1974. Uses the services of music houses and independent songwriters/composers for background music for industrial films and slide presentations, and commercials for radio and TV. Commissions 1-2 composers/year. Pays by the job. Buys all rights.
How to Contact: Submit demo tape of previous work. Prefers cassette or CD. Does not return material; prefers to keep on file. Responds in 3 months.
Music: Uses all styles for industrial videos, slide presentations and TV commercials.

Ⓝ **HOME, INC.**, 731 Harrison Ave., Boston MA 02118. (617)266-1386. Fax: (617)266-8514. E-mail: alanmichel@homeinc.org. Director: Alan Michel. Audiovisual firm and video production company. Clients include cable television, nonprofit organizations, pilot programs, entertainment companies and industrial. Uses the services of music houses and independent songwriters/composers for scoring of music videos, background music and commercials for TV. Commissions 2-5 songwriters/year. Pays up to $200-600/job. Buys all rights and one-time rights.
How to Contact: Submit demo tape of previous work. Prefers cassette with 6 pieces. Does not return material; prefers to keep on file. Responds as projects require.
Music: Mostly synthesizer. Uses all styles of music for educational videos.
Tips: "Have a variety of products available and be willing to match your skills to the project and the budget."

☑ **K&R'S RECORDING STUDIOS**, 28533 Greenfield, Southfield MI 48076. (248)557-8276. E-mail: recordav@knr.net. Website: www.knr.net. **Contact:** Ken Glaza. Scoring service and **jingle/commercial music production house**. Clients include commercial and industrial firms. Services include sound for pictures (music, dialogue). Uses the services of independent songwriters/composers and lyricists for scoring of film and video, commercials and industrials and jingles and commercials for radio and TV. Commissions 1 composer/month. Pays by the job. Buys all rights.

How to Contact: Submit demo tape of previous work. Prefers CD or VHS videocassette with 5-7 short pieces. We rack your tape for client to judge. Does not return material.
Tips: "Keep samples short. Show me what you can do in five minutes. Go to knr.net 'free samples' and listen to the sensitivity expressed in emotional music."

KEN-DEL PRODUCTIONS INC., First State Production Center, 1500 First State Blvd., Wilmington DE 19804-3596. (302)999-1164. Estab. 1950. **Contact:** Edwin Kennedy. A&R Director: Shirl Lotz. General Manager: Edwin Kennedy. Clients include publishers, industrial firms and advertising agencies, how-to's and radio/TV. Uses services of songwriters for radio/TV commercials, jingles and multimedia. Pays by the job. Buys all rights.
How to Contact: "Submit all inquiries and demos in any format to general manager." Does not return material. Will keep on file for 3 years. Generally responds in 1 month.

LAPRIORE VIDEOGRAPHY, 70 James St., Worcester MA 01603. (508)755-9010. **Contact:** Peter Lapriore, owner. Video production company. Clients include corporations, retail stores, educational and sports. Estab. 1985. Uses the services of music houses, independent songwriters/composers for background music for marketing, training, educational videos and TV commercials and for scoring video. "We also own several music libraries." Commissions 2 composers/year. Pays $150-1,000/job. Buys all or one-time rights.
How to Contact: Submit demo tape of previous work. Prefers cassette, CD, or VHS videocassette with 5 songs and lyric sheet. Does not return material; prefers to keep on file. Responds in 3 weeks.
Music: Uses slow, medium, up-tempo, jazz and classical for marketing, educational films and commercials.
Tips: "Be very creative and willing to work on all size budgets."

MALLOF, ABRUZINO & NASH MARKETING, 765 Kimberly Dr., Carol Stream IL 60188. (630)929-5200. Fax: (630)752-9288. E-mail: manm@kwom.com. Website: www.manmarketing.com. **Contact:** Ed Mallof, president. Advertising agency. Works primarily with auto dealer jingles. Estab. 1980. Uses music houses for jingles for retail clients and auto dealers, and commercials for radio and TV. Commissions 5-6 songwriters/year. Pays $600-2,000/job. Buys all rights.
How to Contact: Submit demo tape of previous work. Prefers cassette with 4-12 songs. SASE. Does not return material. Responds if interested.
Tips: "Send us produced jingles we could re-lyric for our customers' needs."

☑ **McCANN-ERICKSON SOUTHWEST**, (formerly McCann-Erickson Worldwide), 14901 Quorum, Suite 800, Dallas TX 75240. (972)991-5518. **Contact:** Mark Daspit, creative director. Advertising agency. Serves all types of clients. Uses services of music houses and independent songwriters for background music for television, jingles for radio, commercials for radio and TV, and videos. Commissions 10 songwriters/year. Pays production cost and registrated creative fee. Arrangement fee and creative fee depend on size of client and size of market. "If song is for a big market, a big fee is paid; if for a small market, a small fee is paid." Buys all rights.
How to Contact: Submit demo tape of previously aired work. Prefers 7½ ips reel-to-reel. "There is no minimum or maximum length for tapes. Tapes may be of a variety of work or a specialization. We are very open on tape content; agency does own lyrics." Does not return material. Responds by phone when need arises.
Music: All types.

☑ **NORTON RUBBLE & MERTZ, INC. ADVERTISING**, 205 W. Walker Dr., Suite 400, Chicago IL 60606. (312)422-9500. Fax: (312)422-9501. Website: www.nrmadv.com. **Contact:** Jason Lambert. Advertising agency. Clients include consumer products, retail, business to business. Estab. 1987. Uses the services of music houses and independent songwriters/composers for jingles and background music for radio/TV commercials. Commissions 2 composers/year. Pays by the job.
How to Contact: Submit tape of previous work; query with résumé of credits. Prefers cassette or CD. Does not return materials; prefers to keep on file. "Please do not call."
Music: Uses up-tempo and pop for commercials.

✓ NOVUS VISUAL COMMUNICATIONS INC., 29 E. 10th St., 5th Floor, New York NY 10003-6157. (212)505-7200. Fax: (212)505-9399. E-mail: novuscom@aol.com. **Contact:** Robert Antonik, president/creative director. Advertising agency. Clients include corporations, interactive products. Estab. 1986. Uses the services of music houses, independent songwriters/composers and lyricists for scoring and background music for documentaries, commercials, multimedia applications, website, film shorts, and commercials for radio and TV. Commissions 2 composers and 4 lyricists/year. Pay varies per job. Buys one-time rights.

How to Contact: Write first to arrange personal interview. Query with résumé. Submit demo of previous work. Prefers cassette or VHS videocassette with 2-3 songs. "Submissions should be short and to the point." Prefers to keep submitted material on file, but will return material if SASE is enclosed. Responds in 6 weeks.

Music: Uses all styles for a variety of different assignments.

Tips: "Always present your best and don't add quantity to your reel, cassette, DAT or other submission. Novus is a full service marketing and communications agency. We work with various public relations, artists managements and legal advisors. We create multimedia events to album packaging and promotion."

N ON-Q PRODUCTIONS, INC., 618 Gutierrez St., Santa Barbara CA 93103. (805)963-1331. President: Vincent Quaranta. Audiovisual firm. Clients include corporate accounts/sales conventions. Uses the services of music houses, independent songwriters/composers and lyricists for scoring, background music and jingles for AV shows. Commissions 1-5 composers and 1-5 lyricists/year. Buys all or one-time rights.

How to Contact: Query with résumé of credits. Prefers cassette or 15 ips reel-to-reel or VHS videocassette. Prefers to keep material on file.

Music: Uses up-tempo music for slide, video and interactive presentations.

✓ RH POWER AND ASSOCIATES, INC., 320 Osuna NE, Bldg. B, Albuquerque NM 87107. Phone/fax: (505)761-3150. E-mail: rhpowr@aol.com. Website: www.rhpower.com. Creative Director: Roger L. Vergara. Advertising agency. Clients include RV, boat and automotive dealers and manufacturers. Estab. 1988. Uses the services of music houses and independent songwriters/composers for background music, and jingles and commercials for radio and TV. Pay varies per job. Buys all rights.

How to Contact: Query with résumé or circular of credits by mail or fax only. Writer first to arrange personal interview. "No need to include a submission package unless contacted from initial résumé or letter contact. Save on costs!" SASE. Responds in 1 week.

Music: Uses contemporary, jazz and up-tempo for jingles, TV and radio, commercials and music-on-hold.

PRICE WEBER MARKETING COMMUNICATIONS, INC., Dept. SM, P.O. Box 99337, Louisville KY 40223. (502)499-9220. Fax: (502)491-5593. E-mail: cfrank@priceweber.com. Website: www.priceweber.com. **Contact:** Charles Frank, associate creative director. Advertising agency and audiovisual firm. Estab. 1968. Clients include Fortune 500, consumer durables, light/heavy industrials and package goods. Uses services of music houses and independent songwriters/composers for scoring of long format videos and corporate shows, jingles for radio and commercials for radio and TV. Commissions 6-8 composers/year. Pays by the job ($5,000-20,000). Buys all or one-time rights.

How to Contact: Submit demo tape of previous work demonstrating composition skills. Prefers CD with 10 or fewer pieces. "Enclose data sheet on budgets per selection on demo tape." SASE. Responds in 2 weeks.

Music: Uses easy listening, up-tempo, pop, jazz, rock and classical for corporate image industrials and commercials.

Tips: "We want fresh music. Budgets run from $5,000 to $20,000. Your music must enhance our message."

QUALLY & COMPANY INC., 2238 Central St. #3, Evanston IL 60201-1457. (847)864-6316. **Contact:** Robert Qually, creative director. Advertising agency. Uses the services of music houses, independent songwriters/composers and lyricists for scoring, background music and jingles for radio and TV commercials. Commissions 2-4 composers and 2-4 lyricists/year. Pays by the job. Buys various rights depending on deal.

How to Contact: Submit demo tape of previous work or query with résumé of credits. Prefers cassette or ¾″ Beta videocassette. SASE, but prefers to keep material on file. Responds in 2 weeks.

Music: Uses all kinds of music for commercials.

Ⓝ RAMPION VISUAL PRODUCTIONS, 125 Walnut St., Watertown MA 02472. (617)972-1777. Fax: (617)972-9157. E-mail: stevent2@aol.com. Website: www.rampion.com. **Contact:** Steven V. Tringali, director/camera. Motion picture multi media production company. Clients include educational, independent producers, corporate clients and TV producers. Estab. 1982. Uses the services of independent songwriters/composers for jingles, background music and scoring to longer form programming. Commissions 4-6 composers/year. Pays by the job. Buys all rights.

How to Contact: Submit demo tape of previous work or query with résumé of credits. Prefers cassette with variety of pieces. Does not return material; prefers to keep on file.

Music: Uses all styles for corporate, educational and original programming.

Tips: "Submit a varied demo reel showing style and client base."

RODEO VIDEO, INC., 412 S. Main St., Snowflake AZ 85937-0412. (520)536-7111. Fax: (520)536-7120. E-mail: kflake@rodeovideo.com. Website: www.rodeovideo.com. **Contact:** Keith Flake, vice president. Video and TV production company. Clients include rodeo contestants and fans. Estab. 1982. Uses the services of music houses, independent songwriters/composers and lyricists for background music for rodeo blooper videos and rodeo documentaries. Commissions 2 composers and 2 lyricists/year. Pay varies. Buys all rights or one-time rights.

How to Contact: Submit demo tape of previous work. Prefers cassette or DAT with any number of songs. Mainly interested in country/western with rodeo theme. Does not return material. Responds only if interested.

Music: Uses country/western for video backgrounds.

Tips: "Looking for uptempo songs with rodeo theme—country/western or rock."

☑ SOTER ASSOCIATES INC., 209 N. 400 W., Provo UT 84601. (801)375-6200. Fax: (801)375-6280. Website: www.soter.net. President: N. Gregory Soter. Vice President: Boyd Karen. Creative Director: Garr Ovard. Advertising agency. Clients include financial, health care, municipal, computer hardware and software. Estab. 1970. Uses services of music houses, independent songwriters/composers and lyricists for background music for audiovisual presentations and jingles for radio and TV commercials. Commissions 1 composer, 1 lyricist/year. Pays by the job. Buys all rights.

How to Contact: Submit tape demonstrating previous work and composition skills. Prefers cassette or VHS videocassette. Does not return submissions; prefers to keep materials on file.

☑ ▣ TRF PRODUCTION MUSIC LIBRARIES, Dept. SM, 747 Chestnut Ridge Rd., Chestnut Ridge NY 10977. (845)356-0800. Fax: (845)356-0895. E-mail: info@trfmusic.com. Website: www.trfmusic.com. **Contact:** Anne Marie Russo. **Music/sound effect libraries.** Estab. 1931. Uses the services of independent composers for all categories of production music for television, film and other media. Pays 50% royalty.

How to Contact: Submit demo tape of new compositions. Prefers audio cassette or CD with 3-7 pieces. Does not return material. Responds in 3 months.

Music: Primarily interested in instrumental and acoustic music for TV, film and AV/multimedia.

☑ ▣ UTOPIAN EMPIRE CREATIVEWORKS, 6055 Robert Dr., Traverse City MI 49684. (231)943-5050. E-mail: lesnmore@aol.com. **Contact:** M'Lynn Hartwell, president. Web design, multimedia firm and motion picture/video production company. Serves commercial, industrial and nonprofit clients. We provide the following services: advertising, marketing, design/packaging, distribution and booking. Uses services of music houses, independent songwriters/composers for jingles and scoring of and background music for multi-image/multimedia, film and video. Negotiates pay. Buys all or one-time rights.

How to Contact: Submit demo tape of previous work, demonstrating composition skills or query with résumé of credits. Prefers CD or good quality cassette. Does not return material; prefers to keep on file. Responds only if interested.

Music: Uses mostly industrial/commercial themes.

VIP VIDEO, Film House, 143 Hickory Hill Circle, Osterville MA 02655. Phone/fax: (508)428-7198. E-mail: moviecast@mediaone.net. Website: www.jeffilms.com. **Contact:** Jeffrey H. Aikman, president. Audiovisual firm. Clients include business, industry and TV stations. Estab. 1983. Uses the services of music houses, independent songwriters/composers and lyricists for scoring andbackground music for motion pictures and home video. Commissions 15-20 composers and 15-20 lyricists/year. Pays by the job, amounts vary depending on the length and complexity of each project. Buys all rights.

How to Contact: Submit demo tape of previous work. Prefers cassette with 1-2 songs. SASE, but prefers to keep material on file unless specifically stated. Responds in 2 months.

Music: Uses easy listening, pop and up-tempo for feature films, TV series, TV pilots and background for videotapes. Currently working on scoring series of 26 feature length silent films. If project is successful, this series will be added to at the rate of 13 per year.

VIS/AID MARKETING/ASSOCIATES, P.O. Box 4502, Inglewood CA 90309-4502. (310)399-0696. **Contact:** Lee Clapp, manager. Advertising agency. Clients include "companies in 23 SIC codes (workable)." Estab. 1965. Uses the services of music houses, independent songwriters/composers and lyricists for background music for films, and commercials, TV jingles for radio/TV and scoring new material. Commissions 1-2 composers and 1-2 lyricists/year. Pay is negotiable. Buys all or one-time rights.

How to Contact: Query with résumé of credits. Call first to arrange personal interview or submit demo tape of previous work. Prefers cassette with 1-2 songs and lyric and lead sheet. "Do not send original material that if misplaced/lost cannot be duplicated." Does not return material. Responds in 2 weeks.

Music: Uses up-tempo, pop, jazz and classical for educational films, slide presentations and commercials.

WARD & AMES, 7500 San Felipe, #350, Houston TX 77063. (713)266-9696. Fax: (713)266-2486. E-mail: names@wardandames.com. Website: www.wardandames.com. **Contact:** Danny Ward and Nancy Ames. Composing and scoring service, **jingle/commercial music production house**, event design and consultancy. Clients include corporations, ad agencies, political entities, TV markets, film studios and production houses. Estab. 1982. Compose and produce custom music packages for scoring of background music, jingles and commercials for all media; also industrials.

How to Contact: Submit project RFP and budget or call to discuss availability. Responds in 3 weeks.

Music: Produces all types for custom productions, jingles, industrials, product launches, ad campaigns, film and recording artists.

SENDING TO A COUNTRY other than your own? Be sure to send International Reply Coupons (IRCs) instead of stamps for replies or return of your materials.

Play Producers & Publishers

Finding a theater company willing to invest in a new production can be frustrating for an unknown playwright. But whether you write the plays, compose the music or pen the lyrics, it is important to remember not only where to start but how to start. Theater in the U.S. is a hierarchy, with Broadway, Off Broadway and Off Off Broadway being pretty much off limits to all but the Stephen Sondheims of the world.

Aspiring theater writers would do best to train their sights on nonprofit regional and community theaters to get started. The encouraging news is there is a great number of local theater companies throughout the U.S. with experimental artistic directors who are looking for new works to produce, and many are included in this section. This section covers two segments of the industry: theater companies and dinner theaters are listed under Play Producers, and publishers of musical theater works are listed under the Play Publishers heading (beginning on page 373). All these markets are actively seeking new works of all types for their stages or publications.

BREAKING IN

Starting locally will allow you to research each company carefully and learn about their past performances, the type of musicals they present, and the kinds of material they're looking for. When you find theaters you think may be interested in your work, attend as many performances as possible, so you know exactly what type of material each theater presents. Or volunteer to work at a theater, whether it be moving sets or selling tickets. This will give you valuable insight into the day-to-day workings of a theater and the creation of a new show. On a national level, you will find prestigious organizations offering workshops and apprenticeships covering every subject from arts administration to directing to costuming. But it could be more helpful to look into professional internships at theaters and attend theater workshops in your area. The more knowledgeable you are about the workings of a particular company or theater, the easier it will be to tailor your work to fit its style and the more responsive they will be to you and your work. (See the Workshops & Conferences section on page 439 for more information.) As a composer for the stage, you need to know as much as possible about a theater and how it works, its history and the different roles played by the people involved in it. Flexibility is the key to successful productions, and knowing how a theater works will only help you in cooperating and collaborating with the director, producer, technical people and actors.

If you're a playwright looking to have his play published in book form or in theater publications, see the listings under the Play Publishers section (page 373). To find play producers and publishers in your area, consult the Geographic Index at the back of this book.

Play Producers

ALLIANCE THEATRE COMPANY, 1280 Peachtree St., Atlanta GA 30309. (404)733-4650. Fax: (404)733-4625. Website: www.alliancetheatre.org. **Contact:** Freddie Ashley, literary associate. Artistic Director: Kenny Lean. Play producer. Estab. 1969. Produces 9-10 plays and 1 new musical/year. Audience is diverse, regional and young. Two performing spaces: 800-seat proscenium and a 200-seat flexible black box. Pays negotiable amount per performance.
How to Contact: Query with synopsis, character breakdown and set description. SASE. Responds in 6 months.

Musical Theater: They are primarily interested in new musicals, but also will consider works for children's theatre. Musicals for young audiences must be no longer than 1 hour in length and have a cast of 8 or fewer.

Productions: *Hot Mikado*, by David Bell/Rob Bowman/Marjorie B. Kellogg (Gilbert & Sullivan's *The Mikado* updated); *Elaborate Lives: The Legend of Aida*, by Elton John and Tim Rice (musical theatre update of legend); and *Soul Possessed*, by Debbie Allen/James Ingram/Arturo Sandoval (musical dance drama set in bayous of Louisiana).

AMERICAN LIVING HISTORY THEATER, P.O. Box 752, Greybull WY 82426. (307)765-9449. Fax: (307)765-9448. E-mail: ludwigunlimited@hotmail.com. **Contact:** Dorene Ludwig, president and artistic director. Play producer. Estab. 1975. Produces 1-2 plays/year. Performs all over U.S.—conventions, schools, museums, universities, libraries, etc. Pays by royalty.
How to Contact: Query first. SASE. Responds in 1 year.
Musical Theater: "We use only primary source, historically accurate material: in music—*Songs of the Civil War* or *Songs of the Labor Movement*, etc.—presented as a program rather than play would be the only use I could foresee. We need music historians more than composers."
Tips: "Do not send fictionalized historical material. We use primary source material only."

☑ **AMERICAN MUSICAL THEATRE OF SAN JOSE**, 1717 Technology Dr., San Jose CA 95110-1305. (408)453-1545. Fax: (408)453-7123. E-mail: mjacobs@amtsj.org. Website: www.amtsj.org. **Contact:** Marc Jacobs, associate artistic director. Play producer. Estab. 1935. Produces 4 mainstage musicals/year. "Our season subscribers are generally upper-middle class families. Our main season is in the 2,500-seat San Jose Center for the Performing Arts. Pays variable royalty.
How to Contact: Submit complete manuscript and tape of songs. SASE. Responds in 6 months.
Musical Theater: "We are not looking for children's musicals, Christmas shows or puppet shows. We are looking for high quality (professional caliber) musicals to develop for our 2,500-seat main stage theatre, a national tour or possible Broadway production. Submissions from composers and writers with some previous track record only, please. The first thing we look for is quality and originality in the music and lyrics. Next we look for librettos that offer exciting staging possibilities. If writing original music to a pre-existing play please be sure all rights have been cleared."
Productions: *Singin' in the Rain* and Barry Manilow's *Copacabana*.
Tips: "We are a company with a $6 million per season operating budget and one of the largest subscription audiences in the country. We are looking for shows we can develop for possible main stage or Broadway productions. Therefore it is advisable that any composers or writers have professional production history before submitting to us."

🔃 **ARIZONA THEATRE COMPANY**, P.O. Box 1631, Tucson AZ 85702. (520)884-8210. Artistic Director: David Goldstein. Professional regional theater company. Members are professionals. Performs 6 productions/year, including 1 new work. Audience is middle and upper-middle class, well-educated, aged 35-64. "We are a two-city operation based in Tucson, where we perform in a 603-seat newly renovated, historic building, which also has a 100-seat flexible seating cabaret space. Our facility in Phoenix, the Herberger Theater Center, is a 712-seat, proscenium stage." Pays 4-10% royalty.
How to Contact: Submit through agent only. SASE. Responds in 4 months.
Musical Theater: Musicals or musical theater pieces. 15-16 performers maximum including chorus. Instrumental scores should not involve full orchestra. No classical or operatic.
Productions: *Five Guys Named Moe*, by Clarke Peters (musical theatre); *The Gershwins' Fascinating Rhythm*, conceived by Mark Lamos/Mel Marvin (musical theatre); and *H.M.S. Pinnafore*, by Gilbert/Sullivan (musical theatre).
Tips: "As a regional theater, we cannot afford to produce extravagant works. Plot line and suitability of music to further the plot are essential considerations."

🔃 **ARKANSAS REPERTORY THEATRE**, 601 Main, P.O. Box 110, Little Rock AR 72203. (501)378-0445. Fax: (501)378-0012. Website: www.therep.org. **Contact:** Brad Mooy. Play producer. Estab. 1976. Produces 8 plays and 4 musicals (1 new musical)/year. "We perform in a 354-seat house and also have a 99-seat blackbox." Pays 5-10% royalty or $75-150 per performance.

How to Contact: Query with synopsis, character breakdown and set description. SASE. Responds in 6 months.
Musical Theater: "Small casts are preferred, comedy or drama and prefer shows to run 1:45 to 2 hours maximum. Simple is better; small is better, but we do produce complex shows. We aren't interested in children's pieces, puppet shows or mime. We always like to receive a tape of the music with the book."
Productions: *Radio Gals*, by Mike Craver/Mark Hardwick; and *Always . . . Patsy Cline*, by Ted Swindley (bio-musical).
Tips: "Include a *good* cassette of your music, *sung well*, with the script."

 BAILIWICK REPERTORY, Bailiwick Arts Center, 1229 W. Belmont, Chicago IL 60657. (773)883-1090. Fax: (773)883-2017. E-mail: bailiwickr@aol.com. Website: www.bailiwick.org. Director: David Zak. Artistic/Managing Director: Debra Hatchett. Play producer. Estab. 1982. Produces 5 mainstage, 5 one-act plays and 1-2 new musicals/year. "We do Chicago productions of new works on adaptations that are politically or thematically intriguing and relevant. We also do an annual director's festival which produces 50-75 new short works each year." Pays 5-8% royalty.
How to Contact: "Send SASE (business size) first to receive manuscript submission guidelines. Material returned if appropriate SASE attached." Responds in 6 months.
Musical Theater: "We want innovative, dangerous, exciting material."
Productions: *The Christmas Schooner*, by John Reeger and Julie Shannon (holiday musical); *Bonnie and Clyde*, by Pomerantz/Eickmann/Herron/Ritchie (Roaring 20s).
Tips: "Be creative. Be patient. Be persistent. Make me believe in your dream."

 BARTER THEATRE, P.O. Box 867, Abingdon VA 24212. (540)628-2281. Fax: (540)619-3335. E-mail: barter@naxs.com. Website: www.bartertheatre.com. **Contact:** Richard Rose, artistic director. Play producer. Estab. 1933. Produces 15 plays and 5-6 musicals (1 new musical)/year. Audience "varies; middle American, middle age, tourist and local mix." 500-seat proscenium stage, 150-seat thrust stage. Pays 5% royalty.
How to Contact: Query with synopsis, character breakdown and set description. SASE. Responds in 1 year.
Musical Theater: "We investigate all types. We are not looking for any particular standard. Prefer sellable titles with unique use of music. Prefer small cast musicals, although have done large scale projects with marketable titles or subject matter. We use original music in almost all of our plays." Does not wish to see "political or very urban material, or material with very strong language."
Productions: *Godspell*, by Stephen Schwartz/John Michael Teblak; *Proposals*, by Neil Simon; *Eleanor: An American Love Story*, by Jonathan Bolt/Thomas Tierney/John Forster; *A Grand Night for Singing*, by Walter Bobbie/Fred Wells; and *The Belle of Amherst*, by William Luce.
Tips: "Be patient. Be talented. Don't be obnoxious. Be original and make sure subject matter fits our audience."

 THE BLOWING ROCK STAGE COMPANY, P.O. Box 2170, Blowing Rock NC 28605. (828)295-9168. Fax: (828)295-9104. E-mail: theatre@blowingrock.com. Website: www.blowingrockstage.com. **Contact:** Robert Warren, producing director. Play producer. Estab. 1986. Produces 2 plays and 2 musicals (1 new musical)/year. "Blowing Rock Stage Company provides a professional summer

**FOR EXPLANATIONS OF THESE SYMBOLS,
SEE THE INSIDE FRONT AND BACK COVERS OF THIS BOOK.**

theatre experience for the residents and the high volume of summer tourists." Performances take place in a 240-seat proscenium summer theater in the Blue Ridge Mountains. Pays flat fee/performance or 5-7% royalty.

How to Contact: Query with synopsis, character breakdown and set description. SASE. Responds in up to 6 months.

Musical Theater: "Casts of ten or less are preferred, with ideal show running time of two hours, intermission included. Limit set changes to three or less; or unit concept. Some comic relief, please. Not producing stark adult themes."

Productions: *Daylight Spirits*, by Charles Thomas (Appalachian music and storyline); *A Grand Night for Singing*, by Rodgers and Hammerstein (review); and *Sophie*, by Karin Baker and Tony Parise (the Sophie Tucker story).

Tips: "We're looking for inspiration. We enjoy supporting projects which are soulful and uplifting. We want light-hearted musicals with some comic relief."

BRISTOL RIVERSIDE THEATRE, Dept. SM, P.O. Box 1250, Bristol PA 19007. (215)785-6664. Fax: (215)785-2762. Website: www.brtstage.org. Artistic Director: Susan D. Atkinson. Business Manager: Jo Lalli. Play producer. Estab. 1986. Produces 5 plays and 2 musicals/year (1 new musical every 2 years) and summer concert series. "302-seat proscenium Equity theater with audience of all ages from small towns and metropolitan area." Pays 6-8% royalty.

How to Contact: Submit complete manuscript, score and tape of songs. SASE. Responds in 18 months.

Musical Theater: "No strictly children's musicals. All other types with small to medium casts and within reasonable artistic tastes. Prefer one-set; limited funds restrict. Do not wish to see anything catering to prurient interests."

Productions: *Sally Blane, World's Greatest Girl Detective*, by David Levy/Leslie Eberhard (spoof of teen detective genre); *Moby Dick*, by Mark St. Germain, music by Doug Katsarous; and *Texas Flyer*, by Larry Gatlin.

Tips: "You should be willing to work with small staff, open to artistic suggestion, and aware of the limitations of newly developing theaters."

WILLIAM CAREY COLLEGE DINNER THEATRE, William Carey College, Hattiesburg MS 39401-5499. (601)582-6454. E-mail: thecom@wmcarey.edu. **Contact:** O.L. Quave, managing director. Play producer. Produces 2 musicals/year. "Our dinner theater operates only in summer and plays to family audiences." Payment negotiable.

How to Contact: Query with synopsis, character breakdown and set description. Does not return material. Responds in 1 month.

Musical Theater: "Plays should be simply-staged, have small casts (8-10 maximum), and be suitable for family viewing; two hours maximum length. Score should require piano only, or piano, synthesizer."

Productions: *Smoke on the Mountain*; *Schoolhouse Rock Live*; and *Pump Boys and Dinettes*.

CENTENARY COLLEGE, Theatre Dept., Shreveport LA 71134-1188. (318)869-5075. Fax: (318)869-5760. E-mail: rbuseick@centenary.edu. **Contact:** Robert R. Buseick, chairman. Play producer. Produces 6 plays (1-2 new musicals)/year. Plays are presented in a 350-seat playhouse to college and community audiences. Pay is negotiable.

How to Contact: Query with synopsis, character breakdown and set description. Does not return material. Responds as soon as possible.

Productions: *Blood Brothers*; *Grand Hotel*; and *Funny Girl*.

Tips: "Keep trying. It's not easy."

CIRCA '21 DINNER PLAYHOUSE, Dept. SM, P.O. Box 3784, Rock Island IL 61204-3784. (309)786-2667. **Contact:** Dennis Hitchcock, producer. Play producer. Estab. 1977. Produces 1-2 plays and 4-5 musicals (1 new musical)/year. Plays produced for a general audience. Three children's works/year, concurrent with major productions. Payment is negotiable.

How to Contact: Query with synopsis, character breakdown and set description or submit complete manuscript, score and tape of songs. SASE. Responds in 3 months.

Musical Theater: "We produce both full length and one act children's musicals. Folk or fairy tale themes. Works that do not condescend to a young audience yet are appropriate for entire family. We're also seeking full-length, small cast musicals suitable for a broad audience." Would also consider original music for use in a play being developed.

Productions: *Forever Plaid*; and the U.S. premier of *Discovering Elvis*.

Tips: "Small, upbeat, tourable musicals (like *Pump Boys*) and bright musically-sharp children's productions (like those produced by Prince Street Players) work best. Keep an open mind. Stretch to encompass a musical variety—different keys, rhythms, musical ideas and textures."

☑ **CROSSROADS THEATRE**, 7 Livingston Ave., New Brunswick NY 08901. (732)249-5800. Fax: (732)249-1861. E-mail: crossroads@iop.com. Website: www.crossroadstheatre.org. **Contact:** Managing Director. Play producer. Estab. 1978. Produces 4 plays/year. 250-300 seat thrust stage. Pay depends on the piece.

How to Contact: Submit synopsis, 10 page sample of book and lyrics/tape. SASE. Responds in 1 month on synopsis; 6-9 months on full manuscript.

Musical Theater: "We tend to produce material for adults and young adults. We focus on works by and about African-Americans. We also produce works that show the intersection of cultures especially with African-American culture." Considers original music for use in a play being developed or for use in a pre-existing play.

Productions: *Homework*, by Kim Coles/Charles Randolph Wright; *Play On!*, by Cheryl L. West/ Sheldon Epps (musical); *Yellow Eyes*, by Migdalia Cruz (drama, world premiere); and *Venice*, by Kathleen McGhee/Anderson (drama world premiere).

THE DIRECTORS COMPANY, 311 W. 43rd St., Suite 307, New York NY 10036. (212)246-5877. Fax: (212)246-5882. Website: www.thedirectorscompany.org. **Contact:** Michael Parva, artistic/ producing director. Play producer. Estab. 1980. Produces 1-2 new musicals/year. Performance space is a 99-seat theatre located in the heart of Manhattan's Theatre District. "It is beautifully equipped with dressing rooms, box office and reception area in the lobby." Pays negotiable rate.

How to Contact: Query first. SASE. Responds in 1 year.

Musical Theater: "The Harold Prince Musical Theatre Program develops new musicals by incorporating the director in the early stages of collaboration. The program seeks cutting edge material that works to break boundaries in music theatre. We produce workshops or developmental productions. The emphasis is on the material, not on production values, therefore, we do not limit cast sizes. However, there are limits on props and production values." No children's musicals or reviews.

Productions: *Bat Boy, The Musical*, by Keythe Farley/Brian Flemming/Lawrence O'Keefe; and *The Passion of Frida Kahlo*, by Dolores Sendler.

ENSEMBLE THEATRE, 1127 Vine St., Cincinnati OH 45210. (513)421-3555. Fax: (513)562-4104. Website: www.cincyetc.com. **Contact:** D. Lynn Meyers, producing artistic director. Play producer. Estab. 1986. Produces 14 plays and at least 1 musical (1 new musical)/year. Audience is multi-generational and multi-cultural. 191 seats, ¾ stage. Pays 5-8% royalty (negotiable).

How to Contact: Query with synopsis, character breakdown and set description. SASE. Responds in 6 months.

Musical Theater: "All types of musicals are acceptable. Cast not over ten; minimum set, please."

Productions: *Cars, Dogs, Money and the Moon*, by David Kisor (musical about growing up in West Virginia); and *Around the World in Eighty Days*, by David Kisor/Joseph McDonough.

Tips: Looking for "creative, inventive, contemporary subjects or classic tales. Send materials as complete as possible."

☑ **THE GASLIGHT THEATRE**, 7010 E. Broadway, Tucson AZ 85710. (520)886-9428. Fax: (520)722-6232. **Contact:** Nancy LaViola, general manager. Play producer. Estab. 1977. Produces 5 musical melodramas (2-3 new musicals)/year. "We cater to family audiences. Our musical melodramas are always fun and never sad. Ages from toddlers to senior citizens come to our shows." Performance space is 20'w × 15'd (not including the apron). Pays for outright purchase.

How to Contact: Query with synopsis, character breakdown, set description. Submit complete ms and score. SASE. Responds in 2 months.

Musical Theater: Prefers musical melodramas of 1 hour and 30 minutes; with an olio of 18-20 minutes. "Our shows always have a hero and villain." Cast size is usually 3 women and 5-6 men. Does not wish to see anything violent or sad. "Family entertainment only." Looking for slapstick comedy. "We always use fun sets, i.e., rolling rocks, underwater adventure, camels that move, horses, etc. Our musical melodrama is followed by a themed olio (song and dance show with jokes). Include lots of music to accompany the show."

Productions: *Zerro Rides Again*; *Robin Hood*; and *Gnatman* (Crime fighter who is a gnat. Take off of Batman), all by Peter Van Slyke.

Tips: "Think fun and comedy! Our productions always have a villian and a hero. In the conflict the hero always wins. Always fun and family entertainment. Lots of music."

THE WILL GEER THEATRICUM BOTANICUM, P.O. Box 1222, Topanga CA 90290. (310)455-2322. Fax: (310)455-3724. E-mail: theatricum@mindspring.com. Website: www.theatricu m.com. **Contact:** Ellen Geer, artistic director. Literary Director: Isreal Baran. Play producer. Produces 4 plays, 1 new musical/year. Plays are performed in "large outdoor amphitheater with 60'x 25' wooden stage. Rustic setting." Pays negotiable royalty.

How to Contact: Query with synopsis, tape of songs and character breakdown. SASE. Responds as soon as can be read.

Musical Theater: Seeking social or biographical works, children's works and full length musicals with cast of up to 10 equity actors (the rest non-equity). Requires "low budget set and costumes. We emphasize paying performers." Would also consider original music for use in a play being developed. Does not wish to see "anything promoting avarice, greed, violence or apathy."

Productions: *Three Penny Opera*, by Brecht; *Robber Bridegroom*, by VHRY/Waldman (country folktale); and *Pie in the Sky*, by Alsop (nuclear/3 Mile Island).

LOS ANGELES DESIGNERS' THEATRE, P.O. Box 1883, Studio City CA 91614-0883. (323)650-9600. T.D.D.: (323)654-2700. Fax: (323)654-3260. E-mail: ladesigners@juno.com. **Contact:** Richard Niederberg, artistic director. Play producer. Estab. 1970. Produces 20-25 plays and 8-10 new musicals/year. Audience is predominantly Hollywood production executives in film, TV, records and multimedia. Plays are produced at several locations, primarily Studio City, California. Pay is negotiable.

How to Contact: Query first. Does not return material. Responds in 4 months. *Send proposals only.*

Musical Theater: "We seek out controversial material. Street language OK, nudity is fine, religious themes, social themes, political themes are encouraged. Our audience is very 'jaded' as it consists of TV, motion picture and music publishing executives who have 'seen it all'." Does not wish to see bland, "safe" material. "We like first productions. In the cover letter state in great detail the proposed involvement of the songwriter, other than as a writer (i.e., director, actor, singer, publicist, designer, etc.). Also, state if there are any liens on the material or if anything has been promised."

Productions: *St. Tim*, by Fred Grab (historical '60s musical); *Slipper and the Rose* (gang musical); and *1593—The Devils Due* (historical musical).

Tips: "Make it very 'commercial' and inexpensive to produce. Allow for non-traditional casting. Be prepared with ideas as to how to transform your work to film or videotaped entertainment."

■ **MANHATTAN THEATRE CLUB**, 311 W. 43rd St., New York NY 10036. (212)399-3000. Fax: (212)399-4329. Website: www.mtc-nyc.org. **Contact:** Clifford Lee Johnson III, director of musical theater program. Associate Artistic Director: Michael Bush. Artistic Director: Lynne Meadow. Play producer. Estab. 1971. Produces 8 plays and sometimes 1 musical/year. Plays are performed at the Manhattan Theatre Club before varied audiences. Pays negotiated fee.

How to Contact: Query first. SASE. Responds in 4 months.

Musical Theater: "Original work."

Productions: *A Class Act*, by Ed Kieban/Lonny Price/Linda Kline; *The Wild Party*, by Andrew Lippa; and *New Yorkers*, by Stephen Weiner/Glenn Slater.

Tips: "Make sure your script is tightly and securely bound."

MIXED BLOOD THEATRE CO., 1501 S. Fourth St., Minneapolis MN 55454. (612)338-7892. E-mail: czar@mixedblood.com. **Contact:** David Kunz, script czar. Play producer. Estab. 1976. Produces 4-5 plays/year and perhaps 1 new musical every 2 years. "We have a 200-seat theater in a converted firehouse. The audience spans the socio-economic spectrum." Pays royalty or per performance.

How to Contact: Query first (1-page cover letter, 1-page synopsis). SASE. Responds on queries in 2 months.

Musical Theater: "We want full-length, non-children's works with a message. Always query first. Never send unsolicited script or tape."

Productions: *Black Belts II*, musical revue (black female vocalists and their music); *Birth of the Boom* (do-wop/hip hop extravaganza); and *Vices* (musical sketch revue).

Tips: "Always query first. The direct approach is best. Be concise. Make it interesting. Surprise us. Contemporary comedies, politically-edged material and sports-oriented shows are usually of interest."

NEW REPERTORY THEATRE, P.O. Box 610418, Newton Highlands MA 02161-0418. (617)332-7058. Fax: (617)527-5217. E-mail: RickNewRep@aol.com. Website: www.NewRep.org. **Contact:** Rick Lombardo, producing artistic director. Play producer. Estab. 1984. Produces 5 plays and 1 musical/year. Audience is Metro-Boston based. Performance space is an intimate, 170-seat thrust stage with minimal space for musicians. Pays negotiable royalty.

How to Contact: Query with synopsis, character breakdown and set description. SASE. Responds in 9 months.

Musical Theater: Seeks small cast (under 7), unusual stories, small orchestra. Full-length with adult themes. Does not wish to see standard musical comedies.

Productions: *Valley Song*, by Athol Fugard (South Africa); *Gifts of the Magi*, by Mark St. Germain and Randy Courrrts (musical of O'Henry); and *Moby Dick*, music by Doug Katsaros, libretto by Mark St. Germain.

Tips: "Be very clever in theatricality and style. Be unconventional."

☑ **NEW YORK STATE THEATRE INSTITUTE**, 37 First St., Troy NY 12180. (518)274-3200. E-mail: nysti@capital.net. Website: www.nysti.org. **Contact:** Patricia Di Benedetto Snyder, producing artistic director. Play producer. Produces 5 plays (1 new musical)/year. Plays performed for student audiences grades K-12, family audiences and adult audiences. Theater seats 900 with full stage. Pay negotiable.

How to Contact: Query with synopsis, character breakdown, set description and tape of songs. SASE. *Do not send ms unless invited.* Responds in 6 weeks for synopsis, 4 months for ms.

Musical Theater: Looking for "intelligent and well-written book with substance, a score that enhances and supplements the book and is musically well-crafted and theatrical." Length: up to 2 hours. Could be play with music, musical comedy, musical drama. Excellence and substance in material is essential. Cast could be up to 20; orchestra size up to 8.

Productions: *A Tale of Cinderella*, by W.A. Frankonis/Will Severin/George David Weiss (adaptation of fairy tale); *The Silver Skates*, by Lanie Robertson/Byron Janis/George David Weiss (adaptation of book); and *The Snow Queen*, by Adrian Mitchell/Richard Peaslee (adaptation of fairy tale).

Tips: "There is a great need for musicals that are well-written with intelligence and substance which are suitable for family audiences."

NEW YORK THEATRE WORKSHOP, 79 E. Fourth St., New York NY 10003. (212)780-9037. Fax: (212)460-8996. **Contact:** James C. Nicola, artistic director. Play producer. Produces 4-6 mainstage plays and approximately 50 readings/year. "Plays are performed in our theater on East Fourth St. Audiences include: subscription/single ticket buyers from New York area, theater professionals, and special interest groups." Pays by negotiable royalty.

How to Contact: Query with synopsis, character breakdown and set description. SASE. Responds in 5 months.

Musical Theater: "As with our nonmusicals, we seek musicals of intelligence and social consciousness that challenge our perceptions of the world and the events which shape our lives. We favor plays that possess a strong voice, distinctive and innovative use of language and visual imagery. Integration of text and music is particularly of interest. Musicals which require full orchestrations would generally be too

big for us. We prefer 'musical theater pieces' rather than straightforward 'musicals' per-se. We often use original music for straight plays that we produce. This music may be employed as pre-show, post-show or interlude music. If the existing piece lends itself, music may also be incorporated within the play itself. Large casts (12 or more) are generally prohibitive and require soliciting of additional funds. Design elements for our productions are of the highest quality possible with our limited funds."
Productions: *The Waves*, adapted from Virginia Woolf's novel, music and lyrics by David Bucknam and text and direction by Lisa Peterson; *My Children! My Africa*, by Athol Fugard; and *Rent*, by Jonathan Larson.
Tips: "Submit a synopsis which captures the heart of your piece; inject your piece with a strong voice and intent and try to surprise and excite us."

ODYSSEY THEATRE ENSEMBLE, Dept. SM, 2055 S. Sepulveda Blvd., Los Angeles CA 90025. (310)477-2055. **Contact:** Sally Essex-Lopresti, director of literary programs. Play producer. Estab. 1969. Produces 9 plays and 1 musical (1-2 new musicals)/year. "Our audience is predominantly over 35, upper middle-class and interested in eclectic brand of theater which is challenging and experimental." Pays negotiable royalty.
How to Contact: Query with synopsis, character breakdown, 8-10 pages of libretto, cassette of music and set description. Query should include résumé(s) of artist(s) and tape of music. SASE. "Unsolicited material is not read or screened at all." Responds to query in 2 weeks; ms in 6 months.
Musical Theater: "We want nontraditional forms and provocative, unusual, challenging subject matter. We are not looking for Broadway-style musicals. Comedies should be highly stylized or highly farcical. Works should be full-length only and not requiring a complete orchestra (small band preferred). Political material and satire are great for us. We're seeking interesting musical concepts and approaches. The more traditional Broadway-style musicals will generally not be done by the Odyssey. If we have a work in development that needs music, original music will often be used. In such a case, the writer and composer would work together during the development phase. In the case of a pre-existing play, the concept would originate with the director who would select the composer."

✅ **THE OPEN EYE THEATER**, P.O. Box 959, Margaretville NY 12455. (914)586-1660. E-mail: openeye@catskill.net. Website: www.theopeneye.org. **Contact:** Amie Brockway, producing artistic director. Play producer. Estab. 1972. Produces approximately 3 full length or 3 new plays for multi-generational audiences. Pays on a fee basis.
How to Contact: Query first. "A manuscript will be accepted and read only if it is a play for all ages and is: 1) Submitted by a recognized literary agent; 2) Requested or recommended by a staff or company member; or 3) Recommended by a professional colleague with whose work we are familiar. Playwrights may submit a one-page letter of inquiry including a very brief plot synopsis. Please enclose a self-addressed (but not stamped) envelope. We will reply only if we want you to submit the script (within several months)."
Musical Theater: "The Open Eye Theater is a not-for-profit professional company working in a community context. Through the development, production and performance of plays for all ages, artists and audiences are challenged and given the opportunity to grow in the arts. In residence, on tour, and in the classroom, The Open Eye Theater strives to stimulate, educate, entertain, inspire and serve as a creative resource."
Productions: *The Weaver and the Sea*, by Julie Steiny (ancient teaching tale); *A Midsummer Night's Dream*, by Shakespeare, music by Robert Cucinotta; and *The Nightingale*, by William E. Black/Annie Brockway, music by Elliot Sokolov (freedom and nature vs. technology).

PLAYHOUSE ON THE SQUARE, 51 S. Cooper, Memphis TN 38104. (901)725-0776. Fax: (901)272-7530. **Contact:** Jackie Nichols, executive producer. Play producer. Produces 12 plays and 4 musicals/year. Plays are produced in a 260-seat proscenium resident theater. Pays $500 for outright purchase.

TO HELP YOU UNDERSTAND and use the information in these listings, see "How to Use *Songwriter's Market* to Get Your Songs Heard," on page 5.

How to Contact: Submit complete manuscript, score and tape of songs. Unsolicited submissions OK. SASE. Responds in 6 months.

Musical Theater: Seeking "any subject matter—adult and children's material. Small cast preferred. Stage is 26' deep by 43' wide with no fly system." Would also consider original music for use in a play being developed.

Productions: *Children of Eden*; and *Tommy*, by The Who.

☑ **PLAYWRIGHTS' ARENA**, 514 S. Spring St., Los Angeles CA 90013. (213)485-1631. E-mail: jrivera923@juno.com. Website: writeaway.net/playrena. **Contact:** Jon Lawrence Rivera, artistic director. Play producer. Estab. 1992. Produces 4 plays and 1 musical (1 new musical)/year. Audience is in their early 20s to 50s. Performance space is 26' deep × 30' wide proscenium stage with fly system. Pays 6% royalty.

How to Contact: Submit complete manuscript, score and tape of songs. SASE. Responds in 6 months.

Musical Theater: Seeking new musicals like *Rent*. Does not want old fashioned musicals.

Productions: *Bitter Homes and Gardens*, by Luis Alfaro; *Last of the Suns*, by Alice Tuan; and *Crawlspace*, by Robert Harders.

☑ **PLAYWRIGHTS HORIZONS**, 416 W. 42nd St., New York NY 10036. (212)564-1235. Fax: (212)594-0296. Website: www.playwrightshorizons.org. **Contact:** Andrea Watson, assistant literary manager. Artistic Director: Tim Sanford. Musical Theatre Associate Producer: Ira Weitzman. Play producer. Estab. 1971. Produces about 4 plays and 1 new musical/year. "Adventurous New York City theater-going audience." Pays general Off-Broadway contract.

How to Contact: Submit complete manuscript and tape of songs. Attn: Musical Theater Program. SASE. Responds in 10 months.

Musical Theater: American writers. "No revivals, one-acts or children's shows; otherwise we're flexible. We have a particular interest in scores with a distinctively contemporary and American flavor. We generally develop work from scratch; we're open to proposals for shows and scripts in early stages of development."

Productions: *The Bubbly Black Girl Sheds Her Chameleon Skin*, by Kirsten Childs; *Floyd Collins*, by Adam Guettel/Tina Landau; and *Violet*, by Brian Crawley/Jeanine Tesori.

☑ **PRIMARY STAGES**, 131 W. 45th St., 2nd Floor, New York NY 10036. (212)840-9705. Fax: (212)840-9725. **Contact:** Casey Childs, artistic director. Play producer. Estab. 1984. Produces 4-5 plays/year. "New York theater-going audience representing a broad cross-section, in terms of age, ethnicity, and economic backgrounds. 99-seat, Off-Broadway theater." Pays $2,000 for a 5-week run.

How to Contact: Query first with synopsis, character breakdown, set description and tape. "No unsolicited scripts accepted. Submissions by agents only." SASE. Responds in up to 8 months.

Musical Theater: "We are looking for work of heightened theatricality, that challenges realism—musical plays that go beyond film and televisions standard fare. We are looking for small cast shows under 8 characters total, with limited sets. We are interested in original works, that have not been produced in New York."

Productions: *I Sent a Letter to My Love*, by Melissa Manchester/Jeffrey Sweet; and *Nightmare Alley*, by Jonathan Brielle.

THE REPERTORY THEATRE OF ST. LOUIS, P.O. Box 191730, St. Louis MO 63119. (314)968-7340. **Contact:** Susan Gregg, associate artistic director. Play producer. Estab. 1966. Produces 9 plays and 1 or 2 musicals/year. "Conservative regional theater audience. We produce all our work at the Loretto Hilton Theatre." Pays by royalty.

How to Contact: Query with synopsis, character breakdown and set description. Does not return material. Responds in 2 years.

Musical Theater: "We want plays with a small cast and simple setting. No children's shows or foul language. After a letter of inquiry we would prefer script and demo tape."

Productions: *Almost September* and *Esmeralda*, by David Schechter and Steve Lutvak; *Jack*, by Barbara Field and Hiram Titus; and *Young Rube*, by John Pielmeier and Nattie Selman.

SECOND STAGE THEATRE, P.O. Box 1807, Ansonia Station, New York NY 10023. (212)787-8302. Fax: (212)877-9886. **Contact:** Christopher Burney, associate artistic director. Play producer. Estab. 1979. Produces 4 plays and 1 musical (1 new musical)/year. Plays are performed in a small, 108-seat Off Broadway House. Pays per performance.
   • Also offers the Constance Klinsky Award for Excellence in the Composition of Musical Theatre. Awarded annually to three composers and/or lyricists. Write for submission guidelines.
How to Contact: Query with synopsis, character breakdown, set description, tape of 5 songs (no more). No unsolicited manuscripts. SASE. Responds in 6 months.
Musical Theater: "We are looking for innovative, unconventional musicals that deal with sociopolitical themes."
Productions: *In a Pig's Valise*, by Eric Overmyer/Kid Creole (spoof on '40s film noir); *A . . . My Name Is Still Alice*, by various (song/sketch revue); and *Saturday Night*, by Stephen Sondheim.
Tips: "Submit through agent; have strong references; always submit the best of your material in small quantities: 5 outstanding songs are better than 10 mediocre ones."

☑ SHENANDOAH INTERNATIONAL PLAYWRIGHTS (A Division of Shenan Arts, Inc.), 717 Quick's Mill Rd., Staunton VA 24401. (540)248-1868. Fax: (540)248-7728. E-mail: theatre @shenanarts.org. Website: www.shenanarts.org. **Contact:** Robert G. Small, artistic director. Play producer. Estab. 1976. Develops 10-12 plays/year for family audience. Pays royalty for full production.
How to Contact: Submit complete manuscript, score and tape of songs. SASE. Responds in 4 months.
Tips: "Submit full materials by February 1."

☑ STAGE ONE, 501 W. Main St., Louisville KY 40202. (502)589-5946. Fax: (502)588-5910. E-mail: stageone@kca.org. Website: www.stageone.org. **Contact:** Moses Goldberg, producing director. Play producer. Estab. 1946. Produces 7-8 plays and 0-2 new musicals/year. "Audience is mainly young people ages 5-18, teachers and families." Pays 5-7% royalty, flat fee or $25-75 per performance.
How to Contact: Submit complete manuscript and tape of songs (cassette preferred). SASE. Responds in 4 months.
Musical Theater: "We seek stageworthy and respectful dramatizations of the classic tales of childhood, both ancient and modern. Ideally, the plays are relevant to young people and their families, as well as related to school curriculum. Cast is rarely more than 12."
Productions: *The Great Gilly Hopkins*, by David Paterson/Steve Liebman (foster home); *Pinocchio*, by Moses Goldberg/Scott Kasbaum (classic tale); and *Jack & the Beanstalk*, by Goldberg/Corrett (fairytale).
Tips: "Stage One accepts unsolicited manuscripts that meet our artistic objectives. Please do not send plot summaries or reviews. Include author's résumé, if desired. In the case of musicals, a cassette tape is preferred. Cast size is not a factor, although, in practice, Stage One rarely employs casts of over 12. Scripts will be returned in approximately 3-4 months, if SASE is included. No materials can be returned without the inclusion of a SASE. Due to the volume of plays received, it is not possible to provide written evaluations."

☑ STAGES REPERTORY THEATRE, 3201 Allen Parkway, Houston TX 77019. (713)527-0220. Fax: (713)527-8669. Website: www.stagestheatre.com. **Contact:** Rob Bundy, artistic director. Play producer. Estab. 1979. Produces 6 plays and 1 musical/year. Performance space includes 170-seat thrust and 230-arena theatre. Pays negotiable royalty.
How to Contact: Query with synopsis, character breakdown and set description. SASE. Responds in 7 months.
Musical Theatre: Prefers edgy, theatrical, non-realistic stories, with a maximum cast size of 10, and single unit set with multiple locations.
Productions: *Nixon's Nixon*, by Russell Lees; *Funny Girl*, by Jules Styne; and *The Pitchfork Disney*, by Philip Ridley.

TADA!, 120 W. 28th St., New York NY 10001. (212)627-1732. Fax: (212)243-6736. E-mail: tada@ta datheater.com. Website: www.tadatheater.com. **Contact:** Janine Nina Trevens, artistic director. Play producer. Estab. 1984. Produces 4 staged readings and 2-4 new musicals/year. "TADA! is a company producing works performed by children ages 6-17 for family audiences in New York City. Performances run approximately 30-45 performances. Pays varying royalty.
   ● Also see the listing for Free Staged Reading Series Playwriting Competition in the Contests and Awards section.
How to Contact: Submit complete manuscript with synopsis, character breakdown, score and tape of songs. SASE. Responds in 1 year.
Musical Theater: "We do not produce plays as full productions. At this point, we do staged readings of plays. We produce original commissioned musicals written specifically for the company."
Productions: *The History Mystery*, by Janine Nina Trevens (kids time traveling through history)' *New York New Year*, by Gary Bagley (a young midwestern girl discovers New York and herself); and *Golly Gee Whiz*, by Erick Rockwell (based on the "Mickey & Judy film classics).
Tips: "Musical playwrights should concentrate on themes and plots meaningful to children and their families as well as consider our young actors' abilities and talents as well. Vocal ranges of children 7-17 should be strongly considered when writing the score."

☑ THEATRE THREE, INC., 2800 Routh St., Suite 168, Dallas TX 75201. (214)871-2933. Fax: (214)871-3139. E-mail: theatre3@airmail.net. Website: www.vline.net/theatre3/. **Contact:** Terry Dobson, musical director. Artistic Director: Jac Alder. Play producer. Estab. 1961. Produces 10-12 plays and 3-4 musicals (1 or 2 new musicals)/year. "Subscription audience of 4,500 enjoys adventurous, sophisticated musicals." Performance space is an "arena stage (modified). Seats 250 per performance. Quite an intimate space." Pays varying royalty.
How to Contact: *Submit through agent only.* SASE. Responds in 2 months.
Musical Theater: "Off the wall topics. We have, in the past, produced *Little Shop of Horrors*, *Angry Housewives*, *Sweeney Todd*, *Groucho*, *A Life in Revue*, *The Middle of Nowhere* (a Randy Newman revue) and *A . . . My Name Is Alice*. We prefer small cast shows, but have done shows with a cast as large as 15. Orchestrations can be problematic. We usually do keyboards and percussion or some variation. Some shows can be a design problem; we cannot do 'spectacle.' Our audiences generally like good, intelligent musical properties. Very contemporary language is about the only thing that sometimes causes 'angst' among our subscribers. We appreciate honesty and forthrightness . . . and good material done in an original and creative manner."
Productions: *I Love You, You're Perfect, Now Change!*, by Jimmy Roberts/Joe Dipietro; *Saturday Night*, by Sondheim/Epstein; and *The World Goes Round*, by Kander/Ebb.

THEATRE WEST VIRGINIA, P.O. Box 1205, Beckley WV 25802. (800)666-9142. E-mail: twv@ cwv.net. Website: wvweb.com/www/TWV. **Contact:** Marina Dolinger, artistic director. Play producer. Estab. 1955. Produces 5 plays and 2 musicals/year. "Audience varies from mainstream summer stock to educational tours (ages K-high school)." Pays 3-6% royalty, negotiable.
How to Contact: Query with synopsis, character breakdown and set description; should include cassette tape. SASE. Responds in 3 months.
Musical Theater: "Theatre West Virginia is a year-round performing arts organization that presents a variety of productions including community performances and statewide educational programs on primary, elementary and secondary levels. This is in addition to our summer, outdoor dramas of *Hatfields & McCoys* and *Honey in the Rock*, now in their 41st year." Anything suitable for school tours. No more than 6 in cast. Play should be able to be accompanied by piano/synthesizer.
Productions: *Beauty and the Beast*, by Kevin Reese/KMR scripts; *Grease*; and *The Wizard of Oz*.

☑ THEATREWORKS/USA, 151 W. 26th St., 7th Floor, New York NY 10003. (212)647-1100. Literary Manager: Michael Alltop. Play producer. Produces 10-13 plays, most are musicals (3-4 are new musicals)/year. Audience consists of children and families. Pays 6% royalty and aggregate of $1,500 commission-advance against future royalties.
How to Contact: Query with synopsis, character breakdown and sample scene and song. SASE. Responds in 6 months.

Musical Theater: "One hour long, 5-6 adult actors, highly portable, good musical theater structure; adaptations of children's literature, historical or biographical musicals, issues, fairy tales—all must have something to say. We demand a certain level of literary sophistication. No kiddy shows, no camp, no fractured fables, no shows written for school or camp groups to perform. Approach your material, not as a writer writing for kids, but as a writer addressing any universal audience. You have one hour to entertain, say something, make them care—don't preach, condescend. Don't forget an antagonist. Don't waste the audience's time. We always use original music—but most of the time a project team comes complete with a composer in tow."

Productions: *Island of the Blue Dolphins*, book/lyrics by Beth Blatt, music by Jennifer Giering (literary adaptation); *The Mystery of King Tut*, book/lyrics by Mindi Dickstein, music by Dan Messé (original historical); and *Gold Rush!*, book by David Armstrong, music by Dick Gallagher, lyrics by Mark Waldrop (original historical).

Tips: "Write a good show! Make sure the topic is something we can market! Come see our work to find out our style."

N. THUNDER BAY THEATRE, 400 N. Second Ave., Alpena MI 49707. (517)354-2267. E-mail: tbt@deepnet.com. Website: www.oweb.com/upnorth/tbt. Artistic Director: Suzanne Konicek. Play producer. Estab. 1967. Produces 12 plays and 6 musicals (1 new musical)/year. Performance space is thrust/proscenium stage. Pays variable royalty or per performance.

How to Contact: Submit complete manuscript, score and tape of songs. SASE. Responds in 3 months.

Musical Theater: Small cast. Not equipped for large sets. Considers original background music for use in a play being developed or for use in a pre-existing play.

Productions: *Wonderful Life*, by Holmes/Knoner/Willison (Christmas); *Smoke On the Mountain* (gospel); and *Forever Plaid*, by Stuart Ross.

UNIVERSITY OF ALABAMA NEW PLAYWRIGHTS' PROGRAM, P.O. Box 870239, Tuscaloosa AL 35487-0239. (205)348-9032. Fax: (205)348-9048. E-mail: pcastagn@woodsquad.as.ua.edu. Website: www.as.ua.edu/theatre/npp.htm. **Contact:** Dr. Paul Castagno, director/dramaturg. Play producer. Estab. 1982. Produces 8-10 plays and 1 musical/year; 1 new musical every other year. University audience. Pays by arrangement. Stipend is competitive. Also expenses and travel.

How to Contact: Submit complete manuscript, score and tape of songs. Submit only August-March. SASE. Responds in 6 months. "Submit before October for Janusfest, which is held in late January."

Musical Theater: Any style or subject (but no children's or puppet plays). No limitations—just solid lyrics and melodic line. Drama with music, musical theater workshops, and chamber musicals.

Productions: *Gospels According to Esther*, by John Erlanger; and *Tempest Tossed*.

Tips: "Take your demos seriously. We really want to do something small scale, for actors, often without the greatest singing ability. While not ironclad by any means, musicals with Southern themes might stand a better chance."

VIRGINIA STAGE COMPANY, P.O. Box 3770, Norfolk VA 23514. (757)627-6988. Fax: (757)628-5958. E-mail: chensley@vastage.com. Website: www.vastage.com. **Contact:** Charlie Hensley, artistic director. Play producer. Estab. 1978. Produces 7-10 plays and 1-2 musicals (0-1 new musical)/year. "We have a diverse audience. As home to a large, well-traveled population from NATO and the U.S. Navy, we serve many sophisticated theatregoers as well as those for whom theatre is not yet a habit. Located in Southeastern Virginia, we also play to a number of people from Southern backgrounds." Performance space is a 670-seat, Beaux-Arts proscenium theatre built in 1913—a national historic landmark. This hemp house features a proscenium opening 36' wide and 28' high with a stage depth of 28'. Pay is negotiable.

How to Contact: Query with synopsis, character breakdown and set description. SASE. Responds in 6 months.

Musical Theater: "We have produced the world premieres of *The Secret Garden* and *Snapshots* (with music by Stephen Schwartz). Our tastes are eclectic and have covered a number of styles. We have recently expanded our programming for young audiences." At this time, shows with less than 20 in the cast have a better chance of production. They have commissioned original music and adaptations for plays including *Hamlet, Twelfth Night, Terra Nova* and *A Christmas Carol*.

Productions: *Appalachian Strings*, by Randal Myler/Dan Wheetman (social history of the Appalachian region); *Snapshots*, by David Stern/Michael Scheman, music by Stephen Schwartz (a middle-aged couple trying to save their marriage); and *Twelfth Night*, by Shakespeare (set in 18th century Ireland with live musicians playing Celtic music).

Tips: "Be patient. We review material as quickly as possible. It also takes time to establish the relationships and resources needed to lead us into full, top-quality productions."

WALNUT STREET THEATRE COMPANY, 825 Walnut St., Philadelphia PA 19107. (215)574-3550, ext. 515. Fax: (215)574-3598. E-mail: wstpc@wstonline.org. Website: www.wstonline.org. **Contact:** Beverly Elliott, literary manager. Play producer. Estab. 1809. Produces 7 plays and 3 musicals/year. Plays produced on a mainstage with seating for 1,078 to a family audience; and in studio theaters with seating for 79-99 to adult audiences. Pays by royalty or outright purchase.

How to Contact: *Does not accept unsolicited scripts from individuals.*

Musical Theater: "We seek musicals with lyrical non-operatic scores and a solid book. We are looking for a small musical for springtime and one for a family audience at Christmas time. We remain open on structure and subject matter and would expect a tape with the script. Cast size: around 20 equity members (10 for smaller musical); preferably one set with variations." Would consider original music for incidental music and/or underscore. This would be at each director's discretion.

Productions: *Singin' in the Rain*, by Betty Conden/Adolph Green (a delightful romantic comedy); *Rags*, by Charles Strouse/Stephen Schwartz (an inspiring musical that celebrates the experience of coming to America); and *A Chorus Line*, by Marvin Hamlisch/Edward Kleban (a loving tribute to the unsung heroes of the chorus).

WEST COAST ENSEMBLE, P.O. Box 38728, Los Angeles CA 90038. (323)876-9337. **Contact:** Les Hanson, artistic director. Play producer. Estab. 1982. Produces 4-8 plays and 1 new musical/year. "Our audience is a wide variety of Southern Californians. Plays will be produced in our theater in Hollywood." Pays $35-50 per performance.

● See the listing for West Coast Ensemble—Musical Stairs in the Contests & Awards section.

How to Contact: Submit complete manuscript, score and tape of songs. SASE. Responds in 8 months.

Musical Theater: "There are no limitations on subject matter or style. Cast size should be no more than 12 and sets should be simple. If music is required we would commission a composer; music would be used as a bridge between scenes or to underscore certain scenes in the play."

Productions: *Cabaret* and *Merrily We Roll Along*.

Tips: "Submit work in good form and be patient. We look for musicals with a strong book and an engaging score with a variety of styles."

N WEST END ARTISTS, 18034 Ventura Blvd. #291, Encino CA 91316. (818)623-0040. Fax: (818)623-0202. E-mail: egaynes@pacbell.net. **Contact:** Edmund Gaynes, artistic director. Play producer. Estab. 1983. Produces 5 plays and 3 new musicals/year. Audience "covers a broad spectrum, from general public to heavy theater/film/TV industry crowds. Pays 6% royalty.

How to Contact: Submit complete manuscript, score and tape of songs. SASE. Responds in 3 months.

MARKET CONDITIONS are constantly changing! If you're still using this book and it is 2003 or later, buy the newest edition of *Songwriter's Market* at your favorite bookstore or order directly from Writer's Digest Books at (800)289-0963.

Musical Theater: "Prefer small-cast musicals and revues. Full length preferred. Interested in children's shows also." Cast size: "Maximum 12; exceptional material with larger casts will be considered."

Productions: *The Taffetas*, by Rick Lewis ('50s nostalgia, received 3 Ovation Award nominations); *Songs the Girls Sang*, by Alan Palmer (songs written for women now sung by men, received 1 Ovation Award nomination); *Crazy Words, Crazy Tunes*(played 2 years to Los Angeles and nationwide).

Tips: "If you feel every word or note you have written is sacred and chiseled in stone and are unwilling to work collaboratively with a professional director, don't bother to submit."

N WESTBETH THEATRE CENTER, 151 Bank St., New York NY 10014. (212)691-2272. Fax: (212)924-7185. E-mail: wbethzach@aol.com. Website: www.westbeththeatre.com. **Contact:** Zachary Morris, curator-new works program. Producing Director: Arnold Engleman. Play producer. Estab. 1977. Produces 1-2 musicals/year. Audience consists of artists, New York professionals and downtown theater goers. "We have five performance spaces, including a music hall and cafe theater." Pay varies. Uses usual New York showcase contract.

How to Contact: Query with résumé, one page project proposal—or one page synopsis with cast and production requirements for scripted plays and any relevant audio/visual material. SASE. Does not return material from outside the US. Responds in 3 months. "Artists must reside in NYC or surrounding areas and be desirous of extensive development and intense collaboration."

Musical Theater: "The New Works Program has expanded its focus to include performance proposals from a range of various disciplines including dancers, playwrights, musicians, and other performance artists. Proposals should be sharp, urban, and contemporary—period pieces or plays set in rural/regional locales will not be considered.

Productions: *20th Century Man*, by Ray Davies (bio of rock group The Kinks); *Almost Famous*, by Bruce Vilanch; and *Exactly Like You*, by Cy Coleman/E. Hutchner (musical comedy).

Tips: "Be open to the collaborative effort. We are a professional theater company, competing in the competitive world of Broadway and off-Broadway, so the work we present must reach for the highest standard of excellence."

☑ WINGS THEATRE CO., 154 Christopher St., New York NY 10014. (212)627-2960. Fax: (212)462-0024. E-mail: jcorrick@wingstheatre.com. Website: www.wingstheatre.com. **Contact:** Tricia Gilbert, literary manager. Artistic Director: Jeffrey Corrick. Play producer. Estab. 1987. Produces 3-5 plays and 3-5 musicals/year. Performance space is a 74-seat O.O.B. proscenium; repertoire includes a New Musicals Series, a gay-play series—we produce musicals in both series. Pays $100 for limited rights to produce against 6% of gross box office receipts.

How to Contact: Submit complete manuscript, score and tape of songs (score is not essential). SASE. Responds in 1 year.

Musical Theater: "Eclectic. Entertaining. Enlightening. This is an O.O.B. theater. Funds are limited." Does not wish to see "movies posing as plays. Television theater."

Productions: *Scott & Zelda*, by Dave Bates (The Fitzgeralds); *Cowboys*, by Clint Jefferies (gay western spoof); and *The Three Musketeers*, by Clint Jefferies (musical adaptation).

Tips: "Book needs to have a well-developed plot line and interesting, fully-realized characters. We place emphasis on well-written scripts, as opposed to shows which rely exclusively on the quality of the music to carry the show. Also be patient—we often hold onto plays for a full year before making a final decision."

☑ WOOLLY MAMMOTH THEATRE CO., M, 917 M. St. NW, Washington DC 20001. (202)289-2446. E-mail: woollymamm@aol.com. **Contact:** Mary Resing, literary manager. Artistic Director: Howard Shalwitz. Play producer. Estab. 1978. Produces 4 plays/year. Royalties vary.

How to Contact: *Submit through agent only.* We do not accept unsolicited manuscripts. SASE. Responds in 6 months.

Musical Theater: "We do unusual works. We have done 1 musical, the *Rocky Horror Show* (very successful). 8-10 in cast. We do not wish to see one-acts."

Productions: *The Dark Kalamazoo*, by Oni Faida Lampley (coming of age/trip to Sierra Leone).

Tips: "Know what we do. Read or see our plays."

Play Publishers

☑ **AMELIA MAGAZINE**, 329 "E" St., Bakersfield CA 93304. (661)323-4064. Fax: (661)323-5326. E-mail: amelia@lightspeed.net. **Contact:** Frederick A. Raborg, Jr., editor. Play publisher. Estab. 1983. Publishes 1 play/year. General audience; one-act plays published in *Amelia Magazine*. The annual Frank McClure One-Act Play Award awards $150 plus publication. Deadline May 15 annually.
How to Contact: Submit complete manuscript and score. Responds in 3 months. "We would consider publishing musical scores if submitted in clean, camera-ready copy—also single songs. Best bet is with single songs complete with clear, camera-ready scoresheets, for regular submissions. We use only first North American serial rights. All performance and recording rights remain with songwriter. Payment same as for fiction—$35 plus copies for regular acceptance. Write for guidelines for McClure Award with SASE." Sample copy: $10.95 ppd.
Tips: "Be polished, professional, and submit clear, clean copy."

N: AMERICAN EASTERN THEATRICAL COMPANY, (formerly Eastern Musicals), % Eastern Musicals, 136 Langley St., Fall River MA 02720. (508)676-3312. President: Raymond Carreiro. Play publisher. Estab. 1996. Publishes 3 musicals/year. Pays standard royalty.
How to Contact: Submit complete ms, score and tape of songs or VHS videocassette. Does not return material. Responds in 3 weeks.
Musical Theater: Seeks rock musicals, classical musicals, contemporary and non-musical theater. "All performances will be at the Associacao Cultural Lusitania."
Publications: *Our Real World*, by Jay Brillient/Maria Esteves; *Dearest Lizzie*, by Raymond Carreiro/Norihiko Hidino (additional lyrics by MaryAnn Thomas); and *A Fifties Christmas Carol*, by Raymond Carreiro/Paul Ponte (music arrangements by Louis Terreira).
Tips: "Looking for new material of all subject matters. No old, dated material."

☑ **BAKER'S PLAYS**, P.O. Box 699222, Quincy MA 02269-9222. (617)745-0805. Fax: (617)745-9891. E-mail: info@bakersplays.com. Website: www.bakersplays.com. **Contact:** John Welch, managing director and chief editor. Play publisher. Estab. 1845. Publishes 15-22 plays and 0-3 new musicals/year. Plays are used by children's theaters, junior and senior high schools, colleges and community theaters. Pays negotiated book and production royalty.
  • See the listing for Baker's Plays High School Playwriting Contest in the Contests & Awards section.
How to Contact: Submit complete manuscript, score and cassette tape of songs. SASE. Responds in 4 months.
Musical Theater: "Seeking musicals for teen production and children's theater production. We prefer large cast, contemporary musicals which are easy to stage and produce. Plot your shows strongly, keep your scenery and staging simple, your musical numbers and choreography easily explained and blocked out. Music must be camera-ready, or at least clean and legible." Would consider original music for use in a play being developed or in a pre-existing play.
Productions: *Oedipus/A New Magical Comedy*, by Bob Johnson.
Tips: "As we publish musicals that can be produced by high school theater departments with high school talent, the writer should know if their play can be done on the high school stage. I recommend that the writer go to performances of original high school musicals whenever possible."

CONTEMPORARY DRAMA SERVICE, 885 Elkton Dr., Colorado Springs CO 80907. (719)594-4422. E-mail: merpcds@aol.com. Website: www.contemporarydrama.com. **Contact:** Arthur Zapel, executive editor. Play publisher. Estab. 1979. Publishes 40-50 plays and 4-6 new musicals/year. "We publish for young children and teens in mainstream Christian churches and for teens and college level in the secular market. Our musicals are performed in churches, schools and colleges." Pays 10-50% book and performance royalty (often up to fixed amount).
How to Contact: *Query first* then submit complete manuscript, score and tape of songs. SASE. Responds in 2 months.
Musical Theater: "For churches we publish musical programs for children and teens to perform at Easter, Christmas or some special occasion. Our school musicals are for teens to perform as class

plays or special entertainments. Cast size may vary from 15-25 depending on use. We prefer more parts for girls than boys. Music must be written in the vocal range of teens. Staging should be relatively simple but may vary as needed. We are not interested in elementary school material. Elementary level is OK for church music but not public school elementary. Music must have full piano accompaniment and be professionally scored for camera-ready publication."

Publications: *Peace in the Kingdom*, by Michael Marion (a musical parable); *The Yankee Doodle Song and Dance Man*, by Bill Francoeur; and *The Velveteen Rabbit*, by Larry Nestor (teenage musical).

Tips: "Familiarize yourself with our market. Send $1 postage for catalog. Try to determine what would fit in, yet still be unique."

ELDRIDGE PUBLISHING CO., INC., P.O. Box 1595, Venice FL 34284. (800)HI-STAGE. E-mail: info@histage.com. Website: www.histage.com. **Contact:** Chris Angermann, musical editor. Play publisher. Estab. 1906. Publishes 60 plays and 2-3 musicals/year. Seeking "large cast musicals which appeal to students. We like variety and originality in the music, easy staging and costuming. Also looking for children's theater musicals which have smaller casts and are easy to tour. We serve the school and church market, 6th grade through 12th; also Christmas and Easter musicals for churches." Would also consider original music for use in a play being developed; "music that could make an ordinary play extraordinary." Pays 50% royalty and 10% copy sales in school market.

How to Contact: Submit manuscript, score or lead sheets and tape of songs. SASE. Responds in 1 month.

Publications: *Hoola Hoops & Halos*, by Jeffrey Smart/Scott Keys ('50s heavenly musical comedy); *Lagooned!*, by Tim Kelly/Lee Ahlin (tropical-pop musical spoof); and *Katastrophe Kate*, by Stephen Murray (a wild-west melodrama).

Tips: "We're always looking for talented composers but not through individual songs. We're only interested in complete school or church musicals. Lead sheets, cassette tape and script are best way to submit. Let us see your work!"

THE FREELANCE PRESS, P.O. Box 548, Dover MA 02030. (508)785-8250. Managing Editor: Narcissa Campion. Play publisher. Estab. 1979. Publishes up to 3 new musicals/year. "Pieces are primarily to be acted by elementary/middle school to high school students (9th and 10th grades); large casts (approximately 30); plays are produced by schools and children's theaters." Pays 10% of purchase price of script or score, 50% of collected royalty.

How to Contact: Query first. SASE. Responds in 6 months.

Musical Theater: "We publish previously produced musicals and plays to be acted by children in the primary grades through high school. Plays are for large casts (approximately 30 actors and speaking parts) and run between 45 minutes to 1 hour and 15 minutes. Subject matter should be contemporary issues (sibling rivalry, friendship, etc.) or adaptations of classic literature for children (*Syrano de Bergerac*, *Rip Van Winkle*, *Pied Piper*, *Treasure Island*, etc.). We do not accept any plays written for adults to perform for children."

Publications: *Tortoise vs. Hare*, by Stephen Murray (modern version of classic); *Tumbleweed*, by Sebastian Stuart (sleepy time western town turned upside down); and *Mything Links*, by Sam Abel (interweaving of Greek myths with a great pop score).

Tips: "We enjoy receiving material that does not condescend to children. They are capable of understanding many current issues, playing complex characters, handling unconventional material, and singing difficult music."

N SAMUEL FRENCH, INC., 45 W. 25th St., New York NY 10010. (212)206-8990. Hollywood office: 7623 Sunset Blvd., Hollywood CA 90046. (323)876-0570. Fax: (323)876-6822. Website: www.samuelfrench.com. President: Charles R. Van Nostrand. Play publisher. Estab. 1830. Publishes 40-50 plays and 2-4 new musicals/year. Amateur and professional theaters.

How to Contact: Query first. SASE. Responds in 10 weeks.

Musical Theater: "We publish primarily successful musicals from the NYC, London and regional stage."

Publications: *Eating Raoul*, by Paul Bartel; *Hello Muddah Hello Faddah*, by Bernstein/Krause; and *Love and Shrimp*, by Judith Viorst.

HEUER PUBLISHING CO., P.O. Box 248, Cedar Rapids IA 52406. (319)364-6311. E-mail: editor @hitplays.com. Website: www.hitplays.com. Publisher: C. Emmett McMullen. Play publisher. Estab. 1928. Publishes plays and musicals for the amateur market including middle schools, junior and senior high schools and church groups. Pays by outright purchase or percentage royalty.
How to Contact: Query with synopsis, character breakdown and set description or submit complete manuscript and score. SASE. Responds in 2 months.
Musical Theater: "We prefer one, two or three act comedies or mystery-comedies with a large number of characters."
Publications: *Brave Buckaroo*, by Renee J. Clark (musical melodrama) and *Pirate Island*, by Martin Follose (musical comedy).
Tips: "We sell almost exclusively to junior and smaller senior high schools. Thus flexible casting is extremely important. We need plays with large, predominantly female casts and if you are writing a musical, we need more choral numbers and solos for girls than boys."

☑ **PIONEER DRAMA SERVICE**, P.O. Box 4267, Englewood CO 80155. (303)779-4035. Fax: (303)779-4315. E-mail: playwrights@pioneerdrama.com. Website: www.pioneerdrama.com. **Contact:** Beth Somers, assistant editor. Play publisher. Estab. 1963. "Plays are performed by junior high and high school drama departments, church youth groups, college and university theaters, semi-professional and professional children's theaters, parks and recreation departments." Playwrights paid 50% royalty (10% sales).
How to Contact: Query first with character breakdown, synopsis and set description. SASE. Responds in 6 months.
Musical Theater: "We seek full length children's musicals, high school musicals and one act children's musicals to be performed by children, secondary school students, and/or adults. As always, we want musicals easy to perform, simple sets, many female roles and very few solos. Must be appropriate for educational market. We are not interested in profanity, themes with exclusively adult interest, sex, drinking, smoking, etc. Several of our full-length plays are being converted to musicals. We edit them, then contract with someone to write the music and lyrics."
Publications: *Sleepy Hollow*, by Vera Morris/Bill Francoeur (adaptation of the classic ghost story by Washington Irving); *Rocky of the Rainforest*, by Jay Mori; and *Let Your Hair Down, Rapunzel*, by Karen Boettdre-Tate/Scott DeTurk (children's musical).
Tips: "Research and learn about our company. Our website and catalog provide an incredible amount of information."

PLAYERS PRESS, INC., P.O. Box 1132, Studio City CA 91614. (818)789-4980. Associate Editor: Karen Flathers. Vice President: Robert W. Gordon. Play publisher, music book publisher, educational publisher. Estab. 1965. Publishes 20-70 plays and 1-3 new musicals/year. Plays are used primarily by general audience and children. Pays variable royalty and variable amount/performance.
How to Contact: Query first. SASE. Responds in 1 year (3 weeks on queries).
Musical Theater: "We will consider all submitted works. Presently musicals for adults and high schools are in demand. When cast size can be flexible (describe how it can be done in your work) it sells better."
Publications: *Rapunzel n' The Witch*, by William-Alan Landes (children's musical); *Song of Love*, by William Alan Landes (musical); and *Curse of the Mummy's Tomb*, by Julian Harries/Pat Witymark (musical).
Tips: "For plays and musicals, have your work produced at least twice. Be present for rehearsals and work with competent people. Then submit material asked for in good clear copy with good audio tapes."

REMEMBER: Don't "shotgun" your demo tapes. Submit only to companies interested in the type of music you write. For more submission hints, refer to Getting Started on page 10.

Classical Performing Arts

Finding an audience is critical to the composer of orchestral music. Fortunately, baby boomers are swelling the ranks of classical music audiences and bringing with them a taste for fresh, innovative music. So the climate is fair for composers seeking their first performance.

Finding a performance venue is particularly important because once a composer has his work performed for an audience and establishes himself as a talented newcomer, it can lead to more performances and commissions for new works.

BEFORE YOU SUBMIT

Be aware that most classical music organizations are nonprofit groups, and don't have a large budget for acquiring new works. It takes a lot of time and money to put together an orchestral performance of a new composition, therefore these groups are quite selective when choosing new works to perform. Don't be disappointed if the payment offered by these groups is small or even non-existent. What you gain is the chance to have your music performed for an appreciative audience. Also realize that many classical groups are understaffed, so it may take longer than expected to hear back on your submission. It pays to be patient, and employ diplomacy, tact and timing in your follow-up.

In this section you will find listings for classical performing arts organizations throughout the U.S. But if you have no prior performances to your credit, it's a good idea to begin with a small chamber orchestra, for example. Smaller symphony and chamber orchestras are usually more inclined to experiment with new works. A local university or conservatory of music, where you may already have contacts, is a great place to start.

All of the groups listed in this section are interested in hearing new works from contemporary classical composers. Pay close attention to the music needs of each group, and when you find one you feel might be interested in your music, follow submission guidelines carefully. To locate classical performing arts groups in your area, consult the Geographic Index at the back of this book.

☑ **AMERICAN OPERA MUSICAL THEATRE CO.**, 400 W. 43rd St. #19D, New York NY 10036. (212)594-1839. Fax: (212)695-4350. E-mail: corto@mindspring.com. **Contact:** Diana Corto, artistic director. Chamber music ensemble, chamber opera and musical theatre producing/presenting organization. Estab. 1994. Members are professionals with varying degrees of experience. Performs 5 concerts/year; 1 or 2 are new works. Audience is sophisticated and knowledgeable about music and theatre. "We rent different performance spaces." Pays negotiable royalty.
How to Contact: Submit tape "of excerpts, not more than 15 minutes." Does not return material. Responds in up to 1 month.
Music: "Must be vocal (for opera or for music theatre) with chamber groups. Cast should not exceed 10. Orchestration should not exceed 22, smaller chamber groups preferred. No rock 'n' roll, brassy pop or theatre material."
Performances: Puccini's *La Boheme* and Verdi's *Rigoletto*.

☑ **AMHERST SAXOPHONE QUARTET**, P.O. Box 29, Buffalo NY 14231-0029. (716)632-2445. Fax: (716)565-0636. E-mail: rosenthl@acsu.buffalo.edu. Website: www.amherstsaxophonequa rtet.buffalo.edu. **Contact:** Steve Rosenthal, director. Chamber music ensemble. Estab. 1978. Performs 80 concerts/year including 10-20 new works. Commissions 1-2 composers or new works/year. "We are a touring ensemble." Payment varies.
How to Contact: Query first. SASE. Responds in 1 month.

Music: "Music for soprano, alto, tenor and baritone (low A) saxophone. We are interested in great music of many styles. Level of difficulty is commensurate with full-time touring ensembles."

Performances: Lukas Foss's *Saxophone Quartet* (new music); David Stock's *Sax Appeal* (new music); and Chan Ka Nin's *Saxophone Quartet* (new music).

Tips: "Professionally copied parts help! Write what you truly want to write."

☑ **ANDERSON SYMPHONY ORCHESTRA**, P.O. Box 741, Anderson IN 46015. (765)644-2111. Fax: (765)644-7703. E-mail: aso@iquest.net or sowers@anderson.edu. Website: www.anderson symphony.org. **Contact:** Dr. Richard Sowers, conductor. Symphony orchestra. Estab. 1967. Members are professionals. Performs 7 concerts/year. Performs for typical mid-western audience in a 1,500-seat restored Paramount Theatre. Pay negotiable.

How to Contact: Query first. SASE. Responds in several months.

Music: "Shorter lengths better; concerti OK; difficulty level: mod high; limited by typically 3 full service rehearsals."

☒ **ARCADY**, P.O. Box 955, Simcoe, Ontario N3Y 5B3 Canada. (519)428-3185. E-mail: arcady@ex eculink.com. Website: www.publish.uwo.ca/~eegraing/arcady. **Contact:** Ronald Beckett, director. Semi-professional chorus and orchestra. Members are professionals, university music majors and recent graduates from throughout Ontario. "Arcady forms the bridge between the student and the professional performing career." Performs 12 concerts/year including 1-2 new works. Commissions 1 composer or new work/year. Pay negotiable.

How to Contact: Submit complete score and tape of piece(s). Does not return material. Responds in 3 months.

Music: "Compositions appropriate for ensemble accustomed to performance of chamber works, accompanied or unaccompanied, with independence of parts. Specialize in repetoire of 17th, 18th and 20th centuries. Number of singers does not exceed 30. Orchestra is limited to strings, supported by a professional quartet. No popular, commercial or show music."

Performances: Ronald Beckett's *I Am . . .* (opera); Ronald Beckett's *John* (opera); and David Lenson's *Prologue to Dido and Aeneas* (masque).

Tips: "Arcady is a touring ensemble experienced with both concert and stage performance."

☒ **AUREUS QUARTET**, 22 Lois Ave., Demarest NJ 07627-2220. (201)767-8704. E-mail: llyandr a2@aol.com. **Contact:** James J. Seiler, artistic director. Vocal ensemble (a cappella). Estab. 1979. Members are professionals. Performs 75 concerts/year, including 12 new works. Commissions 5 composers or new works/year. Pay varies for outright purchase.

How to Contact: Query first. SASE. Responds in 2 months.

Music: "We perform anything from pop to classic—mixed repertoire so anything goes. Some pieces can be scored for orchestras as we do pops concerts. Up to now, we've only worked with a quartet. Could be expanded if the right piece came along. Level of difficulty—no piece has ever been too hard." Does not wish to see electronic or sacred pieces. "Electronic pieces would be hard to program. Sacred pieces not performed much. Classical/jazz arrangements of old standards are great!"

Tips: "We perform for a very diverse audience—luscious, four part writing that can showcase well-trained voices is a must. Also, clever arrangements of old hits from '20s through '50s are sure bets. (Some pieces could take optional accompaniment)."

☑ **BALTIMORE OPERA COMPANY, INC.**, 110 W. Mt. Royal Ave., Suite 306, Baltimore MD 21201. (410)625-1600. Website: www.baltimoreopera.org. **Contact:** James Harp, artistic administrator. Opera company. Estab. 1950. Members are professionals. Performs 16 concerts/year. "The opera audience is becoming increasingly diverse. Our performances are given in the 3,000-seat Lyric Opera House." Pays by outright purchase.

How to Contact: Submit complete score and tapes of piece(s). SASE. Responds in 2 months.

Music: "Our General Director, Mr. Michael Harrison, is very much interested in presenting new works. These works would be anything from Grand Opera with a large cast to chamber works suitable for school and concert performances. We would be interested in perusing all music written for an operatic audience."

Performances: Verdi's *Aida*; Strauss' *Eleletra*; Humperdinck's *Hansel & Gretel*; Gourod's *Faust*; and Puccini's *Turandot*.

Tips: "Opera is the most expensive art form to produce. Given the current economic outlook, opera companies cannot be too avant garde in their selection of repertoire. The modern operatic composer must give evidence of a fertile and illuminating imagination, while also keeping in mind that opera companies have to sell tickets."

 BILLINGS SYMPHONY, 201 N. Broadway., Suite 350, Billings MT 59101-1936. (406)252-3610. Fax: (406)252-3353. E-mail: symphonyub@mcn.net. Website: www.mcn.net/~symphony. **Contact:** Dr. Uri Barnea, music director. Symphony orchestra, orchestra and chorale. Estab. 1950. Members are professionals and amateurs. Performs 12-15 concerts/year, including 6-7 new works. Traditional audience. Performs at Alberta Bair Theater (capacity 1,416). Pays by outright purchase (or rental).

How to Contact: Query first. SASE. Responds in 2 weeks.

Music: Any style. Traditional notation preferred.

Performances: Jerod S. Tate's *Winter Moons* (ballet suite); Alberto Ginastera's *Harp Concerto* (concerto); and Olga Victorova's *Compliments to American Audience* (orchestral piece).

Tips: "Write what you feel (be honest) and sharpen your compositional and craftsmanship skills."

BIRMINGHAM-BLOOMFIELD SYMPHONY ORCHESTRA, 1592 Buckingham, Birmingham MI 48009. (248)645-2276. Fax: (248)645-22760. **Contact:** Felix Resnick, music director and conductor. Executive Director: Carla Lamphere. Symphony orchestra. Estab. 1975. Members are professionals. Performs 6 concerts including 1 new work/year. Commissions 1 composer or new work/year "with grants." Performs for middle-to-upper class audience at Temple Beth El's Sanctuary. Pays per performance "depending upon grant received."

How to Contact: Query first. Does not return material. Responds in 6 months.

Music: "We are a symphony orchestra but also play pops. Usually 3 works on program (2 hrs.) Orchestra size 65-75. If pianist is involved, they must rent piano."

Performances: Brian Belanger's *Tuskegee Airmen Suite* (symphonic full orchestra); and Larry Nazer & Friend's *Music from "Warm"* CD (jazz with full orchestra).

 BRAVO! L.A., 16823 Liggett St., North Hills CA 91343. (818)892-8737. Fax: (818)892-1227. E-mail: info@bravo-la.com. Website: www.bravo-la.com. **Contact:** Dr. Janice Foy, director. An umbrella organization of recording/touring musicians, formed in 1994. Includes the following musical ensembles: Trio of the Americas (piano, clarinet, cello); the New American Quartet (string quartet); Trio Giocosa (string trio); The Ascending Wave (harp, soprano, cello or harp/cello duo); Cellissimo! L.A. (cello ensemble); Musical Combustion (harp, flute, cello); and the Sierra Chamber Players (piano with strings or mixed ensemble). Performs 4 concerts/year, including 1 new work. "We take care of PR and supply a DAT recording. There is also grant money the composer can apply for."

How to Contact: Submit complete score and tape of piece(s). SASE. Responds in a few months.

Music: "Classical, Romantic, Baroque, Popular (including new arrangements done by Shelly Cohen, from the 'Tonight Show Band'), ethnic (including gypsy) and contemporary works (commissioned as well). The New American Quartet has a recording project which features music of Mozart's *Eine Kleine Nachtmusik*, Borodin's *Nocturne*, a Puccini Opera Suite (S. Cohen), Strauss' *Blue Danube Waltz*, *Trepak* of Tschaikovsky, *'El Choclo'* (Argentinian tango), *Csardas!* and arrangements of Cole Porter, Broadway show tunes and popular classics."

**FOR EXPLANATIONS OF THESE SYMBOLS,
SEE THE INSIDE FRONT AND BACK COVERS OF THIS BOOK.**

Performances: Frank Abbinanti's *War & Peace* (cello concerto/rhapsody); Nickolas Driondo's *Gypsy Fantasie* (duo for accordion and cello); and Stephan Chandler's *Cello Concerto* (cello concerto with small chamber orchestra).
Tips: "Please be open to criticism/suggestions about your music and try to appeal to mixed audiences. We also look for innovative techniques, mixed styles or entertaining approaches, such as classical jazz or Bach and pop, or ethnic mixes."

CANADIAN OPERA COMPANY, 227 Front St. E., Toronto, Ontario M5A 1E8 Canada. (416)363-6671. E-mail: sandrag@coc.ca. Website: www.coc.ca. **Contact:** Sandra J. Gavinchuk, associate artistic administrator. Opera company. Estab. 1950. Members are professionals. 50-55 performances, including a minimum of 1 new work/year. Pays by contract.
How to Contact: Submit complete score and tapes of vocal and/or operatic works. "Vocal works please." SASE. Responds in 5 weeks.
Music: Vocal works, operatic in nature. "Do not submit works which are not for voice. Ask for requirements for the Composers-In-Residence program."
Performances: *Henze: Venus and Adonis*; *Burry: The Brother's Grimm*.
Tips: "We have a Composers-In-Residence program which is open to Canadian composers or landed immigrants."

CANTATA ACADEMY, 2441 Pinecrest Dr., Ferndale MI 48220. (248)358-9868. **Contact:** Phillip O'Jibway, business manager. Music Director: Dr. Michael Mitchell. music director. Vocal ensemble. Estab. 1961. Members are professionals. Performs 10-12 concerts/year including 1-3 new works. "We perform in churches and small auditoriums throughout the Metro Detroit area for audiences of about 500 people." Pays variable rate for outright purchase.
How to Contact: Submit complete score. SASE. Responds in 3 months.
Music: Four-part a cappella and keyboard accompanied works, two and three-part works for men's or women's voices. Some small instrumental ensemble accompaniments acceptable. Work must be suitable for forty voice choir. No works requiring orchestra or large ensemble accompaniment. No pop.
Performances: Charles S. Brown's *Five Spirituals* (concert spiritual); Kirke Mechem's *John Brown Cantata*; and Libby Larsen's *Ringeltanze* (Christmas choral with handbells & keyboard).
Tips: "Be patient. Would prefer to look at several different samples of work at one time."

CARMEL SYMPHONY ORCHESTRA, P.O. Box 761, Carmel IN 46032. (317)844-9717. Fax: (317)844-9916. Website: www.ci.carmel.in.us/. **Contact:** Allen Davis, executive director. Symphony orchestra. Estab. 1976. Members are professionals and amateurs. Performs 15 concerts/year, including 1-2 new works. Audience is "40% senior citizens, 85% white." Performs in a 1,500-seat high school performing arts center. Pay is negotiable.
How to Contact: Query first. SASE. Responds in 3 months.
Music: "Full orchestra works, 10-20 minutes in length. Can be geared toward 'children's' or 'Masterworks' programs. 65-70 piece orchestra, medium difficulty."
Performances: Jim Becket's *Glass Bead Jane* (full orchestra); Percy Grainger's *Molly on the Shore* (full orchestra); and Frank Glover's *Impressions of New England* (full orchestra and jazz quartet).

CHARLOTTE PHILHARMONIC ORCHESTRA, P.O. Box 470987, Charlotte NC 28247-0987. (704)846-2788. Fax: (704)847-6043. E-mail: charphilor@aol.com. Website: www.charlottephilharmonic.org. **Contact:** Albert Moehring, music director. Symphony orchestra. Estab. 1991. Members are professionals. Performs 12 concerts/year including 2-4 new works. Audience consists of music lovers, educated and uneducated. "We regularly perform Broadway/movie soundtracks, also standard classical repertoire." Performance spaces are up to 2,500 seats. Pay is negotiable.
 • The Charlotte Philharmonic Orchestra was voted Charlotte's Best Entertainment in 1998.
How to Contact: Submit complete score and tape of piece(s). Does not return material. Responds in 6 weeks.
Music: Seeks full orchestrations, lush strings always popular. Maximum 8-10 minutes. Would review classical styles, but also interested in Boston Pops type selections. Require lyrical music with interest-

ing melodies and good rhythms. "We are not interested in atonal, dissonant styled music. We will neither perform it, nor bother to review it. Our audiences do not like it." Players are professional. Limited rehearsals. String passages playable in limited time. Full orchestra sound—excellent brass players. 75 piece orchestra. Always interested in fine Broadway styled arrangements. Look for strong, smooth transpositions/modulations.

Performances: Davis Brown's arrangement of *Happy Holiday* (Christmas arrangement).

Tips: "With a new composer, we recommend pieces under 10 minutes, lyrical basis with definite melodies. Full use of 75 piece orchestra. Lush strings without exceedingly difficult passages for limited rehearsals. Variety of materials welcomed. Enjoy standard classics, bib band, ballroom dance-type music, ballet style. Also enjoy operatic arrangements. Use our own Philharmonic Chorus as well as regular vocalists. Good choral arrangements with full orchestra always of interest. Appreciate a tape when possible. If a composer submits during a really busy period of performances, please be patient. If there is no response in 4-6 weeks, they may contact us again."

☑ CHATTANOOGA GIRLS CHOIR, P.O. Box 6036, 612 Maclellan Building, Chattanooga TN 37401. (423)266-9422. E-mail: girlschoir@mindspring.com. Website: www.girlschoir.home.min dspring.com. **Contact:** John E. Wigal, artistic director. Vocal ensemble. Estab. 1986. Members are amateurs. Performs 2 concerts/year including at least 1 new work. Audience consists of cultural and civic organizations and national and international tours. Performance space includes concert halls and churches. Pays for outright purchase or per performance.

How to Contact: Query first. SASE. Responds in 6 weeks.

Music: Seeks renaissance, baroque, classical, romantic, twentieth century, folk and musical theatre for young voices of up to 8 minutes. Performers include 5 treble choices: 4th grade (2 pts.); 5th grade (2 pts.) (SA); grades 6-9 (3 pts.) (SSA); grades 10-12 (3-4 pts.) (SSAA); and a combined choir: grades 6-12 (3-4 pts.) (SSAA). Medium level of difficulty. "Avoid extremely high Tessitura Sop I and extremely low Tessitura Alto II."

Performances: Jan Swafford's *Iphigenia Book: Meagher* (choral drama); Penny Tullock's *How Can I Keep from Singing* (Shaker hymn).

COMMONWEALTH OPERA INC., 140 Pine St., Florence MA 01062. (413)586-5026. E-mail: commopr1@aol.com. **Contact:** Richard R. Rescia, artistic director. Opera company. Estab. 1977. Members are professionals and amateurs. Performs 4 concerts/year. "We perform at the Calvin Theatre Northampton in an 1,200-seat opera house. Depending on opera, audience could be family oriented or adult." Pays royalty.

How to Contact: Query first. Does not return material. Response will take months.

Music: "We are open to all styles of opera. We have the limitations of a regional opera company with local chorus. Principals come from a wide area. We look only at opera scores."

Performances: Arnold Black's *The Phantom Tollbooth* (children's opera); *Diefledermaus*, and *The Magic Flute*.

Tips: "We're looking for opera that is accessible to the general public and performable by a standard opera orchestra."

ℕ CONNECTICUT CHORAL ARTISTS/CONCORA, 52 Main St., New Britain CT 06051. (860)224-7500. Website: www.concora.org. **Contact:** Richard Coffey, artistic director. Professional concert choir. Estab. 1974. Members are professionals. Performs 15 concerts/year, including 3-5 new works. "Mixed audience in terms of age and background; performs in various halls and churches in the region." Payment "depends upon underwriting we can obtain for the project."

How to Contact: Query first. "No unsolicited submissions accepted." SASE. Responds in 1 year.

Music: Seeking "works for mixed chorus of 36 singers; unaccompanied or with keyboard and/or small instrumental ensemble; text sacred or secular/any language; prefers suites or cyclical works, total time not exceeding 15 minutes. Performance spaces and budgets prohibit large instrumental ensembles. Works suited for 750-seat halls are preferable. Substantial organ or piano parts acceptable. Scores should be very legible in every way."

Performances: Wm. Schuman's *Carols of Death* (choral SATB); Charles Ives' *Psalm 90* (choral SATB); and Frank Martin's *Mass for Double Chorus* (regional premiere).

Tips: "Use conventional notation and be sure manuscript is legible in every way. Recognize and respect the vocal range of each vocal part. Work should have an identifiable *rhythmic* structure."

☑ **GREAT FALLS SYMPHONY ASSOCIATION**, P.O. Box 1078, Great Falls MT 59403. (406)453-4102. Fax: (406)453-9779. E-mail: info@gfsymphony.org. Website: www.gfsymphony.org. **Contact:** Gordon J. Johnson, music director and conductor. Symphony orchestra. Estab. 1959. Members are nine-member professional core, plus 60 per-service local musicians. Performs 6 concerts (2 youth concerts)/year including 1-2 new works. Commissions 1-2 new works/year. "Our audience is conservative. Newer music is welcome; however, it might be more successful if it were programmatic." Plays in Civic Center Auditorium seating 1,764. Pays per performance.
How to Contact: Query first. Include SASE. Responds in 2 months.
Music: "Compositions should be for full orchestra. Should be composed idiomatically for instruments avoiding extended techniques. Duration 10-20 minutes. Avoid diverse instruments such as alto flute, saxophones, etc. Our orchestra carries 65 members, most of whom are talented amateurs. We have a resident string quartet and woodwind quintet that serve as principals. Would enjoy seeing a piece for quartet or quintet solo and orchestra. Send letter with clean score and tape (optional). We will reply within a few weeks."
Peformances: Bernstein's *Chichester Psalms* (choral and orchestra); Hodkinson's *Boogie, Tango and Grand Tarantella* (bass solo); and Stokes' *Native Dancer.*
Tips: "Music for orchestra and chorus is welcome. Cross cues will be helpful in places. Work should not require an undue amount of rehearsal time (remember that a concerto and symphony are probably on the program as well)."

☑ **GREATER GRAND FORKS SYMPHONY ORCHESTRA**, P.O. Box 7084, Grand Forks ND 58202-7084. (701)777-3359. Fax: (701)777-3320. E-mail: ggfso@und.nodak.edu. **Contact:** Timm Rolek, music director. Symphony orchestra. Estab. 1908. Members are professionals and/or amateurs. Performs 6 concerts/year. "New works are presented in 2-4 of our programs." Audience is "a mix of ages and musical experience. In 1997-98 we moved into a renovated, 450-seat theater." Pay is negotiable, depending on licensing agreements.
How to Contact: Submit complete score or complete score and tape of pieces. SASE. Responds in 6 months.
Music: "Style is open, instrumentation the limiting factor. Music can be scored for an ensemble up to but not exceeding: 3,2,3,2/4,3,3,1/3 perc./strings. Rehearsal time limited to 3 hours for new works."
Performances: Michael Harwood's *Amusement Park Suite* (orchestra); Randall Davidson's *Mexico Bolivar Tango* (chamber orchestra); and John Corigliano's *Voyage* (flute and orchestra); Linda Tutas Maugen's *Fable of Old Turtle* (saxophone concerto).

☑ **HEARTLAND MEN'S CHORUS**, P.O. Box 32374, Kansas City MO 64171-5374. (816)931-3338. Fax: (816)531-1367. E-mail: hmc@hmckc.org. Website: www.hmckc.org. **Contact:** Joseph Nadeau, music director. Men's chorus. Estab. 1985. Members are professionals and amateurs. Performs 3 concerts/year; 9-10 are new works. Commissions 1 composer or new works/year. Performs for a diverse audience at the Folly Theater (1,200 seats). Pay is negotiable.
How to Contact: Query first. SASE. Responds in 2 months.
Music: "Interested in works for male chorus (ttbb). Must be suitable for performance by a gay male chorus. We will consider any orchestration, or a cappella."
Performances: Thomas Pasatieris's *Mornings Innocent* (song cycle); Craig Carnahan's *Nutcracker: Men in Tights* (musical); and Robert Moran's *Night Passage* (opera).
Tips: "Find a text that relates to the contemporary gay experience, something that will touch peoples' lives."

HELENA SYMPHONY, P.O. Box 1073, Helena MT 59624. (406)442-1860. E-mail: hss@ixi.net. Website: www.ixi.net/~hss. **Contact:** Erik Funk, music director and conductor. Symphony orchestra. Estab. 1955. Members are professionals and amateurs. Performs 5-7 concerts/year including new works. Performance space is an 1,800 seat concert hall. Payment varies.
How to Contact: Query first. SASE. Responds in 3 months.

Music: "Imaginative, collaborative, not too atonal. We want to appeal to an audience of all ages. We don't have a huge string complement. Medium to difficult okay—at frontiers of professional ability we cannot do."

Performances: Eric Funk's *A Christmas Overture* (orchestra); Donald O. Johnston's *A Christmas Processional* (orchestra/chorale); and Elizabeth Sellers' *Prairie* (orchestra/short ballet piece).

Tips: "Try to balance tension and repose in your works. New instrument combinations are appealing."

HERSHEY SYMPHONY ORCHESTRA, P.O. Box 93, Hershey PA 17033. (800)533-3088. E-mail: drdackow@aol.com. **Contact:** Dr. Sandra Dackow, music director. Symphony orchestra. Estab. 1969. Members are professionals and amateurs. Performs 8 concerts/year, including 1-3 new works. Commissions "possibly 1-2" composers or new works/year. Audience is family and friends of community theater. Performance space is a 1,900 seat grand old movie theater. Pays commission fee.

How to Contact: Submit complete score and tape of piece(s). SASE. Responds in 3 months.

Music: "Symphonic works of various lengths and types which can be performed by a non-professional orchestra. We are flexible but like to involve all our players."

Performances: Paul W. Whear's *Celtic Christmas Carol* (orchestra/bell choir) and Linda Robbins Coleman's *In Good King Charlie's Golden Days* (overture).

Tips: "Please lay out rehearsal numbers/letter and rests according to phrases and other logical musical divisions rather than in groups of ten measures, etc., which is very unmusical and wastes time and causes a surprising number of problems. Also, please do not send a score written in concert pitch; use the usual transpositions so that the conductor sees what the players see; rehearsal is much more effective this way. Cross cue all important solos; this helps in rehearsal where instruments may be missing."

N HUDSON VALLEY PHILHARMONIC, 11 Cannon St., 1st Floor, Poughkeepise NY 12601. (845)473-5288. Fax: (845)473-4259. E-mail: slamarca@bardavon.org. Website: www.bardavon.org. **Contact:** Gail Schumacher, director of operations. Symphony orchestra. Estab. 1969. Members are professionals. Performs 20 concerts/year including 1-5 new works. Commissions 1 composer or new work every other year. "Classical subscription concerts: older patrons primarily; Pops concerts: all ages; New Wave concerts: baby boomers. New Wave concerts are crossover projects with a rock 'n' roll artist performing with an orchestra. HVP performs in three main theatres which are concert auditoriums with stages and professional lighting and sound." Pay is negotiable.

How to Contact: Query first. SASE. Responds in 8 months.

Music: "HVP is open to serious classical music, pop music and rock 'n' roll crossover projects. Desired length of work between 10-20 minutes. Orchestrations can be varied by should always include strings. There is no limit to difficulty since our musicians are professional. The ideal number of musicians to write for would include up to a Brahms-size orchestra 2222, 4231, T, 2P, piano, harp, strings."

Performances: Joan Tower's *Island Rhythms (serious classical work); Bill Vanaver's P'nai El* (symphony work with dance); and Joseph Bertolozzi's *Serenade* (light classical, pop work).

Tips: "Don't get locked into doing very traditional orchestrations or styles. Our music director is interested in fresh, creative formats. He is an orchestrator as well and can offer good advice on what works well. Songwriters who are into crossover projects should definitely submit works. Over the past four years, HVP has done concerts featuring the works of Natalie Merchant, John Cale, Sterling Morrison, Richie Havens and R. Carlos Nakaì (Native American flute player), all reorchestrated by our music director for small orchestra with the artist."

✓ KENTUCKY OPERA, 101 S. Eighth St. at Main, Louisville KY 40202. (502)584-4500. Fax: (502)584-7484. Website: www.kyopera.org. **Contact:** Kim Cherie Lloyd, director of music. Opera.

THE TYPES OF MUSIC each listing is interested in are printed in **boldface**.

Estab. 1952. Members are professionals. Performs 3 main stage/year. Performs at Whitney Hall, The Kentucky Center for the Arts, seating is 2,400; Bomhard Theatre, The Kentucky Center for the Arts, 620; Macauley Theatre, 1,400. Pays by royalty, outright purchase or per performance.

How to Contact: *Write or call first before submitting. No unsolicited submissions.* Submit complete score. SASE. Responds in 6 months.

Music: Seeks opera—1 to 3 acts with orchestrations. No limitations.

Performances: *Turandot*; *Susannah!*; and *Rigaletto*.

KITCHENER-WATERLOO CHAMBER ORCHESTRA, Box 34015, Highland Hills P.O., Kitchener, Ontario N2N 3G2 Canada. (519)744-3828. **Contact:** Graham Coles, music director. Chamber Orchestra. Estab. 1985. Members are professionals and amateurs. Performs 5-6 concerts/year including 1-2 new works. "We perform mainly baroque and classical repertoire, so any contemporary works must not be too dissonant, long or far fetched." Pays per performance.

How to Contact: "It's best to query first so we can outline what not to send. Include: complete cv—list of works, performances, sample reviews." Include SAE and IRC. Responds in 2 months.

Music: "Musical style must be accessible to our audience and players (3 rehearsals). Length should be under 20 minutes. Maximum orchestration 2/2/2/2 2/2/0/0 Timp/or 1 Percussion String 5/5/3/4/2. We have limited rehearsal time, so keep technique close to that of Bach-Beethoven. We also play chamber ensemble works—octets, etc. We do not want choral or solo works."

Performances: James Grant's *Lament* (string orchestra) and Reynaldo Hahn's *La Fete Chez Therese* (ballet suite).

Tips: "If you want a first-rate performance, keep the technical difficulties minimal."

LAKESIDE SUMMER SYMPHONY, 236 Walnut Ave., Lakeside OH 43440. (419)798-4461. Fax: (419)798-5033. Website: www.lakesideohio.com. **Contact:** G. Keith Addy. Conductor: Robert L. Cronquist. Symphony orchestra. Members are professionals. Performs 8 concerts/year. Performs "Chautauqua-type programs with an audience of all ages (2-102). Hoover Auditorium is a 3,000-seat auditorium."

How to Contact: Query first. SASE. Material should be submitted by October 15. Responds in 6 weeks.

Music: Seeking "classical compositions for symphony composed of 50-55 musicians. The work needs to have substance and be a challenge to our symphony members. No modern jazz, popular music or hard rock."

LAMARCA AMERICAN VARIETY SINGERS, 2655 W. 230th Place, Torrance CA 90505. (310)325-8708. E-mail: kandelpris@hotmail.com. **Contact:** Priscilla Kandel, director. Youth to high school vocal ensembles. Estab. 1979. Members are professionals and amateurs. Performs 10 concerts/year including 3 new works. Performs at major hotels, conventions, community theaters, fund raising events, cable TV, community fairs and Disneyland. Pays showcase only.

How to Contact: Query first. SASE. Responds in 2 weeks.

Music: "Seeks 3-10 or 15 minute medleys; a variety of musical styles from Broadway—pop styles to humorous specialty songs. Top 40 dance music, light rock and patriotic themes. No rap or anything not suitable for family audiences."

Performances: *Disney Movie Music* (uplifting); *Children's Music* (educational/positive); and *Beatles Medley* (love songs).

LEHIGH VALLEY CHAMBER ORCHESTRA, P.O. Box 20641, Lehigh Valley PA 18002-0641. (610)266-8555. Music Director: Donald Spieth. Chamber orchestra. Estab. 1979. Performs 25 concerts/year including 2-3 new works. Members are professionals. Commissions 1-2 composers or new works/year. Typical orchestral audience, also youth concerts. Pays commission for first 2 performances, first right for recording.

How to Contact: Submit complete score and tape of piece(s). SASE. Responds in 4 months.

Music: "Classical orchestral; works for youth and pops concerts. Duration 10-15 minutes. Chamber orchestra 2222-2210 percussion, strings (66442). No limit on difficulty."

Performances: April 2001, Libby Larsen commission (new work for flute, soprano and chamber orchestra—premiere with Eugenia and Arianna Zukermann); and February 2001, Kyle Smith commissioned for new work.

Tips: "Send a sample tape and score of a work(s) written for the requested medium."

☑ LEXINGTON PHILHARMONIC SOCIETY, 161 N. Mill St., Arts Place, Lexington KY 40507. (859)233-4226. Fax: (859)233-7896. Website: www.lexingtonphilharmonic.org. **Contact:** George Zack, music director. Symphony orchestra. Estab. 1961. Members are professionals. Series includes "8 serious, classical subscription concerts (hall seats 1,500); 3 concerts called Pops the Series; 10 outdoor pops concerts (from 1,500 to 5,000 tickets sold); 5-10 run-out concerts (½ serious/ ½ pops); and 10 children's concerts." Pays via ASCAP and BMI, rental purchase and private arrangements.

How to Contact: Submit complete score and tape of piece(s). SASE.

Music: Seeking "good current pops material and good serious classical works. No specific restrictions, but overly large orchestra requirements, unusual instruments and extra rentals help limit our interest."

Performances: Zwillich's *Celebration* (overture); Crumb's *A Haunted Landscape* (tone poem); and Corigliano's *Promenade* (overture).

Tips: "When working on large-format arrangement, use cross-cues so orchestra can be cut back if required. Submit good quality copy, scores and parts. Tape is helpful."

LIMA SYMPHONY ORCHESTRA, 67 Town Square, P.O. Box 1651, Lima OH 45802. (419)222-5701. Fax: (419)222-6587. **Contact:** Crafton Beck, music conductor. Symphony orchestra. Estab. 1953. Members are professionals. Performs 17-18 concerts including at least 1 new work/year. Commissions at least 1 composer or new work/year. Middle to older audience; also Young People's Series. Mixture for stage and summer productions. Performs in Veterans' Memorial Civic & Convention Center, a beautiful hall seating 1,670; various temporary shells for summer outdoors events; churches; museums and libraries. Pays $2,500 for outright purchase (Anniversary commission) or grants $1,500-5,000.

How to Contact: Submit complete score if not performed; otherwise submit complete score and tape of piece(s). SASE. Responds in 3 months.

Music: "Good balance of incisive rhythm, lyricism, dynamic contrast and pacing. Chamber orchestra to full (85-member) symphony orchestra." Does not wish to see "excessive odd meter changes."

Performances: Frank Proto's *American Overture* (some original music and fantasy); Werner Tharichen's *Concerto for Timpani and Orchestra*; and James Oliverio's *Pilgrimage—Concerto for Brass* (interesting, dynamic writing for brass and the orchestra).

Tips: "Know your instruments, be willing to experiment with unconventional textures, be available for in depth analysis with conductor, be at more than one rehearsal. Be sure that individual parts are correctly matching the score and done in good, neat calligraphy."

LITHOPOLIS AREA FINE ARTS ASSOCIATION, 3825 Cedar Hill Rd., Canal Winchester OH 43110-8929. (614)837-8925. **Contact:** Virginia E. Heffner, series director. Performing Arts Series. Estab. 1973. Members are professionals and amateurs. Performs 6-7 concerts/year including 2-3 new works. "Our audience consists of couples and families 30-80 in age. Their tastes run from classical, folk, ethnic, big band, pop and jazz. Our hall is acoustically excellent and seats 400. It was designed as a lecture-recital hall in 1925." Composers "may apply for Ohio Arts Council Grant under the New Works category." Pays straight fee to ASCAP.

How to Contact: Query first. SASE. Responds in 3 weeks.

Music: "We prefer that a composer is also the performer and works in conjunction with another artist, so they could be one of the performers on our series. Piece should be musically pleasant and not too dissonant. It should be scored for small vocal or instrumental ensemble. Dance ensembles have difficulty with 15' high 15' deep and 27' wide stage. We do not want avant-garde or obscene dance routines. No ballet (space problem). We're interested in something historical—national or Ohio emphasis would be nice. Small ensembles or solo format is fine."

Performances: Carole Stephens added verses to *New River Train* (gospel); and Carole Stephens' arrangement of *Christmas Lullaby*.

Tips: "Call in September of 2001 for queries about our 2001-2002 season. We do a varied program. We don't commission artists. Contemporary music is used by some of our artist or groups. By contacting these artists, you could offer your work for inclusion in their program."

☑ **MASTER CHORALE OF WASHINGTON**, 1200 29th St. NW, Suite LL2, Washington DC 20007. (202)471-4050. Fax: (202)471-4051. E-mail: singing@masterchorale.org. Website: www.masterchorale.org. **Contact:** Donald McCullough, music director. Vocal ensemble. Estab. 1967. Members are professionals and amateurs. Performs 8 concerts/year including 1-3 new works. Commissions one new composer or work every 2 years. "Audience covers a wide range of ages and economic levels drawn from the greater Washington DC metropolitan area. Kennedy Center Concert Hall seats 2,400." Pays by outright purchase.

How to Contact: Submit complete score and tape of piece(s). SASE. Responds in 9 months.

Music: Seeks new works for: 1) large chorus with or without symphony orchestras; 2) chamber choir and small ensemble.

Performances: Stephen Paulus' *Mass*; Joonas Kokkonen's *Requiem* (symphonic choral with orchestra); Morten Lauridsen's *Lux Aeterna*; and Donald McCullough's *Let My People Go!: A Spiritual Journey*.

☑ **MILWAUKEE YOUTH SYMPHONY ORCHESTRA**, 929 N. Water St., Milwaukee WI 53202. (414)272-8540. Fax: (414)272-8549. E-mail: general@myso.org. **Contact:** Frances Richman, executive director. Multiple youth orchestras and other instrumental ensembles. Estab. 1956. Members are students. Performs 12-15 concerts/year including 1-2 new works. "Our groups perform in Uihlein Hall at the Marcus Center for the Performing Arts in Milwaukee plus area sites. The audiences usually consist of parents, music teachers and other interested community members, with periodic reviews in the *Milwaukee Journal Sentinel*." Payment varies.

How to Contact: Query first. SASE. Does not return material. Responds in 1 month.

Performances: James Woodward's *Tuba Concerto*.

Tips: "Be sure you realize you are working with *students* (albeit many of the best in southeastern Wisconsin) and not professional musicians. The music needs to be on a technical level students can handle. Our students are 8-18 years of age, in 2 full symphony orchestras, a wind ensemble and 2 string orchestras, plus two flute choirs, advanced chamber orchestra and 15-20 small chamber ensembles."

🅽 **THE MIRECOURT TRIO**, 50 Orchard St., Jamaica Plain MA 02130. (617)524-2495. E-mail: terryk@tiac.net. **Contact:** Terry King. Chamber music ensemble; violin, cello, piano. Estab. 1973. Members are professionals. Performs 2-4 concerts/year including 1 new work. Commissions 1 composer or new work/year. Concerts are performed for university, concert series, schools, societies and "general chamber music audiences of 100-1,500." Pays for outright purchase, percentage royalty or per performance.

How to Contact: Query first. SASE. Responds in 6 months.

Music: Seeks "music of short to moderate duration (5-20 minutes) that entertains, yet is not derivative or clichéd. Orchestration should be basically piano, violin, cello, occasionally adding voice or instrument. We do not wish to see academic or experimental works."

Performances: Otto Leuning's *Solo Sonata* (solo cello); Lukas Foss's *Three American Pieces* (cello, piano premiere); and Coolidge's *Dialectic No. 1 for piano trio*.

Tips: "Submit works that engage the audience or relate to them, that reward the players as well."

🅽 ☙ **MONTREAL CHAMBER ORCHESTRA**, 1155 René Lévesque Blvd. W, Suite 2500, Montreal, Quebec H3B 2K4 Canada. (514)871-1224. Fax: (514)871-8967. Conductor and Music Director: Wanda Kaluzny. Chamber orchestra. Estab. 1974. Members are professionals. Performs 6 concerts including 1-3 new works/year. Commissions various new works/year (Canadian composers only). Audience is mixed ages, mixed income levels. Orchestra performs in Pollack Hall, seating 600. Pays "through the composer's performing arts organization."

How to Contact: Submit complete score. Does not return material. Responds "only if performing the work."

Music: Works with string orchestra (6 / 4 / 2 / 2 / 1), 8-12 min. duration. Strings (6 / 4 / 2 / 2 / 1).

Performances: Stewart Grant's *Chawnne* (string orchestra); Jene René's *Sonata à trois* (string orchestra); and Elegy (string orchestra).

MOZART FESTIVAL ORCHESTRA, INC., 33 Greenwich Ave., New York NY 10014. (212)675-9127. **Contact:** Dr. Baird Hastings, conductor. Symphony orchestra. Estab. 1960. Members are professionals. Performs 1-4 concerts/year including 1-4 new works. Audience members are Greenwich Village residents of all ages, largely professionals. Performances are held at the First Presbyterian Church, Fifth Ave. and 12th St., ("wonderful acoustics"). Payment varies.

How to Contact: Query first. SASE. Responds in 2 weeks.

Music: "We are an established chamber orchestra interested in *unusual* music of all periods, but not experimental. Orchestra size usually under 20 performers."

Performances: Gary Sunden's *Sganarelle* (prelude); and Virgil Thomson's *Portrait* (strings).

NATIONAL ASSOCIATION OF COMPOSERS/USA (NACUSA), P.O. Box 49256, Los Angeles CA 90049. (310)541-8213. E-mail: bia@flash.net. Website: www.thebook.com/nacusa. **Contact:** Marshall Bialosky, president. Chamber music ensemble and composers' service organization. Estab. 1932. Members are professionals. Performs 10-15 concerts/year in L.A.; 10-11 nationally with other chapters—all new works. Usually perform at universities in Los Angeles and at a mid-town church in New York. Paid by ASCAP or BMI (NACUSA does not pay composers).

How to Contact: To submit, you must be a member of NACUSA. Submit complete score and tape of pieces. SASE. Responds in 3 months.

Music: Chamber music for five or fewer players; usually in the 5-20 minute range. "Level of difficulty is not a problem; number of performers is solely for financial reasons. We deal in serious, contemporary concert hall music. No 'popular' music."

Performances: Robert Linn's *Piano Variations*; Aurelio dela Vega's *Transparent Songs* (voice, piano); and Michelle Green's *At Ends* (solo violin).

Tips: "Send in modest-sized pieces—not symphonies and concertos."

N **V** **NORFOLK CHAMBER MUSIC FESTIVAL/YALE SUMMER SCHOOL OF MUSIC**, Box 208246, New Haven CT 06520-8246. (203)432-1966. E-mail: norfolk@yale.edu. Website: www.yale.edu/norfolk. **Contact:** Elaine C. Carroll, festival manager. Summer music festival. Estab. 1941. Members are international faculty/artists plus young professionals. Performs 20 concerts, 15 recitals/year, including 6 new works. Commissions 1 composer or new work/year. Audience is "highly motivated with interests in traditional chamber and serious music." Pays a commission fee. Also offers a Composition Search and Residency biennially. The Norfolk Chamber Music Festival-Yale Summer School of Music seeks new chamber music works from American composers. The goal of this search is to identify promising young composers and to provide a visible and high quality venue for the premiere of their work. A maximum of two winning compositions are selected. Winners are invited to the Norfolk Chamber Music Festival for a week-long residency.

● The Norfolk Chamber Music Festival/Yale Summer School of Music has won an ASCAP/ Chamber Music America award for adventurous programming.

How to Contact: Query first. SASE. Responds in 6 months.

Music: "Chamber music of combinations, particularly for strings, woodwinds, brass and piano."

Performances: Yehudi Wyner's *Epilogue 1996* (commission); Jennifer Higdon's *Autumn Quintet* (Norfolk prize); Martin Bresnick's *The Bucketrider and Be Just!*; and Joan Tower's *Tres Lent*.

V **OPERA ON THE GO**, 1212 Huntcliff Trace, Aiken SC 29803. (803)643-7633. E-mail: jrose14 @bellsouth.net. Website: http://operaonthego.org. **Contact:** Jodi Rose, artistic director. American opera chamber ensemble. Estab. 1985. Members are professionals. Performs about 100 operas/year including 1-2 new works. Commissions variable number of new works/year. "We perform primarily in schools and community theaters. We perform only American contemporary opera. It must be lyrical

in sound and quality as we perform for children as well as adults. We prefer pieces written for children based on fairy tales needing 2-4 singers." Pays royalties of $20-30 per performance. "We also help composers acquire a 'Meet the Composer' grant."
How to Contact: Query first, then submit complete score and tapes of piece(s). SASE. Responds in 2 months.
Music: Need works in all age groups including adults. For older ages the pieces can be up to 60 minutes. Rarely use orchestra. "Keep the music about 45 minutes long since we do a prelude (spoken) and postlude involving the children's active participation and performance. If it is totally atonal it will never work in the schools we perform in."
Performances: Arne Christiansen's *Tumbleweeds* (performed by children); Noel Katz's *Pirate Captains* (opera for 6 grade-adult); and Seymour Barab's *Little Red Riding Hood* (children's opera).
Tips: "Be flexible. Through working with children we know what works best with different ages. If this means editing music to guarantee its performance, don't get offended or stubborn. All operas must have audience participatory sections."

OPERAWORKS, 170 W. 73rd St., New York NY 10023. (212)873-9531. E-mail: operaworksdl@cs.com. Website: www.operaworks.org. **Contact:** David Leighton, music director. Opera producers. Estab. 1983. Members are professionals. Performs 50 times including 5 new works/year. Commissions new composers or new works each year. Diverse audience—classical music enthusiasts and avant-garde art scene. Spaces: 100-400 seat theaters, traditional and experimental. Pay is negotiable.
How to Contact: Submit complete score and tape of piece(s). SASE. Responds in 3 months.
Music: The Virtual Orchestra-realistic orchestral sound produced by state-of-the-art electronic technology.
Performances: Thomas Pasatieri's *The Seagull*; and Louis Gruenberg's *The Emperor Jones*.

ORCHESTRA SEATTLE/SEATTLE CHAMBER SINGERS, 1305 Fourth Ave. #402, Seattle WA 98101. (206)682-5208. E-mail: osscs@osscs.org. Website: www.osscs.org. **Contact:** Andrew Danilchik, librarian. Symphony orchestra, chamber music ensemble and community chorus. Estab. 1969. Members are amateurs and professionals. Performs 8 concerts/year including 2-3 new works. Commissions 1-2 composers or new works/year. "Our audience is made up of both experienced and novice classical music patrons. The median age is 45 with an equal number of males and females in the upper income range. Most concerts now held in Benaroya Hall."
How to Contact: Query first. SASE. Responds in 1 year.
Performances: Robert Kechley's *Psalm 100*; Huntley Beyer's *The Mass of Life and Death*; and Carol Sams's *Marches of Glynn* (choral work); and William Wilde Zeitler's *Beyond the Frontier of the Known* (glass armonica concerto).

☑ **PICCOLO OPERA COMPANY INC.**, 24 Del Rio Blvd., Boca Raton FL 33432-4734. (800)282-3161. Fax: (561)394-0520.E-mail: leejom51@msn.com. **Contact:** Lee Merrill, executive assistant. Traveling opera company. Estab. 1962. Members are professionals. Performs 1-50 concerts/year including 1-2 new works. Commissions 0-1 composer or new work/year. Operas are performed for a mixed audience of children and adults. Pays by performance or outright purchase.
How to Contact: Query first. SASE.
Music: "Musical theater pieces, lasting about one hour, for adults to perform for adults and/or youngsters. Performers are mature singers with experience. The cast should have few performers (up to 10), no chorus or ballet, accompanied by piano or local orchestra. Skeletal scenery. All in English."
Performances: Menotti's *The Telephone*; Mozart's *Cosi Fan Tutte*; and Puccini's *La Boheme* (repertoire of more than a dozen productions).

PRINCETON SYMPHONY ORCHESTRA, P.O. Box 250, Princeton NJ 08542. (609)497-0020. Fax: (609)497-0904. E-mail: pcs7@ix.netcom.com. Website: www.princetonsymphony.org. **Contact:** Mark Laycock, music director. Symphony orchestra. Estab. 1980. Members are professionals. Performs 6-10 concerts/year including some new works. Commissions 1 composer or new work/year. Performs in a "beautiful, intimate 800-seat hall with amazing sound." Pays by arrangement.
How to Contact: Submit through agent only. SASE. Responds in 6 months.

Music: "Orchestra usually numbers 40-60 individuals."

RIDGEWOOD SYMPHONY ORCHESTRA, P.O. Box 176, Ridgewood NJ 07451. (201)612-0118. Fax: (201)445-2762. E-mail: drdackow@aol.com. Website: www.ridgewoodsymphony.org. **Contact:** Dr. Sandra Dackow, music director. Symphony orchestra. Estab. 1939. Members are professionals and amateurs. Performs 4 concerts/year and 2-3 children's concerts including 1-2 new works. Commissions possibly 1 new work/year. Audience is "sophisticated." Performance space is 800-seat school auditorium. Pays commission fee.
How to Contact: Submit complete score and tape of piece(s). SASE. Responds in 3 months ("it depends on how busy we are").
Music: "Symphonic works of various lengths and types which can be performed by a nonprofessional orchestra. We are flexible but would like to involve all of our players; very restrictive instrumentations do not suit our needs."
Performances: Shostakovich's *Festive Overture*; Gerschwin's *Piano Concerto in F*; and Gerschwin's *American in Paris* (rhapsody).
Tips: "Please lay out rehearsal numbers/letters and rests according to phrases and other logical musical divisions rather than in groups of ten measures, etc., which is very unmusical, wastes time and causes a surprising number of problems. Also, please *do not* send a score written in concert pitch; use the usual transpositions so that the conductor sees what the players see. Rehearsal is much more effective this way. Cross cue all important solos; this helps in rehearsal where instruments may be missing."

SACRAMENTO MASTER SINGERS, P.O. Box 215501, Sacramento CA 95821. (916)338-0300. Fax: (916)334-1808. E-mail: rehchoir@aol.com. Website: www.mastersingers.org. **Contact:** Ralph Hughes, conductor/artistic director. Vocal ensemble. Estab. 1984. Members are professionals and amateurs. Performs 9 concerts/year including 5-6 new works. Commissions 2 new works/year. Audience is made up of mainly high school age and older patrons. Performs mostly in churches with 500-900 seating capacity. Pays $200 for outright purchase.
How to Contact: Submit complete score and tape of piece(s). SASE. Responds in 5 weeks.
Music: "A cappella works; works with small orchestras or few instruments; works based on classical styles with a 'modern' twist; multi-cultural music; shorter works probably preferable, but this is not a requirement. We usually have 38-45 singers capable of a high level of difficulty, but find that often simple works are very pleasing."
Performances: Joe Jennings' *An Old Black Woman, Homeless and Indistinct* (SATB, oboe, strings, dramatic).
Tips: "Keep in mind we are a chamber ensemble, not a 100-voice choir."

THE SAINT THOMAS CHOIR OF MEN AND BOYS, One W. 53rd St., New York NY 10019. (212)757-7013. Website: www.saintthomaschurch.org. **Contact:** Dr. Gerre Hancock, organist/director of music, master of choristers. Church choir. Estab. 1919. Performs 4 concerts/year including 1 new work. Commissions 1 composer or new work every other year. Performs for a cosmopolitan New York audience in a Gothic Church. Pays by outright purchase or per performance.
How to Contact: Query first. SASE. Responds in 2 weeks.
Music: "Music for chorus appropriate to religious observances and Anglican liturgies: unaccompanied, organ accompaniment with or without chamber orchestra. The choir consists of 16-20 boy choristers/sopranos (unchanged voices), 4 adult male altos, 4 tenors, 4 basses. All adults are professional singers."
Performances: Gunther Schuller's *Magnificat and Nonc Dimittis (chorus and organ); Randall Thompson's Place of the Blest* (chorus and orchestra); and William Walton's *The Twelve* (chorus and orchestra).

REFER TO THE CATEGORY INDEX (at the end of this section) to find exactly which companies are interested in the type of music you write.

☑ ♬ SAN FRANCISCO GIRLS CHORUS, P.O. Box 15397, San Francisco CA 94115-0397. (415)673-1511. Fax: (415)673-0639. E-mail: info@sfgirlschorus.org. Website: www.sfgirlschorus.org. **Contact:** Susan McMane, artistic director. Vocal ensemble. Estab. 1978. Volunteer chorus with a core of paid professionals. Performs 8-10 concerts/year including 3-4 new works. Commissions 2-3 composers or new works/year. Concerts are performed for "choral/classical music lovers, plus family audiences and audiences interested in international repertoire. Season concerts are performed in a 900-seat church with excellent acoustics and in San Francisco's Davies Symphony Hall, a 2,800-seat state-of-the-art auditorium." Pay negotiable for outright purchase.

• The San Francisco Girls Chorus was a featured guest performer on the San Francisco Symphony's recording of Stravinsky's *Persephone*, which won a 2000 Grammy Award for Best Classical Album and Best Orchestral Performance.

How to Contact: Submit complete score. Does not return material. Responds in 6 months.

Music: "Music for treble voices (SSAA); a cappella, piano accompaniment, or small orchestration; 3-10 minutes in length. Wide variety of styles; 45 singers; challenging music is encouraged."

Performances: Lisa Bielawa's *Letter to Anna (1998)* (a cappella); Jake Heggie's *Patterns* (piano, mezzo-soprano soloist, chorus); and Chen Yi's *Chinese Poems* (a cappella).

Tips: "Choose excellent texts and write challenging and beautiful music. The San Francisco Girls Chorus has pioneered in establishing girls choral music as an art form in the United States. The Girls Chorus is praised for its 'stunning musical standard' (*San Francisco Chronicle*) in performances in the San Francisco Bay Area and on tour. SFGC's annual concert season showcases the organization's concert/touring ensembles, Chorissima and Virtuose, in performances of choral masterworks from around the world, commissioned works by contemporary composers, and 18th-century music from the Venetian Ospedali which SFGC has brought out of the archives and onto the concert stage. Chorissima and Virtuose tour through California with partial support provided by the California Arts Council Touring Program and have represented the U.S. and the City of San Francisco nationally and abroad. The choruses provide ensemble and solo singers for performances and recordings with the San Francisco Symphony and San Francisco Opera, Women's Philharmonic, and many other music ensembles. SFGC's discography includes two 1996 CD recordings, *I Never Saw Another Butterfly* (20th Century music); *A San Francisco Christmas* (Benjamin Britten's *A Ceremony of Carols* and other holiday music); a 1998 release, *Music from the Venetian Ospedali* (18th-century works for girls chorus) (called "fresh" by *The New Yorker*); and a 2000 release, *Crossroads* (a collection of international music)."

SINGING BOYS OF PENNSYLVANIA, P.O. Box 206, Wind Gap PA 18091. (610)759-6002. **Contact:** K. Bernard Schade, Ed. D., director. Vocal ensemble. Estab. 1970. Members are professional children. Performs 100 concerts/year including 3-5 new works. "We attract general audiences: family, senior citizens, churches, concert associations, university concert series and schools." Pays $300-3,000 for outright purchase.

How to Contact: Query first. Does not return material. Responds in 3 weeks.

Music: "We want music for commercials, voices in the SSA or SSAA ranges, sacred works or arrangements of American folk music with accompaniment. Our range of voices are from G below middle C to A (13th above middle C). Reading ability of choir is good but works which require a lot of work with little possibility of more than one performance are of little value. We sing very few popular songs except for special events. We perform music by composers who are well-known and works by living composers who are writing in traditional choral forms. Works which have a full orchestral score are of interest. The orchestration should be fairly light, so as not to cover the voices. Works for Christmas have more value than some other, since we perform with orchestras on an annual basis."

Performances: Don Locklair's *The Columbus Madrigals* (opera).

Tips: "It must be appropriate music and words for children. We do not deal in pop music. Folk music, classics and sacred are acceptable."

☑ SPACE COAST POPS, INC., P.O. Box 3344, Cocoa FL 32924 or 2150 Lake Dr., Cocoa FL 32926. (321)632-7445. Fax: (321)632-1611. E-mail: popsorch@aol.com. Website: http://spacecoastpops.anthill.com. **Contact:** Robert Coleman, music director and conductor. Pops orchestra and chamber music ensemble. Estab. 1986. Members are professionals. Performs 7 concerts/year, including 1-2 new works. Concerts are performed for "average audience—they like familiar works and pops. Concert halls range from 600 to 2,000 seats."

How to Contact: Query first. SASE. Responds in 6 months.

Music: Seeks "pops and serious music for full symphony orchestra, but not an overly large orchestra with unusual instrumentation. We use about 60 musicians because of hall limitations. Works should be medium difficulty—not too easy and not too difficult—and not more than ten minutes long." Does not wish to see avant-garde music.

Performances: Dussich's *First March* (march).

Tips: "If we would commission a work it would be to feature the space theme in our area."

ST. LOUIS CHAMBER CHORUS, P.O. Box 11558, Clayton MO 63105. (636)458-4343. E-mail: maltworm@inlink.com. Website: www.iwc.com/slcc. **Contact:** Philip Barnes, artistic director. Vocal ensemble, chamber music ensemble. Estab. 1956. Members are professionals and amateurs. Performs 6 concerts/year including 5-10 new works. Commissions 1-2 new works/year. Audience is "diverse and interested in unaccompanied choral work and outstanding architectural/acoustic venues." Performances take place at various auditoria noted for their excellent acoustics—churches, synagogues, schools and university halls. Pays by arrangement.

How to Contact: Query first. Does not return material. "Panel of 'readers' submit report to Artistic Director. Responds in 3 months. 'General Advice' leaflet available on request."

Music: "*Only a cappella* writing; no contemporary 'popular' works; historical editions welcomed. No improvisatory works. Our programs are tailored for specific acoustics—composers should indicate their preference."

Performances: Sir Richard Rodney Bennett's *A Contemplation Upon Flowers* (a cappella madrigal); Stuart McIntosh's *Can Thou Lov'st Me, Lady?* (a cappella glee for men's voices); and Sasha Johnson Manning's *Dies Irae* (a cappella motet).

Tips: "We only consider a cappella works which can be produced in five rehearsals. Therefore pieces of great complexity or duration are discouraged."

✓ 🎵 **STAR-SCAPE**, P.O. Box 793, Station F, Toronto, Ontario M4Y 2N7 Canada. (905)951-3155 or (800)437-1454. Fax: (905)951-9712. E-mail: info@sun-scape.com. Website: www.sun-scape.com or www.kennethgmills.com. **Contact:** Ellen Mann, assistant to the conductor. A cappella choir (10-12 voices). Estab. 1976. Members are professionals. Performs 15 concerts/year including over 170 original works. Audience is appreciative of extraordinary technical ability of the ensemble and recognize that "this music, this art opens up the soul." Performances take place in concert halls and churches.

● See the listing for Sun-Scape Enterprises Limited in the Record Companies section.

How to Contact: Query first. SASE.

Performances: Kenneth G. Mills/Christopher Dedrick's *The Fire Mass* and arrangement of *The Battle Hymn of the Republic*; *He's Got The Whole World In His Hands* (spiritual); and Rachmaninoff's *Vespers*.

SUSQUEHANNA SYMPHONY ORCHESTRA, P.O. Box 485, Forest Hill MD 21050. (410)838-6465. E-mail: sbzbair@erols.com. **Contact:** Sheldon Bair, music director. Symphony orchestra. Estab. 1978. Members are amateurs. Performs 6 concerts/year including 1-2 new works. Composers paid depending on the circumstances. "We perform in 1 hall, 600 seats with fine acoustics. Our audience encompasses all ages."

How to Contact: Query first. SASE. Responds in 3 or more months.

Music: "We desire works for large orchestra, any length, in a 'conservative 20th and 21st century' style. Seek fine music for large orchestra. We are a community orchestra, so the music must be within our grasp. Violin I to 7th position by step only; Violin II—stay within 5th position; English horn and harp are OK. Full orchestra pieces preferred."

Performances: Sir Malcolm Arnold's *Symphony No. 9*; Aulis Sallinen's *Sunrise Serenade*; and Gwyneth Walker's *Symphony of Grace* (all orchestral works).

TORONTO MENDELSSOHN CHOIR, 60 Simcoe St., Toronto, Ontario M5J 2H5 Canada. (416)598-0422. Fax: (416)598-2992. Website: www.tmchoir.org. **Contact:** Eileen Keown, manager. Vocal ensemble. Members are professionals and amateurs. Performs 25 concerts/year including 1-3 new works. "Most performances take place in Roy Thomson Hall. The audience is reasonably sophisticated, musically knowledgeable but with moderately conservative tastes." Pays by commission and ASCAP/SOCAN.

How to Contact: Query first or submit complete score and tapes of pieces. SASE. Responds in 6 months.

Music: All works must suit a large choir (180 voices) and standard orchestral forces or with some other not-too-exotic accompaniment. Length should be restricted to no longer than ½ of a nocturnal concert. The choir sings at a very professional level and can sight-read almost anything. "Works should fit naturally with the repertoire of a large choir which performs the standard choral orchestral repertoire."

Performances: Holman's *Jezebel*; Orff's *Catulli Carmina*; and Lambert's *Rio Grande*.

TULSA OPERA INC., 1610 S. Boulder, Tulsa OK 74119-4479. (918)582-4035. Fax: (918)592-0380. Website: www.tulsaopera.com. **Contact:** Carol I. Crawford, general director. Opera company. Estab. 1948. Members are professionals. Performs 3 concerts/year including 1 new work. Commissions 1 composer or new work/year. "We have a contract with the Performing Arts Center. It holds approximately 2,300." Pays for outright purchase or by royalty (negotiable).

How to Contact: Query first. SASE. Responds in 2 months.

Music: "At the present time we are looking for new material for student operas. They need to be approximately 45-50 minutes in length, with piano accompaniment. For our main stage productions we use the Philharmonic Orchestra and our Artistic Director auditions our singers. Our student performances are sometimes done by young artists. The student materials need to be adapted for four-five singers. These young artists are usually just beginning their careers therefore they are limited in difficulty of the music. Our main stage artists are adept in doing more difficult roles and roles of the classic operas."

Performances: Seymour Barab's *Little Red Riding Hood* (children's 1-act opera).

Tips "Our Artistic Director is very open to ideas and materials. She is interested in new works to present for our opera season."

VANCOUVER CHAMBER CHOIR, 1254 W. Seventh Ave., Vancouver, British Columbia V6H 1B6 Canada. E-mail: info@vancouverchamberchoir.com. Website: www.vancouverchamberchoir.com. **Contact:** Jon Washburn, artistic director. Vocal ensemble. Members are professionals. Performs 40 concerts/year including 5-8 new works. Commissions 2-4 composers or new works/year. Pays SOCAN royalty or negotiated fee for commissions.

How to Contact: Submit complete score and tape of piece(s). Does not return material. Responds in 6 months if possible.

Music: Seeks "choral works of all types for small chorus, with or without accompaniment and/or soloists. Concert music only. Choir made up of 20 singers. Large or unusual instrumental accompaniments are less likely to be appropriate. No pop music."

Performances: The VCC has commissioned and premiered over 110 new works by Canadian and international composers, including Alice Parker's *That Sturdy Vine* (cantata for chorus, soloists and orchestra); R. Murray Schafer's *Magic Songs* (SATB a cappella); and Jon Washburn's *A Stephen Foster Medley* (SSAATTBB/piano).

Tips: "We are looking for choral music that is performable yet innovative, and which has the potential to become 'standard repertoire.' Although we perform much new music, only a small portion of the many scores which are submitted can be utilized."

THE DALE WARLAND SINGERS, 119 N. Fourth St., Minneapolis MN 55401-1792. (612)339-9707. Fax: (612)339-9826. E-mail: DWSinger@aol.com. Website: www.dalewarlandsingers.org. **Contact:** Carol Barnett, composer in residence. Choral ensemble. Estab. 1972. Members are professionals. Performs 20-25 concerts/year including 5-10 new works. Commissions 4-8 composers or new works/year. Audience is a typical classical music concert audience; also college and high school students and occasional "popular Christmas" audience. Performance spaces vary, including concert halls, high school/college auditoriums and churches. Pays commission.

How to Contact: Submit complete score and tape of piece(s). SASE. Responds in 6 months.

Music: "A cappella or with small accompanying forces; texts primarily secular; works for concert choir; 5-15 minutes in length (semi-extended)." Does not wish to see "show choir material or gospel."

Performances: Alfred Schuitlke's *Complete This Work* from *The Choral Concerto* (SATB divisi, c. 6 min.); Stanislaw Skrowaczewski's *Christmas Chant* (SATB, oboe, harp, c. 5 min.); and Aaron Jay Kernis's *Dorma, Ador (Sleep, My Beautiful Boy)* (Christmas lullaby; SATB, handbells, c. 5 min.).

Tips: "Keep in mind that there will never be enough rehearsal time. Be clear and concise in notation, and write for the capabilities of the choral voice. We seek from our composers not only craft, but a certain 'magic' quality."

WHEATON SYMPHONY ORCHESTRA, 344 Spring Ave., Glen Ellyn IL 60137. (630)790-1430. Fax: (630)790-9703. **Contact:** Donald C. Mattison, manager. Symphony orchestra. Estab. 1959. Members are professionals and amateurs. Performs 6 summer concerts/year including a varying number of new works. Pays $200/per performance.

How to Contact: Query first. SASE. Responds in 1 month.

Music: "This is a *good* amateur orchestra that wants pieces in a traditional idiom. Large scale works for orchestra only. No avant garde, 12-tone or atonal material. Pieces should be 20 minutes or less and must be prepared in 3 rehearsals. Instrumentation is woodwinds in 3s, full brass 4-3-3-1, 4-5 percussion and strings—minimum instrumentation only. We will read your piece several times and then record it on a cassette. Plays all months except July and August. All union players. Selections for full orchestra only. No pay for reading your piece, but we will record it at our expense."

Performances: Don Draganski's *Overtures and Fanfares* (full orchestra 3-2-2-2/brass 4331/2 percussion/timpani/strings-traditional); John Uth's *Dance Suite* (3-2-3-2/4331/percussion/timpani/strings); and Edward McKenna's *Bagatelles* (3-3-3-3/4331/timpani/percussion/strings-traditional).

Contests & Awards

Participating in contests is a great way to gain exposure for your music. Prizes vary from contest to contest, from cash to musical merchandise to studio time, and even publishing and recording deals. For musical theater and classical composers, the prize may be a performance of your work. Even if you don't win, valuable contacts can be made through contests. Many times, contests are judged by music publishers and other industry professionals, so your music may find its way into the hands of key industry people who can help further your career.

HOW TO SELECT A CONTEST

It's important to remember when entering any contest to do proper research before signing anything or sending any money. We have confidence in the contests listed in *Songwriter's Market*, but it pays to read the fine print. First, be sure you understand the contest rules and stipulations once you receive the entry forms and guidelines. Then you need to weigh what you will gain against what they're asking you to give up. If a publishing or recording contract is the only prize a contest is offering, you may want to think twice before entering. Basically, the company sponsoring the contest is asking you to pay a fee for them to listen to your song under the guise of a contest, something a legitimate publisher or record company would not do. For those contests offering studio time, musical equipment or cash prizes, you need to decide if the entry fee you're paying is worth the chance to win such prizes.

Be wary of exorbitant entry fees, and if you have any doubts whatsoever as to the legitimacy of a contest, it's best to stay away. Songwriters need to approach a contest, award or grant in the same manner as they would a record or publishing company. Make your submission as professional as possible; follow directions and submit material exactly as stated on the entry form.

Contests in this section encompass all types of music and levels of competition. Read each listing carefully and contact them if the contest interests you. Many contests now have websites that offer additional information and even entry forms you can print. Be sure to read the rules carefully and be sure you understand exactly what a contest is offering before entering.

AARON ENTERPRISES SUMMERTIME SONG FESTIVAL, 4411 Red Gate Dr., Disputanta VA 23842. (804)733-5908. **Contact:** Cham Laughlin, song contest director. Estab. 1997. For songwriters in the US. Annual award sponsored by the Aaron Enterprises Songwriters Group, *Songwriter's Monthly*, Red Gate Recordings, Cham Laughlin's Private Studio in the Country, Cham's Music (BMI) and Aaron Enterprises Recordings.
Requirements: "Entries are accepted from March 1st through the postal deadline of June 30th in each contest year. Categories available for entry are: country, folk, rock, pop and R&B, instrumental, inspirational, humorous and song lyric." Deadline: June 30. Send SASE for application. Entry fee: $10 per song.
Awards: "Prizes include T-shirts, certificates of merit, memberships in our songwriter's group, newsletter subscriptions, songwriter's kits, and more." Entries judged by industry professionals.
Tips: "Prepare your entry properly and follow guidelines. Include all information, including zip codes."

N **AFRICAN AMERICAN COMPOSER'S PROGRAM**, (formerly Unisys African American Composer's Residency and National Symposium), 3663 Woodward Ave., Suite 100, Detroit MI 48201-2403. (313)576-5162. Fax: (313)576-5101. **Contact:** Daisy Newman, director of education. Estab. 1989. For composers. Annual award.

Purpose: "Program was designed to identify and perform significant orchestral works by contemporary African American Composers."

Requirements: Send for application. Samples of work upon request. Pieces should be scored for traditional orchestra.

Awards: Applications are judged by Adjudication Committee (conductor and resident conductor).

AGO/ECS PUBLISHING AWARD IN CHORAL COMPOSITION, American Guild of Organists, 475 Riverside Dr., Suite 1260, New York NY 10115. (212)870-2310. Fax: (212)870-2163. E-mail: info@agohq.org. Website: www.agohq.org. **Contact:** Paul Wolfe, program assistant. Biannual award.

Requirements: Work submitted must be unpublished. Approximately 4-8 minutes in length. There is no age restriction. Deadline: TBA. Send for application.

Awards: AGO/ECS Publishing Award in Choral Composition. Details TBA.

N ALEA III INTERNATIONAL COMPOSITION PRIZE, 855 Commonwealth Ave., Boston MA 02215. (617)353-3340. E-mail: kalogeras@aol.com. For composers. Annual award.

Purpose: To promote and encourage young composers in the composition of new music.

Requirements: Composers 40 years of age and younger may apply; 1 score per composer. Works may be for solo voice or instrument or for chamber ensemble up to 15 members lasting between 6 and 15 minutes. All works must be unpublished. Deadline: March 15. Send for application. Submitted work required with application. "Real name should not appear on score; a nom de plume should be signed instead. Sealed envelope with entry form should be attached to each score."

Awards: ALEA III International Composition Prize: $2,500. Awarded once annually. Between 8-10 finalists are chosen and their works are performed in a competition concert by the ALEA III contemporary music ensemble. One grand prize winner is selected by a panel of judges.

Tips: "Emphasis placed on works written in 20th century compositional idioms."

AMERICAN SONGWRITER LYRIC CONTEST, 1009 17th Ave. S., Nashville TN 37212-2201. (615)321-6096 or (800)739-8712. Fax: (615)321-6097. E-mail: contest@americansongwriter.com. Website: www.americansongwriter.com. Contact: Lou Heffernan, managing editor. Estab. 1984. For songwriters and composers. Award for each bimonthly issue of *American Songwriter* magazine, plus grand prize at year-end.

Purpose: To promote the art of songwriting.

Requirements: Lyrics must be typed and a check for $10 (per entry) must be enclosed. Deadlines: January 25, March 22, May 17, July 19, September 20, November 15. Samples are not required. Call for required official form or get it from our website. Lyrics only, no cassettes.

Awards: A Martin guitar to each contest winner. Awards airfare to Nashville and a demo session for yearly winner; certificates to all winners; and top 5 winning lyrics reprinted in each magazine. Lyrics judged by 6-7 industry people—songwriters, publishers, journalists.

Tips: "You do not have to be a subscriber to enter or win. Pick your best lyric (limit three), don't just send them at random."

ARTISTS' FELLOWSHIPS, New York Foundation for the Arts, 155 Avenue of Americas, 14th Floor, New York NY 10013. To receive an application, or contact the fellowship's department, call: (212)366-6900, ext. 217. Fax: (212)366-1778. E-mail: nyfaafp@artswire.org. Website: www.nyfa.org. **Contact:** Jennifer Fell, senior program officer. For songwriters, composers and musical playwrights. Annual award, but each category funded biennially. Estab. 1984.

Purpose: "Artists' Fellowships are $7,000 grants awarded by the New York Foundation for the Arts to individual originating artists living in New York State. The Foundation is committed to supporting artists from all over New York State at all stages of their professional careers. Fellows may use the grant according to their own needs; it should not be confused with project support."

Requirements: Must be 18 years of age or older; resident of New York State for 2 years prior to application; and cannot be enrolled in any graduate or undergraduate degree program. Applications will be available in July. Deadline: October. Samples of work are required with application. 1 or 2 original compositions on separate audiotapes and at least 2 copies of corresponding scores or fully harmonized lead sheets.

Awards: All Artists' Fellowships awards are for $7,000. Payment of $6,300 upon verification of NY State residency, and remainder upon completion of a mutually agreed upon public service activity. Nonrenewable. "Fellowships are awarded on the basis of the quality of work submitted. Applications are reviewed by a panel of 5 composers representing the aesthetic, ethnic, sexual and geographic diversity within New York State. The panelists change each year and review all allowable material submitted."

Tips: "Please note that musical playwrights may submit only if they write the music for their plays—librettists must submit in our playwriting category."

☑ **BAKER'S PLAYS HIGH SCHOOL PLAYWRITING CONTEST**, Baker's Plays, P.O. Box 699222, Quincy MA 02269-9222. (617)745-0805. Fax: (617)745-9891. E-mail: info@bakersplay.c om. Website: www.bakersplays.com. **Contact:** John Welch, managing director & chief editor. Estab. 1990. For high school students. Annual award.

Requirements: Plays should be about the "high school experience," but may also be about any subject and of any length, so long as the play can be reasonably produced on the high school stage. Plays must be accompanied by the signature of a sponsoring high school drama or English teacher, and it is recommended that the play receive a production or a public reading prior to the submission. Multiple submissions and co-authored scripts are welcome. Teachers may not submit a student's work. The manuscript must be firmly bound, typed and come with a SASE. Include enough postage to cover the return of the manuscript. Scripts that do not come with an SASE will not be returned. Do not send originals; copies only. Deadline: January 31, 2002. Send for guidelines.

Awards: 1st Place: $500 and the play will be published by Baker's Plays; 2nd Place: $250 and an Honorable Mention; 3rd Place: $100 and an Honorable Mention.

☑ **BELHAM VALLEY RECORDS SONGWRITING COMPETITION**, P.O. Box 12367, Lahaina HI 96761. Fax: (808)669-5719. E-mail: info@theartscontest.com. Website: www.TheArtsConte st.com. **Contact:** Gary Robilotta, marketing director. Estab. 2000. For songwriters, composers, musical playwrights and performers. Competition is ongoing (based on a limited number of entries per round).

- See the Insider Report in this section with Belham Valley Records Songwriting Competition directors Gary and Carrll Robilotta.

Purpose: The primary objective of the Belham Valley Songwriting Competition is to give new and developing songwriters a forum to compete for significant cash awards, recognition, and exposure to the music industry.

Requirements: Contest is open to amateurs and songwriters earning less than $5,000 per year in songwriting-related royalties. All entries must include a completed and signed entry form, single-song cassette or CD, lyric sheet (if applicable), and an entry fee. Please visit www.TheArtsContest.com for an online entry form and complete instructions. Contest is limited to 15,000 entrants per round of competition. Send for entry form or visit website.

Awards: Songwriters may submit to any of our 20 categories. Grand Prize: $50,000; 2nd overall: $20,000; 3rd overall: $10,000. 1st Prize winners in each of the 20 categories receive $2,000 each; 2nd Place: $1,000; 3rd Place: $500. Grand Prize and First Place (category) winners also have a song released on a CD produced and distributed by Belham Valley Records. Honorable Mention winners in each category receive awards and prizes of varying value. Our judging panel's criteria is based on composition, melody, and lyrics (if applicable). Creativity and originality will also help a song score higher and stand out from the competition.

Tips: "Songs need not be over-produced to score well. In some instances, a song done a cappella or a composition laid out on a single acoustic guitar will sound better than a song performed by a full band or orchestra. While we do not judge on production (sound) quality, a high-quality tape or CD will make your submission 'listenable' and will always make your song sound better. We strongly discourage the use of normal bias tapes. Songwriters should strive to write in the genre and style they most favor; don't compromise your integrity or passion for passing fads or trends. Lastly, if you can't decide what category of music you should enter under, we will select a category for it."

☑ **BILLBOARD SONG CONTEST**, P.O. Box 470306, Tulsa OK 74147-0306. (918)627-0351. Fax: (918)624-2104. E-mail: bbsc@jimhalsey.com. Website: www.billboard.com/songcontest. **Contact:** Ryan Gardenhire, director. Estab. 1988. For songwriters, composers and performing artists. Annual international contest.

Purpose: "To reward deserving songwriters and performers for their talent."

Requirements: Entry fee: $30.

Awards: To be announced. For entry forms and additional information send SASE to the above address or visit website.

Tips: "Participants should understand popular music structure."

☑ **BLANK THEATRE COMPANY YOUNG PLAYWRIGHTS FESTIVAL**, 1301 Lucile Ave., Los Angeles CA 90026. (323)662-7734. Fax: (323)661-3903. E-mail: info@theblank.com. Website: www.youngplaywrights.com. **Contact:** Christopher Steele, producer. Estab. 1993. For musical playwrights. Annual award.

Purpose: "To give young playwrights an opportunity to learn more about playwriting and to give them a chance to have their work produced."

Requirements: Playwrights must be 19 years old or younger on April 1, 2002. Send for application with SASE or via website. Send legible, original plays of any length and on any subject (co-written plays are acceptable provided all co-writers meet eligibility requirements). Submissions must be postmarked by April 1, 2001 and must include a cover sheet with the playwright's name, date of birth, school (if any), home address and home phone number. Pages must be numbered and submitted unbound (unstapled). Manuscripts will not be returned—please do not send originals. Will contact semi-finalists and winners in May.

Awards: Winning playwrights receive a workshop presentation of their work.

▣ **BUSH ARTIST FELLOWS PROGRAM**, E-900 First National Bank Bldg., 332 Minnesota St., St. Paul MN 55101. (651)227-5222. E-mail: kpolley@bushfound.org. Website: www.bushfoundat ion.org. **Contact:** Kathi Polley, program assistant. Estab. 1976. For songwriters, composers and musical playwrights. Applications in music composition are accepted in even-numbered years.

Purpose: "To provide artists with significant financial support that enables them to further their work and their contribution to their communities."

Requirements: Applicant must be a Minnesota, North Dakota, South Dakota or western Wisconsin resident for 12 of preceeding 36 months, 25 years or older, not a student. Deadline: late October. Send for application. Samples of work on cassette required with application. "Music composition applications will not be taken again until the fall of 2002. Applications will be taken in the fall of 2002 in the following areas: music composition, scriptworks (screenwriting and playwriting), literature (creative non-fiction, fiction, poetry) and film/video.

Awards: Fellowships: $40,000 stipend for a period of 12-18 months. "Five years after completion of preceeding fellowship, one may apply again." Applications are judged by peer review panels.

COLUMBIA ENTERTAINMENT COMPANY'S JACKIE WHITE MEMORIAL PLAYWRITING CONTEST, 309 Parkade Blvd., Columbia MO 65202. (573)874-5628. **Contact:** Betsy Phillips, director, CEC contest. For musical playwrights. Annual award.

Purpose: "We are looking for top-notch scripts for theater school use to challenge and expand the talents of our students, ages 10-15. We want good plays with large casts (20-30 characters) suitable for use with our theater school students."

Requirements: "Must be large cast plays, original story lines and cannot have been previously published. Because theater school enrollment is typically composed of more girls than boys, scripts should have at least 50% of characters female. Please write or call for complete rules." Send SASE

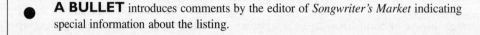

● **A BULLET** introduces comments by the editor of *Songwriter's Market* indicating special information about the listing.

for application; then send scripts to address above. Full-length play, neatly typed. No name on title page, but name, address and name of play on a 3×5 index card and full musical score as well as tape of musical numbers. $10 entry fee. SASE for entry form.

Awards: $250 1st Prize. Production likely but play may not be produced at discretion of CEC. If produced, partial travel expenses will be available to author. Award given after any revisions required are completed. "The judging committee is taken from members of Columbia Entertainment Company's Executive and Advisory boards, and from theater school parents. Readings by at least eight members, with at least three readings of all entries, and winning entries being read by entire committee. We are looking for plays that will work with our theater school students."

Tips: "Remember the play we are looking for will be performed by 10-15 year old students with normal talents—difficult vocal ranges, a lot of expert dancing and so forth will eliminate the play. We especially like plays that deal with current day problems and concerns. However, if the play is good enough, any suitable subject matter is fine. It should be fun for the audience to watch."

COMPOSERS COMMISSIONING PROGRAM, ACF, 332 Minnesota St., #E-145, St. Paul MN 55101. (651)228-1407. Fax: (651)291-7978. E-mail: pblackburn@composersforum.org. Website: www.composersforum.org. **Contact:** Philip Blackburn, program director. Estab. 1979. For songwriters, musical playwrights, composers and performers. Annual award.

Purpose: "CCP provides grants to support the commissioning of new works by emerging composers."

Requirements: Not for students. Deadline: end of July. Application available on website. Samples of work are required with application. Send score/tape.

Awards: 18-22 commissioning grants of $1,500-8,000; each grant good for 5 years. Applications are judged by peer review panel (anonymous).

Tips: "Composers pair up with performers: one party must be based in Minnesota or New York City."

COMPOSERS GUILD ANNUAL COMPOSITION CONTEST, P.O. Box 586, Farmington UT 84025-0586. (801)451-2275. **Contact:** Ruth B. Gatrell, president. Estab. 1963. For songwriters, musical playwrights and composers. Annual award.

Purpose: "To stimulate musical composition and help composers through judge's comments on each composition submitted. Composers can broaden their creative skills by entering different categories. Categories: Arrangements (original in public domain or with composer's permission); music for children; choral; instrumental; jazz/New Age; keyboard; orchestra/band; popular (all types); vocal solo; young composer (18 or under on August 31)."

Requirements: Score and/or cassette. Entry fee: $20 for work 7 minutes or more in length (may include multimovements on compositions), $15 for work less than 7 minutes. Dues are $25/year. Member entry fees: $10 for work 7 minutes or more, $5 less than 7 minutes. Deadline: August 31. Send or call for application.

Awards: Award of Excellence $500; 1st Prize in each category except Award of Excellence category $100; 2nd Prize in each category $50; 3rd Prize in each category $25; Honorable Mention certificate. Judge has a doctorate in music, plus compositions published and performed (usually has vast teaching experience). Same judge never used in successive years.

Tips: "Submit good clear copies of score. Have cassette cued up. Only one composition per cassette (each entry requires separate cassette). No composer names to appear on score or cassette. Enter as many categories and compositions as you wish. Separate entry fee for each. One check can cover all entries and dues."

CRS NATIONAL COMPOSERS COMPETITION, 724 Winchester Rd., Broomall PA 19008. (610)544-5920. Fax: (215)544-5921. E-mail: crsnews@erols.com. Website: www.erols.com/crsnews. **Contact:** Caroline Hunt, administrative assistant. Senior Representative: Jack Shusterman. Estab. 1981. For songwriters, composers and performing artists. College faculty. Annual award.

Requirements: For composers, songwriters, performing artists and ensembles. The work submitted must be non-published (prior to acceptance) and not commercially recorded on any label. The work submitted must not exceed nine performers. Each composer may submit one work for each application submitted. (Taped performances are additionally encouraged.) Composition must not exceed twenty-five minutes in length. CRS reserves the right not to accept a First Prize Winner. Write with SASE for application or visit website. Add $3 for postage and handling. Deadline: October 28. Send a detailed résumé with application form. Samples of work required with application. Send score and parts on cassette or DAT. Application fee $50.

Awards: 1st Prize: Commercial recording grant. Applications are judged by panel of judges determined each year.

CUNNINGHAM PRIZE FOR PLAYWRITING, The Theatre School, DePaul University, 2135 N. Kenmore Ave., Chicago IL 60614. (773)325-7938. Fax: (773)325-7920. E-mail: lgoetsch@wppost. depaul.edu. Website: theatreschool.depaul.edu. **Contact:** Lara Goetsch, director of marketing/public relations. Estab. 1990. For musical playwrights. Annual award.

Purpose: "To recognize and encourage the writing of dramatic works which affirm the centrality of religion, broadly defined, and the human quest for meaning, truth and community. It is the intent of the endowment to consider submissions of new dramatic writing in all genres, including works for children and young people."

Requirements: "The focus for the awarding of the prize is metropolitan Chicago. The candidates for the award must be writers whose residence is in the Chicago area, defined as within 100 miles of the Loop." Deadline: December 1. Send for application with SASE.

Awards: $5,000. "Winners may submit other work for subsequent prize year. The Selection Committee is composed of distinguished citizens including members of DePaul University, representatives of the Cunningham Prize Advisory Committee, critics and others from the theater professions, and is chaired by the Dean of The Theatre School."

N DELTA OMICRON INTERNATIONAL COMPOSITION COMPETITION, 12297 W. Tennessee Place, Lakewood CO 80228. (303)989-2871. Composition Competition Chairman: Judith L. Eidson. For composers. Triennial award.

Purpose: "To encourage composers worldwide to continually add to our wonderful heritage of musical creativity instrumentally and/or vocally."

Requirements: People from college age on (or someone younger who is enrolled in college). Work must be unpublished and unperformed in public. The composition should be for Solo Flute or Flute Quartet with a time length from a minimum of seven minutes to a maximum of fifteen minutes. Manuscripts should be legibly written in ink or processed, signed with *nom de plume*, and free from any marks that would identify the composer to the judges. Entry fee: $25. Deadline: all entries postmarked no later than March 20, 2002. Send for application. Samples of work are required with application.

Awards: 1st Place: $600 and world premiere at Delta Omicron Triennal Conference. Judged by 2-3 judges (performers and/or composers).

☑ EUROPEAN INTERNATIONAL COMPETITION FOR COMPOSERS, 226 E. 2nd St., Suite 5D, New York NY 10009. (212)387-0111. Fax: (212)388-0102. E-mail: iblanyc@aol.com. Website: www.ibla.org. **Contact:** Dr. S. Moltisanti, chairman. Estab. 1995. For songwriters and composers. Annual award.

Purpose: "To promote the winners' career through exposure, publicity, recordings with Athena Records and nationwide distribution with the Empire Group."

Requirements: Deadline: March 15. Send for application. Samples of work are required with application.

Awards: $10,000 to sponsor the promotion of the winners.

☑ FREE STAGED READING SERIES PLAYWRITING COMPETITION, 120 W. 28th St., New York NY 10001. (212)627-1732. Fax: (212)243-6736. E-mail: tada@tadatheater.com. Website: www.tadatheater.com. **Contact:** Janine Nina Trevens, assistant to the artistic director. Estab. 1984. For musical playwrights or anyone wanting to write a play.

Purpose: "The series was initiated to encourage playwrights, composers, and lyricists to write for family audiences and to involve children and their parents in the excitement of the play development process."

Requirements: "Script must be original, unproduced and unpublished. Any age may apply. One act musical or non-musical cast must be primarily youth ages 7-18; children do not play adults—adult actors can be hired. Script must be typed, include character breakdown, set and costume description. Playwrights should adhere to the topic given—teen topics—and take into consideration that they need to not only write for young audiences but young performers as well. Meaningful family topics are also appropriate for this particular staged reading contest with an emphasis on the children's relationship with parents rather than a spotlight on the parents." Deadline: July 15. Send for guidelines.

Tips: "Issues having to do with children and what they are going through in life and good teen issues are especially relevant."

FULBRIGHT SCHOLAR PROGRAM, COUNCIL FOR INTERNATIONAL EXCHANGE OF SCHOLARS, 3007 Tilden St. NW, Suite 5L, Washington DC 20008-3009. (202)686-7877. Fax: (202)362-3442. E-mail: scholars@cies.iie.org. Website: www.cies.org. Estab. 1946. For composers and academics. Annual award.

Purpose: "Awards for university lecturing and advanced research abroad are offered annually in virtually all academic disciplines including musical composition."

Requirements: "U.S. citizenship at time of application; M.F.A., Ph.D. or equivalent professional qualifications; for lecturing awards, university teaching experience (some awards are for professionals non-academic)." Applications become available in March each year, for grants to be taken up 1½ years later. Application deadlines: August 1, all world areas. Write or call for application. Samples of work are required with application.

Awards: "Benefits vary by country, but generally include round-trip travel for the grantee and for most full academic-year awards, one dependent; stipend in U.S. dollars and/or local currency; in many countries, tuition allowance for school age children; and book and baggage allowance. Grant duration ranges from 2 months-1 academic year."

FUTURE CHARTERS, 332 Eastwood Ave., Feasterville PA 19053. (800)574-2986. Phone/fax: (215)953-0952. E-mail: a1foster@aol.com. Website: www.lafay.com/sm. **Contact:** Allen Foster, editor/publisher. Estab. 1993. For songwriters, composers and any aspiring songwriters. Monthly award.

Requirements: To enter, send a clean demo tape of one song with vocals up front, a photo, a bio, lyric sheet, contact information and a SASE (if you'd like your tape returned).

Awards: Winners will receive a writeup in an upcoming issue of *Songwriter's Monthly*, plus a portion of your song will be placed on our 1-800 number so interested parties will be able to call up and listen to part of your song.

Tips: "There is no application form or entry fee. Just send your best song. It doesn't have to be an expensive demo, but it does have to sound clean. Also, be sure to include all materials listed under requirements, as incomplete entry packages will be disqualified."

N HARVEY GAUL COMPOSITION CONTEST, The Pittsburgh New Music Ensemble, Inc., P.O. Box 99476, Pittsburgh PA 15233. Phone/fax: (412)682-2955. E-mail: pnme@pnme.org. Website: www.pnme.org. **Contact:** Kevin Noe, artistic director. For composers. Biennial.

Purpose: Objective is to encourage composition of new music. Winning piece to be premiered by the PNME.

Requirements: "Must be citizen of the US. New works scored for 6 to 16 instruments drawn from the following: flute, oboe, 2 clarinets, bassoon, horn, trumpet, trombone, tuba, 2 violins, cello, bass, 2 percussion, piano, harp, electronic tape." Deadline: April 15. Send SASE for application. Samples of work are required with application. "Real name must not appear on score—must be signed with a 'nom de plume'." Entry fee: $50.

Awards: Harvey Gaul Composition Contest: $3,000.

✓ GREAT AMERICAN SONG CONTEST, PMB 135, 6327-C SW Capitol Hill Hwy., Portland OR 97201-1937. E-mail: info@SongwritersResourceNetwork.com. Website: www.SongwriterResourceNetwork.com. **Contact:** Carla Starrett, event coordinator. Estab. 1998. For songwriters, composers and lyricists. Annual award.

Purpose: To help songwriters get their songs heard by music-industry professionals; to generate educational and networking opportunities for participating songwriters; to help songwriters open doors in the music business.

Requirements: Entry fee: $15. Deadline: November 7, 2001. "Check our website or send SASE along with your mailed request for information." Samples are not required.

Awards: Winners receive a mix of cash awards and prizes. The focus of the contest is on networking and educational opportunities. (All participants receive detailed evaluations of their songs by industry professionals.) Songs are judged by knowledgeable music-industry professionals, including prominent hit songwriters, producers and publishers.

Tips: "The quality of the demo recording is not important. Focus should be on the song—not on fancy production or complex arrangements. Judges will be looking for excellent songwriting, not great performances."

☑ **HENRICO THEATRE COMPANY ONE-ACT PLAYWRITING COMPETITION**, P.O. Box 27032, Richmond VA 23273. (804)501-5100 or (804)501-5138. Fax: (804)501-5284. E-mail: per22@co.henrico.va.us. **Contact:** Amy A. Perdue, cultural arts coordinator. Cultural Arts Assistant: Cindy Warren. For musical playwrights, songwriters, composers and performing artists. Annual award.

Purpose: Original one-act musicals for a community theater organization.

Requirements: "Only one-act plays or musicals will be considered. The manuscript should be a one-act original (not an adaptation), unpublished, and unproduced, free of royalty and copyright restrictions. Scripts with smaller casts and simpler sets may be given preference. Controversial themes and excessive language should be avoided. Standard play script form should be used. All plays will be judged anonymously; therefore, there should be two title pages; the first must contain the play's title and the author's complete address and telephone number. The second title page must contain only the play's title. The playwright must submit two excellent quality copies. Receipt of all scripts will be acknowledged by mail. Scripts will be returned if SASE is included. No scripts will be returned until after the winner is announced. The HTC does not assume responsibility for loss, damage or return of scripts. All reasonable care will be taken." Deadline: July 1st. Send for application first.

Awards: 1st Prize $300; 2nd Prize $200; 3rd Prize $200.

HOLTKAMP-AGO AWARD IN ORGAN COMPOSITION, American Guild of Organists, 475 Riverside Dr., Suite 1260, New York NY 10115. (212)870-2310. Fax: (212)870-2163. E-mail: info@agohq.org. Website: www.agohq.org. **Contact:** Paul Wolfe, program coordinator. For composers and performing artists. Biannual award.

Requirements: Organ solo, no longer than 8 minutes in duration. Specifics vary from year to year. Deadline: May 31 (odd-numbered years). Send for application.

Award: $2,000 provided by the Holtkamp Organ Company; publication by Hinshaw Music Inc.; performance at the biennial National Convention of the American Guild of Organists.

N INDIANA OPERA THEATRE/MACALLISTER AWARDS FOR OPERA SINGERS, 7515 E. 30th St., Indianapolis IN 46219. (317)546-6387. Fax: (317)253-2008. E-mail: opera@iquest.n et. Website: www.macallisterawards.com. Artister/General Director: E. Bookwalter. Estab. 1980. For college and professional opera singers.

Requirements: For professional and amateurs. Send for application or visit website.

INTERNATIONAL CLARINET ASSOCIATION COMPOSITION COMPETITION, Dept. of Music, Miami University, Oxford OH 45056. (513)529-3071. Fax: (513)529-3027. E-mail: gingra m@muohio.edu. Website: miavxl@muohio.edu/~gingram. **Contact:** Michèle Gingras, professor. Estab. 1992. For composers. Annual award.

REFER TO THE GEOGRAPHIC INDEX (at the back of this book) to find listings of companies by state, as well as foreign listings.

Purpose: To expand the clarinet repertoire.

Requirements: Unpublished work, no age limit, no length limit. Submit quintet for clarinet and strings or trio for clarinet, any acoustic instrument and piano. Legit repertoire or legit neo-jazz OK. Submit a tape and score. Entries must be labeled with composer's name, address and phone number on the score and tape. Deadline: April 10 every year. Send score and tape.

Awards: $2,000 and a performance at the annual clarinet congress run by ICA. Applications judged by international jury.

Tips: "Submit recent compositions which would enhance existing 'serious music' clarinet repertoire. Compose a piece which performers want to perform often. Only e-mails and snail mail are guaranteed a response."

N L.A. DESIGNERS' THEATRE MUSIC AWARDS, P.O. Box 1883, Studio City CA 91614-0883. (323)650-9600. (323)654-2700 (T.D.D.). Fax: (323)654-3260. E-mail: ladesigners@juno.com. Artistic Director: Richard Niederberg. For songwriters, composers, performing artists, musical playwrights and rights holders of music.

Purpose: To produce new musicals, operettas, opera-boufes and plays with music, as well as new dance pieces with new music scores.

Requirements: Submit nonreturnable cassette, tape, CD or any other medium by first or 4th class mail. "*We prefer proposals* to scripts." Acceptance: continuous. Submit nonreturnable materials with cover letter. No application form or fee is necessary.

Awards: Music is commissioned for a particular project. Amounts are negotiable. Applications judged by our artistic staff.

Tips: "Make the material 'classic, yet commercial' and easy to record/re-record/edit. Make sure rights are totally free of all 'strings,' 'understandings,' 'promises,' etc. ASCAP/BMI/SESAC registration is OK, as long as 'grand' or 'performing rights' are available."

THE JOHN LENNON SONGWRITING CONTEST, 459 Columbus Ave., Box 120, New York NY 10024. Fax: (212)579-4320. E-mail: info@jlsc.com. Website: www.jlsc.com. **Contact:** Gregg Ross, associate director. Estab. 1996. For songwriters. Annual award.

Purpose: "The purpose of the John Lennon Songwriting Contest is to promote the art of songwriting by assisting in the discovery of new talent as well as providing more established songwriters with an opportunity to advance their careers."

Requirements: Each entry must consist of the following: completed and signed application; audio cassette containing one song only, 5 minutes or less in length; lyric sheet typed or printed legibly (English translation is required when applicable); $30 entry fee. Deadline: August, 2001. Applications can be found in various music-oriented magazines. Prospective entrants can send for an application or contact the contest via e-mail at info@jlsc.com.

Awards: Entries are accepted in the following 12 categories: rock, country, jazz, pop, world, gospel/inspirational, R&B, hip-hop, Latin, electronic, folk and a special category of children's music. 2000 prize packages: 12 Grand Prize winners (one in each category) receive $2,000 in cash, $5,000 in Yamaha project studio equipment, and a $5,000 advance from EMI Music Publishing. One Grand Prize winner receives an additional $20,000 for the "Song of the Year" courtesy of Maxell. Finalists receive $1,000. 72 additional winners receive $100 gift certificates from Guitar Center. Winners are chosen by an Executive Committee comprised of noted songwriters, producers and recording artists. Songs will be judged based upon melody, composition and lyrics (when applicable). The quality of performance and production will not be considered during the adjudication process.

☑ MAXIM MAZUMDAR NEW PLAY COMPETITION, One Curtain Up Alley, Buffalo NY 14202-1911. (716)852-2600. Fax: (716)852-2266. Website: http://alleyway.com. **Contact:** Joanna Brown, literary manager. For musical playwrights. Annual award.

Purpose: Alleyway Theatre is dedicated to the development and production of new works. Winners of the competition will receive production and royalties.

Requirements: Unproduced full-length work not less than 90 minutes long with cast limit of 10 and unit or simple set, or unproduced one-act work less than 40 minutes long with cast limit of 6 and simple set; prefers work with unconventional setting that explores the boundaries of theatricality; limit of submission in each category; guidelines available, no entry form. $5 playwright entry fee. Script, résumé, SASE optional. Cassette mandatory. Deadline: July 1.

Awards: $400, production with royalty and travel and housing to attend rehearsals for full-length play or musical; $100 and production for one-act play or musical.

Tips: "Entries may be of any style, but preference will be given to those scripts which take place in unconventional settings and explore the boundaries of theatricality. No more than ten performers is a definite, unchangeable requirement."

☑ **MCI-SCROLL, INC. ORIGINAL LYRIC COMPETITION**, (formerly Mammoth, Scroll Original Lyric Competition), P.O. Box 562, Swink CO 81077. (719)384-8220. E-mail: scrollpubl@ria. net. **Contact:** C. Gray, promotional manager. Estab. 1995. For songwriters, musicians/all styles and lyric writers. Annual award.

Purpose: Best original artist awarded in 8 categories—blues, country, R&B, rock, inspirational, country rock, folk and pop—will be promoted by top musical producers, commercial ad managers, etc.

Requirements: Tape 2 songs on cassette or CD, bio or discography; performance dates and $25 entry fee, lyric sheet. Deadline: June 2002 and September 2002. Send lyric sheet and cassette or CD/ 2 songs. Samples of work are required with application. Send cassette or CD. May be sent in at anytime up to the deadline dates.

Awards: MCI Scroll, Inc. will award the best of 8 categories: 1 year of free Internet access, 8 home pages, 2 free master CD recordings, and a full length Real Audio recording. They also will give the grand prize winner $25,000 cash and recording contract. Applications are judged by performers, promoters and producers.

Tips: "Send in clear, crisp recordings. Select the best of your original work. If there are vocals involved, let your voice stand out. And never give up."

McKNIGHT VISITING COMPOSER PROGRAM, ACF, 332 Minnesota St., #E-145, St. Paul MN 55101. (651)228-1407. Fax: (651)291-7978. E-mail: pblackburn@composersforum.org. Website: www.composersforum.org. **Contact:** Philip Blackburn, program director. Estab. 1994. For songwriters, musical playwrights and composers. Annual award.

Purpose: "Up to 2 annual awards for non-Minnesota composers to come to Minnesota for a self-designed residency of at least 2 months."

Requirements: Not for Minnesota residents or students. Deadline: March. Send for application. Samples of work are required with application. Send score/tape.

Awards: McKnight Visiting Composer $14,000 stipend. Each award good for 1 year. Applications are judged by peer review panel.

Tips: "Find committed partners in Minnesota with whom to work, and explore diverse communities."

N MID-ATLANTIC SONG CONTEST, 4200 Wisconsin Ave., NW, Washington DC 20016. (800)218-5996 or (301)654-8434. E-mail: masc@saw.org. Website: www.saw.org. For songwriters, performing artists and composers. Estab. 1982. Sponsored by BMI and the Songwriters of Washington. Annual award.

Purpose: "Contest is designed to afford rising songwriters the opportunity of receiving awards/ exposure/feedback of critical nature in an environment of peer competition." Applicants must send for application to Mid-Atlantic Song Contest at above address. Rules and regulations explained— amateur status is most important requirement. Samples of work are required with application: cassette, entry form and 3 copies of lyrics. "Deadline for entries is usually early August—awards given in late fall (November)."

Awards: "Awards usually include cash merchandise and free recording time. Awards vary from year to year. Awards must be used within one calendar year. Winning songs will be placed on a winners CD, which will be distributed to major music publishers. Sponsored by BMI, Songwriters of Washington, TAXI, Omega Recording Studio, Oasis Recording & Duplication and Writer's Digest Books. Winners can perform their songs at the Awards Night Gala.

Requirements: Applications are judged by a panel of 3 judges per category, for 1st Prize, 2nd Prize and Honorable Mentions, to determine top winners in each category and to arrive at the Grand Prize winner. Reduced entry fees are offered for SAW members. Membership also entitles one to a newsletter and reduced rates for special events/seminars.
Tips: "Keep intros short; avoid instrumental solos; get to the chorus quickly and don't bury vocals."

THELONIOUS MONK INTERNATIONAL JAZZ COMPOSERS COMPETITION, sponsored by BMI, 5225 Wisconsin Ave. NW, #605, Washington DC 20015. (202)364-7272. Fax: (202)364-0176. E-mail: sfischer@tmonkinst.org. Website: www.monkinstitute.org. **Contact:** Shelby Fischer, executive producer. Estab. 1993. For songwriters and composers. Annual award.
Purpose: The award is given to an aspiring jazz composer who best demonstrates originality, creativity and excellence in jazz composition.
Requirements: Deadline: August 1. Send for application. Samples of work are required with application. Send cassette. The composition features a different instrument each year.
Awards: $10,000. Applications are judged by panel of jazz musicians. "The Institute will provide piano, bass, guitar, drum set, tenor saxophone, and trumpet for the final performance. The winner will be responsible for the costs of any different instrumentation included in the composition."

☑ MUSEUM IN THE COMMUNITY COMPOSER'S AWARD, P.O. Box 423, Hurricane WV 25526. (304)562-0484. Fax: (304)562-4733. E-mail: info@museuminthecommunity.org. Director of Exhibitions: Kelli Burns. Program Assistants: Lois Payne, Lech Dillenback. For composers. Biennial award.
Purpose: The Composer's Competition is to promote the writing of new works. "Specific type of competition changes. Past competitions have included string quartet, full orchestra and nonet."
Requirements: Work must not have won any previous awards nor have been published, publicly performed or used commercially. Requires 3 copies of the original score, clearly legible and bound. Title to appear at the top of each composition, but the composer's name must not appear. Entry forms must be filled out and a SASE of the proper size enclosed for return of entry. "If you happen to move while competition is underway please let us know." Enclose $25 entry fee (non-refundable). Send for application.
Awards: "Next competition will open in fall 2000. Winning composition announced May 2002 with concert in Fall 2002." Jurors will be 3 nationally known musicologists. Winning composer will be awarded a cash prize of $5,000 and a premiere concert of the composition. Transportation to the premiere from anywhere in the continental United States will be provided by the Museum.
Tips: "Applicants can contact the museum to be put on our mailing list to receive prospectus. Read *and* follow rules listed in Prospectus. Neatness still counts! Enclose SASE if you wish to have your score returned. Please write legibly. Please let us know if you move after you've sent in your entry!"

☑ NACUSA YOUNG COMPOSERS' COMPETITION, Box 49256 Barrington Station, Los Angeles CA 90049. (310)541-8213. Fax: (310)544-1413. E-mail: biaaflash.net. Website: www.theboo k.com/nacusa. **Contact:** Marshall Bialosky, president, NACUSA. Estab. 1978. For composers. Annual award.
Purpose: To encourage the composition of new American concert hall music.
Requirements: Entry fee: $20 (membership fee). Deadline: October 30. Send for application. Samples are not required.
Awards: 1st Prize: $200; 2nd Prize: $50; and possible Los Angeles performances. Applications are judged by a committee of experienced NACUSA composer members.

SAMMY NESTICO AWARD/USAF BAND AIRMEN OF NOTE, 201 McChord St., Bolling AFB, Washington DC 20332-0202. (202)767-1756. Fax: (202)767-0686. E-mail: tyler.kuebler@bolli ng.af.mil. **Contact:** Tyler Kuebler, technical sergeant. Estab. 1995. For composers. Annual award.
Purpose: To carry on the tradition of excellence of Sammy Nestico's writing through jazz composition. The winner will have their composition performed by the USAF Airmen of Note, have it professionally recorded and receive a $1,000 follow up commission for a second work.

Requirements: Unpublished work for jazz ensemble instrumentation (5,4,4,4) style, form and length are unrestricted. Deadline: October 1, 2000. Send for application. Samples of work are required with full score and set of parts (or cassette recording).

Awards: Performance by the USAF Band Airmen of Note; expense paid travel to Washington, DC for the performance; professionally produced recording of the winning composition; and $1,000 follow up commission for second work. Applications are judged by panel of musicians.

☑ **NEW FOLK CONCERTS FOR EMERGING SONGWRITERS**, P.O. Box 29, Kerrville TX 78029. (800)435-8429 or (830)257-3600. Fax: (830)257-8680. E-mail: rod@kerrville-music.com. Website: www.kerrville-music.com. **Contact:** Rod Kennedy, producer. For songwriters. Annual award.

Purpose: "To provide an opportunity for unknown songwriters to be heard and rewarded for excellence."

Requirements: Songwriter enters 2 original previously unrecorded songs on same side of cassette tape with entry fee; no more than one tape may be entered; 6-8 minutes total for 2 songs. No written application necessary; no lyric sheets or press material needed. Deadline: April 6 or first 600 entries received prior to that date. Call to request rules. Entry fee: $16.

Awards: New Folk Award Winner. 32 semi-finalists invited to sing the 2 songs entered during The Kerrville Folk Festival. 6 writers are chosen as award winners. Each of the 6 receives a cash award of $450 or more and performs at a winner's concert during the Kerrville Folk Festival, May 27-28, 2001. Initial round of entries judged by the Festival Producer. 32 finalists judged by panel of 3 performer/songwriters.

Tips: "Make certain cassette is rewound and ready to play. Do not allow instrumental accompaniment to drown out lyric content. Don't enter without complete copy of the rules. Former winners and finalists include Lyle Lovett, Nanci Griffith, Hal Ketchum, John Gorka, David Wilcox, Lucinda Williams and Robert Earl Keen, David Wilcox, Tish Hinojosa, Carrie Newcomer, Jimmy Lafave, etc."

☑ **OMAHA SYMPHONY GUILD INTERNATIONAL NEW MUSIC COMPETITION**, 1605 Howard St., Omaha NE 68102-2705. (402)342-3836, ext. 140. Fax: (402)342-3819. E-mail: bravo@omahasymphony.org. Website: www.omahasymphony.org. **Contact:** Greg Pierson, education and touring manager. For composers with an annual award. Estab. 1976.

Purpose: "The objective of the competition is to promote new music scored for chamber orchestra."

Requirements: Competition open to applicants 25 and up for entry fee of $30. "Follow competition guidelines including orchestration and length of composition." Deadline: April 15, 2001. Write or call for application. Each fall new guidelines and application forms are printed. Follow application guidelines.

Awards: "Monetary award is $3,000. Winners composition will possibly be included in the Omaha Symphony 2002-2003 season. Applications are screened by Omaha Symphony Music Director." Scores will be judged by a panel of respected composers and musicologists.

Tips: "This is an annual competition and each year has a new Symphony Guild chairman; all requests for extra information sent to the Omaha Symphony office will be forwarded. Also, 1,700-1,800 application information brochures are sent to colleges, universities and music publications each fall."

PLAYHOUSE ON THE SQUARE NEW PLAY COMPETITION, 51 S. Cooper, Memphis TN 38104. (901)725-0776. **Contact:** Jackie Nichols, executive director. For musical playwrights. Annual award. Estab. 1983.

Requirements: Send script, tape and SASE. "Playwrights from the South will be given preference." Open to full-length, unproduced plays. Musicals must be fully arranged for piano when received. Deadline: April 1.

Awards: Grants may be renewed. Applications judged by 3 readers.

☑ **PORTLAND SONGWRITERS ASSOCIATION ANNUAL SONGWRITING COMPETITION**, P.O. Box 16985, Portland OR 97292-0985. (503)727-8546. Fax: (503)241-9104. E-mail: info@pdxsongwriters.org. Website: www.pdxsongwriters.org. **Contact:** Judith Adams, president. Vice President: J.C. Tubbs. Estab. 1991. For songwriters and composers. Annual award.

Purpose: To provide opportunities for songwriters to improve their skills in the art and craft of songwriting, to connect our performing songwriters with the public through PSA sponsored venues and to create a presence and an avenue of approach for members' songs to be heard by industry professionals.

Requirements: For information, send SASE. All amateur songwriters may enter. Entries taken between March 1 and August 31. Entry fee: $15 members; $20 nonmembers.

Awards: Multiple awards totaling $1,000 in prizes. All songs will be reviewed by at least three qualified judges, including industry pros. Finalists may have their songs reviewed by celebrity judges.

✓ PULITZER PRIZE IN MUSIC, 709 Journalism, Columbia University, New York NY 10027. (212)854-3841. Fax: (212)854-3342. E-mail: pulitzer@pulitzer.org. Website: www.pulitzer.org. **Contact:** Elizabeth Mahaffey, music secretary. For composers and musical playwrights. Annual award.

Requirements: "For distinguished musical composition of significant dimension by an American that has had its American premiere between March 2 and March 1 of the one-year period in which it is submitted for consideration." Deadline: March 1. Samples of work are required with application, biography and photograph of composer, date and place of performance, score or manuscript and recording of the work, entry form and $50 entry fee.

Awards: "One award: $7,500. Applications are judged first by a nominating jury, then by the Pulitzer Prize Board."

[N] ROCHESTER PLAYWRIGHT FESTIVAL CONTEST, Midwest Theatre Network, 5031 Tongen Ave. NW, Rochester MN 55901. (507)281-1472. E-mail: sweens@uswest.net. **Contact:** Joan Sween, executive director/dramaturg. Estab. 1994. For any person who has created a work that is musical theater. Generally biennial award.

Purpose: To provide exposure, support and promotion of new works for the theatre.

Requirements: Plays must be previously unpublished or never professionally produced. Send SASE or e-mail for information. An audio tape is required with submission of libretto.

Awards: Full production, playwright travel expenses and possible cash. 4-8 plays produced and awarded by a coalition of differing theatres.

Tips: "The closer to performance values the audio tape is, the better."

✓ ROCKY MOUNTAIN FOLKS FESTIVAL SONGWRITER SHOWCASE, P.O. Box 769, Lyons CO 80540. (800)624-2422 or (303)823-0848. Fax: (303)823-0849. E-mail: kahlie@bluegrass.com. Website: www.bluegrass.com. **Contact:** Steve Szymanski, director. Estab. 1993. For songwriters, composers and performers. Annual award.

Purpose: Award based on having the best song and performance.

Requirements: Deadline: June 29. Finalists notified by July 13. Send for rules or find rules available on website. Samples of work are required with application. Send CD or cassette with $10 entry fee.

Awards: 1st Place is a custom Hayes Guitar and Festival Main Stage Set; 2nd: $400; 3rd: $300; 4th: $200; 5th: $100. Applications judged by panel of judges.

RICHARD RODGERS AWARDS, American Academy of Arts and Letters, 633 W. 155th St., New York NY 10032. (212)368-5900. **Contact:** Lydia Kaim, coordinator. Estab. 1978. Deadline: November 1, 2001. "The Richard Rodgers Awards subsidize full productions, studio productions, and staged readings by nonprofit theaters in New York City of works by composers and writers who are not already established in the field of musical theater. The awards are only for musicals—songs by themselves are not eligible. The authors must be citizens or permanent residents of the United States." Guidelines for this award may be obtained by sending a SASE to above address.

OPENNESS TO SUBMISSIONS: ☐ beginners; ◪ beginners and experienced; ◪ experienced only; ◪ no unsolicited submissions/industry referrals only.

ROME PRIZE FELLOWSHIP IN MUSICAL COMPOSITION, American Academy in Rome, 7 E. 60th St., New York NY 10022-1001. (212)751-7200. Fax: (212)751-7220. E-mail: info@aarom.o rg. Website: www.aarome.org. **Contact:** Programs Department. For composers. Annual award.

Purpose: "Rome Prize winners pursue independent projects which vary in content and scope."

Requirements: "Applicants for one-year fellowships must hold a bachelor's degree in music, musical composition or its equivalent." Deadline: November 15. Entry fee: $40. Application guidelines are available to download through the Academy's website. Samples of work are required with application; send CDs and/or tapes and scores.

Awards: Fellowship stipend is up to $20,000 for one year. "Juries convene from January through March to review all work submitted in the competition. In all cases, excellence is the primary criterion for selection, based on the quality of the materials submitted."

☑ **LOIS AND RICHARD ROSENTHAL NEW PLAY PRIZE**, % Cincinnati Playhouse in the Park, P.O. Box 6537, Cincinnati OH 45206-0537. (513)345-2242. Website: www.cincyplay.com **Contact:** Literary Associate. For playwrights and musical playwrights. Annual award.

Purpose: The Lois and Richard Rosenthal New Play Prize was established in 1987 to encourage the development of new plays that are original, theatrical, strong in character and dialogue, and make a significant contribution to the literature of American theatre. Residents of Cincinnati, the Rosenthals are committed to supporting arts organizations and social agencies that are innovative and foster social change.

Requirements: "Plays must be full-length in any style: comedy, drama, musical, etc. Translations, adaptations, individual one-acts and any play previously submitted for the Rosenthal Prize are not eligible. Collaborations are welcome, in which case the prize benefits are shared. Plays must be unpublished prior to submission and may not have received a full-scale, professional production. Plays that have had a workshop, reading or non-professional production are still eligible. Playwrights with past production experience are especially encouraged to submit new work. Submit a two-page maximum abstract of the play including title, character breakdown, story synopsis and playwright information (bio or résumé). Also include up to five pages of sample dialogue. If submitting a musical, please include a tape of selections from the score. All abstracts and dialogue samples will be read. From these, selected manuscripts will be solicited. Do not send a manuscript with or instead of the abstract. Unsolicited manuscripts will not be read. Submitted materials, including tapes, will be returned only if a SASE with adequate postage is provided. The Rosenthal Prize is open for submission from July 1st to December 31st. Only one submission per playwright each year."

Awards: The Rosenthal Prize play receives a full production at Cincinnati Playhouse in the Park as part of the theater's annual season and is given regional and national promotion. The playwright receives a $10,000 award plus travel and residency expenses for the Cincinnati rehearsal period.

☑ **TELLURIDE TROUBADOUR CONTEST**, P.O. Box 769, Lyons CO 80540. (303)823-0848 or (800)624-2422. Fax: (303)823-0849. E-mail: kahlie@bluegrass.com. Website: www.bluegrass.c om. **Contact:** Steve Szymanski, director. Estab. 1991. For songwriters, composers and performers. Annual award.

Purpose: Award based on having best song and performance.

Requirements: Deadline: must be postmarked by April 6; notified April 20, if selected. Send for rules or find rules available on website. Send cassette or CD and $10 entry fee.

Awards: 1st: custom Shanti Guitar and main stage set; 2nd: $400 and Crate acoustic amp; 3rd: $300 and Martin backpacker guitar; 4th: $200 and Martin backpacker guitar; 5th: $100. Applications judged by panel of judges.

THE TEN-MINUTE MUSICALS PROJECT, P.O. Box 461194, West Hollywood CA 90046. **Contact:** Michael Koppy, producer. For songwriters, composers and musical playwrights. Annual award.

Purpose: "We are building a full-length stage musical comprised of complete short musicals, each of which play for between 8-14 minutes. Award is $250 for each work chosen for development towards inclusion in the project, plus a share of royalties when produced."

Requirements: Deadline: August 31. For guidelines, write or phone. Final submission should include script, cassette and lead sheets.
Awards: $250 for each work selected. "Works should have complete stories, with a definite beginning, middle and end."

N "UNISONG" INTERNATIONAL SONG CONTEST, 5198 Arlington Ave., PMB 513, Riverside CA 92504. (213)673-4067 or 44 (0) 208 387 9293 (London). Fax: (818)704-1597. E-mail: entry@unisong.com. Website: www.unisong.com. Co-Founder: Alan Roy Scott. London office: P.O. Box 13383, London, NW3 5ZR United Kingdom. (44)236-4197. Co founder: David Stark. Estab. 1997. For songwriters, composers and lyricists. Annual songwriting contest.
Purpose: "This contest is designed for songwriters by songwriters. We help songwriters around the world by making donations from every entry fee to songwriter organizations internationally and Amnesty International."
Requirements: Deadline: September 1. Send for application or download application from website or request one by phone. Samples of work are required with application. Send cassette, CD or online via mp3. No DATs.
Awards: Grand Prize is participation in the next "Music Bridges" retreat collaboring with celebrity songwriters/artists (i.e., Bonnie Raitt, Diane Warren, Montel Jordan, Mick Fleetwood and Lamont Dozier). Previous destinations for "Music Bridges" have been Ireland, Cuba and Germany. 1st Prize in all 9 categories: $1,500. 2nd Prize in all 9 categories: $500 and various prize packages. 3rd Prize: various services. First level judging by Taxi (professional screening service); second level by established industry professionals. Final level by blue ribbon judging panel. Songs judged on song quality only, not demo.
Tips: "Please make sure your song is professionally presented. Make sure lyrics can be clearly understood. Make sure you are entering song in most appropriate categories."

✓ U.S.A. SONGWRITING COMPETITION, 4331 N. Federal Hwy., Suite 403A, Ft. Lauderdale FL 33308. (954)776-1577. Fax: (954)776-1132. E-mail: info@songwriting.net. Website: www.songwriting.net. **Contact:** Contest Manager. Estab. 1994. For songwriters, composers, performing artists and lyricists. Annual award.
Purpose: "To honor good songwriters/composers all over the world, especially the unknown ones."
Requirements: Open to professional and beginner songwriters. No limit on entries. Each entry must include an entry fee, a cassette tape of song(s) and lyric sheet(s). Judged by music industry representatives. Past judges have included record label representatives and publishers from Arista Records, EMI and Warner/Chappell. Deadline: To be announced. Entry fee: To be announced. Send SASE with request or e-mail for entry forms at any time. Samples of work are not required.
Awards: Prizes include cash and merchandise in 15 different categories: pop, rock, country, Latin, R&B, gospel, folk, jazz, "lyrics only" category, instrumental and many others.
Tips: "Judging is based on lyrics, originality, melody and overall composition. CD quality production is great but not a consideration in judging."

U.S.-JAPAN CREATIVE ARTISTS EXCHANGE FELLOWSHIP PROGRAM, Japan-U.S. Friendship Commission, 1120 Vermont Ave., NW, Suite 925, Washington DC 20005-3523. (202)418-9800. Fax: (202)418-9802. E-mail: artist@jusfc.gov. Website: www.jusfc.gov. **Contact:** Roberta Stewart, secretary. Estab. 1980. For all creative artists. Annual award.
Purpose: "For artists to go as seekers, as cultural visionaries, and as living liaisons to the traditional and contemporary life of Japan."
Requirements: "Artists' works must exemplify the best in U.S. arts." Deadline: June. Send for application and guidelines. Applications available via Internet. Samples of work are required with application. Requires 2 pieces on cassette or CD, cued to the 3-5 minute section to be reviewed.
Awards: Five artists are awarded a six-month residency anywhere in Japan. Awards monthly stipend for living expenses, housing and professional support services; up to $6,000 for pre-departure costs, including such items as language training and economy class roundtrip airfare. Residency is good for 1 year. Applications are judged by a panel of previous recipients of the awards, as well as other arts professionals with expertise in Japanese culture.

Tips: "Applicants should anticipate a highly rigorous review of their artistry and should have compelling reasons for wanting to work in Japan."

🌐 ☑ **U.S.-MEXICO FUND FOR CULTURE**, Londres 16-PB, 3er. Piso, Col. Juarez Mexico City Mexico 06600. (525)592-5386. Fax: (525)566-8071. E-mail: usmexcult@fidemexusa.org.mx. Website: www.fidemexusa.org.mx. **Contact:** Beatriz E. Nava, program officer. Estab. 1991. For composers, choreographers, musical playwrights and performers. Annual award.
Purpose: "The U.S.-Mexico Fund for Culture, an independent body created through a joint initiative of the Bancomer Cultural Foundation, The Rockefeller Foundation and Mexico's National Fund for Culture and the Arts, provides financial support for the development of cultural binational projects in music, theater, dance, visual arts, cultural studies, literary and cultural publications, media arts and libraries."
Requirements: Deadline: April 16, 2001 (postmarked). Send for application with SASE (8½×11 envelope) or contact us at our website. Samples of work are required with application in duplicate.
Awards: Range from $2,000-25,000. Award is good for 1 year. Judged by binational panel of experts in each of the disciplines, one from Mexico and one from the USA.
Tips: "Proposals must be binational in character and have a close and active collaboration with artists from Mexico. The creation of new works is highly recommendable."

WEST COAST ENSEMBLE–MUSICAL STAIRS, P.O. Box 38728, Los Angeles CA 90038. (323)876-9337. **Contact:** Les Hanson, artistic director. For composers and musical playwrights. Annual award.
Purpose: To provide an arena and encouragement for the development of new musicals for the theater.
Requirements: Submit book and a cassette of the score to the above address.
Awards: The West Coast Ensemble Musical Stairs Competition Award includes a production of the selected musical and $500 prize. Panel of judges reads script and listen to cassette. Final selection is made by Artistic Director.
Tips: "Submit libretto in standard playscript format along with professional sounding cassette of songs."

WORDS BY, 332 Eastwood Ave,. Feasterville PA 19053. (800)574-2986. Phone/fax: (215)953-0952. E-mail: a1foster@aol.com. Website: www.lafay.com/sm. **Contact:** Allen Foster, editor/publisher. Estab. 1992. For lyricists. Monthly contest.
Requirements: To enter, send your best lyrics and contact information.
Awards: Winning lyrics will be published along with your address so interested parties may contact you directly. Also, the top lyric for each month receives $25.
Tips: "Due to the large number of submissions we receive each month, you may resubmit a lyric, after two months, if you really believe in that work."

Y.E.S. FESTIVAL OF NEW PLAYS, Northern Kentucky University Dept. of Theatre, FA-205, Highland Heights KY 41099-1007. (606)572-6303. Fax: (606)572-6057. E-mail: forman@nku.edu. **Contact:** Sandra Forman, project director. Estab. 1983. For musical playwrights. Biennial award.
Purpose: "The festival seeks to encourage new playwrights and develop new plays and musicals. Three plays or musicals are given full productions."
Requirements: "Submit a script with a completed entry form. Musicals should be submitted with a piano/conductor's score and a vocal parts score. Scripts may be submitted May 1 through Oct. 31, for the New Play Festival occuring April. Send for application. Samples of work are required with application."
Awards: Three awards of $500. "The winners are brought to NKU at our expense to view late rehearsals and opening night." Applications are judged by a panel of readers.
Tips: "Plays/musicals which have heavy demands for mature actors are not as likely to be selected as an equally good script with roles for 18-25 year olds."

N: YOUNG COMPOSERS AWARDS, % NGCSA and the Hartt School, University of Hartford, 200 Bloomfield Ave., West Hartford CT 06117. (860)768-4451. E-mail: yaffe@mail.hartford.edu or info@natguild.org. Website: www.nationalguild.org. **Contact:** Michael Yaffe, director. For composers. Open to students age 13-18. Annual award.

Purpose: "To encourage young students to write music, so that the art of composition—with no restrictions as to the category of music in which the works are written—will once again occupy the place in the center of music education where it belongs. It takes tons of ore to extract one ounce of gold: by focusing on the inventiveness of many students, the Awards may lead to the discovery of genuine creative talents—that is the eventual goal." Young Composers Awards was established by the late Dr. Herbert Zipperin in 1985 with the initial support of the Rockefeller Foundation. Since 1985, awards in the amount of $42,500 have been granted to 67 young composers.

Requirements: "Applicants must be enrolled in a public or private secondary school, in a recognized musical institution, or be engaged in the private study of music with an established teacher. No compositions will be considered without certification by the applicant's teacher. Student composers must not be enrolled in an undergraduate program when they apply. This competition is open to residents of the United States and Canada. Each applicant may submit only one work. Deadline: all submissions must be postmarked on or before early April 2002. Check website for exact date. Send for application. Samples of work are required with application. Four photocopies of the work must be submitted. All manuscripts must be in legible form and may be submitted on usual score paper or reduced under a generally accepted process. The composer's name must not appear on the composition submitted. The composition must be marked with a pseudonym on the manuscript. Copies must be submitted with a check in the amount of $5 made payable to the Hartt School. One copy of score will be returned if entrant sends SASE with application. Entrants must be certain postage purchased has no expiration date. Composers retain full and all legal rights to their submitted composition. Students who have previously won this award are not eligible to reapply."

Awards: Herbert Zipper Prizes: 2 separate categories—age group 13-15 (Junior) and 16-18 (Senior). 2 prizes are awarded in each of the Senior and Junior categories—Senior: 1st Place: $1,000; 2nd Place: $500. Junior: 1st Place: $500; 2nd Place: $250. A special prize of $1,000 will be awarded in either category for a chamber music composition (defined as a work for at least 2 instruments, intended to be performed with one performer per part). "Announcement of the Awards are made no later than mid-June each year. In the event that no entry is found to be worthy of the $1,000 Prize, the jury may award one or both of the other prizes or none at all. NGCSA appoints an independent jury to review all entries submitted. The jury consists of not less than three qualified judges. Prizes shall be awarded at the discretion of the jury. The decision of the judges is final."

Tips: "Paramount would be neatness and legibility of the manuscript submitted. The application must be complete in all respects."

THE OPENNESS TO SUBMISSIONS INDEX at the back of this book lists all companies in this section by how open they are to submissions.

Resources

Organizations.. 411

Workshops & Conferences........................ 439

Retreats & Colonies.................................... 450

State & Provincial Grants........................ 455

Publications of Interest............................ 458

Websites of Interest.................................... 463

Glossary 469

Organizations

One of the first places a beginning songwriter should look for guidance and support is a songwriting organization. Offering encouragement, instruction, contacts and feedback, these groups of professional and amateur songwriters can help an aspiring songwriter hone the skills needed to compete in the ever-changing music industry.

The type of organization you choose to join depends on what you want to get out of it. Local groups can offer a friendly, supportive environment where you can work on your songs and have them critiqued in a constructive way by other songwriters. They're also great places to meet collaborators. Larger, national organizations can give you access to music business professionals and other songwriters across the country.

Most of the organizations listed in this book are non-profit groups with membership open to specific groups of people—songwriters, musicians, classical composers, etc. They can be local groups with a membership of less than 100 people, or large national organizations with thousands of members from all over the country. In addition to regular meetings, most organizations occasionally sponsor events such as seminars and workshops to which music industry personnel are invited to talk about the business, and perhaps listen to and critique demo tapes.

Check the following listings, bulletin boards at local music stores and your local newspapers for area organizations. If you are unable to locate an organization within an easy distance of your home, you may want to consider joining one of the national groups. These groups, based in New York, Los Angeles and Nashville, keep their members involved and informed through newsletters, regional workshops and large yearly conferences. They can help a writer who feels isolated in his hometown get his music heard by professionals in the major music centers.

In the following listings, organizations describe their purpose and activities, as well as how much it costs to join. Before joining any organization, consider what they have to offer and how becoming a member will benefit you. To locate organizations close to home, see the Geographic Index at the back of this book.

AARON ENTERPRISES SONGWRITERS GROUP, 4411 Red Gate Dr., Disputanta VA 23842. (804)733-5908. **Contact:** Cham Laughlin, founder. Estab. 1997. "Songwriters of all ages, all styles and all skill levels are welcome to join. Applicants must have an interest in songwriting—music writing, lyric writing or co-writing. The main purpose of this organization is to educate songwriters about the business of songwriting, the art and craft of songwriting, lyric writing and structure, musical composition, song structure or arranging and professional presentation of your songs." Offers newsletter, evaluation services, seminars, discounts on demos and leads to publishers. Applications accepted year-round. Membership fee: $25/year with discounts for multiple years.
Tips: "Networking is a very important part of this business. Members are offered a large amount of information and that information is explained to them through free seminars, the newsletter or one-on-one phone consultations to ensure the best possible support network for their songwriting careers."

N ALABAMA SONGWRITER'S GUILD, P.O. Box 272, Garden City AL 35070. (256)352-4873. E-mail: lithics@hiwaay.net. **Contact:** Dennis N. Kahler. Estab. 1992. "The Alabama Songwriter's Guild is comprised of songwriters and their supporters, with no restrictions. We have members who are just beginning to write, and others who have number one hits under their belts on the *Billboard* charts. We welcome all genres of songwriting, and count several non-writers as members of our network efforts. The main purpose of the ASG is to help link Alabama and outside songwriters to information on seminars, showcases, publishing and song-plugging opportunities, local associations, workshops, and other events from one end of the state to the other. We help spread word of the induction ceremonies and other events at the Alabama Music Hall of Fame, report on the annual Frank Brown International Songwriter's Festival in Gulf Shores/Orange Beach every November, and help link writers together with like-minded individuals for co-writes. Any purpose that serves the songwriter is of interest to us." Queries welcomed anytime.

Tips: "Networking is crucial! Wherever you live, develop your network. If you need songwriting contacts in Alabama, contact us."

☑ **ALL SONGWRITERS NETWORK (ASN)**, (formerly American Songwriters Network), Dept A95, Box 23912, Ft. Lauderdale FL 33307. (954)537-3463. E-mail: asn@tiac.net. Website: www.tiac.net/users/asn. **Contact:** Network Manager. Estab. 1995. Serves "professional level songwriters/composers with monthly music industry leads tipsheet. The tipsheet includes the most current listing of producers, A&R managers, record labels, entertainment attorneys, agents and publishing companies looking for specific material for their projects/albums. Any songwriter from any part of the country or world can be a member of this organization. The purpose of this organization is to foster a better professional community by helping members to place their songs." Membership fee: $140/year.

Tips: "Please send SASE or e-mail for application form."

AMERICAN COMPOSERS FORUM, 332 Minnesota St. #E145, St. Paul MN 55101. (651)228-1407. Fax: (651)291-7978. E-mail: mail@composersforum.org. Website: www.composersforum.org. **Contact:** Wendy Montgomery, program manager. Estab. 1973. "The American Composers Forum links communities with composers and performers, encouraging the making, playing and enjoyment of new music. Building two-way relationships between artists and the public, the Forum develops programs that educate today's and tomorrow's audiences, energize composers' and performers' careers, stimulate entrepreneurship and collaboration, promote musical creativity, and serve as models of effective support for the arts. Programs include residencies, fellowships, commissions, producing and performance opportunities, a recording assistance program and a widely-distributed recording label. The Forum's members, more than 1,200 strong, live in 49 states and 16 countries; membership is open to all." Dues: $50, students/seniors: $35.

☑ **AMERICAN MUSIC CENTER, INC.**, 30 W. 26th St., Suite 1001, New York NY 10010-2011. (212)366-5260. Fax: (212)366-5265. E-mail: center@amc.net. Website: www.amc.net. **Contact:** Brian Welsh, administrative associate. Executive Director: Richard Kessler. Administrative Manager: Carlos Camposeco. The American Music Center, founded by a consortium led by Aaron Copland in 1939, is the first-ever national service and information center for new classical and jazz music in the world. The Center, having recently celebrated its 60th anniversary with the creation of a variety of innovative new programs and services, including a montly Internet magazine (www.newm usicbox.org) for new American music, an online catalog of new music for educators specifically targeted to young audiences and a series of professional development workshops. Each month, AMC provides its over 2,500 members with a listing of opportunities including calls for scores, competitions, and other new music performance information. Last year, AMC's Information Services Program fielded over 35,000 requests concerning composers, performers, data, funding, and support programs. AMC Library presently includes over 60,000 scores and recordings, many unavailable elsewhere. AMC also continues to administer several grants programs: the Aaron Copland Fund for Music; the Mary Flagler Cary Charitable Trust/Live Music for Dance; and its own program, The Margaret Fairbank Jory Copying Assistance Program. Members are also eligible to link their artists' pages to the center's website. The American Music Center is not-for-profit and has an annual membership fee.

AMERICAN SOCIETY OF COMPOSERS, AUTHORS AND PUBLISHERS (ASCAP), One Lincoln Plaza, New York NY 10023. (212)621-6000 (administration); (212)621-6240 (membership). E-mail: info@ascap.com. Website: www.ascap.com. President and Chairman of the Board: Marilyn Bergman. CEO: John LoFrumento. Executive Vice President/Membership: Todd Brabec. **Contact:** Member Services at (800)95-ASCAP. **Regional offices: West Coast:** 7920 Sunset Blvd., 3rd Floor, Los Angeles CA 90046, (323)883-1000; **Nashville:** 2 Music Square W., Nashville TN

37203, (615)742-5000; **Chicago:** 4042 N. Pulaski St., Suite 200, Chicago IL 60641, (773)545-5744; **Atlanta:** 541-400 10th St. NW, Atlanta GA 30318, (404)635-1758; **Florida:** 420 Lincoln Rd., Suite 385, Miami Beach FL 33139, (305)673-3446; **United Kingdom:** 8 Cork St., London WIX 1PB England, 011-44-207-439-0909; **Puerto Rico:** 510 Royal Bank Center, 255 Ponce De Leon Ave., Hato Rey, Puerto Rico 00917, (787)281-0782. ASCAP is a membership association of over 111,000 composers, lyricists, songwriters, and music publishers, whose function is to protect the right of its members by licensing and collecting royalties for the nondramatic public performance of their copyrighted works. ASCAP licensees include radio, television, cable, live concert promoters, bars, restaurants, symphony orchestras, new media, and other users of music. ASCAP is the leading performing rights society in the world, with 2000 revenues of more than $576 million. All revenues, less operating expenses, are distributed to members (about 84 cents of each dollar, $400 million, in 1998). ASCAP was the first US performing rights organization to distribute royalties from the Internet. Founded in 1914, ASCAP is the only society created and owned by writers and publishers. The ASCAP Board of Directors consists of 12 writers and 12 publishers, elected by the membership. ASCAP offers a variety of tailor-made benefits to its members, including medical, dental and term insurance, instrument and equipment insurance, and credit union access. ASCAP's Member Benefit cards offers new insurance benefits including studio and tour liability, retail, financial, travel benefits and discounts. A foreign tax credit opportunity saves members over $3 million annually. ASCAP hosts a wide array of showcases and workshops throughout the year, and offers grants, special awards, and networking opportunities in a variety of genres. Visit their website listed above for more information.

☑ **ARIZONA SONGWRITERS ASSOCIATION**, P.O. Box 678, Phoenix AZ 85001-0678. (602)973-1988. Website: www.punkfolker.com. **Contact:** Gavan Wieser, membership director. Estab. 1977. Members are all ages with wide variety of interests; beginners and those who make money from their songs. Most members are residents of Arizona. Purpose is to educate about the craft and business of songwriting and to facilitate networking with business professionals and other local songwriters. Offers instruction, newsletter, lectures, workshops and performance opportunities. Applications accepted year-round. Membership fee: $25/year.

🍁 **ASSOCIATED MALE CHORUSES OF AMERICA**, 773 Cedar Glen Rd., RR1, Dunsford, Ontario K0M 1L0 Canada. E-mail: internationaloffice@ameachorus.org. Website: www.amchorus.org. **Contact:** William J. Bates, executive secretary. Estab. 1924. Serves musicians and male choruses of US and Canada. "Our members are people from all walks of life. Many of our directors and accompanists are professional musicians. Age ranges from high school students to members in their '70s and '80s. Potential members must be supportive of Male Chorus Singing. They do not have to belong to a chorus to join. We have both Associate and Affiliate memberships. Our purpose is to further the power of music, not only to entertain and instruct, but to uplift the spirit, arouse the finest instincts, and develop the soul of man. With so little male chorus music being written, we as a 1,500 member organization provide a vehicle for songwriters, so that the music can be performed." Offers competitions, instruction, lectures, library, newsletter, performance opportunities, social outings and workshops. Also sponsors annual Male Chorus Songwriters Competition Contest. Applications accepted year-round. Membership fees are Chorus Members: $7 (per singer); Affiliate (Individual or Organization) Members: $10; Student Members: $2; Life Members: $125 (one time fee).

☑ 🍁 **ASSOCIATION DES PROFESSIONEL.LE.S DE LA CHANSON ET DE LA MUSI-QUE**, 255 ch. Montréal, Suite 200, Ontario K1L 6C4 Canada. (613)745-5642. Fax: (613)745-1733. E-mail: apcm@sympatico.ca. Website: www.francoculture.ca/musique/apcm. **Contact:** Laurent de Crombruggne, director. Estab. 1989. Members are French Canadian singers and musicians. Members must be French singing and may have a CD/cassette to be distributed. Purpose is to gather French

---

THE FILM & TV INDEX found at the back of this book lists companies placing music in film and TV (excluding TV commercials).

speaking artists (outside of Quebec, mainly in Ontario) to distribute their material, other workshops, instructions, lectures, etc. Offers instruction, newsletter, lectures, workshops, and distribution. Applications accepted year-round. Membership fee: $50 (Canadian).

ASSOCIATION OF INDEPENDENT MUSIC PUBLISHERS, 120 E. 56th St., Suite 1150, New York NY 10022-3607. (212)758-6157. Fax: (212)758-9402. E-mail: aimpny@aol.com. Estab. 1977. Purpose is to educate members on new developments in the music publishing industry and to provide networking opportunities. Offers lectures, workshops and evaluation services. Applications accepted year-round. Membership fee: $75/year.

☑ **AUSTIN SONGWRITERS GROUP**, P.O. Box 2578, Austin TX 78768. (512)442-TUNE. E-mail: asginfo@aol.com. Website: www.austinsongwriter.org. **Contact:** Polk Shelton, president. Vice President of Membership: John Hudson. Estab. 1986. Serves all ages and all levels, from just beginning to advanced. Perspective members should have an interest in the field of songwriting, whether it be for profit or hobby. The main purpose of this organization is "to educate members in the craft and business of songwriting; to provide resources for growth and advancement in the area of songwriting; and to provide opportunities for performance and contact with the music industry." The primary benefit of membership to a songwriter is "exposure to music industry professionals, which increases contacts and furthers the songwriter's education in both craft and business aspects." Offers competitions, instruction, lectures, library, newsletter, performance opportunities, evaluation services, workshops and "contact with music industry professionals through special guest speakers at meetings, plus our yearly 'Austin Songwriters Conference,' which includes instruction, song evaluations, and song pitching direct to those pros currently seeking material for their artists, publishing companies, etc." Applications accepted year-round. Membership fee: $40/year.
Tips: "Our newsletter is top-quality—packed with helpful information on all aspects of songwriting—craft, business, recording and producing tips, and industry networking opportunities."

THE BLACK COUNTRY MUSIC ASSOCIATION, 629 Shady Lane, Nashville TN 37206. (615)227-5570. Co-Founder/Chair: Frankie Staton. Co-Founder/Talent Coordinator: J.J. Jones. Estab. 1997. Members are all ages and all people who perform or support country music. "Purpose is to have a platform for African Americans who love and perform country music in an industry that does not realize how much African-Americans want to participate in this genre. Forming the Black Country Music Showcase, the traveling group of the very best of the BCMA. Appearing at festivals, fairs and other functions." Offers instruction, newsletter, workshops, performance opportunities and evaluation services. Applications accepted year-round. Membership fee: $40.
Tips: "With respect to the Black country artist and songwriter, the BCMA acts as an historical/educational entity. We have a quarterly newsletter. Send all promotional material (picture, bio, tape) to J.J. Jones, 235 Ross Ave., Gallatin TN 37066 (he's the talent co-ordinator)."

THE BOSTON SONGWRITERS WORKSHOP, 14 Skelton Rd., Burlington MA 01803. (617)499-6932. Website: www.laverty.org/BSW. Estab. 1988. "The Boston Songwriters Workshop is made up of a very diverse group of people, ranging in age from late teens to people in their sixties, and even older. The interest areas are also diverse, running the gamut from folk, pop and rock to musical theater, jazz, R&B, dance, rap and classical. Skill levels within the group range from relative newcomers to established veterans that have had cuts and/or songs published. By virtue of group consensus, there are no eligibility requirements other than a serious desire to pursue one's songwriting ventures, and availability and interest in volunteering for the various activities required to run the organization. The purpose of the BSW is to establish a community of songwriters and composers within the greater Boston area, so that its members may better help each other to make further gains in their respective musical careers." Offers performance opportunities, instruction, newsletter, workshops and bi-weekly critique sessions. Applications accepted year-round. Membership: $35/year; newsletter subscription only: $10/year; guest (nonmember) fees: free, limited to two meetings.

BROADCAST MUSIC, INC. (BMI), 320 W. 57th St., New York NY 10019. (212)586-2000; 8730 Sunset Blvd., Los Angeles CA 90069, (310)659-9109. Website: www.bmi.com. **Nashville:** 10 Music

Square East, Nashville TN 37203, (615)401-2000. **Miami:** 5201 Blue Lagoon Dr., Suite 310, Miami FL 33126, (305)266-3636; **United Kingdom:** 84 Harley House, Marylebone Rd., London NW1 5HN, United Kingdom, 011-44-207-486-2036. President and CEO: Frances W. Preston. Senior Vice President, Performing Rights: Del R. Bryant. Vice Presidents, California: Barbara Cane and Doreen Ringer Ross. Vice President, New York: Charlie Feldman. Vice President, Nashville: Paul Corbin. Vice President, London: Phil Graham. Assistant Vice President, Miami: Diane J. Almodovar. BMI is a performing rights organization representing over 250,000 songwriters, composers and music publishers in all genres of music, including pop, rock, country, R&B, rap, jazz, Latin, gospel and contemporary classical. "Applicants must have written a musical composition, alone or in collaboration with other writers, which is commercially published, recorded or otherwise likely to be performed." Purpose: BMI acts on behalf of its songwriters, composers and music publishers by insuring payment for performance of their works through the collection of licensing fees from radio stations, broadcast and cable TV stations, hotels, nightclubs, aerobics centers and other users of music. This income is distributed to the writers and publishers in the form of royalty payments, based on how the music is used. BMI also undertakes intensive lobbying efforts in Washington D.C. on behalf of its affiliates, seeking to protect their performing rights through the enactment of new legislation and enforcement of current copyright law. In addition, BMI helps aspiring songwriters develop their skills through various workshops, seminars and competitions it sponsors throughout the country. Applications accepted year-round. There is no membership fee for songwriters; a one-time fee of $150 is required to affiliate a publishing company. "Visit our website for specific contacts, e-mail addresses and additional membership information."

■ **CALIFORNIA LAWYERS FOR THE ARTS**, 1641 18th St., Santa Monica CA 90404. (310)998-5590. Fax: (310)998-5594. E-mail: usercla@aol.com. Website: www.calawyersforthearts.o rg. Associate Director: Jane Hall. Systems Coordinator: Josie Porter. Estab. 1974. "For artists of all disciplines, skill levels, and ages, supporting individuals and organizations, and arts organizations. Artists of all disciplines are welcome, whether professionals or amateurs. We also welcome groups and individuals who support the arts. We work most closely with the California arts community. Our mission is to establish a bridge between the legal and arts communities so that artists and art groups may handle their creative activities with greater business and legal competence; the legal profession will be more aware of issues affecting the arts community; and the law will become more responsive to the arts community." Offers newsletter, lectures, library, workshops, mediation service, attorney referral service, housing referrals, publications and advocacy. Membership fee: $20 for senior citizens and full-time students; $25 for working artists; $40 for general individual; $55 for panel attorney; $100 to $1,000 for patrons. Organizations: $45 for small organizations (budget under $50,000); $80 for large organizations (budget of $50,000 or more); $100 to $1,000 for corporate sponsors.

■ **CANADA COUNCIL FOR THE ARTS/CONSEIL DES ARTS DU CANADA**, 350 Albert St., P.O. Box 1047, Ottawa, Ontario K1P 5V8 Canada. (613)566-4414, ext. 5060. Website: www.canadacouncil.ca. **Contact:** Maria Martin and Lise Rochon, information officers. Estab. 1957. An independent agency that fosters and promotes the arts in Canada by providing grants and services to professional artists including songwriters and musicians. "Individual artists must be Canadian citizens or permanent residents of Canada, and must have completed basic training and/or have the recognition as professionals within their fields. The Canada Council offers grants to professional musicians to pursue their own personal and creative development. There are specific deadline dates for the various programs of assistance." Call or write for more details.

■ **CANADIAN ACADEMY OF RECORDING ARTS & SCIENCES (CARAS)**, 124 Merton St., Suite 305, Toronto, Ontario M4S 2Z2 Canada. (416)485-3135 or (800)440-JUNO. Fax: (416)485-4978. E-mail: caras@juno-awards.ca. Website: www.juno-awards.ca. President: Daisy C. Falle. Awards and Events Coordinator: Leisa Peacock. Communications Co-ordinator: Tammy Watson. Membership is open to all employees (including support staff) in broadcasting and record companies, as well as producers, personal managers, recording artists, recording engineers, arrangers, composers, music publishers, album designers, promoters, talent and booking agents, record retailers, rack jobbers, distributors, recording studios and other music industry related professions (on approval). Applicants must be affliliated with the Canadian recording industry. Offers newsletter, Canadian artist record discount program, nomination and voting privileges for Juno Awards and discount tickets to Juno awards show. Also discount on trade magazines. "CARAS strives to foster the development of the Canadian music and recording industries and to contribute toward higher artistic standards." Applications accepted year-round. Membership fee is $50/year (Canadian) + GST = $53.50. Applications accepted from individuals only, not from companies or organizations.

CANADIAN COUNTRY MUSIC ASSOCIATION (CCMA), 5 Director Court, Unit 102, Woodbridge, Ontario L4L 4S5 Canada. (905)850-1144. Fax: (905)850-1330. E-mail: country@ccma.org. Website: www.ccma.org. **Contact:** Colleen MacIntyre, membership services coordinator. Executive Director: Sheila Hamilton. Estab. 1976. Members are songwriters, musicians, producers, radio station personnel, managers, booking agents and others. Offers newsletter, workshops, performance opportunities and annual awards. "Through our newsletters and conventions we offer a means of meeting and associating with artists and others in the industry. During our workshops or seminars (Country Music Week), we include a songwriters' seminar. The CCMA is a federally chartered, nonprofit organization, dedicated to the promotion and development of Canadian country music throughout Canada and the world and to providing a unity of purpose for the Canadian country music industry." Send for application.

CANADIAN MUSICAL REPRODUCTION RIGHTS AGENCY LTD., 56 Wellesley St. W, #320, Toronto, Ontario M5S 2S3 Canada. (416)926-1966. Fax: (416)926-7521. E-mail: inquiries@cmrra.ca. Website: www.cmrra.ca. **Contact:** Kevin Shaver, publisher relations. Estab. 1975. Members are music copyright owners, music publishers, sub-publishers and administrators. Representation by CMRRA is open to any person, firm or corporation anywhere in the world, which owns and/or administers one or more copyrighted musical works. CMRRA is a music licensing agency—Canada's largest—which represents music copyright owners, publishers and administrators for the purpose of mechanical and synchronization licensing in Canada. Offers mechanical and synchronization licensing. Applications accepted year-round.

CENTER FOR THE PROMOTION OF CONTEMPORARY COMPOSERS, P.O. Box 631043, Nacogdoches TX 75963. E-mail: cpcc@under.org. Website: www.under.org/cpcc. Director: Dr. Stephen Lias. Estab. 1996. "Our members range from student composers to composers with international reputations." Purpose is to promote the works and activities of contemporary composers by creating custom composer web pages, posting composer opportunities (competitions, calls for scores, grants, faculty openings, etc.), maintaining a catalogue of members' works and a calendar of upcoming performances of new music. Offers competitions, newsletter, performance opportunities and custom web pages and listings in online catalog. Applications accepted year-round. Membership fee: $12 regular; $10/month resident ($120/year).

CENTRAL CAROLINA SONGWRITERS ASSOCIATION (CCSA), 1144 Amber Acres Lane, Knightdale NC 27545. (919)266-5791. Fax: (919)460-6284. E-mail: davisshantel@hotmail.com. Website: www.NCneighbors.com/147/. Founder: Shantel R. Davis. Vice President: Dawn Williams. Estab. 1996. "CCSA welcomes all songwriters and musicians, regardless of age. Our members vary in musical interests, and we cover all types of music. From the beginning songwriter to the experienced professional, all songwriters and musicians can find benefit in joining CCSA. We meet monthly in Raleigh, NC. We are open to all songwriters who could possibly make it to our meetings, or those who are too far away could use our Critique-By-Mail service. All members must be active participants in CCSA for the benefit of the group, as well as for their own benefit, dedicated songwriters/musicians. The main purpose of the CCSA is to provide each songwriter and musician a resourceful organization where members can grow musically by learning and sharing with one another. We want to reach every songwriter we can and attend to his/her musical needs. Our association has partnered with Musical Creations, a local studio, where our vocalists are paid to record vocal tracks on demos. Check it out at www.musicalcreations.com." Offers instruction, newsletter, library, workshops, evaluation services, open-mic nights and musicians/collaborators network. Applications accepted year-round. Dues are $15 per year.

☑ **CENTRAL OREGON SONGWRITERS ASSOCIATION**, 68978 Graham Court, Sisters OR 97759. (541)548-4138. Fax: (541)549-1811. E-mail: cosa@teleport.com. Website: http://COSA4 U.tripod.com. **Contact:** Pat Wilson, secretary/treasurer. Organizer: Earl Richards. President: Barry Stranahan. Estab. 1993. "Our members range in age from their 20s into their 80s. Membership includes aspiring beginners, accomplished singer/songwriter performing artists and all in between. Anyone with an interest in songwriting (any style) is invited to and welcome at COSA. COSA is a nonprofit organization to promote, educate and motivate members in the skills of writing, marketing and improving their craft." Offers competitions, instruction, newsletter, lectures, library, workshops, performance opportunities, songwriters round, awards, evaluation services and collaboration. Applications accepted year-round. Membership fee is $25.
Tips: "COSA enjoys a close association with other like associations, thereby increasing and expanding the benefits of association."

THE COLLEGE MUSIC SOCIETY, 202 W. Spruce St., Missoula MT 59802-4202. (406)721-9616. Fax: (406)721-9419. E-mail: cms@music.org. Website: www.music.org. Estab. 1959. Serves college, university and conservatory professors, as well as independent musicians. "It is dedicated to gathering, considering and disseminating ideas on the philosophy and practice of music as an integral part of higher education, and to developing and increasing communication among the various disciplines of music." Offers journal, newsletter, lectures, workshops, performance opportunities, job listing service, databases of organizations and institutions, music faculty and mailing lists. Applications accepted year-round. Membership fee: $65 (regular dues).

COLORADO MUSIC ASSOCIATION, 200 Logan St., Denver CO 80203-4028. (303)733-2106. E-mail: dolly@coloradomusic.org. Website: http://coloradomusic.org. **Contact:** Dolly Zander, president. Estab. 1999. Members are musicians of all ages and skill levels, songwriters, recording studios, music business merchants, teachers, performers, attorneys, agents, managers, publicists, promoters, venue owners and operators, and others connected to local music communities. Purpose is to support the local music community and encourage the development of skills, creativity and production. Offers instruction, lectures, workshops, performance and showcase opportunities, evaluation services, music directory, and free UPC (barcode) numbers for CD and other music products. Applications accepted year-round. Membership fee: $35/individual; $60/band; $115/business.
Tips: "We meet monthly in Denver and present speakers on topics of interest to the group. Our Internet site is being expanded to provide extensive educational features relative to the music biz.

COMPOSERS GUILD, 40 N. 100 West, P.O. Box 586, Farmington UT 84025-0586. (801)451-2275. **Contact:** Ruth Gatrell, president. Estab. 1963. Serves all ages, including children. Musical skill varies from beginners to professionals. An interest in composing is the only requirement. The purpose of this organization is to "help composers in every way possible through classes, workshops and symposiums, concerts, composition contests and association with others of similar interests." Offers competitions, instruction, lectures, newsletter, performance opportunities, evaluation services and workshops. Applications accepted year-round. Membership fee is $25/year. Associate memberships for child, spouse, parent, grandchild or grandparent of member: $15. "Holds four concerts/year. See our listing in the Contests & Awards section for details."

CONNECTICUT SONGWRITERS ASSOCIATION, 51 Hillcrest Ave., Watertown CT 06795. (860)945-1272. E-mail: paul4csa@aol.com. Website: www.ctsongs.com. **Contact:** Paul Chapin, president. Vice President: Ric Speck. "We are an educational, nonprofit organization dedicated to improving the art and craft of original music. Founded in 1979 by Don Donegan, CSA has grown to over 250 active members and has become one of the best known songwriters' associations in the country. Membership in the CSA admits you to 12-18 seminars/workshops/song critique sessions per year at 3 locations in Connecticut. Out of state members may mail in songs for free critique at our meetings. Noted professionals deal with all aspects of the craft and business of music including lyric writing, music theory, music technology, arrangement and production, legal and business aspects, performance techniques, song analysis and recording techniques. CSA offers 2-3 song screening sessions per year for members (songs which are voted on by the panel). Songs that 'pass' are then eligible for inclusion on the CSA sampler anthology cassette series. Seven 16-20 song tapes have been released so far and are for sale at local retail outlets and are given to speakers and prospective buyers. CSA also offers showcases and concerts which are open to the public and designed to give artists a venue for performing their original material for an attentive, listening audience. CSA benefits help local soup kitchens, group homes, hospice, world hunger, libraries, nature centers, community centers and more. CSA shows encompass ballads to bluegrass and Bach to rock. Our monthly newsletter, *Connecticut Songsmith*, offers free classified advertising for members, and has been edited and published by Bill Pere since 1980. Annual dues: $40; senior citizen and full time students $30; organizations $80. Memberships are tax-deductible as business expenses or as charitable contributions to the extent allowed by law."

☑ **COUNTRY MUSIC ASSOCIATION OF TEXAS**, P.O. Box 549, Troy TX 76579. (254)938-2454. Fax: (254)938-2049. **Contact:** Bud Fisher, founder/director. Estab. 1989. Open to songwriters, singers, pickers, fans and other professionals of all ages from all over the world. Members are interested in country music, especially traditional, classics. Purpose is to promote traditional and independent country music. Offers newsletter, workshops, performance opportunities and evaluation services. Applications accepted year-round. Membership fee: $23.95/year.
Tips: "Membership has grown to over 4,000 fans, musicians and songwriters, making it one of the largest state organizations in America. We hold numerous functions throughout the year and we have helped many local recording artists chart their releases nationwide and in Europe. Texas country music is hot!"

COUNTRY MUSIC SHOWCASE INTERNATIONAL, INC., P.O. Box 368, Carlisle IA 50047. (515)989-3748. Fax: (515)989-0235. E-mail: haroldl@cmshowcase.org. Website: www.cmshowcase.org. **Contact:** Harold L. Luick, president. "We are an online nonprofit website for public use, supported by donations, free will offerings, and operated, maintained entirely by volunteers. We can put you on the Internet with or without you having a computer, so you can advertise, sell, market, promote yourself or your product to Internet buyers and consumers. Ideal for songwriters, musicians, entertainers, bands and music publishers. A great way to do business with the Internet is through our Internet Provider Service. Other services offered are: song critique service, private individual music business consulting service, booking agency service, an Online Music Product Store to market your CD, tapes or product, directory and listings of bands, entertainers, available for hire through our agency, country music festivals, events, stageshows, contests and music activities in the Iowa/Midwest area. We are the #1 traditional, old-time, classic country and Cajun music website destination for search engines in the USA. A non-profit organization for those that believe in keeping country music and Cajun music art forms alive and well. For free brochure/information send a #10 SASE to the above address, e-mail, phone or Fax or visit our website.

☑ **DETROIT MUSIC ALLIANCE**, P.O. Box 24323, Detroit MI 48224. (313)886-7860. Fax: (313)886-7861. E-mail: dmaprez@hotmail.com. Website: www.detroitmusic.com/dma. **Contact:** Sue Summers, vice president. Estab. 1992. Ages 18-40. Members are bands, musicians, songwriters, poets, artists, managers, engineers and music fans. Purpose is to expose Detroit and indie talent, and to educate musicians just starting out as well as musicians who are already in the game. "We are open to helping performers out of state as well." Offers competitions, instruction, newsletter, lectures, library, workshops, performance opportunities, UPC codes, compilation series and evaluation services. Applications accepted year-round. Membership fee: $15/year for individual; $50/year for band.
Tips: "We are looking to network with other music alliances or like-minded organizations across the country."

MARKETS THAT WERE listed in the 2001 edition of *Songwriters Market* but do not appear this year are listed in the General Index with a notation explaining why they were omitted.

☑ **THE FIELD**, 161 Sixth Ave., New York NY 10013. (212)691-6969. Fax: (212)255-2053. E-mail: info@thefield.org. Website: www.thefield.org. **Contact:** Tymberly Canale, associate—career-based programs. Estab. 1986. "The Field gives independent performing artists the tools to develop and sustain their creative and professional lives, while allowing the public to have immediate, direct access to a remarkable range of contemporary artwork. The organization was started by eight emerging artists who shared common roots in contemporary dance and theater. Meeting regularly, these artists created a structure to help each other improve their artwork, and counter the isolation that often comes with the territory of an artistic career. The Field offers a comprehensive program structure similar to an urban artists' residency or graduate program. Participants select from a broad array of services focused in three basic areas: Art, Career and Exploration. These include: workshops and performance opportunities; management training and career development; fundraising consultations, fiscal sponsorship, and informational publications; and residencies. Our goal is to help artists develop their best artwork by deepening the artistic process and finding effective ways to bring that art into the marketplace. Most of our programs cost under $75, and tickets to our performance events average $8. In addition, since 1992, we have coordinated a network of satellite sites in Atlanta, Chicago, Dallas, Houston, Miami, Philadelphia, San Francisco, Seattle, Toronto, Washington D.C. and most recently, Japan. The Field is the only organization in New York that provides comprehensive programming for independent performing artists on a completely non-exclusive basis. This means our programs are open to artists from all disciplines, aesthetic viewpoints, and levels of development." Offers newsletter, workshops and performance opportunities. Applications accepted year-round. Membership fee: $75/year.

☑ **THE FOLK ALLIANCE (North American Folk Music and Dance Alliance)**, 1001 Connecticut Ave. NW, #501, Washington DC 20036. (202)835-3655. Fax: (202)835-3656. E-mail: fa@folk.org. Website: www.folk.org. **Contact:** Tony Ziselberger, programs and services. Executive Director: Phyllis Barney. Estab. 1989. Members are organizations and individuals involved in traditional and contemporary folk music and dance in the US and Canada (in any genre—blues, bluegrass, Celtic, Latino, old-time, singer/songwriter, etc.). The Folk Alliance hosts its annual conference (which includes performance showcases) in late February at different locations in the US and Canada. The conferences include workshops, panel discussions, the largest all folk exhibit hall and showcases. The Folk Alliance also serves members with their newsletter and through education, advocacy and field development. Memberships accepted year-round. Membership fee: $60/year for individual (voting); $140-495/year for organizational. Upcoming conference sites: 2001: Vancouver BC, Canada. 2002: Jacksonville, FL. "We *do not* offer songwriting contests. We are *not* a publisher—no demo tapes, please."

☒ **FORT BEND SONGWRITERS ASSOCIATION**, P.O. Box 1273, Richmond TX 77406. E-mail: mailroom@fbsa.org. Website: www.fbsa.org. President: Gary Taylor. Vice President: Monty West. Estab. 1991. Serves "any person, amateur or professional, interested in songwriting or music. Our members write pop, rock, country, rockabilly, gospel, R&B, children's music and musical plays." Open to all, regardless of geographic location or professional status. The FBSA provides its membership with help to perfect their songwriting crafts. The FBSA provides instruction for beginning writers and publishing and artist tips for the more accomplished writer. The FBSA networks with producers, publishers, music industry professionals and other songwriting groups to help members place songs. Offers competitions, field trips, instruction, lectures, newsletter, performance opportunities, workshops, mail-in critiques and collaboration opportunities. Applications accepted year-round. Membership fees are: Regular: $35; Renewals; $25; Family or Band: $45; Associate: $20; Business: $150; and Lifetime: $250. For more information send SASE.

☑ **FORT WORTH SONGWRITERS ASSOCIATION**, P.O. Box 162443, Fort Worth TX 76161. (817)654-5400. E-mail: info@fwsa.com. Website: www.fwsa.com. President: Bob Bryan. Vice President: Dennis Coble. Estab. 1992. Members are ages 18-75, beginners up to and including published writers. Interests cover gospel, country, western swing, rock, pop, bluegrass and blues. Purpose is to allow songwriters to become more proficient at songwriting; to provide an opportunity for their efforts to be performed before a live audience; to provide songwriters an opportunity to meet co-writers. "We provide our members free critiques of their efforts. We provide a monthly newsletter outlining current happenings in the business of songwriting. We offer competitions and mini workshops with guest speakers from the music industry. We promote a weekly open 'mic' for singers of original material. Our main contest is for Best Song of the Year which is selected by publishers and producers from Nashville. We also offer showcases and web pages for members." Applications accepted year-round. Membership fee: $25.

☑ **GEORGIA MUSIC INDUSTRY ASSOCIATION, INC.**, (formerly Atlanta Songwriters Association, Inc.), P.O. Box 550314, Atlanta GA 30355. (404)266-2666. Website: www.gmia.org. **Contact:** Loretta Peters, president. Estab. 1978. "Members are comprised of all ages from amateur to professionals seeking a career in the music industry." Sponsors songwriting critiques, open mic nights, Music Net studio field trips and seminars on marketing songs, music business, legal issues, recording tips, etc. Produces two annual songwriting competitions: "The Best of Country" Showcase (spring) and the Georgia Music Festival Songwriters Showcase competition (fall). Offers competitions, newsletter, lectures, workshops, performance opportunities and educational panels. Applications accepted year-round. Membership fee: $65/year.

☑ **GOSPEL MUSIC ASSOCIATION**, 1205 Division St., Nashville TN 37203. (615)242-0303. E-mail: joy@gospelmusic.org. Website: www.gospelmusic.org. **Contact:** Joy T. Fletcher, director of member development. Estab. 1964. Serves songwriters, musicians and anyone directly involved in or who supports gospel music. Professional members include advertising agencies, musicians, agents/managers, composers, retailers, music publishers, print and broadcast media, and other members of the recording industry. Associate members include supporters of gospel music and those whose involvement in the industry does not provide them with income. The primary purpose of the GMA is to promote the industry of gospel music, and provide professional development series for industry members. Offers library, newsletter, performance opportunities and workshops. Applications accepted year-round. Membership fee: $75/year (professional) and $50/year (associate).

GOSPEL/CHRISTIAN SONGWRITERS GROUP, 1518 Bennett St., Raleigh NC 27604. (919)834-1707. E-mail: dee.u@usa.net. Website: www.angelfire.com/music/ncgcsg. **Contact:** Deborah E. Ulmer, founder. Estab. 1999. GCSG welcomes all songwriters, lyricists, musicians, singers, poets, music expressionists and industry executives. Our members vary in all styles of Christian music. GCSG is open to all ages, from professional to Church to hobby; in any area of music and the industry. We invite anyone who is in the triangle area to attend our meetings and events. Those who are too far away may join GCSG On The Go, our chapter starting out of town membership. The main purpose of GCSG is to glorify God by ministering to people through music. We want everyone to be able to share their knowledge, learn and work with one another. Offers instruction, newsletter, lectures, workshops, performance opportunities, evaluation services and community events. Applications accepted year-round.

⊕ **THE GUILD OF INTERNATIONAL SONGWRITERS & COMPOSERS**, Sovereign House, 12 Trewartha Rd., Praa Sands, Penzance, Cornwall TR20 9ST England. Phone: (01736)762826. Fax: (01736)763328. E-mail: songmag@aol.com. Website: www.songwriters-guild.c om. **Contact:** C.A. Jones, secretary. Serves songwriters, musicians, record companies, music publishers, etc. "Our members are amateur and professional songwriters and composers, musicians, publishers, studio owners and producers. Membership is open to all persons throughout the world of any age and ability, from amateur to professional. The Guild gives advice and services relating to the music industry. A free magazine is available upon request with an SAE or 3 IRCs. We provide contact information for artists, record companies, music publishers, industry organizations; free copyright service; *Songwriting & Composing Magazine*; and many additional free services." Applications accepted year-round. Annual dues: £38 in the U.K.; £50 in E.E.C. countries; £50 overseas (subscriptions in pounds sterling only).

⊕ **INTERNATIONAL SONGWRITERS ASSOCIATION LTD.**, 37b New Cavendish St., London WI England. (0171)486-5353. E-mail: jliddane@songwriter.iol.ie. Website: www.songwriter.

co.uk. **Contact:** Anna M. Sinden, membership department. Serves songwriters and music publishers. "The ISA headquarters is in Limerick City, Ireland, and from there it provides its members with assessment services, copyright services, legal and other advisory services and an investigations service, plus a magazine for one yearly fee. Our members are songwriters in more than 50 countries worldwide, of all ages. There are no qualifications, but applicants under 18 are not accepted. We provide information and assistance to professional or semi-professional songwriters. Our publication, *Songwriter*, which was founded in 1967, features detailed exclusive interviews with songwriters and music publishers, as well as directory information of value to writers." Offers competitions, instruction, library, newsletter and a weekly e-mail newsletter *Songwriter Newswire*. Applications accepted year-round. Membership fee for European writers is £19.95; for non-European writers, US $30.

N INTERNATIONAL SONGWRITERS GUILD, 108 Louvre Ave., Orlando FL 32812. (407)851-5328. E-mail: l_s_g_2000@yahoo.com. **Contact:** Russ Robinson, president. Estab. 1977.
- Russ Robinson, President of the Guild, played piano for Judy Garland and Frank Sinatra, among others, and was a member of "The Modernairs" (five-part harmony vocals). He is a writer of national commercials, and is well-known in the music and film industry.

Members are lyricists, composers, performers, arrangers, publishers, songwriters of all ages, backgrounds and skill levels. Open to anyone interested in songwriting and in improving their songwriting skills. The main purpose of the organization is to guide and educate those people wanting to write commercial music successfully. We use monthly critiquing sessions of approximately 10 songs, where the top 5 winners are announced in the next monthly newsletter, "Guild Tidings." Offers competitions, lectures, performance opportunities, instruction, evaluation services, newsletters, workshops and industry contacts. Applications accepted year-round. Membership fee: $35 annually.

N JUST PLAIN FOLKS MUSIC ORGANIZATION (www.jpfolks.com), 1315 N. Butler, Indianapolis IN 46219. (317)513-6557. E-mail: JPFolksPro@aol.com. Website: www.jpfolks.com. **Contact:** Jill Sansores (JustPlainJill@aol.com), membership director. Estab. 1998. "We are among the world's largest Music Industry Support and Networking Organization. Our members cover nearly every musical style and professional field, from songwriters, artists, publishers, producers, record labels, entertainment attorneys, publicists and PR experts, performing rights organization staffers, live and recording engineers, educators, music students, musical instrument manufacturers, TV, Radio and Print Media and almost every major Internet Music entity. Representing all 50 US States and over 50 countries worldwide, we have members of all ages, musical styles and levels of success, including winners and nominees of every major music industry award, as well as those just starting out. A complete demographics listing of our group is available on our website. Whether you are a #1 hit songwriter or artist, or the newest kid on the block, you are welcome to join. We're all in this together!" The purpose of this organization is "to share wisdom, ideas and experiences with others who have been there, and to help educate those who have yet to make the journey. Just Plain Folks provides its members with a friendly networking and support community that uses the power of the Internet and combines it with good old-fashioned human interaction. We help promote our members ready for success and educate those still learning." Offers special programs to members, including:
- *Just Plain Notes Newsletter:* Members receive our tri-monthly e-mail newsletter full of expert info on how to succeed in the music business, profiles of members successes and advice, opportunities to develop your career and tons of first-person networking contacts to help you along the way.
- *Just Plain Mentors:* We are in the process of launching real-life chapters worldwide. Some of our Chapter Cities include: Nashville, New York, Los Angeles, Twin Cities, Philadelphia, Atlanta, Seattle, Indianapolis, Chicago, Austin, Boston, Baltimore, Providence, Oklahoma City, Cleveland, as well as International Chapters launching in the United Kingdom, Canada, Australia, Europe and South America. Check our website for current locations nearest you!
- *JPFolks.com Website:* Our home page serves as your pathway to the resources and members of the group worldwide. With message boards, lyric feedback forums, featured members music, member profiles, member contact listings, member links pages, chapter homepages, demographics information, our Internet radio station and all the back issues of our newsletter, "Just Plain Notes."

● *Roadtrips:* We regularly tour the US and Canada, hosting showcases, workshops and friendly member gatherings in each city we visit. We provide opportunities for all our members, at all levels and welcome everyone to our events. Most events are free of charge.

● *Music Awards:* Just Plain Folks has one of the largest and most diverse Member Music Awards programs in the world. The most recent awards involved over 2,500 CDs and 30,000 songs in over 30 genres. Music Award nominees and winners receive featured performance slots at showcases around the world throughout the year. Current submission instructions can be found on the website.

Applications accepted year-round. "To become a member, simply send an e-mail to JPNotes@aol.com with the words 'I Want To Join Just Plain Folks.' In the e-mail, include your name, address, website (if applicable) and phone number for our files." There are currently no membership fees.
Tips: "Our motto is 'We're All In This Together!'"

THE LAS VEGAS SONGWRITERS ASSOCIATION, P.O. Box 42683, Las Vegas NV 89116-0683. (702)223-7255. **Contact:** Betty Kay Miller, president. Secretary: Barbara Jean Smith. Estab. 1980. "We are an educational, nonprofit organization dedicated to improving the art and craft of the songwriter. We want members who are serious about their craft. We want our members to respect their craft and to treat it as a business. Members must be at least 18 years of age. We offer quarterly newsletters, monthly information meetings, workshops three times a month and quarterly seminars with professionals in the music business. We provide support and encouragement to both new and more experienced songwriters. We critique each song or lyric that's presented during workshops, we make suggestions on changes—if needed. We help turn amateur writers into professionals. Several of our songwriters have had their songs recorded on both independent and major labels." Dues: $30/year.

☑ LOS ANGELES MUSIC NETWORK, P.O. Box 8934, Universal City CA 91618-8934. (818)769-6095. E-mail: info@lamn.com. Website: www.lamn.com. **Contact:** Che Wang, membership coordinator. Estab. 1988. "Ours is an association of music industry professionals, i.e., people who work at music companies, in publishing, management, entertainment law, etc. Members are ambitious and interested in advancing their careers. LAMN is an association created to promote career advancement, communication and continuing education among music industry professionals and top executives. LAMN sponsors industry events and educational panels held bi-monthly at venues in the Hollywood area." Offers instruction, newsletter, lectures, seminars, music industry job listings, career counseling, résumé publishing, mentor network, résumé resource guide and many professional networking opportunities. See our website for current job listings and a calendar of upcoming events. Applications accepted year-round. Membership fee is $95 (subject to change without notice).

☑ LOUISIANA SONGWRITERS ASSOCIATION, P.O. Box 80425, Baton Rouge LA 70898-0425. (504)443-5390. E-mail: zimshah@aol.com. Website: www.lasongwriters.org. **Contact:** Connie Zimmerman, membership coordinator. Serves songwriters. "LSA was organized to educate songwriters in all areas of their trade, and promote the art of songwriting in Louisiana. LSA is honored to have a growing number of songwriters from other states join LSA and fellowship with us. LSA membership is open to people interested in songwriting, regardless of age, musical ability, musical preference, ethnic background, etc. "This year marks our 20th anniversary and also a new direction for our organization. Our group is now driven by special projects (short term), which are coordinated and implemented by our membership. This arms our members with the knowledge and experience necessary to succeed within the industry." LSA offers competitions, lectures, library, newsletter, directory, marketing, performance opportunities, workshops, discounts on various music-related books and magazines, discounts on studio time, and we are developing a service manual that will contain information on music related topics, such as copyrighting, licensing, etc." Also offers regular showcases in Baton Rouge and New Orleans. General membership dues: $25/year, 45/2 years.

☑ ☑ MANITOBA AUDIO RECORDING INDUSTRY ASSOCIATION (MARIA), 407-100 Arthur St., Winnipeg, Manitoba R3B 1H3 Canada. (204)942-8650. Fax: (204)942-1555. E-mail: info@manaudio.mb.ca. Website: www.manaudio.mb.ca. **Contact:** Hal Brolund, member services/

office coordinator. Estab. 1987. Organization consists of "songwriters, producers, agents, musicians, managers, retailers, publicists, radio, talent buyers, media, record labels, etc. (no age limit, no skill level minimum). Must have interest in the future of Manitoba's sound recording industry." The main purpose of MARIA is to foster growth in all areas of the Manitoba music industry primarily through education, promotion and lobbying. Offers newsletter, lectures, directory of Manitoba's music industry, workshops and performance opportunities; also presents demo critiquing sessions and comprehensive member discount program featuring a host of participating Manitoba businesses. MARIA is also involved with the Prairie Music Weekend festival, conference and awards show. Applications accepted year-round. Membership fee: $50 (Canadian funds).

✅ **MEET THE COMPOSER**, 2112 Broadway, Suite 505, New York NY 10023. (212)787-3601. Fax: (212)787-3745. E-mail: mtrevino@meetthecomposer.org. Website: www.meetthecomposer.org. Estab. 1974. "Meet The Composer serves composers working in all styles of music, at every career stage, through a variety of grant programs and information resources. A nonprofit organization, Meet The Composer raises money from foundations, corporations, individual patrons and government sources and designs programs that support all genres of music—from folk, ethnic, jazz, electronic, symphonic, and chamber to choral, music theater, opera and dance. Meet The Composer awards grants for composer fees to non-profit organizations that perform, present, or commission original works. This is not a membership organization; all composers are eligible for support. Meet The Composer was founded in 1974 to increase artistic and financial opportunities for composers by fostering the creation, performance, dissemination, and appreciation of their music." Offers grant programs and information services. Deadlines vary for each grant program.

✅ **MEMPHIS SONGWRITERS' ASSOCIATION**, 4500 Summer Ave., Suite #110, Memphis TN 38122. (901)683-5044. Fax: (901)818-9507. E-mail: importer@memphissongwriters.com. Website: www.memphissongwriters.com. **Contact:** Michael Porter, president. Estab. 1973. "MSA is a nonprofit songwriters organization serving songwriters nationally. Our mission is to dedicate our services on a monthly basis to promote, advance, and help songwriters in the composition of music, lyrics and songs; to work for better conditions in our profession; and to secure and protect the rights of MSA songwriters. We offer a correspondence course for all members outside of Memphis. MSA provides a monthly Basic Lyric Writing Course for beginners with a focus on commercial songwriting. We also supply copyright forms, pitch sheets and a collaborator's guide. We offer critique sessions for advanced writers at our monthly meetings. We also have monthly jam sessions to encourage creativity, networking and co-writing. We host an annual songwriter's seminar and an annual songwriter's showcase, as well as a bi-monthly guest speaker series, which provide education, competition and entertainment for the songwriter. In addition, our members receive a bimonthly newsletter to keep them informed of MSA activities, demo services and opportunities in the songwriting field." Annual fee: $35.

MINNESOTA ASSOCIATION OF SONGWRITERS, P.O. Box 581816, Minneapolis MN 55458. (612)649-4636. E-mail: mas@mndir.com. Website: www.isc.net/mas. "Includes a wide variety of members, ranging in age from 18 to 60; types of music are very diverse ranging from alternative rock to contemporary Christian; skill levels range from newcomers to songwriting to writers with published material and songs on CDs in various parts of the country. Main requirement is an interest in songwriting—although most members come from the Minneapolis-St. Paul area, others come in from surrounding cities and nearby Wisconsin. Some members are fulltime musicians, but most represent a wide variety of occupations. MAS is a nonprofit community of songwriters which informs, educates, inspires and assists its members in the art and business of songwriting." Offers instruction, newsletter, lectures, workshops, performance opportunities, evaluation, services and MAS compilation CDs. Applications accepted year-round. Membership fee: $25.

FOR BOOKS ON THE CRAFT AND BUSINESS of songwriting, check out the website for Writer's Digest Books at www.writersdigest.com.

Tips: "Members are kept current on resources and opportunities. Original works are played at meetings and are critiqued by involved members. Through this process, writers hone their skills and gain experience and confidence in submitting their works to others. Members vote to endorse the songs critiqued at meetings."

MISSOURI SONGWRITERS ASSOCIATION, INC., 693 Green Forest Dr., Fenton MO 63026. Phone/fax: (636)343-4765. **Contact:** John G. Nolan, Jr., president. Serves songwriters and musicians. No eligibility requirements. "The MSA (a non-profit organization founded in 1979) is a tremendously valuable resource for songwriting and music business information outside of the major music capitals. Only with the emphasis on education can the understanding of craft and the utilization of skill be fully realized and in turn become the foundation for the ultimate success of MSA members. Songwriters gain support from their fellow members when they join the MSA, and the organization provides 'strength in numbers' when approaching music industry professionals. As a means toward its goals the organization offers: (1) an extremely informative newsletter; (2) Songwriting Contest; prizes include CD and/or cassette release of winners, publishing contract, free musical merchandise and equipment, free recording studio time, plaque or certificate; (3) St. Louis Original Music Celebration featuring live performances, recognition, showcase, radio simulcast, videotape for later broadcast and awards presentation; (4) seminars on such diverse topics as creativity, copyright law, brainstorming, publishing, recording the demo, craft and technique, songwriting business, collaborating, etc.; (5) workshops including song evaluation, establishing a relationship with publishers, hit song evaluations, the writer versus the writer/artist, the marriage of collaborators, the business side of songwriting, lyric craft, etc.; (6) services such as collaborators referral, publisher contracts, consultation, recording discounts, musicians referral, library, etc. The Missouri Songwriters Association belongs to its members and what a member puts into the organization is returned dynamically in terms of information, education, recognition, support, camaraderie, contacts, tips, confidence, career development, friendships and professional growth." Due to various circumstances, some functions or services occasionally may not be active or available. Applications accepted year-round. Tax deductible dues: $30/year.

MUSICIANS CONTACT, P.O. Box 788, Woodland Hills CA 91365. (818)888-7879. Fax: (818)227-5919. E-mail: muscontact@aol.com. Website: www.musicianscontact.com. **Contact:** Sterling, president. Estab. 1969. "The primary source of paying jobs for musicians and vocalists nationwide. Job opportunities arrive by phone and e-mail and are posted daily on the Internet and a 24 hour hotline. Also offers exposure to the music industry for solo artists and complete acts seeking representation."

NASHVILLE SONGWRITERS ASSOCIATION INTERNATIONAL (NSAI), 1701 W. End Ave., 3rd Floor, Nashville TN 37203. (615)256-3354 or (800)321-6008. Fax: (615)256-0034. E-mail: nsai@nashvillesongwriters.com. Website: www.nashvillesongwriters.com. Executive Director: Barton Herbison.
- See the Insider Report in this section with NSAI-Dayton Special Events Coordinator Mick McEvilley.
NSAI is a not-for-profit service organization for both aspiring and professional songwriters in all fields of music. Membership: Spans the United States and several foreign countries. Songwriters may apply in one of four annual categories: Active ($100—for songwriters who have at least one song contractually signed to a publisher affiliated with ASCAP, BMI or SESAC); Associate ($100—for songwriters who are not yet published or for anyone wishing to support songwriters); Student ($80—for full-time college students or for students of an accredited senior high school); Professional ($100—for songwriters who derive their primary source of income from songwriting or who are generally recognized as such by the professional songwriting community); Foreign ($75—for Active, Associate, and Student members residing outside the US). Membership benefits: music industry information and advice, song evaluations by mail, quarterly newsletter, access to industry professionals through weekly Nashville workshop and several annual events, regional workshops, use of office facilities, discounts on books and discounts on NSAI's three annual events. There are also "branch" workshops of NSAI. Workshops must meet certain standards and are accountable to NSAI. Interested coordinators may apply to NSAI.

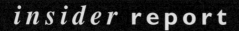

insider report

Songwriter's craft grows along with songwriting organization

Mick McEvilley's journey into songwriting began as a child. "When I was a little kid I had a plastic guitar with plastic strings and I had a few ukuleles, but I finally got my folks to buy me a real guitar in the seventh grade. Within two years, by the time I was fourteen, I had written a love song to my girlfriend." During college, McEvilley wrote and sang in a folk group but "didn't really get anywhere." After college, marriage (to that girlfriend to whom he wrote the love song as a teenager), children and a job limited his musical involvement to " 'Puff the Magic Dragon' about once a month and then putting the guitar away." Then, his neighbor started a recording stu-

Mick McEvilley

dio in his basement and re-awakened McEvilley's songwriting desires. They began playing together. Some years later McEvilley convinced that friend to go guitar-shopping in Nashville, and it was there he realized what he really wanted to do: "I thought I'd died and went to heaven listening to these songwriters at the Bluebird Café play their songs and sing. I decided I absolutely had to get back to songwriting."

McEvilley heard about the Nashville Songwriters Association International (NSAI) and sent for information. He joined and immediately began going to the regional workshops, which offered lessons about the business and craft of songwriting as well as group critiquing of members' songs. After about a year in the group, McEvilley agreed to a leadership position as the special events director for the Dayton/Cincinnati area chapter of NSAI. In this role, McEvilley has been trained and continues to learn both business and craft matters in order to help his fellow songwriters. He shares here some of his thoughts on the benefits of belonging to a songwriters association like NSAI:

What is the mission statement that defines what NSAI is trying to do?
NSAI is an organization for songwriters of all genres of music. It is not just for the aspiring songwriter, but also for the professional songwriter. We want to defend the rights and the future of songwriting and assist songwriters in the craft and business of songwriting. We have lobbied and put up a fight on things like copyright laws to protect the royalties of the songwriter.

What sort of services does NSAI provide?

In addition to the workshops, NSAI has an annual symposium. This is a two-day event where songwriters can go to Nashville and spend time with publishers and managers and have their songs heard and critiqued. One of the most important things they provide is a mail-in critiquing service. A songwriter can put his song on a cassette, send it in, and a professional songwriter will, within three weeks, send a detailed critique of the song back. If the professional songwriter thinks it is good enough, the song can be played at a publishers' night, where it is exposed to the publishers in Nashville. There is almost no other way to get that done from a distance. So while the regional workshops provide a critique from friends and fellow songwriters, you also have a professional songwriter from Nashville as part of the service at any time. That, of course, is very valuable. NSAI also has a full bookshop containing a library of songwriters' books and resources, as well as maps and information about the publishers and music-related companies in Nashville.

How can NSAI help a beginner or someone getting serious about songwriting?

The workshop itself is a tremendous help in getting feedback from other aspiring songwriters. Of course, it's good to get feedback from anybody, but these are people who are very concerned about the craft of songwriting. Some of the suggestions can border on what might be perceived as insulting, and yet you may walk out of the workshop realizing what that person said was correct. You cannot help but write a better song when you have the feedback of friends, other songwriters and people who are concerned about the same things you are.

The music industry is one that attracts many unethical business operators. What difference can a songwriters' association like NSAI make for a beginner in terms of knowing potential traps to avoid?

This is one of the best advantages of membership in a group like NSAI. A common trap for beginners is paying to have their songs published. Anybody who is in NSAI will tell you that there are certain things you never, never pay for. If you are asked to pay to have your songs recorded, then you are not dealing with the kind of people you should be dealing with. NSAI, in addition to the regular workshops, always includes a lesson. Sometimes it is on the craft of songwriting and sometimes it is on the business of songwriting, with information such as this.

What are some of the regional services NSAI offers?

We have been fortunate in our workshops to have people with varying degrees of contacts and experience with Nashville. Just being with people who can answer your questions is helpful, because when you don't know the answers, there are no dumb questions. We also bring in professional songwriters for daylong seminars and concerts. Another service is a regular showcase every other month where our members present their music to the public.

What can a songwriter learn from playing their songs in a live performance?
The first thing you learn is that you probably haven't practiced enough. But it is a tremendous thing to do, because the response you get is going to be one of the greatest sources of information you'll ever have about how well you've done in writing your song. Practicing and becoming a better player can't help but make you a better writer, because the more you play, the more you learn, and the better musician you become. And of course, when the crowd laughs at something you intended to be funny, that's very inspiring.

Have the workshops continued to be helpful to you over the longer term?
Yes, they have. As much as you rewrite over and over again, you always find places where exceptions to the rules work. The continual feedback from your fellow songwriters is invaluable. For example, when I take a song to a workshop, I may not like a phrase or a few words in the song, but I may think, "Well, that's as good as I can get it." When someone else tells me it's no good, then I know my instincts are right, and I have to change it. Or someone will give some terrific hint or clue as to the way he would change it. Writer's block is an ongoing problem, so it's always helpful to go to the workshops and get feedback. The main thing is honesty, because the person who is really interested in advancing his craft will be very impatient with comments like, "Hey, really great song!" Substance—honest feedback—is why we are there.

What environment does Nashville provide that a regional workshop cannot?
I think if a person really wants to be a commercial songwriter and can do it, he or she ought to move to Nashville. They don't call it Music City for nothing. There is music in the air there; there is a community that is songwriter-friendly. You cannot beat the inspiration of being in that atmosphere with all that talent around. It is not just the talent though; it is also the business connections. Often, as coordinator, I get calls from somebody who says, "I understand you are with NSAI. I've got this great song; everybody who hears it says it's going to be a hit. I've just got to get it to the right people." What those people don't understand is that getting it to the right people is only part of the whole process. You have to be in Nashville knocking on doors. *Songwriter's Market* is great for finding who accepts new material, but a lot of songwriting is about making friends and making connections, and Nashville is just where the connections are.

Is there any further advice that you have for aspiring songwriters?
Many of the people who have called to find out about NSAI were referred by other songwriters or businesses in Nashville. I guess the bottom line is that there just isn't any other organization as beneficial to songwriters as this one. I would say, write regularly, practice your musical instrument, and join NSAI.
    —*Amanda Tebbe*

☑ NASHVILLE SONGWRITERS ASSOCIATION INTERNATIONAL-DETROIT, (formerly Michigan Songwriters Association), P.O. Box 26044, Fraser MI 48026. (810)498-7673. Fax: (810)498-8636. E-mail: senecal@earthlink.net. Website: www.homestead.com/nsaidetroit. **Contact:** Terri Senecal, coordinator. Estab. 1967. Serves songwriters, musicians, artists and beginners. "Members are from Detroit with interests in country, pop, rock and R&B. The main purpose of this organization is to educate songwriters, artists and musicians in the business of songwriting." NSAI offers song critique services, instruction, monthly newsletter and 12 meetings/year. Applications accepted year-round. Membership fee: $100/year.

NATIONAL ACADEMY OF POPULAR MUSIC (NAPM), 330 W. 58th St., Suite 411, New York NY 10019-1827. (212)957-9230. Fax: (212)957-9227. E-mail: 73751.1142@compuserve.com. Website: www.songwritershalloffame.org. **Contact:** Bob Leone, projects director. Managing Director: April Anderson. Estab. 1969. "The majority of our members are songwriters, but also on NAPM's rolls are music publishers, producers, record company executives, music attorneys, and lovers of popular music of all ages. Professional members are affiliated with ASCAP, BMI and/or SESAC; or are employed by music industry firms. Associate membership, however, merely requires a completed application and $25 dues. NAPM was formed to determine a variety of ways to celebrate the songwriter (e.g., induction into the Songwriters' Hall of Fame). We also provide educational and networking opportunities to our members through our workshop and showcase programs." Offers newsletter, workshops, performance opportunities, monthly networking meetings with industry pros and scholarships for excellence in songwriting. Applications accepted year-round. Membership fee: $25.
Tips: "Our priority at this time is to locate a site for the re-establishment of the Songwriters' Hall of Fame Museum in New York City."

NATIONAL ACADEMY OF SONGWRITERS (NAS). E-mail: nassong@aol.com. Website: www.nassong.org.
   ● The National Academy of Songwriters and Songwriters Guild of America have merged. National Academy of Songwriter's no longer exists as an organization. Also see the Songwriters Guild of America listing in this section.

THE NATIONAL ASSOCIATION OF COMPOSERS/USA (NACUSA), P.O. Box 49256, Barrington Station, Los Angeles CA 90049. (310)541-8213. President: Marshall Bialosky. Estab. 1932. Serves songwriters, musicians and classical composers. "We are of most value to the concert hall composer. Members are serious music composers of all ages and from all parts of the country, who have a real interest in composing, performing, and listening to modern concert hall music. The main purpose of our organization is to perform, publish, broadcast and write news about composers of serious concert hall music—mostly chamber and solo pieces. Composers may achieve national notice of their work through our newsletter and concerts, and the fairly rare feeling of supporting a non-commercial music enterprise dedicated to raising the musical and social position of the serious composer." Offers competitions, lectures, performance opportunities, library and newsletter. Applications accepted year-round. Membership fee: $20; $40 for Los Angeles, San Francisco, Philadelphia, Tidewater VA, Baton Rouge and New York chapter members.
Tips: "99% of the money earned in music is earned, or so it seems, by popular songwriters who might feel they owe the art of music something, and this is one way they might help support that art. It's a chance to foster fraternal solidarity with their less prosperous, but wonderfully interesting classical colleagues at a time when the very existence of serious art seems to be questioned by the general populace."

☑ NATIONAL SOCIETY OF MEN AND WOMEN OF THE MUSIC BUSINESS (WOMB), P.O. Box 5170, Beverly Hills CA 90209-5170. (323)464-4300. Fax: (323)467-8468. E-mail: wombaccess@aol.com. Website: www.YuleJam.org. **Contact:** Director. Estab. 1996. "WOMB is a non-profit organization of top music industry professionals keeping music education and dreams alive for kids who attend inner-city high schools and community organizations around the U.S. Music industry professionals are encouraged to participate and make a difference in a child's life!" Programs include "WOMB's School Music Network": top music industry professionals volunteer 2-3 hours to visit inner-city high schools; "WOMB's Music for Music": organizes music instrument and material donation drives for schools through corporate sponsorships and events; Yule Jam, a charity concert and music instrument drive with proceeds going to local school music departments. Offers corporate sponsorships, events, performance opportunities and an e-mail newsletter. Future programs include afterschool music programs, college scholarships and special events. Volunteers, music instrument, material donations and corporate sponsorships accepted year-round.

NORTH FLORIDA CHRISTIAN MUSIC WRITERS ASSOCIATION, P.O. Box 61113, Jacksonville FL 32236. (904)786-2372. E-mail: justsongs@aol.com. Website: www.christiansongwriter.com. **Contact:** Jackie Hand, president. Estab. 1974. "Members are people from all walks of life who promote Christian music—not just composers or performers, but anyone who wants to share today's message in song with the world. No age limit. Anyone interested in promoting Christian music is invited to join. If you are talented in several areas you might be asked to conduct a training session or workshop. Your expertise is wanted and needed by our group. The group's purpose is to serve God by using our God-given talents and abilities and to assist our fellow songwriters, getting their music in the best possible form to be ready for whatever door God chooses to open for them concerning their music. Members' works are included in songbooks published by our organization— also biographies." Offers competitions, performance opportunities, field trips, instruction, newsletter, workshops and critiques. This year we offer a new website featuring song clips by members as well as a short bio. Also featured is a special "Memorial Members" list honoring deceased members by keeping their music alive. The one time fee of $100 to place loved ones on the list includes a song clip on our website and entry privileges in our songwriting contest. Applications accepted year-round. Membership fee: $15/year ($20 for outside US), $20 for husband/wife team ($25 for outside US). Make checks payable to Jackie Hand.
Tips: "If you are serious about your craft, you need fellowship with others who feel the same. A Christian songwriting organization is where you belong if you write Christian songs."

NORTHERN CALIFORNIA SONGWRITERS ASSOCIATION, 1724 Laurel St., Suite 120, San Carlos CA 94070. (650)654-3966. Fax: (650)654-2156, or (800)FORSONG (California and Nashville only). E-mail: info@ncsasong.org. Website: www.ncsasong.org. **Contact:** Ian Crombie, executive director. Serves songwriters and musicians. Estab. 1979. "Our 1,200 members are lyricists and composers from ages 16-80, from beginners to professional songwriters. No eligibility requirements. Our purpose is to provide the education and opportunities that will support our writers in creating and marketing outstanding songs. NCSA provides support and direction through local networking and input from Los Angeles and Nashville music industry leaders, as well as valuable marketing opportunities. Most songwriters need some form of collaboration, and by being a member they are exposed to other writers, ideas, critiquing, etc." Offers annual Northern California Songwriting Conference, "the largest event in northern California. This 2-day event held in September features 16 seminars, 50 screening sessions (over 1,200 songs listened to by industry profesionals) and a sunset concert with hit songwriters performing their songs." Also offers monthly visits from major publishers, songwriting classes, competitions, seminars conducted by hit songwriters ("we sell audio tapes of our seminars—list of tapes available on request"), mail-in song-screening service for members who cannot attend due to time or location, a monthly newsletter, monthly performance opportunities and workshops. Applications accepted year-round. Dues: $40/year, student; $75/year, regular membership; $150/year, pro-membership; $250/year, contributing membership.
Tips: "NCSA's functions draw local talent and nationally recognized names together. This is of a tremendous value to writers outside a major music center. We are developing a strong songwriting community in Northern California. We serve the San Jose, Monterey Bay, East Bay, San Francisco and Sacramento areas and we have the support of some outstanding writers and publishers from both Los Angeles and Nashville. They provide us with invaluable direction and inspiration."

SENDING TO A COUNTRY other than your own? Be sure to send International Reply Coupons (IRCs) instead of stamps for replies or return of your materials.

☒ OKLAHOMA SONGWRITERS & COMPOSERS ASSOCIATION, 509 S. Linwood, Cordell OK 73632. E-mail: arf-n-annie@hotmail.com. Website: www.oksongwriters.com. President: G. Colson. Treasurer: Ann Wilson. Estab. 1983. Serves songwriters, musicians, professional writers, amateur writers, college and university faculty, musicians, poets and others. "A nonprofit, all-volunteer organization sponsored by Rose State College providing educational and networking opportunities for songwriters, lyricists, composers and performing musicians. All styles of music. We sponsor major workshops, open-mic nights, demo critiques and the *OSCA News*. Throughout the year we sponsor contests and original music showcases." Applications accepted year-round. Membership fee: $25 for new members, $15 for renewal, $15 for out of state newsletter only.

☑ OPERA AMERICA, 1156 15th St., NW, Suite 810, Washington DC 20005-1704. (202)293-4466. Fax: (202)393-0735. E-mail: frontdesk@operaam.org. Website: www.operaam.org. Membership Services Manager: Ronnie Levine. Membership Services Assistant: Andrew Mariotti. Estab. 1970. Members are composers, librettists, musicians and opera/music theater producers. "OPERA America maintains an extensive library of reference books and domestic and foreign music periodicals, and the most comprehensive operatic archive in the United States. OPERA America draws on these unique resources to supply information to its members." Offers conferences. Publishes online database of opera/music theater companies in the US and Canada. Publishes directory of opera and musical performances world-wide and US. Publishes a directory of new works created and being developed by current-day composers and librettists, to encourage the performance of new works. Applications accepted year-round. Publishes 40-page news bulletin 10 times/year. Membership fee is on a sliding scale.

☒ OUTMUSIC, % The Center, P.O. Box 1422, Old Chelsea Station, New York NY 10113-1422. (212)330-9197. E-mail: info@outmusic.com. Website: www.outmusic.com. Artistic Director: Deian McBryde. Estab. 1990. "OUTMUSIC is comprised of gay men and lesbians. They represent all different musical styles from rock to classical. Many are writers of original material. We are open to all levels of accomplishment—professional, amateur, and interested industry people. The only requirement for membership is an interest in the growth and visibility of music and lyrics created by the gay and lesbian community. We supply our members with support and networking opportunities. In addition, we help to encourage artists to bring their work 'OUT' into the world." Offers newsletter, lectures, workshops, performance opportunities, networking, industry leads and monthly open mics. Sponsors Outmusic Awards. Applications accepted year-round. For membership information go to www.outmusic.com.
Tips: "OUTMUSIC has spawned The Gay Music Guide, The Gay and Lesbian American Music Awards (GLAMA), several compilation albums and many independent recording projects."

OZARK NOTEWORTHY SONGWRITERS ASSOCIATION, INC., 2303 S. Luster, Springfield MO 65804. (417)883-3385. President: Betty Hickory. Vice President: Mary Hickory. Estab. 1992. Purpose is to help songwriters find co-writers, give them updated tip sheets, keep writers updated about what is selling in the music world and explain the copyright law." Offers instruction, newsletter, workshops and performance opportunities. Applications accepted year-round. Membership fee: $30/year. Meets monthly.

☒ PACIFIC MUSIC INDUSTRY ASSOCIATION. (604)873-1914. E-mail: info@pmia.org. Website: www.pmia.org. Estab. 1990. Serves "mostly young adults and up from semi-pro to professional. Writers, composers, performers, publishers, engineers, producers, broadcasters, studios, retailers, manufacturers, managers, publicists, entertainment lawyers and accountants, etc. Must work in some area of music industry." The main purpose of this organization is "to promote B.C. music and music industry; stimulate activity in B.C. industry; promote communication and address key issues." Offers competitions, newsletters, ongoing professional development and directory for the BC music industry. Applications accepted year-round. Membership fee: $50 Canadian (plus 7% GST).

PACIFIC NORTHWEST SONGWRITERS ASSOCIATION, P.O. Box 98564, Seattle WA 98198. (206)824-1568. E-mail: pnsapals@hotmail.com. "PNSA is a nonprofit organization, serving the songwriters of the Puget Sound area since 1977. Members have had songs recorded by national artists on singles, albums, videos and network television specials. Several have released their own albums and the group has done an album together. For only $45 per year, PNSA offers monthly workshops, a quarterly newsletter and direct contact with national artists, publishers, producers and record companies. New members are welcome and good times are guaranteed. And remember, the world always needs another great song!"

THE PHILADELPHIA SONGWRITERS FORUM, 4944 Bingham St., Philadelphia PA 19120. (215)685-0592. *Presently inactive.* **Contact:** Jim Robb, coordinator. Estab. 1986. Membership consists of all ages and levels; an interest in songwriting is the common bond. The main purpose of this organization is to provide information sharing, networking and support for songwriters and lyricists in the Philadelphia area. Offers instruction, newsletter, lectures, workshops, monthly meetings with guest speakers and performance opportunities. "No application necessary. However, we do have a card for you to fill out with basic information such as address, full name and phone number." Membership fee: $10/year.

PITTSBURGH SONGWRITERS ASSOCIATION, 523 Scenery Dr., Elizabeth PA 15037. E-mail: psa@trfn.clpgh.org. Website: trfn.clpgh.org/psa. **Contact:** Van Stragand, president. Estab. 1983. "We are a non-profit organization dedicated to helping its members develop and market their songs. Writers of any age and experience level welcome. Current members are from 20s to 50s. All musical styles and interests are welcome. Our organization wants to serve as a source of quality material for publishers and other industry professionals. We assist members in developing their songs and their professional approach. We provide meetings, showcases, collaboration opportunities, instruction, industry guests, library and social outings. Annual dues: $25. We have no initiation fee. Prospective members are invited to attend two free meetings. Interested parties please call Van Stragand at (412)751-9584."

N POP RECORD RESEARCH, 10 Glen Ave., Norwalk CT 06850. Director: Gary Theroux. Estab. 1962. Serves songwriters, musicians, writers, researchers and media. "We maintain archives of materials relating to music, TV and film, with special emphasis on recorded music (the hits and hitmakers 1877-present): bios, photos, reviews, interviews, discographies, chart data, clippings, films, videos, etc." Offers library and clearinghouse for accurate promotion/publicity to biographers, writers, reviewers, the media. Offers programming, annotation and photo source for reissues or retrospective album collections on any artist (singers, songwriters, musicians, etc.), also music consultation services for film or television projects. "There is no charge to include publicity, promotional or biographical materials in our archives. Artists, writers, composers, performers, producers, labels and publicists are always invited to add or keep us on their publicity/promotion mailing list with career data, updates, new releases and reissues of recorded performances, etc. Fees are assessed only for reference use by researchers, writers, biographers, reviewers, etc. Songwriters and composers (or their publicists) should keep or put us on their publicity mailing lists to ensure that the information we supply others on their careers, accomplishments, etc. is accurate and up-to-date."

☑ PORTLAND SONGWRITERS ASSOCIATION, P.O. Box 16985, Portland OR 97292-0985. (503)727-9072. E-mail: info@pdxsongwriters.org. Website: www.pdxsongwriters.org. Estab. 1991. **Contact:** Judith Adams, president. "The PSA is a nonprofit organization providing education and opportunities that will assist writers in creating and marketing their songs. The PSA offers an annual National Songwriting Contest, monthly workshops, songwriter showcases, special performance venues, quarterly newsletter, mail-in critique service, discounted seminars by music industry pros." Annual dues: $35. Newsletter only: $15 (no eligibility requirements).
Tips: "Although most of our members are from the Pacific Northwest, we offer services that can assist songwriters anywhere. Our goal is to provide information and contacts to help songwriters grow artistically and gain access to publishing, recording and related music markets. For more information, please call, write or e-mail."

☑ RHODE ISLAND SONGWRITERS' ASSOCIATION (RISA), 159, Elmgrove Ave., Providence RI 02906. (401)461-6153. E-mail: rhodysong@aol.com. Website: http://members.aol.com/rhod

ysong. Co-Chairs: Deb DoVale and David Fontaine. Regional Secretary: Michael Khouri. Estab. 1993. "Membership consists of novice and professional songwriters. RISA provides opportunities to the aspiring writer or performer as well as the established regional artists who have recordings, are published and perform regularly. The only eligibility requirement is an interest in the group and the group's goals. Non-writers are welcome as well." The main purpose is to "encourage, foster and conduct the art and craft of original musical and/or lyrical composition through education, information, collaboration and performance." Offers instruction, newsletter, lectures, workshops, performance opportunities and evaluation services. Applications accepted year-round. Membership fee: $25/ year. "The group holds twice monthly critique sessions; twice monthly performer showcases (one performer featured) at a local coffeehouse; songwriter showcases (usually 6-8 performers); weekly open mikes; and a yearly songwriter festival called 'Hear In Rhode Island,' featuring approximately 50 Rhode Island acts, over two days."

SAN DIEGO SONGWRITERS GUILD, 3368 Governor Dr., Suite F-326, San Diego CA 92122. (619)225-2131. E-mail: sdsongwriters@hotmail.com. Website: www.sdsongwriters.org. **Contact:** Joseph Carmel, membership/correspondence. President: Tony Taravella. Vice President: John Dawes. Estab. 1982. "Members range from their early 20s to senior citizens with a variety of skill levels. Several members perform and work full time in music. Many are published and have songs recorded. Some are getting major artist record cuts. Most members are from San Diego county. New writers are encouraged to participate and meet others. All musical styles are represented." The purpose of this organization is to "serve the needs of songwriters and artists, especially helping them in the business and craft of songwriting through industry guest appearances." Offers competitions, newsletter, workshops, performance opportunities, discounts on services offered by fellow members, in-person song pitches and evaluations by publishers, producers and A&R executives. Applications accepted year-round. Membership dues: $45 full; $25 student; $135 corporate sponsorship. Meeting admission for non-members: $20 (may be applied toward membership if joining within 30 days).
Tips: "Members benefit most from participation in meetings and concerts. Generally, one major meeting held monthly on a Monday evening, at the Doubletree Hotel, Hazard Center, San Diego. Call for meeting details. Can join at meetings."

☑ SAN FRANCISCO FOLK MUSIC CLUB, 885 Clayton, San Francisco CA 94117. (415)661-2217. Website: www.idiom.com/~poet/harmony/. Serves songwriters, musicians and anyone who enjoys folk music. "Our members range from ages 2 to 80. The only requirement is that members enjoy, appreciate and be interested in sharing folk music. As a focal point for the San Francisco Bay Area folk music community, the SFFMC provides opportunities for people to get together to share folk music, and the newsletter *The Folknik* disseminates information. We publish two songs by our members an issue (six times a year) in our newsletter, our meetings provide an opportunity to share new songs, and at our camp-outs there are almost always songwriter workshops." Offers library, newsletter, informal performance opportunities, annual free folk festival, social outings and workshops. Applications accepted year-round. Membership fee: $7/year.

SESAC INC., 421 W. 54th St., New York NY 10019. (212)586-3450; 55 Music Square East, Nashville TN 37203. (615)320-0055. Website: sesac.com. President and Chief Operating Officer: Bill Velez. Coordinator-Writer/Publisher Relations: Cindy Brown. SESAC is a selective organization taking pride in having a repertory based on quality rather than quantity. Serves writers and publishers in all types of music who have their works performed by radio, television, nightclubs, cable TV, etc. Purpose of organization is to collect and distribute performance royalties to all active affiliates. As a SESAC affiliate, the individual and the individual's family may obtain group medical and equipment insurance at competitive rates. Tapes are reviewed upon invitation by the Writer/Public Relations dept.

THE SINGER SONGWRITER INFORMATION LINE, 9 Music Square S. #145, Nashville TN 37203. Information Hotline: (800)345-2694. Office: (615)792-2222. Fax: (615)792-1509. E-mail: cjstarlit@aol.com. **Contact:** C.J. Reilly, owner. Estab. 1988. Purpose is to give advice over a free 1-800 number to anyone who writes music. All callers will receive a free publisher's list. Offers instruction, newsletter, performance opportunities and evaluation services.

Tips: "We are a Nashville-based company. When people call, we try to answer questions regarding music publishing and record production."

☑ ☑ **SOCIETY OF COMPOSERS, AUTHORS AND MUSIC PUBLISHERS OF CANADA/SOCIÉTÉ CANADIENNE DES AUTEURS, COMPOSITEURS ET ÉDITEURS DE MUSIQUE (SOCAN)**, Head Office: 41 Valleybrook Dr., Toronto, Ontario M3B 2S6 Canada. (800)55-SOCAN. Fax: (416)445-7108. E-mail: socan.ca. Website: www.socan.ca. CEO: André LeBel. General Manager, Quebec & Atlantic Division and National Licensing: France Lafleur. General Manager, West Coast Division and National Member Services: Kent Sturgeon. The Society licenses public performance of music and distributes performance royalties to composers, lyricists, authors and music publishers. ASCAP, BMI and SESAC license the public performance of SOCAN's repertoire in the US.

☑ ☑ **SODRAC INC.**, 759 Victoria Square, Suite 420, Montreal, Quebec H2Y 2J7 Canada. (514)845-3268. Fax: (514)845-3401. E-mail: sodrac@sodrac.com. Website: www.sodrac.com. **Contact:** George Vuott, membership department (author, composer and publisher) or Diane Lamarre, membership department (visual artist and rights owner). Estab. 1985. "Sodrac was founded in 1985 on the initiative of songwriters and composers in order to manage the reproduction rights of authors, composers and publishers of music works. In September 1997, a new department was created specifically to manage the rights of visual artists. SODRAC represents the musical repertoire of about 83 countries and more than 4,243 Canadian members." Serves those with an interest in songwriting and music publishing no matter what their age or skill level is. "Members must have written or published at least one musical work that has been reproduced on an audio (CD, cassettte, LP) or audio-visual support (TV, video). The new member will benefit of a society working to secure his reproduction rights (mechanicals) and broadcast mechanicals." Applications accepted year-round. "There is no membership fee or annual dues. SODRAC retains a commission currently set at 10% for amounts collected in Canada and 5% for amounts collected abroad. SODRAC is the only Reproduction Rights Society in Canada where both songwriters and music publishers are represented, directly and equally."

☑ **THE SONGWRITERS ADVOCATE (TSA)**, 18 Dortmund Circle, Rochester NY 14624. (716)266-0679. E-mail: jerrycme@aol.com. **Contact:** Jerry Englerth, director. "TSA is a nonprofit educational organization that is striving to fulfill the needs of the songwriter. We offer opportunities for songwriters which include song evaluation workshops to help songwriters receive an objective critique of their craft. TSA evaluates tapes and lyric sheets via the mail. We do not measure success on a monetary scale, ever. It is the craft of songwriting that is the primary objective. If a songwriter can arm himself with knowledge about the craft and the business, it will increase his confidence and effectiveness in all his dealings. However, we feel that the songwriter should be willing to pay for professional help that will ultimately improve his craft and attitude." One-time membership dues: $15. Must be member to receive discounts or services provided.

☑ **SONGWRITERS & LYRICISTS CLUB**, % Robert Makinson, P.O. Box 605, Brooklyn NY 11217-0605. **Contact:** Robert Makinson, founder/director. Estab. 1984. Serves songwriters and lyricists. Gives information regarding songwriting: creation of songs, reality of market and collaboration. Only requirement is the ability to write lyrics or melodies. Beginners are welcome. The primary benefits of membership for the songwriter are opportunities to collaborate and assistance with creative aspects and marketing of songs through publications and advice. Offers newsletter and assistance with lead sheets and demos. *Songwriters & Lyricists Club Newsletter* will be mailed semi-annually to members. Other publications, such as *Climbing the Songwriting Ladder* and *Roster of Songs by Members* are mailed to new members upon joining. Applications accepted year-round. Dues: $35/ year; remit to Robert Makinson. Write with SASE for more information.
Tips: "Plan and achieve realistic goals."

☑ **SONGWRITERS AND POETS CRITIQUE**, P.O. Box 21065, Columbus OH 43226. (614)777-0326. E-mail: spcmusic@yahoo.com. Website: www.songwriterscritique. **Contact:** Brian Preston. Estab. 1985. Serves songwriters, musicians, poets, lyricists and performers. Meets second and fourth Friday of every month to discuss club events and critique one another's work. Offers seminars and workshops with professionals in the music industry. Has established Nashville contacts. "We critique mail-in submissions from long-distance members. Our goal is to provide support and opportunity to anyone interested in creating songs or poetry." Applications are accepted year-round. Annual dues: $30.

[N] SONGWRITERS ASSOCIATION OF WASHINGTON, 4200 Wisconsin Ave. NW, Box 100-137, Washington DC 20016. (301)654-8434. E-mail: president@saw.org. Website: www.saw.org. President: Steve Cutts. Vice President: Michael Sheppard. Estab. 1979. "S.A.W. is a nonprofit organization committed to providing its members with the means to improve their songwriting skills, learn more about the music business and gain exposure in the industry. S.A.W. sponsors various events to achieve this goal, such as workshops, open mics, song swaps, seminars, meetings, member directory with sound bites, showcases and the Mid-Atlantic song contest. S.A.W. publishes *S.A.W. Notes*, a bimonthly newsletter containing information on the music business, upcoming events around the country, tip sheets and provides free classifieds to its members. Joint membership is available with the Washington Area Music Association. For more information regarding membership write or call." Contest information: (800)218-5996.

THE SONGWRITERS GUILD OF AMERICA(SGA), 1560 Broadway, Suite #1306, New York NY 10036. (212)768-7902. Fax: (212)768-9048. E-mail: songnews@aol.com. Website: www.songwriters.org. New Jersey: 1500 Harbor Blvd, Weehawken NJ 07087-6732. (201)867-7603. West Coast: 6430 Sunset Blvd., Suite 705, Hollywood CA 90028, (323)462-1108. Fax: (323)462-5430. Nashville: 1222 16th Ave. S., Nashville TN 37203, (615)329-1782. President: George David Weiss. Executive Director: Lewis M. Bachman. National Projects Director: George Wurzbach. West Coast Regional Director: Aaron Meza. Southern Regional Director: Rundi Ream. Estab. 1931.
  ● Also see the listings for The Songwriters Guild Foundation and The Songwriters Guild of America in the Workshops & Conferences section.
"The Songwriters Guild of America (SGA) is a voluntary songwriter association run by and for songwriters. It is devoted exclusively to providing songwriters with the services and activities they need to succeed in the business of music. The preamble to the SGA constitution charges the board to take such lawful actions as will advance, promote and benefit the profession. Services of SGA cover every aspect of songwriting including the creative, administrative and financial." A full member must be a published songwriter. An associate member is any unpublished songwriter with a desire to learn more about the business and craft of songwriting. The third class of membership comprises estates of deceased writers. Membership dues: $85-450/regular; $70/associate; $70-400/estate. Regular and estate members pay annual dues on a graduated scale, determined by the amount of royalties collected by SGA in the previous year on behalf of that member. The Guild contract is considered to be the best available in the industry, having the greatest number of built-in protections for the songwriter. The Guild's Royalty Collection Plan makes certain that prompt and accurate payments are made to writers. The ongoing Audit Program makes periodic checks of publishers' books. For the self-publisher, the Catalogue Administration Program (CAP) relieves a writer of the paperwork of publishing for a fee lower than the prevailing industry rates. The Copyright Renewal Service informs members a year in advance of a song's renewal date. Other services include workshops in New York and Los Angeles, free Ask-A-Pro sessions with industry pros, critique sessions, collaborator service and newsletters. In addition, the Guild reviews your songwriter contract on request (Guild or otherwise); fights to strengthen songwriters' rights and to increase writers' royalties by supporting legislation which directly affects copyright; offers a group medical and life insurance plan; issues news bulletins with essential information for songwriters; provides a songwriter collaboration service for younger writers; financially evaluates catalogues of copyrights in connection with possible sale and estate planning; operates an estates administration service; and maintains a nonprofit educational foundation (The Songwriters Guild Foundation)."

SONGWRITERS OF OKLAHOMA, P.O. Box 4121, Edmond OK 73083-4121. (405)348-6534. **Contact:** Harvey Derrick, president. Offers information on the music industry: reviews publishing/ artist contracts, where and how to get demo tapes produced, presentation of material to publishers or record companies, royalties and copyrights. Also offers information on the craft of songwriting: co-writers, local songwriting organizations, a written critique of lyrics, songs and compositions on tapes as long as a SASE is provided for return of critique. A phone service is available to answer any questions writers, composers or artists may have. "Calls accepted between 10 and 11 pm CST Tuesday through Thursday only." All of these services are provided at no cost; there is no membership fee.

SONGWRITERS OF WISCONSIN INTERNATIONAL, P.O. Box 1027, Neenah WI 54957-1027. (920)725-1609. E-mail: sowtoner@aol.com. **Contact:** Tony Ansems, president. Workshops Coordinator: Mike Heath. Estab. 1983. Serves songwriters. "Membership is open to songwriters writing all styles of music. Residency in Wisconsin is recommended but not required. Members are encouraged to bring tapes and lyric sheets of their songs to the meetings, but it is not required. We are striving to improve the craft of songwriting in Wisconsin. Living in Wisconsin, a songwriter would be close to any of the workshops and showcases offered each month at different towns. The primary value of membership for a songwriter is in sharing ideas with other songwriters, being critiqued and helping other songwriters." Offers competitions (contest entry deadline: May 15), field trips, instruction, lectures, newsletter, performance opportunities, social outings, workshops and critique sessions. Applications accepted year-round. Membership dues: $20/year.
Tips: "Songwriters of Wisconsin now offers several critique meetings each month. For information call: Fox Valley, Mike Heath (920)722-0122; Milwaukee, Joe Warren (414)475-0314; La Crosse, Jeff Cozy (608)784-4332; Madison, Matt Frazier (608)270-1794; Neillsville, Phil Golembiewski (715)743-4770; S.W. Wisconsin, Bruce Yager (608)987-3544."

☑ **SONGWRITERS RESOURCE NETWORK**, PMB 135, 6327-C SW Capitol Hill, Portland OR 97201-1937. E-mail: info@SongwritersResourceNetwork.com. Website: www.SongwritersResourceNetwork.com. **Contact:** Steve Cahill, president. Estab. 1998. Members are songwriters and lyricists of every kind, from beginners to advanced. No eligibility requirements. Purpose is to help songwriters develop their craft and market their songs and to provide education and helpful information. Sponsors the annual Great American Song Contest, offers marketing tips and website access to music industry contacts. "We provide leads to publishers, producers and other music industry professionals." Applications accepted year-round. Send SASE for more information.

☑ **SOUTHEAST TEXAS BLUEGRASS MUSIC ASSOCIATION**, 130 Willow Run, Lumberton TX 77657-9210. (409)755-0622. E-mail: PickNBow@aol.com. **Contact:** Edy Mathews, editor. Estab. 1976. Members are musicians and listeners of all ages. Purpose is to promote bluegrass, gospel and old time music. Offers newsletter and monthly shows which are free. Applications accepted year-round. Membership fee: $12/year.

☑ **SOUTHERN SONGWRITERS GUILD, INC.**, P.O. Box 52656, Shreveport LA 71136-2656. (318)688-4235. E-mail: songguild@aol.com. Website: www.southernsongwritersguild.org. **Contact:** Cathy Williams, president. Estab. 1984. "The purpose of the Southern Songwriters Guild is to promote the art and craft of songwriting through all available educational and charitable means and to endeavor to uphold its objectives in harmony with society. SSG hosts an annual Awards Banquet that features winners of our 'Song of the Year' contest that provides cash prizes; and to induct new members into 'SSG Songwriters Hall of Fame', who may have local or regional roots in either heritage or career development. SSG has monthly Board and General Membership meetings aimed toward education. Fundraiser benefits are occasionally conducted for specific needs. A small educational scholarship program is infrequently available for those who meet certain criteria for need and purpose. SSG offers an opportunity to network or collaborate with other songwriters and songwriter organizations and encourages dual or multi-memberships with other organizations whose purposes are consistent with those of SSG. A newsletter is distributed to the membership and to non-member related entities. Performance opportunities, open mic sessions, songwriting workshops, clinics, annual family picnic, Christmas party and song critiques are additional functions. Please send SASE for membership application or other information." Applications accepted year-round. Membership fee: $30/year, $25 for each additional family member, $100 for organization or institution.

☑ **SOUTHWEST CELTIC MUSIC ASSOCIATION**, 4340 N. Central Expressway, Suite E104, Dallas TX 75206-6550. (214)821-4173. Fax: (214)824-1009. Website: www.scmatx.org. **Contact:** John Hebley, president. Estab. 1983. Persons interested in promotion and preservation of Celtic music. Musicians and Celtic music lovers are members (not necessary to be a musician to join). No eligibility requirements, although membership is primarily in Texas and surrounding states. Purpose is to promote, preserve and provide education about Celtic music, dance and culture in Texas and the Southwest region of the US. Offers instruction, newsletter, lectures, workshops, performance opportunities and sponsorships and scholarships. Applications accepted year-round. Membership fee: $12/single; $15/family; $25/organization; $50/sponsor; $300/lifetime member.
Tips: "We are the producers of the second largest Irish Festival in the U.S."

SOUTHWEST VIRGINIA SONGWRITERS ASSOCIATION, P.O. Box 698, Salem VA 24153. Phone/fax: (540)586-5000. E-mail: kirasongs@aol.com. **Contact:** Greg Trafidlo. Estab. 1981. 80 members of all ages and skill all levels, mainly country, folk, gospel, contemporary and rock but other musical interests too. "The purpose of SVSA is to increase, broaden and expand the knowledge of each member and to support, better and further the progress and success of each member in songwriting and related fields of endeavor." Offers performance opportunities, evaluation services, instruction, newsletter, workshops, monthly meetings and monthly newsletter. Application accepted year-round. Membership fee: $18/year.

☑ **SPARS (Society of Professional Audio Recording Services)**, 364 Clove Dr., Memphis TN 38117-4009. 1-800-771-7727 or (901)821-9111. Fax: (901)682-9177. E-mail: spars@spars.com. Website: www.spars.com. **Contact:** Larry Lipman, executive director. Estab. 1979. Members are recording studios, manufacturers of audio recording equipment, individual project studio owners, mastering, regular audio engineers, providers of services to the audio recording industry. Call for application/brochure describing membership. Non-profit professional trade organization which unites manufacturers and providers of services in the audio recording industry with users—"Educational Networking and Communition." Offers newsletter, publications, workshops, evaluation services and SPARS test. Applications accepted year-round. Call or write for information.

THE TENNESSEE SONGWRITERS INTERNATIONAL, P.O. Box 2664, Hendersonville TN 37077-2664. TSA Hotline: (615)969-5967. (615)824-4555. Fax: (615)822-2048. E-mail: asktsai@aol. com Website: www.clubnashville.com/tsai.htm. Executive Director: Jim Sylvis. Serves songwriters. "Our membership is open to all ages and consists of both novice and experienced professional songwriters. The only requirement for membership is a serious interest in the craft and business of songwriting. Our main purpose and function is to educate and assist the songwriter, both in the art/ craft of songwriting and in the business of songwriting. In addition to education, we also provide an opportunity for camaraderie, support and encouragement, as well a chance to meet co-writers. We also critique each others' material and offer suggestions for improvement, if needed. We offer the following to our members: Informative monthly newsletters; 'Pro-Rap'—once a month a key person from the music industry addresses our membership on their field of specialty. They may be writers, publishers, producers and sometimes even the recording artists themselves; 'Pitch-A-Pro'—we schedule a publisher, producer or artist who is currently looking for material to come to our meeting and listen to songs pitched by our members; 'Legends Night'—several times a year, a 'legend' in the music business will be our guest speaker. Annual Awards Dinner—honoring the most accomplished of our TSAI membership during the past year; Tips—letting our members know who is recording and how to get their songs to the right people. Workshops are held at Belmont University, Wedgewood Ave., Nashville TN in the Massey Business Center Building, Room 20013 on Wednesday evenings from 7-9 p.m. Other activities—a TSAI summer picnic, parties throughout the year, and opportunities to participate in music industry-related charitable events." Applications accepted year-round. Membership runs for one year from the date you join. Membership fee is $45/year.

TEXAS MUSIC OFFICE, P.O. Box 13246, Austin TX 78711. (512)463-6666. (512)463-4114. E-mail: music@governor.state.tx.us. Website: www.governor.state.tx.us/music. **Contact:** Casey Monahan, director. Estab. 1990. "The main purpose of the Texas Music Office is to promote the Texas music industry and Texas music, and to assist music professionals around the world with information about the Texas market. The Texas Music Office serves as a clearinghouse for Texas music industry information using their seven databases: Texas Music Industry (5,800 Texas music businesses in 94 music business categories); Texas Music Events (700 Texas music events); Texas Talent Register (900 Texas recording artists); Texas Radio Stations (733 Texas stations); U.S. Record Labels; Classical Texas (detailed information for all classical music organizations in Texas); and International (450 foreign businesses interested in Texas music). Provides referrals to Texas music businesses, talent and events in order to attract new business to Texas and/or to encourage Texas businesses and individuals to keep music business in-state. Serves as a liaison between music businesses and other government offices and agencies. Publicizes significant developments within the Texas music industry." Publishes the *Texas Music Industry Directory* (see the Publications of Interest section for more information).

TREASURE COAST SONGWRITERS ASSN. (TCSA), P.O. Box 7382, Port St. Lucie FL 34985-7382. E-mail: gpboley@aol.com. Director: George Boley. Founder/Advisor: Judy Welden. Estab. 1993. A service organization for and about songwriters. Age range of members, 15-80; varying levels of ability, from beginning writer to professional writers with substantial catalogs, publishing track records, radio airplay and releases. Offers competitions, lectures, performance opportunities, evaluation services, instruction and newsletter. Applications accepted year-round. Send SASE. Membership fee: $25.

VICTORY MUSIC, P.O. Box 2254, Tacoma WA 98401. (253)428-0832. Fax: (253)660-3263. E-mail: victory@nwlink.com. Website: www.victorymusic.org. **Contact:** Patrice O'Neill, director. Estab. 1969. All-volunteer organization serves songwriters, audiences and local acoustic musicians of all music styles. Victory Music provides places to play, showcases, opportunities to read about the business and other songwriters, referrals and seminars. Produced 6 albums of NW songwriters. Offers library, magazine (including previews of members' concerts), newsletter, performance opportunities, business workshops, music business books and a musician referral service. Applications accepted year-round. Membership fee: $30/year single; $80/year business; $40/family; $250 lifetime.

VOLUNTEER LAWYERS FOR THE ARTS, 1 E. 53rd St., 6th Floor, New York NY 10022. (212)319-ARTS (2787), ext. 12 (Monday-Friday 9:30-12 and 1-4 EST). Fax: (212)752-6575. E-mail: tcheung@vlany.org or vlany@vlany.org. Website: www.vlany.org. **Contact:** Tina Cheung, director of communications. Estab. 1969. Serves songwriters, musicians and all performing, visual, literary and fine arts artists and groups. Offers legal assistance and representation to eligible individual artists and arts organizations who cannot afford private counsel and a mediation service. VLA sells publications on arts-related issues and offers educational conferences, lectures, seminars and workshops. In addition, there are affiliates nationwide who assist local arts organizations and artists. Call for information.
Tips: "VLA now offers a monthly copyright seminar, 'Copyright Basics,' for songwriters and musicians as well as artists in other creative fields."

WASHINGTON AREA MUSIC ASSOCIATION, 1101 17th St. NW, Suite 1100, Washington DC 20036. (202)338-1134. Fax: (703)237-7923. E-mail: dcmusic@wamadc.com. Website: www.wamadc.com. **Contact:** Mike Schreibman, president. Estab. 1985. Serves songwriters, musicians and performers, managers, club owners and entertainment lawyers; "all those with an interest in the

**FOR EXPLANATIONS OF THESE SYMBOLS,
SEE THE INSIDE FRONT AND BACK COVERS OF THIS BOOK.**

Washington music scene." The organization is designed to promote the Washington music scene and increase its visibility. Its primary value to members is its seminars and networking opportunities. Offers lectures, newsletter, performance opportunities and workshops. WAMA sponsors the annual Washington Music Awards (The Wammies) and The Crosstown Jam or annual showcase of more than 300 artists at 60 venues in the DC area. Applications accepted year-round. Annual dues: $30.

WOMEN IN MUSIC, P.O. Box 441, Radio City Station, New York NY 10101. (212)459-4580. Website: www.womeninmusic.org. **Contact:** Gina Andriolo, president. Estab. 1985. Members are professionals in the business and creative areas: record company executives, managers, songwriters, musicians, vocalists, attorneys, recording engineers, agents, publicists, studio owners, music publishers and more. Purpose is to support, encourage and educate as well as provide networking opportunities. Offers newsletter, lectures, workshops, performance opportunities and business discounts. Presents annual "Touchstone Award" luncheon helping to raise money to support other organizations and individuals through WIM donations and scholarships. Applications accepted year-round. Membership fee: Professional $75; Associate $45; Student $25.

Workshops & Conferences

For a songwriter just starting out, conferences and workshops can provide valuable learning opportunities. At conferences, songwriters can have their songs evaluated, hear suggestions for further improvement and receive feedback from music business experts. They are also excellent places to make valuable industry contacts. Workshops can help a songwriter improve his craft and learn more about the business of songwriting. They may involve classes on songwriting and the business, as well as lectures and seminars by industry professionals.

Get the Most From a Conference

Before You Go:
- **Save money**. Sign up early for a conference and take advantage of the early registration fee. Don't put off making hotel reservations either—the conference will usually have a block of rooms reserved at a discounted price.
- **Become familiar with all the pre-conference literature**. Study the maps of the area, especially the locations of the rooms in which your meetings/events are scheduled.
- **Make a list of three to five objectives you'd like to obtain**, e.g., what you want to learn more about, what you want to improve on, how many new contacts you want to make.

At the Conference:
- **Budget your time**. Label a map so you know where, when and how to get to each session. Note what you want to do most. Then, schedule time for demo critiques if they are offered.
- **Don't be afraid to explore new areas**. You are there to learn. Pick one or two sessions you wouldn't typically attend. Keep your mind open to new ideas and advice.
- **Allow time for mingling**. Some of the best information is given after the sessions. Find out "frank truths" and inside scoops. Asking people what they've learned at the conference will trigger a conversation that may branch into areas you want to know more about, but won't hear from the speakers.
- **Attend panels**. Panels consist of a group of industry professionals who have the capability to further your career. If you're new to the business you can learn so much straight from the horse's mouth. Even if you're a veteran, you can brush up on your knowledge or even learn something new. Whatever your experience, the panelist's presence is an open invitation to approach him with a question during the panel or with a handshake afterwards.
- **Collect everything**: especially informational materials and business cards. Make notes about the personalities of the people you meet to later remind you who to contact and who to avoid.

After the Conference:
- **Evaluate**. Write down the answers to these questions: Would I attend again? What were the pluses and minuses, e.g., speakers, location, food, topics, cost, lodging? What do I want to remember for next year? What should I try to do next time? Who would I like to meet?
- **Write a thank-you letter** to someone who has been particularly helpful. They'll remember you when you later solicit a submission.

Each year, hundreds of workshops and conferences take place all over the country. Songwriters can choose from small regional workshops held in someone's living room to large national conferences such as South by Southwest in Austin, Texas, which hosts more than 6,000 industry people, songwriters and performers. Many songwriting organizations—national and local—host workshops that offer instruction on just about every songwriting topic imaginable, from lyric writing and marketing strategy to contract negotiation. Conferences provide songwriters the chance to meet one on one with publishing and record company professionals and give performers the chance to showcase their work for a live audience (usually consisting of industry people) during the conference. There are conferences and workshops that address almost every type of music, offering programs for songwriters, performers, musical playwrights and much more.

This section includes national and local workshops and conferences with a brief description of what they offer, when they are held and how much they cost to attend. Write or call any that interest you for further information. To find out what workshops or conferences take place in specific parts of the country, see the Geographic Index at the end of this book.

☑ **APPEL FARM ARTS AND MUSIC FESTIVAL**, P.O. Box 888, Elmer NJ 08318. (856)358-2472. Fax: (856)358-6513. E-mail: appelarts@aol.com. Website: www.appelfarm.org. **Contact:** Sean Timmons, artistic director. Estab. Festival: 1989; Series: 1970. "Our annual open air festival is the highlight of our year-round Performing Arts Series which was established to bring high quality arts programs to the people of South Jersey. Festival includes acoustic and folk music, blues, etc." Past performers have included Indigo Girls, John Prine, Ani DiFranco, Randy Newman, Nanci Griffith, Shawn Colvin, Arlo Guthrie and Madeleine Peyroux. In addition, our Country Music concerts have featured Toby Keith, Joe Diffie, Ricky Van Shelton, Doug Stone and others. Programs for songwriters and musicians include performance opportunities as part of Festival and Performing Arts Series. Programs for musical playwrights also include performance opportunities as part of Performing Arts Series. Festival is a one-day event held in June, and Performing Arts Series is held year-round. Both are held at the Appel Farm Arts and Music Center, a 176-acre farm in Southern New Jersey. Up to 20 songwriters/musicians participate in each event. Participants are songwriters, individual vocalists, bands, ensembles, vocal groups, composers, individual instrumentalists and dance/mime/movement. Participants are selected by demo tape submissions. Applicants should send a press packet, demonstration tape and biographical information. Application materials accepted year round. Faculty opportunities are available as part of residential Summer Arts Program for children, July/August.

ARCADY MUSIC FESTIVAL, P.O. Box 780, Bar Harbor ME 04609. (207)288-3151. E-mail: mwilson@acadia.net. Website: www.arcady.org. **Contact:** Dr. Melba Wilson, executive director. Artistic Director: Masanobu Ikemiya. Estab. 1980. Promotes classical chamber music, chamber orchestra concerts, master classes and a youth competition in Maine. Offers programs for performers. Workshops take place year-round in several towns in Eastern Maine. 30-50 professional, individual instrumentalists participate each year. Performers selected by invitation. "Sometimes we premiere new music by songwriters but usually at request of visiting musician."

ASCAP MUSICAL THEATRE WORKSHOP, 1 Lincoln Plaza, New York NY 10023. (212)621-6234. Fax: (212)621-6558. Website: www.ascap.com. **Contact:** Michael A. Kerker, director of musical theatre. Estab. 1981. Workshop is for musical theatre composers and lyricists only. Its purpose is to nurture and develop new musicals for the theatre. Offers programs for songwriters. Offers programs annually, usually April through May. Event took place in New York City. Six musical works are selected. Others are invited to audit the workshop. Participants are amateur and professional songwriters, composers and musical playwrights. Participants are selected by demo tape submission. Send for application. Deadline: mid-March.

☑ **ASCAP WEST COAST/LESTER SILL SONGWRITER'S WORKSHOP**, 7920 Sunset Blvd., 3rd Floor, Los Angeles CA 90046. (323)883-1000. Fax: (323)876-4272. E-mail: rgrimmett@ascap.com. Website: www.ascap.com. **Contact:** Randy Grimmett, director of repertory. Estab. 1963.

Offers programs for songwriters. Offers programs annually. Event takes place mid-January through mid-February. 14 songwriters/musicians participate in each event. Participants are amateur and professional songwriters. Participants are selected by demo tape submission or by invitation. "Send in two songs with lyrics, bio and brief explanation why you'd like to participate." Deadline: November 30.

N ASPEN MUSIC FESTIVAL AND SCHOOL, 2 Music School Rd., Aspen CO 81611. (970)925-3254. Fax: (970)925-3802. E-mail: school@aspenmusic.org. Website: www.aspen.com/mu sicfestival. **Contact:** Shauna Quill, associate artistic administrator. Estab. 1949. Promotes classical music by offering programs for composers, including an advanced master class in composition which meets weekly during the nine-week season. Offers several other music programs as well. School and Festival run June 16 to August 22 in Aspen CO. Participants are amateur and professional composers, individual instrumentalists and ensembles. Send for application. Deadline: February 22. Charges $2,150 for full 9 weeks, $1,425 for one of two 4½ week sessions. Fee: $80 until February 5, $100 February 5-22. Scholarship assistance is available.

✓ BLUESTOCK FESTIVAL, (formerly Bluestock International Music Convention and Festival), P.O. Box 41858, Memphis TN 38174-1858. (901)526-4280. Fax: (901)526-4288. E-mail: info@bluest ock.org. Website: www.bluestock.org. **Contact:** Bertram Lyons, manager/festival director. Estab. 1997. Bluestock's main purpose is to showcase unsigned music talent (blues, soul, blues-based rock, R&B, gospel, etc.) to a host of industry executives and luminaries. Offers programs for songwriters and performers. Offers programs annually. Event takes place at the Memphis Botanic Garden on September 7, 2001. "In addition to showcasing over 100 acts, Bluestock offers educational panels, industry workshops and clinics, heritage and cultural arts, and plenty of networking opportunities." Participants are amateur and professional songwriters, vocalists, instrumentalists and bands. Call for dates, entry fee and application information.

✓ BMI-LEHMAN ENGEL MUSICAL THEATRE WORKSHOP, 320 W. 57th St., New York NY 10019. (212)830-2508. E-mail: jbanks@bmi.com. Website: www.bmi.com. **Contact:** Jean Banks, senior director of musical theatre. Estab. 1961. "BMI is a music licensing company which collects royalties for affiliated writers. We have departments to help writers in jazz, concert, Latin, pop and musical theater writing." Offers programs "to musical theater composers, lyricists and librettists. The BMI-Lehman Engel Musical Theatre Workshops were formed in an effort to refresh and stimulate professional writers, as well as to encourage and develop new creative talent for the musical theater." Each workshop meets 1 afternoon a week for 2 hours at BMI, New York. Participants are professional songwriters, composers and playwrights. "BMI-Lehman Engel Musical Theatre Workshop Showcase presents the best of the workshop to producers, agents, record and publishing company execs, press and directors for possible option and production." Call for application. Tape and lyrics of 3 compositions required with application. "BMI also sponsors a jazz composers workshop. For more information call Burt Korall at (212)586-2000."

BROADWAY TOMORROW PREVIEWS, % Science of Light, Inc., 191 Claremont Ave., Suite 53, New York NY 10027. E-mail: solight@worldnet.att.net. Website: home.att.net/~solight. **Contact:** Elyse Curtis, artistic director. Estab. 1983. Purpose is the enrichment of American theater by nurturing new musicals. Offers series in which composers living in New York city area present scores of their new musicals in concert. 2-3 composers/librettists/lyricists of same musical and 1 musical director/pianist participate. Participants are professional singers, composers and opera/musical theater writers. Submission is by audio cassette of music, synopsis, cast breakdown, résumé, reviews, if any, acknowledgement postcard and SASE. Participants selected by screening of submissions. Programs are presented in fall and spring with possibility of full production of works presented in concert. Membership fee: $50.

✦ ✓ CANADIAN MUSIC WEEK, 5355 Vail Court, Mississauga, Ontario L5M 6G9 Canada. (416)695-9236. Fax: (416)695-9239. Website: www.cmw.net. **Contact:** Neill Dixon, president. Estab. 1985. Offers annual programs for songwriters, composers and performers. Event takes place mid-

March in Toronto. 100,000 public, 400 bands and 1,200 delegates participate in each event. Participants are amateur and professional songwriters, vocalists, composers, bands and instrumentalists. Participants are selected by submitting demonstration tape. Send for application and more information. Concerts take place in 25 clubs and 5 concert halls, and 3 days of seminars and exhibits are provided. Fee: $375 (Canadian).

☑ **CMJ MUSIC MARATHON, MUSICFEST & FILMFEST**, 44 W. 18th St., 6th Floor, New York NY 10011. (877)6-FESTIVAL. Fax: (516)466-7161. E-mail: events@cmj.com. Website: www.c mj.com/Marathon. **Contact:** Kevin McCullough, operations manager. Estab. 1981. Premier annual alternative music gathering of more than 9,000 music business and film professionals. Fall, NYC. Features 4 days and nights of more than 50 panels and workshops focusing on every facet of the industry; exclusive film screenings; keynote speeches by the world's most intriguing and controversial voices; exhibition area featuring live performance stage; over 1,000 of music's brightest and most visionary talents (from the unsigned to the legendary) performing over 4 evenings at more than 50 of NYC's most important music venues. Participants are selected by submitting demonstration tape. Go to website for application.

PETER DAVIDSON'S WRITER'S SEMINAR, P.O. Box 497, Arnolds Park IA 51331. **Contact:** Peter Davidson, seminar presenter. Estab. 1985. "Peter Davidson's Writer's Seminar is for persons interested in writing all sorts of materials, including songs. Emphasis is placed on developing salable ideas, locating potential markets for your work, copyrighting, etc. The seminar is not specifically for writers of songs, but is very valuable to them, nevertheless." Offers programs year-round. One-day seminar, 9:00 a.m.-4:00 p.m. Event takes place on various college campuses. In even-numbered years offers seminars in Minnesota, Iowa, Nebraska, South Dakota, Kansas, Colorado and Wyoming. In odd-numbered years offers seminars in Minnesota, Iowa, Nebraska, South Dakota, Missouri, Illinois, Arkansas and Tennessee. Anyone can participate. Send SASE for schedule. Deadline: day of the seminar. Fee: $40-59. "All seminars are held on college campuses in college facilities—various colleges sponsor and promote the seminars."

FOLK ALLIANCE ANNUAL CONFERENCE, 1001 Connecticut Ave. NW, Suite 501, Washington DC 20036. (202)835-3655. Fax: (202)835-3656. E-mail: fa@folk.org. Website: www.folk.org. Estab. 1989. Conference/workshop topics change each year. Conference takes place mid-February and lasts 4 days at a different location each year. 1,500 attendees include artists, agents, arts administrators, print/broadcast media, folklorists, folk societies, merchandisers, presenters, festivals, recording companies, fans, etc. Artists wishing to showcase should contact the office for a showcase application form. Closing date for application is June 1. Application fee is $35 for members, $75 for nonmembers. $200 on acceptance. Additional costs vary from year to year. Housing is separate for the event, scheduled for Feb. 21-24, 2002 in Jacksonville, FL; Feb. 6-9, 2003 in Nashville, TN; Feb. 26-29, 2004 in San Diego, CA; Feb. 24-27, 2005 in Montreal, Quebec Canada.

N GENESIUS GUILD MONDAY NIGHT PERFORMANCE PROJECT SERIES, P.O. Box 2273, New York NY 10108-2273. (212)946-5625. Fax: (212)865-1723. E-mail: info@genesiusguild.o rg. Website: www.genesiusguild.org. **Contact:** Thomas Morrissey, artistic director. Estab. 1994. Purpose is to create and develop new musical theatre, opera, dance and other musical performance art. Offers programs for songwriters, composers and musical playwrights. Offers programs Mondays September-May including stage reading series, workshops, productions, and roundtable sessions. Event takes place at various venues in New York City. Participants are professional songwriters, vocalists, composers, bands, musical playwrights and instrumentalists. Participants are selected by demo tape submission. Send tape, synopsis and letter. Series takes place at various venues and theatre spaces with 100-200 seats.

TO HELP YOU UNDERSTAND and use the information in these listings, see "How to Use *Songwriter's Market* to Get Your Songs Heard," on page 5.

N I WRITE THE SONGS, PMB 208, 2250 Justin Rd., Suite 108, Highland Village TX 75077-7164. (972)317-2760. Fax: (972)317-4737. E-mail: info@cqkmusic.com. Website: www.cqkmusic.com. **Contact:** Sarah Marshall, administrative director. Estab. 1996. "I Write the Songs is an on-the-air songwriting seminar. It is a syndicated radio talk show available both on the radio and on the Internet. A detailed description of the program and its hosts, Mary Dawson and Sharon Braxton, can be found on the website. The website address will also link you to the Internet broadcasts and list the radio stations that carry the program. I Write the Songs has been created to inspire and instruct aspiring songwriters of all genres of music in the craft and business of songwriting." Offers programs, including weekly programs on radio and the Internet, for songwriters, composers and performers. "Occasionally we hold competitions. All aspiring songwriters earning less than $5,000 annually from song royalties are eligible." I Write the Songs features "Critique Shows" every 4-6 weeks. Songwriters can submit demos on cassette or CD with typed lyric sheet. Does not return material. Featured songs are selected at random. Writers whose songs are selected for a show will receive a taped copy of the program on which their song is critiqued. Mary Dawson conducts songwriting seminars across the country and internationally. For a list of upcoming seminars, check the website.

☑ KERRVILLE FOLK FESTIVAL, Kerrville Festivals, Inc., P.O. Box 291466, Kerrville TX 78029. (830)257-3600. E-mail: staff@kerrville-music.com. Website: www.kerrville-music.com. **Contact:** Rod Kennedy, producer. Estab. 1972. Hosts 3-day songwriters' school, a 4-day music business school and New Folk concert competition sponsored by *Performing Songwriter* magazine. Festival produced in late spring and late summer. Spring festival lasts 18 days and is held outdoors at Quiet Valley Ranch. 110 or more songwriters participate. Performers are professional songwriters and bands. Participants selected by submitting demo, by invitation only. Send cassette, or CD, promotional material and list of upcoming appearances. "Songwriter and music schools include lunch, experienced professional instructors, camping on ranch and concerts. Rustic facilities. Food available at reasonable cost. Audition materials accepted at above address. These three-day and four-day seminars include noon meals, handouts and camping on the ranch. Usually held during Kerrville Folk Festival, first and second week in June. Write for contest rules, schools and seminars information, and festival schedules. Also establishing a Phoenix Fund to provide assistance to ill or injured singer/songwriters who find themselves in distress. Listen to 'Music from Kerrville' 7 pm, Monday through Friday on www.kerrville-music.com."

☑ LAMB'S RETREAT FOR SONGWRITERS presented by SPRINGFED ARTS, a nonprofit organization, P.O. Box 304, Royal Oak MI 48068-0304. (248)589-1594. Fax: (248)589-3913. E-mail: johndlamb@ameritech.net. Website: www.springfed.org. **Contact:** John D. Lamb, director. Estab. 1995. Offers programs for songwriters on annual basis first weekend in November (Thursday-Sunday) at The Birchwood Inn, Harbor Springs, MI. 60 songwriters/musicians participate in each event. Participants are amateur and professional songwriters. Anyone can participate. Send for application or e-mail. Deadline: day before event begins. Fee: $200-400, includes all meals. Facilities are single/double occupancy lodging with private baths; 2 conference rooms and hospitality lodge. Offers song assignments, songwriting workshops, song swaps, open mic and one-on-one mentoring. Faculty are noted songwriters, such as Michael Smith. Partial scholarships may be available by writing: Blissfest Music Organization, % Jim Gillespie, P.O. Box 441, Harbor Springs, MI 49740. Deadline: day before event.

☑ MANCHESTER MUSIC FESTIVAL, P.O. Box 1165, Manchester Center VT 05255. (802)362-1956. Fax: (802)362-0711. E-mail: mmf@vermontel.com. Website: www.mmfvt.org. **Contact:** Robyn Pruett, managing director. Estab. 1974. Offers classical music education and performances. Summer program for young professional musicians offered in tandem with a professional concert series in the mountains of Manchester, VT. Up to 26 young professionals, age 18 and up, are selected by audition for the Young Artists Program, which provides instruction, performance and teaching opportunities, with full scholarship for all participants. Printable application available on website. Application fee: $40. Commissioning opportunities for new music, and performance opportunities for professional chamber ensembles and soloists for both summer and fall/winter concert series. "Celebrating 27 years of fine music."

☑ **MUSIC BUSINESS SOLUTIONS/CAREER BUILDING WORKSHOPS**, P.O. Box 266, Boston MA 02123-0266. (888)655-8335. E-mail: success@mbsolutions.com. Website: www.mbsolutions.com. **Contact:** Peter Spellman, director. Estab. 1991. Workshop titles include "How to Succeed in Music Without Overpaying Your Dues," "How to Release an Independent Record" and "Promoting and Marketing Music Toward the Year 2000." Offers programs for music entrepreneurs, songwriters, musical playwrights, composers and performers. Offers programs year-round, annually and bi-annually. Event takes place at various colleges, recording studios, hotels, conferences. 10-100 songwriters/musicians participate in each event. Participants are both amateur and professional songwriters, vocalists, music business professionals, composers, bands, musical playwrights and instrumentalists. Anyone can participate. Call or write (regular or e-mail) for application. Fee: $50-125. "Music Business Solutions offers a number of other services and programs for both songwriters and musicians including: private music career counseling, business plan development and internet marketing; publication of *Music Biz Insight: Power Reading for Busy Music Professionals*, a bimonthly e-zine chock full of music management and marketing tips and resources. Free subscription with e-mail address."

N NASHVILLE MUSIC FESTIVAL, P.O. Box 291827, Nashville TN 37229-1827. (615)252-8202. Fax: (615)321-0384. E-mail: c4promo@aol.com. Website: www.radiocountry.org (festivals). **Contact:** Ambassador Charlie Ray, director. Estab. 2000. Offers 100 booth spaces for makers of instruments, craftspeople, independent record companies, and unsigned artists; seminars by successful music industry professionals; contests; and stages on which to perform. "Nashville record companies big and small are looking for new talent. A lot of them will have talent scouts at the festival. If they see you on stage and like what they see, you could be signed to a recording contract." Event takes place May 26-28, 2001. "Complete directions to festival location will be mailed with your tickets and posted on our webpage." Fee: $50, adult 3-day ticket.

NATIONAL ACADEMY OF POPULAR MUSIC SONGWRITING WORKSHOP PROGRAM, 330 W. 58th St. Suite 411, New York NY 10019. (212)957-9230. Fax: (212)957-9227. E-mail: 73751.1142@compuserve.com. Website: www.songwritershalloffame.org. **Contact:** Bob Leone, projects director. Managing Director: April Anderson. Estab. 1969. "For all forms of pop music, from rock to R&B to dance." Offers programs for member lyricists and composers including songwriting workshops (beginning to master levels) and songwriters showcases. "The Abe Olman Scholarship for excellence in songwriting is awarded ($1,200) to a student who has been in our program for at least 4 quarters." Offers programs 3 times/year: fall, winter and spring. Event takes place mid-September to December, mid-January to April, mid-April to July (10 2-3 hour weekly sessions) at New York Spaces, 131 W. 72nd St., New York. Also offer monthly networking meetings with industry pros and biweekly open mics. 50 students involved in 4 different classes. Participants are amateur and professional lyricists and composers. Some participants are selected by submitting demonstration tape (pro-song class), and by invitation (master class). Send for application. Deadline: first week of classes. Annual dues: $25. Sponsors songwriter showcases in March, June, September and December.

NEMO MUSIC SHOWCASE & CONFERENCE, Zero Governors Ave. #6, Boston MA 02155. (781)306-0441. Fax: (781)306-0442. E-mail: cavery@ultranet.com. Website: www.nemoboston.com. **Contact:** Candace Avery, founder/director. Estab. 1996. Music showcase and conference, featuring the Boston Music Awards and 3 days/nights of a conference with trade show and more than 200 nightly showcases in Boston. Offers showcases for songwriters. Offers programs annually. Event takes place in April. 1,500 songwriters/musicians participate at conference; 3,000 at awards show; 20,000 at showcases. Participants are professional songwriters, vocalists, composers, bands and instrumentalists. Participants are selected by invitation. Send for application or visit website. Fee: $30.

THE NEW HARMONY PROJECT, 613 N. East St., Indianapolis IN 46202. (317)464-1103. Fax: (317)635-4201. **Contact:** Anna D. Shapiro, artistic director. Estab. 1986. Selected scripts receive various levels of development with rehearsals and readings, both public and private. "Our mission is to nurture writers and their life-affirming scripts. This includes plays, screenplays, musicals and TV scripts." Offers programs for musical playwrights. Event takes place in May/June in southwest Indiana. Participants are amateur and professional writers and media professionals. Send for application.

NEW MUSIC WEST, P.O. Box 308, Delta, British Columbia V4K 3Y3 Canada. (604)684-9338. Fax: (604)684-9337. E-mail: info@newmusicwest.com. Website: www.newmusicwest.com/. Producer: John Donnelly. Associate Producer: James Cowan. Estab. 1990. A four day music festival and conference held May each year in Vancouver, B.C. The conference offers songwriter intensive workshops; demo critique sessions with A&R and publishers; information on the business of publishing; master producer workshops: "We invite established hit record producers to conduct three-hour intensive hands-on workshops with 30 young producers/musicians in studio environments. The festival offers songwriters in the round and 250 original music showcases. Largest music industry event in the North Pacific Rim. Entry fee: $20.

NORFOLK CHAMBER MUSIC FESTIVAL, September-May address: 435 College St., Box 208246, New Haven CT 06520. (203)432-1966. Fax: (203)432-2136. June-August address: Ellen Battell, Stoeckel Estate, Box 545, Norfolk CT 06058. (860)542-3000. Fax: (860)542-3004. E-mail: norfolk@yale.edu. Website: www.yale.edu/norfolk. **Contact:** Elaine C. Carroll, festival manager. Estab. 1941. Festival season of chamber music. Offers programs for composers and performers. Offers programs summer only. Approximately 70 fellows participate. Participants are professional vocalists, composers and instrumentalists. Participants are selected by audition in person or demo tape submission. Auditions are held in New Haven, CT. Send for application. Deadline: February 15. Fee: $50. Situated on the elegant Ellen Battell Stoeckel Estate, the Festival offers a magnificent Music Shed with seating for 1,000, practice facilities, music library, dining hall, laundry and art gallery. Nearby are hiking, bicycling and swimming.

NORTH BY NORTHEAST MUSIC FESTIVAL AND CONFERENCE (NXNE), 189 Church St., Lower Level, Toronto, Ontario M5B 1Y7 Canada. (416)863-6963. Fax: (416)863-0828. E-mail: inquire@nxne.com. Website: www.nxne.com. **Contact:** Leslie Goldthorpe, festival coordinator. Estab. 1995. "Our festival takes place mid-June at over 25 venues and 2 outdoor stages in downtown Toronto, drawing over 2,000 conference delegates, 400 bands and 50,000 music fans. Musical genres include everything from folk to funk, roots to rock, polka to punk and all points in between, bringing exceptional new talent, media front-runners, music business heavies and music fans from all over the world to Toronto." Participants include emerging and established songwriters, vocalists, composers, bands and instrumentalists. Festival performers are selected by submitting a demo tape and package. Send for an application form, or call, fax or e-mail. Submission for 2002 accepted from November 1, 2001 to January 18, 2002. Submissions fee: $20. Conference registration fee: $115-195 (US), $145-250 (Canadian). "Our conference is held at the deluxe Holiday Inn King and the program includes mentor sessions—15-minute one-on-one opportunities for songwriters and composers to ask questions of industry experts. North By Northeast 2001 will be held June 7-9, 2001 and North By Northeast 2002 will be held June 6-8, 2002."

NORTHERN CALIFORNIA SONGWRITERS ASSOCIATION CONFERENCE, 1724 Laurel St., Suite 120, San Carlos CA 94070. (650)654-3966 or (800)FOR-SONG. Fax: (650)654-2156. E-mail: info@ncsasong.org. Website: www.ncsasong.org. **Contact:** Ian Crombie, executive director. Estab. 1980. "Conference offers opportunity and education. 16 seminars, 50 song screening sessions (1,500 songs reviewed), performance showcases, one on one sessions and concerts." Offers programs for lyricists, songwriters, composers and performers. "During the year we have competitive open mics. Winners go into the playoffs. Winners of the playoffs perform at the sunset concert at the conference." Event takes place second weekend in September at Foothill College, Los Altos Hills, CA. Over 500 songwriters/musicians participate in this event. Participants are songwriters, composers, musical playwrights, vocalists, bands, instrumentalists and those interested in a career in the music business. Send for application. Deadline: September 1. Fee: $90-175. "See our listing in the Organizations section."

NSAI SONG CAMPS, 1701 West End Ave., Nashville TN 37023. 1-800-321-6008 or (615)256-3354. Fax: (615)256-0034. E-mail: claudiayoung@nashvillesongwriters.com. Website: www.nashvill esongwriters.com. **Contact:** Claudia Young, director of song camps and cruises. Estab. 1992. Offers programs strictly for songwriters. Event held 5 times/year at Montgomery Bell State Park about 45 minutes west of Nashville, exept for one, which is a cruise ("Song Camp at Sea"). Participants stay, eat meals and hold classes at Montgomery Bell Inn. "We provide most meals and lodging is available. We also bus the campers into town for an evening of music presented by the faculty." Camps are 3 days long, except the cruise, which is 5 days long, with 30-85 participants, depending on the camp. "There are different levels of camps, some having prerequisites. Each camp varies. Please call, e-mail or refer to website. It really isn't about the genre of music, but the quality of the song itself. Song Camp strives to strengthen the writer's vision and skills, therefore producing the better song. Song Camp is known as 'boot camp' for songwriters. It is guaranteed to catapult you forward in your writing! Participants are all aspiring songwriters led by a pro faculty. We do accept lyricists only and composers only with the hopes of expanding their scope. Instrumentalists are not accepted as lyrics are heavily stressed." Participants are selected through submission of 2 songs with lyric sheet. Song Camp is open to NSAI members, although anyone can apply and upon acceptance join the organization. There is no formal application form. See website for membership and event information.

☑ **NSAI SONGWRITERS SYMPOSIUM**, 1701 West End Ave., Nashville TN 37203. (615)256-3354. Fax: (615)256-0034. E-mail: membership@NashvilleSongwriters.com. Website: www.nashvill esongwriters.com. Membership Director: David Mark Thomas. Covers "all types of music. Participants take part in publisher evaluations, as well as large group sessions with different guest speakers." Offers annual programs for songwriters. Event takes place in April in downtown Nashville. 300 amateur songwriters/musicians participate in each event. Send for application. Deadline: March 1. Fee: $225, member; $300, non-member; after March 1: $275 for members; $350 for nonmembers.

🍁 ☑ **ORFORD FESTIVAL**, Orford Arts Centre, 3165 Chemim DuParc, Orford, Quebec J1X 7A2 Canada. (819)843-3981. E-mail: arts.orford@sympatico.ca. Website: www.arts-orford.org. **Contact:** Isabelle Langlois, communications coordinator. Artistic Director: Agnes Grossman. Estab. 1951. "Each year, the Centre d'Arts Orford produces up to 35 concerts in the context of its Music Festival. It receives artists from all over the world in classical and chamber music." Offers master classes for music students, young professional classical musicians and chamber music ensembles. New offerings include master classes for all instruments and voice, opera and jazz workshops. Master classes last 2 months and take place at Orford Arts Centre from June 25 to August 18. 350 students participate each year. Participants are selected by demo tape submissions. Send for application. Closing date for application is March 23. Scholarships for qualified students. Registration fees $50 (Canadian). Tuition fees $250 (Canadian)/week. Accommodations $250 (Canadian)/week.

🆁 **PHILADELPHIA MUSIC CONFERENCE**, P.O. Box 30288, Philadelphia PA 19103. (215)587-9550. Fax: (215)587-9552. E-mail: info@gopmc.com. Website: www.gopmc.com. Show-case Director: Michael Kunze. Estab. 1992. "The purpose of the PMC is to bring together rock, hip hop and acoustic music for three days of panels and four nights of showcases. Offers programs for songwriters, composers and performers, including one-on-one sessions to meet with panelists and song evaluation sessions to have your music heard. "We present 35 panels on topics of all facets of the music industry; 250 showcases at 20 clubs around the city. Also offer a DJ cutting contest." Held annually at the Adam's Mark Hotel in Philadelphia in October. 3,000 amateur and professional songwriters, composers, individual vocalists, bands, individual instrumentalists, attorneys, managers, agents, publishers, A&R, promotions, club owners, etc. participate each year. "As per showcase application, participants are selected by independent panel of press, radio and performing rights organizations." Send for application. Deadline: September 1. Fee(s): $25 showcase application fee; $150 conference registration. "A PMC registration entitles you to access all daytime events, including the panels, daytime showcases, trade show, early evening cocktail party, A&R listening sessions and Mentoring Sessions. Registration also allows you access to all participating Nighttime Showcase venues free of charge. Register easily online! The Philadelphia Music Conference is one of the fastest-growing and exciting events around. Our goal is not just to make the Philadelphia Music Conference one of the biggest in America, but to make it one of the best. 23 artists were signed to major label deals in the first four years of the conference. We will continue to build upon our ideas to keep this an event that is innovative, informative and fun."

N⃞ THE SHIZNIT MUSIC CONFERENCE, P.O. Box 1881, Baton Rouge LA 70821. (225)231-2739. Fax: (225)926-5055. E-mail: staffers@bellsouth.net. Website: www.theshiznit.com. Public Relations: Lee Williams. Vice President: Sedrick Hills. Purpose is to provide performance and networking opportunities for a wide variety of music and music related businesses, from urban to country, from blues to zydeco. Showcases, networking, trade shows and seminars offer information about the music industry. Offers programs annually for songwriters and performers. Event takes place June 22-24, 2001 at over 40 venues in Baton Rouge and New Orleans. 400 songwriters/musicians participate in each event. Participants are amateur and professional songwriters, vocalists and bands. Participants are selected by demo tape audition. Fee: $185. Send for application.

THE SONGWRITERS GUILD FOUNDATION, 6430 Sunset Blvd., Suite 705, Hollywood CA 90028. (323)462-1108. Fax: (323)462-5430. E-mail: lasga@aol.com. Website: www.songwritersorg.com. West Coast Regional Director: B. Aaron Meza. Assistant West Coast Regional Director: Phyllis Osman. Offers a series of workshops with discounts to members. "There is a charge for each songwriting class. Charges vary depending on the class. SGA members receive discounts! Also, the Re-write workshop and Ask-A-Pro/Song Critique are free!"

• Also see the Songwriters Guild of America listing in the Organizations section.

Ask-A-Pro/Song Critique: SGA members are given the opportunity to present their songs and receive constructive feedback from industry professionals. A great chance to meet industry people, make contacts, ask questions and get your song heard! Free to SGA members. Reservations required. Call for schedule. Free.

Jack Segal's Songshop: This very successful 9-week workshop focuses on working a song through to perfection, including title, idea, rewrites and pitching your songs. Please call for more information regarding this very informative workshop. Dates to be announced. Fee.

Phil Swan Country Music Workshop: This 6-week workshop is perfect for those writers who want an inside look into the world of country music. Fee.

Special Seminars and Workshops: Held through the year. Past workshops included Sheila Davis on lyrics, tax workshops for songwriters, MIDI workshops, etc. Call for schedule.

Dr. George Gamez's Creativity Workshop: A 4-week class designed to help songwriters discover their creative possibilities and give them the tools and techniques they need to increase their creative abilities. Fee.

SGA Story Night: Featuring interviews with top guild members. Learn about their experiences in songwriting and perhaps hear a live performance from the pros. Fee.

Vocal Performance Workshop for Singer/Songwriters: Conducted by Berklee College of Music Grad, Phyllis R. Osman, this 4-week performance workshop is held on Saturday mornings at The Songwriters Foundation Office in Hollywood. The class is for all levels of singers and focuses on fundamental breathing exercises and techniques that help the singer/songwriter build stamina and control and help them achieve the sound they desire. Repertoire is also worked on. Fee.

Building a Songwriting Career: A 1-day workshop for songwriters, musicians and recording artists, etc. to help them discover how they can establish a career in the exciting world of songwriting. Features SGA professional songwriters and music business executives in panel discussions about intellectural property, creativity, the craft and business of songwriting and more. No charge for this event.

Re-Write Workshop: Conducted by Michael Allen. Songwriters will have the chance to have their songs critiqued by their peers with an occasional guest critique. Free.

Harriet Schock Songwriting Workshop: A 10-week course consisting of nine lessons which help create a solid foundation for writing songs effortlessly. Fee.

MARKET CONDITIONS are constantly changing! If you're still using this book and it is 2003 or later, buy the newest edition of *Songwriter's Market* at your favorite bookstore or order directly from Writer's Digest Books at (800)289-0963.

Song Critique: New York's oldest ongoing song critique. Guild songwriters are invited to either perform their song live or present a cassette demo for feedback. A Guild moderator is on hand to direct comments. Nonmembers may attend and offer comments. Free.

Street Smarts: Street Smarts is a 3-hour orientation session for new SGA members. It introduces the basics in areas such as: contracts, copyrights, royalties, song marketing and more. The session is free to members and is scheduled whenever there is a minimum of 8 participants.

Pro-Shop: For each of 6 sessions an active publisher, producer or A&R person is invited to personally screen material from professional Guild writers. Participation is limited to 10 writers, and audit of 1 session. Audition of material is required. Coordinator is producer/musician/award winning singer, Ann Johns Ruckert. Fee; $75 (SGA members only).

SGA Week: Held in spring and fall of each year, this is a week of scheduled events and seminars of interest to songwriters. Events include workshops, seminars and showcases. For schedule and details contact the SGA office beginning several weeks prior to SGA Week.

☑ **SONGWRITERS PLAYGROUND**®, 75-A Lake Rd., #366, Congers NY 10920. (845)267-0001. E-mail: heavyhitters@earthlink.net. **Contact:** Barbara Jordan, director. Estab. 1990. "To help songwriters, performers and composers develop creative and business skills through the critically acclaimed programs *Songwriters Playground*®, *The 'Reel' Deal on Getting Songs Placed in Film and Television*, and the *Mind Your Own Business* Seminars. We offer programs year-round. Workshops last anywhere from 2-15 hours. Workshops are held at various venues throughout the United States. Prices vary according to the length of the workshop." Participants are amateur and professionals. Anyone can participate. Send or call for application.

SOUTH BY SOUTHWEST MUSIC AND MEDIA CONFERENCE, P.O. Box 4999, Austin TX 78765. (512)467-7979. Fax: (512)451-0754. E-mail: sxsw@sxsw.com. Website: sxsw.com/sxsw. Estab. 1987. "We have over 1,000 bands perform in over 50 venues over 5 nights featuring every genre of alternative-based music." Offers programs for songwriters and performers. Annual event takes place in March, at the Austin Convention Center, Austin, TX. Participants are songwriters, vocalists, bands, instrumentalists and representatives of almost all areas of the music business. Participants are selected by demo tape audition. Submissions accepted September through mid-November. Fee: $10 early fee; $20 late fee. Application is required. Forms are available by request or on the SXSW website. "We have a mentor program during the conference where participants can have a one-on-one with professionals in the music business. Also of interest to musicians are the SXSW film and interactive/multimedia festivals held the week before the music conference, and the North By Northwest music conference held annually in Autumn in Portland, OR. For more information, see the website."

☑ **THE SWANNANOA GATHERING—CONTEMPORARY FOLK WEEK**, Warren Wilson College, P.O. Box 9000, Asheville NC 28815-9000. (828)298-3434 or (828)771-3761. Fax: (828)299-3326. E-mail: gathering@warren-wilson.edu. Website: www.swangathering.org. Director: Jim Magill. Coordinator: Eric Garrison. "For anyone who ever wanted to make music for an audience, we offer a comprehensive week in artist development, divided into four major subject areas: Songwriting, Performance, Sound & Recording and Vocal Coaching, along with daily panel discussions of other business matters such as promotion, agents and managers, logistics of touring, etc. 2001 staff includes Kate Campbell, Cosy Sheridan, Steve Seskin, Kim and Reggie Harris, John McCutchwon, Ray Chesna, John Smith, Tena Moyer, Penny Nichols, Mae Robertson, Sloan Wainwright and Eric Garrison. For a brochure or other info contact Jim Magill, Director, The Swannanoa Gathering, at the phone number/address above. Tuition: $340. Takes place last week in July. Housing (including all meals): $260. Annual program of The Swannanoa Gathering Folk Arts Workshops."

THE TEN-MINUTE MUSICALS PROJECT, P.O. Box 461194, West Hollywood CA 90046. **Contact:** Michael Koppy, producer. Estab. 1986. Promotes short complete stage musicals. Offers programs for songwriters, composers and musical playwrights. "Works selected are generally included in full-length 'anthology musical'—11 of the first 16 selected works are now in the show

Stories, for instance." Awards a $250 royalty advance for each work selected. Participants are amateur and professional songwriters, composers and musical playwrights. Participants are selected by demonstration tape, script, lead sheets. Send for application. Deadline: August 31st annually.

N. UNDERCURRENTS, P.O. Box 94040, Cleveland OH 44101-6040. (216)397-9921. Fax: (216)932-1143. E-mail: music@undercurrents.com. Website: www.undercurrents.com. **Contact:** John Latimer, president. Estab. 1989. A yearly music industry expo with online exposure featuring seminars, trade show, media center and showcases of rock, alternative, metal, folk, jazz and blues music. Offers programs for songwriters, composers, music industry professionals and performers. Dates for Undercurrents 2001 were May 18-19. Deadline for showcase consideration is February 1. Participants are selected by demo tape, biography and 8×10 photo audition. Send for application. Fee: $25 for 3-day event.

Retreats & Colonies

This section provides information on retreats and artists' colonies. These are places for creatives, including songwriters, to find solitude and spend concentrated time focusing on their work. While a residency at a colony may offer participation in seminars, critiques or performances, the atmosphere of a colony or retreat is much more relaxed than that of a conference or workshop. Also, a songwriter's stay at a colony is typically anywhere from one to twelve weeks (sometimes longer), while time spent at a conference may only run from one to fourteen days.

Like conferences and workshops, however, artists' colonies and retreats span a wide range. Yaddo, perhaps the most well-known colony, limits its residencies to artists "working at a professional level in their field, as determined by a judging panel of professionals in the field." The Brevard Music Center offers residencies only to those involved in classical music. Despite different focuses, all artists' colonies and retreats have one thing in common: They are places where you may work undisturbed, usually in nature-oriented, secluded settings.

SELECTING A COLONY OR RETREAT

When selecting a colony or retreat, the primary consideration for many songwriters is cost, and you'll discover that arrangements vary greatly. Some colonies provide residencies as well as stipends for personal expenses. Some suggest donations of a certain amount. Still others offer residencies for substantial sums but have financial assistance available.

When investigating the various options, consider meal and housing arrangements and your family obligations. Some colonies provide meals for residents, while others require residents to pay for meals. Some colonies house artists in one main building; others provide separate cottages. A few have provisions for spouses and families. Others prohibit families altogether.

Overall, residencies at colonies and retreats are competitive. Since only a handful of spots are available at each place, you often must apply months in advance for the time period you desire. A number of locations are open year-round, and you may find planning to go during the "off-season" lessens your competition. Other colonies, however, are only available during certain months. In any case, be prepared to include a sample of your best work with your application. Also, know what project you'll work on while in residence and have alternative projects in mind in case the first one doesn't work out once you're there.

Each listing in this section details fee requirements, meal and housing arrangements, and space and time availability, as well as the retreat's surroundings, facilities and special activities. Of course, before making a final decision, send a SASE to the colonies or retreats that interest you to receive their most up-to-date details. Costs, application requirements and deadlines are particularly subject to change.

For More Information

For other listings of songwriter-friendly colonies, see *Musician's Resource* (available from Watson-Guptill Publications, 1695 Oak St., Lakewood NJ 08701, 1-800-451-1741), which not only provides information about conferences, workshops and academic programs but also residencies and retreats. Also check the Publications of Interest section in this book for newsletters and other periodicals providing this information.

☑ **BREVARD MUSIC CENTER**, P.O. Box 312, Brevard NC 28712-0312. (828)884-2975. Fax: (828)884-2036. E-mail: bmcadmission@brevardmusic.org. Website: www.brevardmusic.org. **Contact:** Lynn Johnson, admissions coordinator. Estab. 1936. Offers 6-week residencies from the last week in June through the first week of August. Open to professional and student composers, pianists, vocalists and instrumentalists of classical music. A 2-week advanced conducting workshop (orchestral and opera) with David Effron and Gunther Schuller is offered, as well as a collaborative pianist program. 2001 composer in residence is Don Freund. Accommodates 400 at one time. Personal living quarters include cabins. Offers rehearsal, teaching and practice cabins.
Costs: $3,350 for tuition, room and board.
Requirements: Call for application forms and guidelines. $50 application fee. Participants are selected by audition or demonstration tape and then by invitation. There are 60 different audition sites throughout the US.

☑ **BYRDCLIFFE ARTS COLONY**, 34 Tinker St., Woodstock NY 12498. (845)679-2079. Fax: (845)679-4529. E-mail: wguild@ulster.net. Website: www.woodstockguild.org. **Contact:** Carla T. Smith, executive director. Estab. 1991. Offers 1-month residencies June-September. Open to composers, writers and visual artists. Accommodates 10 at one time. Personal living quarters include single rooms, shared baths and kitchen facilities. Offers separate private studio space. Composers must provide their own keyboard with headphone. Activities include open studio, readings, followed by pot luck dinner once a month. The Woodstock Guild, parent organization, offers music and dance performances, gallery exhibits and book signings.
Costs: $500/month. Residents are responsible for own meals and transporation.
Requirements: Send SASE for application forms and guidelines. Accepts inquiries via fax or e-mail. $5 application fee. Submit a score of at least 10 minutes with 2 references, résumé and application.

DORLAND MOUNTAIN ARTS COLONY, P.O. Box 6, Temecula CA 92593. (909)302-3837. Fax: (909)696-2855. E-mail: dorland@ez2.net. Website: www.ez2.net/dorland. **Contact:** Director. Estab. 1979. Offers 1- or 2-month residencies, year-round, on availability. Open to composers, playwrights, writers, visual artists, sculptors, etc. Personal living quarters include 6 individual rustic cottages with private baths and private kitchen facilities. Propane gas is provided for cooking, refrigeration and hot water. Lighting is by kerosene lamps and heat is by wood stoves. There is no electricity. Two Composer studios are equipped with pianos, including 1 concert grand Steinway, and 1 baby grand Chickering.
Costs: $50 non-refundable scheduling fee. Cabin donation: $300 per month (½ non-refundable).
Requirements: Send SASE for application forms and guidelines. Accepts inquiries via fax or e-mail. Deadline: March 1 and September 1.

DORSET COLONY HOUSE, P.O. Box 510, Dorset VT 05251-0510. (802)867-2223. Fax: (802)867-0144. E-mail: theatre@sover.net. Website: www.theatredirectories.com. **Contact:** John Nassivera, executive director. Estab. 1980. Offers up to 1-month residencies September-November and April-May. Open to writers, composers, directors, designers and collaborators of the theatre. Accommodates 8 at one time. Personal living quarters include single rooms with desks with shared bath and shared kitchen facilities.
Costs: $120/week. Meals not included. Transportation is residents' responsibility.
Requirements: Send SASE for application forms and guidelines. Accepts inquiries via fax or e-mail. Submit letter with requested dates, description of project and résumé of productions.

🌐 **THE TYRONE GUTHRIE CENTRE**, Annaghmakerrig, Newbliss, County Monaghan, Ireland. Phone: (353)(47)54003. Fax: (353)(47)54380. E-mail: thetgc@indigo.ie. **Contact:** Regina Doyle, director. Estab. 1981. Offers year-round residencies. Artists may stay for anything from 1 week to 3 months in the Big House, or for up to a year at a time in one of the 5 self-catering houses in the old farmyard. Open to artists of all disciplines. Accommodates 15 at one time. Personal living quarters include bedroom with bathroom en suite. Offers a variety of workspaces. There is a music room for composers and musicians, a large rehearsal and performance space for theatre groups and music ensembles. Activities include informal readings and performances. At certain times of the year it is possible, by special arrangement, to accommodate groups of artists, symposiums, master classes, workshops and other collaborations.

Costs: Artists who are not Irish must pay £600 per week, all found, for a residency in the Big House and £300 per week for one of the self-catering farmyard houses. To qualify for a residency, it is necessary to show evidence of a significant level of achievement in the relevant field. "We are happy to help successful applicants find funding for the fees."

Requirements: Send SAE and IRC for application forms and guidelines. Accepts inquiries via fax or e-mail. Fill in application form with cv to be reviewed by the board members at regular meetings.

■ **THE HAMBIDGE CENTER**, P.O. Box 339, Rabun Gap GA 30568-0339. (706)746-5718. Fax: (706)746-9933. E-mail: hambidge@rabun.net. Website: www.rabun.net/~hambidge. **Contact:** Peggy McBride, residency director. Estab. 1934 (Center); 1988 (residency). Offers 2-week to 2-month residencies year round. Open to all artists. Accommodates 8 at one time. Personal living quarters include a private cottage with kitchen, bath, living/studio space and bedroom. Offers composer/musical studio equipped with piano. Activities include communal dinners April through November and nightly or periodic sharing of works-in-progress.

Costs: $125/week.

Requirements: Send SASE for application forms and guidelines. Accepts inquiries via fax and e-mail. Application fee: $20. Deadline: Applications accepted year-round.

ISLE ROYALE NATIONAL PARK ARTIST-IN-RESIDENCE PROGRAM, 800 E. Lakeshore Dr., Houghton MI 49931-1869. (906)482-0984. Fax: (906)482-8753. E-mail: isro_parkinfo@nps.gov. Website: www.nps.gov/ISRO/. **Contact:** Greg Blust, coordinator. Estab. 1991. Offers 2-3 week residencies from mid-June to mid-September. Open to all art forms. Accommodates 1 artist with 1 companion at one time. Personal living quarters include cabin without electricity; shared outhouse. A canoe is provided for transportation. Offers a guest house at the site that can be used as a workroom. The artist is asked to contribute a piece of work representative of their stay at Isle Royale, to be used by the park in an appropriate manner. During their residency, artists will be asked to share their experience (1 presentation per week of residency, about 1 hour/week) with the public by demonstration, talk, or other means.

Requirements: Send SASE for application forms and guidelines. Accepts inquiries via fax or e-mail. A panel of professionals from various disciplines, and park representatives will choose the finalists. The selection is based on artistic integrity, ability to reside in a wilderness environment, a willingness to donate a finished piece of work inspired on the island, and the artist's ability to relate and interpret the park through their work.

KALANI OCEANSIDE RETREAT, RR 2 Box 4500, Pahoa-Beach Road HI 96778-9724. (808)965-7828. Fax: (808)965-0527. E-mail: kalani@kalani.com. Website: www.kalani.com. **Contact:** Richard Koob, director. Estab. 1980. Offers 2-week to 2-month residencies. Open to all artists who can verify professional accomplishments. Accommodates 80 at one time. Personal living quarters include private cottage or lodge room with private or shared bath. Full (3 meals/day) dining service, also shared kitchens available. Offers shared studio/library spaces. Activities include opportunity to share works in progress, ongoing yoga, hula and other classes; beach, thermal springs, Volcanos National Park nearby; olympic pool/spa on 113-acre facility.

Cost: $55-105/night lodging with 50% stipend. Meals separate at $29/day. Transportation by rental car from $25/day, Kalani service $50/trip, or taxi $70/trip. 50% discount ("stipend") on lodging only.

Requirements: Send SASE for application forms and guidelines. Accepts inquiries via fax or e-mail. $10 application fee.

● **A BULLET** introduces comments by the editor of *Songwriter's Market* indicating special information about the listing.

THE MACDOWELL COLONY, 100 High St., Peterborough NH 03458. (603)924-3886. Fax: (603)924-9142. Website: www.macdowellcolony.org. Admissions Coordinator: Patricia Dodge. Estab. 1907. Offers year-round residencies of up to 2 months (average length is 6 weeks). Open to writers, composers, film/video makers, visual artists, architects and interdisciplinary artists. Personal living quarters include single rooms. Offers private studios on 450-acre grounds.
Cost: None (contributions accepted).
Requirements: Send SASE for application forms and guidelines. Composers should send 2 clearly reproduced scores, one of which was completed in the last 5 years, along with audiocassette (1 piece per cassette) or both works on 1 CD. Application deadline: January 15, April 15 and September 15.

☑ **NORTHWOOD UNIVERSITY ALDEN B. DOW CREATIVITY CENTER**, 4000 Whitring Dr., Midland MI 48640-2398. (517)837-4478. Fax: (517)837-4468. E-mail: creativity@nort hwood.edu. Website: www.northwood.edu/abd. **Contact:** Director. Estab. 1979. Offers 10-week summer residencies (mid-June through mid-August). Fellowship Residency is open to individuals in all fields (the arts, humanities or sciences) who have innovative, creative projects to pursue. Accommodates 4 at one time. Each Fellow is given a furnished apartment on campus, complete with 2 bedrooms, kitchen, bath and large living room. Fellows' apartments serve as their work space as well as their living quarters unless special needs are requested. Fellows are invited to lunch weekdays at the Creativity Center on campus.
Cost: $10 application fee. Room and board is provided plus a $750 stipend to be used toward project costs or personal needs. "We also provide travel to and from the residency. We look for projects which are innovative, creative, unique. We ask the applicant to set accomplishable goals for the 10-week residency."
Requirements: Send for application forms and guidelines. Accepts inquiries via fax or e-mail. Applicants submit 2-page typed description of their project; cover page with name, address, phone numbers plus summary (30 words or less) of project; support materials such as tapes, CDs; personal résumé; facilities or equipment needed; and $10 application fee. Application deadline: December 31 (postmarked).

☑ **SITKA CENTER FOR ART & ECOLOGY**, P.O. Box 65, Otis OR 97368-0065. (541)994-5485. Fax: (541)994-8024. E-mail: info@sitkacenter.org. Website: www.sithacenter.org. **Contact:** Randall Koch, executive director. Estab. 1971. Offers 4-month residencies in October through January or February through May; shorter residencies are available upon arrangement. Open to artists or naturalists who have earned a BA, BS, BFA and/or MA, MS, MFA, PhD degree, or equivalent professional experience. Personal living quarters include 3 living quarters, each self-contained with a sleeping area, kitchen and bathroom. Offers 4 studios. Workshops or presentations are encouraged; an exhibition/presentation to share residents' works is held in January and May.
Cost: The resident is encouraged to hold an open studio or community outreach program at Sitka one day per month during the residency, exceptions by arrangements with the director. The resident is asked to provide some form of community service on behalf of Sitka.
Requirements: Send SASE for application forms and guidelines. Accepts inquiries via fax. Send completed application with résumé, 2 letters of recommendation, work samples and SASE.

☑ **VILLA MONTALVO ARTIST RESIDENCY PROGRAM**, P.O. Box 158, Saratoga CA 95071-0158. (408)961-5822. Fax: (408)961-5850. E-mail: kfunk@villamontalvo.org. Website: www. villamontalvo.org. **Contact:** Dakin Hart, artist residency director. Estab. 1942. "Offers 1- to 3-month residencies year-round. Open to writers (prose, poetry, playwrights, screen writers, etc.), visual artists, musicians and composers, architects, filmmakers. Residents are provided with fully equipped apartments/cottages, with kitchens and baths. Four to five apartments/cottages have pianos. The composer's apartment has a grand piano. Activities include weekly gatherings of the residents.
Cost: Residencies are free, but artists must provide food, materials and transportation. There are 7 fellowships ($400) awarded to highest ranking artists based on panelist's review of work samples.
Requirements: Send self addressed label and 55¢ postage. Accepts inquiries via fax or e-mail. $20 application fee plus work samples as defined by discipline. Application deadline: March 1 and September 1.

VIRGINIA CENTER FOR THE CREATIVE ARTS, Box VCCA, Sweet Briar VA 24595. (804)946-7236. Fax: (804)946-7239. E-mail: vcca@vcca.com. Website: www.vcca.com. **Contact:** Sheila Gulley Pleasants, director of artists' services. Estab. 1971. Offers residencies year-round, typical residency lasts 1 month. Open to originating artists: composers, writers and visual artists. Accommodates 22 at one time. Personal living quarters include 20 single rooms, 2 double rooms, bathrooms shared with one other person. All meals are served. Kitchens for fellows' use available at studios and residence. Activities include trips in the VCCA van twice a week into town. Fellows share their work regularly. Three studios have pianos.
Cost: No transportation costs are covered. The suggested daily fee is $30 which includes meals.
Requirements: Send SASE for application forms and guidelines or call the above number. Applications are reviewed by a panel of judges. Application fee: $20. Deadline: May 15 for October-January residency; September 15 for February-May residency; January 15 for June-September residency.

YADDO ARTISTS' COMMUNITY, P.O. Box 395, Union Ave., Saratoga Springs NY 12866-0395. (518)584-0746. Fax: (518)584-1312. E-mail: yaddo@yaddo.org. Website: www.yaddo.org. **Contact:** Lesley M. Leduc, centennial and public affairs coordinator. Estab. 1900. Offers residencies of 2 weeks to 2 months, year-round except for a brief 2-3 week period in September. Open to those working at a professional level in their field, as determined by a judging panel of professionals in the field. Accommodates 12-15 in winter, up to 35 in spring and summer at one time. Personal living quarters include private rooms and studios, some with private baths and some with shared baths. All meals are provided; breakfast and dinner are communal; lunches packed in lunch pails. Offers composers' studios equipped with pianos. Several small libraries are available on the grounds; guests have access to a college and municipal library nearby.
Cost: No fees are charged for any services. Limited help with travel expenses available.
Requirements: Send SASE with 55¢ postage for application forms and guidelines. Accepts inquiries via fax or e-mail. $20 non-refundable filing fee, work samples required (2 musical scores and audio cassette of one of the scores) and 2 letters of support sent directly to Yaddo by the sponsors. Deadline: January 15 and August 1.

Get Your 2003 Edition Delivered Right to Your Door—and Save!

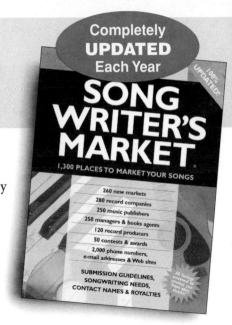

Completely UPDATED Each Year

SONG WRITER'S MARKET

1,300 PLACES TO MARKET YOUR SONGS

260 new markets
280 record companies
250 music publishers
250 managers & books agents
120 record producers
50 contests & awards
2,000 phone numbers,
e-mail addresses & Web sites

SUBMISSION GUIDELINES,
SONGWRITING NEEDS,
CONTACT NAMES & ROYALTIES

Finding the right markets for your songs is crucial to your success! With constant changes in the music industry, staying informed as to who, where and why is a challenge. That's why every year the most savvy songwriters turn to the new edition of *Songwriter's Market* for the most up-to-date information on the people and places that will get their songs heard. This indispensable guide includes more than 2,000 listings of music publishers, record producers, managers, booking agents and more. You'll also find insider tips from industry professionals which will further increase your opportunities.

2003 Songwriter's Market will be published and ready for shipment in August 2002.

Through this special offer, you can reserve your 2003 *Songwriter's Market* at the 2002 price—just $23.99. Order today and save!

Turn over for more books to help write and market your songs!

☐**Yes!** I want the most current edition of *Songwriter's Market*. Please send me the 2003 edition at the 2002 price—$23.99. (#10789-K)

# 10789-K	$ 23.99

(NOTE: *2003 Songwriter's Market* will be shipped in August 2002.)

I also want these books listed on back:

Book	Price
# -K	$
# -K	$
# -K	$
# -K	$
Subtotal	$
Postage & Handling	$

In the U.S., please add $3.95 s&h for the first book, $1.95 for each additional book. In OH and NY add applicable sales tax. In Canada, add US$5.00 for the first book, US$3.00 for each additional book, and 7% GST. Payment in U.S. funds must accompany order.

Total	$

Credit card orders call
TOLL FREE 1-800-221-5831
or visit
www.writersdigest.com/catalog

☐ Payment enclosed $ _____ (or)
Charge my: ☐ VISA ☐ MC ☐ AmEx Exp._____

Account # _____

Signature _____

Name _____

Address _____

City_____

State/Prov._____ ZIP/PC_____

☐ Check here if you do not want your name added to our mailing list.

30-Day Money Back Guarantee on every book you buy!

ZAH01B4

Mail to: Writer's Digest Books • PO Box 9274 • Central Islip, NY 11722-9274

More Great Books to Help You Market Your Songs!

You Can Write Song Lyrics
by Terry Cox
An experienced and successful lyric writer guides you
step by step through the process of lyric writing. Learn
about basic song components, collaborative song-writing
and creative ways to come up with song ideas. Cox also walks
you through the stages of writing lyrics for a song — from
choosing a title, to the chorus, verses and bridge. You'll even
find valuable information on the next steps of getting the song
performed and recorded.
#10685-K/$14.99/112 p/pb

The Craft and Business of Songwriting
2nd Edition
by John Braheny
Want to be a professional songwriter? Then get Braheny's
must-have insider info on being competitive in this crowded
market. You'll learn how to overcome writer's block, focus
ideas, handle business concerns, and much more. Plus, up-to-
date Web references, video info and software advice.
#10767-K/$22.99/322 p/pb

**The Musician's Guide to Making &
Selling Your Own CDs & Cassettes**
by Jana Stanfield
Learn how to produce the kind of recordings that will
launch your music career. It doesn't take a major label to be
successful in the music industry. Stanfield shows you how she
made it to the top, and how you can too.
#10522-K/$18.99/160 p/pb

**The Songwriter's Market Guide to Song and
Demo Submission Formats**
by the editors of Songwriter's Market
Get your foot in the door with knock-out query letters,
slick demo presentation, and the best advice for dealing
with every player in the industry!
#10401-K/$19.99/160 p/hc

Writing Better Lyrics
by Pat Pattison
Make every song sizzle using this unique, in-depth approach to
lyric writing. You'll examine extraordinary songs to determine
what makes them so effective; work through more than 30
language exercises to find snappy rhymes and create meaningful
metaphors and similes.
#10742-K/$15.99/192 p/pb

Order these helpful references today from your local bookstore,
or use the handy order card on the reverse side.

State & Provincial Grants

Arts councils in the United States and Canada provide assistance to artists (including poets) in the form of fellowships or grants. These grants can be substantial and confer prestige upon recipients; however, **only state or province residents are eligible**. Because deadlines and available support vary annually, query first (with a SASE).

UNITED STATES ARTS AGENCIES

Alabama State Council on the Arts, *201 Monroe St., Montgomery AL 36130-1800. (334)242-4076. E-mail: staff@arts.state.al.us. Website: www.arts.state.al.us.*

Alaska State Council on the Arts, *411 W. Fourth Ave., Suite 1-E, Anchorage AK 99501-2343. (907)269-6610. E-mail: info@aksca.org. Website: www.aksca.org.*

Arizona Commission on the Arts, *417 W. Roosevelt, Phoenix AZ 85003-1326. (602)255-5882. E-mail: general@arizonaarts.org. Website: az.arts.asu.edu/artscomm/.*

Arkansas Arts Council, *1500 Tower Bldg., 323 Center St., Little Rock AR 72201. (501)324-9766. E-mail: info@dah.state.ar.us. Website: www.arkansasarts.com.*

California Arts Council, *1300 I St., Suite 930, Sacramento CA 95814. (916)322-6555. E-mail: cac@cwo.com. Website: www.cac.ca.gov/.*

Colorado Council on the Arts, *750 Pennsylvania St., Denver CO 80203-3699. (303)894-2617. E-mail: coloarts@state.co.us. Website: www.coloarts.state.co.us.*

Connecticut Commission on the Arts, *755 Main St., 1 Financial Plaza, Hartford CT 06103. (860)566-4770. Website: www.ctarts.org.*

Delaware Division of the Arts, *Carvel State Office Building, 820 N. French St., Wilmington DE 19801. (302)577-8278. E-mail: delarts@artswire.org. Website: www.artsdel.org.*

District of Columbia Commission on the Arts & Humanities, *410 Eighth St. NW, 5th Floor, Washington DC 20004. (202)724-5613. Website: www.dcarts.dc.gov.*

Florida Arts Council, *Division of Cultural Affairs, Florida Dept. of State, The Capitol, Tallahassee FL 32399-0250. (850)487-2980. Website: www.dos.state.fl.us/dca.*

Georgia Council for the Arts, *260 14th St. NW, Suite 401, Atlanta GA 30318-5793. (404)685-2787. E-mail: goarts@arts-ga.com. Website: www.arts-ga.com*

Hawaii State Foundation on Culture & Arts, *44 Merchant St., Honolulu HI 96813. (808)586-0300. E-mail: sfca@sfca.state.hi.us. Website: www.state.hi.us/sfca.*

Idaho Commission on the Arts, *P.O. Box 83720, Boise ID 83720-0008. (208)334-2119. E-mail: mestrada@ica.state.id.us. Website: www2.state.id.us/arts.*

Illinois Arts Council, *100 W. Randolph, Suite 10-500, Chicago IL 60601. (312)814-6750. E-mail: info@arts.state.il.us. Website: www.state.il.us/agency/iac.*

Indiana Arts Commission, *402 W. Washington St., Indianapolis IN 46204-2741. (317)232-1268. E-mail: arts@state.in.us. Website: www.state.in.us/iac.*

Iowa Arts Council, *600 E. Locust, Capitol Complex, Des Moines IA 50319-0290. (515)281-4451. Website: www.culturalaffairs.org/iac.*

Kansas Arts Commission, *Jay Hawk Tower, SW 700 Jackson, Suite 1004, Topeka KS 66603. (785)296-3335. E-mail: KAC@arts.state.ks.us. Website: www.arts.state.ks.us.*

Kentucky Arts Council, *300 W. Broadway, Old Capital Annex, Frankfort KY 40601-1942. (502)564-3757.*

Louisiana State Arts Council, *P.O. Box 44247, Baton Rouge LA 70804-4247. (225)342-8180.*
E-mail: arts@crt.state.la.us. Website: www.crt.state.la.us/arts.

Maine Arts Commission, *55 Capitol St., 25 State House Station, Augusta ME 04333-0025. (207)287-2724.*
E-mail: jan.poulin@state.me.us. Website: www.mainearts.com.

Maryland State Arts Council, *175 West Ostend Street, Suite E, Baltimore MD 21230. (410)767-6555.*
E-mail: tcolvin@mdbusiness.state.md.us. Website: www.msac.org.

Massachusetts Cultural Council, *10 St. James Ave., 3rd Floor, Boston MA 02116-3803. (617)727-3668.*
E-mail: web@art.state.ma.us. Website: www.massculturalcouncil.org.

Michigan Council for Arts & Cultural Affairs, *Dept. of Consumer & Industry, 525 W. Ottawa, P.O. Box 30004,*
Lansing, MI 48909. (517)373-1820. E-mail: artsinfo@cis.state.mi.us.
Website: www.commerce.state.mi.us/arts/home.htm.

Minnesota State Arts Board, *Park Square Court, 400 Sibley St., Suite 200, St. Paul MN 55101-1949.*
(651)215-1600. E-mail: msab@state.mn.us. Website: www.arts.state.mn.us.

Mississippi Arts Commission, *239 N. Lamar St., Suite 207, Jackson MS 39201. (601)359-6030.*
E-mail: hedgepet@arts.state.ms.us. Website: www.arts.state.ms.us.

Missouri Arts Council, *111 N. Seventh St., Suite 105, St. Louis MO 63101-2188. (314)340-6845.*
E-mail: moarts@mail.state.mo.us. Website: www.missouriartscouncil.org.

Montana Arts Council, *P.O. Box 202201, Helena MT 59620-2201. (406)444-6430. E-mail: mac@state.mt.us.*
Website: www.art.state.mt.us.

National Endowment for the Arts, *1100 Pennsylvania Ave. NW, Washington DC 20506. (202)682-5400.*
E-mail: webmgt@arts.endow.gov. Website: www.arts.endow.gov.

Nebraska Arts Council, *3838 Davenport St., Omaha NE 68131-2329. (402)595-2122.*
E-mail: cmalloy@nebraskaartscouncil.org. Website: www.nebraskaartscouncil.org.

Nevada State Council on the Arts, *716 Carson St., Carson City NV 89703. (775)687-6680.*
E-mail: kjodonne@clan.lib.nv.us. Website: www.dmla.clan.lib.nv.

New Hampshire State Council on the Arts, *40 N. Main St., Concord NH 03301-4974. (603)271-2789.*
E-mail: mdurkee@nharts.state.nh.us. Website: www.state.nh.us/nharts.

New Jersey State Council on the Arts, *P.O. Box 306, 225 W. State St., Trenton NJ 08625. (609)292-6130.*
E-mail: njsca@arts.sos.state.nj.us. Website: www.njartscouncil.org.

New Mexico Arts Division, *228 E. Palace Ave., Santa Fe NM 87501. (505)827-6490.*
Website: www.nmmnh-abq.mus.nm.us/arts/html.

New York State Council on the Arts, *915 Broadway, New York NY 10010. (212)387-7000.*
E-mail: pinfo@nysca.org. Website: www.nysca.org.

North Carolina Arts Council, *Department of Cultural Resources and Service Center 4632,*
Raleigh NC 27699-4632. (919)733-4834. Website: www.ncarts.org.

North Dakota Council on the Arts, *418 E. Broadway, Suite 70, Bismarck ND 58501-4086. (701)328-3954.*
E-mail: comserv@state.nd.us. Website: www.state.nd.us/arts/index.html.

Ohio Arts Council, *727 E. Main St., Columbus OH 43205. (614)466-2613. E-mail: wlawson@mail.oac.ohio.gov.*
Website: www.oac.state.oh.us.

Oklahoma Arts Council, *P.O. Box 52001-2001, Oklahoma City OK 73152-2001. (405)521-2931.*
E-mail: okarts@arts.state.ok.us. Website: www.state.ok.us/~arts.

Oregon Arts Commission, *775 Summer St. NE, Suite 350, Salem OR 97310. (503)986-0088.*
E-mail: oregon.artscomm@state.or.us. Website: www.art.econ.state.or.us.

Pennsylvania Council on the Arts, *Room 216, Finance Bldg., Harrisburg PA 17120. (717)787-6883.*
E-mail: mcaszatt@state.pa.us. Website: www.artsnet.org/pca.

Institute of Puerto Rican Culture, *Apartado Postal 4184, San Juan PR 00902-4184. (809)725-5137.*

Rhode Island State Council on the Arts, *83 Park St., 6th Floor, Providence RI 02903. (401)222-3880.*
E-mail: info@risca.state.ri.us. Website: www.risca.state.ri.us.

South Carolina Arts Commission, *1800 Gervais St., Columbia SC 29201. (803)734-8696.*
E-mail: burnette@state.sc.us. Website: www.state.sc.us/arts.

South Dakota Arts Council, *800 Governors Dr., Pierre SD 57501. (605)773-3131. E-mail: sdac@stlib.state.sd.us. Website: www.state.sd.us/deca/sdarts.*

Tennessee Arts Commission, *401 Charlotte Ave., Nashville TN 37243-0780. (615)741-1701. Website: www.arts.state.tn.us/index.html.*

Texas Commission on the Arts, *P.O. Box 13406, Austin TX 78711-3406. (512)463-5535. E-mail: front.desk@arts.state.tx.us. Website: www.arts.state.tx.us.*

Utah Arts Council, *617 E. South Temple, Salt Lake City UT 84102-1177. (801)236-7555. E-mail: swadding@arts.state.ut.us. Website: www.dced.state.ut.us/arts/index.html.*

Vermont Arts Council, *136 State St., Drawer 33, Montpelier VT 05633-6001. (802)828-3291. E-mail: info@arts.vca.state.vt.us. Website: www.vermontartscouncil.org.*

Virgin Islands Council on the Arts, *41-42 Norre Gada, P.O. Box 103, St. Thomas VI 00804. (340)774-5984. E-mail: vicouncil@islands.vi.*

Virginia Commission for the Arts, *Lewis House, 2nd Floor, 223 Governor St., Richmond VA 23219. (804)225-3132. E-mail: vacomm@artswire.org. Website: www.artswire.org/~vacomm/.*

Washington State Arts Commission, *P.O. Box 42675, Olympia WA 98504-2675. (360)753-3860. E-mail: joslet@arts.wa.gov. Website: www.arts.wa.gov.*

West Virginia Arts Commission, *Cultural Center, 1900 Kanawha Blvd. E., Charleston WV 25305-0300. (304)558-0220. E-mail: barbie.anderson@wvculture.org. Website: www.wvculture.org.*

Wisconsin Arts Board, *101 E. Wilson St., 1st Floor, Madison WI 53702. (608)266-0190. E-mail: artsboard@arts.state.wi.us. Website: www.arts.state.wi.us.*

Wyoming Arts Council, *2320 Capitol Ave., Cheyenne WY 82002. (307)777-7742. Website: spacr.state.wy.us/cr/arts.*

CANADIAN PROVINCES ARTS AGENCIES

Alberta Foundation for the Arts, *901 Standard Life Centre, 10405 Jasper Ave., 9th Floor, Edmonton, Alberta T5J 4R7. (780)427-6315. E-mail: afa@mcd.gov.ab.ca. Website: www.affta.ab.ca.*

British Columbia Arts Council, *P.O. Box 9819, Stn Prov Govt, Victoria, British Columbia V8W 9W3. (250)356-1728. E-mail: csbinfo@tbc.gov.bc.ca. Website: www.bcartscouncil.gov.bc.ca.*

Manitoba Arts Council, *525 - 93 Lombard Ave., Winnipeg, Manitoba R3B 3B1. (204)945-2237. E-mail: manart1@mb.sympatico.ca. Website: www.artscouncil.mb.ca.*

New Brunswick Department of Economic Development, Tourism & Culture, *Arts Branch, P.O. Box 6000, Fredericton, New Brunswick E3B 5H1. (506)453-3984. Website: www.gnb.ca/Inv-Evp/index.htm.*

Newfoundland & Labrador Arts Council, *P.O. Box 98, St. John's, Newfoundland A1C 5H5. (709)726-2212. E-mail: nlacmail@newcomm.net. Website: www.nlac.nf.ca.*

Nova Scotia Arts Council, *P.O. Box 1559, CPO, Halifax, Nova Scotia B3J 2Y3. (902)422-1123. E-mail: nsartcouncil@ns.sympatico.ca. Website: www.novascotiaartscouncil.ns.ca.*

The Canada Council, *350 Albert St., P.O. Box 1047, Ottawa, Ontario K1P 5V8. (613)566-4414. Website: www.canadacouncil.ca.*

Ontario Arts Council, *151 Bloor St. W., 6th Floor, Toronto, Ontario M5S 1T6. (416)961-1660. E-mail: info@arts.on.ca. Website: www.arts.on.ca/.*

Prince Edward Island Council of the Arts, *115 Richmond, Charlottetown, Prince Edward Island C1A 1H7. (902)368-6176. E-mail: artscouncil@pei.aibn.com.*

Saskatchewan Arts Board, *3475 Albert St., Regina, Saskatchewan S4S 6X6. (306)787-4056.*

Yukon Arts Branch, *Box 2703, Whitehorse, Yukon Y1A 2C6. (867)667-8589. E-mail: arts@gov.yk.ca. Website: www.artsyukon.com.*

Publications of Interest

Knowledge about the music industry is essential for both creative and business success. Staying informed requires keeping up with constantly changing information. Updates on the evolving trends in the music business are available to you in the form of music magazines, music trade papers and books. There is a publication aimed at almost every type of musician, songwriter and music fan, from the most technical knowledge of amplification systems to gossip about your favorite singer. These publications can enlighten and inspire you and provide information vital in helping you become a more well-rounded, educated, and, ultimately, successful musical artist.

This section lists all types of magazines and books you may find interesting. From songwriters' newsletters and glossy music magazines to tip sheets and how-to books, there should be something listed here that you'll enjoy and benefit from.

PERIODICALS

THE ALBUM NETWORK, *120 N. Victory Blvd., Burbank CA 91502. (818)955-4000. Website: www.musicbiz. com. Weekly music industry trade magazine.*

AMERICAN SONGWRITER MAGAZINE, *1009 17th Ave. S., Nashville TN 37212-2201. (615)321-6096. E-mail: info@americansongwriter.com. Website: www.americansongwriter.com. Bimonthly publication for and about songwriters.*

BACK STAGE and BACK STAGE WEST, *P.O. Box 5026, Brentwood TN 37024. (800)437-3183. Website: www.back stage.com. Weekly East and West Coast performing artist trade papers.*

BASS PLAYER, *2800 Campus Dr., San Mateo CA 94403. (650)513-4300. Fax: (650)513-4642. E-mail: bassplayer@ musicplayer.com. Website: www.bassplayer.com. Monthly magazine for bass players with lessons, interviews, articles, and transcriptions.*

BILLBOARD, *1515 Broadway, New York NY 10036. (800)745-8922. E-mail: bbstore@billboard.com. Website: www. billboard.com. Weekly industry trade magazine.*

CANADIAN MUSICIAN, 23 Hannover Dr., Suite 7, St. Catharines, Ontario L2W 1A3 Canada. (877)746-4692. Website: www.canadianmusician.com. *Bimonthly publication for amateur and professional Canadian musicians.*

CHART, *200-41 Britain St., Toronto, Ontario M5A 1R7 Canada. (416)363-3101. E-mail: chart@chartnet.com. Website: www.chartnet.com. Monthly magazine covering the Canadian and international music scenes.*

CMJ NEW MUSIC REPORT, *11 Middle Neck Rd., Suite 400, Great Neck NY 11021-2301. (800)CMJ-WKLY or (516)466-6000. E-mail: subscriptions@cmj.com. Website: www.cmjmusic.com. Weekly college radio and alternative music tip sheet.*

CONTEMPORARY SONGWRITER, *P.O. Box 25879, Colorado Springs CO 80936-5879. E-mail: contemposong@ yahoo.com. Website: www.contemposong.bigfoot.com. Monthly songwriter's magazine.*

COUNTRY LINE MAGAZINE, *P.O. Box 17245, Austin TX 78760. (512)292-1113. E-mail: editor@countrylinemaga zine.com. Website: http://countrylinemagazine.com. Monthly Texas-only country music cowboy and lifestyle magazine.*

DAILY VARIETY, *5700 Wilshire Blvd., Suite 120, Los Angeles CA 90036. (323)857-6600. Website: www.variety.com. Daily entertainment trade newspaper.*

DRAMALOGUE, *1456 N. Gordon, Hollywood CA 90028. L.A.-based entertainment newspaper with an emphasis on theatre and cabaret.*

THE DRAMATIST, *1501 Broadway, Suite 701, New York NY 10036. (212)398-9366. Fax: (212)944-0420. Website: www.dramaguild.com. The quarterly journal of the Dramatists Guild, the professional association of playwrights, composers and lyricists.*

ENTERTAINMENT LAW & FINANCE, *New York Law Publishing Co., 345 Park Ave. S., 8th Floor, New York NY 10010. (917)256-2115. E-mail: leader@ljextra.com. Monthly newsletter covering music industry contracts, lawsuit filings, court rulings and legislation.*

EXCLAIM!, *7-B Pleasant Blvd., Suite 966, Toronto, Ontario M4T 1K2 Canada. (416)535-9735. E-mail: exclaim@ex claim.ca. Website: http://exclaim.ca. Canadian music monthly covering all genres of non-mainstream music.*

FAST FORWARD, *Disc Makers, 7905 N. Rt. 130, Pennsauken NJ 08110-1402. (800)468-9353. Website: www.disc makers.com/music/ffwd. Quarterly newsletter featuring companies and products for performing and recording artists in the independent music industry.*

THE GAVIN REPORT, *140 Second St., 5th Floor, San Francisco CA 94105. (415)495-1990. Website: www.gavin.com. Weekly listing of radio charts.*

GUITAR PLAYER, *2800 Campus Dr., San Mateo CA 94403. (650)513-4300. Fax: (650)513-4646. E-mail: guitplyr@m usicplayer.com. Website: www.guitarplayer.com. Monthly guitar magazine with transcriptions, columns, and interviews, including occasional articles on songwriting.*

HITS MAGAZINE, *14958 Ventura Blvd., Sherman Oaks CA 91403. (818)501-7900. Website: www.hitsmagazine.com. Weekly music industry trade publication.*

JAZZTIMES, *P.O. Box 99050, Collingswood NJ 08108. (888)279-7444. Website: http://jazztimes.com. 10 issues/year magazine covering the American jazz scene.*

THE LEADS SHEET, *Allegheny Music Works, 1611 Menoher Blvd., Johnstown PA 15905. (814)535-3373. Monthly tip sheet.*

LYRICIST REVIEW, *P.O. Box 2167, North Canton OH 44720-0167. E-mail: lyricaslit@aol.com. Website: www.lyricist review.com. Quarterly commentaries on song lyrics and previously unpublished lyrics available to performing musicians.*

MUSIC BOOKS PLUS, *P.O. Box 670, 240 Portage Rd., Lewiston NY 14092. (800)265-8481. E-mail: mail@nor.com. Website: www.musicbooksplus.com.*

MUSIC BUSINESS INTERNATIONAL MAGAZINE, *1 Penn Plaza, 11th Floor, New York NY 10119. (212)615-2925. E-mail: mbi@dotmusic.com. Bimonthly magazine for senior executives in the music industry.*

MUSIC CONNECTION MAGAZINE, *4731 Laurel Canyon Blvd., N. Hollywood CA 91607. (818)755-0101. E-mail: mc@musicconnection.com. Website: www.musicconnection.com. Biweekly music industry trade publication.*

MUSIC MORSELS, *P.O. Box 672216, Marietta GA 30006-0037. (770)850-9560. Fax: (770)850-9646. E-mail: musmor sels@aol.com. Website: www.serge.org/musicmorsels.htm. Monthly songwriting publication.*

MUSIC ROW MAGAZINE, *P.O. Box 158542, Nashville TN 37215. (615)321-3617. E-mail: news@musicrow.com. Website: www.musicrow.com. Biweekly Nashville industry publication.*

OFFBEAT MAGAZINE, *OffBeat Publications, 421 Frenchman St., Suite 200, New Orleans LA 70116-2506. (504)944-4300. E-mail: editor@offbeat.com. Website: www.offbeat.com. Monthly magazine covering Louisiana music and artists.*

PERFORMANCE MAGAZINE, *1101 University Dr., Suite 108, Fort Worth TX 76107-3000. (817)338-9444. Fax: (817)877-4273. E-mail: performmag@aol.com. Website: www.performancemagazine.com. Weekly publication on touring itineraries, artist availability, upcoming tours, and production and venue news.*

THE PERFORMING SONGWRITER, *2805 Azalea Place, Nashville TN 37204. (800)883-7664. E-mail: order@perf ormingsongwriter.com. Website: www.performingsongwriter.com. Bimonthly songwriters' magazine.*

PRODUCER REPORT, *415 S. Topanga Canyon Blvd., Suite 114, Topanga CA 90290. (310)455-0888. Fax: (310)455-0894. E-mail: web@mojavemusic.com. Website: www.mojavemusic.com. Semimonthly newsletter covering which producers are working on which acts, and upcoming, current and recently completed projects.*

PROFESSIONAL SOUND, *23 Hannover Dr., Suite 7, St. Catharine's, Ontario L2W 1A3 Canada. (800)265-8481. Fax: (905)641-1648. E-mail: mail@nor.com. Website: www.professional-sound.com. Bimonthly publication for professionals in the sound and light industry.*

PUBLIC DOMAIN REPORT, *P.O. Box 3102, Margate NJ 08402. (609)822-9401. Website: www.pubdomain.com. Monthly guide to significant titles entering the public domain.*

RADIO AND RECORDS, *10100 Santa Monica Blvd., 5th Floor, Los Angeles CA 90067-4004. (310)553-4330. Fax: (310)203-9763. E-mail: mailroom@rronline.com. Website: www.rronline.com. Weekly newspaper covering the radio and record industries.*

RADIR, *Radio Mall, 2412 Unity Ave. N., Dept. WEB, Minneapolis MN 55422. (800)759-4561. E-mail: info@bbhsoftwar e.com. Website: www.bbhsoftware.com. Quarterly radio station database on disk.*

SING OUT!, *P.O. Box 5460, Bethlehem PA 18015. (888)SING-OUT. Fax: (610)865-5129. E-mail: info@singout.org. Website: www.singout.org. Quarterly folk music magazine.*

SONGCASTING, *15445 Ventura Blvd. #260, Sherman Oaks CA 91403. (818)377-4084. Monthly tip sheet.*

SONGLINK INTERNATIONAL, *23 Belsize Crescent, London NW3 5QY England. E-mail: david@songlink.com. Website: www.songlink.com. 10 issues/year newsletter including details of recording artists looking for songs; contact details for industry sources; also news and features on the music business.*

SONGWRITER MAGAZINE, *P.O. Box 25879, Colorado Springs CO 80936. Monthly magazine especially for songwriters.*

SONGWRITER PRODUCTS, IDEAS AND NECESSITIES, *2520 CR 427 North, Suite 100, Longwood FL 32750. (407)834-8555. Fax: (407)834-9997. Website: www.songwriterproducts.com. Free semi-annual catalog of songwriting tips, tools and accessories, including tapes, CDs, duplication products and music business career packages.*

SONGWRITER'S MONTHLY, The Stories Behind Today's Songs, *332 Eastwood Ave., Feasterville PA 19053. (215)953-0952. E-mail: a1foster@aol.com. Website: www.lafay.com. Monthly songwriters' magazine.*

THE TEXAS POLKA NEWS, *P.O. Box 800183, Houston TX 77280. (281)480-8624. Fax: (713)462-7213. Website: www.angelfive.com/folk/polka/news.html. Monthly publication on Texas dancehalls, record releases, festival and dance listings, and radio station information.*

VARIETY, *5700 Wilshire Blvd., Suite 120, Los Angeles CA 90036. (323)857-6600. Fax: (323)857-0494. Website: www.variety.com. Weekly entertainment trade newspaper.*

WORDS AND MUSIC, *41 Valleybrook Dr., Don Mills, Ontario M3B 2S6 Canada. (416)445-8700. Website: www. socan.ca. Monthly songwriters' magazine.*

BOOKS & DIRECTORIES

88 SONGWRITING WRONGS & HOW TO RIGHT THEM, *by Pat & Pete Luboff, Writer's Digest Books, 1507 Dana Ave., Cincinnati OH 45207. (800)289-0963. Website: www.writersdigest.com.*

THE A&R REGISTRY, *by Ritch Esra, SRS Publishing, 7510 Sunset Blvd. #1041, Los Angeles CA 90046-3418. (800)377-7411 or (800)552-7411. E-mail: musicregistry@compuserve.com.*

ATTENTION: A&R, *by Teri Muench and Susan Pomerantz, Alfred Publishing Co. Inc., P.O. Box 10003, Van Nuys CA 91410-0003. (818)892-2452. Website: www.alfredpub.com.*

THE BILLBOARD GUIDE TO MUSIC PUBLICITY, *revised edition, by Jim Pettigrew, Jr., Billboard Books, 1695 Oak St., Lakewood NJ 08701. (800)344-7119.*

BREAKIN' INTO NASHVILLE, *by Jennifer Ember Pierce, Madison Books, University Press of America, 4720 Boston Way, Lanham MD 20706.*

CMJ DIRECTORY, *11 Middle Neck Rd., Suite 400, Great Neck NJ 11021-2301. (516)466-6000. Website: www.cmj.com.*

CONTRACTS FOR THE MUSIC INDUSTRY, *P.O. Box 952063, Lake Mary FL 32795-2063. (407)834-8555. E-mail: info@songwriterproducts.com. Website: www.songwriterproducts.com. Book and computer software of a variety of music contracts.*

THE CRAFT AND BUSINESS OF SONGWRITING, *by John Braheny, Writer's Digest Books, 1507 Dana Ave., Cincinnati OH 45207. (800)289-0963. Website: www.writersdigest.com.*

THE CRAFT OF LYRIC WRITING, *by Sheila Davis, Writer's Digest Books, 1507 Dana Ave., Cincinnati OH 45207. (800)289-0963. Website: www.writersdigest.com.*

CREATING MELODIES, *by Dick Weissman, Writer's Digest Books, 1507 Dana Ave., Cincinnati OH 45207. (800)289-0963. Website: www.writersdigest.com.*

DIRECTORY OF INDEPENDENT MUSIC DISTRIBUTORS, *by Jason Ojalvo, Disc Makers, 7905 N. Rt. 130, Pennsauken NJ 08110. (800)468-9353. E-mail: discman@discmakers.com. Website: www.discmakers.com.*

FILM/TV MUSIC GUIDE, *by Ritch Esra, SRS Publishing, 7510 Sunset Blvd. #1041, Los Angeles CA 90046-3418. (800)552-7411. E-mail: musicregistry@compuserve.com or srspubl@aol.com.*

FINDING FANS & SELLING CDs, *by Veronique Berry and Jason Ojalvo, Disk Makers, 7905 N. Rt. 130, Pennsauken NJ 08110-1402. (800)468-9353. E-mail: discman@diskmakers.com. Website: www.discmakers.com.*

GUIDE TO INDEPENDENT MUSIC PUBLICITY, *by Veronique Berry, Disc Makers, 7905 N. Rt. 130, Pennsauken NJ 08110-1402. (800)468-9353. E-mail: discman@discmakers.com.*

GUIDE TO MASTER TAPE PREPARATION, *by Dave Moyssiadis, Disk Makers, 7905 N. Rt. 130, Pennsauken NJ 08110-1402. (800)468-9353. E-mail: discman@discmakers.com.*

HOLLYWOOD CREATIVE DIRECTORY, *3000 W. Olympic Blvd. #2525, Santa Monica CA 90404. (800)815-0503. Website: www.hcdonline.com. Lists producers in film and TV.*

THE HOLLYWOOD REPORTER BLU-BOOK PRODUCTION DIRECTORY, *5055 Wilshire Blvd., Los Angeles CA 90036. (323)525-2150. Website: www.hollywoodreporter.com.*

HOT TIPS FOR THE HOME RECORDING STUDIO, *by Hank Linderman, Writer's Digest Books, 1507 Dana Ave., Cincinnati OH 45207. (800)289-0963. Website: www.writersdigest.com.*

HOW TO PROMOTE YOUR MUSIC SUCCESSFULLY ON THE INTERNET, *by David Nevue, Midnight Rain Productions, P.O. Box 21831, Eugene OR 97402. Website: www.rainmusic.com.*

HOW YOU CAN BREAK INTO THE MUSIC BUSINESS, *by Marty Garrett, Lonesome Wind Corporation, P.O. Box 2143, Broken Arrow OK 74013-2143. (800)210-4416. Website: www.telepath.com/bizbook.*

LOUISIANA MUSIC DIRECTORY, *OffBeat, Inc., 421 Frenchmen St., Suite 200, New Orleans LA 70116. (504)944-4300. Website: www.offbeat.com.*

MUSIC ATTORNEY LEGAL & BUSINESS AFFAIRS REGISTRY, *by Ritch Esra and Steve Trumbull, SRS Publishing, 7510 Sunset Blvd. #1041, Los Angeles CA 90046-3418. (800)552-7411. E-mail: musicregistry@compuserve.com or srspubl@aol.com.*

MUSIC DIRECTORY CANADA, *seventh edition, Norris-Whitney Communications Inc., 23 Hannover Dr., Suite 7, St. Catherines, Ontario L2W 1A3 Canada. (877)RING-NWC. E-mail: mail@nor.com. Website: http://nor.com.*

MUSIC LAW: HOW TO RUN YOUR BAND'S BUSINESS, *by Richard Stin, Nolo Press, 950 Parker St., Berkeley CA 94710-9867. (510)549-1976. Website: www.nolo.com.*

MUSIC, MONEY AND SUCCESS: THE INSIDER'S GUIDE TO THE MUSIC INDUSTRY, *by Jeffrey Brabec and Todd Brabec, Schirmer Books, 1633 Broadway, New York NY 10019. Website: http://w3.mlr.com/mlr/schirmer.*

THE MUSIC PUBLISHER REGISTRY, *by Ritch Esra, SRS Publishing, 7510 Sunset Blvd. #1041, Los Angeles CA 90046-3418. (800)552-7411. E-mail: musicregistry@compuserve.com or srspubl@aol.com.*

MUSIC PUBLISHING: A SONGWRITER'S GUIDE, *revised edition, by Randy Poe, Writer's Digest Books, 1507 Dana Ave., Cincinnati OH 45207. (800)289-0963. Website: www.writersdigest.com.*

THE MUSICIAN'S GUIDE TO MAKING & SELLING YOUR OWN CDs & CASSETTES, *by Jana Stanfield, Writer's Digest Books, 1507 Dana Ave., Cincinnati OH 45207. (800)289-0963. Website: www.writersdigest.com.*

MUSICIANS' PHONE BOOK, THE LOS ANGELES MUSIC INDUSTRY DIRECTORY, *Get Yourself Some Publishing, 28336 Simsalido Ave., Canyon Country CA 91351. (805)299-2405. E-mail: mpb@earthlink.net. Website: www.musiciansphonebook.com.*

NASHVILLE MUSIC BUSINESS DIRECTORY, *by Mark Dreyer, NMBD Publishing, P.O. Box 120675, Nashville TN 37212. Phone/Fax: (615)826-4141. E-mail: nashvillemusicbusinessdirectory@juno.com.*

NASHVILLE'S UNWRITTEN RULES: INSIDE THE BUSINESS OF THE COUNTRY MUSIC MACHINE, *by Dan Daley, Overlook Press, 2568 Rt. 212, Woodstock NY 12498. (914)679-6838.*

NATIONAL DIRECTORY OF INDEPENDENT RECORD DISTRIBUTORS, *P.O. Box 452063, Lake Mary FL 32795-2063. (407)834-8555. E-mail: info@songwriterproducts.com. Website: www.songwriterproducts.com.*

THE OFFICIAL COUNTRY MUSIC DIRECTORY, *P.O. Box 7000, Rancho Mirage CA 92270. (760)773-0995.*

RADIO STATIONS OF AMERICA: A NATIONAL DIRECTORY, *P.O. Box 452063, Lake Mary FL 32795-2063. (407)834-8555. E-mail: info@songwriterproducts.com. Website: www.songwriterproducts.com.*

THE REAL DEAL—HOW TO GET SIGNED TO A RECORD LABEL FROM A TO Z, *by Daylle Deanna Schwartz, Billboard Books, 1695 Oak St., Lakewood NJ 08701. (800)344-7119.*

RECORDING INDUSTRY SOURCEBOOK, *Music Books Plus, P.O. Box 670, 240 Portage Rd., Lewiston NY 14092. (800)265-8481. Website: www.musicbooksplus.com.*

THE SONGWRITERS IDEA BOOK, *by Sheila Davis, Writer's Digest Books, 1507 Dana Ave., Cincinnati OH 45207. (800)289-0963. Website: www.writersdigest.com.*

SONGWRITER'S MARKET GUIDE TO SONG & DEMO SUBMISSION FORMATS, *Writer's Digest Books, 1507 Dana Ave., Cincinnati OH 45207. (800)289-0963. Website: www.writersdigest.com.*

SONGWRITER'S PLAYGROUND—INNOVATIVE EXERCISES IN CREATIVE SONGWRITING, *by Barbara L. Jordan, Creative Music Marketing, 1085 Commonwealth Ave., Suite 323, Boston MA 02215. (617)926-8766.*

SONGWRITING AND THE CREATIVE PROCESS, *by Steve Gillette, Sing Out! Publications, P.O. Box 5253, Bethlehem PA 18015-0253. (888)SING-OUT. E-mail: singout@libertynet.org. Website: www.singout.org/sopubs.html.*

SONGWRITING: ESSENTIAL GUIDE TO LYRIC FORM AND STRUCTURE, *by Pat Pattison, Berklee Press, 1140 Boylston St., Boston MA 02215. (617)747-2146. Website: www.www.berkleepress.com.*

THE SOUL OF THE WRITER, *by Susan Tucker with Linda Lee Strother, Journey Publishing, P.O. Box 92411, Nashville TN 37209. (800)776-4231. Website: www.journeypublishing.com.*

SUCCESSFUL LYRIC WRITING, *by Sheila Davis, Writer's Digest Books, 1507 Dana Ave., Cincinnati OH 45207. (800)289-0963. Website: www.writersdigest.com.*

THIS BUSINESS OF MUSIC MARKETING AND PROMOTION, *by Tad Lathrop and Jim Pettigrew, Jr., Billboard Books, Watson-Guptill Publications, 1515 Broadway, New York NY 10036-8986. (800)344-7119.*

TIM SWEENEY'S GUIDE TO RELEASING INDEPENDENT RECORDS, *by Tim Sweeney, TSA Books, 21213-B Hawthorne Blvd. #5255, Torrance CA 90503. (310)542-1322. Website: www.tsamusic.com.*

TIM SWEENEY'S GUIDE TO SUCCEEDING AT MUSIC CONVENTIONS, *by Tim Sweeney, TSA Books, 21213-B Hawthorne Blvd. #5255, Torrance CA 90503. (310)542-1322. Website: www.tsamusic.com.*

TEXAS MUSIC INDUSTRY DIRECTORY, *Texas Music Office, Office of the Governor, P.O. Box 13246, Austin TX 78711. (512)463-6666. E-mail: music@governor.state.tx.us. Website: www.governor.state.tx.us/music.*

TUNESMITH: INSIDE THE ART OF SONGWRITING, *by Jimmy Webb, Hyperion, 114 Fifth Ave., New York NY 10011. (800)343-9204.*

VOLUNTEER LAWYERS FOR THE ARTS GUIDE TO COPYRIGHT FOR MUSICIANS AND COMPOSERS, *One E. 53rd St., 6th Floor, New York NY 10022. (212)319-2787.*

WRITING BETTER LYRICS, *by Pat Pattison, Writer's Digest Books, 1507 Dana Ave., Cincinnati OII 45207. (800)289-0963. Website: www.writersdigest.com.*

THE YELLOW PAGES OF ROCK, *The Album Network, 120 N. Victory Blvd., Burbank CA 91502. (818)955-4000.*

Websites of Interest

The Internet can provide a wealth of information for songwriters and performers, and the number of sites devoted to music grows each day. Below is a list of some websites that can offer you information, links to other music sites, contact with other songwriters and places to showcase your songs. Since the online world is changing and expanding at such a rapid pace, this is hardly a comprehensive list, and some of these addresses may be obsolete by the time this book goes to print. But it gives you a place to start on your journey through the Internet to search for opportunities to get your music heard.

ABOUT.COM MUSICIANS' EXCHANGE: *http://musicians.miningco.com*
Site featuring headlines and articles of interest to independent musicians, as well as numerous links.

AMERICAN MUSIC CENTER: *www.amc.net*
Classical/jazz archives, includes a list of composer organizations and contacts.

AMERICAN SOCIETY OF COMPOSERS, AUTHORS AND PUBLISHERS (ASCAP) *www.ascap.com*
Database of performed works in ASCAP's repertoire. Also includes songwriter, performer and publisher information, ASCAP membership information and industry news.

AMPCAST.COM: *www.ampcast.com*
Online musicians community and music hosting site.

ARCANA, Artist Research, Composer's Aid & Network Access: *www.musicnotes.com*
Reference site for classical composers and musicians, including collaboration opportunities, contests and music archives, in addition to industry news.

ASSOCIATION FOR INDEPENDENT MUSIC: *www.afim.org*
AFIM's mission is to establish channels of effective communication for independent distribution. They sponsor an annual convention of retailers, distributors, labels and artists.

BANDADVERTISING.COM: *www.bandadvertising.com*
Site offering members help with promotion, including online radio play, free banner rotation on sponsoring websites, free advice and webpage design for online music sites.

THE BANDIT A&R NEWSLETTER: *www.banditnewsletter.com*
Offers newsletter to help musicians target demos and press kits to labels, publishers, managers and production companies actively looking for new talent.

BANDSTAND: *www.bandstand.com*
Music news and links.

THE BARD'S CRIER: *http://thebards.net/crier/*
A free guerilla music marketing e-zine.

THE BLUES FOUNDATION: *www.blues.org*
Information on the foundation, its membership and events.

BROADCAST MUSIC, INC. (BMI): *www.bmi.com*
Offers lists of song titles, songwriters and publishers of the BMI repertoire. Also includes BMI membership information, and general information on songwriting and licensing.

THE BUZZ FACTOR: *www.thebuzzfactor.com*
Offers press kit evaluation, press release writing, guerrilla music marketing, tips and weekly newsletter.

CDBABY: *www.cdbaby.com*
An online CD store dedicated solely to independent music.

CDSTREET.COM: *www.cdstreet.com*
Offers secure online ordering support to artist websites for a 15% commission.

CHILDREN'S MUSIC WEB: *www.childrensmusic.org*
Website dedicated to music for kids.

CHORUS AMERICA: *www.chorusamerica.org*
The website of Chorus America, a national service organization for professional and volunteer choruses, including job listings and professional development information.

COMPOSERS CONCORDANCE: *www.musicnotes.com*
The website of the ARCANA-sponsored group which promotes performance of new American music through concert series and public awareness.

COUNTRY SONGWRITER: *www.countrysongwriter.com*
Monthly online music magazine with articles on the music business and the songwriting process.

CPCC: *www.under.org/cpcc*
Website for the Center for the Promotion of Contemporary Composers.

CREATIVE MUSICIANS COALITION (CMC): *www.aimcmc.com*
Website of the CMC, an international organization dedicated to the advancement of independent musicians, links to artists, and tips and techniques for musicians.

DIY TOUR GUIDE: *http://industrial.org/tour.html*
Directory of venues and promoters.

ENSEMBLE 21: *www.ensemble21.com/e21.html*
Website of the New York contemporary music performance group dedicated to promotion and performance of new orchestral compositions.

FILM MUSIC: *www.filmmusic.com*
Website relating to film and TV music composition.

FOURFRONT MEDIA AND MUSIC: *www.knab.com*
This site by music industry consultant Christopher Knab offers in-depth information on product development, promotion, publicity and performance.

GAJOOB MAGAZINE: *www.gajoob.com*
Online magazine offering information on labels looking for artists, radio stations looking for independent artists, festivals, publications, collaborations, etc.

GETSIGNED.COM: *www.getsigned.com*
Interviews with industry executives, how-to business information and more.

GOVERNMENT LIAISON SERVICES: *www.trademarkinfo.com*
An intellectual property research firm. Offers a free online trademark search.

GUITAR NINE RECORDS: *www.guitar9.com*
Offers articles by music professionals and insiders.

HARRY FOX AGENCY: *www.nmpa.org/hfa/licensing.html*
Offers a comprehensive FAQ about licensing songs for use in recording, performance and film.

INDEPENDENT ARTISTS' SERVICES: *www.idiom.com/~upend/*
Full of information including searchable databases of bands and booking/touring information and other resources.

INDEPENDENT DISTRIBUTION NETWORK: *www.idnmusic.com/*
Website of independent bands distributing their music, with advice on everything from starting a band to finding labels.

INDEPENDENT SONGWRITER WEB MAGAZINE: *www.independentsongwriter.com*
Independent music reviews, classifieds, message board and chat sessions.

INDIE CENTRE: *www.indiecentre.com*
An independent label information site created to share ideas on releasing albums, including creating a label, distribution and touring.

INDIE CORNER: *http://theglobalmuse.com/indiecorner/index.html*
Offers tips and articles on promotion and marketing, demos, dealing with A&R persons and designing a website geared toward promoting and selling your music.

INDIE-MUSIC.COM: *http://indie-music.com*
Full of how-to articles, record label directory, radio links and venue listing.

INTERNET UNDERGROUND MUSIC ARCHIVE (IUMA): *www.iuma.com*
Online musicians community and music hosting site.

JAZZ COMPOSERS COLLECTIVE: *www.jazzcollective.com*
Industry information on composers, projects, recordings, concerts and events.

JAZZ CORNER: *www.jazzcorner.com*
Website for musicians and organizations featuring links to 70 websites for jazz musicians and organizations and the Speakeasy, an interactive conference area.

JUST PLAIN FOLKS: *www.jpfolks.com*
Online songwriting organization featuring messageboards, lyric feedback forums, member profiles, featured members' music, contact listings, chapter homepages, and an Internet radio station. (See the Just Plain Folks listing in the Organizations section).

KATHODE RAY MUSIC: *www.kathoderaymusic.com*
Specializes in marketing and promotion consultation and offers a business forum, e-newsletter and a free classified ads board.

LAW CYBERCENTER: *www.hollywoodnetwork.com/Law/music/survival2.html*
Tips on negotiating and dealing with songwriting contracts.

LI'L HANK'S GUIDE FOR SONGWRITERS IN L.A.: *www.halsguide.com*
Website for songwriters with information on clubs, publishers, books, etc. as well as links to other songwriting sites.

LIVECONCERTS.COM: *www.liveconcerts.com*
Features interactive interviews with artists, concert dates and industry news.

LOS ANGELES GOES UNDERGROUND: *www.primenet.com/~matthew/lagu/*
Website dedicated to underground rock bands from Los Angeles and Hollywood.

LOS ANGELES MUSIC ACCESS (LAMA): *http://lama.com*
Database of Los Angeles bands, clubs and resources sponsored by a group that promotes independent artists.

LYRICAL LINE: *www.lyricalline.com*
Offers places to market your songs, critique service, industry news and more.

LYRICIST.COM: *www.lyricist.com*
Jeff Mallet's songwriter site offering contests, tips and job opportunities in the music industry.

MEDIA BUREAU: *www.mediabureau.com*
Live Internet radio programs where guests perform and talk about songwriting.

MISERYLOVES RECORDS COPYRIGHT TUTORIAL: *www.miseryloves.com/law.htm*
Copyright information and contract pages devoted to music law issues.

MI2N (THE MUSIC INDUSTRY NEWS NETWORK): *www.mi2n.com*
Offers news on happenings in the music industry and career postings.

MP3.COM: *www.mp3.com*
Currently the most well-known online musicians community and music hosting site with thousands of songs available for free download.

THE MUSE'S MUSE: *www.musesmuse.com*
Classifieds, catalog of lyric samples, songwriting articles, organizations and chat room.

MUSIC & AUDIO CONNECTION: *www.vaxxine.com/music*
Guide to Canadian artists, associations and other resources from Norris-Whitney Communications, Inc.

MUSIC INDUSTRY PAGES: *www.musicindustry.com*
Listings of labels, magazines, products, music schools, retailers, etc.

MUSIC PUBLISHERS ASSOCIATION: *http://host.mpa.org*
Provides a copyright resource center, directory of member publishers and information on the organization.

MUSIC YELLOW PAGES: *www.musicyellowpages.com*
Phone book listings of music-related businesses.

MUSICIANS ASSISTANCE SITE (MAS): *www.musicianassist.com*
Features site reviews and databases of venues, contacts, promoters, manufacturers and record labels. Also includes an archive of music business articles, columns, and pre-made contracts and agreements.

THE MUSICIANS GUIDE THROUGH THE LEGAL JUNGLE: *www.legaljungleguide.com/resource.htm*
Offers articles on copyright law, music publishing and talent agents.

NASHVILLE PUBLISHERS NETWORK: *www.songnet.com/npn*
Website dedicated to networking in the Nashville music community.

NATIONAL ASSOCIATION OF COMPOSERS USA (NACUSA): *www.music-usa.org/nacusa*
Website of the organization dedicated to promotion and performance of new music by Americans, featuring a young composers' competition, concert schedule, job opportunities and more.

NATIONAL MUSIC PUBLISHERS ASSOCIATION: *www.nmpa.org*
The organization's online site with information about copyright, legislation and other concerns of the music publishing world.

ONLINE ROCK: *www.onlinerock.com*
Offers e-mail, marketing and free webpage services. Also features articles, chat rooms, links, etc.

OPERA AMERICA: *www.operaam.org*
Website of Opera America, featuring information on advocacy and awareness programs, publications, conference schedules and more.

OUTERSOUND: *www.outersound.com*
Information on finding a recording studio, educating yourself in the music industry, and a list of music magazines to advertise in or get reviewed by.

PUBLIC DOMAIN MUSIC: *www.pdinfo.com*
Articles on public domain works and copyright, including public domain song lists, research resources, tips and a FAQ.

RES ROCKET SURFER: *www.resrocket.com or www.rocketnetwork.com*
Offers collaboration opportunities and industry news.

RHYTHM NET: *www.rhythmnet.com*
Information on artists, labels, entertainment establishments and more.

SESAC INC.: *www.sesac.com*
Includes SESAC performing rights organization information, songwriter profiles, organization news, licensing information and links to other sites.

SONG SHARK: *www.geocities.com/songshark*
Website of information on known song sharks.

SONGCATALOG.COM: *www.songcatalog.com*
Online song catalog database for pitching and licensing.

SONGFILE.COM: *www.songfile.com*
Online song catalog database for pitching and licensing.

SONGLINK: *www.songlink.com*
Offers opportunities to pitch songs to music publishers for specific recording projects, also industry news.

SONGPITCH.COM:
Online song catalog for pitching to music publishers and producers.

SONGSCAPE: *www.songscape.com*
Music database and music industry news service.

SONGSCOPE.COM: *www.songscope.com*
Online song catalog database for pitching and licensing.

SONGWRITER PRODUCTS IDEAS & NECESSITIES (SPIN): *www.songwriterproducts.com*
Offer songwriting tips, tools and accessories, including tapes, CDs, duplication products and music business career packages.

SONGWRITER'S GUILD OF AMERICA (SGA): *www.songwriters.org*
Offers industry news, members services information, newsletters, contract reviews and more.

SONGWRITER'S RESOURCE NETWORK: *www.songwritersresourcenetwork.com*
Online information and services designed especially for songwriters.

THE SONGWRITING EDUCATION RESOURCE: *www.craftofsongwriting.com*
An educational site for Nashville songwriters offering discussion boards, articles and links.

SONIC NET: *www.sonicnet.com*
Music news, chat and reviews.

STOMPINGGROUND: *www.stompinground.com*
Provides bands with Real Audio concerts, free listings, promotion and a list of record labels.

STUDIO FINDER: *www.studiofinder.com*
Locate more than 5,000 recording studios anywhere in the U.S.

TAXI: *www.taxi.com*
Independent A&R vehicle that shops tapes to A&R professionals.

ULTIMATE BAND LIST: *www.ubl.com*
Lists record labels and their artists, posts calendar of events, festivals and club dates for artists nationwide; also includes chart information and artist news.

UNITED STATES COPYRIGHT OFFICE: *http://lcweb.loc.gov/copyright*
The homepage for the U.S. copyright office, offering information on registering songs.

YAHOO!: *www.yahoo.com/Entertainment/Music/*
Use this search engine to retrieve over 20,000 music listings.

ONLINE SHOWCASES

These sites offer places for you to post your music for a fee as a way of marketing your songs to music executives.

ARTIST UNDERGROUND: *www.aumusic.com*

BILLBOARD TALENT NET: *www.billboardtalentnet.com*

BROADBAND TALENT NET: *www.broadbandtalent.com*

INTERNET UNDERGROUND MUSIC ARCHIVE (IUMA): *www.iuma.com.*

KALEIDOSPACE: *http://kspace.com*

MUSIC SPOTLIGHT WEB: *www.musicspotlight.com*

ONLINE AUDITIONS, INC.: *http://newbands.net*

SOUND ARTIST: *www.soundartist.com*

Contributors to the Insider Reports

ANNE BOWLING is editor of *Novel & Short Story Writer's Market* and a Cincinnati-based free-lance writer.

CYNTHIA LAUFENBERG was editor of *Songwriter's Market* from 1992 to 1997. She lives in Princeton, New Jersey.

AMANDA TEBBE was last published in her eighth-grade creative writing class, but hopes for better luck soon. She is a recent graduate of Xavier University.

Glossary

A cappella. Choral singing without accompaniment.

AAA form. A song form in which every verse has the same melody; often used for songs that tell a story.

AABA, ABAB. A commonly used song pattern consisting of two verses, a bridge and a verse, or a repeated pattern of verse and bridge, where the verses are musically the same.

A&R Director. Record company executive in charge of the Artists and Repertoire Department who is responsible for finding and developing new artists and matching songs with artists.

A/C. Adult contemporary music.

Advance. Money paid to the songwriter or recording artist, which is then recouped before regular royalty payment begins. Sometimes called "up front" money, advances are deducted from royalties.

AFIM. Association for Independent Music (formerly NAIRD). Organization for independent record companies, distributors, retailers, manufacturers, etc.

AFM. American Federation of Musicians. A union for musicians and arrangers.

AFTRA. American Federation of Television and Radio Artists. A union for performers.

AIMP. Association of Independent Music Publishers.

Airplay. The radio broadcast of a recording.

AOR. Album-Oriented Rock. A radio format that primarily plays selections from rock albums as opposed to hit singles.

Arrangement. An adaptation of a composition for a recording or performance, with consideration for the melody, harmony, instrumentation, tempo, style, etc.

ASCAP. American Society of Composers, Authors and Publishers. A performing rights society. (See the Organizations section.)

Assignment. Transfer of rights of a song from writer to publisher.

Audio Visual Index (AVI). A database containing title and production information for cue sheets which are available from a performing rights organization. Currently, BMI, ASCAP, SOCAN, PRS, APRA and SACEM contribute their cue sheet listings to the AVI.

Audiovisual. Refers to presentations that use audio backup for visual material.

Background music. Music used that creates mood and supports the spoken dialogue of a radio program or visual action of an audiovisual work. Not feature or theme music.

b&w. Black and white.

Bed. Prerecorded music used as background material in commercials. In rap music, often refers to the sampled and looped drums and music over which the rapper performs.

Black box. Theater without fixed stage or seating arrangements, capable of a variety of formations. Usually a small space, often attached to a major theater complex, used for workshops or experimental works calling for small casts and limited sets.

BMI. Broadcast Music, Inc. A performing rights society. (See the Organizations section.)

Booking agent. Person who schedules performances for entertainers.

Bootlegging. Unauthorized recording and selling of a song.

Business manager. Person who handles the financial aspects of artistic careers.

Buzz. Attention an act generates through the media and word of mouth.

b/w. Backed with. Usually refers to the B-side of a single.

C&W. Country and western.

Catalog. The collected songs of one writer, or all songs handled by one publisher.

CD. Compact Disc (see below).

CD-R. A recordable CD.

CD-ROM. Compact Disc-Read Only Memory. A computer information storage medium capable of holding enormous amounts of data. Information on a CD-ROM cannot be deleted. A computer user must have a CD-ROM drive to access a CD-ROM.

Chamber music. Any music suitable for performance in a small audience area or chamber.

Chamber orchestra. A miniature orchestra usually containing one instrument per part.

Chart. The written arrangement of a song.

Charts. The trade magazines' lists of the best-selling records.

CHR. Comtemporary Hit Radio. Top 40 pop music.

Collaboration. Two or more artists, writers, etc., working together on a single project; for instance, a playwright and a songwriter creating a musical together.

Compact disc. A small disc (about 4.7 inches in diameter) holding digitally encoded music that is read by a laser beam in a CD player.

Composers. The men and women who create musical compositions for motion pictures and other audio visual works, or the creators of classical music composition.

Co-publish. Two or more parties own publishing rights to the same song.

Copyright. The exclusive legal right giving the creator of a work the power to control the publishing, reproduction and selling of the work. Although a song is technically copyrighted at the time it is written, the best legal protection of that copyright comes through registering the copyright with the Library of Congress.

Copyright infringement. Unauthorized use of a copyrighted song or portions thereof.

Cover recording. A new version of a previously recorded song.

Crossover. A song that becomes popular in two or more musical categories (e.g., country and pop).

Cut. Any finished recording; a selection from a LP. Also to record.

DAT. Digital Audio Tape. A professional and consumer audio cassette format for recording and playing back digitally-encoded material. DAT cassettes are approximately one-third smaller than conventional audio cassettes.

DCC. Digital Compact Cassette. A consumer audio cassette format for recording and playing back digitally-encoded tape. DCC tapes are the same size as analog cassettes.

Demo. A recording of a song submitted as a demonstration of a writer's or artist's skills.

Derivative work. A work derived from another work, such as a translation, musical arrangement, sound recording, or motion picture version.

Distributor. Wholesale marketing agent responsible for getting records from manufacturers to retailers.

Donut. A jingle with singing at the beginning and end and instrumental background in the middle. Ad copy is recorded over the middle section.

E-mail. Electronic mail. Computer address where a company or individual can be reached via modem.

Engineer. A specially-trained individual who operates recording studio equipment.

Enhanced CD. General term for an audio CD that also contains multimedia computer information. It is playable in both standard CD players and CD-ROM drives.

EP. Extended play record or cassette containing more selections than a standard single, but fewer than a standard album.

Exploit. To seek legitimate uses of a song for income.

Final mix. The art of combining all the various sounds that take place during the recording session into a two-track stereo or mono tape. Reflects the total product and all of the energies and talents the artist, producer and engineer have put into the project.

Fly space. The area above a stage from which set pieces are lowered and raised during a performance.

Folio. A softcover collection of printed music prepared for sale.

Following. A fan base committed to going to gigs and buying albums.

Foreign rights societies. Performing rights societies other than domestic which have reciprocal agreements with ASCAP and BMI for the collection of royalties accrued by foreign radio and television airplay and other public performance of the writer members of the above groups.

Harry Fox Agency. Organization that collects mechanical royalties.

Grammy. Music industry awards presented by the National Academy of Recording Arts and Sciences.

Hip-hop. A dance oriented musical style derived from a combination of disco, rap and R&B.

Hit. A song or record that achieves top 40 status.

Hook. A memorable "catch" phrase or melody line that is repeated in a song.

House. Dance music created by remixing samples from other songs.

Hypertext. Words or groups of words in an electronic document that are linked to other text, such as a definition or a related document. Hypertext can also be linked to illustrations.

Indie. An independent record label, music publisher or producer.

Infringement. A violation of the exclusive rights granted by the copyright law to a copyright owner.

Internet. A worldwide network of computers that offers access to a wide variety of electronic resources.

ips. Inches per second; a speed designation for tape recording.

IRC. International reply coupon, necessary for the return of materials sent out of the country. Available at most post offices.

Jingle. Usually a short verse set to music designed as a commercial message.

Lead sheet. Written version (melody, chord symbols and lyric) of a song.

Leader. Plastic (non-recordable) tape at the beginning and between songs for ease in selection.

Libretto. The text of an opera or any long choral work. The booklet containing such text.

Listing. Block of information in this book about a specific company.

LP. Designation for long-playing record played at 33⅓ rpm.

Lyric sheet. A typed or written copy of a song's lyrics.

Market. A potential song or music buyer; also a demographic division of the record-buying public.

Master. Edited and mixed tape used in the production of records; the best or original copy of a recording from which copies are made.

MD. MiniDisc. A 2.5 inch disk for recording and playing back digitally-encoded music.

Mechanical right. The right to profit from the physical reproduction of a song.

Mechanical royalty. Money earned from record, tape and CD sales.

MIDI. Musical instrument digital interface. Universal standard interface that allows musical instruments to communicate with each other and computers.

Mini Disc. (See **MD** above.)

Mix. To blend a multi-track recording into the desired balance of sound, usually to a 2-track stereo master.

Modem. MOdulator/DEModulator. A computer device used to send data from one computer to another via telephone line.

MOR. Middle of the road. Easy-listening popular music.

MP3. File format of a relatively small size that stores audio files on a computer. Music saved in a MP3 format can be played only with a MP3 player (which can be downloaded onto a computer).

Ms. Manuscript.

Multimedia. Computers and software capable of integrating text, sound, photographic-quality images, animation and video.

Music bed. (See **Bed** above.)

Music jobber. A wholesale distributor of printed music.

Music library. A business that purchases canned music, which can then be bought by producers of radio and TV commercials, films, videos and audiovisual productions to use however they wish.

Music publisher. A company that evaluates songs for commercial potential, finds artists to record them, finds other uses (such as TV or film) for the songs, collects income generated by the songs and protects copyrights from infringement.

Music Row. An area of Nashville, TN, encompassing Sixteenth, Seventeeth and Eighteenth avenues where most of the major publishing houses, recording studios, mastering labs, songwriters, singers, promoters, etc. practice their trade.

NARAS. National Academy of Recording Arts and Sciences.

The National Academy of Songwriters (NAS). The largest U.S. songwriters' association. (See the Organizations section.)

Needle-drop. Refers to a type of music library. A needledrop music library is a licensed library that allows producers to borrow music on a rate schedule. The price depends on how the music will be used.

Network. A group of computers electronically linked to share information and resources.

NMPA. National Music Publishers Association.

One-off. A deal between songwriter and publisher which includes only one song or project at a time. No future involvement is implicated. Many times a single song contract accompanies a one-off deal.

One-stop. A wholesale distributor of who sells small quantities of records to "mom and pop" record stores, retailers and jukebox operators.

Operetta. Light, humorous, satiric plot or poem, set to cheerful light music with occasional spoken dialogue.

Overdub. To record an additional part (vocal or instrumental) onto a basic multi-track recording.

Parody. A satirical imitation of a literary or musical work. Permission from the owner of the copyright is generally required before commercial exploitation of a parody.

Payola. Dishonest payment to broadcasters in exchange for airplay.

Performing rights. A specific right granted by U.S. copyright law protecting a composition from being publicly performed without the owner's permission.

Performing rights organization. An organization that collects income from the public performance of songs written by its members and then proportionally distributes this income to the individual copyright holder based on the number of performances of each song.

Personal manager. A person who represents artists to develop and enhance their careers. Personal managers may negotiate contracts, hire and dismiss other agencies and personnel relating to the artist's career, review material, help with artist promotions and perform many services.

Piracy. The unauthorized reproduction and selling of printed or recorded music.

Pitch. To attempt to solicit interest for a song by audition.

Playlist. List of songs a radio station will play.

Points. A negotiable percentage paid to producers and artists for records sold.

Producer. Person who supervises every aspect of a recording project.

Production company. Company specializing in producing jingle packages for advertising agencies. May also refer to companies specializing in audiovisual programs.

Professional manager. Member of a music publisher's staff who screens submitted material and tries to get the company's catalog of songs recorded.

Proscenium. Permanent architectural arch in a theater that separates the stage from the audience.

Public domain. Any composition with an expired, lapsed or invalid copyright, and therefore belonging to everyone.

Purchase license. Fee paid for music used from a stock music library.

Query. A letter of inquiry to an industry professional soliciting his interest.

R&B. Rhythm and blues.

Rack Jobber. Distributors who lease floor space from department stores and put in racks of albums.

Rate. The percentage of royalty as specified by contract.

Release. Any record issued by a record company.

Residuals. In advertising or television, payments to singers and musicians for use of a performance.

RIAA. Recording Industry Association of America.

Royalty. Percentage of money earned from the sale of records or use of a song.

RPM. Revolutions per minute. Refers to phonograph turntable speed.

SAE. Self-addressed envelope (with no postage attached).

SASE. Self-addressed stamped envelope.

SATB. The abbreviation for parts in choral music, meaning Soprano, Alto, Tenor and Bass.

Score. A complete arrangement of all the notes and parts of a composition (vocal or instrumental) written out on staves. A full score, or orchestral score, depicts every orchestral part on a separate staff and is used by a conductor.

Self-contained. A band or recording act that writes all their own material.

SESAC. A performing rights organization, originally the Society of European Stage Authors and Composers. (See the Organizations section.)

SFX. Sound effects.

Shop. To pitch songs to a number of companies or publishers.

Single. 45 rpm record with only one song per side. A 12″ single refers to a long version of one song on a 12″ disc, usually used for dance music.

Ska. Fast tempo dance music influenced primarily by reggae and punk, usually featuring horns, saxophone and bass.

SOCAN. Society of Composers, Authors and Music Publishers of Canada. A Canadian performing rights organization. (See the Organizations section.)

Solicited. Songs or materials that have been requested.

Song plugger. A songwriter representative whose main responsibility is promoting uncut songs to music publishers, record companies, artists and producers.

Song shark. Person who deals with songwriters deceptively for his own profit.

SoundScan. A company that collates the register tapes of reporting stores to track the actual number of albums sold at the retail level.

Soundtrack. The audio, including music and narration, of a film, videotape or audiovisual program.

Space stage. Open stage that features lighting and, perhaps, projected scenery.

Split publishing. To divide publishing rights between two or more publishers.

Staff songwriter. A songwriter who has an exclusive agreement with a publisher.

Statutory royalty rate. The maximum payment for mechanical rights guaranteed by law that a record company may pay the songwriter and his publisher for each record or tape sold.

Subpublishing. Certain rights granted by a U.S. publisher to a foreign publisher in exchange for promoting the U.S. catalog in his territory.

Synchronization. Technique of timing a musical soundtrack to action on film or video.

Take. Either an attempt to record a vocal or instrument part, or an acceptable recording of a performance.

Tejano. A musical form begun in the late 1970s by regional bands in south Texas, its style reflects a blended Mexican-American culture. Incorporates elements of rock, country, R&B and jazz, and often features accordion and 12-string guitar.

Thrust stage. Stage with audience on three sides and a stagehouse or wall on the fourth side.

Top 40. The first 40 songs on the pop music charts at any given time. Also refers to a style of music which emulates that heard on the current top 40.

Track. Divisions of a recording tape (e.g., 24-track tape) that can be individually recorded in the studio, then mixed into a finished master.

Trades. Publications covering the music industry.

12″ Single. A 12-inch record containing one or more remixes of a song, originally intended for dance club play.

Unsolicited. Songs or materials that were not requested and are not expected.

VHS. ½″ videocassette format.

Vocal score. An arrangement of vocal music detailing all vocal parts, and condensing all accompanying instrumental music into one piano part.

Website. An address on the World Wide Web that can be accessed by computer modem. It may contain text, graphics and sound.

Wing space. The offstage area surrounding the playing stage in a theater, unseen by the audience, where sets and props are hidden, actors wait for cues, and stagehands prepare to chance sets.

World music. A general music category which includes most musical forms originating outside the U.S. and Europe, including reggae and calypso. World music finds its roots primarily in the Caribbean, Latin America, Africa and the south Pacific.

World Wide Web (WWW). An Internet resource that utilizes hypertext to access information. It also supports formatted text, illustrations and sounds, depending on the user's computer capabilities.

Indexes

Openness to Submissions Index.......... 476

Film & TV Index................................. 484

Geographic Index............................. 485

General Index................................... 502

Openness to Submissions Index

Use this index to find companies open to your level of experience. Be sure to read the Openness to Submissions sidebar on page 8 for more information. It is recommended to use this index in conjunction with the Category Indexes found at the end of the following sections: Music Publishers, Record Companies, Record Producers, Managers & Booking Agents. Once you have compiled a list of companies open to your experience and music, read the information in these listings, paying close attention to **How to Contact**

◯ OPEN TO BEGINNERS

Music Publishers
Abalone Publishing
Alco Music
Alexander Sr. Music
Alexis
Alias John Henry Tunes
All Rock Music
Allegheny Music Works
American Heartstring Publishing
Antelope Publishing Inc.
ARAS Music
Audio Music Publishers
Avalon Music
Barkin' Foe the Master's Bone
Barren Wood Publishing
Bay Ridge Publishing Co.
Black Stallion Country Publishing
Bradley Music, Allan
Brewster Songs, Kitty
BSW Records
Buried Treasure Music
California Country Music
Clevère Musikverlag, R.D.
Corelli's Music Box
Country Rainbow Music
Cupit Music
Dagene Music
Dapmor Publishing
Delev Music Company
Door Knob Music Publishing
Doss Music, Buster
Dream Seekers Publishing
Duane Music, Inc.
Earitating Music Publishing
East Coast Music Publishing
Edition Rossori
Emandell Tunes
Emstone, Inc. Music Publishing
Faverett Group

Fifth Avenue Media, Ltd.
Fresh Entertainment
Frick Enterprises, Bob Scott
Furrow Music
Gary Music, Alan
Glad Music Co.
Golden Music, August
Goodland Music Group Inc., The
Hammel Associates, Inc., R.L.
Hickory Valley Music
His Power Productions and Publishing
Hitsburgh Music Co.
Holy Spirit Music
Indie-Go Music
Interplanetary Music
Iron Skillet Music
Ja/Nein Musikverlag GmbH
Jerjoy Music
JPMC Music Inc.
Kansa Records Corporation
Kaupps & Robert Publishing Co.
Leigh Music, Trixie
Les Music Group
Lindsay Publishing, Doris
Mayfair Music
McConkey Artists Agency Music Publishing
McCoy Music, Jim
Mellow House Music
Mighty Blue Music Machine, The
Moon June Music
Mymit Music Productions, Chuck
Newcreature Music
Ontrax Companies
Otto Publishing Co.
Pecos Valley Music
PEN Music Group, Inc.
Peters Music, Justin
Portage Music
Prejippie Music Group
Prescription Company
QUARK, Inc.

R.T.L. Music
Rustron Music Publishers
Sabteca Music Co.
Salt Works Music
Samuels Publishing, R.
Scott Music Group, Tim
Silicon Music Publishing Co.
Simply Grand Music, Inc.
Sound Cellar Music
Southern Most Publishing Company
Succes
Tedesco Music Co., Dale
Third Wave Productions Limited
Tiki Enterprises, Inc.
Ultimate Peak Music
Wemar Music Corp.
Wengert, Berthold (Musikverlag)
White Cat Music
World Famous Music Co.
Yorgo Music

Record Companies
A.P.I. Records
Airplay Label, The
Albatross Records
Alco Recordings
Allegheny Music Works
Amigos Music & Marketing
Anisette Records
Ariana Records
Atlan-Dec/Grooveline Records
Avalon Recording Group
Avenue Communications
Aware Records
babysue
Belham Valley Records
Beluga Records
Big Beat Records
Blue Gem Records
Blue Wave
BSW Records
Cellar Records
Chattahoochee Records
Collector Records
Com-Four Distribution
Comstock Records Ltd.
Coral Records LLC
Creative Improvised Music Projects Records
Dagene/Cabletown Company
Dale Productions, Alan
Deadeye Records
Deep South Entertainment
Discmedia
Discos Fuentes/Miami Records & Edimusica
   USA
Drool Records
Edmonds Record Group
Emerald City Records

Enterprize Records-Tapes
First Power Entertainment Group
Flood Recording Corp.
Flying Heart Records
Fountain Records
Fresh Entertainment
Front Row Records
Golden Triangle Records
Goldwax Record Corporation
Gonzo! Records Inc.
Gotham Records
Grass Roots Record & Tape/LMI Records
Gueststar Records, Inc.
Hacienda Records & Recording Studio
Hi-Bias Records Inc.
Hottrax Records
Imaginary Records
Keeping It Simple and Safe, Inc.
L.A. Records (Michigan)
Landmark Communications Group
Lock
Loconto Productions/Sunrise Studio
Megaforce Worldwide Entertainment
Merlin Records of Canada
Missile Records
Modal Music, Inc.™
MOR Records
North Star Music
OCP Publications
Omega Record Group, Inc.
Only New Age Music, Inc.
P.M. Records
P. & N. Records
Plateau Music
PMG Records
Powerblast Recordings
Presence Records
Radical Records
Rags to Records, Inc.
Rampant Records
Redemption Records
Road Records
Roll On Records®
Rotten Records
Rowena Records
Rustron Music Productions
Sabre Productions
Sabteca Record Co.
Safire Records
Satellite Music
Sealed Fate Records
Sims Records, Jerry
Sonar Records & Production
Songgram Music
sonic unyon records canada
Southland Records, Inc.
SunCountry Records
Synergy Records

Tangent® Records
Texas Rose Records
Third Wave Productions Ltd.
Triple X Records
28 Records
UAR Records
World Beatnik Records
X.R.L. Records/Music
Yellow Jacket Records

Record Producers
Aberdeen Productions
ACR Productions
Angel Films Company
Avalon Productions
Big Sky Audio Productions
Blues Alley Records
Celt Musical Services, Jan
Coachouse Music
Cupit Productions, Jerry
DAP Entertainment
Dixon III, Philip D., Attorney at Law
Haworth Productions
Jay Jay Publishing & Record Co.
Kovach, Robert R.
L.A. Entertainment, Inc.
Landmark Communications Group
Lark Talent & Advertising
Lazy Bones Productions/Recordings, Inc.
Linear Cycle Productions
Loconto Productions
Mac-Attack Productions
Magid Productions, Lee
Mathews, d/b/a Hit or Myth Productions, Scott
Merlin Productions
Mona Lisa Records/Bristol Studios
Musicland Productions, Inc.
Neu Electro Productions
New Vizion Studios, The
Omni 2000 Inc.
Panio Brothers Label
Philly Breakdown Recording Co.
Prejippie Music Group
Prescription Co., The
R&D Productions
Reel Adventures
Road Records
Rustron Music Productions
SAS Productions/Hit Records Network
Satkowski Recordings, Steve
Sound Works Entertainment Productions Inc.
Studio Seven
Studio Voodoo Music
Swift River Productions
Syndicate Sound, Inc.
Tamjam Productions
Tari, Roger Vincent
Theoretical Reality
TMC Productions

Trinity Studio, The
Vickers Music Association, Charles
Weisman Production Group, The

Managers & Booking Agents
Afterschool Publishing Company
Bassline Entertainment, Inc.
Black Stallion Country, Inc.
Blue Wave Productions
Butler Music, Bill
Conscience Music
Cox Promotions & Management, Stephen
Creative Star Management
D&R Entertainment
Detko Management, Bill
DMR Agency
Earth Tracks Artists Agency
Ellis International Talent Agency, The
Endangered Species Artist Management
Evans Productions, Scott
Exclesisa Booking Agency
Golden City International
Gueststar Entertainment Agency
Hardison International Entertainment
   Corporation
Horizon Management Inc.
Kickstart Music Ltd.
Kuper Personal Management
Loggins Promotion/Backstage Entertainment
Lowell Agency
M.E.G Management
Martin Productions, Rick
Merlin Management Corp.
Merri-Webb Productions
Music Marketing & Promotions
Nash-One Management Inc.
On Stage Management
On the Level Music!
Outlaw Entertainment International
Precision Management
Pro Talent Consultants
RadioActive
Renaissance Entertainment Group
Rock of Ages Productions
Rock Whirled Music Management
Rustron Music Productions
Sea Cruise Productions, Inc.
Spoon Agency L.L.C., The
Stevens & Company Management
T.J. Booker Ltd.
Total Acting Experience, A
Universal Music Marketing
Wagner Agency, William F.
Walls & Co. Management/Showbiz Kidz!
Wilder Artists' Management, Shane
Wood Artist Management, Richard

✔ PREFERS EXPERIENCED, BUT OPEN TO BEGINNERS

Music Publishers

Activate Entertainment LLC
AlliSongs Inc.
Alpha Music Inc.
Amen, Inc.
Americatone International
Aquarius Publishing
Audio Images Two Thousand Music Publishing
Bagatelle Music Publishing Co.
Baird Music Group
Bal & Bal Music Publishing Co.
Bernard Enterprises, Inc., Hal
Better Than Sex Music
Big Fish Music Publishing Group
Blue Dog Publishing and Records
BME Publishing
Branson Country Music Publishing
Cherri/Holly Music Inc.
Christmas & Holiday Music
Christopher Publishing, Sonny
Cornelius Companies, The
De Miles Music Company, The Edward
Doré Records
Earthscream Music Publishing Co.
Ever-Open-Eye Music
First Time Music (Publishing) U.K.
Fricon Music Company
Frozen Inca Music
G Major Music
Happy Melody
High-Minded Moma Publishing & Productions
Hitsource Publishing
Inside Records/OK Songs
Jae Music, Jana
Jasper Stone Music (ASCAP)/JSM Songs (BMI)
Jolson Black & White Music, Al
Juke Music
KeyShavon Music Publishing
Largo Music Publishing
Lari-Jon Publishing
Lexington Alabama Music Publishing
Lilly Music Publishing
Lineage Publishing Co.
Luick & Associates Music Publisher, Harold
Magic Message Music
Makers Mark Gold
Manuiti L.A.
Marvin Publishing, John Weller
Mento Music Group
Musikuser Publishing
New Rap Jam Publishing, A
Northwest Alabama Music Publishing
Orchid Publishing

Piano Press
Pollybyrd Publications Limited
Presser Co., Theodore
Pritchett Publications
R.J. Music
Rock N Metal Music Publishing Co.
Rocker Music/Happy Man Music
Rockford Music Co.
Sci-Fi Music
Scrutchings Music
Shawnee Press, Inc.
Shu'Baby Montez Music
Silver Thunder Music Group
Sinus Musik Produktion, Ulli Weigel
Spradlin/Gleich Publishing
Starbound Publishing Co.
Stellar Music Industries
Stuart Music Co., Jeb
Sunsongs Music/Dark Son Music
T.C. Productions/Etude Publishing Co.
Tower Music Group
Transamerika Musikverlag KG
Transition Music Corporation
Vaam Music Group
Valet Publishing Co.
Vokes Music Publishing
Weaver of Words Music
Westwood Music Group
Whiting Music
Wilcom Publishing
Zettitalia Music International
Zomba Music Publishing

Record Companies

A.A.M.I. Music Group
Afterschool Records, Inc.
All Star Record Promotions
Alpha Beat
Americatone Records International USA
AMP Records & Music
Awal.com
Bagatelle Record Company
Bankroll Records Inc.
Belmont Records
Big Wig Productions
Bolivia Records
Broken Note Records
C.P.R.
Candyspiteful Productions
CAPP Records
Capricorn Records
Capstan Record Production
Cherry Street Records
Chiaroscuro Records
CKB Records/Helaphat Entertainment
Cleopatra Records
Dapmor Records

Deary Me Records
Del-Fi Records, Inc.
DM/Bellmark/Critique Records
Don't Records
Drumbeat Indian Arts, Inc.
Dwell Records
EMF Productions
EMF Records & Affiliates
Evil Teen Records
Fireant
First Time Records
Fish of Death Records and Management
Garrett Entertainment, Marty
Gig Records
Gold City Records, Inc.
Happy Man Records
Hot Wings Entertainment
Idol Records
Kaupp Records
L.A. Records (Canada)
Lamar Music Marketing
Landslide Records
Lari-Jon Records
Lark Record Productions, Inc.
Magnum Music Corp. Ltd.
Major Entertainment, Inc.
Makoché Recording Company
Mayfair Music
MCB Records/Pepe
Mighty Records
Nation Records Inc.
Neurodisc Records, Inc.
Omni 2000 Inc.
Orillyon Entertainment
Outstanding Records
Pacific Time Entertainment
Paint Chip Records
Permanent Press Recordings/Permanent Wave
PGE Platinum Groove Entertainment
Pickwick/Mecca/International Records
Platinum Entertainment, Inc.
Playbones Records
Pop Record Research
PPL Entertainment Group
Pravda Records
Q Records
Quark Records
RA Records
Radioactive Records
Red-Eye Records
Reiter Records Ltd.
Relativity Records
Rhiannon Records
Rival Records
Ruf Records
Salexo Music
Siltown Records
Silver Wave Records

Silvertone Records
Sin Klub Entertainment, Inc.
Smithsonian Folkways Recordings
Sound Gems
Spinball Music and Video
Spotlight Records
St. Francis Records
Stardust
Stone Age Records
Suisonic Records
Sun-Scape Enterprises Limited
Surface Records
Sweet June Music
Take 2 Records
Thump Records, Inc.
Topcat Records
Valtec Productions
Vander-Moon Entertainment
Vokes Music Record Co.
Wall Street Music
Warehouse Creek Recording Corp.
Winchester Records
Worldwide Recordings Limited/
    Worldrecords.com
Xemu Records
Young Country Records/Plain Country Records

Record Producers
"A" Major Sound Corporation
Alco Productions
Baird Enterprises, Ron
Bal Records
Birthplace Productions
Candyspiteful Productions
Coffee and Cream Productions
Collector Records
Craig, Douglas
DeLory and Music Makers, Al
Eiffert, Jr., Leo J.
Esquire International
Gallway Bay Music
Hailing Frequency Music Productions
Heart Consort Music
Integrated Entertainment
Interstate Records
Janoulis Productions, Alexander/Big Al Jano
    Productions
John Productions, David
JSB Groupe Management Inc.
June Productions Ltd.
Kane Producer/Engineer, Karen
Known Artist Productions
Lari-Jon Productions
Luick & Country Music Showcase Intl.
    Associates, Harold
Magnetic Oblivion Music Co.
Makers Mark Music Productions
Martin, Pete/Vaam Music Productions
Mega Truth Records

Mittelstedt, A.V.
Moffet, Gary
New Experience Records
Ormsby, John "Buck"/Etiquette Productions
Pacific North Studios Ltd.
Parker, Patty
Pierce, Jim
Rainbow Recording
Shu'Baby Montez Music
Silver Thunder Music Group
Sound Arts Recording Studio
Sphere Group One
Valtec Productions
Westwires Digital USA
WIR (World International Records)
Wilbur Productions
Willson, Frank
WLM Music/Recording
World Records
Wytas Productions, Steve
Y-N-A/C.D.T. Productions

Managers & Booking Agents
Air Tight Management
Alert Music, Inc.
All Star Management
All Star Talent Agency
American Artists Entertainment
American Independent Artists
Anderson Associates Communications Group
Ardenne Int'l Inc.
Big J Productions
Blackground
Blank & Blank
Blowin' Smoke Productions/Records
Bouquet-Orchid Enterprises
Brothers Management Associates
CBA Artists
Chucker Music Inc.
Circuit Rider Talent & Management Co.
Class Act Productions/Management
Clockwork Entertainment Management Agency
Clousher Productions
Cody Entertainment Group
Concept 2000 Inc.
Concerted Efforts, Inc./Foggy Day Music
Corvalan-Condliffe Management
Countdown Entertainment
Countrywide Producers
Crawfish Productions
Criss-Cross Industries
Crossfire Productions
D&M Entertainment Agency
DCA Productions
Dinwoodie Management, Andrew
Direct Management
Doss Presents, Col. Buster
EAO Music Corporation of Canada
Evergreen Entertainment Services

Fenchel Entertainment Agency, Fred T.
First Time Management
Godtland Management, Inc., Eric
Greif-Garris Management
Hale Enterprises
Hall Entertainment & Events, Bill
Hansen Enterprises, Ltd.
Hawkeye Attractions
Immigrant Music Inc.
J & V Management
Jacobson Talent Management
Jae Enterprises, Jana
James Management, Roger
Kagan International, Sheldon
KKR Entertainment Group
Klein, Joanne
Knight Agency, Bob
Lari-Jon Promotions
Lawrence, Ltd., Ray
Levinson Entertainment Ventures International, Inc.
Lindsay Productions, Doris/Successful Productions
Live-Wire Management
Magnum Music Corporation Ltd.
Management Plus
Management Trust Ltd., The
Mayo & Company, Phil
McDonnell Group, The
Media Management
Mega Music Productions
Mirkin Management
Montgomery Management, Gary F.
Original Artists' Agency
Outland Productions
Pillar Records
Rainbow Collection Ltd.
Rainbow Talent Agency
Right-On Management
Riohcat Music
Risavy, Inc., A.F.
Rothschild Productions Inc., Charles R.
Saffyre Management
Sa'Mall Management
Shute Management Pty. Ltd., Phill
Siddons & Associates
Skorman Productions, Inc., T.
Sound Management Direction
Southeastern Attractions
SP Talent Associates
Sphere Group One
Staircase Promotion
Stander Entertainment
Starkravin' Management
Steinman Management, Obi
Stewart Management, Steve
Stormin' Norman Productions
Strictly Forbidden Artists

Surface Management Inc.
T.L.C. Booking Agency
Tas Music Co./Dave Tasse Entertainment
Texas Sounds Entertainment
315 Beale Studios/Taliesyn Entertainment
Tiger's Eye Entertainment Management &
    Consulting
Tutta Forza Music
Twentieth Century Promotions
Umpire Entertainment Enterprizes
Varrasso Management, Richard
Vokes Booking Agency
Warner Productions, Cheryl K.
Wemus Entertainment
Williams Management, Yvonne
World Park Productions
World Wide Management
WorldSound, LLC
Zane Management, Inc.

◙ ONLY OPEN TO PREVIOUSLY PUBLISHED SONGWRITERS/WELL-ESTABLISHED ACTS

Music Publishers
Baitstring Music
Brian Song Music Corp.
Flying Red Horse Publishing
Goodnight Kiss Music
Lyrick Studios
Markea Music/Gina Pie Music
Montina Music
Paden Place Music
Pegasus Music
Segal's Publications
Sellwood Publishing
Slanted Circle Music
Sun Star Songs
Winston & Hoffman House Music Publishers

Record Companies
American Recordings
Arkadia Entertainment Corp.
Broken Records International
Cambria Records & Publishing
Cantilena Records
Griffin Music
Heads Up Int., Ltd.
Kingston Records
Lucifer Records, Inc.
Malaco Records
Monticana Records
Trac Record Co.

Record Producers
Kingston Records and Talent
Marenco, Cookie

Monticana Productions
Segal's Productions
Texas Fantasy Music Group
Trac Record Co.

Managers & Booking Agents
Blue Cat Agency, The
Buxton Walker P/L
Capital Entertainment
DAS Communications, Ltd.
De Miles Company, The Edward
Levy Management, Rick
Management by Jaffe
Northern Lights Management
Noteworthy Productions
Prestige Artistes
Serge Entertainment Group
Van Pol Management, Hans

◙ DOES NOT ACCEPT UNSOLICITED MATERIAL/ ONLY ACCEPTS MATERIAL REFERRED BY AN INDUSTRY SOURCE

Music Publishers
A Ta Z Music
ALLRS Music Publishing Co.
Bixio Music Group/IDM Ventures, Ltd.
Bourne Co. Music Publishers
Brentwood-Benson Music Publishing
Cheavoria Music Co. (BMI)
CTV Music (Great Britain)
Famous Music Publishing Companies
Green One Music
Heupferd Musikverlag GmbH
Hickory Lane Publishing and Recording
Lake Transfer Productions & Music
Maverick Music
Melody Hills Ranch Publishing Co.
Music Bridge, The
Music Room Publishing Group, The
Naked Jain Records
Old Slowpoke Music
Omni 2000, Inc.
Pas Mal Publishing Sarl
Perla Music
Rainbow Music Corp.
Ren Zone Music
S.M.C.L. Productions, Inc.
Silver Blue Music/Oceans Blue Music
Warner/Chappell Music Canada Ltd.
Wipe Out Music Ltd.

Record Companies
Arista Records
Astralwerks

Atlantic Records
Avita Records
Big Heavy World
Brentwood Records/Diadem Records
Capitol Records
Columbia Records
Cosmotone Records
Curb Records
DreamWorks Records
Elektra Records
Epic Records
Geffen/DGC Records
Green Bear Records
Groove Makers' Recordings
Heart Music, Inc.
Hollywood Records
Horizon Records, Inc.
Interscope/Geffen/A&M Records
Island/Def Jam Music Group
Jive Records
LaFace Records
Leatherland Productions
London Sire Records
Maverick Records
MCA Records
Moody Productions, Doug
Motown Records
NPO Records, Inc.
Pointblank Records
Priority Records
Qwest Records
RAVE Records, Inc.
Razor & Tie Entertainment
RCA Records
Reprise Records
Robbins Entertainment LLC
Sahara Records and Filmworks Entertainment

Street Records
Strugglebaby Recording Co.
Sureshot Records
Tommy Boy Records
Universal Records
VAI Distribution
Verve Music Group, The
Virgin Records
Warner Bros. Records
Waterdog Music
Windham Hill Records
Wind-Up Entertainment
Word Records & Music

Record Producers
Allyn, Stuart J.
Appell Productions, Inc., Jonathan
Bernard Enterprises, Inc., Hal
Cupit Productions, Jerry
De Miles, Edward
Diamond Entertainment, Joel
Doss Presents, Col. Buster
Eternal Song Agency, The
Final Mix Music
Jag Studio, Ltd.
Jay Bird Productions
KMA
Poku Productions

Managers & Booking Agents
Bacchus Group Productions, Ltd.
Barnard Management Services (BMS)
GCI, Inc.
Harrell & Associates, M.
International Entertainment Bureau
Noteworthy Enterprises
Richards World Management, Inc., Diane
Sendyk, Leonard & Co. Inc.

Film & TV Index

This index lists companies who place music in motion pictures and TV shows (excluding commercials). To learn more about their film/TV experience, read the information under **Film & TV** in their listings. It is recommended to use this index in conjunction with the Openness to Submissions Index on page 476.

Music Publishers
Abalone Publishing
ALLRS Music Publishing Co.
Alexander Sr. Music
Alpha Music Inc.
Better Than Sex Music
Big Fish Music Publishing Group
Bixio Music Group/IDM Ventures, Ltd.
Brentwood-Benson Music Publishing
BSW Records
Christmas & Holiday Music
CTV Music (Great Britain)
De Miles Music Company, The Edward
Famous Music Publishing Companies
Fresh Entertainment
Golden Music, August
Goodnight Kiss Music
Heupferd Musikverlag GmbH
Holy Spirit Music
Largo Music Publishing
Lilly Music Publishing
Lyrick Studios
Manuiti L.A.
Markea Music/Gina Pie Music
McConkey Artists Agency Music Publishing
Naked Jain Records
Old Slowpoke Music
Pas Mal Publishing Sarl
PEN Music Group, Inc.
Presser Co., Theodore
QUARK, Inc.
Rainbow Music Corp.
Shu'Baby Montez Music
Silver Blue Music/Oceans Blue Music
Succes

Tedesco Music Co., Dale
Tower Music Group
Transamerika Musikverlag KG
Transition Music Corporation
Warner/Chappell Music Canada Ltd.
Winston & Hoffman House Music Publishers
Zettitalia Music International

Record Companies
CAPP Records
Sahara Records and Filmworks Entertainment

Record Producers
Craig, Douglas
Texas Fantasy Music Group

Managers & Booking Agents
American Artists Entertainment
Hansen Enterprises, Ltd.
Total Acting Experience, A

Advertising, Audiovisual & Commercial Music Firms
AGA Creative Communications
Angel Films Company
Cantrax Recorders
Cinevue/Steve Postal Productions
Disk Productions
D.S.M. Producers Inc.
Entertainment Productions, Inc.
Film Classic Exchange
TRF Production Music Libraries
Utopian Empire Creativeworks
Vis/Aid Marketing/Associates

Geographic Index

This Geographic Index will help you locate companies by state, as well as those in countries outside of the U.S. It is recommended to use this index in conjunction with the Openness to Submissions Index on page 476. Once you find the names of companies in this index you are interested in, check the listings within each section for addresses, phone numbers, contact names and submissions details.

ALABAMA

Music Publishers
Baitstring Music
Cheavoria Music Co.
Lexington Alabama Music Publishing
Northwest Alabama Music Publishing

Record Producers
Known Artist Productions

Managers & Booking Agents
Southeastern Attractions

Advertising, Audiovisual & Commercial Music Firms
Ensemble Productions

Play Producers & Publishers
University of Alabama New Playwrights' Program

Organizations
Alabama Songwriter's Guild

ARIZONA

Music Publishers
Spradlin/Gleich Publishing
White Cat Music

Record Companies
Ariana Records
Comstock Records Ltd.
Drumbeat Indian Arts, Inc.
Suisonic Records

Record Producers
Parker, Patty

Advertising, Audiovisual & Commercial Music Firms
Rodeo Video, Inc.

Play Producers & Publishers
Arizona Theatre Company
Gaslight Theatre, The

Organizations
Arizona Songwriters Association

ARKANSAS

Music Publishers
G Major Music

Play Producers & Publishers
Arkansas Repertory Theatre

CALIFORNIA

Music Publishers
Activate Entertainment LLC
Alexis
American Heartstring Publishing
Audio Music Publishers
Avalon Music
Bal & Bal Music Publishing Co.
Big Fish Music Publishing Group
Black Stallion Country Publishing
Bradley Music, Allan
California Country Music
CAPP Records
Cherri/Holly Music Inc.
Christmas & Holiday Music
Dagene Music
Doré Records
Duane Music, Inc.
Emandell Tunes
Famous Music Publishing Companies
Goodnight Kiss Music
Kaupps & Robert Publishing Co.
Lake Transfer Productions & Music
Magic Message Music
Manuiti L.A.
Maverick Music
McConkey Artists Agency Music Publishing
Mellow House Music
Music Bridge, The
Music Room Publishing Group, The
Musikuser Publishing

GEOGRAPHIC INDEX

Naked Jain Records
PEN Music Group, Inc.
Piano Press
Pollybyrd Publications Limited
Ren Zone Music
Sabteca Music Co.
Samuels Publishing, R.
Sellwood Publishing
Silver Blue Music/Oceans Blue Music
Tedesco Music Co., Dale
Tiki Enterprises, Inc.
Transition Music Corporation
Vaam Music Group
Wemar Music Corp.
Wilcom Publishing
Winston & Hoffman House Music Publishers
Zettitalia Music International
Zomba Music Publishing

Record Companies
American Recordings
Arista Records
Atlantic Records
Avenue Communications
Awal.com
Big Beat Records
Blue Gem Records
Broken Note Records
Cambria Records & Publishing
Cantilena Records
CAPP Records
Capitol Records
Chattahoochee Records
Cleopatra Records
Columbia Records
Coral Records LLC
Curb Records
Dagene/Cabletown Company
Deadeye Records
Discmedia
DreamWorks Records
Drool Records
Dwell Records
Edmonds Record Group
Elektra Records
EMF Records & Affiliates
Epic Records
Flood Recording Corp.
Geffen/DGC Records
Gonzo! Records Inc.
Grass Roots Record & Tape/LMI Records
Hollywood Records
Horizon Records, Inc.
Interscope/Geffen/A&M Records
Island/Def Jam Music Group
Jive Records
Kaupp Records
LaFace Records

London Sire Records
Maverick Records
MCA Records
MOR Records
Moody Productions, Doug
Motown Records
Only New Age Music, Inc.
Outstanding Records
Permanent Press Recordings/Permanent Wave
Pointblank Records
PPL Entertainment Group
Priority Records
Qwest Records
Radioactive Records
Rampant Records
RCA Records
Relativity Records
Reprise Records
Road Records
Roll On Records®
Rotten Records
Rowena Records
Sabteca Record Co.
St. Francis Records
Siltown Records
Silvertone Records
Sims Records, Jerry
Sureshot Records
Tangent® Records
Thump Records, Inc.
Trac Record Co.
Triple X Records
Universal Records
Valtec Productions
Verve Music Group, The
Virgin Records
Warner Bros. Records
Windham Hill Records
Young Country Records/Plain Country Records

Record Producers
Bal Records
Diamond Entertainment, Joel
Eiffert, Jr., Leo J.
Final Mix Music
Gallway Bay Music
Hailing Frequency Music Productions
L.A. Entertainment, Inc.
Linear Cycle Productions
Magid Productions, Lee
Magnetic Oblivion Music Co.
Marenco, Cookie
Martin, Pete/Vaam Music Productions
Mathews, d/b/a Hit or Myth Productions, Scott
Mega Truth Records
Prescription Co., The
Road Records
SAS Productions/Hit Records Network
Studio Voodoo Music

Tamjam Productions
Trac Record Co.
Valtec Productions
Weisman Production Group, The

Managers & Booking Agents
Barnard Management Services
Black Stallion Country, Inc.
Blackground
Blowin' Smoke Productions/Records
Blue Cat Agency, The
Class Act Productions/Management
Corvalan-Condliffe Management
Cox Promotions & Management, Stephen
Crawfish Productions
Criss-Cross Industries
Detko Management, Bill
Godtland Management, Inc., Eric
Golden City International
Greif-Garris Management
Jacobson Talent Management
KKR Entertainment Group
Lawrence, Ltd., Ray
Levinson Entertainment Ventures International,
    Inc.
Live-Wire Management
Loggins Promotion/Backstage Entertainment
M.E.G Management
Media Management
Merri-Webb Productions
Pro Talent Consultants
Saffyre Management
Sa'Mall Management
Sendyk, Leonard & Co. Inc.
Siddons & Associates
Stander Entertainment
Starkravin' Management
Steinman Management, Obi
Stewart Management, Steve
Total Acting Experience, A
Varrasso Management, Richard
Wagner Agency, William F.
Williams Management, Yvonne
WorldSound, LLC

Advertising, Audiovisual & Commercial Music Firms
Ad Agency, The
Cantrax Recorders
Creative Support Services
Entertainment Productions, Inc.
ON-Q Productions, Inc.
Vis/Aid Marketing/Associates

Play Producers & Publishers
Amelia Magazine
American Musical Theatre of San Jose
French, Inc., Samuel
Geer Theatricum Botanicum, The Will
Los Angeles Designers' Theatre

Odyssey Theatre Ensemble
Players Press, Inc.
Playwrights' Arena
West Coast Ensemble
West End Artists

Classical Performing Arts
BRAVO! L.A.
Lamarca American Variety Singers
National Association of Composers/USA
    (NACUSA)
Sacramento Master Singers
San Francisco Girls Chorus

Contests & Awards
Blank Theatre Company Young Playwrights
    Festival
L.A. Designers' Theatre Music Awards
NACUSA Young Composers' Competition
Ten-Minute Musicals Project, The
"Unisong" International Song Contest
West Coast Ensemble—Musical Stairs

Organizations
American Society of Composers, Authors and
    Publishers (ASCAP)
California Lawyers for the Arts
Los Angeles Music Network
Musicians Contact
National Academy of Songwriters
National Association of Composers/USA
    (NACUSA), The
National Society of Men and Women of the
    Music Business (WOMB)
Northern California Songwriters Association
San Diego Songwriters Guild
San Francisco Folk Music Club
Songwriters Guild of America, The

Workshops & Conferences
ASCAP West Coast/Lester Sill Songwriter's
    Workshop
Northern California Songwriters Association
    Conference
Songwriters Guild Foundation, The
Ten-Minute Musicals Project, The

Retreats & Colonies
Dorland Mountain Arts Colony
Villa Montalvo Artist Residency Program

COLORADO

Record Companies
Silver Wave Records

Play Producers & Publishers
Contemporary Drama Service
Pioneer Drama Service

Contests & Awards
Columbia Entertainment Company's Jackie
    White Memorial Children's Playwriting
    Contest
Delta Omicron International Composition
    Competition
MCI-Scroll, Inc. Original Lyric Competition
New Folk Concerts for Emerging Songwriters
Playhouse on the Square New Play Competition
Rocky Mountain Folks Festival Songwriter
    Showcase
Telluride Troubadour Contest

Organizations
Colorado Music Association

Workshops & Conferences
Aspen Music Festival and School

CONNECTICUT
Music Publishers
Antelope Publishing Inc.

Record Company
Pop Record Research

Record Producers
John Productions, David
New Vizion Studios, The
Wytas Productions, Steve

Managers & Booking Agents
Air Tight Management
Martin Productions, Rick
Rustron Music Productions
Tutta Forza Music

Classical Performing Arts
Connecticut Choral Artists/Concora
Norfolk Chamber Music Festival/Yale Summer
    School of Music

Contests & Awards
Young Composers Awards

Organizations
Connecticut Songwriters Association
Pop Record Research

Workshops & Conferences
Norfolk Chamber Music Festival

DELAWARE
**Advertising, Audiovisual & Commercial
Music Firms**
Ken-Del Productions Inc.

DISTRICT OF COLUMBIA
Record Companies
Orillyon Entertainment
Rags to Records, Inc.

Smithsonian Folkways Recordings

Managers & Booking Agents
Capital Entertainment

Play Producers & Publishers
Woolly Mammoth Theatre Co.

Classical Performing Arts
Master Chorale of Washington

Contests & Awards
Fulbright Scholar Program, Council for
    International Exchange of Scholars
Mid-Atlantic Song Contest
Monk International Jazz Composers
    Competition, Thelonious
Nestico Award, Sammy/USAF Band Airmen of
    Note
U.S.-Japan Creative Artists Exchange Fellowship
    Program

Organizations
Folk Alliance
Opera America
Songwriters Association of Washington
Washington Area Music Association

Workshops & Conferences
Folk Alliance Annual Conference

FLORIDA
Music Publishers
Alco Music
ARAS Music
Audio Images Two Thousand Music Publishing
Emstone, Inc. Music Publishing
Mighty Blue Music Machine, The
Otto Publishing Co.
Pritchett Publications
Rocker Music/Happy Man Music
Rustron Music Publishers
Stuart Music Co., Jeb

Record Companies
Alco Recordings
Discos Fuentes/Miami Records & Edimusica
    USA
DM/Bellmark/Critique Records
Happy Man Records
Loconto Productions/Sunrise Studio
Neurodisc Records, Inc.
PGE Platinum Groove Entertainment
Pickwick/Mecca/International Records
Rustron Music Productions
Stone Age Records
28 Records

Record Producers
Alco Productions
Esquire International

Jay Jay Publishing & Record Co.
Loconto Productions
Mac-Attack Productions
Musicland Productions, Inc.
Rustron Music Productions
Satkowski Recordings, Steve
Vickers Music Association, Charles

Managers & Booking Agents
Anderson Associates Communications Group
Concept 2000 Inc.
Evans Productions, Scott
Levy Management, Rick
Mega Music Productions
Noteworthy Enterprises
Rainbow Collection Ltd.
Rock of Ages Productions
Rustron Music Productions
Skorman Productions, Inc., T.
Walls & Co. Management/Showbiz Kidz!

Advertising, Audiovisual & Commercial Music Firms
Cinevue/Steve Postal Productions

Play Producers & Publishers
Eldridge Publishing Co., Inc.

Classical Performing Arts
Piccolo Opera Company Inc.
Space Coast Pops, Inc.

Organizations
All Songwriters Network (ASN)
International Songwriters Guild
North Florida Christian Music Writers
    Association
SPARS
Treasure Coast Songwriters Assn. (TCSA)

GEORGIA
Music Publishers
Fresh Entertainment
Frozen Inca Music
Orchid Publishing
Stellar Music Industries

Record Companies
Atlan-Dec/Grooveline Records
babysue
Capricorn Records
Fresh Entertainment
Goldwax Record Corporation
Hottrax Records
LaFace Records
Landslide Records
Platinum Entertainment, Inc.

Record Producers
Janoulis Productions, Alexander/Big Al Jano
    Productions

Kovach, Robert R.

Managers & Booking Agents
Bouquet-Orchid Enterprises
Montgomery Management, Gary F.
Outland Productions
Serge Entertainment Group

Play Producers & Publishers
Alliance Theatre Company

Organizations
Georgia Music Industry Association, Inc.

Retreats & Colonies
Hambidge Center, The

HAWAII
Record Companies
Belham Valley Records

Contests & Awards
Belham Valley Records Songwriting
    Competition

Retreats & Colonies
Kalani Oceanside Retreat

IDAHO
Record Companies
Big Wig Productions

ILLINOIS
Music Publishers
De Miles Music Company, The Edward
Dream Seekers Publishing
Jerjoy Music
Sound Cellar Music

Record Companies
Aware Records
Bankroll Records Inc.
Beluga Records
Broken Records International
Cellar Records
Griffin Music
Modal Music, Inc.™
Nation Records Inc.
Pravda Records
Sahara Records and Filmworks Entertainment
UAR Records
Waterdog Music

Record Producers
Coachouse Music
De Miles, Edward
Neu Electro Productions

Managers & Booking Agents
Bacchus Group Productions, Ltd.
Conscience Music

De Miles Company, The Edward
Risavy, Inc., A.F.

Advertising, Audiovisual & Commercial Music Firms
Geter Advertising Inc.
Mallof, Abruzino & Nash Marketing
Norton Rubble & Mertz, Inc. Advertising
Qually & Company Inc.

Play Producers & Publishers
Bailiwick Repertory
Circa '21 Dinner Playhouse

Classical Performing Arts
Wheaton Symphony Orchestra

Contests & Awards
Cunningham Prize for Playwriting

Organizations
American Society of Composers, Authors and
Publishers (ASCAP)

INDIANA
Music Publishers
Hammel Associates, Inc., R.L.
Hickory Valley Music
Interplanetary Music
Ontrax Companies

Record Companies
Dale Productions, Alan
P.M. Records
Yellow Jacket Records

Managers & Booking Agents
De Miles Company, The Edward
Hale Enterprises
Harrell & Associates, M.
Hawkeye Attractions
International Entertainment Bureau

Advertising, Audiovisual & Commercial Music Firms
Caldwell Vanriper/Marc

Classical Performing Arts
Anderson Symphony Orchestra
Carmel Symphony Orchestra

Contests & Awards
Indiana Opera Theatre/MacAllister Awards for
Opera Singers

Organizations
Just Plain Folks

Workshops & Conferences
New Harmony Project, The

IOWA
Music Publishers
Luick & Associates Music Publisher, Harold
Rock N Metal Music Publishing Co.

Record Producers
Heart Consort Music
Luick & Country Music Showcase Intl.
Associates, Harold

Managers & Booking Agents
Fenchel Entertainment Agency, Fred T.

Play Producers & Publishers
Heuer Publishing Co.

Organizations
Country Music Showcase International, Inc.

Workshops & Conferences
Davidson's Writer's Seminar, Peter

KANSAS
Music Publishers
Dave Music, Jof
Kansa Records Corporation

KENTUCKY
Music Publishers
Holy Spirit Music

Advertising, Audiovisual & Commercial Music Firms
Price Weber Marketing Communications, Inc.

Play Producers & Publishers
Stage One

Classical Performing Arts
Kentucky Opera
Lexington Philharmonic Society

Contests & Awards
Y.E.S. Festival of New Plays

LOUISIANA
Music Publishers
Dapmor Publishing
Melody Hills Ranch Publishing Co.

Record Companies
Dapmor Records
EMF Productions

Managers & Booking Agents
Big J Productions
GCI, Inc.
Sea Cruise Productions, Inc.

Advertising, Audiovisual & Commercial Music Firms
Disk Productions

Play Producers & Publishers
Centenary College, Theatre Department

Organizations
Louisiana Songwriters Association
Southern Songwriters Guild, Inc.

Workshops & Conferences
Shiznit Music Conference, The

MAINE
Workshops & Conferences
Arcady Music Festival

MARYLAND
Music Publishers
Leigh Music, Trixie

Record Companies
First Power Entertainment Group

Managers & Booking Agents
Noteworthy Productions

Advertising, Audiovisual & Commercial Music Firms
dbF A Media Company

Classical Performing Arts
Baltimore Opera Company, Inc.
Susquehanna Symphony Orchestra

MASSACHUSETTS
Music Publishers
East Coast Music Publishing
Scott Music Group, Tim
Segal's Publications

Record Companies
Anisette Records
Belmont Records
Fish of Death Records and Management
Keeping It Simple and Safe, Inc.
Sealed Fate Records

Record Producers
Mona Lisa Records/Bristol Studios
Segal's Productions

Managers & Booking Agents
Clockwork Entertainment Management Agency
Concerted Efforts, Inc./Foggy Day Music

Advertising, Audiovisual & Commercial Music Firms
Communications for Learning
Film Classic Exchange
Home, Inc.
Lapriore Videography
Rampion Visual Productions
VIP Video

Plays Producers & Publishers
American Eastern Theatrical Company
Baker's Plays
Freelance Press, The
New Repertory Theatre

Classical Performing Arts
Commonwealth Opera, Inc.
Mirecourt Trio, The

Contests & Awards
ALEA III International Composition Prize
Baker's Plays High School Playwriting Contest

Organizations
Boston Songwriters Workshop, The

Workshops & Conferences
Music Business Solutions/Career Building Workshops
NEMO Music Showcase & Conference

MICHIGAN
Music Publishers
Abalone Publishing
Prejippie Music Group

Records Companies
Afterschool Records, Inc.
Gueststar Records, Inc.
L.A. Records (Michigan)
PMG Records
RAVE Records, Inc.
Wall Street Music

Record Producers
Prejippie Music Group
Theoretical Reality
World Records

Managers & Booking Agents
Afterschool Publishing Company
Gueststar Entertainment Agency
J & V Management
Right-On Management

Advertising, Audiovisual & Commercial Music Firms
K&R's Recording Studios
Utopian Empire Creativeworks

Play Producers & Publishers
Thunder Bay Theatre

Classical Performing Arts
Birmingham-Bloomfield Symphony Orchestra
Cantata Academy

Contests & Awards
African American Composer's Program

Organizations
Detroit Music Alliance
Nashville Songwriters Association International-Detroit

Workshops & Conferences
Lamb's Retreat for Songwriters

Retreats & Colonies
Isle Royale National Park Artist-in-Residence Program

Northwood University Alden B. Dow Creativity
    Center

MINNESOTA
Music Publishers
Portage Music

Record Producers
Rainbow Recording

*Advertising, Audiovisual & Commercial
Music Firms*
Butwin & Associates, Inc.

Play Producers & Publishers
Mixed Blood Theatre Co.

Classical Performing Arts
Warland Singers, The Dale

Contests & Awards
Bush Artist Fellows Program
Composers Commissioning Program
McKnight Visiting Composer Program
Rochester Playwright Festival Contest

Organizations
American Composers Forum
Minnesota Association of Songwriters

MISSISSIPPI
Music Publishers
Bay Ridge Publishing Co.

Record Companies
Malaco Records
Missile Records

Managers & Booking Agents
Exclesisa Booking Agency

Play Producers & Publishers
Carey College Dinner Theatre, William

MISSOURI
Music Publishers
Blue Dog Publishing and Records
Green One Music
Lineage Publishing Co.
Southern Most Publishing Company

Record Companies
Capstan Record Production
Green Bear Records

Record Producers
Angel Films Company
Haworth Productions

Managers & Booking Agents
Original Artists' Agency
Staircase Promotion

*Advertising, Audiovisual & Commercial
Music Firms*
Angel Films Company

Play Producers & Publishers
Repertory Theatre of St. Louis, The

Classical Performing Arts
Heartland Men's Chorus
St. Louis Chamber Chorus

Contests & Awards
Columbia Entertainment Company's Jackie
    White Memorial Children's Playwriting
    Contest

Organizations
Missouri Songwriters Association, Inc.
Ozark Noteworthy Songwriters Association, Inc.

MONTANA
Classical Performing Arts
Billings Symphony
Great Falls Symphony Association
Helena Symphony

Organizations
College Music Society, The

NEBRASKA
Music Publishers
Lari-Jon Publishing

Record Companies
Lari-Jon Records
Redemption Records

Record Producers
Lari-Jon Productions

Managers & Booking Agents
Lari-Jon Promotions

Contests & Awards
Omaha Symphony Guild International New
    Music Competition

NEVADA
Music Publishers
Pollybyrd Publications Limited

Record Companies
Americatone Records International USA

Record Producers
Sound Works Entertainment Productions Inc.

Managers & Booking Agents
Hansen Enterprises, Ltd.
Wilder Artists' Management, Shane

Organizations
Las Vegas Songwriters Association, The

NEW HAMPSHIRE
Record Companies
Kingston Records

Record Producers
Kingston Records and Talent
Reel Adventures

Retreats & Colonies
MacDowell Colony, The

NEW JERSEY
Music Publishers
Gary Music, Alan
Omni 2000, Inc.
Perla Music
T.C. Productions/Etude Publishing Co.
Westwood Music Group
Yorgo Music

Record Companies
A.P.I. Records
Airplay Label, The
Gig Records
Lucifer Records, Inc.
Omni 2000 Inc.
Presence Records
Ruf Records
Songgram Music

Record Producers
Omni 2000 Inc.
Sphere Group One
Tari, Roger Vincent

Managers & Booking Agents
American Artists Entertainment
Brothers Management Associates
Renaissance Entertainment Group
Sphere Group One
Stormin' Norman Productions
Surface Management Inc.

Classical Performing Arts
Aureus Quartet
Princeton Symphony Orchestra
Ridgewood Symphony Orchestra

Organizations
Songwriters Guild of America, The

Workshops & Conferences
Appel Farm Arts and Music Festival

NEW MEXICO
Music Publishers
Pecos Valley Music

Record Companies
SunCountry Records

Managers & Booking Agents
Northern Lights Management

Advertising, Audiovisual & Commercial Music Firms
Power and Associates, Inc., RH

NEW YORK
Music Publishers
ALLRS Music Publishing Co.
Alpha Music Inc.
Better Than Sex Music
Bixio Music Group/IDM Ventures, Ltd.
BMG Music Publishing
Bourne Co. Music Publishers
Famous Music Publishing Companies
Fifth Avenue Media, Ltd.
Indie-Go Music
Jasper Stone Music/JSM Songs
JPMC Music Inc.
Largo Music Publishing
Mymit Music Productions, Chuck
Prescription Company
QUARK, Inc.
Rainbow Music Corp.
Rockford Music Co.
Sunsongs Music/Dark Son Music
Zomba Music Publishing

Record Companies
Amigos Music & Marketing
Arista Records
Atlantic Records
Blue Wave
C.P.R.
Candyspiteful Productions
Capitol Records
Chiaroscuro Records
Columbia Records
Com-Four Distribution
Creative Improvised Music Projects (CIMP)
Discos Fuentes/Miami Records & Edimusica
    USA
DreamWorks Records
Elektra Records
Epic Records
Evil Teen Records
Geffen/DGC Records
Gold City Records, Inc.
Gotham Records
Hollywood Records
Hot Wings Entertainment
Interscope/Geffen/A&M Records
Island/Def Jam Music Group
Jive Records
Lamar Music Marketing
Major Entertainment, Inc.
MCA Records
Mighty Records
Motown Records
NPO Records, Inc.

Omega Record Group, Inc.
Pacific Time Entertainment
Paint Chip Records
Priority Records
Quark Records
Qwest Records
Radical Records
Razor & Tie Entertainment
RCA Records
Relativity Records
Reprise Records
Robbins Entertainment LLC
Silvertone Records
Tommy Boy Records
Universal Records
VAI Distribution
Verve Music Group, The
Virgin Records
Warner Bros. Records
Windham Hill Records
Wind-Up Entertainment
Xemu Records

Record Producers
Allyn, Stuart J.
Appell Productions, Inc., Jonathan
Candyspiteful Productions
KMA
Prescription Co., The
Wilbur Productions
Y-N-A/C.D.T. Productions

Managers & Booking Agents
Anderson Associates Communications Group
Bassline Entertainment, Inc.
Blue Wave Productions
Chucker Music Inc.
Countdown Entertainment
DAS Communications, Ltd.
DCA Productions
DMR Agency
Earth Tracks Artists Agency
Endangered Species Artist Management
Horizon Management Inc.
Klein, Joanne
Knight Agency, Bob
Management by Jaffe
On the Level Music!
RadioActive
Rainbow Talent Agency
Richards World Management, Inc., Diane
Rothschild Productions Inc., Charles R.
Sound Management Direction
Wilder Artists' Management, Shane
Wood Artist Management, Richard
World Wide Management

Advertising, Audiovisual & Commercial Music Firms
D.S.M. Producers Inc.
Fine Art Productions/Richie Suraci Pictures, Multimedia, Interactive
Fitzmusic
Novus Visual Communications Inc.
TRF Production Music Libraries

Play Producers & Publishers
Crossroads Theatre
Directors Company, The
French, Inc., Samuel
Manhattan Theatre Club
New York State Theatre Institute
New York Theatre Workshop
Open Eye Theater, The
Playwrights Horizons
Primary Stages
Second Stage Theatre
Tada!
Theatreworks/USA
Westbeth Theatre Centre
Wings Theatre Co.

Classical Performing Arts
American Opera Musical Theatre Co.
Amherst Saxophone Quartet
Hudson Valley Philharmonic
Mozart Festival Orchestra, Inc.
Operaworks
Saint Thomas Choir of Men and Boys, The

Contests & Awards
AGO/ECS Publishing Award in Choral Composition
Artists' Fellowships
European International Competition for Composers
Free Staged Reading Series Playwriting Competition
Holtkamp-AGO Award in Organ Composition
Lennon Songwriting Contest, The John
Mazumdar New Play Competition, Maxim
Pulitzer Prize in Music
Rodgers Awards, Richard
Rome Prize Fellowship in Musical Composition

Organizations
American Music Center, Inc.
American Society of Composers, Authors and Publishers (ASCAP)
Association of Independent Music Publishers
Broadcast Music, Inc. (BMI)
Field, The
Meet the Composer
National Academy of Popular Music (NAPM)
Outmusic
SESAC Inc.
Songwriters Advocate, The (TSA)

Songwriters & Lyricists Club
Volunteer Lawyers for the Arts
Women in Music

Workshops & Conferences
ASCAP Musical Theatre Workshop
BMI-Lehman Engel Musical Theatre Workshop
Broadway Tomorrow Previews
CMJ Music Marathon, MusicFest & FilmFest
Genesius Guild Monday Night Performance
    Project Series
National Academy of Popular Music Songwriting
    Workshop Program
Songwriters Playground®

Retreats & Colonies
Byrdcliffe Arts Colony
Yaddo Artists' Community

NORTH CAROLINA
Music Publishers
Lindsay Publishing, Doris

Record Companies
Deep South Entertainment
Fountain Records
Salexo Music

Record Producers
Jag Studio, Ltd.
WLM Music/Recording

Advertising, Audiovisual & Commercial Music Firms
Hodges Associates, Inc.

Play Producers & Publishers
Blowing Rock Stage Company, The

Classical Performing Arts
Charlotte Philharmonic Orchestra

Organizations
Central Carolina Songwriters Association
    (CCSA)
Gospel/Christian Songwriters Group

Workshops & Conferences
Swannanoa Gathering—Contemporary Folk
    Week, The

Retreats & Colonies
Brevard Music Center

NORTH DAKOTA
Record Companies
Makoché Recording Company

Classical Performing Arts
Greater Grand Forks Symphony Orchestra

OHIO
Music Publishers
Alexander Sr. Music
Barkin' Foe the Master's Bone

Barren Wood Publishing
Bernard Enterprises, Inc., Hal
Marvin Publishing, John Weller
New Rap Jam Publishing, A
Salt Works Music
Scrutchings Music

Record Companies
All Star Record Promotions
Deary Me Records
Emerald City Records
Heads Up Int., Ltd.
Powerblast Recordings
Rival Records
Sin Klub Entertainment, Inc.
Spotlight Records
Strugglebaby Recording Co.

Record Producers
Bernard Enterprises, Inc., Hal
DAP Entertainment
Eternal Song Agency, The
New Experience Records
Syndicate Sound, Inc.

Managers & Booking Agents
All Star Management
Concept 2000 Inc.
Creative Star Management
Lowell Agency

Play Producers & Publishers
Ensemble Theatre

Classical Performing Arts
Lakeside Summer Symphony
Lima Symphony Orchestra
Lithopolis Area Fine Arts Association

Contests & Awards
International Clarinet Association Composition
    Competition
Rosenthal New Play Prize, Lois and Richard

Organizations
Songwriters and Poets Critique

Workshops & Conferences
Undercurrents

OKLAHOMA
Music Publishers
Branson Country Music Publishing
Furrow Music
Jae Music, Jana
Old Slowpoke Music

Record Companies
Cherry Street Records
Garrett Entertainment, Marty
Lark Record Productions, Inc.

GEOGRAPHIC INDEX

Record Producers
Lark Talent & Advertising
Studio Seven

Managers & Booking Agents
D&R Entertainment
Jae Enterprises, Jana

Classical Performing Arts
Tulsa Opera Inc.

Contests & Awards
Billboard Song Contest

Organizations
Oklahoma Songwriters & Composers
    Association
Songwriters of Oklahoma

OREGON

Music Publishers
Earitating Music Publishing
High-Minded Moma Publishing & Productions
Moon June Music

Record Companies
Flying Heart Records
OCP Publications

Record Producers
Celt Musical Services, Jan

Managers & Booking Agents
American Independent Artists

Contests & Awards
Great American Song Contest
Portland Songwriters Association Annual
    Songwriting Competition

Organizations
Central Oregon Songwriters Association
Portland Songwriters Association
Songwriters Resource Network

Retreats & Colonies
Sitka Center for Art & Ecology

PENNSYLVANIA

Music Publishers
Allegheny Music Works
Baird Music Group
Delev Music Company
Makers Mark Gold
Presser Co., Theodore
Shawnee Press, Inc.
Shu'Baby Montez Music
Vokes Music Publishing

Record Companies
Allegheny Music Works
Golden Triangle Records

Megaforce Worldwide Entertainment
Q Records
Reiter Records Ltd.
Sound Gems
Vokes Music Record Co.

Record Producers
Baird Enterprises, Ron
Big Sky Audio Productions
Coffee and Cream Productions
Integrated Entertainment
Makers Mark Music Productions
Philly Breakdown Recording Co.
Shu'Baby Montez Music
Westwires Digital USA

Managers & Booking Agents
Blank & Blank
Clousher Productions
Countrywide Producers
Hall Entertainment & Events, Bill
McDonnell Group, The
Rock Whirled Music Management
Vokes Booking Agency
Zane Management, Inc.

Advertising, Audiovisual & Commercial Music Firms
Advertel, Inc.
BRg Music Works
Fredrick, Lee & Lloyd

Play Producers & Publishers
Bristol Riverside Theatre
Walnut Street Theatre Company

Classical Performing Arts
Hershey Symphony Orchestra
Lehigh Valley Chamber Orchestra
Singing Boys of Pennsylvania

Contests & Awards
CRS National Composers Competition
Future Charters
Gaul Composition Contest, Harvey
Words By

Organizations
Philadelphia Songwriters Forum, The
Pittsburgh Songwriters Association

Workshops & Conferences
Philadelphia Music Conference

RHODE ISLAND

Record Companies
North Star Music

Managers & Booking Agents
D&M Entertainment Agency
Twentieth Century Promotions
World Park Productions

Organizations
Rhode Island Songwriters' Association

SOUTH CAROLINA
Music Publishers
Brian Song Music Corp.

Record Companies
Street Records

Classical Performing Arts
Opera on the Go

TENNESSEE
Music Publishers
Alias John Henry Tunes
AlliSongs Inc.
Avalon Music
BMG Music Publishing
Brentwood-Benson Music Publishing
Buried Treasure Music
Cornelius Companies, The
Country Rainbow Music
Cupit Music
Door Knob Music Publishing
Doss Music, Buster
Famous Music Publishing Companies
Faverett Group
Frick Enterprises, Bob Scott
Fricon Music Company
Golden Music, August
Goodland Music Group Inc., The
Hitsburgh Music Co.
Iron Skillet Music
Jolson Black & White Music, Al
Juke Music
Markea Music/Gina Pie Music
Newcreature Music
NSAI Song Camps
Paden Place Music
Peters Music, Justin
Silver Thunder Music Group
Simply Grand Music, Inc.
Sun Star Songs
Tower Music Group
Ultimate Peak Music
Whiting Music

Record Companies
Arista Records
Atlantic Records
Avalon Recording Group
Avita Records
Brentwood Records/Diadem Records
Capitol Records
Columbia Records

Curb Records
DreamWorks Records
Epic Records
Imaginary Records
Island/Def Jam Music Group
Jive Records
Landmark Communications Group
MCA Records
MCB Records/Pepe
Plateau Music
RCA Records
Stardust
Take 2 Records
Vander-Moon Entertainment
Warner Bros. Records
Word Records & Music

Record Producers
Aberdeen Productions
Avalon Productions
Birthplace Productions
DeLory and Music Makers, Al
Doss Presents, Col. Buster
Interstate Records
Landmark Communications Group
Pierce, Jim
Silver Thunder Music Group
Swift River Productions

Managers & Booking Agents
All Star Talent Agency
Circuit Rider Talent & Management Co.
Doss Presents, Col. Buster
Hardison International Entertainment
    Corporation
Nash-One Management Inc.
Riohcat Music
315 Beale Studios/Taliesyn Entertainment
Warner Productions, Cheryl K.

Play Producers & Publishers
Playhouse on the Square

Classical Performing Arts
Chattanooga Girls Choir

Contests & Awards
American Songwriter Lyric Contest
Playhouse on the Square New Play Competition

Organizations
American Society of Composers, Authors and
    Publishers (ASCAP)
Black Country Music Association, The
Broadcast Music, Inc. (BMI)
Gospel Music Association
Memphis Songwriters' Association
Nashville Songwriters Association International
SESAC Inc.
Singer Songwriter Information Line, The
Songwriters Guild of America, The

Tennessee Songwriters International, The

Workshops & Conferences
Bluestock Festival
Nashville Music Festival
NSAI Songwriters Symposium

TEXAS

Music Publishers
Amen, Inc.
Bagatelle Music Publishing Co.
BSW Records
Christopher Publishing, Sonny
Earthscream Music Publishing Co.
Flying Red Horse Publishing
Glad Music Co.
His Power Productions and Publishing
Les Music Group
Lyrick Studios
Silicon Music Publishing Co.
Starbound Publishing Co.

Record Companies
Albatross Records
Arista Records
Bagatelle Record Company
BSW Records
CKB Records/Helaphat Entertainment
Cosmotone Records
Enterprize Records-Tapes
Front Row Records
Groove Makers' Recordings
Hacienda Records & Recording Studio
Heart Music, Inc.
Idol Records
Sabre Productions
Sonar Records & Production
Southland Records, Inc.
Surface Records
Sweet June Music
Texas Rose Records
Topcat Records
World Beatnik Records

Record Producers
ACR Productions
Dixon III, Philip D., Attorney at Law
Mittelstedt, A.V.
R&D Productions
Sound Arts Recording Studio
Texas Fantasy Music Group
TMC Productions
Trinity Studio, The
Willson, Frank

Managers & Booking Agents
Butler Music, Bill
Crossfire Productions
Direct Management

Kuper Personal Management
Management Plus
Mirkin Management
SP Talent Associates
Spoon Agency L.L.C., The
Stevens & Company Management
Texas Sounds Entertainment
Umpire Entertainment Enterprizes
Universal Music Marketing
Wemus Entertainment

Advertising, Audiovisual & Commercial Music Firms
Bridge Enterprises
McCann-Erickson Southwest
Ward & Ames

Play Producers & Publishers
Stages Repertory Theatre
Theatre Three, Inc.

Contests & Awards
New Folk Concerts for Emerging Songwriters

Organizations
Austin Songwriters Group
Center for the Promotion of Contemporary Composers
Country Music Association of Texas
Fort Bend Songwriters Association
Fort Worth Songwriters Association
Southeast Texas Bluegrass Music Association
Southwest Celtic Music Association
Texas Music Office

Workshops & Conferences
I Write the Songs
Kerrville Folk Festival
South by Southwest Music and Media Conference

UTAH

Advertising, Audiovisual & Commercial Music Firms
Soter Associates, Inc.

Contests & Awards
Composers Guild Annual Composition Contest

Organizations
Composers Guild

VERMONT

Music Publishers
A Ta Z Music

Record Companies
Big Heavy World

Managers & Booking Agents
Evergreen Entertainment Services
Mayo & Company, Phil

Workshops & Conferences
Manchester Music Festival

Retreats & Colonies
Dorset Colony House

VIRGINIA

Music Publishers
Slanted Circle Music
Weaver of Words Music

Record Companies
Leatherland Productions
Warehouse Creek Recording Corp.

Managers & Booking Agents
Cody Entertainment Group
Precision Management

Play Producers & Publishers
Barter Theatre
Shenandoah International Playwrights
Virginia Stage Company

Contests & Awards
Aaron Enterprises Summertime Song
    Festival
Henrico Theatre Company One-Act Playwriting
    Competition

Organizations
Aaron Enterprises Songwriters Group
Southwest Virginia Songwriters Association

WASHINGTON

Music Publishers
Corelli's Music Box
Valet Publishing Co.

Record Producers
Lazy Bones Productions/Recordings, Inc.
Ormsby, John "Buck"/Etiquette Productions

Managers & Booking Agents
T.L.C. Booking Agency

Classical Performing Arts
Orchestra Seattle/Seattle Chamber Singers

Organizations
Pacific Northwest Songwriters Association
Victory Music

WEST VIRGINIA

Music Publishers
McCoy Music, Jim

Record Companies
Winchester Records

Record Producers
Blues Alley Records

Play Producers & Publishers
Theatre West Virginia

Contests & Awards
Museum in the Community Composer's
    Award

WISCONSIN

Music Publishers
KeyShavon Music Publishing

Record Companies
Don't Records
Safire Records

Managers & Booking Agents
Ellis International Talent Agency, The
Tas Music Co./Dave Tasse Entertainment
Tiger's Eye Entertainment Management &
    Consulting

*Advertising, Audiovisual & Commercial
Music Firms*
AGA Creative Communications

Classical Performing Arts
Milwaukee Youth Symphony Orchestra

Organizations
Songwriters of Wisconsin International

WYOMING

Play Producers & Publishers
American Living History Theater

AUSTRALIA

Managers & Booking Agents
Buxton Walker P/L
Dinwoodie Management, Andrew
Music Marketing & Promotions
Shute Management Pty. Ltd., Phill

AUSTRIA

Music Publishers
Aquarius Publishing
Edition Rossori
Hit-Fabrik Musikverlag

Record Producers
WIR (World International Records)

BELGIUM
Music Publishers
Happy Melody
Inside Records/OK Songs
Succes

Record Producers
Jump Productions

CANADA
Music Publishers
Hickory Lane Publishing and Recording
Lilly Music Publishing
Mayfair Music
Montina Music
S.M.C.L. Productions
Sci-Fi Music
Third Wave Productions Limited
Warner/Chappell Music Canada Ltd.

Record Companies
Hi-Bias Records Inc.
L.A. Records (Canada)
Magnum Music Corp. Ltd.
Mayfair Music
Merlin Records of Canada
Monticana Records
P. & N. Records
RA Records
Spinball Music and Video
Sun-Scape Enterprises Limited
sonic unyon records canada
Synergy Records
Third Wave Productions Ltd.
Worldwide Recordings Limited/
    Worldrecords.com

Record Producers
"A" Major Sound Corporation
Jay Bird Productions
JSB Groupe Management Inc.
Kane Producer/Engineer, Karen
Merlin Productions
Moffet, Gary
Monticana Productions
Pacific North Studios Ltd.
Panio Brothers Label
Poku Productions

Managers & Booking Agents
Alert Music, Inc.
Ardenne Int'l Inc.
EAO Music Corporation of Canada
Immigrant Music Inc.
Kagan International, Sheldon

Magnum Music Corporation Ltd.
Management Trust Ltd., The
Merlin Management Corp.
Outlaw Entertainment International
Strictly Forbidden Artists
T.J. Booker Ltd.

Classical Performing Arts
Arcady
Canadian Opera Company
Kitchener-Waterloo Chamber Orchestra
Montreal Chamber Orchestra
Star-Scape
Toronto Mendelssohn Choir
Vancouver Chamber Choir

Organizations
Associated Male Choruses of America
Association des Professionel.le.s de la chanson
    et de la musique
Canada Council for the Arts/Conseil des Arts du
    Canada
Canadian Academy of Recording Arts &
    Sciences (CARAS)
Canadian Country Music Association
Canadian Musical Reproduction Rights Agency
    Ltd.
Manitoba Audio Recording Industry Association
    (MARIA)
Pacific Music Industry Association
Society of Composers, Authors and Music
    Publishers of Canada/Société canadienne
    des auteurs, compositeurs et éditeurs de
    musique (SOCAN)
SODRAC Inc.

Workshops & Conferences
Canadian Music Week
New Music West
North by Northeast Music Festival and
    Conference
Orford Festival

FRANCE
Music Publishers
Pas Mal Publishing Sarl

GERMANY
Music Publishers
BME Publishing
Clevère Musikverlag, R.D.
Heupferd Musikverlag GmbH
Ja/Nein Musikverlag GmbH
Mento Music Group
Sinus Musik Produktion, Ulli Weigel
Transamerika Musikverlag KG
Wengert, Berthold (Musikverlag)

Record Companies
Playbones Records

IRELAND
Retreats & Colonies
Guthrie Centre, The Tyrone

JAPAN
Contests & Awards
U.S.-Japan Creative Artists Exchange Fellowship
    Program

MEXICO
Contests & Awards
U.S.-Mexico Fund for Culture

THE NETHERLANDS
Music Publishers
All Rock Music

Record Companies
A.A.M.I. Music Group
Collector Records

Record Producers
Collector Records

Managers & Booking Agents
CBA Artists
Van Pol Management, Hans

NEW ZEALAND
Music Publishers
Pegasus Music

PUERTO RICO
Organizations
American Society of Composers, Authors and
    Publishers (ASCAP)

SCOTLAND
Music Publishers
Brewster Songs, Kitty
Jammy Music Publishers Ltd.

UNITED KINGDOM
Music Publishers
CTV Music (Great Britain)
Ever-Open-Eye Music
First Time Music (Publishing) U.K.
R.T.L. Music
Wipe Out Music Ltd.

Record Companies
AMP Records & Music
First Time Records
Lock
Red-Eye Records
Rhiannon Records
Satellite Music
X.R.L. Records/Music

Record Producers
June Productions Ltd.

Managers & Booking Agents
Circuit Rider Talent & Management Co.
First Time Management
James Management, Roger
Kickstart Music Ltd.
Prestige Artistes

Organizations
American Society of Composers, Authors and
    Publishers (ASCAP)
Guild of International Songwriters &
    Composers, The
International Songwriters Association Ltd.

General Index

Use this index to locate specific markets and resources. Also, we list companies that appeared in the 2001 edition of *Songwriter's Market*, but do not appear this year. Instead of page numbers beside these markets you will find two-letter codes in parenthesis that explain why these markets no longer appear. The codes are: **(ED)**—Editorial Decision, **(NS)**—Not Accepting Submissions, **(NR)**—No (or late) Response to Listing Request, **(OB)**—Out of Business, **(RR)**—Removed by Listing's Request, **(UC)**—Unable to Contact.

A

A.A.M.I. Music Group 172
"A" Major Sound Corporation 255
A.P.I. Records 173
A Ta Z Music 100
A&M Records 173
Aaron Enterprises Songwriters Group 411
Aaron Enterprises Summertime Song Festival 393
Abalone Publishing 100
Aberdeen Productions 255
ABL Records (UC)
Academy of Country Music (NR)
Acadiana Symphony Orchestra (NR)
ACR Productions 256
Activate Entertainment LLC 101
Ad Agency, The 344
Adrian Symphony Orchestra (NR)
Advertel, Inc. 345
African American Composer's Program 393
Afterschool Publishing Company 292
Afterschool Records, Inc. 173
AGA Creative Communications 345
AGO/ECS Publishing Award in Choral Composition 394
Air Tight Management 292
Airplay Label, The 173
Airtrax (UC)
AKO Productions (UC)
Alabama Songwriter's Guild 411
Albatross Records 174
Alco Music 101
Alco Productions 256
Alco Recordings 174
ALEA III International Composition Prize 394
Alert Music, Inc. 293
Alexander Sr. Music 102
Alexis 102
Alias John Henry Tunes 102
All Rock Music 102
All Songwriters Network (ASN) 412

All Star Management 293
All Star Record Promotions 174
All Star Talent Agency 293
Allegheny Music Works 103
Allegheny Music Works 174
Allen Entertainment Development, Michael (NR)
Alliance Theatre Company 359
AlliSongs Inc. 103
ALLRS Music Publishing Co. 101
Allyn, Stuart J. 256
Almo Music Corp./Almo Sounds (RR)
Alpha Music Inc. 103
AlphaBeat 174
AMAJ Records (NR)
AMAS Musical Theatre, Inc. (NR)
Amelia Magazine 373
Amen, Inc. 103
American Artists Entertainment 293
American Bands Management (NR)
American Boychoir, The (NR)
American Classics Media, Inc. (RR)
American Composers Forum 412
American Eastern Theatrical Company 373
American Heartstring Publishing 104
American Independent Artists 293
American Living History Theater 360
American Music Center, Inc. 412
American Musical Theater Festival (NR)
American Musical Theatre of San Jose 360
American Opera Musical Theatre Co. 376
American Recordings 175
American Society of Composers, Authors and Publishers (ASCAP) 412
American Songwriter Lyric Contest 394
American Stage Festival (NR)
Americatone International 104
Americatone Records International USA 175
Amherst Saxophone Quartet 376
Amigos Music & Marketing 175
Amok Artists Agency (NR)

AMP Records & Music 175
Anderson Associates Communications Group 294
Anderson Symphony Orchestra 377
Angel Films Company 256
Angel Films Company 345
Angel/EMI Records (UC)
Anisette Records 176
Antelope Publishing Inc. 104
Appel Farm Arts and Music Festival 440
Appell Productions, Inc., Jonathan 256
Aquarius Publishing 104
AR Management (UC)
ARAS Music 104
Arcady Music Festival 440
Arcady 377
Ardenne Int'l Inc. 294
Ariana Records 176
Arista Records 176
Arizona Songwriters Association 413
Arizona Theatre Company 360
Arkadia Entertainment Corp. 176
Arkansas Repertory Theatre 360
Artist Representation and Management (NR)
Artists' Fellowships 394
Artists' Legal & Accounting Assistance (ALAA) (NR)
ASCAP Musical Theatre Workshop 440
ASCAP West Coast/Lester Sill Songwriter's Workshop 440
Aspen Music Festival and School 441
Associated Male Choruses of America 413
Association des Professionel.le.s de la chanson et de la musique 413
Association of Independent Music Publishers 414
Astralwerks 177
Atch Records and Productions (NR)
Atlan-Dec/Grooveline Records 177
Atlanta Pops Orchestra (NR)
Atlanta Young Singers of Collanwolde, The (NR)
Atlantic Canadian Composers Association (NR)
Atlantic Entertainment Group (NR)
Atlantic Records 177
Audio Images Two Thousand Music Publishing 105
Audio Music Publishers 105
Aureus Quartet 377
Austex Music (NR)
Austin Songwriters Group 414
Avalon Music 105

Avalon Productions 257
Avalon Recording Group 178
Avenue Communications 178
Avita Records 178
Awal.com 178
Aware Records 178

B
Babylon Entertainment Inc. (NR)
babysue 179
Bacchus Group Productions, Ltd. 294
Backstage Entertainment/Loggins Promotions (NR)
Backstreet Booking (NR)
Bagatelle Music Publishing Co. 105
Bagatelle Record Company 179
Bailiwick Repertory 361
Baird Enterprises, Ron 257
Baird Music Group 106
Baitstring Music 106
Baker's Plays High School Playwriting Contest 395
Baker's Plays 373
Bal & Bal Music Publishing Co. 106
Bal Records 257
Baltimore Opera Company, Inc. 377
Bamn Management (NR)
Bandstand (International) Entertainment Agency (OB)
Bankroll Records Inc. 179
Barkin' Foe the Master's Bone 106
Barnard Management Services (BMS) 294
Barren Wood Publishing 107
Barrett Rock 'N' Roll Enterprises (NR)
Barter Theatre 361
Bassline Entertainment, Inc. 295
Baxter Management, Dick (NR)
Bay Ridge Publishing Co. 107
BC Productions (NR)
Belham Valley Records Songwriting Competition 395
Belham Valley Records 179
Belmont Records 180
Beluga Records 180
Bernard Enterprises, Inc., Hal 107
Bernard Enterprises, Inc., Hal 257
Better Than Sex Music 108
Big Beat Records 180
Big Fish Music Publishing Group 108
Big Heavy World 180
Big J Productions 295

Big Sky Audio Productions 258
Big Wig Productions 181
Billboard Song Contest 396
Billings Symphony 378
Birmingham Children's Theatre (NR)
Birmingham-Bloomfield Symphony Orchestra 378
Birthplace Productions 258
Bixio Music Group/IDM Ventures, Ltd. 108
Black Country Music Association, The 414
Black Rock Coalition, The (NR)
Black Stallion Country, Inc. 295
Black Stallion Country Publishing 109
Blackground 295
Blank & Blank 296
Blank Theatre Company Young Playwrights Festival 396
Blind Records (ED)
Blowin' Smoke Productions/Records 296
Blowing Rock Stage Company, The 361
Blue Cat Agency, The 296
Blue Dog Publishing and Records 109
Blue Gem Records 181
Blue Planet Music (NR)
Blue Wave Productions 296
Blue Wave 181
Blues Alley Records 258
Bluestock Festival 441
BME Publishing 109
BMG Music Publishing 109
BMI-Lehman Engel Musical Theatre Workshop 441
Bohemian Entertainment Group (NR)
Bolivia Records 181
Boston Songwriters Workshop, The 414
Boulevard Music & Publishing (NR)
Bouquet-Orchid Enterprises 296
Bourne Co. Music Publishers 109
Bozell Kamstra (NR)
BRAVO! L.A. 378
Bradley Music, Allan 110
Branson Country Music Publishing 110
Brentwood Records/Diadem Records 182
Brentwood-Benson Music Publishing 110
Brevard Music Center 451
Brewster Songs, Kitty 111
BRg Music Works 345
Brian Song Music Corp. 111
Bridge Enterprises 346
Bristol Riverside Theatre 362
Broadcast Music, Inc. (BMI) 414
Broadway on Sunset (NR)
Broadway Tomorrow Previews 441
Broken Note Records 182
Broken Records International 182

Brothers Management Associates 297
BSW Records 111, 182
Buried Treasure Music 111
Burns Talent Agency, Dott (NR)
Bush Artist Fellows Program 396
Butler Music, Bill 297
Butwin & Associates, Inc. 346
Buxton Walker P/L 297
Byrdcliffe Arts Colony 451

C
C.P.R. 183
Caldwell Vanriper/Marc 346
Calgary Boys Choir (NR)
California Country Music 112
California Lawyers for the Arts 415
Callner Music (OB)
Cambria Records & Publishing 183
Canada Council for the Arts/Conseil des Arts du Canada 415
Canadian Academy of Recording Arts & Sciences (CARAS) 415
Canadian Country Music Association 416
Canadian Music Week 441
Canadian Musical Reproduction Rights Agency Ltd. 416
Canadian Opera Company 379
Candyspiteful Productions 183, 258
Cantata Academy 379
Cantilena Records 183
Cantrax Recorders 346
Capital Entertainment 297
Capitol Records 183
CAPP Records 184
Capricorn Records 184
Capstan Record Production 184
Carey College Dinner Theatre, William 362
Carmel Symphony Orchestra 379
Carson City Symphony (NR)
Casaro Records (NR)
Cascade Sympphony Orchestra (NR)
Case Entertainment Group/C.E.G. Records, Inc. (NR)
CBA Artists 298
Cellar Records 185
Celt Musical Services, Jan 258
Centenary College, Theatre Department 362
Center for the Promotion of Contemporary Composers 416
Central Carolina Songwriters Association (CCSA) 416
Central Oregon Songwriters Association 417
Chamber Orchestra of South Bay/Carson-Dominiquez Hills Symphony (NR)
Charlotte Philharmonic Orchestra 379

Chattahoochee Records 185
Chattanooga Girls Choir 380
Cheavoria Music Co. (BMI) 112
Cherri/Holly Music Inc. 112
Cherry Street Records 185
Cheyenne Symphony Orchestra (NR)
Chiaroscuro Records 185
Chicago Alliance for Playwrights (NR)
Chicago String Ensemble, The (NR)
Christmas & Holiday Music 112
Christopher Publishing, Sonny 116
Chucker Music Inc. 298
Cimarron Circuit Opera Company (NR)
Cinevue/Steve Postal Productions 347
Circa '21 Dinner Playhouse 362
Circuit Rider Talent & Management Co. 298
CITA Communications Inc. (NR)
CKB Records/Helaphat Entertainment 186
Class Act Productions/Management 299
Cleopatra Records 186
Clevère Musikverlag, R.D. 116
Clockwork Entertainment Management Agency
   299
Clousher Productions 299
CMJ Music Marathon, MusicFest & FilmFest
   442
Coachouse Music 259
Cody Entertainment Group 299
Coffee and Cream Productions 259
Coffer Management, Raymond (NR)
Collector Records 186, 259
College Music Society, The 417
Colorado Music Association 417
Columbia Entertainment Company's Jackie
   White Memorial Playwriting Contest 396
Columbia Management Corp. (NR)
Columbia Records 186
Com-Four Distribution 189
Commonwealth Opera, Inc. 380
Communications for Learning 347
Composers Commissioning Program 397
Composers Guild Annual Composition Contest
   397
Composers Guild 417
Comstock Records Ltd. 189
Concept 2000 Inc. 299
Concerted Efforts, Inc./Foggy Day Music 300
Connecticut Choral Artists/Concora 380
Connecticut Songwriters Association 417
Conscience Music 300
Contemporary Drama Service 373

Coppin, Johnny/Red Sky Records (NR)
Coral Records LLC 190
Corelli's Music Box 116
Cornelius Companies, The 116
Corvalan-Condliffe Management 300
Cosmotone Records 190
Countdown Entertainment 300
Countdown Records (NR)
Country Breeze Music (UC)
Country Legends Association (NR)
Country Music Association of Texas 418
Country Music Showcase International, Inc. 418
Country Rainbow Music 116
Country Showcase America (NR)
Countrywide Producers 301
Cox Promotions & Management, Stephen 301
Craig, Douglas 259
Crank! A Record Company (NR)
Crawfish Productions 301
Creative Improvised Music Projects (CIMP) Re-
   cords 190
Creative Star Management 301
Creative Support Services 347
Creede Repertory Theatre (NR)
Crescent Recordign Corporation (NR)
Criss-Cross Industries 302
Crossfire Productions 302
Crossroads Theatre 363
CRS National Composers Competition 397
CTV Music (Great Britain) 117
Cunningham Prize for Playwriting 398
Cupit Music 117
Cupit Productions, Jerry 260
Curb Records 191
Cycle of Fifths Management, Inc. (OB)

D

D.S.M. Producers Inc. 347
DAP Entertainment 260
Dagene Music 117
Dagene/Cabletown Company 191
Dale Productions, Alan 191
D&D Talent Associates (ED)
D&M Entertainment Agency 302
D&R Entertainment 302
Dapmor Publishing 117
Dapmor Records 191
DAS Communications, Ltd. 303
Dave Music, Jof 118
Davidson's Writer's Seminar, Peter 442
Daylo Music (RR)

GENERAL INDEX

dbF A Media Company 348
DCA Productions 303
De Miles Company, The Edward 303
De Miles, Edward 260
De Miles Music Company, The Edward 118
Deadeye Records 191
Deary Me Records 192
Deep South Entertainment 192
Delev Music Company 118
Del-Fi Records, Inc. 192
DeLory and Music Makers, Al 260
Delta Omicron International Composition Competition 398
Demi Monde Records & Publishing Ltd. (NR)
Desert Chorale (NR)
Detko Management, Bill 303
Detroit Music Alliance 418
Diamond Entertainment, Joel 260
Dinwoodie Management, Andrew 304
Direct Management 304
Directors Company, The 363
Discmedia 193
Discos Fuentes/Miami Records & Edimusica USA 193
Disk Productions 348
Dixon III, Philip D., Attorney at Law 261
DM/Bellmark/Critique Records 193
DMR Agency 304
Don't Records 193
Door Knob Music Publishing 118
Doré Records 119
Dorland Mountain Arts Colony 451
Dorset Colony House 451
Doss Music, Buster 119
Doss Presents, Col. Buster 261, 304
Dramatists Guild of America, The (NR)
Dream Seekers Publishing 119
DreamWorks Records 193
Drive Entertainment (NR)
Drive Music (NR)
Drool Records 194
Drumbeat Indian Arts, Inc. 194
Duane Music, Inc. 119
Dunner Talent Management (NR)
Dúo Clásico (NR)
Dwell Records 194

E

EAO Music Corporation of Canada 304
Earitating Music Publishing 119
Earth Tracks Artists Agency 305
Earthscream Music Publishing Co. 120
East Coast Music Publishing 120
Edition Rossori 120
Edmonds Record Group 194

Eiffert, Jr., Leo J. 261
Eldridge Publishing Co., Inc. 374
Elektra Records 194
Ellis International Talent Agency, The 305
Emandell Tunes 120
Emerald City Records 195
EMF Productions 195
EMF Records & Affiliates 195
Emstone, Inc. Music Publishing 121
Endangered Species Artist Management 305
Ensemble Productions 348
Ensemble Theatre 363
Enterprize Records-Tapes 196
Entertainment Productions, Inc. 348
Entourage Music Group (NR)
Epic Records 196
Erwin Music (OB)
Esquire International 261
Eternal Song Agency, The 262
European International Competition for Composers 398
European Union Chamber Orchestra (NR)
Evans Productions, Scott 306
Evergreen Entertainment Services 306
Ever-Open-Eye Music 121
Evil Teen Records 196
Exclesisa Booking Agency 306

F

Factory Beat Records, Inc. (NR)
Famous Music Publishing Companies 121
Faverett Group 122
Feldman & Associates, S.L. (NR)
Fenchel Entertainment Agency, Fred T. 306
Fiedler Management, B.C. (NR)
Field, The 419
Fifth Avenue Media, Ltd. 122
Film Classic Exchange 353
Final Mix Music 262
Fine Art Productions/Richie Suraci Pictures, Multimedia, Interactive 353
Fireant 196
First Power Entertainment Group 197
First Time Management 307
First Time Music (Publishing) U.K. 122
First Time Records 197
Fish of Death Records and Management 197
Fitzmusic 353
Five Star Entertainment (NR)
550 Music (NR)
Flash Point Records (ED)
Flinter Music (NR)
Flood Recording Corp. 198
Flying Heart Records 198
Flying Red Horse Publishing 122

Folk Alliance Annual Conference 442
Folk Alliance 419
Fontana Concert Society (NR)
Fools Company, Inc. (NR)
Fort Bend Songwriters Association 419
Fort Worth Children's Opera (NR)
Fort Worth Songwriters Association 419
Fountain Records 198
Fountain Theatre (NR)
Fox Management Inc., Mitchell (NR)
Fredrick, Lee & Lloyd 354
Free Staged Reading Series Playwriting Competition 398
Freedman & Smith Entertainment (NR)
Freelance Press, The 374
French, Inc., Samuel 374
Fresh Entertainment 122, 198
Frick Enterprises, Bob Scott 123
Fricon Music Company 123
Front Row Records 199
Frozen Inca Music 123
Fulbright Scholar Program, Council for International Exchange of Scholars 399
Furrow Music 123
Future Charters 399
Future Star Entertainment (NR)

G
G Major Music 124
Gallery II Records/Jumpin' Jack Records (NR)
Gallway Bay Music 262
Garrett Entertainment, Marty 199
Gary Music, Alan 124
Gaslight Theatre, The 363
Gaul Composition Contest, Harvey 399
GCI, Inc. 307
Geer Theatricum Botanicum, The Will 364
Geffen/DGC Records 199
Generic Records, Inc. (NR)
Genesius Guild Monday Night Performance Project Series 442
Georgia Music Industry Association, Inc. 420
Geter Advertising Inc. 354
Gig Records 199
Glad Music Co. 124
GMI Entertainment Inc. (NR)
Godtland Management, Inc., Eric 307
Gold City Records, Inc. 200
Golden City International 307
Golden Guru Entertainment (NR)
Golden Music, August 124

Golden Triangle Records 200
Goldwax Record Corporation 200
Gonzo! Records Inc. 201
Gonzo/Vireo Records (NS)
Goodland Music Group Inc., The 125
Goodnight Kiss Music 125
Gospel Music Association 420
Gospel/Christian Songwriters Group 420
Gotham Records 201
Grace Praise Records (NR)
Grass Roots Record & Tape/LMI Records 201
Great American Song Contest 399
Great Falls Symphony Association 381
Greater Grand Forks Symphony Orchestra 381
Green Bear Records 201
Green One Music 125
Greif-Garris Management 307
Griffin Music 202
Groove Makers' Recordings 202
G-String Publishing (UC)
Gueststar Entertainment Agency 308
Gueststar Records, Inc. 202
Guild of International Songwriters & Composers, The 420
Gurley & Co. (NR)
Guthrie Centre, The Tyrone 451

H
Hacienda Records & Recording Studio 202
Hailing Frequency Music Productions 262
Hale Enterprises 308
Hall Entertainment & Events, Bill 308
Hambidge Center, The 452
Hammel Associates, Inc., R.L. 126
Hammerhead Records, Inc. (NS)
Hansen Enterprises, Ltd. 309
Happy Man Records 203
Happy Melody 126
Hardison International Entertainment Corporation 309
Harlow Sound (NR)
Harrell & Associates, M. 309
Hartford Stage Company (NS)
Hawkeye Attractions 309
Haworth Productions 263
Heads Up Int., Ltd. 203
Heart Consort Music 263
Heart Music, Inc. 203
Heartland Men's Chorus 381
Heartland Symphony Orchestra (NR)
Helena Symphony 381

GENERAL INDEX

Hendersonville Symphony Orchestra (NR)
Henrico Theatre Company One-Act Playwriting
   Competition 400
Hermann Sons German Band (NR)
Hershey Symphony Orchestra 382
Heuer Publishing Co. 375
Heupferd Musikverlag GmbH 126
Hi-Bias Records Inc. 203
Hickory Lane Publishing and Recording 126
Hickory Valley Music 126
High-Minded Moma Publishing & Productions
   127
His Power Productions and Publishing 127
Hit Parade/New Faith Record Co., Inc. (NR)
Hit-Fabrik Musikverlag 127
Hitsburgh Music Co. 127
Hitsource Publishing 128
Hodges Associates, Inc. 354
Hollywood Records 204
Holtkamp-AGO Award in Organ Composition
   400
Holy Spirit Music 128
Home, Inc. 354
Horizon Management Inc. 309
Horizon Records, Inc. 204
Horizon Theatre (NR)
Hot Wings Entertainment 204
Hottrax Records 204
Hudson Valley Philharmonic 382
Huge Production, Inc., A (NR)
Hupp Enterprises, Joe (NR)

I
I Write The Songs 443
Idol Records 205
Imaginary Records 205
IMI Records (NR)
Immigrant Music Inc. 310
Indiana Opera Theatre/MacAllister Awards for
   Opera Singers 400
Indianapolis Songwriters Association, Inc., The
   (NR)
Indie-Go Music 128
Inner Soul Records, Inc. (NR)
Inside Records/OK Songs 128
Inside Sounds (NR)
Integrated Entertainment 263
International Bluegrass Music Association
   (IBMA) (NR)
International Clarinet Association Composition
   Competition 400
International Entertainment Bureau 310
International Songwriters Association Ltd. 420
National Songwriters Guild 421
Planetary Music 128

Interscope/Geffen/A&M Records 205
Interstate Records 263
Intrepid Records (NR)
Invictus Music Group/Records/Productions (ED)
Iron Skillet Music 129
Island/Def Jam Music Group 206
Isle Royale National Park Artist-in-Residence
   Program 452
Its Happening Now (ED)

J
J & V Management 310
Jacobson Talent Management 310
Jae Enterprises, Jana 311
Jae Music, Jana 129
Jag Studio, Ltd. 264
Jam Down Entertainment, LLC (UC)
James Management, Roger 311
Jammy Music Publishers Ltd. 129
Ja/Nein Musikverlag GmbH 129
Janoulis Productions, Alexander/Big Al Jano
   Productions 264
Jasper Stone Music (ASCAP)/JSM Songs (BMI)
   130
Jay Bird Productions 264
Jay Jay Publishing & Record Co. 264
Jericho Sound Lab (NR)
Jerjoy Music 130
Jewish Repertory Theatre (NS)
Jive Records 206
John Productions, David 264
Jolson Black & White Music, Al 130
JPMC Music Inc. 131
JSB Groupe Management Inc. 265
Juke Music 131
Jump Productions 265
June Productions Ltd. 265
Juniper Music Productions (NR)
Just Plain Folks Music Organization 421

K
Kagan International, Sheldon 311
Kalani Oceanside Retreat 452
K&R's Recording Studios 354
Kane Producer/Engineer, Karen 265
Kansa Records Corporation 131
Kaupp Records 206
Kaupps & Robert Publishing Co. 131
Kaylee Music Group, Kaylee (NR)
Keeping It Simple and Safe, Inc. 206
Ken-Del Productions Inc. 355
Kentucky Opera 382
Kerrville Folk Festival 443
Kerrville Music Foundation Inc. (OB)

KeyShavon Music Publishing 132
Kickstart Music Ltd. 311
Kill Rock Stars (NR)
Kingston Records and Talent 266
Kingston Records 207
Kitchener-Waterloo Chamber Orchestra 383
KKR Entertainment Group 311
Klein, Joanne 312
KMA 266
Knight Agency, Bob 312
Known Artist Productions 266
Kovach, Robert R. 266
Kuper Personal Management 312

L

L.A. Designers' Theatre Music Awards 401
L.A. Entertainment, Inc. 267
L.A. Records (Canada) 207
L.A. Records (Michigan) 207
La Jolla Playhouse (NR)
LaFace Records 208
Lake Transfer Productions & Music 132
Lakeside Summer Symphony 383
Lamar Music Marketing 208
Lamarca American Variety Singers 383
Lamb's Retreat for Songwriters 443
Lamon Records (NR)
Landmark Communications Group 208, 267
Landslide Records 208
Lapriore Videography 355
Largo Music Publishing 132
Lari-Jon Productions 267
Lari-Jon Promotions 312
Lari-Jon Publishing 133
Lari-Jon Records 209
Lark Record Productions, Inc. 209
Lark Talent & Advertising 267
Las Vegas Songwriters Association, The 422
Lawrence, Ltd., Ray 313
Lazy Bones Productions/Recordings, Inc. 267
Leatherland Productions 209
Legacy Sound & Entertainment (NR)
Legend Artists Management (NR)
Lehigh Valley Chamber Orchestra 383
Leigh Music, Trixie 133
Lennon Songwriting Contest, The John 401
Lenthall & Associates (NR)
Les Music Group 133
Levinson Entertainment Ventures International, Inc. 313
Levy Management, Rick 313

Lexington Alabama Music Publishing 133
Lexington Philharmonic Society 384
Lilly Music Publishing 133
Lima Symphony Orchestra 384
Lindsay Productions, Doris/Successful Productions 313
Lindsay Publishing, Doris 134
Lineage Publishing Co. 134
Linear Cycle Productions 268
Lithopolis Area Fine Arts Association 384
Little Miller Music Co. (OB)
Live-Wire Management 313
Living Eye Productions (NR)
Lock 209
Loconto Productions 268
Loconto Productions/Sunrise Studio 209
Loggins Promotion/Backstage Entertainment 314
London Sire Records 210
Los Angeles Designers' Theatre 364
Los Angeles Music Network 422
Louisiana Songwriters Association 422
Lowell Agency 314
Lucifer Records, Inc. 210
Luick & Associates Music Publisher, Harold 134
Luick & Country Music Showcase Intl. Associates, Harold 268
Lutz Entertainment Agency, Richard (NR)
Lyric Opera of Chicago (NR)
Lyrick Studios 134
LyricsReview.com Music Publishing Co. (UC)

M

M.E.G Management 314
Mac-Attack Productions 268
MacDowell Colony, The 453
MacPherson Productions, Don and Pat (NR)
Magic Message Music 135
Magic Theatre (NR)
Magid Productions, Lee 269
Magnetic Oblivion Music Co. 269
Magnum Music Corp. Ltd. 210, 314
Major Entertainment, Inc. 210
Makers Mark Gold 135
Makers Mark Music Productions 269
Makoché Recording Company 211
Malaco Records 211
Mallof, Abruzino & Nash Marketing 355
Management by Jaffe 315
Management Plus 315
Management Trust Ltd., The 315

Manchester Music Festival 443
Manhattan Theatre Club 364
Manitoba Audio Recording Industry Association
    (MARIA) 422
Manuiti L.A. 135
Marenco, Cookie 270
Markea Music/Gina Pie Music 135
Martin, Pete/Vaam Music Productions 270
Martin Productions, Rick 315
Marvin Publishing, John Weller 136
Marvin Taylor Playwriting Award (OB)
Master Chorale of Washington 385
Mathes Productions, David (NR)
Mathews, d/b/a Hit or Myth Productions, Scott
    270
Maverick Music 136
Maverick Records 211
Mayfair Music 136, 211
Mayo & Company, Phil 315
Mazumdar New Play Competition, Maxim 401
Mazur Public Relations (NR)
M.B.H Music Management (NR)
MCA Records 211
MCB Records/Pepe 212
McCann-Erickson Southwest 355
McConkey Artists Agency Music Publishing 136
McCoy Music, Jim 136
McDonnell Group, The 316
MCI-Scroll, Inc. Original Lyric Competition 402
McKnight Visiting Composer Program 402
McLaren Comedy Playwriting Competition (RR)
Media Management 316
Meet the Composer 423
Mega Music Productions 316
Mega Truth Records 271
Megaforce Worldwide Entertainment 212
Mellow House Music 137
Melody Hills Ranch Publishing Co. 137
Memphis Songwriters' Association 423
Mento Music Group 137
Merlin Management Corp. 316
Merlin Productions 271
Merlin Records of Canada 212
Merri-Webb Productions 317
Metal Blade Records (NR)
Metro Talent Group, Inc. (NR)
MHM Recordings (NR)
Mid-Atlantic Song Contest 402
Mighty Blue Music Machine, The 137
Mighty Records 213
Mill Mountain Theatre (NR)
    er & Company, Thomas J. (NR)
    kee Youth Symphony Orchestra 385
    Association of Songwriters 423
    Trio, The 385

Mirkin Management 317
Missile Records 213
Missouri Songwriters Association, Inc. 424
Mittelstedt, A.V. 271
Mixed Blood Theatre Co. 365
MJJ Music (OB)
Modal Music, Inc.™ 213
Moffet, Gary 271
Mohawk Trail Concerts (NR)
Mona Lisa Records/Bristol Studios 272
Monk International Jazz Composers Competi-
    tion, Thelonious 403
Monopoly Management (NR)
Montgomery Management, Gary F. 317
Monticana Productions 272
Monticana Records 214
Montina Music 138
Montreal Chamber Orchestra 385
Moody, David (NR)
Moody Music Group (NR)
Moody Productions, Doug 214
Moon June Music 138
Moore Compositions, Patrick (NR)
MOR Records 214
Motown Records 214
Mozart Festival Orchestra, Inc. 386
Museum in the Community Composer's Award
    403
Music Bridge, The 138
Music Business Solutions/Career Building
    Workshops 444
Music In The Right Keys Publishing Company
    (ED)
Music Marketing & Promotions 317
Music Room Publishing Group, The 138
Music Services & Marketing (ED)
Music Wise Inc. (NR)
Musicians Contact 424
Musicland Productions, Inc. 272
Musikuser Publishing 138
Mymit Music Productions, Chuck 138
Mystic Music (NR)

N
NACUSA Young Composers' Competition 403
Naked Jain Records 139
Nash-One Management Inc. 317
Nashville Music Festival 444
Nashville Songwriters Association International-
    Detroit 428
Nashville Songwriters Association International
    (NSAI) 424
Nation Records Inc. 214
National Academy of Popular Music (NAPM)
    428

National Academy of Popular Music Songwriting Workshop Program 444
National Academy of Songwriters 428
National Association of Composers/USA (NACUSA) 386, 428
National Society of Men and Women of the Music Business (WOMB) 428
National Songwriter's Network Contests (NR)
Nelson Entertainment Inc., Brian (NR)
Nelson Promotions & Management Co., Lou (ED)
NEMO Music Showcase & Conference 444
Nestico Award, Sammy/USAF Band Airmen of Note 403
Neu Electro Productions 272
Neurodisc Records, Inc. 214
New Experience Records 272
New Folk Concerts for Emerging Songwriters 404
New Harmony Project, The 444
New Music West 445
New Rap Jam Publishing, A 139
New Repertory Theatre 365
New Vizion Studios, The 273
New York State Theatre Institute 365
New York Theatre Workshop 365
Newcreature Music 139
Nik Entertainment (NR)
Nilsson Production, Christina (NR)
Nocturnal Records (NR)
Norfolk Chamber Music Festival 445
Norfolk Chamber Music Festival/Yale Summer School of Music 386
North Arkansas Symphony Orchestra (ED)
North by Northeast Music Festival and Conference 445
North Florida Christian Music Writers Association 429
North Shore Music Theatre (NR)
North Star Music 215
Northern California Songwriters Association Conference 445
Northern California Songwriters Association 429
Northern Lights Management 318
Northern Lights Playhouse (NR)
Northwest Alabama Music Publishing 140
Northwood University Alden B. Dow Creativity Center 453
Norton Rubble & Mertz, Inc. Advertising 355
Noteworthy Enterprises 318
Noteworthy Productions 318

Novus Visual Communications Inc. 356
NPO Records, Inc. 215
NSAI Song Camps 445
NSAI Songwriters Symposium 446
NSP Music Publishing Inc. (RR)

O
OCP Publications 215
Odyssey Theatre Ensemble 366
Oklahoma Songwriters & Composers Association 430
Old School Records (RR)
Old Slowpoke Music 140
Omaha Symphony Guild International New Music Competition 404
Omega Record Group, Inc. 215
Omni 2000, Inc. 140, 216, 273
On Stage Management 318
On the Level Music! 318
Only New Age Music, Inc. 216
ON-Q Productions, Inc. 356
Ontrax Companies 140
Open Eye Theater, The 366
Opera America 430
Opera Festival of New Jersey (NR)
Opera Memphis (NR)
Opera on the Go 386
Operaworks 387
Orchestra Seattle/Seattle Chamber Singers 387
Orchid Publishing 141
Oregon Symphony (NR)
Orford Festival 446
Original Artists' Agency 319
Orillyon Entertainment 216
Orinda Records (NR)
Ormsby, John "Buck"/Etiquette Productions 273
OTA Productions (NR)
Otto Publishing Co. 141
Outland Productions 319
Outlaw Entertainment International 319
Outmusic 430
Outpost Recordings (NR)
Outstanding Records 216
Ozark Noteworthy Songwriters Association, Inc. 430

P
P. & N. Records 217
P.M. Records 217
Pacific Music Industry Association 430

Pacific North Studios Ltd. 273
Pacific Northwest Songwriters Association 430
Pacific Time Entertainment 217
Paden Place Music 141
Paint Chip Records 217
Pandyamonium/William Tenn Artist Management (NR)
Panio Brothers Label 274
Parker, Patty 274
Pas Mal Publishing Sarl 141
Pecos Valley Music 141
Pegasus Music 142
PEN Music Group, Inc. 142
Perla Music 142
Permanent Press Recordings/Permanent Wave 218
Peters Music, Justin 142
PGE Platinum Groove Entertainment 218
Philadelphia Music Conference 446
Philadelphia Songwriters Forum, The 431
Philly Breakdown Recording Co. 274
Phil's Entertainment Agency Limited (NR)
Piano Press 142
Piccolo Opera Company Inc. 387
Pickwick/Mecca/International Records 218
Pierce, Jim 274
Pillar Records 319
Pioneer Drama Service 375
Pittsburgh Songwriters Association 431
Planet Dallas Recording Studios (RR)
Plateau Music 219
Platinum Entertainment, Inc. 219
Playbones Records 219
Players Press, Inc. 375
Playhouse on the Square New Play Competition 404
Playhouse on the Square 366
Playwrights' Arena 367
Playwrights Horizons 367
PMG Records 219
Pointblank Records 220
Poku Productions 275
Pollybyrd Publications Limited 143
Poole Agency Limited, Gordon (NR)
Pop Record Research 220, 431
Portage Music 143
Portland Songwriters Association Annual Songwriting Competition 404
Portland Songwriters Association 431
Power and Associates, Inc., RH 356
Powerblast Recordings 220
...lay Entertainment (NR)
...tainment Group 221
...ords 221
... Management 320

Prejippie Music Group 143, 275
Prescription Company 144, 275
Presence Records 221
Presser Co., Theodore 144
Prestige Artistes 320
Prestige Management (NR)
Price Weber Marketing Communications, Inc. 356
Primary Stages 367
Princeton Symphony Orchestra 387
Priority Records 221
Prism Saxophone Quartet (NR)
Pritchett Publications 144
Pro Talent Consultants 320
Publishing Central (RR)
Pulitzer Prize in Music 405

Q
Q Records 222
Qually & Company Inc. 356
QUARK, Inc. 144
Quark Records 222
Qwest Records 222

R
R.J. Music 145
R.T.L. Music 146
RA Records 222
Radical Records 222
Radioactive Records 223
RadioActive 320
Rags to Records, Inc. 223
Rainbow Collection Ltd. 321
Rainbow Music Corp. 145
Rainbow Recording 275
Rainbow Talent Agency 321
Rampant Records 223
Rampion Visual Productions 357
R&D Productions 275
RAVE Records, Inc. 224
Razco (NR)
Razor & Tie Entertainment 224
RCA Records 224
Redemption Records 224
Red-Eye Records 224
Reel Adventures 276
Regis Records Inc. (UC)
Reiter Records Ltd. 225
Relativity Records 225
Ren Zone Music 145
Renaissance Entertainment Group 321
Reno Chamber Orchestra (NR)
Repertory Theatre of St. Louis, The 367
Reprise Records 225

Rhiannon Records 225
Rhino Entertainment (NR)
Rhode Island Songwriters' Association 431
Richards World Management, Inc., Diane 321
Ridgewood Symphony Orchestra 388
Right-On Management 321
Riohcat Music 322
Risavy, Inc., A.F. 322
Rival Records 226
Road Records 226, 276
Roadshow Music Corp. (RR)
Robbins Entertainment LLC 226
Rochester Playwright Festival Contest 405
Rock N Metal Music Publishing Co. 145
Rock 'N' Roll Management (NR)
Rock of Ages Productions 322
Rock Whirled Music Management 322
Rocker Music/Happy Man Music 145
Rockford Music Co. 146
Rocky Mountain Folks Festival Songwriter
   Showcase 405
Rodeo Video, Inc. 357
Rodgers Awards, Richard 405
Rogue Management (NR)
Roll On Records® 226
Rome Prize Fellowship in Musical Composition
   406
Rosenman, Mike (RR)
Rosenthal New Play Prize, Lois and Richard 406
Rothschild Productions Inc., Charles R. 323
Rotten Records 227
Rowena Records 227
RPM Management Services Pty Ltd. (NR)
RR&R Records/Music Productions, Inc. (NR)
Ruf Records 227
Rustron Music Productions 227, 276, 323
Rustron Music Publishers 146

S
S.M.C.L. Productions, Inc. 150
Sabre Productions 228
Sabteca Music Co. 147
Sabteca Record Co. 228
Sacramento Master Singers 388
Saddlestone Publishing (RR)
Saffyre Management 323
Safire Records 228
Sahara Records and Filmworks Entertainment
   229
St. Francis Records 233
Saint John Artists (NR)

St. Louis Chamber Chorus 390
Saint Thomas Choir of Men and Boys, The 388
Salexo Music 229
Salt Lake Symphonic Choir (NR)
Salt Works Music 147
Sa'Mall Management 323
Samuels Publishing, R. 147
San Diego Songwriters Guild 432
San Francisco Folk Music Club 432
San Francisco Girls Chorus 389
SAS Productions/Hit Records Network 277
Satellite Music 229
Satkowski Recordings, Steve 277
Sault Ste. Marie Symphony Orchestra (NR)
Sci-Fi Music 147
Scott Entertainment, Craig (NR)
Scott Music Group, Tim 147
Scrutchings Music 148
SDM, Inc./Sunset Boulevard Entertainment (NR)
Sea Cruise Productions, Inc. 324
Seafair/Bolo Records (NR)
Sealed Fate Records 229
Second Stage Theatre 368
Secret Agent Entertainment Group, Ltd. (NR)
Segal's Productions 277
Segal's Publications 148
Sellwood Publishing 148
Sendyk, Leonard & Co. Inc. 324
Serge Entertainment Group 324
SESAC Inc. 432
Shakespeare Santa Cruz (NR)
Shawnee Press, Inc. 148
Shenandoah International Playwrights 368
Shiznit Music Conference, The 447
Shu'Baby Montez Music 149, 277
Shute Management Pty. Ltd., Phill 324
Siddons & Associates 325
Siegel Entertainment Ltd. (NR)
Silicon Music Publishing Co. 149
Siltown Records 230
Silver Blue Music/Oceans Blue Music 149
Silver Bow Productions/Management (NR)
Silver Thunder Music Group 149, 278
Silver Wave Records 230
Silvertone Records 230
Simply Grand Music, Inc. 150
Sims Records, Jerry 230
Sin Klub Entertainment, Inc. 230
Singer Songwriter Information Line, The 432
Singermanagement, Inc. (NR)
Singing Boys of Pennsylvania 389

Sinus Musik Produktion, Ulli Weigel 150
Sitka Center for Art & Ecology 453
Skorman Productions, Inc., T. 325
Slanted Circle Music 150
Smeltzer Productions, Gary (NR)
Smithsonian Folkways Recordings 231
Society of Composers, Authors and Music Publishers of Canada/Société canadienne des auteurs, compositeurs et éditeurs de musique (SOCAN) 433
SODRAC Inc. 433
Solana Records (NR)
Soli Deo Gloria Cantorum (NR)
Song Farm Music (NR)
Sonar Records & Production 231
Songgram Music 231
Songwriters Advocate, The (TSA) 433
Songwriters & Lyricists Club 433
Songwriters and Poets Critique 433
Songwriters Association of Nova Scotia (NR)
Songwriters Association of Washington 434
Songwriters Guild Foundation, The 447
Songwriters Guild of America, The 434
Songwriters of Oklahoma 434
Songwriters of Wisconsin International 435
Songwriters Playground® 448
Songwriters Resource Network 435
Sonic Records, Inc./SRI Records, Inc. 231
sonic unyon records canada 232
Soter Associates, Inc. 357
Sound and Serenity Management (NR)
Sound Arts Recording Studio 278
Sound Cellar Music 151
Sound Gems 232
Sound Management Direction 325
Sound Works Entertainment Productions Inc. 278
South by Southwest Music and Media Conference 448
Southeast Texas Bluegrass Music Association 435
Southeastern Attractions 325
Southern Arizona Symphony Orchestra (NR)
Southern Made Records (NR)
Southern Most Publishing Company 151
Southern Songwriters Guild, Inc. 435
Southland Records, Inc. 232
Southwest Celtic Music Association 436
Southwest Virginia Songwriters Association 436
Talent Associates 326
Coast Pops, Inc. 389
436
up One 278, 326
and Video 233
(NS)
ency L.L.C., The 326

Spotlight Records 233
Spradlin/Gleich Publishing 151
Stage One 368
Stages Repertory Theatre 368
Staircase Promotion 326
Stander Entertainment 327
Starbound Publishing Co. 151
Stardust 233
Starfish Records (OB)
Starkravin' Management 327
Star-Scape 390
Starstruck Writers Group (NR)
Stay Gold Productions (NR)
Steinman Management, Obi 327
Stellar Music Industries 152
Stevens & Company Management 327
Stewart Management, Steve 328
Stone Age Records 233
Stormin' Norman Productions 328
Strawberry Productions, Inc. (NR)Strictley Business Music Management (NR)
Street Records 234
Strictly Forbidden Artists 328
Strugglebaby Recording Co. 234
Stuart Music Co., Jeb 152
Studio Seven 279
Studio Voodoo Music 279
Succes 152
Suisonic Records 234
Sun Star Songs 152
SunCountry Records 234
Sun-Scape Enterprises Limited 235
Sunsongs Music/Dark Son Music 153
Supreme Enterprises Int'l Corp. (NR)
Sureshot Records 235
Surface Management Inc. 328
Surface Records 235
Survivor Records/Ten of Diamonds Music (NR)
Susquehanna Symphony Orchestra 390
Swannanoa Gathering—Contemporary Folk Week, The 448
Sweet June Music 235
Swift River Productions 279
Swine Palace Productions (NR)
Symphony of the Americas (NR)
Syndicate Management (NR)
Syndicate Sound, Inc. 279
Synergy Records 236

T
T.C. Productions/Etude Publishing Co. 153
T.J. Booker Ltd. 328
T.L.C. Booking Agency 329
Tabitha Music, Ltd. (NR)
Tada! 369

Take 2 Records 236
Take Out Management (NR)
Talbot Music Group (RR)
Tamjam Productions 280
Tangent® Records 236
Tari, Roger Vincent 280
Tas Music Co./Dave Tasse Entertainment 329
Tedesco Music Co., Dale 153
Telluride Troubadour Contest 406
Ten-Minute Musicals Project, The 406, 448
Tennessee Songwriters International, The 436
Texas Accountants & Lawyers for the Arts (NR)
Texas Cherokee Music (RR)
Texas Fantasy Music Group 280
Texas Music Office 436
Texas Rose Records 237
Texas Sounds Entertainment 329
Theatre Three, Inc. 369
Theatre West Virginia 369
Theatrevirginia (NR)
Theatreworks/USA 369
Theoretical Reality 281
Third Wave Productions Limited 153
Third Wave Productions Ltd. 237
315 Beale Studios/Taliesyn Entertainment 329
Thump Records, Inc. 237
Thunder Bay Theatre 370
Tiger's Eye Entertainment Management & Consulting 329
Tiki Enterprises, Inc. 154
Time Art Records (RR)
Time Out Productions/Bramla Music (RR)
TMC Productions 281
Tom Willett/Tommark Records (OB)
Tommy Boy Records 237
Tommy Overstreet Music Companies (ED)
Topcat Records 238
Toronto Mendelssohn Choir 391
Toronto Musicians' Association (NR)
Total Acting Experience, A 330
Tough Guy Booking (NR)
Touring Concert Opera Co. Inc. (NR)
Tower Music Group 154
Trac Record Co. 238, 281
Transamerika Musikverlag KG 154
Transatlantic Management (NR)
Transition Music Corporation 155
Traveler Enterprises (ED)
Treasure Coast Records (RR)
Treasure Coast Songwriters Assn. (TCSA) 437
TRF Production Music Libraries 357

Triangle Talent, Inc. (NR)
Trinity Studio, The 281
Triple X Records 238
Tulsa Opera Inc. 391
Tutta Forza Music 330
Twentieth Century Promotions 330
28 Records 238

U
U.S.A. Songwriting Competition 407
U.S.-Mexico Fund for Culture 408
U.S.-Japan Creative Artists Exchange Fellowship Program 407
UAR Records 239
Ultimate Peak Music 155
Umbrella Artists Management, Inc. (NR)
Umpire Entertainment Enterprizes 331
Undercurrents 449
"Unisong" International Song Contest 407
Universal Music Marketing 331
Universal Records 239
University of Alabama New Playwrights' Program 370
Unknown Source Music (RR)
Up Front Management (ED)
Utopian Empire Creativeworks 357

V
Vaam Music Group 155
VAI Distribution 239
Valet Publishing Co. 155
Valtec Productions 239, 282
Van Pol Management, Hans 331
Vancouver Chamber Choir 391
Vander-Moon Entertainment 240
Varrasso Management, Richard 331
Vector Sound (NR)
Verve Music Group, The 240
Vickers Music Association, Charles 282
Victor Valley Symphony Association (NR)
Victory Music 437
Villa Montalvo Artist Residency Program 453
VIP Video 358
Virgin Records 240
Virginia Center for the Creative Arts 454
Virginia Opera (NR)
Virginia Stage Company 370
Vis/Aid Marketing/Associates 358
Vital Sounds Entertainment (NR)
Vokes Booking Agency 331

Companies that appeared in the 2001 edition of *Songwriter's Market*, but do not appear this year, are listed in this General Index with the following codes explaining why these markets were omitted: (ED)—Editorial Decision, (NS)—Not Accepting Submissions, (NR)—No (or late) Response to Listing Request, (OB)—Out of Business, (RR)—Removed by Listing's Request, (UC)—Unable to Contact.

Vokes Music Publishing 155
Vokes Music Record Co. 240
Volunteer Lawyers for the Arts 437
VVV Music Record Co./Productions (ED)

W

Wagner Agency, William F. 332
Walbash River and Broken Arrow Productions (NR)
Wall Street Music 241
Walls & Co. Management/Showbiz Kidz! 332
Walnut Street Theatre Company 371
Ward and Ames 358
Warehouse Creek Recording Corp. 241
Warland Singers, The Dale 391
Warner Bros. Records 241
Warner Productions, Cheryl K. 332
Warner/Chappell Music Canada Ltd. 156
Washington Area Music Association 437
Waterdog Music 241
Waterloo Community Playhouse (NR)
We Don't Need No Stinkin' Dramas (NR)
We Records & Management (NR)
Weaver of Words Music 156
Weisman Production Group, The 282
Wemar Music Corp. 156
Wemus Entertainment 332
Wengert, Berthold (Musikverlag) 156
West Coast Ensemble 371
West Coast Ensemble—Musical Stairs 408
West End Artists 371
Westbeth Theatre Centre 372
Westminster Presbyterian Church (NR)
Westwires Digital USA 282
Westwood Entertainment Group (NR)
Westwood Music Group 156
Wheaton Symphony Orchestra 392
White Cat Music 157
White Hat Management (NR)
Whitewing Music (NR)
Whiting Music 157
Wich Audio Services (NR)
Wilbur Productions 283
Wilcom Publishing 157
Wilder Artists' Management, Shane 333
Williams Management, Yvonne 333

Willson, Frank 283
Wilma Theater, The (NR)
Winchester Records 242
Windham Hill Records 242
Wind-Up Entertainment 242
Wings Theatre Co. 372
Winston & Hoffman House Music Publishers 157
Wipe Out Music Ltd. 158
WIR (World International Records) 283
WLM Music/Recording 283
Women in Music 438
Women's Project and Productions (NR)
Wood Artist Management, Richard 333
Woolly Mammoth Theatre Co. 372
Word Records & Music 242
Words By 408
Work Group (OB)
World Beatnik Records 242
World Entertainment Service, Inc. (NR)
World Famous Music Co. 158
World Park Productions 333
World Records 283
World Wide Management 334
WorldSound, LLC 334
Worldwide Recordings Limited/Worldrecords.com 243
Wytas Productions, Steve 284

X

X.R.L. Records/Music 243
Xemu Records 244

Y

Y.E.S. Festival of New Plays 408
Yaddo Artists' Community 454
Yellow Jacket Records 244
Y-N-A/C.D.T. Productions 284
Yorgo Music 158
Young Composers Awards 409
Young Country Records/Plain Country Records 244

Z

Zane Management, Inc. 334
Zettitalia Music International 158
Zomba Music Publishing 159